ny event on the timeline could be placed in more than one category. Some scholars claim that globalization has been happening for a long time, and others say has only been happening for a relatively short time. As you read through this timeline, think about how current events happening in your social world are part f this larger process of global change.

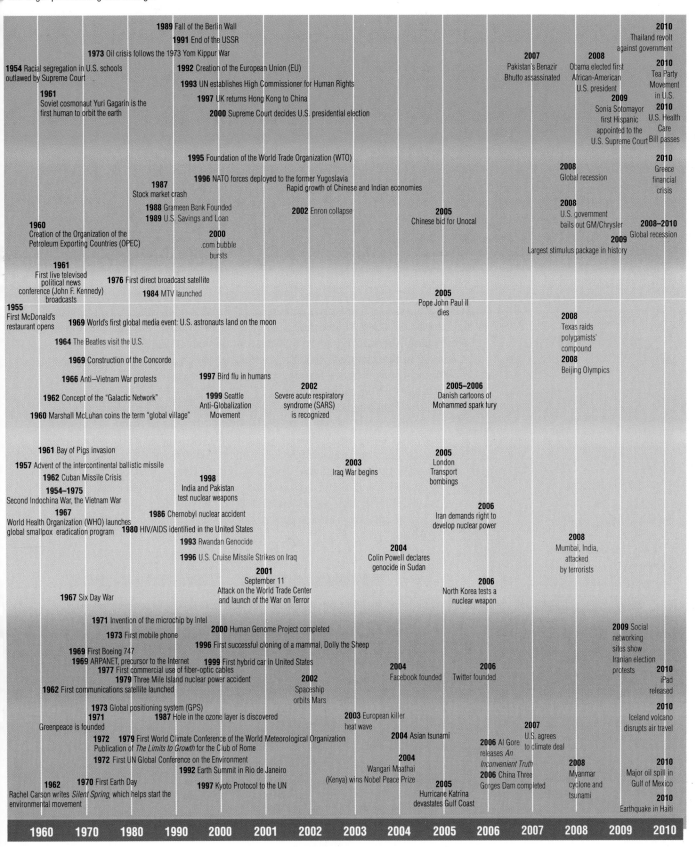

MODERN ERA

THIRD EDITION

OUR SOCIAL WORLD

Condensed Version

Introduction to Sociology

Jeanne H. Ballantine | Keith A. Roberts

To the Student

Chapter-opening visual representations of the **social world model**—streamlined for clarity and simplicity—display the micro, meso, and macro levels for that chapter's topic, with **"Think About It"** questions to focus your thinking on key ideas and **"What's coming in this chapter?"** to guide you through the chapter organization. These features provide active learning opportunities to encourage you to further engage with the subject matter.

"**Thinking Sociologically**" features throughout the text challenge your understanding of core concepts. Found at the end of major sections or features, these questions ask you to apply the material to your own life. Chapter-ending review materials include **"What Have We Learned?"** and an overview of chapter **key points** to ensure mastery of each chapter's core material, and discussion questions to continue the analysis of material in the chapter. Also, suggestions are offered for volunteer work, internships, or career possibilities doing *public sociology* in **"Contributing to Our Social World."**

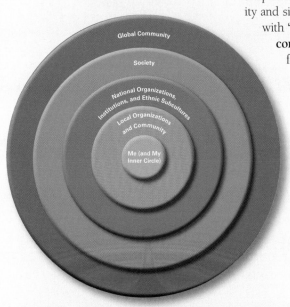

Thinking Sociologically

Identify several dyads, small groups, and large organizations to which you belong. Did you choose to belong, or were you born into membership in the group? How does each group influence decisions you make?

Think About It	
Micro: Self and Inner Circle	How can sociology help me understand my own life and my sense of self?
Micro: Local Community	How can sociology help me to be a more effective employee and citizen in my community?
Meso: National Institutions; Complex Organizations; Ethnic Groups	How do sociologists help us understand and even improve our lives in families, classrooms, and health care organizations?
Macro: National Society	How do national loyalty and national policies affect my life?
Macro: Global Community	How might global events impact my life?

st issue, then, is how we gather data that inform how ...derstand and influence the social world. When we ...ow something about society, how is it that we know?

What is considered evidence in sociology, and what lens (theory) do we use to interpret the data? These are the central issues of the next chapter.

Contributing to Our Social World: What Can We Do?

At the end of this and all subsequent chapters, you will find suggestions for work, service learning, internships, and volunteering that encourage you to apply the concepts, principles, and ideas discussed in the chapter in practical contexts.

At the Local Level:

• Soc... ...nts' *student organizations or clubs.* You ...

At the Regional and National Levels:

• *The American Sociological Association (ASA)* is the leading professional organization of sociologists in the United States. It has several programs and initiatives of special interest to students. Visit the ASA website at www.asanet .org and click on the "Teaching & Learning/Students: Undergraduate" link at the top of the page. Read the ...

What Have We Learned?

We live in a complex social world with many layers of interaction. If we really want to understand our own lives, we need to comprehend the various levels of analysis that affect our lives and the dynamic connections between those levels. Moreover, as citizens of democracies, we need to understand how to influence our social environments, from city councils, school boards, and state legislatures to congressional, presidential, and other organizations with major policy makers. To do so wisely, we need both objective lenses for viewing this complex social world and accurate, valid information (facts) about the society. As the science of society, sociology can provide both tested empirical data and a broad, analytical perspective.

lives and personal troubles are shaped by historical and structural events outside of our everyday lives. It also prods us to see how we can influence our society. (See pp. 9–10.)

• Sociology is a social science and, therefore, uses the tools of the sciences to establish credible evidence to understand our social world. As a science, sociology is scientific and objective rather than value laden. (See pp. 10–13.)

• Sociology has pragmatic applications, including those that are essential for the job market. (See pp. 13–17.)

• Sociology focuses on social units or groups, on social structures such as institutions, on social processes that give a social unit its dynamic character, and on their environments. (See pp. 17–20.)

Key Points:

• Humans are, at their very core, social animals—more ...ack or herd animals than to individual... ...izing theme of this

Excerpt From Review in *Teaching Sociology*

"It is exciting to see a new offering such as Our Social World *that is innovative in its pedagogical choices. It is an exceptionally well-organized and well-written text, and as such is an exciting new option for any introductory sociology class. This text strikes us as particularly effective at engaging students. It becomes quite evident that these two award-winning coauthors understand where students are coming from and which questions are most likely to engage them and push them to think analytically."*

—Reviewed by Catherine Fobes and Laura von Wallmenich,
Alma College, in *Teaching Sociology*, Vol. 36, 2008 (April:161–184)

Student Praise for *Our Social World*

"It's been one of my favorite textbooks to read!"

"I felt the text was speaking 'my language.'"

"I liked that it explains what careers come from sociology. I love the real-life examples to explain key words. This really helped me understand how sociology applies to life."

"I really enjoyed how it started off with a story as an example of what sociology is . . . I formed a picture in my mind that stayed there throughout the chapter."

"It helped me relate my life and personal experiences to the concepts in sociology . . . . It made me concentrate on what was happening to others instead of worrying whether I could get through all the reading. I stayed focused."

"The chapters provide a good overview of the concepts of sociology."

"The charts/diagrams are very helpful in understanding the topics."

"The 'Thinking Sociologically' questions are a great way to stop and reflect because you remember what you read so much better when you have a chance to make it personal."

"It made me become more aware of why people are the way they are and do the things they do. It taught me to view the world with a different outlook. . . . . By being aware of the various social groups out there, I can become a better person."

"Overall, I found this to be one of the most interesting things I have ever been forced to read, and I mean that in a good forced way."

"I really enjoy the book. It is clear to understand, funny at times, and has great examples!"

"I enjoyed how a real person's story was told at the opening of the chapters. It made sociology seem pertinent to real life."

To the Instructor

An Innovative Intro Text for a New Generation of Students . . .
Incredibly Successful in Its First Two Editions and Now Even Better!

Written by two award-winning sociology instructors who are passionate about excellence in teaching, this textbook has been adopted at a variety of community colleges, four-year colleges, and comprehensive research universities, and these schools have used it in traditional as well as online Introduction to Sociology courses. Some of the many schools that have adopted the book include

- American River College
- Boise State University
- Buffalo State College
- Cape Cod Community College
- Capital Community College
- Capital University
- Chaffey College
- Cleveland State University
- College of Staten Island, The City University of New York
- Drexel University
- Hanover College
- Hofstra University
- Indiana University
- Indiana University of Pennsylvania
- Ithaca College
- La Salle University
- Le Moyne College
- Long Island University
- Messiah College
- Minot State University
- Monroe County Community College
- New Mexico State University
- The Ohio State University
- Pennsylvania State University
- Quinebaug Valley Community College
- St. Cloud State University
- San Francisco State University
- Shippensburg University
- Sinclair Community College
- The State University of New York
- Stevenson University
- Tennessee State University
- Towson University
- University of Akron
- University of Central Oklahoma
- University of Maryland
- University of Nebraska
- University of the Ozarks
- University of Richmond
- University of Tennessee
- Wright State University

. . . and many, many more! We would like to say THANK YOU to our loyal adopters who chose *Our Social World* in its previous editions, making it such an overwhelming success. We hope you find the third edition of *Our Social World, Condensed* even more exciting.

Instructor Praise for *Our Social World*

"Unlike most textbooks that I have read, the breadth and depth of coverage . . . is very impressive. This text forces the students deep into the topics covered and challenges them to see the interconnectedness of them."
—Keith Kerr, Texas A&M University

"I love the global emphasis, the applied material, and the emphasis on solutions to social problems."
—Gina Carreno, Florida Atlantic University

"So often students ask, 'What can I do with sociology?' Having this applied information interspersed in the text allows them to get answers to that question over and over again."

"Finally, a text that brings sociology to life! . . . This is so well written that I'm not sure the students will even realize they are learning theory!"
—Martha Shockey-Eckles, St. Louis University

"This is an excellent textbook . . . it has definitely made life easier, and the ancillary material is extremely helpful."
—Jamie M. Dolan, Carroll College

New to This Edition!

- Increased attention to public sociology, including a description of the work of at least one public sociologist per chapter in a "Sociologists in Action" feature
- Increased attention to the sociology of disabilities, especially a feature on the deaf subculture in the United States
- Major topics listed at the start of each chapter
- New discussion questions at the end of each chapter
- Seventeen new featured essays
- Revised and new "Engaging Sociology" features, with more opportunity for data analysis by students
- Clarified and often simplified definitions and updating of the glossary, and a separate section with glossary terms and definitions
- Scores of new examples
- Reorganization of the religion, education, groups and organizations, and other chapters
- Discussion of new social movements and the 2012 election
- Nearly 100 new and updated tables, plus 800 new references, dozens of new photos, and a dozen new or updated maps
- "Contributing to Our Social World" feature with additional ideas for volunteer work, internships, and careers

Engaging Sociology

How to Read a Research Table

A statistical table is a researcher's labor-saving device. Quantitative data presented in tabular form are more clear and concise than the same information presented in several written paragraphs. A good table has clear signposts to help the reader avoid confusion. For instance, the table below shows many of the main features of a table, and the list that follows explains how to read each feature.*

Table 2.1 Educational Attainment by Selected Characteristic: 2009, for Persons 25 Years Old and Over Reported in Thousands

Characteristic	Population (1,000)	Not a High School Graduate	High School Graduate	Some College, but No Degree	Associate's Degree[1]	Bachelor's Degree	Advanced Degree
Age							
25–34 yrs old	40,520	11.7	28.0	19.2	8.9	22.8	9.3
35–44 yrs old	41,322	11.7	28.7	16.6	10.2	21.4	11.4
45–54 yrs old	44,366	10.9	32.2	17.0	10.8	18.8	10.4
55–64 yrs old	34,289	11.1	30.2	17.8	9.2	18.6	13.1
65–74 yrs old	20,404	17.7	36.4	15.5	5.9	13.9	10.5
75 yrs or older	17,384	26.3	36.6	13.7	4.9	11.4	7.0
Sex							
Male	95,518	13.8	31.4	16.8	7.9	19.0	11.1
Female	102,767	12.9	30.8	17.3	10.0	19.0	10.1
Race							
White[2]	162,079	12.9	31.2	16.9	9.1	19.3	10.7
Black[2]	22,598	15.9	35.4	20.3	9.0	12.7	6.6
Other	13,608	14.3	22.3	13.9	7.8	25.8	16.0
Hispanic origin							
Hispanic	25,956	38.1	29.3	13.3	6.1	9.6	3.6
Non-Hispanic	172,329	9.6	31.3	17.6	9.4	20.4	11.6
Region							
Northeast	36,572	11.8	33.3	13.1	8.6	19.9	13.3
Midwest	43,163	10.2	34.4	17.1	9.8	18.2	9.7
South	72,720	15.0	31.8	16.9	8.6	17.9	9.8
West	45,829	14.8	25.1	19.9	9.1	20.7	10.5

Source: U.S. Census Bureau (2011b).

1. Includes vocational degrees.
2. For persons who selected this race group only.
*Features of the table adapted from Broom and Selznick (1963).

Photo Essay

Houses as Part of a Society's Material Culture

Homes are good examples of material culture. Their construction is influenced by local materials, but also ideas of what a home is. Homes shape the context in which family members interact. Indeed, in some cases, homes become status symbols that are far larger than the family needs, but the family is making a prestige statement about their socioeconomic standing.

The invention of the plow was essential for agricultural societies to develop, and in the early period of agriculture, plows were pushed by people and then pulled by animals. The harnessing of energy was taken to another level when gasoline engines could pull the plow and cultivate thousands of acres. This represents the beginning of industrialization. Modern machinery such as this harvester has pushed farming into the new level of productivity.

This Japanese schoolgirl might think that eating with a fork or spoon is quite strange. She has been well socialized to know that polite eating involves competent use of chopsticks.

Thinking Sociologically

Identify several dyads, small groups, and large organizations to which you belong. Did you choose to belong, or were you born into membership in the group? How does each group influence decisions you make?

Finally, here is a text that engages students. *Our Social World, Condensed* uses a unique, dynamic approach to focus on developing sociological skills of analysis, problem solving, and critical thinking rather than simply emphasizing memorization of basic ideas and concepts.

The text is both personal and global. It introduces sociology clearly, with the updated social world model providing a clear and cohesive framework that lends integration and clarity to the course. With the theme of globalization intertwined throughout the text and an emphasis on deep learning and the public side of sociology, *Our Social World, Condensed*, Third Edition, inspires both critical thinking and community participation.

Teach Students the Basics of Sociology via the Newly Simplified, Visually Compelling "Social World Model"

This model, which provides the organizing framework for the text and visually introduces each chapter, illustrates the levels of analysis related to each topic (from micro to meso to macro), and addresses how each topic can be seen through these different levels and how the levels are interrelated.

Engage Students . . . With Engaging Sociology

Active learning exercises keep sociology fun, drawing students into an analysis of a relevant table, the application of a population pyramid to the business world, or an interactive survey on the differences in social and cultural capital for first-generation students. Some of these involve interpretation of a map, and others engage students in quantitative data analysis of tables or figures.

Introduce a Global Perspective, Asking Students to Be Citizens of the World

This text uniquely weaves a truly global perspective into each part of the book, challenging students to think of themselves as global citizens rather than as local citizens looking out at others in the world. "Sociology Around the World" features introduce fascinating historical or global examples of key concepts.

Encourage Deep Learning and Critical Thinking with Uniquely Effective Pedagogy

"Thinking Sociologically" questions, "What Have We Learned?" end-of-chapter summaries and discussion questions, and "Sociology in Our Social World" features encourage critical thought, challenging students to reflect on how the material is relevant and applicable to their lives.

Inspire an Active Engagement in Sociology Using Motivating Chapter Features

"Contributing to Our Social World: What Can We Do?" suggestions include work and volunteer opportunities in which students can apply their newfound sociological knowledge right away. "Sociologists in Action" boxes introduce students to a variety of people with sociological degrees, illuminating bachelor's through PhD career options.

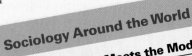

Sociology Around the World

Tunisian Village Meets the Modern World

This is a story of change as macro-level innovations enter a small traditional village. It illustrates how the social world model and the three levels of analysis enter into sociological analysis. As you read, try to identify both the units and levels of analysis being discussed and the impact of globalization on a community that cannot know what these changes will bring.

The workday began at dawn as usual in the small fishing village on the coast of Tunisia, North Africa. Men prepared their nets and boats for the day, while women prepared breakfast and dressed the young children for school. About 10 A.M., it began—the event that would [...] this picturesque village forever. Bulldozers [...] followed by trench diggers and cement [...]

beautiful village; others viewed the changes as destroying a lifestyle that was all they and generations before them had known.

Today, the village is dwarfed by the huge hotel, and the locals are looked on as quaint curiosities by the European tourists. Fishing has become a secondary source of employment to working in the hotel and casino or selling local crafts and trinkets to souvenir-seeking visitors. Many women are now employed outside the home by the hotel, creating new family structures as grandparents, unemployed men, and other relations take over child-rearing responsibilities.

To understand the changes in this one small village [...]

Sociology in Our Social World

Burnouts and Jocks in a Public High School

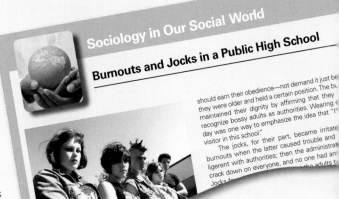

should earn their obedience—not demand it just because they were older and held a certain position. The burnouts maintained their dignity by affirming that they recognize bossy adults as authorities. Wearing a [...] day was one way to emphasize the idea that "I'm a visitor in this school."

The jocks, for their part, became irritated with burnouts when the latter caused trouble and made administrators crack down on everyone, and no one had any [...] jocks [...]

What Have We Learned?

Theories serve as lenses to help us make sense of the data that we gather with various research strategies. However, the data themselves can be used to test the theories, so there is an ongoing reciprocal relationship between theory (the lens for making sense of the data) and the research (the evidence used to test the theories). The most important ideas in this chapter are what sociology considers evidence and how sociology operates as a science. These ideas form the framework for the content of sociology.

Key Points:

[...] derstand society have existed for at [...]

(through secondary sources or through content ana [...] (See pp. 37–40.)

- Use of multiple methods—triangulation—in [...] confidence in the findings. (See p. 39.)

- Scientific confidence in results also requires rep [...] tive samples, usually drawn randomly. (See pp [...]

- Sociology has three strong traditions: One st [...] objective nature of science; another emph [...] uniquely human qualities, such as human [...]

Contributing to Our Social World: What Can We Do?

At the Local Level:

- *Local service organizations*, found in every community, work to provide for unmet needs of community members: housing, legal aid, medical care, elder care, and so on. United Way works with most local service organizations. Volunteer to work with the organization to learn more about its needs assessment research and research methods that are used.

At the Meso Level:

[...] *Applied and Clinical Sociol* [...]

At the National and Global Levels:

- The *U.S. Bureau of the Census* is best known for [...] nial (occurring every 10 years) enumeration of [...] lation, but its work continues each year as [...] special reports, population estimates, and r [...] lications (including *Current Population Repo* [...] Census Bureau's website at www.census.gov [...] the valuable and extensive amount of qua [...] and other information available, or vis [...] Census Bureau office to discuss volunteer [...]

Ancillaries

For the Instructor

The password-protected Instructor Site at **www.sagepub.com/oswcondensed3e** gives instructors access to a full complement of resources to support and enhance their courses. The following assets are available on the Instructor Site:

- A **test bank** with multiple choice, true/false, and critical answer essay questions. The test bank is provided on the site in Word format as well as in Respondus
- **PowerPoint** slides for each chapter, for use in lectures and review. Slides are integrated with the book's distinctive features and incorporate key graphics, talking points, and information utilize maximum chapter review.
- **Lecture notes/chapter outlines** are provided to aid in further chapter review and lectures.
- **Sample course syllabi** for semester and quarter courses provide suggested models for instructors use when creating the course syllabi.
- **Chapter-specific discussion questions** help launch classroom interaction by prompting students to engage with the material and by reinforcing important content.
- Lively and stimulating **ideas for class activities** that can be used in class to reinforce active learning. The activities apply to individual or group projects.
- A list of **recommended readings** provide a jumping-off point for course assignments, papers, research, group work, and class discussion.
- EXCLUSIVE! Access to certain full-text **SAGE journal articles** that have been carefully selected for each chapter. Each article supports and expands on the concepts presented in the chapter. This feature also provides questions to focus and guide student interpretation. Combine cutting-edge academic journal scholarship with the topics in your course for a robust classroom experience.
- Carefully selected, web-based **video links** feature relevant interviews, lectures, personal stories, inquiries, and other content for use in independent or classroom-based explorations of key topics.
- Each chapter includes **audio links** related to important topics and designed to supplement key points within the text.
- **Reference Links** for each chapter includes links to relevant articles from SAGE handbooks and encyclopedias.
- SAGE's **course cartridges** provide you with flexible, editable content in formats that import easily into your learning management system. Course cartridges include banks, PowerPoint® slides, and links to multimedia assets help you build an engaging, comprehensive course. SAGE's course cartridges are compatible with many popular learning management systems.
- And more!

For the Student

To maximize students' understanding and promote critical thinking and active learning, we have provided the following chapter-specific student resources at **www.sagepub.com/oswcondensed3e**. The open-access Student Study Site includes the following:

- EXCLUSIVE! Access to certain full-text **SAGE journal articles** have been carefully selected for each chapter. Each article supports and expands on the concepts presented in the chapter. This feature also provides questions to focus and guide your interpretation.

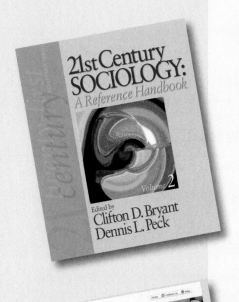

- Carefully selected, **video links** feature relevant interviews, lectures, personal stories, inquiries, and other content for use in independent or classroom-based explorations of key topics.
- Each chapter includes **audio links**, covering important topics and designed to supplement key points within the text.
- **Reference Links** for each chapter includes links to relevant articles from SAGE handbooks and encyclopedias.
- **Study questions** reinforce key concepts in each chapter for self-review.
- Mobile-friendly **eFlashcards** reinforce understanding of key terms and concepts that have been outlined in the chapters.
- Mobile-friendly **web quizzes** allow for independent assessment of progress made in learning course material.
- **Internet activities** direct both instructors and students to useful and current web sites, along with creative activities to extend and reinforce learning or allow for further research on important chapter topics.

Interactive eBook

Our Social World: Condensed Version, Third Edition is also available as an Interactive eBook, which can be packaged free with the book or purchased separately. Ideal for students in online and traditional courses who prefer a more contemporary, multimedia-integrated presentation for learning, this incredibly interactive eBook provides students with the identical content and page layout of the traditional printed book in a flexible electronic format. Users of the eBook can link directly from the page to video, audio, journal, and additional enrichment readings, glossary terms, and other relevant resources that brings Sociology to life. Students will also have immediate access to study tools such as highlighting, bookmarking, and note-taking.

 Sage Journal Video  Audio Icon Reference

SAGE Teaching Innovations and Professional Development Awards Fund

Largely inspired by the authors of *Our Social World*, SAGE has created this awards fund to help graduate students and pretenure faculty attend the annual American Sociological Association preconference teaching workshop, hosted by the Section on Teaching and Learning in Sociology, with grants of $500 per recipient. In its first year, there were 13 award recipients. Since that time, 23 additional authors have joined the program as cosponsors, and in the seven years of the program, 152 recipients have benefited from this award. In 2008, the ASA's Section on Teaching and Learning in Sociology awarded SAGE with a glass plaque to honor the publisher and its participating authors and editors—including the authors of *Our Social World*—for their commitment to excellence in teaching.

About the Authors

Jeanne H. Ballantine (far right) is Professor Emerita of Sociology at Wright State University, a state university of about 17,000 students in Ohio. She has also taught at several four-year colleges, including an "alternative" college and a traditionally black college, and with international programs in universities abroad. Jeanne has been teaching introductory sociology for more than 30 years with a mission to introduce the uninitiated to the field and to help students see the usefulness and value in sociology. Jeanne has been active in the teaching movement, shaping curriculum, writing and presenting research on teaching, and offering workshops and consulting in regional, national, and international forums. She is a Fulbright Senior Scholar and serves as a Departmental Resources Group consultant and evaluator.

Jeanne has written several textbooks, all with the goal of reaching the student audience. As the original director of the Center for Teaching and Learning at Wright State University, she scoured the literature on student learning and served as a mentor to teachers in a wide variety of disciplines. Local, regional, and national organizations have honored her for her teaching and for her contributions to helping others become effective teachers. In 1986, the American Sociological Association's Section on Undergraduate Education (now called the Section on Teaching and Learning in Sociology) recognized her with the Hans O. Mauksch Award for Distinguished Contributions to Undergraduate Sociology. In 2004, she was honored by the American Sociological Association with its Distinguished Contributions to Teaching Award. In 2010, the North Central Sociological Association awarded her the J. Milton Yinger Lifetime Award for a Distinguished Career in Sociology.

Keith A. Roberts (top left) is Emeritus Professor of Sociology at Hanover College, a private liberal arts college of about 1,100 students in Indiana. He has been teaching introductory sociology for more than 37 years with a passion for active learning strategies and a focus on "deep learning" by students that transforms the way students see the world. Prior to teaching at Hanover, he taught at a two-year regional campus of a large university. Between them, these authors have taught many types of students at different types of schools.

Keith has been active in the teaching movement, writing on teaching and serving as a consultant to sociology departments across the country in his capacity as a member of the American Sociological Association Departmental Resources Group. He is the coauthor of a very popular textbook in the sociology of religion (with David Yamane), has coauthored a book on writing in the undergraduate curriculum, and for 22 years ran an annual workshop for high school sociology teachers. He has chaired the Selection Committee for the SAGE Teaching Innovations and Professional Development Awards since the program's inception. He has been honored for his teaching and teaching-related work at local, state, regional, and national levels. The American Sociological Association's Section on Teaching and Learning awarded him the Hans O. Mauksch Award for Distinguished Contributions to Undergraduate Sociology in 2000. In 2010 he was awarded the American Sociological Association's Distinguished Contributions to Teaching Award. In 2012, the North Central Sociological Association awarded Keith the J. Milton Yinger Lifetime Award for a Distinguished Career in Sociology.

2004 AMERICAN SOCIOLOGICAL ASSOCIATION

DISTINGUISHED CONTRIBUTIONS TO TEACHING AWARD

2010 AMERICAN SOCIOLOG\ICAL ASSOCIATION

DISTINGUISHED CONTRIBUTIONS TO TEACHING AWARD

Visit www.sagepub.com for valuable Intro to Sociology supplemental texts
1-800-818-SAGE (7243)
www.sagepub.com

The world is condensing, and it will be a different social place for our children and grandchildren.

It is in that spirit that we dedicate this book to our respective grandchildren:

Hannah Ballantine, Caleb Ballantine, Kai Jolly-Ballantine, Ayla Jolly-Ballantine, Zainakai Blair-Roberts, and others "on the way to becoming." May the condensed global society they inhabit be an increasingly humane one.

OUR SOCIAL WORLD

Condensed Version

THIRD EDITION

Jeanne H. Ballantine
Wright State University

Keith A. Roberts
Hanover College

Los Angeles | London | New Delhi
Singapore | Washington DC

Los Angeles | London | New Delhi
Singapore | Washington DC

FOR INFORMATION:

SAGE Publications, Inc.
2455 Teller Road
Thousand Oaks, California 91320
E-mail: order@sagepub.com

SAGE Publications Ltd.
1 Oliver's Yard
55 City Road
London EC1Y 1SP
United Kingdom

SAGE Publications India Pvt. Ltd.
B 1/I 1 Mohan Cooperative Industrial Area
Mathura Road, New Delhi 110 044
India

SAGE Publications Asia-Pacific Pte. Ltd.
3 Church Street
#10-04 Samsung Hub
Singapore 049483

Acquisitions Editor: Jeff Lasser
Associate Editor: Nathan Davidson
Assistant Editor: Megan Koraly
Editorial Assistant: Lauren Johnson
Production Editor: Brittany Bauhaus
Copy Editor: Melinda Masson
Typesetter: C&M Digitals (P) Ltd.
Proofreader: Wendy Jo Dymond
Indexer: Scott Smiley
Cover Designer: Gail Buschman
Marketing Manager: Erica DeLuca

Printed in Canada

A catalog record of this book is available from the Library of Congress.

9781452275758

This book is printed on acid-free paper.

13 14 15 16 17 10 9 8 7 6 5 4 3 2 1

Brief Contents

Preface: To Our Readers   xxi

Instructors: How to Make This Book Work for You   xxiii

A Personal Note to the Instructor   xxvii

Acknowledgments   xxx

PART I. UNDERSTANDING OUR SOCIAL WORLD: THE SCIENTIFIC STUDY OF SOCIETY   1

Chapter 1 • Sociology: A Unique Way to View the World   2

Chapter 2 • Examining the Social World: How Do We Know?   28

PART II. SOCIAL STRUCTURE, PROCESSES, AND CONTROL   55

Chapter 3 • Society and Culture: Hardware and Software of Our Social World   56

Chapter 4 • Socialization: Becoming Human and Humane   88

Chapter 5 • Interaction, Groups, and Organizations: Connections That Work   112

Chapter 6 • Deviance and Social Control: Sickos, Weirdos, Freaks, and Folks Like Us   140

PART III. INEQUALITY   171

Chapter 7 • Stratification: Rich and Famous—or Rags and Famine?   172

Chapter 8 • Race and Ethnic Group Stratification: Beyond "We" and "They"   208

Chapter 9 • Gender Stratification: She/He—Who Goes First?   242

PART IV. INSTITUTIONS   277

Chapter 10 • Family: Partner Taking, People Making, and Contract Breaking   284

Chapter 11 • Education and Religion: Answering "What?" and "Why?"   310

Chapter 12 • Politics and Economics: Penetrating Power and Privilege   358

PART V. SOCIAL DYNAMICS   393

Chapter 13 • Population and Health: Living on Spaceship Earth   394

Chapter 14 • The Process of Change: Can We Make a Difference?   428

References   R-1

Credits   C-1

Glossary   G-1

Index   I-1

Detailed Contents

Preface: To Our Readers   xxi

Instructors: How to Make This Book Work for You   xxiii

A Personal Note to the Instructor   xxvii

Acknowledgments   xxx

Part I. Understanding Our Social World: The Scientific Study of Society   1

Chapter 1 • Sociology: A Unique Way to View the World   2

What Is Sociology?   6
   Ideas Underlying Sociology   6
   Sociology Versus Common Sense   7
   Social Science Findings and
      Commonsense Beliefs   8
   The Sociological Imagination   10
   Questions Sociologists Ask—and Don't Ask   10
   The Social Sciences: A Comparison   11
Why Does Sociology Matter?   12
   Why Study Sociology?   12

Sociology in Our Social World—Burnouts and
Jocks in a Public High School   13
   What Do Sociologists Do?   14
   What Employers Want   15
The Social World Model   16
   Social Structures   18
   Social Processes   19
   The Environment of Our Social World   19
   Studying the Social World: Levels of Analysis   19
      Micro-Level Analysis   20
      Meso-Level Analysis   20
      Macro-Level Analysis   20
   The Social World Model and This Book   22

Engaging Sociology—Micro–Meso–Macro   23

Sociology Around the World—Tunisian Village
Meets the Modern World   24

Engaging Sociology—Micro–Meso–Macro:
An Application Exercise   25

What Have We Learned?   26

Contributing to Our Social World:
What Can We Do?   27

Chapter 2 • Examining the Social World: How Do We Know?   28

Ideas Underlying Science   31
Empirical Research and Social Theory   32
How Sociologists Study the Social World   33
   Planning a Research Study   33
   Designing the Research Method and
      Collecting the Data   34

Sociology in Our Social World—Being
Clear About Causality   35
   Making Sense of the Data: Analysis   38
   Ethical Issues in Social Research   39
The Development of Sociology as a Social Science   39

Engaging Sociology—How to Read
a Research Table   40
   Early Sociological Thought   41
   Conditions Leading to Modern Sociology   42
   The Purposes of Sociology   43
Sociology's Major Theoretical Perspectives   44
   Micro- to Meso-Level Theories: Symbolic
      Interaction and Rational Choice   44
      Symbolic Interaction Theory   44

Sociology in Our Social World—Human Language
and the Marvel of a College Classroom   45
      Rational Choice (Exchange) Theory   46
   Meso- and Macro-Level Theories:
      Structural-Functional,
      Conflict, and Feminist   47
      Structural-Functional Theory   47
      Conflict Theory   48
      Multilevel Analysis   50
   Using Different Theoretical Perspectives   52

\What Have We Learned?   53

Contributing to Our Social World:
What Can We Do?   54

Part II. Social Structure, Processes, and Control 55

Chapter 3 • Society and Culture: Hardware and Software of Our Social World 56

Society: The Hardware 59
Evolution of Societies 59
Hunter-Gatherer Societies 60
Herding and Horticultural Societies 61
Agricultural Societies 61
Industrial Societies 62
Postindustrial or Information Societies 63

Engaging Sociology—Demographics of Internet Users 64

Sociologists in Action—Creativity, Community, and Applied Sociology 65
Culture: The Software 66
Ethnocentrism and Cultural Relativity 67
The Components of Culture: Things and Thoughts 70
Material Culture: The Artifacts of Life 70
Nonmaterial Culture: Beliefs, Values, Rules, and Language 70

Sociology Around the World—Life and Death in a Guatemalan Village 73
Society, Culture, and Our Social World 78
Microcultures: Micro-Level Analysis 78
Subcultures and Countercultures: Meso-Level Analysis 78

Sociology in Our Social World—Deaf Subculture in the United States 80
National and Global Cultures: Macro-Level Analysis 81
National Society and Culture 82
Global Society and Culture 82
Theories of Culture 83
Cultural Theory at the Micro Level 83
Symbolic Interaction Theory 83
Cultural Theories at the Meso and Macro Levels 84
Structural-Functional Theory 84
Conflict Theory 85
The Fit Between Hardware and Software 86

What Have We Learned? 86

Contributing to Our Social World: What Can We Do? 87

Chapter 4 • Socialization: Becoming Human and Humane 88

Nature *Versus* Nurture—or *Both* Working Together? 91

The Importance of Socialization 91
Isolated and Abused Children 92
Socialization and the Social World 93
Development of the Self: Micro-Level Analysis 94
The Looking-Glass Self and Role-Taking 94
Parts of the Self 95

Sociology in Our Social World—Black Men and Public Space 96
Stages in the Development of the Self 97
The Self and Connections to the Meso Level 98
Socialization Throughout the Life Cycle 99
The Process of Resocialization 101
Agents of Socialization: The Micro-Meso Connection 102
Micro-Level Socialization 102

Sociology in Our Social World—Gender Socialization in American Public Schools 103
Meso-Level Socialization 104
Social Class 104
Electronic Media 105

Engaging Sociology—Media Exposure and Socialization 106
Socialization and Macro-Level Issues 107
Sense of Self Versus the "Other": Diverse Global Societies 107
Policy and Practice 108

What Have We Learned? 109

Contributing to Our Social World: What Can We Do? 110

Chapter 5 • Interaction, Groups, and Organizations: Connections That Work 112

Networks and Connections in Our Social World 115
Networks at the Micro, Meso, and Macro Levels 115

Engaging Sociology—Examining Your Social Networks 117
The Process of Interaction: Connections at the Micro Level 117
The Elements of Social Interaction 118
Theoretical Perspectives on the Interaction Process 120
Symbolic Interaction Theory 120
Rational Choice Theory 121
Social Status: The Link to Groups 121
The Relationship Between Status and Role 123
Role Strain and Role Conflict 124
Groups in Our Social World: The Micro-Meso Connection 125
The Importance of Groups for the Individual 125
Anomie and Suicide 125
Types of Groups 126

Organizations and Bureaucracies: The Meso-Macro Connection 129

Modern Organizations and Their Evolution 129

Sociology Around the World—The McDonaldization of Society 130

Modern Organizations and Modern Life 131

Characteristics of Bureaucracy 131

Issues in Bureaucracies 132

Professionals in Bureaucracies 132

Diversity and Equity in Organizations 133

Organizational Dysfunctions 133

National and Global Networks: The Macro Level 134

Policy Issues: Women and Globalization 134

Sociologists in Action—Using Sociology in International Travel and Intercultural Education 135

What Have We Learned? 137

Contributing to Our Social World: What Can We Do? 138

Chapter 6 • Deviance and Social Control: Sickos, Weirdos, Freaks, and Folks Like Us 140

What Is Deviance? 142

Engaging Sociology—Who Is Deviant? 143

Crime: Deviance That Violates the Law 145

What Causes Deviant Behavior? Theoretical Perspectives 146

Micro-Level Explanations of Deviance: Rational Choice and Interactionist Perspectives 146

Rational Choice Approaches to Deviance 146

Symbolic Interaction Approaches to Deviance 148

Meso- and Macro-Level Explanations of Deviance 150

Structural-Functional Approaches to Deviance 150

Sociology in Our Social World— Stigmatizing Fatness 151

Conflict Theory of Deviance 153

Feminist Theory of Deviance 153

Crime and Individuals: Micro-Level Analysis 154

How Much Crime Is There? 154

Types of Crime 155

Predatory or Street Crimes 155

Crimes Without Victims 156

Hate Crimes 156

Crime and Organizations: Meso-Level Analysis 157

Crimes Involving Organizations and Institutions 157

Organized Crime 157

Occupational Crime 158

National and Global Crime: Macro-Level Analysis 159

Cross-National Comparison of Crimes 160

Global Crimes 161

Controlling Crime: Social Policy Considerations 162

Dealing With Crime: The Criminal Justice Process 163

Prisons and Jails 163

The Purposes of Prisons 164

Alternative Forms of Social Control 166

Sociologists in Action—Police and Delinquent Youth: Changing Stereotypes and Making Peace 167

What Have We Learned? 169

Contributing to Our Social World: What Can We Do? 170

Part III. Inequality 171

Chapter 7 • Stratification: Rich and Famous—or Rags and Famine? 172

The Importance of Social Stratification 176

Micro-Level Prestige and Influence 176

Meso-Level Access to Resources 177

Macro-Level Factors Influencing Stratification 177

Theoretical Explanations of Stratification 177

Micro-Level Theory 178

Symbolic Interaction 178

Rational Choice Theory 178

Meso- and Macro-Level Theories 179

Structural-Functional Theory 179

Conflict Theory 179

The Evolutionary Theory of Stratification: A Synthesis 181

Individuals' Social Status: The Micro Level 182

Individual Life Chances 183

Education 183

Health, Social Conditions, and Life Expectancy 183

Engaging Sociology—Life Expectancy, Per Capita Income, and Infant Mortality 184

Individual Lifestyles 184

Attitudes Toward Achievement 185

Religious Membership 185

Political Behavior 185

Status Inconsistency 185

Social Mobility: The Micro-Meso Connection 186

Types of Social Mobility 186

How Much Mobility Is There? Measures of Social Mobility 187

Factors Affecting an Individual's Mobility 188

Family Background, Socialization, and Education 188

Economic Vitality and Shifting Jobs 189
Population Trends 189

Engaging Sociology—First-Generation College Students:
Issues of Cultural Capital and Social Capital 190
    Gender and Ethnicity 191
    *The Interdependent Global Market and International
    Events* 192
  Is There a "Land of Opportunity"? Cross-Cultural
  Mobility 192

**Major Stratification Systems:
Macro-Level Analysis 193**
  Ascribed Status: Caste and Estate Systems 193
  Achieved Status: Social Class Systems 194

Sociology Around the World—The Outcastes of India 195
    The Property (Wealth) Factor 194
    The Power Factor 196
    The Prestige Factor 197
  Social Classes in the United States 197

**Poverty: Determinants and Social
Policy 199**

**National and Global Digital Divide:
Macro-Level Stratification 201**

Sociology in Our Social World—The Functions
of Poverty 202
  The Global "Digital Divide" and Social Policy 204

What Have We Learned? 205

Contributing to Our Social World: What Can We Do? 206

Chapter 8 • Race and Ethnic Group Stratification: Beyond "We" and "They" 208

Sociologists in Action—Stopping Slavery in the 21st
Century 212

**What Characterizes Racial and Ethnic
Groups? 213**
  Minority Groups 213
  The Concept of Race 213
    Origins of the Concept of Race 214
    *Social Construction of Race: Symbolic
    Interaction Analysis* 215
    The Significance of Race Versus Class 216
  Ethnic Groups 217
  Biracial and Multiracial Populations:
  Immigration, Intermarriage, and Personal
  Identification 217

Prejudice: Micro-Level Analysis 219
  The Nature of Prejudice 219

Sociology in Our Social World—Anti-Muslim
Sentiments in the United States 220
    Explanations of Prejudice 221
  Racial Bigotry and Its Forms 222

**Discrimination:
Meso-Level Analysis 223**

Engaging Sociology—Using and
Relating Key Concepts 225

**Dominant and Minority Group Contact:
Macro-Level Analysis 226**
  Theoretical Explanations of Dominant-Minority
  Group Relations 228

Sociology in Our Social World—Pluralism:
A Long-Standing History in the United States
229
    Structural-Functional Theory 229
    Conflict Theory 230

**The Effects of Prejudice, Racism, and
Discrimination 231**
  The Costs of Racism 231
  Minority Reactions to Prejudice, Discrimination,
  and Racism 232
    Micro-Level Coping Strategies 232
    *Meso- and Macro-Level Efforts to Bring Change:
    Nonviolent Resistance* 233

**Policies Governing Minority and Dominant
Group Relations 234**
  Individual or Small-Group Solutions 234
  Group Contact 235
  Institutional and Societal Strategies to Improve
  Group Relations 235
  Affirmative Action 235

Engaging Sociology—Preference Policies at the
University of Michigan 237
  Global Movements for Human Rights 238

What Have We Learned? 239

Contributing to Our Social World: What Can We Do? 240

Chapter 9 • Gender Stratification: She/He—Who Goes First? 242

**Sex, Gender, and the Stratification
System 244**
  Sex 245
  Gender 246
  Sexuality 247
  Sex, Gender, and Sexuality: The Micro Level 247
  Sex, Gender, and Sexuality: The Meso Level 248
    Empowerment of Women 249

Sociologists in Action—Sociology Students Engage With
Microfinance 250
  Sex, Gender, and Sexuality: The Macro Level 250

**Gender Socialization: Micro- and
Meso-Level Analyses 252**
  Stages in Gender Socialization 252
    Infancy 252
    Childhood 252

Sociology in Our Social World—The Boy Code 253

**Meso-Level Agents of Gender
Socialization 254**
  Corporations 254
  Mass Media 255
  Educational Systems 256

Religious Organizations 227

Gender Stratification: Meso- and Macro-Level Processes 258

Engaging Sociology—Masculinity and Femininity in Our Social World 259
    Women and Men at Work: Gendered Organizations 260
        Institutionalized Gender Discrimination 261
    Gender Differences in Internet Use 262

Gender Stratification: Micro- to Macro-Level Theories 263
    Symbolic Interaction Theory: Micro-Level Analysis 263
    Structural-Functional and Conflict Theories: Meso- and Macro-Level Analyses 264
    Structural-Functional Theory 264

Sociology in Our Social World—Gender and Food 265
        Conflict Theory 266
        Feminist Theory 266

Sociology in Our Social World—Rape and the Victims of Rape 268
        The Interaction of Class, Race, and Gender 269

Gender, Homosexuality, and Minority Status 269

Costs and Consequences of Gender Stratification 271
    Psychological and Social Consequences: Micro-Level Implications 271
    The Results of Gender Role Expectations 272
    Societal Costs and Consequences: Meso- and Macro-Level Implications 272

Changing Gender Stratification and Social Policy 273

What Have We Learned? 275

Contributing to Our Social World: What Can We Do? 276

Part IV. Institutions 277

Chapter 10 • Family: Partner Taking, People Making, and Contract Breaking 284

What Is a Family? 287

Engaging Sociology—The Ideal Family 288

Theoretical Perspectives on Family 289
    Micro-Level Theories of Family and the Meso-Level Connection 289
    Symbolic Interaction Theory 289
    Rational Choice Theory 290
    Meso- and Macro-Level Theories of the Family 291
    Structural-Functional Theory 291
    Conflict Theory 293
    An Alternative Theory for Analysis of the Family 293
    Feminist Theory 293

Family Dynamics: Micro-Level Processes 294
    Mate Selection: How Do New Families Start? 294
    Norms Governing Choice of Marriage Partners: Societal Rules and Intimate Choices 294
    Finding a Mate 295
    Who Holds the Power? Authority in Marriage 297
    Decision Making in Marriage 297
    Who Does the Housework? 297

Engaging Sociology—Household Tasks by Gender 298

The Family as an Institution: Meso-Level Analysis 299
    Marriage and Family Structure: The Components of Family as an Institution 299
    Types of Marriages 299
    Extended and Nuclear Families 300

National and Global Family Issues: Macro-Level Analysis 301
    Cohabitation 301
    Same-Sex Relationships and Civil Unions 302
    Divorce—Contract Breaking 303

Sociology in Our Social World—Debunking Misconceptions About Divorce 304
    Divorce and Its Social Consequences 305
    Global Family Patterns and Policies 306

Sociology Around the World—Cross-Cultural Differences in Family Dissolution 307

What Have We Learned? 308

Contributing to Our Social World: What Can We Do? 309

Chapter 11 • Education and Religion: Answering "What?" and "Why?" 310

Education: The Search for Knowledge 312
    State of the World's Education: An Overview 313
    Who Does What? Micro-Level Interactions in Educational Organizations 314
    Micro-Level Theories: Individuals Within Schools 314
    Statuses and Roles in the Educational System 315

Sociology in Our Social World—Where the Boys Are: And Where Are the Boys? 317
    The Informal System: What Really Happens Inside Schools? 318
    After the School Bell Rings: Meso-Level Analysis 319
    Formal Education Systems 319
    The Bureaucratic School Structure 320
    Educational Decision Making at the Meso Level 321

Sociology in Our Social World—Disability and Inequality 322
    Education, Society, and the Road to Opportunity: The Macro Level 322
    Why Societies Have Education Systems: Macro-Level Theories 323

Engaging Sociology—Consequences of High or Low Numbers of Bachelor's Degrees 325
    Can Schools Bring About Equality in Societies? 327

Who Gets Ahead and Why? The Role of Education in
   Stratification   327

Engaging Sociology—Test Score Variations by Gender and
Ethnicity   328
   Education and Social Policy Issues   329
   Global Policy Issues in Education   329

Sociologists in Action—Geoffrey Canada and the Harlem
Children's Zone   330

Religion: The Search for Meaning   333
   What Does Religion Do for Us?   333
   Components of Religion   334
      Meaning System   334
      Belonging System   334
      Structural System   335
   Becoming Part of a Faith Community: Micro-Level
      Analysis   336
      Symbols and the Creation of Meaning: A Symbolic
         Interactionist Perspective   337
      Seeking Eternal Benefits: A Rational Choice
         Perspective   340
   Religion and Modern Life: Meso-Level Analysis   340
      Types of Religious Associations   340
      New Religious Movements or Cults   342

Sociology in Our Social World—Islam, Mosques, and
Organizational Structure   343

Sociology in Our Social World—Witchcraft in the
United States   344
   Religion in Society: Macro-Level Analysis   345
      The Contribution of Religion to Society: A Structural-
         Functional Perspective   345
      The Link Between Religion and Stratification: A Conflict
         Perspective   346

Sociology in Our Social World— Red Sex, Blue Sex   347

Engaging Sociology—Women and Spirituality   350
   Religion and Secularization: Micro-, Meso-, and
      Macro-Level Discord   351
   Religion in the Contemporary Global Context   353
      Religion and Peace   353
      Religion, Technology, and the World Wide Web   354

What Have We Learned?   355

Contributing to Our Social World: What Can We Do?   357

**Chapter 12 • Politics and Economics:
Penetrating Power and Privilege   358**

What Is Power?   361
**Power and Privilege in Our Social
World   361**
**Theoretical Perspectives on Power and
Privilege   362**
   Micro- and Meso-Level Perspectives:
      Legitimacy of Power   362

Sociology in Our Social World—The Flag, Symbolism, and
Patriotism   363
   Social Construction of Politics: Legitimacy,
      Authority, and Power   364

How Do Leaders Gain Legitimate Power?   364
   Self-Interest as a Path to Legitimacy   365
   Macro Perspectives: Who Rules?   365
      Pluralist Theory   366
      Elite Theory   366

**Micro-Level Analysis: Individuals, Power,
and Participation   367**
   Participation in Democratic Processes   367
      Ideology and Attitudes About
         Politics and Economics   368
      Levels of Participation in Politics   368

Sociology Around the World—Women and
Political Change in Postgenocide Rwanda   369

Sociology in Our Social World—The 2012 Presidential
Election and the Youth Vote   371

**Meso-Level Analysis: Distributions
of Power and Privilege Within
a Nation   372**
   What Purposes Do Political and Economic
      Institutions Serve?   372
   Meso- and Macro-Level Systems of Power and
      Privilege   373
      Types of Political Systems   374

Sociology Around the World—The Khmer Rouge Revolution:
A Totalitarian Regime   375
      Technology and Democracy   376
      Types of Economic Systems   377

**Macro-Level Analysis:
National and Global Systems
of Power and Privilege   379**
   Power and the Nation-State   379
   Revolutions and Rebellions   380

Sociology Around the World—Social Networking and
Political Protests   381
   The Meso-Macro Political Connection   382
   Global Interdependencies: Cooperation and
      Conflicts   383

Engaging Sociology—Political Decisions: Social Processes
at the Micro, Meso, and Macro Levels   383
      Violence on the Global Level   384
      Why Do Nations Go to War?   385
      How Might Nations Avoid War?   387
      Terrorism   388

What Have We Learned?   390

Contributing to Our Social World: What Can We Do?   391

Part V. Social Dynamics   393

**Chapter 13 • Population and Health:
Living on Spaceship Earth   394**

**Macro-Level Patterns in World Population
Growth   398**
   Patterns of Population Growth Over Time   398
   Predictors of Population Growth   399

Population Patterns: Theoretical Explanations 402
Malthus's Theory of Population 402
Demographic Transition: Explaining Population Growth and Expansion 403
Conflict Theorists' Explanations of Population Growth 404

Meso-Level Institutional Influences on Population Change 405

Institutional Factors Affecting Fertility Rates 405
Economic Factors and Population Patterns 406
Political Systems and Population Patterns 407
Religion and Population Patterns 408
Education and Population 408

Mortality Rates: Social Patterns of Health, Illness, and Death 409
Life Expectancy and Infant Mortality 409

Sociology in Our Social World—The Significance of the Baby Boom 410
Mortality From the Spread of Diseases and Plagues 411

Sociology Around the World—"Ring Around the Rosie" and the Plague 412
Globalization and the Mobility of Disease 413

Sociology Around the World—Comparing Health Care Systems: The Canadian Model 414

Migration: Where and Why People Move 415
International Migration 416
Internal Migration in the United States 417

Micro-Level Population Patterns and Our Everyday Lives 419

Engaging Sociology—World Urbanization Trends 420

Engaging Sociology—Population Pyramids and Predicting Community Needs and Services 423

Environmental and Demographic Policy Issues 423

Population Patterns and Economic Development 423
The Environment and Urban Ecosystems 424

What Have We Learned? 425

Contributing to Our Social World: What Can We Do? 426

Chapter 14 • The Process of Change: Can We Make a Difference? 428

The Complexity of Change in Our Social World 431

Change at the Individual Level: Micro-Level Analysis 431
Change at the Institutional Level: Meso-Level Analysis 432

Change at the National and Global Levels: Macro-Level Analysis 432
Society-Level Change 432
Global Systems and Change 434

Social Change: Process and Theories 434

The Process of Social Change 434
Theories of Social Change 436
Micro-Level Theories of Change 436

Sociology in Our Social World—Technology and Change: The Automobile 437
Meso- and Macro-Level Theories of Change 439

Collective Behavior: Micro-Level Behavior and Change 441

Theories of Collective Behavior 442
Types of Collective Behavior 443

Planned Change in Organizations: Meso-Level Change 444

How Organizations Plan for Change 445
Models for Planning Organizational Change 445
The Process of Planned Change 449

Social Movements: Macro-Level Change 446

What Is a Social Movement? 446
Types of Social Movements 447
Globalization and Social Movements 449

Engaging Sociology—Micro to Macro: Change From the Bottom Up 450

Technology, Environment, and Change 451

Technology and Science 452
Technology and Change 453

Engaging Sociology—Making a Difference 455

What Have We Learned? 456

Contributing to Our Social World: What Can We Do? 457

References R-1

Credits C-1

Glossary G-1

Index I-1

Preface

To Our Readers

This book asks you to think outside the box. Why? The best way to become a more interesting person, to grow beyond the old familiar thoughts and behaviors, and to make life exciting is to explore new ways of thinking about the world around you. The world in which we live is intensely personal and individual in nature, with much of our social interaction occurring in intimate circles of friends and family. Our most intense emotions and most meaningful links to others are at this "micro" level of social life.

However, these intimate micro-level links in our lives are influenced by larger social structures and global trends. At the start of the second decade of the 21st century, technological advances make it possible to connect with the farthest corners of the world. Multinational corporations cross national boundaries, form new economic and political unions, and change job opportunities of people everywhere. Some groups embrace the changes, while others try to protect their members from the rapid changes that threaten to disrupt their traditional lives. Even our most personal relationships or what we eat tonight may be shaped by events on the other side of the continent or the globe. From the news headlines to family and peer interactions, we confront sociological issues daily. The task of this book and of your instructor is to help you see world events and your personal life from a sociological perspective. Unless you learn how to look at our social world with an analytical lens, many of its most intriguing features will be missed.

The social world you face in the job markets of the 21st century is influenced by changes and forces that are easy to miss. Like the wind, which can do damage even if the air is unseen, social structures are themselves so taken for granted that it is easy to miss them. However, their effects can be readily identified. Sociology provides new perspectives, helping students understand their families, their friends their work lives, their leisure, and their place in a diverse and changing world.

A few of you will probably become sociology majors. Others will find the subject matter of this course relevant to your personal and professional lives. Some of the reasons the authors of this book and your own professor chose to study sociology many years ago are the factors that inspire undergraduates today to choose a major in sociology: learning about the social world from a new perspective; working with people and groups; developing knowledge, inquiry, and interpersonal skills; and learning about social life, from small groups to global social systems. As the broadest of the social sciences, sociology has a never-ending array of fascinating subjects to study. This book touches only the surface of what the field has to offer and the exciting things you can do with this knowledge. These same considerations motivated us and gave us direction in writing this introductory book.

Where This Book Is Headed

A well-constructed course, like an effective essay, needs to be organized around a central question, one that spawns other subsidiary questions and intrigues the participants. The problem with introductory courses in many disciplines is that there is no central question and thus no coherence to the course. They have more of a flavor-of-the-week approach (a different topic each week), with no attempt at integration. We have tried to correct that problem in this text.

The Social World Model

For you to understand sociology as an integrated whole rather than a set of separate chapters in a book, we have organized the chapters in this book around the *social world model:* a conceptual model that demonstrates the relationships between individuals (micro level); organizations, institutions, and subcultures (meso level); and national societies and global structures (macro level). At the beginning of each chapter, a visual diagram of the model will illustrate this idea as it relates to the topic of that chapter, including how issues related to the topic have implications at various levels of analysis in the social world. For example, socialization is explored in Chapter 4 as a part of the whole social world, influencing and being affected by other parts of society. No aspect of society exists in a vacuum. On the other hand, this model does not assume that everyone always gets along or that relationships are always harmonious or supportive. Sometimes, different parts of the society are in competition for resources, and intense conflict and hostility may be generated.

This micro- to macro-level analysis is a central concept in the discipline of sociology. Many instructors seek first and foremost to help students develop a *sociological imagination,* an ability to see the complex links between various levels of the social system from the micro level of close relationships to the macro level of globalization. This is a key goal of this book. Within a few months, you may not remember all of the specific concepts or terms that have been introduced, but if the way you see the world has been transformed during this course, a key element of deep learning has been accomplished. Learning to see things from alternative perspectives is a precondition for critical thinking. This entire book attempts to help you recognize connections between your personal experiences and problems and larger social forces of society. Thus, You will be learning to take a new perspective on the social world in which you live.

A key element of that social world is diversity. We live in societies in which there are people who differ in a host of ways: ethnicity, socioeconomic status, religious background, political persuasion, gender, sexual orientation, and so forth. Diversity is a blessing in many ways to a society because the most productive and creative organizations and societies are those that are highly diverse. This is the case because people with different backgrounds solve problems in very different ways. When people with such divergences come together, the outcome of their problem solving can create new solutions to vexing problems. However, diversity often creates challenges as well. Misunderstanding and "we" versus "they" thinking can divide people. These issues are explored throughout this book. We now live in a global village, and in this book, you will learn something about how people on the other side of the village live and view the world.

We hope you enjoy the book and get as enthralled with sociology as we are. It genuinely is a fascinating field of study.

Jeanne H. Ballantine

Jeanne H. Ballantine
Wright State University

Keith A. Roberts

Keith A. Roberts
Hanover College

Your authors—teaching "outside the box."

Instructors

How to Make This Book Work for You

Special features woven throughout each chapter support the theme of the book. These will help students comprehend and apply the material and make the material more understandable and interesting. These features are also designed to facilitate deep learning, to help students move beyond rote memorization and increase their ability to analyze and evaluate information.

For students to understand both the comparative global theme and sociology as an integrated whole rather than as a set of separate chapters in a book, we have organized the chapters in this book around the *social world model*: a conceptual model that demonstrates the relationships between individuals (micro level); organizations, institutions, and subcultures (meso level); and national societies and global structures (macro level). At the beginning of each chapter, a visual diagram of the model illustrates this idea as it relates to the topic of that chapter, including how issues related to the topic have implications at various levels of analysis in the social world.

"Think About It"

So that students can become curious, active readers, we have posed questions at the outset of each chapter that we hope are relevant to everyday life but that are also tied to the micro-meso-macro levels of analysis that serve as the theme of the book. The purpose is to transform students from passive readers who run their eyes across the words into curious, active readers who read to answer a question and to be reflective. Active or deep reading is key to comprehension and retention of reading material. Instructors can also use this feature in or out of class to encourage students to think critically about the implications of what they have read. Instructors might want to ask students to write a paragraph about one of these questions before coming to class each day. These questions might also provide the basis for in-class discussions.

Students should be encouraged to start each chapter by reading and thinking about these questions, looking at the topics in the chapter, and asking some questions of their own. This will mean they are more likely to stay focused, remember the material long-term, and be able to apply it to their own lives.

"What's Coming in This Chapter?"

Each chapter begins with a simple listing of the key topic headings. Research on deep reading shows that if students have an overview of what is to come and begin to ask questions and become active as readers at the outset, they comprehend and retain more of the material. This new feature is added in response to requests by reviewers of the text.

A Global Perspective and the Social World Model

We are part of an ever-shrinking world, a global village. What happens in distant countries not only is news the same day but also affects relatives living in other countries, the cost of goods, work and travel possibilities, and the balance of power in the world. Instead of simply including cross-cultural examples of strange and different peoples, this book incorporates a global perspective throughout. This is done so students can see how others live different but rewarding lives and so they can see the connections between others' lives and their own. Students will need to think about and relate to the world globally in future roles as workers, travelers, and global citizens. Our analysis illustrates the interconnections of the world's societies and their political and economic systems, and demonstrates that what happens in one part of the world affects others. For instance, if a major company in the area moves much of its operations to another country with cheaper labor, jobs are lost, and the local economy is hurt.

This approach attempts to instill interest, understanding, and respect for different groups of people and their lifestyles. Race, class, and gender are an integral part of understanding the diverse social world, and these features of social life have global implications. The comparative global theme is carried throughout the book in headings and written text, in examples, and in boxes and selection of photos. As students read this book, they should continually think about how the experiences in their private world are influenced by and may influence events at other levels: the community, organizations and institutions, the nation, and the world.

Opening Vignettes

Chapters typically open with an illustration relevant to the chapter content. For instance, in Chapter 2, "Examining the Social World," the case of Hector, a Brazilian teenager living in poverty in a *favela*, is used to illustrate research methods and theory. In Chapter 4, "Socialization," there is the case of Phoebe Prince, a 15-year-old immigrant from Ireland, who was so harassed and bullied by peers that she hung herself. Chapter 7 begins with a discussion of the royal wedding of Prince William and Kate Middleton. Chapter 8 begins with an actual account of trafficking in body parts, examining the ethnic implications of the practice. These vignettes are meant to interest students in the upcoming subject matter by helping them relate to a personalized story. In several cases, including Hector's story, the vignettes serve as illustrations throughout the chapters.

"Thinking Sociologically" Questions

Following major topics, students will find questions that ask them to think critically and apply the material just read to some aspect of their lives or the social world. The purpose of this feature is to encourage students to apply the ideas and concepts in the text to their lives and to develop critical thinking skills, shown to help understanding and retention. These questions can be the basis for in-class discussions and can be assigned as questions to start interesting conversations with friends and families to learn how the topics relate to students' own lives. Note that some of these questions have a miniature icon—a small version of the chapter-opening

model—signifying that these questions reinforce the theme of micro, meso, and macro levels of social influence.

"Engaging Sociology"

Perhaps the most innovative feature is called "Engaging Sociology"—and the double entendre is intentional. We want students to think of sociology as engaging and fun, and these features are designed to engage—to draw students into active analysis of a table, application of a population pyramid to the business world, taking a survey to understand why differences in social and cultural capital make first-generation students feel alienated on a college campus, and reading a map and learning to analyze the patterns. This feature offers opportunities for students to engage in some quantitative data analysis—a major new emphasis in teaching sociology.

Key Concepts, Examples, and Writing Style

Key terms that are defined and illustrated within the running narrative and that appear in the Glossary are in **bold**. Other terms that are defined but are of less significance are italicized. The text is rich in examples that bring sociological concepts to life for student readers. Each chapter has been student tested for readability. Both students and reviewers describe the writing style as reader-friendly, often fascinating, and not watered down.

Special Features

Although there are numerous examples throughout the book, featured inserts provide more in-depth illustrations of the usefulness of the sociological perspective to understand world situations or events with direct relevance to a student's life. There are four kinds of special features. "Sociology in Our Social World" features focus on a sociological issue or story, often with policy implications. "Sociology Around the World" features take readers to another part of the globe to explore how things are different from (or the same as) what they might experience in their own lives. "Sociologists in Action" features appear in many chapters and examine profiles of contemporary sociologists who are working in the field. This helps students grasp what sociologists can actually do with sociology.

Technology and Society

Nearly every chapter examines issues of technology that are relevant to that chapter. We have especially sought out materials that have to do with the Internet and with communications technology.

Social Policy and Becoming an Active Citizen

Some chapters include discussion of social policy issues: an effort to address the concerns about public sociology and the relevance of sociological findings to current social debates. Further, because students sometimes feel helpless to know what to do about social issues that concern them at macro and meso levels, we have concluded every chapter with a few ideas about how they might become involved as active citizens, even as undergraduate students. Suggestions in the "Contributing to Our Social World: What Can We Do?" sections may be assigned as service learning or term projects or simply used as suggestions for ways students can get involved on their own time.

Summary Sections and Discussion Questions

Each chapter ends with a brief "What Have We Learned?" summary to ensure mastery of the chapter's core material. The summary is followed with probing questions that ask students to go beyond memorization of terms to apply and use sociology to think about the world. Research indicates that unless four discrete sections of the brain are stimulated, the learning will not be long term and deep but short term and surface (Zull 2002). These questions are carefully crafted to activate all four critical sections of the brain.

A Little (Teaching) Help From Our Friends

Whether the instructor is new to teaching or an experienced professor, there are some valuable ideas that can help invigorate and energize the classroom. The substantial literature on teaching methodology tells us that student involvement is key to the learning process. Built

into this book are discussion questions and projects that students can report on in class. In addition, there are a number of suggestions in the supplements and teaching aids for active learning in large or small classes.

Instructor Resources Site

The Instructor Resources Site (**www.sagepub.com/osw condensed3e**) contains a number of helpful teaching aids, from goals and objectives for chapters to classroom lecture ideas, active learning projects, collaborative learning suggestions, and options for evaluating students. Suggestions for the use of visual materials—videos, transparencies, and multimedia—are also included.

Test Bank

The test bank allows for easy question sorting and exam creation. It includes multiple-choice, true-false, short-answer, and essay questions. In keeping with the deep-learning thrust of this book, however, the test questions will have more emphasis on application skills than on rote memorization—the latter being a too-common characteristic of test banks.

PowerPoint Slides

Because visuals are an important addition to classroom lectures, recognizing the varying learning styles of students, PowerPoint slides that include lecture outlines and relevant tables, maps, diagrams, pictures, and short quotes are included in the Instructor Resources Site for instructors to use in the classroom.

Student Study Site

To further enhance students' understanding of and interest in the material, we have created a student website to accompany the text. This website includes the following:

- **Podcasts and audio clips** that cover important topics and are designed to supplement key points within the text;
- Carefully selected, web-based **video resources** for use in independent or classroom-based explorations of key topics;

- **Flashcards** that allow for easy reviewing of key terms and concepts;
- **Self-quizzes** that can be used to check students' understanding of the material or can be sent in to the professor for a grade;
- **Web exercises** that direct students to various sites on the web and ask them to apply their knowledge to a particular topic;
- *This American Life* radio segments that illustrate each chapter's concepts;
- **"Learning From Journal Articles"** features that include original research from SAGE journal articles and teach students how to read and analyze a journal article;
- Interesting and relevant **recommended readings** for course assignments, papers, research, group work, and class discussion;
- A list of **recommend websites** that students can explore for research or their own edification;
- Information on how to create **photo essays**;
- and much more!

Visit **www.sagepub.com/oswcondensed3e**.

What Is Different About This *Condensed* Edition?

The title of this book, like the subtitles of each chapter, plays on double entendre. The world has indeed condensed—becoming more accessible and interconnected, with communication and transportation making possible contacts with and travel to the most remote parts of the globe. That reality comes through in this book. However, this book is also a condensed version of our longer introductory book, *Our Social World*. We did surveys of sociologists to find out what was essential and what was dispensable. The one thing that was not dispensable was the thematic nature of the book—that we absolutely not turn this into another "core concepts" book that focuses on memorization of concepts rather than transformative learning through perspective taking. We were committed to making this a book that avoids the typical cross between a dictionary and an encyclopedia. Like the more comprehensive book, this is a coherent essay on the sociological imagination, understood globally. Moreover, many "brief" books are edited and reduced by developmental editors rather than by the authors. That is not true of this volume. The authors used a fine scalpel to refine use of language, cut some boxed features, reduced the size and number of photos, and kept an eye on both quality of the text and cost to students of the final product.

There are 17 new boxed features in this book. The "Applied Sociologists at Work" feature has been replaced by "Sociologists in Action"—with more emphasis on policy work in many of the new additions.

In this revision we have reorganized several chapters and updated all data, added many new studies, and included new emphases in sociology. The addition of discussions on deaf subcultures in the chapter on culture (Chapter 3) and obesity in several chapters are examples of this. Most chapters have *extensive* updates involving nearly 800 new references. Chapter 11, for example, has new material with more than 120 new citations (dozens of dated references were dropped); Chapter 10 has 84 new ones; Chapter 13 has 93. There are also dozens of new photos in this edition.

The section opener that more clearly frames "institutions" was new to the last edition. It has been well received and has undergone minor improvements. We had discovered that our first editions—and almost all other introductory texts—have done a notoriously poor job of defining institutions; we have focused on clarifying this important concept. Considerable attention has also been given to clarifying and simplifying definitions throughout the book and determining what should be in the glossary. The core elements of the book—with the unifying theme and the social world model at the beginning of every chapter—have not changed.

Finally, although we have been told that the writing was extraordinarily readable, we have tried to simplify sentence structure in a number of places. In short, we have tried to respond to what we heard from all of you—both students and instructors (and, yes, we *do* hear from students)—to keep this book engaging and accessible.

A Personal Note to the Instructor

We probably share many of the same reasons for choosing sociology as our careers. Our students also share these reasons for finding sociology a fascinating and useful subject: learning about the social world from a new perspective; working with people and groups; developing a range of knowledge, inquiry, and interpersonal skills; and learning the broad and interesting subject matter of sociology, from small groups to societies. In this book, we try to share our own enthusiasm for the subject with students. The following explains what we believe to be unique features of this book and some of our goals and methods for sharing sociology. We hope you share our ideas and find this book helps you meet your teaching and learning goals.

What Is Distinctive About This Book?

What is truly distinctive about this book? This is a text that tries to break the mold of the typical textbook synthesis, the cross between an encyclopedia and a dictionary. *Our Social World, Condensed* is a unique course text that is a coherent essay on the sociological imagination—understood globally. We attempt to radically change the feel of the introductory book by emphasizing coherence, an integrating theme, and current knowledge about learning and teaching, as we present traditional content. Instructors will not have to throw out the well-honed syllabus and begin from scratch, but they can refocus each unit so it stresses understanding of micro-level personal troubles within the macro-level public issues framework. Indeed, in this book, we make clear that the public issues must be understood as global in nature.

Here is a text that engages students. *They* say so! From class testing, we know that the writing style, the structure of chapters and sections, the "Thinking Sociologically" features, the wealth of examples, and other pedagogical aids help students stay focused, think about the material, and apply it to their lives. It neither bores them nor insults their intelligence. It focuses on deep learning rather than memorization. It develops sociological skills of analysis rather than emphasizing memorization of vocabulary. Key concepts and terms are introduced but only in the service of a larger focus on the sociological imagination. The text is both personal and global. It speaks to sociology as a science as well as addressing public or applied aspects of sociology. It has a theme that provides integration of topics as it introduces the discipline. This text is an analytical essay, not a disconnected encyclopedia.

As one of our reviewers noted,

Unlike most textbooks I have read, the breadth and depth of coverage in this one is very impressive. It challenges the student with college-level reading. Too many textbooks seem to write on a high school level and give only passing treatment to most of the topics, writing in nugget-sized blocks. More than a single definition and a few sentences of support, the text forces the student deep into the topics covered and challenges them to see interconnections.

Normally, the global-perspective angle within textbooks, which seemed to grow in popularity in the mid-to-late 1990s, was implemented by using brief and exotic examples to show differences between societies—a purely comparative approach rather than a globalization treatment. They gave, and still give to a large extent, a token nod to diversity. This textbook, however, forces the student to take a broader look at similarities and differences in social institutions around the world and at structures and processes operating in all cultures and societies.

So our focus in this book is on deep learning, especially expansion of students' ability to role-take or "perspective-take." Deep learning goes beyond the content of concepts and terms and cultivates the habits of thinking that allow one to think critically. Being able to see things from the perspective of others is essential to doing sociology, but it is also indispensible to seeing weaknesses in various theories or recognizing blind spots in a point of view. Using the sociological imagination is one dimension of role-taking because it requires a step back from the typical micro-level understanding of life's events and fosters a new comprehension of how meso- and macro-level forces—even global ones—can shape the individual's life. Enhancement of role-taking ability is at the core of this book because it is a *prerequisite* for deep learning in sociology and it is the core competency needed to "*do*" sociology. One cannot do sociology unless one can see things from various positions and points of view in on the social landscape.

This may sound daunting for some student audiences, but we have found that instructors at every kind of institution have had great success with the book because of the writing style and teaching tools used throughout. We have made some strategic decisions based on these principles of learning and teaching. We have focused much of the book on higher-order thinking skills rather than on memorization and regurgitation. We want students to learn to think sociologically: to apply, analyze, synthesize, evaluate, and comprehend the interconnections of the world through a globally informed sociological imagination. However, we think it is also essential to do this with an understanding of how students learn.

Many introductory-level books offer several theories and then provide a critique of the theory. The idea is to teach critical thinking. We have purposefully refrained from extensive critique of theory (although some does occur) for several reasons. First, providing critique to beginning-level students does not really teach critical thinking. It trains them to memorize someone else's critique. Furthermore, it simply confuses many of them, leaving students with the feeling that sociology is really just contradictory ideas and the discipline really does not have anything firm to offer. Teaching critical thinking needs to be done in stages, and it needs to take into account the building steps that occur before effective critique is possible. That is why we focus on the concept of deep learning. We are working toward building the foundations that are necessary for sophisticated critical thought at upper levels in the curriculum.

Therefore, in this beginning-level text, we have attempted to focus on a central higher-order or deep-learning skill—synthesis. Undergraduate students need to grasp this before they can fully engage in evaluation. Deep learning involves understanding of complexity, and some aspects of complexity need to be taught at advanced levels. While students at the introductory level are often capable of synthesis, complex evaluation requires some foundational skills. Thus, we offer contrasting theories in this text, and rather than telling what is wrong with each one, we encourage students through "Thinking Sociologically" features to analyze the use of each and to focus on honing synthesis and comparison skills.

Finally, research tells us that learning becomes embedded in memory and becomes long-lasting only if it is related to something that learners already know. If they memorize terms but have no unifying framework to which they can attach those ideas, the memory will not last until the end of the course, let alone until the next higher-level course. In this text, each chapter is tied to the social world model that is core to sociological thinking. At the end of a course using this book, we believe that students will be able to explain coherently what sociology is and construct an effective essay about what they have learned from the course as a whole. Learning to develop and defend a thesis, with supporting logic and evidence, is another component of deep learning. A text that is mostly a dictionary does not enhance that kind of cognitive skill.

Organization and Coverage

Reminiscent of some packaged international tours, in which "it is Day 7 so this must be Paris," many introductory courses seem to operate on the principle that it is Week 4 so this must be deviance week. Students do not sense any integration, and at the end of the course, they have trouble remembering specific topics. This book is different. A major goal of the book is to show the integration between topics in sociology and between parts of the social world. The idea is for students to grasp the concept of the interrelated world. A change in one part of the social world affects all others, sometimes in ways that are mutually supportive and sometimes in ways that create intense conflict.

Although the topics are familiar, the textbook is organized around levels of analysis, explained through the social world model. This perspective leads naturally to a comparative approach and discussions of diversity and inequality.

Each chapter represents a part of the social world structure (society, organizations and groups, and institutions) or a process in the social world (socialization, stratification, and change). Chapter order and links between chapters clarify this idea. Part I (Chapters 1 and 2) introduces the student to the sociological perspective and tools of the sociologist: theory and methods. Part II (Chapters 3–6) examines "Social Structure, Processes, and Control," exploring especially processes such as socialization, interaction, networks, and the *rationalization* of society. Part III (Chapters 7–9) covers the core issue of inequality in society, with emphasis on class, race or ethnicity, and gender. Part IV (Chapters 10–12) turns to the structural dimensions of society, as represented in institutions. Unlike most section openers, which are limited to one page, the section opener on institutions is more substantial, and we recommend that you include the section opener in your assignments regardless of which institutions you cover. It defines institutions, examines their contribution to society at the meso level, and explains the strong ties between them. Rather than trying to be all-encompassing, we examine family, education and religion, and politics and economics to help students understand how structures affect their lives. We do not cover sports, science, mass media, health, or military in separate chapters, but aspects of emerging institutions are woven into many chapters. It was a painful decision to cut our coverage of material from the comprehensive book, but attention to length and cost required hard choices. Part V (Chapters 13 and 14) turns to social dynamics: how societies change. Population patterns, urbanization and environmental issues, social movements, technology, and other aspects of change are included.

As instructors and authors, we value books that provide students with a well-rounded overview of approaches to the field. Therefore, this book takes an eclectic theoretical approach, drawing on the best insights of various theories and stressing that multiple perspectives enrich our understanding. We give attention to most major theoretical perspectives in sociology: structural-functional and conflict theories at the meso and macro levels of analysis and symbolic interaction and rational choice theories at the micro and meso levels of analysis. Feminist, postmodern, and ecological theories are discussed where relevant to specific topics. Each of these is integrated into the broad social world model, which stresses development of a sociological imagination.

The book includes 14 chapters plus additional online materials, written to fit into a semester or quarter system. It allows instructors to use the chapters in order or to alter the order, because each chapter is tied into others through the social world model. We strongly recommend that Chapter 1 be used early in the course because it introduces the integrating model and explains the theme. Otherwise, the book has been designed for flexible use. Instructors may also want to supplement the core book with other materials, such as those suggested in the Instructors' Resources on CD-ROM. Each chapter, for example, has an online exercise that helps students grasp the practical, public implications of sociology. While covering all of the key topics in introductory sociology, the cost and size of a "condensed" book allows for this

flexibility. Indeed, for a colorful introductory-level text, the cost of this book is remarkably low—roughly a third of the cost of some other popular introductory texts.

A Unique Program Supporting Teaching of Sociology

There is one more way in which *Our Social World* has been unique among introductory sociology textbooks. In 2007, the authors teamed with SAGE to start a new program to benefit the entire discipline. Using royalties from *Our Social World* and *Our Social World, Condensed,* there is a new award program called the SAGE Teaching Innovations and Professional Development Awards Fund. It is designed to prepare a new generation of scholars within the teaching movement in sociology. People in their early career stages (graduate students, assistant professors, newly minted PhDs) can be reimbursed $500 each for expenses entailed while attending the daylong American Sociological Association (ASA) Section on Teaching and Learning in Sociology's pre-conference workshop. The workshop is the day before ASA meetings. In 2007, 13 people received this award and benefited from an extraordinary workshop on learning and teaching. Subsequently joined by 23 other SAGE authors who support this program from textbook royalties, a total of 152 young scholars have been beneficiaries by 2013. We are pleased to have had a hand in initiating and continuing to support this program.

We hope you find this book engaging. If you have questions or comments, please contact us.

Jeanne H. Ballantine

Jeanne H. Ballantine
Wright State University
jeanne.ballantine@gmail.com

Keith A. Roberts

Keith A. Roberts
Hanover College
robertsk@hanover.edu

Acknowledgments

Knowledge is improved through careful, systematic, and constructive criticism. The same is true of all writing. This book is of much greater quality because we had such outstanding critics and reviewers. We, therefore, wish to honor and recognize the outstanding scholars who served in this capacity. These scholars are listed on this page and the next.

We also had people who served in a variety of other capacities: drafting language for us for special features, doing library and Internet research to find the most recent facts and figures, and reading or critiquing early manuscripts. Contributors include Khanh Nguyen, Kate Ballantine, Jessica Hoover, Kelly Joyce, Justin Roberts, Kent Roberts, Susan Schultheis, and Vanessa M. Simpson. Authors of original essays written specifically for this book include Jackie Bergdahl, Jeremy Castle, Leslie Elrod, Thomas Horejes, Melanie Hughes, Wendy Ng, Mike Norris, Robert Pellerin, Elise Roberts, and Saher Selod. The religion chapter has some new approaches to denominationalism and to church polity, and David Yamane drafted early versions of much of that. Perhaps the most important contributor to this edition was Kathleen Korgan. She helped revise the discussion of public and applied sociology, wrote or found authors for "Sociologists in Action" features (many from her coauthored books, *Sociologists in Action* and *The Engaged Sociologist*), revised and updated the "Contributing to Our Social World" features, wrote the discussion questions at the end of each chapter, and designed exercises that are online and involve students in thinking about and even doing public sociology.

Both of us are experienced authors, and we have worked with some excellent people at other publishing houses. However, the team at SAGE Publications was truly exceptional in support, thoroughness, and commitment to this project. Our planning meetings have been fun, intelligent, and provocative. Ben Penner, former SAGE acquisitions editor, signed us for this project; he was followed by Jeff Lasser, who continued to provide excellent support. Other folks who have meant so much to the quality production of this book include Lauren Johnson, the sociology editorial assistant; Brittany Bauhaus, our production manager; Melinda Masson, copy editor extraordinaire and in reality a research assistant; John O'Neill, permissions editor; Jonathan Mason, sociology marketing manager; Erica DeLuca, senior marketing manager; Claudia Hoffman, managing editor; Scott Hooper, manufacturing manager; Ravi Balasuriya, art director; Steven Martin, vice president—production; Michele Sordi, vice president and editorial director—books acquisitions; Helen Salmon, former director—books marketing; David Horwitz, vice president—sales; Tom Taylor, vice president—marketing and sales; and Blaise Simqu, president and chief executive officer. We have become friends and colleagues with the staff at SAGE Publications. They are all greatly appreciated.

Thanks to the following reviewers:

Sabrina Alimahomed
University of California at Riverside

Richard Ball
Ferris State University

Fred Beck
Illinois State University

David L. Briscoe
University of Arkansas at Little Rock

Jamie M. Dolan
Carroll College (MT)

Obi N. I. Ebbe
The University of Tennessee at Chattanooga

Lance Erickson
Brigham Young University

Stephanie Funk
Hanover College

Loyd R. Ganey, Jr.
Western International University

Mary Grigsby
University of Missouri at Columbia

Chris Hausmann
University of Notre Dame

Todd A. Hechtman
Eastern Washington University

Keith Kerr
Blinn College

Elaine Leeder
Sonoma State University

Jason J. Leiker
Utah State University

Stephen Lilley
Sacred Heart University

David A. Lopez
California State University at Northridge

Ali Akbar Mahdi
Ohio Wesleyan University

Gerardo Marti
Davidson College

Laura McCloud
The Ohio State University

Meeta Mehrotra
Roanoke College

Melinda S. Miceli
University of Hartford

Leah A. Moore
University of Central Florida

Katy Pinto
California State University at Dominguez Hills

R. Marlene Powell
University of North Carolina at Pembroke

Suzanne Prescott
Central New Mexico Community College

Olga Rowe
Oregon State University

Paulina Ruf
Lenoir-Rhyne University

Sarah Samblanet
Kent State University

Martha L. Shockey-Eckles
Saint Louis University

Toni Sims-Muhammad
University of Louisiana at Lafayette

Terry L. Smith
Harding University

Frank S. Stanford
Blinn College

Tracey Steele
Wright State University

Rachel Stehle
Cuyahoga Community College

Amy Stone
Trinity University

John Stone
Boston University

Stephen Sweet
Ithaca College

Ruth Thompson-Miller
Texas A&M University

Timothy A. Ulrich
Seattle Pacific University

Thomas L. VanValey
Western Michigan University

Connie Veldink
Everett Community College

Chaim I. Waxman
Rutgers University

Debra Welkley
*California State University
at Sacramento*

Debra Wetcher-Hendricks
Moravian College

Deborah J. White
Collin County Community College

Jake B. Wilson
University of California at Riverside

Laurie Winder
Western Washington University

Robert Wonser
College of the Canyons

Luis Zanartu
Sacramento City College

John Zipp
University of Akron

PART I

Understanding Our Social World

The Scientific Study of Society

Would you like to know why friends and family get along (or do not), how groups form and who becomes a leader, and where your country fits into the world? What can we learn from studying our everyday lives? Can understanding sociology make our lives better?

Studying sociology takes us on a trip to a deeper level of understanding of ourselves and our social world. Like your sociology professor, this book argues that sociology is valuable because it gives us new perspectives on our personal and professional lives and because sociological insights and skills can help all of us make the world a better place. It is relevant to everything we do—enhancing our competence and our quality of life.

By the time you finish reading the first two chapters, you should have an initial understanding of what sociology is, how it can help you understand your social world, why the field is worth taking your time to explore, and how sociologists know what they know. We invite you to take a seat and come to see our social world through the fascinating lens of sociology.

CHAPTER 1

Sociology

A Unique Way to View the World

Sociology involves a transformation in the way one sees the world—learning to recognize the complex connections between our intimate personal lives, large organizations, national structures, and global events.

Our Social World Model

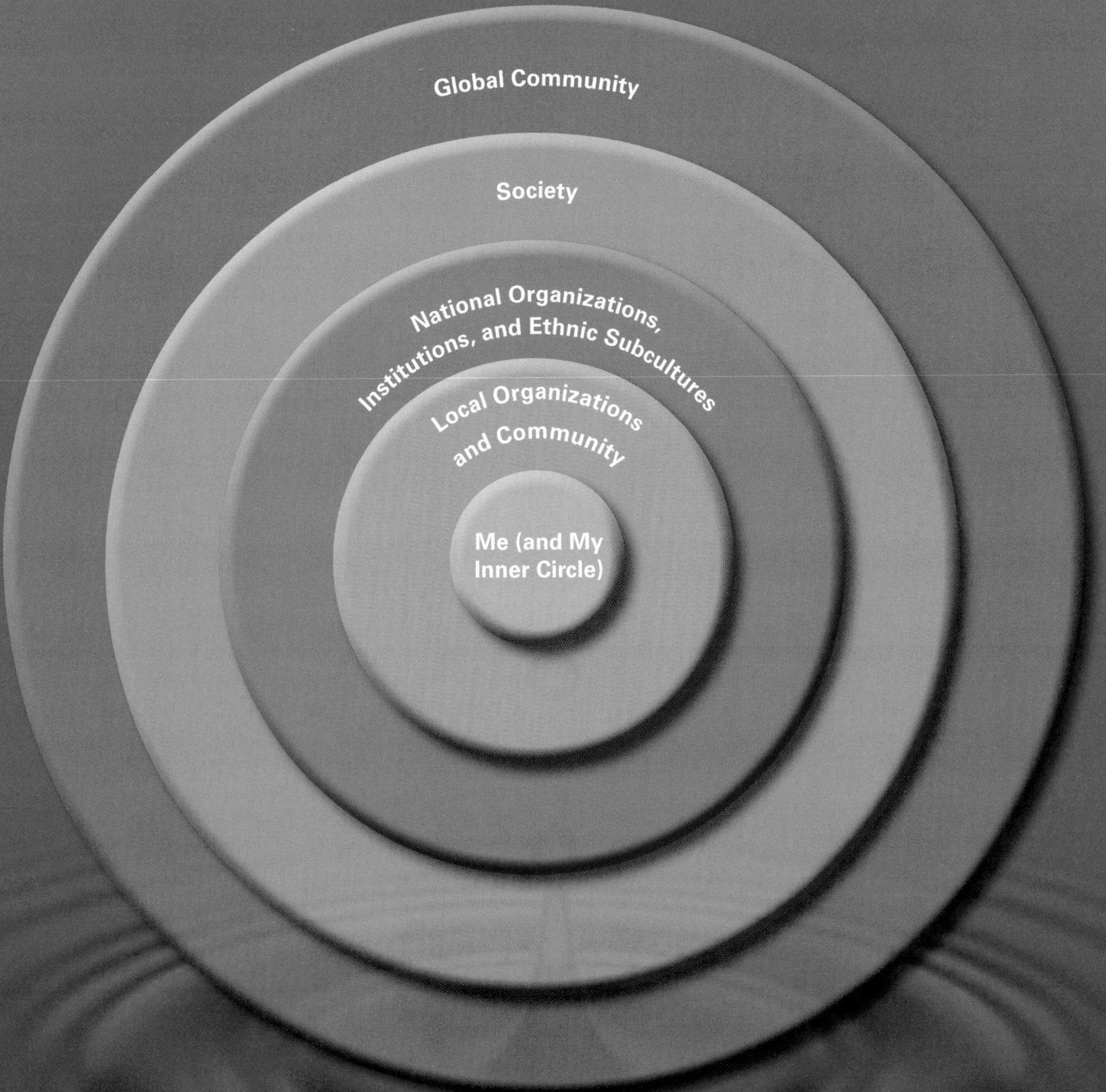

Global Community

Society

National Organizations,
Institutions, and Ethnic Subcultures

Local Organizations
and Community

Me (and My
Inner Circle)

This model illustrates a core idea carried throughout the book—the way in which your own life is shaped by your family, community, society, and world, and how it influences them in return. Understanding this model can make you more aware of your social world and a more knowledgeable and effective person.

Think About It	
Micro: Self and Inner Circle	How can sociology help me understand my own life and my sense of self?
Micro: Local Community	How can sociology help me to be a more effective employee and citizen in my community?
Meso: National Institutions; Complex Organizations; Ethnic Groups	How do sociologists help us understand and even improve our lives in families, classrooms, and health care organizations?
Macro: National Society	How do national loyalty and national policies affect my life?
Macro: Global Community	How might global events impact my life?

What's coming in this chapter?

What Is Sociology?

Why Does Sociology Matter?

The Social World Model

It may win the prize for the strangest place to get a back massage, but according to a recent scientific article, twins experience a lot of back rubs while still in the womb (Weaver 2010). Scientists studied the movement of five pairs of twin fetuses using ultrasonography, a technique that visualizes internal body structures, and found that by the fourth month of gestation, twin fetuses begin reaching for their "womb-mates." By 18 weeks, they spend more time touching their neighbors than themselves or the walls of the uterus. Fetuses that have single-womb occupancy also tend to touch the walls of the uterus a good deal to make contact with the mother. Nearly 30% of the movement of twins is directed toward their companions. Movements toward the partner, such as stroking the back of the head, are more sustained and more precise than movements toward themselves, such as touching their own mouths or other facial features. As the authors put it, they are "wired to be social" (Castiello et al. 2010). In short, humans are innately social creatures.

Strange as it may seem, the social world is not merely something that exists outside of us. As the story of the twins illustrates, the social world is also something we carry inside of us. We are part of it, we reflect on it, and we are influenced by it, even when we are alone. The patterns of the social world engulf us in ways both subtle and obvious, with profound implications for how we create order and meaning in our lives. The point is that we need others—and that is where sociology enters.

Sometimes it takes a dramatic and shocking event for us to realize just how deeply embedded we are in a social world that we take for granted. "It couldn't happen in the United States," read typical world newspaper accounts. "This is something you see in Bosnia, Kosovo, the Middle East, Central Africa, and other war-torn areas. . . . It's hard to imagine this happening in the economic center of the United States." Yet on September 11, 2001, shortly after 9 A.M., a commercial airliner crashed into a New York City skyscraper, followed a short while later by another pummeling into the paired tower. This mighty symbol of financial wealth—the World Trade Center—collapsed. After the dust settled and the rescue crews finished their gruesome work, nearly 3,000 people were dead or unaccounted for. The world as we knew it changed forever that day. This event taught U.S. citizens how integrally connected they are with the international community.

Following the events of September 11, the United States launched its highly publicized War on Terror, and many

Within hours of their birth in October 2010, Jackson and Audrey became highly fussy if the nurses tried to put them in separate bassinets. At one point shortly after birth, both babies were put in a warmer, and Jackson cried until he found Audrey, proceeding to intertwine his arms and legs with hers. Twins, like all humans, are hardwired to be social and in relationships with others.

These signs were put up right after the September 11 attacks on the World Trade Center by people looking for missing loved ones. The experience of New Yorkers was alarm, fear, grief, and confusion—precisely the emotions that the terrorists sought to create. Terrorism disrupts normal social life and daily routines and undermines security. It provides an effective tool for those with less power.

terrorist strongholds and training camps were destroyed. Still, troubling questions remain unanswered. Why did this extremist act occur? How can such actions be deterred in the future? How do the survivors recover from such a horrific event? Why was this event so completely disorienting to Americans and to the world community? These terrorist acts horrified people because they were unpredicted and unexpected in a normally predictable world. They violated the rules that foster our connections to one another. They also brought attention to the discontent and disconnectedness that lie under the surface in many societies—discontent that can come to the surface and express itself in hateful violence. Such discontent and hostility are likely to continue until the root causes are addressed.

Terrorist acts represent a rejection of the modern civil society we know. The terrorists themselves see their acts as justifiable, but few outside their inner circle can sympathize with their behavior. When terrorist acts occur, we struggle to fit such events into our mental picture of a just, safe, comfortable, and predictable social world. The events of September 11 forced U.S. citizens to realize that, although they may see a great diversity among themselves, people in other parts of the world view them as all the same. U.S. citizens may also be despised for what they represent—consumerism, individualism, freedom of religion, and tolerance of other views. The United States is a world power, yet its values challenge and threaten the views of many people around the world. For many U.S. citizens, a sense of loyalty to the nation was deeply stirred by the events of 9/11. Patriotism abounded. So, in fact, the nation's people became more connected as a reaction to an act against the United States.

Most of the time, we live with social patterns that we take for granted as routine, ordinary, and expected. These social patterns, or social facts, characterize social groups. The social expectations are external to each individual (unlike motivations or drives), but they still guide (or constrain) our behaviors and thoughts. Without shared expectations between humans about proper patterns of behavior, life would be chaotic. Connections require some basic rules of interaction, and these rules create routine and safe normality in everyday interaction. For the people in and around the World Trade Center, the social rules governing everyday life broke down that awful day.

Socialization and Norms

This chapter examines the social ties that make up our social world, as well as sociology's focus on those connections. We will learn what sociology is and why it is valuable to study it, how sociologists view the social world and what they do, how studying sociology can help us in our everyday life, and how the social world model is used as a framework to understand the topics we will study throughout this book.

What Is Sociology?

According to the American Sociological Association (2009:5),

> **Sociology** is *the study of social life, social change, and the social causes and consequences of human behavior.* Sociologists investigate the structure of groups, organizations, and societies and how people interact within these contexts. Since all human behavior is social, the subject matter of sociology ranges from the intimate family to the hostile mob; from organized crime to religious traditions; from the divisions of race, gender, and social class to the shared beliefs of a common culture.

Sociologists conduct scientific research on social relationships and problems that range from tiny groups of two people to national societies and global social networks.

An athletic team teaches members to interact, cooperate, develop awareness of the power of others, and deal with conflict. Here, children experience ordered interaction in the competitive environment of a football game. What values, skills, attitudes, and assumptions about life and social interaction do you think these young boys are learning?

Unlike the discipline of psychology, which focuses on attributes, motivations, and behaviors of individuals, sociology tends to focus on group patterns. Whereas a psychologist might try to explain behavior by examining the personality traits of individuals, a sociologist would examine the position of different people within the group and how positions influence what individuals do. Sociologists seek to analyze and explain why people interact with others and belong to groups, how groups work, why some groups have more power than other groups, how decisions are made, and how groups deal with conflict and change. From the early beginnings of their discipline (discussed in Chapter 2), sociologists have asked questions about the rules that govern group behavior; about the causes of social problems, such as child abuse, crime, and poverty; and about why nations declare war and kill each other's citizens.

Two persons interacting—*dyads*—are the smallest units sociologists study. Examples of dyads include roommates discussing their classes, a professor and a student going over an assignment, a husband and a wife negotiating their budget, and two children playing. Next in size are small groups consisting of three or more interacting people—a family, a neighborhood or peer group, a classroom, a work group, or a street gang—where most people know each other. Then come increasingly larger groups—organizations such as sports or scouting clubs, neighborhood associations, and local religious congregations. Among the largest groups contained within nations are ethnic groups and national organizations, including economic, educational, religious, health, and political systems. Nations themselves are still larger and can sometimes involve hundreds of millions of people. In the past several decades, social scientists have also pointed to globalization, the process by which the entire world is becoming a single interdependent entity. Of particular interest to sociologists are how these various groups are organized, how they function, why they sometimes conflict, and how they influence one another.

Thinking Sociologically

Identify several dyads, small groups, and large organizations to which you belong. Did you choose to belong, or were you born into membership in the group? How does each group influence decisions you make?

Ideas Underlying Sociology

Most people share certain ideas with others that they all take for granted. For example, the idea that one action can cause something else is a core idea in all science. Sociologists also share several principles that they take for granted about the social world. These ideas about humans and social life are supported by considerable evidence and considered to be true. Understanding these core principles helps us see how sociologists approach the study of people in groups.

People are social by nature. This means that humans seek contact with other humans, interact with each other, and influence and are influenced by the behaviors of one another. Furthermore, humans need groups to survive. Although a few individuals may become socially isolated as adults, they could not have reached adulthood without sustained interactions with others. The central point here is that we become who we are because other people and groups constantly influence us.

People live much of their lives belonging to social groups. It is in social groups that we interact with family, friends, and work groups; learn to share goals and to cooperate with others; develop identities that are influenced by our group affiliations; obtain power over others—or are relatively powerless; and have conflicts with others over resources. Our individual beliefs and behaviors, our experiences, our observations, and the problems we face are derived from connections to our social groups.

Interaction between the individual and the group is a two-way process in which each influences the other. In our family or on a sports team, we can influence the shape and direction of groups, just as the group provides the rules and establishes the expected behaviors for individuals.

Recurrent social patterns, ordered behavior, shared expectations, and common understandings among people characterize groups. Consider the earlier example of the chaos created by 9/11. This event was so troubling because it was unexpected and out of the normal range of expectations. Normally, a degree of continuity and recurrent behavior is present in human interactions, whether in small groups, large organizations, or society.

The processes of conflict and change are natural and inevitable features of groups and societies. No group can remain unchanged and hope to perpetuate itself. To survive, groups must adapt to changes in the social and physical environment. Yet rapid change often comes at a price. It can lead to conflict within a society— between traditional and new ideas and between groups that have vested interests in particular ways of doing things. Rapid change can give rise to protest activities; changing in a controversial direction or failing to change fast enough can spark conflict, including revolution. The recent Arab Spring demonstrations illustrate the desire for rapid change from long-standing dictatorships, springing from citizens' discontent with corrupt or authoritarian rule. The problem

is finding acceptable replacement governments to take over what has been overthrown.

As you read this book, keep in mind these basic ideas that form the foundation of sociological analysis: People are social; they live and carry out activities largely in groups; interaction influences both individual and group behavior; people share common behavior patterns and expectations; and processes such as change and conflict are always present. In several important ways, sociological understandings provide new lenses for looking at our social world.

Sociology Versus Common Sense

Common sense refers to ideas that are so completely taken for granted that they have never been seriously questioned and seem to be sensible to any reasonable person.

A Palestinian and an Israeli work together. Although their governments are hostile to one another, the people themselves often have very different sentiments toward those on the other side of the divide.

 Understanding Social Patterns   Sociological Perspective

Commonsense interpretations based on personal experience are an important means of processing information and deciding on a course of action. Although all of us hold such ideas and assumptions, that does not mean they are accurate. Sociologists assume human behavior can be studied scientifically; they use scientific methods to test the accuracy of commonsense beliefs and ideas about human behavior and the social world. Would our commonsense notions about the social world be reinforced or rejected if examined with scientifically gathered information? Many commonsense notions are actually contradictory:

Birds of a feather flock together	Opposites attract
Absence makes the heart grow fonder	Out of sight, out of mind
Look before you leap	He who hesitates is lost
You can't teach an old dog new tricks	It's never too late to learn
Above all to thine own self be true	When in Rome, do as the Romans do
Variety is the spice of life	Never change horses in midstream
Two heads are better than one	If you want something done right, do it yourself
You can't tell a book by its cover	The clothes make the man
Haste makes waste	Strike while the iron is hot
There's no place like home	The grass is always greener on the other side

Source: Eitzen and Zinn (1998).

These are examples of maxims that people use as "absolute" guides to live by. They become substitutes for real analysis of situations. The fact is that all of them are accurate *at some times, in some places, about some things.* Sociological thinking and analysis are about studying the conditions in which maxims such as these hold and do not hold (Eitzen and Zinn 1998).

Human tragedy can result from false commonsense beliefs. For example, the Nazi genocide and the existence of slavery both have their roots in false beliefs about racial superiority. Often citizens interpret news stories through a "commonsense" lens rather than digging deeper for better analysis.

The difference between common sense and sociology is that sociologists test their beliefs by gathering information and analyzing the evidence in a planned, objective, systematic, and replicable (repeatable) scientific way. Indeed, they set up studies to see if they can disprove what they think is true. This is the way science is done. Consider the following examples of commonsense beliefs about the social world and some research findings about these beliefs.

Thinking Sociologically

What are some other commonsense sayings you know that contradict one another? You may also want to take the common sense quiz online at **www.sagepub.com/oswcondensed3e.** Do some of the answers surprise you? Why?

Social Science Findings and Commonsense Beliefs

Sometimes we hold commonsense beliefs that are a part of common knowledge. However, sometimes these beliefs are disproven by research. Here are some examples:

Belief: Most of the differences in the behaviors of women and men are based on "human nature"; men and women are just plain different from each other. Research shows

The Wodaabe society in Niger in sub-Saharan Africa illustrates that our notions of masculinity and femininity—which common sense tells us are innate and universal—are actually socially defined, variable, and learned. Wodaabe men are known for their heavy use of makeup to be attractive to women.

that biological factors certainly play a part in the behaviors of men and women, but the culture (beliefs, values, rules, and way of life) that people learn as they grow up determines who does what and how biological tendencies are played out. A unique example illustrates this: In the nomadic Wodaabe tribe in Africa, women do most of the heavy work while men adorn themselves with makeup, sip tea, and gossip (Beckwith 1983; Loftsdottir 2004). Each year the group holds a festival where men show their white teeth and the whites of their eyes to attract a marriage partner. Such dramatic variations in behavior of men and women around the world are so great that it is impossible to attribute behavior simply to biology or human nature alone.

Belief: As developing countries modernize, the lives of their female citizens improve. This is generally false. In fact, the status of women in many developed and developing countries is getting worse. Women make up roughly 51% of the world's approximately 7 billion people and account for two thirds of the world's hours at work (National Geographic Society 2011). However, in no country for which data are available do they earn what men earn, and sometimes the figures show women earning less than 50% of men's earnings for similar work. Women hold many unpaid jobs in agriculture, and they own only 1% of the world's property. Furthermore, of the world's 775 million illiterate adults, two thirds are women (World Factbook 2012c). Only 79.7% of the world's women over age 15 can read and write compared to 88.6% of men. Illiteracy rates for women in South Asia, sub-Saharan Africa, and the Middle East are highest in the world, implying lack of access to education. These are only a few examples of the continuing poor status of women in many countries (World Factbook 2012c). The "commonsense" idea is clearly wrong.

Belief: Given high divorce rates in the United States and Canada, marriages are in serious trouble. The highest divorce rates in the United States are found among those below the average on education and who live in poverty. Those who are middle class or higher tend to have extremely stable marriages (Luscombe 2010; Pew Research Center 2010). Although overall the divorce rate in North America is high, the rate of marriage is also one of the highest in the world. If the fear-of-commitment hypothesis were true, it is unlikely the marriage rate would be so high. Moreover, even those who have been divorced tend to remarry. Despite talk about decline and despite genuine concern about high levels of marital failure, Americans now spend more years of their lives in marriage than at any other time in history. Divorce appears to be seen as rejection of a particular partnership rather than as rejection of marriage itself (Coontz 2011a; Wallerstein and Blakeslee 1996). The divorce rate reached a peak in the United States in 1982 and has declined modestly since that time (Newman 2009).

Literacy is a major issue for societies around the globe. These Chinese children are learning to read, but in many developing countries, boys have more access to formal education than girls have. The commonsense notion is that most children in the world, boys and girls, have equal access to education, yet many children, especially girls, do not gain literacy.

As these examples illustrate, many of our commonsense beliefs are challenged by social scientific evidence. On examination, the social world is often more complex than our commonsense understanding of events, which is based on limited evidence. Throughout history, there are examples of beliefs that seemed obvious at one time but have been shown through scientific study to be mistaken. Social scientific research may also confirm some common notions about the social world. For example, the unemployment rate among African Americans in the United States is higher than that among most other groups; women with similar education and jobs earn less income than men with the same education and jobs; excessive consumption of alcohol is associated with high levels of domestic violence; and people tend to marry others who are of a similar social class. The point is that the discipline of sociology provides a method to assess the accuracy of our commonsense assumptions about the social world.

To improve lives of individuals in societies around the world, decision makers must rely on an accurate understanding of the society. Accurate information gleaned from sociological research can be the basis for more rational and just social policies—policies that better meet the needs of all groups in the social world. The sociological perspective, discussed in the following, helps us gain reliable understanding.

Theory and Practice

The Sociological Imagination

Events in our social world affect our individual lives. If we are unemployed or lack funds for our college education, we may say this is a personal problem. Yet broader social issues are often at the root of our situation. The sociological perspective holds that we can best understand our personal experiences and problems by examining their broader social context—by looking at the big picture.

Individual problems (or private troubles) are rooted in social or public issues (what is happening in the social world outside of one's personal control). C. Wright Mills (1959) called the ability to understand this *complex inter-active relationship between micro-level individual experiences and macro-level public issues* the **sociological imagination**. For Mills, many personal experiences can and should be interpreted in the context of large-scale forces in the wider society.

Consider, for example, the personal trauma caused by being laid off from a job. This personal trauma is a common situation in today's economy. The unemployed person often experiences feelings of inadequacy or lack of worth. This, in turn, may produce stress in a marriage or even result in divorce. These conditions not only are deeply troubling to the person most directly affected but also are related to wider political and economic forces in society. The unemployment may be due to corporate downsizing or to a corporation taking operations to another country where labor costs are cheaper and where there are fewer environmental regulations on companies. People may blame themselves or each other for personal troubles such as unemployment or a failed marriage, believing that they did not try hard enough. Often, they do not see the connection between their private lives and larger economic forces beyond their control. They fail to recognize the public issues that create private troubles.

Families also experience stress as partners have, over time, assumed increasing responsibility for their mate's and their children's emotional and physical needs. Until the second half of the 20th century, the community and the extended family unit—aunts, uncles, grandparents, and cousins—assumed more of that burden. Extended families continue to exist in countries where children settle near their parents, but in modern urban societies, both the sense of community and the connection to the extended family are greatly diminished. There are fewer intimate ties to call on for help and support. Divorce is a very personal condition for those affected, but it can be understood far more clearly when considered in conjunction with the broader social context of economics, urbanization, changing gender roles, lack of external support, and legislated family policies.

As we learn about sociology, we will come to understand how social forces shape individual lives, and this will help us understand aspects of everyday life we take for granted. In this book, we will investigate how group life influences our behaviors and interactions and why some individuals follow the rules of society and others do not. A major goal is to help us incorporate the sociological perspective into our way of understanding the social world and our place in it. Indeed, the notion of sociological imagination—connecting events from the global and national level to the personal and intimate level of our own lives—is the core organizing theme of this book.

Thinking Sociologically

How does poverty, a war, or a recession cause personal troubles for someone you know? Give examples of situations in which it is not adequate to explain the causes of personal troubles by examining only the personal characteristics of those affected.

Questions Sociologists Ask—and Don't Ask

Sociologists ask questions about human behavior in social groups and organizations—questions that can be studied scientifically. Sociologists, like other scientists, cannot answer certain questions—philosophical questions about the meaning of life, the existence of God, the ethical implications of stem cell research, or the morality of physician-assisted suicide. What sociologists *do* ask are questions about people in social groups and organizations—questions that can be studied scientifically. How people feel about the above issues can be determined (the percentage of people who approve of stem cell research, for example), but sociologists cannot say what are right and wrong answers to such value-driven opinions. What effect does holding certain ideas or adhering to certain ethical standards have on the behavior and attitudes of people? For example, are people more likely to obey rules if they believe that there are consequences for their actions in an afterlife? Sociologists might ask who gets an abortion, why do they do so, and how does society as a whole view abortion? These are matters of fact that a social scientist can explore. However, sociologists avoid making ethical judgments about whether abortion is sometimes acceptable or always wrong. Such a judgment is a question of values, not one that can be answered through scientific analysis. The question about the morality of abortion is very important to many people, but it is based on philosophical or theological rationale, not on sociological findings.

Financial Crisis

Likewise, what are the circumstances around individuals becoming drunk and drunken behavior? This question is often tied more to social environment than to alcohol itself. Note that a person might be very intoxicated at a fraternity party but behave differently at a wedding reception, where the expectations for behavior are very different. The researcher does not make judgments about whether use of alcohol is good or bad or right or wrong and avoids—as much as possible—opinions regarding responsibility or irresponsibility. The sociologist does, however, observe variations in the use of alcohol in social situations and resulting behaviors. The focus is on facts and on causality.

The Social Sciences: A Comparison

Not so long ago, our views of people and social relationships were based on stereotypes, intuition, superstitions, supernatural explanations, and traditions passed on from one generation to the next. Natural sciences first used the scientific method, a model later adopted by social sciences. Social scientists, including anthropologists, psychologists, economists, cultural geographers, historians, and political scientists, apply the scientific method to study social relationships, to correct misleading and harmful misconceptions about human behaviors, and to guide policy decisions. Consider the following examples of specific studies a social scientist might conduct. These are followed by a brief description of the focus of sociology as a social science.

Consider anthropological studies that focus on garbage, studying what people discard to understand their patterns of life (Bond 2010). Anthropology is closely related to sociology. In fact, the two areas have common historical roots. *Anthropology* is the study of humanity in its broadest context. There are four subfields within anthropology: physical anthropology (which is related to biology), archaeology, linguistics, and cultural anthropology (sometimes called *ethnology*). This last field has the most in common with sociology. Cultural anthropology focuses on the culture, or way of life, of the society being studied, and uses methods appropriate to understanding culture.

A political scientist studies opinion poll results to predict who will win the next election, how various groups of people are likely to vote, or how elected officials will vote on proposed legislation. *Political science* is concerned with government systems and power—how they work, how they are organized,

What is acceptable or unacceptable drinking behavior varies according to the social setting. Binge drinking, losing consciousness, vomiting, or engaging in sexual acts while drunk may be a source of storytelling at a college party but be offensive at a wedding reception. Sociologists study different social settings and how the norms of acceptability vary in each, but they do not make judgments about those behaviors.

forms of government, relations between governments, who holds power and how they obtain it, how power is used, and who is politically active. Political science overlaps with sociology, particularly in the study of political theory and the nature and the uses of power.

After wiring research subjects to a machine that measures their physiological reaction to a violent film

The Meth Epidemic

Psychology as a discipline tends to focus on individuals, including such fields as sensation, perception, memory, and thought processes. In this study, the researcher is using specialized equipment and a computer to measure how the eye and the brain work together to help create depth perception.

clip, a psychologist asks them questions about what they were feeling. *Psychology* is the study of individual behavior and mental processes (e.g., sensation, perception, memory, and thought processes). It differs from sociology in that it focuses on individuals, rather than on groups, institutions, and societies as sociology does. Although there are different branches of psychology, most psychologists are concerned with individual motivations, personality attributes, attitudes, perceptions, abnormal behavior, mental disorders, and stages of normal human development.

An economist studies the banking system and market trends, trying to determine what will remedy the global recession. *Economists* analyze economic conditions and explore how people organize, produce, and distribute material goods. They are interested in supply and demand, inflation and taxes, prices and manufacturing output, labor organization, employment levels, and comparisons of industrial and nonindustrial nations.

What these examples of social sciences—sociology, anthropology, psychology, political science, and economics—have in common is that they study aspects of human behavioral and social life. Social sciences share many common topics, methods, concepts, research findings, and theories, but each has a different focus or perspective on the social world. Each of these social sciences relates to topics studied by sociologists, but sociologists focus on human interaction, groups, and social structure, providing the broadest overview of the social world.

Thinking Sociologically

Consider issues such as the condition of poverty in developing countries or homelessness in North America. What question(s) might different social sciences ask about these problems?

Why Does Sociology Matter?

Sociology is important not only to understand our relationships with other people and because it can inform social policy decisions, but because one can also pursue a career in sociology or use skills developed through sociology in a wide range of career fields.

Why Study Sociology?

The sociological perspective helps us to be more effective as we carry out our roles as significant others, workers, friends, family members, and citizens. For example, an employee who has studied sociology may better understand how to work with groups and how the structure of the workplace affects individual behavior, how to approach problem solving, and how to collect and analyze data. Likewise, a schoolteacher trained in sociology may have a better understanding of classroom management, student motivation, causes of poor student learning that have roots outside the school, and other variables that shape the professional life of teachers and the academic success of students. Consider the example in the next "Sociology in Our Social World," which explores how each high school clique's behavior might be quite logical in certain circumstances. *Burnouts and Jocks in a Public High School* explores a social environment very familiar to most of us.

Two ingredients are essential to the study of our social world: a keen ability to observe what is happening in the social world and a desire to find answers to the question of why it is happening. The value of sociology is that it affords us a unique perspective from which to examine the social world, and it provides methods to answer important questions about human interaction, group behavior, and social structure. The practical significance of the sociological perspective is that it

- fosters greater self-awareness, which can lead to opportunities to improve one's life;
- encourages a more complete understanding of social situations by looking beyond individual explanations to include group analyses of behavior;

Dress Codes

Sociology in Our Social World

Burnouts and Jocks in a Public High School

High schools are big organizations made up of smaller friendship networks and cliques; a careful examination can give us insight into the tensions that exist as the groups struggle for resources and power in the school.

Sociologist Penelope Eckert (1989) focused on two categories of students that exist in many high schools in North America: "burnouts" and "jocks." The burnouts defied authorities, smoked in the restrooms, refused to use their lockers, made a public display of not eating in the school cafeteria, and wore their jackets all day. Their open and public defiance of authority infuriated the jocks—the college prep students who participated in choir, band, student council, and athletics and who held class offices. The burnouts were disgusted with the jocks. In their view, by constantly sucking up to the authorities, the jocks received special privileges and, by playing the goody-two-shoes role, made life much more difficult for the burnouts.

Despite their animosity toward one another, the goal of both groups was to gain more autonomy from the adult authorities who constantly bossed students around. As the burnouts saw things, if the jocks would have even a slight bit of backbone and stand up for the dignity of students as adults, life would be better for everyone. The burnouts believed that school officials should earn their obedience—not demand it just because they were older and held a certain position. The burnouts maintained their dignity by affirming that they did not recognize bossy adults as authorities. Wearing coats all day was one way to emphasize the idea that "I'm just a visitor in this school."

The jocks, for their part, became irritated at the burnouts when the latter caused trouble and were belligerent with authorities; then the administration would crack down on everyone, and no one had any freedom. Jocks found that if they did what the adults told them to do—at least while the adults were around—they got a lot more freedom. When the burnouts got defiant, however, the principal got mad and removed everyone's privileges.

Sociologist Eckert (1989) found that the behavior of both groups was quite logical for their circumstances and ambitions. Expending energy as a class officer or participating in extracurricular activities is a rational behavior for college preparatory students because those leadership roles help students get into the college of their choice.

However, those activities do not help students get a better job in a factory in town. In fact, hanging out at the bowling alley makes far more sense. For the burnouts, having friendship networks and acquaintances in the right places is more important to achieving their goals than a class office listed on their résumé.

Eckert's (1989) method of gathering information was effective in showing how the internal dynamics of schools—conflicts between student groups—were influenced by outside factors such as working- and upper-middle-class status. Continuing research in this field upholds Eckert's findings on the importance cliques play in shaping school behavior (Gallup and Hern'ndez 2005). Like Eckert, Bonnie Barber, Jacquelynne Eccles, and Margaret Stone (2001) followed various friendship cliques starting in 10th grade in a Michigan high school. The jocks in their study were the most integrated to mainstream society in adult life. The burnouts (or criminals, as they are labeled in Barber's research) were most likely to have been arrested or incarcerated, showing that the propensity to defy authority figures may carry on into adult life.

These studies show that sociological analysis can help us understand some ways that connections between groups—regardless of whether they are in conflict or harmony—shape the perceptions, attitudes, and behaviors of people living in this complex social world.

- helps people understand and evaluate problems by enabling them to view the world systematically and objectively rather than in strictly emotional or personal terms;
- cultivates an understanding of the many diverse cultural perspectives and how cultural differences are related to behavioral patterns;
- provides a means to assess the impact of social policies;
- reveals the complexities of social life and provides methods of inquiry to study them; and
- provides useful skills in interpersonal relations, critical thinking, data collection and analysis, problem solving, and decision making.

What Do Sociologists Do?

Your first encounter with a sociologist is probably in the classroom. About three quarters of sociologists work in higher education settings, teaching and doing research. However, sociologists are employed in a variety of other settings as well. Table 1.1 illustrates that a significant portion of sociologists work in business, government, and social service agencies (American Sociological Association 2006).

College graduates with a bachelor of arts degree in sociology who seek employment immediately after college are most likely to find their first jobs in social services, administrative assistantships, or some sort of management position. The first jobs of sociology majors are indicated in Figure 1.1. With a master's or a doctorate degree, graduates usually become college teachers, researchers, clinicians, or consultants.

Consider your professor. The duties of professors vary depending on the type of institution and the level of courses offered. In addition to teaching classes, other activities include preparing for classes, preparing and grading exams and assignments, advising students, serving on committees, keeping abreast of new research in the field, and conducting and publishing research studies. This "publish or perish" task is deemed the most important activity for faculty in some universities.

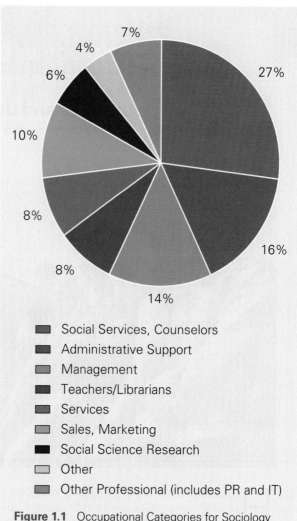

- ■ Social Services, Counselors
- ■ Administrative Support
- ■ Management
- ■ Teachers/Librarians
- ■ Services
- ■ Sales, Marketing
- ■ Social Science Research
- ■ Other
- ■ Other Professional (includes PR and IT)

Figure 1.1 Occupational Categories for Sociology Graduates' First Jobs

Source: Based on *21st Century Careers With an Undergraduate Degree in Sociology* by American Sociological Association (2009).

Sociologists who work outside of academia, applied sociologists, use their knowledge and research skills to address the needs of businesses, nonprofit organizations, and government. In government jobs, they provide data such as population projections for education and health care planning. In social service agencies, such as police departments, they help address causes of deviant behavior, and in health agencies, they may be concerned with doctor-patient interactions. Public and applied sociology are important aspects of the field. The "Sociologists in Action" features you will find throughout the book provide some examples of what one can do with a sociology degree. In addition, at the end of most chapters you will find a section discussing policy examples and implications related to that chapter topic. Table 1.2 provides some ideas of career paths for graduates with a degree in sociology.

Table 1.1 Where Sociologists Are Employed

Place of Employment	Percentage Employed
College or university	75.5
Government (all positions)	7.1
Private, for-profit business	6.2
Not-for-profit public service organizations	7.6
Self-employed	0.4

Source: American Sociological Association (2006).

Table 1.2   What Can You Do With a Sociology Degree?

Business or Management	Human Services	Education
Market researcher	Social worker	Teacher
Sales manager	Criminologist	Academic research
Customer relations	Gerontologist	Administration
Manufacturing representative	Hospital administrator	School counselor
Banking or loan officer	Charities administrator	Policy analyst
Data processor	Community advocate or organizer	College professor
Attorney		Dean of student life
Research	**Government**	**Public Relations**
Population analyst	Policy advisor or administrator	Publisher
Surveyor	Labor relations	Mass communications
Market researcher	Legislator	Advertising
Economic analyst	Census worker	Writer or commentator
Public opinion pollster	International agency representative	Journalist
Interviewer	City planning officer	
Policy researcher	Prison administrator	
Telecommunications researcher	Law enforcement	
	FBI agent	
	Customs agent	

Source: American Sociological Association (2009).

Note: Surveys of college alumni with undergraduate majors in sociology indicate that this field of study prepares people for a broad range of occupations. Notice that some of these jobs require graduate or professional training. For further information, contact your department chair or the American Sociological Association in Washington, D.C., for a copy of *21st Century Careers With an Undergraduate Degree in Sociology.*

Thinking Sociologically

From what you have read so far, how might sociological topics (e.g., social interaction skills and knowledge of how groups work) be useful to you in your anticipated major and career?

What Employers Want

Ask employers what they want in a new hire, and the focus is likely to be on writing, speaking, and analytical skills—especially when the new employee will be faced with complex problems. In addition, acceptance of other cultures, the ability to work effectively in diverse teams, and the ability to gather and interpret quantitative information are key needs. Table 1.3 on page 16 indicates in the left column what employers want from college graduates; the right column indicates the skills and competencies that are part of most sociological training. Compare the two, noting the high levels of overlap.

These competencies show that skills stressed in the sociology curriculum are also those sought by employers: an ability to understand and work with others, research and computer skills, planning and organizing, oral and written communication competency, and critical thinking skills (WorldWideLearn 2007).

We now have a general idea of what sociology is and what sociologists do. It should be apparent that sociology is a broad field of interest; sociologists study all aspects of human social behavior. The next section of this chapter shows how the parts of the social world that sociologists study relate to each other, and it outlines the model you will follow as you continue to learn about sociology.

Thinking Sociologically

Imagine that you are a mayor, legislator, police chief, or government official. You make decisions based on information gathered by social science research rather than on your own intuition or assumptions. What are some advantages to this decision-making method?

Table 1.3   What Employers Want and What Sociology Majors Can Deliver

Employers Who Want Colleges to "Place More Emphasis" on Essential Learning Outcomes		Traits and Knowledge That Are Developed in Most Sociological Training
Knowledge of human culture	**% Seeking**	**Skills and Competencies**
1. Global issues	72	➤ Knowledge of global issues. ➤ Sensitivity to diversity and differences in cultural values and traditions.
2. The role of the United States in the world	60	➤ Sociological perspective on the United States and world.
3. Cultural values and traditions— U.S. and global	53	➤ Understanding diversity. ➤ Working with others (ability to work toward a common goal).
Intellectual and practical skills	**% Seeking**	**Skills and Competencies**
4. Teamwork skills in diverse groups	76	➤ Effective leadership skills (ability to take charge and make decisions). ➤ Interpersonal skills (working with diverse coworkers).
5. Critical thinking and analytic reasoning	73	➤ Analytical and research skills. ➤ Organizing thoughts and information. ➤ Planning effectively (ability to design, plan, organize, and implement projects and to be self-motivated).
6. Written and oral communication	73	➤ Communication skills (listening, verbal and written communication). ➤ Working with peers. ➤ Effective interaction in group situations.
7. Information literacy	70	➤ Knowledge of how to find information one needs—online or in a library.
8. Creativity and innovation	70	➤ Flexibility, adaptability, and multitasking (ability to set priorities, manage multiple tasks, adapt to changing situations, and handle pressure).
9. Complex problem solving	64	➤ Ability to conceptualize and solve problems. ➤ Ability to be creative (working toward meeting the organization's goals).
10. Quantitative reasoning	60	➤ Computer and technical literacy (basic understanding of computer hardware and software programs). ➤ Statistical analysis.
Personal and social responsibility	**% Seeking**	**Skills and Competencies**
11. Intercultural competence (teamwork in diverse groups)	76	➤ Personal values (honesty, flexibility, work ethic, dependability, loyalty, positive attitude, professionalism, self-confidence, willingness to learn). ➤ Working with others Start (ability to work toward a common goal).
12. Intercultural knowledge (global issues)	72	➤ Knowledge of global issues.

Source: American Sociological Association (2009), Hansen and Hansen (2003) and WorldWideLearn (2007).

The Social World Model

Think about the different groups you depend on and interact with on a daily basis. You wake up to greet members of your family or your roommate. You go to a larger group—a class—that exists within an even larger organization—the college or university. Understanding sociology and comprehending the approach of this book requires a grasp of **levels of analysis**, that is, *social groups from the smallest to the largest.* It may be relatively easy to picture small groups such as a family, a sports team, or a sorority or fraternity.

These men carry the supplies for a new school to be built in their local community—Korphe, Pakistan. The trek of more than 20 miles up mountainous terrain was difficult, but their commitment to neighbors and children of the community made it worthwhile. The project was a local one (micro level), but it also was made possible by an international organization—Central Asia Institute.

It is more difficult to visualize large groups such as corporations—the Gap, Abercrombie & Fitch, Eddie Bauer, General Motors Company, or Starbucks—or organizations such as local or state governments. The largest groups include nations or international organizations, such as the sprawling networks of the United Nations or the World Trade Organization. Groups of various sizes shape our lives. Sociological analysis involves understanding these groups at various levels of analysis, and the connections between them.

The **social world model** helps us picture *the levels of analysis in our social surroundings as an interconnected series of small groups, organizations, institutions, and societies.* Sometimes, these groups are connected by mutual support and cooperation, but sometimes, there are conflicts and power struggles over access to resources. What we are asking you to do here and throughout this book is to develop a sociological imagination—the basic lens used by sociologists. Picture the social world as connected levels of increasingly larger circles. To understand the units or parts in each circle of the social world model, look at the social world model shown to the right and at the beginning of each chapter.

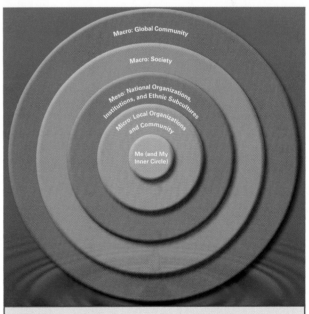

This social world model will be used throughout our book to illustrate how each topic fits into the big picture—our social world. The social world also has two main parts that occur at each level—social structures and social processes.

Social Structures

Picture the human body, held together by bones and muscles. The units that make up that body include the brain, heart, lungs, and kidneys. In a similar manner, **social units** are *interconnected parts of the social world ranging from small groups to societies.* These connect to make the **social structure**—*the stable patterns of interactions, statuses, roles, and organizations that provide stability for the society and bring order to individuals' lives.* Those social units include dyads, two people such as a husband and wife; small groups like the members of a family; community organizations including schools and faith communities; large-scale organizations such as political parties or state and national governments; and global societies such as the United Nations. All of these social units combine to make up a system that brings order to our lives. Think about these parallels

between the structure that holds together the human body and the structure that holds together societies and their parts.

Sometimes, however, the units in the social structure conflict. For example, a religion that teaches that birth control is wrong may conflict with the health care system regarding how to provide care to women. This issue has been in the news lately as many religious organizations have fought against the 2010 Affordable Care Act in the United States, which requires that employers provide birth control to those who wish to receive it.

Social institutions are the largest units that make up every society—*organized, patterned, and enduring sets of social structures that provide guidelines for behavior and help each society meet its basic survival needs.* Think about the idea that all societies have some form of family, education, religion, politics, economics, science, sports, health care, and military. These are the institutions that provide the setting for activities essential to human and societal survival. For example, we cannot survive without an economic institution to provide guidelines and a structure for meeting our basic needs of food, shelter, and clothing. Likewise, we would never make it to adulthood as functioning members of society without the family, the most basic of all institutions. Most social units you can think of fall under one of these institutions. Like the system of organs that make up our bodies—heart, lungs, kidneys, bladder—all social institutions are interrelated. Just as a change in one part of the body affects all others, a change in one institution affects the others.

The **national society**, one of the largest social units in our model, includes *a population of people, usually living within a specified geographic area, who are connected by common ideas and are subject to a particular political authority.* It also features a social structure with groups and institutions. In addition to having relatively permanent geographic and political boundaries, national societies have one or more languages and a unique way of life. In most cases, national societies involve countries or large regions where the inhabitants share a common identity as members. In certain other instances, such as contemporary Great Britain, a single national society may include several groups of people who consider themselves distinct nationalities (e.g., Welsh, English, Scottish, and Irish within the United Kingdom). Such multicultural societies may or may not be harmonious. Although a national society is one of the largest social units, it is still a subsystem of the interdependent global system.

This refugee mother and child from Mozambique represent the smallest social unit, a dyad. In this case, they are trying to survive with help from larger groups such as the United Nations.

Thinking Sociologically

Think about how a major conflict or change in your family (micro level) might affect your education, economic situation, or health care. How might change in one national institution such as health care affect change in another institution (such as the family or the economy)?

Social Processes

If social structure is similar to the human body's skeletal structure, social processes are similar to what keeps the body alive—beating heart, lungs processing oxygen, stomach processing nutrients. **Social processes** *take place through actions of people in institutions and other social units.* The process of socialization teaches individuals how to become productive members of society. It takes place through actions of families, educational systems, religious organizations, and other social units. Socialization is essential for the continuation of any society because it teaches members the thoughts and actions needed to survive in their society. Another process, conflict, occurs between individuals or groups over money, jobs, and other needed resources. The process of change is also a continuous pattern in every social unit; change in one unit affects other units of the social world, often in a chain reaction. For instance, change in the quality of health care can affect the workforce; a beleaguered workforce can affect the economy; instability in the economy can affect families, as breadwinners lose jobs.

Sociologists generally do not judge these social processes as good or bad. Rather, sociologists try to identify, understand, and explain processes that take place within social units. Picture these processes as overlying and penetrating our whole social world, from small groups to societies. Social units would be lifeless without the action brought about by social processes, just as body parts would be lifeless without the processes of electrical impulses shooting from the brain to each organ or the oxygen transmitted by blood coursing through our arteries to sustain each organ.

The Environment of Our Social World

Surrounding each social unit is an **environment**. It *includes everything that influences the social unit, such as its physical and organizational surroundings and technological innovations.* This does not refer to just our physical environment, but is actually much broader. Each unit has an environment to which it must adjust, just as each individual has a unique environment, including family, friends, and other social units.

Some parts of the environment are more important to the individual or social unit than others. Your local church, synagogue, or mosque is located in a community environment. That religious organization may seem autonomous and independent, but it depends on its national organization for guidelines and support; the local police force to protect the building from vandalism; and the local economy to provide jobs to members so that the members, in turn, can support the organization. If the religious education program is going to train children to understand the scriptures, the local schools are needed to teach the

children to read. A religious group may also be affected by other religious bodies, competing with one another for potential members from the community. These religious groups may work cooperatively—organizing a summer program for children or jointly sponsoring a holy-day celebration—or they may dfine one another as evil, each trying to stigmatize the other. Moreover, one local religious group may be composed primarily of professional and business people, and another group mostly of laboring people. The religious groups may experience conflict in part because they each serve different socioeconomic constituencies. The point is that to understand a social unit or the human body, we must consider the structure and processes within the unit, as well as the interaction with that unit's surrounding environment. A perfect relationship or complete harmony between the social units is unusual. Social units are often motivated by self-interests and self-preservation, with the result that they compete with other groups and units for resources (time, money, skills, energy of members). Therefore, social units within the society are often in conflict. Whether groups are in conflict or mutually supportive does not change their interrelatedness; units are interdependent. The nature of that interdependence is likely to change over time and can be studied using the scientific method.

Studying the Social World: Levels of Analysis

Picture for a moment your sociology class as a social unit in your social world. Students (individuals) make up the class, the class (a small group) is offered by the sociology department, the sociology department (a large group) is part of the college or university, the university (an organization) is located in a community and follows the practices approved by the social institution (education) of which it is a part, and education is an institution located within a nation. Practices the university follows are determined by a larger accrediting agency that provides guidelines and oversight for institutions. The national society, represented by the national government, is shaped by global events—technological and economic competition between nations, natural disasters, global warming, wars, and terrorist attacks. Such events influence national policies and goals, including policies for the educational system. Thus, global tensions and conflicts may shape the curriculum taught in the local classroom.

Each of these social units—from the smallest (the individual student) to the largest (society and the global system)—is referred to as a level of analysis (see Table 1.4 on page 20). These levels are illustrated in the social world model at the beginning of each chapter, and their relation to that chapter's content is shown through examples in the model.

 Advertising

 A Social Theory of War

Table 1.4   The Structure of Society and Levels of Analysis

	Level	Parts of Education
Micro-level analysis	Interpersonal	Sociology class; study group cramming for an exam
	Local organizations	University; sociology department
Meso-level analysis	Organizations and institutions	State boards of education; National Education Association
	Ethnic groups within a nation	Islamic madrassas or Jewish yeshiva school systems
Macro-level analysis	Nations	Policy and laws governing education
	Global community	World literacy programs

 MICRO-LEVEL ANALYSIS

A focus on *individual or small-group interaction in specific situations* is called **micro-level analysis**. Micro-level analysis is important because face-to-face interaction forms the basic foundation of all social groups and organizations to which we belong, from families to corporations to societies. We are members of many groups at the micro level.

To understand micro-level analysis, consider the problem of spousal abuse. Why does a person remain in an abusive relationship, knowing that each year thousands of people are killed by their lovers or mates and millions more are severely and repeatedly battered? To answer this, several possible micro-level explanations can be considered. One view is that the abusive partner has convinced this person that she is powerless in the relationship or that she "deserves" the abuse. Therefore, she gives up in despair of ever being able to alter the situation. The abuse is viewed as part of the interaction—of action and reaction—and the partners come to see abuse as what comprises "normal" interaction.

Another explanation for remaining in the abusive relationship is that the person may have been brought up in a family situation where battering was an everyday part of life. However unpleasant and unnatural this may seem to outsiders, it may be seen by the abuser or by the abused as a "normal" and acceptable part of intimate relationships.

Another possibility is that an abused woman may fear that her children will be harmed or that she will be harshly judged by her family or church if she "abandons" her mate. She may have few resources to make leaving the abusive situation possible. To study each of these possible explanations involves analysis at the micro level because each focuses on interpersonal interaction factors rather than on society-wide trends or forces. Meso-level analysis leads to quite different explanations for abuse.

 MESO-LEVEL ANALYSIS

Meso-level analysis involves looking at intermediate-sized *units smaller than the nation but larger than the local community or even the region*. This level includes national institutions (e.g., the economy of a country, the national educational system, or the political system within a country); nationwide organizations (e.g., a political party, a soccer league, or a national women's rights organization); nationwide corporations (e.g., Ford Motor Company or IBM); and ethnic groups that have an identity as a group (e.g., Jews, Mexican Americans, or the Lakota Sioux in the United States). Organizations, institutions, and ethnic communities are smaller than the nation or global social forces, but they are still beyond the everyday personal experience and control of individuals. They are intermediate in the sense of being too large for members to know everyone in the group, but they are not nation-states. For example, states in the United States, provinces in Canada, prefectures in Japan, or cantons in Switzerland are more accessible and easier to change than the national bureaucracies of countries. Thus, they are meso-level.

In discussing micro-level analysis, we used the example of domestic violence. We must be careful not to "blame the victim"—in this case, the abused person—for getting into an abusive relationship and for failing to act in ways that stop the abuse. To avoid blaming victims for their own suffering, many social scientists look for broader explanations of spousal abuse, such as the social conditions at the meso level of society that cause the problem (Straus, Gelles, and Steinmetz 2006). When a pattern of behavior in society occurs with increasing frequency, it cannot be understood solely from the point of view of individual cases or micro-level causes. Remember the sociological imagination. For instance, sociological findings show that fluctuations in spousal or child abuse at the micro level are related to levels of unemployment at the meso and macro levels. Frustration resulting in abuse erupts within families when poor economic conditions make it nearly impossible for people to find stable and reliable means of supporting themselves and their families. The message here is that economic issues must be addressed if violence in the home is to be lessened.

 MACRO-LEVEL ANALYSIS

Studying the largest social units in the social world, called **macro-level analysis**, involves looking at *entire nations*,

 Gastronationalism

global forces, and international social trends. Macro-level analysis is essential to our understanding of how larger societal forces and global events shape our everyday lives. A natural disaster, such as the 2011 tsunami off the coast of Japan or Hurricane Sandy on the east coast of the United States in 2012, can disrupt both production and supply chains. Because much of our cuisine is now imported from other parts of the world, something as simple as what we are able to put on our family dinner table may be affected by such a global event. Map 1.1 shows some of the most deadly natural disasters of the past few years. Likewise, a political conflict on the other side of the planet can lead to war, which means that a member of your family may be called up to active duty and sent into harm's way more than 7,000 miles from your home. Each member of the family may experience individual stress, have trouble concentrating, and feel ill with worry. The entire globe has become an interdependent social unit. If we are to prosper and thrive in the twenty-first century, we need to understand connections that go beyond our local communities.

Even patterns such as domestic violence, considered as micro- and meso-level issues earlier, can be examined at the macro level. Violence against women (especially rape) occurs at very different rates in different societies, with some societies being completely free of rape and others having a "culture

This photo depicts the damage following the catastrophic earthquake that hit Haiti on January 12, 2010. This event not only changed the lives of people in Haiti—one of the poorest countries in the world—but had ripple effects on economic exchange, relief efforts around the globe, and international trade. Those, in turn, can affect the cost of various products such as the foods you put on your table.

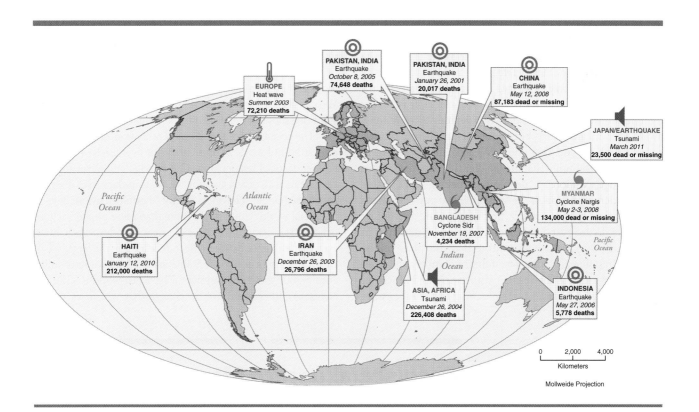

Map 1.1   The Deadliest Natural Disasters From January 2001 to April 2013

Source: EM-DAT emergency events database, Center for Research on the Epidemiology of Disasters. Map by Anna Versluis.

of rape" (Kristof and WuDunn 2009). Consider the 2013 case of a medical student in India who was gang-raped on a bus and subsequently died, creating an outpouring of concern about abuse of women. The most consistent predictor of violence against women is a macho conception of masculine roles and personality. A society or subgroup within society that teaches males that the finest expression of their masculinity is physical strength and domination is very likely to have battered women (Burn 2011; Lindow 2009). Societies that do not define masculinity in terms of dominance and control are virtually free of domestic violence and rape.

The point is that understanding individual human behavior often requires investigation of larger societal beliefs that support that behavior. Worldwide patterns may tell us something about a social problem and offer new lenses for understanding variables that contribute to a problem. Try the next "Engaging Sociology" activity to test your understanding of levels of analysis and the sociological imagination.

Thinking Sociologically

What factors influenced you to take this sociology class? Micro-level factors might include your advisor, your schedule, and a previous interest in sociology. At the meso and macro levels, what other factors influenced you?

Distinctions between each level of analysis are not always sharply delineated. The micro level shades into the meso level, and the lines between the meso level and the macro level are blurry. Still, it is clear that in some micro-level social units, you know everyone, or at least every member of the social unit is only two degrees of relatedness away. That means every person in the social unit knows someone whom you also know. We also all participate in meso-level social units that are smaller than the nation but can be huge. Millions of people may belong to the same religious denomination or the same political party. We have connections with those people, and our lives are affected by people we do not even know. Consider political activities in the United States and other countries that take place on the Internet. In political campaigns, millions of individuals join organizations such as the Tea Party movement and MoveOn.org. People living thousands of miles from one another were united financially and in spirit to support Obama-Biden or Romney-Ryan in the 2012 U.S. presidential election. Thus, the meso level is different from the micro level, but both influence us. The macro level is even more removed from the individual, but its impact can change our lives.

The social world model presented in the chapter opening illustrates the interplay of micro-, meso-, and macro-level forces, and Figure 1.2 shows how this micro-to-macro model should be seen as a continuum. In the next "Sociology Around the World" we examine a village in Tunisia to see how macro-level forces influence a meso-level local community and individual micro-level lives.

Thinking Sociologically

Place the groups to which you belong in a hierarchy from micro to meso to macro levels. Note how each social unit and its subunits exist within a larger unit until you reach the level of the entire global community.

The Social World Model and This Book

Throughout this book, the social world model will be used as the framework for understanding the social units, social processes, and surrounding environment. Each social unit and process is taken out, examined, and returned to its place in the interconnected social world model so that you can comprehend the whole social world and its parts, like putting a puzzle together. Look for the model at the beginning of every chapter. You can also expect the micro-, meso-, and macro-level dimensions of issues to be explored throughout the text.

The social world engulfs each of us from the moment of our birth until we die. Throughout our lives, each of us is part of a set of social relationships that provide guidelines for how we interact with others and how we see ourselves. This does not mean that human behavior is strictly determined by our links to the social world. Humans are more than mere puppets whose behavior is programmed by social structure. It does mean, however, that influence between the individual and the larger social world is reciprocal. We are influenced by and we have influence on our social environment. The social world is a human creation, and we can and do change that which we create.

Micro social units   Meso social units   Macro social units

Figure 1.2 The Micro-to-Macro Continuum

  Vaccinations   Linking Micro, Meso, and Macro

Engaging Sociology

Micro-Meso-Macro

Look at the list of various groups and other social units below. Identify which group would belong in each level—(1) micro, (2) meso, or (3) macro. The definitions should help you make your decisions, but keep in mind that not all social units fall clearly into one level. Answers are found online at www.sagepub.com/oswcondensed3e.

Micro-level groups: Small, local community social units in which everyone knows everyone or knows someone whom you also know.

Meso-level groups: Social units of intermediate size, usually large enough that many members may never have heard the names of many other members and may have little access to the leaders, yet not so large as to seem distant or the leaders unapproachable. If members do not know a leader themselves, they probably know someone who is friends with the leader.

Macro-level groups: Large social units, usually quite bureaucratic, which operate at a national or a global level. Most members are unlikely to know or have communicated with the leaders personally or know someone who knows them. The "business" of these groups is of international import and implication. A macro-level system is one in which *most* of the members are within at least five degrees of relatedness to each other—that is, they know someone who knows someone who knows someone who knows someone who knows the person in question.

Engaging with Sociology

Indicate for each item below the correct category: 1, 2, or 3.

1. Micro social units

_____ Your nuclear family

_____ The United Nations

_____ A local chapter of the Lions Club or the Rotary Club

_____ Your high school baseball team

_____ India

_____ NATO (North Atlantic Treaty Organization)

_____ The First Baptist Church in Muncie, Indiana

_____ The World Bank

_____ A family reunion

_____ Google, Inc. (international)

_____ The Department of Education for the Commonwealth of Kentucky

_____ The show choir in your local high school

_____ African Canadians

_____ The Dineh (Navajo) people

2. Meso social units
3. Macro social units

_____ Canada

_____ The Republican Party in the United States

_____ The World Court

_____ A fraternity at your college

_____ The International Monetary Fund (IMF)

_____ The Ministry of Education for Spain

_____ The Roman Catholic Church (with its headquarters at the Vatican in Rome)

_____ Australia

_____ The Chi Omega National Sorority

_____ Boy Scout Troop #3 in Marion, Ohio

_____ Al-Qaeda (an international alliance of terrorist organizations)

_____ The provincial government for the Canadian province of Ontario

_____ The United States of America

Most of these fall into clear categories, but some are "on the line," and one could legitimately place them in more than one group. See how your authors rate these at **www.sagepub.com/oswcondensed3e**. There is a second exercise online that asks you to apply these categories to identify some connections.

Sociology Around the World

Tunisian Village Meets the Modern World

This is a story of change as macro-level innovations enter a small traditional village. It illustrates how the social units of the social world model and the three levels of analysis enter into sociological analysis. As you read, try to identify both the units and levels of analysis being discussed and the impact of globalization on a community that cannot know what these changes will bring.

The workday began at dawn as usual in the small fishing village on the coast of Tunisia, North Africa. Men prepared their nets and boats for the day, while women prepared breakfast and dressed the young children for school. About 10 A.M., it began—the event that would change this picturesque village forever. Bulldozers arrived first, followed by trench diggers and cement mixers, to begin their overhaul of the village.

Villagers had suspected something was afoot when important-looking officials arrived two months earlier with foreign businessmen, followed by two teams of surveyors. Without their approval, the government had sold land that the village had held communally for generations to the foreigners so they could build a multimillion-dollar hotel and casino. When concerned citizens asked what was happening in their village, they were assured that their way of life would not change. The contractor from the capital city of Tunis said they would still have access to the beach and ocean for fishing. He also promised them many benefits from the hotel project—jobs, help from the government to improve roads and housing, and a higher standard of living.

The contractor had set up camp in a trailer on the beach, and word soon got around that he would be hiring some men for higher hourly wages than they could make in a day or even month of fishing. Rivalries soon developed between friends over who should apply for the limited number of jobs.

As the bulldozers moved in, residents had mixed opinions about the changes taking place in their village and their lives. Some saw the changes as exciting opportunities for new jobs and recognition of their beautiful village; others viewed the changes as destroying a lifestyle that was all they and generations before them had known.

Today, the village is dwarfed by the huge hotel, and the locals are looked on as quaint curiosities by the European tourists. Fishing has become a secondary source of employment to working in the hotel and casino or selling local crafts and trinkets to souvenir-seeking visitors. Many women are now employed outside the home by the hotel, creating new family structures as grandparents, unemployed men, and other relations take over child-rearing responsibilities.

To understand the changes in this one small village and other communities facing similar change, a sociologist uses the sociological imagination. This involves understanding the global, political, and economic trends that are affecting this village and its inhabitants (macro-level analysis). It requires comprehension of transformation of social institutions within the nation (meso-level analysis). Finally, sociological investigation explores how change impacts the individual Tunisian villagers (micro-level analysis).

To sociologically analyze the process of change, it is important to understand what is going on in this situation. The government officials and the international business representatives negotiated a lucrative deal to benefit both Tunisia and the business corporation. The community and its powerless residents presented few obstacles to the project from the point of view of the government, and in fact, government officials reasoned that villagers could benefit from new jobs. However, economic and family roles of the villagers—how they earned a living and how they raised their children—changed dramatically with the disruption to their traditional ways. The process of change began with the demand of people far from Tunisia for vacation spots in the sun. Ultimately, this process reached the village's local environment, profoundly affecting the village and everyone in it. For this Tunisian village, the old ways are gone forever.

It acts on us, and we act on it. In this sense, social units are not static but are constantly emerging and changing in the course of human action and interaction.

The difficulty for most of us is that we are so caught up in our daily concerns that we fail to see and understand the social forces that are at work in our personal environments. What we need are the conceptual and methodological tools to help us gain a more complete and accurate perspective on the social world. The ideas, theories, methods, and levels of analysis employed by sociologists are the very tools that will help give us that perspective. To use an analogy, each different lens of a camera gives the photographer a unique view of the world. Wide-angle lenses, close-up lenses, tele-photo lenses, and special filters each serve a purpose in creating a distinctive picture or frame of the world. No one lens will provide the complete picture. Yet, the combination of images produced by various lenses allows us to examine in detail aspects of the world we might ordinarily overlook. That is what the sociological perspective gives us: a unique set of tools to see the social world with more penetrating clarity. In seeing the social world from a sociological per-spective, we are better able to use that knowledge construc-tively, and we are better able to understand who we are as social beings. Try identifying the levels of analysis in the following "Engaging Sociology."

Building and staffing of this resort in Tunisia—which is patronized by affluent people from other continents (global)—changed the local economy, the culture, the social structures of family (meso level), and individual lives (micro level) in the local community.

Engaging Sociology

Micro-Meso-Macro: An Application Exercise

Imagine that there has been a major economic downturn (recession) in your local community. Identify three possible events at each level (micro, meso, and macro) that might contribute to the economic troubles in your town.

The micro (local community) level:

1. _____
2. _____
3. _____

The meso (intermediate—state, organizational, or ethnic subculture) level:

1. _____
2. _____
3. _____

The macro (national/global) level:

1. _____
2. _____
3. _____

 Social Construction of Reality

Social Units as Product of Human action

The next issue, then, is how we gather data that inform our understanding and influence on the social world. When we say we know something about society, how is it that we know? What is considered evidence in sociology, and what lens (theory) do we use to interpret the data? These are the central issues of the next chapter.

What Have We Learned?

- *How can sociology help me understand my own life, who I am, and how I relate to others?* A version of this question was posed at the beginning of the chapter. Throughout this book you will find ideas and examples that will help answer these questions and expand on the *sociological imagination.* These ideas will illustrate how sociology can help you communicate more effectively and understand your interactions with others.

- *How do sociologists help us understand and even improve our lives?* Understanding organizations and bureaucracies can make us better family members, more effective citizens, and more adept at getting along with coworkers. As citizens of democracies, we need to understand how to influence our social environments, from city councils, school boards, health care systems, and state legislatures to congressional, presidential, and other governmental organizations.

- *How do national policies and global events influence my life?* As the world changes, we need to be aware of global issues and how they affect us, from our job changes and lost jobs to skills demanded in the 21st century.

- We live in a complex social world with many layers of interaction. If we really want to understand our own lives, we need to comprehend the levels of analysis that affect our lives and the connections between those levels. To do so wisely, we need both objective lenses for viewing this complex social world and accurate, valid information (facts) about the society. As the science of society, sociology can provide both tested empirical data and a broad, analytical perspective, as you will

learn in the next chapter. Here is a summary of points from Chapter 1.

Key Points:

- Humans are, at their very core, social animals—more akin to pack or herd animals than to individualistic cats. (See pp. 6–7.)

- A core concept in sociology is the *sociological imagination.* It requires that we see how our individual lives and personal troubles are shaped by historical and structural events outside of our everyday lives. It also prods us to see how we can influence our society. (See p. 10.)

- Sociology is a social science and, therefore, uses the tools of the sciences to establish credible evidence to understand our social world. As a science, sociology is scientific and objective rather than value laden. (See pp. 11–12.)

- Sociology has pragmatic applications, including those that are essential for the job market. (See pp. 12–16.)

- Sociology focuses on social units or groups, on social structures such as institutions, on social processes that give a social unit its dynamic character, and on their environments. (See pp. 16–19.)

- The social world model is the organizing theme of this book. Using the sociological imagination, we can understand our social world best by clarifying the interconnections between micro, meso, and macro levels of the social system. Each chapter of this book will examine society at these three levels of analysis. (See pp. 19–22.)

Discussion Questions

1. Think of a problem that impacts you personally (e.g., the high cost of tuition, unemployment, divorce) and explain how you would make sense of it differently if you viewed it as (a) a personal problem or (b) a public issue. How do possible solutions to the problem differ depending on how you view it?

2. How can sociology help you become a more informed citizen and better able to understand how government policies impact society?

3. What are three ways the sociological perspective can help you to succeed in college and the workforce?

4. Think of some of the ways the social institutions of government and education interconnect. Why is it in the interest of the government to support higher education? How has government support (or lack of support) impacted your college experience?

5. Imagine you would like to look at reasons behind the college dropout rate in the United States. How might the questions you ask differ based on whether your analysis was on the micro, meso, or macro level? Why?

Contributing to Our Social World: What Can We Do?

At the end of this and all subsequent chapters, you will find suggestions for work, service learning, internships, and volunteering that encourage you to apply the ideas discussed in the chapter. Suggestions for Chapter 1 focus on student organizations for sociology majors and nonmajors.

At the Local Level

- *Student organizations and clubs* enable students to meet other students interested in sociology, carry out group activities, get to know faculty members, and attend presentations by guest speakers. These clubs are usually not limited to sociology majors. If no such organization exists, consider forming one with the help of a faculty member. Sociologists also have an undergraduate honors society, Alpha Kappa Delta (AKD). Visit the AKD website at http://alphakappadelta.org to learn more about the society and what it takes to form a chapter.

At the Regional, National, and Global Levels

- *The American Sociological Association (ASA)* is the leading professional organization of sociologists in the United States. Visit the ASA website at www.asanet.org, and take a look around it. You will find many programs and initiatives of special interest to students. If you are interested in becoming a sociologist, be sure to look at the links under the heading "News on the Profession."

The organization also sponsors an Honors Program at the annual meeting that introduces students to the profession and gives students a heads-up on being successful in sociology and graduate education. For more information go to http://www.asanet.org/students/honors.cfm.

- *State and regional sociological associations* are especially student-friendly and feature publications and sessions at their annual meetings specifically for undergraduates. The ASA lists organizations and their website addresses, with direct links to their home pages, at http://www.asanet.org/about/Aligned_Associations.cfm.

- *The International Sociological Association (ISA)* serves sociologists from around the world. Every four years, the organization sponsors a large meeting (Yokohama, Japan, in July 2014). Specialty groups within ISA hold smaller conferences throughout the world during the other years. Check out www.isa-sociology.org.

Visit **www.sagepub.com/oswcondensed3e** for online activities, sample tests, and other helpful information. Select "Chapter 1: Sociology" for chapter-specific activities.

Examining the Social World

How Do We Know?

Science is about knowing through scientific research. Pictured here are scientists: archaeologists, a sociologist, a geologist, and a biologist. Sociology is a social science because of the way we gather scientific evidence.

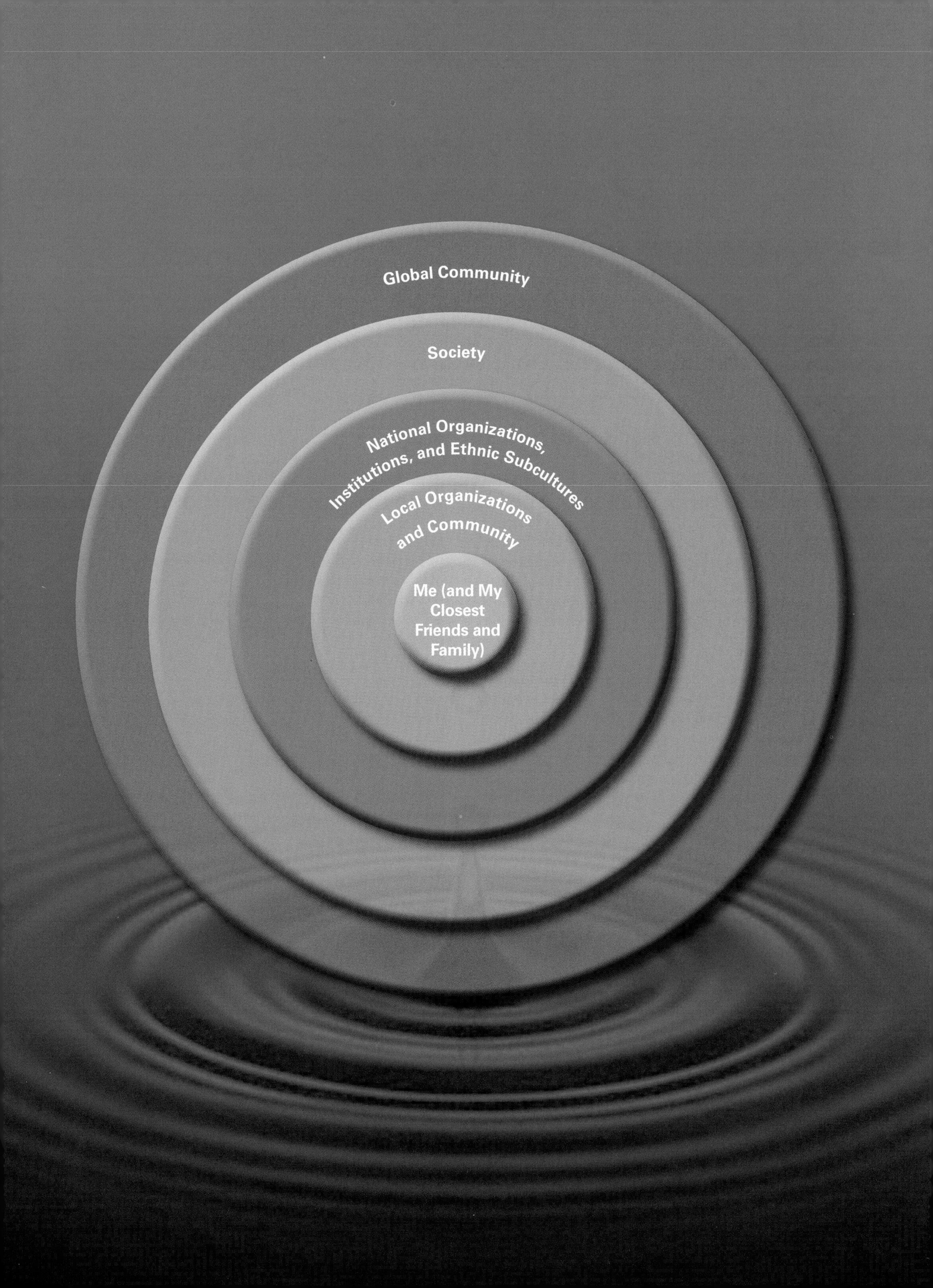

Global Community

Society

National Organizations,
Institutions, and Ethnic Subcultures

Local Organizations
and Community

Me (and My
Closest
Friends and
Family)

Think About It

Micro: Me (and My Closest Friends/ Family)	When you are talking with friends and you say that you know something, how do you know it?
Micro: Local Community	When you are trying to convince neighbors or people in your community to accept your opinion, why are accurate facts and evidence important?
Meso: National Institutions; Complex Organizations; Ethnic Groups	How do sociologists gather dependable data about families, educational institutions, or ethnic groups?
Macro: National Society	How do social scientists study national political or economic patterns scientifically?
Macro: Global Community	How can theories about global interactions help us understand our own lives at the micro level?

What's coming in this chapter?

Ideas Underlying Science

Empirical Research and Social Theory

How Sociologists Study the Social World

The Development of Sociology as a Social Science

Sociology's Major Theoretical Perspectives

Slum dwellers of São Paulo, Brazil. Hector lives in a neighborhood with shelters made of available materials such as boxes, no electricity or running water, and poor sanitation.

Let us travel to the Southern Hemisphere to meet a teenage boy, Hector. He is a 16-year-old living in a favela (slum) on the outskirts of São Paulo, Brazil. He is a polite, bright boy, but his chances of getting an education and a steady job in his world are limited. Like millions of other children around the world, he comes from a poor rural farm family that migrated to an urban area in search of a better life. However, his family ended up in a crowded slum with only a shared spigot for water and one string of electric lights along the dirt road going up the hill on which they live. The sanitary conditions in his community are appalling—open sewers, no garbage collection, contagious diseases. His family is relatively fortunate, for they have cement walls and wood flooring, although no bathroom, running water, or electricity. Many adjacent dwellings are little more than cardboard walls with corrugated metal roofs and dirt floors.

Hector wanted to stay in school but was forced to drop out to help support his family. Since leaving school, he has picked up odd jobs—deliveries, trash pickup, janitorial work, gardening—to help pay the few centavos for the family's dwelling and to buy food to support his parents and six siblings. Even when he was in school, Hector's experience was discouraging. He was not a bad student, and some teachers encouraged him to continue, but other students from the city teased the favela kids and made them feel unwelcome because they were poor and sometimes dirty. Most of his friends dropped out before he did. Hector often missed school because of other obligations—opportunities for part-time work, a sick relative, or a younger sibling who needed care. The immediate need to put food on the table outweighed the long-term value of staying in school. What is the bottom line for Hector and millions like him? Because of his limited education and work skills, obligations to his family, and limited opportunities, he most likely will continue to live in poverty. Sociologists are interested in what influences the social world of children like Hector: family, friends, school, community, and the place of one's nation in the global political and economic systems. Because of many previous studies of poverty and theories as to why it occurs, sociologists have some understanding of Hector's problems.

To understand how sociologists study poverty and many other social issues, we consider the theories and methods they use to do their work. Understanding the *how* helps us see that sociology is more than guesswork or opinion. Rather, it involves the use of scientific methods based on a systematic process for expanding knowledge of the social world. Some of the ideas and terms in this chapter may be new to you, but they are important as they lay the foundation for future chapters.

Whatever our area of study or job interests, we are likely to find ourselves asking sociological questions. Consider some examples: How do we select our mates? Why do we feel so strongly about our preferred sports team? Why is there binge drinking on college campuses? Do sexually explicit videos and magazines reinforce sexist stereotypes or encourage sexual violence? Do tough laws and longer prison sentences deter people from engaging in criminal conduct? How do we develop our religious and political outlooks? How are the Internet and other technologies affecting everyday life for people around the world? Knowing what is involved in a good study and the tools to carry out a study will help us understand how sociologists answer these questions.

This chapter will introduce you to the basic tools used to plan studies and gather dependable information on topics of interest. It will also help you understand how sociology approaches research questions. To this end, we will consider ideas underlying science, what social research and social theory entail, how sociologists study the social world, the development of sociology as a discipline, sociology's major theoretical perspectives, ethical issues, and practical applications and uses of sociological knowledge. We start with some background on the origins of sociology to provide a better understanding of how sociology developed.

Ideas Underlying Science

Throughout most of human history, people came to "know" the world by traditions being passed down from one generation to the next. Things were so because authoritative people in the culture said they were so. Often, there was reliance on magical or religious explanations of the forces in nature, and these explanations became part of tradition. It was little more than 260 years ago that people thought lightning storms were a sign of an angry god, not electricity caused by meteorological forces. With advances in the natural sciences, observations of cause-and-effect processes became more systematic and controlled. As ways of knowing about the world shifted, tradition and magic as primary means to understand the world were challenged.

The scientific approach is based on several core ideas: First, there is a real social world that can be studied scientifically. Second, there is a certain order to the world with identifiable patterns that results from a series of causes and effects. The world is not a collection of unrelated random events but rather is a collection of events that are causally related and patterned. Third, the way to gain knowledge of the world is to subject it to empirical testing. **Empirical knowledge** *means that the facts have been objectively (without opinion or bias) gathered and carefully measured and that what is being measured is the same for all people who observe it.*

For knowledge to be scientific, it must come from phenomena that can be observed and measured. Phenomena that cannot be subject to measurement are not within the realm of scientific inquiry. The existence of God, the devil,

Lightning has been understood as a form of electricity rather than a message from an angry god only since 1752, thanks to an experiment by Benjamin Franklin.

Scientific Method

heaven, hell, and the soul cannot be observed and measured and therefore cannot be examined scientifically.

Finally, science is rooted in **objectivity**; that is, one must take steps *to ensure that one's personal opinions or values do not bias or contaminate data collection and analysis.* **Evidence** *refers to facts and information that are confirmed through systematic testing using the five senses, sometimes enhanced with research tools.* Moreover, scientists are obliged not to distort their research findings so as to promote a particular point of view. Scientific research is judged first on whether it passes the test of being conducted objectively, without bias.

One way to evaluate evidence is to see whether the research does or does not support what the researcher thinks is true. The failure to disprove one's ideas offers evidence to support the findings. For example, if we wish to study whether gender is a major factor in a person being altruistic (helpful to others), then we must plan the research study so that we can either support or disprove our hypothesis (our educated guess or prediction).

A failure to meet these standards—empirical knowledge, objectivity, and scientific evidence—means that a study is not scientific. Someone's ideas can seem plausible and logical but still not be supported by the facts. This is why evidence is so important. Sociology is concerned with having accurate evidence, and it is important to know what is or is not considered accurate evidence. Perhaps you have seen an episode of the *CSI: Crime Scene Investigation* or *Bones* series on television. The shows in these series depict the importance of careful collection of data and commitment to objective analysis. Sociologists deal with different issues, but the same sort of concern for accuracy in gathering data guides their work.

Sociologists have come a long way from the early explanations of the social world that were based on the moral judgments of the 18th- and 19th-century social philosophers. Part of the excitement of sociology today comes from the challenge to improve the scientific procedures applied to the study of humans and social behavior and to base policy on carefully collected data.

Thinking Sociologically

If you wanted to learn something about the morale of one of your university's athletic teams or of a Greek sorority or fraternity, which of the following would produce better results: (a) interviewing those who have quit the organization, (b) interviewing a wide range of campus athletes or Greek members, or (c) interviewing students who are neither athletes nor Greeks? Why? Why might some of those approaches end up with bias in the results and not give the full story?

Empirical Research and Social Theory

We all have beliefs about how our social world works. Social researchers use the scientific method to examine these beliefs about society. They assume that (a) there are predictable social relations in the world, (b) social situations will recur in certain patterns, and (c) social situations have causes that can be understood. Just as individuals develop preferences for different religious or political beliefs that guide their lives, sociologists develop preferences for different explanations of the social world, called social theories. The main difference between individual beliefs and social theories is that the latter are subject to ongoing, systematic empirical testing.

Theories are *statements or explanations regarding how or why two or more facts are related to each other and the connections between these facts.* Theories try to explain social interactions, behaviors, and problems. A good theory helps the scientist to make predictions about the social world. Which theory a sociologist uses to study the social world depends in part on the level of analysis to be studied, as illustrated in Figure 2.1.

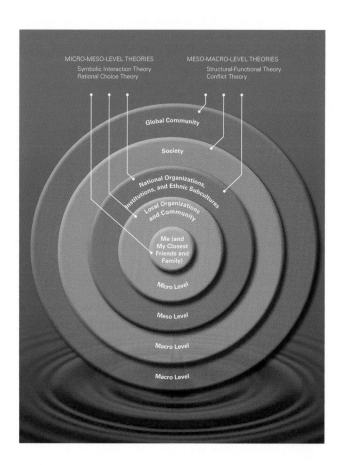

Each of the major theories discussed in this chapter gives a perspective on the way the social world works. To study Hector's life in Brazil, researchers might focus on the micro-level interactions between Hector and his family members, peers, teachers, and employers as factors that contribute to his situation. For example, why does Hector find some activities (e.g., working) more realistic or immediately rewarding than others (such as attending school)? A meso-level focus might examine organizations and institutions—such as the business world, the schools, and the religious communities in Brazil—to see how they shape the forces that affect Hector's life. Alternatively, the focus might be on macro-level analysis—the class structure (rich to poor) of the society and the global forces such as trade relations between Brazil and other countries that influence opportunities for the Brazilians who live in poverty.

Scientists, including sociologists, often use theories to predict why things happen and under what conditions they are likely to happen. Explanations about the relationships between social variables need to be tested by collecting data. This is where research methods—the procedures one uses to gather data—are relevant. Theory and research are used together and are mutually dependent. The facts (data) must be carefully gathered and are then used to assess the accuracy of the theory. If a theory is not supported by the data, it must be reformulated or discarded. We turn first to a discussion of how we gather data.

How Sociologists Study the Social World

How do we know? Suppose you have a research question related to your work or community. Presented here is a skeleton of the research process that sociologists and other social scientists use. A researcher follows a number of logically related steps.

I. Planning A Research Study

    Step 1: Define a topic or problem that can be studied scientifically.

    Step 2: Review existing relevant research studies and theories to refine the topic and define variables.

    Step 3: Formulate hypotheses or research questions and determine how to measure variables.

II. Designing The Research Plan And Method For Collecting The Data

    Step 4: Design the research method that specifies how the data will be gathered.

    Step 5: Select a sample of people or groups from the population to study.

    Step 6: Collect the data using appropriate research methods.

III. Making Sense Of The Data: Analysis

    Step 7: Analyze the data, figuring out exactly what the study says about the research question(s).

    Step 8: Draw conclusions and present the final report, including suggestions for future research.

Each of these steps is very important, whether you become a professional sociologist or do a study for a local organization or your workplace. To introduce the research process, we provide a quick summary of how sociologists conduct research: designing a research plan; selecting a method for collecting data; doing analysis of the data; and drawing conclusions.

Planning a Research Study

Planning a research study involves three main steps: (1) define the topic or problem clearly, (2) review existing research studies and theories to find out what is already known about the topic, and (3) formulate hypotheses (educated guesses) or research questions with clear definitions and ways to measure variables.

Step 1, the most important step, is to *define a topic or problem* that can be investigated scientifically. Without a clear problem, the research will go nowhere.

Specific research topics, ones that can be measured and tested, are usually posed in the form of questions: Why is it that, in some countries, large segments of the population live in poverty? What causes some students—especially those in poor families such as Hector—to drop out of school? Why are there disproportionate numbers of women and people of color living in poverty? Are people who are poor more vulnerable to excessive drug or alcohol use? The research question must be asked in a precise way. Otherwise, it cannot be tested empirically.

Thinking Sociologically

Pick a topic of interest to you. Now, write a research question based on your topic.

Step 2 in planning the research is *reviewing existing relevant research studies and theories* to determine what other researchers have already learned about the topic. One needs to know how the previous research was done, how terms

Gathering data—through interviews, direct observations of behavior, experiments, and other methods—is part of the science of sociological investigation.

were defined, and the strengths and limitations of that research. Social scientists can then link their study to existing findings to build the knowledge base. This step usually involves combing through scholarly journals and books on the topic. In the case of Hector, researchers would need to identify what previous studies have said about why impoverished young people drop out of school.

In *Step 3*, based on the review of the literature on the topic, social scientists often formulate **hypotheses**—*reasonable, educated guesses about how variables are related to each other, including causal relationships. These speculations do not yet have supporting data.* An example of a hypothesis to study Hector's situation might be as follows: "Poverty is a major cause of favela teenagers dropping out of school because they need to earn money for the family." Again, *a hypothesis provides a statement to be tested.*

Researchers then identify the key concepts, or ideas, in the hypothesis (e.g., poverty and dropping out of school). These concepts can be measured by collecting facts or data. **Variables** are *concepts (ideas) that can vary in frequency of occurrence from one time, place, or person to another.* Examples include levels of poverty, percentage of people living in poverty, and number of years of formal education. Variables can then be measured by collecting data to test hypothesized relationships between variables. The process of determining how to measure variables is very important. Researchers must link social concepts such as poverty to specific measurement indicators. Using the preceding hypothesis, concepts such as dropouts and poverty can be measured by determining the number of times they occur. Dropouts, for instance, might be defined by the number of days of school missed in a designated period of time according to school records. Poverty could be defined as

having an annual income that is less than half of the average income for a similar size of family in the country or by assessing ownership of property such as cattle, automobiles, and indoor plumbing. It is important to be clear, precise, and consistent about how one measures the variables in one's hypothesis.

Thinking Sociologically

Considering your research question, write a hypothesis, and identify your variables in the hypothesis.

The relationship between variables is central to understanding *causality*, and because use of language is so important, the elements of causal reasoning are discussed in the next Sociology in Our Social World.

Designing the Research Method and Collecting the Data

After the researcher has carefully planned the study, *Step 4* is to *select appropriate data collection methods.* Because every research study should be replicable—capable of being repeated—enough information must be given to ensure that another researcher could repeat the study and compare results. The appropriate data collection method depends on the levels of analysis of the research question (micro, meso, or macro) the researcher is asking. If researchers want to answer a macro-level research question, such as the effect of poverty on students dropping out of school in Brazil, they are likely to focus on large-scale social and economic data sources such as the Brazilian census. To learn about micro-level issues such as the influence of peers on an individual's decision to drop out of school, researchers will focus on small-group interactions at the micro level. Figure 2.2 on page 38 illustrates different levels of analysis.

The primary methods used to collect data for research studies include surveys (both questionnaires and structured interviews), observation studies, controlled experiments, and use of existing information. Our discussion cannot go into detail about how researchers use these techniques, but a brief explanation gives an idea of why they use these primary methods.

Surveys. The **survey method** is *used when sociologists want to gather information directly from a number of people regarding how they think or feel or what they do.* Two forms of surveys are common: the structured interview and the questionnaire. Both involve a series of questions asked of respondents.

Interviews are conducted by talking directly with people and asking questions in person or by telephone. The term *structured interview* simply means that specific questions

Sociology in Your Social World

Being Clear About Causality

S ociology as a science tries to be very careful about language—more precise than we usually are in our everyday conversations. What do we really mean when we say that something causes something else? At the heart of the research process is the effort to find causal relationships (i.e., one variable causes another one to change—they do not just vary together, called covariations). The following key terms are important in understanding how two variables (concepts that vary in frequency and can be measured) are related:

CORRELATION

- **Correlation** *refers to a relationship between variables (such as poverty and low levels of education), with change in one variable associated with change in another.* The hypothesis above predicts that poverty and teenagers dropping out of school are related and vary together. That is, when poverty level is high, dropping out of school is also high. If we claim that there is a correlation, however, that is only the first step. We have not yet established that change in one variable *causes* a change in the other.

CAUSE-AND-EFFECT VARIABLES

- **Cause-and-effect relationships** *occur when there is a relationship between variables so that one variable stimulates a change in another.* Once we have determined that there is probably a relationship, or correlation (the fact that the two variables, such as poverty and dropping out of school, both occur in the same situation), we need to take the next step: figuring out which comes first and seeing if one variable causes change in another. The **independent variable** *is the variable in a cause-and-effect relationship that comes first in a time sequence and causes a change in another variable—the* **dependent variable.** If we hypothesize that

poverty causes Hector and others to drop out of school, *poverty* is the independent variable in this hypothesis and *dropping out of school* is the dependent variable, dependent on the poverty. In determining cause and effect, the independent variable must always precede the dependent variable in time sequence if we are to say that one variable causes another.

SPURIOUS RELATIONSHIPS

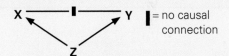

- **Spurious relationships** *occur when there is no causal relationship between the independent and dependent variables, but they vary together, often due to a third variable affecting both of them.* For example, if the quantity of ice cream consumed is highest during those weeks of the year when most drownings occur, these two events are correlated. However, eating ice cream did not cause the increase in deaths. Indeed, hot weather may have caused more people both to purchase ice cream and to go swimming, with the larger number of swimmers resulting in more drowning incidents. The connection between ice cream and drownings is a *spurious relationship*.

CONTROLS

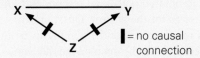

- **Controls** *are steps used by researchers to eliminate all variables except those related to the hypothesis—especially those variables that might be spurious.* Using controls helps ensure that the relationship is not spurious. Using the ice cream example, we might have studied beaches where lots of ice cream is sold and beaches where none is available in order to compare water death incidents.

The months when ice cream is consumed the most are the same months when the most drownings occur. However, this is not because of a causal connection. Both variables are related to another factor—hot weather.

Micro Level

Individual	Hector
Small group	Hector's family and close friends
Local community	The *favela;* Hector's local school, church, neighborhood organizations

Meso Level

Organizations	Brazilian corporations, Catholic Church, and local school system in Brazil
Institutions	Family; education; political, economic, and health systems in the region or nation of Brazil
Ethnic subcultures	Native peoples, African-Brazilians

Macro Level

National society	Social policies, trends, and programs in Brazil
Global community of nations	Status of Brazil in global economy; trade relations with other countries; programs of international organizations or corporations

Figure 2.2 The Social World Model and Levels of Analysis

are asked—as in an opinion poll—and respondents chose among specific choices for the answer. Questionnaires are written questions to which respondents reply in writing. In both cases, questions may be open-ended, allowing the respondent to say or write whatever comes to mind, or closed-ended, requiring the respondent to choose from a set of possible answers.

One method to study school dropouts is to survey teenagers about what caused them to leave school. The researcher would have to evaluate whether an interview or a questionnaire would provide the best information. Interviews are more time consuming and labor intensive than questionnaires but are better for gathering in-depth information. However, if the researcher wants information from a large number of teenagers, questionnaires are often more practical and less costly.

Thinking Sociologically

How would you word questions objectively (without bias) in a survey about the effects of peer influence on dropping out of school? How could you find out whether your questions are good ones?

One example of a survey is the census, done in the United States and many other countries every 10 years. Sometimes it is difficult to gather accurate data on the entire population. In this situation, the census worker is counting homeless people in Penn Station in New York City.

Observation Studies. **Observation studies** (also called field research) *involve systematic, planned observation and recording of interactions or human behavior in natural settings.* They can take different forms: observations in which the researcher actually participates in the activities of the group being studied, or observations in which the researcher is not involved in group activities but observes or videotapes the activity. The important thing is for observers to avoid altering group functioning and interaction by their presence. The researcher must also be aware that interpretation of the social scene is subject to misunderstanding. Despite these potential problems, observation remains a useful way of obtaining information.

Some methods of gathering data produce data that are called qualitative because they provide valuable information that is rich in detail and describes the context of the situation, such as the dynamics of the favela or Hector's classroom. Observation studies as well as unstructured interviews, which allow respondents to answer questions in a more open-ended manner, are referred to as *qualitative* research. The research evolves in response to what the researcher learns as the research progresses. Unlike research driven by hypotheses to be tested, this method allows the researcher to respond to new ideas that come up during the research. Quantitative research, on the other hand, provides hard data such as percentages or other numbers that answer the researcher's questions and can be illustrated in neat tables (Creswell 2009). Many sociologists use surveys to gain qualitative data.

Experiments. In **experiments**, *all variables except the one being studied are controlled so researchers can study the effects of the variable under study.* An experiment usually requires an **experimental group**, in which *subjects in the group are exposed to the variable being studied to test the effects of that variable on human behavior,* and a **control group**, in which *the subjects are not exposed to the variable the experimenter wants to test.* The control group provides a baseline to which the experimental group can be compared. Experiments are powerful because they are the most accurate test of cause and effect, since they make it more possible to control variables, determine the sequence in which variables affect each other, and identify spurious relationships.

The problem is that many sociological questions cannot be studied in controlled settings because they cannot be placed in a controlled situation like the lab pictured above. For example, Hector's situation in the favela cannot be studied in a laboratory setting. Thus, there are many variables that social scientists cannot introduce in the laboratory.

Existing Sources. **Existing sources** *refer to use of materials that already exist.* Two important approaches to using existing sources are secondary analysis and content analysis. **Secondary analysis** *uses existing data, information that has already been collected by other researchers in other studies.* Often, large data-collecting organizations such as the United Nations or a country's census bureau, a country's national education department, or a private research organization will make data available for use by researchers. Consider the question of the dropout rate in Brazil. Ministries or departments of education often collect such data. Likewise, if we want to compare modern dropout rates with the rates of an earlier time, we may find data from previous decades to be invaluable. Secondary analysis can be an excellent way to

Experiments are especially effective at controlling all of the variables to be able to know which outcomes result from the independent variable. Of course, they are not as effective as observation studies in terms of being real-life situations, and they are more subject to researcher effects—that is, respondents being influenced by the researcher or the research setting.

do meso- or macro-level studies that reveal large-scale patterns in the social world.

Content analysis *involves systematic categorizing and recording of information from written or recorded sources.* With content analysis (a common method in historical research and study of organizations), sociologists can gather the data they need from printed materials (books, magazines, newspapers, laws, letters), videos, archived radio broadcasts, or even artworks. A researcher studying variations in levels of concern about child abuse over time could do a content analysis of popular magazines to see how many pages or stories were devoted to child abuse each decade from the 1960s to the present. Content analysis has the advantage of being relatively inexpensive and easy to do. It is also unobtrusive, meaning that the researcher does not influence the subjects being investigated by having direct contact. Furthermore examining materials in historical sequence can be effective in recognizing patterns over time.

Thinking Sociologically

What method(s) would be appropriate to collect data on your research question? Why?

Triangulation *refers to the utilization of two or more methods of data collection to enhance the amount and type of data for analysis and the accuracy of the findings.* To study Hector's situation, a research study could use macro-level quantitative data on poverty and on educational statistics in

Social scientists are not the only professionals who use triangulation. Journalists also consult a variety of sources including social scientists to put together news broadcasts.

Brazil and micro-level qualitative unstructured interviews with Hector and his peers to determine their goals and their attitudes toward education. If all findings point to the same conclusion, the researcher can feel much more confident about the study results. Data collection techniques—survey, observation study, controlled experimentation, and analysis of existing sources—represent the dominant methods used to collect data for sociological research.

Step 5 involves selecting a sample. It would be impossible to survey the reasons for poverty or for dropping out of school for every teenager in Brazil. Researchers must select a representative group to study that will help them to understand the larger group. A part of the research design is determining how to make sure the study includes people who are typical of the total group. When the research study involves a survey or field observation, sociologists need to decide who will be observed or questioned to provide a group representative of the whole. This involves careful selection of a **sample**, *a group of systematically chosen people in survey research who represent a much larger group.* The objective of sampling is to select a group that accurately represents the characteristics of the entire group (or population) being studied.

Researchers use many types of samples. A common one, the *representative sample,* attempts to accurately reflect the group being studied so that the sample results can be generalized or applied to the larger population. In the case of Hector's favela, a sample for a study could be drawn from all 13- to 16-year-olds in his region or city in Brazil.

The most common form of representative sample is the *random sample.* People from every walk of life and every group within the population have an equal chance of being selected for the study. By observing or talking with this smaller group selected from the total population under study, the researcher can get an accurate picture of the total population and have confidence that the findings apply to the larger group. Developing an effective sampling technique is often a complex process, but it is important to have a sample that represents the group being studied.

Step 6 involves collecting the data. Researchers have selected the appropriate research method for collecting data and the sample to study. The researcher's next step is to collect the data and then analyze those data and see what they say about the research questions and hypotheses.

Making Sense of the Data: Analysis

Step 7 involves making sense of our data. Now that we have, say, 100 interviews from residents of Hector's favela, plus a notebook full of field observation notes from "hanging out" with the youth there, what do we do with the data? Social researchers use multiple techniques to analyze data, but whatever techniques they use, they look for patterns in the data. For example, are dropout rates among Hector's friends related to their grades in school or other factors? Sociology is not guesswork or speculation. It involves careful, objective analysis of specific data. *Step 8* involves discussion of results and drawing conclusions for the analysis. A report is developed, outlining the research project and analysis of the data collected. The final section of the report presents a discussion of results, draws conclusions as to whether or not the hypotheses were supported, interprets the results, and makes recommendations from the researcher's point of view, if appropriate. As part of the presentation and discussion of results, the report may contain tables or figures presenting summaries of data that are useful in understanding the data. The next "Engaging Sociology" on pages 40 and 41 provides useful tips on reading research tables found in journal articles, books, and newspapers.

Given that social science research focuses on humans and humans are changeable, it is difficult to say that any single study has definitively proved the hypothesis or answered a research question with finality. Indeed, the word *prove* is never used to describe the interpretation of findings in the social and behavioral sciences. Rather, social scientists say that findings tend to support or reject hypotheses. Systematic, scientific research, does, however, bring us much closer to the reality of the social world than guesswork and opinions. Having supportive findings from numerous studies, not just one, builds a stronger case to support a theory and conclusions. The search for truth is ongoing—a kind of mission in life for those of us who do research. Furthermore, as we get closer to accurate understanding of society, our social policies can be based on the most accurate knowledge available.

What makes a discipline scientific is not the subject matter. It is how we conduct our research and what we consider valid evidence. To have credible findings, scientists always consider the possibility that they have overlooked alternative explanations of the data and alternative ways to view the problem. This is one of the hardest principles to grasp, but it is one of the most important in reaching the truth. Science is a process that is made possible by a social exchange of ideas, a clash of opinions, and a continual search for truth. Knowledge in the sciences is created by vigorous debate. Rather than just memorizing concepts in this book to take a test, we hope you will engage in the creation of knowledge by entering into these debates.

Ethical Issues in Social Research

Sociologists and other scientists are bound by ethical codes of conduct governing research. This is to protect any human subjects used in research from being harmed by the research. The following standards are a part of the American Sociological Association's code of ethics:

- How will the findings from the research be used? Will the information hurt individuals, communities, or nations if they get into the hands of "enemies"? Can they be used to aggravate hostilities? In whose interest is the research being carried out?
- How can the researcher protect the privacy and identities of respondents and informants? Is the risk to subjects justified by an anticipated outcome of improved social conditions?
- Is there informed consent among the people being studied? This issue relates to the issue of deception by social scientists. If the public learns that social scientists have actively deceived them, what will be the consequences for trusting researchers at a later time when a different study is being conducted?
- Will there be any harm to the participants—including injury to self-esteem or feelings of guilt and self-doubt?
- How much invasion of privacy is legitimate in the name of research? How much disclosure of confidential information, even in disguised form, is acceptable?

Codes of ethics provide general guidelines. In addition, most universities and organizations where research is common have human subjects review boards whose function is to ensure that human participants are not harmed by the research.

Thinking Sociologically

What might be some ethical problems in the research project you are thinking about as you read this chapter? What, for example, might be the ethical issues of studying a setting or situation but not informing those people involved that you are studying them?

The Development of Sociology as a Social Science

Throughout recorded history, humans have been curious about how and why people form groups. That should not be surprising because the groups we belong to are so central to human existence and to a sense of satisfaction in life.

Engaging Sociology

How to Read a Research Table

A statistical table is a researcher's labor-saving device. Quantitative data presented in tabular form are more clear and concise than the same information presented in several written paragraphs. A good table has clear signposts to help the reader avoid confusion. For instance, Table 2.1 shows many of the main features of a table, and the list that follows explains how to read each feature.*

Table 2.1 Educational Attainment by Selected Characteristic: 2010, for Persons 25 Years Old and Over Reported in Thousands

Characteristic	Population (1,000)	Percent of Population—Highest Level					
		Not a High School Graduate	High School Graduate	Some College, but No Degree	Associate's Degree[1]	Bachelor's Degree	Advanced Degree
Total persons	199,928	12.9	31.2	16.8	9.1	19.4	10.5
Age							
25–34 yrs old	41,085	11.6	27.2	18.9	9.5	24.0	8.9
35–44 yrs old	40,447	11.7	28.6	16.3	10.3	21.9	11.2
45–54 yrs old	44,387	10.4	32.8	16.7	10.6	19.0	10.4
55–64 yrs old	35,359	10.4	31.3	17.3	9.2	18.6	13.1
65–74 yrs old	20,956	17.0	35.4	15.7	6.6	14.1	11.1
75 yrs or older	17,657	24.6	37.6	14.0	4.6	11.9	7.3
Sex							
Male	96,325	13.4	31.9	16.5	8.0	19.4	10.9
Female	103,603	12.4	30.7	17.1	10.2	19.4	10.2
Race							
White[2]	163,083	12.4	31.3	16.7	9.2	19.6	10.7
Black[2]	22,969	15.8	35.2	19.8	9.4	13.3	6.5
Other	13,876	13.0	23.5	13.0	8.1	26.6	15.7
Hispanic origin							
Hispanic	26,375	37.1	29.6	12.9	6.5	10.1	3.8
Non-Hispanic	173,553	9.2	31.5	17.4	9.5	20.8	11.5
Region							
Northeast	36,834	11.4	33.7	13.0	8.4	20.6	12.9
Midwest	43,380	10.1	34.6	17.6	10.0	18.2	9.5
South	73,682	14.5	31.9	16.9	8.7	18.1	9.8
West	46,032	14.0	25.0	19.0	9.5	21.6	10.8

Source: U.S. Census Bureau (2011).

1. Includes vocational degrees.

2. For persons who selected this race group only.

*Features of the table adapted from Broom and Selznick (1963).

TITLE: The title provides information on the major topic and variables in the table.

"Educational Attainment by Selected Characteristic: 2010"

HEADNOTE (or Subtitle): Many tables will have a headnote or subtitle under the title, giving information relevant to understanding the table or units in the table.

For this table, the reader is informed that this includes all persons over the age of 25, and they will be reported in thousands.

HEADINGS AND STUBS: Tables generally have one or two levels of headings under the title and headnotes. These instruct the reader about what is in the columns below.

In this table, the headings indicate the level of education achieved so the reader can identify the percentage with a specified level of education.

The table also has a stub: the far-left column. This lists the items that are being compared according to the categories found in the headings. In this case, the stub indicates population of various characteristics: age, sex, race, Hispanic origin, and region.

MARGINAL TABS: In examining the numbers in the table, try working from the outside in. The marginals, the figures at the margins of the table, often provide summary information.

In this table, the first column of numbers is headed "Population (1,000)," indicating (by thousands) the total number of people in each category who were part of the database. The columns to the right indicate—by percentages—the level of educational attainment for each category.

CELLS: To make more detailed comparisons, examine specific cells in the body of the table. These are the boxes that hold the numbers or percentages.

In this table, the cells contain data on age, sex, racial/ethnic (white, black, Hispanic), and regional differences in education.

UNITS: Units refer to how the data are reported. It could be in percentages, in number per 100 or 1,000, or in other units.

In this table, the data are reported first in raw number in thousands and then in percentages.

FACTS FROM THE TABLE: After reviewing all of the above information, the reader is ready to make some interpretations about what the data mean.

In this table, the reader might note that young adults are more likely to have a college education than older citizens. Likewise, African Americans and Hispanics are less likely than whites to have college or graduate degrees, but the rate for "Other" is even higher than that for whites, probably because it includes Asian Americans. People in the Northeast and West have the highest levels of education. What other interesting patterns do you see?

FOOTNOTES: Some tables have footnotes, usually indicating something unusual about the data or where to find more complete data.

In this table, two footnotes are provided so the reader does not make mistakes in interpretation.

SOURCE: The source note, found under the table, points out the origin of the data. It is usually identified by the label "source."

Under this table, the source note says "U.S. Census Bureau (2012e)."

Early Sociological Thought

Religion influenced the way individuals thought about the world and their social relationships. Christianity dominated European thought systems during the Middle Ages, from the end of the Roman Empire to the 1500s, while Islamic beliefs ruled in much of the Middle East and parts of Africa. North African Islamic scholar Ibn Khaldun (1332–1406) is generally considered the first social scientist as he was the first on record to suggest a systematic approach to explain the social world. Influenced by Aristotle's work, Khaldun wrote about the processes of social and political change; the rise and fall

Family Dinner

Science

of societies, cities, and economic life; and the feelings of solidarity that held tribal groups together during his day, a time of great conflict and wars. He discussed the importance of individuals identifying with their groups and subordinating their own interests to their societies and kinship groups. He felt that this subordination made societies possible and allowed for the rule of monarchs, seen as the natural ruling structure at his time (Alatas 2006; Hozien n.d.).

Sociology has its modern roots as a scientific discipline in the ideas of 19th-century European philosophers, who laid the groundwork for the scientific study of society. Until the 19th century, social philosophers provided the primary approach to understanding society, one that invariably had a strong moral tone. Their opinions were derived from abstract reflection about how the social world works. Often, they advocated forms of government that they believed would be just and good, denouncing those they considered inhumane or evil. Even today, people still debate the ideal communities proposed by Plato, Aristotle, Machiavelli, Thomas More, and other philosophers from the past.

Conditions Leading to Modern Sociology

Several conditions in the 19th century gave rise to the emergence of sociology: First, Europeans wanted to learn more about the people in their new colonies. Second, they sought to understand the social revolutions taking place and changes brought about by the Industrial Revolution. Finally, advances in the natural sciences demonstrated the value of the scientific method, and some wished to apply this scientific method to understand the social world.

The social backdrop for the earliest European sociologists was the Industrial Revolution (which began around the middle of the 1700s) and the French Revolution (1789–1799). No one had clear, systematic explanations for why the old social structure, which had lasted since the early Middle Ages, was collapsing or why cities were exploding with migrants from rural areas. French society was in turmoil, and new rules of justice were taking hold. Churches were subordinate to the state, equal rights under the law were established for citizens, and democratic rule emerged. These dramatic changes marked the end of the traditional monarchy and the beginning of a new social order. Leaders in France relied on the social philosophies of the time to react to the problems that surrounded them, philosophies not informed by facts about social life.

It was in this setting that the scientific study of society emerged. Two social thinkers, Henri Saint-Simon (1760–1825) and Auguste Comte (1798–1857), decried the lack of systematic data collection or objective analysis in social thought. These Frenchmen are considered the first to suggest that a science of society could help people understand

and perhaps control the rapid changes and unsettling revolutions taking place. Comte officially coined the term *sociology* in 1838. Just as the natural sciences provided basic facts about the physical world, so too there was a need to gather scientific knowledge about the social world. Only then could leaders systematically apply this scientific knowledge rather than use religious or philosophical speculation to improve social conditions.

Comte asked two basic questions: What holds society together and gives rise to a stable order in lieu of anarchy? Further, why and how do societies change? Comte conceptualized society as divided into two parts. *Social statics* referred to aspects of society that give rise to order, stability, and harmony. *Social dynamics* referred to change and evolution in society over time. Simply stated, Comte was concerned with what contemporary sociologists and the social world model in this book refer to as *structure* (social statics) and *process* (social dynamics). By understanding these aspects of the social world, Comte felt leaders could strengthen society and could respond appropriately to change. His optimistic belief was that sociology would be the "queen of sciences," guiding leaders to construct a better social order.

Massive social and economic changes in the 18th and 19th centuries brought about restructuring and sometimes the demise of political monarchies, aristocracies, and feudal lords. Scenes of urban squalor were common in Great Britain and other industrializing European nations. Machines replaced both agricultural workers and cottage (home) industries because they produced an abundance of goods faster, better, and cheaper. Peasants were pushed off the land by the new technology and migrated to urban areas to find work at the same time that a powerful new social class of capitalists was emerging. Industrialization brought

Industrialization had a number of positive outcomes, including the expansion of prosperity to a larger class of people, but it also had some high costs in exploitation of workers and slums in places like London.

the need for a new skilled class of laborers, putting new demands on an education system that had served only the elite. Families now depended on wages from their labor in the industrial sector to stay alive.

These changes stimulated other social scientists to study society and its problems. Writings of Émile Durkheim, Karl Marx, Harriet Martineau, Max Weber, W. E. B. Du Bois, and many other early sociologists set the stage for development of sociological theories. Accompanying the development of sociological theory was the utilization of the scientific method—systematic gathering and recording of reliable and accurate data to test ideas.

The Purposes of Sociology

There are three long-standing approaches to sociology that speak to the purpose of sociology and the relationship between research and theory: scientific sociology, humanistic sociology, and activist public sociology (Buechler 2008). Keep in mind that all three approaches have been around for almost as long as sociology has existed. The founders of sociology sometimes combined the approaches, which lay the foundation for most modern theories we use today.

Scientific Sociology. One approach, strongly influenced by the ideas of Auguste Comte, Émile Durkheim, and other early sociologists, stresses *scientific sociology*—being objective and modeling the discipline after the natural sciences. Sociology was to stick to pure science: fact-finding and testing hypotheses.

Humanistic Sociology. A second view of the discipline is called *humanistic sociology:* "When scientific sociologists do science, they emphasize the word *science*, linking it to other sciences. When humanistic sociologists do social science, they emphasize the word *social*, separating it from other sciences" (Buechler 2008:326). This tradition puts much more emphasis on the unique capacity of humans to create *meaning* in their lives—the way humans interpret their social world. However, when one is studying meaning—what does a handshake, a kiss, or a cross symbolize for people?—it is virtually impossible to produce objective quantitative data, which are often the standard of the natural sciences. Humanistic sociologists argue that studying humans is qualitatively different from research in the natural sciences, and that focusing only on rigorous methods and standards of objectivity causes researchers to miss some of the most interesting and important dimensions of human social behavior.

Public Sociology. The third view stresses the relevance of sociology to society. Most early sociologists—beginning with Lester Ward, the first president of the American Sociological Association—promoted sociology as means for improving society (Calhoun 2007). These **public sociologists** *strive to better understand how society operates and to make practical use of their sociological findings* (ASA Task Force 2005). In advocating for public sociology, president of the American Sociological Association Michael Burawoy wrote: "As a mirror and conscience of society, sociology must define, promote and inform public debate about deepening class and racial inequality, new gender regimes, environmental degradation, market fundamentalism, state and non-state violence" (Burawoy 2005:4). The idea is to consider what *might* be and what would make a better world.

One aspect of public sociology has received increased attention in recent years because there are job opportunities in this area: applied sociology. *Applied sociologists* use sociological knowledge and research skills to address organizational needs or problems in government, education, health care settings, social service agencies, and business organizations; often the client determines the research questions. Depending on their positions, they may be known as sociological practitioners, applied sociologists, clinical sociologists, policy analysts, program planners, or evaluation researchers, among other titles. They focus on pragmatic ways to improve organizations, sometimes recommending major changes and sometimes proposing modest policy proposals. Their careers take them outside of academia.

Throughout the history of the discipline, sociologists have debated their proper role in society. However, like physicists, chemists, and geologists, many sociologists believe that there are both important practical applications of the discipline and many policy issues that need to be informed by good science (Pickard and Poole 2007).

Table 2.2 outlines the key differences between basic (pure) scientific sociology and public sociology. In most chapters, you will find a feature called "Sociologists in Action,"

Table 2.2   Scientific Versus Public Sociology

	Scientific Sociology	*Public/Applied Sociology*
Orientation	Theory building, hypothesis testing	Program effects, focus on consequences of practices
Goal	Knowledge production	Knowledge utilization, problem solving
Source	Self- or discipline-generated; supported by grants	Self- or discipline-generated (public sociology) or client-generated (applied sociology)

Source: Adapted with permission from the NTL Institute (DeMartini 1982).

which describes a sociologist with a bachelor's, master's, or doctoral degree working in the topic area being discussed.

Sociology's Major Theoretical Perspectives

A **theoretical perspective** is a *basic view of society that guides sociologists' ideas and research. Theoretical perspectives are the broadest theories in sociology, providing overall approaches to understanding the social world and social problems.* Sociologists draw on major theoretical perspectives at each level of analysis to guide their research and to help them understand social interactions and social organizations.

Recall the description of the social world model presented in Chapter 1. It stresses the levels of analysis—smaller units existing within larger social systems. Some theories are especially effective in understanding micro-level interactions, and others illuminate macro-level structures, although the distinctions are not absolute. Either type of theory—those most useful at the micro or macro levels—can be used at the meso level, depending on the research question being asked. To illustrate how a social problem is approached differently by four major theoretical perspectives, we will further delve into our examination of Hector's circumstances that we described at the beginning of this chapter (Ashley and Orenstein 2009). Keep in mind that sociologists use many theories, some of which are introduced when relevant in future chapters.

Micro- to Meso-Level Theories: Symbolic Interaction and Rational Choice

If we want to study Hector's interaction with his friends and their influence on him (micro level) or his school performance, successes, and failures, theories at the micro and meso levels will help guide our research. Two theories that are most often used at the micro and meso levels of analysis are discussed in this section.

Symbolic Interaction Theory

Symbolic interaction theory (also called social construction or interpretative theory) *sees humans as active agents who create shared meanings of events and symbols and then interact on the basis of those meanings.* For example, Hector interacts with his family and friends in the favela in ways that he has learned are necessary for survival there. In Hector's world of poverty, the informal interactions of the street and the more formal interactions of the school carry different sets of meanings that guide Hector's behavior.

Symbolic interaction theory assumes that groups form around interacting individuals. Through these interactions, people learn to share common understandings and learn what to expect from others. They make use of **symbols**, *actions or objects that represent something else and therefore have meaning beyond their own existence*—such as flags, wedding rings, words, and nonverbal gestures—to interpret interactions with others. Symbolic communication (e.g., language) helps people construct a meaningful world. This implies that humans are not merely passive agents responding to their environments. Instead, they are actively engaged in creating their own meaningful social world based on their constructions and interpretations of the social world. Many people accept the social definitions and interpretations of others, saving themselves the effort of interpreting symbols and making sense of the stimuli around them (Blumer 1969; Fine 1990). Still, more than any other theory in the social sciences, symbolic interaction theory stresses *human agency*—the active role of individuals in creating their social environment.

George Herbert Mead (1863–1931) is prominently identified with the symbolic interaction perspective (Mead [1934] 1962). Mead explored the mental processes associated with how humans define situations. He placed special emphasis on human interpretations of gestures and symbols (including language) and the meanings we attach to our actions. He also examined how we learn our social roles in society such as mother, teacher, and friend and how we learn to carry out these roles. Indeed, as we will see in Chapter 4, he insisted that our notion of who we are—our self—emerges from social experience and interaction with others. Language is critical to this process, for it allows us to step outside of our own experience and reflect back on

Micro-level interactions occur in classrooms every day, both among peers and between teacher and students.

Abstinence-Based Sex Education

how others see us. Indeed, human language is a unique and powerful human trait, as is illustrated in the next "Sociology in Our Social World."

These ideas of how we construct our individual social worlds and maintain some control over them have come from the Chicago School of symbolic interaction theory. Another symbolic interaction approach—the Iowa School—makes an explicit link between individual identities and positions within organizations. If we hold several positions—honors student, club president, daughter, sister, student, athlete, thespian, middle-class person—those positions form a relatively stable core—our *self*. We will interpret new situations in light of our social positions, some of which are very important and anchor how we see the social world. Once a core self is established, it guides and shapes the way we interact with people in many situations—even new social settings

Sociology in Our Social World

Human Language and the Marvel of a College Classroom

A college classroom is a magical place, and this is true mostly because of human language. All other species communicate with a fairly limited number of sounds they can make. We can learn to recognize when our dog is hungry, when it needs to go to the bathroom, or when it is alarmed by an unrecognized person in the yard. Human language is distinctive. Except for humans and perhaps dolphins, whales, and chimpanzees, other animals only communicate about something that is happening in the present time and location (Phillips 2013).

Humans as infants can make hundreds of sounds—perhaps as many as a thousand. Each language identifies about 50 of those sounds that come to be designated as meaningful language sounds. In English, this includes such sounds as *sss, mmm, nnn, ttt, kkk, bbb*, and *ooo*. We take this designated collection of sounds and combine them in various ways to make words: *cat, dog, college, student*. This ability to combine sounds into words and words into sentences is called a *distinctive feature system*. A distinctive feature system allows you to say something to your instructor that she or he has never heard any other human say before. The sounds are familiar, as are the words themselves, but you may combine them in a novel way that causes a new idea to occur to your listener. This is actually the root of much humor: You say a sentence or tell a story that has such a surprising ending that it causes the listener to laugh.

Now your animal companions at home clearly have memory. They can recognize you when you get home. Your dog may well remember the other pups in his litter. However, they cannot remember together. They cannot gather to recall and share stories about good old dad the way you can recall the quirky traits of your professors with friends. Your dogs and cats cannot plan for the future—planning a litter reunion for next summer, for example.

The fact that our communication is a *distinctive feature system* allows something unique: temporal and spatial sharing. We can remember together our experiences of the past, and we can pass ideas from one person to another. We can discuss the ideas of people who have died and have perhaps been gone for more than a century. A mare cannot transmit to her colt the racing ideas of Man o' War, the great race horse of the 1920s, let alone the experiences of horses involved in the Trojan War, or even the more recent derby winner Secretariat. However, whether in a classroom or a pub, humans can discuss the ideas of Plato, or Muhammad, or Karl Marx. Further, humans, because of words, can take other perspectives—to vicariously visit the other side of the planet or to go back in history to experience a time when an entirely different set of ideas about life was common.

When we come into a classroom, something mysterious, something amazing, happens. Language allows us to see things from a new point of view. What a remarkable gift that we can share ideas and see things through the eyes of someone different from ourselves, and it is largely because of the human *distinctive feature system* of communication. What an interesting species to study! What a marvel that we can do so in a classroom.

(M. Kuhn 1964). Thus, if you are president of an organization and have the responsibility for overseeing the organization, part of your self-esteem, your view of responsible citizenship, and your attitude toward life will be shaped by that position. The Iowa School of symbolic interaction places a bit less emphasis on individual choice but more on recognizing the link between the micro, meso, and macro levels of society (Carrothers and Benson 2003; Stryker 1980).

The following principles summarize the modern symbolic interaction perspective and how individual action results in groups, organizations, and institutions, in societies (Ritzer 2007):

- Humans are endowed with the capacity for thought, shaped by social interaction.
- In social interaction, people learn the meanings and symbols that allow them to exercise thought and participate in human action.
- People modify the meanings and symbols as they struggle to make sense of their situations and the events they experience.
- Interpreting the situation involves seeing things from more than one perspective, and choosing one course of action.
- These patterns of action and interaction make up the interactive relations that we call groups, institutions, and societies.
- Our positions or memberships in these groups, organizations, and societies may profoundly influence the way we define our *selves* and may lead to fairly stable patterns of interpretation of our experiences and of social life.

To summarize, the modern symbolic interaction theory emphasizes the process each individual goes through in creating or changing his or her social reality and identity within a social setting. Without a system of shared symbols, humans could not coordinate their actions with one another, and hence society as we understand it would not be possible.

Theorists from the symbolic interaction perspective have made significant contributions to understanding the development of social identities and interactions as the basis for groups, organizations, and societies.

Rational Choice (Exchange) Theory

According to **rational choice theory**, *humans are fundamentally concerned with self-interests, (exchange) making rational decisions based on weighing costs and rewards of the projected outcome.* People act in ways that maximize their rewards and minimize their costs as they make their choices. Where the balance lies determines our behavior. Women may decide to stay in abusive relationships if they think the costs of leaving the relationship are higher than the costs of staying. In considering a divorce, for example, do the rewards of escaping a conflicted, abusive

marriage outweigh the costs of daily economic and emotional stresses related to going it alone? Rational choice (also called exchange) theory has its roots in several disciplines—economics, behavioral psychology, anthropology, and philosophy (Cook, O'Brien, and Kollock 1990). Social behavior is seen as an exchange activity—a transaction in which resources are given and received (Blau 1964; Homans 1974). Every interaction involves an exchange of something valued—money, time, material goods, attention, sex, allegiance. People stay in relationships because they get something from the exchange, and they leave relationships that cost them without providing adequate benefits. They constantly evaluate whether there is reciprocity or balance in a relationship so that they are receiving as much benefit as they give. Simply stated, people are more likely to act if they see some reward or success coming from their behavior. The implication is that self-interest for the individual is the guiding element in human interaction.

Applying the rational choice theory to Hector's situation, we could examine how he evaluates his life options. What are the costs and rewards for staying in school versus those associated with dropping out and earning money from temporary jobs? For Hector, the immediate benefit of earning a meager income to put food on his family's table comes at a cost—the loss of a more hopeful and prosperous future. When hungry, the reward of being paid for odd jobs may outweigh the cost of leaving school and losing long-term opportunities.

In summary, rational choice theory involves the following key ideas:

- Human beings are mostly self-centered and are driven in their behavior by self-interest.
- Humans calculate costs and benefits (rewards) in making decisions.
- Humans are rational in that they weigh choices in order to maximize their own benefits and minimize costs.
- Every interaction involves exchanges entailing rewards and penalties or expenditures.
- A key element in exchanges is reciprocity—a balance in the exchange of benefits.
- People keep a mental ledger in their heads about whether they owe someone else or that person owes them.

Thinking Sociologically

How can symbolic interaction and rational choice perspectives help explain dating behavior? For example, how might a "hookup" mean something different to females as opposed to males? How would each micro theory above answer this question a bit differently?

Fear of Germs

Meso- and Macro-Level Theories: Structural-Functional, Conflict, and Feminist

Meso- and macro-level theories consider larger units in the social world, including organizations (e.g., General Motors or the Episcopal Church), institutions (e.g., education, religion, health care, politics, or economics), societies (Canada or Mexico), or global systems (the World Trade Organization [WTO] or the United Nations [UN]). For example, Hector lives in a modernizing country, Brazil, which is struggling to raise the standard of living of its people and compete in the world market. The decisions that are made by Hector's government at a national and an international level affect his life in a variety of ways. As Brazil industrializes, the nature of jobs and the modes of communication change. Local village cultures modify as the entire nation gains more uniformity of values, beliefs, and norms. Similarly, resources such as access to clean water in Tanzania may be allotted at the local level, but local communities need national and sometimes international support, as illustrated in the photo of Tanzanian tribal elders. We can begin to understand how the process of modernization influences Hector in Brazil, and other people around the globe, by looking at two major macro-level perspectives: structural-functional and conflict theories.

The Tanzanian village elders in this photo continue to have authority to make local (micro-level) decisions about the traditional irrigation canals that are being improved in their village, but their expanded water supply is possible in part because of international financial support (meso- and macro-level decisions).

Structural-Functional Theory

Structural-functional theory (also called **functional theory**) *assumes that all parts of the social structure (including groups, organizations, and institutions), the culture (values and beliefs), and social processes (e.g., social change or child rearing) work together to make the whole society run smoothly and harmoniously.* To understand the social world from this perspective, we must look at how the parts of society (structure) fit together and how each part contributes to the maintenance of society. For instance, two functions of the family include reproducing children and teaching them to be members of society. These and other functions help perpetuate society, for without reproducing and teaching new members to fit in, societies would collapse.

Émile Durkheim (1858–1917) further developed functionalism by theorizing that society is made up of necessary parts that fit together into a working whole. Durkheim felt that individuals conform to the rules of societies because of a collective conscience—the shared beliefs in the values of a group (Durkheim 1947). People grow up sharing the same values, beliefs, and rules of behavior as those around them. Gradually, these shared beliefs and rules are internalized. A person's behavior is, in a sense, governed from within because it feels right and proper to behave in accordance with what is expected. As such, the functionalist perspective of Durkheim and subsequent theorists places emphasis on social consensus, which gives rise to stable and predictable patterns of order in society. Because people need groups for survival, they adhere to the group's rules so that they fit in. This means that most societies run in an orderly manner with most individuals fitting into their positions in society.

Two influential 20th-century functional theorists were Talcott Parsons (1902–1979) and Robert Merton (1910–2003). While Parsons developed a grand, all-encompassing theory and analysis of society, Merton focused on "middle range theories," those that could be studied using empirical data. Both played major roles in developing structural-functional theory (Merton 1938, [1942] 1973).

Functions (contributions or consequences) can be manifest or latent. **Manifest functions** are *the planned outcomes of social organizations or institutions.* The function of the microwave oven, for instance, has been to allow people to prepare meals quickly and easily, facilitating life in overworked and stressed modern families. **Latent functions** are *unplanned or unintended consequences of actions or of social structures* (Merton 1938). Some of the unplanned consequences of microwave ovens were the creation of a host of new jobs and stimulation of the economy as people wrote new cookbooks and as businesses were formed to produce microwavable cookware and prepared foods for the microwave.

Dysfunctions are *those actions that undermine the stability or equilibrium of society* (Merton 1938). By allowing people to cook meals without using a convection oven, the microwave oven has contributed to some young people having no idea how to cook, thus making them highly dependent on expensive technology and processed foods.

From a functionalist perspective, it is important to examine the possible functional and dysfunctional aspects of the different parts of society in terms of the maintenance and harmony of society as a whole.

To summarize the structural-functional perspective, the following points are key:

- It examines the macro-level organizations and patterns in society.
- It focuses on what holds societies together and enhances social continuity.
- It considers the consequences or "functions" of each major part in society.
- It focuses on the way the structure (groups, organizations, institutions), the culture, and social processes work together to make society function smoothly.
- It considers manifest functions (which are planned), latent functions (which are unplanned or secondary), and dysfunctions (which undermine stability).

Functionalism has had a profound impact on social science analysis. Still, functionalism in the 21st century fails to explain many contemporary social situations—wars, overthrow of dictators, and racial conflicts—according to proponents of a rival macro-level perspective, conflict theory.

Thinking Sociologically

Are existing social arrangements in a society necessarily desirable? Is dramatic change necessarily dysfunctional as suggested by functional theory?

A Masai family works together as a unit, and in so doing, they enhance the stability and continuity of their entire society by following its cultural expectations.

Conflict Theory

Conflict theory *contends that conflict is inevitable in any group or society.* Conflict theorists claim that inequality and injustice are the source of conflicts that permeate society. Because resources and power are distributed unequally in society, some members have more money, goods, and prestige than others. The rich protect their positions by using the power they have accumulated to keep those less fortunate in their places. From the perspective of poor people such as Hector, it seems the rich get all the breaks. Because most of us want more of the resources in society (money, good jobs, nice houses, and cars), conflict erupts between the haves and the have-nots. Therefore, conflict can sometimes bring about a change in the society.

Modern conflict theory has its origins in the works of Karl Marx (1818–1883), a German social philosopher who lived in England during the height of 19th-century industrial expansion. He recognized the plight of exploited underclass workers in the new industrial states of Europe and viewed the ruling elites and the wealthy industrial owners as exploiters of the working class. Marx wrote about the new working class crowded in urban slums, working long hours every day, not earning enough money for decent housing and food, and living and working in conditions that were appalling. Few of the protections enjoyed by workers today—such as retirement benefits, health coverage, sick leave, the 40-hour workweek, and restrictions against child labor—existed in Marx's time.

Capitalism emerged as the dominant economic system in Europe. *Capitalism* is an economic system in which (a) the equipment (machinery) and property (factory and land) for producing goods are owned privately by wealthy individuals, who have the right to use these resources however they want, and (b) the market system (supply and demand) determines the distribution of resources and the levels of income (including wages, rents, and profits). Although there are various forms of capitalism, the core principles involve private ownership of industries and nonintervention by government (Heilbroner and Milberg 2012).

Marx believed that two classes, the capitalists (also referred to as bourgeoisie or "haves") who owned the **means of production** (*property, machinery, and cash owned by capitalists*) and the workers (also referred to as proletariat or "have-nots"), would continue to live in conflict until the workers shared more equally in the profits of their labor. The more workers came to understand their plight, the more awareness they would have of the unfairness of the situation. Eventually, Marx believed that workers would rise up and overthrow capitalism, forming a new classless society. Collective ownership—shared ownership of the means of production—would be the new economic order (Marx and Engels [1848] 1969).

The idea of the *bourgeoisie* (the capitalist exploiters who own the means of production, such as factories) and the *proletariat* (the exploited workers who do not own the means of production and sell their labor to survive) has carried over into analysis of modern-day conflicts between labor and management, between women's and men's interests, and between warring factions in places such as Sudan in Africa and Muslim religious sects in the Middle East and North Africa. From a conflict perspective, Hector in Brazil and millions like him in other countries are part of the reserve labor force—a cheap labor pool that can be called on when labor is needed or disregarded when demand is low, thus meeting the changing labor needs of industry and capitalism. This pattern results in permanent economic insecurity and poverty for Hector and those like him.

Many branches of the conflict perspective have grown from the original ideas of Marx. Here, we mention several contributions to conflict theory, those of American sociologists Harriet Martineau ([1837] 1962, 1838), W. E. B. Du Bois ([1899] 1967), and Ralf Dahrendorf (1959). As you can see, social conflict has been a major focus of sociological investigation for more than a century.

Harriet Martineau (1802–1876), generally considered the first female sociologist, wrote several books that contributed to our understanding of modern sociological research methods and provided a critique of America's failure to live up to its democratic principles, especially as they related to women (Martineau 1838). In her work, published before Karl Marx and Friedrich Engels's *Communist Manifesto* ([1848] 1969), she points out that social life is guided by general laws and that these are influenced by population dynamics and what is happening in the natural physical environment. Her work is a precursor to current feminist and conflict theories.

Another early American conflict theorist was W. E. B. Du Bois (1868–1963), the first African American to receive a doctorate from Harvard University. Du Bois felt that sociology should be active in bettering society, that although research should be scientifically rigorous and fair-minded, the ultimate goal of sociological work was social improvement—not just human insight. He saw the conflict between haves and have-nots as being based largely on race in the United States, not just social class.

Du Bois not only wrote on these issues but also acted on them. He was one of the cofounders of the National Association for the Advancement of Colored People (NAACP). He stressed the need for minority ethnic groups to create conflict—to object loudly when those in power do something to disadvantage minorities—and to change the society toward greater equality and participation (Du Bois [1899] 1967). He was, and continues to be, an inspiration to many sociologists who believe that their findings should have real applications and should be used to create a more humane social world (Mills 1956).

A half-century later, in 1959, Ralf Dahrendorf (1929–2009) argued that society is always in the process of change and affected by forces that bring about change. Dahrendorf refined Marx's ideas in several ways. First, he pointed out that the overthrow of capitalism that Marx predicted had not come about because of changes in conditions for workers (employee organizations, unions). Instead, a middle class developed, some workers became part owners, stockholders

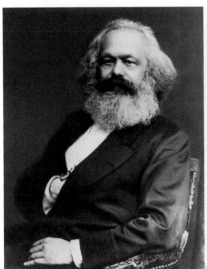

Karl Marx (left) was a social analyst who is often identified as the central figure establishing conflict theory. Harriet Martineau's work preceded Marx's, but she (center) was not taken seriously as a scholar for more than a century because she was female—an early feminist theorist. W. E. B. Du Bois (right) was an outstanding contributor to the development of conflict theory and was among the first to apply that theory to American society, especially to race and ethnic relations.

Conflict Theory

dispersed the concentration of wealth, and a higher standard of living was achieved for workers. Second, he proposed that class conflict occurs between the haves and the have-nots, and the have-nots develop consciousness of their situation and feel that change is possible.

Interest groups, such as members of Hector's favela, share a common situation or interests, including a desire for sanitation, running water, electricity, and a higher standard of living. From within such interest groups, conflict groups arise to fight for changes. There is always potential for conflict when those without power realize their common position and form interest groups. How much change or violence is brought about depends on how organized those groups become.

Dahrendorf's major contribution is the recognition that class conflict over resources results not just in a conflict between proletariat and bourgeoisie but in a multitude of interest groups including old people versus young people, rich versus poor, one region of the country versus another, Christians versus non-Christians, men versus women, and so forth. This acknowledges multiple rifts in the society based in interest groups.

Whereas Marx emphasized the divisive nature of conflict, other theorists have offered a modified theory. American theorist Lewis Coser (1913–2003) took a very different approach to conflict from that of Marx, arguing that it can strengthen societies and organizations within them. According to Coser, problems in a society or group lead to complaints or conflicts—a warning message to the group that all is not well. Resolution of the conflicts shows that the group is adaptable in meeting the needs of its members, thereby creating greater loyalty to the group. Thus, conflict provides the message of what is not working to meet people's needs, and the system adapts to the needs for change because of the conflict (Coser 1956; Simmel 1955).

In summary, conflict theorists advance the following key ideas:

- Conflict and the potential for conflict underlie all social relations.
- Groups of people look out for their self-interest and try to obtain resources and make sure they are distributed primarily to members of their own group.
- Social change is desirable, particularly changes that bring about a greater degree of social equality.
- The existing social order reflects powerful people imposing their values and beliefs upon the weak.

Thinking Sociologically

Imagine you are a legislator. You have to decide whether to cut funding for a senior citizens' program or slash a scholarship program for college students. You want to be reelected, and you know that approximately 90% of senior citizens are registered to vote and that most actually do. You also know that less than half of college-age people are likely to vote. These constituencies are about the same size. What would you do, and how would you justify your decision? How does this example illustrate conflict theory? Why are these meso-level questions?

Multilevel Analysis

Many of the more contemporary theorists try to bridge the gap between micro and macro levels of analysis, offering insights that are relevant at each level.

Max Weber's Contributions. Max Weber's contributions (1864–1920) have had a lasting effect on sociology and other social sciences. Weber (pronounced *Veber*) cannot be pigeonholed easily into one of the theoretical categories, for his contributions include both micro- and macro-level analyses. His emphasis on *Verstehen*, meaning deep empathetic understanding, gives him a place in micro-level theory, and his discussions of Karl Marx and of bureaucracies give him a place in meso- and macro-level theory (Weber 1946).

Verstehen stems from the interpretations or meanings individuals at the micro level give to their social experiences. These subjective interpretations help individuals to understand their lives. Following in Weber's footsteps, sociologists try to understand both people's behaviors and the meanings that people attach to their experiences. In this work, Weber is a micro theorist having set the stage for symbolic interaction theorists. However, the goal-oriented, efficient new organizational form called *bureaucracy* was the focus of much of Weber's writing at the meso level. This organizational form was based on rationality rather than long-standing tradition. In other words, decisions were based on what would best accomplish the organization's goals, not individual benefit. Hiring and promotion on the basis of individual merit (getting the most qualified person rather than hiring a friend or relative) is one example of this rational decision making. This is a principle we take for granted now, but it was not always so. The entire society becomes transformed through a change in how individuals make decisions on behalf of a bureaucratic organization.

Opportunities for jobs were changed, the culture became more geared to merit as a basis for decisions, and organizational life became more governed by rules and routines. All of this came from a redefinition of appropriate ways to make decisions. Weber's ideas about society at the meso level have laid the groundwork for theoretical understanding of modern organizations.

Weber also attempted to understand macro-level processes. For instance, he asked how capitalists understood the world around them, resulting in his famous book, *The Protestant Ethic and the Spirit of Capitalism* (Weber [1904–1905] 1958). His work was influenced by Marx's writings, but while Marx focused on economic conditions as the key factor shaping history and power relations, Weber argued that Marx's focus was too narrow and that politics, economics, religion, psychology, and the military all help explain the social world, power relationships, and conflict. In short, Weber thought that society was more complex than Karl Marx's core notion that two groups—the haves and the have-nots—are in conflict over economic resources.

Thinking Sociologically

To what extent are we human beings free to create our own social world and come up with our own ideas about what our lives should be? To what extent are our lives determined or greatly shaped by our culture, by the society around us, and by our positions in the economic and political system?

Feminist Theory. **Feminist theory** *critiques the hierarchical power structures, which feminists argue treat women and other minorities unfairly* (Cancian 1992; P. Collins 2009). Feminists argue that sociology has been dominated by a male perspective and that the male perspective does not give a complete view of the social world. Much of feminist theory, then, has foundations in the conflict perspective. Women are viewed as disadvantaged by the hierarchical way that society is arranged, whereas men experience privilege because of those arrangements. Men become an interest group intent on preserving their privileges. In this sense, feminist theory is an expression of macro-level conflict theory.

Some branches of feminist theory, however, are not based on Marx's writings. Instead, their ideas come from interaction perspectives, emphasizing the way gender cues and symbols shape the nature of much human interaction. Thus, feminist theory moves from meso- and macro-level analysis (e.g., looking at national and global situations that give privileges to men) to micro-level analysis (e.g., looking at inequality between husbands and wives in marriage). In particular, feminist theory points to the importance of gender as a variable influencing social patterns.

Males learn early in their lives that vulnerability must be avoided so that one is not exploited by others. This, according to feminist theorists, influences the way men think about society. For example, rational choice theory maintains that each individual is out to protect self-interests and to make choices that benefit the self. This theory is based on a male view of society. Men are also more likely to view hierarchical social arrangements as normal, contributing to their difficulty in recognizing how patriarchal society actually is. Also, some feminists claim that most people are blind to the fact that gender roles are socially created, not biologically determined. As a result of these differences in experience and in socialization, women's views on issues of justice, morality, and society lend a different interpretation to society and can present a more

Michelle Obama has a law degree from an Ivy League university, has had a successful legal career, and has called herself "Mom-in-Chief." She is unapologetic about believing that men and women should be treated equally and about being called feminist.

inclusive view of the world (Brettell and Sargent 2009; Burn 2011; Kramer 2010; Lorber 2009).

Many people are excluded from full citizenship because of many possible factors, and it is the interplay of these factors that interested Patricia Hill Collins. An important contemporary scholar, Collins examined the discrimination and oppression people face because of their race, class, gender, sexuality, or nationality, all of which are interconnected.

Patricia Hill Collins is an innovative feminist scholar who has challenged sociologists to look at the ways race, social class, gender, and sexuality can work alone or in combination to provide privilege or not to certain citizens—sometimes without the awareness of the persons involved.

Feminist Theory

Black women are often restricted in their opportunities because of other people's definitions of who and what they should be. In response, people who face discrimination due to one or more social or physical traits often create their own self-definitions and self-images. The idea of *intersectionality*—multiple identities (e.g., race, class, and gender) being intertwined and affecting individuals' life chances—is a particularly powerful concept in sociology (Collins 2005, 2009).

It is interesting that many women today will begin a sentence with the disclaimer "I am not a feminist, but . . ." This is in response to the negative reaction of some men and conservative women to the equal rights movement, the strident style of some feminists, and the focus on men as the cause of problems. Yet not all feminists are strident or focus on men as oppressors. Indeed, many men call themselves feminists, for a feminist is someone who believes that men and women should be given equal standing and equal opportunities in society. Feminists have opened the door to understanding how social structures can bind and inhibit the freedom of both men and women.

Using Different Theoretical Perspectives

Each of the theoretical perspectives described in this chapter begins from a set of assumptions about humans. Each makes a contribution to our understanding, but each has limitations or blind spots, such as not taking into account other levels of analysis (Ritzer 2007). Figure 2.3 provides a summary of cooperative versus competitive perspectives to illustrate how the theories differ.

It is important to understand that there are several different and useful theories to explain society. None of these is right or wrong. Rather, a particular theory may be more or less useful when studying some level of analysis or aspect

	Macro analysis	Micro analysis
Humans viewed as cooperative (people interact with others on the basis of shared meanings and common symbols)	*Structural-Functional Theory*	*Symbolic Interactionism Theory*
Humans viewed as competitive (behavior governed by self-interest)	*Conflict Theory* (group interests)	*Rational Choice Theory* (individual interests)

Figure 2.3   Cooperative Versus Competitive Perspectives

of society. It is also important to learn how each major theoretical perspective can be used to provide a framework and viewpoint to guide research. The micro-, meso-, and macro-level social world model used in this book does not imply that one of these theories is better than another. Each theoretical perspective focuses on a different aspect of society and level of analysis and gives us a different lens through which to view our social world. The social world model helps us picture the whole system and determine which theory or synthesis of theories best suits our needs in analyzing a specific social process or structure.

Thinking Sociologically

Consider the issue of homelessness in cities around the world. How could each of the theories discussed in this chapter be used to help us understand the problem of homelessness?

So far, we have focused on what sociology is and how sociologists know what they know. The rest of the book examines aspects of our social world. The next chapter explores how you can understand your culture and society at the various levels of analysis in our social world.

Ethics in Research

What Have We Learned?

Theories serve as lenses to help us make sense of the data that we gather with various research strategies. However, the data themselves can be used to test the theories, so there is an ongoing reciprocal relationship between theory (the lens for making sense of the data) and the research (the evidence used to test the theories). The most important ideas in this chapter are what sociology considers evidence and how sociology operates as a science. These ideas form the framework for the content of sociology.

Key Points:

- Attempts to understand society have existed for at least 2.5 millennia, but gathering of scientific evidence to test hypotheses and validate claims is a rather modern idea. (See pp. 32–33.)

- As a science, sociology uses eight systematic steps to gather data and test theories about the social world. (See p. 33.)

- In most cases, planning a research study requires that we identify causes (independent variables) and effects (dependent variables) and that we make sure correlations of variables are not spurious; the simultaneous occurrence of two variables can be accidental or noncausal. (See p. 35.)

- Major methods for gathering data in sociology include surveys (e.g., structured interviews and questionnaires), observation studies (direct observation of a natural setting), controlled experiments, and analysis of existing sources (through secondary sources or through content analyses). (See pp. 37–38.)

- Use of multiple methods—triangulation—increases confidence in the findings. (See p. 38.)

- Scientific confidence in results also requires representative samples, usually drawn randomly. (See pp. 38–39.)

- Debates have raged over the purpose of sociology: One approach stresses the objective nature of science; another emphasizes the uniquely human qualities, such as humans making meaning, and argues that complete objectivity is never fully attained; and a third stresses practical or public applications of research to make a more humane, just, and compassionate society. Each of these has a long tradition within sociology. (See pp. 38–44.)

- Theories are especially important to science because they raise questions for research and explain relationships between facts. Sociology has four primary overriding theoretical perspectives or paradigms: symbolic interaction theory, rational choice theory, structural-functional theory, and conflict theory. Other perspectives, such as feminist theory, serve to modify the main paradigms. Most of these theories are more applicable at the micro to meso level or at the meso to macro level. (See pp. 44–52.)

Discussion Questions

1. Why do research questions have to be asked in a precise way? Give an example of a precise research question. How does it make it possible for you to test and measure your topic?

2. If you were to conduct a study to measure student satisfaction with a particular academic department on campus, what research method(s) would you use? Why? How would the method(s) you might select vary according to (a) the size of the department and (b) the type of information you sought?

3. As stated in this chapter, "sociologists must be continually open to having their findings reexamined and new interpretations proposed. Describe a time when you changed your mind due to new information. Was it difficult for you to change your mind? Why or why not?

4. Why is the ability to be open to new ideas and interpretations so vital to the scientific perspective? Do you think you could carry this aspect of the scientific process out successfully—no matter what the topic? Why or why not?

5. If you were to examine the relationship between the government and the economy in the United States today, which of the four major theoretical perspectives outlined in the chapter would be most helpful? Why?

6. Imagine you would like to conduct a sociological study of the students with whom you attended the fourth grade, to determine what key factors influenced their academic achievements. Which of the four major theoretical perspectives would you employ in your study? Why?

Contributing to Our Social World: What Can We Do?

At the Local Level:

- *Local service organizations,* found in every community, work to provide for unmet needs of community members: housing, legal aid, medical care, elder care, and so on. United Way works with most local service organizations. Volunteer to work with the organization in its needs assessment research and learn more about the sociological principles and research methods that are used.

At the Meso Level:

- *The Association for Applied and Clinical Sociology (AACS)* represents sociologists interested in the "application of sociological knowledge." The mission statement of the organization stresses sociologists' ability to work "for beneficial social change through scholarly, educational, programmatic, community, and policy activities" (AACS 2013). Check out the organization's website at www.aacsnet.net.

At the National and Global Levels:

- *The U.S. Bureau of the Census* is best known for its decennial (occurring every 10 years) enumeration of the population, but its work continues each year as it prepares special reports, population estimates, and regular publications (including *Current Population Reports*). Visit the Census Bureau's website at www.census.gov and explore the valuable and extensive amount of quantitative data and other information available, or visit your local Census Bureau office to discuss volunteer work.

Visit **www.sagepub.com/oswcondensed3e** for online activities, sample tests, and other helpful information. Select "Chapter 2: Examining the Social World" for chapter-specific activities.

PART II

Social Structure, Processes, and Control

Picture a house. First there is the wood frame and then the walls and roof. This provides the framework or structure. Within that structure, activities or processes take place—electricity allows for turning on lights and appliances, water is available to wash in and drink, and people carry out these processes. If something goes wrong in the house, we take steps to control the damage and repair it.

Whether we are building a house or a society, the process of constructing our social world is parallel. Social structure is the framework of society with its organizations, and social processes are the dynamic activities of the society. This section begins with a discussion of the structure of society, followed by the processes of culture and socialization through which individuals are taught cultural rules—how to function and live effectively within their society. Although socialization takes place primarily at the micro level, we will explore its implications at the meso and macro levels as well.

If we break the social structure into parts, like the wood frame, walls, and roof of a house, it is the groups and organizations that make up the structure. To work smoothly, these organizations depend on people's loyalty so that they do what society and its groups need to survive. However, smooth functioning does not always happen. Things break down. Those in control of societies try to control disruptions and deviant individuals in order to maintain control and function smoothly.

As we explore the next chapters, we will continue to examine social life at the micro, meso, and macro levels, for each of us as an individual is profoundly shaped by social processes and structures at larger and more abstract levels, all the way to the global level.

CHAPTER 3

Society and Culture

Hardware and Software of Our Social World

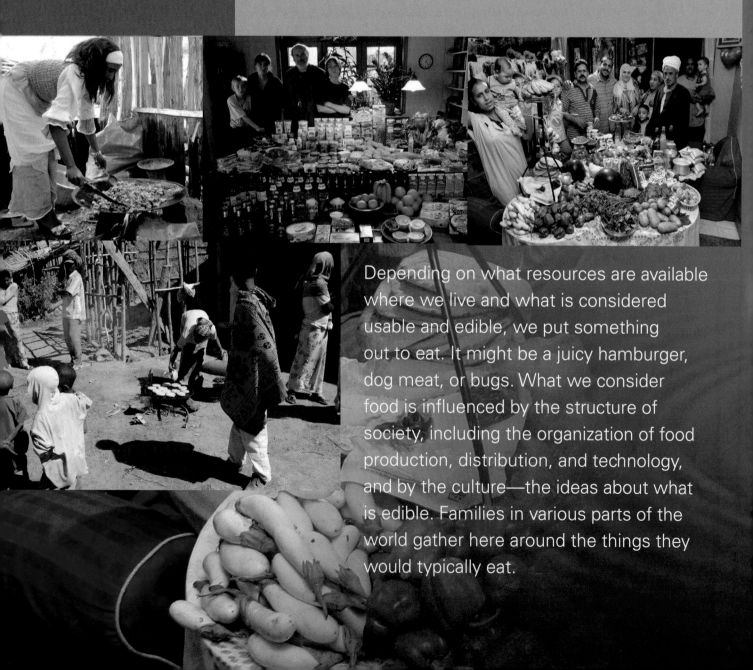

Depending on what resources are available where we live and what is considered usable and edible, we put something out to eat. It might be a juicy hamburger, dog meat, or bugs. What we consider food is influenced by the structure of society, including the organization of food production, distribution, and technology, and by the culture—the ideas about what is edible. Families in various parts of the world gather here around the things they would typically eat.

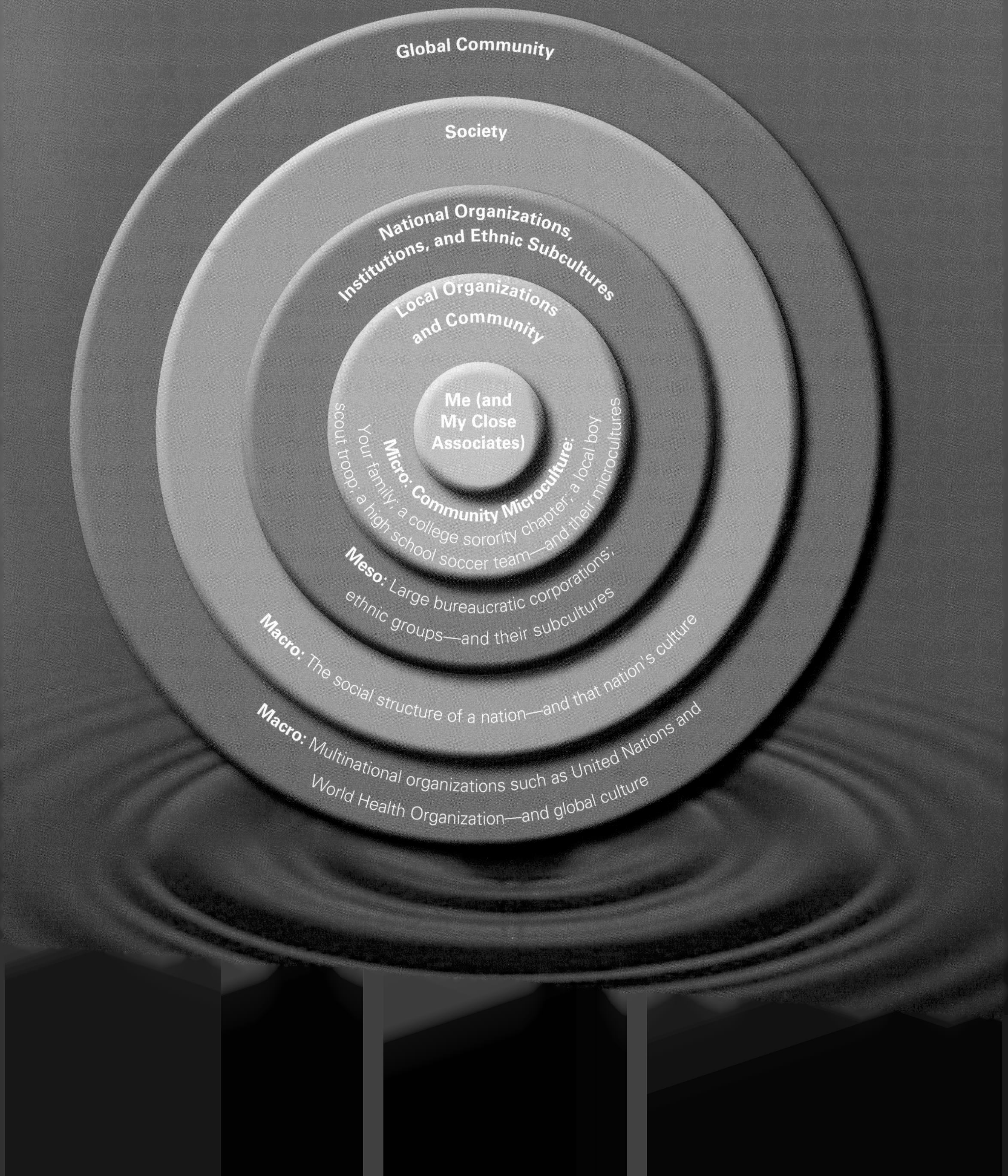

Global Community

Society

National Organizations, Institutions, and Ethnic Subcultures

Local Organizations and Community

Me (and My Close Associates)

Micro: Community Microculture: Your family; a local boy scout troop; a college sorority chapter; a high school soccer team—and their microcultures

Meso: Large bureaucratic corporations; ethnic groups—and their subcultures

Macro: The social structure of a nation—and that nation's culture

Macro: Multinational organizations such as United Nations and World Health Organization—and global culture

Think About It	
Micro: Self and Inner Circle	Could you be human without culture?
Micro: Local Community	How do microcultures—the values and beliefs in your fraternity, choir, or athletic team—affect you?
Meso: National Institutions; Complex Organizations; Ethnic Groups	How do subcultures and countercultures shape the character of the nation and influence your own life?
Macro: National Society	How do the nation's social structures and culture impact you, and how can you influence the national structures and culture?
Macro: Global Community	Why do people live so differently in various parts of the world, and how can those differences be relevant to your own country?

What's coming in this chapter?

Society: The Hardware

Culture: The Software

The Components of Culture: Things and Thoughts

Society, Culture, and Our Social World

Theories of Culture (at the Micro, Meso, and Macro Levels)

The Fit Between Hardware and Software

What do people around the world eat? To answer this question, researchers asked families to buy food supplies for a week. They then took pictures of families with their weekly diets laid out. The differences in these foods and what each family paid to eat give us an insight into differences in one aspect of cultures around the world (Menzel and D'Aluisio 1998).

Mrs. Ukita, the mom in the Ukita family, rises early to prepare a breakfast of miso soup and a raw egg on rice. The father and two daughters eat quickly and rush out to catch their early morning trains to work and school in Kodaira City, Japan. The mother cares for the house, does the shopping, and prepares a typical evening meal of fish, vegetables, and rice for the family.

The Ahmed family lives in a large apartment building in Cairo, Egypt. The 12 members of the extended family include the women who shop for and cook the food—peppers, greens, potatoes, squash, tomatoes, garlic, spices, and rice along with pita bread and often fish or meat.

In the Breidjing refugee camp in Chad, many Sudanese refugees eat what relief agencies can get to them—and that food source is not always reliable. Typical for the Aboubakar family, a mother and five children, is rice or another grain, oil for cooking, dried legumes, occasionally some root plants or squash that keep longer than

fresh fruits and vegetables, and a few spices. The girls and women go into the desert to fetch firewood for cooking and to get water from whatever source has water at the time. This is a dangerous trip as they may be attacked and raped or even killed outside of the camps.

The Walker family from Norfolk, Virginia, grabs dinner at a fast-food restaurant on their way to basketball practice and an evening meeting. Because of their busy schedules and individual activities, they cannot always find time to cook and eat together.

Although most diets include some form of grain and starch, locally available fruits and vegetables, and perhaps meat or fish, broad variations in food consumption exist even within one society. Yet all of these differences have something in common: Each represents a society that has a unique culture that includes what people eat. Food is only one aspect of our way of life and what is necessary for survival. Ask yourself why you sleep on a bed, brush your teeth, or listen to music with friends. Our way of life is called culture.

Culture *refers to the way of life shared by a group of people—the knowledge, beliefs, values, rules or laws, language, customs, symbols, and material products (e.g., food, houses, and transportation) within a society that help meet human needs.* Culture provides guidelines for living. Learning our culture puts our social world in an understandable framework, providing a tool kit with a variety of "tools" we can use to help us construct the meaning of our world (Bruner 1996; Nagel 1994). We compare culture to *software* because it is the human ideas and input that make the society work. Otherwise, society would just be structures, like the framework of a house.

A **society** is *an organized and interdependent group of individuals who live together in a specific geographic area, who interact more with each other than they do with outsiders, and who cooperate for the attainment of common goals.* Each society includes key parts called institutions—such as family, education, religion, politics, economics, and health—that meet basic human needs. This structure that makes up society is what we refer to here as the *hardware* as in a computer.

Culture and Food

Two of the photos on the opening page of this chapter show families from several countries gathered around a typical week's food supply. Members of the Aboubakar family of Sudan gather here in front of their tent with a week's worth of food. Note the differences of foods between these family groups.

Increasingly in the United States, where both parents work, dinner is a fast-food takeout or ready-to-cook packaged meal—a quick dash for nourishment in front of the TV rather than a communal event.

The way people think and behave in any society is largely prescribed by its shared culture, which is learned, reshaped, and transmitted from generation to generation. All activities in the society, whether educating young members, preparing and eating dinner, selecting leaders for the group, finding a mate, or negotiating with other societies, are guided by cultural rules and expectations. In each society, culture provides the social rules for how individuals carry out necessary tasks.

While culture provides the "software" for the way people live, society represents the "hardware"—the structure that gives organization and stability to group life. Society—organized groups of people—and culture—the people's way of life—are interdependent. The two are not the same thing, but they cannot exist without each other, just as computer hardware and software are each useless without the other.

This chapter explores the ideas of society and culture and discusses how they relate to each other. We will look at the following: what society is and how it is organized, how it influences and is influenced by culture, what culture is, how and why culture develops, the components that make up culture, and cultural theories. The first part of the chapter focuses on the hardware: society. After reading this chapter we will have a better idea of how we as individuals fit into society and learn our culture.

Society: The Hardware

Families, groups of friends, neighborhoods or communities, and workplace and school groups all provide the structure of society. All societies have geographical boundaries or borders and individuals who live together in families and communities and who share a culture. The structures that make up society include the interdependent positions we hold (parents, workers), the groups to which we belong (family, work group, clubs), and the institutions in which we participate. This "hardware" (structure) of our social world provides the framework for "software" (culture) to function.

Societies differ because they exist in different places with unique resources—mountains, coastal areas, jungles. Societies change over time with new technology and leadership. Although human societies have become more complex, especially in recent human history, people have been hunters and gatherers for 99% of human existence. Only a few groups remain hunters and gatherers today.

Evolution of Societies

The Saharan desert life for the Tuareg tribe is pretty much as it has been for centuries. In simple traditional societies, individuals are assigned to comparatively few social positions or statuses. Today, however, few societies are isolated from global impact. Even the Tuareg are called on to escort adventurous tourists through the desert for a currency new to them and unneeded until recently. In 2012, members of al-Qaeda in the Islamic Magreb challenged the Tuareg's control over their desert homeland in a war in northern Mali, Africa.

In such traditional societies, men teach their sons everything they need to know, for all men do much the same jobs, depending on where they live—hunting, fishing, or farming and protecting the community from danger. Likewise, daughters learn their jobs from their mothers—such as child care, fetching water, food preparation, farming, weaving, and perhaps house building. By contrast,

The Tuareg live a traditional life in the Saharan desert in the Sahel region of Niger and Mali (Africa), and their social structure has few social positions except those defined by gender. Their pattern of life is slowly changing with the influence of globalization.

more complex societies, such as industrial or "modern" societies, have thousands of interdependent job statuses based on complex divisions of labor with designated tasks. An interesting question is how traditional societies such as the Tuareg change into new types of societies that are more complex, less personal, more technologically dependent, and more bureaucratic.

Émile Durkheim ([1893] 1947), an early French sociologist, pictured a continuum between simple and complex societies. He described simple premodern societies as held together by **mechanical solidarity**, or *cohesion and integration based on the similarity of individuals in the group, including beliefs, values, and emotional ties between members of the group.* Furthermore, the division of labor is based largely on male-female distinctions and age groupings. Members of premodern societies tend to think the same way on important matters, and everyone fulfills his or her expected social positions. This provides the glue that holds the society together. The entire society may involve only a few hundred people, with no meso-level institutions, organizations, or subcultures. Prior to the emergence of nation-states, there was no macro level either—only tribal groupings.

According to Durkheim ([1893] 1947), as societies transform, they become more complex through increasingly complex divisions of labor and changes in the ways people carry out necessary tasks for survival. **Organic solidarity** refers to *cohesion and integration based on differences of individuals in the group so that they are interdependent. The society has a substantial division of labor, with each member playing*

a highly specialized role in the society and each person being dependent on others due to interdependent, interrelated tasks. The society has cohesion regardless of whether people have common values and shared outlooks.

Prior to the factory system, for example, individual cobblers made shoes to order. With the Industrial Revolution, factories took over the process, with many individuals carrying out interdependent tasks. The division of labor is critical because it leads to new forms of social cohesion (glue) based on interdependence, not emotional ties. Durkheim called this organic solidarity because he likened the interdependence of people in different social positions to the interdependence of an animal's internal organs; if any one organ ceases to work, other organs may malfunction, and the animal may die. This is also true of a society. Changes from mechanical (traditional) to organic (modern) society also involve harnessing new forms of energy and finding more efficient ways to use them (Nolan and Lenski 2010). For example, the use of steam engines and coal for fuel triggered the Industrial Revolution, leading to the development of industrial societies.

As societies changed toward organic solidarity, they developed more levels, and the meso level—institutions and large bureaucratic organizations—became more influential. Still, as recently as 200 years ago, even large societies had little global interdependence, and life for the typical citizen was influenced mostly by events at the micro and meso levels. Keep in mind that it was less than 250 years ago when American colonies selected representatives to form a loosely federated government that came to be called the United States.

As you read about each of the following types of societies, from the simplest to most complex, notice the presence of these variables: division of labor, interdependence of people's positions, increasingly advanced technologies, and new forms and uses of energy. Although none of these variables appears *sufficient* to trigger evolution to a new type of society, they may all be *necessary* for a transition to occur.

According to Durkheim ([1893] 1947), then, in traditional societies with mechanical solidarity, interpersonal interaction and community life at the micro level are the most important aspects of social life. Societies have developed as a result of changes toward more organic solidarity. As societies become more complex, meso- and macro-level institutions become more important and have more profound impacts on the lives of individuals.

Hunter-Gatherer Societies

Life in hunter-gatherer societies is organized around kinship ties and *reciprocity*—that is, mutual assistance—for the well-being of the whole community. When a large animal is killed, people gather from a wide area to share in the bounty, and great care is taken to ensure that the meat is

A mother in Côte d'Ivoire (West Africa), carrying her load on her head, returns to the village with her daughter after gathering wood. Carrying wood and water is typically women's work. In this hunter-gatherer society, the primary social cohesion is mechanical solidarity.

distributed fairly. In **hunter-gatherer societies,** *people rely on vegetation and animals occurring naturally in their habitat to sustain life.* People make their clothing, shelter, and tools from available materials or obtain goods through trade with other nearby groups. People migrate seasonally to new food sources. Population size remains small as the number of births and deaths in the society is balanced.

From the beginning of human experience until recently, hunting and gathering (or foraging) were the sole means of sustaining life. Other types of societies emerged only recently (Nolan and Lenski 2010), and today, only a handful of societies still rely on hunting and gathering. The hunter-gatherer lifestyle is becoming extinct.

Herding and Horticultural Societies

Herding societies *have food-producing strategies based on domestication of animals, whose care is the central focus of their activities.* Domesticating animals has replaced hunting them. In addition to providing food and other products, cattle, sheep, goats, pigs, horses, and camels represent forms of wealth that result in more social prestige for some members of the group.

Horticultural societies *are those in which the food-producing strategy is based on domestication of plants, using digging sticks and wooden hoes to cultivate small gardens.* They may also keep domesticated animals, but they focus on primitive agriculture or gardening. They cultivate tree crops, such as date palms or bananas, and plant garden plots, such as yams, beans, taro, squash, or corn. This is more efficient than gathering wild vegetables and fruits.

Both herding and horticultural societies differ from hunter-gatherer societies in that they make their living by cultivating food and have some control over its production (Ward and Edelstein 2009). The ability to control food sources was a major turning point in human history. Societies became more settled and stored surpluses of food, which led to increases in population size. A community could contain as many as 3,000 individuals. More people, surplus food, and greater accumulation of possessions encouraged the development of private property and created new status differences between individuals and families. Forms of social inequality became even more pronounced in agricultural societies.

The end of the horticultural stage saw advances in irrigation systems, fertilization of land, crop rotation, more permanent settlements, land ownership, human modification of the natural environment, higher population density (cities), and power hierarchies. However, the technological breakthrough that moved many societies into the agricultural stage was the plow, introduced more than 6,000 years ago. It marked the beginning of the Agricultural Revolution and brought massive changes in social structures to many societies.

Agricultural Societies

Like horticulturalists, **agricultural societies** *rely primarily on raising crops for food but make use of technological advances*

Masai men in Kenya herd their cattle, leading them to water or better grazing. The strategy of domesticating cattle rather than hunting game has been a survival strategy for the Masai, but it also affects the culture in many other ways.

such as the plow, irrigation, animals, and fertilization to continuously cultivate the same land, thus permitting permanent settlements and greater food surpluses. Through time, the size of population centers increased to as much as a million or more. Agricultural societies are more efficient in utilizing energy than foraging societies. The plow circulates nutrients better than a digging stick, and when an animal is used to pull the plow, strength beyond that of a person is marshaled.

As surpluses accumulated, land in some societies became concentrated in the hands of a few individuals. Wealthy landowners built armies and expanded their empires and could control the labor sources and acquire serfs or slaves. Thus, the feudal system was born. Serfs (the peasant class) were forced to work the land for their

The invention of the plow was essential for agricultural societies to develop, and in the early period of agriculture, plows were pushed by people and then pulled by animals. The harnessing of energy was taken to another level when gasoline engines could pull the plow and cultivate thousands of acres. This represents the beginning of industrialization. Modern machinery such as this harvester has pushed farming into the new level of productivity.

survival. Food surpluses also allowed some individuals to leave the land and to trade goods or services in exchange for food. For the first time, social inequality became extensive enough that we could refer to social classes. At this point, religion, political power, a standing army, and other meso-level institutions and organizations came to be independent of the family. The meso level became well established.

As technology advanced, goods were manufactured in cities. Peasants moved from farming communities where land could not support the large population to rapidly growing urban areas where the demand for labor was great. It was not until the mid-1700s in England that the next major transformation of society took place, resulting largely from technological advances and harnessing of energy.

Industrial Societies

The Industrial Revolution brought the harnessing of steam power and gasoline engines, permitting machines to replace human and animal power; a tractor can plow far more land in a week than a horse, and an electric pump can irrigate more acres than an ox-driven pump. As a result of the new technologies, raw mineral products such as ores, raw plant products such as rubber, and raw animal products such as hides could be transformed into mass-produced consumer goods. The Industrial Revolution brought enormous changes in occupations, division of labor, specialization, products, and social structures.

Industrial societies *rely primarily on mechanized production for subsistence, resulting in greater division of labor based on expertise.* Economic resources were distributed more widely among individuals in industrial societies, but inequities between owners and laborers persisted. Wage earning gradually replaced slavery and serfdom, and highly skilled workers earned higher wages, leading to the rise of a middle class. Farmworkers moved from rural areas to cities to find work in factories, which produced consumer goods. Cities came to be populated by millions of people.

Family and kinship patterns at the micro level also changed. Agricultural societies need large, land-based extended family units to do the work of farming, but industrial societies need individuals with specific skills, ability to move to where the jobs are, and smaller families to support. Family roles have changed. For example, children are an asset in agricultural societies and begin work at an early age. However, from a purely economic perspective, children become a liability in an industrial society because they contribute less to the finances of the family.

Meso- and macro-level dimensions of social life expand in industrializing societies and become more influential in the lives of individuals. National institutions and multinational organizations develop. Today, for example, global organizations such as the World Bank, the

World Court, the United Nations, and the World Health Organization address social problems and sometimes even make decisions that change policies within a nation. Medical organizations such as Doctors Without Borders work cross-nationally, corporations such as Nike and Gap become multinational (located in many countries), and voluntary associations such as Amnesty International lobby for human rights around the globe.

Perhaps the most notable characteristic of the industrial age is the rapid rate of change compared to other stages of societal development. The beginning of industrialization in Europe was gradual, based on years of population movement, urbanization, technological development, and other factors in modernization. Today, however, societal change occurs so rapidly that societies at all levels of development are being drawn together into a new age—the postindustrial era.

Postindustrial or Information Societies

The difference between India and the United States is "night and day"—literally. As Keith and Jeanne finished chapters for this book, they were sent to India in the evening and returned typeset by morning, a feat made possible by the time difference. Efficiency of overnight electronic delivery and cost of production have led many publishing companies to turn to businesses halfway around the world for much of the book production process. As India and other

This Buddhist monk uses modern technology, including a laptop that can connect him with colleagues on the other side of the globe. In a postindustrial or information society, even rather traditional positions can be affected.

developing countries increase their trained, skilled labor force, they are being called on by national and multinational companies to carry out global manufacturing processes. India has some of the world's best technical training institutes and the most modern **technology**—*the practical application of tools, skills, and knowledge to meet human needs and extend human abilities*. Although many people in India live in poverty, a relatively new middle class is rapidly emerging in major business centers around the country.

Postindustrial societies are *those that have moved from human labor and manufacturing to automated production and service jobs, largely processing information*. This shift, first occurring in the United States, Western Europe, and Japan, was characterized by movement from human labor to automated production and from a predominance of manufacturing jobs to a growth in service jobs, such as computer operators, bankers, scientists, teachers, public relations workers, stockbrokers, and salespeople. More than two thirds of all jobs in the United States now reside in organizations that produce and transmit information, thus the reference to the "information age." Daniel Bell (1973, 1999) described this transformation of work, information, and communication as "the third technological revolution" after industrialization based on steam (which he calls the first technological revolution) and the invention of electricity (the second technological revolution). According to Bell, the third technological revolution was the development of the computer, which has led to this postindustrial era or the information age.

As is true in other types of societies, postindustrial societies are undergoing significant structural changes. For example, postindustrial societies require workers with high levels of technical and professional education. Those without technical education are less likely to find rewarding employment in the technological revolution (Drori 2006; Tapscott 1998). This results in new class lines being drawn, based in part on skills and education in new technologies. To examine these issues more fully, look at Table 3.1 in the next "Engaging Sociology" feature on page 68 and conduct the interviews suggested.

Postindustrial societies rely on new sources of power, such as atomic, wind, thermal, and solar energy, and new uses of computer automation, such as computer-controlled robots, which eliminate the need for human labor other than highly skilled technicians. In an age of global climate change, there is also a lot of interest in technologies that reduce pollution, such as hybrid buses. The core issue in a postindustrial society is this: Control of information and ability to develop technologies or provide services, rather than control of money or capital, becomes most important.

Values of 21st-century postindustrial societies favor scientific and creative approaches to problem solving, research, and development, along with attitudes that support the globalization of world economies. Satellites, cell

Engaging Sociology

Demographics of Internet Users

Below is the percentage of each group of American adults who use the Internet, according to a February 2012 Pew Research Center survey. For instance, 79% of women use the Internet.

Table 3.1   Internet Use Variation

	Percent who use the Internet
All adults	80
Men	81
Women	79
Race/Ethnicity	
White, non-Hispanic	83
Black, non-Hispanic	71
Hispanic (English- and Spanish-speaking)	71
Age	
18–29	94
30–49	88
50–64	79
65+	48
Household income	
Less than $30,000/yr.	65
$30,000–$49,999	85
$50,000–$74,999	94
$75,000+	98
Educational attainment	
No high school diploma	45
High school grad	73
Some college	91
College+	97

Source: Pew Internet and American Life Project tracking survey conducted January 20-February 19, 2012. N = 2,253 adults age 18 and older, including 901 interviews conducted by cell phone. Interviews were conducted in both English and Spanish.

Engaging With Sociology

Interview 10 people you know to find out about their Internet use, keeping records on the gender, age, ethnicity, educational attainment, and income bracket of each. Then compare your figures with those in this table. Are they similar? If not, what are possible geographic or other social factors that might cause your figures to be different from those in this national survey?

phones, fiber optics, and especially the Internet are further transforming postindustrial societies of the information age.

In a study of postmodern communities, sociologist Richard Florida links creativity to the local cultural climate and to economic prosperity. His research has important applied dimensions and is useful to policy makers in local communities. As his research in the next "Sociologists in Action" makes clear, the organization of the society and the means of providing the necessities of life have a profound impact on values, beliefs, lifestyle, and other aspects of culture.

Sociologists in Action— Richard Florida

Creativity, Community, and Applied Sociology

Like the transformations of societies from the hunter-gatherer to the horticultural stage or from the agricultural to the industrial stage, our own current transformation seems to have created a good deal of "cultural wobble" in society. How does one identify the elements or the defining features of a new age while the transformation is still in process? This was one of the questions that intrigued sociologist Richard Florida, who studied U.S. communities.

Professor Florida (2002, 2012a) combined several methods. First, he traveled around the country to communities that were especially prosperous and seemed to be on the cutting edge of change in U.S. society. In these communities, he did both individual interviews and focus-group interviews. Focus-group interviews are semistructured group interviews with seven or eight people in which their views and ideas can be generated by asking open-ended questions. Professor Florida recorded the discussion and analyzed the transcript of the discussion. The collected data helped him identify the factors that caused people to choose a place to live. His informants discussed quality of life and the way they make decisions. As certain themes and patterns emerged, he tested the ideas by comparing statistical data for regions that were vibrant, had growing economies, and seemed to be integrated into the emerging information economy. He used another method to compare communities and regions of the country—analyzing already existing archival data collected by various U.S. government agencies, especially the U.S. Bureau of Labor Statistics and the U.S. Census Bureau.

Florida argues that the economy of the 21st century is largely driven by creativity, and creative people often decide where to live based on certain features of the society. Currently, more than one third of the jobs in the United States—and almost all of the extremely well-paid professional positions—require creative thinking. These include not just the creative arts but scientific research, computer and mathematical occupations, educational and library science positions, and many media, legal, and managerial careers. People in this "creative class" are given an enormous amount of autonomy; in their work, they have problems to solve and freedom to figure out how to do so. Florida found that modern businesses flourish when they hire highly creative people. Thus, growing businesses tend to seek out places where creative people locate.

Through his research, Florida identified regions and urban areas that are especially attractive to the creative class. Florida found that creative people thrive on diversity—ethnic, gender, religious, and otherwise—for when creative people are around others who think differently, it tends to spawn new avenues of thinking and problem solving. Tolerance of difference and even the enjoyment of individual idiosyncrasies are a hallmark of thriving communities. Interestingly, Florida is now very much in demand as a consultant to mayors and urban-planning teams, and his books have become required reading for city council members. Some elected officials have decided that fostering an environment conducive to creativity that attracts creative people leads to prosperity because business will follow. Key elements for creative communities are local music and art festivals, the presence of organic food grocery stores, legislation that encourages interesting mom-and-pop stores (and keeps out large "box stores" that crush such small and unique endeavors), encouragement of quaint locally owned bookstores and distinctive coffee shops, provisions for bike and walking paths throughout the town, and ordinances that establish an environment of tolerance for people who are "different."

* * * * * * *

Note: Richard Florida heads the Martin Prosperity Institute at the Rotman School of Management at the University of Toronto. He also runs the private Creative Class Group. He earned his bachelor's degree from Rutgers University and his doctorate in urban planning from Columbia University.

Thinking Sociologically

What are likely to be the growth areas for jobs in your society? What competencies and skills will be essential in the future for you to find employment and be successful on the job?

What will the future bring? Among the many ideas for the future, technological advances dominate the field. Predictions include the increasing use of cell phones, connecting the poorest corners of the globe with the rest of the world. One billion mobile phone users are predicted for China by 2020, with 80% of the population having phones. With discovery and efficient use of energy being central to sociocultural evolution, alternative energy sources from wind and solar power to hydrogen will become essential to meet demand. Plug-in hybrids, natural gas, and electric batteries may replace gasoline motors. One million hydrogen-fueled cars are predicted for the United States by the year 2035, and far more for Europe and Japan

(*News of Future* 2012). Rechargeable batteries that will run for 40 hours without recharging will run most home appliances by 2030. Those who are paralyzed will find help from brain-computer interfaces, giving them ability to control their environments. Many advances will occur in space travel, and medical advances will result in stem cell breakthroughs that can develop into various types of body tissue (Future for All 2013; National Institutes of Health 2012). These are just a few of the many predictions that will affect societies and alter some human interactions. The point is that rapid change is inevitable, and the future looks exciting.

In much of this book, we focus on complex, multilevel societies, for this is the type of system in which most of us reading this book now live. Much of this book also focuses on social interaction and social structures, including interpersonal networking, the growth of bureaucratic structures, social inequality within the structures, and the core institutions necessary to meet the needs of individuals and society. In short, "hardware"—society—is the focus of many subsequent chapters. The remainder of this chapter focuses primarily on the "software" dimension (culture).

Culture: The Software

I sleep on a bed. Perhaps you sleep on a tatami mat. I brush my teeth with a toothbrush and toothpaste. Perhaps you chew on a special stick to clean your teeth. I speak English, along with 328 million native English speakers. You may be a native speaker of one of the many other languages in the world, as are over 1.2 billion Chinese speakers (mostly Mandarin); 221 million Arabic speakers; 182 million Hindustani speakers in India, and many others around the world; and 329 million Spanish speakers in 23 countries in which Spanish is the official language (*World Almanac* 2013). English is the top Internet language around the world with 536.9 million users; Chinese has 444.9 million, Spanish 153.3 million, and Japanese 99.1 million. Many other languages are also used on the Internet (Internet World Stats 2010).

I like meat and veggies. Perhaps you like tofu and grasshoppers. I wear jeans and a T-shirt. Perhaps you wear a sari or burqa. In the United States, proper greetings include a handshake, a wave, or saying "hello" or "hi." The greeting ceremony in Japan includes bowing, with the depth of the bow defined by the relative status of each individual. The proper greeting behavior in many European countries calls for men as well as women to kiss acquaintances on both cheeks.

The point of these examples is to show that the culture—the ideas and "things" that are passed on from one generation to the next in a society, including the knowledge, beliefs, values, rules and laws, language, customs, symbols, and material products—varies greatly as we travel the globe. Each social unit of cooperating and interdependent people, whether at the micro, meso, or macro level, develops a unique way of life. This culture provides guidelines for the actions and interaction of individuals and groups within the society. The cultural guidelines that people follow when they greet another person are examples. As you can see, the sociological definition of culture refers to far more than "high culture"—such as fine art, classical music, opera, literature, ballet, and theater—and also far more than "popular culture"—such as reality TV, professional wrestling, YouTube, and other mass entertainment.

All people share a culture with others in their society. Culture provides the rules, routines, patterns, and expectations for carrying out daily rituals and interactions. Within a society, the process of learning how to act is called socialization (discussed in detail in Chapter 4). From birth, we learn the patterns of behavior approved in our society.

Culture evolves over time and is adaptive. What is normal, proper, and good behavior in hunter-gatherer societies, where cooperation and communal loyalty are critical to the hunt, differs from appropriate behavior in an information age, where individualism and competition may be encouraged and enhance one's position and well-being.

The creation of culture is ongoing and cumulative. Individuals and societies continually build on existing culture to adapt to new challenges and opportunities. The behaviors, values, and institutions that seem natural to you are actually shaped by your culture. Culture is so much a part of life that you may not even notice behaviors that outsiders find unusual or even abhorrent. You may not think about handing food to someone with your left hand, but in some other cultures, such acts may be defined as disgusting and rude.

The transmission of culture is the feature that most separates humans from other animals. Some societies of higher primates have shared cultures but do not systematically enculturate (teach a way of life to) the next generation. Primate cultures focus on behaviors relating to food getting, use of territory, and social status. Human cultures have significantly more content and are mediated by language. Humans are the only mammals with cultures that enable them to adapt to and even modify their environments so they can survive on the equator, in the Arctic, or even beyond the planet.

Online Lives

This Japanese family might think that eating with a fork or spoon or that sitting on a chair for dinner is quite strange. The children have been well socialized into their culture to know that polite eating involves competent use of chopsticks and kneeling on pillows.

Ethnocentrism and Cultural Relativity

As scientists, sociologists must rely on careful use of the scientific method to understand behavior. The scientific method calls for objectivity, the practice of considering observed behavior independently of one's own beliefs and values. The study of social behavior thus requires both sensitivity to a wide variety of human social patterns and a perspective that reduces bias. This is more difficult than it sounds because sociologists themselves are products of society and culture. All of us are raised in a particular culture that we view as normal or natural. Yet, not every culture views the same things as "normal."

The Arapesh of New Guinea, a traditional and stable society, encourage premarital sex. Margaret Mead found that it is a way for a girl to prove her fertility, which makes her more attractive as a potential marriage partner (Mead [1935] 1963). Any babies born out of wedlock are simply absorbed into the girl's extended family. The baby's care, support, belonging, and lineage are not problems for the Arapesh. The babies are simply accepted and welcomed as new members of the mother's family because the structure is able to absorb them. For the Arapesh, sexual behavior outside of marriage is not a moral issue. Mead's findings have been questioned, but the fact that societies have many

different views on premarital sex and pregnancy remains (Library of Congress 2010).

From studies of societies documented in the *Human Relations Area Files,* scientists have found that about 42% of the 154 included societies encourage premarital sex, whereas 29% forbid such behavior and punish those who disobey this rule (Ford 1970). The remainder fall in between. As you can see, social values, beliefs, and behaviors can vary dramatically from one society to the next. Differences can be threatening and even offensive to people who judge others according to their own perspectives, experiences, and values.

The tendency to view one's own group and its cultural expectations as right, proper, and superior to others is called **ethnocentrism**. If you were brought up in a society that forbids premarital or extramarital sex, for instance, you might judge the Arapesh—or many Americans—to be immoral. In a few Muslim societies, people who violate this taboo may be severely punished, or even executed, because premarital sex is seen as an offense against the faith and the family and as a weakening of social bonds. It threatens the lineage and inheritance systems of family groups. In turn, the Arapesh would find rules of abstinence to be strange and even wrong. Societies instill some degree of ethnocentrism in their members because ethnocentric beliefs hold groups together and help members feel that they belong to the group. Ethnocentrism promotes loyalty, unity, high morale, and conformity to the rules of society. Fighting for one's country, for instance, requires some degree of belief in the rightness of one's own society and its causes. Ethnocentric attitudes also help protect societies from rapid, disintegrating change.

In 1923, members of the Hollywood Association started a campaign to expel the Japanese from their community. Signs like these were prominent throughout Hollywood and other California communities. They illustrate ethnocentrism.

If most people in a society did not believe in the rules and values of their own culture, the result could be widespread dissent, deviance, or crime.

Ethnocentrism can take many forms (see, for example, how you react to Map 3.1). Unfortunately, ethnocentrism often leads to misunderstandings between people of different cultures. In addition, the same ethnocentric attitudes that strengthen ties between people may also encourage hostility, racism, war, and even genocide against others—even others within the society—who are different. Virtually all societies tend to "demonize" their adversary—in movies, the news, and political speeches—especially when a conflict is most intense. Dehumanizing another group with labels makes it easier to torture or kill its members or to perform acts of discrimination and brutality. We see this in current Afghanistan conflicts in which both sides in the conflict feel hatred for the other combatants. However, as we become a part of a global social world, it

becomes increasingly important to accept those who are "different." Bigotry and attitudes of superiority do not enhance cross-national cooperation and trade—which is what the increasing movement toward a global village and globalization entail.

U.S. foreign relations also illustrate how ethnocentrism can produce hostility. Many U.S. citizens are surprised to learn that the United States—great democracy, world power, and disseminator of food, medicine, and technological assistance to developing nations—is despised in many countries. One cause is the political dominance of the United States and the threat it poses to other people's way of life (Hertsgaard 2003). U.S. citizens are regarded by some as thinking ethnocentrically and only about their own welfare as their country exploits weaker nations. U.S. tourists are often seen as loudmouthed ignoramuses whose ethnocentric attitudes prevent them from seeing value in other cultures or from learning other languages.

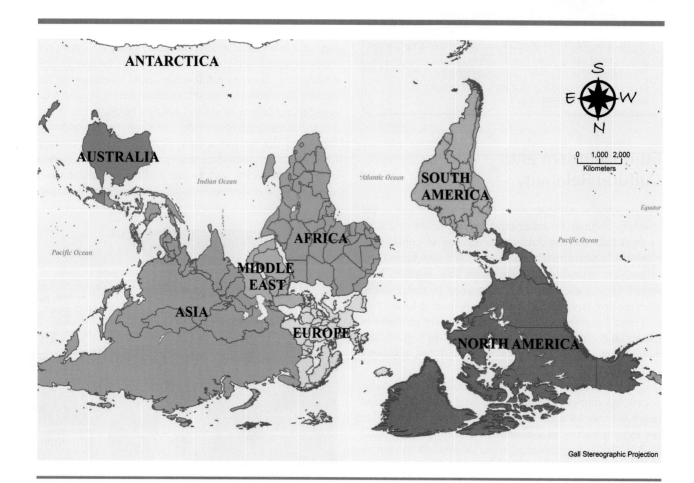

Map 3.1 "Southside Up" Global Map

Source: Map by Anna Versluis.

Note: This map illustrates geographic ethnocentrism. Americans tend to assume it is natural that the north should always be "on top." The fact that this map of the world is upside-down, where south is "up," seems incorrect or disturbing to some Americans, yet it too illustrates an ethnocentric view of the world. Most people think of their countries or regions as occupying a central and larger part of the world.

Anti-U.S. demonstrations in South America, the Middle East, and Asia have brought this reality to life through television. Indeed, politicians in several Latin American and European countries have run for office on platforms aimed at reducing U.S. influence. Thus, U.S. ethnocentrism may foster anti-American ethnocentrism by people from other countries. Note that even referring to citizens of the United States as "Americans"—as though people from Canada, Mexico, and South America do not really count as Americans—is seen as ethnocentric by many people from these other countries. *America* and the *United States* are not the same thing, but many people in the United States, including some presidents, fail to make the distinction, much to the dismay of other North and South Americans.

Not all ethnocentrism is hostile; some is just reactions we have to the strange ways of other cultures. An example is making judgments about what is proper food to eat and what is just not edible. While food is necessary for survival, there are widespread cultural differences in what people eat, as noted in the first part of this chapter. Some people in New Guinea tribes savor grasshoppers; Europeans and Russians relish raw fish eggs (caviar); Inuit children may find seal eyeballs a treat; some Indonesians eat dog; and some Nigerians prize termites. Whether it is from another time period or another society, variations in food can be shocking to us.

In contrast to ethnocentrism, **cultural relativism** *requires setting aside cultural and personal beliefs and prejudices to understand another group or society through the eyes of a member of that community using its own standards.* Cultural relativism requires that we shrug our shoulders and admit, "Well, they are getting vitamins, proteins, and other nutrients, and it seems to work for them." Instead of judging cultural practices and social behavior as good or bad according to one's own cultural practices, the goal is to be impartial in learning the purposes and consequences of practices and behaviors in the group under study. Just as we may have preferences for certain software programs to do analyses or word processing, we can recognize that other software programs are quite good, may have some features that are better than the one we use, and are ingeniously designed.

Yet, being tolerant and understanding is not always easy; even for the most objective observer, differences in other cultures can be difficult to understand. The idea of being "on time," which is so much a part of the cultures of the United States, Canada, Japan, and parts of Europe, is a rather bizarre concept in many societies. Among many Native American people, such as the Dineh (Apache and Navajo), it is ludicrous for people to let a piece of machinery such as a timepiece that one wears on one's arm or a cell phone in one's pocket govern the way one lives life. The Dineh orientation to time—that one should do things according to a natural rhythm of the body and not according to an artificial electronic mechanism—is difficult for many North Americans to grasp. Misunderstandings occur when those of European heritage think "Indians are always late" and jump to an erroneous conclusion that "Indians" are undependable. Native Americans, on the other hand, think whites are neurotic about letting some instrument control them (Basso 1979; Farrer 2011; E. Hall 1959, 1983).

In the United States, dogs are family members and are highly cherished, with dog care becoming a growth industry. In Nanking, China, dogs are valued more as a culinary delicacy and a good source of protein. If you feel a twinge of disgust, that is part of the ethnocentrism we may experience as our perspectives conflict with those elsewhere in the world.

Values

Cultural relativism does not require that social scientists accept or agree with all the beliefs and behaviors of the societies or groups they study. Certain behaviors, such as infanticide, cannibalism, slavery, female genital mutilation (removal of part of the female anatomy), forced marriage, or genocide, may be regarded as unacceptable by almost all social scientists. Yet, it is still important to try to understand those practices in the social and cultural contexts in which they occur. Many social scientists take strong stands against violations of human rights, environmental destruction, and other social policies. They base their judgments on the concept of universal human rights and the potential for harm to individuals. Still, most Western democracies are adaptations to systems that thrive on values of extreme individualism, differentiation, and competition that are consistent with a very complex society. Other societies do not always think our ideas of "universal rights" are universal. They are based on ideas of individualism that some other cultures do not use as the basis of their values, with the needs of communities having higher priority than individual rights.

Thinking Sociologically

Small, tightly knit societies with no meso or macro level often stress cooperation, conformity, and personal sacrifice for the sake of the community. Complex societies with established meso- and macro-level linkages are more frequently individualistic, stressing personal uniqueness, achievement, individual creativity, and critical thinking. Why might this be so?

The Components of Culture: Things and Thoughts

Things and thoughts—these make up much of our culture. **Material culture** *includes all the objects (things) we can see or touch including the artifacts of a group of people.* **Nonmaterial culture** includes *our thoughts, language, feelings, beliefs, values, and attitudes that make up much of our culture.* Together they provide the guidelines for our lives.

Material Culture: The Artifacts of Life

Material culture includes all the human-made objects we can see or touch, all the artifacts of a group of people—their grindstones for grinding cassava root, microwave ovens for cooking, bricks of mud or clay for building shelters, hides or woven cloth for making clothing, books or computers for conveying information, tools for reshaping their environments, vessels for carrying and sharing food, and weapons for dominating and subduing others.

Some material culture is from the local community—it is of micro-level origin. The kinds of materials with which homes are constructed and the materials used for clothing often reflect the geography and resources of the local area. Likewise, types of jewelry, pottery, musical instruments, or clothing reflect tastes that emerge at the micro and meso levels of family, community, and ethnic subculture. At a more macro level, national and international corporations interested in making profits work hard to establish trends in fashion and style that may cross continents and oceans.

Material culture in many ways drives the globalization process. Many of our clothes are now made in Asian or Central American countries. Our shoes may well have been produced in the Philippines. The oil used to make plastic water bottles and devices in our kitchens likely came from the Middle East. Even food is imported year-round from around the planet. That romantic diamond engagement ring—a symbol that represents the most intimate tie—may well be imported from a South African mine using low-paid or even slave labor. Our cars are assembled from parts produced on nearly every continent. Moreover, we spend many hours in front of a piece of material culture—our computers—surfing the World Wide Web.

Thinking Sociologically

Think of examples of material culture that you use daily: stove, automobile, cell phone, computer, refrigerator, clock, money, and so forth. How do these material objects influence your way of life and the way you interact with others? How would your behavior be different if these material objects, say iPhones or cars, did not exist?

Nonmaterial Culture: Beliefs, Values, Rules, and Language

Saluting the flag, saying a blessing before meals to express gratitude for abundance in one's life, flashing someone an obscene gesture, and a football coach signaling the defense what defensive formation to run for the next play are all symbolic acts. In the case of the salute and the prayer, the acts undergird a belief about the nation or about a higher spiritual presence. In each case something is communicated, yet each of these acts refers to something deeper than any material object.

Photo Essay

Houses as Part of a Society's Material Culture

Homes are good examples of material culture. Their construction is influenced by local materials, but also ideas of what a home is. Homes shape the context in which family members interact. Indeed, in some cases, homes become status symbols that are far larger than the family needs, but the family is making a prestige statement about their socioeconomic standing.

Nonmaterial culture refers to *the thoughts, language, feelings, beliefs, values, and attitudes that make up much of our culture.* They are the invisible and intangible parts of culture; they are of equal or even greater importance than material culture for they involve the society's rules of behavior, ideas, and beliefs that shape how people interact with others and with their environment. Although we cannot touch the nonmaterial components of our culture, they pervade our life and are instrumental in determining how we think, feel, and behave. Nonmaterial culture is complex, comprising four main elements: values, beliefs, norms or rules, and language. **Values** are *shared judgments about what is desirable or undesirable, right or wrong, good or bad.* They express the basic ideals of any group of people. In industrial and postindustrial societies, for instance, a good education is highly valued. That you are in college shows you have certain values toward learning and education. Gunnar Myrdal (1964), a Swedish sociologist and observer of U.S. culture, referred to the U.S. value system as the "American creed." Values become a creed when they are so much a part of the way of life that they acquire the power of absolute conviction. We tend to take our core values for granted, including freedom, equality, individualism, democracy, free enterprise, efficiency, progress, achievement, and material comfort (Macionis 2012; R. Williams 1970).

At the macro level, conflicts may arise between groups in society because of differing value systems. For example, there are major differences between the values of the dominant culture and those of various native or "First Nations" peoples (Lake 1990; H. Sharp 1991). Consider the story in the next "Sociology Around the World" about Rigoberta Menchú Tum and the experiences of Native American populations living in Guatemala.

The conflict in values between First Nations and national cultures of Canada, the United States, and many Latin American countries has had serious consequences. Cooperation is a cultural value that has been passed on through generations of Native Americans in both North and South America. This is because group survival has always depended on group cooperation in the hunt, in war, and in daily life. The value of cooperation can place native children at a disadvantage in North American schools that emphasize competition. Native American and Canadian First Nation children experience more success in classrooms that stress cooperation and sociability over competition and individuality (Lake 1990; Mehan 1992).

Another Native American value is the appreciation of and respect for nature. Conservation of resources and protection of the natural environment—Mother Earth—have always been important because of the people's dependence on nature for survival. Today, we witness disputes between native tribes and governments of Canada, the United States, Mexico, Guatemala, Brazil, and other countries over raw resources found on native reservations. While many other North and South Americans also value cooperation and respect for the environment, these

values do not govern decision making in most communities (D. Brown 2001; Marger 2012). The values honored by governments and corporations are those held by the people with power, prestige, and wealth.

Beliefs are *more specific ideas we hold about life, about the way society works, and about where we fit into the world.* They are expressed as specific statements that we hold to be true. Many Hindus, for example, believe that fulfilling behavioral expectations of one's own social caste will be rewarded in one's next birth, or incarnation. In the next life, good people will be born into a higher social status. In contrast, some Christians believe that one's fate in the afterlife depends on whether one believes in certain ideas—for instance, that Jesus Christ is one's personal savior. Beliefs come from traditions established over time, sacred scriptures, experiences people have had, and lessons given by parents and teachers or other individuals in authority. Beliefs influence the choices we make. They tend to be based on values, which are broader and more abstract notions of something desirable. A value might be that the environment is worth preserving, but a belief might be that humans have caused global warming. Another value might be eternal life, but a belief might be that this occurs through reincarnation and eventually nirvana.

Values and beliefs, as elements of nonmaterial culture, are expressed in two forms: an ideal culture and a real culture. **Ideal culture** consists of *practices, beliefs, and values that are regarded as most desirable in society and are consciously taught to children.* Not everyone, however, follows the approved cultural patterns, even though they may say they do. **Real culture** refers to *the way things in society are actually done.* For the most part, we hardly question these practices and beliefs that we see around us. Rather like animals that have always lived in a rain forest and cannot imagine a treeless desert, we often fail to notice how our culture helps us make sense of things. Because of this, we do not recognize the gap between what we tell ourselves and what we actually do.

For example, the ideal in many societies is to ban extramarital sex. Sex outside marriage can raise questions of paternity (who is the father) and inheritance (who is in line to inherit wealth), besides leading to spousal jealousy and family conflict. In the United States, about one fourth of all married men and one in seven married women report that they have had at least one extramarital affair (National Opinion Research Center 2010; D. Newman 2009). While in ideal culture we claim that we believe in marital fidelity and this is at the core of family morality, actual behavior or real culture is frequently different.

Norms are *rules of behavior shared by members of a society and rooted in the value system.* All of our rather routine behaviors—from saying "hi" to people we meet to obeying traffic signs—are examples. Norms range from religious warnings such as "Thou shalt not kill" to the expectation in many societies that young people will complete their high school education. Sometimes, the origins of particular norms are quite clear. Few people wonder, for instance, why there is a norm to stop

🎧 Material Culture

Sociology Around the World

Life and Death in a Guatemalan Village

In her four decades of life, Rigoberta Menchú Tum experienced the closeness of family and cooperation in village life. These values are very important in Chimel, the Guatemalan hamlet where she lives. She also experienced great pain and suffering with the loss of her family and community. A Quiche Indian, Menchú became famous throughout the world in 1992 when she received the Nobel Peace Prize for her work to improve the conditions for Indian peoples.

Guatemalans of Spanish origin hold the most power in Guatemala and have used Indians almost as slaves. Some of the natives were cut off from food, water, and other necessities, but people in Menchú's hamlet helped support each other and taught children survival techniques. Most people had no schooling. Menchú's work life in the sugarcane fields began at age 5. At 14, she traveled to the city to work as a domestic servant. While there, she learned Spanish, which helped her be more effective in defending the rights of the indigenous population in Guatemala. Her political coming of age occurred at age 16 when she witnessed her brother's assassination by a group trying to expel her people from their native lands.

Menchú's father started a group to fight repression of the indigenous and poor, and at 20, Menchú joined the movement, *Comité de Unidad Campesina* (CUC), which the government claimed was communist inspired. Her father was murdered during a military assault, and her mother was tortured and killed. Menchú moved to Mexico with many other exiles to continue the nonviolent fight for rights and democracy.

The values of the native population represented by Menchú focus on respect for and a profound spiritual relationship with the environment, equality of all people, freedom from economic oppression, the dignity of her culture, and the benefits of cooperation over competition. The landowners tended to stress freedom of people to pursue their individual self-interests (even if inequality resulted), the value of competition, and the right to own property and to do whatever one desired to exploit that property for economic gain. Individual property rights were thought to be more important than preservation of indigenous cultures. Economic growth and profits were held in higher regard than religious connectedness to the earth.

The values of the native population and landowners are in conflict. Only time will tell if the work of Indian activists such as Rigoberta Menchú Tum and her family will make a difference in the lives of this indigenous population.

and look both ways at a stop sign. Other norms, such as the rule in many societies that women should wear skirts but men should not, have been passed on through the generations and become unconsciously accepted patterns and a part of tradition. Sometimes we may not know how norms originated or even be aware of norms until they are violated.

Thinking Sociologically

The experiences of Rigoberta Menchú Tum illustrate clashes between powerful and powerless groups. What are other ways that different cultural values cause problems between Native Americans and dominant groups?

Norms are generally classified into three categories—folkways, mores, and laws—based largely on how important the norms are in the society and people's response to the breach of those norms. *Folkways* are customs or desirable behaviors, but they are not strictly enforced: Some examples are responding politely when introduced to someone, not scratching your genitals in public, or using proper table manners. Violation of these norms causes people to think you are weird or even uncouth but not necessarily immoral or criminal.

Mores are norms that most members observe because they have great moral significance in a society. Conforming to mores is a matter of right and wrong, and violations of many mores are treated very seriously. The person who deviates from mores is considered immoral or bordering on criminal. Being honest, not

Material and Nonmaterial Culture

cheating on exams, and being faithful in a marriage are all mores. Table 3.2 provides examples of folkway and more violations.

Taboos are the strongest form of mores. They concern actions considered unthinkable or unspeakable in the culture. For example, most societies have taboos that forbid incest (sexual relations with a close relative) and prohibit eating a human corpse. Taboos are most common in societies that do not have centralized governments to enforce laws and maintain jails.

Taboos and other moral codes may be of the utmost importance to a group, yet behaviors that are taboo in one situation may be acceptable at another time and place. The *incest taboo*, a prohibition against sex with a close relative, is an example found in all cultures, yet application of the incest taboo varies greatly across cultures (D. E. Brown 1991). In medieval Europe, if a man and a woman were within seven degrees of relatedness and wanted to marry, the marriage could be denied by the priest as incestuous. (Your first cousin is a third degree of relatedness from you.) On the other hand, the Balinese permit twins to marry because it is believed they have already been intimately bonded together in the womb (Leslie and Korman 1989). In some African and Native American societies, one cannot marry a sibling but might be expected to marry a first cousin. As Table 3.3 illustrates, the definition of what is and what is not incest varies even from state to state in the United States.

Laws are norms that have been formally encoded by those holding political power in society, such as laws

Table 3.2 Violations of Norms

Folkways: Conventional Polite Behaviors
Violations viewed as "weird":
Swearing in house of worship
Wearing blue jeans to the prom
Using poor table manners
Picking one's nose in public
Mores: Morally Significant Behaviors
Violations viewed as "immoral":
Lying or being unfaithful to a spouse
Buying cigarettes or liquor for young teens
Having sex with a professor as a way to increase one's grade
Parking in handicap spaces when one is in good physical condition

against stealing property or killing another person. The violator of a law is likely to be perceived not just as a weird or an immoral person but as a criminal who deserves formal punishment. Many mores are passed into law, and some folkways are also made into law. Formal punishments are imposed. Spitting on the sidewalk is not a behavior that has high levels of moral contempt, yet it results in fines in some cities. Furthermore, behaviors may be folkways in one situation and mores in another. For example, nudity or

Table 3.3 Incest Taboos in the United States: States That Allow First-Cousin Marriage

Alabama	Connecticut	Hawaii	New Mexico	South Carolina
Alaska	District of Columbia	Maryland	New York	Tennessee
California	Florida	Massachusetts	North Carolina	Vermont
Colorado	Georgia	New Jersey	Rhode Island	Virginia

States that allow it only under certain conditions such as marriage after a *certain age or inability to bear children:* Arizona, Illinois, Indiana, Utah, and Wisconsin.

Marriage of half cousins: Kansas, Maine, Montana, Nebraska, Nevada, and Oklahoma.

Marriage of adopted cousins: Louisiana, Mississippi, Oregon, and West Virginia.

States that do not allow first-cousin marriage: All other U.S. states disallow marriages to first cousins within the state: Arkansas, Delaware, Idaho, Iowa, Kentucky, Michigan, Minnesota, Missouri, New Hampshire, North Dakota, Ohio, Pennsylvania, South Dakota, Texas, Washington, and Wyoming.

Historically, in the United States, incest laws forbid in-law marriages far more than first-cousin marriages.

Source: National Conference of State Legislatures (2013).

Nudity may be considered a violation of law, or mores, or folkways, or it may simply be accepted as normal, as in the case of this nude beach.

various stages of near nudity may be only mildly questionable in some social settings (the beach or certain fraternity parties) but would be quite offensive in others (a four-star restaurant or a house of worship) and against the law in others, incurring a penalty or sanction.

Sanctions *reinforce norms through rewards and penalties.* **Formal sanctions** *are rewards or punishments conferred by recognized officials to enforce the most important norms.* Fines for parking illegally, lowered grades on an assignment for plagiarism, and expulsion for bringing drugs or weapons to school are formal negative sanctions your school might impose. Honors and awards are formal positive sanctions. **Informal sanctions** *are unofficial rewards or punishments such as smiles, frowns, or ignoring unacceptable behaviors.* A private word of praise by your professor after class about how well you did on your exam would be an informal positive sanction; gossip or ostracism by other students because of clothes you are wearing would be an informal negative sanction. Sanctions vary with the importance of the norm and can range from a parent frowning at a child who misbehaves to a prison term or death sentence. Similarly, when we obey norms, we are rewarded, sometimes with simple acts such as jokes and pats on the back that indicate solidarity with others. Most often, adherence to norms is ingrained so deeply that our reward is

simply "fitting in." Folkways and many mores are enforced through informal sanctions, yet sometimes penalties for deviant behavior can be severe.

When a society faces change, especially from war, rapid urbanization, industrialization, and modernization, traditional norms that have worked for the society for centuries are challenged. In the past few decades, examples have been seen in many Islamic countries in which modernization has met with a resurgence of religious fundamentalism. A case in point is Iran where rapid modernization and social changes in the post–World War II era were met by a backlash from religious fundamentalists. Radio music and drinking of alcoholic beverages were banned, and women were required to again wear the veil. Afghanistan and other Muslim nations are currently struggling with the conflicts between traditional religious and cultural values and those related to pressures from Western nations for modernization.

Communication is often mediated and enhanced through nonverbal indicators such as tone of voice, inflection, facial expressions, or other gestures that communicate emotion. In e-mail, the words are just words without context. To establish norms, many electronic mailing lists now have rules for polite communication to avoid "flaming" someone—insulting him or her with insensitive words by a faceless person. The development of emoticons (such as smileys) has allowed for adding combinations of characters that represent the emotional context of the message. Norms of Internet communication are still emerging, and you probably have experienced times when messages have been misunderstood because the norms of communication are ambiguous.

Thinking Sociologically

One of the problems of Internet communication has been that many norms of civil discourse are ignored and new norms emerge. What do you see as the current rules for Internet and Twitter communication? When dealing with conflict, how do these norms differ from verbal norms of communication?

Language *is the foundation of every culture. It conveys verbal and nonverbal messages among members of society.* The mini-drama between infant and adult is played out every day around the world as millions of infants learn the language of the adults who care for them. In the process, they acquire an essential part of culture, which is learned. Although many animals can communicate with a limited repertoire of sounds, the ability to speak a language is unique to humans (Phillips 2013). Transport a baby from France to the Arapesh tribe in New Guinea and another baby from New Guinea to France, and each will learn to speak the language and adhere to the culture in which it is brought up. Through the use of language, members of culture can pass on essential knowledge to children and can share ideas with other members of their society. Work can be organized; the society can build on its experiences and plan its future.

Language takes three primary forms: spoken, written, and nonverbal. There are an estimated 5,000 languages spoken in the world. The most common ones are Chinese (with 1.2 billiion speakers), Spanish (329 million speakers), English (328 million speakers), Hindu-Urdu (242 million speakers), and Arabic (221 million speakers) (Infoplease 2012; The World Almanac 2013).

Written language enables humans to store ideas for future generations, accelerating the accumulation of ideas on which to build. It also makes possible communication over distances. Members of a society learn to read these shared symbols, some of which are displayed in Figure 3.1.

Nonverbal language consists of gestures, facial expressions, and body postures. This mode of communication may carry as much as 90% of the meaning of a message (Samovar and Porter 2003). Every culture uses nonverbal language to communicate, and just like verbal language, those cues may differ widely among cultures.

The power to communicate nonverbally is illustrated in American Sign Language, designed for the hearing-challenged and the mute. Complex ideas can be transmitted without vocalizing a word. Indeed, one can argue that the deaf have a distinctive culture of their own rooted in large part in the unique sign language that serves them. In addition, technology has aided communication among the hearing-impaired through text messaging.

Misinterpretation of nonverbal signals can also occur between males and females in Western societies. Consider the differences in meaning of a nod of the head. When women nod their heads in response to a person who is talking, they

福
Поздравляю!
Θεος
לחם שר בא
-십 시요
العربية
राम

Figure 3.1 Societies Use Various Symbols to Communicate Their Written Language

often are encouraging the speaker to continue, signaling that they are listening and that they want the speaker to carry on with clarification and explanation. It does not signal agreement. When men nod their heads when another person is speaking, they typically assume the message is "I agree with what you are saying." This can lead to awkward, confusing, and even embarrassing miscues when men and women talk to one another, with a man mistakenly confident that the woman agrees with his ideas (Stringer 2006).

Thinking Sociologically

Explain a situation of miscommunication between you and a member of a different sex. What nonverbal messages were involved, and what happened?

Language development is extremely important to becoming fully human, and it happens very rapidly from about the first year of life. Still, babies learn to communicate in a variety of other ways. Note how these infants communicate emotions nonverbally. What does each of them seem to be communicating?

Language and Labels

Language also plays a critical role in perception and in thought organization. The *linguistic relativity theory* (Sapir 1929, 1949; Whorf 1956) posits that the people who speak a specific language make interpretations of their reality—they notice certain things and may fail to notice certain other things. "A person's 'picture of the universe' or 'view of the world' differs as a function of the particular language or languages that person knows" (Kodish 2003:384). While most scientists agree that language does not totally determine thinking, it does influence thinking (Casasanto 2008; Gumperz and Levinson 1996; Levinson 2000). For example, in some Native Alaskan cultures where life is dependent on the elements, there are a number of words for snow, each giving members of the group a description that could mean life or death—wet snow, dry snow, heavy snow, melting snow. Children in each different culture will learn about the world within the framework provided by their language.

To use another example, in the English language people tend to associate certain colors with certain qualities in a way that may add to the problem of racist attitudes (Levinson 2000). The definition of the word *black* includes "dismal," "boding ill," "hostile," "harmful," "inexcusable," "without goodness," "evil," "wicked," "disgrace," and "without moral light." The word *white*, on the other hand, is defined as "honest," "dependable," "morally pure," "innocent," and "without malice" (*Webster's Unabridged English Dictionary*, 1989). If the linguistic relativity thesis is correct, it is more than a coincidence that bad things are associated with the *black sheep* of the family, the *blacklist*, or *Black Tuesday* (when the U.S. stock market dropped dramatically and crashed in 1929).

This association of blackness with negative images and meanings is not true of all languages. The societies that have negative images for black and positive images for white are the same societies that associate negative qualities with people of darker skin. The use of *white* as a synonym for "good" or "innocent"—as in reference to a "white noise machine" or a "white lie"—may contribute to a cultural climate that devalues people of color. In essence, the language may influence our perception of color in a manner that contributes to racism. Interestingly, there is empirical evidence supporting this claim of color symbolism. Athletic teams that wear black uniforms have more penalties called on them than are teams with lighter colored uniforms (Frank and Gilovich 1988).

White and black as colors have symbolic meaning—with phrases like "blackballed from the club" or "black sheep of the family" indicating negative judgment associated with blackness. Research shows that teams wearing black are called for more fouls than are teams wearing white, which raises questions about how pervasive this association is in our perception.

Thinking Sociologically

The words *bachelor* and *spinster* are supposedly synonymous terms, referring to unmarried adult males and females, respectively. Generate a list of adjectives that describe each of these words and that you frequently hear associated with them (e.g., *eligible, swinging, old, unattractive*). Are the associated words positive or negative in each case? How are these related to the position of the unmarried in societies?

Neither culture nor society stands alone; they are interdependent. In the next section we examine the connections between society and culture at each level of analysis: micro, meso, and macro.

For additional visual support for understanding material and nonmaterial cultural patterns, see the table "Material and Nonmaterial Cultural Patterns in Sport" on our webpage at **www.sagepub.com/oswcondensed3e**.

Society, Culture, and Our Social World

Whether their people are eating termite eggs, fish eggs, or chicken eggs, societies always have a culture, and culture is always linked to a society. Culture provides guidelines for behaviors and actions that take place at each level of society, from the global system to the individual family. The social world model at the beginning of the chapter, with its concentric circles, represents the micro to macro levels of society. Smaller social units such as schools operate within larger social units such as the community, which is also part of a region of the country. What takes place in each of these units is determined by the culture. There is a social unit—structural *hardware*—and a culture, or *software,* at each level.

Microcultures: Micro-Level Analysis

Micro-level analysis focuses on social interactions in small groups. To apply this idea to culture, we look at **microcultures**, *groups that affect only a small segment of one's life or influence a limited period of one's life*, such as membership in a Girl Scout troop, a boarding school, or prayer group (Gordon 1970). Other classic examples from sociology include a street gang, a college sorority, a business office, or a summer camp group.

Hospitals are organizations for the care and treatment of the sick and injured, providing centralized medical knowledge and technology for treatment of patients. They are communities of people with a microculture. People in different-colored uniforms scurry around carrying out their designated tasks, part of the division of labor in the organization, each having symbolic significance indicating positions at the hospital. Hospital workers interact among themselves to attain goals of patient care. They have a common in-group vocabulary, a shared set of values, a hierarchy of positions with roles and behaviors for each position, and a guiding system of regulations for the organization—all of which shape interactions during the hours that each member works in the hospital. Yet, the hospital microculture may have little relevance to the rest of the employees' everyday lives. Microcultures may survive over time, with individuals coming in and leaving as workers and patients, but in a complex society no one lives his or her entire life within a microculture. The values, rules, and specialized language used by the hospital staff continue as one shift ends and other medical personnel enter and sustain that microculture.

Every organization, club, and association is a social group and therefore must have a culture (a microculture) with its own set of rules and expectations. Organizational microcultures may last for many years, but some microcultures exist for a limited time or for a special purpose. A summer camp microculture may develop but exists only for that summer. The following summer, a very different culture may evolve because of new counselors and campers. A girls' softball team may develop its own cheers, jokes, insider slang, and values regarding competition or what it means to be a good sport, but next year, the girls may be realigned into different teams, and the transitory culture of the previous year may change. In contrast to microcultures, subcultures continue across a person's life span.

Subcultures and Countercultures: Meso-Level Analysis

A **subculture** is *the culture of a meso-level subcommunity that distinguishes itself from the dominant culture of the larger society.* A subculture is the way of life of a group that is smaller than the nation but, unlike a microculture, large enough to support people throughout their life span. A subculture is unique to that group yet at the same time shares the culture of the dominant society (Arnold 1970; Gordon 1970). Many ethnic groups within the larger society have their own subculture with their own sets of conventions and expectations. For example, picture a person who is African Canadian, Chinese Canadian, or Hispanic Canadian, living within an ethnic community that provides food, worship, and many other resources. Despite unique cultural traits, that person and the group are still good Canadian citizens, living within the national laws and way of life. It is just that their life has guidelines from the subculture in addition to the dominant culture of the society.

Because the social unit, such as any of the ethnic groups mentioned above, plays a more continuous role in the life span of group members than a summer camp or a sorority (microcultures), we analyze subcultures at the meso level. (Table 3.4 illustrates the connection between the social unit at each level and the type of culture at that level.)

Note that many categories into which we group people are not subcultures. For example, redheads, left-handed people, individuals who read *Wired* magazine, people who are single, and visitors to Chicago do not make up subcultures because they do not interact as social units or share a common way of life. A motorcycle gang, a college fraternity, and a summer camp are also not subcultures because microcultures affect only a

 Culture

 Camp Culture

Table 3.4   Social Units of Society and Levels of Culture

Social Unit (the People who interact and feel they belong)	Culture (the Way of life of that social unit)
Dyads; small groups; local community	Microculture
Ethnic community or social class community	Subculture
National society	Culture of a nation
Global system	Global culture

segment of one's life (Gordon 1970; Yablonski 1959). A subculture, by contrast, influences a person throughout life. You may participate in many different microcultures in a single day (the choir, a Greek organization, an athletic team, a classroom), but you are likely to live your entire life within the same subculture. Consider some examples, such as those that follow.

In the United States, subcultures include ethnic groups, such as Mexican Americans and Korean Americans, and social class groups, including the exclusive subculture of the elite upper class on the East and West coasts of the United States. The superwealthy have networks, exclusive clubs, and the Social Register, which lists names and phone numbers of the elite so they can maintain contact with one another. They have a culture of opulence that differs from middle-class culture, and this culture is part of their experience throughout their lives.

Another example is Hasidic Jews, who adhere to the same laws as other Americans but follow additional rules specific to their religion. Clothing and hairstyles follow strict rules; men wear beards and temple locks (*payos*), and married women wear wigs. Their religious holidays are different from those of the dominant Christian culture. Hasidic Jews observe dietary restrictions such as avoiding pork and shellfish, and they observe the Sabbath from sunset Friday to sunset Saturday. They are members of a subculture in the larger society of which they are citizens. In today's world, this is a global subculture maintained through websites of, by, and for Hasidic Jews. Again, one can live one's entire life under the influence of the values and rules of the subculture, and this is certainly true for Hasidic Jews.

Many societies have subcultures that are based on ethnicity or religion or other historical characteristics, but broad-based subcultures with extensive social networks can emerge in other ways as well. Perhaps the most fascinating is the deaf subculture in the United States, which is explained in the next "Sociology in Our Social World" on page 80 by a scholar eminently qualified to discuss it.

A give-and-take exists between subcultures and the dominant culture, with each contributing to and influencing

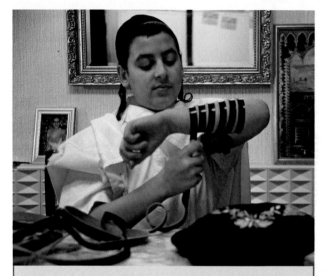

A young Orthodox Jewish boy prepares to pray according to Jewish law by wrapping the leather strap of his tefillin around his arm and a tallit (prayer shawl) around his shoulders. He is part of a subgroup of the larger society, the Jewish faith community. This community will affect his values throughout life—from infancy to death. It is a subculture.

the other. Hispanic Americans have brought many foods to American cuisine, for example, including tacos, burritos, and salsa.

Subcultural practices can cause tensions with the dominant group, which has the power to determine cultural expectations in society. When conflict with the larger culture becomes serious and important norms of the dominant society are violated, a different type of culture emerges. A **counterculture** is *a group with expectations and values that contrast sharply with the dominant values of a particular society* (Yinger 1960).

An example of a counterculture is the Old Order Amish of Pennsylvania and Ohio. The Amish drive horse-drawn buggies and seldom use electricity or modern machines. They reject many mainstream notions of success and replace them with their own work values and goals. Conflicts between federal and state laws and

Hippie Subculture

Sociology in Our Social World

Deaf Subculture in the United States

by Thomas P. Horejes

The deaf subculture possesses its own language, norms, and social networks that are unique to the deaf. American Sign Language (ASL) has its own conversational rules and social norms such as mandatory eye gaze, appropriate facial expressions, and proper ways to interject ideas. Like other subcultures, the deaf subculture celebrates its own arts and entertainment, including Deaf View/Image Art (De'VIA), deaf poetry (ASL Slam), deaf music (Signmark), deaf theater (National Theatre of the Deaf & Deaf West Theater), and deaf cinema (World Deaf Cinema festival). The arts and entertainment of the deaf subculture are often expressed visually through perspectives, experiences, and/or metaphors only understood by those who are fluent in ASL and a part of the deaf subculture. For example, *"true biz have VP? GA to SK no more? PAH!"* would probably get a chuckle from someone who is immersed in the deaf subculture. Additionally, there are social gatherings and events by associations within the deaf subculture that host annual conferences and tournaments ranging from the Deaf World Softball Championships, to the National Black Deaf Advocates, to the Rainbow Alliance of the Deaf (an LGBT organization). As with other subcultures, there is a deaf history and heritage that is passed on from generation to generation.

For many of the 5% to 10% of deaf children who are born to deaf parents, they are immediately enculturated into their own deaf subculture. In contrast, a large majority (over 90%) of deaf children (including myself, born to hearing parents) start with an identity from the larger world (hearing society). As we progress throughout life, however, our identities become negotiated as we become more aware of a subculture—a deaf subculture that each of us has embraced quite differently. Some reject the deaf subculture in favor of total immersion into hearing society while others navigate in the deaf subculture, but in different ways. In addition to those born deaf, there are many individuals who become deaf later in life whether it is due to age, illness, or even prolonged exposure to loud sounds.

Regardless of how one becomes deaf, some individuals rely on technology (hearing aids or cochlear implants), communicate with hearing individuals via spoken/written English or through an ASL interpreter, and express willingness to work in the workplace dominated by members of the hearing society. Other deaf individuals become fully immersed into the deaf subculture or what they call the deaf "world." They may attempt to be a part of a counterculture departing from the hearing culture by rejecting values and beliefs possessed by the hearing society such as assistive-listening devices, speech therapy, and not placing their deaf child into hearing schools. There are also numerous people who become situated on the margins and/or the borderlands between the hearing world and the deaf subculture. They do not seem fully welcome in either social space.

It is possible to navigate through the deaf social landscapes in different phases of one's life. For example, some deaf people may immerse themselves into the counterculture at one time in their lives after being isolated from the dominant culture. Others come from a strong deaf culture and deaf "world" (those whose entire family is deaf) and are later immersed into the hearing world with peers from a different culture. Still others grow up being the only deaf person in a family, not having learned any sign language. One common denominator in shaping deaf identity and deaf subculture is language: the incorporation or lack of sign language in the deaf individual's life.

****

Dr. Horejes received his PhD at Arizona State University in justice studies and teaches sociology at Gallaudet University, the world's only university with programs and services specifically designed to accommodate deaf and hard of hearing students. He is author of *Constructions of Deafness: Examining Deaf Languacultures in Education.*

Amish religious beliefs have produced compromises by the Amish on issues of educating children, using farm machinery, and transportation. The Old Order Amish prefer to educate their children in their own communities, insisting that their children not go beyond an eighth-grade education in the public school curriculum. They also do not use automobiles or conventional tractors. The Amish are pacifists and will not serve as soldiers in the national military.

Other types of countercultures seek to withdraw from society or to operate outside its economic and legal systems or even to bring about the downfall of the larger society. Examples are survivalist groups such as racist militia and skinheads, who reject the principles of democratic pluralism.

Countercultures of all types have existed throughout history. The "old believers" of 17th-century Russia committed group suicide rather than submit to the authority of the czar of Russia on matters of faith and lifestyle (Crummey 1970). There are now Russian old believer communities in Oregon, northern Alberta, and the Kenai Peninsula of Alaska. Some of their villages are so isolated that they are virtually inaccessible by car, and visitors are greeted with "no trespassing" signs.

Some countercultures continue over time and can sustain members throughout their life cycle—such as the Amish. Like subcultures they operate at the meso level, but reject mainstream culture. However, most countercultural groups, such as punk rock groups or violent and deviant teenage gangs, are short-lived or are relevant to people only at a certain age—operating only at the micro level.

Members of countercultures do not necessarily reject all of the dominant culture, and in some cases, parts of their culture may eventually come to be accepted by the dominant culture. For example, a counterculture in Ohio in the mid-1800s established a communal living utopian society and a very alternative college—the first college in the world to be both racially integrated and coeducational. The idea of men and women attending the same college was unacceptable in the larger society, and no one thought whites and blacks could be in the same college classrooms. This college—Oberlin College—started a radical idea in 1833, but is now mainstream. Most colleges are coeducational (there are only three all-male colleges that are not either Jewish religious schools or military academies), and racial segregation has become unacceptable. Thus, the countercultural ideas of this college from 1833 are now absorbed into the larger society.

Countercultures are not necessarily bad for society. According to the conflict theory, which was introduced in Chapter 2, the existence of counterculture groups is clear evidence that there are contradictions or tensions within a society that need to be addressed. Countercultures often challenge unfair treatment of groups in society that do not hold power and sometimes develop into social organizations or protest groups. Extremist religious and political groups, whether Christian, Islamic, Hindu, or other, may best be understood as countercultures against Western or global influences that they perceive as threatening to their way of life. Figure 3.2 illustrates the types of cultures in the social world and the relationship between countercultures and their national culture. Countercultures, as depicted, view themselves and are viewed by others as "fringe" groups—partial outsiders within a nation.

Thinking Sociologically

Describe a counterculture group whose goals are at odds with those of the dominant culture. Do you see evidence that the group is influencing behavioral expectations and values in the larger society? What effect, if any, does it have on your life?

National and Global Cultures: Macro-Level Analysis

Canada is a national society, geographically bounded by the mainland United States to the south, the Pacific Ocean and Alaska to the west, the Atlantic Ocean to the east, and the Arctic to the north. The government in Ottawa passes laws that regulate activities in all provinces (which are similar

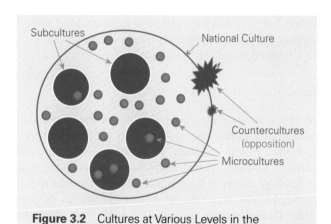

Figure 3.2 Cultures at Various Levels in the Social World

Amish Culture   Counterculture

to states or prefectures), and each province passes its own laws on regional matters. These geographic boundaries and political structures make up the national society of Canada.

National Society and Culture

The **national society** is *a population of people, usually living within a specified geographic area, who are connected by common ideas, cooperate for the attainment of common goals, and are subject to a particular political authority*. Within the nation, there may be smaller groups, such as ethnic, regional, or tribal subcultures made up of people who identify closely with each other. Most nations have a **national culture** of *common values and beliefs that tie citizens of a nation together*. The national culture affects the everyday lives of most citizens. For example, within some countries of Africa and the Middle East that became self-governing nations during the 20th century by breaking their colonial ties, local ethnic or religious loyalties are much stronger than any sense of national culture. In fact, subcultural differences divide many nations. Consider the loyalties of Shiites, Sunnis, and Kurds to their subcultures in Iraq, where the national culture struggles for influence over its citizens through laws, traditions, and military force.

In colonial America, people thought of themselves as Virginians or Rhode Islanders rather than as U.S. citizens. Even during the "War Between the States" of the 1860s, the battalions were organized by states and often carried their state banners into battle. The fact that some Southern states still call it the War Between the States rather than the Civil War communicates the struggle over whether to recognize the nation or states as the primary social unit of loyalty and identity. People in the United States today are increasingly likely to think of themselves as U.S. citizens (rather than as Iowans or Floridians), yet the national culture determines only a few of the specific guidelines for everyday life. Nonetheless, the sense of nation has grown stronger in most industrialized societies over the past century, and primary identity is likely to be a "United States" or "Canadian" citizen.

Global Society and Culture

Several centuries ago, it would have been impossible to discuss a global culture, but with expanding travel, economic interdependence of countries, international political linkages, global environmental concerns, and technology allowing for communication throughout the world, people now interact across continents in seconds. **Globalization** refers to *the process by which the entire world is becoming a single sociocultural entity—more uniform, more integrated, and more interdependent* (Pieterse 2004; Robertson 1997; Stutz and Warf 2005). Globalization is not a product or an object but a process

of increased connectedness, uniformity, and interdependency across the planet (Eitzen and Zinn 2012).

Western political and economic structures dominate in the development of this global society, largely as a result of the domination of Western (European and U.S.) worldviews and Western control over resources. For example, the very idea of governing a geographic region with a bureaucratic structure known as a nation-state is a fairly new notion. Formerly, many small bands and tribal groupings dominated areas of the globe. However, with globalization, nation-states now exist in every region of the world.

Global culture includes *behavioral standards, symbols, values, and material objects that have become common across the globe*. Global beliefs are unspoken, unquestioned, internal assumptions we hold (International Beliefs and Values Institute 2012). We need to understand global culture to engage in human rights issues, global education, conflict resolution, sustainability, and religious and cultural understanding. For example, beliefs that monogamy is normal; that marriage should be based on romantic love; that people have a right to life, liberty, and the pursuit of happiness; that people should be free to choose their leaders; that women should have rights such as voting; that wildlife and fragile environments should be protected; and that everyone should have a cell phone and television set are spreading across the globe (Leslie and Korman 1989; D. Newman 2009).

During the 20th century and up to the present, the idea of the primacy of individual rights, civil liberties, and human rights spread around the world, creating conflicts with nations that traditionally lack democratic institutions and processes. Backlashes against these and other Western ideas also can be seen in acts of groups that have embraced terrorism (Eitzen and Zinn 2012; Kurtz 2007; B. Turner 1991a, 1991b). This has resulted in Western societies scapegoating, or blaming, certain groups for economic

There are many simple norms or beliefs about how to behave in public that are now becoming increasingly global—like staying seated in an airplane or waiting in line to be served at a bank or a post office.

Pop Culture   Globalization

and social crises (Morey and Yaqin 2011; "Muslims and Multicultural Backlash" 2011).

Still, these trends are aspects of the emerging global culture. Even 100 years ago, notions of global culture would have seemed quite bizarre (Lechner and Boli 2005). However, in nations all over the globe, people who travel by plane know they must stand in line, negotiate airport security, and stay seated in the plane until they are told they can get up (Lechner and Boli 2005). Regardless of nationality, we know how to behave in any airport in the world.

Nations are accepted as primary units of social control, and use of coercion is perfectly normal if it is done by the government. We compete in Olympic Games as citizens of nations, and the winners stand on the platform while their national anthems are played. Across the globe the idea of nations seems "normal," yet only a few centuries ago, the notion of nations would have seemed very strange (Lechner and Boli 2005).

As the world community becomes more interdependent and addresses issues that can only be dealt with at the global level (e.g., global warming, pirates from Somalia and other countries, massive human rights violations as in the Syrian revolution or Sudanese war, international terrorism, and global financial crises), the idea of a common "software" of beliefs, social rules, and common interests takes on importance. Common ideas for making decisions allow for shared solutions to conflicts. Global culture at the macro level affects our individual lives, and its influence will only increase.

However, global culture is not the only pattern that is new. Today, we are seeing a counterculture at the global level. Stateless terrorist networks such as al-Shabaab, al-Qaeda, and the Taliban reject the values of international organizations such as the World Court, the Geneva Convention, and other international systems designed to resolve disputes. Terrorists do not recognize the sovereignty of nations and do not acknowledge many values of respect for life or for civil discourse. This counterculture at the global level is a more serious threat than those at the micro and meso levels, in part because it does not fit into the global system and its norms.

Thinking Sociologically

Make a list of social units of which you are a part. Place each group into one of the following categories: microculture, subculture, national culture, and global culture. Consider which of them affects only a portion of your day or week (like your place of work) or only a very limited time in your entire life span. Consider which groups are smaller than the nation but will likely influence you over much of your life. To what cross-national (global) groups do you belong?

Theories of Culture

So social structure and culture operate at each of the levels of society. Various theories about culture help illuminate further the way culture operates in the society; we turn now to the main theories.

Cultural Theory at the Micro Level

To understand our interactions with family and friends, we turn to the micro level of analysis. Although external forces at the national and global (macro) levels shape us in many ways, that is not the whole story as we see when we examine the symbolic interaction approach to culture.

Symbolic Interaction Theory

How amazing it is that babies learn to share the ideas and meanings of complex cultures with others in those cultures. *Symbolic interaction theory* considers how we learn to share meanings of symbols, whether material or nonmaterial. Culture is about symbols, such as rings, flags, and words that stand for or represent something. A ring means love and commitment. A flag represents national identity and is intended to evoke patriotism and love of country. A phrase such as *middle class* conjures up images and expectations of what the phrase means, and we share this meaning with others in our group. Together in our groups and societies, we define what is real, normal, and good.

Symbolic interaction theory maintains that our humanness comes from the impact we have on each other through these shared understandings of symbols that humans have created. When people create symbols, such as a new greeting ("give me five") or a symbolic shield for a fraternity or sorority, symbols come to have an existence and importance for a group. Symbolic interaction theory pictures humans as consciously and deliberately creating their personal and collective histories. The theory emphasizes the part language and gestures play in the shared symbols of individuals and the smooth operation of society. More than any other theory in the social sciences, symbolic interaction stresses the active decision-making role of individuals—the ability of individuals to do more than conform to the larger forces of the society.

Many of our definitions of what is "normal" are shaped by what others around us define as "normal" or "good." The **social construction of reality** is *the process by which individuals and groups shape reality through social interaction.* One illustration of this is the notion of what is beautiful or ugly. In the late 18th and early 19th centuries, in Europe and the

 Global Culture and Identity   Symbolic Interaction

United States, beaches were considered eyesores since there was nothing there but crushed stone and dangerous water. A beach was not viewed as a place to relax in a beautiful environment. Likewise, when early travelers to the West encountered the Rocky Mountains, with soaring granite rising to snow-capped peaks, the idea was that these were incredibly ugly wounds in the earth's surface. The summits were anything but appealing. Still, over time, some individuals began to redefine these crests as breathtakingly beautiful. We now see both as beautiful, but the social construction of scenery has not always been so (Lofgren 1999, 2010).

This notion that individuals shape culture and that culture influences individuals is at the core of symbolic interaction theory. Other social theories tend to focus at the meso and macro levels.

Thinking Sociologically

Recall some of the local "insider" symbols that you used as a teenager—such as friendship bracelets. What are some of the symbols you have exchanged with close friends or romantic partners to signify your ties to one another?

Cultural Theories at the Meso and Macro Levels

How can we explain such diverse world practices as eating termites and worshipping cows? Why have some societies allowed men to have four wives whereas others—such as the Shakers—prohibited sex between men and women entirely? Why do some groups worship their ancestors while others have many gods or believe in a single divine being? How can societies adapt to extremes of climate and geographical terrain—hot, cold, dry, wet, mountainous, flat? Humankind has evolved practices so diverse that it would be hard to find a practice that has not been adopted in some society at some time in history.

To explain cultural differences, we will examine two already familiar perspectives that have made important contributions to understanding culture at the meso and macro levels: structural-functional and conflict theories.

Structural-Functional Theory

Structural-functional theorists ask why members of an ethnic subculture or a society engage in certain practices. To answer, structural-functionalists look at how those practices contribute to the survival or social solidarity of the group

In the late 1700s and early 1800s, these beach and mountain views would have been considered eyesores—too ugly to enjoy. The social construction of reality—the definition of what is beautiful in our culture—has changed dramatically over the past two centuries.

or society as a whole. An example is the reverence for cattle in India. The "sacred cow" is protected, treated with respect, and not slaughtered for food. The reasons relate to India's ancient development into an agricultural society that required sacrifices (M. Harris 1989). Cattle were needed to pull plows and to provide a source of milk and dried dung for fuel. Cows gained religious significance because of their importance for the survival of early agricultural communities. They must, therefore, be protected from hungry people for the long-term survival of the group. Protecting cows was functional; that is, the practice served a purpose for society.

Functionalists view societies as composed of interdependent parts, each fulfilling certain necessary functions or purposes for the total society (Radcliffe-Brown 1935). Shared norms, values, and beliefs, for instance, serve the function of holding a social group together. At a global macro level, functionalists see the world moving in the direction of having a common culture, potentially reducing "we" versus "they" thinking and promoting unity across boundaries. Synthesis of cultures and even the loss of some cultures are viewed as a natural result of globalization.

Although most cultural practices serve positive functions for the maintenance and stability of the society, some practices, such as slavery, may be functional for those in power (those using child labor) but dysfunctional for minority groups or individual members of society. Some critics argue that functional theory overemphasizes the need for consensus and integration among different parts of society, thus ignoring conflicts that may point to problems such as inequality in societies (Dahrendorf 1959).

Conflict Theory

Whereas functionalists assume consensus because all people in society have learned the same cultural values, rules, and expectations, conflict theorists do not view culture as having this uniting effect. Conflict theorists describe societies as composed of meso level groups—class, ethnic, religious, and political—vying for power. Each group protects its own self-interests and struggles to make its own cultural ways dominant in the society. Instead of consensus, the dominant groups may impose their cultural beliefs on minorities and other subcultural groups, thus laying the groundwork for conflict. Conflict theorists identify tension between meso and macro levels, whereas functionalists tend to focus on harmony and smooth integration between those levels.

Actually, conflict may contribute to a smoother-running society in the long run. The German sociologist Georg Simmel (1955) believed that some conflict could serve a positive purpose by alerting societal leaders to problem areas that need attention. This view is illustrated by the political changes taking place in several North African and Middle Eastern countries such as Tunisia, Egypt, Yemen, and Libya. The Republican primary to select a presidential

Conflict theorists believe that society is composed of groups, each acting to meet its own self-interests, and those groups struggle to make their own cultural values supreme in the society. The conflict in Egypt in 2012 over who won a presidential election and where the country is headed in the future is one recent example.

candidate for the U.S. elections in 2012 witnessed candidates throwing insults at opponents, pointing out what they felt were problems in the U.S. system that needed fixing.

Conflict theorists argue that the people with privilege and power in society manipulate institutions such as religion and education. In this way, common people learn the values, beliefs, and norms of the privileged group and foster beliefs that justify the dominant group's self-interests, power, and advantage. The needs of the privileged are likely to be met, and their status will be secured. For instance, schools that serve lower-class children usually teach obedience to authority, punctuality, and respect for superiors— behaviors that make for good laborers. The children of the affluent, meanwhile, are more likely to attend schools stressing divergent thinking, creativity, and leadership, attributes that prepare them to occupy the highly rewarded positions in their society. Conflict theorists point to this control of the education process by those with privilege as part of the overall pattern by which the society benefits the rich.

Conflict theory can also help us understand global dynamics. Many poor nations feel that the global system protects the self-interests of the richest nations and that those rich nations impose their own culture, including their ideas about economics, politics, and religion, on the poor nations of the Global South.

Some scholars believe there is great richness in local customs that is lost when homogenized by cultural domination of the powerful nations (Eitzen and Zinn 2012; Ritzer 2007). Conflict theory is useful for analyzing relationships

Social Change

between societies (macro level) and between subcultures (meso level) within complex societies. It also helps illuminate tensions in a society when local (micro-level) cultural values clash with national (macro-level) trends. Conflict theory is not as successful, however, in explaining simple, well-integrated societies in which change is slow to come about and cooperation is an organizing principle.

The Fit Between Hardware and Software

Computer software cannot work with incompatible machines. Some documents cannot be easily transferred to another piece of hardware, although sometimes a transfer can be accomplished with significant modification in the formatting of the document. The same is true with the hardware of society and the software of culture. For instance, consider the size of families: The value (software) of having

large extended families, typical in agricultural societies, does not work well in the structure (hardware) of industrial and postindustrial societies, which are mostly urban and crowded. Children in urban settings are generally a liability compared to those who work on the farm in agricultural societies. In short, there are limits to what can be transferred from one type of society to another, and the change of "formatting" may mean the new beliefs transferred to a different social setting are barely recognizable.

Attempts to transport U.S.-style "software" (culture)—individualism, capitalism, freedom of religion, and democracy—to other parts of the world illustrate that these ideas are not always successful in other settings. The hardware of other societies may be able to handle more than one type of software or set of beliefs, but there are limits to the adaptability. Thus, we should not be surprised when our ideas are transformed into something quite different when they are imported to another social system. If we are to understand the world in which we live and if we want to improve it, we must first fully understand other societies and cultures.

Because there is such variation between societies and cultures in what they see as normal, how do we ever adjust to our society's expectations? The answer is addressed in the next chapter. Humans go through a lifelong process of socialization to learn social and cultural expectations.

What Have We Learned?

Individuals and small groups cannot live without the support of a larger society, the hardware of the social world. Without the software—culture—there could be no society, for there would be no norms to guide our interactions with others in society. Humans are inherently social and learn their culture from others. Furthermore, as society has evolved into more complex and multileveled social systems, humans have learned to live in and negotiate conflicts between multiple cultures, including those at micro, meso, and macro levels. Life in an information age society demands adaptability to different sociocultural contexts and tolerance of different cultures and subcultures. This is a challenge to a species that has always had tendencies toward ethnocentrism.

Key Points:

- *Society* refers to an organized and interdependent group of individuals who live together in a specific geographic area, interact with each other more than with outsiders, cooperate to attain goals, and share a common culture. Each society has a *culture*, the way of life shared by

a group of people, including ideas and "things" that are passed on from one generation to the next in the society; the culture has both material and nonmaterial components. (See p. 58.)

- Societies evolve from very simple societies to more complex ones, from the simple hunter-gatherer society to the information societies of the postindustrial world. (See pp. 59–66.)

- The study of culture requires that we try to avoid ethnocentrism (judging other cultures by the standards of our culture), taking a stance of cultural relativity instead so that the culture can be understood from the standpoint of those inside it. (See pp. 67–70.)

- Just as social units exist at various levels of our social world, from small groups to global systems, cultures exist within different levels of the social system—microcultures, subcultures, national cultures, and global cultures. Some social units at the micro or meso level stand in opposition to the dominant national culture, and they are called countercultures. (See pp. 70–83.)

- Various theories offer different lenses for understanding culture. While symbolic interaction illuminates the way humans bring meaning to events (thus generating culture), the functionalist and conflict paradigms examine cultural harmony and conflict between cultures, respectively. (See pp. 83–86.)

- The metaphor of hardware (society's structure) and software (culture) describes their interdependent relationship, and as with computers, there must be some compatibility between the structure and the culture. If there is none, either the cultural elements that are transported into another society will be rejected, or the culture will be "reformatted" to fit the society. (See p. 86.)

Discussion Questions

1. Think about the evolution of societies described in this chapter. In which type of society (hunter-gatherer, herding, horticultural, agricultural, industrial, postindustrial) would you prefer to live? Why? In which would you most likely be (a) economically successful and (b) content? Why?

2. This chapter points out that material culture now, in many ways, "drives the globalization process." Look around at what your classmates are wearing and carrying and come up with some examples that support that point.

3. Think of a subculture to which you belong. What are the norms, values, and material artifacts that distinguish members of your subculture from those who do not belong to it?

4. Every classroom has norms of behavior. Some are mores, and some are folkways. Describe two of each in a typical classroom at your school. How are both enforced? How do you help enforce these norms?

5. Are you part of a counterculture? Why or why not? In what ways might a counterculture benefit a society?

Contributing to Our Social World: What Can We Do?

At the Local and National Levels

- *Ethnic group* organizations and clubs focus on the interests of specific ethnic groups: Arabic, Chinese, Italian, Polish, and other Canadian and U.S. citizens. You may have one or more on your own campus. Contact one of these groups (of your own background or, even more interesting, of a background that differs from your own). Arrange to attend one of the group's meetings, and learn about the activities in which its members are involved. To find an ethnic association on campus, call your campus activities office. To find one in your local area, try Googling the name of the ethnic group, "club," and the name of your town or city.

- *Immigrant aid groups* are ethnically oriented organizations that assist recent immigrants in dealing with adjustment to U.S. life, especially those from Mexico and other Spanish-speaking countries, Arabic-speaking countries of the Middle East, and East and South Asian countries such as China, Vietnam, the Philippines, Korea, and India. Contact one of these groups, and explore the possibility of volunteering or serving as an intern. You should be able to determine if one is in your area by Googling the name of your town or city, the name of the ethnic group, and "immigrant aid group."

At the Global Level

- *The United Nations Permanent Forum on Indigenous Issues* assists indigenous people around the world in

facing threats to their cultures, languages, and basic rights as the process of globalization accelerates. We have experienced this in North America in relation to Native American and Inuit populations, but it is occurring throughout the world. Visit the forum's website at http://social.un.org/index/IndigenousPeoples.aspx, and contact the forum about the possibility of volunteering or interning.

- *Nongovernmental organizations (NGOs)* are nonprofit, voluntary citizens' groups that are organized on a local, national, or international level (www.ngo.org/ngoinfo/define.html). One example is Cultural Survival (www.cs.org), an organization that partners with indigenous people to secure rights, promote respect, ensure their participation, and assure rights to land. Another organization that works for the rights of indigenous peoples and acts as a representative for them and unrecognized nations is UNPO (Unrepresented Nations and Peoples Organization). You can learn more about UNPO at www.unpo.org.

Visit **www.sagepub.com/oswcondensed3e** for online activities, sample tests, and other helpful information. Select "Chapter 3: Society and Culture" for chapter-specific activities.

Socialization

Becoming Human and Humane

Whether at the micro, meso, or macro level, our close family and friends plus various organizations help us learn how to be human and humane in our society. Skills are taught, as are values such as loyalty and compassion.

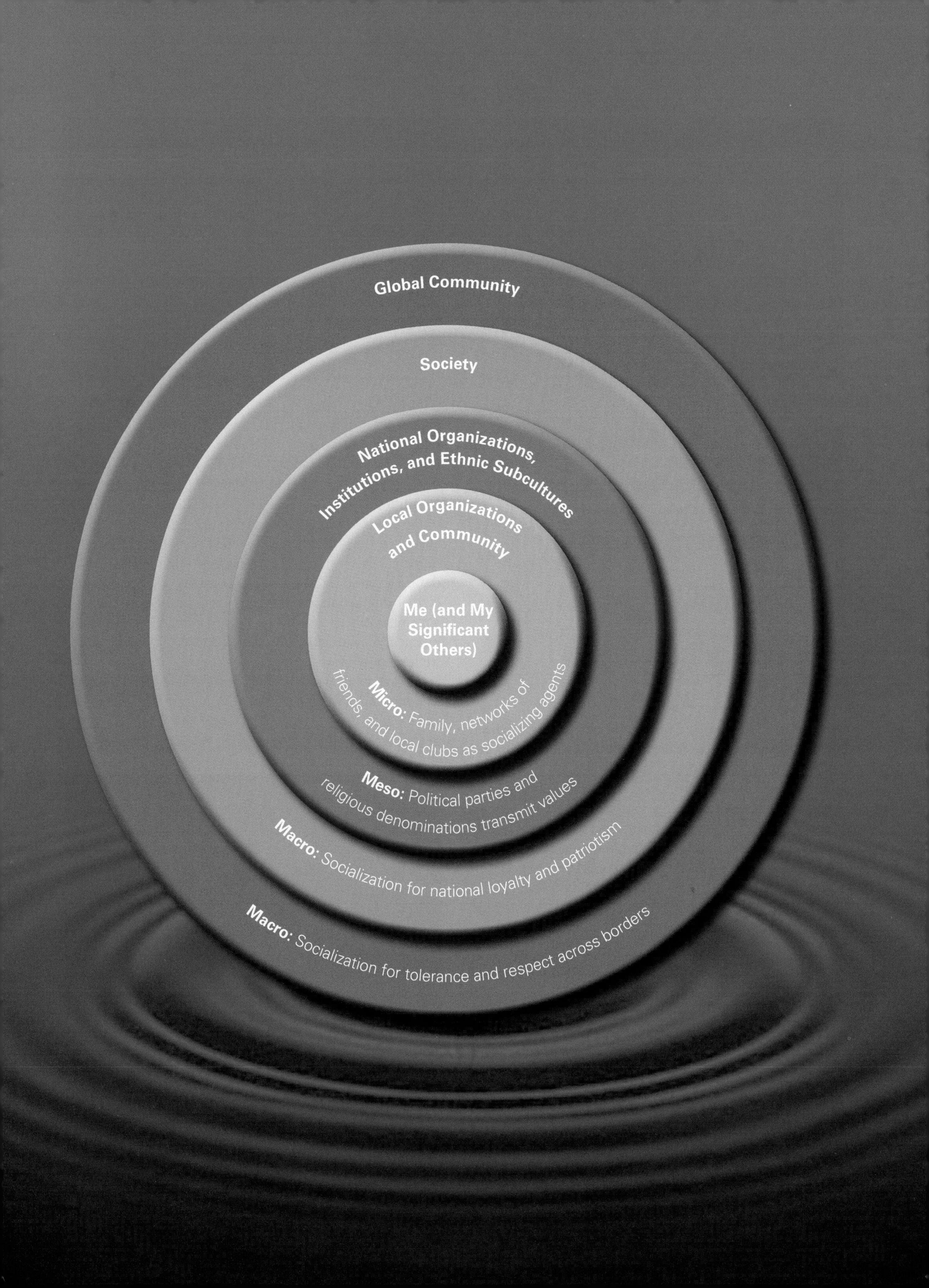

Global Community

Society

National Organizations,
Institutions, and Ethnic Subcultures

Local Organizations
and Community

Me (and My
Significant
Others)

Micro: Family, networks of
friends, and local clubs as socializing agents

Meso: Political parties and
religious denominations transmit values

Macro: Socialization for national loyalty and patriotism

Macro: Socialization for tolerance and respect across borders

Think About It	
Micro: Self and Inner Circle	What does it mean to have a "self"? How would you be different if you had been raised in complete isolation from other people?
Micro: Local Community	How have your local religious congregation and schools shaped who you are?
Meso: National Institutions; Complex Organizations; Ethnic Groups	How do various subcultures or organizations of which you are a member (your political party, your religious affiliation) influence your position in the social world?
Macro: National Society	What would you be like if you were raised in a different country? How does your sense of national identity influence the way you see things?
Macro: Global Community	How might globalization or other macro-level events—such as the terrorist attack of 9/11—impact you and your sense of self?

What's coming in this chapter?

Nature *Versus* Nurture—or *Both* Working Together?

The Importance of Socialization

Socialization and the Social World

Development of the Self: Micro-Level Analysis

Socialization Throughout the Life Cycle

Agents of Socialization: The Micro-Meso Connection

Socialization and Macro-Level Issues

Policy and Practice

P hoebe Prince was a 15-year-old immigrant from Ireland. She and her family had recently settled in South Hadley, Massachusetts, and she enrolled in the high school. Unfortunately, she made a mistake! She dated a popular senior on the football team. This was not acceptable to a clique of girls who had it out for Phoebe. These "mean girls" sent her threatening text messages, threw things at her, called her "Irish slut" and "whore" on social networking sites such as Facebook and Twitter, and engaged in other bullying behaviors. Other students and even faculty who were aware of the bullying did nothing. After months of enduring this treatment, the "mean girls" threw a can at her—and she went home and hanged herself (Crime Library 2012).

Phoebe's story and stories of hundreds of other bullied and abused children point to a problem in the process of socialization, both what the victim is experiencing and what the perpetrators are doing. In this chapter we will examine the process of socialization, how it involves development of our "self," and what can happen when socialization goes wrong.

Socialization is *the lifelong process of learning to become a member of the social world, beginning at birth and continuing until death.* It is a major part of what the family, education, religion, and other institutions do to prepare individuals to be members of their social world. Each of us learns the values and beliefs of our culture. From the day they are born, infants are interactive, ready to be socialized into members of the social world. As they cry, coo, or smile, they gradually learn that their behaviors elicit responses from other humans. This exchange of messages—this *interaction*—is the basic building block of socialization. Out of this process of interaction, a child learns its culture and becomes a member of society. This process of interaction shapes the infant into a human being with a social self—perceptions we have of who we are.

Three main elements provide the framework for socialization: human biological potential, culture, and individual experiences. Babies enter this world unsocialized, totally dependent on others to meet their needs, and completely

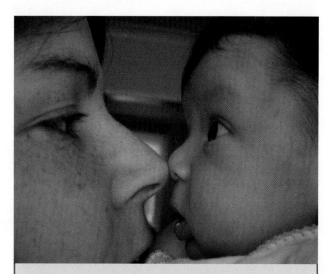

Babies interact intensively with their parents, observing and absorbing everything around them and learning what kinds of sounds or actions elicit response from the adults. Socialization starts at the beginning of life.

The Cruelty of Children

lacking in social awareness and an understanding of the rules of their society. Despite this complete vulnerability, they have the potential to learn the language, norms, values, and skills needed in their society. They gradually learn who they are and what is expected of them. Socialization is necessary not only for the survival of the individual but also for the survival of society and its groups. The process continues in various forms throughout our lives as we enter and exit various positions—from school to work to retirement to death.

In this chapter, we will explore the nature of socialization and how individuals become socialized. We consider why socialization is important. We also look at development of the self, socialization through the life cycle, who or what socializes us, macro-level issues in the socialization process, and a policy example illustrating socialization. First, we briefly examine an ongoing debate: Which is more influential in determining who we are—our genes (nature) or our socialization into the social world (nurture)?

Nature *Versus* Nurture—or *Both* Working Together?

What is it that most makes us who we are? Is it our biological makeup or the family and community in which we are raised that guides our behavior and the development of our self? One side of the contemporary debate regarding nature versus nurture seeks to explain the development of the self and human social behaviors—violence, crime, academic performance, mate selection, economic success, gender roles, and other behaviors too numerous to mention here—by examining biological or genetic factors (J. Harris 2009; Winkler 1991). Sociologists call this sociobiology, and psychologists refer to it as evolutionary psychology. The theory claims that our human genetic makeup wires us for social behaviors (Wilson et al. 1978).

The idea is that we perpetuate our own biological family and the human species through our social behaviors. Human groups develop power structures, are territorial, and protect their kin. A mother ignoring her own safety to help a child, soldiers dying in battle for their comrades and countries, communities feeling hostility toward outsiders or foreigners, and neighbors defending property lines against intrusion by neighbors are all examples of behaviors that sociobiologists claim are rooted in genetic makeup of the species. Sociobiologists would say these behaviors continue because they result in an increased chance of survival of the species as a whole (Lerner 1992; Lumsden and Wilson 1981; E. Wilson 1980, 1987).

Most sociologists believe that sociobiology and evolutionary psychology explanations have flaws. If social behavior is genetically programmed, then it should manifest itself regardless of the culture in which humans are raised. Yet there are vast differences between cultures, especially in gender behaviors and traits. The range of differences would not occur if we were biologically hardwired to certain behaviors. In Chapter 1, for example, we saw that in some societies men wear makeup and are gossipy and vain, violating our stereotypes. The key is that what makes humans unique is not our biological heritage but our ability to learn the complex social arrangements of our culture.

Most sociologists recognize that individuals are influenced by biology, which limits the range of human responses and creates certain needs and drives, but they believe that nurture is far more important. Some sociologists propose theories that consider both nature and nurture. Alice Rossi has argued that we need to build both biological and social theories—or biosocial theories—into explanations of social processes such as parenting (Rossi 1984). Currently several sociologists are developing an approach called evolutionary sociology that takes seriously the way our genetic makeup—including a remarkable capacity for language—shapes our range of behaviors. However, it is also very clear from biological research that living organisms are often modified by their environments and the behaviors of others around them—with even genetic structure changing due to social interaction and experiences (Lopreato 2001; Machalek and Martin 2010).

In short, biology influences human behavior, but human action and interaction can also modify biological traits. Indeed, nutritional history of grandparents can affect the metabolism of their grandchildren, and what the grandparents ate was largely shaped by cultural ideas about food (BBC's Science and Nature 2009; Freese, Powell, and Steelman 1999; Rossi 1984). What we eat today and whether we share food with the less privileged in our society are shaped by our cultural values. The point is that socialization is key in the process of "becoming human and humane."

The Importance of Socialization

If you have lived on a farm, watched animals in the wild, or seen television nature shows, you probably have noticed that many animal young become independent shortly after birth. Horses are on their feet in a matter of hours, and the parents of turtles are long gone by the time the babies hatch from eggs. Many species in the animal kingdom do not require contact with adults to survive because their behaviors are inborn and instinctual. Generally speaking, the more intelligent the species, the longer the period of gestation and of nutritional and social dependence on the mother and family. Humans clearly take the longest time to socialize their young. Even among primates, human infants have the longest gestation and dependency period, generally 6 to 8 years. Chimpanzees, very similar to humans in their DNA, take only 12 to 28 months. This extended dependency period for humans—what some have referred to as the *long childhood*—allows each human being time to learn the complexities of culture. This suggests that biology and social processes work together.

Normal human development involves learning to sit, crawl, stand, walk, think, talk, and participate in social interactions. Ideally, the long period of dependence allows children the opportunity to learn necessary skills, knowledge, and social roles through affectionate and tolerant interaction with people who care about them. Yet, what happens if children are deprived of adequate care or even human contact? The following section illustrates the importance of socialization by showing the effect of deprivation and isolation on normal socialization.

Intense interaction by infants and their caregiver, usually a parent, occurs in all cultures and is essential to becoming a part of the society and to becoming fully human. This African father shares a tender moment with his son.

Isolated and Abused Children

What would children be like if they grew up without human contact? Among the most striking examples are cases of severely abused and neglected children whose parents kept them isolated in cellars or attics for years without providing even minimal attention and nurturing. When these isolated children were discovered, typically they suffered from profound developmental disorders that endured throughout their lives (Curtiss 1977; Davis 1947). Most experienced great difficulty in adjusting to their social world's complex rules of interaction, which are normally learned from infancy onward.

In case studies comparing two girls, Anna and Isabelle, who experienced extreme isolation in early childhood, Kingsley Davis found that even minimal human contact made some difference in their socialization (Davis 1947). Both "illegitimate" girls were kept locked up by relatives who wanted to keep their existence a secret. Both were discovered at about age 6 and moved to institutions where they received intensive training. Yet, the cases were different in one significant respect: Prior to her discovery by those outside her immediate family, Anna experienced virtually no human contact. She saw other individuals only when they left food for her. Isabelle lived in a darkened room with her deaf-mute mother, who provided some human contact. Anna could not sit, walk, or talk and learned little in the special school in which she was placed. When she died from jaundice at age 11, she had learned the language and skills of a 2- or 3-year-old. Isabelle, on the other hand, progressed. She learned to talk and played with her peers. After 2 years, she reached an intellectual level approaching normal for her age but remained about 2 years behind her classmates in skill and competency levels (Davis 1940, 1947).

Cases of children who come from war-torn countries, are forced into slavery or fighting wars, live in orphanages, or are neglected or abused illustrate less extreme isolation. Although not totally isolated, these children also experience problems and disruptions in the socialization process, and in physical and psychological development. These neglected children's situations have been referred to as abusive, violent, and dead-end environments that are socially toxic because of their harmful developmental consequences for children (War Child 2013).

What is the message? These cases illustrate the devastating effects on socialization of isolation, neglect, and abuse early in life. Humans need more from their environments than food and shelter. They need positive contact, a sense of belonging, affection, safety, and someone to teach them knowledge and skills. This is children's socialization into the world through which they develop a self. Before we examine the development of the self in depth, however, we consider the complexity of socialization in the multileveled (micro, meso, and macro) social world.

Music and Development

Socialization and the Social World

Ram, a first grader from India, had been attending school in Iowa for only a couple of weeks. The teacher was giving the first test. Ram did not know much about what a test meant, but he rather liked school, and the red-haired girl next to him, Elyse, had become a friend. He was catching on to reading a bit faster than she, but she was better at the number exercises. They often helped each other learn while the teacher was busy with a small group in the front of the class.

The teacher gave each child the test, and Ram saw that it had to do with numbers. He began to do what the teacher instructed the children to do with the worksheet, but after a while, he became confused. He leaned over to look at the page Elyse was working on. She hid her sheet from him, an unexpected response. The teacher looked up and asked what was going on. Elyse said that Ram was "cheating." Ram was not quite sure what that meant, but it did not sound good. The teacher's scolding of Ram left him baffled, confused, and entirely humiliated.

This incident was Ram's first lesson in the individualism and competitiveness that govern Western-style schools. He was being socialized into a new set of values. In his parents' culture, competitiveness was discouraged, and individualism was equated with selfishness and rejection of community. Athletic events were designed to end in a tie so that no one would feel rejected. Indeed, a well-socialized person would rather lose in a competition than cause others to feel bad because they lost.

At the *micro level*, most parents teach children proper behaviors to be successful in life, and **peer groups,** *who are roughly equal in some status within the society, such as age or occupation,* influence children to "fit in" and have fun. Individual development and behavior occur in social settings. Interaction theory, focusing on the micro level, forms the basis of this chapter, as you will see.

At the *meso level*, religious denominations and political groups teach their versions of the Truth, and educational systems teach the knowledge and skills necessary for functioning in society. At the nationwide *macro level*, television ads encourage viewers to buy products that will make them better and happier people. From interactions with our significant others to dealing with government bureaucracy, most activities are part of the socialization experience that teaches us how to function in our society. Keep in mind that socialization is a lifelong process. Even your grandparents are learning how to live at their stage of life. The process of socialization takes place at each level, linking the parts. Groups at each level have a stake in how we are socialized because they all need trained and loyal group members to survive.

Most perspectives on socialization focus on the micro level because socialization takes place in each individual. Meso- and macro-level theories add to our understanding of how socialization prepares individuals for their roles in the larger social world. Structural-functional perspectives of socialization tend to see organizations at different levels supporting each other. For example, families often organize holidays around patriotic themes, such as a national independence day, or around religious celebrations. These values are compatible with preparing individuals to support national political and economic systems.

At the meso level, the purposes and values of organizations or institutions are sometimes in direct contrast with one another or are in direct conflict with other parts of the social system. From the conflict perspective, the linkages between various parts of the social world are based on competition with or even direct opposition to another part. Demands from organizations for individuals' time, money, and energy may leave little to give to our religious communities or even our families. Each organization and unit competes to gain our loyalty in order to claim some of our resources.

Conflict can occur in the global community as well. For example, religious groups often socialize their members to identify with humanity as a whole ("the family of God"). However, in some cases, nations do not want their citizens socialized to identify with those beyond their borders. If religion teaches that all people are "brothers and sisters" and if religious people object to killing, the nation may have trouble mobilizing its people to arms when the leaders call for war.

Conflict theorists believe that those who have power and privilege use socialization to manipulate individuals in the social world to support the power structure and the self-interests of the elite. Although individuals may not realize it, most individuals have little power to control and decide their futures.

Whether we stress harmony in the socialization process or conflict rooted in power differences, the development of a sense of self through the process of socialization is an ongoing, lifelong process. Having considered the multiple levels of analysis and the issues that make socialization complex, let us focus specifically on the micro level: Where does the development of self originate?

Thinking Sociologically

Give examples of family, community, subcultural, national, or global events that might have influenced how you were socialized or that might influence how you would socialize your child.

Development of the Self: Micro-Level Analysis

A baby is born with the potential to develop a self, but that self can evolve in many directions. Think of a baby you have observed; what is influencing that baby from birth? Can you see how those influences contribute to the developing self? The main product of the socialization process is *the self*. Fundamentally, **self** refers to *the perceptions we have of who we are*. Throughout the socialization process, our self develops largely from the way others respond to us—praising us, disciplining us, ignoring us. The development of the self allows individuals to interact with other people and to learn to function at each level of the social world.

Humans are not born with a sense of self. It develops gradually, beginning in infancy and continuing throughout adulthood. Selfhood emerges through interaction with others. Individual biology, culture, and social experiences all play a part in shaping the self. The hereditary blueprint each person brings into the world provides broad biological outlines, including particular physical attributes, temperament, and a maturational schedule. Each person is also born into a family that lives within a particular culture, illustrating that nature is shaped by nurture. This hereditary blueprint, in interaction with family and culture, helps create each unique person, different from any other person yet sharing the types of interactions by which the self is formed.

Most sociologists, although not all (Irvine 2004), believe that we humans are distinct from other animals in our ability to develop a self and to be aware of ourselves as individuals or objects. Consider how we refer to ourselves in the first person—*I* am hungry, *I* feel foolish, *I* am having fun, *I* am good at basketball. We have a conception of who we are, how we relate to others, and how we differ from and are separate from others in our abilities and limitations. We have an awareness of the characteristics, values, feelings, and attitudes that give us our unique sense of self (W. James [1890] 1934; Mead [1934] 1962).

Thinking Sociologically

Who are some of the people who have been most significant in shaping your *self*? How have their actions and responses helped shape your self-conception as musically talented, athletic, intelligent, kind, assertive, or any of the other hundreds of traits that make up your *self*?

The Looking-Glass Self and Role-Taking

The theoretical tradition of symbolic interaction offers important insights into how individuals develop the self. Charles H. Cooley believed the self is a social product, shaped by interactions with others from the time of birth. He likened interaction processes to looking in a mirror wherein each person reflects an image of the other:

> Each to each a looking-glass
>
> Reflects the other that doth pass.
>
> (Cooley [1909] 1983:184)

For Cooley ([1909] 1983), the **looking-glass self** *is a reflective process that develops the self based on our interpretations and on our internalization of the reactions of others.* In this process, Cooley believed that there are three principal elements, shown in Figure 4.1. We experience feelings such

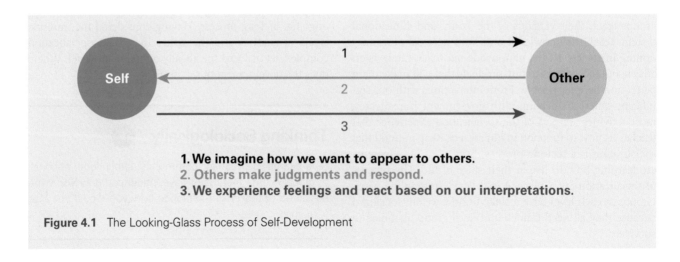

1. **We imagine how we want to appear to others.**
2. **Others make judgments and respond.**
3. **We experience feelings and react based on our interpretations.**

Figure 4.1   The Looking-Glass Process of Self-Development

Our sense of self is often shaped by how others see us and what is reflected back to us by the interactions of others. Cooley called this process, operating somewhat like a mirror, the "looking-glass self."

another person. For Mead, role-taking is prerequisite for the development of sense of self. The next "Sociology in Our Social World" illustrates the looking-glass self process for African American males. This situation experienced by Brent Staples vividly illustrates the impact of others on us.

Thinking Sociologically

First, read the essay on page 96. Brent Staples goes out of his way to reassure others that he is harmless. What might be some other responses to this experience of having others assume one is dangerous and untrustworthy? How might one's sense of self be influenced by these responses of others? How are the looking-glass self and role-taking at work in this scenario?

as pride or shame based on this imagined judgment and respond based on our interpretation. Moreover, throughout this process, we actively try to manipulate other people's view of us to serve our needs and interests. This is one of the many ways we learn to be boys or girls—the image that is reflected back to us lets us know whether we have behaved in ways that are socially acceptable according to gender expectations. The issue of gender socialization in particular will be discussed in Chapter 9. Of course, this does not mean our interpretation of the other person's response is correct, but our interpretation does determine how we respond.

Our self is influenced by the many "others" with whom we interact, and each of our interpretations of their reactions feeds into our self-concept. Recall that the isolated children failed to develop this sense of self precisely because they lacked interaction with others.

Taking the looking-glass self idea a step further, George Herbert Mead ([1934] 1962) explained that *individuals take others into account by imagining themselves in the position of that other, a process called* **role-taking**. When children play mommy and daddy, doctor and patient, or firefighter, they are imagining themselves in another's shoes. Role-taking allows humans to view themselves from the standpoint of others. This requires mentally stepping out of our own experience to imagine how others experience and view the social world. Through role-taking, we begin to see who we are from the standpoint of others. In short, role-taking allows humans to view themselves as objects, as though they are looking at themselves through the eyes of

Mead also argued that role-taking is possible because humans have a unique ability to use and respond to symbols. **Symbols**, first described in Chapter 2, *are actions or objects that represent something else and therefore have meaning beyond their own existence:* Language and gestures are examples, for they carry specific meaning for members of a culture. Symbols such as language allow us to give names to objects in the environment and to infuse those objects with meanings. Once the person learns to symbolically recognize objects in the environment, the self can be seen as one of those objects. This starts with possessing a name that allows us to see our self as separate from other objects. When we say the name LeBron James most listeners would immediately think of the same person: an extraordinary athlete who largely turned around the fortunes of the Miami Heat professional basketball team to win the NBA championship.

Using symbols is unique to humans. In the process of symbolic interaction, we take the actions of others and ourselves into account. We may blame, encourage, praise, punish, or reward ourselves. An example would be a basketball player missing the basket because the shot was poorly executed and thinking, "What did I do to miss that shot? I'm better than that!" A core idea is that the self has *agency*—it is an initiator of action and a maker of meaning, not just a passive responder to external forces.

Parts of the Self

According to the symbolic interaction perspective, the self is composed of two distinct but related parts—dynamic parts in interplay with one another (G. Mead [1934] 1962). The most basic element of the self is what George Herbert Mead refers to as the **I**, *the spontaneous, unpredictable, impulsive, and largely unorganized aspect of the self.* These spontaneous,

Sociology in Our Social World

Black Men and Public Space

By Brent Staples

Many stereotypes—rigid images of members of a particular group—surround the young African American male in the United States. How these images influence these young men and their social world is the subject of this feature. Think about the human cost of stereotypes and their effect on the socialization process as you read the following essay. If your sense of self is profoundly influenced by the ways others respond to you, how might the identity of a young African American boy be affected by public images of black males?

My first victim was a woman—white, well dressed, probably in her early 20s. I came upon her late one evening on a deserted street in Hyde Park, a relatively affluent neighborhood in an otherwise mean, impoverished section of Chicago. As I swung onto the avenue behind her . . . she cast back a worried glance. To her, the youngish black man—broad, six feet, two inches tall; with a beard and billowing hair; both hands shoved into the pockets of a bulky military jacket—seemed menacingly close. After a few more quick glimpses, she picked up her pace and was running in earnest. Within seconds, she disappeared into a cross street.

That was more than a decade ago. I was 22 years old, a graduate student newly arrived at the University of Chicago. It was in the echo of that terrified woman's footfalls that I first began to know the unwieldy inheritance I'd come into. . . . It was clear that she thought herself the quarry of a mugger, a rapist, or worse. Suffering a bout of insomnia, however, I was stalking sleep, not defenseless wayfarers. . . . I was surprised, embarrassed, and dismayed all at once. Her flight . . . made it clear that I was indistinguishable from the muggers who occasionally seeped into the area from the surrounding ghetto. That first encounter, and those that followed, signified that a vast, unnerving gulf lay between nighttime pedestrians—particularly women—and me. And I soon gathered that being perceived as dangerous is a hazard in itself. I only needed to turn a corner into a dicey situation; crowd some frightened, armed person in a foyer somewhere; or make an errant move after being pulled over by a policeman. Where fear and weapons meet—and they often do in urban America—there is always the possibility of death.

In that first year, my first away from my hometown, I was to become thoroughly familiar with the language of fear. At dark, shadowy intersections, I could cross in front of a car stopped at a traffic light and elicit the thunk, thunk, thunk, thunk of the driver—black, white, male, or female—hammering down the door locks. On less-traveled streets after dark, I grew accustomed to but never comfortable with people crossing to the other side of the street rather than pass me. Then there was the standard unpleasantness with policemen, doormen, bouncers, cabdrivers, and those whose business it is to screen out troublesome individuals before there is any nastiness.

After dark, on the warren-like streets of Brooklyn where I live, I often see women who fear the worst from me. They seem to have set their faces on neutral, and with their purse straps strung across their chests bandolier style, they forge ahead as though bracing themselves against being tackled. I understand, of course, that . . . women are particularly vulnerable to street violence and young black males are drastically overrepresented among the perpetrators of that violence. Yet these truths are no solace against the kind of alienation that comes of being ever the suspect. . . .

Over the years, I learned to smother the rage I felt at so often being taken for a criminal. Not to do so would surely have led to madness. I now take precautions to make myself less threatening. I move about with care, particularly late in the evening. I give a wide berth to nervous people on the subway platforms during the wee hours. . . . I have been calm and extremely congenial on those rare occasions when I've been pulled over by the police.

On late-evening constitutionals, I employ what have proved to be excellent tension-reducing measures: I whistle melodies from Beethoven and Vivaldi and the more popular classical composers. Even steely New Yorkers hunching toward nighttime destinations seem to relax, and occasionally they even join in the tune. Virtually everybody seems to sense that a mugger wouldn't be warbling bright, sunny selections from Vivaldi's *Four Seasons*. It is my equivalent of the cowbell that hikers wear when they know they are in bear country.

Source: Staples 2001.

undirected impulses of the *I* initiate or give propulsion to behavior without considering the possible social consequences. We can see this at work in the "I want it now" behavior of a newborn baby or even a toddler. Cookie Monster on the children's television program *Sesame Street* illustrates the *I* in every child, gobbling cookies at every chance, and insisting on more *now*.

The *I* continues as part of the self throughout life, tempered by the social expectations that surround individuals. In stages, humans become increasingly influenced by interactions with others who instill society's rules. Children develop the ability to see the self as others see them (role taking) and critique the behavior of the *I*. Mead called this reflective capacity of the self the *Me*. The **Me** *is the part of the self that has learned the rules of society through interaction and role-taking, and it controls the* I *and its desires*. Just as the *I* initiates the act, the *Me* gives direction to the act. In a sense, the *Me* channels the impulsive *I* in an acceptable manner according to societal rules and restraints, yet meets the needs of the *I* as best it can. When we stop ourselves just before saying something and think to ourselves, "I'd better not say that," it is our *Me* monitoring and controlling the *I*. Notice that the *Me* requires the ability to take the role of the other, to anticipate the other's reaction.

Stages in the Development of the Self

The process of developing a social self occurs gradually and in stages. Mead identified three critical stages: the imitation stage, the play stage, and the game stage, each of which requires the unique human ability to engage in role-taking (G. Mead [1934] 1962). In the **imitation stage**, *children under 3 years old are preparing for role-taking by observing others and imitating their behaviors, sounds, and gestures.*

The **play stage** involves *a child, usually from 3 to 5, having the ability to see things (role-take) from the perspective of one person at a time; simple role-taking or play-acting.* Listen to children who are 3 to 5 years old play together. You will notice that they spend most of their time telling each other what to do. One of them will say something like "You be the mommy, and I can be the daddy, and Julie, you be the dog. Now you say, 'Good morning, Dear,' and I'll say, 'How did you sleep?' and Julie, you scratch at the door like you want to go out." They will talk about their little skit for 15 minutes and then enact it, with the actual enactment taking perhaps one minute. Small children mimic or imitate role-taking based on what they have seen.

A child who is playing mommy or daddy with a doll is playing at *taking the role* of parent. The child is directing activity toward the doll in a manner imitative of how the parents direct activity toward the child. The child often

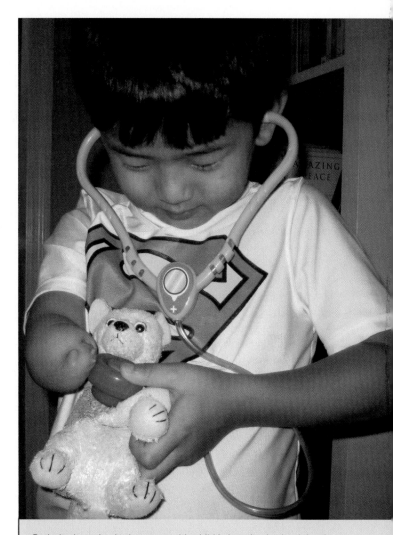

By imitating roles he has seen, this child is learning both adult roles and empathy with others. This kind of role enactment is an important prerequisite to the more complex interaction of playing a game with others.

does not know what to do when playing the role of a parent "going off to work" because children can play only roles with which they are familiar. They do not know what the absent parent does at work. The point is that this "play" is actually extremely important "work" for children because they need to observe and imitate the relationships between roles and they do this by observation and imitation (Handel, Cahill, and Elkin 2007).

Society and its rules are initially represented by **significant others**—*parents, guardians, relatives, or siblings whose primary and sustained interactions with the child are especially influential*. That is why much of the play stage involves role-taking based on these significant people in the child's life. The child does not yet understand the complex relations and multiple role players in the social world outside the immediate family. Children may have a sense of how their mommy or daddy sees them, but children are not yet able to comprehend how they are seen by the larger social world. Lack of role-taking ability is apparent when children say inappropriate things such as "Why are you so fat?"

The **game stage** in the process of developing a social self is when *a child develops the ability to take the role of multiple others concurrently and conform to societal expectations.* The child goes beyond the significant other such as the parent to value the opinion of all peers or expectations of the community.

Have you ever watched a team of young children play T-ball (a pre–Little League baseball game in which the children hit the ball from an upright rubber device that holds the ball), or have you observed a soccer league made up of 6-year-olds? If so, you have seen Mead's point illustrated vividly. In soccer (or football), 5- or 6-year-old children will not play their positions despite constant urging and cajoling by coaches. They all run after the ball, with little sense of their interdependent positions. Likewise, a child in a game of T-ball may pick up a ball that has been hit, turn to the coach, and say, "Now what do I do with it?" Most still do not quite grasp throwing it to first base, and the first-base player may actually have left the base to run for the ball. It can be hilarious for everyone except the coach, as a hit that goes 7 feet turns into a home run because everyone is scrambling for the ball.

When the children enter the game stage at about age 7 or 8, they will be developmentally able to play the roles of various positions and enjoy a complex game. Each child learns what is expected and the interdependence of roles because she or he is then able to respond to the expectations of several people simultaneously (Hewitt 2007; Meltzer 1978). This allows the individual to coordinate his or her activity with others.

In moving from the play stage to the game stage, children's worlds expand from family and day care to neighborhood playmates, school, and other organizations. *This process gradually builds up a composite of societal expectations that the child learns from family, peers, and other organizations*—what Mead refers to as the **generalized other**. The child learns to internalize the expectations of society—the generalized other—over and above the expectations of any "significant others." Behavior comes to be governed by abstract rules ("no running outside of the baseline" or "no touching the soccer ball with your hands unless you are the goalie") rather than guidance from and emotional ties to a "significant other." Children become capable of moving into new social situations such as school, organized sports, and (eventually) the workplace to function with others in both routine and novel interactions. Individuals are active in shaping their social contexts, the self, and the choices they make about the future.

As we grow, we identify with new in-groups such as a neighborhood, a college sorority, or the military. We learn new ideas and expand our understanding. Some individuals ultimately come to think of themselves as part of the global human community. Thus, for many individuals, the social world expands through socialization. However, some individuals never develop this expanded worldview, remaining narrowly confined and drawing lines between themselves and others who are different. Such narrow boundaries often result in prejudice against others.

Very young children who play soccer do not understand the role requirements of games. They all—including the goalie—want to chase after the ball. Learning to play positions is a critical step in socialization, for it requires a higher level of role-taking than children can do at the play stage.

Thinking Sociologically

Who are you? Write down 15 or 20 roles or attributes that describe who you are. How many of these items are characteristics associated with the *Me*—nouns such as *son, mother, student,* or *employee*? Which of the items are traits or attributes—adjectives such as *shy, sensitive, lonely, selfish,* or *vulnerable*? How do you think each of these was learned or incorporated into your conception of your *self*?

The Self and Connections to the Meso Level

In the preceding "Thinking Sociologically" exercise, we asked you to think about how you see yourself and what words you might use to portray yourself. If you were describing yourself for a group of people you did not know, we suspect that you would use mostly nouns or adjectives describing a status or a social position within

Socialization and Sports

the society: *student, employee, athlete, violinist, daughter, sister, Canadian, Lutheran,* and so forth. To a large extent, our sense of who we are is rooted in social positions that are part of organizations and institutions in the society (Kuhn 1964; Stryker 1980). This is a key point made by what is referred to as the Iowa School of symbolic interaction: Selfhood is relatively stable because we develop a core self—a stable inner sense of who we are regardless of the immediate setting in which we find ourselves. This core often centers on the most important social positions we hold in the larger structure of society. You may think of yourself as politically or religiously conservative or liberal, and that may influence the way you conduct yourself in a wide range of situations and social settings. It may shape your sexual behavior, the honesty with which you conduct business with others, and whether you are willing to cheat on an exam—even though you may not be around other people of your moral or political persuasion at the time (Kuhn 1964; Turner 2003; Stryker 1980, 2000; Stryker and Stratham 1985).

The Chicago School of symbolic interactionism emphasizes the role of the *I* and focuses on individuals' involvement in their own development and their agency in creating their world. The Iowa School places somewhat more emphasis on the *Me*—on the role of others and the external social environment in shaping us (Carrothers and Benson 2003).

Socialization Throughout the Life Cycle

Markers in many societies point to rites of passage that mark movement from one stage to the next in the socialization process: birth; naming ceremonies or christenings; starting school at age 5 or 6; officially joining a church or temple at early puberty; obtaining a driver's license; becoming eligible for military draft; being able to vote and drink alcohol; getting a job; marriage; having children; and retiring from the workforce. Most social scientists emphasize the importance of *rites of passage*—celebrations or public recognitions when individuals shift from one status to another. The importance of this shift resides in how others come to perceive the individual differently, the different expectations that others hold for the person, and changes in how the person sees himself or herself.

Socialization is a lifelong process with many small and large passages. Infants begin the socialization process at birth. In childhood, one rite of passage is a child's first day at school—entrance into a meso-level institution. This turning point marks a child's entry into the larger world. The standards of performance are now defined by the child's teachers, peers, friends, and others outside the home. Adolescence is an important stage in Western

Rites of passage are often celebrated with religious rituals, such as this baptism into the Christian faith.

industrial and postindustrial societies, but this stage is far from universal. Indeed, it is largely an invention of complex societies over the past two centuries, characterized by extensive periods of formal education and dependency on parents (Papalia and Feldman 2011). In many agricultural societies teens are working on the farms and taking on adult responsibilities. Adolescence is, in a sense, a structurally produced mass identity crisis because Western societies lack clear rites of passage for adolescents. Teens come to view themselves as a separate and distinct group with their own culture, slang vocabulary, clothing styles, and opinions about appropriate sexual behavior and forms of recreation.

Most of our adult years are spent in work and home life, including marriage and parenting roles. It is not surprising, then, that graduation from one's final alma mater (whether it be high school, college, or graduate school), marriage, and acceptance of one's first full-time job are rites of passage into adulthood in modern societies. Even the retired and elderly members of society are constantly undergoing socialization and resocialization in the process of developing their sense of self. The type of society influences the socialization experience of the elderly and how they carry out their roles, as well as their status in society. Consider the changes that have taken place in the lifetimes of those born before 1945. They were born "before television, before polio shots, frozen foods, Xerox, plastic, contact lenses, Frisbees and the Pill . . . before credit cards, split atoms, laser beams and ball point pens; before pantyhose, dishwashers, clothes dryers, electric blankets, air conditioners . . . ," and many other familiar "necessities" of today (Grandpa Junior 2006). There are increasing numbers of people in the elder category, with the percentage of citizens in the United States older than 65 reaching 13% in 2012 (M. Brandon 2012). The average life expectancy in 1929 was only 57 years. Today, in the United States it is 78.7 years (81.7% for women), and 50 countries have even higher average life expectancies than the United States (Data360 2012; Landau 2009).

Thinking Sociologically

Find someone who has grown up in a different culture and ask her or him about rites of passage from adolescence to adulthood. How are the patterns similar to or different from your own?

The elderly are vitally important to the ongoing group in more settled agricultural societies. They are the founts of wisdom and carry group knowledge, experiences, and traditions that are valued in societies where little change takes place. In industrial and postindustrial countries, the number of elderly is growing rapidly as medical science keeps people alive longer, diets improve, and diseases are brought under control. Yet, in modern systems, social participation by the elderly often drops after retirement. Retirement is a rite of passage to a new status, like that of marriage or parenthood, for which there is little preparation. As a result, retired people sometimes feel a sense of uselessness when they abruptly lose their occupational status. Retirees in Western societies generally have 20, even 30 or more, years of life yet to live. Many retirees develop hobbies, enjoy sports, or have new jobs they can pursue.

Dying is the final stage of life (Kübler-Ross 1997). Death holds different meanings in different cultures: passing into another life, a time of judgment, a waiting for rebirth, or a void and nothingness. In some religious groups, people work hard or do good deeds because they believe they will

Death rituals differ depending on the culture and religion of the group. In India (top left), this body is being cremated by the holy Ganges River to release the soul from earthly existence. The closest relative lights the funeral pyre. The top right photo shows the Muslim tradition of washing and wrapping the dead before burial in Najaf, Iraq. At the bottom, a U.S. Honor Guard carries a casket with the remains of U.S. Air Force personnel at Arlington National Cemetery. A U.S. Honor Guard (bottom left) carries a basket with the remains of U.S. Air Force personnel at Arlington National Cemetery. A celestial burial master (bottom right) feeds the body of a dead Tibetan to the vultures in northwest China's Qinghai province. In Tibetan religions, the practice is known as jhator, *which literally means "giving alms to the birds," as people believe in rebirth and there is no need to preserve the body.*

 Death

be rewarded in an afterlife or with rebirth to a better status in the next life on earth. Thus, beliefs about the meaning of death can affect how people live their lives and how they cope with dying and death.

Each stage of the life cycle involves socialization into new roles in the social world. Many social scientists have studied these developmental stages and contributed insights into what happens at each stage (Clausen 1986; Erikson 1950; Freud [1923] 1960; Gilligan 1982; Handel et al. 2007; Kohlberg 1971; Papalia and Feldman 2011; Piaget 1989). Although examination of this topic is beyond the scope of this chapter, it is important to know that developmental theorists have detailed stages in the growth process.

Death ends the lifelong process of socialization, a process of learning social rules and roles and adjusting to them. When the individual is gone, society continues. New members are born, are socialized into the social world, pass through roles once held by others, and eventually give up those roles to younger members. Cultures provide guidelines for each new generation to follow; the social world perpetuates itself and outlives the individuals who populate it.

The Process of Resocialization

If you have experienced life in the military, a boarding school, a convent, a mental facility, or a prison or had a major transition in your life such as a divorce or the death of a spouse or child, you have experienced resocialization. **Resocialization** is *the process of shedding one or more positions and taking on others, which involves learning new norms, behaviors, and values suitable to the newly acquired status*. It involves changing from established patterns learned earlier in life to new ones suitable to the newly acquired status (Goffman 1961). Resocialization may take place in a **total institution**—*a place that cuts people off from the rest of society and totally controls their lives in the process of resocialization*. These include prisons, mental hospitals, monasteries, concentration camps, boarding schools, and military barracks. Bureaucratic regimentation and the manipulation of residents for the convenience of the staff are part of the routine (Goffman 1961).

We often associate resocialization with major changes in adult life—leaving home to go to college, marriage, having a baby, divorce, retirement, and widowhood. Changes in status present opportunities to move in new and often exciting directions, such as going to college. Resocialization can also mean adjusting to living alone, raising children alone, loneliness, and possible financial problems. One divorcée of 3 years told the authors: "There are many things to commend the single life, but I still have not adjusted to eating alone and cooking for myself. Worse than that are Sunday afternoons. That is the loneliest time." Sometimes resocialization refers to individuals who are

The primary socialization unit for young children is the family, but as they become teenagers, peers become increasingly important as a reference group, shaping their norms, values, and attitudes.

forced to correct or reform behaviors that are defined as undesirable or deviant. Prison rehabilitation programs provide one example. However, research suggests the difficulty in resocializing prisoners is rooted in the nature of the prison environment itself. Prisons are often coercive and violent environments, which may not provide the social supports necessary for bringing about positive change in a person's attitudes and behaviors.

Although resocialization is the goal of self-help groups such as Alcoholics Anonymous, Gamblers Anonymous, Parents Anonymous, drug rehabilitation groups, and weight-loss groups, relapse is a common problem among participants. These groups and organizations aim to substitute new behaviors and norms for old undesirable ones, but the process of undoing socialization and achieving resocialization is difficult.

There are multiple individuals, groups, and institutions involved in the socialization process. These socialization forces are referred to as agents of socialization.

Thinking Sociologically

As you read the next section that discusses socializing agents, make a list of the agents discussed in these pages. Indicate two or three central messages each agent of socialization tries to instill in you and in other people you know. Consider which agents are micro, meso, or macro agents. Are there different kinds of messages at each level? Do any of them conflict? If so, why, and what problems are caused?

Agents of Socialization: The Micro-Meso Connection

Agents of socialization are the *transmitters of culture—the people, organizations, and institutions that help us define our identity and teach us how to thrive in our social world*. Agents are the mechanism by which the self learns the values, beliefs, and behaviors of the culture. Agents of socialization help new members find their place, just as they prepare older members for new responsibilities in society. At the micro level, one's family, one's peer group, and local groups and organizations help people know what is expected. At the meso level, formal sources of learning—education, religion, politics, economics, and health—and other informal sources of learning such as the media and books are all agents that contribute to socialization. They transmit information to children and to adults throughout people's lives.

In early childhood, the family acts as the primary agent of socialization, passing on messages about respect for property and authority, and the value of love and loyalty, for example (Handel et al. 2007). Peer groups are also important, especially during the teenage years. Some writers even argue that the peer group is most important in the socialization process of children and teens (Aseltine 1995; J. Harris 2009). Each agent has its own functions (purposes) and is important at different stages of the life cycle, but meso-level institutions play a more active role as one matures. For example, schools and religious bodies become more involved in socialization as children become 6 years old compared to when they were preschool age. The next "Sociology in Our Social World" discusses socialization in schools by exploring an important and widely cited research project—the issue of how schools reinforce notions of gender.

Thinking Sociologically

Recall your own playground days or watch a sibling or another child on the playground. What do your observations tell you about the role of play in gender socialization?

Lessons from one agent of socialization generally complement those of other agents. Parents work at home to support what school and religion teach. However, at times agents provide conflicting lessons. For example, family and faith communities often give teens messages that conflict with those of peer groups regarding sexual activity and drug use. This is an instance of mixed messages given by formal and informal agents.

Formal agents of socialization are *official or legal agents (e.g., families, school, teachers, religious training) whose purpose it is to socialize the individual into the values, beliefs, and behaviors of the culture*. Formal agents usually have some official or legal responsibility for instructing individuals. For example, a primary goal of families is to teach children to speak and to learn proper behavior. In addition, school-teachers educate by giving formal instruction, and religious training provides moral instruction. (These formal agents of socialization are discussed in Chapters 10 and 11.)

Informal agents of socialization are *unofficial forces that shape values, beliefs, and behaviors in which socialization is not the express purpose*. Examples include the media, books, advertising, and the Internet. They bring us continuous messages even though their primary purpose is not socialization but entertainment or selling products. Children watch countless advertisements on television, many with messages about what is good and fun to eat and how to be more attractive, more appealing, smarter, and a better person through the consumption of products. This bombardment is a particularly influential part of socialization at young ages.

This distinction between formal, intentional socialization and informal socialization has important implications for the kinds of messages that are presented and for how such messages are received.

Thinking Sociologically

What confusion might be created for children when the formal and informal agents of socialization provide different messages about values or acceptable behaviors? Is this contradiction something that parents should be concerned about? Why or why not?

Micro-Level Socialization

Perhaps the most important micro-level formal agent of socialization is the family—parents, siblings, and other family members. One way in which families teach children what is right and wrong is through rewards and punishments, called *sanctions*. Children who steal cookies from the cookie jar may receive a verbal reprimand or a slap on the hand, be sent to their room, have "time out," or receive a severe spanking, depending on differences in child-rearing practices in different families. These are examples of negative sanctions. Conversely, children may be rewarded for good behavior with a smile, praise, a cookie, or a special event. These are examples of positive sanctions. The number and types of sanctions dispensed in the family shape the socialization process, including development of the self and the perceptions we have of who we are. Note that family influence varies from one culture to another.

In the United States, most parents value friendliness, cooperation, orientation toward achievement, social competence, responsibility, and independence as qualities their children should learn, in contrast to values of conformity and fitting into the group espoused in Japan. However, sub-cultural values and socialization practices may differ within

Prisoners

Role Taking

Agents of Socialization

Sociology in Our Social World

Gender Socialization in American Public Schools

Pause for a moment as you pass a school yard, and observe the children at play. Children's behavior on the school playground translates into a powerful agent of gender socialization in a world that is very complex. Consider the evidence reported in the ethnographic study of Barrie Thorne, recounted in her award-winning book, *Gender Play* (1993).

Many people assume that gender differences are natural and that we are "born that way." By contrast, Thorne provides evidence that gender differences are social constructions, influenced by the setting, the players involved in the situation, and the control people have over the situation. She is suggesting that we need to look at well-known everyday patterns from a fresh point of view.

As an astute observer and researcher, Thorne suspected that girls and boys have complex relations that play out in the classroom and school yard. She chose the playground as the focus of her observation of the separate worlds of girls and boys. As her research strategy, she points out that "when adults seek to learn about and from children, the challenge is to take the closely familiar and to render it strange."

Through systematic participant observation she found that children and adults play an active role in defining and shaping gender expectations through the collective practices of forming lines, choosing seats, teasing, gossiping, and participating in selected activities.

Thorne used two schools for her research—one in a small California city and another in a Midwest suburb. She entered the world of the children, sometimes sitting apart on the playground taking notes, sometimes participating in their activities such as eating and talking in the lunchroom. In each setting, she recorded her observations and experiences. For example, she noted what children call themselves and how they think of themselves. She was intrigued by the reference to the *opposite sex*—a term that stresses difference and opposition rather than similarity and a sense of "we." Thorne was struck by the active meaning construction of children as they gained a notion of "normal" gender behavior. The real focus of her work is in taking seriously how children themselves make sense of sex differences—and how they sometimes ignore any difference as irrelevant to their activities.

Previous studies concluded that boys tend to interact in larger, more age-heterogeneous groups and in more rough-and-tumble play and physical fighting. Thorne also found that boys' play involves a much larger portion of the playground, and their play space was generally farther from the building, making them less subject to monitoring and sanctioning. In addition, boys would often run "sneak invasions" into the girls' space to take things belonging to the girls. Many boys felt they had a right to the geographical space that was occupied by females. Girls played close to the buildings in much smaller areas and rarely ventured into the boys' area.

Girls' play tended to be characterized by cooperation and turn-taking. They had more intense and exclusive friendships, which took shape around keeping and telling secrets, shifting alliances, and indirect ways of expressing disagreement. Instead of direct commands, girls more often used words like *let's* or *we gotta*. However, Thorne found that these notions of "separate girls' and boys' worlds" used in most previous studies miss the subtleties in the situation—race, class, and other factors.

In follow-up research, Valerie Ann Moore examined children at a summer day camp (Moore 2001). Like Thorne, she watched the children play and interact with one another, and found that children also use play to construct the meaning of gender, race, and age. The boys in the camp showed their independence by defying the adults' rules, which unified them across racial and age boundaries. The girls at the camp, on the other hand, were much more likely to separate by age and by race when interacting with other campers. Narratives of romance were likely to break the physical boundaries among older campers (Moore 2001). These romances, however, emphasize gender differences. The camp counselors reinforced this difference by constantly creating and maintaining gender boundaries to prohibit romances from forming between the teens.

The major contribution of these two studies is to alert us to the complexity of the gender socialization process, helping us see the extent to which children are active agents creating their own definitions of social relations, not just short automatons who enact adult notions of what gender means.

Japanese fathers and their sons eat lunch during a festival. While mothers are the key agents of socialization in Japan, fathers also have a role, especially during special events in the life of the child.

the diverse groups in the U.S. population. Conceptions of what makes a "good person" or a "good citizen" and different goals of socialization bring about differences in the process of socialization around the world.

In addition, the number of children in a family and the placement of each child in the family structure can influence the unique socialization experience of the child. In large families, parents typically have less time with each additional child. Where the child falls in the hierarchy of siblings can also influence the development of the self. In fact, birth order is a very strong predictor of social attitudes—perhaps more so than race, class, or gender—according to some studies, and firstborns are typically the highest achievers (Benokraitis 2008; "First Born Children" 2008). Younger children may be socialized by older siblings as much as by parents, and older siblings often serve as models that younger children want to emulate.

Meso-Level Socialization

Meso-level agents are at work socializing people into specific cultural values and to the roles they must learn to fulfill. Education and religion are two obvious influences—both being institutions with primary responsibility for socialization. We will discuss those in more detail in Chapter 11, and here we will illustrate meso-level socialization influences with a focus on social class and the media.

Social Class

Our education level, our occupation, the house we live in, what we choose to do in our leisure time, the foods we eat, and what we believe in terms of religion and politics are just a few aspects of our lives that are affected by socialization. Applying what we know from sociological research, the evidence strongly suggests that socialization varies by **social class**, or *the wealth, power, and prestige rankings that individuals hold in society* (Pearce 2010). Meso-level patterns of distribution of resources—based in part on the economic opportunities created by state and national policies—affect who we become. Upper-middle-class and middle-class parents in the United States usually have above-average education and managerial or professional jobs. They tend to pass on to their children skills and values necessary to succeed in the subculture of their social class. Subcultures, you will recall, operate at the meso level of the social system. Autonomy, creativity, self-direction (the ability to make decisions and take initiative), responsibility, curiosity, and consideration of others are especially important for middle-class success and are part of middle-class subculture (Kohn 1989). If the child misbehaves, for example, middle-class parents typically analyze the child's reasons for misbehaving, and punishment is related to these reasons. Sanctions often involve instilling guilt and denying privileges.

Working-class parents using meso-level family patterns tend to pass on to children their cultural values of respect for authority and conformity to rules, lessons that will be useful if the children also have blue-collar jobs (Kohn 1989). Immediate punishment with no questions asked if a rule is violated functions to prepare children for positions in which obedience to rules is important to success. They are expected to be neat, clean, well-mannered, honest, and obedient students (MacLeod 2008). Socialization experiences for boys and girls are often different, following traditional gender-role expectations of the working-class subculture. Moreover, these differences in behavior across social classes and parenting styles are apparent between different societies as well (Leung, Lau, and Lam 1998). What conclusions can we draw from these studies? Members of each class are socializing their children to be successful in their social class and to meet expectations for adults of that class. Schools, like families, participate in this process. Although the extent to which schools create or limit opportunities for class mobility is debated, what is clear is that children's social class position on entering school has an effect on the socialization experiences they have in school (Ballantine and Hammack 2012). Families and schools socialize children to adapt to the settings in which they grow up and are likely to live.

Social class, however, is only one of many influencing agents. As we saw in *Black Men and Public Space*, race and ethnicity are very important factors in socialization, as is gender. Gender socialization is discussed in more detail in Chapter 9, but we note here that race, class, and gender act as structural constraints on some members of the population. People from different social classes, ethnic and racial groups, and genders receive different messages about who they are and how they should behave. Therefore, it is important to recognize the interplay of these variables in people's lives.

These parents pass on a love for the piano to their young son. Because of the social class of this father, his son is likely to receive many messages about creativity, curiosity, and self-direction.

Electronic Media

Television and computers are important informal agents of socialization at the meso level. They are intermediate-sized social units—larger than a local community, but smaller than a nation. They impact both nation-states and global agencies at the macro level by shaping public attitudes, and they affect family notions of what is normal or not normal at the micro level. In developed countries, there is scarcely a home without a television set, and more than 75% of homes have computers and Internet access (WebSiteOptimization.com 2010).

Researchers have collected nearly five decades of information on how television has become a way of life in homes. By the time an average child in the United States reaches age 18, he or she will have spent more time watching television than doing any other single activity besides sleeping. On average, children between ages 8 and 18 spend three hours a day watching television, one hour and 11 minutes watching videos or DVDs, one hour and 44 minutes with audio

media, one hour using computers, and 49 minutes playing video games, with a total media exposure in a typical day of eight hours and 33 minutes. The next "Engaging Sociology" feature on page 106 shows total media exposure of children by several variables. Examine this issue in more depth by answering the questions following Tables 4.1 and 4.2.

The moguls of mass media—a meso-level social system—are able to influence socialization within the most intimate of environments. Children in the United States use computers at very young ages. More than 80% of children younger than 5 use the Internet weekly (Kessler 2011). Seventy-nine percent of people in the United States and Canada now use the Internet, and they make up 11.4% of the world Internet users. Forty-five percent are from Asia and 22% from Europe (Internet World Stats 2013).

A serious concern related to socialization centers on the messages children receive from television and computer games, along with the behavioral effects of these messages. There is ample evidence that children are affected in negative ways by excessive television viewing, especially television violence, but a direct causal link between television viewing and behavior is difficult to establish (National Science Foundation 2005). Researchers know, however, that parents who play an active role in helping children understand the content of television shows can have a powerful effect on mitigating television's negative impacts and enhancing the positive aspects of television shows. The television-viewing habits of parents—length of viewing time, types of shows watched, times of day—can also influence how their children respond to television.

A more alarming concern with Internet socialization is its role in radicalizing young people and involving them in terrorism. The Tsarnaev brothers—Tamerlan and Dzhokhar—were apparently well-adjusted teens while in high school, but they were deeply influenced by Internet exchanges and by political websites. Eventually they teamed together to plot the Boston Marathon bombings on April 15, 2013. Three people were killed, and roughly 280 people were injured, many losing limbs. The actions of these young men were spawned when they adopted ideologies deeply antagonistic to the United States through Internet socialization. In a country that values free speech, controlling such antisocial influences is a real dilemma (Crary and Lavoie 2013).

Perhaps the most important aspect of television and computers is something that we do not fully understand but that has frightening potential. For the first time in human history, we have powerful agents of socialization in the home from a child's birth onward. Time spent attending to television or computer games means less time spent engaging in interaction with caregivers and peers. Intimate family bonds formed of affection and meaningful interaction are being altered by the dominant presence of electronic media in the home. In addition, those who control the flood of mass media messages received by children may have interests and concerns that are very much at odds with those of parents. A significant part of the informal socialization process occurs with the assistance

Advertising

Social Media's Influence

Engaging Sociology

Media Exposure and Socialization

Examine Tables 4.1 and 4.2 and respond to the questions below.

Table 4.1 Total Media Exposure (Average Hours and Minutes per Day)

Age	8–10 years old	7:51
	11–14 years old	11:53
	15–18 years old	11:23
Gender	Boys	11:12
	Girls	10:17
Race	White	8:36
	Black	12:59
	Hispanic	13:00
Parent education	High school or less	11:26
	Some college	11:30
	College graduate	10:00

Table 4.2 Average Amount of Time per Day Spent With Each Medium: 8- to 18-Year-Olds

Medium	1999	2009
Television	3:47	4:29
Music/audio	1:48	2:31
Computer	:27	1:29
Video games	:26	1:13
Print	:43	:38
Movies	:18	:25
Total media exposure	7:29	10:45
Multitasking proportion	16%	29%

Sociological Data Analysis:

1. Considering the data in Tables 4.1 and 4.2, how would you describe television-watching and other media-engaged patterns among different groups?

2. Are the trends in media exposure over the first decade of the 21st century a matter of concern? Why or why not?

3. How might media time affect other aspects of socialization of children?

4. What might be the social consequences of ethnic minorities (blacks and Hispanics) and those children whose parents do not have a college education having so much higher media exposure each day than whites who are more highly educated?

5. Do your conclusions cause any concerns about your society? Why or why not?

Source: Kaiser Family Foundation (2010); Rideout, Foehr, and Roberts (2010).

of electronic equipment within the home that commands a significant portion of a child's time and attention.

With globalization, global knowledge and understanding also become important parts of school curricula and media coverage, and we move next to a discussion of some of the national and global processes that impact socialization.

Thinking Sociologically

What other agents of socialization in addition to family, social class, and electronic media are important in teaching us our roles, norms, values, and beliefs? What is the impact, for example, of friendship networks or peer groups?

Socialization and Macro-Level Issues

Although socialization that involves acculturation is a lifelong micro-level process of an individual becoming a member of the social world, it is clearly influenced by (and it affects) macro trends and forces.

Sense of Self Versus the "Other": Diverse Global Societies

Immigration patterns and ethnic conflicts around the world have resulted in a fairly new phenomenon: transnationalism. **Transnationalism** is *the process by which immigrants create multinational social relations that link together their original societies with their new locations. This means that an individual or a family has national loyalty to more than one country* (Levitt 2001, 2007; Levitt and Waters 2006). Often, it occurs after migration of war refugees, when one's roots lie in the country of origin and many of one's close family members may continue to live there. Consider transnational children raised in war-torn countries. In the Palestinian territories, especially Gaza, and in Israeli settlements along the border, children grow up with fear and hatred, major influences on their socialization. Some war refugees spend childhoods in refugee camps and may never return to their native countries.

For people experiencing transnationalism, there are conflicting messages about culturally appropriate behaviors and the obligations of loyalty to family and nation. However, one need not migrate to another country to experience global pressures. The Internet and cell phones have increasingly created a sense of connectedness to other parts of the world and an awareness of global interdependencies (Brier 2004; Roach 2004). Some commentators have even

suggested that the Internet is a threat to the nation-state as it allows individuals to maintain traditions and loyalties to relatives and friends in more than one country (Drori 2006). Ideas of social justice or progress in many parts of the world are shaped not just by the government that rules the country but by international human rights organizations and ideas that are obtained from media that cross borders, such as the World Wide Web. In recent uprisings in some Middle Eastern and North African countries, social networking kept movement participants in touch with others in the uprisings and with outside media and supporters. So socialization can include agents that are beyond the local community and beyond the national boundaries.

Access to international information and friendships across borders and boundaries are increasingly possible as more people have access to the Internet. Map 4.1 (page 108), on Internet use around the world, illustrates not only variability of access but also how widespread this access is becoming. One interesting question is how access or lack of access will influence the strength of "we" versus "they" feelings.

At a time when people lived in isolated rural communities and did not interact with those unlike themselves, there was little price to pay for being bigoted or chauvinistic toward those who were different. However, we now live in a global village where we or our businesses will likely interact with very different people in a competitive environment. If we hold people in low regard because they are unlike us, there may be a high cost for this animosity toward those who are not like us. Among other problems, terrorism is fermented where people feel alienated. Therefore, training in cultural sensitivity toward those "others" has become an economic and political issue.

The reality is that children in the 21st century are being socialized to live in a globalized world. Increasingly, children around the world are learning multiple languages to enhance their ability to communicate with others. Some college campuses are requiring experiences abroad as part of the standard curriculum because faculty members and administrators feel that a global perspective is essential in our world today and part of a college education. Socialization to global sensitivity and tolerance of those who were once considered "alien" has become a core element of our day (Robertson 1992; Schaeffer 2003; Snarr and Snarr 2008).

Sometimes, global events can cause a different turn: away from tolerance and toward defensive isolation. When 19 young men from Saudi Arabia and other Middle Eastern countries crashed planes into the World Trade Center in New York City and into the Pentagon in Washington, D.C., the United States was shocked and became mobilized to defend itself and its borders. The messages within schools and from the government suddenly took a more patriotic turn. Then U.S. secretary of defense Donald Rumsfeld stated that the problem with the United States is that citizens do not have a strong enough sense of "we" versus "they." So this event and other terrorist acts, clearly tragedies rooted in

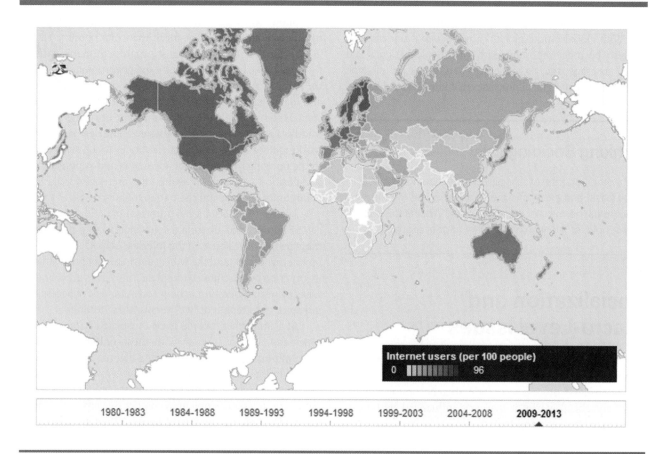

Map 4.1   Internet Users per 100 People

Source: World Bank (2011).

global political conflicts, can intensify boundaries between people and loyalty to the nation-state. Global forces are themselves complex and do not always result in more tolerance.

Indeed, the only thing we can predict with considerable certainty is that in this age of sharing a small planet, the socialization of our citizens will be influenced by events at the macro level, whether national or global.

Policy and Practice

Should preschoolers living in poverty be socialized in day care settings? Should adolescents work while going to school? Should we place emphasis in high school and college on in-group loyalty and patriotism or on developing a

sense of global citizenship? Should new parents be required to take child-rearing classes? How should job-training programs be structured? How can communities use the talents and knowledge of retirees? Can the death process be made easier for the dying person and the family? These are all policy questions—issues of how to establish governing principles that will enhance our common life.

These policy questions rely on an understanding of socialization—how we learn our beliefs and our positions in society. For example, making decisions about how to provide positive early childhood education experiences at a time when young children are learning the ways of their culture relies on understanding the socialization they receive at home and at school. The quality of child care we provide for young children will affect not only how effective our future workforce is but also whether children turn out to be productive citizens or a drain on society. These are also all questions sociologists can help to answer.

Now that we have some understanding of the process of socialization, we look next at the process of interaction and how individuals become members of small groups, networks, and large complex organizations.

What Have We Learned?

Human beings are not born to be noble savages or depraved beasts. As a species, we are remarkable in how many aspects of our lives are shaped by learning—by socialization. Human socialization is pervasive, extensive, and lifelong. We cannot understand what it means to be human without comprehending the impact of a specific culture on us, the influence of our close associates, and the complex interplay of pressures from micro, meso, and macro levels. Indeed, without social interaction, there would not even be a *self*. We humans are, in our most essential natures, social beings. The purpose of this chapter has been to open our eyes to the ways in which we become the individuals we are.

Key Points:

- Human beings must work with their biological makeup, but most of what makes us uniquely human has to do with things we learn from our culture and society—our socialization. Humans who live in isolation from others do not receive the socialization necessary to be part of culture and are sometimes barely human. (See pp. 91–92.)

- The self consists of the interaction of the *I*—the basic impulsive human with drives, needs, and feelings—and the *Me*—the reflective self one develops by role-taking to see how others might see one. (See pp. 95–97.)

- The self is profoundly shaped by others, but it also has agency—it is an initiator of action and the maker of meaning. (See pp. 97–101.)

- The self develops through stages, from mimicking others (the play stage) to more intellectually sophisticated abilities to role-take and to see how various roles fit together—the play and game stages. (See pp. 97–98.)

- Although the self is somewhat flexible in adjusting to different settings and circumstances, there is also a self that is part of meso-level organizations and institutions in which the self participates. (See pp. 98–99.)

- The self is modified as it moves through life stages, and some of those stages require major resocialization—shedding old roles and taking on new ones as one enters new statuses in life. (See p. 101.)

- A number of agents of socialization are at work on each of our lives, communicating messages that are relevant at the micro, the meso, or the macro level of social life. At the meso level, for example, we may receive different messages about what it means to be a "good" person depending on our ethnic, religious, or social class subculture. (See pp. 101–107.)

- Some of these messages may be in conflict with each other, as when global messages about tolerance for those who are different conflict with a nation's desire to have absolute loyalty and a sense of superiority. (See pp. 107–108.)

Discussion Questions

1. Cooley's idea of the "looking-glass self" helps us understand how we think other people view us and how that can influence our view of ourselves. How has your sense of your ability to succeed in college been influenced by the feedback you have processed from those around you (particularly teachers, peers, and family members)?

2. Socialization occurs throughout the life cycle. Into what role have you been socialized most recently? Who were the primary agents in this socialization process? Did you find the process relatively easy or difficult? Why?

3. Sociological studies have shown that middle-class and working-class parents tend to socialize their children differently. Explain the differences and describe how they relate to how you were socialized by your family of origin.

4. How has your socialization been influenced by television and video games? Do you think the extent to which these informal agents of socialization influence children these days has a positive or negative impact on our society? Why or why not?

5. If you were asked to create a government policy to promote positive socialization experiences that would strengthen our society, what might you propose? Why?

Contributing to Our Social World: What Can We Do?

At the Local Levels

In every community, numerous opportunities exist for volunteer work helping children from economically and otherwise disadvantaged backgrounds to succeed in school.

- *Tutoring or mentoring in the local schools.* Contact an education faculty member for information.

- *Volunteering in Head Start centers for poor preschool children.* See the program's website at www.nhsa.org.

- *Helping in a local Boys and Girls Club* that provides socialization experiences for children through their teens. You can find a club near you by going to http://www.bgca .org/whoweare/Pages/FindaClub.aspx.

- *Taking service learning course credits.* Locate the service learning office at your college or university to learn about service learning programs on your campus that help disadvantaged children.

At the National and Global Levels

Literacy is a vital component of socialization, yet remains an unmet need in many parts of the world, especially in the less developed countries of Africa and Asia.

- *World Education* provides training and technical assistance in nonformal education in economically disadvantaged communities worldwide. Go to the organization's website at www.worlded.org to learn about its wide variety of projects and volunteer/work opportunities.

- *CARE International* (www.care-international.org) and *Save the Children* (www.savethechildren.org) provide funding for families to send children to school and to receive specialized training.

- *Free the Children* (www.freethechildren.com), an organization that empowers young people to help other young people, has built more than 650 schools and school rooms for children in various parts of the world.

- *UNESCO (United Nations Educational, Scientific and Cultural Organization)* promotes literacy around the world in many ways. Learn more about its efforts at www .unesco.org/new/en/education. Opportunities exist for fundraising, internships, and eventually jobs with these organizations.

Visit **www.sagepub.com/oswcondensed3e** for online activities, sample tests, and other helpful information. Select "Chapter 4: Socialization" for chapter-specific activities.

5

Interaction, Groups, and Organizations

Connections That Work

Human interaction results in connections—
networks—that make life more fulfilling and
make our economic efforts more productive.
These connections are critical in our social
world—from small micro-level groups to large
bureaucratic organizations.

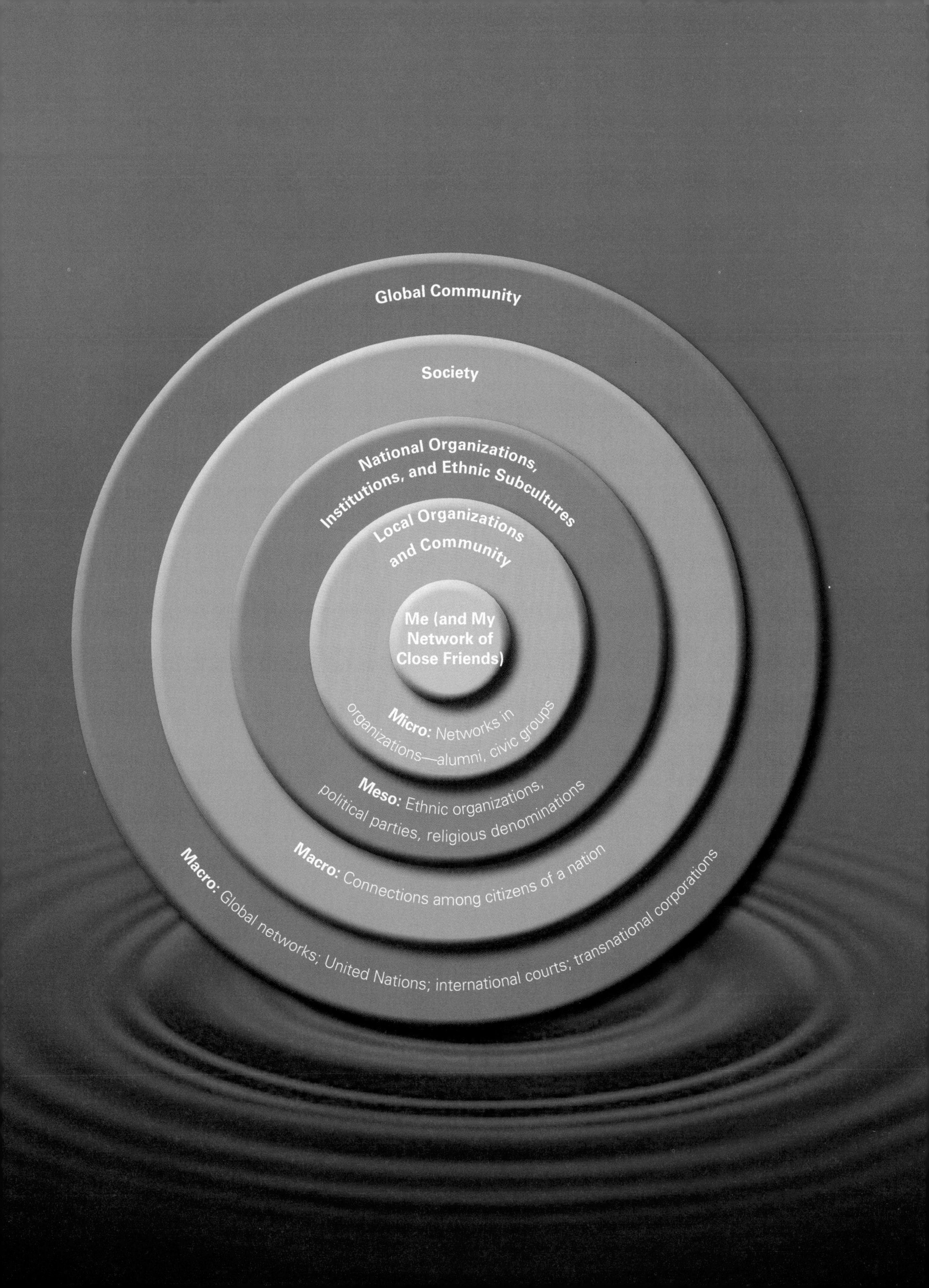

Global Community

Society

National Organizations,
Institutions, and Ethnic Subcultures

Local Organizations
and Community

Me (and My
Network of
Close Friends)

Micro: Networks in
organizations—alumni, civic groups

Meso: Ethnic organizations,
political parties, religious denominations

Macro: Connections among citizens of a nation

Macro: Global networks; United Nations; international courts; transnational corporations

Think About It	
Micro: Self and Inner Circle	Are you likely to meet your perfect mate over the Internet?
Micro: Local Community	How does interaction with family and friends affect who you are and what you believe?
Meso: National Institutions; Complex Organizations; Ethnic Groups	Is bureaucratic red tape both necessary and inevitable?
Macro: National Society	What are some ways national trends—such as the spread of fast-food chains and "box stores"—influence your quality of life?
Macro: Global Community	What are some ways networks across the globe affect you, your education, and your job?

What's coming in this chapter?

Networks and Connections in Our Social World

The Process of Interaction: Connections at the Micro Level

Groups in Our Social World: The Micro-Meso Connection

Organizations and Bureaucracies: The Meso-Macro Connection

National and Global Networks: The Macro Level

Policy Issues: Women and Globalization

Peaceful demonstrators, gathered to contest the 2009 election in Iran, were confronted with massive police forces. They were driven to disperse, many were beaten and arrested, and some were killed. Although the government imposed a news blackout and crackdown on communications, demonstrators used their cell phones, blogs, Twitter, and Facebook to send pictures and video footage around the world, documenting the events. Some have referred to this as the "Twitter Revolution." This cyber inspiration has spread to protesters in other countries such as Tunisia, Yemen, Egypt, Oman, Bahrain, and Libya. Cyberspace links people around the world in seconds in ways that few governments can stop (Stone and Cohen 2009). There is no need to wait for the mail or even talk on the phone. The information superhighway is opening new communication routes and allowing individuals with common interests to engage in networking.

Only a few decades ago, we read about cyberspace in science fiction novels written by authors with a little science background and a lot of imagination. Indeed, the word *cyberspace* was coined in 1984 by science fiction writer William Gibson. The implications of the rapidly expanding links in cyberspace are staggering. We cannot even anticipate some of them because change is so rapid.

For entertainment, we can talk with friends on electronic mailing lists or with people we have "met" through cyber social groups. Some of these acquaintances have never left their own country, which may be on the other side of the planet.

Universities now communicate with students and employees by computer. You may be able to register for class by "talking" to the computer. Computers track your registration and grades, and they may even send you computer-generated letters, emails, and texts about your status. They also monitor employee productivity. For doing certain types of research, library books are becoming secondary to the World Wide Web.

The purpose of this chapter is to lay the groundwork for understanding how we fit into the structure of our social world—exploring the link between the individual and the social structure. The process starts when we are born and continues with group activities as we join

No longer are paper and pencil the media of academics. Most universities are now requiring students to have laptops or access to computers on campus. Almost all colleges now provide Wi-Fi Internet access, thus expanding the modes of teaching, learning, and communicating.

playgroups, preschool groups, and kindergarten groups. It broadens as we become members of larger organizations and bureaucracies within universities, workplaces, national political parties, and national and international religious organizations. First, we consider how networks and connections link individuals and groups to different levels of analysis. Then, we focus on micro-level interactions, meso-level groups, and meso- and macro-level organizations and bureaucracies. Finally, we consider macro-level national and global networks.

Networks and Connections in Our Social World

Try imagining yourself at the center of a web, as in a spider's web. Attach the threads that spread from the center first to family members and close friends, next to peers, then to friends of friends. Some thread connections are close and direct. Others are more distant but connect more and more people in an ever-expanding web.

Perhaps you have heard it said that every American is only six steps (or degrees removed) from any other person in the country. This assertion is rooted in a study with evidence to support it. Stanley Milgram and his associates studied social networks by selecting several target people in different cities (Korte and Milgram 1970; Milgram 1967; Travers and Milgram 1969). Then they identified "starting persons" in cities more than 1,000 miles away. Each starting person was given a folder with instructions and the target person's name, address, and occupation, as well as a few other facts. The starting person was instructed to mail the folder to someone he or she knew on a first-name basis who lived closer to or might have had more direct networks with the target person than the starting person. Although many folders never arrived at their destination, one third did. The researchers were interested in how many steps were involved in the delivery of the packages that did arrive. The number of links in the chain to complete delivery ranged from two to ten, with most having five to seven intermediaries. This is the source of the reference to "six degrees of separation."

More recently, research by scientists at Facebook and the University of Milan showed that the average number of acquaintances separating any two people in the world is now 4.74; within the United States the separation is only 4.37 people (Markoff and Sengupta 2011). Clearly, networks are powerful linkages and create a truly small world.

Our **social networks**, then, refer to individuals linked together by one or more social relationships connecting them to the larger society. We use our social network to get jobs or favors, often from people who are not very far removed from us in the web. Networks begin with micro-level contacts and exchanges between individuals in private interactions and expand to small groups, then to large (even global) organizations (Granovetter 2007; Tolbert and Hall 2009). The stronger one's networks are, the more influential they can be in a person's life. The web in Figure 5.1 illustrates that individuals are linked to other people, groups, organizations, and nations in the social world through networks.

Although network links can be casual and personal rather than based on official positions and channels, they place a person within the larger social structure, and it is from these networks that group ties emerge. People in networks talk to each other about common interests. This communication process creates linkages between clusters of people. For example, cyber networks on the Internet bring together people with common interests.

Networks at the Micro, Meso, and Macro Levels

At the micro level, you develop close friends in college—bonds that may continue for the rest of your life. You introduce your friends from theater to your roommate's friends from the soccer team, and the network expands. These acquaintances may have useful information about which professors to avoid, how to make contacts to study abroad, and how to get a job in your field. Food cooperatives, self-help groups such as Alcoholics Anonymous and Weight Watchers, and computer-user groups are examples of networks that connect individuals with common interests.

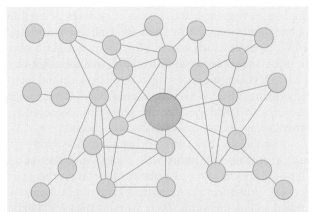

The yellow circle represents an individual—perhaps you—and the blue dots represent your friends and acquaintances. Your network looks a bit like a web but is less complete in terms of every point connected to the adjacent point, since some of your friends do not know each other.

Figure 5.1   Networks: A Web of Connections

Social Media

Thinking Sociologically

Map your social network web. What advantages do you get from your network? What economic benefits might your connections have for you? How have you tried to expand your network? What Internet sites help you network?

Network links create new types of organizational forms at the meso level, such as those in the opening example of cyberspace and the Internet. These networks cross societal, racial, ethnic, religious, and other lines that divide people. Networks also link groups at different levels of analysis. In fact, you are linked through networks to (a) micro-level local civic, sports, and religious organizations; (b) meso-level formal complex organizations such as a political party or a national fraternity and ethnic or social class subcultures; (c) the macro-level nation of which you are a citizen and to which you have formal obligations (such as the requirement that you go to war as a draftee if the government so decides); and (d) global entities such as the United Nations, which use some of your donated resources or taxes to help impoverished people, tsunami victims, and earthquake survivors elsewhere in the world. These networks may open opportunities, but they also may create obligations that limit your freedom to make your own choices. As we move from the micro level to the larger meso and macro levels, interactions tend to become more formal. Formal organizations are explored in the latter half of this chapter.

By linking individuals to people around the globe, Internet users have redefined networking through the creation of blogs, chat rooms, message boards, electronic mailing lists, newsgroups, and dozens of websites devoted to online networking ("Five Rules for Online Networking" 2005). Websites such as LinkedIn, Xing, and Plaxo offer business and professional networking, whereas other sites such as Myspace and Facebook focus on personal and social networking. There is even an international journal, *Social Networks*, that publishes interdisciplinary studies about the structure and impact of social networks and sites.

Probably the most famous networking site is Facebook, and it became even more well known with the recent film—*The Social Network*—about Mark Zuckerberg, its founder. With members from all ages and places, Facebook truly does link the world. There are more than 1.15 billion active users around the world, with 1 in 7.7 people in the world having a Facebook account and 125 billion "friendships." The time logged per month on this single system exceeds 700 billion minutes. Users share blogs, news, web links, notes, photos, and more. About 80% of users are outside of the home base, the United States, and Facebook is translated into 70 languages. Thirty-nine percent of business owners planned to market on Facebook in 2012.

Some analysts argue that Facebook is changing the way we interact and connect with people (Bullas 2012; Facebook .com 2013).

Thinking Sociologically

Compare the way you communicate with your friends and the way your parents or grandparents communicate with their friends. Are there differences, and what are the advantages and disadvantages of each? Does one method result in closer relationships than another?

As a way of examining your own networks, try the exercise in the next "Engaging Sociology" feature.

An even more recent development is the rapidly increasing popularity of Twitter, a microblogging website that allows users to post 140-character messages ("tweets") using their personal computer or the text messaging function on their mobile phone. Messages are mostly conversational (37.6%) and "pointless babble" (40%), but they also pass along news as well as self-promotion, and have been used by protesters to mobilize reform movements in countries with oppressive governments (Infographics 2012). Interestingly, users have played a crucial role in developing Twitter, including inventing "hashtags" that indicate the subject of the tweet and allowing others to search for all tweets on the same topic (S. Johnson 2009).

The irony, of course, is that electronic technology has changed interactions by making them both more intimate and accessible—and less so. We can network through Facebook, and we can keep in touch constantly through text messaging. However, this means that people spend more time interacting with a piece of technology and less time interacting face-to-face. How ironic it is to see people at adjacent desks or offices, or with friends down the hall in the dorm, talking on cell phones or texting other friends. Likewise, distance learning courses are in one sense less intimate—the instructor and the student may never meet face-to-face. Yet through Internet contact, the students may have more access to the ideas and the personal counsel of a professor than they would if they were in a large lecture class. We are only beginning to understand the implications of this technology on human interaction and on interpersonal skills.

Thinking Sociologically

How do Facebook and Twitter shape your interactions with friends?

 Social Networks

 Social Networks

Engaging Sociology

Examining Your Social Networks

If you are on Facebook, go to your Facebook account and note the number of friends you have listed. Then look at them carefully to see if you can answer the following questions:

What is the age range of the friends on your list?

What is the gender composition of your list?

How many members of each of the following racial or ethnic groups are on your list?

___ African Americans

___ Whites of predominantly European heritage

___ Hispanics

___ Asians

___ Other/Multiracial

Indicate the number of friends that have each of the following economic characteristics:

___ Blue-collar (families in which the primary wage earner[s] works for an hourly wage)

___ Middle class (families in which the primary wage earner[s] earns a salary of less than $100,000 per year)

___ Professional (families in which the primary wage earner[s] earns a salary of $100,000 to $500,000 per year)

___ Highly affluent corporate executives (families in which the primary wage earner[s] earns a salary of $500,000 to $10 million per year)

___ Upper class (families in which much of the wealth is inherited and annual income is in the multimillions)

Engaging with sociological data:

- Now look at the data you have collected. What have you learned about your own networks?
- How much socioeconomic, age, and ethnic diversity do the data reveal about your networks?

The Process of Interaction: Connections at the Micro Level

Each morning as you rouse yourself and prepare for the challenges ahead, you consider what the day might bring, what activities and obligations are on your calendar, and to whom you will talk. As you lift your limp, listless body from a horizontal to an upright position and blood begins coursing through your veins, thoughts of the day's events begin to penetrate your semiconscious state. A cup of caffeine, cold water on the face, and a mouth-freshening brush bring you to the next stage of awareness. You evaluate what is in store for you, what roles you will play during the day, and with whom you are likely to interact.

Should you wear the ragged but comfortable jeans and T-shirt? No, there is that class trip to the courthouse today. Something a bit less casual is in order. Then, you are meeting with your English professor to discuss the last essay you wrote. What approach should you take? You could act insulted that she failed to think of you as a future J. K. Rowling. Maybe a meek, mild "Please tell me what I did wrong; I tried so hard" approach would work. She seems a nice, sympathetic sort. After class, there is a group of students who chat in the hall. It would be nice to meet them. What strategy should you use? Try to enter the conversation? Tell a joke? Make small talk? Talk to the students individually so you can get to know each before engaging the whole group? Each of these responses is a strategy for interaction, and each might elicit different reactions.

The Elements of Social Interaction

"Let's have a drink!" Such a simple comment might have many different meanings. We could imagine two children playing together, men going to a bar after work, a couple of friends getting together to celebrate an event, fraternity brothers at a party, or a couple on a date. In all these cases, **social interaction** consists of *two or more individuals purposefully relating to each other*.

"Having a drink," like all interaction, involves action on the part of two or more individuals, is directed toward a goal that people hope to achieve, and takes place in a social context that includes cultural norms and rules governing the situation, the setting, and other factors shaping the way people perceive the circumstances. The action, goal, and social context help us interpret the meaning of statements such as "Let's have a drink."

The norms governing the particular social context tell us what is right and proper behavior. Recall from Chapter 3 that *norms* are rules that guide human interactions. People assume that others will share their interpretation of a situation. These shared assumptions about proper behavior provide the cues for your own behavior that become a part of your social self. You look for cues to proper behavior and rehearse in your mind your actions and reactions. In the "Let's have a drink" scenario, you assume that the purpose of the interaction is understood. What dress, mannerisms,

speech, and actions you consider appropriate depend on expectations from your socialization and past experience in similar situations, for in modern societies a range of behaviors and responses is possible in any social situation (Parsons 1951).

Although most people assume that talking, or verbal communication, is the primary means of communication between individuals, words themselves are actually only a part of the message. In most contexts, they make up less than 50% of the communication, and only 35% of the emotional content of the message (Birdwhistell 1970). **Nonverbal communication**—*interactions without words using facial expressions, the head, eye contact, body posture, gestures, touch, walk, status symbols, and personal space*—makes up the rest, estimated to be between 50% and 70% of all communication (Cherry 2012; Givens 2012). These important elements of communication are learned through socialization as we grow up.

People who travel to a country other than their own often use gestures to be understood. Like spoken language, nonverbal gestures vary from culture to culture, as illustrated in the photos on the next page. Communicating with others in one's own language can be difficult enough. Add to this the complication of individuals with different languages, cultural expectations, and personalities using different nonverbal messages, and misunderstandings are likely. Although one may master another written and verbal language, nonverbal messages are the hardest part of another language to master because they are specific to a culture and learned through socialization.

Consider the following example: You are about to wrap up a major business deal. You are pleased with the results of your negotiations, so you give your hosts the thumb-and-finger A-OK sign. In Brazil, you have just grossly insulted your hosts—it is the equivalent of giving them "the finger." In Japan, you have asked for a small bribe. In the south of France, you have indicated the deal is worthless. Although your spoken Portuguese, Japanese, or French may have been splendid, your nonverbal language did not cut the deal. Intercultural understanding is more than being polite and knowing the language.

Another example of nonverbal language involves personal space. Most people have experienced social situations, such as parties, where someone gets too close. One person backs away, the other moves in again, and the first backs away again—into a corner or a table with nowhere else to go. Perhaps the person approaching was aggressive or rude, but it is also possible that the person held different cultural norms or expectations in relation to personal space.

The amount of personal space an individual needs to be comfortable or proper varies with the cultural setting, gender, status, and social context of the interaction. Individuals from Arab countries are comfortable at very close range. However, people from Scandinavia or the United States

The words "Let's have a drink" may have very different meanings in different social interaction contexts. Humans must learn not only the language but also how to interpret the messages.

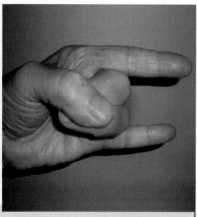

Gestures are symbolic forms of interaction. However, these gestures can have entirely different meanings in different cultures. A friendly gesture in one culture may be obscene in the next. The photo on the far right is how one would signal that one wanted four of something in China.

need a great deal of personal space. Consider the following four categories of social distance and social space based on a study of U.S. middle-class people. Each category applies to particular types of activity (E. Hall and Hall 1992):

1. *Intimate distance:* from zero distance (touching, embracing, kissing) to 18 inches. Children may play together in such close proximity, and adults and children may maintain this distance, but between adults, this intimate contact is reserved for private and affectionate relationships.

2. *Personal distance:* from 18 inches to 4 feet. This is the public distance for most friends and for informal interactions with acquaintances.

3. *Social distance:* from 4 feet to 12 feet. This is the distance for impersonal business relations, such as a job interview or class discussions between students and a professor. This distance implies a more formal interaction or a significant difference in the status of the two people.

4. *Public distance:* 12 feet and beyond. This is the distance most public figures use for addressing others, especially in formal settings and in situations in which the speaker has very high status.

Personal space also communicates one's position in relation to others. The higher one's position is, the more one is in control of her or his personal space. In social situations, individuals with higher positions spread out, prop their feet up, put their arms out, and use more sweeping gestures. Women and men differ with regard to personal space and other forms of nonverbal language. For instance,

women tend to be more sensitive to subtle cues such as status differences and the use of personal space (Henley, Hamilton, and Thorne 2000; Knapp and Hall 1997).

Sociologists study interactions, including verbal and nonverbal communication, to explain this very basic link between humans and the group. The following theoretical perspectives focus on the micro level of analysis in attempting to explain interactions.

A more formal setting calls for a distance of 4 to 12 feet. If the distance is quite large, the situation can feel very formal and intimidating. What is the message at this meeting?

Bourdieu's Theory of Space and Social Distance

When a famous or powerful person speaks in a public setting, listeners are expected to keep themselves at a distance of about 12 feet or more. When President Barack Obama speaks, it is not only the Secret Service that keeps people at a formal distance; it is also a sense of awed respect for the office of the president.

Thinking Sociologically

What are some complications that you or your friends have had in interactions involving cross-cultural contacts or male-female miscommunication? What might help clarify communication in these cases?

Theoretical Perspectives on the Interaction Process

How many people do you interact with each day, and what happens in each of these interactions? You probably have not given the question much thought or analysis, but that process is exactly what fascinates interaction theorists. Why do two people interact in the first place? What determines whether the interaction will continue or stop? How do two people know how to behave and what to say around each other? What other processes are taking place as they "talk" to each other? Why do people interact differently with different

people? What governs the way they make sense of messages and how they respond to them? These questions address the basic interaction processes that result in group formations that range in size from dyads (two people) to large organizations. The following section explores theories that attempt to provide explanations for interactions.

Symbolic Interaction Theory

Symbolic interaction theory focuses on how individuals interpret situations, such as "Let's have a drink," and how this, in turn, affects their actions. Symbolic interactionism is based on the idea that our humanness derives from the mutual impact we have upon each other. Humans act toward things on the basis of the meanings those things have for them. The meanings are derived by individuals as they interact with others. Hence, humans are above all symbol-creating and symbol-modifying creatures, for symbols have meaning beyond their own fleeting existence. Symbols are the key to understanding human life, for we go about the task of fitting our actions together because of shared perceptions or shared meanings. Meaning is not inherent in the events of life; it is created by individuals and communicated among them. Through our mental manipulation of symbols and interpretation of meaning, we *define situations* and determine how we should act in a given situation or how we should make sense of it (Charon 2010; Hewitt and Shulman 2011).

Symbolic interactionists see humans as active agents who consciously, deliberately, and directly fashion their personal and collective histories. These theorists emphasize the part that language and gestures play in the formation of the mind, the self, and society. More than any other theory in the social sciences, symbolic interactionism stresses the agency—the active decision-making role—of humans within their societies (Charon 2010; Hewitt and Shulman 2011).

In ambiguous situations, humans look to others to see how they have made sense of the situation or interaction taking place—is it frightening, funny, annoying, boring, or inspiring? If someone behaves in a manner that is unconventional—that is weird or strange—it could be cause for alarm or humor or disgust. Once one person defines the situation and acts, especially if that person is highly regarded or very self-confident, others will often accept that response as "normal." This is how social interaction is involved in the social construction of reality—the social process of defining what is true or real or valid (Berger and Luckmann 1966; Hewitt and Shulman 2011; J. O'Brien 2011).

One approach to interaction analysis is called *dramaturgy,* analyzing life as a play or drama on a stage, with scripts and props and scenes to be played. The play we put on creates an impression for our audience. In everyday life, individuals learn new lines to add to their scripts through the socialization process, including influence from family, friends, films, and television. They perform these scripts for social audiences in order to maintain certain images, much like the actors in a play.

Every day in high schools, thousands of teenagers go on stage—in the classroom or the hallway with friends and peers and with adult authorities who may later be giving grades or writing letters of reference. The props these students use include their clothing, a backpack with paper and pen, and a smile or "cool" look. The set is the classroom, the cafeteria, and perhaps the athletic field. The script is shaped by the actors, with teachers establishing an authoritarian relationship, with classmates engaging in competition for grades, or with peers seeking social status among companions. The actors include hundreds of teens struggling with issues of identity, changing bodies, and attempts to avoid humiliation. Each individual works to assert and maintain an image through behavior, clothing, language, and friends.

As individuals perform according to society's script for the situation, they take into consideration how their actions will influence others. By carefully managing the impression they wish the acquaintance to receive—a process called *impression management*—people hope to create an impression that works to their advantage. In other words, they are trying to manipulate how others see them, especially as it relates to others' opinion of them.

Most of the time, we engage in front-stage behavior, the behavior safest with casual acquaintances because it is scripted and acted for the public to create an impression. At home or with close friends with whom we are more intimate, we engage in backstage behavior, letting our feelings show and behaving in ways that might be unacceptable for other audiences (Goffman [1959] 2001, 1967). Each part or character an individual plays, as well as each audience, requires a different script. Dramaturgical analysis can be a useful approach to broadening our understanding of interactions.

Thinking Sociologically

What are some ways your life feels like a dramatic production—with a front-stage presentation and a backstage presence?

Rational Choice Theory

Rational choice or exchange theorists look at a different aspect of interaction—why relationships continue. Focusing on the rewards and costs of interaction to the individual, they argue that choices we make are guided by reason. If the benefits of the interaction are high and if the costs are low, the interaction will be valued and sustained. Every interaction involves calculations of self-interest, expectations of reciprocity (a mutual exchange of favors), and decisions

to act in ways that have current or eventual payoff for the individual (Smelser 1992).

Reciprocity is a key concept for rational choice theorists. The idea is that if a relationship is imbalanced over a period of time, it will become unsatisfying. As theorists from this perspective see human interaction, each person tends to keep a mental ledger of who "owes" whom. If I have done you a favor, you owe me one. If you have helped me in some way, I have an obligation to you. If I then fail to comply, or even do something that hurts you, you will likely view it as a breach in the relationship and have negative feelings toward me. Moreover, if there is an imbalance in what we each bring to the relationship, one person may have more power in the relationship.

In the study of families, scholars utilize the "principle of least interest," which says that the person with the least interest in the relationship has the most power. The person with the least interest is the person who brings more resources to the relationship and receives less. That person could easily leave. The person who offers less to the relationship or who has fewer assets (physical, financial, social, personal) is more dependent on the relationship. This person is likely to give in when there is a disagreement, so the person with less interest gets her or his way. Lack of reciprocity can be important for how relationships develop. Sometimes a person may engage in a behavior where there is little likelihood of reciprocity from the other person—as in cases where the behavior is altruistic or self-giving. Rational choice theorists would argue that there is still a benefit. It might be enhanced feelings of self-worth, recognition from others, hope for a place in heaven, or just the expectation of indirect reciprocity. This later notion is that the person I help might not help me, but if I were in a similar situation, I would hope for and expect someone to come to my assistance (Gouldner 1960; J. Turner 2003).

Social Status: The Link to Groups

As you recall from Chapter 4, a **social status** is *a social position in society*. We interact with others and they react to us based in part on the statuses we hold. We interact differently when in the daughter status with our parents, in a student status with our professor, or in friend status with our peers. Each individual holds many statuses, and this combination held by any individual is called a status set: daughter, mother, worker, teammate, student.

Statuses affect the type of interactions individuals have. In some interactions (as with classmates), people are equals. In other situations, individuals have interchanges with people who hold superior or inferior statuses. If you are promoted to supervisor, your interaction with subordinates will change. Consider the possible interactions shown in Figure 5.2, in which the first relationship is between equals and the others are between those with unequal statuses.

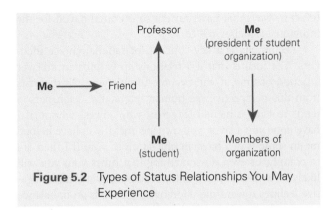

Figure 5.2   Types of Status Relationships You May Experience

between males and females find that gender, power, and hierarchical relationships are important in determining interaction patterns. The more powerful person, such as one who has more wealth or privilege, can interrupt in a conversation with his or her partner and show less deference in the interaction (Kim et al. 2007; Reid and Ng 2006; Wood 2008).

People have no control over certain statuses they hold. These **ascribed statuses** are often *assigned at birth and do not change during an individual's lifetime.* Some examples are gender and race or ethnicity. Ascribed statuses are assigned to a person without regard for personal desires, talents, or choices. In some societies, one's caste, or the social position into which one is born (e.g., a slave), is an ascribed status because it is usually impossible to change.

Achieved status, on the other hand, *is chosen or earned by decisions one makes and sometimes by personal ability.* Attaining a higher education, for example, improves an individual's occupational opportunities and hence his or her achieved status. Being a guitarist in a band is an achieved

With a friend, these status relationships are constantly being negotiated and bargained: "I'll do what you want tonight, but tomorrow I choose." By contrast, when individuals are in dominant or subordinate positions, power or deference affects their interactions. Studies of interaction

Positions people carry out in different cultures depend on tasks important in that culture. Upper left: The two women from Ghana carry yams, a staple food, from the fields. Upper right: The market for these Asian women is on the water. Lower left: Men in China use traditional methods to keep the roads open. Lower right: Fishermen in India pull in a catch for their livelihood.

status, and so is being a prisoner in jail, for both are earned positions based on the person's own decisions and actions.

At a particular time in life or under certain circumstances, one of an individual's statuses may become most important and take precedence over others, called a **master status**. Whether it is an occupation, parental status, or something else, it dominates and shapes much of an individual's life, activities, self-concept, and position in the community for a period of time. For a person who is very ill, for instance, that illness may occupy a master status, needing constant attention from doctors, influencing social relationships, and determining what that person can do in family, work, or community activities.

Thinking Sociologically

What are your statuses? Which ones are ascribed, and which are achieved statuses? Do you have a master status? How do these statuses affect the way you interact with others in your network of relationships?

The Relationship Between Status and Role

Every status (position) in your network includes certain behaviors and obligations as you carry out **roles**, *the expected behaviors, rights, obligations, responsibilities, and privileges assigned to a social status*. Roles are the dynamic, action part of statuses in a society. They define how each individual in an interaction is expected to act (Linton 1937). The roles of a person holding the status of "college student" include behaviors and obligations such as attending classes, studying, taking tests, writing papers, and interacting with professors and other students. Individuals enter most statuses with some knowledge of how to carry out the roles dictated by their culture. Through the process of socialization, individuals learn roles by observing others, watching television and films, reading, and being taught how to carry out the status. Both statuses (positions) and roles (behavioral obligations of the status) form the link with other people in the social world because they must be carried out in relationships with others. A father has certain obligations (or roles) toward his children and their mother. The position of father exists not on its own but in relationship to significant others who have reciprocal ties.

Your status of student requires certain behaviors and expectations, depending on whether you are interacting with a dean, a professor, an adviser, a classmate, or a prospective employer. This is because the role expectations of the status of student vary as one interacts with specific people in other statuses. Within a group, individuals may hold both formal and informal statuses. One illustration is the formal status of high school students, each of whom plays a number of informal roles in cliques that are not part of the formal school structure. One student may be known as a preppy, a goth, a hick, a clown, a jock, or an outcast. Each of these roles takes place in a status relationship with others: teacher-student, peer-peer, coach-athlete. The connections between statuses and roles are illustrated in Table 5.1.

Social networks may be based on ascribed characteristics such as age, race, ethnicity, and gender or on achieved status such as education, occupation, or common interests (House 1994). These links, in turn, form the basis for social interactions and group structures (R. Hall 2002). However, at times, individuals cannot carry out their roles as others expect them to, creating role strain or conflict.

Thinking Sociologically

In your web, detail your network from close family and friends to distant acquaintances. Include your statuses and roles in each part of the network with family members, friends, and school and work acquaintances. What does your network tell you about yourself?

Table 5.1   The Relationship Between Statuses and Roles

Status (position in structure)	Role (behavior, rights, obligations)
Student	*Formal*
	Study, attend class, turn in assignments
	Informal
	Be a jock, clown, cut-up; abuse alcohol on weekends
Parent	*Formal*
	Provide financial support, child care
	Informal
	Be a playmate, lead family activities
Employee	*Formal*
	Work responsibilities: punctuality, doing one's tasks
	Informal
	Befriend coworkers, join lunch group, represent company in bowling league

Office Politics

Role Strain and Role Conflict

Every status carries role expectations, the way the status is supposed to be carried out according to generally accepted societal or group norms. Most people have faced times in their lives when they simply could not carry out all the obligations of a status such as student—write two papers, study adequately for two exams, complete the portfolio for the studio art class, finish the reading assignments for five classes, and memorize lines for the oral interpretation class, all in the same week. In these cases, individuals face **role strain**, *tension between roles within one of the statuses*. Role strain causes the individual to be pulled in many directions by various obligations of the single status, as in the example regarding the status of "student." Another such strain is often experienced by first-time fathers as they attempt to reconcile their role expectations of fathering with ideas held by their wives.

To resolve role strain, individuals cope in one of several ways: pass the problem off lightly (and thus not do well in classes), consider the dilemma humorous, become highly focused and pull a couple of all-nighters to get everything done, or become stressed, tense, fretful, and immobilized because of the strain. Most often, individuals set priorities based on their values and make decisions accordingly: "I'll work hard in the class for my major and let another one slide."

Role conflict refers to *conflict between the roles of two or more social statuses*. It differs from role strain in that conflict is between the roles of two or more statuses, rather than tension between roles within one of the statuses. The conflict can come from within an individual or be imposed from outside. College athletes face role conflicts from competing demands on their time (Adler and Adler 1991, 2004). They must complete their studies on time, attend practices and be prepared for games, perhaps attend meetings of a Greek house to which they belong, and get home for a little brother's birthday. Similarly, a student may be going to school, holding down a part-time job to help make ends meet, and raising a family. If the student's child gets sick, the status of parent comes into conflict with that of student and worker. In the case of role conflict, the person may choose—or be informed by others—which status is the master status. Figure 5.3 illustrates the difference between role conflict and role strain.

Statuses and the accompanying roles come and go. You will not always be a student, and someday, you may be a parent and hold a professional job. Certainly, you will retire from your job. For instance, as people grow older, they disengage from some earlier statuses in groups and engage in new and different statuses and roles.

Our statuses connect us and make us integral parts of meso- and macro-level organizations. Our place within the social world, then, is guaranteed, even obligatory, because of statuses we hold—within small groups (family and peers), in larger groups and organizations (school and work organizations), in institutions (political parties or religious

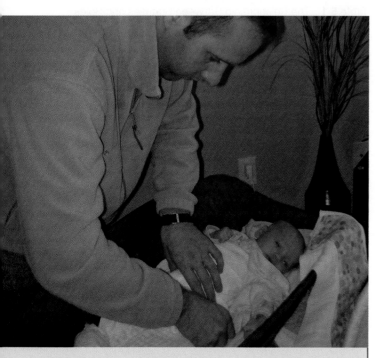

Parenting roles often need to be negotiated. In some traditional families in the past, the status had clearer role expectations, and fathers were rarely expected to change diapers.

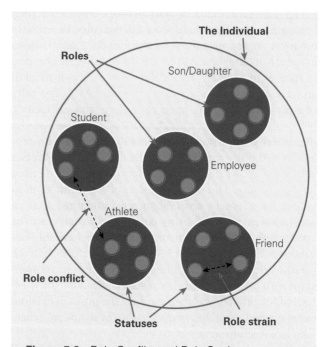

Figure 5.3   Role Conflict and Role Strain

Each individual has many statuses: a status set. Each status has many roles: a role set. A conflict between two roles of the same status is a role strain. A conflict between the roles of two different statuses is a role conflict.

Role Strain

denominations), and ultimately as citizens of the society and the world (workers in global corporations). Each of these statuses connects us to a group setting.

Thinking Sociologically

Using Figure 5.3, fill in the statuses you hold in your social world and roles you perform in these statuses. In your diagram, list three examples of role conflicts and three examples of role strains that you experience.

Groups in Our Social World: The Micro-Meso Connection

Groups refer to *units involving two or more people who interact with each other because of shared common interests, goals, experiences, and needs* (Drafke 2008). Few of us could survive without others. Most of us constantly interact with the people around us. We are born into a family group. Our socialization occurs in groups. We depend on the group for survival. Groups are necessary for protection, to obtain food, to manufacture goods, and to get jobs done. Groups meet our social needs for belonging and acceptance, support us throughout our lives, and place restrictions on us. Groups can be small, intimate environments—micro-level interactions with family or a group of friends—or they can become quite large as they morph into meso-level organizations. In any case, it is through our group memberships that the micro and meso levels are linked.

Not all collections of individuals are groups. For instance, your family is a group, but people shopping at a mall or waiting for a bus are not a group because they do not regularly interact or acknowledge shared common interests.

Groups form through a series of succeeding steps. Consider people forming a soccer team. The first step is initial interaction. If membership is rewarding and meets individuals' needs, the individuals will attempt to maintain the benefits the group provides (T. Mills 1984). A group of people interact to form this team. In the second step, a collective goal emerges. For example, team members work together to plan practice and game schedules, buy uniforms, and advertise the games. Groups establish their own goals and pursue them, trying to be free from external controls or constraints. In the third and final step, the group attempts to expand its collective goals by building on the former steps and by pursuing new goals. For example, the team may reach out to new players, to coaches, and to supporters for funding.

The Importance of Groups for the Individual

Groups are essential parts of human life (micro level) and of organizational structures (meso and macro levels). They establish our place in the social world, providing us with support and a sense of belonging. Few individuals can survive without groups. This becomes clear when we consider two problems: anomie and suicide.

Anomie and Suicide

Who commits suicide? Did you know that the answer to this is closely related to an individual's group affiliations? With the rapid changes and continued breakdown of institutional structures in Afghanistan as rival warlords vie for power over territory and in Libya as religious and political groups vie for power, horrific problems abound. Civil disorder, conflicts for power, suicide bombings, murder of police officers, and looting are frequent occurrences. Social controls (police and military forces) are strained, and leaders struggle to cope with the chaos. The result of this breakdown in norms is **anomie**, *the state of normlessness that occurs when the rules for behavior in society break down under extreme stress from rapid social change or conflict* (Merton 1968a).

Early sociologist Émile Durkheim took a unique approach to understanding suicide. In his volume, *Suicide*, he discussed the social factors contributing to suicide (Durkheim [1897] 1964). Using existing statistical data to determine suicide rates in European populations, Durkheim

Even Buddhist nuns, who spend much of their lives devoted to private meditation, need the support and solidarity of a group.

looked at such variables as sex, age, religion, nationality, and the season in which suicide was committed. His findings were surprising to many, and they demonstrate that individual problems cannot be understood without also understanding the group context in which they occur.

Durkheim found that Protestants committed suicide more often than Catholics, urban folks more often than people living in small communities, people in highly developed and complex societies more frequently than those in simple societies, and people who lived alone more than those situated in families. The key variable linking these findings was the degree to which an individual was integrated into the group—that is, the degree of social bond with others. During war, for instance, people generally felt a sense of common cause and belonging to their country. Thus, suicide rates were greater during peacetime because the social climate offered less cause for feeling that bond.

Durkheim describes three distinct types of suicide. *Egoistic suicide* occurs when the individual feels little social bond to the group or society and lacks ties such as family or friends that might prevent suicide. Egoistic suicide is a result of personal despair and involves the kind of motive most people associate with suicide.

Suicide seems like it would always be an individual act, committed because of personal problems, but this is not always the case. *Anomic suicide* occurs when a society or one of its parts is in disorder or turmoil and lacks clear norms and guidelines for social behavior. This situation is likely during major social change or economic problems such as a severe depression. Rapid changes in society brought on by industrialization can also contribute to anomie and loss of meaning. Until the late 1900s, South Korea's elderly parents typically lived with their eldest son's family. As Korean society became economically successful, family life also changed. Many young people moved away from rural areas to economic centers, and the assumption that the elderly would live out their lives in their son's care have changed. The government has also cut back on support for the elderly, leaving many in this vulnerable elderly group to live out their years in poverty. The consequence is a mismatch between remarkable economic success of the nation and vulnerability of some populations. Suicides in South Korea among people 65 and older ballooned from 1,161 in 2000 to 4,378 in 2010—and growing, and scholars attribute this to anomie (Sang-Hun 2013).

Durkheim's third pattern, *altruistic suicide,* differs from the others in that it involves such a strong bond and group obligation that the individual is willing to die for the group. Self-survival becomes less important than group survival (Durkheim [1897] 1964). Examples of altruistic suicide include the young suicide bombers in Iraq, Afghanistan, and Pakistan committing suicide missions against their country's police forces and sometimes against American military forces, which they have defined as invading forces. These suicides usually occur in societies or religious groups that have very clear norms and high levels of consensus about values arising from their religious or political commitments. Another example is illustrated in the photo of Jorge Parra. These are suicides rooted in extraordinarily high integration into a political or religious group.

Many sociologists have studied suicide, and while not all studies support Durkheim's original findings, they do support the general finding that suicide rates are strongly influenced by social and psychological factors that can operate at the meso or macro level. Suicide is not a purely individualistic decision (R. Hall 2002; Nolan, Triplett, and McDonough 2010; Pescosolido and Georgianna 1989).

No individual is an island. The importance of groups and social influence from various levels in the system is an underlying theme of this text. Groups are essential to human life, but to understand them more fully, we must understand the various kinds of groups in which humans participate.

Jorge Parra was disabled in a General Motors plant in Colombia, and he was subsequently fired. He and more than a dozen other injured workers protested outside the U.S. Embassy in Colombia for more than a year, and in the fall of 2012 they went on a hunger strike. They sewed their mouths closed so they could ingest only liquids. They were so tightly bonded that Jorge decided he would fast until death, if necessary, to protest the injustices they face. He had gone more than 70 days without food by January 2013, when the United Auto Workers agreed to help negotiate a solution, provided he end his death fast. The willingness to die voluntarily as part of solidarity with a group is called altruistic suicide.

Types of Groups

Each of us belongs to several types of groups. Some groups provide intimacy and close relationships, whereas others do not. Some are required affiliations, and others are voluntary. Some provide personal satisfaction, and others are obligatory or necessary for survival. The following discussion

Darfur

points out several types of groups and reasons individuals belong to them.

Primary groups are *characterized by cooperation among people in close, intimate relationships*—the most micro level. Your family members, best friends, school classmates, and close work associates are all of primary importance in your everyday life. Primary groups provide a sense of belonging and shared identity. Group members care about you, and you care about the other group members, creating a sense of loyalty. Approval and disapproval from the primary group influence the activities you choose to pursue. Belonging to the group is the main reason for membership. The group is of intrinsic value—enjoyed for its own sake—rather than for some utilitarian value such as making money.

For individuals, primary groups provide an anchor point in society. You were born into a primary group—your family. You may hold many statuses and play a variety of roles in primary relationships—those of spouse, parent, child, sibling, relative, close friend, and so on. You meet with other members face-to-face or keep in touch on a regular basis and know a great deal about their lives. What makes them happy or angry? What are sensitive issues? In primary groups you share values, say what you think, let down your hair, dress as you like, and share your concerns and emotions, as well as your successes and failures (Goffman [1959] 2001, 1967). Charles H. Cooley, who first discussed the term *primary group*, saw these relationships as the source of close human feelings and emotions—love, cooperation, and concern (Cooley ([1909] 1983).

Secondary groups are *those with formal, impersonal, and businesslike relationships, often temporary, and based on a specific limited purpose or goal.* In the modern world, people cannot always live under the protective wing of primary group relationships. Secondary groups are usually large and task oriented because they have a specific purpose to achieve and focus on accomplishing a goal. As children grow, they move from the security and acceptance of primary groups—the home and neighborhood peer group—to the large school classroom, where each child is one of many students vying for the teacher's approval and competing for rewards. Similarly, the job world requires formal relations and procedures: applications, interviews, contracts, and so on. Employment is based on specific skills, training, and job knowledge, and there may be a trial period. In Western cultures, we assume that people should be hired not because of personal friendship or nepotism but rather for their competence to carry out the role expectations in the position.

Because each individual in secondary groups carries out a specialized task, communication between members is often specialized as well. Contacts with doctors, store clerks, and even professors are generally formal and impersonal parts of organizational life. Sometimes associations with secondary groups are long lasting, and sometimes they are of short duration—as in the courses you are taking this term.

These teens—a primary group of friends—enjoy one another's company during a cookout at the beach. Their interpersonal connections are valued for intrinsic reasons.

Secondary groups operate at the meso and macro levels of our social world, but they affect individuals at the micro level.

As societies modernize, they evolve from small towns and close, primary relationships to predominantly urban areas with more formal, secondary relationships. In the postindustrial world, as family members are scattered across countries and around the world, secondary relationships have come to play ever greater roles in people's lives. Large work organizations may provide day care, health clinics, financial planning, courses to upgrade skills, and sports leagues.

The small micro- and large macro-level groups often occur together. Behind most successful secondary groups are primary groups. These relationships help individuals feel a part of larger organizations, just as residents of large urban areas have small groups of neighborhood friends.

Megachurches began in the 1950s. They have more than 10,000 members, with the largest church in the world (Yoido Full Gospel Church in South Korea) having between 850,000 and 1 million members. About half of all megachurches are nondenominational Protestant, and the rest are related to evangelical or Pentecostal groups. The focus of programming is on creating small support groups (primary groups) within the huge congregation (PBS 2012; Thumma and Travis 2007).

Table 5.2 on page 128 summarizes some of the dimensions of primary and secondary groups.

Problems in primary groups can affect performance in secondary groups. Consider the problems of a student who has an argument with a significant other or roommate or experiences a failure of his or her family support system due to divorce or other problems. Self-concepts and social skills diminish during times of family stress and affect group relationships in other parts of one's life.

Table 5.2   Primary and Secondary Group Characteristics

	Primary Group	*Secondary Group*
Quality of relationships	Personal orientation	Goal orientation
Duration of relationships	Usually long-term	Variable, often short-term
Breadth of activities	Broad, usually involving many activities	Narrow, usually involving few largely goal-directed activities
Subjective perception of relationships	As an end in itself (friendship, belonging)	As a means to an end (to accomplish a task, earn money)
Typical examples	Families, close friendships	Coworkers, political organizations

Reference groups are *composed of members who act as role models and establish standards against which members measure their conduct.* Individuals look to reference groups to set guidelines for behavior and decision making. The term is often used to refer to models in one's chosen career field. Students in premed, nursing, computer science, business, or sociology programs watch the behavior patterns of those who have become successful professionals in their chosen career. When people make the transition from student to professional, they adopt clothing, time schedules, salary expectations, and other characteristics from reference groups. Professional organizations such as the American Bar Association or American Sociological Association set standards for behavior and achievements.

However, it is possible to be an attorney or an athlete and not aspire to be like others in the group if they are unethical or abuse substances such as steroids. Instead, a person might be shaped by the values of a church group or a political group with which he or she identifies. Not every group one belongs to is a reference group. It must provide a standard by which one evaluates his or her behavior for it to be a reference group. For example, ethnic groups provide some adolescents with strong reference group standards by which to judge themselves. The stronger the ethnic pride and identification, the more some teens may separate themselves from contact with members of other ethnic groups (Schaefer and Kunz 2008). This can be functional or dysfunctional for the teens, as shown in the next section on in-groups and out-groups.

An **in-group** is *one to which an individual feels a sense of loyalty and belonging.* It also may serve as a reference group, since any group may fit into more than one category of groups. An **out-group** is *one to which an individual does not belong, but more than that, it is a group that is often in competition or in opposition to an in-group.*

Membership in an in-group may be based on sex, race, ethnic group, social class, religion, political affiliation, the school one attends, an interest group such as the fraternity or sorority one joins, or the area where one lives. People tend to judge others according to their own in-group identity. Members of the in-group—for example, supporters of a

Bloods gang members in Los Angeles use their in-group hand signal to identify one another.

high school team—often feel hostility toward or reject out-group members, boosters of the rival team. The perceived outside threat or hostility is often exaggerated, but it does help create the in-group members' feelings of solidarity.

Unfortunately, these feelings can result in prejudice and ethnocentrism, overlooking the individual differences between in-group members. Teen groups or gangs such as the Bloods and the Crips are examples of in-groups and out-groups resulting in gang conflicts and killings.

Thinking Sociologically

What are some examples of your own group affiliations: Primary groups? Secondary groups? Peer groups? Reference groups? In-groups and out-groups?

Organizations and Bureaucracies: The Meso-Macro Connection

Our days are filled with activities that involve us with complex organizations: from the doctor's appointment to college classes; from the political rally for the issue we are supporting to Sabbath worship in our church, temple, or mosque; from paying state sales tax for our toothpaste to buying a sandwich at a fast-food franchise. Figure 5.4 shows institutions of society, each made up of thousands of organizations and each following the cultural norms of our society. We have statuses and roles in each group, and these link us to networks and the larger social world.

How did these organizational forms develop? Let us consider briefly the transformations of organizations into their modern forms and the characteristics of meso-level organizations today.

Modern Organizations and Their Evolution

Empires around the world have risen and fallen since the dawn of civilization. Some economic, political, and religious systems have flourished while others have withered. We cannot understand our social world at any historical or modern time without comprehending the organizational structures and processes present at that time. Recall the discussion of types of societies, from hunter-gatherer to postindustrial, in Chapter 3. Each type of society entails different organizational structures, from early cities and feudal manors to craft guilds, heavy industries, and today's information- and web-based companies (Blau 1956; Nolan and Lenski 2010).

The development of modern organizations began with industrialization in the 1700s and became the dominant form of organization by the 1800s. What Max Weber called **rationalization of social life**—*the attempt to maximize efficiency by creating rules and procedures focused solely on accomplishing goals*—was thought to be the best way to run organizations (Weber 1947). People were expected to behave in purposeful, coordinated ways that advanced the organization. No longer were decisions made by tradition, custom, or the whim of a despot. Instead, trained leaders planned policies, tasks became more specialized, and some manual jobs were taken over by machines.

Standardization of products allowed for greater productivity, precision, and speed. **Formal organizations** (also called modern rational organizations) are *comprised of complex secondary groups deliberately formed to pursue and achieve certain goals.* They are called "formal organizations" because of the written charters, constitutions, bylaws, and procedures that govern them. The Red Cross, Ford Motor Company, the National Basketball Association (NBA), the Republican Party, and your university are all formal organizations.

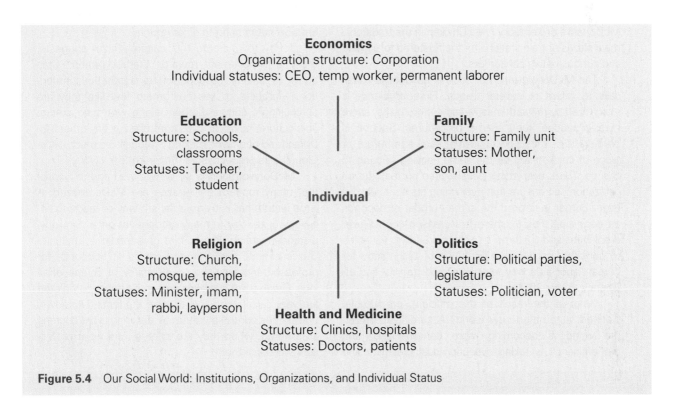

Figure 5.4 Our Social World: Institutions, Organizations, and Individual Status

Bureaucracies are *specific types of very large formal organizations that have the purpose of maximizing efficiency. They are characterized by formal relations between participants, clearly laid-out procedures and rules, and pursuit of stated goals.* Bureaucratization evolved as the most efficient way of producing products economically for mass markets (Ritzer 2013b).

An example of bureaucracies is found in the fast-food empires springing up around the world. The next "Sociology Around the World" describes the trend toward the "McDonaldization of Society"—Ritzer's pop culture term for rationalization in organizations.

Thinking Sociologically

Can anything be done to protect the locally owned mom-and-pop businesses, or are they destined to be eliminated by the "McCompetition"?

Sociology Around the World

The McDonaldization of Society

The process of rationalization described by Max Weber—the attempt to reach maximum bureaucratic efficiency—comes in a new modern version, expanded and streamlined, as exemplified by the fast-food restaurant business and the chain "box" stores found around the world. Efficient, rational, predictable sameness is sweeping the world—from diet centers such as Weight Watchers and Nutrisystem to 7-Eleven and Walmart to Gap clothing stores with their look-alike layouts. Most major world cities feature McDonald's or Kentucky Fried Chicken in the traditional main plazas or train stations for the flustered foreigners and curious native consumers.

The McDonaldization of society, as George Ritzer calls it, refers to several trends: First, *efficiency* is maximized by the sameness—same store plans, same mass-produced items, same procedures. Second is *predictability*, the knowledge that each hamburger or piece of chicken will be the same, leaving nothing to chance. Third, everything is *calculated* so that the organization can ensure that everything fits a standard—every burger is cooked the same number of seconds on each side. Fourth, there is *increased control* over employees and customers so there are fewer variables to consider—including substitution of technology for human labor as a way to ensure predictability and efficiency (Ritzer 2013b).

What is the result of this efficient, predictable, planned, automated new world? According to Ritzer, the world is becoming more dehumanized, and the efficiency is taking over individual creativity and human interactions. The mom-and-pop grocery, bed and breakfasts, and local craft or clothing shops are rapidly becoming a thing of the past, giving way to the McClones like In-N-Out Burger. This process of the McDonaldization of society, meaning principles of efficiency and rationalization exemplified by fast-food chains, is coming to dominate more and more sectors of our social world (Ritzer 2013b). While there are aspects of this predictability that we all like, there is also a loss of the uniqueness and local flavor that individual entrepreneurs bring to a community.

To try to re-create this culture, Ritzer suggests, there is a movement toward "Starbuckization." Starbucks is unique because of its aesthetic contribution. Starbucks makes customers feel like they are purchasing a cultural product along with their coffee. This culture, however, is as controlled as any other McDonaldized endeavor, making Starbucks as much a McClone as its predecessors (Ritzer 2013b).

McDonaldization is so widespread and influential that many modern universities are McDonaldized. A large lecture hall is a very efficient way of teaching sociology or biology to many students at once. Similarly, distance learning, PowerPoint presentations, multiple-choice exams, and a limited choice of textbooks for professors increase the predictability of course offerings. Grade point averages and credit hours completed are very calculated ways to view students. Moreover, universities control students by deciding what courses are offered, when they are offered, and what professors will teach them.

Modern Organizations and Modern Life

Organizations and modern life are almost synonymous. Live in one, and you belong to the other. Think about the many organizations that regularly affect your life: the legal system that passes laws, your college, your workplace, and voluntary organizations to which you belong. Human interactions take place in modern organizations, and modern organizations require human interaction to meet their organizational needs. Some organizations, such as the local chapter of the Rotary Club or a chapter of a sorority, are small enough to function at the micro level. Everyone is in a face-to-face relationship with every other member of the organization. However, those local chapters are part of a nationwide meso-level organization. At the macro level, the federal government is a complex modern organization that influences the lives of every citizen and every organization within it. Meanwhile, transnational corporations and entities such as the United Nations are global in their reach.

Some organizations provide us with work necessary for survival. Others are forced on us—prisons, mental hospitals, military draft systems, and even education up until a certain age. Still others are organizations we believe in and voluntarily join—scouts, environmental protest groups, sports leagues, and religious organizations (Etzioni 1975). Membership in voluntary organizations is higher in the United States than in many other countries (D. Johnson and Johnson 2006), yet in recent years, membership in many voluntary organizations has dropped.

The hospital setting is an example of a modern organization that not only is governed by formal rules and impersonal relations but also increasingly involves extensive communication via computers.

Some analysts argue that new types of affiliations and interactions, including the Internet, are replacing some older organizational affiliations.

Thinking Sociologically

Make a list of your activities in a typical day. Which of these activities are, and which are not, associated with large (meso-level) modern organizations?

Still, it is the bureaucracy that is the most modern type of structure; it has enormous impact on our lives. So what are the characteristics of bureaucracy?

Characteristics of Bureaucracy

To get a driver's license, pay school fees, or buy tickets for a popular concert or game, you may have to stand in a long line or fill out a form online. Finally, after waiting in line or online, you may discover that you have forgotten your Social Security number or cannot pay with a credit card. The rules and red tape can be irksome. Yet what is the alternative? Some institutions have adopted telephone and online registration or ticket purchases, but even with this automated system, problems can occur.

If you have been to a Caribbean, African, Asian, or Middle Eastern market, you know that the bartering system is used to settle on a mutually agreeable price. This system is more personal and involves intense interaction between the seller and the buyer, but it also takes more time, is less efficient, and can be frustrating to the uninitiated visitor accustomed to the relative efficiency and predictability of bureaucracy. As societies transition, they tend to adopt bureaucratic forms of organization. Most organizations in modern society—hospitals, schools, churches, government agencies, industries, banks, and even large clubs—are bureaucracies. Therefore, understanding these modern organizations is critical to understanding the modern social world in which we live.

At the beginning of the 20th century, Max Weber (1864–1920) looked for reasons behind the massive changes taking place that were causing the transition from traditional society to bureaucratic, capitalistic society. He wanted to understand why the rate of change was more rapid in some parts of Europe than others and why bureaucracy came to dominate forms of organization in some countries. Whereas traditional society looked to the past for guidance, bureaucratic industrial society required a new form of thinking and behavior, a change in attitude toward rationality. Weber observed that leadership in business and government was moving from traditional forms

McDonaldization

with powerful families and charismatic leaders toward more efficient and less personal bureaucracy.

Weber's *concept of the ideal-type bureaucracy* refers to the dominant and essential characteristics of our modern organizations that are designed for reliability and efficiency (Weber 1947). The term describes an organization with a particular set of common traits, not a good or perfect organization. Any one bureaucracy is unlikely to have all of the characteristics in the ideal type, but the degree of bureaucratization is measured by how closely an organization resembles the core characteristics of the ideal type. The following characteristics of Weber's ideal-type bureaucracy provide an example of how these characteristics relate to schools:

1. *Division of labor based on technical competence:* Administrators lead but do not teach, and instructors teach only in areas of their certification; staff are assigned positions for which credentials make them most qualified, and recruitment and promotion are governed by formal policies.

2. *Administrative hierarchy:* There is a specified chain of command and designated channels of communication, from school board to superintendent to principal to teacher.

3. *Formal rules and regulations:* Written procedures and rules—perhaps published in an administrative manual—spell out system-wide requirements, including discipline practices, testing procedures, curricula, sick days for teachers, penalties for student tardiness, field trip policies, and other matters.

4. *Impersonal relationships:* Formal relationships tend to prevail between teachers and students and between teachers and administrative staff (superintendents, principals, counselors); written records and formal communication provide a paper trail for all decisions.

5. *Emphasis on rationality and efficiency to reach goals:* Established processes are used, based on the best interests of the school. Efficiency is defined in terms of lowest overall cost to the organization in reaching a goal, not in terms of personal consequences.

6. *Provision of lifelong careers:* Employees may spend their entire careers working for the same organization, working their way up the hierarchy through promotions.

Although the list of characteristics makes bureaucracies sound formal and rigid, informal structures allow organizational members to deviate from rules both to meet goals of the bureaucracy more efficiently and to humanize an otherwise uncaring and sterile workplace. A teacher may help a student outside the formal class structure and curriculum, even though it is not part of his or her contract to do so. The *informal structure,* then, includes the unwritten norms and the interpersonal networks that people use within an organization to carry out roles. Likewise, although bylaws, constitutions, or contracts spell out the way things are supposed to be done, people often develop unwritten shortcuts to accomplish goals.

Informal norms are not always compatible with those of the formal organization. Consider the following example from a famous classical study. In the Western Electric plant near Chicago, the study found that new workers were quickly socialized to do "a fair day's work," and those who did more or less than the established norm—what the work group thought was fair—were considered "rate busters" or "chiselers" and experienced pressure from the group to conform. These informal mechanisms gave informal groups of workers a degree of power in the organization (Roethlisberger and Dickson 1939).

Thinking Sociologically

How closely does each of Weber's characteristics of ideal-type bureaucracy describe your college or your work setting? Is your college highly bureaucratized, with many rules and regulations? Are decisions based on efficiency and cost-effectiveness, educational quality, or both? To what extent is your work setting characterized by hierarchy and formal rules governing your work time? To what extent by informal relationships?

Issues in Bureaucracies

Bureaucratic inefficiency and red tape are legendary. Yet, bureaucracies are likely to stay, for they are the most efficient form of modern organization yet devised. Nonetheless, several individual and organizational problems created by bureaucratic structures are important to understand. These can be due to our roles in organizations or our interactions with organizations. Some examples follow.

Professionals in Bureaucracies

Doctors, lawyers, engineers, and professors are considered to be *professionals* because they have particular attributes: high status, knowledge-based occupations that are characterized by specialized knowledge, authority and autonomy on the job, and self-regulation. This generally involves advanced and specialized education, strong commitment to their field, a service orientation and commitment to the needs of the client, and a sense of intrinsic satisfaction from the work (rather than motivation rooted mainly in external rewards, such as salary).

By claiming authority and control in their work, professionals may face conflicting loyalties to their profession and to the bureaucratic organization in which they are

Bureaucracies

employed (Tolbert and Hall 2009). A scientist hired by a tobacco company faced a dilemma when his research findings did not support the company position that nicotine is not addictive. His superiors wanted him to falsify his research, which would be a violation of professional ethics. Should he publicly challenge the organization? Several professional whistle-blowers have done so but lost their jobs as a result. Bureaucracy, some argue, can be the number-one enemy of professionalism because the goals may be in conflict.

The potential clash between professionals and bureaucracy raises key concerns as universities, hospitals, and other large organizations are governed increasingly by bureaucratic principles (Roberts and Donahue 2000). Alienation among professionals occurs when they are highly regulated rather than when they have some decision-making authority and are granted some autonomy (Tolbert and Hall 2009). For example, high-tech companies find that hierarchical structures undermine productivity, whereas factors such as intrinsic satisfaction, flexible hours, and relaxed work environments are central to creative productivity (Florida 2002, 2012b; Friedman 2005).

Diversity and Equity in Organizations

Women and other minorities in bureaucracies often face barriers that keep them from reaching high levels of management. The result is that individuals from these groups are found disproportionately in midlevel positions with little authority and less pay than others with similar skills and credentials (Arulampalam, Booth, and Bryan 2007). When employees have little chance for promotion, they have less ambition and loyalty to the organization (Kanter 1977). This hurts the organization. For example, research indicates that women executives bring valuable alternative perspectives to organizational leadership. They share information readily, give employees greater autonomy, and stress interconnectedness between parts of the organization, resulting in a more democratic type of leadership style (Kramer 2010). The more women in an organization's senior positions, the more likely newcomers are to find support.

The interaction of people who see things differently because of religious beliefs, ethnic backgrounds, and gender experiences increases productivity in many organizations. Having a wide range of perspectives can lead to better problem solving, increased productivity, and reduction in the barriers to promotion that are dysfunctional for organizations (Florida 2004, 2012a). Thus, anything that reduces diversity—such as barriers to promotion based in discrimination—is harmful to the organization and to the society.

Organizational Dysfunctions

Although bureaucracies are far more efficient and functional than many other ways of organizing large groups of people,

Women in many countries have low-paid, dead-end jobs that make them feel uninvolved and unconnected. Such jobs result in alienation, but these women need the work and have little choice but to accept them.

they can also be frustrating and unproductive. Three of the more common problems are alienation, the tendency to oligarchy, and goal displacement.

Alienation, *feeling uninvolved, uncommitted, unappreciated, and unconnected to the group or the society*, occurs when workers experience routine, boring tasks or dead-end jobs with no possibility of advancement. Marx believed that alienation is a structural feature of capitalism with serious consequences: Workers lose their sense of purpose and seem to become dehumanized and objectified in their work, creating a product that they often do not see completed, that they feel no pride in, and for which they do not get the profits (Marx [1844] 1964). Dissatisfaction comes from low pay and poor benefits; routine, repetitive, and fragmented tasks; lack of challenge and autonomy, leading to boredom; and poor working conditions. Workers who see possibilities for advancement put more energy into the organization, but those stuck in their positions are less involved and put more energy into activities outside the workplace (Kanter 1977).

Thinking Sociologically

How might participation in decision making and increased autonomy for workers enhance commitment and productivity in your place of work or in your college? What might be some risks or downsides to such worker input and freedom?

Oligarchy, *the concentration of power in the hands of a small group*, is a common occurrence in organizations. In the early 1900s, Robert Michels, a French sociologist, wrote about the iron law of oligarchy, the idea that power becomes concentrated in the hands of a small group of self-perpetuating leaders in political, business, voluntary, or other organizations. Initially, organizational needs, more than the motivation for power, cause these few stable leaders to emerge. As organizations grow, a division of labor emerges so that only a few leaders have access to information, resources, and the overall picture. This, in turn, causes leaders who enjoy their elite positions of power to become entrenched (Michels [1911] 1967). Yet recent events in the Middle East and North Africa illustrate that concentrated authority is being challenged. Likewise, in the United States, Wall Street high rollers felt immune from interference in their insulated world, but the public demanded the reinstatement of some regulations to limit their power and make them accountable to someone for their actions.

Goal displacement *occurs when the original motives or goals of the organization are displaced by new secondary goals.* Organizations form to meet specific goals. Religious organizations are founded to worship a deity and serve humanity on behalf of that deity; schools are founded to educate children; and social work agencies are organized to serve the needs of citizens who seem to have fallen between the cracks. Yet, over time, original goals may be met or become less important as other motivations and interests emerge (Merton 1968b; Whyte 1956).

Thinking Sociologically

In what areas of your college or workplace do you see goal displacement? In other words, where do you see decisions being driven by goals other than the original purpose of the organization?

National and Global Networks: The Macro Level

Understanding people who are unlike us, networking with people who have different cultures, and making allowances for alternative ideas about society and human behavior have become core competencies in our globalizing social world. Increasingly, colleges have study-abroad programs, jobs open up for teaching English as a second language, and corporations seek employees who are multilingual and culturally competent in diverse settings. One young college graduate with a sociology degree found that she could use her sociology skills in leading groups of college-age students in international travel experiences. She explains this applied use of sociology in the next "Sociologists in Action."

With modern communication and transportation systems and the ability to transfer ideas and money with a touch of the keyboard, global networks are superseding national boundaries. Multinational corporations now employ citizens from around the world and can make their own rules because there is no legally recognized worldwide oversight body.

A wide range of products can be obtained through Internet orders from websites that have no geographical home base. In some cases, there are no actual warehouses or manufacturing plants, and there might not be a home office. Some businesses are global and exist in the Ethernet, not in any specific nation (Ritzer 2007). This reality makes one rethink national and global loyalties and boundaries.

Family loyalties are considered less important than the needs of the corporation. Feelings are subordinated while efficiency and calculability are highly prized in multinational corporations. However, as these Western notions of how public life should operate are exported to other countries, a severe backlash has occurred. In many Middle Eastern Islamic countries, for example, these values clash with Muslim loyalties and priorities. The result has been high levels of anger at the United States and Western Europe. Many scholars believe that Middle Eastern anger at the United States is based not on opposition to freedom and democracy, as our politicians sometimes say, but on what some Middle Easterners see as the crass greed and impersonal organizational structures we try to import into their micro-, meso-, and macro-level worlds. They feel that their very culture is threatened (Ritzer 2007).

Thinking Sociologically

How do you think global interaction will be transformed through Internet technology? How will individual connections at the micro level be affected by these transformations at the macro levels of our social world?

Policy Issues: Women and Globalization

Women in much of the world are viewed as second-class citizens, the most economically, politically, and socially marginalized people on the planet, caught in expectations of religion, patriarchy, and roles needed to sustain life (Schneider and Silverman 2006). They account for 70% of

Sociologists in Action— Elise Roberts

Using Sociology in International Travel and Intercultural Education

After graduating from college with a bachelor's degree in sociology, I left the country to backpack through Mexico and Central America. My studies helped me be more objective and aware as I experienced other societies. My international travel helped me examine my own societal assumptions and further understand how society creates so much of one's experience and view of the world. I found a job leading groups of teenagers on alternative education trips abroad. I was excited to get the job, but I was soon to learn that leading groups of teenagers in other countries is actually very hard work.

What struck me on meeting my first group was that I had very few students who initially understood this socio-logical perspective that I took for granted and that was so helpful in dealing with others. At times, my students would make fun of the way things were done in other countries, calling them "weird" or "stupid." They would mock the local traditions, until we discussed comparable traditions in American culture. These students were not mean or unintelligent. In fact, they loved the places we were seeing and the people we were meeting. They just thought everything was factually, officially weird. They had been socialized to understand their own society's ways as "right" and "normal." They were fully absorbed in the U.S. society, and they had never questioned it before.

It was rewarding to apply concepts from my textbooks to the real world. My coleaders and I learned to have fun while encouraging our students to become more socially conscious and analytical about their travel experience. We sent the groups out on scavenger hunts, and they would inevitably come back proudly announcing what they had paid for a rickshaw ride—only to learn that they had paid 10 times the local price. We would use this experience to talk about the role of foreigners, the assumptions that the local population made due to our skin color, and the culture of bartering. They had to learn to understand "odd" gestures, like pointing with the lips or side-to-side nodding. We would use these experiences to discuss nonverbal communication and gestures that each culture takes for granted.

We would encourage our novice travelers to interact with the people around them, which helped them understand the struggles facing immigrants and non-English speakers in countries such as the United States. We would force them to have conversations while standing toe-to-toe with each other, and they would finish with backaches from leaning away from one another. We would not allow them to explain their behavior with "because it's creepy to stand so close together," even though this was the consensus. "Why do you feel uncomfortable?" we would ask. "Why is this weird?" The answer has to do with social constructions of what is "normal" in any society.

Of course, while traveling internationally, one is surrounded by various other sociological issues, such as different racial or ethnic conflicts, gender roles, or class hierarchies, and learning about these issues was a part of our program as well. Without realizing it, many group conversations and meetings began to remind me of some of my favorite Macalester College classes. "Study sociology!" I would say, plugging my major to the most interested students.

I have always thought that travel is an incredibly useful means not only to learn about the society and culture one is visiting but also to learn much about oneself and one's home society. For teenagers who otherwise might never step back to think about the role of being a foreigner or the traditions and social patterns they take for granted, it is even more important. Traveling abroad on my own and leading programs abroad were such extremely rich and rewarding experiences not only due to the cross-cultural exchanges and the intense personal examination that I saw in my students but also because it was fascinating and rewarding to be able to use my sociology degree every day on my job.

* * * * * * *

Note: Elise Roberts graduated from Macalester College with a major in sociology. Her postcollege travels took her through Central America, the South Pacific, and many parts of Asia. She competed a master's degree from Columbia University in international social work and is now a regional coordinator for Witness for Peace.

Around the world, two-thirds of the poorest adults are women, even though women produce more than two thirds of food supplies in the world. A Laotian woman works in the field (top) and an Indian woman transports goods to market (bottom).

Because women are often more vulnerable and have historically been exploited, global organizations like UN Women and microfinance groups like the Grameen Bank and FINCA have provided loans and other supports for women to begin their own business enterprises. When women are assisted, it usually has a marked improvement on the circumstances of children.

the world's population living in absolute poverty (Global Fund for Women 2012). To help their children survive, women do whatever their situation allows to make money: street-selling, low-paying factory assembly line work, piece-work (e.g., sewing clothing in their homes), prostitution and sex work, and domestic service.

Women produce 80% to 90% of the food crops in sub-Saharan Africa, and almost 50% in the world (Diouf 2010–2011). They run households and are often the main support for children in poor countries. Yet, due to the "feminization of poverty," two out of three poor adults are women (Enloe 2006). Causes of the many problems facing women are found at each level of analysis and will be discussed throughout this book.

One macro-level organization with policies to help raise the status of women through development is the United Nations. Each decade since the 1960s, this global organization has set forth plans to improve conditions for women. Early plans made by some international organizations to help poor countries were driven by interests of capitalist countries in the first world. This left women out of the equation and planning. Women suffered greatly under

some of these plans because their positions and responsibilities did not change. Conditions got worse as development money went to large corporations with the idea that profits would trickle down to the local level, an idea that did not materialize in most countries. Today organizations concerned with women's status advocate more ownership or control of land and a larger role in agriculture, estimating that this could boost food production by 20% to 30% (Boulding and Dye 2002; Global Fund for Women 2012).

The United Nations sponsors conferences on the status of women. In July 2010, the organization launched a new division, United Nations Women, headed by former Chilean president Michelle Bachelet. UN Women initiates policies to help educate local women in health, nutrition, basic first aid, and business methods.

A world development report by the World Bank outlines four priorities for improving the conditions for women: "reducing excess female mortality and closing education gaps, improving access to economic opportunities for women, increasing women's voice and agency in the household and society, and limiting the reproduction of

Bank Mergers

gender inequality across generations" (World Development Report 2011:286). Many projects have been spawned, including micro-lending organizations (Grameen Bank, SEWA, FINCA, CARE), allowing individuals and groups of women to borrow money to start cooperatives and other small-business ventures. These initiatives can have very beneficial effects if they are used wisely by policy makers who care about the people involved. In the next few chapters, we will learn about factors that cause some individuals and countries to be poorer than others.

Our networks play a major role in setting our norms and controlling our behaviors, usually resulting in our conformity to the social expectations of those in our networks. This, of course, contributes to stability of the entire social system because deviation can threaten the existence of "normal" patterns, as we see in the next chapter.

What Have We Learned?

Each of us has a network of people and groups that surround us. The scope of our networks has broadened with increased complexity and includes the global social world. Indeed, it is easy not to recognize how extensively our networks reach. Although some of our social experiences are informal (unstructured), we are also profoundly affected by another phenomenon of the past three centuries—highly structured bureaucracies. As a result of both, our intimate experiences of our personal lives are far more extensively linked to meso- and macro-level events and to people and places on the other side of the globe than was true for our parents' generation. If we hope to understand our lives, we must understand this broad context. Although it may have been possible to live without global connections and bureaucratic systems several centuries ago, these networks are intricately woven into our lifestyles and our economic systems today. The question is whether we control these networks or they control us.

Key Points:

- People in the modern world are connected through one acquaintance to another in a chain of links, referred to as networks. (See pp. 114–115.)

- Increasingly our electronic technology is creating networks that span the globe, but this same impersonal technology is used to enhance friendship networks and to meet a romantic life partner. (See pp. 115–117.)

- Interpersonal interactions at the micro level are affected by unspoken assumptions that are understood due to the social context, by nonverbal communication, and by the physical space between people. (See pp. 118–119.)

- Many of our behaviors are shaped by the statuses (social positions) we hold and the roles (expectations associated with a status) we play. However, our multiple status occupancy can create role conflicts (between the roles of two statuses) and role strains (between the role expectations of a single status). (See pp. 123–125.)

- When the norms of behavior are unclear, we may experience anomie (normlessness), and this ambiguity compromises our sense of belonging and is linked to reasons for individuals performing one of the most personal of acts—suicide. (See pp. 125–126.)

- Various types of groups affect our behavior—from primary and secondary groups to peer groups and reference groups. (See pp. 126–129.)

- At the meso level, we find that formal organizations in the contemporary modern world are ruled by rational calculation of the organization's goals rather than by tradition or emotional ties. These modern formal organizations expand, are governed by impersonal formal rules, and stress efficiency and rational decision making. They have come to be called bureaucracies. (See pp. 129–130.)

- Bureaucracies often involve certain issues that may make them inefficient or destructive. (See pp. 131–133.)

- While bureaucratization emerged at the meso level as the defining element of the modern world, it is also found at the national and global levels where people do not know each other on a face-to-face basis. (See p. 133.)

- Some scholars think that this impersonal mode of organizing social life—so common in the West for several centuries now—is a critical factor in anti-American and anti-Western resistance movements. (See p. 134.)

Discussion Questions

1. Think about your social network. How useful might it be in helping you get a job (or a better job) once you graduate from college? Why?

2. During a typical day, when, respectively, do you engage in front- and back-stage behavior? Why? With whom do you engage in each? Why?

3. Have you ever experienced role strain because of your status as a student? Explain why or why not. If so, how did/do you cope with it?

4. Most college students, particularly those with family, work, and/or sports team obligations, deal with role conflict. Describe a time when you dealt with a conflict between roles you carry out and what you did about it. How might colleges and universities diminish role conflict among students?

5. To what primary and secondary groups do you belong? How does your involvement (or lack thereof) in primary groups on your campus impact your feelings of attachment to your school?

6. Would you rather live in a bureaucratic society or in a society without bureaucratic forms of organizations? Why? How does the informal structure at your college or university impact how the school functions? Does it do more to help or hurt students? Why?

Contributing to Our Social World: What Can We Do?

At the Local Level

• *Tutoring and mentoring* programs help students struggling with their studies. Contact your local student affairs or tutoring office and arrange to observe and/or volunteer in a program. Helping students build *social capital*, which includes their knowledge of ways to obtain the help they need, can increase their chances of success.

• Workers' centers for *low*-wage workers not represented by unions have developed in many metropolitan areas, often with the aid of local clergy. Workers' centers help these workers, many of whom are not being protected by current labor laws, organize and develop the social capital to obtain better wages, benefits, and workplace dignity. For a list of workers' centers, go to www.iwj.org/worker-center-network/locations.

At the Organizational or Institutional Level

• The social capital theory can also be applied to meso-level community organizations: *Community organizations* that work to build power and implement social change, such as the *IAF* (*Industrial Areas Foundation* at www.industrialareasfoundation.org), *Gamaliel* (www.gamaliel.org), and *PICO National Network* (www.piconetwork.org), provide their members with social capital. Find an organization affiliated with one of these organizations near you.

• *Unions* also develop social capital for their members. Although far fewer Americans are unionized today than in past decades, membership in a union can make a significant improvement in the economic prospects of workers. For some workers, this can make the difference between living in poverty and obtaining a living wage. At 2.1 million members, the Service Employees International Union (SEIU) is the fastest growing union in North America. Internships with unions like SEIU are a great way to learn about organizing social capital.

• *The Anti-Defamation League* (www.adl.org), *the American-Arab Anti-Discrimination Committee* (www.adc.org), and the *National Association for the Advancement of Colored People* (www.naacp.org) are examples of organizations that defend the rights of minority groups. These organizations often use volunteers or interns and can provide you with the opportunity to learn about the extent to which social contacts and networks play a role in managing social conflict.

At the National or Global Level

• Well-run *microfinance organizations* can help poor people, particularly women, gain social capital and economic independence. Three well-known and respected groups are *CRS* (Catholic Relief Services at http://crs.org/microfinance), *FINCA* (www.finca.org), and *Kiva* (www.kiva.org). Check out their websites to learn how you can support their efforts.

Visit **www.sagepub.com/oswcondensed3e** for online activities, sample tests, and other helpful information. Select "Chapter 5: Interaction, Groups, and Organizations" for chapter-specific activities.

CHAPTER 6

Deviance and Social Control

Sickos, Weirdos, Freaks, and Folks Like Us

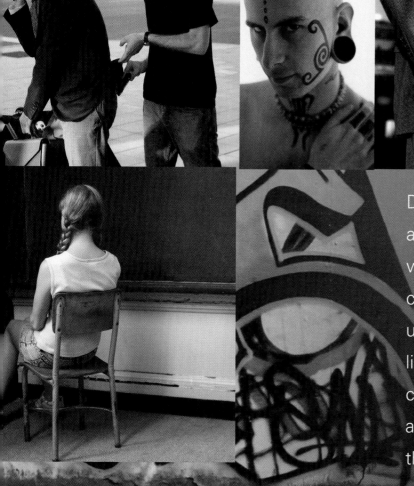

Deviants are often thought of as perverts and rule breakers without consciences. We often contrast them to people like us, but the reality is that the line between deviants and conformists is frequently vague, and we may be surprised to learn that often "deviants are us."

Global Community

Society

National Organizations, Institutions, and Ethnic Subcultures

Local Organizations and Community

Me (and My Deviant Friends)

Micro: Violations of local ordinances: theft, burglary, local corruption

Meso: Violations of state laws; crimes within and by corporations

Macro: Federal crimes (treason, tax fraud); state crimes (domestic terrorism); Internet fraud

Macro: Global environmental destruction; international terrorism; human rights violations

Think About It	
Micro: Me (and My Deviant Friends)	Are you deviant? Who says so?
Micro: Local Community	Why do some people in your community become deviant?
Meso: National Institutions; Complex Organizations; Ethnic Groups	What are the consequences of organized crime or occupational crime in large bureaucratic organizations?
Macro: National Society	What are the costs—and the benefits—of deviance for the nation?
Macro: Global Community	How can a global perspective on crime enhance our understanding of international criminal activities?

What's coming in this chapter?

What Is Deviance?

What Causes Deviant Behavior? Theoretical Perspectives

Crime and Individuals: Micro-Level Analysis

Crime and Organizations: Meso-Level Analysis

National and Global Crime: Macro-Level Analysis

Controlling Crime: Social Policy Considerations

Wafa Idris grew up as other girls do, but she was destined to make world headlines on January 27, 2002—as the first female suicide bomber in the Palestinian-Israeli conflict. She was the age of most university students reading this book, but she never had an opportunity to attend college. The story sounds simple: She was to take explosives across the Israeli border for the intended bomber, her brother. Instead, she blew up herself and an Israeli soldier. She was declared a martyr, a *sahida*, by the al-Aqsa Martyrs Brigade, which took credit for the attack. Her act was given approval by the group's political leadership, opening the way for other women to follow. Why did this happen? What motivated her to commit suicide and take another life in the process? Was she driven by ideology to participate in the Palestinian-Israeli struggle? Were there social and structural factors that affected her decision? Most important, was she criminally deviant in carrying out this act, and according to whom?

Wafa grew up in Palestine. She was married at a young age but did not produce children. As a result, her husband divorced her and remarried. She had no future and little role to play without children, for who would want a barren, divorced woman in a society that values women for their purity and their childbearing ability? She was a burden to her family. Her way out of an impossible and desperate situation was to commit suicide, bringing honor and wealth to her family and redeeming herself in the process.

Other women who followed Wafa have similar stories: Most shared an inability to control their own lives in the patriarchal (male-controlled) society (Handwerk 2004; Victor 2003). Terrorist cells in Palestine saw this as an opportunity to recruit other vulnerable women with nothing to lose, and this was one more way that women came to be exploited (Victor 2003).

Our question is this: Are these women deviant criminal terrorists, mentally ill "crazies," invisible victims in a patriarchal society, or martyrs who should be honored for their acts? Who says so? Each of these views is held by commentators on the situation. From this opening example, we can begin to see several complexities that arise when considering deviance, and some of these ideas may encourage new ways of looking at what and who is deviant. In this chapter, we will consider who is deviant, under what circumstances, and in whose eyes. We will find that most people around the world conform to social norms of their societies most of the time, and we will explore why some turn to deviance.

In this chapter, we discuss **deviance**—*the violation of social norms*—and the social control mechanisms that keep most people from becoming deviant. We also explore **crime**, *deviant actions for which there are severe formal penalties imposed by the government*, penalties like fines, jail, and prison sentences. The content of this chapter may challenge some of your deeply held assumptions about human behavior and defy some conceptions about deviance. In fact, it may convince you that we are all deviant at some times and in some places. The self-test in the next "Engaging Sociology" illustrates this point. Try taking it to see whether you have committed a deviant act.

What Is Deviance?

Deviance refers to violation of the society's norms, which then evokes negative reactions from others. The definition is somewhat imprecise because of constantly changing ideas and laws about what acts are considered deviant. Some

Deviance

Engaging Sociology

Who Is Deviant?

Please jot down your answers to the following self-test questions. There is no need to share your responses with others.

Have you ever engaged in any of the following acts?

☐ 1. Stolen anything, even if its value was less than $10

☐ 2. Used an illegal drug

☐ 3. Misused a prescription drug

☐ 4. Run away from home prior to age 18

☐ 5. Used tobacco prior to age 18

☐ 6. Drunk alcohol prior to age 21

☐ 7. Engaged in a fistfight

☐ 8. Carried a knife or gun

☐ 9. Used a car without the owner's permission

☐ 10. Driven a car after drinking alcohol

☐ 11. Forced another person to have sexual relations against his or her will

☐ 12. Offered sex for money

☐ 13. Damaged property worth more than $10

☐ 14. Been truant from school

☐ 15. Arrived home after your curfew

☐ 16. Been disrespectful to someone in authority

☐ 17. Accepted or transported property that you had reason to believe might be stolen

☐ 18. Taken a towel from a hotel room after renting the room for a night

All of the above are delinquent acts (violations of legal standards), and most young people are guilty of at least one infraction. However, few teenagers are given the label of *delinquent*. If you answered yes to any of the preceding questions, you have committed a crime in many states. Your penalty or sanction for the infraction would range from a stiff fine to several years in prison—*if* you got caught!

Engaging With Sociology

1. Do you think of yourself as being deviant? Why or why not?

2. Are deviants only those who get caught? For instance, if someone steals your car but avoids being caught, is he or she deviant?

3. Who is considered deviant—and by whom?

acts are deviant in most societies most of the time: murder, assault, robbery, and rape. Deviant acts may be overlooked or even viewed as understandable by some, as in the case of looting by citizens following Hurricane Katrina along the Gulf Coast in August 2005. Killing innocent people, looting, and burning houses during a civil or tribal war, like the one that has been occurring in Syria since 2011, may also seem reasonable to those committing the atrocities. Harmful behavior can often be rationalized.

Other acts of deviance are considered serious offenses in one society but tolerated in another. Examples include prostitution, premarital or extramarital sex, gambling, corruption, and bribery. Even within a single society, different groups may define deviance and conformity quite differently.

Hurricane Katrina

The state legislature may officially define alcohol consumption by 19-year-olds as deviant, but on a Saturday night at the fraternity party, the 19-year-old "brother" who does *not* drink may be viewed as deviant by his peers. What do these cases tell us about what deviance is?

Deviance is socially constructed. This means that members of groups in societies define what is deviant. Consider the phenomenon of today's young people getting tattoos, studs, and rings anywhere on the body they can place them. Is this deviant? It depends on who is judging. Are tattoos, studs, and rings symbols of independence and rebellion, a "cool" and unique look that is a way to tell one's personal story? What if many people begin to adopt the behavior? Is it still a sign of independence, or does it become conformity to a group? When The Beatles started the long-hair rage in the 1960s, this was deviant behavior to many. Today, we pay no special attention to men with long hair.

Some acts are deviant at one time and place and not at others. Stem cell research was viewed as unacceptable and a violation of U.S. law because of ethical concerns about using or destroying human cells. However, that policy changed with the change of president and administration. In many other countries, there are no moral restrictions on stem cell research, and scientists are proceeding with research in this field.

Definitions of deviance vary depending on the social situation or context in which the behavior occurs (Clinard and Meier 2004; McCaghy et al. 2006). If we take the same behavior and place it in a different social context, perceptions of whether the behavior is deviant may well change. In Greece, Spain, and other Mediterranean countries, the clothing norms on beaches are very different from those in most of North America. Topless sunbathing by women is not at all uncommon, even on beaches designated as family beaches. The norms vary, however, even within a few feet of the beach. Women will sunbathe topless, lying only 10 feet from the boardwalk where concessionaires sell beverages, snacks, and tourist items. If these women become thirsty, they cover up, walk the 15 feet to purchase a cola, and return to their beach blankets, where they again remove their tops. To walk onto the boardwalk topless would be highly deviant.

An individual's status or group may be defined as deviant. Some individuals have a higher likelihood of being labeled deviant because of the group into which they were born, such as a particular ethnic group, or because of a distinguishing mark or characteristic, such as a deformity. Others may escape being considered deviant because of their dominant status in society. The higher one's status, the less likely one is to be suspected of violating norms and characterized as "criminal."

Are any of these people deviant? Why or why not?

Death as Deviance

Even the looting that happened following Hurricane Katrina was addressed differently when it was done by whites rather than African Americans (Huddy and Feldman 2006; Thompson 2009). (An image of a "looter" in New Orleans appears in the center photo on page 144.) The media showed photos of black "looters" who "stole food," but the same media described whites who "broke into grocery stores" in search of food as "resourceful." Likewise, gays and lesbians are often said to be deviant and accused of flaunting their sexuality. Heterosexuals are rarely accused of "flaunting" their sexuality, regardless of how overtly flirtatious or underdressed they are. So one's group membership or ascribed traits may make a difference in whether or not one is defined as deviant.

Deviance represents a breakdown in norms. However, according to structural-functional theory, it can be functional as well as problematic for society. Deviance serves vital functions by setting examples of what is considered unacceptable behavior, providing guidelines for behavior that is necessary to maintain the social order, and bonding people together through their common rejection of the deviant behavior. Deviance is also functional because it provides jobs for those who deal with deviants—police, judges, social workers, and so forth (Gans 2007). Furthermore, deviance can signal problems in society that need to be addressed and can therefore stimulate positive change. Sometimes, deviant individuals break the model of conventional thinking, thereby opening the society to new and creative paths of thinking. Scientists, inventors, activists, and artists have often been rejected in their time but have been honored later for accomplishments that positively affected society. Famous artist Vincent van Gogh, for example, lived in poverty and mental turmoil during his life because many people did not recognize his genius, but he became recognized as a renowned painter after his death, with his paintings selling for millions of dollars. Likewise, Martin Luther King Jr. and Mahatma Gandhi were once considered deviant and dangerous, but are now considered social justice heroes.

Our tasks in this chapter are to understand what deviance is, what causes it, and where it fits in the social world. We look at theoretical perspectives that help explain deviance, how some deviant acts become crimes, and what policies might be effective in controlling or reducing crime.

Some sociologists point out that crime can be "functional" because it creates jobs for people like those above, and it unifies the society against the nonconformists.

Thinking Sociologically

Think of examples in your life that illustrate the relative nature of deviance. For instance, are some of your behaviors deviant in one setting but not in another, or were they deviant when you were younger but not deviant now?

Crime: Deviance That Violates the Law

Laws reflect opinions of what is considered right or wrong at a particular time and place in a society. Like all other norms, laws change over time, reflecting changing public opinion based on social conditions or specific events. Still, there are formal sanctions—punishments—that the government imposes for violation of laws, and the social disapproval associated with these deviant acts results in being identified as "criminal."

 Workplace Deviance

In the United States up until 1967, this couple would have been violating the law in roughly half of the states, and their families would have been "illegitimate." Interracial marriages were illegal until the Supreme Court decided otherwise. Change in definitions of what is illegal has been common in the past 50 years.

How did this happen? Was Helena born with a biological propensity toward deviance? Does she have psychological problems? Is the problem in her social environment? Helena's situation is, of course, only one unique case. Sociologists cannot generalize from Helena to other cases, but they do know from their studies that there are thousands of teens with problems like Helena's.

Throughout history, people have proposed explanations for why some members of society "turn bad"—from biological explanations of imbalances in hormones and claims of innate personality defects to social conditions within individual families or in the larger social structure. Biological and psychological approaches focus on personality disorders or abnormalities in the body or psyche of individuals, but they generally do not consider the social context in which deviance occurs.

Sociologists examine why certain acts are defined as deviant, why some people engage in deviant behavior, and how other people in the society react to deviance. Sociologists place emphasis on understanding the interactions, social structure, and social processes that lead to deviant behavior, rather than on individual characteristics. They consider the socialization process and interpersonal relationships, group and social class differences, cultural and subcultural norms, and power structures that influence individuals to conform to or deviate from societal expectations (Liska 1999). Theoretical explanations about why people are deviant influence social policy decisions about what to do with deviants.

This section explores several approaches to understanding deviance. Some theories explain particular types of crime better than others (say, theft as opposed to sexual assault). Some illuminate micro-, meso-, or macro-level processes better than others. Taken together, these theories help us understand a wide range of deviant and criminal behaviors.

At the end of the 1920s, 42 of the 48 U.S. states had laws forbidding interracial marriage (Coontz 2005). Legislatures in half of these states removed those restrictions by the 1960s, but 16 states still had antimiscegenation laws on the books before the 1967 U.S. Supreme Court *Loving v. Virginia* ruling that made these laws unconstitutional. Today, this legal bar on interracial marriage has been eliminated completely, illustrating that most laws change to reflect the times and sentiments of the majority of people.

What Causes Deviant Behavior? Theoretical Perspectives

Helena is a delinquent. Her father deserted the family when Helena was 10, and before that, he had abused Helena and her mother. Her mother has all she can cope with just trying to survive financially and keep her three children in line. Helena gets little attention and little support or encouragement in her school activities. Her grades have fallen steadily. As a young teen, she sought attention from boys, and in the process, she became pregnant. Now, the only kids who have anything to do with her are others who have been in trouble and labeled delinquent. Helena's schoolmates, teachers, and mother see her as a delinquent troublemaker, and it would be hard for Helena to change their views and her status.

Micro-Level Explanations of Deviance: Rational Choice and Interactionist Perspectives

No one is born deviant. Individuals learn to be law-abiding citizens or to be deviant through the process of socialization and as they develop their social relationships. *Social control theory* contends that most people are law-abiding citizens because the desire to fit into the group encourages conformity with the norms. Then why do some people become deviant and others follow the norms of society? *Rational choice* and *symbolic interaction* theories focus primarily on micro-level answers to this question.

Rational Choice Approaches to Deviance

The basic idea behind rational choice theory, as noted in previous chapters, is that when individuals make decisions,

Nonconformity

Rational choice theories hold that people weigh the possible negative consequences against the benefits, and if the benefits outweigh the costs, then violating official rules or expectations may be worth it. This would suggest that the cost must be increased to deter deviance. This little boy is weighing the costs and benefits of taking cookies from the cookie jar on the counter, and the benefits are looking pretty sweet!

they calculate the costs and benefits to themselves. They consider the balance between pleasure and pain. Those who use rational choice theory focus on the cost-benefit analysis of one's choices about deviance or conformity. Social control to prevent deviance comes from shifting the balance toward more pain and fewer benefits for those who deviate from norms—jail time, fines, community service, embarrassment, a public record of deviance. However, some members of society find crime to be to their advantage within their situations and opportunities, the product of a conscious, rational, calculated decision made after weighing the costs and benefits of alternatives. Often they choose lives of crime after failure in school or work or after seeing others succeed in crime.

Rational choice theorists believe punishment—imposing high "costs" for criminal behavior, such as fines, imprisonment, or even the death penalty—is the way to dissuade criminals from choosing crime. When the cost outweighs the potential benefit and opportunities are restricted, it deters people from thinking crime is a "rational" choice (Earls and Reiss 1994; Winslow and Zhang 2008). Even just changing the perception of the cost-benefit balance can be important in lowering crime. Criminals make decisions based on the situational constraints and opportunities in their lives (Schmalleger 2012).

Social Control Theory. One of sociology's central concepts is social control—why people obey norms (Gibbs 1989; Hagan 2011). A specific rational choice application, control theory focuses on why most people conform most of the time and do not commit deviant acts. If human beings were truly free to do whatever they wanted, they would likely commit more deviant acts. Yet, to live near others and with others requires individuals to control their behaviors based on social norms and sanctions—in short, social control.

A perpetual question in sociology is the following: How is social order possible in the context of rapidly changing society? A very general answer is that social control results from norms that promote order and predictability in the social world. When many people fail to adhere to these norms or when the norms are unclear, the stability and continuance of the entire social system may be threatened, as is happening in some countries of the world such as Somalia.

Control theory contends that people are bonded to others by four powerful factors:

1. *Attachment* to other people who respect the values and rules of the society. Individuals do not want to be rejected by those to whom they are close or whom they admire.

2. *Commitment* to conventional activities (e.g., school and jobs) that they do not want to jeopardize.

3. *Involvement* in activities that keep them so busy with conventional roles and expectations that they do not have time for mischief.

4. *Belief* in the social rules of their culture, which they accept because of childhood socialization and indoctrination into conventional beliefs.

Should these factors be weakened, there is an increased possibility that the person could commit deviant acts (Hirschi [1969] 2002). In short, these factors increase the benefit of conformist behavior and the cost of deviance, so control theory is often considered one type of rational choice explanation.

Two primary factors shape our tendency to conform. The first is internal controls, those voices within us that tell us when a behavior is acceptable or unacceptable, right or wrong. The second is external controls, society's formal or informal controls against deviant behavior. Informal external controls include smiles, frowns, hugs, and ridicule from close acquaintances (Gottfredson and Hirschi 1990). Formal external controls come from the legal system through police, judges, juries, and social workers. In both cases, the cost-benefit ratio shifts, making either conformity or deviance a rational choice.

Thinking Sociologically

Think of a time when you committed a deviant act or avoided doing so despite a tempting opportunity. What factors influenced whether you conformed to societal norms or committed a deviant act?

Symbolic Interaction
Approaches to Deviance

How a group influences an individual's social construction of reality is the focus of another approach, based in symbolic interaction theory. The core issue is how people define reality and how they are influenced by the society in constructing who they are and what is acceptable behavior in society. One approach, differential association, emphasizes that people learn to commit delinquent acts through their social relationships with peers and family members. Another, labeling theory, stresses that if they adopt a deviant lifestyle that is stigmatized by others, including law enforcement, they come to be *labeled* deviant after committing a deviant act. Because symbolic interaction theorists stress variables other than pure self-interest—like getting rich quick—they are less inclined to think that increasing the penalties or changing the costs will change behavior and reduce deviance. The first symbolic interaction approach, differential association, focuses on how individuals learn deviant behavior.

Differential Association Theory. If someone offered you some heroin, what would determine whether you took it? First, would you define sticking a needle in your arm and injecting heroin as a good way to spend your afternoon? Second, do you typically hang around with others who engage in this type of behavior and define it as "the thing to do"? Third, would you know the routine—how to cook the heroin to extract the liquid—if you had never seen it done? You likely would not know the proper technique for how to prepare the drug or how to inject it. Why? Being a drug user depends on whether you have associated with drug users and whether your family and friends define drug use as acceptable or deviant.

Differential association theory refers to two processes that can result in individuals learning to engage in crime. First, association with others who share criminal values and commit crimes results in learning how to carry out a criminal act (Sutherland, Cressey, and Luckenbil 1992). Second, learning in a particular social context—socialization into a counterculture—results in reinforcement of criminal behavior (Hagan 2011).

Differential association theory focuses on the process of learning deviance from family, peers, fellow employees, political organizations, neighborhood groups such as gangs, and other groups in one's surroundings (Hagan 2011; Sutherland et al. 1992). Helena, for example, came to be surrounded by people who made dropping out of school and other delinquent acts seem normal. If her close friends and siblings were sexually active as teens, her teen pregnancy might not be remarkable and might even be a source of some prestige with her group of peers.

According to differential association theory, the possibility of becoming deviant depends on four factors related

Shooting drugs as a way of spending time and money is a way of life for some young people. Yet most teens would not know the technique for preparing and injecting illegal drugs, nor would they have learned from associates that this is a fun or acceptable way to spend one's time.

to associating with a deviant group: the duration of time spent with the group, the intensity of interaction, the frequency of interaction, and the priority of the group in one's friendship networks (Sutherland et al. 1992). If deviant behavior exists in people's social circles and if the individuals are exposed to deviance regularly and frequently (duration and intensity), especially if they are in close association with a group that accepts criminal behavior, they are more likely to learn deviant ways. Furthermore, individuals learn motives, drives, rationalizations, and attitudes, and they develop techniques that influence behavior and cause them to commit deviant acts.

Some theorists contend that life in poverty often involves a distinctive subculture in which delinquent behavior patterns are transmitted through socialization. The values, beliefs, norms, and practices that have evolved in poor communities over time can often lead to violation of laws. These values and norms have been defined by those in power as deviant. Just as upper-class youth seem to be expected and destined to succeed, lower-class youth may learn other behaviors that those with privilege have defined as delinquent and criminal (Bettie 2003; Chambliss 1973). For some inner-city youth, the local norms are to be tough and disrespectful of authority, to live for today, to seek excitement, and to be "cool"—these are survival techniques.

Today, we know that members of all social classes commit crimes, and no socioeconomic class has a monopoly on violence, graft, corruption, or dishonesty. However, *labeling* explains why some individuals and groups are more likely to be caught and punished for deviance.

Labeling Theory. Labeling theory is *a symbolic interaction approach that focuses on how people define deviance—what or who is or is not "normal"—and society's response to unacceptable behaviors, labeling as deviant those who violate society's norms.* Labels (such as "juvenile delinquent") are symbols that have meanings that affect an individual's self-concept and the way others see the individual. The basic assumption underlying labeling theory is that no behavior or individual is intrinsically deviant. Behavior is deviant because individuals in society label it deviant.

The basic social process of labeling someone is as follows: Members of society create deviance by defining certain behaviors as deviant—smoking pot, wearing long hair, holding hands in public, or whatever is seen as inappropriate at a particular time and place. They then react to the deviance by rejecting the deviant person or by imposing penalties.

Labeling theorists define two stages in the process of becoming a deviant. **Primary deviance** is *a violation of a norm that may be an isolated act or an initial act of rule breaking,* such as a young teenager shoplifting something on a dare by friends. Most people commit acts of primary deviance. However, many of us are able to avoid being labeled "deviant" when we commit one of these primary acts. Remember how you marked the deviant behavior test that you took at the beginning of this chapter? If you engaged in deviant acts, you were probably not labeled deviant for the offense. If you were labeled, you would likely not be in college or taking this class, but be cooling your heels in jail or juvenile detention.

If an individual continues to violate a norm and begins to take on a deviant identity because of being labeled deviant, this is referred to as **secondary deviance**. Secondary deviance becomes publicly recognized, and the individual is identified as deviant, beginning a deviant career. If a teenager such as Helena in the opening example is caught, her act becomes known, perhaps publicized in the newspaper. She may spend time in a juvenile detention center, and parents of other teens may not want their children associating with her. Employers and store managers may refuse to hire her. Soon, there are few opportunities open to her because others *expect* her to be delinquent. The teen may continue the deviant acts and delinquent acquaintances, in part because few other options are available. Society's reaction, then, is what defines a deviant person (Lemert 1951, 1972).

Shoplifting is often done by young people who have not been caught and arrested for anything—a form of primary deviance.

The process of labeling individuals and behaviors takes place at each level of analysis, from individual to society. If community or societal norms define a behavior as deviant, individuals are likely to believe it is deviant. Sanctions for juvenile delinquents can have the effect of reinforcing the deviant behavior by (a) increasing alienation from the social world, (b) forcing increased interaction with deviant peers, and (c) motivating juvenile delinquents to positively value and identify with the deviant status (Kaplan and Johnson 1991).

Self-fulfilling prophecy occurs when *a belief or a prediction becomes a reality, in part because of the prediction.* Individuals may come to see themselves as deviant because of harassment, ridicule, rejection by friends and family, and negative sanctions. James is 8 years old and already sees himself as a failure because his parents, teachers, and peers tell him he is "dumb." In keeping with the idea of self-fulfilling prophecy, James accepts the label and acts accordingly. Unless someone—such as an insightful teacher—steps in to give him another image of himself, the label is unlikely to change.

Thinking Sociologically

What labels do you carry, and how do they affect your self-concept and behavior?

A major explanation of why certain individuals and groups are labeled as deviant has to do with their status and power in society—a concern of conflict theory. Those who are on the fringes, away from power and nonparticipants in the mainstream, are more likely to be labeled as deviants—the poor, minorities, members of new religious movements, or those who in some way do not fit into the dominant system. Because the powerful have the influence to define what is acceptable, they protect themselves from being defined as deviants. People from different subcultures, social classes, or religious groups may be accorded deviant labels.

A study by William J. Chambliss illustrates the process of labeling in communities and groups and the relationship between interaction and conflict theories (Chambliss 1973). Chambliss looked at the behavior of two groups of boys and at the reactions of community members to their behavior. The Saints, boys from "good" families, were some of the most delinquent boys at Hannibal High School. Although the Saints were constantly occupied with truancy, drinking, wild driving, petty theft, and vandalism, none were officially arrested for any misdeed during the two-year study. The Roughnecks, who were from less affluent families, were constantly in trouble with police and community residents, even though their rate of delinquency was about equal to that of the Saints.

What was the cause of the disparity between these two groups? Community members, police, and teachers alike labeled the boys based on their perceptions of the boys' family backgrounds and social class. The Saints came from stable, white, upper-middle-class families; were active in school affairs; and were precollege students everyone expected would become professionals. The general community feeling was that the Roughnecks would amount to nothing. They carried around a label that was hard to change, and that label was realized.

Labels are powerful and can stigmatize an individual—branding the person as disgraceful or reprehensible. This process can be extended to a number of issues, including fatness, as the next "Sociology in Our Social World" illustrates.

Thinking Sociologically

You have a friend who is getting into drugs. From what you know about the preceding theories, what might be the reason why this is happening, and what, if anything, can you do for your friend?

Meso- and Macro-Level Explanations of Deviance

While micro-level interactions can lead to becoming deviant and being labeled deviant, many sociologists believe that meso- and macro-level analyses create greater understanding of the societal factors leading to deviance. Meso-level analysis focuses on ethnic subcultures, national organizations, and institutions. Macro-level theories focus on national and global social systems.

Structural-Functional Approaches to Deviance

We look first at structural-functional theories of deviance, those with the longest history in sociology. They include two themes: (a) anomie, the breakdown of the norms guiding behavior, which leads to social disorganization; and (b) strain created by the difference between definitions of success (goals) and the means available to achieve those goals.

Anomie and Social Disorganization. Villagers from industrializing countries in Africa, Asia, and Latin America were pushed off marginally productive rural lands and were pulled by the lure of the city to seek better lives and means for survival. They flocked to population centers with industrial opportunities, excitement, and a chance to change their lives, but when they arrived, they were often disappointed. Poor, unskilled, and homeless, they moved into crowded apartments or shantytowns of temporary shacks and tried to adjust to the new style of life that often included unemployment.

Many industrializing countries face structural changes as their economies move from agriculture to industry or service economies. Young men in particular leave behind strong bonds and a common value system that encourage conformity to norms. In cities, individuals melt into the crowd and live anonymously. Old village norms that have provided the guidelines for proper behavior crumble, sometimes without clear expectations emerging to take their place. The lack of clear norms in the rapidly changing urban environment leads to high levels of social disorganization and deviant behavior.

Sociologists use the term **anomie**, or *the state of normlessness that occurs when rules for behavior in society break down under extreme stress from rapid social change or conflict* (Merton 1968a). When norms are absent or conflicting, deviance increases as the previous example illustrates. Émile Durkheim (1858–1917) first described this normlessness as a condition of weak, conflicting, or absent norms and values that arise when societies are disorganized. This situation is typical in rapidly urbanizing, industrializing societies; at times of sudden prosperity or depression; during rapid technological change; during a war; or when a government is overthrown. Anomie affects

Sociology in Our Social World

Stigmatizing Fatness

By Leslie Elrod

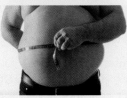

The United States is now the fattest country in the world. "American society has become 'obesogenic,' characterized by environments that promote increased food intake, nonhealthful food, and physical inactivity. . . . One in seven low-income preschool children is obese" (Centers for Disease Control and Prevention [CDC] 2009). The CDC has found that more than 60% of American adults are classified as overweight or obese, and 25% of children are classified as obese. Deviation from the idealized image of physical thinness allows others to judge and condemn nonconforming individuals, resulting in embarrassment, severe isolation, or alienation. According to Cooley's theory of the looking-glass self, because we tend to define ourselves by others' attitudes toward us and our interaction with others, individuals who are obese may suffer lower self-esteem and have negative self-images, thus creating heightened levels of psychological distress (Cooley 1902, [1909] 1983). When a physical attribute is assigned social significance, violators of this norm are likely to endure negative labeling because of perceived physical imperfections. The obese, labeled as self-indulgent, gluttonous, lazy, sloppy, and mean, experience social condemnation. Obese women tend to experience greater discrimination than obese men.

Women are taught that their physical appearance is a valuable commodity, in both the public and private spheres. Ascertaining the degree to which they fit the media models of female perfection, women attempt to adapt their appearance to reach this standard of beauty. Holding up an image of female perfection, such as slenderness, daintiness, or being demure, the media insinuate that women themselves somehow fall short of that perfection. This is exemplified in print ads, magazines, television programming, and movies as well as merchandising directed toward females of all ages. The "feminine failing" not only jeopardizes a woman's happiness but also challenges her femininity. The appearance discrepancy is based on the fact that over the course of the past century, as real women grew heavier, models and "beautiful" women were portrayed as increasingly thinner. An example of the change in media imagery is that of the White Rock mineral girl, portrayed as 5 feet 4 inches tall and 140 pounds in 1950. More recently, she is 5 feet 10 inches tall, weighing 110 pounds (Phipher 1994).

While much of the research on women's obsession with weight assumes that all women and girls are affected by the culture of thinness, there is some evidence to suggest that not all women are affected equally. Obesity rates are highest among minorities, the poor, and the disenfranchised. Yet "few black women seem to have eating disorders . . . and less emphasis [is placed] on eating and weight in general among black college students compared to white students" (Powell and Kahn 1995:190). When compared to black females, white women feel greater social pressure to be thin. One researcher, though, found that eating disorders, an outcome of dissatisfaction with one's body, are no longer confined to upper-class white females, indicating that the effects of body mass on self-esteem may be changing (Hesse-Biber 2007). Because the obese are victims of prejudice and discrimination resulting from social norm violation, they are less likely than their nonobese counterparts to be involved in various organizational and social activities. Weight-based embarrassment was indicated as a reason that obese people shied away from social obligations. Several clinical studies have documented that obese women even delay seeking medical care and participating in preventative medical techniques. Some obese people reject the stigmatizing "fat identity," using a variety of coping mechanisms such as avoidance of others who stigmatize them or coping through immersion in supportive subcultures. Those who suffer from low self-esteem may actively seek out activities and relationships that have the capacity to improve their self-esteem. While not all obese persons experience and internalize fat stigmatization, a statistically significant number of overweight and obese juveniles do indicate poor body image and diminished self-esteem. Many experts suggest that individuals should take a proactive approach by seeking medical or psychological help, joining support groups, and dealing with the problem if it is impairing their activities.

****

Leslie Elrod is an assistant professor of sociology at University of Cincinnati Blue Ash College. Two of her specialties are sociology of the body and deviance.

Yemeni army soldiers try to stop antigovernment protesters demanding the resignation of the autocratic Yemeni president, Ali Abdullah Saleh. In response the president ordered a crackdown on Arab Spring protesters, and at least 120 people were killed in just one city in Yemen.

urban areas first but may eventually affect the whole society. Macro-level events, such as economic recessions or wars, show how important social solidarity is to an individual's core sense of values.

Strain Theory. *Strain theory* examines the breakdown of norms caused by the lack of shared, achievable goals and the lack of socially approved means to achieve those goals (Merton 1938). Most people in a society share similar values and goals, but those with poor education and few resources have less opportunity to achieve shared goals than others. When legitimate routes to success are cut off, frustration and anger can result, and deviant methods may be used to achieve goals. Strain theory, primarily a macro-level theory, focuses on contradictions and tensions between the shared values and goals of a society on the one hand and the opportunity structures of the society on the other.

Strain theory suggests that the gap between an individual's or the society's *goals* and legitimate ways of attaining the goals—*the means*—can lead to strain in the society (Merton 1968b). Individuals may agree with society's definition of goals for success (say, financial affluence) but not be able to achieve it using the socially prescribed means of achieving that success. The strain that is created can lead to deviance. Merton uses U.S. society as an example because it places a heavy emphasis on success, measured by wealth and social standing. He outlines five ways individuals adapt to the strain. Figure 6.1 shows these five types and their relationship to goals and means.

To illustrate these, we trace a lower-class student who realizes the value of an education and knows it is necessary to get ahead, but who has problems financing education and competing in the middle class–dominated school setting.

1. *Conformity* means embracing the society's definition of success and adhering to the established and approved means of achieving success. The student works hard despite the academic and financial obstacles, trying to do well in school to achieve success and a good job placement. She uses legitimate, approved means—education and hard work—to reach goals that the society views as worthy.

2. *Innovation* refers to use of illicit means to reach approved goals. Our student uses illegitimate means to achieve her education goals. She may cheat on exams or get papers from Internet sources. Success in school is all that matters, not how she gets there.

3. *Ritualism* involves strict adherence to the culturally prescribed rules, even though individuals give up on the goals they hope to achieve. The student may give up the idea of getting good grades and graduating from college but, as a matter of pride and self-image, continue to try hard and to take classes. She conforms to expectations, for example, but with no sense of purpose. She just does what she is told.

4. *Retreatism* refers to giving up on both the goals and the means. The student either bides her time, not doing well, or drops out, giving up on future job goals. She abandons or retreats from the goals of a professional position in society and the means to get there. She may even turn to a different lifestyle—for example, becoming a user of drugs and alcohol—as part of the retreat.

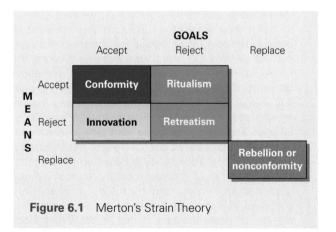

Figure 6.1 Merton's Strain Theory

5. *Rebellion* entails rejecting the socially approved ideas of success and the means of attaining that success. It replaces those with alternative definitions of success and alternative strategies for attaining the new goals. Rebelling against the dominant cultural goals and means, the student may join a radical political group or a commune, intent on developing new ideas of how society should be organized and what a "truly educated" person should be.

Deviant behavior results from retreatism, rebellion, and innovation. According to Merton, the reasons individuals resort to these behaviors lie in the social conditions that prevent access to success, not in their individual biological or psychological makeup.

The macro-level structural-functional approaches to deviance focus on what happens if deviance disrupts the ongoing social order. They explore what causes deviance, how to prevent disruptions, how to keep change slow and nondisruptive, and how deviance can be useful to the ongoing society. However, anomie and strain theories fail to account for class conflicts, inequities, and poverty, which conflict theorists argue underlie deviance.

Conflict Theory of Deviance

Conflict theorists assume that conflict between groups is inevitable. Because many societies today are heterogeneous groupings of people, the differences in goals, resources, norms, and values between interest groups and groups in power often cause conflict. Conflict theory focuses on meso- and macro-level analysis of deviance, looking at deviance as a result of social inequality or of the struggle between groups for power.

For conflict theorists, deviance is often seen as related to social class status, interest groups, or cultural conflict between the dominant group and ethnic, religious, political, regional, or gender groups. Wealthy and powerful elites want to maintain their control and their high positions (Domhoff 2009). They have the power to pass laws and define what is deviant, sometimes by effectively eliminating opposition groups. The greater the cultural difference between the dominant group and other groups in society, the greater the possibility of conflict. This is because minority groups and subcultures challenge the norms of the dominant groups and threaten the consensus in a society (Huizinga, Loeber, and Thornberry 1994).

Some conflict theorists blame capitalist systems for unjust administration of law and unequal distribution of resources, arguing that the ruling class uses the legal system to further the capitalist enterprise (Quinney 2002). The dominant or ruling class defines deviance, applies laws to protect its interests, represses any conflict or protest and, in effect, may force those in subordinate classes to carry out

People hold signs during a Tea Party protest in Freedom Plaza in Washington, D.C. The Tea Party has taken a strident oppositional position to stop governmental growth and any possible increase in taxes. This event coincided with the day that American citizens are required to file their national income tax. Conflict theorists believe that society is made up of groups with different self-interests, and this often leads to deviance.

actions that the dominant class has defined as deviant. These deviant actions are necessary for survival when legitimate avenues to resources are restricted by the affluent. Activities that threaten the interests and well-being of the wealthy capitalist class and those in power become defined as deviant. By subordinating certain groups and then defining them as deviant or criminal, the dominant group consolidates its powerful position. Because the dominant class is usually of one ethnic group and those of other races or ethnicities tend to be in the subordinate class, conflict often has racial and ethnic implications as well as social class dimensions. The fact that, for the same offenses, subordinate class or race members are arrested and prosecuted more often than are dominant class or race members provides evidence to support this contention, according to conflict theorists (Quinney 2002). When people feel they are not treated fairly by the society, they have less loyalty to the society and to its rules. This may result in activities considered deviant by those in power. To reduce deviance and crime, conflict theorists believe that we must change the structure of society.

Feminist Theory of Deviance

Feminists argue that traditional theories do not give an adequate picture or understanding of women's situations. Although there are several branches of feminist theory, most see the macro-level causes of abuses suffered by women as rooted in the capitalist patriarchal system. Feminist theorists look for explanations for violence against women and the secondary status of most women in gender relations and social structures. They include the following ideas: (a) Women are faced with a division of labor resulting from their sex, (b) separation between public (work) and private (home) spheres of social activity create "we" versus "they" thinking between men and women, and (c) socialization of children into gender-specific adult roles has implications for how males and females perceive and relate to each other.

One result of women's status is that they are often victims of crime. The type of victimization varies around the globe, from sex trafficking to rape (Bales 2004; Bales and Trodd 2008). Women are less often in a position to commit serious crimes. Deviant acts by women have traditionally fallen into the categories of shoplifting, credit card or welfare fraud, writing bad checks (in developed societies), prostitution, and in some countries adultery or inappropriate attire. Many Western feminist theorists contend that until women around the world are on an equal footing with men, crimes against women are likely to continue. Consider the case of intimate partner violence, including rape. Until recent years, there have been few serious consequences for the offenders in many countries (especially during times of anomie or war), and women often were blamed or blamed themselves for "letting it happen" (Boy and Kulczycki 2008). In some cultures, women fear reporting violence. Unfortunately, from recent data collected by the United Nations, we know that up to 59% of women will experience violent attacks at some point in their lives. Data also show that 16% to 52% of married women in the Middle East were assaulted in one year, compared to 1.3% to 12% in Europe and North America (United Nations 2010).

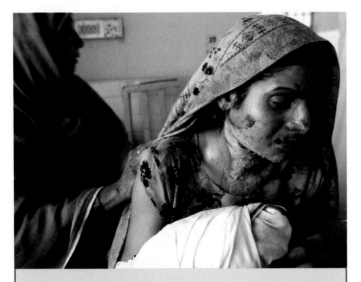

Ishrat Abdullah sits in her hospital bed after her husband threw sulfuric acid over her during a domestic dispute. She has burns inflicted to more than 30% of her body. Such abuse is the concern of feminist activists and scholars.

Feminist theorists argue that we learn our gender roles, part of which is men learning to be aggressive. Women's status in society often results in their being treated as sex objects, to be used for men's pleasure. Women's race and class identification become relevant in the exploitation of poor ethnically distinct women from developing countries as they become victims of human trafficking. Some branches of feminist theory argue that men exploit women's labor power and sexuality to continue their dominance. The system is reproduced through new generations that are socialized to maintain the patriarchy and to view inequality between the sexes as "normal" and "natural." Women who deviate from the cultural expectations of "normal" behavior are condemned.

No one theory of why deviance occurs can explain all deviance. Depending on the level of analysis of the questions sociologists wish to study (micro, meso, or macro), they select the theory that best fits the data they find. In the following sections, we explore in more detail the micro-meso-macro connections as they apply to one manifestation of deviance—crime. This illustrates how the sociological imagination can be applied to deviance at each level in the social system.

Thinking Sociologically

Meso- and macro-level social forces can be even more powerful than micro-level forces in explaining deviance. What might be the factors that contribute to deviance at the meso and macro levels? Pick a recent example of deviance now in the news. Which sociological theories help explain this deviance?

Crime and Individuals: Micro-Level Analysis

Crimes that affect the individual or primary group seem most threatening to us and receive the most attention in the press and from politicians. Yet, these micro-level crimes are only a portion of the total crime picture and, except for hate crimes, are not the most dysfunctional or dangerous crimes. In the United States, more than 2,800 acts are listed as federal crimes. These acts fall into several types of crime, some of which are discussed in the following. First, we analyze how crime rates are measured.

How Much Crime Is There?

How do sociologists and law enforcement officials know how much crime occurs? Not all crime is reported to the police, and when crime is reported, the methods of collecting data may differ. Each country has its own methods of keeping crime records. For instance, the official record of crime in the United States is found in the Federal Bureau of Investigation's *Uniform Crime Reports* (UCRs). The FBI relies on information submitted voluntarily by law enforcement agencies and divides crimes into two categories: Type I and Type II offenses. Type I offenses, also known as *FBI Index Crimes,* include murder, forcible rape, robbery, aggravated assault, burglary, larceny theft, motor vehicle theft, and arson. Type II offenses include fraud, simple assault, vandalism, driving under the influence of alcohol or drugs, and running away from home. In fact, there are hundreds of Type II crimes. The Crime Clock in Figure 6.2 summarizes UCR records on Type I offenses.

To examine trends in crime, criminologists calculate a rate of crime, usually per 100,000 individuals. Recent data indicate that the rate of violent crime in the United States has been dropping since the mid-1990s (U.S. Department of Justice 2011c). In 1992 there were 757.7 violent crimes per 100,000 residents; in 2002 that number was 494.4; by 2011 the number had dropped to 386.3. The most prevalent violent crimes were aggravated assault (751,131) and robbery (354,396). Moreover, black men were 6 times as likely to be homicide victims as white men (Stout 2009).

Although the UCR data provide a picture of how much crime gets reported to the police and leads to arrest, they do not provide information on how much crime there is in the United States because not all crimes go through the criminal justice system. An alternative measurement is the *National Incident-Based Reporting System* (NIBRS) that reports incident-driven crime, meaning that the FBI gathers more detailed information and categories on victim and offender characteristics. Reports include the type of offense, whether a weapon was used, location, whether drugs were a factor, and any motivations related to race, religion, or gender. This system provides more detailed and accurate crime statistics.

Another technique to assess crime rates is *self-reporting surveys*—asking individuals what criminal acts they have committed. Criminal participation surveys typically focus on adolescents and their involvement in delinquency. Yet another approach is *victimization surveys*—surveys that ask people how much crime they have experienced. The most extensively gathered victimization survey in the United States is the National Crime Victimization Survey, conducted by the Bureau of Justice Statistics. According to these records, the tendency to report crime to the police varies by the type of crime, with violent victimizations having the highest reporting rate. The victimization survey corroborates the findings of the UCR, showing that violent crime rates have declined since the early 1990s (Truman and Planty 2012; U.S. Department of Justice 2011c).

Each measurement instrument provides a different portion of the total picture of crime. By using several data-gathering techniques (triangulation), a more accurate picture of crime begins to emerge. Most of the crimes that concern average citizens of countries around the world are violent crimes committed by individuals or small groups. The following are some examples of these types of micro-level crimes.

Thinking Sociologically

Imagine that you work for the Bureau of Justice Statistics as many sociologists do. Congress asks you to predict how many FBI agents will be needed to deal with different types of crime. How would you go about determining this, and what databases might you use?

Types of Crime

Crimes range from petty theft of a candy bar or a fistfight in a bar to rape and murder. The following outlines several major types of crime as designated by the FBI.

Predatory or Street Crimes

Public opinion holds *predatory crimes* committed against individuals or property to be the most serious crimes. In the United States, the Uniform Crime Reports list eight serious index crimes used to track crime rates: predatory acts against people (murder, robbery, assault, and rape) and property (burglary, arson, theft, and auto theft).

Citizens in the United States are increasingly afraid of violent predatory crime. Many citizens feel they cannot trust others. Some keep guns. Some, especially women, African

A Violent Crime occured every	**25.3 seconds**
One Murder every	35.6 minutes
One Forcible Rape every	6.2 minutes
One Robbery every	1.4 minutes
One Aggravated Assault every	40.5 seconds
A Property Crime occured every	**3.5 seconds**
One Burglary every	14.6 seconds
One Lanceny-theft every	5.1 seconds
One Motor Vehicle Theft every	42.8 seconds

Figure 6.2 2011 Crime Clock Statistics

Source: U.S. Department of Justice (2011a).

Americans, older Americans, and low-income individuals, are afraid to go out near their homes at night. Because one's property and bodily safety are at stake, the public fixates on these crimes as the most feared and serious. The good news is that the total violent crime victimization rate declined by 13% in 2010 and another 4% in 2011, part of a two-decade drop in violent crime rates (FBI 2012; Truman 2011). In the following we discuss crimes committed by individuals —but stay tuned because most criminologists feel there are more serious crimes to be discussed under meso- and macro-level deviance.

Crimes Without Victims

Acts committed by or between individual consenting adults are known as **victimless** or **public order crimes**. Depending on the laws of countries, these can include prostitution, homosexual acts, gambling, smoking marijuana and using drugs, drunkenness, and some forms of white-collar crime. Participants involved do not consider themselves to be victims, but the offense is mostly an affront to someone else's morals. These illegal acts may be tolerated as long as they do not become highly visible. Some prostitution is overlooked in major cities of the world, but if it becomes visible or is seen as a public nuisance, authorities crack down, and it is controlled. Even though these acts are called victimless, there is controversy over whether individuals are victims even when consenting to the act and whether others such as family members are victims dealing with the consequences of the illegal activities.

A man lights up a marijuana pipe in Holland's Cannabis Castle, which provides some of the most potent strains of the herbal drug. Smoking pot is legal in the Netherlands. The Dutch think that because there is no victim, there should be no prohibition on the behavior.

Societies respond to victimless crimes such as using and selling drugs with a variety of policies, from execution in Iran and hanging in Malaysia to legalization in Holland. Long prison terms in the United States mean that 3 out of every 10 prison cells are now reserved for the user, the addict, and the drug seller—yet the problem has not diminished (E. Goode 2012). Proposals to legalize drugs, gambling, prostitution, and other victimless crimes meet with strong opinions both for and against. Although in many countries current policies and programs toward drugs are not working to reduce use and crime connected with use of drugs, the various consequences of alternative proposals are also uncertain.

Thinking Sociologically

Can a person be victimized by drugs even if he willingly uses them? Many prostitutes only consent to sex acts because poverty leaves them with few other options and because, like many women without resources, they are vulnerable to domination by men. Are they victims, or are these crimes without victims? Why?

Hate Crimes

Ethnic violence around the world results in hate crimes in communities, between ethnic groups, at workplaces, and on college campuses. **Hate crimes** are *criminal offenses committed against a person, property, or a group that are motivated by the offender's bias against a religion, an ethnic or racial group, a national origin, a gender, or a sexual orientation.* This is another micro-level crime since it affects primarily individuals. The Uniform Crime Reports in the United States indicate that hate crimes account for 11.5% of total criminal offenses. Most hate crimes are directed against property and involve destruction, damage, or vandalism; others involve direct intimidation. In 2010, a total of 6,628 hate crimes were reported. Hate crimes were categorized as racial bias, the largest percentage of hate crimes at 47.3%; 20% involve religious bias; 19.3% sexual-orientation bias; 12.8% ethnicity/nationality bias; and 0.6% disability bias (U.S. Department of Justice 2011b). Hate crimes are often vicious and brutal because the perpetrators feel rage against the victim as a representative of a group they despise. The crimes are committed by individuals or small vigilante groups (Blee 2008). Consider the case of Matthew Shepard, the gay college student who was robbed, tied to a fence post, beaten, and left to die in the cold Wyoming night. Nearly 16% of hate crimes are against those with different sexual orientations. Victims often form supportive in-groups to protect themselves from others who create a "culture of hate" (Levin and McDevitt 2003). The examples above represent only three of the many types of

In Munich, Germany, advocates of a hate-free world express their support for the LGBT community in the Christopher Street Day parade, an annual European celebration held in cities across Europe for the rights of LGBT people. Others (right) express their sentiment that Matthew Shepard, a gay student who was beaten and left to die in a Wyoming hate crime, was a deviant who had no moral standing and, seemingly, no right to live.

micro-level crimes, characterized by individual or small-group actions. We now turn to crime in organizations and institutions. Not only is crime rooted in complex organizations at the meso level, but crimes themselves are committed within or by organizations.

Crime and Organizations: Meso-Level Analysis

As societies modernize, there is an almost universal tendency for crime rates to increase dramatically due to anomie affecting new migrants whose old norms are no longer relevant (Merton 1968a). Societies become more reliant on formal or bureaucratic mechanisms of control—in other words, development of a criminal justice system at the meso level of our social world.

Crimes Involving Organizations and Institutions

Some crimes are committed by highly organized, hierarchically structured syndicates that are formed for the purpose of achieving their economic objectives in any way possible. A high-profile area of fraud is the medical system. Health care costs and insurance premiums have been rising at alarming rates, and one of the contributing factors is fraud in Medicaid and Medicare. Medicare fraud is estimated at $98 billion in 2011, with 20% of every Medicare dollar

going to fraud (Konrad 2012; PolitiFact.com 2009). For example, in South Florida, criminals open storefronts claiming to sell medical equipment; often fake offices are located in dying strip malls, and after the criminals have sent in false claims for Medicare payments, sometimes amounting to millions of dollars, they close the storefronts and cannot be traced.

Although the federal government has a small number of investigators, they are hardly a match for the fast-moving criminals with their get-rich-quick schemes (CBS News 2010). Such fraudulent organizations intentionally flout the law. On the other hand, some crime is done by legitimate corporations that cross the line. Their crimes are very serious, but the public image of such organizations is not criminal, so they are not always suspected or caught. We look first at organized criminal organizations and then at crime committed by people within their legitimate occupations.

Organized Crime

Organized crime refers to *ongoing criminal enterprises by an organized group whose ultimate purpose is economic gain through illegitimate means* (Siegel 2013). They engage in violence and corruption to gain and maintain power and profit. Our image of this type of crime is sometimes glamorized, coming from stereotypes in films such as *No Country for Old Men, The Godfather, Goodfellas, Gangs of New York,* and many others. On television, *The Sopranos* is the ultimate media "mob" depiction. Despite the alluring view of these idealized stories, organized crime is a serious problem in many countries. It is essentially a counterculture with a

Films like The Godfather romanticize and "domesticate" organized crime, creating a false image in the minds of the public about how dangerous this form of crime can really be.

hierarchical structure, from the boss down to underlings. The organization relies on power, control, fear, violence, and corruption. This type of crime is a particular problem when societies experience anomie and social controls break down.

Marginalized ethnic groups that face discrimination may become involved in a quest to get ahead through organized crime. Early in U.S. history, Italians were especially prominent in organized crime, but today, many groups are involved. Organized crime around the world has gained strong footholds in countries in transition (Siegel and Nelen 2008). For example, in Russia, the transition from a socialist economy to a market economy has provided many opportunities for criminal activity. The *Mafiya* is estimated to be over 100,000 people, and some estimate members control 70% to 80% of all private business and 40% of Russia's wealth (Lindberg and Markovic n.d.; Schmalleger 2012).

Organized crime usually takes one of three forms: (a) the sale of illegal goods and services, including gambling, loan sharking, trafficking in drugs and people, selling stolen goods, and prostitution; (b) infiltrating legitimate businesses and unions through threat and intimidation and using bankruptcy and fraud to exploit and devastate a legitimate company; or (c) racketeering, the extortion of funds in exchange for protection (i.e., not being hurt). Activities such as running a casino or trash collection service often appear to be legitimate endeavors on the surface but may be cover operations for highly organized illegal crime rings.

Although the exact cost of organized crime in the United States is impossible to determine precisely, the estimated annual gross income of organized crime activity is at least $50 billion, more than 1% to 2% of the gross national

product. Some scholars estimate earnings as high as $90 billion per year (CNBC 2010; Siegel 2013). Internationally, criminal proceeds for all recorded criminal activities are 3.6% of global gross domestic product, or $2.1 trillion. Drug trafficking and illicit drugs are 20% of proceeds (Fedotov 2012). Money laundering is estimated at 2% to 5% of the world's GDP (Bjelopera and Finklea 2012).

Transnational organized crime takes place across national boundaries, using sophisticated electronic communications and transportation technologies. Experts identify several major crime clans in the world: (a) Hong Kong–based triads, (b) South American cocaine cartels, (c) Italian mafia, (d) Japanese *Yakuza,* (e) Russian *Mafiya,* and (f) West African crime groups. Organized crime is responsible for thousands of deaths a year through drug traffic and murders, and it contributes to a climate of violence in many cities (Siegel 2013).

The value of the global illicit drug market, for example, is estimated at more than $322 billion at the retail level (based on retail prices). The largest market is cannabis, followed by cocaine, opiates, and other markets such as methamphetamine, amphetamine, and ecstasy (P. Smith 2009). Many people survive off of the drug trade, from the poppy farmers in Afghanistan, who grow more than 90% of the world's poppies, to the street drug dealers. In 2011, the acreage devoted to growing poppies was the highest ever, especially in southern and western Afghanistan (Afghanistan Opium Survey 2011; "Global Opium Production" 2011; Shah and Rubin 2012). This problem is not likely to end soon because farmers are in debt to the Taliban and are therefore forced to continue growing poppies. The Taliban profit from the sales by more than $100 million per year, which helps keep them in power. Thus, Westerners who use opium drugs help financially sustain the Taliban (National Public Radio 2008).

Add other types of crimes (transporting migrants, selling human organs, trafficking in women and children for the sex industry, and sales of weapons and nuclear material), and the estimates of profits for international crime cartels are from $650 billion to more than $1.5 trillion a year ("Transnational Crime in the Developing World" 2011).

Occupational Crime

A violation of the law committed by an individual or a group in the course of a legitimate, respected occupation or financial activity is called **white-collar or occupational crime** (Coleman 2006; Hagan 2011). Occupational crime receives less attention than violent crimes because it is less visible and because it is frequently committed by people in positions of substantial authority and prestige, as opposed to reports of violent crimes that appear on the television news each night. Yet, it is far more costly in currency, health, and lives. Victims of financial scams who have lost their life savings are well aware of this. Occupational crimes include embezzlement, pilfering, bribery, tax evasion, price fixing, obstruction of justice, and various forms of fraud.

Although the Madoff financial scandal became public knowledge in December 2008, the details unfolded for the next several months. Bernard (Bernie) Madoff, former chair of the NASDAQ stock exchange, had developed a Ponzi scheme that is probably the largest investment fraud Wall Street has ever seen. The scheme defrauded and wrecked thousands of investors, public pension funds, charitable foundations, and universities, with over $65 billion missing from investor accounts. Named after Charles Ponzi, the first to be caught (in 1919), Ponzi schemes involve promises of large returns on investments, paying old investors with money from new investors. Money is shifted between investors (*Wall Street Journal* 2009).

Annual economic losses from white-collar crimes in the United States are estimated to be 10 times those from all other crimes reported to the police (Coleman 2006). The collapse of the savings and loan industry cost the public billions of dollars. Antitrust violations cost $250 billion, tax fraud $150 billion, and health care industry fraud $100 billion. Employee theft adds an estimated 2% to the retail purchase price of products we buy (Coleman 2006).

The list of cybercrimes is long, but they include identity theft, embezzlement, international illegal transfers of money, illegal stock trades, sales of illegal or inferior products, creation of computer viruses, and computer hacking. As technology advances, it facilitates new and currently unimaginable opportunities for dishonest people to take advantage of technology for personal gain (Schmalleger 2012).

Sociologists divide occupational crimes into four major categories: (1) against the company, (2) against employees, (3) against customers, and (4) against the general public and other organizations (Hagan 2011). *Crimes against the company* include pilfering (using company resources such as the photocopy machine for personal business) and employee theft ("borrowing company property," taking from the till, and embezzlement).

Three types of corporate crime are often done on behalf of the company, and the victims are employees or members of the larger society. *Crimes against employees* refer to corporate neglect of worker safety. *Crimes against customers* involve acts such as selling dangerous foods or unsafe products, consumer fraud, deceptive advertising, and price fixing (setting prices in collusion with another producer). *Crimes against the general public* include acts by companies that negatively affect large groups of people. One example is companies surreptitiously dumping pollutants into landfills, streams, or the air. Pollutants from industrial waste have caused high rates of miscarriages, birth defects, and diseases among residents (Coleman 2006).

The bottom line is that white-collar crime committed by company executives is by far our most serious crime problem. The economic cost of white-collar crime is vastly greater than the economic cost of street crime. White-collar criminals kill considerably more people than all violent street criminals put together (Coleman 2006).

Thinking Sociologically

Why are meso-level (such as occupational/white-collar) crimes considered by scholars to be more dangerous and more costly to the public than micro-level crimes? Why do they get so much less attention?

National and Global Crime: Macro-Level Analysis

National boundaries are blurring as people migrate around the globe and corporations have no loyalty to any boundaries. Crime syndicates are international as goods and people are moved surreptitiously across borders. Terrorist organizations, too, have no boundaries. Let us now explore crime at the national and global macro level.

Terrorism is *the planned use of random, unlawful (or illegal) violence or threat of violence against civilians to create (or raise) fear and intimidate citizens in order to advance the terrorist group's political or ideological goals* (U.S. Department of Defense 2011). Add to that international terrorism practiced in a foreign country, and terrorism becomes a worldwide problem. According to the U.S. State Department, the number of international terrorist attacks in 2012 was 6,771, with 32,750 people killed or wounded (U.S. Department of State 2013).

Terrorist groups can be religious, state-sponsored, left- or right-wing, or nationalist. Table 6.1 on page 160 shows types of terrorist groups.

Crime is a national and global issue as illustrated by *state-organized crime,* acts defined by law as criminal but committed by state or government officials in the pursuit of their jobs. For example, a government might be complicit in smuggling, assassination, or torture, acting as an accessory to crime that is then justified in terms of "national defense." Government offices may also violate laws that restrict or limit government activities such as eavesdropping. In some countries, political prisoners, such as the Guantánamo Bay detainees held in Cuba by the United States, have been held for long periods without charges, access to lawyers, and trials, and some have been tortured, violating both national

Corporate Crime

Table 6.1   Types of Terrorist Groups

Nationalist	Irish Republican Army, Basque Fatherland and Liberty, Kurdistan Workers' Party
Religious	Al-Qaeda, Hamas, Hezbollah, Aum Shinrikyo (Japan)
State-sponsored	Hezbollah (backed by Iran), Abu Nidal Organization (Syria, Libya), Japanese Red Army (Libya)
Left-wing	Red Brigades (Italy), Baader-Meinhof Gang (Germany), Japanese Red Army
Right-wing	Neo-Nazis, skinheads, white supremacists
Anarchist	Some contemporary antiglobalization groups

Source: Schmalleger (2006:347).

and international laws. The Obama administration planned to shut down the Guantánamo Bay facility in 2010, but that has not happened. Although the number of detainees has dropped from 245 in January 2009 to 166 in March 2013, those remaining are complicated legal cases (White House 2011; Reilly 2013). In several U.S. Supreme Court rulings (2006 and 2008), the verdict was that the rights of these people have been violated by the U.S. administration (Global Security 2009). Although countries may violate their own laws, it is difficult to prosecute when the guilty party is the government.

Bribery and corruption are the way of life in many governments and businesses. The percentage of persons who said they had paid a bribe to obtain services is as high as 79% in Nigeria, 72% in Cambodia, and 71% in Albania (Transparency International 2012).

Detainees sit in a holding area at the naval base in Guantánamo Bay, Cuba, during in-processing to the "temporary" detention facility. It violates U.S. law, but it continues to hold prisoners and to operate.

Thinking Sociologically

Sometimes, government officials and even heads of state are the perpetrators of crimes. Is there a difference in crime if it is done by an official and justified as necessary for national defense? Why or why not? Is it ever justified for a military or an intelligence agency to violate its own country's laws?

Cross-National Comparison of Crimes

The vending machine was on the corner near the Ballantines' house in Japan. The usual cola, candy, and sundries were displayed, along with cigarettes, beer, whiskey, sake, and pornographic magazines. Out of curiosity, Jeanne and her family watched to see who purchased what from the machines, and not once did they see teenagers sneaking the beer, cigarettes, or porn. It turns out the Ballantines were not the only ones watching! The neighbors also kept an eye on who did what, the neighborhood watch being an effective form of social control in Japan. Because of the **stigma**—*social disapproval that discredits a person's claim to a "normal" identity*—teens understand the limits, and vigilant neighbors help keep the overall amount of deviance low. The neighborhood watch sends a signal that deviant behavior is unacceptable and provides social control of behaviors of those who might be tempted to commit crimes.

Japan and the United States are both modern, urban, industrial countries, but their crime rates and the way they deal with deviant behavior and crime differ dramatically. Japan had 0.5 murders for every 100,000 people, whereas the United States had a rate 10 times higher—5.0 per 100,000 residents (Cowen and Williams 2012; Spacey 2012).

How can these extreme differences in crime rates be explained? Researchers look at cultural differences: Japan's low violent crime rate is due in part to Japan's tight-knit,

Japanese vending machines carry a wide range of products that are not freely available in the United States—such as pornographic magazines. However, young people do not purchase these products that are not meant for them, for they know the neighbors are watching and to do so would bring shame and embarrassment on them and on their families.

Table 6.2 Crime Rates per 100,000 People in Selected Countries

Country	Murders	Rapes	Burglaries	Robberies
Mexico	18.1	13.3	156	607
United States	5.0	28.6	515	133
Israel	2.1	17.5	611	40
Canada	1.8	1.4	611	96
New Zealand	1.5	30.6	1386	52
Australia	1.2	91.9	1283	18
England & Wales	1.1	27.7	986	137
Denmark	0.9	6.4	1939	73
Germany	0.8	8.9	456	60
Japan	0.5	1.1	117	4

Source: Cowen and Williams (2012).

due in part to the much higher disparity in income between rich and poor and the heterogeneity of populations.

Thinking Sociologically

Study Table 6.2. Which countries have especially striking crime rates—either high or low? Why? Why might the differences between the rankings on countries for violent crimes (the first two columns) and economic crimes (the third and fourth columns) be so dramatic?

Although comparing cross-national data on crime is difficult because there are variations in the definitions of crime and measurements used, comparisons do give us insight into what types of crimes are committed, under what circumstances, and how often. Two sources of international data are Interpol (the International Criminal Police Organization) and the United Nations. One problem is that they have no way to check accuracy of the data they receive from countries.

Global Crimes

Increasingly, crimes are global in nature. Some crimes are committed by transnational conglomerates and may involve organized crime and the smuggling of illegal goods and humans. Other crimes violate international laws, treaties, and agreements such as protection of the global environment, laws that are ignored when contrary to the self-interests of governments or corporations. The international community

homogeneous society—inequality between citizens is not great. Further, success is not as focused on material possessions and consumption, Japanese people are loyal to a historic tradition of cooperation that provides a sense of moral order, and Japanese do not carry guns. The Japanese government spends far less of its gross national product on police, courts, and prisons, and police in Japan want to be thought of as kind and caring rather than threatening. For many crimes in Japan, the offender may simply be asked to write a letter of apology. The humiliation of writing an apology and the fear of shame and embarrassing one's family are strong enough to curb deviant behavior (Lazare 2004).

Table 6.2 provides information on crimes in selected countries, and it allows you to see differences in crime rates per 100,000 individuals in the population. Differences are

has the capacity to try people, organizations, and countries for violation of human rights or international laws, but the process is difficult and politically charged.

Some scholars use world systems theory to understand global crime, arguing that the cause lies in the global economy, inequalities between countries, and competition between countries for resources and wealth. As a result of the capitalist mode of production, an unequal relationship has arisen between core nations (developed, wealthy ones in the Global North) and peripheral nations (in the Global South). Core nations often take unfair advantage of peripheral nations. Peripheral nations, in turn, must find ways to survive in this global system, and they sometimes turn to illegal methods—such as violating global environmental standards—to achieve their goals (Chase-Dunn and Anderson 2006). Semiperipheral nations benefit from extensive trade, making them less vulnerable than the poorest nations. Map 6.1 shows where core, peripheral, and semiperipheral nations are located.

As you look at this map, note that the developed or affluent countries are almost all located in the Northern Hemisphere. Although some poor countries are north of the equator, the pattern is obvious. Furthermore, the phrase "gone south" is often a colloquialism for an economy that is not strong. To avoid some misleading implications of the words *developed* and *developing*, many scholars now prefer the term *Global South* to refer to less affluent nations. If you see or hear the term *Global South*, this map should help you see why it refers to developing or poor countries.

One example of global crime and corruption is computer crimes. As noted above, Internet deviance or cyberspace crime is growing faster than a cybergeek can move a mouse. This new world of crime ranges from online identity theft and pornography to hate sites and hacking into government and military files (Thio, Taylor, and Schwartz 2012). As one team of researchers reports, "fraudsters can tap into an international audience from anyplace in the world" (Sager et al. 2006:261).

Controlling Crime: Social Policy Considerations

When people are afraid to walk the streets because they might be assaulted and when a significant number of individuals are dropping out of society and taking up deviant lifestyles, deviance becomes a topic of great concern.

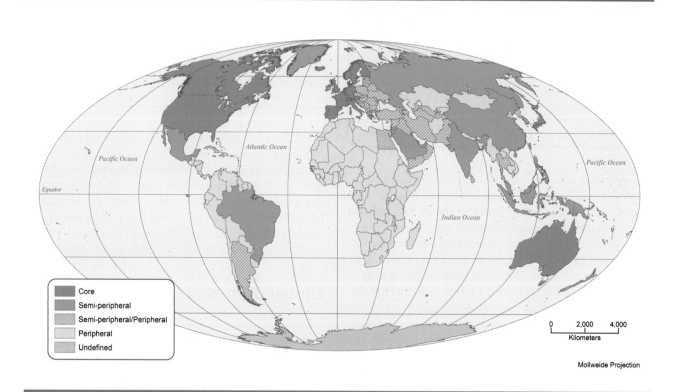

Map 6.1   Core, Peripheral, and Semiperipheral Countries of the World

Source: Map by Anna Versluis.

Most governments pass laws and make policies to keep deviance from disrupting the smooth functioning of society. This section discusses mechanisms used by societies to control the amount of deviance.

Dealing With Crime: The Criminal Justice Process

Every society has a process for dealing with criminals. Sometimes the ground rules and processes of justice respect human rights and represent blind justice, meaning that all people are treated equally, but often they do not. Structural-functionalists see the justice system as important to maintaining order in society. Some conflict theorists argue that the criminal justice system depicts crime as a threat from poor people and minorities, which creates fear of victimization in members of society. It is in the interests of those in power to maintain the image that crime is primarily the work of outsiders and the poor. This deflects citizen discontent and hostility from the powerful and helps them retain their positions (Reiman and Leighton 2010a, 2010b). Conflict theorists point out that there will always be a certain percentage of crime in society because the powerful will make sure that something is labeled deviant. Based on these theories, policy might focus on how to deter deviant acts or on how to correct the injustices of the system. In both cases, prisons and jails are currently a primary means of controlling individual criminal behavior.

Prisons and Jails

There is money to be made by locking up prisoners. Farming prisoners out to the private sector, often in other states, costs less than a state running its own prisons, according to advocates for privatization. Private prisons save on labor costs by not paying the high benefits that states must pay to employees. Advocates claim that private enterprise is always more efficient since businesses are driven by profit motive and competition.

Those against privatization argue that incarcerating (imprisoning) people for profit is a bad idea, morally and financially. They point out that costs per prisoner often rise after the initial contract with the state, and some states must incarcerate a certain number of people due to contracts with private prisons, thereby manipulating the criminal justice system. People in poverty may lose access to family members if prisoners are sent out of state. When profit motive is the bottom line, quality of food and other treatment of inmates deteriorates. These are but a few of the arguments for and against private prisons, but they provide a taste of the controversies surrounding our high prison population (Current.com 2012; Michael n.d.).

Protecting the public from offenders often means locking up criminals in prison, a form of *total institution* that completely controls the prisoners' lives and regulates all of their activities. Inmates' lives are drastically changed through the processes of *degradation,* which marks the individual as deviant, and *mortification,* which breaks down the individual's original self as the inmate experiences *resocialization* (Irwin and Owen 2007). The inmate is allowed no personal property. There is little communication, and verbal abuse of inmates by guards is common. Heterosexual activity is prohibited, uniforms and standard buzz cuts are required, and the inmates' schedules are totally controlled.

Social systems that develop within the prison often involve rigid roles, norms, and privileges. In a famous study that simulated a prison situation, researchers illustrated the social organization that develops and the roles that individuals play within the prison system. Students were assigned to roles as prisoners or prison guards. Within a short time, the individuals in the study were acting out their roles. The students playing the role of "guard" became cruel and sadistic, causing the researcher, Philip Zimbardo, to end the experiment prematurely because abuse was

Time in jails or prisons is often the formal sanction applied to enforce the rules passed by legitimate officials. This woman is consulting with her lawyer about legal options.

beginning to have alarming consequences (Zimbardo et al. 1973). The abuse of prisoners in Iraq and at Guantánamo prison in Cuba parallel the findings from Zimbardo's earlier study. In short, the authoritarian situation can lead to abuse; it is not a matter of maladjusted individuals in those roles (Zimbardo 2009).

Jails in local communities have been called "asylums for poor people." Most people in jails are there for their "rabble existence"—including petty hustlers, derelicts, junkies, "crazies," and outlaws, but mostly disorganized and economically marginal members of society (Irwin and Owen 2007). Jails in Europe and the United States house disproportionate numbers of immigrants (especially those with non-European features and skin tones), young men, and members of the poorest class of the citizenry.

Conflict theorists believe that these figures are strong evidence that jails and prisons are mostly about controlling or "managing" the minorities and poor people, not about public safety. African American males, for example, are more than 6 times as likely to be incarcerated as white men (Fathi 2009; Sentencing Project 2012a; West, Sabol, and Greenman 2009). More African American males are in prison today than were slaves in 1850. Among female prisoners, African Americans were 2.9 times as likely to be incarcerated than whites, and Hispanic women were 1.5 times as likely to spend time in prison (Sentencing Project 2012a). As a result, in the United States only 39% of the incarcerated population is white, even though whites comprise 68% of the total population (Guerino, Harrison, and Sabol 2011). Yet many scholars are convinced that, when white-collar crimes are included, whites do not commit fewer crimes than do blacks (M. Alexander 2011; Farley 2010). The makeup of U.S. prisons is presented in Table 6.3.

Thinking Sociologically

From what you have learned so far in this chapter, why are the people who get sent to jail disproportionately young, poor, immigrants, or racial and ethnic minorities?

The Purposes of Prisons

People are sent to prison for a variety of reasons. Why do we, unlike people in many societies, lock people up for long periods?

From the functional perspective prisons serve several purposes for society: (1) the desire for revenge or retribution; (2) removing dangerous people from society; (3) deterring would-be deviants; and (4) rehabilitating through counseling, education, and work training programs inside prisons (R. Johnson 2002). However, in prison, inmates are exposed to more criminal and antisocial behavior, so rehabilitation and deterrence goals are often undermined by the nature of prisons. According to a recent Bureau of Justice Statistics report, roughly 5% of prison inmates are sexually assaulted by other prisoners or prison guards, and 12% of youth in juvenile detention facilities are victims, often in gang rapes ("New Federal Report" 2010). This ongoing problem of assault, rape, and threat of violence in prison so brutalizes inmates that it becomes difficult for them to reenter society as well-adjusted citizens ready to conform to the conventional society they feel has brutalized them. Many prisoners suffer from mental health problems and have difficulty reintegrating into society (Fathi 2009).

Compared to the rates in other countries, the U.S. incarceration rate is much higher. With less than 5% of the world's population, one quarter of the world's prison population is in the United States. The median rate in all countries in the world is 125 per 100,000 citizens, one-sixth the rate in the United States. One reason is that the United States incarcerates people for lesser crimes and longer periods than do most other countries (Liptak 2008). Table 6.4 compares the rates of incarceration.

The disturbing reality is that, despite the high rates of incarceration in the United States, **recidivism rates**—*the likelihood that someone who is arrested, convicted, and imprisoned will later be a repeat offender*—are also very high. More than half of all men who do time in prison will be confined again for a crime. This means that as a specific deterrent or for rehabilitation, imprisonment does not work very well (Quinney 2002; Siegel 2013). What options does the government have? In the following sections, we discuss the death penalty and alternatives to prisons.

Table 6.3 Characteristics of People in Prison

	Makeup of U.S. Prison Population	*Makeup of U.S. Population*	*Ratio of the Population 30–34 Years Old in Prison*	*Chance of Spending Time in Prison During Lifetime*
Black	38%	12.4%	1:10	32%
Hispanic	22%	14.1%	1:26	17%
White	32%	68%	1:61	6%

Source: Sentencing Project (2012a).

Table 6.4   2011 World Comparative Rates of Incarceration (per 100,000 People)

Top 11 Countries	
United States	716
Rwanda	595
Russia	568
Brazil	253
Spain	159
Australia	133
France	96
Germany	85
Sweden	78
Denmark	74
India	32

Source: Sentencing Project (2012b:3).

The Death Penalty

All modern societies provide some means of protecting individuals from criminals, especially those considered dangerous. People convicted of murder, assault, robbery, and rape usually receive severe penalties. The most controversial (and irreversible) method of control is for the state to put the person to death. The most common argument for using the death penalty, more formally known as capital punishment, is to deter people from crime. The idea is that not only will the person who has committed the crime be punished, but also others will be deterred from committing such a crime because they know that the death penalty is a possibility for them too.

Sixty-one percent of the American public favor a punishment other than the death penalty for homicide and other severe crimes, and 88% of criminal justice experts feel the death penalty does not deter murder (Alarcon and Mitchell 2011; Radelet and Lacock 2009). In addition, the costs to execute any one of the 3,199 death row criminals in the United States is exorbitant. A study in California shows that more than $4 billion has been spent on 13 executions there since 1978, a cost of $308 million per execution. The cost of capital trials, various appeals processes (many of which are mandated by law to avoid mistakes), and special death row incarceration requirements is much greater than that for life imprisonment (Alarcon and Mitchell 2011). While U.S. states with the death penalty assume that those contemplating crimes will be deterred, studies on the deterrent effects of capital punishment do not support this assumption. Inmates who had committed three or more violent crimes indicated that their crimes were

not planned, that "things went wrong," and that they were not thinking about the possible penalty when committing their crimes (Wilcox and Steele 2003). Murder is also more likely to happen in states with the death penalty. In fact, the 20 states with the highest murder rates in 2008 all had the death penalty (Death Penalty Information Center 2012). Despite this, 37 states still have death penalty clauses for at least some crimes. Why is this severe penalty by which the state is authorized to take someone's life still utilized?

Most Global North countries do not use the death penalty, and in 2007 the United Nations passed a resolution calling on all nations to abolish it as "cruel and unusual punishment" (Amnesty International 2012; UN News Centre 2010). However, as you can see from Map 6.2 on page 166, the United States is one of the 20 countries that utilize the death penalty out of 198 where records are available (Amnesty International 2013). Only China and Yemen officially recorded more executions in 2010 than the United States (World Coalition 2012).

Thinking Sociologically

How can you explain higher murder rates in U.S. states that have the death penalty?

There is evidence that the death penalty is deeply influenced by race and class status of the prisoner. In most U.S. states with capital punishment, a disproportionate number

Prisoners awaiting the death penalty are held in a separate isolation unit known as "death row." More than 70% of the members of the United Nations have abolished the death penalty, including all of the European nations.

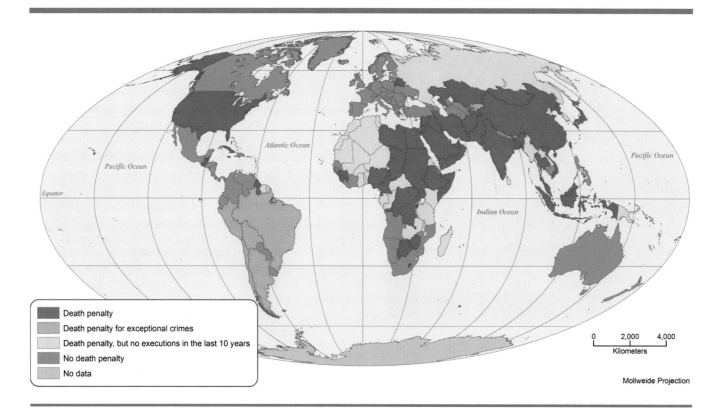

Map 6.2   Global Status of the Death Penalty in 2011

Source: Amnesty International. Map by Anna Versluis.

of minority and lower-class individuals are put to death. Of those executed since 1976, 56% have been white and 34% black. Yet the percentage of blacks in the total population is less than 13%.

Furthermore, the death penalty is usually imposed if a white person has been murdered. Homicides in which African Americans, Latinos and Latinas, Native Americans, and Asian Americans are killed are much less likely to result in a death penalty for the murderer, implying that people in society view their loss of life as less serious (Amnesty International 2006). In addition, mistakes are made. As of August 2013, 311 prisoners have been exonerated, or found not guilty due to further evidence or DNA samples (Innocence Project 2013). DNA tests are acquitting other death row prisoners and have found that some people who have already been executed were actually innocent.

The cost of the death penalty combined with the facts that the death penalty sometimes kills innocent people, that it is often racially discriminatory, and that it is not an effective deterrent has led to a search for alternative means to deter crime and has spurred policy analysts to rethink assumptions about what factors are effective in controlling human behavior.

Alternative Forms of Social Control

Based on the assumptions that most criminal behavior is learned through socialization, that criminals can be resocialized, and that tax dollars can be saved, several sociological theories of crime suggest early community intervention to reduce crime rates. Some of these ideas include high-quality schools, to prevent young people entering the criminal justice system in the first place, and methods of treatment other than brutalizing incarceration for those who do find themselves in trouble with the law. The goals are to provide alternative routes to success for those living in poverty, reduce the number of individuals who go to prison, and cut the number who are rearrested after being released—*the recidivism rate*. Improving the social capital of potential offenders is one approach.

Social capital refers to social networks, shared norms, values, and understanding that facilitates cooperation within or among groups and access to important resources (Flavin 2004). Social capital encompasses relationships, support systems and services, and access to community resources (Jarrett, Sullivan, and Watkins 2005). Increasing an individual's social capital by increasing educational attainment, job skills, and ability to take advantage of available resources such as job opportunities can reduce the

Perfect Evidence

chances of that person going to prison in the first place and of recidivism, or repeat offenses and incarceration.

The tendency to think that the way to control human behavior is through more severe punishments is based on a rational choice theory. If the cost is high enough for committing deviant acts, so the idea goes, people will conform. Yet despite severe punishments, crime rates generally remain higher in the United States than in other countries. One public sociologist, Susan Guarino-Ghezzi, found that hostile relations between young delinquents and police officers had developed into a cycle that simply made for more crime. She explains in the next "Sociologists in Action" how a different strategy was effective in transforming the dynamic that led to crime.

Sociologists in Action— Susan Guarino-Ghezzi

Police and Delinquent Youth: Changing Stereotypes and Making Peace

In the 1990s, I conducted research in Boston on two groups of people—police and gang-involved male juvenile offenders held at the Massachusetts Department of Youth Services (DYS). I was interested in how each group defined encounters with one another. Police and juveniles were each frustrated by the relentless violence and record homicide rate, and they blamed one another for the situation. Within both groups were subcultures that reinforced fallacies and stereotypes. These misunderstandings were perceived as "real" and locked each group into routine, ritualized behaviors, guaranteeing that they would clash.

My goal was to uncover these patterns, expose misleading stereotypes, and use these new understandings to change behaviors on both sides. Previous research I had conducted with others revealed that the youths who were the most alienated from police had the most frequent encounters with them (Guarino-Ghezzi and Carr 1996; Guarino-Ghezzi and Kimball 1996). Negative encounters with police were at the center of their lives, and I came to realize that while the offenders claimed to hate police, they actually looked forward to negative confrontations as opportunities to reinforce peer bonds.

At the same time, I learned that police painted ex–juvenile offenders with the same brush. If a juvenile offender returned to the community after a long program of rehabilitation, regardless of his or her willingness to reform, the individual was still a juvenile offender as far as the police were concerned. If a juvenile offender became a victim of crime, the police showed less sympathy than if the juvenile were a law-abiding victim.

I contacted the deputy superintendent of the experimental neighborhood-policing district in Boston and shared my concerns. Together, with some other police officers, we established a program called Make Peace With Police (MPWP), which arranged communication sessions, role-plays, and other nonconfrontational encounters between police and gang-involved juveniles. As executive director, I oversaw 41 group meetings run by MPWP facilitators on a weekly basis. These sessions helped us to understand the sources of hostility on both sides, but more importantly, they helped to create useful dialogue between juveniles and police.

A key finding of the MPWP project was that without sincere efforts to establish relationships, juveniles lacking positive social bonds learn to define police negatively from their social environments. While some of the most defiant and hostile-seeming youths were biased against police based on their peer subcultures, our sessions became turning points for developing positive relationships.

Police told us that they were surprised to learn that young gang members were really "just kids." An officer who arrived at a session feeling tough and somewhat angry at the youths quickly attached to a youth who was visibly upset when mentioning a death in his family during the session. The officer offered to help the youth find a job when he was released from the DYS facility. When asked what made him change, the officer explained that he had no idea how young and vulnerable the youths were because he'd never looked beyond the "street tough" exteriors that were so common among groups of youths in high-crime communities.

Another officer received a surprise one weekend when a youth he had met in the detention facility recognized him in his cruiser and went out of his way to initiate a pleasant conversation. It was especially fulfilling because the boy was one of a small number who refused to even speak to police in his first MPWP session. The communication sessions provided a necessary "bridge" for redefining social norms.

* * * * * * *

Note: This excerpt is adapted from Korgen, White, and White's *Sociologists in Action: Sociology, Social Change, and Social Justice* (2013). Susan Guarino-Ghezzi is a professor of sociology and criminology at Stonehill College. She is the former director of research of the Massachusetts Department of Youth Services, and is a frequent consultant on juvenile crime.

What works in one country cannot necessarily be imported directly into another country. Not many people think that the apology technique used in Japan would work as a deterrent to crimes in the United States. On the other hand, there is a wide range of options available for dealing with crime other than harsh (and expensive) punishments. Seeing how crime is controlled in other countries may challenge assumptions in one's own country, causing authorities to come up with creative new solutions that do work. For example, many criminologists argue that the United States should concentrate on the serious criminals and reduce the number of minor offenders in jails by providing less expensive and longer impact alternatives to prison time. They also suggest a number of alternatives to sending offenders to jail and prisons such as community service, work release, and educational training programs.

Prison reforms, rehabilitation, training programs, shock probation, work release, halfway houses, and other alternative programs are intended to integrate the less serious offenders into the community in a productive way and help them regain social capital. If we can integrate the potential criminal into the community, reduce discrimination, and teach at-risk youth acceptable behavior patterns, we may reduce crime and gain productive citizens. Some state penal systems provide education from basic skills to college courses, provide counseling and therapy programs, and allow conjugal and family stays to help keep families together (U.S. Bureau of Justice Statistics 2003).

Sociologists help design programs and evaluate their effectiveness by researching whether the programs have met their goals and made a difference. For example, evidence shows that prison education programs reduce recidivism rates dramatically. Approximately 1 in 100 U.S. citizens are in prison (Science Daily 2011b). The three-year recidivism rate (those returning to prison within three years of release) is estimated at about 52%. Yet research studies show that education and job opportunities reduce that rate: Earning a GED (high school equivalency) cuts recidivism below 50%; an associate's degree reduces recidivism to only 13.7%, a bachelor's degree to 5.6%, and a master's degree to 0% recidivism (Pew Center on the States 2011). Data such as these cause many criminologists to think that other factors besides harsh punishments may be important in reducing crime rates.

Thinking Sociologically

Do you think changing the "cost-benefit" ratio so the costs of crime to the criminal are higher will deter crime, or are other policies or methods more effective in enticing nonviolent offenders to be responsible, contributing members of society? Why?

One of the dominant characteristics of modern society is social inequality, often an issue in criminal activity. Indeed, many of our social problems are rooted in issues of inequality. Extreme inequality may even be a threat to the deeper values and dreams of the society, especially ones that stress individualism and achievement. In the following three chapters, we look at three types of inequality: socioeconomic, ethnic or racial, and gender-based inequity.

What Have We Learned?

Perhaps the answers to some of the chapter's opening questions—what is deviance, why do people become deviant, and what should we do about deviance?—have now taken on new dimensions. Deviance has many possible explanations, and there are multiple interpretations about how it should be handled. Deviance and crime are issues for any society, for they can be real threats to stability, safety, and sense of fairness that undermine the social structure. The criminal justice system tends to be a conservative force in society and is often championed by the "haves" of society because of its focus on ensuring social conformity. Still, there may be positive aspects of deviance for any society, from uniting society against deviant behavior to providing creative new ways to solve problems.

Key Points:

- Deviance—the violation of social norms, including those that are formal laws—is a complex behavior that has both positive and negative consequences for individuals and for society. (See pp. 142–145.)

- Deviance is often misunderstood because of simplistic and popular misconceptions. (See pp. 145–146.)

- Many theories try to explain deviance—rational choice and social control and symbolic interaction's anomie and labeling theories at the micro level, along with macro-level structural explanations: structural-functional theory's differential association and strain theory, and conflict and feminist theory. (See pp. 146–154.)

- Many of the formal organizations concerned with crime (e.g., the FBI and the media) focus on crimes involving individuals—predatory crimes, crimes without victims, and hate crimes—but the focus on these crimes may blind us to crimes that actually are more harmful and more costly. (See pp. 154–157.)

- At the meso level, organized and occupational crimes may cost billions of dollars and create great risk to thousands of lives. Occupational crime may be against the company, employees, customers, or the public. (See pp. 157–159.)

- At the macro level, national governments sometimes commit state-organized crimes, sometimes in violation of their own laws or in violation of international laws. These crimes may be directed against their own citizens (usually minorities) or people from other countries. (See pp. 159–161.)

- Also at the macro level, some crimes are facilitated by global networks and by global inequities of power and wealth. (See pp. 161–162.)

- Controlling crime has generated many policy debates, from the use of prisons to the death penalty and even to alternative approaches to control of deviance. (See pp. 162–168.)

Discussion Questions

1. List five acts that were once considered deviant but are now considered acceptable or even courageous. Have you ever committed a deviant act because you believed it was the moral thing to do? If yes, please explain why. If not, in what sort of situation might you consider carrying out a deviant act?

2. Have you ever been labeled deviant? Why or why not? How does your social class, level of education, gender, race or ethnicity, and nation of origin impact the chances you will be considered deviant in your country?

3. Which of the following theories of deviance described in the chapter—rational choice, differential association, labeling theory, anomie and social disorganization, strain theory, and conflict theory—best explain the increase in cheating among college students? Why?

4. Why is occupational crime not given as much attention as violent crime? What are some examples of occupational crimes that hurt millions of Americans every day? What would you suggest policy makers do to curb these crimes?

5. How do conflict theorists explain the demographic makeup of prisoners in the U.S. prison system? Do you agree with their explanation? Why or why not?

6. How can social capital help keep people out of prison and help former prisoners avoid returning to prison? How will your social capital help you conform (or not) to the norms of society?

Contributing to Our Social World: What Can We Do?

At the Local Level

- *LGBT groups* support students who are lesbian, gay, bisexual, and/or transgender. The Consortium of Higher Education LGBT Resource Professionals, a national organization of college and university groups, maintains a website at www.lgbtcampus.org. Regardless of your own sexual identity/orientation, consider contacting your campus LGBT group, attending meetings, and participating in its support and public education activities.

- *Boys and Girls Clubs* provide local programs and services to promote healthy development by instilling a sense of competence, usefulness, belonging, and influence in young people. Organizations for youth like Boys and Girls Clubs need interns and volunteers to provide role models for youth. Consider volunteering to help children with homework or activities. You can find a club near you by going to www.bgca.org/whoweare/Pages/FindaClub.aspx.

At the Organizational or Institutional Level

The extensive and rapidly growing *criminal justice system* in the United States focuses on crime prevention, law enforcement, corrections, and rehabilitation. Identify the aspect of the system that interests you most and, using faculty and community contacts, select an appropriate organization for volunteer work, an internship, or a job.

- *Criminal courts* play a central role in the administration of criminal justice, and trials are often open to the public. Attending a trial and/or contacting a judge or magistrate could provide a good introduction to the court system and some of the people who work within it.

- *Crime prevention programs* are designed to reduce crime. Information can be found from the National Crime Prevention Council at www.ncpc.org/programs. In order to obtain a better understanding as to what types of crime prevention programs are most effective, go to the Center for the Study and Prevention of Violence's (CSPV) Blueprints for Healthy Youth Development website at www.colorado.edu/cspv/blueprints.

At the National and Global Levels

- *The Polaris Project* works to reduce global trafficking in women and children (www.polarisproject.org). Volunteers participate in letter-writing campaigns, support antitrafficking legislation, and conduct research on the problem.

Visit **www.sagepub.com/oswcondensed3e** for online activities, sample tests, and other helpful information. Select "Chapter 6: Deviance and Social Control" for chapter-specific activities.

PART III

Inequality

Why are you affluent, while others in your sociology class are poor—or vice versa? Why do some people rise to the top of society with wealth, power, and prestige at their fingertips and others languish near the bottom? Does ethnicity, race, or gender affect your position in society? The focus of the next three chapters is inequality, the process of stratification through which some people "make it" and others do not. At the very bottom of the human hierarchy are those starving and diseased world citizens who have no hope of survival for themselves or their families. This compares with corporate executives, bankers, and some world politicians or royalty who have billions of dollars at their disposal.

Social inequality is one of the most important processes in modern societies, and the implications extend from the individual all the way to the global social network. Sometimes, the inequality is based on one's socioeconomic status, but the basis of differential treatment is often found in other characteristics: race, ethnicity, gender, sexual orientation, religion, or age. These differences often result in strong "we" versus "they" thinking. Patterns of inequality have implications for social interaction at the micro, meso, and macro levels of analysis. In this section, we do not try to cover all forms of inequality; rather, we illustrate the patterns by exploring issues of social class, race, ethnicity, and gender.

CHAPTER 7

Stratification

Rich and Famous—or Rags and Famine?

In rich countries, such as the United States, Canada, Japan, and Western European nations, we assume there are many economic opportunities, and we like to believe that anyone can become rich and famous. The reality, however, is that our social world is very brutal for many people, and what they experience is rags and famine.

Global Community

Society

National Organizations,
Institutions, and Ethnic Subcultures

Local Organizations
and Community

Me (and My
Rags or
Riches)

Micro: How I am regarded by my peers

Meso: Institutions support the
privilged. Ethnic subcultures often disadvantaged

Macro: The privileged control resources,
health care, economic markets, and tax rates

Macro: Rich and poor countries in global system

Think About It	
Micro: Me (and My Inner Circle)	Why do you buy what you buy, believe what you believe, and live where you live?
Micro: Local Community	Why are some people in your community rich and others poor?
Meso: National Institutions; Complex Organizations; Ethnic Groups	How do institutions—such as education, the family, religion, health, and the economy—help keep people in the class they were born into?
Macro: National Society	Why are some nations affluent and others impoverished?
Macro: Global Community	How does the fact that we live in a global environment affect you and your social position?

What's coming in this chapter?

The Importance of Social Stratification

Theoretical Explanations of Stratification

Individuals' Social Status: The Micro Level

Social Mobility: The Micro-Meso Connection

Major Stratification Systems: Macro-Level Analysis

Poverty: Determinants and Social Policy

National and Global Digital Divide: Macro-Level Stratification

Pomp and circumstance surrounded the April 29, 2011, royal wedding of Duke of Cambridge, William (heir to the British throne), and Catherine (Kate) Middleton, Duchess of Cambridge. All eyes in Britain and many eyes around the world were glued to TVs or lined the royal route to the palace. Few commoners will

Prince William and the Duchess of Cambridge, Kate Middleton, were married in 2011 in Westminster Abbey with all the trappings of British royalty. They are in line to inherit the throne of England.

Lives of the Rich

experience this lifestyle. The royal couple was thrust into the limelight again with the birth of their son and the next heir to the throne—His Royal Highness George Alexander Louis—on July 22, 2013.

Not just anyone can belong to a royal family. One must be born as royalty or marry into it. Members of royal families—such as Prince William and Prince Harry of Britain—grow up in a world of the privileged: wealth, prestige, and access to power. Their lifestyles include formal receptions, state affairs, horse races, polo games, royal hunts, state visits, and other social and state functions. The family has several elegant residences at its disposal. However, like most royalty, William, Harry, and now Kate also live within the confines of their elite status, with its strict expectations and limitations. They cannot show up for a beer at the local pub or associate freely with commoners, and their family problems or casual antics are subject matter for front pages of tabloids, as seen in antics of Pippa Middleton (Kate's sister) in a trip to Paris with friends that thrilled the paparazzi and dismayed the royal household. In today's world, some royalty are figureheads with little political power; others—such as the Ashanti chiefs in West Africa, King Bhumibol Adulyadej of Thailand, and Emperor Akihito in Japan—have great influence in state affairs.

While there is no official royalty in the United States, in Newport, Rhode Island, spacious mansions are nestled along the coast, with tall-masted sailboats at the docks. These are the summer homes of the U.S. aristocracy. Members of this class have an elegant social life, engage in elite sports such as fencing and polo, patronize the arts, and are influential behind the scenes in business and politics.

On the other hand, hidden from the public eye in each country are people with no known names and no swank addresses; some have no address at all. We catch glimpses of their plight through vivid media portrayals, such as those of refugees in Darfur, Sudan, and of impoverished victims of Hurricane Katrina in 2005 along the U.S. Gulf of Mexico coast, and through news stories of famines occurring in Somalia and other poor countries. The earthquake and tsunami in Japan in March 2011 affected people from all socioeconomic levels, but many poor and working-class people lived in more vulnerable

Newport, Rhode Island, has long been one of the most affluent cities in North America, a community where mansions and yachts line the seacoast.

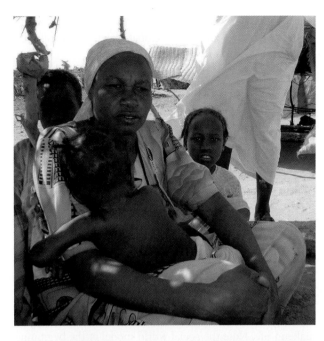

Poor people around the world find shelter wherever they can. A woman and her children displaced by war sit beneath a temporary shelter at a refugee camp in South Darfur. Even in affluent North America, some people are homeless and spend nights on sidewalks, in parks, or in homeless shelters.

areas where floods were more likely. That quake triggered 35-foot waves that left 16,447 people dead and 4,666 missing. Most victims were people who lived in poverty (Diep 2011; Vervaeck and Daniell 2011).

Economic hard times have pushed many lower-income people from their rural homes to cities in hopes of finding jobs. However, with few jobs for unskilled and semiskilled workers in today's postindustrial service economies, many of the poor are left behind and homeless. They live in abandoned buildings or sleep in unlocked autos, on park benches, under bridges, on beaches, or anywhere they can stretch out and hope not to be attacked or harassed. Beggars stake out spots on city sidewalks, hoping citizens and tourists will give them a handout. In the United States, cities such as Houston, Texas; Los Angeles; Washington, D.C.; and New York try to cope with the homeless by setting up sanitary facilities and temporary shelters, especially in bad weather. Cities rely on religious and civic organizations such as churches and the Salvation Army to run soup kitchens.

In some areas of the world, such as India and sub-Saharan Africa, the situation is much more desperate, and many families are starving. At daybreak, a cattle cart traverses the city of Kolkata (Calcutta), India, picking up bodies of diseased and starved homeless people who have died on the streets during the night. Mother Teresa, who won the Nobel Peace Prize for her work with those in dire poverty, established a home in India where these people could die with dignity. She also founded an orphanage for children who would otherwise wander the streets begging or die. These efforts are noble but only a drop in the world bucket of misery.

Of the 1.9 billion children in the world, 2.2 million mostly from Global South countries die every year (6,000 a day) from malnutrition, diseases related to unsafe water,

poor sanitation, and inadequate health care. According to a 2012 report on urban children, 1 in 3 city dwellers live in a slum, but that ratio is as high as 6 in 10 in Africa (UN News Centre 2012). These urban children grow up in poverty, with lack of electricity, clean water, education, sanitation, health care, or adequate food. They die of preventable diseases. These humans are at the bottom of the social hierarchy.

This chapter discusses (a) why stratification is important, (b) why people are rich or poor (stratification systems), (c) the importance and consequences of social rankings for individuals, (d) whether one can change social class positions (social mobility), (e) characteristics of major

Class Structure

stratification systems, (f) poverty and social policies to address problems, and (g) the global digital divide between rich and poor countries.

The Importance of Social Stratification

Consider your own social ranking in your community and society. You were born into a family that holds a position in society—upper, middle, or lower class. The position of your family influences the neighborhood in which you live and where you shop, go to school, and attend religious services. Most likely, you and your family carry out the tasks of daily living in your community with others of similar position. Your position in the stratification system affects the opportunities available to you and the choices you make in life. Note the social world model at the beginning of the chapter provides a visual image of the social world and socioeconomic stratification. The stratification process affects everything from individuals' social rankings at the micro level of analysis to positions of countries in the global system at the macro level.

Social stratification *refers to how individuals and groups are layered or ranked in society according to how many valued resources they possess.* Stratification is an ongoing process of sorting people into different levels of access to resources, with the sorting legitimated by cultural beliefs about why the inequality is justifiable. This chapter focuses on socioeconomic stratification, and subsequent chapters examine ethnic and gender stratification.

Three main assumptions underlie the concept of stratification: (a) people are divided into ranked categories; (b) there is an unequal distribution of things people want and need, meaning that some members of society possess more valued resources and others possess less; and (c) each society determines what it considers to be valued resources. In an agricultural society, members are ranked according to how much land or how many animals they own. In an industrial society, age, occupational position, and income are three of the criteria for ranking. Most Japanese associate old age with wisdom, honor, and high rank, whereas Americans often admire and offer high status to people for their youthful vigor and beauty. In postindustrial information societies knowledge of technology is key to rankings, and this usually favors the young.

What members of each society value and the criteria they use to rank other members depend on events in the society's history, its geographic location, its level of development in the world, its political philosophy, and the decisions of those in power. Powerful individuals are more likely to get the best positions, the most desirable mates, and the greatest opportunities. They may have power because of birth status, personality characteristics, age, physical attractiveness, education, intelligence, wealth, race, family background, occupation, religion, or ethnic group—whatever the basis for power is in that particular society. Those with power have advantages that perpetuate their power, and they try to hold onto those advantages through laws, custom, power, or ideology.

The social world model at the beginning of the chapter provides a visual image of socioeconomic stratification. The stratification process affects everything from individuals' social rankings at the micro level of analysis to positions of countries in the global system at the macro level.

Micro-Level Prestige and Influence

Remember how some of your peers on the playground were given more respect than others? Their high regard may have come from belonging to a prestigious family, having a dynamic or domineering personality, or owning symbols that distinguished them—"cool" clothing or shoes, a desirable bicycle, expensive toys, or a fancy car. This is stratification as children experience it at its beginning stage.

Property, power, and prestige are accorded to those individuals who have *cultural capital* (knowledge and access to important information in the society) and *social capital* (networks with others who have influence). Individual qualities such as leadership, personality, sense of humor, self-confidence, quick-wittedness, physical attractiveness, or ascribed characteristics—such as gender or ethnicity or age—influence cultural and social capital.

Even the sports one plays—such as polo—are greatly influenced by social class and convey different kinds of social and cultural capital. Polo clearly requires a good deal of economic capital in order to play.

Meso-Level Access to Resources

Often, our individual status in the society is shaped by our access to resources available through meso-level organizations and institutions. Our status is learned and reinforced in the family through the socialization process. Then we move on to learn grammar and manners that affect our success in school. Educational organizations treat children differently according to their social status, and our religious affiliation is likely to reflect our social status as well. Political systems, including laws, the courts, and police, reinforce the stratification system. Access to health care often depends on one's position in the stratification system. Our position and connections in organizations have a profound impact on how we experience life and how we interact with other individuals and groups.

Macro-Level Factors Influencing Stratification

The economic system, which includes the occupational structure, level of technology, and distribution of wealth in a society, is often the basis for stratification. Haiti, located on the island of Hispaniola in the Caribbean, is the poorest country in the Western Hemisphere and one of the poorest countries in the world, with little technology, few resources, ineffective government, and an occupational structure based largely on subsistence farming. Even its forest resources are almost gone as desperately poor people cut down the last trees for firewood and shelters, leaving the land to erode (Diamond 2005). The economy is in a downward cycle, resulting in many already poor people still more destitute and on the lowest rungs of the world's stratification system. Adding to the economic woes in Haiti, people faced further misery brought about by the 2010 earthquake and floods; people were driven from what meager shelters they had, and in addition faced a cholera epidemic. The economic position and geographic location of nations such as Haiti affect the opportunities available to individuals in those societies. There are simply no opportunities for most Haitians to get ahead. Thus, macro-level factors can shape the opportunity structure and distribution of resources to individuals.

One problem for Haiti is that it has few of the resources that many other countries in the global system take for granted—a strong educational system, well-paying jobs in a vibrant economy, productive land, an ample supply of water, money to pay workers, and access to the most efficient and powerful technology and resources wanted by the world community. Almost all societies stratify members, and societies themselves are stratified in the world system, so each individual and nation experiences the world in unique ways related to its position. Stratification

Look at all those forks and knives. Some people know what to do with each of them! Knowing which fork or knife to use for each course of a meal could influence someone's acceptance into elite society or chances of success on a job interview for certain kinds of positions.

is one of the most powerful forces that we experience, but we are seldom conscious of how it works or how pervasive it is in our lives. This is the driving question sociologists ask when developing theories of stratification: How does it work?

Thinking Sociologically

Place yourself in the center of the social world model. Working outward from micro-level interactions toward the meso-level institutions and the macro-level global stratification system, indicate what has influenced where you fall in the stratification system.

Theoretical Explanations of Stratification

Why is the distribution of resources so uneven? Is unequal distribution normal, inevitable, or healthy for society? Sociologists have developed explanations—theories that help explain stratification. Recall that theories provide a framework for asking questions to be studied. Just as your interpretation of a question may differ from your friends' ideas, sociologists have developed different explanations

Global Banking

for stratification and tested these with research data. These explanations of social rankings range from individual micro-level to national and global macro-level theories.

Micro-Level Theory

Our now familiar theories that relate to the micro level help us again, this time to understand differences between individuals in the stratification hierarchy.

Symbolic Interaction

Most of us have been at a social gathering, perhaps at a swank country club or in a local bar, where we felt out of place. Each social group has norms that members learn through the socialization process. These norms are recognized within that group and can make clueless outsiders feel like space aliens. People learn what is expected in their groups—family, peer group, social class—through interaction with others. For instance, children are rewarded or punished for behaviors appropriate or inappropriate to their social position. This process transmits and perpetuates our positions in the social stratification system. Learning our social position means learning values, speech patterns, consumption habits, appropriate group memberships (including religious affiliation), and even our self-concept. In this way, children's home experiences and education help reproduce the social class systems (Ballantine and Hammack 2012). It also provides us with the cultural capital we carry into our social positions.

Cultural capital *refers to the language patterns, values, experiences, and knowledge that children learn at home and bring with them to school.* Schools place children into courses and academic groups, influenced in part by the labels children receive due to their cultural capital. Home environments develop cultural capital of children. Some home environments teach children to obey rules and authority, and to develop skills repairing houses and cars. Other families teach children by expanding vocabularies; developing good grammar; experiencing concerts, art, and theater; visiting historical sites; providing reading materials; and modeling engagement with reading. The higher-class parents tend to stress thinking skills as opposed to simply learning to obey authority figures. The result of this learning at home is that all children attain cultural capital, but children from the middle and upper classes or higher castes are more likely to get the best education, setting them up to be future leaders with better life chances. In this way, children's home experiences and education help *reproduce the social class systems*, that is, to perpetuate the family's social class position in society (Ballantine and Hammack 2012).

Symbols often represent social positions. Clothing, for example, sets up some people as special and privileged.

In India, many people must bathe every day in public in whatever water supply they can find. Even many people with homes would not have their own water supply. Privacy for one's cleanliness and grooming is a symbol of privilege for the affluent.

In the 1960s, wearing blue jeans was a radical act by college students to reject status differences—showing solidarity with and support for the working class. Today, the situation has changed, as many young people wear expensive designer jeans that low-income people cannot afford. Drinking wine rather than beer, driving a Jaguar rather than a less expensive set of wheels, and living in a home that has six or eight bedrooms and 5,000-plus square feet is an expression of *conspicuous consumption*—displaying goods in a way that others will notice and that will presumably earn the owner respect (Veblen 1902). Thus, purchased products become symbols that are intended to define the person as someone of high status.

In most of the Global North, one symbol of middle-class "decency" is the right to bathe and do one's grooming in privacy. Indeed, many young people in the United States expect to have their own bedrooms and expect no interruptions when sprucing up for the day. Homeless people in the United States do not have this luxury, and in India, bathing on the streets is not uncommon. So, even privacy is a symbol of affluence.

Rational Choice Theory

As discussed in previous chapters, rational choice theorists focus on individuals and the way they make decisions regarding their own self-interest. From this view, people are always making decisions based on their perception of costs and benefits. Some people evaluate potential benefits with a view to the long term. They are willing to endure short-term expense or "pain" if the long-term gains are substantial. In order to take this view, one needs a sense of *delayed gratification*—delaying rewards or benefits until a later time. People who are willing or in a position to do this—living austerely now in order to experience prosperity later—may be more likely to have upward mobility and to experience greater affluence at a later time. While your friend from high school may have a job and drive a nicer car than you can afford, you may be building debts and living in a drab dormitory in hopes of a better future. Thus, rational choice theorists would focus on how our personal choices influence our place in the social system. The idea is that one's socioeconomic position is shaped largely by individual decisions.

In high school, many college prep students make decisions to become involved in athletic programs, the Spanish Club, leadership roles in National Honor Society, or the junior prom committee because they want to list those involvements on college applications. They commit effort now—sometimes in activities that they care little about—in hopes of having a payoff in scholarships or even just admission to the college of their choice. Those same students become discouraged with classmates who will not help with the prom decorations or with building the junior class float. However, for young people whose parents have never gone to college, and who spend time at the local pool hall or bowling alley where they might meet people who could help them get a job in the local factory, spending time decorating a float makes no sense. Thus, the way one evaluates costs and benefits may actually be influenced by the social position one already holds.

Meso- and Macro-Level Theories

Micro-level theories help us understand how individuals learn and live their positions in society. Next, we consider theories that examine the larger social structures, processes, and forces that affect stratification and inequality: structural-functional and various forms of conflict theory.

Structural-Functional Theory

Structural-functionalists (sometimes simply called functionalists) view stratification within societies as an inevitable—and probably necessary—part of the social world. The stratification system provides each individual with a place or position in the social world and motivates individuals to carry out their roles. Societies survive by having an organized system into which each individual is born, where each is raised and where each contributes some part to the maintenance of the society.

The basic elements of the structural-functional theory of stratification were explained by Kingsley Davis and Wilbert Moore, and their work still provides the main ideas of the theory today. Focusing on stratification by considering different occupations and how they are rewarded, Davis and Moore argue the following:

1. *Value of positions:* Positions in society are neither equally valued nor equally pleasant to perform. Some positions—such as physicians—are more highly technical and valued because people feel they are very important to society and the public is dependent on this expertise. Therefore, societies must motivate talented individuals to prepare for and occupy the most important and difficult positions, such as being physicians.

2. *Preparation requires talent, time, and money:* To motivate talented individuals to make the sacrifices necessary to prepare for and assume difficult positions such as becoming a physician, differential rewards of income, prestige, power, or other valued goods must be offered. Thus, a doctor receives high income, prestige, and power as incentives.

3. *Unequal distribution of rewards:* The differences in rewards such as pay lead to the unequal distribution of resources for occupations in society. Some people get richer. Therefore, stratification is inevitable. The unequal distribution of status and wealth in society motivates individuals to fill necessary positions—such as willingness to undertake the stress of being chief executive officer of a corporation in a highly competitive field. (Davis and Moore 1945)

In the mid-20th century, functional theory provided sociologists with a valuable framework for studying stratification, but things do change. In the 21st century, new criteria such as controlling information and access to information systems have become important for determining wealth and status, making scientists and technicians a new class of elites. The society also experiences conflict over distribution of resources that functionalism does not fully explain (Tumin 1953).

Conflict Theory

Conflict theorists see stratification as the outcome of struggles for dominance and scarce resources, with some individuals in society taking advantage of others. Individuals and groups act in their own self-interest by trying to exploit others, leading inevitably to a struggle between those who have advantages and want to keep them and those who want a larger share of the pie.

Conflict theory developed in a time of massive economic transformation. With the end of the feudal system, economic displacement of peasants, and the rise of urban factories as major employers, a tremendous gap between

Class Consciousness

the rich and the poor evolved. This prompted theorists to ask several basic questions related to stratification: (a) How do societies produce necessities—food, clothing, shelter? (b) How are relationships between rich and poor people shaped by this process? and (c) How do many people become alienated in their routine, dull jobs in which they have little involvement and no investment in the end product?

Karl Marx (1818–1883), considered the father of conflict theory, lived during this time of industrial transformation. Marx described four possible ways to distribute wealth, according to (a) what each person needs, (b) what each person wants, (c) what each person earns, or (d) what each person can take. It was this fourth way, Marx believed, that was dominant in competitive capitalist societies (Cuzzort and King 2002; Marx and Engels 1955).

Marx viewed the stratification structure as composed of two major economically based social classes: the haves and the have-nots. The haves consisted of the capitalist bourgeoisie, whereas the have-nots were made up of the working-class proletariat. Individuals in the same social class had similar lifestyles, shared ideologies, and held common outlooks on social life. The struggle over resources between haves and have-nots is the cause of conflict (Hurst 2013).

The haves control what Marx called the means of production—money, materials, and factories (Marx [1844] 1964). The haves dominate because the lower-class have-nots cannot accumulate enough money to change their positions. The norms and values of the haves dominate the society because of their power and ability to make the distribution of resources seem "fair" and justified. Laws, religious beliefs, educational systems, political structures and policies, and police or military force ensure continued control by the haves. This keeps the have-nots from understanding their own self-interests and is why working-class people often support politicians whose policies really favor the rich 1%. The unorganized lower classes can be exploited as long as they do not develop a *class consciousness*—a shared awareness of their poor status. Marx contended that, with the help of intellectuals who believed in the injustice of the exploited poor, the working class would develop a class consciousness, rise up, and overthrow the haves, culminating in a classless society in which wealth would be shared (Marx and Engels 1955).

Thinking Sociologically

How can conflict theory help us understand the uprisings, led primarily by youth, in Egypt, Libya, Syria, and other Middle Eastern and North African countries? Can it help us understand the Occupy Wall Street protests? Explain.

Selena Gomez was one of the Glamour Women of the Year in 2012. Although she is just 20 and has little education, she is paid millions of dollars each year to entertain the public with acting and singing. Meanwhile the public school teacher in the bottom photo would take 30 years of teaching hundreds of children to read before her total cumulative income for her entire career would add up to $1 million.

Underclass

Unlike the structural-functionalists, then, conflict theorists maintain that money and other rewards are not necessarily given to those in the most important positions in the society. Can we argue that a rock star or a baseball player is more necessary for the survival of society than a teacher or a police officer? Yet the pay differential is tremendous.

Not all of Karl Marx's predictions have come true. However, some developments have moved toward wider distribution of the resources. Labor unions arose to unite and represent the working class and put its members in a more powerful position vis-à-vis the capitalists, manager and technician positions emerged to create a large middle class, some companies moved to employee ownership, and workers gained legal protection from government legislative bodies in most industrial countries (Dahrendorf 1959). Still, no truly classless societies have developed, in part because those in power protect their positions, perpetuating class distinctions.

Even societies that claim to be classless, such as China, have privileged classes and poor peasants. In recent years, the Chinese government has allowed more private ownership of shops, businesses, and other entrepreneurial efforts, motivating many Chinese citizens to work long hours at their private businesses to "get ahead." The only classless societies are a few small hunter-gatherer groups that have no extra resources that would allow some members to accumulate wealth and rise in economic status.

Some theorists criticize Marx for his focus on only the economic system, pointing out that noneconomic factors enter into the stratification struggle as well. Max Weber (1864–1920), an influential theorist, amended Marx's theory. He agreed with Marx that group conflict is inevitable, that economics is one of the key factors in stratification systems, and that those in power try to perpetuate their positions. However, he added two other influential factors that he argued determine stratification in modern industrial societies: power and prestige. Sometimes, these are identified as the "three Ps"—property, power, and prestige. Recent theorists suggest that using the three Ps, we can identify five classes—capitalists, managers, small business owners or the petty bourgeoisie, workers, and the underclass—rather than just haves and have-nots. *Capitalists* own the means of production, and they purchase and control the labor of others. *Managers* sell their labor to capitalists and manage the labor of others for the capitalists. The *petty bourgeoisie,* such as small shop or business owners, own some means of production but control little labor of others; nevertheless, they have modest prestige, power, and property (Sernau 2010). *Workers* sell their labor to capitalists and are low in all three Ps. The *underclass* has virtually no property, power, or prestige.

In the modern world, as businesses become international and managerial occupations continue to grow, conflict theorists argue that workers are still exploited but in different ways. Owners and chief executive officers (CEOs) get more income than many analysts feel is warranted by their responsibilities and greater education. For example, the CEO of Oracle received $84.5 million in 2009 (Barr and Goldman 2010). Despite the severe recession and unemployment at the time, executives at the 500 biggest companies in the United States received a collective 16% pay raise in 2010, amounting to $5.2 billion. These figures contrast with average U.S. workers' raise of 3% (DeCarlo 2012).

Moreover, the labor that produces our clothes, cell phones, digital cameras, televisions, and other products is increasingly provided by impoverished people around the world working for low wages at multinational corporations (Bonacich and Wilson 2005). In rich countries, service providers receive low wages at fast-food chains and box stores such as Walmart (Ehrenreich 2001, 2005). Conflict theorists contend that multinational corporations are not really bringing opportunity to poor countries, but exploiting them to enhance the wealth of the already-wealthy (Wallerstein 2004).

The Evolutionary Theory of Stratification: A Synthesis

Evolutionary theory borrows assumptions from both structural-functional and conflict theories in an attempt to determine how scarce resources are distributed and how that distribution results in stratification (Lenski 1966; Nolan and Lenski 2010). The basic ideas are as follows: (a) To survive, people must cooperate; (b) despite this, conflicts of interest occur over important decisions that benefit one individual or group over another; (c) valued items such as money and status are always in demand and in short supply; (d) there is likely to be a struggle over these scarce goods; and (e) customs or traditions in a society often prevail over rational criteria in determining distribution of scarce resources. After the minimum survival needs of both individuals and the society are met, power determines who gets the surplus: prestige, luxury living, the best health care, and so forth. Lenski believes that privileges (including wealth) flow from having power, and prestige usually results from having access to both power and privilege (Hurst 2013).

Lenski tested his theory by studying societies at different levels of technological development, ranging from simple to complex. He found that the degree of inequality increases with technology until it reaches the advanced industrial stage. For instance, in subsistence-level hunter-gatherer societies, little surplus is available, and everyone's needs are met to the extent possible. As surplus accumulates in agrarian societies, those who acquire power also control surpluses such as more land and servants, and they use this to benefit their friends and relations. However, even if laws are made by those in power, the powerful must share some of the wealth or fear being overthrown. Interestingly, when societies finally reach the advanced industrial stage there is less inequality. This happens because people in various social classes enjoy greater political participation and because more resources are available to be shared in the society.

Lenski's theory explains many different types of societies by synthesizing elements of both structural-functional and conflict theory (Lenski 1966; Nolan and Lenski 2010). For instance, evolutionary theory takes into consideration an idea shared by structural-functional and rational choice theorists—that talented individuals need to be motivated to make sacrifices. This produces motivated, competent, and well-educated people in the most important social statuses. The theory also recognizes exploitation leading to inequality, a factor that conflict theorists find in capitalist systems of stratification.

The reality is that while some inequality may be useful in highly complex societies, extraordinary amounts of inequality may undermine motivation and productivity. Upward mobility may seem so impossible that the most talented people do not necessarily get the most demanding and responsible jobs. So Nolan and Lenski conclude that the size of the inequality gaps in a society does matter (Nolan and Lenski 2010). Huge differentials in access to resources, they believe, are unhealthy to vigorous democratic societies.

The amount of inequality differs in societies, according to evolutionary theorists, because of different levels of technological development. Industrialization brings surplus wealth, a division of labor, advanced technology, and interdependence among members of a society. No longer can one control all the important knowledge, skills, or capital resources. This should eliminate the extreme gaps between haves and have-nots because resources would normally be more evenly distributed.

The symbolic interaction, structural-functional, conflict, and evolutionary theories provide different explanations for understanding stratification in modern societies. These theories are the basis for micro- and macro-level discussions of stratification. Our next step is to look at some factors that influence an individual's position in a stratification system and the ability to change that position.

Thinking Sociologically

Why is the income gap between rich and poor individuals currently increasing in the United States? How might conflict and functional theories each explain this pattern?

Individuals' Social Status: The Micro Level

You are among the world's elite. Less than 7% of the world has a college degree ("6.7% of World Has College Degree" 2010). However, that number is expanding rapidly as countries such as China provide higher education opportunities to more students to support their growing economies. In fact, enrollment of Chinese students in higher education has now surpassed the percentage enrolled in the United States (People's Daily Online 2011).

Because the demand for a college education far exceeds the opportunity in China, many Chinese college students are studying abroad, adding to their opportunities and enhancing China's knowledge of the world. In fact, Chinese students make up the largest number of international students studying in the United States—160,000 in 2012 (*Huffington Post* 2012b; Wong 2012).

Being able to afford the time and money for college is a luxury with little relevance to those struggling to survive each day. It is beyond the financial or personal resources of most people in the Global South. Considered in this global perspective, college students learn professional skills and have advantages that billions of other world citizens will never know or even imagine.

In the United States, access to higher education is greater than in many other countries because there are more levels of entry—including technical colleges, community colleges, large state universities, and private four-year colleges. However, with limited government help, most students must have financial resources to cover tuition and the cost of living. Many students do not realize that the prestige of the college they choose makes a difference in their future

For some people living in poverty, the standard of wealth is ownership of a single horse. The boys above travel to their village in Afghanistan, where they must work every day rather than going to school.

opportunities. Those students born into wealth can afford better preparation for entrance exams as well as tutors or courses to increase SAT or ACT scores. Some attend private prep schools and gain acceptance to prestigious colleges that open opportunities not available to those attending the typical state university or nonelite colleges (Persell 2005).

Ascribed characteristics, such as gender, can also affect one's chances for success in life. Embedded gender stratification systems may make it difficult for women to rise in the occupational hierarchy. Many Japanese women, for example, earn college degrees but leave employment after getting married and having children (Globe Women 2013). Issues of gender stratification are examined in more depth in Chapter 9, but they intersect with socioeconomic class and must be viewed as part of a larger pattern resulting in inequality in the social world.

Individual Life Chances

Life chances refer to one's opportunities based on both achieved and ascribed status in society. That you are in college, that you probably have health insurance and access to health care, and that you are likely to live into your late 70s or beyond, compared to people in some poor countries whose average life span is in the 40s, are factors directly related to your life chances. Let us consider several examples of how placement in organizations and institutions at the meso level affects individual experiences and has global ramifications.

Education

Although education is valued by most individuals, the cost of books, clothing, shoes, transportation, child care, and time taken from income-producing work may be an insurmountable barrier to attendance from grade school through college. Economically disadvantaged students in most countries are more likely to attend less prestigious and less expensive institutions if they attend high school or university at all. Globally speaking, girls are particularly disadvantaged (Lewis and Lockheed 2006).

One's level of education affects many aspects of life, not just income. The higher levels of education affect political, religious, and marital attitudes and behavior: The more active individuals are in political life, the more mainstream or conventional their religious affiliation will be, the more likely they are to marry into a family with both economic and social capital, the more stable the marriage will be, and the more likely they are to have good health.

Health, Social Conditions, and Life Expectancy

If you have a sore throat, you go to see your doctor. Yet, many people in the world will never see a doctor. Access to

health care requires doctors and medical facilities, money for transportation and treatment, access to child care, and released time from other tasks to get to a medical facility. The poor sometimes do not have these luxuries. By contrast, the affluent eat better food, are less exposed to polluted water and unhygienic conditions, and are able to pay for medical care and drugs when they do have ailing health. Even causes of death illustrate the differences between people at different places in the stratification hierarchy. For example, in poor Global South countries, shorter life expectancies and deaths, especially among children, are due to controllable infectious diseases such as cholera, typhoid, AIDS, tuberculosis, and other respiratory ailments. By contrast, in affluent countries, coronary heart disease, stroke, and lung cancer are the most common causes of death, and most deaths are of people older than the age of 65 (U.S. Census Bureau, Population Division, International Programs Center 2011). So whether considered locally or globally, access to health care resources makes a difference in life chances. To an extent, the chance to have a long and healthy life is a privilege of the elite. Again, globally speaking, if you are reading this book as part of a college course, you are part of the elite.

By studying Table 7.1 in the next "Engaging Sociology" feature, you can compare life expectancy with two other measures of life quality for the poorest and richest countries: the gross domestic product (GDP) per capita income—the average amount of money each person has per year—and the infant mortality rates (death rates for babies). Note that

People living in poverty around the world often get health care at clinics or emergency rooms, if they have access to care, where they wait for hours to see a health care provider as shown in this mother-child health clinic in Kisumu, Kenya.

Health and Class

Engaging Sociology

Life Expectancy, Per Capita Income, and Infant Mortality

Analyzing the meaning of data can provide an understanding of the health and well-being of citizens around the world. A country's basic statistics including life expectancy, per capita gross national product, and infant mortality tell researchers a great deal about its status.

Quantitative Data Analysis:

1. What questions do the data in Table 7.1 raise regarding differences in mortality and life expectancy rates around the world?

2. Considering what you know from this and previous chapters and from Table 7.1, what do you think are some differences in the lives of citizens in the richest and poorest countries?

Table 7.1 Life Expectancy, Per Capita Income, and Infant Mortality for Selected Poor and Rich Countries, 2012

Poor Countries	Life Expectancy (in years)	Infant Mortality (deaths per 1,000 births)	Per Capita GDP ($)	Rich Countries	Life Expectancy (in years)	Infant Mortality (deaths per 1,000 births)	Per Capita GDP ($)
Chad	48.7	93.6	1,900	Singapore	83.8	2.7	60,500
Afghanistan	49.7	121.6	1,000	Hong Kong	82.1	2.9	49,800
Zimbabwe	50.8	28.2	500	Australia	81.9	4.6	40,800
Somalia	50.8	103.7	600	France	81.5	3.7	35,600
Mozambique	52.0	76.9	1,100	Canada	81.5*	4.9*	41,100
Nigeria	52.0	74.3	800	Sweden	82.2	2.7	40,900
Zambia	52.6	64.6	1,600	Switzerland	81.2	4.0	43,900
Mali	53.0	109	1,100	Iceland	81.0	3.2	38,500
Niger	53.8	110.0	800	New Zealand	80.7	4.7	28,000
Ethiopia	56.6	75.3	1,100	United Kingdom	80.2	4.6	36,600
Liberia	57.4	72.4	500	United States	78.5**	6.0**	49,000

Source: World Factbook (2012b), (2012e) for life expectancy and infant mortality; World Factbook (2012d) for per capita income.

Note: Infant mortality is per 1,000 live births.

*Canada is 12th in life expectancy and 41st in infant mortality rates.

**United States is 50th in life expectancy and 49th in infant mortality rates.

as of this writing average life expectancy in poor countries is as low as 49.07 years, income is as low as $0 a year (many of the people in these populations, such as Kosovo, are subsistence farmers), and infant mortality is estimated to be as high as 119.41 deaths and as low as 1.81 deaths in the first year of life for every 1,000 births (World Factbook 2012a, 2013d, 2013e). Numbers for the richest countries are dramatically different.

The United States has much larger gaps between rich and poor people than do most other wealthy countries, resulting in higher poverty rates (more people at the bottom rungs of the stratification ladder).

Thinking Sociologically

What factors at the micro, meso, and macro levels affect your life expectancy and that of your family members?

Individual Lifestyles

Your individual **lifestyle** includes *your attitudes, values, beliefs, behavior patterns, and other aspects of your place in the*

Wealth

world, shaped by socialization. As individuals grow up, the behaviors and attitudes consistent with their culture and their family's status in society become internalized through the process of socialization. Lifestyle is not a simple matter of having money. Acquiring money—say, by winning a lottery—cannot buy a completely new lifestyle (Bourdieu and Passeron 1977). This is because values and behaviors are ingrained in our self-concept from childhood. A person may gain material possessions, but that does not mean she has the lifestyle of the upper-class rich and famous. Consider some examples of factors related to your individual lifestyle: attitudes toward achievement, political involvement, and religious membership.

Attitudes Toward Achievement

Attitudes differ by social status and are generally closely correlated with life chances. Motivation to get ahead and beliefs about what you can achieve are in part products of your upbringing and the opportunities you see as available to you. These attitudes differ greatly depending on the opportunity structure around you, including what your family and friends see as possible and desirable. Consider the situation of children from poor countries and poor families. Their primary concern may be to help put food on the family's table. Even attitudes toward primary and secondary education reflect the luxury and inaccessibility that schooling is for some children. In Global North countries, opportunity is available for most children to attend school through high school and beyond. However, some students do not learn to value achievement in school due to poor self-concepts, difficulty in school, peer pressures, lack of support from family members and poor role models, poor schools and teaching, language differences, cultural differences, and many other factors (Ballantine and Hammack 2012).

Religious Membership

Religious affiliation also correlates with social status variables of education, occupation, and income. For instance, in the United States, upper-class citizens are found disproportionately in Episcopalian, Unitarian, Presbyterian, and Jewish religious groups, whereas lower-class citizens are attracted to Nazarene, Southern Baptist, Jehovah's Witness, and other holiness and fundamentalist sects. Each religious group attracts members predominantly from one social class, as is illustrated in Chapter 11 in the section on religion. Those who attend the same religious group tend to share other values and attitudes about their lives and society, they tend to have different worship styles, and they have different ways of expressing religiosity. For example, people in higher socioeconomic statuses tend to know more about scripture and attend religious services more frequently, but those at the lower ends are more likely to pray daily (Roberts and Yamane 2012).

Political Behavior

What political preferences we hold and how we vote are also affected by several key variables: our orientation on issues of public policy; our assessment of the performance of government; and our evaluation of personal traits of the candidates. In addition, one's party identification and general ideological dispositions affect voting, and are in turn affected by social factors such as race, religion, region of the country, social class, gender, marital status, and age (Interuniversity Consortium for Political and Social Research 2011). Around the world, upper middle classes are most supportive of elite or procapitalist agendas because these agendas support their way of life, whereas lower- and working-class members are least supportive (E. Wright 2000). Generally, the lower the social class, the more likely people are to vote for liberal parties, and the higher the social status, the more likely people are to vote conservative on economic issues—consistent with protecting their wealth (Domhoff 2005; Kerbo 2008).

In the United States, members of the lower class tend to vote liberal on economic issues, favoring government intervention to improve economic conditions. However, those with lower levels of education and income vote conservatively on many social issues relating to minorities and civil liberties (e.g., rights for homosexuals, gay marriage, and abortion) (Gilbert 2011; Kerbo 2008). In the 2012 election, many voters had to make choices about economic policies they liked and whether those policies were more important than their preferences on some of the social issues.

Status Inconsistency

The reality is that some people experience high status on one trait, especially a trait that is achieved through education and hard work, but may experience low status in another area. For example, a professor may have high prestige but low income. Max Weber called this unevenness in one's social standing *status inconsistency*. Individuals who experience such status inconsistency, especially if they are treated as if their lowest ascribed status is the most important one, are likely to be very liberal and to experience discontent with the current system (Weber 1946).

As noted earlier, people tend to associate with others like themselves, perpetuating and reinforcing lifestyles. In fact, people often avoid contact with others whose lifestyles are outside their familiar and comfortable patterns. This desire for familiarity also means that most people remain in the same social class because they have learned the "subculture" and it is comfortable and familiar.

Life chances and lifestyles are deeply shaped by the type of stratification system that is prevalent in the nation. Such life experiences as hunger, the unnecessary early death of family members, or the pain of seeing one's child denied opportunities are all experienced at the micro level, but their causes are usually rooted in events and actions at other levels of the social world. This brings us to our next question: Can an individual change positions in a stratification system?

Thinking Sociologically

Describe your own lifestyle and life chances. How do these relate to your socialization experience and your family's position in the stratification system? What difference do they make in your life?

Social Mobility: The Micro-Meso Connection

The LeBron Jameses and Peyton Mannings of the world make millions of dollars—at least for the duration of their playing careers. For professional athletes, each hoop, goal, or

This young street basketball player slam-dunks his ball in a milk-crate hoop as he dreams of glory on the courts. Despite grand dreams by young minorities, few experience dramatic social mobility through sports.

touchdown throw is worth thousands of dollars. These riches give hope to those in rags that if they "play hard," they too may be on the court or field making millions. The problem is that the chances of making it big are so small that such hopes are some of the cruelest hoaxes faced by young African Americans and others in the lower or working class. Therefore, it is a false promise to think of sports as the road to opportunity (Dufur and Feinberg 2007; Edwards 2000). The chances of success or even of moving up a little in the social stratification system through sports are very small.

Those few minority athletes who do "make it big" and become models for young people experience "stacking," holding certain limited positions in a sport. When retired from playing, few black athletes rise in the administrative hierarchy of the sports of football and baseball, although basketball has a better record of hiring black coaches and managers. Thus, when young people put their hopes and energies into developing their muscles and physical skills, they may lose the possibility of moving up in the social class system, which requires developing their minds and their technical skills. Even those young players who make it into the National Basketball Association or other major leagues may have done so by leaving college after a single year. This thwarts their postathletic career opportunities.

The whole idea of changing one's social position in the stratification system is called social mobility. **Social mobility** refers to *the extent of individual movement up or down in the class system, changing one's social position in society—especially relative to one's parents* (Gilbert 2011). What is the likelihood that your status will be different from that of your parents over your lifetime? Will you start a successful business? Marry into wealth? Win the lottery? Experience downward mobility due to loss of a job, illness, or inability to complete your education? What factors at different levels of analysis might influence your chances of mobility? These are some of the questions addressed in this section and the next.

Four issues dominate the analysis of mobility: (a) types of social mobility, (b) methods of measuring social mobility, (c) factors that affect social mobility, and (d) whether there is a "land of opportunity" for those wishing to improve their lot in life.

Types of Social Mobility

Mobility can be up, down, or sideways, as described below. *Intergenerational mobility* refers to change in class status compared to one's parents' status, usually resulting from education and occupational attainment. If you are the first to go to college in your family and you become an engineer, this would represent intergenerational mobility. The amount of intergenerational mobility—that is, the number of children who move up or down in the social structure compared to where their parents are—measures the degree to which a society has an *open class system*. The more movement there is between classes, meaning that you could move up or down in comparison with your parents in the stratification system, the more open the class system is. This type of movement is not possible in many societies. If you change positions at the same level in the stratification system, say a postal service job to a police position, it is called *horizontal mobility*.

Intragenerational mobility (not to be confused with *intergenerational mobility*) refers to the change within a position in a single individual's life. For instance, if you begin your career as a teacher's aide and end it as a school superintendent, that is upward intragenerational mobility. However, mobility is not always up. *Vertical mobility* refers to movement up or down in the hierarchy and sometimes involves changing social classes. You may start your career as a waitress, go to college part-time, get a degree in engineering, and get a more prestigious and higher-paying job, resulting in upward mobility. Alternatively, you could lose a job and take one at a lower status, a reality for many when the economy is doing poorly. In the current global economic downturn, people at all levels of the occupational structure are experiencing layoffs and downward intragenerational mobility because they often have problems finding new positions at comparable levels and pay.

How Much Mobility Is There? Measures of Social Mobility

Can one move up in the class system? One traditional method of measuring mobility is to compare fathers with sons, and in more recent research with daughters. Surveys ask men about their occupations and those of their fathers or sons. Table 7.2 reflects data collected from U.S. fathers about their sons' and daughters' mobility.

Several conclusions can be derived from this table:

1. There is a high level of occupational inheritance—sons following fathers into jobs at the very same occupational level.

2. The higher the father's occupational level, the better the son's chances for occupational achievement.

3. There is also considerable movement up and down the occupational ladder from one generation to the next.

4. Sons are more likely to move up than down.

5. Daughters are even more likely to move up than sons. (Gilbert 2011)

Table 7.2 Outflow From Father's Occupation to Son's or Daughter's Occupation

	Son's Occupation (in percent) in Blue Daughter's Occupation (in percent) in Red					
	Upper-White Collar	**Lower-White Collar**	**Upper Manual**	**Lower Manual**	**Farm**	**Total**
Father's Occupation						
Upper White-Collar	42	31	12	15	1	100
	54	33	9	3	*	
Lower White-Collar	34	33	13	19	1	100
	49	34	11	6	*	
Upper Manual	20	20	29	29	2	100
	35	37	18	8	1	
Lower Manual	20	22	20	36	12	100
	32	39	19	9	1	
Farm	16	18	19	35	3	100
	34	28	22	14	2	
Total (N = 3,398)	27	25	19	27	1	100
	27	25	19	27	3	

Source: Gilbert (2011:131, 135).

Note: Rows but not columns add to 100%. For example, read across the row that begins with "lower manual" on far left to trace the sons of fathers who held unskilled "lower manual jobs." While 20% rose to upper-white-collar (professional or managerial) positions, the largest group (36%) followed their fathers into unskilled manual jobs.

Something for Nothing

Thinking Sociologically

Indicate where your father falls in the occupational categories in Table 7.2. Compare this with your intended occupation and likely social class position in a few years. What can you conclude about your chances for mobility?

Determining the mobility of women is more difficult because they often have lower-level positions and their mothers may not have worked full-time, but a conclusion that can be drawn is that both women's and men's occupational attainment is powerfully influenced by class origins.

Factors Affecting an Individual's Mobility

Why are some people successful at moving up the ladder while others lag behind? Mobility is driven by many factors, from your family's background to global economic variables. One's chances to move up depend on micro-level factors—one's family "cultural capital," socialization, personal characteristics, and education—and macro-level factors such as the occupational structure and economic status of countries, population changes, the numbers of people vying for similar positions, discrimination based on gender or ethnicity, and the global economic situation.

The study of mobility is complicated because these key variables are interrelated. Macro-level forces (e.g., the economy and occupational structure in a country) are related to meso-level factors (e.g., access to education and job opportunities) and micro-level factors (e.g., socialization, family background, and education level) (Blau and Duncan 1967). An individual's background accounts for nearly half of the factors affecting occupational attainment (Jencks 1979).

Family Background, Socialization, and Education

Our family background socializes us into certain behavior patterns, language usage, and occupational expectations (Sernau 2010). Let us consider language. Parents in professional families use three times as many different words at home as parents in low-income families. By the time the children of professional families are 3 years old, they have a vocabulary of about 1,100 words and typically use 297 different words per hour. Children in working-class families have a 700-word vocabulary and use 217 words per hour, while children from low-income families have 500 words accessible to them and use 149 per hour. These numbers represent a gap in the range of words they hear at home (Hart and Risley 2003).

Thinking Sociologically

How might differences in one's vocabulary affect one's success in school? How might an expanded vocabulary affect one's opportunities in life and impress a potential employer?

College is one expectation, if not requirement, for upward mobility in the Global North countries. Although not all those with a college degree are successful in finding a job and moving up the success ladder, few in Global North countries have a chance to be successful without a college degree (Lareau 2003). College education is the most important factor for high-income status, and the rewards of college degrees have increased. Those with degrees become richer than those without, largely because of new types of jobs in the computer information age. The demand is now for specialists who work with ideas, knowledge, and technology rather than manufacturing (Hurst 2013). We can see from Table 7.3 that most students in the United States with high ability from high-status families go to college, while high-ability students from low-status families go to college much less often (83% vs. 51%).

When we look at actual college degrees awarded, the pattern is more extreme, with diplomas going disproportionately to students in the top status groups (50%), compared to only 10% of students from the bottom half of income levels. If American society were truly a **meritocracy**, *positions would be allocated in a social group or organization according to individuals' abilities and credentials, as in level of education attained.* One would expect cognitive ability to be the most important variable, and that is spread across social classes (Gilbert 2011). Despite claims that the United States is a meritocracy, these data raise doubts about that assertion.

Even when a young person is admitted to a college or university, she or he may be at a disadvantage in the classroom and alienated from past social ties. The culture

Table 7.3   College Attendance by Social Class and Cognitive Ability (percent in college)

Cognitive Ability Quartile	Family Socioeconomic Status Quartile			
	Top	Third	Second	Lowest
Top	83	74	63	51
Second	69	51	42	33
Third	57	40	24	23
Lowest	35	20	13	13

Source: Gilbert (2011:149).

Money and Behavior

These men hold very different positions in society; one can offer his family more cultural capital to spend in influential positions and can provide more opportunities because of his education, family background, and networks with others in positions of influence. One of the two has a law degree.

of college is often the culture of the well-educated upper middle class, and everything from values to knowledge base to sense of humor may be different and uncomfortable. However, two-year community colleges can bridge the gap to four-year colleges, easing the transition. This alienation experienced at four-year colleges is explored in more detail in the next "Engaging Sociology" on pages 190–191.

Many poor people lack education and skills such as interviewing for jobs and obtaining recommendations needed to get or change jobs in the postindustrial occupational structure (Ehrenreich 2001, 2005; MacLeod 2008). Isolated from social networks in organizations, they lack contacts, or social capital, to help in the job search. The type of education system one attends also affects mobility. In Germany, Britain, France, and some other European countries, children are "streamed" (tracked) into either college preparatory courses or more general curricula, and the rest of their occupational experience usually reflects this early placement decision in school. In the United States, educational opportunities remain more open to those who can afford them—at least this is what is supposed to happen.

Economic Vitality and Shifting Jobs

The economic vitality of a country affects the chances for individual mobility, since there will be fewer positions at the top if the economy is stagnant. As agricultural work decreases and technology jobs increase, these changes in the composition and structure of occupations affect individual opportunity (Hurst 2013). Thus, macro-level factors such as a country's economy and its place in the global system shape employment chances of individuals. The global economic downturn that started in 2008 illustrates the vulnerability of both macro-level nations whose banks and companies are failing and micro-level individuals living in those nations who are losing their jobs.

Population Trends

The fertility rates, or number of children born at a given time, are a macro-level trend that influences the number of people who will be looking for jobs. The U.S. nationwide baby boom that occurred following World War II resulted in a flood of job applicants and downward intergenerational mobility for the many who could not find work comparable to their social class at birth. By contrast, the smaller group following the baby boomer generation had fewer competitors for entry-level jobs. Baby boomers hold many of the executive and leadership positions today, so promotion has been hard for the next cohort. As baby boomers retire, opportunities will open up, and mobility should increase.

Recession

Engaging Sociology

First-Generation College Students: Issues of Cultural Capital and Social Capital

Socioeconomic classes develop subcultures that can be quite different from each other, and when one changes subcultures, it can be confusing and alienating. College campuses provide an example. Generally they are dominated by middle-class cultures. Young people from blue-collar backgrounds and those who are first-generation college students often find themselves in a world as alien to them as another country. Students whose parents went to college are more likely to have "cultural or social capital" that helps them adjust and helps them to understand their professors who are generally part of the middle-class culture. Answer the following survey questions. How might your own cultural or social capital cause you to feel at home or alienated, privileged or disprivileged, hopeful or despairing?

A. Which of the following experiences were part of your childhood?

   ◊ Had a library of books (at least 50 adult books) at your childhood home
   ◊ Had a subscription to a newspaper that was delivered to the home
   ◊ Had news magazine subscriptions that came to the home (*Time, Newsweek, The Economist*)
   ◊ Listened to music as a family, including classical or instrumental music such as harp or flute
   ◊ Traveled to at least 20 other states or to at least 5 other countries.
   ◊ Took regular trips to the library
   ◊ Took regular trips to museums
   ◊ Attended movies
   ◊ Attended plays (theater productions)
   ◊ Attended concerts
   ◊ Played a musical instrument
   ◊ Took dance lessons
   ◊ Listened to National Public Radio (NPR)
   ◊ Watched PBS (Public Broadcasting Station) on television

B. Which of the following *relationships* were part of your childhood?

   ◊ My parents knew at least two influential people in my community on a first-name basis—such as the mayor, members of the city council, the superintendent of schools, members of the school board, the local county sheriff, the chief of police, the prosecuting attorney, the governor, and the district's representative to Congress.
   ◊ The regional leader of my religious group—church, temple, or mosque—knew and respected my family.
   ◊ My parents knew on a first-name basis at least three chief executive officers (CEOs) of corporations.
   ◊ When I entered new situations in high school, it was likely that my parents were known by the coaches, music directors, summer camp counselors/directors, or other authority figures who were "running the show."
   ◊ When I came to college, one or more professors and administrators at the college knew my parents, a sibling, or another family member.
   ◊ I have often interacted directly and effectively (in a nonadversarial way) with authority figures.

Engaging in Sociological Analysis:

1. If you experienced many of the items in Question A at home, you had fairly high cultural capital. If you marked most of the items in Question B, you had a lot of social capital. If you did not, you may find the culture of a college campus to be alien and even confusing. How well does your background match with the cultural capital of a college?

2. Which of the following makes a first-generation college student feel most alienated at your college and even within this sociology course: *economic* capital (money), *social* capital (networks with those who have resources), or *cultural* capital (knowledge of important aspects of the culture)? Why?

Source: Survey constructed in part using ideas from Morris and Grimes (1997).

Answer the three questions below and then read the sociological explanations.

1. Which of the following makes a first-generation college student feel most alienated at your college and even within this sociology course: *economic* capital (money), *social* capital (networks with those who have resources), or *cultural* capital (knowledge of important aspects of the culture)? Why?

2. What did "doing well" in school mean in your family? Did they stress education, and if so, how?

3. What did it mean within your family to be "independent" when you were in high school?

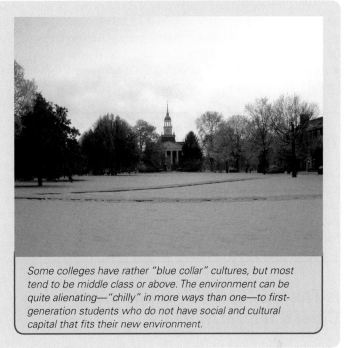

Some colleges have rather "blue collar" cultures, but most tend to be middle class or above. The environment can be quite alienating—"chilly" in more ways than one—to first-generation students who do not have social and cultural capital that fits their new environment.

Gender and Ethnicity

Many women and ethnic minority groups, locked in a cycle of poverty, dependence, and debt, have little chance of changing their status. Women in the U.S. workforce, for instance, are more likely than men to be in dead-end clerical and service positions with no opportunity for advancement. In the past three decades, the wage gap between women and men has narrowed, and women who are employed full time now earn 80% of what men earn compared to 60% in 1980 (Fitzpatrick 2010; U.S. Department of Labor 2011). African American women make 68% of what white men earn in comparable jobs (Fitzpatrick 2010). Table 7.4 shows the earnings for white males and the percentage of those earnings for other gender and ethnic groups.

Special circumstances such as war have often allowed women and others who were denied access to good jobs to get a "foot in the door" and actually enhance their upward mobility. Another factor affecting career success of women is that today in the United States more females than males are earning college degrees. Women represent 51 percent of the nation's PhDs, 67 percent of college graduates, and more than 70 percent of 2012 valedictorians. In addition, women run over 10 million businesses with combined annual sales of $1.1 trillion (DeBoskey 2012).

Some people experience privilege, whereas some experience disprivilege due to socioeconomic status, ethnicity, gender, or a combination of these. Be aware that various

Table 7.4 Median Annual Earnings by Race/Ethnicity and Sex

Race/Gender	Earnings	Wage Ratio
White men	$44,200	100.0%
White women	35,578	80.4
Black men	32,916	74.4
Black women	30,784	69.6
Hispanic men	29,120	65.9
Hispanic women	26,416	59.7
Gender wage gap		81.2%
All men	$42,848	
All women	34,788	

Source: U.S. Department of Labor, 2011.

forms of inequality intersect in many societies in highly complex ways.

The Interdependent Global Market and International Events

If the Chinese or Japanese stock markets hiccup, it sends ripples through world markets. If high-tech industries in Japan or Europe falter, North American companies in Silicon Valley, California, may go out of business, costing many professionals their lucrative positions. In ways such as these, the interdependent global economies affect national and local economies, and that affects individual families.

Whether individuals move from "rags to riches" is not determined solely by their personal ambition and work ethic. Mobility for the individual, a micro-level event, is linked to a variety of events at other levels of the social world, and one cannot assume that the unemployed individual is just lazy or incompetent.

Thinking Sociologically

Can you identify family members or friends who have lost jobs because of economic slowdowns at the meso or macro level or who have gotten jobs because of economic booms and opening opportunities? What changes have occurred in their mobility and social class?

Is There a "Land of Opportunity"? Cross-Cultural Mobility

Countless immigrants have sought better opportunities in new locations. Perhaps, your parents or ancestors did just this. The question for this section concerns your realistic chances for mobility: Do you have a better chance to improve your status in England, Japan, the United States, or some other country? The answer is not simple. If there is a land of opportunity where individuals can be assured of improving their economic and social position, it is not easy to identify, as many variables affect the opportunity structure. The reality of the "land of opportunity" depends on the historical period when immigrants first came to the country, the economic conditions, the attitudes toward foreigners when new immigrants arrive, immigrants' personal skills, and the newcomer's ability to blend into the new society.

During economic growth periods, many immigrants have found great opportunities for mobility in the United States and Europe. Early industrial tycoons in railroads, automobiles, steel, and other industries are examples of success stories. Today, fortunes are being made in the high-tech industries of China, India, and other countries, and in energy resources in Russia. The number of millionaires and billionaires in the world is increasing dramatically, yet this is still a very small percentage of the world's population. In 2010, there were 1,011 billionaires globally. The richest man was Carlos Slim Helú with $69 billion from América Movíl, a telecom company. Close behind was Bill Gates with $61 billion from Microsoft, and Warren Buffett with $47 billion from Berkshire Hathaway company (*Forbes* 2012). China is the dramatic success story, reaching an estimated 260 billionaires, including many women, in 2009, doubling the number in one year. At current growth rates it will soon top the list of countries with the most billionaires (France 24 International News 2009; Spero News 2009). Such wealth eludes most people who immigrate and must work multiple low-paying jobs just to feed their families and stay out of poverty.

Opportunities for upward mobility have changed significantly with globalization. Many manufacturing jobs in the global economy have moved from the Global North to the Global South to take advantage of cheap labor. This has reduced the number of unskilled and low-skilled jobs available in Global North countries. Multinational corporations look for the cheapest sources of labor in the Global South with low taxes, no labor unions, few regulations, and many workers needing jobs. This has drained away low-skilled jobs from the United States, making it even more essential to have advanced educational credentials (such as a diploma, a college degree, or a master's degree).

Why the changes in the job structure? The increase in international trade results in demand for high-tech products from the United States but fewer manufacturing jobs. New technologies and automation leave low-skilled workers in Global North countries without jobs. The minimum-wage and low-wage jobs are all that is available to lower-skilled workers, and labor unions with declining memberships and political clout have less influence on the wages and working conditions of the remaining manufacturing workers today (Gilbert 2011). High-tech positions are good news for those with college degrees and technical skills, but the replacement of laboring positions with service jobs in fast-food and box store chains (e.g., Walmart, Meijer, Home Depot, Lowe's) means a severe loss of genuine opportunity for living wages.

Although the new multinational industries springing up in Global South countries such as Malaysia, Thailand, and the Philippines provide opportunities for mobility to those of modest origins, much of the upward mobility in the world is taking place among those who come from small, highly educated families with individualistic achievement-oriented values and people who see education as a route to upward mobility (Featherman and Hauser 1978; Rothman 2005). They are positioned to take advantage of the changing occupational structure and high-tech jobs. As the gap between rich and poor individuals and countries widens, more individuals in the United States begin to move down rather than up in the stratification system.

Thinking Sociologically

What social factors in your society limit or enhance the likelihood of upward social mobility for you and your generation? Explain.

Major Stratification Systems: Macro-Level Analysis

Imagine being born into a society in which you have no choices or options in life because of your family background, age, sex, or ethnic group. You cannot select an occupation that interests you, you cannot choose your mate, and you cannot live in the part of town you choose. You see wealthy aristocrats parading their advantages and realize that this will never be possible for you. You can never own land or receive the education of your choice.

This situation is reality for millions of people in the world—they are born this way and will spend their lives in this plight. In **ascribed stratification systems**, *characteristics beyond the control of the individual—such as family background, age, sex, and race—determine one's position in society.* In contrast, **achieved stratification systems** allow individuals to earn positions through their ability, efforts, and choices. In an open class system it is possible to achieve a higher ranking by working hard, obtaining education, gaining power, or doing other things that are highly valued in that culture.

The futures of these Aboriginal boys in Australia are determined by their ethnic group and family of birth, making it unlikely that they will ever experience much affluence in Australian society.

Ascribed Status: Caste and Estate Systems

Caste systems are *the most rigid ascribed stratification systems. Individuals are born into a status, which they retain throughout life. That status is deeply imbedded in religious, political, and economic norms and institutions.* Caste members have predetermined occupational positions, marriage partners, residences, social associations, and prestige levels. A person's caste is easily recognized through clothing, speech patterns, family name and identity, skin color, or other distinguishing characteristics. From their earliest years, individuals learn their place in society through the process of socialization. To behave counter to caste prescriptions would be to go against religion and social custom and to risk not fitting into society. That can be a death sentence in some societies.

Religious ideas dictate that one's status after death (in Christian denominations) or one's next *reincarnation* or rebirth (in the Hindu tradition) also might be in jeopardy. Stability in Hindu societies is maintained in part by the belief that people can be reborn into a higher status in the next life if they fulfill expectations in their ascribed position in this life. Thus, believers in both religions work hard in hopes of attaining a better life after death or in the next

reincarnation. The institution of religion works together with the family, education, and economic and political institutions to shape (and sometimes reduce) both expectations and aspirations and to keep people in their prescribed places in caste systems.

The clearest example of a caste system is found in India. The Hindu religion holds that individuals are born into one of four *varna*, broad caste positions, or into a fifth group below the caste system, the *outcaste* group. The outcaste encompasses profoundly oppressed and broken people—"a people put aside"—referred to as untouchables, outcastes, *Chandalas* (a Hindu term), and *Dalits* (the name preferred by many "untouchables" themselves). Although the Indian Constitution of 1950 granted full social status to these citizens and a law passed in 1955 made discrimination against them punishable, deeply rooted traditions are difficult to change. Caste distinctions are still very prevalent, especially in rural areas, as seen in the discussion in the next "Sociology Around the World."

Estate systems are characterized by the concentration of economic and political power in the hands of a small minority of political-military elite, with the peasantry tied to the land (Rothman 2005). Based on ownership of land, the position one is born into, or military strength, estate systems are rigid as are caste systems in stratifying individuals. An individual's rank and legal rights are clearly spelled out, and arranged marriages and religion bolster the system. During the Middle Ages, knights defended the realms and the religion of the nobles. Behind every knight in shining armor were peasants, sweating in the fields and paying for the knights' food, armor, and campaigns. For farming the land owned by the nobility, peasants received protection against invading armies and enough of the produce to survive. Their life was often miserable. If the crops were poor, they ate little. In a good year, they might save enough to buy a small parcel of land. A very few were able to become independent in this fashion.

Estate systems existed in ancient Egypt, the Incan and Mayan civilizations, Europe, China, and Japan. Today, similar systems exist in some Central and South American, Asian, and African countries on large banana, coffee, cacao, and sugar plantations. Over time, development of a mercantile economy resulted in modifications in the early estate systems, and now peasants often work the land in exchange for the right to live there and receive a portion of the produce.

Achieved Status: Social Class Systems

Class systems *allow individuals the possibility to earn positions through their ability, efforts, and choices.* The system is supposedly completely open to social mobility and achievement based on merit, though we have already seen that there are many constraints on mobility. Still, the system has an ideal of meritocracy and does offer more mobility than do ascribed systems.

Members of the same social class have similar income, wealth, and economic position and they share styles of life, levels of education, culture, and patterns of social interaction. In a class system our life circumstances and social respect are based in large measure on what we achieve in our lives. Most of us are members of class-based stratification systems, and we take advantage of opportunities available to our social class. Our families, rich or poor, educated or unskilled, provide us with an initial social ranking and socialization experience. We tend to feel a kinship and sense of belonging with those in the same social class—our neighborhood and work group, our peers and friends. We think alike, share interests, and probably look up to the same people as a reference group. Our social class position is based on the three main factors determining positions in the stratification system: (1) property, (2) power, and (3) prestige.

This is the trio—the "three Ps"—that, according to Max Weber (1946, 1947), determines where individuals rank in relation to each other. By *property* (wealth), Weber refers to owning or controlling the means of production. *Power*, the ability to control others, includes not only the means of production but also the position one holds. *Prestige* involves the esteem and recognition one receives, based on wealth, position, or accomplishments. Table 7.5 on page 196 gives examples of households in the upper and lower social classes by illustrating the variables that determine a person's standing in the three areas of the stratification system.

Although these three dimensions of stratification are often found together, this is not always so. Recall the idea of *status inconsistency:* An individual can have a great deal of prestige yet not command much wealth; consider winners of the prestigious Nobel Peace Prize such as Wangari Maathai, a Kenyan environmentalist who won the prize for starting a movement to plant trees and for her political activism; Rigoberta Menchú Tum of Guatemala (see "Sociology Around the World" on page 73 in Chapter 3); or Betty Williams and Mairead Corrigan of Northern Ireland, founders of the Community of Peace People to find a peaceful end to their country's problems. None of them is rich, but each has made contributions to the world that brought universal prestige. Likewise, some people gain enormous wealth through crime or gambling, but this wealth may not be accompanied by respect or prestige (Weber 1946).

Compared with systems based on ascribed status, achieved status systems maintain that everyone is born with common legal status; everyone is equal before the law. In principle, all individuals can own property and choose their own occupations. However, in practice, most class systems pass privilege or poverty from one generation to the next. Individual upward or downward mobility is more difficult than the ideology invites people to believe.

The Property (Wealth) Factor

One's income, property, and total assets comprise one's **wealth**. These lie at the heart of class differences. The contrast between the splendor of aristocrats and royalty and the daily struggle for survival of those in poverty is an example of the differences extreme wealth creates. Another example is shown in the income distribution in the United States by quintiles (see Table 7.6 on page 196). In 2012, the median household income in the United States was $50,020, 7.8% less than it was when the economic downturn began in December 2007 (Safdar 2012). Likewise, the 2010 poverty rate was 15.1% of the population, up from 12.5% of the population in 2007 (World Hunger Education Service 2013a). Of children younger than 18, 22% live in poverty (World Hunger Education Service 2013a).

Thinking Sociologically

Explain the trends found in Table 7.6 on page 196. What evidence do you see of increased or decreased inequality?

Poverty

Sociology Around the World

The Outcastes of India

The Dalits—*sometimes called "untouchables"—are the most impoverished people in India and some of the most impoverished in the world. While they live in incredible hardship, they are beginning to mobilize and demand rights as citizens of India and the world.*

The village south of Madras (now known as Chennai) in the state of Tamil Nadu was on an isolated dirt road, one kilometer from the nearest town. It consisted of a group of mud and stick huts with banana leaf–thatched roofs. As our group of students arrived, the *Dalit* villagers lined the streets to greet us—and stare. Many had never seen Westerners. They played drums and danced for us and threw flower petals at our feet in traditional welcome.

Through our translator, we learned something of their way of life. The adults work in the fields long hours each day, plowing and planting with primitive implements, earning about 8 cents from the landowner, often not enough to pay for their daily bowl of rice. Occasionally, they catch a frog or bird to supplement their meal. In the morning, they drink rice gruel, and in the evening, they eat a bowl of rice with some spices. Women and children walk more than a kilometer to the water well—but the water is polluted during the dry season. There are no privies but the fields. As a result of poor sanitation, inadequate diet, and lack of health care, many people become ill and die from health problems that are easily cured in Western societies. For instance, lack of vitamin A, found in many fruits and vegetables to which they have little access, causes blindness in many village residents. Although the children have the right to go to the school in the closest village, many cannot do so because they have no transportation, shoes, or money for paper, pencils, and books. Also, the families need them to work in the fields alongside their parents or help care for younger siblings just to survive.

Many taboos rooted in tradition separate the *Dalits* from other Indians. For instance, they are forbidden to draw water from the village well, enter the village temple, or eat from dishes that might be used later by people of higher castes. The latter prohibition eliminates most dining at public establishments. About 95% are landless and earn a living below subsistence level.

Dalits who question these practices have been attacked and their houses burned. In one instance, 20 houses were burned on the birthday of B. R. Ambedkar, a leader in the *Dalit* rights movement. Official records distributed by the Human Rights Education Movement of India state that every hour, two *Dalits* are assaulted, three *Dalit* women are raped, two *Dalits* are murdered, and two *Dalit* houses are burned (Dalit Liberation Education Trust 1995; Thiagaraj 2007; K. Wilson 1993). Violence is used to control *Dalits* who try to uplift themselves and thus create threats to the social status and dominance of higher caste groups (Karthikeyan 2011). This group on the bottom rung of the stratification system has a long fight ahead to gain the rights that many of us take for granted.

A few *Dalits* have migrated to cities, where they blend in, and some of these have become educated and are now leading the fight for the rights and respect guaranteed by law. Recently, unions and interest groups have been representing the *Dalits*, and some members have turned to religious and political groups that are more sympathetic to their plight, such as Buddhists, Christians, or Communists.

One social activist, Henry Thiagaraj, has committed his life to improving conditions for the *Dalits*. Thiagaraj works on micro, meso, and macro levels. On the micro level, he suggests that those in power form *Dalit* youth and women's *sangams* (activist groups) and organize the people who live in *Dalit* slums. At the meso level, Thiagaraj and other *Dalit* activists work to initiate microlending to the *Dalits* and improve their education and labor training. On the macro level, Thiagaraj works with nongovernmental organizations to increase support for *Dalit* interests. He also works to improve media coverage of the *Dalits* to raise awareness of their experiences. Thiagaraj's (2007) book, *Human Rights From the Dalits' Perspective*, provides an outstanding retrospective of how India has addressed caste discrimination since the 1980s.

Table 7.5   Basic Dimensions of Social Stratification

	Property Variables	*Prestige Variables*	*Power Variables (Political-Legal)*
	Income	Occupational prestige	Political participation
	Wealth	Respect in community	Political attitudes
	Occupation	Consumption	Legislation and governmental benefits
	Education	Participation in group life	Distribution of justice
	Family stability	Evaluations of race, religion, and ethnicity	
Households in the upper social class	Affluence: economic security and power, control over material and human investment, income from work but mostly from property	More integrated personalities, more consistent attitudes, and greater psychic fulfillment due to deference, valued associations, and consumption	Power to determine public policy and its implementation by the state, thus giving control over the nature and distribution of social values
Households in the lower social class	Destitution: worthlessness on economic markets	Unintegrated personalities, inconsistent attitudes, sense of isolation and despair, sleazy social interaction	Political powerlessness, lack of legal recourse or rights, socially induced apathy

Source: Rossides (1997:15).

Table 7.6   Share of Household Income in Quintiles

	1980	*1990*	*2000*	*2010*
Lowest quintile	4.2	3.8	3.6	3.3
Second quintile	10.2	9.6	8.9	8.5
Third quintile	16.8	15.9	14.9	14.6
Fourth quintile	24.7	24.0	23.0	23.4
Highest quintile	44.1	46.6	49.8	50.2

Source: Johnson (2011); U.S. Census Bureau (2009b).

Note: The lowest quintile has an income under $20,000 year; the highest quintile has an income over $100,066 a year. Each quintile has 23.7 million households.

Some analysts see the middle class in the United States today as dividing the haves and the have-nots with few actually in the "middle." The median household incomes dropped 2.3% between 2009 and 2010. The highest quintile (richest 20%) controls 84% of the wealth in the United States, and the richest 400 families have the same net worth as the bottom 50%. One in six households are now in poverty, and there is an increase in numbers at both extremes of the income scale (P. Harris 2011).

The Power Factor

Power refers to *the ability of a person or group to realize its own will in groups, even against the resistance of others.*

Positions of power are gained through family inheritance, family connections, political appointments, education, hard work, or friendship networks.

We discussed previously the conflict theorists' view that those who hold power are those who control the economic capital and the means of production in society (Ashley and Orenstein 2009). Consistent with Marx, many recent conflict theorists have focused on a **power elite model** in which *power is held by top leaders in corporations, politics, and the military. These interlocking elites make major decisions guiding nations* (Domhoff 2005; Mills 1956). These people interact with each other and have an unspoken agreement to protect their positions and ensure to that their power is not threatened. Each tends to protect the power of the other. The idea is that those who are not in this interlocking elite group do not hold real power and have little chance of breaking into the inner circles (Dye 2002a, 2002b).

Pluralist model of power, on the other hand, argue that *power is not held exclusively by an elite group but is shared among many power centers, each of which has its own self-interests to protect* (Ritzer and Goodman 2004). Well-financed special-interest groups (e.g., dairy farmers' or truckers' trade unions) and professional associations (e.g., the American Medical Association) have considerable power through collective action. From the pluralist perspective, officials who hold political power are vulnerable to pressure from influential interest groups, and each interest group competes for power with others. Creating and maintaining this power through networks and pressure on legislators is the job of lobbyists. For example, in the intense U.S. debate over health care legislation, interest groups from the medical community, insurance lobbies, and citizens' groups wielded their power to influence the outcome, but because these major interests conflict and no one group has the most power, a resolution was extremely difficult to reach. The core idea of pluralist theorists, then, is that many centers of power create at least some checks and balances on those in elite positions

The Prestige Factor

Prestige refers to *the esteem, recognition, and respect one receives, based on wealth, position, or accomplishments.* An individual's prestige ranking is closely correlated with the value system of society. Chances of being granted high prestige improve if one's patterns of behavior, occupation, and lifestyle match those that are valued in the society. Among high-ranked occupations across nations are scientists, physicians, military officers, lawyers, and college professors. Table 7.7 on page 198 shows selected occupational prestige rankings in the United States.

Note the correlation between recent news events—such as 9/11 and the Boston Marathon bombings—and the increased rankings of occupations in which people have been portrayed as "heroes" in the United States. Being a hero, obtaining material possessions, or increasing one's educational level can boost prestige but in itself cannot change class standing.

Thinking Sociologically

Describe your own wealth, power, and prestige in society. Does your family have one factor but not others? What difference does each of the factors make in your life? What part would you like these factors to play in your future, and what might you do to achieve your goal?

Social Classes in the United States

In the current U.S. economic structure, most people are middle class and identify themselves as such, but the middle class is shrinking. There is slight movement to the upper class and somewhat more movement to the lower class. As noted previously, the U.S. system allows for mobility within the middle class, but there is little movement at the very top and very bottom of the social ladder. People in the top rung often use their power and wealth to insulate themselves and protect their elite status, and the bottom group is isolated because of vicious cycles of poverty that are hard to break

Power elite theorists believe that most power is held by the leaders in corporations (like the one depicted here), politics, and the military. These interlocking elites call the shots within a country and control the resources.

Table 7.7 Prestige Rankings of 20 Professions and Occupations

Occupations (Base: All Adults)	% Who Said Very Great Prestige	% Who Said Hardly Any Prestige at All
Firefighter	62%	5%
Scientist	57	7
Doctor	56	3
Nurse	54	4
Military officer	51	4
Teacher	51	10
Police officer	44	7
Priest/minister/ clergyman	41	10
Engineer	39	5
Farmer	36	14
Architect	29	10
Member of Congress	28	22
Business executive	23	26
Athlete	21	19
Journalist	17	22
Union leader	17	30
Entertainer	19	25
Banker	16	18
Accountant	11	19
Real estate agent/ broker	5	30

Source: Harris Interactive (2009).

(Gilbert 2011). Figure 7.1 illustrates the social class structure in the United States.

The middle class, as defined by sociologists, makes up about 30% of the population in the United States, depending on what economic criteria are used. Whereas about half of citizens in the United States identify themselves as middle class, two thirds of the British population identify themselves as "working class" (Cashell 2007; Gilbert 2011). How we identify ourselves expresses our feelings about our placement in the stratification system and also our class "culture." Classes have distinctive values, beliefs, and attitudes toward education, religion, politics, and what makes a good life in general. Often what we define as "normal" is actually what is affirmed by others in our socioeconomic status. A number of scholars have written about the cultural shock they experienced when moving from their blue-collar experiences

as children to becoming professors. The shift in cultures was like entering a new country (Dews and Law 1995; Morris and Grimes 1997). Even the differences in vocabulary usage, discussed earlier in this chapter, represent part of the cultural difference (Hart and Risley 2003).

Since the 1970s, wealth has become increasingly concentrated in the hands of the richest 1% of households. The income gap between the top 5% and bottom 40% of the U.S. population is increasing, and the number of full-time workers in poverty is rising. There has been no reduction in poverty since the 1970s, and in fact it has grown in recent years, yet the proportion of families exceeding $100,000 in annual income has also been growing (Gilbert 2011).

Wages and salaries in the middle classes have declined since the 1980s, but those of the upper classes have risen. Reasons for middle-class decline include downsizing and layoffs of workers, global shifts in production, technological innovations that displace laborers, competition, trade deficits between countries, and deregulation (removing restrictions or regulations). All of these are macro-level economic forces that mean lower incomes for middle-class workers. The wealthiest 1% earned 21.5% of income gains in the last economic expansion, resulting in two thirds of income gains going to the top 1%—hence the phrase "the 1%" and "the 99%" from the Occupy Wall Street movement (Feller and Stone 2009). The upward movement among the few who have received huge gains in earning power is causing wages and earnings to become more unequal.

Upper-middle-class families typically have high income, high education, high occupational level (in terms of prestige and other satisfactions), and high participation in political life and voluntary associations. Families enjoy a stable life, stressing companionship, privacy, pleasant surroundings in safe neighborhoods, property ownership, and stimulating associations. They stress internalization of moral standards of right and wrong, taking responsibility for their own actions, learning to make their own decisions, and training their children for future leadership positions.

The *lower-middle class* includes small-business owners and farmers; middle-management personnel, both private and public; and sales and clerical workers in comfortable office settings. Families in this class are relatively stable. They participate in community life, and although they are less active in political life than the upper classes, they are more politically involved than those in classes below them. Children are raised to work hard and obey authority. Therefore, child-rearing patterns more often involve swift physical punishment for misbehavior than talk and reasoning, which is typical of the upper-middle class.

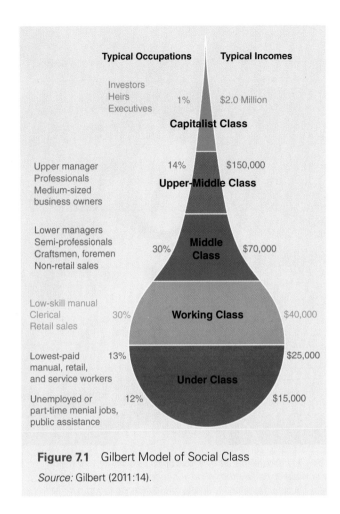

Figure 7.1 Gilbert Model of Social Class

Source: Gilbert (2011:14).

Thinking Sociologically

How does today's popular culture on TV and in films, magazines, and popular music reflect interests of different social classes? How are the rich and poor people depicted in media? Who is responsible for their wealth or poverty—the individuals, the society, or some other combination? Do any of these depictions question the U.S. class system?

Poverty: Determinants and Social Policy

Stories about hunger and famine in Global South countries fill the newspapers. Around the world, nearly 870 million people, or roughly 15% of people living in the Global South, go to bed hungry every night (World Hunger Education

Service 2013c). Of the 10.9 million deaths of children each year, 5 million are directly related to malnutrition (World Hunger Education Service 2013c). These numbers have risen steadily since 1995. Figure 7.2 shows where most of the world hunger occurs. One third of all deaths—18 million people each year or 50,000 per day—are due to poverty-related causes (Vivat International 2012).

One hardly expects to see hunger in rich countries, yet 17.2 million U.S. households, or 14.5% of households (1 in 7), did not have enough food and were skipping meals during the 2010 year, the highest ever recorded in the United States (Coleman-Jensen et al. 2011). Demand at food pantries was up 20%, and the Supplemental Nutrition Assistance Program (SNAP) served a record 35 million recipients in 2010 (World Hunger Education Service 2012a). Twenty-five percent of Americans are afraid they will not be able to afford food at some point in the year (Casteel 2011).

Most people living in poverty have no property-based income and no permanent or stable work, only casual or intermittent earnings in the labor market. They are often dependent on help from government agencies or private organizations to survive. In short, they have personal troubles in large part because they have been unable to establish linkages and networks in the meso- and macro-level organizations of our social world. They have no collective power and, thus, little representation of their interests and needs in the political system.

Thinking Sociologically

Explain how your family's ability to provide food for its members at the micro level is largely dependent on its connectedness to the meso and macro levels of society.

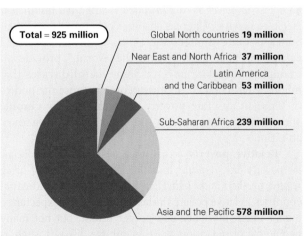

Figure 7.2 Distribution of Hunger in the World

Source: World Hunger Education Service (2011c).

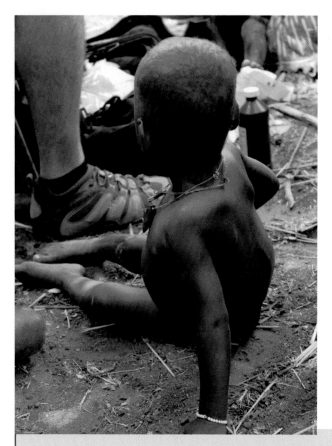 

This little boy (left) sits at the feet of an aid worker. How much power do you imagine this little African boy's parents have to make sure their child's needs are met? This boy and his family have personal troubles because the meso and macro systems of his society have failed to work effectively for individuals and poor families. Compare his circumstances to those of the little girl (right) with her cell phone who is riding in a limousine.

Sociologists recognize two basic types of poverty: absolute poverty and relative poverty. **Absolute poverty**, *not having resources to meet basic needs, means no prestige, no access to power, no accumulated wealth, and insufficient means to survive.* Whereas absolute poverty in the United States is quite limited, the *Dalits* of India, described earlier in "Sociology Around the World," provide an example of absolute poverty. Some die of diseases that might be easily cured in other people because the bodies of those in absolute poverty are weakened by chronic and persistent hunger and almost total lack of medical attention.

Relative poverty *occurs when one's income falls below the poverty line, resulting in an inadequate standard of living relative to others in the individual's country.* In most industrial countries, relative poverty means shortened life expectancy, higher infant mortality, and poorer health, but not many people die of starvation or easily curable diseases, such as influenza.

The *feminization of poverty* refers to the trend in which single females, increasingly younger and with children, make up a growing proportion of those in poverty.

Vicki's situation provides one example. After her parents divorced, she quit high school to take odd jobs to help her mother pay the bills. At 18, she was pregnant, and the baby's father was out of the picture, so Vicki lived on government aid because without a high school degree she could not get a job that paid enough to support her and her baby or to pay for health insurance. She eventually could not pay her rent and lived out of her car, which did not run because she lacked the money to repair it. Her life spiraled out of control, and her daughter has now been placed in foster care.

The feminization of poverty in the United States is heightened as many middle-class women are pushed into poverty through divorce. Some of them have sacrificed their own careers for husbands and family, so their earning power is reduced, yet many divorced women are unable to collect child support from the fathers. This results in low-income supplemental families—mother and children living under the poverty line.

Girls who grow up in female-headed households or foster homes, without a stable family model, are more likely to become single teen mothers and to live in

While these men may look impoverished by North American standards, they are relatively well-off in comparison to many urban neighbors in India, for they own a method of transportation that can earn a cash income, providing food and shelter for their families. Their poverty is not absolute.

poverty, causing disruption in their schooling and setting limits on their employment possibilities and marital opportunities. Conflict theorists argue that poor women, especially women of color, in capitalistic economic systems are used as a reserve labor force that can be called on when labor is needed and dismissed when not needed (Aguirre and Baker 2007; Ehrenreich 2001). They are an easily exploited group, living under constant stress that can cause mental or physical breakdowns and alienation from the social system. Some turn to alcohol or drugs to escape the pressure and failure or to crime to get money to pay the bills. Poor physical and mental health, inadequate nutrition, higher mortality rates, obesity, low self-esteem, feelings of hopelessness, daily struggle to survive, and dependence on others are a few of the individual consequences of poverty within our social world. Costs to the larger society are great:

- The loss of talents and abilities that these people could contribute.
- Expenditure of tax dollars to address their needs or to regulate their lives with social workers and police.
- The contradictions of their lives with cultural values: The United States claims that all citizens "are created equal" and are worthy of respect, yet not all can "make it" in U.S. society.

Welfare programs in affluent countries are only one of a number of kinds of government assistance programs. In the United States, some people think of such programs as unearned giveaways for the poor; however, there are massive programs of government support for people at all levels of the social system. Some of these include tax breaks for business owners, farmers, oil companies, and financial institutions. In other affluent countries, all citizens are provided with universal health insurance, and in some of these countries, university students pay little or nothing to attend college. Government assistance in many countries, including the United States, is clearly not just for the poor. The question is whether affluence and prosperity are viewed as collectively created and shared, rather than as individual achievements. Ignoring the importance of either individual responsibility and initiative or how social systems collectively produce affluence (or poverty) is a mistake. Both are at work.

Thinking Sociologically

Are tax breaks and bailouts for business owners and wealthy companies "unearned giveaways"? Are programs that help the poor "unearned giveaways"? What is the difference?

For most societies, poverty means loss of labor, a drain on other members in society to support the poor, and extensive health care and crime prevention systems. Those working with people in poverty generally argue that the elimination of poverty takes money and requires choices by policy makers to *do* something about poverty. Some argue that poverty will never be eliminated because poor people are needed in society. Consider the position put forth in the next "Sociology in Our Social World."

National and Global Digital Divide: Macro-Level Stratification

Mamadou from Niger and Eric from Ghana answer their cell phones to the sound of chimes from London's Big Ben clock tower and a Bob Marley song. One speaks in Kanuri and French and the other in Twi to friends thousands of miles away. They are the future generation of elites from the Global South, fluent in the languages of several countries, adept in computer software, and at the forefront of their countries in digital technology. Many of their fellow citizens

Sociology in Our Social World

The Functions of Poverty

Surely wealthy countries such as the United States have the means to eliminate poverty if they choose to do so. Its persistence invites debate. Some sociologists argue that poverty serves certain purposes or *functions* for society, and these make it difficult to address the problem directly and systematically. Some people actually benefit from having poor people kept poor (Gans 1971, 1995). Consider the following points:

1. The fact that some people are in poverty provides us with a convenient scapegoat—someone to blame for individual and societal problems. We have individuals to blame for poverty—the poor individuals themselves—and can ignore meso- and macro-level causes of poverty that would be expensive to resolve.

2. Having poor people creates many jobs for those who are not poor, including "helping" professions such as social workers, as well as law enforcement jobs such as police, judges, and prison workers.

3. The poor provide an easily available group of laborers to do work, and they serve as surplus workers to hire for undesirable jobs.

4. The poor serve to reinforce and legitimate our own lives and institutions. Their existence allows

the rest of us to feel superior to someone, enhancing our self-esteem.

5. Their violation of mainstream values helps remind us of those values, thereby constantly reaffirming the values among the affluent.

This perspective can be extended to poverty on the global scale.

1. Just as poor U.S. laborers can be hired for undesirable jobs, the global poor work at very low wages to provide consumers in wealthy nations with low-cost goods.

2. The gifted and talented individuals in poor societies often migrate to wealthier nations, creating a brain drain that removes human capital from poor states and increases it in wealthy states.

3. The poor of the world are blamed for macro-level social problems such as overpopulation and terrorism. As with our local poor, their existence allows us to overlook the macro-level causes of poverty.

From this perspective, the poor serve a role in the structure of society. Therefore, some groups of people, be it individuals or nations, will always be at the bottom of the stratification ladder.

in Niger and Ghana in Africa are not so fortunate. They live subsistence lives and have little contact with the digital world swirling overhead through satellite connections. This represents the *digital divide,* the gap between those with knowledge and access to information technology and those without it. The lines of the divide are drawn by the position of the country in the world, socioeconomic status, minority group membership, and urban versus rural residence (Mehra, Merkel, and Bishop 2004).

The world economic and political institutions are increasingly based on producing and transmitting

information through digital technology. Few tools are more important in this process than the computer, the Internet, cell phones, and iPods. In nearly every salaried and professional position, computer knowledge and ability to navigate the Internet are critical employment skills. Individuals with insufficient access to computers and lack of technical skills face barriers to many professions and opportunities. Because computer skills are important for personal success, this is an important micro-level issue. The digital divide is breaking down for some young and elite members of developing societies such as Mamadou and Eric, but many individuals and Global South countries have insufficient technology and educated citizens to participate in this new economy (Drori 2006). Still, the number of Internet users around the globe increased from 250 million in 2000 to 2 billion in 2011. In fact, as 2012 approached nearly 33% of the world's population had Internet usage, and as of June 2012 that percentage had risen to more than 34% (Internet World Stats 2013; Renick 2011). As Table 7.8 makes clear, this varies greatly by region of the world.

Researchers have laid out three tiers in the digital divide, based on the following: (1) personal computers per 100 in the population, (2) Internet users per 100 in the population, and (3) Internet bandwidth per person. Using these standards, all developed countries plus some additional countries in the Caribbean, Eastern Europe, and the Middle East are Tier 1—the places with most access. The second tier includes Brazil, Russia, China, and some smaller countries in South America. African nations account for the majority of members in the lowest tier, reflecting disadvantage of the continent in lack of computers, computer use, and bandwidth ("International Digital Divide" 2011).

On the other hand, cell phone users around the world rose from 500 million in 2000 to nearly 6 billion (Read 2011). The rapid increase is fueled by the boom of mobile cellular telephone subscriptions in Global South countries, resulting in a total global user rate of 87% (Renick 2011).

South Korea is the most wired country in the world. The United States is in the top tier as well, but many poor people in the United States do not have access to computers or mentors to teach them how to use computers. This digital divide is beginning to close with active efforts by schools and libraries to provide accessibility. According to a recent sociological study, "black and Latino youth use media more than ever, outpacing white and Asian youth, but there's a big difference in *how* they use media," creating challenges for bridging the digital divide (National Public Radio 2011). African American youth are on the cutting edge of Twitter and other social media. Blacks and Latinos are as likely to be on Facebook as other groups, and use their mobile devices to listen to music, play games, and do social networking. However, the African American and Latino kids are less likely to be the ones on the cutting edge of technology, using it for creating and designing digital content. Some kids use technology to interact with friends, and others use it for interest-based reasons such as knowledge and hobbies (National Public Radio 2011).

An additional difficulty is that because most websites and email services use English, many computer keyboards are designed with a Western alphabet, and some of the digital systems in computers are established on the basis of English symbols and logic. It is sometimes difficult to use the Internet in other languages—a fact that many of us may not think about as we use the system (Drori 2006). For people who are struggling for the very survival of their culture, the dominance of English may feel like a threat, one more example of Western dominance. So where there is resistance to the use of computers and the Internet, it is more than a matter of finances or technology. There may be cultural objections as well.

Policy decisions at the international level affect the status of the Global South. The United Nations, the International Monetary Fund, and other international organizations have pressured countries to develop their Internet capacities. Indeed, this is sometimes used as a criterion for ranking countries in terms of their "level of modernization" (Drori 2006). Countries that have not been able to get "in the game" of Internet technology cannot keep pace with a rapidly evolving global economy.

Digital technology is an example of one important force changing the micro- to macro-level global stratification system—a spectrum of people and countries from the rich and elite to the poor and desperate.

Table 7.8   Internet Use: Distribution by World Regions, 2013

World Regions	Internet Penetration (% Population)	% of Total Global Internet Users
Africa	15.6	7.0
Asia	27.5	44.8
Europe	63.2	21.5
Middle East	40.2	3.7
North America	78.6	11.4
Latin America/ Caribbean	42.9	10.6
Oceania/Australia	67.6	1.0
WORLD TOTAL	34.3	100.0

Source: Internet World Stats (2013).

Thinking Sociologically

What evidence of the digital divide do you see in your family, community, nation, and world? For instance, can your grandparents program their DVD players? Do they know how to work a cell phone or navigate the Internet? Could they create their own Facebook page if asked to do so? If not, does this have any consequences for their lives?

Digital Divide

The Global "Digital Divide" and Social Policy

Bangalore is home to India's booming digital industries, and provides an example of India's successful competition in the global high-tech market. Yet, many villages and cities in India illustrate the contrasts between the caste system and the emerging class system. In rural agricultural areas, change is extremely slow despite laws forbidding differential treatment of outcastes and mandating change. In urban industrial areas, new opportunities are changing the traditional caste structures, as competition for wealth and power is increasing with the changes in economic, political, and other institutional structures. The higher castes were the first to receive the education and lifestyle that create industrial leaders. Now, shopkeepers, wealthy peasants, teachers, and others are vying for power. Within the world system, India is generally economically poor but developing certain economic sectors rapidly. Thus, India is in transition both internally and in the global system.

As poor countries become part of the electronic age, some such as India are making policies that facilitate rapid modernization. They are passing over developmental stages that rich countries went through. As an illustration, consider the telephone. Most telephones in the world are cell phones, many using satellite connections. Some countries never did get completely wired for landlines, thus eliminating one phase of phone technology. With the satellite technology now in place, some computer and Internet options will be available without expensive intermediate steps (Drori 2006). Cell phones that originated for the business elite have become a personal item. Use in poor countries has boomed, giving people access to health care and other services. By the end of 2011, there were almost 6 billion mobile phone subscribers—and the world's population is 7 billion. Cell phone subscriptions have grown 45% annually for the past 4 years (Whitney 2012). The point here is that there is a global digital divide, but that divide is narrowing in some areas of technology.

The One Laptop per Child foundation is helping fund efforts to distribute efficient small laptops to children around the world. Linux and Novatium, to name

In the Global North, computers are seen as necessary equipment in homes. Yet in rural villages throughout much of the world, people may never see a computer and lack the reliable electricity and other support systems for Internet technology. This is part of the digital divide in the global system.

just two companies, are developing $100 computers, and some governments are buying large numbers for their schools (One Laptop per Child 2011; Rubenstein 2007). Engineers in India, working through an organization called Simputer Trust, have been designing a simple computer (a "simputer") that will be less expensive and will have more multilingual capacities than the PC. Such efforts will enhance access of poor countries to the computer and Internet and will provide the means for children in poor countries to become part of the competitive global stratification system. Technology has the potential to level the world playing field.

We leave this discussion of stratification systems, including class systems, with a partial answer to the question posed at the beginning of this chapter: Why are some people rich and others poor? In the next two chapters, we expand the discussion to include other variables in stratification systems—race and ethnicity and gender. By the end of these chapters, the answer to the opening question should be even clearer.

What Have We Learned?

Perhaps you have a better understanding of why you are rich or poor—and what effect your socioeconomic status has on what you buy, what you believe, and where you live. Perhaps you have gained some insight into what factors affect your ability to move up in the social class system. The issue of social stratification calls into question the widely held belief in the fairness of our economic system. By studying this issue, we better understand why some individuals are able to experience prestige (respect) and to control power and wealth at the micro, meso, and macro levels of the social system while others have little access to those resources. Few social forces affect your personal life at the micro level as much as stratification. That includes the decisions you make about what you wish to do with your life or who you might marry. Indeed, stratification influenced the fact that you are reading this book.

Key Points:

- Stratification—the layering or ranking of people within society—is one of the most important factors shaping the life chances of individuals. This ranking is influenced by micro, meso, and macro forces and resources. (See pp. 176–177.)

- Various theories of stratification disagree on whether inequality is functional or destructive to society and its members. The evolutionary perspective suggests ways stratification can be positive, but much of the inequality currently experienced creates problems for individuals and societies. (See pp. 177–182.)

- For individuals, personal respect (prestige) is experienced as highly personal, but it is influenced by the way the social system works at the meso and macro level—from access to education and the problems created by gender and ethnic discrimination to population trends and the vitality of the global economy. (See pp. 182–185.)

- People without adequate capital and connections to the meso and macro levels are likely to experience less power, wealth, and prestige. (See pp. 186–193.)

- Some macro systems stress ascribed status (assigned to one, often at birth, without consideration of one's individual choices, talents, or intelligence). Other systems purport to be open and based on achieved status (dependent upon one's contributions to the society and one's personal abilities and decisions). Unlike the caste system, the class system tends to stress achieved status, although it does not always perform openly. (See pp. 193–196.)

- The elements of stratification are complex, with property, power, and prestige having somewhat independent influences on the system of inequality and on one's standing. (See pp. 196–200.)

- Poverty itself is a difficult problem, one that can be costly to a society as a whole. However, various solutions at the micro, meso, and macro levels have had mixed results, partially, perhaps, because it is in the interests of those with privilege to have an underclass to do the unpleasant jobs. (See pp. 200–202.)

- Technology is both a contributor and a possible remedy to inequality, as the digital divide creates problems for the poor, but electronic innovations may create new opportunities in the social structure for networking and connections to the meso and macro levels—even for those in the Global South, the poor regions of the world. (See pp. 202–204.)

Discussion Questions

1. Were you surprised to learn that among rich nations, life expectancy in the United States is among the lowest? Explain. What sociological theory best explains this fact? Support your answer.

2. How has the social class of your parents and your upbringing influenced your success in school and your professional aspirations?

3. What is the social status of most of the people with whom you hang out? Why do you think you tend to associate with people from this social status?

4. Describe factors at the (a) micro, (b) meso, and (c) macro levels that impact your ability to move up the social class ladder.

5. How do the forces that have led to the shrinking of the middle class impact your chance of becoming (or remaining) a member of the (a) middle, (b) upper-middle, or (c) upper class after you graduate from college?

6. How can bridging the global digital divide lead to a decrease in inequality across the world? How does your ready access (or lack of access) to a computer and the Internet impact *your* life chances?

Contributing to Our Social World: What Can We Do?

At the Local Level

- *Volunteer to serve a meal* at an area soup kitchen. Your campus activities office should be able to help you find one in your area and even connect you with a group on campus that regularly volunteers at one.

- *Tip service people in cash.* Housekeepers in hotels and motels, maids, meal servers at restaurants, and food delivery employees may depend on tips to survive. In order to make it more likely that they receive the tips intended for them, be sure to tip in cash, rather than using a credit card.

At the Organizational or Institutional Level

- *Habitat for Humanity* pairs volunteers with current and prospective home owners in repairing or constructing housing for little or no cost. Habitat projects are under way or planned for many communities in the United States and around the world. See the organization's website at www.habitat.org for more details and to see if you can volunteer for a project in your area.

- *AmeriCorps* founded in the early 1990s, includes a variety of programs from intensive residential programs to part-time volunteer opportunities in communities across the United States. For more information, go to the organization's website at www.nationalservice.gov/programs/americorps.

At the National and Global Levels

- *The Peace Corps* involves a serious, long-term commitment, but most who have done it agree that it is well worth the time and energy. The Peace Corps is an independent agency of the U.S. government, founded in 1961. Volunteers work in foreign countries throughout the world, helping local people improve their economic conditions, health, and education. The Peace Corps website (www.peacecorps.gov) provides information on the history of the organization, volunteer opportunities, and reports of former and present volunteers.

- *Grameen Bank* (www.grameen-info.org or www.grameenfoundation.org), a microcredit organization, was started in Bangladesh by Professor Muhammad Yunus, winner of the 2006 Nobel Peace Prize. It makes small business loans to people who live in impoverished regions of the world and who have no collateral for a loan. Consider doing a local fundraiser with friends for the Grameen Bank or other microcredit organizations, such as FINCA (www.finca.org), Kiva (www.kiva.org), and CARE International (www.care-international.org).

- *Free the Children* is a youth-focused organization whose international programs help free people across the globe from the cycle of poverty by providing clean water, schools, health care, and sanitation. You can learn more about this organization and how you can join its efforts at www.freethechildren.com.

Visit **www.sagepub.com/oswcondensed3e** for online activities, sample tests, and other helpful information. Select "Chapter 7: Stratification" for chapter-specific activities.

Race and Ethnic Group Stratification

Beyond "We" and "They"

As we travel around our social world, the people we encounter gradually change appearance. As human beings, we are all part of "we," but there is a tendency to define those who look different as "they."

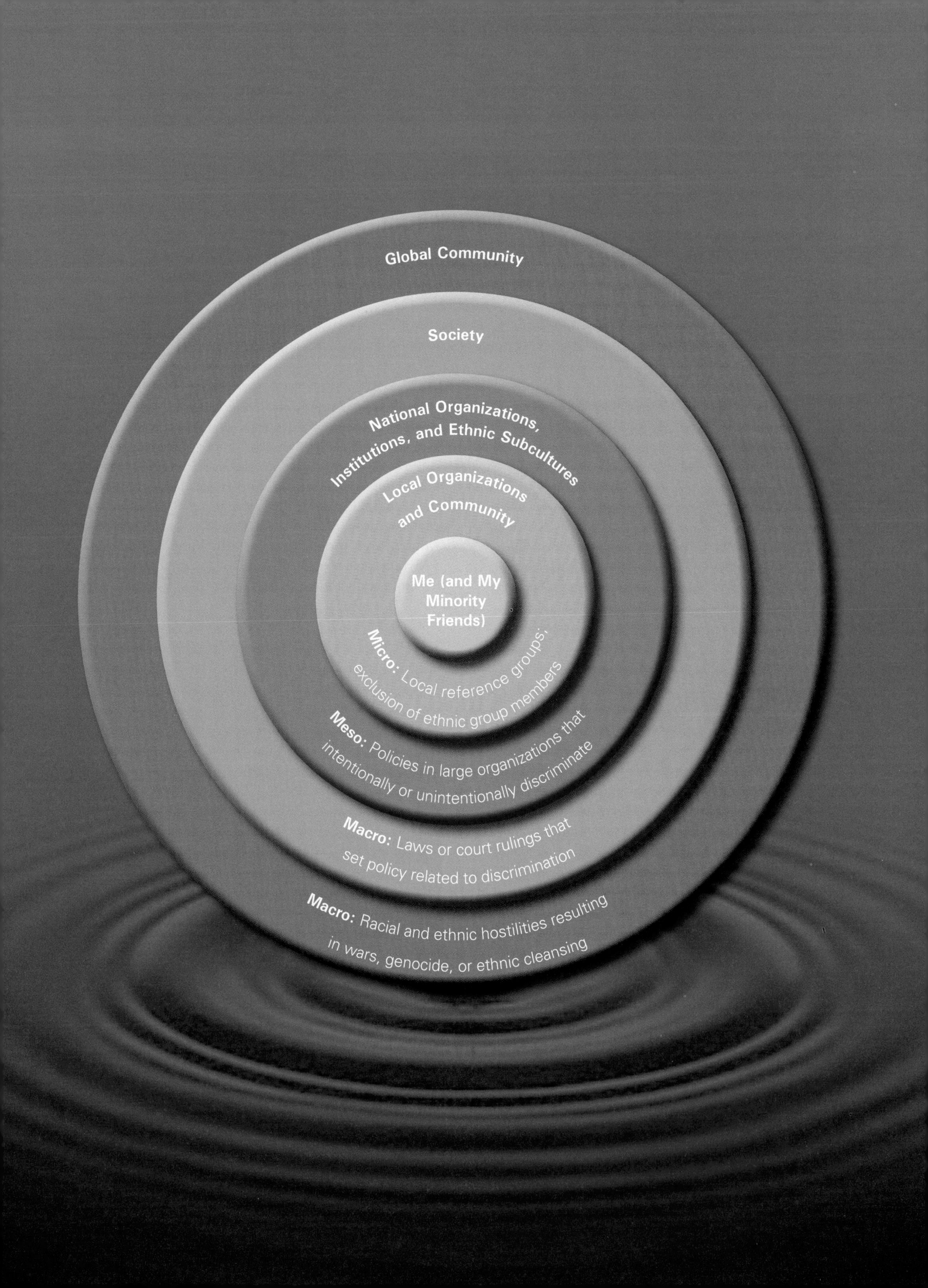

Global Community

Society

National Organizations, Institutions, and Ethnic Subcultures

Local Organizations and Community

Me (and My Minority Friends)

Micro: Local reference groups; exclusion of ethnic group members

Meso: Policies in large organizations that intentionally or unintentionally discriminate

Macro: Laws or court rulings that set policy related to discrimination

Macro: Racial and ethnic hostilities resulting in wars, genocide, or ethnic cleansing

Think About It	
Micro: Me (and My Ethnically Diverse Friends)	Do you look different from those around you? If not, why do you think you are surrounded by people who look like you? What relevance do these differences have for your life?
Micro: Local Community	Why do people in the local community categorize "others" into racial or ethnic groups?
Meso: National Institutions; Complex Organizations; Ethnic Groups	How are advantages and disadvantages embedded in institutions so that they operate independently of personal bias or prejudice?
Macro: National Society	Why are minority group members in most countries economically poorer than dominant group members?
Macro: Global Community	In what ways might ethnicity or race shape international negotiations and global problem solving? What can you do to make the world a better place for all people?

What's coming in this chapter?

What Characterizes Racial and Ethnic Groups?

Prejudice: Micro-Level Analysis

Discrimination: Meso-Level Analysis

Dominant and Minority Group Contact: Macro-Level Analysis

The Effects of Prejudice, Racism, and Discrimination

Micro-Level Coping Strategies

Meso- and Macro-Level Efforts to Bring Change: Nonviolent Resistance

Policies Governing Minority and Dominant Group Relations

The unnamed adult female was brought to the UK by an organized gang with the intention of removing her organs and selling them to those desperate for a transplant. It is unclear whether the plot was uncovered before the organ removal took place, but campaigners said it was the first such case they had seen in Britain. The case is now the subject of a police investigation, but represents a sinister development in the already disturbing trade in human trafficking [and sale of organs] . . .

According to the World Health Organization as many as 7,000 kidneys are illegally obtained by traffickers each year around the world. While there is a market for organs such as hearts, lungs and livers, kidneys are the most sought after organs because one can be removed from a patient under proper medical conditions without any ill effects. (M. Evans 2012)

It may surprise you to know that *slaves*—individuals or families bound in servitude as the property of a person or household, bought and sold, and forced to work—continue to be exploited around the world,

including the United States and Canada (Free the Slaves 2013). The United Nations estimates that 2.4 million people around the world were victims of human trafficking in 2012 alone; that's 1.8 people per 1,000 inhabitants in the world, and 3 per 1,000 in Asia and the Pacific ("Human Trafficking" 2012). Eighty percent of these were in sexual services, and most were women and girls. Human trafficking is lucrative—a $32 billion market (Lederer 2012). The global market for child trafficking involves more than 1.2 million child

In Calcutta's red-light district, more than 7,000 women and girls work as prostitutes. Only one group has a lower standing: their children. Zana Briski first began photographing prostitutes in Calcutta in 1998. Living in the brothels for months at a time, she quickly developed a relationship with many of the kids who, often terrorized and abused, were drawn to the rare human companionship she offered. Because the children were fascinated by her camera, Zana taught photography to the children of prostitutes. Learn more about her organization, Kids With Destiny, at www.kidswithdestiny.org.

Slavery

victims (Stop Child Trafficking Now 2012). New markets in human body parts may be the largest growth area (Evans 2012). Can you imagine being so desperate for income—in part because of your ethnic background—that you had to sell your body parts—or even your daughter?

Around the stadiums of international events such as the Olympics, major soccer matches, and Super Bowls, cheap hotels and brothels buy and sell child prostitutes (Elam 2011). Young foreign girls are brought in from other countries—chosen for sex slaves because they are exotic, are free of AIDS, and cannot escape due to insufficient money and knowledge of the language or the country to which they are exported. Sometimes, poor families sell their daughters for the promise of high wages and perhaps money sent home. As a result, girls as young as 6 are held captive as prostitutes or as domestic workers. Child labor, a problem in many parts of the world, requires poor young children to do heavy labor for long hours in agriculture as well as brick-making, match-making, and carpet factories. Although they earn little, sometimes their income helps families pay debts. Much of the cacao (used to make chocolate) and coffee (except for Fair Trade Certified products) that we buy also supports slavery. Young girls and boys work up to 80 hours a week in cacao plantations, but are not paid (Nall 2012). They are given a choice of unpaid hard labor (with beatings for any disobedience) or death by starvation or shooting (Bales 2000, 2012). Very little chocolate is produced *without* slave labor.

Debt bondage is another form of modern-day slavery. Extremely poor families—often people with differences in appearance from those with power—work in exchange for housing and meager food. Severe debt, passing from generation to generation, may also result when farmers borrow money because they face drought or need cash to keep their families from starving. The only collateral they have on the loan is themselves—put up for bondage until they can pay off the loan. No one but the wealthy landowner keeps accounting records, which results in there being no accountability. In the slavery of the 19th century, slaves were expensive, and there was at least some economic incentive to care about their health and survival so that they could be productive workers. In the new slavery, humans are cheap and replaceable. There is little concern about working them to death, especially if they are located in remote sugar, cacao, or coffee plantations. By current dollars, a slave in the southern United States prior to the Civil War would have cost as much as $40,000, but contemporary slaves are cheap. They can be procured from poor countries for an average of $90 (Bales 2012). The cost is $40 in Mali for a young male and $1,000 in Thailand for an HIV-free female (Free the Slaves 2013).

Just as the issue of slavery mobilized people to start abolition movements in the first half of the 19th century, it is a cause for action by some public sociologists. The sociologist most at the forefront of the current movement to abolish slavery is featured in the next "Sociologists in Action."

Much of the work on cacao plantations is done by child slaves from poor countries who were smuggled, bought, or coerced with promises of a better life. The photo at the right shows children working at a coffee plantation in Panama. The children have no childhood and often no schooling. This plantation does not have fair trade practices.

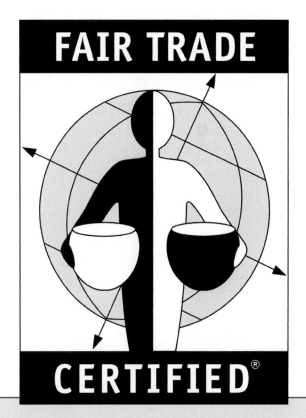

The Fair Trade Certified symbol signifies that products such as coffee, tea, and chocolate (made from cacao) meet sustainable development goals, help support family farmers at fair prices, and are not produced by slave labor. Much cacao plantation labor is done by child slaves smuggled in from poor countries. Fair trade requires respect for the dignity and autonomy of the workers.

Sociologists in Action— by Kevin Bales

Stopping Slavery in the 21st Century

In the following excerpt from "Confronting Slavery With the Tools of Sociology" Kevin Bales describes how he has used his sociological training to draw attention to and work to combat modern slavery, living the life of a public sociologist.

* * * * * * *

Becoming an abolitionist sociologist crept up on me. The first tiny prodding was a leaflet I picked up at an outdoor event in London. The front of the leaflet read "There are Millions of Slaves in the World Today." I was a university professor, and I confess to an unpleasant mixture of pride and hubris in my reaction to the bold title of the leaflet. Having been involved in human rights for many years, I thought, "How could this be true if I don't know about it already?"

Something began to itch in my mind . . . what if? What if there were millions of people in slavery? What if almost all of us, governments, human rights groups, the media, the public, were simply unaware? Millions of hidden slaves seemed unlikely, but my nagging thought was that if there were millions of people in slavery, then finding them was the job of a social researcher. If there weren't millions of slaves, this type of literature needed debunking.

I pulled in students to help dig and sift through information, and paid one researcher to look further afield. As a faint picture of global slavery began to emerge, I came to understand why this issue was invisible. Slavery was hidden under a thick blanket of ignorance, concealed by the common assumption that it was extinct. With slavery illegal in every country, criminal slaveholders kept their activities hidden.

As I built up a picture of slavery, every new set of facts generated new questions. I began to realize that a large-scale research project was needed and I went in search of modern slavery, traveling to India, Pakistan, Thailand, Mauritania, and Brazil—often going undercover as I studied slave-based businesses in each country. The result was the book, *Disposable People: New Slavery in the Global Economy* (1999, 2004, 2012).

Some years later, I was able to build a database of slave prices over time that showed that slaves had been high-ticket capital purchase items in the past (even though occasional gluts caused prices to dip) and are normally low cost disposable inputs today.

In 2000, I, with three others, helped found Free the Slaves, the American sister-organization of Anti-Slavery International, the world's oldest (1787) and original human rights group. Free the Slaves works with local partners to liberate slaves around the world and change the systems that allow slavery to exist. In addition to addressing the crime of enslavement, this work often involves confronting gender inequality, racism, ethnic and religious discrimination, and the negative outcomes of global economic growth. We have learned that freedom and empowerment are viral, and that freed slaves will stop at nothing to stay free and help others to liberty.

Not every part of liberation and reintegration requires sociological training, but it would be very hard to be successful without it. Without carefully constructed longitudinal surveys of villages in slavery we could never have demonstrated the "freedom dividend," the powerful and positive economic change that comes to whole communities when slavery is abolished. Without training in the empathetic understanding of a social researcher we could never have developed the "slavery lens," a way of seeing this hidden crime, that the U.S. government now requires of all its foreign aid program workers. Without learning about the complex interplay of culture, society, economics, politics, and social vulnerability, we would never be able to build the unique methodologies of liberation tailored to specific and culturally rooted forms of slavery. And there is nothing like the ugly reality of a crime like slavery to push young sociologists to do their best work—using solid social science to change the world.

* * * * * * *

Kevin Bales is a sociologist and professor of contemporary slavery at the Wilberforce Institute for the Study of Slavery and Emancipation (WISE), University of Hull, and cofounder of Free the Slaves, Washington. This excerpt is taken from *Sociologists in Action: Sociology, Social Change, and Social Justice* (Korgen, White, and White 2013).

Thinking Sociologically

Poor people around the world often lose control over their lives. What situations can lead to this condition, and what are the consequences for these people?

What is the significance of slavery for our discussion of race and ethnic group stratification? What all of these human bondage situations have in common is that poor minority groups are victimized. Because many slaves are members of ethnic, racial, religious, tribal, gender, age, caste, or other minority groups with little cultural capital, are generally very poor, and have obvious physical or cultural distinctions from the people who exploit them, they are at a distinct disadvantage in the stratification system. Historical conditions and conflicts rooted in religious, social, political, and historical events set the stage for dominant or minority status, and people are socialized into their dominant or subservient group.

Minority or dominant group status affects most aspects of people's experiences and stratification position in the social world. These include status in the community, socialization experience, residence, opportunities for success in education and occupation, the religious group to which they belong, and the health care they receive. In fact, it is impossible to separate minority status from position in the stratification system (Aguirre and Turner 2011; Farley 2010; Rothenberg 2010).

In this chapter, we explore characteristics of race and ethnic groups that lead to differential placement in stratification systems, including problems at the micro, meso, and macro levels—prejudice, racism, and discrimination. The next chapter considers ascribed status based on gender. The topics in this chapter and the next continue the discussion of stratification: who is singled out for differential treatment, why they are singled out, results for both the individuals and the society, and some actions or policies that deal with differential treatment.

What Characterizes Racial and Ethnic Groups?

Migration, war and conquest, trade, and intermarriage have left virtually every geographical area of the world populated by groups of people with varying ethnicities. In this section, we consider characteristics that set groups apart, especially groups that fall at the lower end of the stratification system.

Minority Groups

Minority groups are *groups in a population that differ from others in some characteristics and are therefore subject to less power, fewer privileges, and discrimination.* Several factors characterize minority groups and their relations with dominant groups in society (Dworkin and Dworkin 1999). Minority groups

1. are distinguishable from dominant groups due to factors that make them different from the group that holds power;

2. are excluded or denied full participation at the meso level of society in economic, political, educational, religious, health, and recreational institutions;

3. have less access to power and resources within the nation and are evaluated less favorably based on their characteristics as minority group members;

4. are stereotyped, ridiculed, condemned, or otherwise defamed, allowing dominant group members to justify and not feel guilty about unequal and poor treatment; and

5. develop collective identities among members to insulate themselves from the unaccepting world. This in turn perpetuates their group identity by creating ethnic or racial enclaves, intragroup marriages, and segregated group institutions such as religious congregations.

Thinking Sociologically

Based on the preceding list of minority group characteristics, how might some people be affected at the micro, meso, or macro levels of society, depending on their membership in dominant or minority groups?

Because minority status changes with time, power shifts, and ideology, the minority group may be the dominant group in a different time or society. Throughout England's history, wars and assassinations changed the ruling group from Catholic to Protestant and back several times. In Iraq, Shiite Muslims are dominant in numbers and now also in power, but they were a minority under Saddam Hussein's Sunni rule.

Dominant groups are not always a numerical majority. In the case of South Africa, advanced European weapons placed the native African Bantu population under the rule of a relatively small number of white British and Dutch descendants in a system called *apartheid.* Until recently, each major group in South Africa—white, Asian, colored, and black—had its own living area, and members carried identification cards showing the "race" to which they belonged. In this case, racial classification and privilege were defined by the laws of the dominant group.

The Concept of Race

A racial minority is one of the three types of minority groups that we will discuss and that are most common in the social world. **Race** is *a socially created concept that identifies a group as "different" based on certain biologically inherited physical characteristics.* This allows them to be singled out for dissimilar treatment. Most attempts at racial classifications have been based on combinations of appearance, such as skin color and shade, stature, facial features, hair color and texture, head form, nose shape, eye color and shape, height, and blood or gene type. Our discussion of race focuses on three issues: (a) origins of the concept of race, (b) the social construction of race, and (c) the significance of race versus class.

A Class Divided

Origins of the Concept of Race

In the 18th and 19th centuries, scientists attempted to divide humans into four major groupings—Mongoloid, Caucasoid, Negroid, and Australoid—and then into more than 30 racial subcategories. In reality, few individuals fit clearly into any of these types.

From the earliest origins thought to be in Ethiopia, Africa, about 200,000 years ago, *Homo sapiens* slowly spread around the globe, south through Africa, north to Europe, and across Asia. Original migration patterns of early humans over thousands of years are shown in Map 8.1. As the map shows, many scholars believe humans crossed Asia and the Bering Strait to North America around 20,000 BCE and continued to populate North and South America (J. Diamond 1999). Physical adaptations of isolated groups to their environments originally resulted in some differences in physical appearance—skin color, stature, hair type—but mixing of peoples over the centuries has left few if any genetically isolated people.

Thus, the way societies choose to define race has come about largely through what is culturally convenient for the dominant group.

In the 1970s, the United Nations, concerned about racial conflicts and discrimination based on scientifically inaccurate beliefs, issued a "Statement on Race" prepared by a group of eminent scientists from around the world. This and similar statements by scientific groups point out the harmful effects of racist arguments, doctrines, and policies. The conclusion of this document upheld that (a) all people are born free and equal both in dignity and in rights, (b) racism stultifies personal development, (c) conflicts (based on race) cost nations money and resources, and (d) prejudice foments international conflict. Racist doctrines lack any scientific basis, as all people belong to the same species and have descended from the same origin. In summary, problems arising from race relations are social, not biological, in origin; differential treatments of groups based on "race" falsely claim a scientific basis for classifying humans. Biologically speaking, a "race" exists in any life

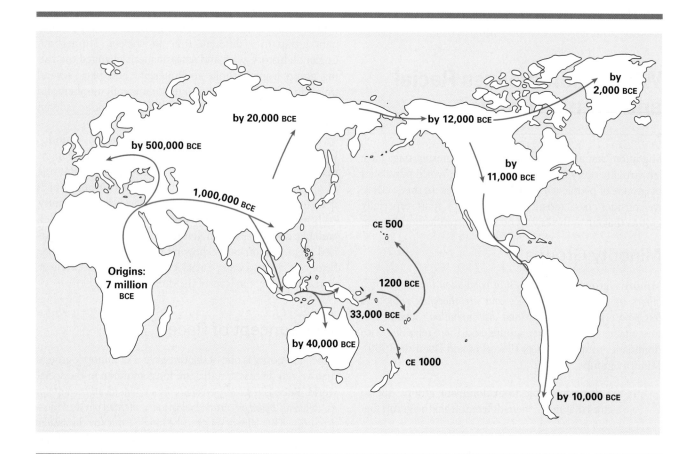

Map 8.1   The Spread of Humans Around the World

Source: J. Diamond (1999:37).

This map shows the historical spread of humans around the globe and the approximate periods of the movements.

Race Relations

form when the two groups cannot interbreed and where, if they do, the offspring are infertile or sterile. This is not true of any group of human beings. So what is the problem?

Social Construction of Race: Symbolic Interaction Analysis

Why are sociologists concerned about a concept that has little scientific accuracy and is ill defined? The answer is its social significance. The social reality is that people are defined or define themselves as belonging to a group based in part on physical appearance. As individuals try to make meaning of the social world, they may learn from others that some traits—eye or nose shape, hair texture, or skin color—are distinguishing traits that make people different. Jean Piaget, the famous cognitive psychologist, described the human tendency to classify objects as one of our most basic cognitive tools (Piaget and Inhelder [1955] 1999). This inclination has often been linked to classifying "racial" groups. Once in place, racial categories provide individuals with an identity based on ancestry—"my kind of people have these traits."

Symbolic interaction theory contends that if people believe something is real, it may become real in its consequences. It does not matter whether scientists say that attempts to classify people into races are inaccurate and that the word is biologically meaningless. People on the streets of your hometown think *they* know what the word *race* means. That people *think* there are differences based on appearance has consequences. As a social concept, race has not only referred to physical features and inherited genes but also carried over to presumed psychological and moral characteristics, thus justifying discriminatory treatment. The following examples illustrate the complex problems in trying to classify people into "races."

With the enactment of apartheid laws in 1948, the white government in South Africa institutionalized differential laws based on its definitions of racial groups and specified the privileges and restrictions allotted to each group (Marger 2012). Bantu populations (the native Africans) and coloreds (those of mixed blood) were restricted to separate living areas and types of work. Asians (mostly descendants of immigrants from India) received higher salaries than the Bantu groups but less than whites, while whites of European descent, primarily Dutch and English, had the highest living standard and best residential locations. Under the apartheid system, race was determined by tracing ancestry back for 14 generations. A single ancestor who was not Dutch or English might have caused an individual to be considered "colored" rather than white—the "one drop of blood" rule made people a minority if they had any ancestry from another group. Physical features mattered little. Individuals carried a card indicating their race based on genealogy. Although this system began to break down

in the 1990s due to international pressure and under the leadership of the first black president (Nelson Mandela, elected in 1994), vestiges of these notions of "reality" will take generations to change.

By contrast, in Brazil an individual's race is based on physical features—skin tone, hair texture, facial features, eye color, and so forth—rather than on the "one drop of blood" rule that existed in South Africa. Brothers and sisters who have the same parents and ancestors may be classified as belonging to different races. The idea of race is based on starkly contrasting criteria in Brazil and South Africa, illustrating the arbitrary nature of racial classification attempts (Kottak 2010).

Before civil rights laws were passed in the United States in the 1960s, a number of states had laws that spelled out differential treatment for racial groups. These were commonly referred to as Jim Crow laws. States in the South passed laws defining who was African American or Native American. In many cases, it was difficult to determine to which category an individual belonged. For instance, African Americans in Georgia were defined as people with any ascertainable trace of "Negro" blood in their veins. In Louisiana, 1/32 "Negro" blood defined one as black. Differential treatment was spelled out in other states as well. In Texas, for example, the father's race determined the race of the child. In West Virginia, a newborn was classified as "black" if either parent was considered black. Until recently, several U.S. states still attempted to classify the race of newborns by the percentage of black blood or parentage (Lopez 1996). Federal law now prohibits discrimination on the

This house in the Chicago slums is not atypical of the quality of homes in segregated America in the 1940s.

basis of "racial" classifications, and most state laws that are explicitly racial have been challenged and dropped.

The Significance of Race Versus Class

From the time of slavery in the Americas until the 21st century, race has been the determining factor regarding opportunities for people of African descent. Whether this is changing in the 21st century is a question that has occupied sociologists, politicians, educators, and other scientists in recent years. Some scholars argue that race is a primary cause of different placement in the stratification system, whereas others insist that race and social class are both at work, with socioeconomic factors (social class) more important than race.

Influential sociologist William Julius Wilson writes that the racial oppression that characterized the African American experience throughout the 19th century was caused first by slavery and then by a lingering caste structure that severely restricted upward mobility. However, the breakdown of the plantation economy and the rise of industrialism created more opportunities for African Americans to participate in the economy (W. J. Wilson 1978, 1993a, 1993b).

Wilson argues that after World War II, an African American class structure developed with characteristics similar to those of the white class structure. Occupation and income took on ever greater significance in social position, especially for the African American middle class. However, as black middle-class professionals moved up in the stratification structure, lower-class African American ghetto residents became more isolated and less mobile. Limited unskilled job opportunities for the lower class have resulted in poverty and stagnation so severe that some families are almost outside of the functioning economic system. Wilson calls this group the *underclass* (W. J. Wilson 1978, 1984, 1993a).

Some researchers assert that the United States cannot escape poverty because well-paid, unskilled jobs are disappearing from the economy and because the poor are concentrated in segregated urban areas (Massey 2007; Massey and Denton 1998). Poorly educated African American teenagers and young adults see their job prospects limited to the low-wage sector (e.g., fast-food work paying minimum wage), and they experience record levels of unemployment. Movement out of poverty becomes almost impossible (Farley 2010; E. O. Wilson 1987).

When Wilson did his research in the 1980s and 1990s, his point was illustrated by the fact that more than 2 in 5 African Americans were middle-class, compared to 1 in 20 in 1940. On the other hand, many adults in inner-city ghetto neighborhoods are not employed in a typical week. Thus, children in these neighborhoods may grow up without ever seeing someone go to work (W. J. Wilson 1996). The new global economic system is a contributing factor as unskilled jobs go abroad to cheaper labor (Friedman 2008; Massey 2007). Without addressing these structural causes of poverty, we cannot expect to reduce the number of people in the underclass—regardless of race or ethnicity.

The situation for black Americans—including the black middle class—deteriorated since the economic crisis that began in 2007. White median household net worth in 2010 was $110,729, while net worth of blacks was $4,995, and of Hispanics, $7,424. In other words, white wealth was 22 times the wealth of blacks and 15 times that of Hispanics in 2010 compared to 12 times for blacks and 8 times for Hispanics prior to the recession. Median household net worth fell during the recession by about 60% for all except whites; the wealth of whites slipped by 23% (Luhby 2012). By 2009, the black unemployment rate was 16.2%, and only 56% of black men over 20 were working. Many people lost their homes, but that involved 4.5% of whites and 8% of blacks (Washington 2011).

With these dismal figures in mind, a big debate among scholars surrounds the following question: Has race declined in significance and class become more important in determining placement in the stratification system? Tests of Wilson's thesis present us with mixed results (Jencks 1992). Thirty-three percent of whites are college graduates, compared to 19.8% of blacks (U.S. Census Bureau 2012b). More important, African Americans earn less than whites in the same occupational categories. As Table 8.1 makes clear, income levels for African Americans and whites are not even close to being equal. So economics alone does not seem a complete answer to who is in the underclass. Although racial bias has decreased at the micro (interpersonal) level, it is still a significant determinant in the lives of African Americans, especially those in the lower class. The data are complex, but we can conclude that for upwardly mobile African Americans, class may be more important than race.

Table 8.1 Income by Educational Level and Race/Ethnicity

Education	White	Black	Hispanic
Not a high school graduate	$20,457	$18,936	$19,816
High school graduate	31,429	26,970	25,998
Some college, no degree	33,119	29,129	29,836
College graduate	57,762	47,799	49,017
Master's degree	73,771	60,067	71,322
Professional degree	127,942	102,328	79,228

Source: U.S. Census Bureau (2012f).

Thinking Sociologically

Considering the data and discussion above about whether race or class has a greater impact on one's ability to succeed in U.S. society today, what is your opinion, and why?

Ethnic Groups

The next major type of minority group—the **ethnic group**—is based *on cultural factors: language, religion, dress, foods, customs, beliefs, values, norms, a shared group identity or feeling, and sometimes loyalty to a homeland, monarch, or religious leader.* Members are grouped together because they share a common cultural heritage, often connected with a national or geographical identity. Some social scientists prefer to call racial groups "ethnic groups" because the term *ethnic* encompasses most minorities, avoiding problems with the term *race.* It is also true that the ideas often go together (Aguirre and Turner 2011).

Visits to ethnic enclaves in large cities around the world give a picture of ethnicity. Little Italy, Chinatown, Greek Town, and Polish neighborhoods may have non-English street signs and newspapers, ethnic restaurants, culture-specific houses of worship, and clothing styles that reflect the ethnic subculture. Occasionally, ethnic groups share power in pluralistic societies, but most often such groups hold a minority status with little power.

How is ethnicity constructed or defined? Many very different ethnic groups have been combined in government categories, such as censuses conducted by countries, yet they speak different languages and often have very different religions. For example, in North America, native ethnic group members often do not view themselves as "Indian" or "Native American." Instead, they use 600 independent tribal nation names to define themselves, including the Ojibwa (Chippewa), the Dineh (Navajo), the Lakota (Sioux), and many others. Likewise, in the U.S. census, Koreans, Filipinos, Chinese, Japanese, and Malaysians come from very different cultures but are identified as *Asian Americans.* People from Brazil, Mexico, and Cuba are grouped together in a category called *Hispanics* or *Latinos.* When federal funds for social services were made available to Asian Americans or American Indians, these diverse people began to think of themselves as part of a larger grouping for political purposes (Esperitu 1992). The federal government essentially created an ethnic group by naming and providing funding to that group. If people wanted services (health care, legal rights, etc.), they had to become a part of a particular group—such as "Asian Americans." This process of merging many ethnic groups into one broader category—called *panethnicity*—emphasizes that ethnic identity is itself socially shaped and created.

Ethnic enclaves have a strong sense of local community, holding festivals from the old country and developing networks in the new country. Such areas, called "ghettos," are not necessarily impoverished. This photo depicts a street in San Francisco's Chinatown.

Biracial and Multiracial Populations: Immigration, Intermarriage, and Personal Identification

Our racial and ethnic identities are becoming more complex as migration around the world brings to distant shores new immigrants in search of safety and a new start. Keep in mind that our racial and ethnic identities come largely from external labels placed on us by governments and our associates but reinforced by our own self-identification.

Many European countries are now host to immigrants from their former colonies, making them multiracial. France hosts many North and West Africans, and Great Britain hosts large populations from Africa, India, and Pakistan. The resulting mix of peoples has blurred racial lines and created many multiracial individuals. The patterns shown in Map 8.1 on page 214 illustrate that "push" factors drive people from some countries and "pull" them to other countries. The most common push-pull factors today are job opportunities, desire for security, individual liberties, and availability of medical and educational opportunities. The target countries of migrants are most often in North America, Australia, or Western Europe, and the highest emigration rates (leaving a country) are from Africa, Eastern Europe, Central Asia, and South and Central America.

The United States was once considered a biracial country, black and white (which, of course, disregarded the Native American population). However, the nation currently accepts more new immigrants than any other country (700,000 per year) and has the second-highest rate of immigration (behind Canada) in terms of immigrants per 1,000 residents (Farley 2010). Immigration from every continent has led to a more diverse population, with 12% of the U.S. population (36.7 million residents) born elsewhere and another 11% (33 million) having at least one foreign-born parent (UPI.com 2010). With new immigration, increasing rates of intermarriage, and many more individuals claiming multiracial identification, the picture is much more complex today, and the color lines have been redrawn (DaCosta 2007; Lee and Bean 2004, 2007). One in forty individuals claims multiracial status today, and estimates are that one in five will do so by 2050 (Lee and Bean 2004). For the first time in 2008, the United States elected a biracial president, although the application of the "one drop of blood" rule in the United States has caused many people to refer to President Obama as "black."

Census data are used in countries to determine many characteristics of populations. In the United States, questions about race and ethnic classification have changed with each 10-year study. The important point is that government-determined categories thereafter define the racial and ethnic composition of a country. In the 2000 census, citizens were for the first time given the option of picking more than one racial category. By 2010, 9 million people reported mixed race background, a 32% growth since 2000 (Basu 2012). *Latinos,* sometimes called Hispanics, made up 16.3% (50.5 million) of the total U.S. population (308.7 million) in 2010 (Perez 2011). Hispanics accounted for 56% of the nation's growth since the 2000 census, up from 35.3% in 2000 (Pew Hispanic Center 2011). Among Latinos, Mexicans made up roughly 65.1%, Puerto Ricans 9.3%, Cubans 3.6%, Central Americans 8.4%, and South Americans 5.7% (U.S. Census Bureau 2012b). Blacks follow Latinos with 12.6% (38.9 million) of the U.S. population. Non-Hispanic whites make up 63.7% (196.8 million), whites (including Hispanic whites) 72.4%, Asians 4.8%, and Native Americans/Native Alaskans 0.9% of the total U.S. population (Day 2011; Humes, Jones, and Ramirez 2011). Figure 8.1 illustrates the ethnic group distribution and projections for the future for the United States.

Arbitrary socially constructed classifications of people into groups are frequently used as justification for treating individuals differently, despite the lack of scientific basis for such distinctions (G. Williams 1996). The legacy of "race" remains even in countries where discrimination based on race is illegal. The question remains: Why is a multiracial baby with any African, Native American, or other minority heritage classified by the minority status, not as a member of the majority?

Thinking Sociologically

Identify one dominant and one minority group in your community or on campus. Where do that group's members fit into the stratification or prestige system of your community or campus? How are the life chances of individuals in these groups influenced by factors beyond their control?

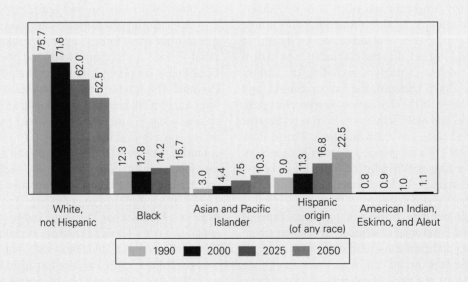

Figure 8.1 Percent of the United States Population, by Race and Hispanic Origin: 1990, 2000, 2025, and 2050

Source: U.S. Census Bureau (2012).

Prejudice: Micro-Level Analysis

Have you ever found yourself in a situation in which you were viewed as different, strange, undesirable, or "less than human"? Perhaps you have felt the sting of rejection, based not on judgment of you as a person but solely on the ethnic group into which you were born. Then again, you may have been insulated from this type of rejection if you grew up in a homogeneous community; you may have even learned some negative attitudes about those different from yourself. It is sobering to think that where and when in history we were born determines how we are treated, our life chances, and many of our experiences and attitudes.

When minority groups are present within a society, prejudice influences dominant-minority group relations. **Prejudice** refers to *attitudes that prejudge a group, usually negatively and not based on facts*. Prejudiced individuals lump together people with certain characteristics as an undifferentiated group without considering individual differences. Although prejudice can refer to positive attitudes and exaggerations (as when patriots are prejudiced in thinking their society is superior), in this chapter we refer to the negative aspects of prejudice. We also focus on the adverse effects brought on minority group members by prejudice. While prejudice can be stimulated by events such as conflicts at the institutional level and war at the societal level, attitudes are held by individuals and can be best understood as a micro-level phenomenon.

If prejudiced attitudes become actions, they are referred to as **discrimination**, *differential treatment of and harmful actions against minorities*. These actions at the micro level might include refusal to sell someone a house because of the religion, race, or ethnicity of the buyer or employment practices that treat some candidates less well based on their minority status (Feagin and Feagin 2010). However, discrimination operates largely at the meso or macro level, discussed later in the chapter. For now, note that individual animosity toward those of another racial category is not the same thing as racism.

The Nature of Prejudice

Prejudice is an understandable response of humans to their social environment. To survive, every social group or unit— a sorority, a sports team, a civic club, or a nation—needs to mobilize the loyalty of its members. Each organization needs to convince people to voluntarily commit energy, skills, time, and resources so the organization can meet its needs. Furthermore, as people commit themselves to a group, they invest a portion of themselves in the group.

Individual commitment to a group influences one's perception and loyalties, creating preference or even bias for the group. This commitment is often based on stressing distinctions from other groups and deep preference for one's own group. However, these loyalties may be dysfunctional for out-group members and the victims of prejudice.

One reason people hold prejudices is that it is easier to pigeonhole the vast amount of information and stimuli coming at us in today's complex societies and to sort information into neat, unquestioned categories than to evaluate each piece of information separately for its accuracy. When prejudiced individuals use distorted, oversimplified, or exaggerated ideas to categorize a group of people and attribute personal qualities to them based on their dress, language, skin color, or other identifying features, it is called *stereotyping*. Stereotypes are not just generalizations; they are by definition misleading overgeneralizations that result in prejudice and cause harm.

In wartime, the adversary may be the victim of racial slurs, or members of the opponent society may be depicted in films or other media as villains. During World War II, American films often showed negative stereotypes of Japanese and German people. These depictions likely reinforced the decision to intern more than 110,000 Japanese Americans, the majority of whom were U.S. citizens, in detention camps following the bombing of Pearl Harbor. Similar issues and stereotypes have arisen for American citizens with Middle Eastern ancestry since the attacks on the New York World Trade Center on September 11, 2001.

Note that there has been an increase in attacks on U.S. Muslims and an uproar over the plans to build a mosque for

On December 7, 1941, Japan bombed Pearl Harbor in Hawaii, prompting President Franklin D. Roosevelt to sign an executive order designating the West Coast as a military zone from which "any or all persons may be excluded." Although not specified in the order, Japanese Americans were singled out for evacuation, and more than 110,000 were removed from many western states and sent to 10 relocation camps. Barber G. S. Hante points proudly to his bigoted sign against people of Japanese origin.

Sociology in Our Social World

Anti-Muslim Sentiments in the United States

By Saher Selod

On September 11, 2001, the United States experienced the largest terrorist attack on U.S. soil. Four airplanes were hijacked by terrorists. Two of the airplanes were flown into the World Trade Center, causing the two buildings to collapse. Another airplane crashed into the Pentagon, and the fourth plane crashed due to a revolt by the passengers on board. The attacks claimed the lives of close to 3,000 Americans. The terrorists were Muslims from Saudi Arabia, United Arab Emirates, and Egypt. These horrific events changed the lives of all Americans, including Muslim Americans and immigrants.

A few sociologists studied the impact 9/11 had on Muslims living in the United States (Bakalian and Bozorgmehr 2009; Cainkar 2009; Peek 2011). Some of the findings reveal Muslims have become targets for antiterrorist laws and policies, which were a part of a government-led campaign known as the "War on Terror" (Cainkar 2009). For example, a little over a month after the attacks, the USA PATRIOT Act (Uniting and Strengthening America by Providing Appropriate Tools Required to Intercept and Obstruct Terrorism Act) was signed into law. This 300-page document restricted the civil liberties of Muslims and any other Americans who could be connected to terrorism. The document loosely defined terrorism, justifying the surveillance of Muslims due to an inaccurate association of Islam with terrorism. As a result, mass deportations of Muslim immigrants for minor infractions of their visas were hidden from the public by the Patriot Act. There was also an increase in visitations of Muslims by the Federal Bureau of Investigation.

Another policy passed after 9/11 was the National Security Entry-Exit Registration System, initiated in September 2002 by the Immigration and Naturalization Service. This law required noncitizen men over the age of 16 from 25 countries (of which 24 were Muslim) to register with the government. Muslim men were forced to submit fingerprints and had their photos taken as if they were potential criminals. One of the consequences of these laws and policies is that they have created an environment where innocent people are treated as if they are guilty due to their shared religious identity with the perpetrators of the terrorist attacks. Since 9/11, over a thousand Muslims (mostly noncitizens) have been detained even though no connection to terrorism was determined. Furthermore, these policies have encouraged the distrust of Muslims by their fellow citizens.

Muslims living in the United States have reported a rise in prejudice and discrimination. Lori Peek's study, *Behind the Backlash: Muslim Americans After 9/11*, highlights the backlash experienced by Muslims living in New York City and Colorado in the few weeks after 9/11. Although it has been over 10 years since the terrorist attacks, anti-Muslim sentiments remain strong today. According to a Gallup report published in 2010, 43% of Americans admitted to feeling some prejudice toward Muslims, and 31% of Americans view Islam unfavorably (Gallup Center for Muslim Studies 2010). These rising anti-Muslim sentiments have had a direct impact on the everyday life of the Muslim population. Statistics compiled by the FBI reveal hate crimes against Muslims increased by almost 50% from 2009 to 2010 (Southern Poverty Law Center 2012). In August 2012, a mosque in Joplin, Missouri, was burned to the ground by an arsonist. As a consequence of government policies targeting Muslims and the perpetuation of stereotypes that Muslims are a threat to national security and American cultural values, Muslims are living with a new racialized identity. Fortunately, organizations such as the Council on American-Islamic Relations (CAIR) and the American Civil Liberties Union (ACLU) are heralding the fight against bigotry and discrimination against Muslims living in the United States.

* * * * * * *

Saher Selod is an assistant professor of sociology at Simmons College. Her areas of research are race and ethnicity and sociology of religion—especially the Muslim experience in the United States.

peace near the 9/11 site. Sociologist Saher Selod examines factors that have contributed to intensified bigotry toward Muslims in the previous "Sociology in Our Social World."

Explanations of Prejudice

We have all met people who express hostility toward others. They tell jokes about minorities, curse them, and even threaten action against them. Why do these individuals do this? The following theories have attempted to explain the prejudiced individual.

Frustration-aggression theory. In Greensboro, North Carolina, in 1978, a group of civil rights activists and African American adults and children listened as a guitarist sang freedom songs. A nine-car cavalcade of white Ku Klux Klan (KKK) and American Nazi Party members arrived. The intruders unloaded weapons from the backs of their cars, approached the rally, and opened fire for 88 seconds. Then they left as calmly as they had arrived.

Four white men and a black woman were dead (Greensboro Justice Fund 2005). According to frustration-aggression theory, many of the perpetrators of this and other heinous acts feel angry and frustrated because they cannot achieve their work or other goals. They blame any vulnerable minority group—religious, ethnic, sexual orientation—and members of that group become targets of their anger. Frustration-aggression theory focuses largely on poorly adjusted people who express their frustration though aggressive attacks on others. Hate groups evolve from like-minded individuals, often because of prejudice and frustration (see Map 8.2).

Scapegoating. When it is impossible to vent frustration toward the real target—one's boss, one's teachers, the economic system—frustration can take the form of aggressive action against people who are vulnerable—scapegoats. The word *scapegoat* comes from the Bible, Leviticus 16:5–22. Once a year, a goat (which was obviously innocent) was laden with parchments on which people had written their sins.

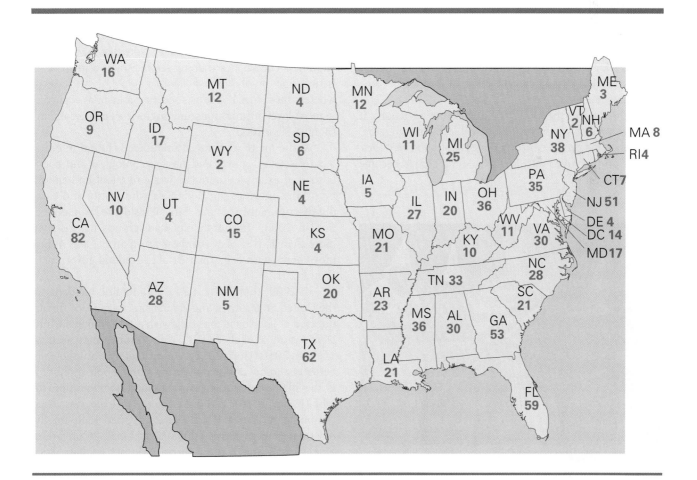

Map 8.2   Active Hate Groups in 2012

Source: Reprinted by permission of the Southern Poverty Law Center (2012).

Muslim Americans

The goat was then sent out to the desert to die. This was part of a ritual of purification, and the creature took the blame for others.

Scapegoating occurs when a minority group is blamed for the failures of others. It is difficult to look at oneself to seek reasons for failure but easy to transfer the cause for one's failure to others. Individuals who feel they are failures in their jobs or other aspects of their lives may blame minority groups. From within such a prejudiced mind-set, even violence toward the out-group becomes acceptable.

Today, jobs and promotions are harder for young adults to obtain than they were for the baby boom generation. The reason is largely demographic, but also a result of the changing economic system. The baby boom of the 1940s and 1950s resulted in a bulge in the population. There are many people in the workforce at the higher steps on the ladder, and it will be another few years before those baby boomers retire in large numbers. Given the economic downturn, potential retirees may further put off retirement, resulting in a good deal of frustration about the occupational stagnation. It is easier—and safer—to blame others, including minorities or affirmative action programs, than to vent frustration at the next-oldest segment of the population—one's grandparents—for having a large family or for working beyond age 65. Blacks, Hispanics, and other minorities become easy scapegoats.

Although this theory helps explain some situations, it does not predict when frustration will lead to aggression, why only some people who experience frustration vent their feelings on the vulnerable, and why some groups become targets (Marger 2012).

Klansmen in traditional white robes demonstrate in front of a courthouse in New York City in 1999. They carried a flag sewn together from parts of American and Confederate flags, a symbol of their blended loyalties.

Racial Bigotry and Its Forms

A bigot is someone who blindly insists that certain other people are so different that they are inferior—even less human. Hate groups in the United States, Europe, and many other countries justify themselves on the basis of such bigotry.

Another pattern of racial and ethnic bigotry at the micro level is more subtle—*"color blind" prejudice*. In this case, individuals insist that they are not prejudiced or racist—that they are color-blind and committed to equality. At the same time, they oppose any social policies (such as scholarships specifically for minorities) that would reduce historically based disadvantage and make equality of opportunity possible (Farley 2010). People who display this pattern claim to reject the idea that race and racism are present but also fail to correct any problems that are created because racism is still embedded in our social system.

Color-blind prejudice allows discrimination that is hidden within the society's institutions to remain in place. Symbolic bigots reject ideological bigotry as blatant, crude, and ignorant, but fail to recognize that their own actions may perpetuate inequalities at the institutional or meso level. (This will be discussed later.) Note that many people without social science training see racism as a micro-level issue—one involving *individual* actions or attitudes—whereas most social scientists see the problem as occurring in meso-level organizations and macro-level policies or laws (Bonilla-Silva 2003).

At the micro level racial prejudice is found in either form discussed above and has psychological and social costs. For example, there is a waste of talent and energy, both for minorities and for those who justify and carry out discriminatory actions. Since President Obama's election in 2008, the number of hate groups has risen to more than 1,018. Many of these are "patriot" and militia movements with deep distrust of the federal government (Potok 2012).

In 2009, there were 1,211 anti-Semitic incidents in the United States involving vandalism, assaults, or threats directed at Jewish citizens or Jewish establishments (Anti-Defamation League 2010). This number increased to 1,239 in 2010 (Horn 2011). Unfortunately, until there are better economic opportunities for more people, prejudice is the likely consequence of economic competition for jobs (Farley 2010). Although micro-level theories (frustration-aggression and scapegoating) shed light on the most extreme cases of individual or small-group prejudice, there is much these theories do not explain. They say little about the everyday hostility and reinforcement of prejudice that most of us experience or engage in, and they fail to deal with discrimination that is embedded in institutions.

Discrimination: Meso-Level Analysis

DeBrun was a well-liked African American college student, actively involved in extracurricular activities. Like many college students, he enjoyed both alcohol consumption on weekends and the outrageous things that happened when people were inebriated. However, DeBrun's anger, normally kept in check, tended to surface when he was drunk. One weekend, some racial slurs were thrown around at a party, and when one of the perpetrators pushed DeBrun too far—including a sucker punch—DeBrun exploded in a fury of violence. No one died, but there were some serious injuries—the worst inflicted by the muscular DeBrun—and at one point a weapon was pulled. DeBrun was expelled from the university, and felony charges were leveled against him. Because there had been a weapon—one that did not belong to DeBrun but at one point ended up in his hand—the university president would not consider readmission. The local white prosecutor, who saw a powerfully built young black man who had tattoos and dreadlocks, assumed that this campus leader was a "thug" and insisted on the most severe felony charges and penalties. DeBrun, who had no previous encounters with law enforcement, ended up with a felony record and two years in prison. Because of both state and federal laws, the felony charges meant that he no longer qualified for any federal financial aid. As his family had very few resources, his hopes for a college degree were crushed. As a convicted felon, he would not be able to vote for the rest of his life in many states, his future employment prospects were greatly diminished, and his family's hopes that he would be their first college graduate were crushed. The president of the college was not a bigot, but the professors who know DeBrun well were convinced that neither his expulsion, nor his arrest, nor his conviction of a serious felony would have occurred had he been white.

This recent incident represents a way that black males can experience a different United States of America than middle-class white males. The cause is not necessarily personal bigotry by people in power. *Discrimination*, differential treatment and harmful actions against minorities, can sometimes occur at individual and small-group levels, but is particularly problematic at the organizational and institutional levels—the meso level of analysis.

Discrimination is based on race, ethnicity, age, sex, sexual orientation, nationality, social class, religion, or whatever other category members of a society choose to make significant (Feagin and Feagin 2010). Discrimination involves actions taken against a person or group by another, often because of minority group membership. It can take many forms, from avoiding contact by excluding individuals from one's club, neighborhood, or even country to

physical violence against minorities as seen in hate crime attacks on immigrant Americans perceived to be taking jobs from white Americans.

Racism is *any meso-level institutional arrangement that favors one racial group over another; this favoritism may result in intentional or unintentional consequences for minority groups* (Farley 2010). Racism is mostly embedded in institutions of society and often is supported by people who are not aware of the social consequence of their actions, as in the case of color-blind prejudice discussed above. So racism has nothing to do with being a nasty or mean-spirited person; it usually operates independently of prejudice (Bonilla-Silva 2003; Rothenberg 2011).

Racism, as sociologists use the concept, involves discrimination as a normal or routine part of the way an organization operates that systemically disadvantages members of one group. It can include intentional actions, such as laws restricting minorities, as well as unintentional actions that have consequences restricting minorities. This kind of system discrimination is built into organizations and cultural expectations in the social world. Even nonprejudiced people can participate in racism of this sort quite unintentionally. For example, many schools place students in academic tracks based on standardized test results. Minority children end up disproportionately in lower tracks because the tests have biases that favor middle-class whites. Thus, a policy that is meant to give all children an equal chance ends up legitimizing the channeling of many minority group students into the lower-achieving classroom groupings.

Jim Crow laws, passed in the late 1800s in the United States, and laws that barred Jews in Germany from working in certain places are examples of intentional discrimination embedded in organizations. By contrast, much discrimination is unintentional, resulting from policies that have the unanticipated consequence of favoring one group and disadvantaging another. In this case there is discrimination "in fact" even if not in intent—entirely separated from personal ill will. This type of discrimination can be more damaging than that imposed by individuals because it is often done by people who are not the least bit prejudiced and may not recognize the effects of their actions (Merton 1949).

Unintentional discrimination usually occurs through one of two processes: side-effect discrimination or past-in-present discrimination (Feagin and Feagin 1986; Rydgren 2004). **Side-effect discrimination** refers to *practices in one institutional area that have a negative impact because they are linked to practices in another institutional area; because institutions are interdependent, discrimination in one results in unintentional discrimination in others.* Figure 8.2 on page 224 illustrates this idea. Each institution uses information from the other institutions to make decisions. Thus, discrimination in the criminal justice system, which has in fact been well documented, may influence discrimination in education or health care systems.

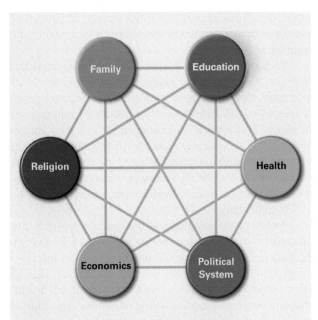

Figure 8.2 Side-Effect Discrimination

Each circle represents a different institution—family, education, religion, health, political-legal system, and economics. These meso-level systems are interdependent, using information or resources from the others. If discrimination occurs in one institution, the second institution may unintentionally borrow information that results in discrimination. In this way, discrimination occurs at the meso level without awareness by individuals at the micro level.

Children play on the porch of their rustic home with no plumbing in the rural Alaskan village of Akhiok, among the Aleutian Islands. Finding jobs through the Internet is not an option from this location.

Consider the following examples of side-effect discrimination. The first is in the criminal justice and employment systems. In an interview conducted by one of the authors, a probation officer in a moderate-size city in Ohio said that he had never seen an African American in his county get a not-guilty verdict and that he was not sure it was possible. He had known of cases in which minorities had pleaded guilty to a lesser charge even though they were innocent because they did not think they could receive a fair verdict in that city. When people apply for jobs, however, they are required to report the conviction on the application form. By using information about someone's criminal record, employers who clearly do not intend to discriminate end up doing so whether or not the individual was guilty. The side-effect discrimination is unintentional discrimination; the criminal justice system has reached an unjust verdict, and the potential employer is swayed unfairly.

A second example of side-effect discrimination shows that the Internet also plays a role in institutionalized discrimination and privilege. For example, in Alaska, 20% of the population is Native, but Natives hold only 5% of state jobs, and 27.3% of Native men and 16% of Native women are unemployed (AAANativeArts 2013; U.S. Census Bureau 2009a, 2011a). Consider that the state of Alaska uses the Internet as its primary means of advertising and accepting applications for state jobs (State of Alaska 2006). However, Internet access is unavailable in 164 predominantly Native villages in Alaska—a state so large and spread out that it is 2.2 times the size of Texas and has 229 Native groups (Denali Commission 2001, 2011). Other options for application include requesting applications by mail, but a person must first know about the opening. The usefulness of this process is limited, however, by the reliability and speed of mail service to remote villages and the often short application periods for state jobs. State officials may not intentionally use the mechanism to prevent Aleuts, Inupiats, Athabaskans, or other Alaska Natives from gaining access to state jobs, but the effect can be institutionalized discrimination. Here, Internet access plays a role in participation of minorities in the job market (Nakamura 2004).

The point is that whites, especially affluent whites, benefit from privileges not available to low-income minorities. The privileged members may not purposely disadvantage others and may not be prejudiced, but the playing field is not level, even though discrimination may be completely unintentional (Rothenberg 2011). Consider the following privileges that most of us who are part of the dominant group take for granted (McIntosh 2002:97–101):

- I can avoid spending time with people who mistrust people of my color.
- I can protect my children most of the time from people who might not like them.
- I can criticize our government and talk about how I fear its policies and behavior without being seen as a cultural "outsider."

- I can easily buy posters, postcards, picture books, greeting cards, dolls, toys, and children's magazines featuring people of my race.
- I can arrange my activities so that I will never have to experience feelings of rejection owing to my race.

Now imagine *not* being able to take these and many other privileges for granted. What would your reaction be, and what could you do about it?

Thinking Sociologically

Imagine someone in your hometown who runs a business that is hiring people. In order to make a decision about whom to hire, she uses information that has been provided by another institution or organization. How might some of that information be a source of unintended side-effect discrimination for a minority group member? How might the employer discriminate in hiring against a minority group person without realizing it?

Past-in-present discrimination refers to *practices from the past that may no longer be allowed but that continue to have consequences for people in the present* (Feagin and Feagin 1986; Verbeek and Penninx 2009).

In Mississippi in the 1950s, state expenditures to educate a white child averaged $147 per pupil, whereas the average was $34 per black pupil in segregated schools (Luhman and Gilman 1980). Such blatant segregation and inequality in use of tax dollars is no longer legal. This may seem like ancient history, yet some African Americans who were in school in the 1950s and 1960s are receiving low Social Security checks because their earning power was diminished and they cannot help to pay for their grandchildren to go to college. To those who received a substandard education and did not have an opportunity for college, this is not ancient history; it affects their opportunities today.

Remember that prejudice is an attitude, discrimination an action. If neighbors do not wish to have minority group members move onto their block, that is prejudice. If they try to organize other neighbors against the newcomers or make the situation unpleasant once the minority family has moved in, that is discrimination. If minorities cannot afford to live in the neighborhood because of discrimination in the marketplace, that is institutionalized discrimination. An opportunity to clarify and to recognize interrelationships between some of these sociological terms can be explored in the next "Engaging Sociology" feature.

In the United States things seem to have changed since 2008 when a biracial president was elected. Conservative commentators and many journalists are fond of saying that this means we have entered a postracial society—that race has become irrelevant. While it is true that President Obama is the nation's first biracial president, it is also true that

Engaging Sociology

Using and Relating Key Concepts

A lot of terms in this chapter have related to issues of prejudice, discrimination, and racism and how they operate at micro and meso levels. Figure 8.3 indicates the levels at which each issue operates.

	Micro Level	*Meso Level*
Conscious and Intended	Prejudice: explicit bigotry	Institutionalized discrimination (explicit)
Unconscious and Unintended	Color-blind prejudice	Indirect institutionalized discrimination
		Side-effect discrimination
		Past-in-present discrimination

Figure 8.3   Understanding Key Concepts

Engaging With Sociology

1. Define and give an example of each term.

2. Identify which two cells represent *racism* as sociologists use the term.

3. Identify ways that each of these elements of intergroup conflict might foster the others.

only two senators (out of 100) are black in 2013—and one of them was appointed rather than elected. We have also seen in Table 8.1 on page 216 that college-educated blacks earn $10,000 a year less than white college graduates. Whites with a professional degree earn about $128,000 per year while Hispanics with the same degree earn $79,000. In a poor economy, blacks and other minorities continue to have higher unemployment than whites. Note also that on a typical Sunday morning, whites and blacks worship separately, with multiracial churches being rare (Emerson 2006; Emerson and Smith 2000; Marti 2009). As long as differences divide the United States, it is hard to support the notion that it is a "postracial" society.

Thinking Sociologically

Think of some events in history that have an effect on particular groups today. Why might the events cause intergroup hostility or cooperation? How does discrimination, as discussed above, help us understand world conflicts, such as the intense hostility between Palestinians and Jews in Israel?

Dominant and Minority Group Contact: Macro-Level Analysis

Economic hard times hit Germany in the 1930s, following that nation's loss in World War I. To distract citizens from the nation's problems, a scapegoat was found—the Jewish population. The German states began restricting Jewish activities and investments. Gradually, hate rhetoric intensified, but even then, most Jews had little idea about the fate that awaited them. Millions perished in gas chambers because the ruling Nazi party defined them as an undesirable race (although being Jewish is actually a religious or ethnic identification, not a biological category).

Mexico, Guatemala, and other Central American governments face protests by their Indian populations, descendants of Aztecs, Mayans, and Inca, who have distinguishing features and are today generally relegated to servant positions. These native groups have been protesting against government policies and their poor conditions—usurping of their land, inability to own land, absentee landownership, poor pay, and discrimination by the government (DePalma 1995). One result of discrimination against Central and South American native groups is that their numbers are diminishing and some groups, such as those in Tierra del Fuego, Chile, have died out.

These examples illustrate two of the patterns of contact between governments and minority groups. The Jews in

Germany faced genocide while First Nations in Latin America in the past century have faced forced relocation to new geographical areas. The form that policies toward minority groups take depends on

1. which group has more power;
2. the needs of the dominant group for labor or other resources (e.g., land) that could be provided by the minority group;
3. the cultural norms of each group, including level of tolerance of out-groups;
4. the social histories of groups, including their religious, political, racial, and ethnic differences;
5. the physical and cultural identifiers that distinguish the groups; and
6. the times and circumstances (wars, economic strains, recessions).

Where power between groups in society is unequal, the potential for differential treatment is always present. Yet, some groups live in harmony whether their power is equal or unequal. Whether totally accepting or prone to conflict, dominant-minority relations depend on time, place, and circumstances. Figure 8.3 indicates the range of dominant-minority relationships and policies (Kitano, Aqbayani, and de Anda 2005).

Genocide is *the systematic effort of one group, usually the dominant group, to destroy a minority group.* Christians were thrown to the lions in ancient Rome. Hitler sent Jews and other non-Aryan groups into concentration camps to be

One of the most horrific racial or ethnic policies was the Holocaust, the murder of 11 million people, including 6 million Jews, by the Nazi government in Germany under Adolf Hitler. This photo is horrible to view, but this is the consequence of bigotry that leads to genocide.

Culture

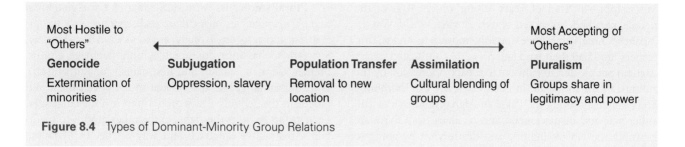

Most Hostile to "Others"				Most Accepting of "Others"
Genocide	**Subjugation**	**Population Transfer**	**Assimilation**	**Pluralism**
Extermination of minorities	Oppression, slavery	Removal to new location	Cultural blending of groups	Groups share in legitimacy and power

Figure 8.4 Types of Dominant-Minority Group Relations

gassed. Iraqis used deadly chemical weapons against the Kurdish people within their own country. Members of the Serbian army massacred Bosnian civilians to rid towns of Bosnian Muslims, an action referred to as "ethnic cleansing" that has been used more recently in Darfur, Africa (Cushman and Mestrovic 1996; T. Evans 2010). In Rwanda, people of the Tutsi and Hutu tribes carried out mass killings against each other in the late 1990s. In 2011, some politicians argued for intervention in Libya because of the threat of genocide against civilians. More recently, the Syrian dictator Bashar al-Assad and his military have killed many who defied his rule by demonstrating; most were Sunni Muslims, different from Assad's ruling group, the Alawites. Members of the international community intervened, but did so amid controversy. Genocide has existed at many points in history, and as illustrated, it still exists today. These examples show the lethal consequences of racism, one group at the meso level systematically killing off another, often a minority, to gain control and power.

Subjugation refers to *the subordination of one group to another that holds power and authority.* Haiti and the Dominican Republic are two countries sharing the island of Hispaniola in the Caribbean. Because many Haitians are poor, they are lured by promises of jobs in the sugarcane fields of the Dominican Republic. However, they are forced to work long hours for little pay and are not allowed to leave until they have paid for housing and food, which may be impossible to do on their low wages.

Slavery is one form of subjugation that has existed throughout history. When the Roman Empire defeated other lands, captives became slaves. This included ancient Greeks, who also kept slaves at various times in their history. African tribes enslaved members of neighboring tribes, sometimes selling them to slave traders, and slavery has existed in Middle Eastern countries such as Saudi Arabia. As mentioned in the opening story for this chapter, slavery is flourishing in many parts of the world today (Bales 2000, 2007, 2012).

Segregation, a specific type of subjugation, separates minorities from the dominant group and deprives them of access to the dominant institutions. Jim Crow laws, instituted in the southern United States after the Civil War, legislated separation between groups—separate facilities,

These children in Sudan play outside their "home"—a tent at Andalus refugee camp. Some people have survived in refugee camps with almost no food and little water, but the alternative was to be killed in their homeland.

schools, and neighborhoods (Alexander 2010; Feagin and Feagin 2010; Massey and Denton 1998). **Population transfer** refers to *the removal, often forced, of a minority group from a region or country.* Generally, the dominant group wants land or resources. Due to the ongoing conflicts discussed above, an ongoing example of population transfer has been taking place in Darfur and South Sudan in Africa. Members of the population there must move from their villages or be burned out of their homes or get caught in the cross fire. Even in refugee camps women and children are subject to rape and other atrocities when they seek water or wood for fires outside of the camps. The Sudanese military forces and their subsidiaries have been forcing residents of the non-Arab parts of Sudan to leave their land; they have no place to go but refugee camps.

Other examples of population transfers are numerous: Native Americans in the United States were removed to reservations. The Cherokee people were forced to walk from Georgia and North Carolina to new lands west of the

Population Transfer ▶

Mississippi—a "Trail of Tears" along which 40% of the people perished. As noted above, during World War II, Japanese Americans were forcibly moved to "relocation centers" and had their land and property confiscated. Many Afghani people fled to Pakistan to escape oppression by the ruling Taliban and again in 2001 to escape U.S. bombing. Today, civilians along the Pakistan-Afghanistan border still suffer war and displacement, and civilians from Syria are escaping the violent fighting and destruction by going to refugee camps in neighboring Turkey, Lebanon, and Jordan.

Assimilation refers to *the structural and cultural merging of minority and majority groups, a process by which minority members may lose their original identity but contribute to their new society* (Kitano, Aqbayani, and de Anda 2005; Marger 2012). Forced assimilation occurs when a minority group is forced to suppress its identity. This happened in Spain around the time of World War II, when the Basque people were forbidden by the central government to speak or study the Basque language. For several centuries—ending only a few decades ago—the British government tried to stamp out the Welsh language from Wales. However, assimilation is often a voluntary process in which a minority chooses to adopt the values, norms, and institutions of the dominant group.

Assimilation is more likely to occur when the minority group is culturally similar to the dominant group. For instance, in the United States, the closer a group is to being white, English speaking, and Protestant, or "WASP" (white Anglo-Saxon Protestant), the faster its members will be assimilated into the society, adopting the culture and blending in biologically through intermarriage.

The notion that we should be a "color-blind" nation is really a call for assimilation, for the only way we can ignore real differences between people is to obliterate the differences. This means that people of color would have to give up their cultures and become like the dominant Euro-American culture (Dalton 2012; Dyer 2012). It is for this reason that some minorities see assimilation policy as oppressive and an effort to destroy them.

The United States is becoming increasingly diverse and pluralistic. This billboard ad for McDonald's first appeared in August 2012 in St. Paul, Minnesota—in the Hmong language.

Pluralism occurs *when each ethnic or racial group in a country maintains its own culture and separate set of institutions but has recognized equity in the society.* For example, Switzerland has four dominant cultural language groups: French, German, Italian, and Rommansh (or Rumantsch). Four official languages are spoken in the government and taught in the schools. Laws are written in four languages. Each group respects the rights of the other groups to maintain a distinctive language and way of life. In Malaysia, three groups share power—Malays, Chinese, and Indians. Although the balance is not completely stable because Chinese and Indians have higher levels of education and hold more political and economic power than the native Malays, there is a desire to maintain a pluralistic society. While tensions do exist, both Switzerland and Malaysia represent examples of pluralist societies. Legal protection of smaller or less powerful groups is often necessary to have pluralism. In the United States, pluralism as a policy was first embraced by the nation's first president, George Washington, as explained in the next "Sociology in Our Social World."

Many individuals in the world face disruptions during their lifetimes that change their position in the society. The dominant-minority continuum illustrates the range of relations with dominant groups that can affect people's lives as transitions take place.

Thinking Sociologically

Think of examples from current news stories of positive and harmful intercultural contact. Where do your examples fit on the continuum from genocide to pluralism? What policies might address issues raised in your examples?

Theoretical Explanations of Dominant-Minority Group Relations

Are humans innately cruel, inhumane, greedy, aggressive, territorial, or warlike? Some people think so, but the evidence is not very substantial. To understand prejudice in individuals or small groups, psychological and social-psychological theories are most relevant. To understand discrimination that is embedded in institutions, studying meso-level organizations is helpful, and to understand the pervasive nature of prejudice and stereotypes over time in various societies, cultural explanations are useful. Although aspects of macro-level theories relate to micro- and meso-level analysis, their major emphasis is on understanding the national and global systems of group relations.

Sociology in Our Social World

Pluralism: A Long-Standing History in the United States

This Jewish synagogue, the oldest in the United States, proudly displays a letter from George Washington enshrining pluralism in the new nation's policies.

It is no mistake that the oldest Jewish synagogue in the United States is in Rhode Island, for separation of church and state and tolerance of other religious traditions was a founding principle of Rhode Island. After George Washington was elected president of the new nation, he received a letter from that early Jewish congregation in Newport, Rhode Island, asking about his policies of pluralism or multiculturalism (though those words had not been coined yet). In response in 1790, Touro Synagogue received a handwritten letter signed by President Washington (and now proudly on display by the synagogue) embracing an open and "liberal" policy to all American citizens, regardless of origin or religious affiliation. In this letter, George Washington affirmed a policy of pluralism from the very beginning of the country's existence as a nation. Passages from that letter follow.

* * * * * * *

The Citizens of the United States of America have a right to applaud themselves for having given to mankind examples of an enlarged and liberal policy: a policy worthy of imitation. . . . It is now no more that toleration is spoken of, as if it was by the indulgence of one class of people, that another enjoyed the exercise of their inherent natural rights. For happily the Government of the United States, which gives to bigotry no sanction, to persecution no assistance, requires only that they who live under its protection should demean themselves as good citizens.

. . . May the children of the Stock of Abraham, who dwell in this land, continue to merit and enjoy the good will of the other Inhabitants; while every one shall sit in safety under his own vine and figtree, and there shall be none to make him afraid. May the father of all mercies scatter light and not darkness in our paths, and make us all in our several vocations useful here, and in his own due time and way everlastingly happy.

G. Washington

Structural-Functional Theory

From the structural-functional perspective, maintaining a cheap pool of laborers who are in and out of work serves several purposes for society. Low-paying and undesirable jobs for which no special training is needed—busboys, janitors, nurse's aides, street sweepers, and fast-food service workers—are often filled by minority group members of societies, including immigrant populations.

Not only does this cheap pool of labor function to provide a ready labor force for dirty work or the menial unskilled jobs; these individuals also serve other functions for society. They make possible occupations that service the poor, such as social work, public health, criminology, and the justice and legal systems. They buy goods others do not want—day-old bread, old fruits and vegetables, secondhand clothes. They set examples for others of what not to be, and they allow others to feel good about giving to charity (Gans 1971, 1994).

Thomas Sowell contends that circumstances of the historical period and the situation into which one is born create the major differences in the social status of minority groups. He believes that minority individuals must work hard to make up for their disadvantages. His contentions are controversial in part because of the implication that meso-level discrimination embedded in institutions can be overcome by hard work (Sowell 1994). Conflict theorists counter his argument by saying that discrimination that reduces opportunities is built into institutions and organizations and must be dealt with through meso- and macro-level structural change. They argue that hard work is necessary, but not sufficient, for minorities to succeed. Prejudice, discrimination, and institutionalized racism are dysfunctional for society, resulting in loss of human resources, costs to societies due to poverty and crime, hostilities between groups, and disrespect for those in power (Schaefer 2012).

Conflict Theory

In the 1840s, as the United States set out to build a railroad, large numbers of laborers emigrated from China to do the hard manual work. When the railroad was completed and competition for jobs became tight, the once-welcomed Chinese became targets of bitter prejudice, discrimination, and sometimes violence. Between 1850 and 1890, whites in California protested against Chinese, Japanese, and Chicano workers. Members of these minority groups banded together in towns or cities for protection, founding

Chinese men were invited and encouraged to come to North America to help build railroads. However, prejudice was extremely prevalent, especially once the railroads were completed and the immigrants began to settle into other jobs in the U.S. economy.

the Chinatowns we know today (Kitano, Aqbayani, and de Anda 2005). Non-Chinese Asian groups suffered discrimination as well because the prejudiced generalizations were applied to all Asians (Son 1992; Winders 2004).

Why does discrimination occur? Conflict theorists argue that creating a "lesser" group protects the dominant group's advantages. Because privileges and resources are usually limited, those who have them want to keep them. One strategy used by privileged people, according to conflict theory, is to perpetrate prejudice and discrimination against minority group members. A case in point is the *Gastarbeiter* (guest workers) in Germany and other Western European countries, who immigrate from Eastern Europe, the Middle East, and Africa to fill positions in European economies. They are easily recognized because of cultural and physical differences and are therefore ready targets for prejudice and discrimination, especially in times of economic competition and slowing economies. This helps keep many of them in low-level positions. Today some European countries are considering laws to limit immigration, in part because of their weak economies.

Karl Marx argued that exploitation of the lower classes is built into capitalism because it benefits the ruling class. Unemployment creates a ready pool of labor to fill the marginal jobs, with the pool often made up of identifiable minority groups. This pool protects those in higher-level positions from others moving up in the stratification system and threatening their jobs.

Several theories stemming from conflict theory help explain minority relations. One is discussed below, *"the development of hostilities between groups."*

Three critical factors contribute to *hostility between groups*, according to one conflict theorist (Noel 1968): First, if two groups of people can each be identified by their appearance, clothing, or language, then we-versus-they thinking and ethnocentrism may develop. However, this by itself does not mean there will be long-term hostility between the groups. Second, if the two groups conflict over scarce resources that both want, hostilities are very likely to arise. The resources might be the best land, the highest-paying jobs, access to the best schools for one's children, energy resources such as oil, or positions of prestige and power. If the third element is added to the mix—one group having much more power than the other—then intense dislike between the two groups and misrepresentation of each group by the other are almost certain to occur. What happens is that the group with more power uses that power to ensure that its members (and their offspring) get the most valued resources. However, because they do not want to see themselves as unfair and brutish people, they develop stereotypes and derogatory characterizations of "those other people," so the lack of access provided to "them" seems reasonable and justified. Discrimination (often at the macro level) comes first, and bigoted attitudes and beliefs (at the micro level) come later to justify the discrimination (Noel 1968). Thus, macro- and meso-level conflicts can lead to micro-level attitudes. Stereotypes, then, are the consequence of hostility between groups—not the cause.

Conflict theory has taught us a great deal about racial and ethnic stratification. However, conflict theorists often focus on people with power quite intentionally oppressing others to protect their own self-interests. They depict the dominant group as made up of nasty, power-hungry people. As we have seen in the meso-level discussion of side-effect and past-in-present discrimination, privilege and discrimination are often subtle and unconscious, which means they can continue without ill will among those in the dominant group. Their privilege has been institutionalized. Conflict theorists sometimes miss this important point.

Thinking Sociologically

What are some micro-, meso-, and macro-level factors that enhance the chances that minority persons can move up the social ladder to better jobs?

The Effects of Prejudice, Racism, and Discrimination

Pictures of starving orphans from Sudan and Ethiopia and broken families from war-torn Bosnia remind us of the human toll resulting from prejudice and discrimination. This section discusses the results of prejudice, racism, and discrimination for minority groups and for societies.

The Costs of Racism

Individual victims of racism suffer from the destruction of their lives, health, and property, especially in societies where racism leads to poverty, enslavement, conflict, or war. Poor self-concept and low self-esteem stem from constant reminders of a devalued status in society. Moreover, 7.6 million children of color died in 2010 from malnutrition, and 1 in 8 children in sub-Saharan Africa die before age 5 (World Hunger Education Service 2012b).

Prejudice and discrimination result in costs to organizations and communities as well as to individuals. First, organizations and communities lose the talents of individuals who could be productive and contributing members. Because of poor education, substandard housing, and inferior medical care, these citizens cannot use their full potential to contribute to society. In 2010, 50.7 million or 16.7% of U.S. citizens did not have health insurance (Wolf 2010). The inequities in health care coverage are

Sudanese children wait in line to receive food in the Sudanese refugee camp of Narus.

striking: 11.6% of whites are without care, but the figure is 19.9% for African Americans and 41.5% for Hispanics (Newport and Mendes 2009).

Second, government subsidies cost millions in the form of welfare, food stamps, and imprisonment, but they are made necessary in part by the lack of opportunities for minority individuals. Representation of ethnic groups in the U.S. political system can provide a voice for concerns of groups. Table 8.2 shows the representation of ethnic groups in Congress, but even this understates the lack of representation. In the entire history of the United States, the number of senators from minority ethnic groups is extremely small.

Thinking Sociologically

How might lack of access to health care and insurance affect other aspects of a person's life (work, family life, education)?

Table 8.2 Representation in the U.S. Congress, 2013–2014

	Native American	Asian	Black	Hispanic
Senate	0	2 (2%)	2 (2%)	3 (3%)
House	1 (0.2%)	9 (2%)	44 (10%)	30 (6.7%)
% of Population	0.9%	4.8%	12.6%	16.3%

Source: Ethnic Majority (2012); U.S. Senate (2013).

Continued attempts to justify discrimination by stereotyping and labeling groups have cultural costs, too. There are many talented African American athletes who are stars on college and professional sports teams, but very few of them have been able to break into the ranks of coaches and managers (Sage and Eitzen 2012). That said, there has been more opportunity in basketball than in other sports where 14 of 30 National Basketball Association head coaches are black in a sport with 80% black players (Mahoney 2012). The number of African American and Mexican American actors and artists has increased, but the number of black playwrights and screenwriters who can get their works produced or who have become directors remains limited. African American musicians have found it much more difficult to earn royalties, and therefore most cannot compose full-time (V. Alexander 2003). Because these artists must create and perform their art "as a sideline," they are less able to contribute their talents to society. The rest of us are poorer for it.

Minority Reactions to Prejudice, Discrimination, and Racism

How have minority groups dealt with their status? Five different reactions are common: assimilation, acceptance, avoidance, aggression, and change-oriented actions directed at the social structure. The first four are micro-level responses. They do not address the meso- and macro-level issues.

Micro-Level Coping Strategies

Assimilation is an accommodation to prejudice and discrimination. Some minority group members attempt to pass or assimilate as members of the dominant group so as to avoid bigotry and discrimination. Although this option is not open to many because of their distinguishing physical characteristics, this strategy usually involves abandoning their own culture and turning their back on family roots and ties, a costly strategy in terms of self-esteem and sense of identity. People who select this coping strategy are forced to deny who they are as defined by their roots and to live their lives in constant anxiety, feeling as though they must hide something about themselves.

In the 1960s, popular items advertised in African American magazines included "whitening creams" or "skin bleaches." Some light-colored people with African ancestry would bleach their skin to pass as white. Skin-whitening creams are still popular in some Asian countries. Dissatisfaction with one's body has an impact on one's self-concept. *Passing*—pretending to be a member of the privileged group when one is not fully a part of that community—is one strategy used to enhance assimilation and avoid the stigma of belonging to a minority group. It has also been a common response of gays and lesbians who are afraid to come out. Homosexuals experience the costly impact on self-esteem and the constant fear that they may be discovered. Likewise, assimilated Jews have changed their religion and their names to be accepted. Despite the wrenching from their personal history, passing has allowed some individuals to become absorbed into the mainstream. *Acceptance* is another common reaction to minority status. Some minority groups have learned to live with their minority status with little overt challenge to the system. They may or may not hold deep-seated hostility, but they ultimately conclude that change in the society is not very likely, and acceptance may be the rational means to survive within the existing system.

There are many possible explanations for this seeming indifference. For example, religious beliefs allow poor Hindus in India to believe that if they accept their lot in life, they will be reincarnated in a higher life-form. If they rebel, they can expect to be reincarnated into a lower life-form. Their religion is a form of social control.

Unfortunately, many children are socialized to believe that they are inferior or superior because minority group members are expected by the dominant group to behave in certain ways and often live up to that expectation because of the self-fulfilling prophecy (Farley 2010). Evidence to support stereotypes is easily found in individual cases—"inferior" kids live in shabby houses, dress less well, and speak a different dialect. At school and on the job, minority position is reaffirmed by these characteristics.

Avoidance means shunning all contact with the dominant group. This can involve an active and organized attempt to leave the culture or live separately as some political exiles have done. In the United States, Marcus Garvey organized a Back-to-Africa movement in the 1920s, encouraging blacks to give up on any hope of justice in American society and to return to Africa. Native Americans continually moved west in the 19th century—trying to or being forced to get away from white Anglo settlers who brought alcohol and deadly diseases. In some cases, withdrawal may mean dropping out of the society as an individual—escaping by obliterating consciousness in drugs or alcohol. The escape from oppression and low self-concept is one reason why drug use is higher in minority ghettos and alcohol abuse is rampant on Native American reservations.

Avoidance that is not so destructive—more withdrawal and isolation—is also used by the Roma (sometimes called Gypsies—of which there are about a million in the United States) and by Native American groups that seek to preserve their cultures. Among some groups of isolated Apaches in New Mexico and Arizona, nearly half of the older population speaks no English and has no need or desire to learn it. They live according to old cultural ways in rather isolated desert climates. They have simply withdrawn from contact with the larger society (Farrer 2011).

Aggression resulting from anger and resentment over minority status and from subjugation may lead to retaliation or violence. Because the dominant group holds significant power, a direct route such as voting against the dominant group or defeating oppressors in war is not always possible. Indeed, direct confrontation can be very costly to those lacking political or economic power. Suicide bombers from Palestine represent the many Palestinians who are frustrated and angry over their situation in relation to Israel but have few options to express their anger.

Aggression usually takes one of two forms, indirect aggression or displaced aggression. Indirect aggression includes biting assertiveness in the arts—literature, art, racial and ethnic humor, and music—and in job-related actions such as inefficiency and slowdowns by workers. Displaced aggression, on the other hand, involves hostilities directed toward individuals or groups other than the dominant group, as happens when youth gangs attack other ethnic gangs in nearby neighborhoods. They substitute aggression against the dominant group by acting against the other minority group to protest their frustrating circumstances.

The four responses discussed thus far address the angst and humiliation that individual minorities feel. Each strategy allows an individual person to try to cope, but none addresses the structural causes of discrimination. The final strategy is change-oriented action: Minority groups pursue social change in the meso- and macro-level structures of society, as discussed in the following.

Meso- and Macro-Level Efforts to Bring Change: Nonviolent Resistance

Another technique for bringing about change at the meso and macro levels is nonviolent resistance by minority groups. The model for this technique comes from India where, in the 1950s, Mahatma Gandhi led the struggle for independence from Britain. Although Britain clearly had superior weapons and armies, boycotts, sit-ins, and other forms of resistance eventually led to British withdrawal as the ruling colonial power. This strategy has been used successfully by workers and students to bring about change in many parts of the world.

In the United States, Martin Luther King Jr. followed in the nonviolent resistance tradition of India's Gandhi, who sought to change India's laws so minorities could have equal opportunities within the society. King's strategy involved nonviolent popular protests, economic boycotts, and challenges to the current norms of the society. The National

Mahatma Gandhi, leader of the Indian civil disobedience revolt, marched to the shore to collect salt, a clear violation of the law that he felt was inhumane and unjust. On the right is a woman lieutenant in his nonviolent resistance movement.

Association for the Advancement of Colored People sought to bring about legal changes through lawsuits that create new legal precedents supporting racial equality. Often, these lawsuits address side-effect discrimination—a meso-level problem. Many other associations for minorities—including the Anti-Defamation League (founded by Jews) and La Raza Unida (a Chicano organization)—also seek to address problems both within organizations and institutions (meso level) and in the nation as a whole (macro level). Like Dr. King, who had an undergraduate degree in sociology, many sociologists have used their training to address the issues of discrimination and disprivilege through empowerment and change.

The Occupy Wall Street movement (sometimes called "We Are the 1%") began on September 17, 2011, and has spread from New York to many cities around the world. Members of the 99% minority (called a minority since they have less power and fewer resources than the top 1%) have protested against the lack of resource distribution in the United States, setting up encampments in city parks

The Occupy Wall Street movement is a very current example of a nonviolent strategy for change. The members of this movement are protesting on behalf of the 99%, since two thirds of income gains since 2000 have gone to the wealthiest 1%. Occupy appears to have less centralized organization than most such movements, with no clear leader.

and marching against what they feel is inequity in the job and tax structure. They reject use of violence, but they want their voice to be heard. On the opposite side of the political spectrum is the Tea Party Patriots, which focuses largely on smaller government and decreases in taxes for all—including the rich—because (1) they feel that this will stimulate the economy more and result in growth, and (2) they seek freedom for individuals to spend their resources however they please. So movements on both sides can use similar strategies to try to influence the direction of the society's policies (Tea Party Patriots 2012). Nonviolent resistance movements such as these illustrate continuing efforts to bring about change.

Sometimes the minority effort to bring change results in assimilation, but often, the goal is to create a pluralistic society in which cultures can be different yet have economic opportunities open to all.

Thinking Sociologically

The preceding discussion presents five types of responses by minorities to the experience of discrimination and rejection. Four of these are at the micro level, and only one is at the meso and macro levels. Why do you suppose most of the coping strategies of minorities are at the micro level?

Policies Governing Minority and Dominant Group Relations

From our social world perspective, we know that no problem can be solved by working at only one level of analysis. A successful strategy must bring about change at every level of the social world—individual attitudes, organizational discrimination, cultural stereotypes, societal stratification systems, and national and international structures. However, most current strategies focus on only one level of analysis. The types of problems and their solutions at each level of the social system are discussed below and illustrated in Figure 8.5.

Individual or Small-Group Solutions

Programs to address prejudice and stereotypes through human relations workshops, group encounters, and therapy can achieve goals with small numbers of people. For instance, black and white children who are placed in interracial classrooms in schools are more likely to develop close interracial friendships (Ellison and Powers 1994). Beyond that, education gives a broader, more universal outlook; reduces misconceptions and prejudices; shows that many issues do not have clear answers; and encourages

Types of Problems at Each Level	Types of Solutions or Programs
Individual level: stereotypes and prejudice	Therapy, tolerance-education programs
Group level: negative group interaction	Positive contact, awareness by majority members of their many privileges
Societal level: institutionalized discrimination	Education, media, legal-system revisions
Global level: deprivation of human rights	Human rights movements, international political pressures

Figure 8.5   Problems and Solutions

This Louisianan waits at a shelter as Hurricane Isaac bears down on the Louisiana coast in the summer of 2012. Minorities are more often living in vulnerable areas and therefore more often victimized. The solution proposed by some nongovernmental organizations is to address problems and suffering with volunteer work and donations. Others think the government should have a major role.

multicultural understanding. Two groups with strong multicultural education programs are the Anti-Defamation League and the Southern Poverty Law Center's Teaching Tolerance program. Both groups provide schools and community organizations with their literature, videos, and other materials aimed at combating intolerance and discrimination toward others.

However, these strategies do not address the social conditions underlying the problems because they reach only a few people achieving only limited results. They also do not begin to address dilemmas that are rooted in meso- and macro-level causes of problems.

Group Contact

Some social scientists advocate organized group contact between dominant and minority group members to improve relations and break down stereotypes and fears. Although not all contact reduces prejudice, many studies have shown the benefits of contact. Some essential conditions for success are equal status of participants, noncompetitive and nonthreatening contact, and projects or goals on which to cooperate (Farley 2010).

In a classic study of group contact, social psychologists Muzafer Sherif and Carolyn Sherif (1953) learned that the most effective strategy to reduce group prejudice is to introduce a superordinate goal that can be achieved only if everyone cooperates. As groups work together, established stereotypes begin to fade away. The key, then, is to find common interests that can only be satisfied if all parties are seen as partners in solving some larger problem, and the outcome is win-win for all.

Positive group contact experiences can be effective in improving relations in groups at a micro level by breaking down stereotypes, but negative or ineffective group contact may also affect "the many cognitive, affective, situational and institutional barriers to positive contact" (Pettigrew and Tropp 2000:93). To solidify the positive gains, we must also address institutionalized inequalities, discussed next.

Institutional and Societal Strategies to Improve Group Relations

Sociologists contend that group, institutional, and societal approaches to reduce discrimination get closer to the core of the problems and affect larger numbers of people than do micro-level strategies. For instance, voluntary advocacy organizations pursue political change through lobbying, watchdog monitoring, rallies, and boycotts (Minkoff 1995).

The U.S. Civil Rights Commission and the Equal Employment Opportunity Commission are government organizations that protect rights and work toward equality for all citizens. These agencies oversee practices and hear complaints relating to racial, sexual, age, and other forms of discrimination. Legislation, too, can modify behaviors. Laws requiring equal treatment of minorities have resulted in increased tolerance of those who are "different" and have opened doors that previously were closed to minorities.

Affirmative action laws, first implemented during Lyndon Johnson's administration, have been used to fight pervasive institutional racism, but they are controversial (Crosby 2004; Farley 2010).

Affirmative Action

One of the most contentious policies in the United States has been affirmative action. The following discussion addresses the goals and forms of the policy. A societal policy for change, affirmative action actually involves three different policies. Its simplest and original form, which we call *strict affirmative action,* involves affirmative or positive steps to make sure that unintentional discrimination does not occur. It requires, for example, that an employer who receives federal monies must advertise a position widely and not just through internal or friendship networks. If the job requires an employee with a college education, then by federal law, employers must recruit through minority and women's colleges as well as state and private colleges in the region. If employers are hiring in the suburbs, they are obliged to contact unemployment agencies in poor and minority communities as well as those in the affluent neighborhoods. After taking these required extra steps, employers are expected to hire the most qualified candidate who applies, regardless of race, ethnicity, sex, religion, or other external characteristics. The focus is on providing opportunities for the best-qualified people. For many people, this is the meaning of affirmative action, and it is inconceivable that this could be characterized as reverse discrimination, for members of the dominant group will be hired if they are in fact the most qualified. These policies do not overcome the problem that qualified people who have been marginalized may be competent but do not have the traditional paper credentials that document their qualifications (Gallagher 2004).

A *quota system,* the second policy, is a requirement that employers *must* hire a certain percentage of minorities. For the most part, quotas are now unconstitutional. They apply only in cases in which a court has found a company to have a substantial and sustained history of discrimination against minorities and in which the employment position does not have many requirements (if the job entails sweeping floors and cleaning toilets, there would not be an expectation of a specific academic degree or a particular grade point average).

Preference policies are the third form and the one that has created the most controversy among opponents of affirmative action. Preference policies are based on the concept of equity, the belief that sometimes people must be treated differently in order to be treated fairly. This policy was enacted to level the playing field, which was not rewarding highly competent people because of institutional racism.

The objectives of preference policies are to (1) eliminate qualifications that are not substantially related to the job but that unwittingly favor members of the dominant group and (2) foster achievement of objectives of the organization that are only possible through enhanced diversity. To overcome these inequalities and achieve certain objectives, employers and educational institutions take account of race or sex by making special efforts to hire and retain workers or accept students from groups that have been underrepresented. In many cases, these individuals bring qualifications others do not possess. Consider the following examples.

A goal of the medical community is to provide access to medical care for underserved populations. There is an extreme shortage of physicians on the Navajo reservation. Thus, a Navajo applicant for medical school might be accepted, even if her scores are slightly lower than those of another candidate, because she speaks Navajo and understands the culture. One could argue that she is more qualified to be a physician on the reservation than someone who knows nothing about Navajo society but has a slightly higher grade point average or test score. Some argue that tests should not be the only measure to determine successful applicants.

Likewise, a black police officer may have more credibility in a minority neighborhood and may be able to defuse a delicate conflict more effectively than a white officer who scored slightly higher on a paper-and-pencil placement test. Sometimes, being a member of a particular ethnic group can actually make one more qualified for a position.

Many colleges and universities admit students because they need an outstanding point guard on the basketball team, an extraordinary soprano for the college choir, or a student from a distant state for geographic diversity. These students are shown preference by being admitted with lower test scores than some other applicants because they are "differently qualified." Many colleges also give preference to male students to achieve gender balance, even if more qualified females apply. The controversy about whether minority students should be given preference follows this same reasoning. Consider the following example.

A lawsuit filed in Detroit alleged that the University of Michigan gave unlawful preference to minorities in undergraduate admissions and in law school admissions. In this controversial case, the court ruled that undergraduate admissions were discriminatory because they used numbers rather than individualized judgments to make the admissions determination (Alger 2003). Consider the next "Engaging Sociology" feature and decide whether you think the policy was fair and whether only race and ethnicity should have been deleted from the preferences allowed.

Predictions were that 25 years after the Michigan cases racial preferences would no longer be necessary to achieve the affirmative action goals. In 2013 the Supreme Court ruled on another case involving affirmative action, this time at the University of Texas (*Fisher v. University of Texas*). The court ruled that diversity in educational institutions is so important that race may need to be considered as a basis for preference in admissions. However, the court raised the standard for such policies, insisting that universities must show that they have unsuccessfully tried other race-neutral policies to achieve the same end (Liptak 2013). For example, three fourths of the University of Texas first-year students are admitted because a state law requires that the top students—usually the top 10%—must be admitted. The state of Texas is 38% Hispanic and 12% African American, and many of its schools are overwhelmingly of one race (Farley 2010; Lewin 2012). Unlike most states that have a smaller minority population, this policy may be sufficient to create substantial diversity. So the *Fisher* case affirmed the need for preference policies, but insisted that colleges must demonstrate they have tried other options.

In California, doing away with preferences reduced the number of minority students, especially African Americans and Latinos, in higher education (Liptak 2012; National Public Radio 2010). Thus far California has not discovered other options that will ensure similar levels of diversity in the college classroom.

The question remains: Should preferences be given to accomplish diversity? Some people feel that programs involving any sort of preference are reverse discrimination. Others believe such programs have encouraged employers, educational institutions, and government to look carefully

Engaging Sociology

Preference Policies at the University of Michigan

To enhance diversity on the campus—a practice that many argue makes a university a better learning environment and enhances the academic reputation of the school—many colleges have preference policies in admissions. However, the University of Michigan was sued by applicants who felt they were not admitted because others replaced them on the roster due to their racial or ethnic background.

The University of Michigan is a huge university where a numbering system is needed to handle the volume (tens of thousands) of applicants; admissions staff cannot make a decision based on personal knowledge of each candidate. Thus, they give points for each quality they deem desirable in the student body. A maximum of 150 points is possible, and a score of 100 would pretty much ensure admission. The university feels that any combination of points accumulated according to the following formula will result in a highly qualified and diverse student body.

For academics, up to 110 points are possible:

- 80 points for grades (a particular grade point average in high school results in a set number of points; a 4.0 results in 80 points; a 2.8 results in 56 points)
- 12 points for standardized test scores (ACT or SAT)
- 10 points for the academic rigor of high school (so all students who go to tougher high schools earn points)
- 8 points for the difficulty of the curriculum (e.g., points for honors curriculum vs. keyboarding courses)

For especially desired qualities, including diversity, up to 40 points are possible for any combination of the following (but no more than 40 in this "desired qualities" category):

- Geographical distribution (10 for Michigan resident; an additional 6 for underrepresented Michigan county)
- Legacy—a relative has attended Michigan (4 points for a parent; 1 for a grandparent or sibling)
- Quality of submitted essay (3 points)
- Personal achievement—a special accomplishment that is noteworthy (up to 5 points)
- Leadership and service (5 points each)
- Miscellaneous (only one of these can be used):
  __Socioeconomic disadvantage (20 points)
  __Racial or ethnic minority (20 points; disallowed by the court ruling)
  __Men in nursing (5 points)
  __Scholarship athlete (20 points)
  __Provost's discretion (20 points; usually the son or daughter of a large financial donor or of a politician)

In addition to ethnicity being given preference, athleticism, musical talent, having a relative who is an alum, or being the child of someone who is noteworthy to the university are also considered. Some schools also give points for being a military veteran. The legal challenge to this admissions system was based only on the racial and ethnic preference given to some candidates, not on the other items that are preferenced.

* * * * * * *

Engaging With Sociology

1. Does this process seem reasonable as a way to get a diverse and highly talented incoming class of students? Why or why not?

2. Does it significantly advantage or disadvantage some students? Explain.

3. How would you design a fair system of admissions, and what other factors would you consider?

at hiring policies and minority candidates and that many more competent minority group members are working in the public sector as a result of these policies.

Global Movements for Human Rights

A unique coalition of world nations has emerged from the terrorist attack of September 11, 2001. In this attack on the World Trade Center in New York City, a center housing national and international businesses and workers, citizens

Some human rights movements have justice issues in countries around the world as their focal point. Amnesty International is one such movement, which has strong support at many college campuses.

from 90 countries were killed when two hijacked commercial jetliners flew into the towers.

The rights granted to citizens of any nation used to be considered the business of each sovereign nation, but after the Nazi Holocaust, German officers were tried at the Nuremberg trials, and the United Nations passed the Universal Declaration of Human Rights. Since that time, many international organizations have been established, often under the auspices of the United Nations, to deal with health issues, world poverty and debt, trade, security, and many other issues affecting world citizens—World Health Organization, World Bank, World Trade Organization, and numerous regional trade and security organizations.

The United Nations, several national governments (Britain, France, and Canada), and privately funded advocacy groups speak up for international human rights as a principle that transcends national boundaries. The most widely recognized private group is Amnesty International, a watchdog group that does lobbying on behalf of human rights and supports political prisoners and ethnic group spokespersons. When Amnesty International was awarded the Nobel Peace Prize in 1997, the group's visibility was dramatically increased. Some activist sociologists have formed Sociologists Without Borders, or SSF (*Sociólogos sin Fronteras;* www.sociologistswithoutborders.org), a transnational organization committed to the idea that "all people have equal rights to political and legal protections, to socioeconomic security, to self-determination, and to their personality."

Everyone can make a positive difference in the world, and one place to start is in our own communities (see "Contributing to Our Social World"). We can counter prejudice, discrimination, and socially embedded racism in our own groups by teaching children to see beyond "we" and "they" and by speaking out for fairness and against stereotypes and discrimination.

Inequality is not limited to social classes, race or ethnic groups, or religious communities. "We" and "they" thinking can invade some of the most intimate settings. It can infect relations between men and women in everything from the home to the boardroom and from the governance of nations to the decisions of global agencies. We will explore this in the next chapter: "Gender Stratification."

What Have We Learned?

Why are minority group members in most countries poorer than dominant group members? This and other chapter-opening questions can be answered in part by considering the fact that human beings have a tendency to create "we" and "they" categories and to treat those who are different as somehow less human. The categories can be based on physical appearance, cultural differences, religious differences, or anything the community or society defines as important. Once people notice differences, they are more inclined to hurt "them" or to harbor advantages for "us" if there is competition over resources that both groups want. Even within a nation, where people are supposedly all "us," there can be sharp differences and intense hostilities.

Key Points:

- Although the concept of race has no real meaning biologically, race is a social construction because people *believe* it is real. (See pp. 213–216.)

- Minority group status—having less power and less access to resources—may occur because of racial status or because of ethnic (cultural) factors. (See pp. 217–218.)

- Prejudice operates at the micro level of society and is closest to people's own lives, but it has much less impact on minorities than discrimination. Color-blind prejudice has become more of a problem—the denial of overt prejudice but the rejection of any policies that might correct inequities. (See pp. 219–222.)

- At the meso level, institutionalized discrimination operates through two processes: side-effect and past-in-present. These forms of discrimination are unintended and unconscious—operating quite separate from any prejudice of individuals in the society. (See pp. 223–226.)

- When very large ethnic groups or even nations collide, some people are typically displaced and find themselves in minority status. (See p. 219.)

- The policies of the dominant group may include genocide, subjugation, population transfer, assimilation, or pluralism. (See pp. 226–228.)

- The costs of racism to the society are high, including loss of human talent and resources, and the costs make life more difficult for the minority group members. (See pp. 231–232.)

- Coping devices used by minorities include five strategies, only one of which addresses the meso and macro-level causes. These strategies are assimilation, acceptance, avoidance, aggression, and organizing for societal change. (See pp. 232–234.)

- Policies to address problems of prejudice and discrimination range from individual and small-group efforts at the micro level to institutional, societal, and even global social movements. (See pp. 234–235.)

- Affirmative action policies are one approach, but the broad term *affirmative action* includes three different sets of policies that are quite distinct and have different outcomes. (See pp. 235–238.)

Discussion Questions

1. Before you read this chapter, were you aware that slavery still exists throughout the world? If yes, describe how you learned about it and your reaction to this fact. If not, think about *how* your social location led to your learning about it for the first time in this course.

2. Have you ever experienced being stereotyped because of your race or ethnicity? Why or why not? How can racial stereotypes harm societies, as well as groups and individuals?

3. What is the difference between blatant bigotry and color-blind prejudice? Why is it so difficult to recognize and address color-blind prejudice in the United States today?

4. Give two examples, respectively, of both side-effect discrimination and past-in-present discrimination. How have they impacted you and your life chances? Why?

5. We know that efforts to reduce prejudice, racism, and discrimination must take place at all levels (micro, meso, and macro). Most organizations, though, must choose one level on which to focus their particular efforts. If you were going to start an organization to decrease racial or ethnic prejudice, would you focus on the micro, meso, or macro level? Why? Explain what your organization would do.

(Continued)

(Continued)

6. Do you agree with the Supreme Court ruling that upheld preferences for college applicants at the University of Michigan who were scholarship athletes or the sons or daughters of a large donor or a politician, but not for racial or ethnic minorities? Why or why not? How might each type of preference benefit (a) the university and (b) the larger society?

Contributing to Our Social World: What Can We Do?

At the Local Level

- *African American Student Associations, Arab American Student Associations, and Native American Student Associations* are all examples of student organizations dedicated to fighting bigotry and promoting understanding and the rights of racial minorities. Identify one of these groups on your campus and arrange to attend a meeting. If appropriate, volunteer to help with its work.

At the Organizational or Institutional Level

- *The Leadership Conference on Civil and Human Rights* is a national coalition dedicated to combating racism and its effects. It maintains a website that includes a directory of its membership of more than 200 organizations (www.civilrights.org). On its website you can find a "take action" link that will help you to explore ways in which you can participate in its efforts.

- *Teaching Tolerance* (www.splcenter.org/center/tt/teach.jsp), a program of the Southern Poverty Law Center, has curriculum materials for teaching about diversity and a program for enhancing cross-ethnic cooperation and dialogue in schools. Check into internship opportunities in local primary and secondary schools, and explore ways in which the Teaching for Tolerance approach can be incorporated into the curricula in your school district with local teachers and administrators.

At the National and Global Levels

- *Anti-Defamation League* (www.adl.org): The ADL acts to "stop the defamation of the Jewish people and to secure justice and fair treatment to all." They develop and implement educational programs on interfaith/intergroup understanding, scrutinize and call attention to hate groups, monitor hate speech on the Internet, and mobilize communities to stand up to bigotry throughout the United States and abroad. Job listings, summer internships, and opportunities in Israel and other locations are listed on their website.

- *National Relief Charities* strive "to help Native American people improve the quality of their lives by providing opportunities for them to bring about positive changes in their communities." To do so, it partners with tribal and other groups on the ground in the tribal regions of the Plains and Midwest. You can find out how to support their work and the work of their partner organizations by going to www.nrcprograms.org.

- *Cultural Survival and the UN Permanent Forum on Indigenous Issues* (www.cs.org and www.un.org/esa/socdev/unpfii) provide opportunities for combating racism globally. Also, consider purchasing only Fair Trade Certified (packages are clearly marked as such) coffee, and especially chocolate, and encouraging your school to sell Fair Trade products. You can learn more about Fair Trade products and issues by reading the article at www.nytimes.com/2012/09/28/business/media/green-mountain-coffee-begins-fair-trade-campaign-advertising.html and looking at educational materials provided by the Fair Trade Resource Network online at www.fairtraderesource.org.

- *Amnesty International* campaigns for internationally recognized human rights. It relies heavily on volunteers organized into chapters, many of them campus-based. You can join the organization and learn how to participate in its action through its website at www.amnesty.org. Consider joining or starting one on your campus.

Visit **www.sagepub.com/oswcondensed3e** for online activities, sample tests, and other helpful information. Select "Chapter 8: Race and Ethnic Group Stratification" for chapter-specific activities.

CHAPTER 9

Gender Stratification

She/He—Who Goes First?

Social inequality is especially evident in gender relations, and although in some societies women are treated with deference, they are rarely given first access to positions of significant power or financial reward. While they may hold many work roles, they often carry the load of child care by themselves, causing more role strains. The photos presented here focus on women's roles.

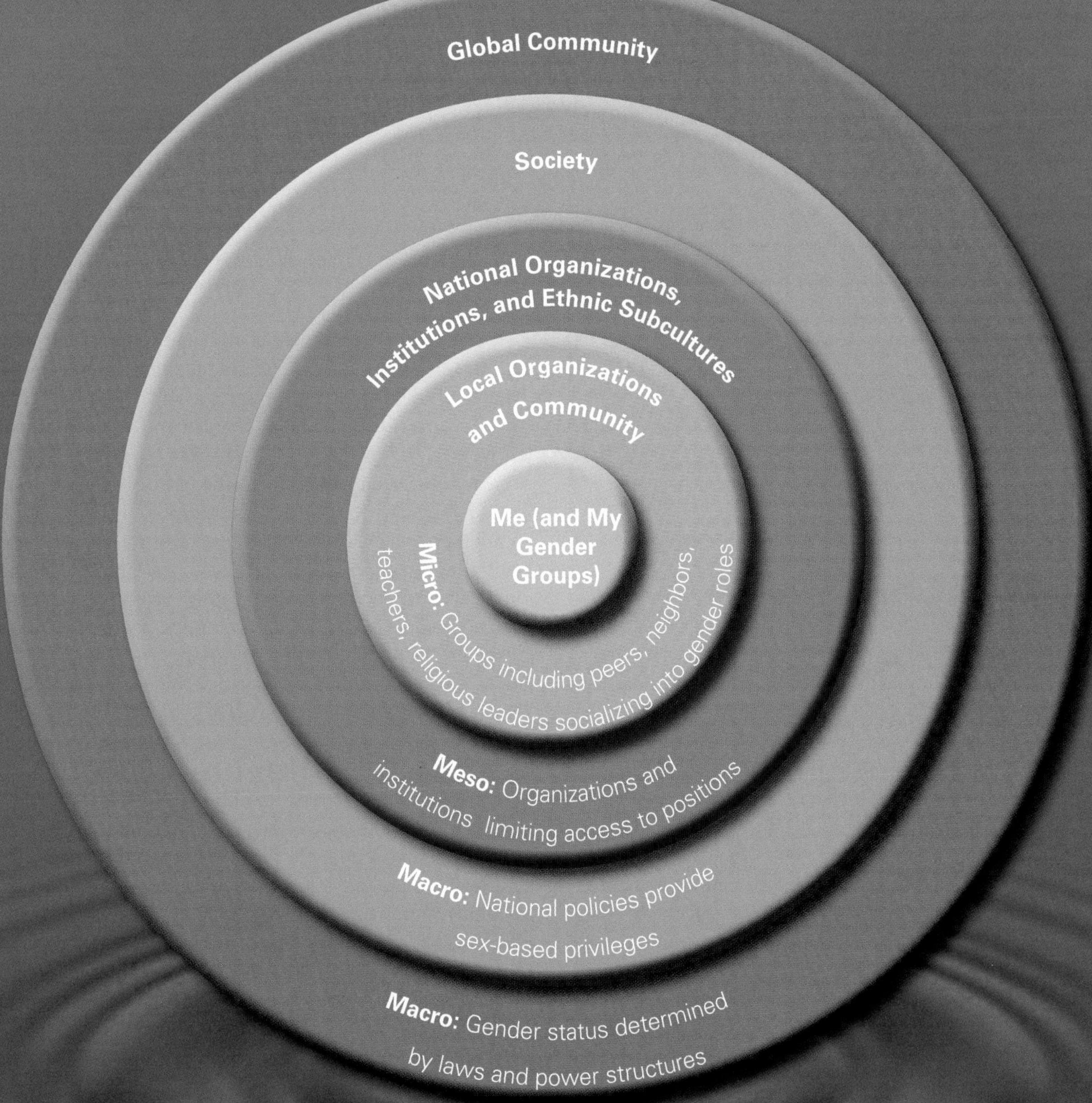

Global Community

Society

National Organizations, Institutions, and Ethnic Subcultures

Local Organizations and Community

Me (and My Gender Groups)

Micro: Groups including peers, neighbors, teachers, religious leaders socializing into gender roles

Meso: Organizations and institutions limiting access to positions

Macro: National policies provide sex-based privileges

Macro: Gender status determined by laws and power structures

Think About It	
Micro: Self and Inner Circle	How does being female or male affect your thoughts and behaviors?
Micro: Local Community	Why do some people face violence in their homes and communities because of their gender or sexuality?
Meso: National Institutions; Complex Organizations; Ethnic Groups	Can anything be done in our organizations and institutions to make men and women more equal?
Macro: National Society	Why do women have second-class status in many societies?
Macro: Global Community	How is gender inequality an issue in this new age of globalization?

What's coming in this chapter?

Sex, Gender, and the Stratification System

Gender Socialization: Micro- and Meso-Level Analyses

Meso-Level Agents of Gender Socialization

Gender Stratification: Meso- and Macro-Level Processes

Gender Stratification: Micro- to Macro-Level Theories

Gender, Homosexuality, and Minority Status

Costs and Consequences of Gender Stratification

Changing Gender Stratification and Social Policy

As women around the world wake up to International Women's Day 2013, their lives are radically different, yet each woman holds the same basic goals: a trusting and happy relationship; the option of having healthy, educated children with a fair chance in life; enough food on the table; self-respect; access to health care; and whatever individual desires are relevant in her society. Consider the following example from a Global North country that illustrates the problems some women face in meeting basic goals:

Jocelyn, who lives in the United States, is now retired and is having trouble making ends meet. After training in nursing, including a master's degree, she married and dropped her career to raise her family. The marriage did not work out, and 15 years after her college training she found herself with no credit, two children, little job experience, and mounting expenses. She is a conscientious and hard worker, but with two children and meager child support from their father, she could not put much away for retirement. Nursing does not pay well in her town in the Midwest, but there had been few other career options for females in the early 1960s when she was getting her education.

Moreover, after her divorce she had worked a full-time job and done all the housework for 22 years. Two decades does not build a very large retirement annuity, and she had never been able to buy an adequate home on her income. If she had been a typical male with a master's degree, her *lifetime* earnings would have been more than $1 million in cumulative income (Catalyst 2013; U.S. Census Bureau 2012f). Her life chances were clearly affected by the fact that she was female.

Due to changes in gender roles and opportunities over the past 50 years, Jocelyn's granddaughter Emma will have a range of opportunities that were beyond consideration for her grandma. Ideas about sex, gender, and appropriate roles for women and men not only transform over time; they vary a great deal from one society to the next. Some practices of your own society may seem very strange to women and men in another society. Gender identities and roles are not stagnant; they change slowly over time, reflecting the economic, political, and social realities of the society. For instance, women in today's India seldom commit *sati* (suicide) on their husband's funeral pyre, but before the practice of *sati* was outlawed, it was a common way to deal with widows who no longer had a social role or means of support (Ahmad 2009).

In this chapter, we explore the concepts of sex, gender, and sexuality. We combine these issues with race and class for further understanding of the stratification system, or why people hold the positions they do in society. Although gender refers to a range of social behaviors, more emphasis will be on women's status and roles than men's as this is generally more relevant to our concern about stratification and minorities. At the micro level, we consider gender socialization or how girls learn to be women in their respective societies. At the meso and macro levels we consider gender stratification, or placement of women and men in the society's stratification system. A discussion of costs and consequences of gender stratification ends this chapter.

Sex, Gender, and the Stratification System

Variations around the world show that most roles and identities are not biological but rather socially constructed. In Chapter 7, we discussed factors that stratify individuals into social groups (castes and classes), and in Chapter 8, we discussed the roles race and ethnicity play in stratification. Add the concepts of sex and gender, and we have a more complex and complete picture of how class, race and ethnicity, and gender together influence experiences that make us who we are and our positions in society. Consider the following examples from societies that illustrate some human social constructions based on sex and gender that may seem unusual to most reading this text. These examples illustrate that gender roles are created by humans to meet needs of their societies. We will then move to more familiar societies.

Men of the Wodaabe society in Niger, Africa, are nomadic cattle herders and traders who would be defined as effeminate by most Western standards because of their behavior patterns. The men are like birds, showing their colorful feathers to attract females. They take great care in doing their hair, applying makeup, and dressing to attract women. They also gossip with each other while sipping their tea. Meanwhile, the women are cooking meals, caring for the children, cleaning, tending to the animals, planting small gardens, and preparing for the next move of this nomadic group (Beckwith 1993; Saharan Vibe 2007). These patterns have developed over time and carry on as traditions. The point is that groups have developed cultural norms over time that make gender behaviors differ widely.

Women of the Tchambuli (now *Chambri*) in New Guinea seem unacceptably aggressive, assertive, business-like, and competitive to people of the nearby Arapesh tribe, where gentleness and nonaggression are the rule for both women and men. Men of the Tchambuli exhibit expressive, nurturing, and gossipy behavior. The Mbuti and !Kung peoples of Africa value gender equality in their division of labor and treatment of women and men, and among the Agta of the Philippines, women do the hunting. In West African societies such as the Ashanti and Yoruba kingdoms, women control much of the market system (Dahlberg 1981; Mead [1935] 1963; Turnbull 1962). Each tradition has evolved over time to meet certain needs of society.

Under the Taliban rule in Afghanistan at the turn of this century—and still today in some areas—women could not be seen in public without total body covering that met strict requirements. Anyone not obeying could be stoned to death. If they became ill, women could not be examined by a physician because all doctors were male. Instead, they had to describe their symptoms to a doctor through a screen (Makhmalbaf 2003).

Certain tasks must be carried out by individuals and organizations in each society for members to survive. Someone must be responsible for raising children, someone must provide people with the basic necessities (food, clothing, shelter), someone needs to lead, someone must defend the society, and someone must help resolve conflicts. One's sex and age are often used to determine who holds what positions and who carries out what tasks. Each society develops its own way to meet its expectations, and its own interpretations of right and wrong gender role behaviors.

Wodaabe men in Niger (Africa) go to great pains with makeup, hair, and jewelry to ensure that they are highly attractive, a pattern that is thought by many people in North America to be associated with females.

This results in gender role variations from one society to the next. If the genders are identified as fundamentally different, distinguishing symbols such as dress, head coverings, and hairstyle become important for each gender's identity.

Thinking Sociologically

Why did groups in different corners of the globe develop such radically different ways of organizing their gender roles?

Sex

At birth, when doctors say, "It's a . . . ," they are referring to the distinguishing primary characteristics that determine sex—the penis or vagina. **Sex** is generally seen as a term referring to *ascribed genetic, anatomical, and hormonal*

Muslim girls in some parts of the world cover their faces when in public. The display of skin, even in a college classroom, would be immoral to many Muslims. However, in other Muslim countries such coverings would be unusual.

differences between males and females, right? This is actually only partially true. Sex is also "a determination made through the application of socially agreed upon biological criteria for classifying persons as females or males" (West and Zimmerman 1987:127). In other words, occasionally this binary male-female categorization by biological criteria is not clear. Occasionally, babies are born with ambiguous genitalia, not fitting the typical definition of male or female (the *intersexed*). Up to five variations in sexes have been identified including about 1.7% of babies born with unusual sex chromosomes, internal procreative organs, and external genitalia in a variety of combinations (Fausto-Sterling 2000). In Global North countries, these babies often undergo surgeries to "clarify" their sex, with hormonal treatments later in life (Chase 2000). Where medical interventions are not possible, people with sex anomalies may have special status, such as the transgendered *Hijras* (or *Aravanis*) in India. These unique people are called on for special religious observances and other ceremonial occasions (Gannon

2009). Whether male, female, or intersexed, anatomical differences or chromosomal typing results in cultural attempts to categorize sex. Still, the word *sex* when applied to a person refers largely to elements of one's anatomy.

Great lengths are taken to identify the sex of an infant. Why is this an issue? The reality is that sex constitutes a major organizing principle in most societies. Despite emphasis on "achieved status" in modern societies, expectations guiding people's behavior are largely determined by their sex. Our attraction to others is expressed by our sexuality and our sexual identity, with most people categorized as heterosexual (other sex), homosexual (same sex), bisexual (both sexes), or "varied" (such as transgendered). Our identities are defined by the cultural expectations held in most societies that a "normal" girl or boy will be sexually attracted to and eventually have sex with someone of the other sex (Lorber and Moore 2011). However, the point is that sex is not always a straightforward distinction and is as social as it is biological.

In adolescence, secondary characteristics further distinguish the sexes, with females developing breasts and hips and males developing body hair, muscle mass, and deep voices. Individuals are then expected to adopt the behaviors appropriate to their anatomical features as defined by society. In addition, a few other physical conditions are commonly believed to be sex linked, such as a prevalence of color blindness, baldness, learning disabilities, autism, and hemophilia in males. Yet, some traits that members of society commonly link to sex are actually learned through socialization. There is little evidence, for instance, that emotions, personality traits, or ability to fulfill most social statuses is determined by inborn physical sex differences. The social messages urging people to conform to expectations for their sex category are strong, however.

Consider the ideal male body as depicted in popular magazines in contemporary Western cultures: "over 6 feet tall, 180 to 200 pounds, muscular, agile, with straight white teeth, a washboard stomach, six-pack abs, long legs, a full head of hair, a large penis (discreetly shown by a bulge), broad shoulders and chest, strong muscular back, clean shaven, healthy, and slightly tanned if White, or a lightish brown if Black or Hispanic" (Lorber and Moore 2011:89–90). We grow up learning what is appealing.

A person's sex—male, female, or other—is a basis for stratification around the globe, used in every society to assign positions and roles to individuals. However, what is defined as normal behavior for a male, a female, or an intersexed person in one society could get one killed in another.

Gender

Gender refers to *a society's notions of masculinity and femininity—socially constructed meanings associated with being male or female—and how individuals construct their identity*

Gender and Socialization

in terms of gender within these constraints. Gender identity, then, is how individuals form their identity using the categories of sex and gender and negotiating the constraints they entail. The examples at the beginning of this section illustrate some differences in how cultures are structured around gender.

These gender meanings profoundly influence the statuses we hold within the social structure and placement in the stratification system (Rothenberg 2010). Individuals are expected to fulfill positions appropriate for their sex category. Statuses are positions within the structures of society, and roles are expected behaviors within those statuses. **Gender roles**, then, *are those commonly assigned tasks or expected behaviors linked to an individual's sex-determined statuses* (Lips 2010). Members of each society learn the structural guidelines and positions expected of males and females (West and Zimmerman 1987). Our positions—which affect access to power and resources—are embedded in institutions at the meso level with culture defining what is right and wrong. The point is that there is not some global absolute truth governing gender or gender roles. While both vary across cultures, gender is a learned cultural idea, while gender roles are part of the structural system of roles and statuses in a society.

Sexuality

Sexuality refers to *culturally shaped meanings both of sexual acts and of how we experience our own bodies—especially in relation to the bodies of others.* Strange as it may seem, sexuality is also *socially constructed.* A sex act is a "social enterprise," with cultural norms defining what is normal and acceptable in each society, how we should feel, and hidden assumptions about what the act means (Steele 2005). Even what we find attractive is culturally defined. For a period in China, men found tiny feet a sexual turn-on—hence, bound feet in women. In some cultures, legs are the attraction, and in others, men are fascinated by breasts.

The struggles that some individuals have with their sexual identity are reflected in the studies of *transgender:* when intersexed individuals do not fit clearly into female or male sex classifications (Leeder 2004). Transgender refers to "identification as someone who is challenging, questioning, or changing gender from that assigned at birth to a chosen gender—male-to-female, female-to-male, transitioning between genders, or gender 'queer' (challenging gender norms)" (Lorber and Moore 2007:6). Transgendered individuals are of interest to sociologists because of their life on the boundaries. Due to the pressure to fit in, most transgendered people change themselves, sometimes through surgery, to fit into their chosen gender.

In summary, although the terms *sex, gender,* and *sexuality* are often used interchangeably, they do have distinct meanings. The connections between these social realities

are not always as clear as the public thinks. One can be a masculine heterosexual female, a masculine homosexual male, or any of a number of possible combinations. As individuals continually negotiate the meanings attached to gender and sexuality, they are *doing gender,* a process discussed later in this chapter ("Doing Gender" 2011; West and Zimmerman 1987).

Sex, Gender, and Sexuality: The Micro Level

"It's a boy!" brings varying cultural responses. In many Western countries, that exclamation results in blue blankets, toys associated with males, roughhousing, and gender socialization messages. In some societies, boys are sources for great rejoicing whereas girls may be seen as a burden. In China and India, *female infanticide* (killing of newborn girls) is sometimes practiced especially in rural areas, in part because of the cost to poor families of raising a girl and the diminished value of girls. Abortion rates are also much higher when ultrasound tests show that the fetus is female ("Gendercide" 2010). In China, the male preference system is exacerbated by the government's edict that most couples may have only one child. As a result of government policy and female infanticide and abortion, the sex imbalance is growing and causing other consequences.

At the micro level we trace stages in an individual's life as a female or male: early childhood socialization, school and community activities and experiences, adult statuses and roles of females and males, language patterns, and so on through the life cycle. Beginning at birth, each individual passes through many stages. At each, there are messages that reinforce appropriate gender behavior in that society. These gender expectations are inculcated into children from birth by parents, siblings, grandparents, neighbors, peers, and even day care providers. If we fail to respond to the expectations of these significant people in our lives, we may experience negative sanctions: teasing, isolation and exclusion, harsh words, and stigma. To avoid these informal sanctions, children usually learn to conform, at least in their public behavior.

The lifelong process of gender socialization continues once we reach school age and we become more involved in activities separate from our parents. Other people—teachers, religious leaders, coaches—begin to influence us. We are grouped by sex in many of these social settings, and we come to think of ourselves as like *this* group and unlike *that* group: boys versus girls, us versus them. Even if our parents are not highly traditional, we still experience many influences from peers, school, and other sources at the micro level to conform to traditional gender notions.

With adulthood, differential treatment and stratification of the sexes take new forms. Men traditionally have more networks and statuses, as well as greater access to resources outside of the home. This has resulted in many women having less power because they are more dependent on husbands or fathers for resources. Even spousal abuse is related to imbalance of power in relationships. Lack of connections to the larger social system makes it difficult for many women to remove themselves from abusive relationships.

The subtitle of this chapter asks, "Who goes first?" When it comes to the question of who walks through a door first, the answer is that in many Western societies, *she* does—or at least, formal etiquette would suggest this is proper. The strong man steps back and defers to the weaker female, graciously holding the door for her (Walum 1974). Yet, when it comes to who walks through the metaphorical door to the professions, it is the man who goes first. Women are served first at restaurants and at other micro-level settings, but this seems little compensation for the fact that doors are often closed to them at the meso and macro levels of society.

Language can be powerful in shaping the behavior and perceptions of people, as discussed in the chapter on culture. Women often end sentences with tag questions, a pattern that involves ending a declarative statement with a short tag that turns it into a question: "That was a good idea, don't you think?" This pattern may cause male business colleagues to think women are insecure or uncertain about themselves. The women themselves may view it as an invitation to collaboration and dialogue. Yet, a perception of insecurity may prevent a woman from getting the job or the promotion. On the flip side, when women stop using these "softening" devices, they may be perceived by men as strident, harsh, or "bitchy" (Sandberg 2013; Wood and Reich 2006). Another aspect of men's and women's language usage is that women tend to use more words related to psychological and social processes, while men prefer more discussion of objects and impersonal topics (Newman et al. 2008)

Other aspects of language may also be important. The same adverb or adjective, when preceded by a male or female pronoun, can take on very different meanings. When one says, "He's easy" or "He's loose," it does not generally mean the same thing as when someone says, "She's easy" or "She's loose." Likewise, there are words such as *slut* for women for which there are no equivalents for men. There is no female equivalent for *cuckold,* the term describing a man whose wife is making a fool of him by having an affair. Why is that? To use another example, the word *spinster* is supposed to be the female synonym for *bachelor,* yet it has very different connotations. Even the more newly coined *bachelorette* is not usually used to describe an appealing, perhaps lifelong, role.

Those who invoke the biological argument that women's options are limited by pregnancy, childbirth, or breastfeeding from participating in public affairs and politics ignore the fact that in most societies these biological roles are time limited and women play a variety of social roles. The biological argument also ignores those societies in which males are deeply involved in nurturing activities such as child rearing.

Thinking Sociologically

Some people always write *he* first when writing "he and she." Others sometimes put she first. Does language influence how we view gender roles, or does it just describe what exists? Explain.

Sex, Gender, and Sexuality: The Meso Level

By whatever age is defined as adulthood in our society, we are expected to assume leadership roles and responsibilities in the institutions of society. Our roles in these institutions often differ depending on our sex (Brettell and Sargent 2009). This makes it difficult—but not impossible—for women to attain the most powerful positions in a society.

In most societies, sex and age stipulate when and how we experience *rites of passage,* rituals and ceremonies in institutions that mark a change of status in the family and community—the meso levels of society. These rites include any ceremonies or recognitions that admit one to adult duties and privileges. Rites of passage are institutionalized in various ways: religious rituals such as the Jewish male bar mitzvah or female bat mitzvah ceremonies; educational celebrations such as graduation ceremonies, which often involve caps and gowns of gender-specific colors or place females on one side of the room and males on the other; and different ages at which men and women are permitted to marry.

Other institutions also segregate us by sex. Orthodox Jewish synagogues, for example, do not have families seated together. Men sit on one side of the sanctuary, and women on the other. Many institutions, including religious, political, and economic organizations, have historically allowed only males to have leadership roles. Only men are to teach the scriptures to the young among traditional Jews, but few men fill that role in contemporary Christian congregations.

Women's reduced access to power in micro-level settings has to do with a lack of power and status in meso-level organizations and institutions. This is why gender roles are important. This is also a reason why policy makers concerned about gender equality have focused so much on inclusion of women in social institutions.

Some women today are in major leadership positions. India's recently elected president Pratibha Patil (left) is the first woman to hold the post in her country, and she won the election with about twice the votes of the opposition candidate. Cristina Fernández de Kirchner was reelected president of Argentina in 2011, also with a landslide victory. Ellen Johnson Sirleaf is president of Liberia and the first elected female head of state in Africa. She is serving her second term as president and was one of the cowinners of the Nobel Prize for Peace in 2011. These are able women leaders, but they are often criticized for being strong and showing leadership.

Empowerment of Women

Thirty village women gather regularly to discuss issues of health, crops, their herds, the predicted rains, goals for their children, and how to make ends meet. They are from a subsistence farming village in southern Niger on the edge of the Sahara desert. Recently, a microcredit organization was established with a small grant of $1,500 from abroad. With training from CARE International, an international nongovernmental organization (NGO), the women selected a board of directors to oversee the loans. Groups of five or six women have joined together to explain their projects to the board and request small loans. Each woman is responsible for paying back a small amount on the loan each week once the project is established and bringing in money.

Typical microcredit participants are women with several children, living at or below poverty, and sharing shelter with other families. With loans, women can make and sell items and build businesses to feed, clothe, and educate children (Foundation for Women 2012). A loan of between $20 and $50 from the microcredit organization is a tremendous sum considering that for many of these women it is equivalent to 6 months' earnings. Strong social norms are instituted to encourage repayment. Women who repay their loans promptly often decide who is eligible for future loans. Participation in the program encourages women and grants them economic and social capital otherwise unavailable to them.

With the new possibilities for their lives, they have big plans: For instance, one group plans to buy a press to make peanut oil, a staple for cooking in the region. Currently, people pay a great deal for oil imported from Nigeria. Another group will buy baby lambs, fatten them, and sell them for future festivals at a great profit. Yet another group plans to set up a small bakery. Women are also discussing the possibility of making local craft products to sell to foreign fair trade organizations such as Ten Thousand Villages (a fair trade organization that markets products made by villagers and returns the profits back to the villagers).

Some economists and social policy makers claim that grassroots organizations such as microcredits may be the way out of poverty for millions of poor families and that women are motivated to be small entrepreneurs to help support their families and buy education and health care for their children. Indeed, in 2006, Muhammad Yunus, who founded Grameen Bank—a microcredit lender for the very poor—received the Nobel Prize for Peace.

Microcredit lenders build significant economic and social capital for their participants, but critics suggest that there is an under-researched downside to microlending. As they see it, despite its success, the solution is a micro-level attempt to address a macro-level problem. Macro economists such as Linda Mayoux question whether or not the program will address the gender inequalities in the developing nations they target Mayoux (2002, 2008). Examples such as that above show that microloans may shift relations between husbands and wives, leaving men in a less powerful position within marriages, and changing gender dynamics. Most economists agree that microlending works best alongside macro-level initiatives seeking to address national economic problems.

Thinking Sociologically

How might women's lack of positions and authority in organizations and institutions in some societies—the meso level—influence females at the micro level? How might it influence their involvements at the macro level?

Microcredit banks have provided places for public sociologists to be involved in a variety of ways. For example, the next "Sociologists in Action" feature describes how one class of undergraduate students got involved in trying to raise money and awareness of how meso-level organizations—banks—can impact people at the micro level.

Sex, Gender, and Sexuality: The Macro Level

People around the world engage in going to school, driving a car, and working, but in some parts of the world, schooling, driving, and working are forbidden for women.

Sociologists in Action—Donna Yang, Christian Agurto, Michelle Benavides, Brianne Glogowski, Deziree Martinez, and Michele Van Hook

Sociology Students Engage With Microfinance

Students at William Paterson University describe their participation in a microcredit organization and how they used the sociological tools they gained in their Principles of Sociology course. They educated their classmates about Kiva.org, a microfinance project designed to aid women and diminish poverty globally, and raised money for the organization's efforts.

Kiva is an international microfinance organization dedicated to helping ordinary people across the globe become lenders to beginning entrepreneurs. After enrolling in an introductory sociology course, we collaborated to complete a group assignment that was designed to utilize various sociological concepts. We sought not only to raise money toward a Kiva loan, but—more importantly—to generate awareness about microfinance's ability to empower women and help fight poverty. The website, www.Kiva.org, is designed to facilitate partnerships between everyday people willing to give and low-income entrepreneurs seeking financial services. Kiva loans typically range from $25 to $3,000, and are temporarily financed by Kiva users who have browsed the profiles of potential entrepreneurs uploaded on the website.

Although gender inequality was central to our Kiva project, we used many other key sociological ideas. The purpose of the assignment was to promote the application of two important ideas from sociology, using a sociological eye and promoting social activism. Utilizing our collective sociological eye, we were able to look beneath the surface of society and recognize patterns of inequality intersecting along both class and gender lines. We realized that social stratification has created hierarchies through which women are marginalized economically, politically, and socially. Microfinance programs such as Kiva seek to mitigate this unequal access to wealth by creating greater accessibility for low-income individuals, mostly women, to financial services. In this way, they help to redistribute the accessibility of wealth across a wider spectrum of social classes. As a group, we felt passionate about Kiva.org because of its commitment to improve society by providing more equal lending opportunities.

We raised more than $150 toward a group loan for the communal bank "Mujeres Progresistas" (Progressive Women) in Cuenca, Ecuador. This bank is comprised of eleven women, and our specific loan was distributed to two women—both mothers of four seeking loans to help finance their personal businesses in order to help support their families. Maria Huerta will use this second loan to invest in buying chickens and chicken feed to begin running a chicken farm. Maria Suqui will be using the loan to help establish a snack shop through which she hopes to earn enough money to eventually own a home.

In order to promote awareness about our project and Kiva.org's initiatives, we also created informational pamphlets and distributed them to students on our college campus. The pamphlets explained microfinance, how Kiva utilizes this process of lending to help low-income individuals around the globe, and how they can get involved. Additionally, we presented our project to peers enrolled in a Principles of Sociology class in hopes of inspiring other peer members to join Kiva's efforts. This project helped us to realize the importance of sociology, its applicability within everyday life, and our obligation to act as socially conscious individuals in order to help promote greater social justice.

* * * * * * *

Note: This excerpt is adapted from Korgen and White's *The Engaged Sociologist: Connecting the Classroom to the Community* (2013).

A 14-year-old Pakistani girl was shot and severely wounded for both going to school and speaking out for other girls to have educational opportunity (Mehsud 2012). The Taliban, a regional organization that extends beyond the local boundaries, is opposed to girls going to school.

When we turn to the national and global level, we again witness inequality between the sexes that is quite separate from any form of personal prejudice or animosity toward women. Patterns of social action that are embedded in the entire social system may influence women and men, providing unrecognized privileges or disadvantages (McIntosh 1992). This is called *institutionalized privilege* or *disprivilege.*

The winds of change are influencing the roles of women in many parts of the world, as is seen in governing structures. Although women are still denied the right to vote in a few countries, voting is a right for most. In the United States, women have voted for a little more than 90 years. Yet, in the entire history of the United States, only 45 women have served in the U.S. Senate, and a total of 297 women have served in Congress since the first one was elected in 1917. As of 2013, the number is at an all-time high, with 20 out of 100 senators being women, and with 78 women out of 435 representatives in the House—women comprising 18.3% of all national representatives. Only four states (Delaware, Iowa, Mississippi, and Vermont) have never sent a woman to a congressional seat (Center for American Women and Politics 2013).

Even with changes, the United States is far behind many other countries in women's representation in governing bodies. In fact, the global average for women in national parliaments is 18.4%, so the United States is slightly below the average of female representation in national governments. The nation with the highest percentage of women in national parliament or congress is Rwanda (sub-Saharan Africa) with 56.3% women—one of only two countries to reach or surpass 50%. Canada is tied for 50th among nations, and the United States ranks 93rd—well below Global North countries like Sweden (#4), Denmark (#13), Spain (#20), and Germany (#27) and trailing Global South countries like Afghanistan (#40), Iraq (#47%), and Saudi Arabia (#83) (Inter-Parliamentary Union 2013). (See Table 9.1.)

Thinking Sociologically

What factors might affect the ranking of countries on women in national governments, as shown in Table 9.1? What factors might explain why the United States and Canada rank so poorly in representation of women in their governments?

Table 9.1 Women in National Governments (Selected Countries), 2013

		Lower Chamber or Single Chamber	Upper Chamber or Senate
1	Rwanda	56.3	38.5
2	Andorra	50.0	—
3	Cuba	48.9	—
4	Sweden	44.7	—
5	Seychelles	43.8	—
6	Senegal	42.7	—
7	Finland	42.5	—
8	South Africa	42.3	32.1
9	Nicaragua	40.2	—
10	Iceland	39.7	—
11	Norway	39.6	—
12	Mozambique	39.2	—
13	Denmark	39.1	—
14	Netherlands	38.7	36.0
20	Spain	36.0	—
27	Germany	32.9	—
29	New Zealand	32.2	—
40	Afghanistan	27.7	27.5
47	Iraq	25.2	—
50	Australia	24.7	38.2
50	Canada	24.7	37.9
60	China	23.4	—
66	United Kingdom	22.5	22.6
83	Saudi Arabia	19.9	—
93	United States of America	17.8	20.0

Source: Inter-Parliamentary Union (2013). Reprinted with permission of the Inter-Parliamentary Union.

Note: To examine the involvement of women in other countries or to see even more recent figures, go to http://www.ipu.org/wmn-e/classif.htm.

Several factors have been especially effective in increasing women's positions in national parliaments in many African countries: the existence of a matriarchal culture (where women may have increased authority and power in decision making, political systems that stress proportional representation, and the adoption of gender quotas for government positions (Yoon 2008, 2011a, 2011b). Without such systems and quotas, democratization of governmental systems is sometimes linked to a *decrease* in representation by women, a sad reality for those committed to establishing democracy around the world (Yoon 2001). Globally, women's access to power and prestige is highly variable, with African and Northern European countries having a position of leadership when it comes to gender equity in government. As you study Table 9.1, note that researchers find that the needs and interests of women are not fully represented unless a critical mass of female representatives is reached, and that critical mass is usually about 35% (Yoon 2011b).

Cross-cultural analyses confirm that gender roles either evolve over centuries or are transformed by sweeping reform laws such as voting rights, accompanied by proportional representation or quotas, and other legal protections for women. The fact that women in China generally work outside the home whereas women in some Muslim societies hardly venture from their homes is due to differences in cultural norms about gender roles that are dictated by governments or tradition and learned through the socialization process.

Gender Socialization: Micro- and Meso-Level Analyses

Socialization into gender roles is the process by which people learn the cultural norms, attitudes, and behaviors appropriate to their gender. That is, they learn how to think and act as boys or girls, women or men. As noted earlier, socialization reinforces the "proper" gender behaviors and punishes the improper behaviors. In many societies, traits of gentleness, passivity, and dependence are associated with femininity, whereas boldness, aggression, strength, and independence are identified with masculinity. For instance, in most Western societies, aggression in women is considered unfeminine, if not inappropriate or disturbing (Sandberg 2013). Likewise, the gentle, unassertive male is often looked on with scorn or pity, stigmatized as a "wimp." Gender stereotypes in the United States are less rigid than in the past, but they are still a big part of popular culture and provide guidelines for parents, and especially for boys' behavior. Girls' norms of femininity have expanded more than norms of masculinity, and more girls have aspirations for law and medical school than boys have for nursing. Girls have more flexibility in sports they choose and in toys they can play with ("Gender Stereotypes" 2011). Expectations related to these stereotypes are rigid in many societies (Pollack 1999).

Stages in Gender Socialization

Bounce that rough-and-tumble baby boy and cuddle that precious, delicate little girl. Thus begins gender socialization, starting at birth and taking place through a series of life stages, discussed in Chapter 4 on socialization. Examples from infancy and childhood show how socialization into gender roles takes place.

Infancy

Learning how to carry out gender roles begins at birth. Parents in the United States describe their newborn daughters as soft, delicate, fine-featured, little, pretty, cute, and resembling their mothers. They depict their sons as strong, firm, alert, and well coordinated (Lindsey 2011; Rubin 1974). Clothing, room decor, and toys also reflect notions of gender. In Spain, parents and grandparents dress babies and their carriages in pink or blue depending on gender, proudly showing off the little ones to friends as they promenade in the evenings. Although gender stereotypes have declined in recent years, they continue to affect the way we handle and treat male and female infants. The interesting thing is that only a century ago pink was considered the "manly" color and self-respecting men were steered away from the very soft feminine color—blue (*New York Times* 1893). A trade publication, *Earnshaw's Infants' Department*, published an article in June 1918 advising parents that "The generally accepted rule is pink for the boys, and blue for the girls. The reason is that pink, being a more decided and stronger color, is more suitable for the boy, while blue, which is more delicate and dainty, is prettier for the girl." In 1927, *Time* magazine printed a chart showing sex-appropriate colors for children: pink is for boys—blue for girls (Maglaty 2011). Moreover, prior to the 20th century both boys and girls in the United States were dressed mostly in frilly dresses until they were about 6 (Maglaty 2011).

Childhood

Once they are out of infancy, research shows that many boys are encouraged to be more independent and exploratory whereas girls are protected from situations that might prove harmful. More pressure is put on boys to behave in "gender appropriate" ways (Kramer 2010). Boys are socialized into "the boy code" that provides rigid guidelines as described in the next "Sociology in Our Social World." Cross-cultural studies show boys often get more attention than girls because of their behavior, with an emphasis on achievement, autonomy, and aggression for boys (Kimmel and Messner 2009).

Thinking Sociologically

First, read "The Boy Code" on pages 253 and 254. Is there evidence of the boy code when you observe your friends and relatives? What is the impact of the boy code? Is there a similar code for girls?

Fairy Tales

Sociology in Our Social World

The Boy Code

Boys and girls begin to conform to gender expectations once they are old enough to understand that their sex is rather permanent, that boys are not capable of becoming "mommies." They become even more conscious of adhering to norms of others in their gender category.

The Old Boy network in American society favors adult men over women through a system of networks. This system actually starts with "the boy code," the rules about boys' proper behavior. Young boys learn "the code" from parents, siblings, peers, teachers, and society in general. They are praised for adhering to the code and punished for violating its dictates. William Pollack writes that boys learn several stereotyped behavior models exemplifying the boy code:

1. "The sturdy oak": Men should be stoic, stable, and independent; a man never shows weakness.

2. "Give 'em hell": From athletic coaches and movie heroes, the consistent theme is extreme daring, bravado, and attraction to violence.

3. "The 'big wheel'": Men and boys should achieve status, dominance, and power; they should avoid shame, wear the mask of coolness, and act as though everything is under control.

4. "No sissy stuff": Boys are discouraged from expressing feelings or urges perceived as feminine—dependence, warmth, empathy (Pollack 1999).

The boy code is ingrained in society; by 5 or 6 years of age, boys are less likely than girls to express hurt or distress. They have learned to be ashamed of showing feelings and of being weak. This gender straitjacket, according to Pollack, causes boys to conceal feelings in order to fit in and be accepted and loved. As a result, some boys, especially in adolescence, become silent, covering any vulnerability and masking their true feelings. This affects boys' relationships, performance in school, and ability to connect with others. It also causes young males to put on what Jackson Katz calls the "tough guise," when young men and boys emphasize aggression and violence to display masculinity (Katz 2006). Moreover, if fathers emphasize competition and toughness, their sons are much more likely to become bullies and are likely to have few deep friendships, especially in the later teen years (Kindlon and Thompson 2000; Way 2011).

With the women's movement and shifts in gender expectations have come new patterns of male behavior. Some men are forming more supportive and less competitive relationships with other men, and there are likely to be continued changes in and broadening of "appropriate" behavior for men (Kimmel and Messner 2009; Way 2011).

Kindlon and Thompson found that although boys are innately as capable of expressing emotion as girls, they

(Continued)

(Continued)

learn to suppress emotions—except for anger, which is legitimate (Kindlon and Thompson 2000). This inability to share feelings has serious repercussions for inner well-being and for healthy relationships. Niobe Way found a more complex pattern. Just as many girls resist the mainstream culture's messages of passivity and obsession with appearance as core to being female, many boys are also a part of a resistance movement (Way 2011). They have quite intimate relationships with male friends—sharing emotions, vulnerabilities, and secrets—especially during childhood and early adolescence. Sadly, Way found that while most boys in her sample deeply valued intimate same-sex friendships, those ties weakened considerably by late adolescence, and many boys struggled privately with the loss. The important finding in Way's study was that boys do not just accept the boy code blindly. Many resist aspects of that code and try to resist the culture's definitions of masculinity.

Stereotypes for girls in a majority of societies label feminine behaviors as soft, nonaggressive, and noncompetitive. Consider that boys act out their aggressive feelings, but girls are socialized to be nice, nurturing, and not aggressive. In a study about how schoolgirls express aggression, Simmons finds that girls express "relational aggression," aggression that affects girls' social contacts indirectly through rumors, name-calling, giggling, ignoring, backbiting, exclusion, and manipulation of victims. Friendship and needing to belong are the weapons, rather than sticks and stones. This form of bullying is subtle and hard to detect, but it can have long-lasting effects (Girls Health 2009; Simmons 2002).

Names for children also reflect stereotypes about gender. Boys are more often given strong, hard names that end in consonants. The top 10 boys' names include Jacob, Mason, Ethan, Noah, William, Liam, Jayden, Michael, Alexander, and Aiden. Girls are more likely to be given soft, pretty names with vowel endings such as most of the top 10: Sophia, Emma, Isabella, Olivia, Ava, Emily, Abigail, Mia, Madison, and Elizabeth (Social Security Administration 2012b).

Alternatively, girls may be given feminized versions of boys' names—Roberta, Jessica, Josephine, Nicole, Michelle, or Donna. Sometimes, traditional boys' names are given to girls without first feminizing them. Names such as Lynn, Stacey, Tracey, Faye, Dana, Jody, Lindsay, Robin, Carmen, Kelly, Kim, Beverly, Ashley, Dana, Carol, Shannon, and Leslie used to be names exclusively for men, but within a decade or two after they were applied to girls, parents stopped using them for boys (Kean 2007). So a common name for males may for a time be given to either sex, but then it is given primarily to girls. The pattern rarely goes the other direction. Once feminized, the names seem to have become unacceptable for boys (Lieberson, Dumais, and Bauman 2000).

In the early childhood years, children become aware of their own gender identity. As they reach school age, they learn that their sex is permanent, and they begin to categorize behaviors that are appropriate for their sex. As children are rewarded for performing proper gender roles, these roles are reinforced. That reinforcement solidifies gender roles, setting the stage for gender-related interactions, behaviors, and choices in later life.

Meso-Level Agents of Gender Socialization

Clues to proper gender roles surround children in materials produced by corporations (books, toys, games), in mass media images, in educational settings, and in religious organizations and beliefs. In Chapter 4 on socialization, we learned about agents of socialization. Those agents play a major role in teaching children proper gender roles. The following examples demonstrate how organizations and institutions in our society teach and reinforce gender assumptions and roles.

Corporations

Corporations produce many materials that help socialize children into proper conduct. Publishers, for example, produce books that present images of expected gender behavior. The language and pictures in preschool picture books, elementary children's books, and school textbooks are steeped in gender role messages reflecting society's expectations and stereotypes. In a classic study of award-winning children's books from the United States that have sold more than 3 million copies, the researchers found very substantial differences in how males and females were depicted, with females passive and dependent (Weitzman et al. 1972). More recent studies have found some correction of this pattern—even an overcorrection in some cases—but many children's books, especially those about nonhumans, still show stereotyped images of females (Anderson and Hamilton 2005; Diekman and Murmen 2004; Houlis 2011).

Producers of toys and games also contribute to traditional messages about gender. Store-bought toys fill rooms in homes of children in the Western world. Each toy or game prepares children for future gender roles. Choices ranging from college major and occupational choice to activities that depend on visual-spatial and mathematical abilities appear to be affected by these early choices and childhood learning experiences (Tavris and Wade 1984).

Defining Gender Roles

Girls and boys quickly pick up messages—from parents, other children, and the media—about what kinds of toys are appropriate for someone of their sex. Many books and toys, like Barbie dolls and construction toys, have very explicit gender messages.

Boys have more experience manipulating blocks, Tinkertoys, LEGO bricks, and Erector Sets—toys paralleling masculinized activities outside the home in the public domain, from constructing and building trades to military roles and sports. Girls prepare for domestic roles with toys relating to domestic activities. Barbie dolls stress physical appearance, consumerism, and glamour. Only a few Barbies are in occupational roles. This supports the prevailing cultural stereotype that girls play with Barbies and boys with trucks. Toy stores are generally divided into distinct boys' and girls' sections, shaping parents' and children's choices, and girls' and boys' future skills and interests (C. Williams 2006). Each toy or game prepares children through anticipatory socialization for future gender roles. Toys that require building, manipulating, and technical skills provide experiences for later life.

Mass Media

It is Friday night at the game store; groups of adolescent males gather to play games. Their two favorites are the card game *Magic: The Gathering* (MTG or Magic), and the online game, *World of Warcraft* (WoW). WoW is played with many online players, and the individual players can sit in front of their computers alone, interacting only online. Popular video games that attract primarily boys include *Grand Theft Auto: Vice City* (adventure), *Halo 2* (action), *Gran Turismo 3: A-Spec* (driving), and *Madden NFL* (sports). The bottom line is that gender portrayals are unequal and the few females presented are in stereotypical roles—supporting, needing rescue, or sexually alluring. Research shows that adolescents identify with their characters, often as role models (Mou and Peng 2009). Girls are generally missing or peripheral to the play. Notice the next time you are in a video game room that the fighting characters are typically male and often in armor. When fighting women do appear, they are usually clad in skin-revealing bikini-style attire— odd clothing in which to do battle!

Thinking Sociologically

Why are video and role-playing games primarily a boy thing? Where are the girls? What effect might girls' and boys' different activities have on their futures?

Mass media comes in many forms—magazines, ads, films, music videos, Internet sites—and is a major agent of socialization into gender roles. Young men and women, desiring to fit in, are influenced by messages from the media. For instance, the epidemic of steroid use among boys in attempts to stimulate muscle growth results from desire to be successful in sports and have an appealing body image. One issue that is media driven for girls is an obsession with thinness (Dixon 2011). A study of more than 2,000 10- to 14-year-old girls found that almost 30% were trying to lose weight and 10.5% had eating disorders (McVey, Tweed, and Blackmore 2004). Dieting among girls, driven in part by ads, is a health concern in the United States and some other countries (Taub and McLorg 2010). Yet manufacturers advertise food products with promises to remake teens into more attractive people.

Some recent action films include adventurous and competent girls and women, helping counter media images of sexy and helpless females. The *Hunger Games* heroine, Katniss Everdeen, has become a brave idol for teenage girls; Mattel has even made a Barbie version of the heroine. *The Girl With the Dragon Tattoo* and other films in that series present an extremely clever and unique heroine in Lisbeth. These are only a few examples of young women in strong leadership roles. Despite the changes that have occurred, highly competent females are seen less frequently than men.

Television is another powerful socializing agent. Children in the United States spend—on average—3 to 4 hours a day watching television. This is more time than

Gender Advertising

they will have spent in the classroom by the time they graduate from high school ("Children and Watching TV" 2011). Television presents a simple, stereotyped view of life, from advertisements to situation comedies to soap operas. Women in soap operas and ads, especially those working outside the home, are often depicted as having problems in carrying out their role responsibilities (Boston Women's Health Book Collective 2006). Even the extraordinary powers of superheroes on Saturday morning television depict the female characters as having gender-stereotyped skills such as superintuition.

How do social scientists know that television affects gender role socialization? Studies have shown that the more television children watch, the more gender stereotypes they hold. From cartoons to advertisements, television in many countries provides enticing images of a world in which youth is glorified, old age is scorned, and female and male roles are stereotyped and/or unattainable (Kilbourne 2000; Witt 2000). However, research has also found that these

media images have a much greater impact on white girls than on black girls (Milkie 1999).

Thinking Sociologically

Think of recent mass media examples that you have seen. How do they depict women and men? How might these meso-level depictions affect young men and women at the micro level?

Educational Systems

Girls and boys often have very different experiences in school. As noted in the examples below, educational systems are socialization agents of children through classroom, lunchroom, and playground activities; students' popularity and recognition; sports and Title IX programs; and teachers' attitudes and expectations. For example, boys are encouraged to join competitive team sports and girls to support them (Gilligan 1982; Kramer 2010). Some argue that this simulates hierarchical adult roles of boss/secretary and physician/nurse.

Children's separate experiences in grade and middle school reinforce boundaries of "us" and "them" in classroom seating and activities, in the lunchroom, and in playground activities, as girls and boys are seated, lined up, and given assignments by sex (Sadker and Sadker 2005). Those who go outside the boundaries, especially boys, are ridiculed by peers and sometimes teachers, reinforcing stereotypes and separate gender role socialization (Sadker and Sadker 2005; Thorne 1993).

Part of the issue of male-female inequality in schools is tied to the issue of popularity, which seems to have less to do with being liked than with being known and visible. If everyone knows a person's name, she or he is popular (Eder, Evans, and Parker 1995). At the middle school level, there are more ways that boys can become known. In sports, even when there are both boys' and girls' basketball teams, many spectators come to the boys' contests and very few to the girls' games. Thus, few people know the female athletes by name. In fact, a far more visible position is cheerleader—standing on the sidelines cheering for the boys—because those girls are at least seen (Eder, Evans, and Parker 1995; Milner 2006).

High schools are breeding grounds for status consciousness. Which lunch table one sits at, with whom one goes to the prom, who holds the popular positions (such as cheerleader and football player), and what clothing one wears are all status-enhancing activities and symbols needed to be cool (Milner 2006). Girls are visible or known because of their physical appearance, a major standard of

Olsen twins Mary-Kate and Ashley (left) pose together in front of their new star on the Walk of Fame in Hollywood. Like most glamorous stars, they must conform to the image of very thin, shapely femininity.

American Steroids   Body Image

High school and college athletics are much less reliable paths for women to become known on campus since so few people come to the games. Even this college game with a winning team has sparse attendance (top photo). By contrast, women in very sexy outfits are highly visible and can even become local celebrities when they perform as cheerleaders in front of 80,000 fans at men's sporting events (bottom photo).

popularity and esteem (Eder, Evans, and Parker 1995). The bottom line is that there are far more visible positions for the boys than for girls in middle and high school, allowing them to be recognized and become leaders.

Title IX of the U.S. Education Amendments of 1972 was a major legislative attempt to level the educational and sports playing field. Passed in order to bar gender discrimination in schools receiving federal funds, this legislation mandates equal opportunity for participation in school-sponsored programs (Lindsey 2011). The law has reduced or eliminated blatant discrimination in areas ranging from admissions to counseling and housing. However, the biggest impact of Title IX legislation has been in athletics.

Women's athletic programs and scholarship opportunities have grown since 1972, but still lag behind men's levels. By 2011, the number of girls competing in high school sports had climbed to almost 3.2 million, yet opportunities for girls are still 1.3 million fewer than for boys. In collegiate sports, the number has grown from fewer than 30,000 to about 200,000. Men's sports both bring in and receive more money and have more airtime on TV (Dusenbery and Lee 2012). Participation in athletics, especially team sports, is important because sports can foster skills in teamwork, thinking about strategy, and anticipating counteractions by a competitor, all of which are useful skills in business and government.

Religious Organizations

Religious organizations serve as agents of socialization by defining, reinforcing, and perpetuating gender role stereotypes and cultural beliefs. Religious teachings provide explanations of all aspects of life, including proper male and female roles. The three major monotheistic religions—Christianity, Islam, and Judaism—are traditionally patriarchal, stressing separate female and male spheres (Kramer 2010). The following are examples of some of these traditional role expectations and the status of women in various religions.

Some interpretations of the Adam and Eve creation story in the Hebrew Bible (the Old Testament in the Christian Bible) state that because man was created first, men are superior. Because Eve, created from the rib of man, was a sinner, her sins keep women forever in an inferior, second-class position. Thus, in some branches of these religions, women are restricted in their roles within family and religious organizations. They cannot be priests in Catholic churches and cannot vote on business matters in some religious organizations. However, recent work by feminist scholars is challenging the notion of patriarchy in Judaic and Christian history, pointing out that women may have played a much broader role in religious development than is often recognized (Hunter College Women's Studies Collective 2005). Even *Yahweh*—the name for God in the Hebrew Bible—had both male and female connotations, and when God was referred to as a source of wisdom, feminine pronouns and references were used (Borg 1994). Increasingly, denominations are granting women greater roles in the religious hierarchies of major religious groups.

Women in Judaism lived for centuries in a patriarchal system where men read, taught, and legislated (Lindsey 2011). Today, three of the five main branches of Judaism allow women equal participation, illustrating that some religious practices change over time. However, Hasidic and Orthodox Jews have a division of labor between men and women following old laws, with designated gender roles.

Some Christian teachings have treated women as second-class citizens, even in the eyes of God. For this reason, some Christian denominations have excluded women from a variety of leadership roles and told them they must be subservient to their husbands. Other Christians point to the admonition by Saint Paul that, theologically speaking, "there is neither . . . male nor female, for you are all one in Christ Jesus" (Galatians 3:28). This suggests that women and men are not spiritually different.

Traditional Hindu religion painted women as seductresses, strongly erotic, and a threat to male spirituality and asceticism. To protect men from this threat, women were kept totally covered in thick garments and veils and seen only by men in their immediate families. Today, Hinduism comes in many forms, most of which honor the domestic sphere of life—mothers, wives, and homemakers—while accepting women in public roles (Lindsey 2011).

Traditional Islamic beliefs also portrayed female sexuality as dangerous to men, although many women in Islamic societies today are full participants in the public and private sphere. The Quran (also spelled Qur'an or Koran), the Muslim sacred scripture, includes a statement that men are superior to women because of the qualities God has given men. Hammurabi's Code, written in the Middle East between 2067 and 2025 BCE, is the earliest recorded legal system. The laws about women's status were written to distinguish between decent women, belonging to one man, and indecent or public women. Some aspects of these traditional beliefs have carried over to present times. Sharia law, or strict Islamic law, adopted in several Islamic countries and among some groups, has been used to punish women accused of violating its rules. Recent cases include a woman in Nigeria who had a child out of wedlock and another woman in Pakistan who was a rape victim. Both women were sentenced to death by stoning, but their sentences have not been carried out because of protests from within and outside the countries. Some Muslim women in Britain have tried to get an Islamic divorce, but a Sharia council must approve. Women who are in forced marriages and who are abused have little recourse as Sharia councils grant few of these divorces (Proudman 2012). These women suffer social humiliation, degradation, and potential death, but they also reinforce the social expectations for others who might stray from the laws (Mydans 2002).

Women in fundamentalist Muslim societies such as Algeria, Iran, Syria, and Saudi Arabia are separated from men (except for fathers and brothers) in work and worship. They generally remain completely covered (Ward and Edelstein 2009). Today, some women point out that they wear the veil for modesty, for cosmetic purposes, or to protect themselves from stares of men. Others claim that the veil represents oppression and subservience, showing that women must keep themselves in submissive positions. Still, religious rules often provide the justifications to keep women servile, and public shaming and threat of severe punishments reinforce the laws.

Meso-level religious systems influence how different societies interpret proper gender roles and how sometimes these belief systems change with new interpretations of scriptures. (Further discussion of the complex relationship between religion and gender appears in Chapter 11.) From family and education to media and religion, meso-level agents of socialization reinforce "appropriate" gender roles in each society.

Thinking Sociologically

What are some books, toys, games, television shows, school experiences, and religious teachings that influenced your gender role socialization? In what ways did they do so?

Gender Stratification: Meso- and Macro-Level Processes

The phrase *glass ceiling* generally applies to processes that limit progress to the highest job or status positions because of invisible barriers that bar promotion within an organization. Although a woman may have superior skills or experience, she is passed over. "The *glass ceiling* keeps women from reaching the highest levels of corporate and public responsibility, and the 'sticky floor' keeps the vast majority of the world's women stuck in low-paid jobs" (Hunter College Women's Studies Collective 2005:393). The reasons this is a big deal is loss of talent, unfair discrimination, and the impact on salaries. Although there are high-profile women as chief executive officers and in government leadership positions in the United States, they occupy only 4.2% of the *Fortune* 500 CEO positions ("Gendercide" 2010). Although women now represent 51% of the U.S. PhDs and 67% of college graduates, women earn only about 80 cents to every dollar earned by men (C. Berman 2010; DeBoskey 2012; U.S. Bureau of Labor Statistics 2012).

Men, on the other hand, often experience the "invisible escalator," especially in traditionally female occupations. Even if they do not seek to climb in the organizational hierarchy, occupational social forces push them up the job ladder into higher echelons. However, minority men may not experience the same escalator effect as white men (Wingfield 2009). The next "Engaging Sociology" provides an exercise to think about how our ideas about leadership may subtly maintain the glass ceiling and the invisible escalator.

American Porn

Engaging Sociology

Masculinity and Femininity in Our Social World

1. Mark each characteristic with an "M" or an "F" depending on whether you think it is generally defined by society as a masculine or a feminine characteristic.

   — achiever

   — aggressive

   — analytical

   — caring

   — confident

   — deferential (defers to others; yields with courtesy)

   — devious

   — dynamic

   — intuitive

   — loving

   — manipulative

   — nurturing

   — organized

   — passive

   — a planner

   — powerful

   — relationship-oriented (makes decisions based on how others will feel)

   — rule oriented (makes decisions based on abstract procedural rules)

   — sensitive

   — strong

2. Next, mark an "X" just to the right of 10 characteristics that you think are the essential qualities for a leadership position in a complex organization (business, government, etc.). You might want to ask 20 of your acquaintances to do this and then add up the scores for "masculinity," "femininity," and "leadership trait."

3. Do you (and your acquaintances) tend to view leadership as having the same traits as those marked "masculine" or "feminine"? What are the implications of your findings for the "glass ceiling" or the "invisible escalator"?

4. How might correlations between the traits of leadership and gender notions help to explain the data on income in Table 9.2?

Table 9.2   U.S. Income by Educational Level and Sex—Full-Time Workers

Education	Men	Women
Not a high school graduate	$33,194	$23,478
High school graduate	$43,140	$32,227
College graduate (bachelor's)	$79,003	$53,524
Master's degree	$102,295	$72,073
Doctorate	$125,104	$97,124
Professional degree	$163,234	$109,619

Source: U.S. Census Bureau (2012e).

Women and Men at Work: Gendered Organizations

How can I do it all—marriage, children, career, social life? This is a question that many college students ask. They already anticipate a delicate balancing act. Work has been central to the definition of masculinity in U.S. society, and for the past half-century, women have been joining the workforce in ever greater numbers (Kramer 2010). Today, women outnumber men in the workforce, with 800,000 more women than men on payrolls in January 2010, according to the U.S. Department of Labor. Figure 9.1 shows how men's and women's incomes vary in the United States for several career fields. The graph shows the average pay for women in an occupation as a ratio of what men earn. For example, women who are personal financial advisors earn 58.7% of what men in that occupation earn. The pattern of unequal pay is true in a number of Global North countries (20-First 2010).

Working is necessary for many women, especially single mothers, to support their families, and many women want to work and use their education and skills. Among countries of the Global North, Sweden has the highest percentage of working women at more than 8 out of 10 women participating in the labor force. Yet, even in Sweden, with

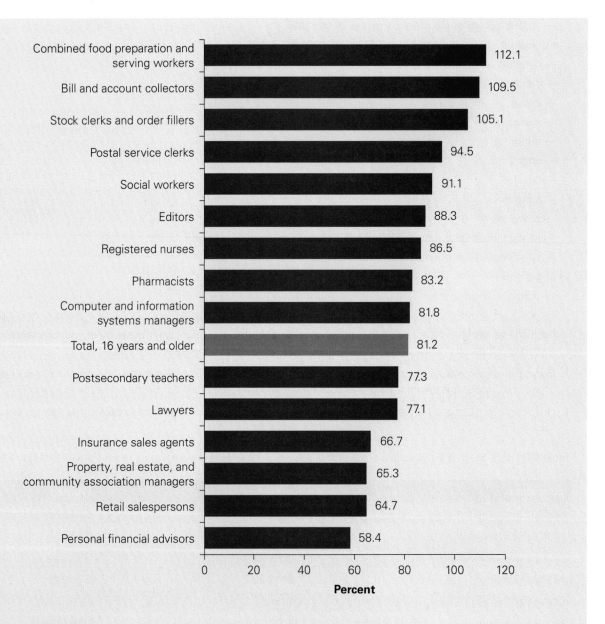

Figure 9.1 Ratio of Women's to Men's Earnings for Selected Occupations, 2010

Source: Derek Thompson, "How Women in the Workforce Are Changing America." *The Atlantic*, March 9, 2011.

Although public school teachers are disproportionally women and although serving in the classroom is the normal channel for working into high administrative posts, principals and superintendents—with higher pay and more authority—are disproportionally men. This is an example of a gendered organization.

its parental leave and other family-friendly policies, women feel pressures of work and family responsibilities (Eshleman and Bulcroft 2010). Dual-career marriages raise questions about child rearing, power relations, and other factors in juggling work and family.

Every workplace has a gendered configuration: ratios of female to male workers; gender reflected in subordinate-supervisor positions; and distribution of positions between men and women. This, in turn, affects our experiences in the workplace. Consider the example of mothers who are breast-feeding their babies. Must they quit their jobs or alter their family schedules if the workplace does not provide a space for breast-feeding? Some workplaces accommodate family needs, but many do not.

Research shows that workers are more satisfied when the sex composition of their work group and the distribution of men and women in power are balanced (Britton 2000). Feminists propose ideas to minimize gender differences in organizations—that is, to "degender" organizations so that all members have equal opportunities (Britton 2000).

Thinking Sociologically

If corporate structures were reversed so that women structured and organized the workplace, how might the workplace environment change?

Institutionalized Gender Discrimination

Gender stratification at the meso level—like race and ethnic stratification—can occur quite independently of any overt prejudice or ill will by others. It becomes part of the social system, and we are not even conscious of it, especially if we are one of the privileged members of society. *Discrimination* is built into organizations and cultural expectations and includes intentional actions as well as actions or structures that unintentionally have consequences that restrict minorities. It is embedded in institutions.

Recall from the previous chapter that *side-effect discrimination* involves practices in one institutional area that have negative impact because they are linked to practices in another institutional area; because institutions are interdependent, discrimination in one can result in unintentional discrimination in others. For example, if roles of women in family life are determined by rigid gender expectations, as research shows, then women find it more difficult to devote themselves to gaining job promotions. In addition, as long as little girls learn through socialization to use their voices and to hold their bodies and to gesture in ways that communicate deference, employers assume a lack of the self-confidence necessary for major leadership roles. If women are paid less despite the same levels of education (see Table 9.2 on page 259), they are less likely to have access to the best health care or to be able to afford a $40,000 down payment for a house, unless they are married. This makes women dependent on men in a way that most men are not dependent on women.

A factor affecting differences in income is the type of academic degree that men and women receive (engineering

Little girls learn to use their voices and to hold their bodies and to gesture in ways that communicate deference. This little girl does not look very powerful or confident. When women tilt their heads—either forward or to one side—they also look like they lack confidence, and this hurts their chances of promotion in the corporate world.

rather than education, for example). However, even when these differences are factored in, men still make considerably more on average than women with the same levels of experience and training.

Past-in-present discrimination refers to practices from the past that may no longer be allowed but that continue to affect people today. For example, at an appliance industry in the Midwest investigated by one of the authors, there is a sequence of jobs one must hold to be promoted up the line to foreman. This requirement ensures that the foreman understands the many aspects of production at the plant. One of the jobs involves working in a room with heavy equipment that cuts through and bends metal sheets. The machine is extremely powerful and could easily cut off a leg or hand if the operator is not careful. Because of the danger, the engineers designed the equipment so it would not operate unless three levers were activated at the same time. One lever was triggered by stepping on a pedal on the floor. The other two required reaching out with one's hands so that one's body was extended. When one was spread-eagled to activate all three levers, there was no way one could possibly have a part of one's body near the blades.

It was brilliant engineering, but there was one unanticipated problem: The hand-activated levers were 5 feet 10 inches off the ground and 5 feet apart. Few women had the height and arm span to run this machine, and therefore, no women had yet made it through the sequence of positions to the higher-paying position of foreman. The equipment cost millions of dollars, so it was not likely to be replaced. Neither the engineers who designed the machine nor the upper-level managers who established the sequence of jobs to become foreman had deliberately tried to exclude women. Indeed, they were perplexed when they looked at their employee figures and saw so few women moving up through the ranks. The cause of women's disadvantage was not mean-spirited men but features of the system that had unintended consequences resulting in past-in-present discrimination. A machine built in the past but still in use continues to disqualify women for an important job. The barriers women face, then, are not just matters of socialization or other micro-level social processes. The nature of sexism is often subtle yet pervasive in the society, operating at the meso and macro levels as institutional discrimination.

Earlier in this chapter we discussed inequalities and stereotypes in children's books. Although more recent books show expansion in the roles of males and females, the tens of thousands of older, classic books in public and school libraries mean that a parent or child picking a book off of the shelf is still likely to select a book that has old stereotypical views of boys and girls. This is an example of how prejudices and discrimination in the past can still affect us in the present.

Men often get defensive and angry when people talk about sexism in society because they feel they are being attacked or asked to correct injustices of the past. However, the empirical reality is that the playing field is not level for men and women. Most men do not do anything to intentionally harm women, and they may not feel prejudiced toward women, but sexism operates so that men are given privileges they never asked for and may not even recognize.

Gender Differences in Internet Use

Consider gender differences in Internet use. Internet-related gender stratification exhibits itself not just in terms of *whether* a person uses the Internet but also in terms of *how* a person uses the Internet. Even within industrialized countries such as the United States, women tend to use mostly the e-mail services, with the intent of keeping up with family and friends (Shade 2004). Women's use focuses on personal growth, maintaining a social group, getting information about products and brands, and sites offering anonymity not available on Facebook and Twitter. A recent Nielsen study shows that 75.8% of women who are online use social networking sites compared to 69.7% of men. Globally, women account for 47.9% of visitors to social networking sites, and spend 30% more time on social networking sites than men (ComScore 2010; Morrison 2010).

For men, the Internet is used to gather information and to exchange ideas, knowledge of events in the world, job skills, awareness of job openings, networks that extend beyond national borders, and facts relevant to professional activities. Thus, "women are using the Internet to reinforce their private lives and men are using the Internet for engaging in the public sphere" (Shade 2004:63). The

In some countries, there is a huge gender digital divide. In others, nearly as many women as men use computers. However, research shows that women tend to use computers in different ways. These women in Iraq are learning computer skills.

difference also reflects differences in the professional positions men and women hold. For men, the Internet is enhancing their careers. This is less true for women.

In Chapter 7, we explored global differences in Internet usage and found that the largest variance was based on wealth of the country and access to technology. The same principle holds for women's usage in the Global North and South. African countries may have only a small percent of the population online, but in none of the African countries do women have more than 15% of that tiny share (Drori 2006). Fewer than 7 out of 10,000 African women had used the Internet as of 2006; however, that number is growing rapidly. Still, the majority of African women are "out of the digital loop," and competency in use of the Internet has become an extremely important resource in the contemporary global economy.

The story is different in the United States, where women have recently caught up with or outpaced their male peers. The direction of U.S. usage parallels that of other Global North countries and may predict the future in other countries (Madden and Zickuhr 2011).

Thinking Sociologically

Ask several people from different generations and different genders how they use computer technology and the Internet and how they learned these skills. What do you conclude about differences between women and men?

Gender Stratification: Micro- to Macro-Level Theories

In recent years, some biologists and psychologists have considered whether there are innate differences in the makeup of women and men. For instance, males produce more testosterone, a hormone found to be correlated with aggression. Research shows that in many situations, males tend to be more aggressive and concerned with dominance, whether the behavior is biologically programmed or learned or both. Other traits, such as nurturance, empathy, and altruism, show no clear gender difference (Fausto-Sterling 1992; Sapolsky 2011).

Although biological and psychological factors are part of the difference between females and males, our focus here is on the major contribution that social factors make in social statuses of males and females in human society. This section explores social theories that explain gender differences.

Symbolic Interaction Theory: Micro-Level Analysis

Traditional notions of gender are hard to change. Confusion over proper masculine and feminine roles creates anxiety and even anomie in a society. People want guidelines. Thus, it is easier to adhere to traditional notions of gender that are reinforced by religious or political dogmas, making those ideas appear sacred, absolute, and beyond human interference. Absolute answers are comforting to those who find change disconcerting. Others believe the male prerogatives and privileges of the past were established by men to protect their rights. Any change in concepts of gender or of roles assigned to males and females will be hard to bring about precisely because they are rooted in the meaning system and status and power structures present in the social world. Symbolic interactionists look at gender as socially constructed. Sex is the biological reality of different "plumbing" in our bodies, and interactionists are interested in how those physical differences come to be symbols, resulting in different social rights and rewards. This chapter's discussions of micro-level social processes have pointed out that the meaning assigned to one's sex is connected to notions of masculinity and femininity. The symbolic interaction perspective has been forceful in insisting that notions of proper gender behavior are not intrinsically related to a person's sex. The bottom line is that gender is a socially created or constructed idea.

Symbolic interaction—more than any other theory—stresses the idea of human agency, the notion that humans not only are influenced by the society in which they live but actively help create it (Charon 2010; Hewitt and Shulman 2011). In a study of elementary children in classrooms and especially on playgrounds, Barrie Thorne found that while teachers influenced the children, the children themselves were active participants in creating the student culture that guided their play. As children played with one another, Thorne noticed the ways in which they created words, nicknames, distinctions between one another, and new forms of interaction (Thorne 1993). This is a very important point: Humans do not just passively adopt cultural notions about gender; they *do gender.* They create it as they behave and interact with others in ways that define "normal" male or female conduct (West and Zimmerman 1987). "Doing gender" is an everyday, recurring, and routine occurrence. It is a constant ongoing process that defines each situation, takes place in organizations and between individuals, and becomes part of institutional arrangements. Social movements such as civil rights and the women's movement challenge these arrangements and can bring about change. Understanding the process of doing gender helps us understand why we think and act as we do.

When children are in an ambiguous situation, they may spontaneously define their sex as the most relevant trait

Some cultures suggest that women are helpless and need the door held for them, and women's stylish attire—such as many forms of shoes and dresses—actually does make them more vulnerable and helpless in certain situations. In these decisions and behaviors, men and women are "doing gender."

and although this process begins at a micro level, it has implications all the way to the global level.

Thinking Sociologically

How do you *do gender*? How did you learn these patterns of behavior? Are they automatic responses, or do you think about "who opens the door" and other gender behaviors?

One example of *doing gender* is illustrated in the following "Sociology in Our Social World." This is one example of how gender socialization affects our attitudes toward everyday events that we take for granted.

Structural-Functional and Conflict Theories: Meso- and Macro-Level Analyses

Structural-Functional Theory

From the structural-functional perspective, each sex has a role to play in the interdependent groups and institutions of society. Some early theorists argued that men and women carry out different roles that have developed since early human history. Social relationships and practices that have proven successful in the survival of a group are likely to continue and be reinforced by society's norms, laws, and religious beliefs. Thus, relationships between women and men that are believed to support survival are maintained. In traditional hunter-gatherer, horticultural, and pastoral societies, for instance, the division of labor is based on sex and age. Social roles are clearly laid out, indicating who performs which everyday survival tasks. The females often take on the primary tasks of child care, gardening, food preparation, and other duties near the home. Men do tasks that require movements farther from home, such as hunting, fishing, or herding.

As societies industrialize, roles and relationships change due to structural changes in society. Émile Durkheim described a gradual move from traditional societies held together by *mechanical solidarity* (the glue that holds society together through shared beliefs, values, and traditions) to modern societies that hold together due to *organic solidarity* (social coherence based on division of labor, with each member playing a highly specialized role) (Durkheim [1893] 1947). According to early functionalists, gender division of labor exists in modern societies because it is efficient and useful to have different but complementary male and female roles. They believed this accomplishes essential tasks and maintains societal stability (Lindsey 2011).

More recent structural-functional theorists describe society as an integrated system of roles that work together

about themselves or others. Indeed, even when children act as if gender matters, they are helping make it a reality for those around them. This process helps make the notion of gender more concrete and real to the other children. As the next child adopts the "definition of reality" from the first, acting as if sex is more important than hair color or eye color or earlobe attachment to the cheek, this makes gender the most prominent characteristic in the mind of the next child. Yet each child, in a sense, could choose to ignore gender and decide that something else, like nationality, is more important. This is part of human agency—the freedom to define reality differently than others. The same principle applies to adults. When a person "chooses" to recognize gender as a critical distinction between two individuals or two groups, that person is "doing gender." We do gender all the time, every day. In fact, we cannot avoid it. It is present in our interactions, and we are conscious that we will be judged by others. That judgment could be harsh if we go outside accepted boundaries of gender behavior. Thus, little girls and boys learn to do their appropriate gender roles (Hewitt and Shulman 2011; J. O'Brien 2011; Schoepflin 2011). Through interaction, people do gender,

Sociology in Our Social World

Gender and Food

By Jacqueline Bergdahl

Behavior is generally considered *gendered* when it has symbolic meaning that differs for men versus women. Driving is gendered—men operate motor vehicles differently than women. Men are more likely to drive at night and after drinking, to tailgate more, and to speed more; therefore, they are more likely to die in car crashes than are women.

Food is also gendered—embedded with symbolic meanings. In food preparation, women are more likely than men to be the primary food preparer in households, while there are more male professional chefs than female ones. Women are more likely to bake than men, and men are more likely to grill than women. Food practices are shaped by gender, even though we prefer to think that what and how we eat are due to personal preferences, rather than larger social forces.

Some food items are considered to have a gender. Meat, potatoes, and coffee are foods that many people consider to be masculine, while yogurt and fruit are feminine, and chicken and oranges are gender neutral (Rappoport, 2003). McPhail, Beagan, and Chapman asked subjects to sort the pictures of food items into men's foods and women's foods. Salad, fish, couscous, and stir-fry were generally considered women's foods while pizza, hot dogs, macaroni and cheese, pot roast, and bacon cheeseburgers were considered men's foods (McPhail, Beagan, and Chapman 2012).

Food preferences are also gendered. Salads are considered food for women, while men require red meat. Women are said to eat daintily and men heartily. Part of these differences could be argued to be biological, as men generally require more calories to maintain their greater muscle mass than women, but generally these expectations about who eats what have more to do with cultural gender constructions than the physicality of bodies.

In the 2012 study by McPhail, Beagan, and Chapman, food was considered women's food when it was colorful, delicate, in smaller portions, lighter, or healthier. Part of the attribution of foods to women had to do with weight control. Women were perceived as needing to be more concerned with maintaining or losing weight. Men were thought to prefer both heartier fare and larger portions—little worrying about controlling their food intake or weight. Most of the women expressed concern about eating healthily and watching their weight, although there were a few men who also expressed these concerns.

Women were more adventurous than men when it came to food choices, while ease of preparation and consumption were felt to be the primary considerations for men. Men were also found to be less concerned about their health, more reluctant to eat vegetables, and more likely to prefer spicy foods. Most participants in the study considered meat, and particularly red meat, to be men's food.

Some foods were less gendered. Fish was generally considered women's food as it was healthy and light, but many considered fish to be men's food because more men than women like to catch and eat their own fish. Sushi was seen by some as women's food because of its appearance but as men's food by others because it contained raw fish. Despite all these clearly gendered ideas about food, all of McPhail and colleagues' subjects denied that their eating was gendered. All identified their food preferences as a matter of individual choice, not the result of social patterns or forces (McPhail, Beagan, and Chapman 2012).

Why is it important to understand that food is gendered—that it has symbolic as well as nutritional substance? It allows us to see that our behavior is under the influence of larger structural forces. We may recognize the influence generally (in this case by being willing to sort food photographs into piles according to gender), but we prefer to view our own behavior as simply a matter of choice. Until we acknowledge the effects of gender in all spheres, it will be difficult to eradicate gender inequality. Thinking about how food is gendered is a way of seeing the effects of gender in our lives and would make interesting dinner conversation.

* * * * * * *

Jacqueline Bergdahl is an associate professor of sociology at Wright State University. She studies food, gender, and obesity among other topics.

to carry out the necessary tasks in society. In the version of "traditional family" that was common for much of the 20th century, the father works, the mom stays at home, and they have 2 children. The female plays the expressive role through childbearing, nursing, and caring for family members in the home. The male carries out the instrumental role by working outside the home to support the family (Dilon 2009; Parsons and Bales 1953). Although this pattern was relevant during the Industrial Revolution and again after World War II, as of 2011 it characterized only 23% of U.S. families. Today more children are being raised by single moms than married couples (Aulette 2010; Coontz 2011b). In addition, substantial numbers of families today thrive with two adult partners of the same sex.

In reality, gender segregation has seldom been total because in most cultures, women's work has combined their labor in the public sphere—that is, outside the home—with their work in the private sphere—inside the home (Lopez-Garza 2002). Poor minority women in countries around the world must often work in low-paying service roles in the public sphere and carry the major burden for roles in the private sphere. Gender analysis through a structural-functional perspective stresses efficiencies that are believed to be gained by specialization of tasks (Waite and Gallagher 2000).

Conflict Theory

Conflict theorists view males as the haves—controlling the majority of power positions and most wealth—and females as the have-nots. Women have less access to power and have historically depended on males for survival. This is the case

By contrast to the clothing and gestures that create vulnerability in women, men are encouraged to use gestures that communicate strength and self-assurance, and their clothing and shoes allow them to defend themselves or flee danger.

even though they raise the next generation of workers and consumers, provide unpaid domestic labor, and ensure a pool of available, cheap labor during times of crisis, such as war. By keeping women in subordinate roles, males control the means of production and protect their privileged status.

A classical conflict explanation of gender stratification is found in the writings of Karl Marx's colleague, Friedrich Engels ([1884] 1942). In traditional societies, where size and strength were essential for survival, men were often dominant, but women's roles were respected as important and necessary to the survival of the group. Men hunted, engaged in warfare, and protected women. Over time, male physical control was transformed into control by ideology, by the dominant belief system itself. Capitalism strengthened male dominance by making more wealth available to men and their sons. Women became dependent on men, and their roles were transformed into "taking care of the home" (Engels [1884] 1942).

Ideologies based on traditional beliefs and values have continued to be used to justify the social structure of male domination and subjugation of women. It is in the interest of the dominant group, in this case men, to maintain positions of privilege. Conflict theorists believe it is unlikely that those in power by virtue of sex, race, class, or political or religious ideology will voluntarily give up their positions as long as they are benefiting from them. By keeping women in traditional gender roles, men maintain control over institutions and resources (R. Collins 1971).

Feminist Theory

Feminist theorists agree with Marx and Engels that gender stratification is based on power struggles, not biology. On the other hand, some feminist theorists argue that Marx and Engels failed to consider fully a key variable in women's oppression: patriarchy. Patriarchy involves a few men dominating and holding authority over all others, including women, children, and less powerful men (Arrighi 2000; Lindsey 2011). According to feminist theory, women will continue to be oppressed by men until patriarchy is eliminated.

A distinguishing characteristic of most feminist theory is that it actively advocates change in the social order, whereas many other theories we have discussed try only to explain the social world (Anderson 2006; Lorber 1998). There is a range of feminist theories. However, all feminist theories argue for bringing about a new and equal ordering of gender relationships to eliminate the patriarchy and sexism of current gender stratification systems (Kramer 2010).

Feminist theorists try to understand the causes of women's lower status and seek ways to change systems to provide educational and work opportunities, to improve the standard of living, and to give women control over their bodies and reproduction. Feminist theorists also feel that little

Tough Guise

Men who play cards, games, or sports together or who join men's-only clubs develop networks that enhance their power and their ability to "close deals." When women are not part of the same networks, they are denied the same insider privileges. Even if it is not intentional, this works against women, people of color, and the laboring classes. Most conflict theorists and some feminist theorists would argue that leaving women out is purposeful.

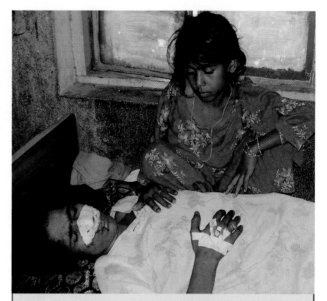

When women have less power at the meso level, they may also be more vulnerable at home. This girl attends to her injured mother at a hospital in Hyderabad, Pakistan, after the woman's husband chopped off her nose with an axe and broke all her teeth. According to the Pakistan Institute of Medical Sciences, more than 90% of married women report being severely abused when husbands are dissatisfied with their cooking or cleaning or when the women give birth to a girl instead of a boy or are unable to bear a child at all.

change will occur until group consciousness is raised so that women understand the system that limits their options (Sapiro 2003). In addition to awareness, women need the networks that open occupational doors for many men.

As societies become technologically advanced and need an educated workforce, women of all social classes and ethnic groups around the world are likely to gain more equal roles. Women are entering institutions of higher education in record numbers, and evidence indicates they are needed in the world economic system and the changing labor force of most countries. Societies in which women are not integrated into the economic system generally lag behind other countries. Feminist theorists examine these global and national patterns, but they also note the role of patriarchy in interpersonal situations—such as domestic violence.

Violence against women perpetuates gender stratification, as is evident in the intimate environment of many homes. Because men have more power in the larger society, they often have more resources within the household as well (an example of side-effect discrimination). Women are often dependent on the man of the house for his resources, meaning they are willing to yield on many decisions. Power differences in the meso- and macro-level social systems also contribute to power differentials and vulnerability of women in micro-level settings. In addition, women who

lack stable employment have fewer options when considering whether to leave an abusive relationship. Although there are risks of staying with a violent partner, many factors enter into a woman's decision to stay or leave (Scott, London, and Myers 2002). The following "Sociology in Our Social World" discusses one form of violence around the world that is perpetuated predominantly against women: rape.

In summary, feminist analysis finds gender patterns embedded in social institutions of family, education, religion, politics, economics, and health care. If the societal system is ruled by men, the interdependent institutions are likely to reflect and support this system. Feminist theory helps us understand how patriarchy at the meso and macro levels can influence patriarchy at the micro level and vice versa.

Thinking Sociologically

First, read the essay about rape on page 268. Why do women and men stay in abusive relationships? If these behaviors are hurtful or destructive, what might be done to change the situation, or what policies might be enacted to address the problems?

Sociology in Our Social World

Rape and the Victims of Rape

For many women around the world, rape is the most feared act of violence and the ultimate humiliation. Rape is a sexual act but closely tied to macho behavior. Rape is often a power play to intimidate, hurt, and dominate women. As a weapon of war, rape humiliates the enemies who cannot protect their women (Larsen 2013; Sanday and Goodenough 1990). Some societies are largely free from rape whereas others are prone toward rape. What is the difference?

When a society is relatively tolerant of interpersonal violence, holds beliefs in male dominance, and strongly incorporates ways to separate women and men, rape is more common ("Male Dominance Causes Rape" 2008; Sanday and Goodenough 1990). Rape is also more common when gender roles and identities are changing and norms about interaction between women and men are unclear.

An alarming problem is rape on college campuses in the United States. What does this say about the United States, where 1 in 4 to 5 college women will be raped or survive a rape attempt during her college years (Burn 2011; One in Four, Inc. n.d.)? That is one every 21 hours. Ninety percent occur under the influence of alcohol.

Eighteen percent of women in the United States have survived a complete or an attempted rape—22 million women. In the United States, someone is sexually assaulted or raped every 2 minutes, averaging more than 2,000 rapes daily. Annually, there are 169,370 female, 15,020 male, and a total of 272,350 rapes or sexual assaults (Truman 2011a). The U.S. Justice Department estimates that only 26% of rapes and attempted rapes are reported (Anti-Violence Resource Guide 2012; National Center for Injury Prevention and Control 2011).

The fallout from rape and attempted rape is that victims "often experience anxiety, guilt, nervousness, phobias, substance abuse, sleep disturbances, depression, alienation, sexual dysfunction, aggression, and distrust of others." Physical disorders are also common, including sexually transmitted diseases

(Anti-Violence Resource Guide 2012). All of this indicates that rape and sexual assault really do intimidate a significant portion of the population, making the targeted group feel vulnerable and less confident. The net result means a reduction of power, as pointed out by feminist theory.

Women report being sexually assaulted whereas many males who are sexually aggressive toward women do not define their behavior as rape. This discrepancy points to the stereotypes and misunderstandings that can occur because of different beliefs and attitudes. Rape causes deep and lasting problems for women victims as well as for men accused of rape because of "misreading" women's signals. Some college men define gang rape as a form of male bonding. To them, it is no big deal. The woman is just the object and instrument. Her identity is immaterial (Martin and Hummer 1989; Sanday and Goodenough 1990).

Men who hold more traditional gender roles view rape very differently than women and less traditional men. The former tend to attribute more responsibility to the female victim of a rape, believe sex rather than power is the motivation for rape, and look less favorably on women who have been raped. In a strange twist of logic, one study showed that some men actually believe that women want to be forced into having involuntary sex (Szymanski et al. 1993). Researchers have found that societies with widespread gender stratification report more gendered violence (Palmer 1989; Sanday 1996, 2007).

Many citizens and politicians see rape as an individualized, personal act, whereas social scientists tend to see it as a structural problem that stems from negative stereotypes of women, subservient positions of women in society, and patriarchal systems of power. The rape culture in the war-torn parts of Sudan and the Congo are examples. A number of sociologists and anthropologists believe that rape will not be substantially reduced unless our macho definitions of masculinity are changed (McEvoy and Brookings 2008; Sanday and Goodenough 1990).

The Interaction of Class, Race, and Gender

Zouina is Algerian, but she was born in France to her immigrant parents. She lived with them in a poor immigrant suburb of Paris until she was forced to return to Algeria for an arranged marriage to a man who already had one wife. That marriage ended, and she returned to her "home" in France. Since she returned to France, Zouina has been employed wherever she can find work. The high unemployment and social and ethnic discrimination, especially against foreign women, makes life difficult. An estimated 200,000 people, including children, live in up to 20,000 polygamous families, a practice that is illegal in France ("Polygamy in France" 2010).

The situation is complex. Muslim women from Tunisia, Morocco, and Algeria, former French colonies, living in crowded slum communities outside Paris face discrimination in the workplace and their community (Lazaridis 2011). Expected to be both good Muslim women and good family coproviders—which necessitates working in French society—they face ridicule when they wear their *hijabs* (coverings) to school or to work. However, they encounter derision in their community if they do not wear them. They are caught between two cultures and may be the scapegoats for frustrated young men who cannot find work.

Because of high unemployment in the immigrant communities, many youth roam the streets. Gang rapes by North African youth against young women have been on the rise in France and elsewhere abroad. These rapes mean that North African women are faced with rejection and disdain in France, in their immigrant community, and in their original North African communities. With the conflicting messages due to their ethnic differences (race), their poor status (class), and their gender, these women attempt to construct their identities under grueling circumstances (Killian 2006).

Feminist theory seeks explanations for the conditions women face (Walby 1990). One current trend in feminist interpretation, illustrated in the previous example, is to view the social world as an intersection of class, race, and gender (Anderson and Collins 2006). In this way, one can look at the variety of ways that many common citizens are controlled by those who have a monopoly on power and privilege.

The reality is that some women are quite privileged and wealthy. Not all women live in poverty. However, even privileged women often have less power than their husbands or other men in their lives. It is also true that some women in the world are privileged because of their race or ethnicity (Rothenberg 2010). In many respects, they have more in common with men of their own ethnicity or race than they do with women of less esteemed groups, and they may choose to identify with those statuses that enhance their privilege.

Consider another example of the intersection of race, class, and gender. Income for men and women varies significantly depending on ethnicity within the United States, and this means that minority women are even more disprivileged. However, even when ethnicity is held constant, women get paid less than men (see Table 9.3).

Table 9.3 Median Usual Weekly Earnings of Full-Time Wage and Salary Workers by Sex, Race, and Percent of Men's Earnings by Women, 2011

Race and Ethnicity	Male	Female	Women's % of Men's Earnings
Asian American	$970	$751	77%
White	$856	$703	82%
African American	$653	$595	91%
Hispanic or Latino	$571	$518	90%

Source: U.S. Department of Labor, Bureau of Labor Statistics (2012).

These examples illustrate that race, class, and gender have crosscutting lines that may affect one's status in the society. Sexual orientation, age, nationality, and other factors also have the effect of either diminishing or increasing minority status of specific women, and theorists are paying increasing attention to these intersections (Rothenberg 2010). Chapter 8 discussed the fact that race and class lines may be either crosscutting or parallel in a given society, and the patterns affect ethnic relations. In the case of gender, there are always crosscutting lines with race and social class. Gender always affects one's prestige and privilege within that class or ethnic group. Thus, these three variables—race, class, and gender—should be considered simultaneously.

Gender, Homosexuality, and Minority Status

We have learned that sex, gender, and sexuality are not simple opposites, the range of sexuality and gender being much more complex than that. Societal expectations developed over time that have imposed categories on both gender and human sexuality.

Heterosexism is the notion that the society reinforces heterosexuality and marginalizes anyone who does not conform to this norm. Heterosexism focuses on social processes that define homosexuality as deviant and legitimize heterosexuality as the only normal lifestyle (Oswald 2000, 2001). In short, heterosexism operates often at the meso and macro levels of society, through privileges such as rights to health care and jobs granted to people who are heterosexual and sometimes denied to those who are not. Despite this, homosexuality and transgendered people have always existed. They have been accepted and even required at some times and places and rejected or outlawed in others. In some cases, homosexuals and transgendered individuals have been placed in a separate sexual category with special roles. For example, the *Hijras* in India and some other areas in South Asia are usually physiological males who have feminine gender identity. Many live in *Hijra* communities and have designated roles in Indian festivals and celebrations.

Some societies ignore the existence of LGBTQ (lesbian, gay, bisexual, transsexual/transgender and queer/questioning) members of the community. Some consider it a psychological illness or form of depraved immorality. A few even consider these forms of sexuality a crime (as in some Muslim societies today and in most states in the United States during much of the 20th century). In a recent global controversy in Uganda, Africa, the parliament proposed a bill to outlaw homosexuality and even put homosexuals to death. This move was fueled in part by an American evangelist who is accused of fomenting antigay hysteria that resulted in persecution, arrest, torture, and even murder of homosexuals in Uganda. Human rights outcries kept the bill from passing in 2009, but the bill has since been reintroduced (Goodstein 2012). In each case around the world, the government or dominant religious group determines the status of homosexuals. The reality is that deviation from a society's gender norms, such as attraction to a member of the same sex, may cause one to experience minority status.

Homophobia—intense fear and hatred of homosexuality and homosexuals, whether male or female—is highly correlated with and perhaps a cause of people holding traditional notions of gender and gender roles (Shaw and Lee 2005). The issue of homophobia focuses on prejudice held and transmitted by individuals, and it therefore operates only at the micro level.

Some homosexuals deviate from traditional notions of masculinity and femininity and therefore from significant norms of many societies. This may result in hostile reactions and stigma from the dominant group. Indeed, homosexual epitaphs are often used to reinforce gender conformity and to intimidate anyone who would dare to be different from the norm. Because in most societies women are economically dependent on men, their status in society is typically based on their relationship with men. Therefore, lesbians—women who are attracted to other women—go against norms of societies and are in some instances perceived as dangerous, unnatural, or a threat to men's power (Burn 2011; Ward and Edelstein 2009).

The mass media has begun to include LGBT characters in films such as *A Single Man* (2009), *Milk* (2008), *Shelter* (2007), *Brokeback Mountain* (2005), and *Latter Days* (2003). Television features such as *Ellen* and *Will and Grace* have also become popular (Ayers 2010). In addition, there are many well-known gay news commentators and show hosts illustrating popular culture's change in acceptance of homosexuals. Gallup polls reveal that U.S. public acceptance of homosexuals surpassed 50% in 2010, and those calling homosexuality "morally wrong" dropped to 43%. Fifty-eight percent felt relations between consenting adults should be legal (Saad 2010). More than 90% of the U.S. population now supports equal opportunity for homosexuals on the job (P. Johnson 2005). Despite these indications of greater openness in attitudes, in 2010 it was still legal in 29 states to fire someone based on his or her sexuality (Topix.com 2010).

Still, homosexuality—especially same-sex marriage—was a hot topic in the elections of 2012. Views on both extremes were presented, and this social issue seemed to split the country between the religious right and the liberal left. In several states bans on same-sex marriage have been passed, yet the public opinion is inching toward more acceptance. Most states have "Defense of Marriage Acts" or constitutional amendments prohibiting same-sex marriage, but laws are changing (Hamilton 2012; National Conference of State Legislatures 2012). In short, many institutions including family, economics and work, politics, religion, and health care have been influenced by this debate over sexuality and gender. Note how meso-level institutions such as government and religion control personal relationships—even trying to restrain whom one can love.

The LGBTQ community does not have many of the rights that heterosexuals have, a discrepancy based on sexual preferences. Heterosexuals in the United States have a variety of rights—ranging from insurance coverage and inheritance rights for lifelong partners to jointly acquired

The movement among gays, lesbians, bisexuals, and transsexuals for equal rights and recognition is not just a North American or European phenomenon. These Nepalese transsexuals are among hundreds from across the country who gathered in Kathmandu, the capital, to demand official recognition and political representation in Nepal. This is a global movement.

property, hospital visitation rights as family, rights to claim the body of a deceased partner, and rights to have the deceased prepared for burial or cremation. The U.S. federal government confers 1,138 rights on heterosexuals that they normally take for granted, but often, these rights do not extend to same-sex partners in a long-term committed relationship. Most states also bestow more than 200 specific rights to persons who "marry," but because most states do not allow same-sex marriages, homosexuals do not have these same rights (Michon 2013; U.S. General Accounting Office 2004). In Canada and many European countries, citizens do have a right to same-sex marriage, and this has reduced the number of discrepancies in the rights of homosexuals and heterosexuals.

Thinking Sociologically

The concept of *homophobia* focuses on micro-level processes—prejudice. The notion of *heterosexism* is most relevant at the meso and macro level—discrimination in law, social structures, and culture. Which of these concepts reveals the most about issues faced by the lesbian and gay community? Why?

Liberals tend to see limited rights for LGBTQ communities as prejudice against persons for a characteristic that is unchangeable. They assume that homosexuality is an inborn trait—present from birth. Conservatives argue that homosexuality is a choice that has moral implications. They tend to see homosexuality as a behavior that is acquired through socialization; therefore, acceptance of homosexuality will likely increase the numbers of people who engage in this lifestyle. Social conservatives see politically liberal notions about homosexuality and gender roles as a threat to society and family, a threat to the moral social order, whereas liberals often feel that sexuality within a committed relationship is not a moral issue. The real moral issue for them is bigotry—lack of tolerance of other lifestyles. Thus, the two groups have socially constructed the meaning of morality along different lines.

While some religions do not accept homosexuality, some mainstream Christian denominations have developed policies supportive of lesbian, gay, and bisexual persons in local churches: More Light (Presbyterian), Open and Affirming (United Church of Christ and Christian Church), Reconciling in Christ (Lutheran), and Reconciling Ministries (Methodist). These designations apply to approximately 300 congregations that wish to be known as gay and lesbian friendly (www.mlp.org). A new denomination, the Universal Fellowship of Metropolitan

Community Churches, affirms homosexuality as a legitimate lifestyle for Christians (Metropolitan Community Churches 2013; Rodriguez and Ouellette 2000). It has more than 300 local churches in the United States, with 17 in the conservative state of Texas. In short, cultural notions about gender and sexuality are influencing the structure of society at the meso level, including institutions such as family, politics, and religion. Gender is very personal and private but also a public issue with macro-level implications.

Costs and Consequences of Gender Stratification

In rapidly changing modern societies, role confusion abounds. Men hesitate to offer help to women, wondering if gallantry will be appreciated or scorned. Women are torn between traditional family roles on the one hand, and working to support the family and fulfill career goals on the other. As illustrated in the following examples, sex- and gender-based stratification limits individual development and causes problems in education, health, work, and other parts of the social world.

Psychological and Social Consequences: Micro-Level Implications

For both women and men, rigid gender stereotypes can be very constraining. Individuals who hold highly sex-typed attitudes feel compelled to behave in stereotypic ways, ways that are consistent with the pictures they have in their heads of proper gender behavior (Kramer 2010). However, individuals who do not identify rigidly with masculine or feminine gender types tend to have a broad acceptable repertoire of behaviors and know how to cope with changing situations (Cheng 2005). They are more flexible in thoughts and behavior, score higher on intelligence tests, have greater spatial ability, and have higher levels of creativity. Because they allow themselves a wider range of behaviors, they have more varied abilities and experiences and become more tolerant of others' behaviors. High masculinity in males sets up rigid standards for male behavior and has been correlated with anxiety, guilt, and neuroses, whereas less rigid masculine expectations are associated with emotional stability, sensitivity, warmth, and enthusiasm (Bellisari 1990). Rigid stereotypes and resulting sexism affect everyone and can curtail our activities, behaviors, and perspectives.

The Results of Gender Role Expectations

Women in many societies are expected to be beautiful, youthful, and sexually interesting and interested, while at the same time preparing the food, caring for the children, keeping a clean and orderly home, sometimes bringing in money to help support the family, and being competent and successful in their careers. Multiple, sometimes contradictory, expectations for women can cause stress and even serious psychological problems. The resulting strain contributes to depression and certain health problems such as headaches, nervousness, and insomnia (Wood 2008).

Gender expectations also affect women's self-concepts and body images. As noted earlier, beautiful images jump out at us from billboards, magazine covers, and TV and movie screens. Some of these images are unattainable because they have been created through surgeries and eating disorders—and even by the use of airbrushing on photographs. Disorders, including anorexia and bulimia nervosa, relate to societal expectations of the ideal woman's appearance (Taub and McLorg 2010).

Thinking Sociologically

If females are encouraged to spend money, energy, and attention on how they look to ensure that they are physically appealing to others, how might this affect their view of themselves, their health, their use of time, and their access to positions of power?

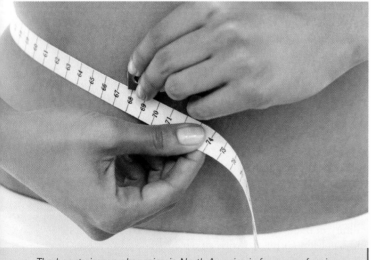

The beauty-image obsession in North America is far more of an issue with white Anglos than African Americans or Latinas, but especially with young white women it results in disorders relative to eating. Obsessed with thinness, some young women consider a small salad a complete dinner.

Perhaps 10% of men also have eating disorders, and fitness magazines picture the "perfect" male body and advertise exercise equipment and steroids ("Eating Disorder Statistics" 2008). In addition, men die earlier than women, in part due to environmental, psychological, and social factors. Problems in Global North countries such as heart disease, stroke, cirrhosis, cancers, accidents, and suicides are linked in part to the role expectations that males should appear tough, objective, ambitious, unsentimental, and unemotional—traits that require men to assume great responsibility and suppress their feelings (Leit, Gray, and Pope 2002).

Societal Costs and Consequences: Meso- and Macro-Level Implications

Gender stratification creates costs for societies around the world in a number of ways. Poor education achievement of female children leads to the loss of human talents and resources of half of the population, a serious loss for societies. *Social divisiveness*—we-they thinking based on sex—can also create alienation, if not hostility, and this can result in aggression. Discrimination and violence against women, whether physical or emotional, have consequences for all institutions in a society.

Consider how the ratio of women to men in an occupational field affects the prestige of the occupation. As more men enter predominantly female fields such as nursing and library science, the fields gain higher occupational prestige, and salaries tend to increase. It seems that men take their gender privilege with them when they enter female professions. However, the evidence indicates that as women enter male professions such as law, the status tends to become lower, making women's chances of improving their position in the stratification system limited (Kramer 2010).

Gender stratification has often meant loss of the talents and brainpower of women, and that is a serious loss to modern postindustrial societies because human capital—the resources of the human population—is central to social prosperity in this type of system. Yet, resistance to expanding women's public sphere and professional roles is often strong. For example, Japanese women make up close to 50% of the workforce, but only 10.1% hold managerial positions and many leave the workplace when they marry (Fackler 2007). A poll of major Japanese corporations found that most want to use women's talents as women are well educated, but in fact only a small number (5.4%) of lower-level management positions in companies were held by women (Gaijinpot 2010). Although their education levels are generally high, Japanese women earn wages that are about 66% of their male counterparts' wages (Japan Institute for Labour Policy and Training 2009; Kumlin 2006). Breaking through the glass ceiling continues to be a barrier for individual women but also a challenge for entire societies that could benefit from abilities never fully maximized.

Changing Gender Stratification and Social Policy

One global policy issue has to do with multinational corporations that create a dilemma for women: Is it better for a woman in the Global South to have a poor-paying job and poor working conditions, or no job? On the one hand, few wage-paying jobs are available in some areas, and most of those positions in manufacturing and assembly positions that do become available are held by women. Yet women in factories around the globe face dangerous conditions and low pay. Sweatshops exist because poor women and sometimes men have few other job options to support their families and because people in rich countries want to buy the cheap products that perpetuate the multinational corporate system. For example, more than 1 million Mexicans work in *maquiladoras* (foreign-owned manufacturing and assembly plants) in Mexican border towns.

The maquiladoras are owned by U.S., European, and Japanese conglomerates, and hire primarily unskilled young women who work for as little as 50 cents an hour; skilled workers may get $1 to $2 an hour. The employees produce electronic equipment, clothing, plastics, furniture, appliances, and auto parts, most of which are shipped to the United States (Rosenberg 2012). The hours worked per week range from 50 to 75, with some maquiladoras paying $40 to $50 for a 60-hour week. Women and children often make less than men ("Misery of the Maquiladoras" 2011). Workers are not paid a living wage in most maquiladoras and in other multinational corporations in the Global South.

One result of low wages and poor working conditions is exploitation of women in other parts of the world. Another is loss of income for workers in the United States, including men. Manufacturers within the United States are starting to hire after the recession, but the wages they are offering are $10 to $15 an hour less than before the economic recession (Kelber 2012). So the "race to the bottom" by multinationals (seeking the lowest price for labor)

The collapse of a garment building in Bangladesh—a sweatshop providing clothing for top clothing brands around the world—illustrates the vulnerability of women. Twelve women died in a building that the owners knew was unsafe. Bangladesh has 5,000 such factories and is the second leading exporter of clothing in the world.

Women in Thailand produce shoes for extremely low pay. These jobs are better than no employment at all, but before pressures from Western societies changed their cultures, most people were able to feed their families on farms in small villages. Changes in the entire world system have made that form of life no longer feasible, but working for multinational corporations also keeps these women impoverished.

is affecting earnings of men and women in the United States. We really live in an interconnected world.

What can be done about the abusive treatment of women workers around the world? This is a tough issue: Governments have passed legislation to protect workers, but governments also want the jobs that multinational corporations bring and therefore do little to enforce regulations. International labor standards are also difficult to enforce because multinational corporations are so large and located in many different parts of the world. Trade unions have had little success attracting workers to join because companies squash their recruiting efforts immediately.

One way activist groups protest for fair wages and conditions for workers is to adopt practices that have worked for other groups facing discrimination in the past. Consider the following strategies used by these groups to bring about change: holding nonviolent protests, sit-down strikes, and walkouts to protest unequal and unfair treatment; working together in support groups to help children, neighborhoods, and communities; encouraging companies to help the communities in which they are located; using the Internet to carry a message to others; carrying out boycotts against companies that mistreat employees; using the arts, storytellers, and teachers to mobilize resistance; and building on traditions of community and religious activism (P. Collins 2000). Most of these strategies require organized movements, but such efforts face the possibility of antagonizing the companies so that they move to other countries. It is a delicate balance.

Thinking Sociologically

Take a look at the clothing in your closet and your drawers. Figure out where it was made either by reading the label or by looking up the company's factories on the Internet. Would you be willing to pay more for that clothing so that other people could have better conditions? What about your friends? Should you be concerned about these workers' lives or not? Why?

Most United Nations member countries have at least fledgling women's movements fighting for improved status of women and their families. The movements attempt to change laws that result in discrimination, poverty, abuse, and low levels of education and occupational status. One example is the Better Factories movement in Cambodia (Kampuchea) that works to address worker problems. Although the goals of eliminating differential treatment of women, especially minority women, are jointly affirmed by most women's groups, the means to improve conditions for women are debated between women's groups. Whether any of these efforts will change women's individual lives and the lives of their children is unknown. We would be too optimistic to predict that grassroots efforts or boycotts against those who are enjoying the fruits of poor women's labor will change the system. The best hope may lie in increased opportunities for women as countries modernize and in efforts to enforce labor laws and improve conditions and wages for workers (Better Factories 2012).

Inequality based on class, race, ethnicity, and gender is taking place at all levels of analysis, but is often entrenched at the meso level within institutions—family, education, religion, politics, economics, and health care.

In complex societies, there are other core institutions including science and technology, sport, and the military. We turn now to a discussion of institutions in our social world.

What Have We Learned?

In the beginning of this chapter, we asked how being born female or male affects our lives. Because sex is a primary variable on which societies are structured and stratified, being born female or male affects our public- and private-sphere activities, our health, our ability to practice religion or participate in political life, our opportunities for education, and just about everything we do. Gender inequality clearly exists. What should be done to alleviate problems related to gender stratification is a matter of debate.

Key Points:

- Whereas sex is biological, notions of gender identity and gender roles are socially constructed and therefore variable. (See pp. 245–247.)

- Notions of gender are first taught at the micro setting—the intimacy of the home—but they are reinforced and even sacralized at the meso and macro levels. (See pp. 247–252.)

- While "she" may go first in micro-level social encounters (served first in a restaurant or the first to enter a doorway), "he" goes first in meso and macro settings—with the doors open wider for men to enter leadership positions in organizations and institutions. (See pp. 246–252.)

- Greater access to resources at the meso level makes it easier to have entrée to macro-level positions, but it also influences respect in micro settings. (See pp. 254–258.)

- Much of the gender stratification today is unconscious and unintended—not caused by angry or bigoted men who purposefully oppress women. Inequality is rooted in institutionalized privilege and disprivilege. (See pp. 258–263.)

- Various social theories shed different light on the issues of gender roles assigned to various sexes and inequality. (See pp. 263–269.)

- For modern postindustrial societies, there is a high cost for treating women like a minority group—both individually for the people who experience it and for the society, which loses the intelligence, skills, and commitment of highly competent people. (See pp. 271–273.)

Discussion Questions

1. Describe some of the ways socializing agents (e.g., family, peers, the media, religion, teachers) encouraged you to conform to traditional gender norms. Do you think you will encourage (or have you encouraged) your own children to conform to traditional gender norms? Why or why not?

2. Give two examples of side-effect gender discrimination that leads to economic inequality between men and women.

3. How does gender socialization influence who runs for office and for whom we vote? How are female politicians treated by the media, compared to male politicians? How has that impacted your own perception of female politicians?

4. How does gender discrimination harm society? What could be done on your campus to improve the status of women? How might you join these efforts?

5. What are your career goals? Do they follow traditional gender roles? Why or why not? How has your gender socialization impacted your career plans?

6. More women than men are now in college. How do you think this fact will impact gender roles on campus and in the larger society?

Contributing to Our Social World: What Can We Do?

At the Local Level

- *To learn about gender discrimination on your campus*, schedule an interview with the director or other staff members of the human resources or affirmative action office on your campus to learn about your school's policies regarding gender discrimination. What procedures exist for hiring? Do women and men receive the same salaries, wages, and benefits for equal work? Explore the possibility of your working as a volunteer or intern in the office, specifically in the area of gender equity.

At the Organizational and National Levels

- *The National Organization for Women (NOW)* is the world's leading advocate for gender equity. It deals with issues such as abortion and reproductive rights, legislative outreach, economic justice, ending sex discrimination, and promoting diversity. Several internship programs are listed on the organization's website, www.now.org, along with contact information, state and regional affiliates, and "NOW on Campus" links.

- *Sociologists for Women in Society (SWS)*, an organization that "works to improve women's lives through advancing and supporting feminist sociological research, activism and scholars" provides many resources for students. SWS provides students with scholarships, opportunities to be mentored, and an award to recognize students who improve the lives of women through activism.

At the Global Level

- *MADRE*, an international women's rights organization, works primarily in less developed countries. You can find numerous opportunities for working on issues of justice, human rights, education, and health on its website at www.madre.org.

- *Equality Now*, an international nongovernmental organization, provides many venues for those interested in promoting equality for women and curbing gender violence and discrimination. You can find more about this organization at www.equalitynow.org.

- *The United Nations Inter-Agency Network on Women and Gender Equality* works on global issues, including violence against women and women's working conditions. Its WomenWatch website at www.un.org/womenwatch contains news, information, and ideas for contributing to the worldwide campaign for women's rights.

Visit **www.sagepub.com/oswcondensed3e** for online activities, sample tests, and other helpful information. Select "Chapter 9: Gender Stratification" for chapter-specific activities.

PART IV

Institutions

Picture a house, a *structure* in which you live. Within that house there are the action and activities that bring the house alive—the *processes*. Flip a switch, and the lights go on because the house is well wired. Adjust the thermostat, and the room becomes more comfortable as the structural features of furnace or air-conditioning systems operate. If the structural components of the plumbing and water heating systems work, you can take a hot shower when you turn the knob. These actions taken within the structure make the house livable. If something breaks down, you need to get it fixed so that everything works smoothly.

Institutions, too, provide a *structure* for society—a framework that promotes stability. *Processes* are the actions within institutions—the activities that take place. They include the interactions between people, decision making, and other actions in society. These processes can lead to significant change within the structure—like a decision about whether new homeowners should remodel their kitchen. Institutions are meso-level structures because they are larger in scope than the face-to-face social interactions of the micro level, yet they are smaller than the nation or the global system.

Institutions—such as family, education, religion, politics, economics, and health care—include certain patterns and expectations that differ in each society. They are interdependent and mutually supportive, just as the plumbing, heating system, and electricity in a house work together to make a home functional. However, breakdown in one institution affects the whole society, just as a malfunction in the electrical system may shut the furnace off and cool down the water heater.

The Importance of Institutions

Institutions are not anything concrete that you can see, hear, touch, or smell. The concept of "institutions" is an abstraction—a way of understanding how society works. For example, the institution of family meets certain needs that are found in almost all societies. Family as an institution refers to the behavior of thousands of people who—taken as a whole—form a social structure. Think of your own family. It has unique ways of interacting and raising children, but it is part of a community with many families. Those many families, in turn, are part of a national set of patterned behaviors we call "the family." This pattern meets basic needs of the society for producing and socializing new members and providing an emotionally supportive environment.

Institutions do not dictate exactly how you will carry out the roles within your family. However, they do specify certain individual needs that families will meet and statuses (spouse/partner, parent, child) that will relate to each other in certain mutually caring ways to fill important family roles. An institution provides a blueprint (much like a local builder needs a blueprint to build a house), and in your local version of the institution you may make a few modifications to the plans to meet your individual micro-level needs. Still, through this society-encompassing structure and interlocking set of statuses, basic needs—for individuals at the micro level and for society at the macro level—are met.

Institutions, then, *are organized, patterned, and enduring sets of social structures that provide guidelines for behavior and help each society meet its basic survival needs*. While institutions operate mostly at the meso level, they also act to integrate micro and macro levels of society. Let us look more deeply at this definition.

1. *Organized, patterned, and enduring sets of social structures* do not represent the bricks and mortar of buildings but refer to a complex set of groups or organizations, statuses within those groups, and norms of conduct that guide people's behavior. These structures

ensure socialization of children, education of the young, sense of meaning in life, companionship, and production and distribution of needed goods (food, clothing, automobiles, iPods, cell phones) for the members of the society. If this patterned behavior were missing, these needs might not be addressed. At the local level, we may go to a neighborhood school, or we may attend worship at a congregation we favor. These are local organizations—local franchises, if you will—of a much more encompassing structure (education or religion) that provides guidelines for education or addresses issues of meaning of life for an enormous number of people. The Catholic Church in your town, for example, is a local "franchise" of an organization that is transnational in scope and global in its concerns.

2. *Guidelines for behavior* help people know how to conduct themselves to obtain basic needs. Individuals and local organizations actually carry out the institutional guidelines in each culture; the exact ways the guidelines are carried out vary by locality. In local "franchises" of the political system, people know how to govern and how to solve problems at the local level because of larger norms and patterns provided by the political institution. Individual men and women operate a local hospital or clinic (a local "franchise" of the medical institution) because a national blueprint of how to provide health care informs local expectations and decisions. The specific activities of a local school, likewise, are influenced by the guidelines and purposes of the larger notions of "formal education" in a given nation.

3. *Meeting basic survival needs* is a core component of institutions because societies must meet needs of their members; otherwise the members die or the society collapses. Institutions, then, are the structures that support social life in a large bureaucratized society. Common to all industrialized societies are family, education, religion, economics, and politics. These institutions are discussed in the following three chapters.

Integrating micro and macro levels of society is also critical because one of the collective needs of society is coherence and stability—including some integration between the various levels of society. Institutions help provide that integration for the entire social system. They do this by meeting needs at the local franchise level (food at the grocery, education at the local school, health care at the local clinic) at the same time they coordinate national and global organizations and patterns.

Again, if all of this sounds terribly abstract, that is because institutions are abstractions. You cannot touch institutions, yet they are as real as air or love or happiness. In fact, in the modern world institutions are as necessary to life as is air, and they help provide love and happiness that make life worth living.

The Development of Modern Institutions

If we go all the way back to early hunting and gathering societies, there were no meso or macro levels to their social experience. People lived their lives in one or two villages, and while a spouse might have come from another village or one might have moved to a spouse's clan, there was no national or state governance and certainly no awareness of a global social system. In those simple times, family provided whatever education was needed, produced and distributed goods, paid homage to a god or gods, and solved conflicts and disputes through a system of familial (usually patriarchal) power distribution. One social unit—the family—served multiple functions. As societies have become more complex and differentiated, not only have multiple levels of the social system emerged, but various new institutions have emerged. Sociology textbooks in the 1950s identified only "five basic institutions": family, economic systems, political systems, religion, and education (formal public education only having been created in the mid-19th century). These five institutions were believed to be the core structures that met the essential needs of individuals and societies in an orderly way.

Soon thereafter, *medicine* moved from the family and small-town doctors to be recognized as an institution. Medicine had become bureaucratized in hospitals, medical labs, professional organizations, and other complex structures that provided health care. *Science* is also now something more than flying kites in thunderstorms in one's backyard. It is a complex system that provides training, funding, research institutes, peer review, and professional associations to support empirical research. New information is the lifeblood of an information-based or postindustrial society. Science, discussed in Chapter 14, is now an essential institution. Although it is arguable whether sports are an essential component for social viability, sports have clearly become highly structured in the past 50 years, and many sociologists consider sports an institution. The mass media and military also fall into the category of institutions in more advanced countries. There are gray areas as to whether or not something is considered an institution, but the questions to ask are (a) whether the structure meets basic needs of the society for survival, (b) whether it has become a complex organization providing routinized structures and guidelines for society, and (c) whether it is national or even global in its scope, while also having pervasive local (micro) impact.

The Interconnections Between Institutions

The global economic crisis that began in 2008 illustrates the forces that bring about changes through interconnections between institutions. As described by "the sociological imagination," our individual problems such as loss of a job are tied to the macro-level changes in the economy. So the family is affected, and citizens expect the government to intervene and fix the problem. Religious congregations have increased demands at their food banks, soup kitchens, and thrift shops run for low-income people, yet religious contributions are more difficult in tough economic times. Schools also suffer from lack of income from the economic downturn. Table IV.1 illustrates these connections.

Table IV.1   The Impact of Institutions at Each Level of Analysis

	Family	Education	Economic Systems	Political Systems	Religion	Medicine
Macro (national and global social systems and trends)	Kin and marriage structures, such as monogamy versus polygamy; global trends in family such as choice of partners rather than arranged marriages	National education system; United Nations Girls' Education Initiative	Spread of capitalism around the world; World Bank; International Monetary Fund; World Trade Organization	National government; United Nations; World Court; G8 (most powerful 8 nations in the world)	Global faith-based movements and structures: National Council of Churches; World Council of Churches; World Islamic Call Society; World Jewish Congress	National health care system; World Health Organization; transnational pandemics
Meso (institutions, complex organizations, ethnic subcultures, state/ provincial systems)	The middle-class family; the Hispanic family; the Jewish family	State/provincial department of education; American Federation of Teachers*	State/provincial offices of economic development; United Auto Workers*	State/provincial governments; national political parties; each state or province's supreme court	National denominations/ movements: e.g., United Methodist Church or American Reform Judaism	HMOs; American Medical Association*
Micro (local "franchises" of institutions)	Your family; local parenting group; local Parents Without Partners; county family counseling clinic	Your teacher; local neighborhood school; local school board	Local businesses; local chamber of commerce; local labor union chapter	Neighborhood crime watch program; local city or county council	Your local religious study group or congregation	Your doctor and nurse; local clinic; local hospital

*These organizations are national in scope and membership, but they are considered meso level here because they are complex organizations *within* the nation.

Thinking Sociologically

Using Table IV.1, try placing other institutions (mass media, science, sports, the military) in the framework.

Interconnections between meso-level institutions are a common refrain in this book. The following two examples serve to illustrate the types of interconnections that hold our social world together.

Education, Family, and Other Linkages

When children enter kindergarten or primary school, they bring their prior experience, including socialization experiences from their families. Family background, according to many sociologists, is the single most important influence on children's school achievement (Jencks 1972). Children succeed in large part because of what their parents do to support them in education (MacLeod 2008; Schneider and Coleman 1993).

Most families stress the importance of education, but they do so in different ways. Middle-class parents in the Global North tend to manage their children's education, visiting schools and teachers, having educational materials in the home, and holding high expectations for their children's achievement. In these families, children learn the values of hard work, good grades, and deferred gratification for reaching future goals.

Involvement of parents from lower socioeconomic status and first-generation immigrant families can have significant impact on their children's educational outcomes; however, many of these parents tend to look to schools as the authority (Bankston 2004; Domina 2005). They are less involved in their children's schooling, leaving decisions to the school. Yet, children who must make educational decisions without familial guidance are more likely to do poorly or to drop out of school (Bridgeland, Dilulio, and Morison 2006; Kalmijn and Kraaykamp 1996).

Moreover, when economic times are rough, employment instability and uncertainty, economic strain, and deprivation can cause strained family relations. Low-income families, especially single-parent families headed by women, are particularly hard-hit and often have to struggle for survival (R. Staples 1999; Willie 2003). In some cases, families are so financially devastated that they become homeless—a difficult life, especially for children. Even if the family is not homeless, the trend toward the "feminization of poverty"—where single motherhood is widespread—can mean that children have less support for schoolwork at home (B. Williams, Sawyer, and Wahlstrom 2013). Single mothers experience dual roles as workers and mothers, lower earnings than men, and irregular paternal support payments, so they may have less time to be attentive to academic needs of their children. Thus, the economic health of the family affects its stability and the number of stressors it faces. These stressors, in turn, may affect the ability of the family to support a child's achievement

in school. If the child does not get a good education, she or he is less likely to be a strong contributor to the economy in the future and is less likely to vote or be politically involved. Thus, family, education, economics, and politics become interrelated.

Religion and the Economy

Religion and the economy are intertwined and interdependent as you will note in Chapter 11. Here we illustrate how each can affect the other using a classic study of these two institutions. In fact, one sociologist felt that religious beliefs helped create the economic system that dominates most of the Global North. Why do most of us study hard, work hard, and strive to get ahead? Why are we sacrificing time and money now—taking this and other college courses—when we might spend that money on an impressive new car? Our answers probably have something to do with our moral attitudes about work, about those who lack ambition, and about convictions regarding the proper way to live. Max Weber ([1904–1905] 1958) believed that the economic system, particularly capitalism, and many of our attitudes about economic behavior are rooted in religious ideas about work and sacrifice.

Weber's study, *The Protestant Ethic and the Spirit of Capitalism,* became a classic in the field. Noting that the areas of Europe where the Calvinists had strong followings were the same areas where capitalism grew fastest, Weber ([1904–1905] 1958) argued that four elements in the Calvinist Protestant faith created the moral and value system necessary for the growth of capitalism: predestination, a calling, self-denial, and individualism.

1. *Predestination* meant that one's destiny was predetermined. Nothing anyone could do would change what was to happen. Because God was presumed to be perfect, he was not influenced by human deeds. Those people who were chosen by God were referred to as the *elect* and were assumed to be a small group. Therefore, people looked for signs of their status—salvation or damnation. High social status was sometimes viewed as a sign of being among the elect, so motivation was high to succeed in *this* life.

2. The *calling* referred to the concept of doing God's work. Each person was put on Earth to serve God, and each had a task to do in God's service. One could be called by God to any occupation, so the key was to work very hard and with the right attitude. Because work was a way to serve God, laziness or lack of ambition was viewed as a sin. These ideas helped create a society in which people's self-worth and their evaluation of others were tied to a work ethic. Protestants became workaholics.

3. *Self-denial* involved living a simple life. If one had a good deal of money, one did not spend it on a lavish home, expensive clothing, or various forms of entertainment. Such consumption would be offensive to God. Therefore, if people worked hard and began to accumulate resources, they simply saved them or invested them in a business. This self-denial was tied to an idea that we now call *delayed gratification,* postponing the satisfaction of one's present wants and desires in exchange for a future reward. The reward these people sought was in the afterlife.

4. *Individualism* meant that each individual faced his or her destiny alone before God. This stark individualism of Calvinistic theology stressed that each individual was on his or her own before God. Likewise, in the economic system that was emerging, individuals were on their own. The person who thrived was an individualist who planned wisely and charted his or her own course. Religious individualism and economic individualism reinforced one another.

For capitalism to develop, there was a need for individualistic entrepreneurs who had a strong work ethic, strong motivation based on delayed gratification and a hope for the future, and a pool of capital to invest (which was generated in part by the tendency to simple lifestyles). This combination of factors was fostered by the teachings of Luther, Calvin, and other early Protestant reformers. Religion contributed to major changes in cultural values, which, in turn, transformed the economic system. Weber ([1904–1905] 1958) saw the religious and economic systems as dynamic, interrelated, and ever-changing.

Gradually, the capitalistic system, stimulated by the Protestant Ethic, spread to other countries and to other religious groups. Many of the attitudes about work and delayed gratification no longer have supernatural focus, but they are part of our larger culture nonetheless. They influence our feelings about people who are not industrious and our ideas about why some people are poor.

Thus, religious beliefs may have had some influence in creating a particular type of economic system, but we know that the influence runs the other direction as well. People join religious groups that have values and attitudes compatible with their present socioeconomic status. Our social class standing influences our decisions about church, temple, or mosque membership (Bowles and Gintis 1976; Pew Forum on Religion and Public Life 2008; Weber 1946).

These examples give an idea of the interconnectedness between institutions at the meso level. We next consider theories that help us understand meso-level dynamics.

Theories Explaining Institutions

Various theoretical lenses look at institutions, and each has something worthwhile to teach us. Functional theorists speak of the essential *functions* carried out by institutions to meet societal needs. As society becomes more complex, there are more institutions needed, as in the case of science, an institution that has allowed humans to land on the moon and develop new forms of energy to power our technologies, which helps many of our institutions work. If any institution fails, the entire social system is in severe jeopardy. If all institutions fail, the basic needs of society will not be met, and the society will collapse—or there will be a massive overthrow of the existing system. While functionalists may overemphasize the role of stability, institutions do provide guidelines for each society. Functionalists help us identify the purposes of each institution.

Conflict theorists focus on the inequities and inequalities created by institutions that have been developed and run by powerful members of society.

In this process, less powerful groups can be exploited. Powerful elites do try to maintain stability in societies as they have a vested interest in keeping things from changing too dramatically, because their own privileges are rooted in the existing structure.

We have pointed out that all institutions are interconnected and interdependent, with radical change in one potentially upsetting the balance in the others. This is a cause for concern for conflict theorists, since it constrains social change. For example, religious institutions help make family sacred through marriage ceremonies. In doing so, this sacred status makes it harder to change the system—even if the system treats women or homosexuals unfairly. Educational institutions build loyalty in political systems, for example, by requiring a pledge of allegiance at the outset of the day. The political system often makes the existing economic system seem indisputably right and fair. Note also how thoroughly sports have become involved in fostering patriotism through halftime shows and ongoing comments about national loyalty by the announcers. So institutions have a conservative bias because stability in the larger social system enhances stability of each institution making up the society. This serves the interests of those in leadership roles within each institution. Conflict theorists are concerned that institutions will maintain stability even if that stable system is oppressive to some members of the society. It is precisely that conserving role that is seen as dysfunctional to those who favor social change to enhance equality.

Interaction theorists argue that the micro-level interactions that shape our lives are based on patterns that we take for granted. These patterns are shaped by our perceptions of what is "normal," and these perceptions in turn come largely from the institutions that surround us. Generally we do what we have observed is right and acceptable in a particular status we occupy within an organization (officer in a corporation, for example) or within an institution (father, for example). So institutions affect the way we interact, how we treat people, and whether we expect deference from others. On the other hand, interaction theorists do not think our lives are totally determined by our surroundings. We do have *agency*—the possibility of being active and creative beings within our social settings. So a woman in a leadership role in an organization may redefine how leadership is understood by changing people's *definition of the situation*—their *social construction of reality.* Here we see, on the one hand, that people at the micro level are shaped by the meso-level norms; on the other hand, those meso-level norms can be changed by dynamic individuals who see things differently.

Rather than trying to be all-encompassing in this book, we attempt to illustrate how various aspects of society work. The next three chapters provide examples of institutions and how these structures make up societies. The first and most basic institution is family, discussed in Chapter 10. Next we consider two institutions that play a major role in our socialization, belonging, and meaning systems—education and religion. Finally, our example of the political-economic system illustrates institutions that impact the macro level but also affect us at the micro level. As you read these chapters, notice that change in one institution affects others. Sociologists studying the legal system, mass media, medicine, the military, science, and sports as institutions would raise similar questions and would want to know how the institution influences the micro, meso, and macro levels of a society. We begin with family—an institution that is such an intimate part of our lives that it is often called the "most basic" institution of society.

CHAPTER 1

Family

Partner Taking, People Making, and Contract Breaking

Appearing in rich variety, the family is often referred to as the "most basic" institution. In this social relationship, we take partners and "make people"—both biologically and socially speaking. In the modern world, these intimate "basic" unions often experience conflict, violence, and contract breaking as well.

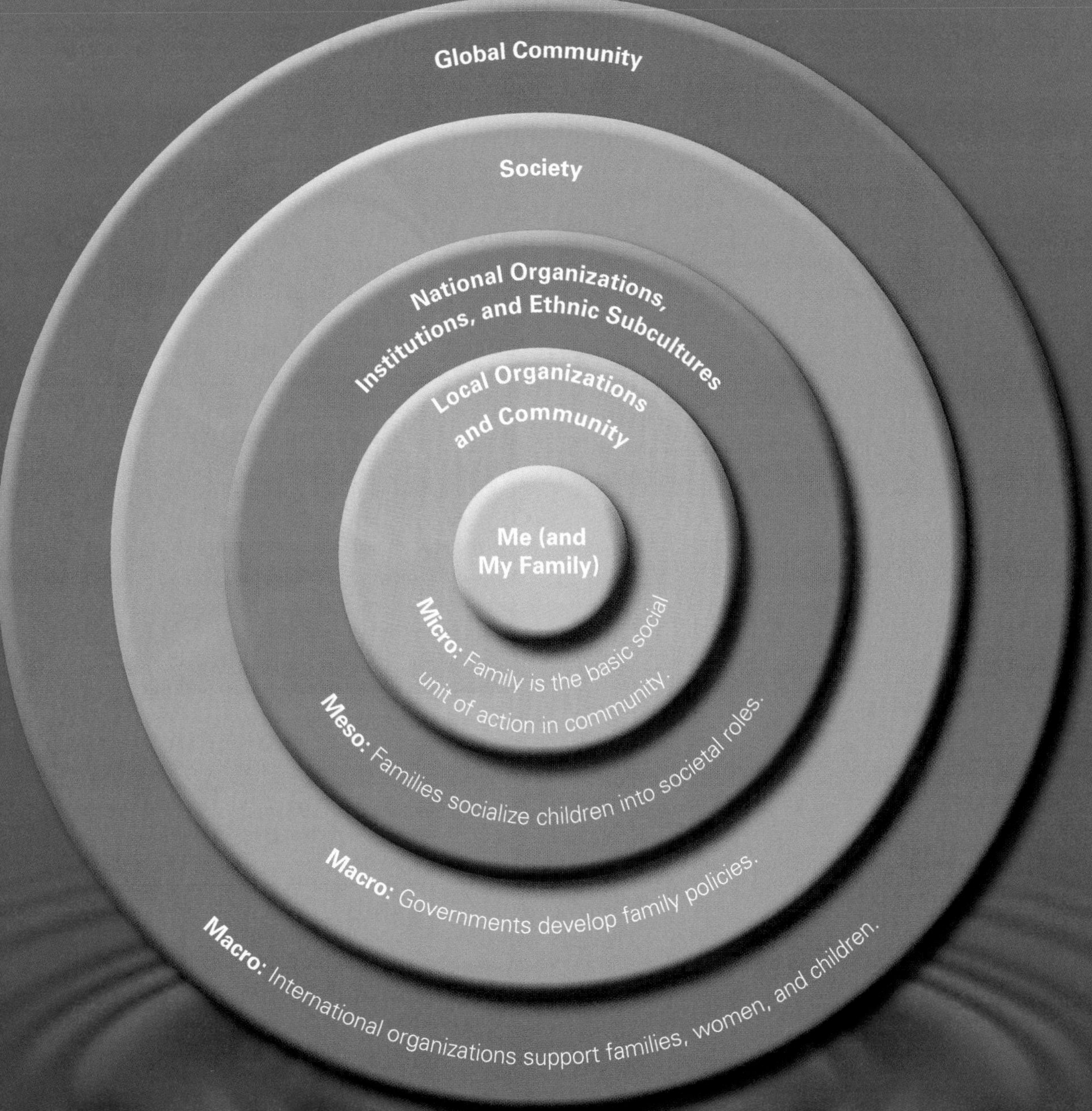

Global Community

Society

National Organizations,
Institutions, and Ethnic Subcultures

Local Organizations
and Community

Me (and
My Family)

Micro: Family is the basic social
unit of action in community.

Meso: Families socialize children into societal roles.

Macro: Governments develop family policies.

Macro: International organizations support families, women, and children.

Think About It	
Micro: Self and Inner Circle	Why is family important to you?
Micro: Local Community	How do people find life partners?
Meso: National Institutions; Complex Organizations; Ethnic Groups	Why is family seen as the core or basic institution of society?
Macro: National Society	What, if anything, should be done by government to strengthen families?
Macro: Global Community	Why are families around the world so different?

What's coming in this chapter?

What Is a Family?

Theoretical Perspectives on Family

Family Dynamics: Micro-Level Processes

The Family as an Institution: Meso-Level Analysis

National and Global Family Issues: Macro-Level Analysis

A Guatemalan family in a rural village prepares for the day's chores. Maria prepares the breakfast as Miguel cares for the animals. The children fix their lunches of tortillas, beans, rice, and banana to take to school. When they return home, they will help with the farm chores. They live together with their extended family, several generations of blood relatives living side by side.

It is morning in Sweden. Anders and Karin Karlsson are rushing to get to their offices on time. The children, a 12-year-old son and an 8-year-old daughter, are being hurried out the door to school. All will return in the evening after a full day of activities and join together for the evening meal. In this dual-career family, common in many postindustrial societies, both parents are working professionals.

The gossip at the village water well this day in Niger, Africa, is about the rich local merchant, Abdul, who has just taken his fourth and last wife. She is a young, beautiful girl of 15 from a neighboring village. She is expected to help with household chores and bear children for his already extensive family unit. Several of the women at the well live in affluent households where the husband has more than one wife.

Tom and Jackson in Minneapolis, Minnesota, recently adopted Ty into their family. The couple share custody of the 5-year-old boy. Ty's two fathers attend his school events and teach him what all parents are expected to teach their children. Adoption by same-sex couples is legal in only 21 U.S. states and the District of Columbia (Human Rights Campaign 2013). However, both political candidates in the 2012 U.S. presidential campaign supported a policy allowing gay couples to adopt children (Cronkite 2012).

Dora, a single mom, lives next door with her two children. She bundles them off to school before heading to her job. After school she has an arrangement with Tom and Jackson to care for the children until she gets home.

What do these very different scenes have in common? Each describes a family, yet there is controversy about what constitutes a family. Those groupings that are officially recognized as families by governments tend to receive hundreds of privileges and rights, such as health insurance and inheritance rights, but not every group that thinks it is a family is defined as "family" by the society (DeGenova, Stinnett, and Stinnett 2011). In this chapter, we discuss characteristics of families, theoretical perspectives on family, family dynamics, family as an institution, family issues, and policies regarding marriage and family dissolution.

Families come in many shapes, sizes, and color combinations. We begin our exploration of this institution with a discussion of what *is* family.

In recent decades, the definition of family has broadened. No longer is it necessarily limited to heterosexual couples. These gay men are parents to this baby.

What Is a Family?

Who defines what constitutes a family: each individual, the government, or religious groups? Is a family just Ma, Pa, and the kids? Let us consider several definitions. The U.S. government defines the family as "two people or more (one of whom is the householder) related by birth, marriage, or adoption and residing together; all such people (including related subfamily members) are considered as members of one family" (U.S. Census Bureau 2012a). Thus, a family in the United States might be composed of siblings, cousins, a grandparent and grandchild, or other groupings. Some sociologists define family more broadly, saying a *family* is "two or more individuals who maintain an intimate relationship that they expect will last indefinitely—or in the case of parent and child, until the child reaches adulthood—and who usually live under the same roof and pool their incomes and household labor" (Cherlin 2010:14). This definition would include same-sex couples and many cohabiting heterosexuals as families. Some religious groups define family as a mother, a father, and their children, whereas others include several spouses and even parents and siblings living under the same roof.

How do you define the ideal family? Answering the questions in the next "Engaging Sociology" on page 288 will indicate the complexity of this question.

As noted earlier, the family is often referred to as the most basic *institution* of any society. First, the place where we learn many of the norms for functioning in the larger society is the family, so it serves as the institution that helps us function in all other institutions. This makes it pretty basic to us and to the society. Second, most of us spend our lives in the security of a family. People are born and raised in families, and many will die in a family setting. Through good and bad, sickness and health, most families provide for our needs, both physical and psychological. Therefore, families meet our primary, most basic needs. Third, major life events—marriages, births, graduations, promotions, anniversaries, religious ceremonies, holidays, funerals—take place within the family context and are celebrated with family members. In short, family is where we invest the most emotional energy and spend much of our leisure time. Fourth, in many nonindustrial societies and in some ethnic groups within modern cultures, the family is the key to social organization, for in such societies, one's status and identity are determined almost entirely by one's family. Finally, the family is capable of satisfying a range of social needs—belonging to a group, economic support, education or training, raising children, religious socialization, resolution of conflicts, and so forth. One cannot conceive of the economic system providing emotional support for each individual or the political system providing socialization and personalized care for each child. Family carries out these functions.

This Romanian family does not have much money, but the children learn many survival skills, and the most basic needs of the children, physical and psychological, are met.

The family is the place where we confirm our partnerships as adults, and it is where we *make people*—not just biologically but also socially. In the family, we take an organism that has the potential to be fully human, and we mold this tiny bit of humanity into a caring, compassionate, productive person.

Thinking Sociologically

What purposes does your family serve for its members? What role does each member play in the family? Why might this be important for the larger society?

In most Global North societies, individuals are born and raised in the **family of orientation**, *the family into which we are born*. This family consists of parent(s) and possibly sibling(s); individuals are born and raised in this family, receive early socialization, and learn the language, norms, core values, attitudes, and behaviors of the community and society. A **family of procreation** *is the family we create ourselves*. We find a life mate and/or have children. The transmission of values, beliefs, and attitudes from our family of orientation to our family of procreation preserves and stabilizes the family system. Because family involves emotional investment, we have strong feelings about what form it should take.

Whether we consider families at micro, meso, or macro levels, sociological theories can help us understand the role of families in the social world.

Family Planning

Engaging Sociology

The Ideal Family

What is "the ideal family"? Does it have one adult woman and one adult man? One child or many? Grandparents living with the family? First, complete the following survey yourself. Then ask a friend or relative to also answer the questions below.

1. How many adults should the ideal family contain? _____

2. How many children should the ideal family contain? _____

3. What should be the sex composition of the adults in an ideal family? (check all that apply)
   a. One female and one male
   b. Male-male or female-female
   c. Several males and several females
   d. Other (write in) _____

4. What should be the sexes of the child(ren) in the ideal family? _____

5. Who should select the marriage partner? (check all that apply)
   a. The partners should select each other.
   b. The parents or close relatives should select the partner.
   c. A matchmaker should arrange the marriage.
   d. Other _____

6. What is the ideal number of generations living in the same household?
   a. One generation: partners and no children
   b. Two generations: partners and children
   c. Three or more generations: partners, children, grandparents, and great-grandparents
   d. Other _____

7. With whom should the couple live?
   a. By themselves
   b. With parents
   c. With brothers or sisters
   d. With as many relatives as possible

8. What should the sexual arrangements be? (check all that apply)
   a. Partners have sex only with each other.
   b. Partners can have sex outside of marriage if it is not "disruptive" to the relationship.
   c. Partners are allowed to have sex with all other consenting adults.
   d. Male partners can have sex outside marriage.
   e. Female partners can have sex outside marriage.
   f. Other _____

9. Which person(s) in the ideal family should work to help support the family?
   a. Both partners
   b. Male only
   c. Female only
   d. Both, but the mother only after children are in school
   e. Both, but the mother only after children graduate from high school
   f. All family members including children
   g. Other _____

10. Should the couple have sex before marriage if they wish? Yes ___ No ___ Other_____

11. Should physically disabled aging parents
    a. Be cared for in a child's home?
    b. Be placed in a nursing care facility?
    c. Other _____

Why do you hold these particular views of "the ideal family"? Are your answers different from those of your friend or relative? Why might others in your society have answered differently?

Note: All of these options can be found in some societies.

No other institution can fulfill the functions of the family, but the family can fulfill many functions of other institutions. On the left, a family works together as an economic team to produce food. On the right, a family in the United States prays together before lunch.

Theoretical Perspectives on Family

Consider the case of Felice, a young mother locked into a marriage that provides her with little satisfaction. For the first year of marriage, Felice tried to please her husband, Tad, but gradually he seemed to drift further away. He began to spend evenings out. Sometimes, he came home drunk and yelled at her or hit her. Felice became pregnant shortly after their marriage and had to quit her job. This increased the financial pressure on Tad, and they fell behind in paying the bills.

Then came the baby. They were both ecstatic at first, but Tad soon reverted to his old patterns. Felice felt trapped. She was afraid and embarrassed to go to her parents. They had warned her against marrying so young without finishing school, but she was in love and had gone against their wishes. She and Tad had moved away from their hometown, so she was out of touch with her old support network and had few friends in her new neighborhood. Her religious beliefs told her she should try to stick it out, suggesting that the trouble was partly her fault for not being a "good enough wife." Lacking a job or skills to get a job that paid more than minimum wage, she could not live on her own with a baby. She thought of marriage counseling, but Tad refused to consider this and did not seem interested in trying to work out the problems. He had his reasons for behaving the way he did, including feeling overburdened with the pressure of caring for two dependents. The web of this relationship seems difficult to untangle. Sociological theories provide us with tools to analyze such family dynamics.

Micro-Level Theories of Family and the Meso-Level Connection

Micro-level theories focus on the interpersonal interactions within families. Symbolic interaction and rational choice theories stress different processes and focus on different factors as most important in this intimate social context.

Symbolic Interaction Theory

Symbolic interaction theory can help us understand Felice's situation by explaining how individuals learn their particular behavior patterns and ways of thinking. Our role relationships are developed through socialization and interaction with others. Felice developed certain expectations and patterns of behavior by modeling her experiences on her *family of orientation* (the family into which she was born), observing others, and developing expectations from her initial interactions with Tad. He developed a different set of expectations for his role of husband, modeled after his father's behavior. His father had visited bars after work, had affairs with other women, and expected "his woman" at home to accept this without question.

Two related concepts in symbolic interaction theory are the *social construction of reality* and the *definition of a situation*. What we define as real or as normal is shaped by what significant others around us accept as ordinary or acceptable. Children who grow up in homes where adults hit one another or argue using sarcastic put-downs may come to think of this behavior as typical or a normal part of family life. They simply have known no other type of interaction. Thus, they may create a similar pattern of family interaction in their own *families of procreation* (the families they create).

Thinking Sociologically

Concepts such as *family*, *spouse*, and *parenting* carry meaning to you and your siblings but may mean something very different to the person sitting beside you in class or to a potential mate. Ask several people you know to explain the words *husband*, *wife*, *partner*, and *parenting* and what they mean to them.

One of the great challenges of newlyweds is meshing their ideas about division of labor, family holidays, discipline of children, spousal relations, and economic necessities, along with their assumptions about being in a committed relationship. A new couple socially constructs a new relationship, blending the models of life partnership from their own childhood homes or creating an entirely new model as they jointly define their relationship. Furthermore, the meaning of one's identity and one's obligations to others changes dramatically when one becomes a parent. This brings us back to a central premise of symbolic interaction theory: Humans are active agents who create their social structure through

Introduction of a baby to a household changes the interpersonal dynamics, the topics of conversation, the amount of sleep people are able to get, the sense of responsibility for the future, relationships to the larger community (including schools), and many other aspects of social life.

interaction. We not only learn family patterns; we *do family* just as we do *gender* in the sense that we create roles and relationships and pass them on to others as "normal."

Our individual identities and family patterns are shaped by institutional arrangements at the meso level: Corporations, religious bodies, legal systems, and other government entities define the roles of "wife" and "husband." For example, each U.S. state actually spells out in its legal codes the duties of husbands and wives. Those who do not fulfill these duties may be in "neglect of duty." These family roles are embedded in the larger structure in ways that many people do not realize.

Rational Choice Theory

Rational choice theory can also shed light on Felice's situation, helping us understand why people seek close relationships and why they stay in abusive relationships. As discussed in Chapter 2, rational choice theory asserts that individuals evaluate the costs and rewards of engaging in interaction. We look for satisfaction of our needs—emotional, sexual, and economic—through interaction. Patterns in the family are reinforced to the extent that exchanges are beneficial to members. When the costs outweigh the rewards, the relationship is unlikely to continue. Women in abusive relationships weigh the costs of suffering abuse against the rewards of having social legitimacy, income, religious approval, a home, and companionship. Many factors enter into the complex balance of the exchange. Indeed, costs and benefits of various choices are often established by meso-level organizations and institutions: insurance programs, health care options, and legal regulations that make partnering decisions easy or difficult.

Another core dimension of this cost-benefit consideration is that in interaction, humans constantly consider whether there is reciprocity—"if you scratch my back, I will scratch yours." According to this view, humans will not extend assistance to others unless they think there will be a payback and some balance in the relationship. If people feel like they give more than they receive, the relationship turns sour. This pattern, rational choice theorists assert, is no less true of family relationships than any other human interactions. Humans are ultimately seen in this perspective as focused on self-interest.

According to rational choice theorists, even the mate selection process is shaped by a calculation of exchange. People estimate their own assets—physical, intellectual, social, and economic—and try to find the "best deal" they can make, with attention to finding someone with at least the level of resources they possess, even if those assets are in different areas. If someone marries a person with far more assets, the one with fewer assets is likely to have little power and to feel dependent on that relationship, often putting up with things that equal partners would not tolerate. Cost

 Family Roles

and benefit, according to this view, affect the forming of the relationship and the power and influence later in the relationship.

Thinking Sociologically

What situations can you identify within your family when cost and benefit calculations seemed to drive decisions? When is reciprocity the norm in family relationships?

Meso- and Macro-Level Theories of the Family

Meso- and macro-level theories focus on the link between family as an institution and other components of the society. Structural-functional, conflict, and feminist theories each illuminate different aspects of the tie.

Structural-Functional Theory

Why do all societies have families? One answer is that families fulfill certain purposes, or functions, for societies that enhance survival of individuals and societies. Traditionally, there have been at least six ways the family has helped stabilize the society, according to structural-functional theory:

Sexual regulation. Physically speaking, any adult human could engage in sex with any other human. However, in practice, no society allows total sexual freedom. Every society attempts to regulate the sexual behavior of its members in accordance with its own particular values. This is most often accomplished through marriage. Regulation ensures that the strong biological drive is satisfied in an orderly way that does not create ongoing disruption, conflict, or jealousy. Certain people are "taken" and "off-limits" (Ward and Edelstein 2009).

Reproduction and replacement. Societies need children to replace members who die, leave, or are incapacitated. Reproduction is controlled to keep family lineage and inheritance clear. Parent and caretaker roles are clearly defined and reinforced in many societies by ceremonies: baby showers, birth announcements, christenings, and naming ceremonies that welcome the child as a member of the family. In some places, such as New Guinea, procreation is so important that a young girl who has had children before marriage is more desirable because she has established her fertility. This practice is possible in matriarchal societies where the child is absorbed into the female side of the family.

Socialization. The family is the main training ground for children. In our families, we begin to learn values and norms, proper behavior, roles, and language. Later socialization in most societies is carried out by schools, religious organizations, and other institutions, but the family remains the most important initial socializing agent to prepare us for roles in society. Much of the socialization is done by parents, but siblings, grandparents, and other relatives are important as well.

Emotional support and protection. Families are the main source of love and belonging in many societies, giving us a sense of identity, security, protection, and safety from harm. The family is one place where people may experience unqualified acceptance and feelings of being cherished. Problems of children in youth shelters and incidents of family violence and neglect are reminders that this function is not always successfully provided in families. Still, the family is usually the environment most capable of meeting this need.

Status assignment. Our family of birth is the most important determinant of our social status, life chances, and lifestyles. It strongly affects our educational opportunities, access to health care, religious and political affiliations, and values. In fact, in societies with caste systems, the ascribed position at birth is generally the position at death. Although in class societies individuals may achieve new social statuses, our birth positions and the early years of socialization have a strong impact throughout life on who and what we are.

This woman in New Guinea became more attractive to men as a potential wife after she had proved her fertility by having children.

Siblings often provide some of the emotional support and part of the socialization for younger siblings. This is especially true in the poor Global South, where mothers often must work or carry water for the family from distant water sources. This sister cares for her younger sister in Soweto, South Africa.

Economic support. Historically, the family was a unit of production—running a farm or a bakery or a cobbler shop. Although this function is still predominant in many societies, the economic function carried out in individual families has pretty much disappeared in most Global North families. However, the family remains an economic unit of consumption. Who paid for your clothing, food, and other needs as you were growing up? Who helps many of you pay your college tuition and expenses? Taxing agencies, advertising and commercial enterprises, workplaces, and other social organizations also treat the family as the primary economic unit.

Functional theorists recognize ways that the micro-level processes of the family (e.g., socialization of Japanese children to be cooperative and of members of groups and of U.S. children to be competitive and individualistic) are compatible with structural needs of society at the meso and macro levels (e.g., in most Global North countries, the need for motivated workers who thrive on competition). Each part of the system, according to functionalists, works with other parts to create a functioning society.

Changing family functions. In some societies, the family is the primary unit for bearing and educating children, practicing religion, structuring leisure time activities, caring for the sick and aged, and even conducting politics. However, as societies modernize, many of these functions are transferred to other institutions.

As societies change, so do family systems. The sociohistorical perspective of family tells us that changes in intimate relationships—sexuality, marriage, and family patterns—have occurred over the centuries. Major transitions from agricultural to industrial to postindustrial societal systems change all of the institutions within those societies. Families in agricultural societies are often large and self-sufficient, producing their own food and providing their own shelter, but this is not the case in contemporary urban societies. Industrialization and urbanization typical in 18th- and 19th-century Europe and the United States created a distinct change in roles. The wife and child became dependent on the husband who "brought home the bread." The family members became consumers rather than independent and self-supporting coworkers on a farm.

In addition to evolving roles, other changes in society have brought shifts to the family. Improved technology, for example, brought medical technology advances, new knowledge and skills to be passed on in schools, recreation outside of the family unit organized according to age groups, and improved transportation.

As many families moved to urban areas, the economic function has moved to the factory, store, and office. Socialization is increasingly done in schools, and in some cases teachers have become substitute parents. The traditional protection and care function has been partially replaced by police, reform schools, unemployment compensation, Social Security, health care systems (e.g., Medicare and Medicaid), and other types of services provided by the state. Little League baseball, industrial bowling teams, aerobic exercise groups, television, and computer games have replaced the family as the source of leisure activities and recreation. Although many would argue that the family still remains the center of caring and affection and is the socially recognized place for producing children, one does not have to look far to discover that these two functions are also increasingly found outside the boundaries of the traditional family unit.

These changes have made the family's functions more specialized, though family remains a critical institution in society. Most families still function to provide stable structures to carry out early childhood socialization and to sustain love, trust, affection, acceptance, and an escape from the impersonal world.

Thinking Sociologically

Does reduction of traditional family functions mean a decline in the importance of family or merely an adaptation of the family to changes in society? Is the modern family—based largely on emotional bonds rather than structural interdependency—a healthier system, or is it more fragile?

Conflict Theory

Conflict theorists study both individual family situations and broad societal family patterns. They argue that conflict in families is natural and inevitable. It results from the struggle for power and control in the family unit and in the society at large. As long as there is an unequal allocation of resources, conflict will arise.

Family conflicts take many forms. For instance, conflicts occur over allocation of resources, a struggle that may be rooted in conflict between men and women in the society: Who makes decisions, who gets money for clothes or a car, and who does the dishes? On the macro level, family systems are a source of inequality in the general society, sustaining class inequalities by passing on wealth, income, and educational opportunities to their own members or perpetuating disadvantages such as poverty and lack of cultural capital.

Yet, some conflict theorists argue that conflict within the family can be important because it forces constant negotiation among individual family members and may bring about change that can strengthen the unit as a whole. Believing that conflict is both natural and inevitable, these theorists focus on root causes of conflict and how to deal with the discord. For conflict theorists, there is no assumption of a harmonious family. The social world is characterized more by tension and power plays than by social accord.

An Alternative Theory for Analysis of the Family

One approach to analysis of family and the place of family within the society is sometimes a micro and sometimes a macro-level theory; it offers a different lens for understanding interaction within family structures: feminist theory.

Feminist Theory

Because women often occupy very different places in society than men, feminist theorists argue the need for a feminist perspective to understand family dynamics. Feminist scholars begin by placing women at the center, not to suggest their superiority but to spotlight them as subjects of inquiry and as active agents in the working of society. The biases rooted in patriarchal assumptions are uncovered and examined (Eshleman and Bulcroft 2010).

A micro-level branch of feminist theory, the interpretive approach, considers women within their social contexts—the interpersonal relations and everyday reality facing women. It does not ignore economic, political, social, and historical factors but focuses on the ways women construct their reality, their opportunities, and their place in the community. According to feminist theorists, this results in a more realistic view of family and women's lives than many other theories provide.

Applying this feminist approach to understand Felice's situation, the theorists would consider the way she views her social context and the way she assesses her support systems. This approach is similar to Max Weber's concept of *Verstehen*—understanding people and social units from within the experience—and has much in common with symbolic interaction theory, since it focuses on what interaction means to the women themselves. Felice's religious background, her reference group of close women friends, and her parents and siblings can have a profound effect on how she understands marriage, her rights and responsibilities within family roles, and her view of herself as mistreated or not. Many feminists have been effective in helping to analyze how women cope and how they resist their treatment in overt or covert ways.

Many branches of feminist theory have roots in conflict theory and are therefore more macro in focus. These theorists argue that patterns of patriarchy and dominance lead to inequalities for women. One of the earliest conflict theorists, Friedrich Engels (Karl Marx's close associate), argued that the family was the chief source of female oppression and that until basic resources were reallocated within the family, women would continue to be oppressed. However, he said that as women become aware of their collective interests and oppression, they will insist on a redistribution of power, money, and jobs (Engels [1884] 1942).

One vivid example of how women and men can be viewed as groups with competing interests is through a

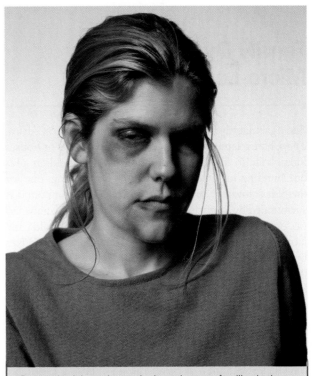

Domestic violence is a major issue in many families in the United States, with an average of three women and one man actually killed each day by a spouse or a partner.

feminist analysis of domestic violence. In the United States, one in four women have experienced domestic violence in their lifetimes. With an estimated 1.3 million women assaulted by an intimate partner each year, there is an incident of domestic violence every 25 seconds in the United States. Eighty-five percent of the victims of those acts of domestic violence are women (Domestic Violence Resource Center 2012). Boys who witness domestic violence are more than twice as likely to abuse their own wives later in life. Thirty-five percent of female murder victims were murdered by a spouse or boyfriend, with three women and one man killed each day by a spouse or an intimate partner (Domestic Violence Resource Center 2012; Federal Bureau of Investigation 2009).

Women are most severely exploited in societies that treat them as property and in which the family is a key political unit for power and status. For example, in some societies such as the Masai of East Africa and in some communities in Brazil, a husband is expected to beat his wife if he is dissatisfied with her cooking, housekeeping, or child care or for violating gender expectations (Rani, Bonu, and Diop-Sidibe 2004). The woman's life is valuable primarily as it relates to her economic value and the needs of men. Changes in the patriarchal family structure, education and employment opportunities for women, and child care availability can lead to greater freedom of choice, equality, and autonomy for women, according to feminist theorists (Shaw and Lee 2005).

Family Dynamics: Micro-Level Processes

The Agabi family belongs to the Hausa tribe of West Africa. They share a family compound composed of huts or houses for each family unit of one wife and her young children, plus one building for greeting guests, one for cooking, one for the older children, and one for washing. The compound is surrounded by an enclosure. Each member of the family carries out certain tasks: food preparation, washing, child care, farming, herding—whatever is needed for the group. Wives live with their husbands' families. Should there be a divorce, the children generally belong to the husband's household because the family lineage is through the father's side.

The eldest male is the leader and makes decisions for the group. When a child is born, the eldest male within the family presides over a ceremony to name and welcome the child into the group. When the child reaches marrying age, the eldest male plays a major role in choosing a suitable mate. Upon his death, the power he has held passes to his eldest son, and his property is inherited by his sons.

However, the eldest Agabi son has moved away from the extended family to the city, where he works in a factory to support himself. He lives in a small room with several other migrants. He has met a girl from another tribe and may marry her, but he will do so without his family's blessing. He will probably have a small family because of money and space pressures in the city. His lifestyle and even his values have already altered considerably. The trend toward the Global North model of industrialization and urbanization is altering cultures around the world and changing family life.

In summary, families can be studied at each level of analysis: as interdependent micro-level social units with family members in the immediate household; as meso-level institutions that can be seen as economic units; and as an influential force in macro-level social systems. Many individual family issues that seem very intimate and personal are actually affected by cultural norms and forces at other levels (e.g., migration and urbanization), and decisions of individuals at the micro level affect meso- and macro-level social structures (e.g., size of families). Individual families are, in essence, local franchises of a larger social phenomenon.

Thinking Sociologically

What kinds of changes in families would you anticipate as societies change from agricultural to industrial to information technology economies and as individuals move from rural to urban areas? What changes has your family undergone over several generations?

Mate Selection: How Do New Families Start?

At the most micro level, two people get together to begin a new family unit. In 2011 the world population reached 7 billion people, but our partners are not randomly selected from the entire global population. Even in Global North societies, where we think individuals have free choice of marriage partners, mate selection is not an entirely individual choice. Indeed, mate selection is highly limited by geographical proximity, ethnicity, age, social class, and a host of other variables. As we shall see, micro-level and macro-level forces influence each other in a process as personal as mate selection.

Norms Governing Choice of Marriage Partners: Societal Rules and Intimate Choices

A number of cultural rules—meso- and macro-level expectations—govern the choice of a mate in any society. Most are unwritten norms. One of the cultural rules is **exogamy**—*norms governing the choice of a mate that require individuals to*

Fathers

marry outside of their own immediate group. The most universal form of exogamy is the incest taboo, including restrictions against father-daughter, mother-son, and brother-sister marriages. Some countries, as well as about half the U.S. states, forbid first cousins to marry (see Table 3.3 on page 74), whereas others, such as some African groups and many Syrian villages, encourage first-cousin marriages to solidify family ties and property holdings. Some societies require village exogamy (marriage outside the village) because it bonds together villages and reduces the likelihood of armed conflict between neighboring groups. The reasons for exogamy range from recognition of the negative biological results of inbreeding to necessity for families to make ties with outside groups for survival (Williams, Sawyer, and Wahlstrom 2013).

One clear issue is that rights to sexual access can cause jealousy that rips a social unit apart. If father and son became jealous about who was sleeping with the wife/mother or sister, relationships would be destroyed and parental authority sabotaged. Likewise, if the father went to the daughter for sexual satisfaction, the mother and daughter bond would be severely threatened (Davis 1960; Williams, Sawyer, and Wahlstrom 2013). No society can allow this to happen to its family system. Any society that has failed to have an incest taboo self-destructed long ago.

On the other hand, norms of **endogamy** *require individuals to marry inside certain boundaries, whatever the societal members see as protecting the homogeneity of the group*. The purpose is to encourage group bonding and solidarity, and to help minority groups survive in societies with different cultures. Endogamous norms may require individuals to select mates of the same race, religion, social class, ethnic background, or clan (Williams, Sawyer, and Wahlstrom 2013). Examples of strictly endogamous religious groups include the Armenian Iranians, Orthodox Jews, Old Order Amish, Jehovah's Witnesses, and the Parsi of India. The result is less biologically diversified groups but protection of the minority identity (Belding 2004). Whether marriages are arranged or entered into freely, both endogamy and exogamy limit the number of possible mates. In addition to marrying within a group, most people choose a mate with similar social characteristics—age, place of residence, educational background, political philosophy, moral values, and psychological traits—a practice called *homogamy*.

Going outside the expected and accepted group in mate selection can make things tough for newlyweds who need family and community support. Few take this risk. For instance, in the United States, close to 80% to 90% marry people with similar religious values (Williams, Sawyer, and Wahlstrom 2013). About 80% to 90% of Protestants marry other Protestants, and 64% to 85% of Catholics marry within their religious faith. For Jews, the figure has been as high as 90% but has dropped in recent decades to as low as 50% for more liberal groups of Jews (Newman 2009). In Canada, only one person in five marries across religious boundaries (British Columbia Ministry of Labour & Citizens' Services 2006). With increased tolerance for differences, cross-denominational marriage is more likely today than a century ago.

Interracial marriages also challenge norms of endogamy, yet the practice is becoming more common with every passing year. Of marriages in the United States, 14.6% involve a spouse from a different race or ethnic group (Inniss 2010). Also, one in five has a close relative in a mixed-race marriage, and one half of the dating population has dated someone of a different race (Carroll 2010).

Each group may have different definitions of where the exogamy boundary is. For Orthodox Hasidic Jews, marriage to a Reform Jew is exogamy—strictly forbidden. Marriage of a Hopi to a Navajo is also frowned on—even though many Anglos would think of this as an endogamous marriage of two Native Americans.

So cultural norms of societies limit individual decisions about micro-level matters such as choice of a spouse, and they do so in a way that most individuals do not even recognize. Exogamy and endogamy norms and expectations generally restrict the range of potential marriage partners, even though some of these norms are weakening. Still, the question remains: How do we settle on a life partner?

Finding a Mate

In most societies, mate selection is achieved through arranged marriages, free-choice unions, or some combination of the two. In either case, selection is shaped by cultural rules of the society.

Arranged marriages *involve a pattern of mate selection in which someone other than the couple—elder males, parents, a matchmaker—selects the marital partners*. This method of mate selection is most common in traditional, often patriarchal, societies. Some examples follow.

For many traditional girls in Muslim societies, marriage is a matter of necessity, for girls' support comes from the family system. Economic arrangements and political alliances between family groups are solidified through marriage. Daughters are valuable commodities in negotiations to secure these ties between families (Burn 2011). Beauty, youth, talent, and pleasant disposition bring a high price and a good match. Should the young people like each other, it is icing on the cake. Daughters must trust that the male elders in their families will make the best possible matches for them. Clearly, the men hold the power in this vital decision.

Seated front and center with the bride and groom at many Japanese weddings is the matchmaker, the person responsible for bringing the relationship into being. After both families agree to the arrangement, the couple meets over tea several times to decide whether the match suits them. Today, about 30% of marriages in Japan are still arranged this way, the rest being called "love marriages" ("Getting Married in Japan" 2013).

Arranged Marriages

Japanese weddings are very formal and colorful events, and in many cases they still involve the parental selection of spouse, often with the help of a matchmaker.

emphasis on romantic love and the process of attracting a mate than most other societies. For example, 86% of U.S. college students say they would not marry without love, the figure being higher for men than for women. Romantic love is most common in countries where individualism is emphasized over community interests (Eshleman and Bulcroft 2010).

E-romance on the Internet is helping facilitate mate selection in modern societies. What those in arranged marriage systems find bewildering about free-choice systems is how people meet possible mates. Many of the e-dating services claim that their profiles and processes are based on social science research. Several popular sites are Match.com, PerfectMatch.com, Chemistry.com, and eHarmony.com (Consumer Rankings 2012). For example, according to eHarmony, each day approximately 15,000 individuals fill out the site's extensive 258-question questionnaire to create a personality profile that the company claims is a "scientifically proven" compatibility-matching system. More than 33 million users from 150 countries hope for one or more matches from the system. If the reported average of 236 members who marry every day is an indication, many would-be mates are finding their partners (eHarmony 2012). Many specialized services have sprung up based on race, religion, sexual orientation, and other interests such as DatingforAtheists.com and ConservativeDates.com.

Thinking Sociologically

Is e-dating a modern-day form of the matchmaker? Is it replacing other forms of finding a mate? Why or why not?

Starting with the assumption that eligible people are most likely to meet and be attracted to others who have similar values and backgrounds, sociologists have developed various mate selection theories, several of which view dating as a three-stage process. (See Figure 10.1.)

1. Stimulus: We meet someone to whom we are attracted by appearance, voice, dress, similar ethnic background, sense of humor, or other factors. Something serves as a stimulus that makes us take notice. Of course, sometimes the stimulus is simply knowing the other person is interested in us.

2. Value comparison: As we learn about the other's values, we are more likely to find that person compatible if she or he affirms our own beliefs and values toward life, politics, religion, and roles of men and women in society and marriage. If values are

Where arranged marriages are the norm, love has a special meaning. The man and woman may never have set eyes on each other before the wedding day, but respect and affection generally grow over time as the husband and wife live together. People from societies with arranged marriages are assured a mate and have difficulty comprehending marriage systems based on love, romance, and courtship, factors that they believe to be insufficient grounds for a lifelong relationship. They wonder why anyone would want to place himself or herself in a marriage market, with all of the uncertainty and rejection. Such whimsical and unsystematic methods would not work in many societies, where the structure of life is built around family systems.

Free-choice marriage is *a pattern of mate selection in which the partners select each other based primarily on romance and love.* Sonnets, symphonies, rock songs, poems, and plays have been written to honor love and the psychological and physiological pain and pleasure that the mating game brings. However impractical romance may seem, marriage choice based on *romantic love*, the idea that each person has the right to choose a partner with minimal interference from others, is becoming more prevalent. As societies around the world become more Westernized, women gain more rights and freedoms, and families exert less control over their children's choice of mates (Eshleman and Bulcroft 2010). Industrial and postindustrial societies tend to value love and individualism and tend to have high marriage rates, low fertility rates, and high divorce rates.

Free-choice mate selection is found in most Western societies. Couples in the United States tend to put more

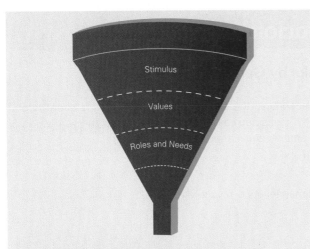

Figure 10.1 Mate Selection "Filtering"

The notion of mate selection described above is sometime referred to as a filter theory. It is as though you were filtering specs of gold, and the first filter holds out the large stones, the second filter holds back pebbles, the third filter stops sand, but the flakes of gold come through. Each stage in the mate selection process involves filtering some people out of the process. For you there may be other filter factors as well—such as religious similarities or common ethnicity.

not compatible, the person does not pass through our filter. We look elsewhere.

3. Roles and needs stage: Another filter comes when the couple explores roles of companion, parent, housekeeper, and lover. This might involve looking for common needs, interests, and favored activities. If roles and needs are not complementary to one's own, desire for a permanent relationship wanes.

The mate selection process varies somewhat from person to person, but social scientists believe that a sequential series of decisions, in a pattern such as that described above, is often part of the process (Eshleman and Bulcroft 2010; Murstein 1987). For you there may be other filter factors as well—such as religious similarities or common ethnicity.

Who Holds the Power? Authority in Marriage

Power relations, another micro-level issue shaped by cultural norms at the macro level, affect the interactions and decision making in individual families. Two areas that have received particular sociological attention are decision making in marriage and work roles.

Decision Making in Marriage

Cultural traditions establish the power base in society and family: patriarchy, matriarchy, or egalitarianism. The most typical authority pattern in the world is *patriarchy*, or male authority. *Matriarchy*, female authority, is rare. Even where the lineage is traced through the mother's line, males usually dominate decision making. Egalitarian family patterns—in which power, authority, and decision making are shared between the spouses and perhaps with the children—are emerging, but they are not yet a reality in most households. For example, research indicates that in many U.S. families, decisions concerning vacation plans, car purchases, and housing are reached democratically. Still, most U.S. families are not fully egalitarian. Males generally have a disproportionate say in major decisions (Lindsey 2011). However, social scientists find no evidence that there are any inherent intellectual or personality foundations for male authority as opposed to female authority (Kramer 2010; Ward and Edelstein 2009).

Resource theory attempts to explain power relations by arguing that the spouse with the greater resources—education, occupational prestige, and income—has the greater power. In many societies, income is the most important factor because it represents identity and power. If only one spouse brings home a paycheck, the other is usually less powerful (Tichenor 1999). In families in which the wife is a professional, factors other than income, such as persuasion and egalitarian values, may enter into the power dynamic (Lindsey 2011). Regardless of who has greater resources, men in two-earner couples tend to have more say in financial matters and less responsibility for children and household tasks.

Who Does the Housework?

The *second shift*, a term coined by Arlie Hochschild, refers to the housework and child care that employed women do after their first-shift jobs (Hochschild 1989). Studies indicate that women work doing household activities 2.6 hours per day or about 18 hours per week, whereas men work 2.0 hours per day. Men spend more time doing leisure activities (U.S. Bureau of Labor Statistics 2013). On an average day, 82% of women and 65% of men spend some time doing housework (U.S. Bureau of Labor Statistics 2013). The next "Engaging Sociology" on page 298 shows the breakdown in percentages spent by men and women at various household activities.

Employment schedules also affect the amount of time each spouse contributes to household tasks. Husbands who are at home during hours when their wives are working tend to take on more tasks. Employment, education, and earnings give women more respect and independence and a power base for a more equitable division of labor across tasks (Cherlin 2010; Kramer 2010). Recent research also clearly shows a narrowing of the gap in time

Engaging Sociology

Household Tasks by Gender

In many families, household tasks are highly gendered. As recently as the 1980s, wives and daughters spent two or three times as much time as fathers and sons in household tasks such as cleaning and laundry and yard work. However, the tides have been shifting, and while they are not entirely equal, they are more balanced.

Sociological Data Analysis:

- What is the division of labor (by gender) for household maintenance in your family?
- How did it evolve?
- Is it considered fair by all participants?
- How does it compare to the data in Figure 10.2?

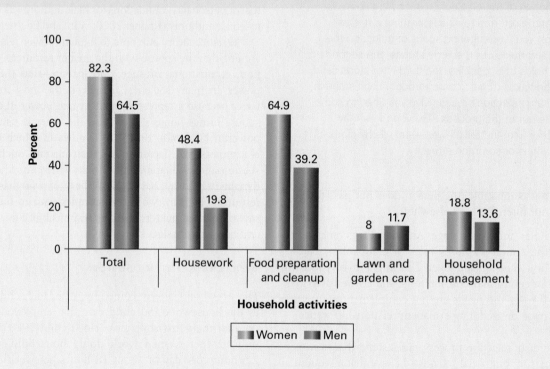

Figure 10.2   Percent of Men and Women Engaging in Some Type of Household Task Each Day

Source: U.S. Bureau of Labor Statistics (2013).

spent by men and women on household tasks, though such factors as presence and the ages of children, how many years the mother has worked outside the home, and socioeconomic status of the family influence how involved men are and how much real "free time" each experiences. When women do have free time, it is much more likely to be interrupted than is true for men (Kan, Sullivan, and Gershuny 2011; Mattingly and Sayer 2006; Saxbe, Repetti, and Graesch 2011).

Interestingly, husbands who do an equitable share of the household chores actually report higher levels of satisfaction with the marriage, and the couple is less likely to divorce (Lorillard 2011). The success or failure of a marriage depends in large part on patterns that develop early in the marriage for dealing with the everyday situations including power relationships and division of labor.

While women generally are more economically dependent on men, men are more often dependent on women

Men are increasingly sharing the household tasks such as cooking and cleaning.

emotionally, for they are less likely to have same-sex friends with whom they share feelings and vulnerabilities. Men bond with one another, but they seldom develop truly intimate ties that provide support in hard times. So women are not entirely without power. It is just that their power frequently takes a different form (and results in fewer privileges) (Newman 2009).

The Family as an Institution: Meso-Level Analysis

We experience family life at a very personal level, but the sum total of hundreds of thousands of families interacting in recognizable patterns results in "the family" as an institution at the meso level.

Marriage and Family Structure: The Components of Family as an Institution

Although the family is an institution in the larger social system, it does vary in interesting ways from one society to another. One example is how many mates one should have.

Some societies believe that several wives provide more hands to do the work and establish useful political and economic alliances between family groups. They bring more children into the family unit and provide multiple family members for emotional and physical support and satisfaction. On the other hand, having one spouse per adult probably meets most individuals' social and emotional needs very effectively, is less costly, and eliminates the possibility of conflict or jealousy among spouses. It is also easier to relocate a one-spouse family to urban areas, a necessity for many families in industrial and postindustrial societies. Let us examine the issue of adult partners in a family. Institutions lay out the general framework for families in any society and include types of marriages, extended and nuclear families, and other structural models of families. Individual families are local expressions of a larger corporate enterprise.

Types of Marriages

Monogamy and polygamy are the main forms of marriage found around the world. **Monogamy** refers to *marriage of two individuals* and is the most familiar form of marriage in industrial and postindustrial societies. **Polygamy**, *marriage of one person to more than one partner at the same time*, is most often found in agricultural societies where multiple spouses and children mean more help with the farmwork. There are two main forms of polygamy—polygyny and polyandry. Anthropologist George Murdock (1967) found that **polygyny**, *a marital system in which a husband can have more than one wife*, was allowed (although not always practiced) in 709 of the 849 tribal groups and societies he cataloged in his classic *Ethnographic Atlas*. Only 16% (136 societies) were exclusively monogamous (Barash 2002). Polygyny is limited because it is expensive to maintain a large family, brides must be acquired at high prices in some

This polyandrous family poses for a photo in front of their tent in northwest China. Fraternal polyandry means that brothers share a common wife. When children are born, they call the oldest brother father and all other brothers uncle, regardless of who the biological father is. China's marriage law does not officially permit polyandry.

societies, and there is a global movement toward monogamy. Polygyny does increase at times of war when the number of men is reduced due to war casualties.

Polyandry, *a marital system in which a wife can have more than one husband*, is practiced in less than 1% of the world's societies. Among the Todas of Southern India, for example, brothers can share a wife (O'Connel 1993). This usually happens when the men are poor and must share a single plot of land to eke out a meager livelihood, so they decide to remain a single household with one wife.

Members of Global North societies often find the practice of polygamy hard to understand, just as those from polygamous societies find monogamy strange. Some societies insist on strict monogamy: Marriage to one other person is lifelong, and deviation from that standard is prohibited. Yet, most Global North societies practice what could be called a variation of polygamy—serial monogamy. With high divorce and remarriage rates, Western societies have developed a system of marrying several spouses, but one at a time. One has spouses in a series rather than simultaneously.

Extended and Nuclear Families

The typical ma-pa-and-kids monogamous model that is familiar in many industrialized parts of the world is not as typical as it appears. From a worldwide perspective, it is only one of several structural models of family.

An **extended family** *includes two or more adult generations that share tasks and living quarters*. This may include brothers, sisters, aunts, uncles, cousins, and grandparents. In most extended family systems, the eldest male is the authority figure. This is a common pattern around the world, especially in agricultural societies. Some ethnic groups in the United States, such as Mexican Americans and some Asian Americans, live in extended monogamous families with several generations under one roof. This is financially practical and helps group members maintain their traditions and identity by remaining somewhat isolated from Anglo society.

As societies become more industrialized and fewer individuals and families engage in agriculture, the **nuclear family**, *consisting of two parents and their children—or any two of the three*—becomes more common. This worldwide trend toward nuclear family occurs because more individuals live in urban areas where smaller families are more practical, mate selection is based on love, couples establish independent households after marriage, marriage is less of an economic arrangement between families, fewer marriages take place between relatives such as cousins, and equality between the sexes increases (Burn 2011; W. Goode 1970).

No matter in what form the family manifests itself in a society, the family as an institution is interdependent at the meso level with each of the other major institutions.

For example, if the economy goes into a recession and jobs are not available, families experience stress, abuse rates increase, and marriages are more likely to become unstable. When husbands lose jobs, it often makes their primary role in the family ambiguous, causing sense of failure by the husband and stress in the relationship. In single-parent families in which the mother is the custodial parent, the loss of her job can be financially devastating. In worst-case scenarios, families that lose their incomes may become homeless.

Thinking Sociologically

Under what social circumstances would an extended family be helpful? Under what circumstances would it be a burden? What are strengths and weaknesses of nuclear families?

Family is a diverse and complex social institution. It interacts with other institutions and in some ways reinforces them. Families prepare the next generation. Adult family members teach national loyalty, tutor children in reading and math, and mentor their progeny on the use of money. Families pray together and provide care of disabled, infirm, or sick members. As a basic institution, the family plays a role in the vitality of the entire nation. So it should not be surprising that at the macro level, many national and global policy decisions concern how to strengthen the family.

In many societies, the family is still the primary unit of economic production. These family members in Myanmar are selling the goods they produced as a family.

Polygamy

National and Global Family Issues: Macro-Level Analysis

An effective way to explore macro-level issues pertaining to families is through policy matters that affect the family or that are intended to strengthen families. After exploring issues of national concern—cohabitation, homosexual relationships, and divorce—we look at some global trends in marriage and family life.

Cohabitation

Cohabitation—living together in a sexual relationship without marriage—is a significant macro-level trend in many countries that has implications for national family laws, tax laws, work benefits, and other macro-level issues. In the United States, "unmarried couples, both single and opposite sex, living together rose from 7.1 million in 2009 to more than 8.1 million in 2010" (Kreider 2010). There was an unusually large 13% increase (868,000 couples) in cohabiting couples between 2009 and 2010, in large part influenced by the economic downturn (Jayson 2011; Kreider 2010). The overall trend in the number of "unmarried households" has been a dramatic rise for several decades. Two thirds of couples married in the past decade

lived together for an average of two years before marriage (Jay 2012; Kreider and Elliott 2009).

Some argue that a newly emerging pattern for young adults between 25 and 34 is serial cohabitation (Lichter, Turner, and Sassler 2010). As Figure 10.3 shows, the increases in cohabiting households (same-sex and different-sex couples) in the United States more than 50 years are dramatic. Still, at any given point in time, only about 9% of the population in the United States is cohabiting (Benokraitis 2012; Lamanna and Riedmann 2010).

Thinking Sociologically

Why do couples decide to cohabit? Is it usually with expectation of marriage, or is something else at work? Ask some friends or family members who are cohabiting their reasons and compile a list of motivations.

Countries in Europe with the highest percentages of cohabiting couples between the ages of 20 and 34 include Denmark (28.6%), Estonia (23.5%), Finland (28.3%), France (21.3%), Netherlands (21.9%), Norway (22.7%), and the United Kingdom (22.2%) (OECD Family Database 2010). Latin American and Caribbean surveys

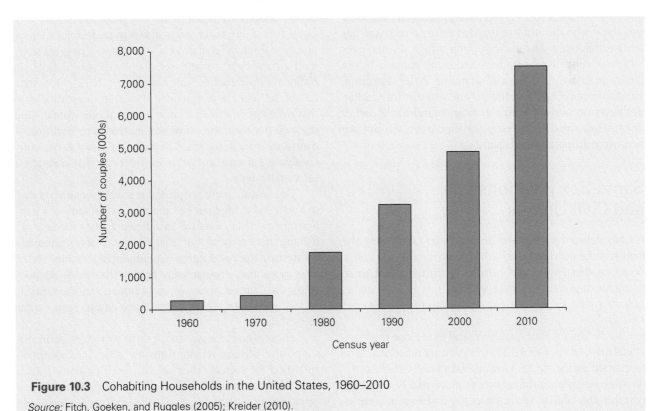

Figure 10.3 Cohabiting Households in the United States, 1960–2010

Source: Fitch, Goeken, and Ruggles (2005); Kreider (2010).

have indicated that more than one in four women between the ages of 15 and 49 are in relationships they call consensual unions, living together without official sanction. Such women typically have far less legal protection than European women during or after such unions.

Rates and reasons for marriage versus cohabitation vary significantly by ethnicity. For whites in the United States, cohabitation is often a precursor to marriage. For blacks, it may be an alternative to marriage. Financial problems encourage cohabitation in African American families because many African American men avoid marriage if they do not think they can support a family and fulfill the breadwinner role. Although childbearing increases the chance of marriage, it is a much stronger impetus for white than for black cohabitants.

We might assume that cohabiting would allow couples to make more realistic decisions about entering permanent relationships if they do get married. However, studies show that this is not always the case. When couples have different objectives for cohabiting, or have not discussed the future of the relationship before moving in together, problems may arise, and divorce may result. For many decades, cohabitation prior to marriage was linked to higher rates of divorce (Sassler and Miller 2011; Stanley and Rhoades 2009).

That strong relationship between cohabiting couples and likelihood of divorce has declined dramatically, however, in the past decade or so. Recent research indicates that the fairly large gap in divorce rates between cohabiters and those who did not live together prior to marriage has nearly evaporated. The one exception is high divorce rates for "serial cohabiters" who have had many partners before finally marrying (Cohen and Manning 2010; Manning, Longmore, and Giordano 2007). Note also that this decline in the connection between cohabitation and likelihood of divorce happened at precisely the time when the divorce rates were dropping significantly.

Same-Sex Relationships and Civil Unions

A hotly debated macro-level policy matter concerning the family is the official status of homosexual couples. Policy decisions affect rights and benefits for partners, but there is intense disagreement over whether this issue is about human rights or about divinely determined rights and wrongs.

In the United States, at the federal level alone marriage grants married couples 1,138 rights that are not available to unmarried partners (U.S. General Accounting Office 2004). As same-sex relationships become more widely acknowledged in the Global North, many gay and lesbian couples are living together openly as families. Denmark was the first

country to recognize same-sex unions in 1989, granting legal rights to couples. In 2001, the Netherlands was the first country to allow same-sex marriages. Eleven countries now allow same-sex marriages, including Canada. However, some other countries have threatened punishment—even death—for openly gay individuals (Goodstein 2012; Martin and Thompkins 2009).

As reported by the U.S. Census Bureau, in 2010 there were approximately 594,000 same-sex couple households in the United States, or about 1% of all couple households (Lofquist 2011). Most scholars acknowledge that this is probably an underreporting because of the stigma in many parts of the country of reporting that one is gay or lesbian. One out of every nine unmarried cohabiting couples are gay or lesbian, and one quarter of gay couples are raising children (Benokraitis 2012; S. James 2011).

On the other hand, as of the summer of 2013, 13 states and Washington, D.C., have legalized same-sex marriage. These include California, Connecticut, Delaware, Iowa, Maine, Maryland, Massachusetts, Minnesota, New Hampshire, New York, Rhode Island, Vermont, and Washington (Freedom to Marry 2013). Some states have passed this through the legislatures, and in other cases it has been a ruling by a court that the ban is discriminatory and denies people equal rights. The battle between court rulings and votes by the populace has raged for almost a decade, but in 2012, a federal district court in California ruled that the proposition banning same-sex marriage (passed in 2008) violated the equal protection provisions of the U.S. Constitution. Six other states also legalized same-sex relationships through "civil unions"—contracts that grant state-level spousal rights to same-sex couples (*Boston Globe* 2012; National Conference of State Legislatures 2012). More than half of the states have amended their state constitutions so that marriage is limited to one man and one woman, and most do not recognize same-sex marriages or civil unions contracted in other states. The Supreme Court is currently considering a case on same-sex marriage that may affect some states' laws.

One reason many people in the *lesbigay* community are so intent on having same-sex marriage is that same-sex partnerships or civil unions are "insufficiently institutionalized," making them somewhat less stable and creating ambiguity about their roles and rights (Cherlin 1978; Stewart 2007). They argue that if we actually believe that stable relationships and families make for a healthier and more stable society, then families with same-sex adults need public recognition.

Those who favor gay and lesbian marriages claim that supportive lifelong relationships are good for individuals and good for society. They see the fact that homosexuals want stable socially sanctioned relationships as an encouraging sign about how important the family is to society and how homosexuals want to fit in. Moreover, because many

Gay Issues   Marriage Contracts

societies offer tax benefits, insurance coverage, and other privileges to married couples, the denial of marriage on the basis of one's gender attraction is discriminatory and may be costly to partners who are denied rights, and to societies that must care for the needs of the uninsured or unemployed.

Those opposed argue that marriage has been a function of the church, temple, and mosque for centuries. Marriage was historically governed in Europe by the church or temple until Martin Luther insisted that the government would play a role. Gradually after that time, marriage came to be monitored and recorded by governments (Kephart 1977). Still, that did not happen in England until as recently as 1837, so religious groups have defined marriage for most of Western history (Ancestry.co.uk 2013). None of the religious traditions have historically recognized gay relationships as legitimate (although a few are doing so now). Some opponents appeal to biology with the assertion that marriage is a legitimate way to propagate the species. Because homosexual unions do not serve this purpose, they do not serve the society, according to the opponents of same-sex marriage. However, many same-sex couples are providing homes for children, their own or adopted.

In the backyard of their home in Beverly Hills, comedian Ellen DeGeneres, left, and Portia de Rossi got married during one of the short windows when same-sex marriage was legal in California. Same-sex marriage is once again legal in California as of 2013.

Divorce—Contract Breaking

Is the family breaking down? Is it relevant in today's world? Although most cultures extol the virtues of family life, the reality is that not all partnerships work. Support is not forthcoming for the partner, trust is violated, abuse is present, and relationships deteriorate. So we cannot discuss family life without also recognizing the often painful side of family life that results in contract breaking.

Some commentators view divorce rates as evidence that the family is losing importance. They see enormous problems created by divorce. There are costs to adults who suffer guilt and failure, to children from divided homes, and to the society that does not have the stabilizing force of intact lifelong partnerships. Many children around the world are raised without both natural parents present. For example, in the United States, 69% of children younger than 18 live in two-parent households, 31% live with one parent, and nearly half live at least part of their lives in single-parent families (Kreider and Ellis 2011; U.S. Census Bureau 2007). Considering single-parent families by race and ethnicity, in 2010 66% of African American, 52% of American Indian, 16% of Asian and Pacific Islander, 41% of Hispanic or Latino, and 24% of white children lived in single-parent households (Kids Count Data Center 2010).

Others argue that marriage is not so much breaking down as adapting to a different kind of social system. Indeed, more people today express satisfaction with marriage than at any previous period, and there are more golden (50-year) wedding anniversaries now than ever before (Kain 2005). Late in the 19th century, the average length of a marriage was only 13 years—mostly because life expectancy was so short. "Till death do us part" was not such a long time then as it is today, when average life expectancy is in the late 1970s (Coontz 2005). There are many misconceptions about divorce in the 21st century as well, and the next "Sociology in Our Social World" on page 304 addresses some of those.

Thinking Sociologically

Micro-level issues of divorce may be easier to identify since they are usually rooted in the personalities and relationship factors of the individuals. Talk with friends and family who have divorced about micro-level factors that contributed. Now, based on the previous discussion, make a list of meso-level factors (e.g., religious, economic, legal, educational) that contribute to or reduce divorce rates.

Macro-level social issues also contribute to divorce. These in turn result in micro-level individual family problems. The reason for the dramatic increases in the

Sociology in Our Social World

Debunking Misconceptions About Divorce

By David Popenoe

Divorce Fallacy 1: Because people learn from their bad experiences, second marriages tend to be more successful than first marriages.

Fact: Although many people who divorce have successful subsequent marriages, the divorce rate of remarriages is in fact higher than that of first marriages.

Divorce Fallacy 2: Having a child together will help a couple to improve their marital satisfaction and prevent a divorce.

Fact: Many studies have shown that the most stressful time in a marriage is after the first child is born. Couples who have a child together have a slightly decreased risk of divorce compared to couples without children, but the decreased risk is far less than it used to be.

Divorce Fallacy 3: When parents don't get along, children are better off if their parents divorce than if they stay together.

Fact: A recent large-scale, long-term study suggests that while parents' marital unhappiness and discord have a broad negative impact on virtually every dimension of their children's well-being, so does going through a divorce. It was only the children in very high-conflict

homes who benefited from a divorce. In lower-conflict marriages that ended in divorce—as many as two thirds of the divorces—the situation of the children was made much worse following a divorce. Therefore, except in high-conflict marriages it is better for the children if their parents stay together and work out their problems than if they divorce.

Divorce Fallacy 4: Being very unhappy at certain points in a marriage is a good sign that the marriage will eventually end in divorce.

Fact: All marriages have their ups and downs. Recent research using a large national sample found that 86 percent of people who were unhappy in their marriages but stayed with the marriage indicated five years later that they were happy. Indeed, three fifths of the formerly unhappily married couples rated their marriages as either "very happy" or "quite happy."

Divorce Fallacy 5: It is usually men who initiate divorce proceedings.

Fact: Two thirds of all divorces are initiated by women.

Source: Copyright 2002 by David Popenoe, the National Marriage Project, University of Virginia. Reprinted by permission of David Popenoe.

U.S. divorce rate after the early 1970s was a policy change: no-fault divorce laws. For centuries in the United States, one had to prove that the other party was in breach of contract. Marriage was a lifelong contract that could only be severed by one party having violated the terms of the contract. When U.S. divorce laws became more lenient in the 1970s, there was a boomlet of divorces, stimulated by the increasing number of women who entered the labor force and changed family dynamics. As the U.S. family adapted to the new reality of women's changing roles, one adaptation was to pool income from both spouses. In addition, many couples wait longer to marry. Because dual-income families are generally more educated, they have economic stability and more marriage stability.

All this makes divorce in the United States much easier to obtain than in previous years. However, some ask if divorces are being sought for the slightest offense. Some critics believe this ease has led to a *divorce culture*—a society in which people assume that marriages are fragile rather than assuming that marriages are for life (a *marriage culture*). Divorce rates for most groups in the United States have been dropping since 1996 (Cherlin 2010; Clarkson 2011). It dropped from 15.9 divorces per 1,000 citizens each year in 1980 to 3.6 in 2011 (Centers for Disease Control and Prevention/National Center for Health Statistics [CDC/NCHS] 2013). Despite this, the United States still has one of the highest rates of divorce in Global North countries (U.S. Bureau of Labor Statistics 2008). Currently, macro-level

Divorce

A security guard checks people for weapons before they board Miami-Dade County's Family Division Circuit Court bus, which was dubbed "The Divorce Bus." More than two dozen uncontested divorce cases were heard in fewer than 45 minutes. This does seem to give new meaning to the idea of divorce made convenient.

factors such as the poor housing market and slow economy inhibit some couples from divorcing because they cannot afford the expenses of two homes and child support (Divorce Rate 2011).

The quality of health care has improved over the past two centuries, and as a result people are living much longer—another macro trend. Because of this, people may live much longer in a marriage than in the past. If we grant that not everyone will be able to sustain a nurturing marriage for 50 years, and if we acknowledge that people do change over time, what would be an acceptable divorce rate for our society—5% of all marriages, 20%, or 30%? This is difficult for governments to decide, but many people feel that the current rate (3.6 divorces per 1,000 people each year) is too high (CDC/NHCS 2013; Religious Tolerance 2009). In any case, health systems that contribute to longevity may also contribute to people being in more than one marriage over a lifetime.

Thinking Sociologically

Is divorce really a problem, or is it a solution to a worse problem? Does divorce have lasting consequences for spouses and children? What evidence supports your position?

Divorce and Its Social Consequences

The highest rates of divorce are among young couples. In the United States, the highest rates are for women in their teens and men between 20 and 24. The rate of divorce has dropped since 1981, as shown in Table 10.1. In Canada, roughly 40% of first marriages end in divorce, with around 70,000 divorces in the country in a given year. The peak in Canada was also in the 1980s (CBC News 2010).

The emotional aspects of divorce are for many most difficult. Divorce is often seen as a failure, rejection, and even punishment. Moreover, a divorce often involves a splitting with family and many close friends; with one's church, mosque, or synagogue; and from other social contexts in which one is known as part of a couple (Amato 2000). No wonder divorce is so wrenching. Unlike simple societies, most modern societies have no ready mechanism for absorbing people back into stable social units such as clans.

Adjustment to divorced status varies by gender: Men typically have a harder time emotionally adjusting to singlehood or divorce than do women. Divorced men must often leave not only their wives but also their children, and whereas many women have support networks, fewer men have developed or sustained friendships outside of marriage. Finances, on the other hand, are a bigger problem for divorced women and their children than for men. Women were more likely to be living in poverty than men across all racial and ethnic groups, with more than 24 million women living below the poverty line in 2009 (Reason 2011). Single mothers were twice as likely to be in poverty as single fathers, and over 35% experienced food insecurity (not enough food) in 2010 (Gray 2012).

Support from the noncustodial parent can help relieve the poverty, yet one quarter of custodial parents receive no help at all. Of the remaining 75%, 70.8% receive some or all of what is owed, with 41.2% of those receiving full child support (U.S. Census Bureau 2011b).

Table 10.1 U.S. Divorce Rate Trends

Year	Divorces per 1,000 Population
1950	2.6
1960	2.2
1970	3.5
1980	5.2
1981	5.3 (Highest rate)
1990	4.7
2000	4.0
2010	3.6
2011	3.6

Source: CDC/NCHS (2013).

Gay Divorce

Men often find emotional adjustment to divorce especially difficult since they often leave the children and they have fewer intimate friendships outside of marriage.

There are also costs for children whose lives are often turned upside down: Many children move to new houses and locations, leave one parent and friends, and make adjustments to new schools and to reduced resources.

On the other hand, some studies find that children who are well adjusted to begin with have an easier time with divorce, especially if they can remain in their home and in their familiar school, with both parents part of their lives, and if they maintain their friendship networks. Grandparents, too, can provide stability during these traumatic times.

Thinking Sociologically

Would making it harder to get a divorce create stronger and healthier families? Would it create more stable but less healthy and nurturing families? If you were making divorce policies, what would you do? What are the positive and negative aspects of your policy?

Global Family Patterns and Policies

Family systems around the world are changing in similar ways, pushed by industrialization and urbanization, by migration to new countries or refugee status, by changing kinship and occupational structures, and by influences from outside the family. The most striking changes include greater choice of spouse, more equal status for women, equal rights in divorce, neolocal residency (when partners

in a married couple live separate from either set of parents), bilateral kinship systems (tracing lineage through both parents), and pressures for individual equality (McKie and Callan 2012). However, countermovements in some parts of the world call for strengthening of marriage through modesty of women, separation of the sexes (in both public and private spheres), and rejection of high divorce rates and other Western practices.

Do marriage and divorce rates indicate the family is in crisis all across the globe? To answer these questions, we need information on current patterns, historical trend lines, and patterns in other parts of the world. The next "Sociology Around the World" provides cross-cultural data on marriage and divorce ratios.

Family life, which seems so personal and intimate, is actually linked to global patterns. Global aid is activated when drought, famine, or other disasters affect communities and a country is not able to provide for families. In such cases, international organizations such as the United Nations, Doctors Without Borders, Oxfam, and the Red Cross mobilize to support families in crises. Support varies from feeding starving children to opposing the slavery that occurs when parents are reduced to selling their bodies or children to survive. International crises can lead to war, perhaps removing the main breadwinner from the family or taking the life of a son or daughter who was drafted to fight. Homes and cultivated fields may be destroyed and the families forced into refugee status.

We have been talking about global and national trends (divorce rates) regarding an institution (the family) and the consequences they have for individuals. Processes at the macro and meso levels affect the micro level of society, and decisions at the micro level (i.e., to dissolve a marriage) affect the community and the nation. The various levels of the social world are indeed interrelated in complex ways.

Global forces, such as ethnic holocausts that create refugees, can strain and destroy families. This is a scene of a refugee camp in Syria following that country's struggle for freedom.

Single Parenting

Marriage and Poverty

Sociology Around the World

Cross-Cultural Differences in Family Dissolution

How do families cope with changing national and global demands? Family conflict and disorganization occur when members of the family unit do not or cannot carry out roles expected of them by spouses, other family members, the community, or the society. This may be due to voluntary departure (divorce, separation, desertion), involuntary problems (illness or other catastrophe), a crisis caused by external events (war or deteriorating economic conditions), or failure to communicate role expectations and needs. Many of these role failures are a direct consequence of societal changes due to globalization. Once again, the social world model helps us understand macro-level trends and patterns that affect us in micro-level contexts.

Divorce is still very limited in some parts of the world, and it may be an option for only one gender. In some Arab countries, only the husband has the right to declare "I divorce thee" in front of a witness on three separate occasions, after which the divorce is complete. The wife returns, sometimes in disgrace, to her family of orientation, while the husband generally keeps the children in the patriarchal family and is free to take another wife. Only recently is divorce initiated by the wife coming to be accepted in some countries, although the grounds for divorce by women may be restricted (Khazaleh 2009). Despite a seemingly easy process for men to divorce, the rate remains rather low in many Global South countries because family ties and allegiances are severely strained when divorces take place. Thus, informal pressures and cultural attitudes restrain tendencies to divorce.

Still, when family turmoil and conflict are too great to resolve or when the will to save the family disappears, the legal, civil, and religious ties of marriage may be broken. The methods for dissolving marriage ties vary, but most countries have some form of divorce. Table 10.2 compares marriage and divorce rates in selected industrial countries. Notice that while the divorce rate in countries such as the United States is quite high, the marriage rate is also high.

Table 10.2 Marriage and Divorce Rates in Selected Countries, 1980–2008

Country	Marriages per 1,000 Persons in Population				Divorces per 1,000 Persons in Population			
	1980	1990	2000	2008	1980	1990	2000	2008
USA	15.9	14.9	12.5	10.6	7.9	7.2	6.2	5.2
Canada	11.5	10.0	7.5	6.4	3.7	4.2	3.1	na
Japan	9.8	8.4	9.2	na	1.8	1.8	3.1	na
Denmark	8.0	9.1	10.8	10.3	4.1	4.0	4.0	4.1
France	9.7	7.7	7.9	6.6	2.4	2.8	3.0	na
Germany	X	8.2	7.6	6.9	X	2.5	3.5	3.5
Ireland	10.9	8.3	7.6	na	na	na	1.0	na
Italy	8.7	8.2	7.3	6.3	0.3	0.7	1.0	1.3
Netherlands	9.6	9.4	8.2	6.7	2.7	2.8	3.2	2.9
Spain	9.4	8.5	7.9	6.2	na	0.9	1.4	3.5
Sweden	7.1	7.4	7.0	8.3	3.7	3.5	3.8	3.5
United Kingdom	11.6	10.0	8.0	na	4.1	4.1	4.0	na

Source: U.S. Census Bureau (2012d), Table 1335.

Note: na = not available; X = country was two nations at that time.

The next two chapters continue to examine institutions and their interconnections. As children grow up and branch out from the embrace of the family, the social environments they experience first are usually the local school and a religious congregation. It is to education and religion that we turn next.

What Have We Learned?

Despite those who lament the weakening of the family, the institution of family is here to stay. Its form may alter as it responds and adapts to societal changes, and other institutions will continue to take on functions formerly reserved for the family. Still, the family is an institution crucial to societal survival, and whatever the future holds, the family will adapt in response to changes in other parts of the social world. It is an institution that is sometimes vulnerable and needs support, but it is also a resilient institution—the way we partner and "make people" in any society.

Our happiest and saddest experiences are integrally intertwined with family. Family provides the foundation, the group through which individuals' needs are met. Societies depend on families as the unit through which to funnel services. It is the political, economic, health, educational, religious, and sexual base for most people. These are some of the reasons family is important to us.

Key Points:

- Families are diverse entities at the micro level, having a wide range of configurations, but families also collectively serve as a core structure of society—institutions—at the meso and macro levels. (See pp. 287–289.)

- The family is sometimes called the most basic unit of society, for it is a core unit of social pairing into groups (partner taking), a primary unit of procreation and socialization (people making), and so important that when it comes unglued (contract breaking), the whole social system may be threatened. (See pp. 289–290.)

- Various theories—rational choice, symbolic interactionism, functionalism, conflict theory, and feminist theory—illuminate different aspects of family and help us understand conflicts, stressors, and functions of families. (See pp. 290–294.)

- At the micro level, people come together in partner-taking pairs, but the rules of partner taking (exogamy/endogamy, free choice/arranged marriage, polygamy/monogamy) are meso-level rules. (See pp. 294–301.)

- Power within a partnership—including distribution of tasks and authority—is assigned through intimate processes that are again largely controlled by rules imposed from another level in the social system. (See pp. 298–299.)

- At the macro level, nations and even global organizations try to establish policies that strengthen families. Issues that are of concern to some analysts include cohabitation patterns that seem a threat to family, same-sex households (including same-sex marriage), and contract breaking (divorce). (See pp. 301–307.)

Discussion Questions

1. What do you believe is the ideal makeup of a family? Why? How does your description relate to the functions the family performs in society?

2. Which of the main theoretical perspectives discussed in this chapter (functional, conflict, and feminist) is most useful when examining the families with which you are familiar? Why?

3. A majority of Americans and a strong majority of young Americans (those younger than 30) now support same-sex marriages. What are some cultural and structural changes that have led to this increase in support for marriage equality over the past decade?

4. Does (or did) your family expect you to marry someone of a particular (a) race or ethnicity, (b) social class, (c) educational background, or (d) religion? Why or why not? How do you think endogamous norms impact (a) individual marriages and (b) society?

5. How does your family's income influence the (a) amount and (b) quality of time family members spend together? How might (a) more or (b) less money influence your family members' relationships with one another? Why?

6. Do you think the establishment of no-fault divorce laws have been good or bad for (a) the institution of the family in the United States, (b) married couples, and (c) children? Explain your answers.

Contributing to Our Social World: What Can We Do?

At the Local Level

- *Support groups for married or partnered students* respond to the needs of an ever-increasing number of undergraduate students living on or near campus with spouses, partners, and children. If your campus has a support group, arrange to attend a meeting and work with members to help them meet the challenges associated with their family situation. If such a group does not exist, consider forming one.

- Is there *day care available on your campus*? Day care on campus can be invaluable for parents. If there is, look at the cost and availability of care for the children of faculty, staff, and students. If there is not a day care, look at the possibilities of creating, funding, and staffing one. How might it benefit the college or university, as well as the families it will serve?

At the Organizational or Institutional Level

- *Support groups for multigeneration households* provide an important opportunity to support this growing population. Approximately one in five households contain more than one generation of adults. *House builders* have begun to change how they design some houses in order to meet the needs of such households. Contact your local *Habitat for Humanity chapter* (www.habitat.org) and ask if you can help create more homes suitable for multigeneration households. You can find some ideas for such homes at http://www.chicagotribune.com/special/primetime/chi-primetime-multigen-091412,0,4957985.story.

At the National and Global Levels

- *Influencing marriage policies* is another way for sociology students to make a difference in our social world. Select a family-related issue about which you feel strongly—pro or con (for example, covenant marriage, no-fault divorce options, or same-sex marriage policies). Find out about the laws of the United States or your state regarding the issue. Next, identify your members in the U.S. House of Representatives (www.house.gov), the U.S. Senate (www.senate.gov), and/or your state legislature (www.ncsl.org/about-us/ncslservice/state-legislative-websites-directory.aspx). Contact those people via letter or email, stating your views.

- *Voices* is a multi-issue advocacy group for children with member organizations across the nation. The organization strives to improve the lives of children and their families, particularly those most at risk. You can learn about the issues on which the group is working and join its efforts, if you would like to do so, by going to www.voices.org.

- *Hofstra University* maintains a resource site on international family law at http://people.hofstra.edu/lisa_a_spar/intlfam/intlfam.htm where you can learn more about the field.

Visit **www.sagepub.com/oswcondensed3e** for online activities, sample tests, and other helpful information. Select "Chapter 10: Family" for chapter-specific activities.

Education and Religion

Answering "What?" and "Why?"

Whether in schools or houses of worship, "What happened?" and "Why did that happen?" are commonly asked questions. In schools, the answers may have to do with experimenting (science) or with plot (literature). When the questions are asked in a religious setting, the answers are likely to focus on the meaning of the event for one's life or for human history.

Global Community

Society

National Organizations,
Institutions, and Ethnic Subcultures

Local Organizations
and Community

Me (and My
Teacher and
Classmates)

Micro: Classrooms in schools;
neighborhood and city school systems

Meso: State funding and
regulations governing education

Macro: National policies to improve schools

Macro: United Nations policies and programs to improve education in poor countries

Think About It	
Micro: Self and Inner Circle	What did you personally learn—both formally and informally—in schools and in houses of worship?
Micro: Local Community	How do role expectations of people in a local school—student, teacher, principal—affect the learning that occurs in that school?
Meso: National Institutions; Complex Organizations; Ethnic Groups	How does the institution of government influence schools and faith communities?
Macro: National Society	How are education and religion changing in your nation?
Macro: Global Community	Why are education and religion of major concern around the world?

What's coming in this chapter?

Education: The Search for Knowledge

   State of the World's Education

   Who Does What? Micro-Level Interactions in Educational Organizations

   After the School Bell Rings: Meso-Level Analysis

   Education, Society, and the Road to Opportunity: The Macro Level

   Education and Social Policy Issues

   Global Policy Issues in Education

Religion: The Search for Meaning

   What Does Religion Do for Us?

   Components of Religion

   Religion and Modern Life: Meso-Level Analysis

   Religion in Society: Macro-Level Analysis

   Religion in the Contemporary Global Context

Aastik, in his home country of Nepal, goes to school most days of the week, where he learns not only skills like reading, writing, and mathematics, but the meaning of citizenship in his country and the history and geography of his nation. He also attends religious services with his family one day a week and on holiday occasions. With this faith community he learns about how those who share this religious perspective view the meaning of life, define the role of God in human existence, and characterize ethical behaviors and moral prohibitions. In both of these institutions, Aastik is experiencing socialization.

Think about your own childhood. What were the most influential factors in shaping you into who you are today? You probably think of family members; your school, teachers, and best friends; and your religious group. This chapter discusses two institutions whose main purpose is to socialize us; after family, they are crucial to our early socialization.

Both educational institutions and religious ones ask questions about the "what" and the "why" of our lives. Education tends to focus on answers that have to do with knowledge—causality and the relationship of facts—while religion tends to address ultimate meaning in life and values that shape our decision making. Both help shape who we are through socialization throughout our lives. We begin with an examination of education; the second half of the chapter explores religion.

Education: The Search for Knowledge

Tomás is a failure. At 9 years old, he cannot read, write, or get along with his peers, and out of frustration, he sometimes misbehaves. He has been a failure since he was 3, but his failure started earlier than that. His parents have told Tomás over and over that he will not amount to anything if he does not shape up. His teachers have noticed that he is slow to learn and has few friends. So two strikes against him are the judgments of his parents and his teachers. The third strike is Tomás's own acceptance of the label "failure." He has little evidence to contradict their judgment. Tomás is an at-risk child, identified as having characteristics inclining him toward failure in school and society. Probably he will not amount to anything, and he may even get in trouble with the law unless caring people intervene, encouraging him to realize his abilities.

Tomás goes to school in Toronto (Ontario), Canada, but he could live in any country. Although successful children develop a positive self-concept that helps them deal with disappointments and failures, the Tomáses internalize failures. Successful children negotiate the rules and regulations of school, and school provides them with necessary skills for future occupations. Tomás carries a label with him that will shape his life because, next to home, schools play the biggest role in affecting children's self-concepts and attitudes toward achievement. What factors could

Religion and Academics

change educational outcomes for students like Tomás? The following discussion of the institution of education may shed some light on experiences of children in the educational system.

Schooling—learning skills such as reading and math in a building via systematic instruction by a trained professional—is a luxury some children will never know. On the other hand, in most urban areas around the world and in affluent countries, formal education is necessary for success—and even for survival. Education of the masses in a school setting is a modern concept that became necessary when literacy and math skills emerged as essential to many jobs, even if just to read instructions for operating machinery. Literacy is also necessary to democratic governments, where an informed citizenry elects officials and votes on public policies.

In this part of the chapter, we will explore the state of the world's education, theoretical perspectives on education, micro-level interactions in educational organizations, what happens in schools after the school bell rings, whether education is the road to opportunity, and global educational social policy issues.

Overcrowding in classrooms is not uncommon in poor countries, as seen in this very poor school in a Darfur refugee camp. Note that the students are primarily boys.

State of the World's Education: An Overview

Every society educates its children. In most societies, national education systems carry out this task. Global organizations concerned with education also contribute. Over the past 50 years, UNESCO (the United Nations Educational, Scientific and Cultural Organization) has become the "global center for discussion and implementation of educational ideas and organization models" (Boli 2002:307). It provides teacher training, curricular guidance, and textbook sources, and it gathers international statistics on educational achievement. Many countries in Africa, Asia, Europe, Latin America, and the Middle East have adopted UNESCO global standards, including the organizational model of six years of primary school and three years apiece for intermediate and secondary school, with an emphasis on comprehensive rather than specialized training (UNESCO Institute for Statistics 2012).

Education has become a global issue. What is considered essential knowledge to be taught in schools is based largely on a country's level of development, cultural values, political ideology, and guidelines from international standards. Country leaders believe that a literate population is necessary for economic development and expansion, a thriving political system, and the well-being of the citizenry. "Education has become a global social process that both reflects and helps create the global society that is under formation" (Boli 2002:312).

Formal education—schooling that takes place in a formal setting with the goal of teaching a predetermined curriculum—has expanded dramatically in the

past several decades as higher percentages of students in many countries attend school. Although major educational gaps still exist between the elite and the poor and between females and males, these gaps are narrowing. Enrollment among girls rose from 32% of school enrollees in 1950 to almost 50% in 2010 (World Bank 2013b). Some countries lag behind in the number of boys in primary and secondary school compared to the number of girls; for every 100 boys, 66 girls are in school in Afghanistan, 69 in the Central African Republic, and 68 in Chad, Africa (World Bank 2013b). In Global North countries, women are entering male-dominated fields of higher education and attending university at levels equal to or exceeding those of men.

Still, an estimated 775 million adults and 122 million children in our global village cannot read or write, and have no experience with technology. The result is that they cannot participate in the global economy, unemployment is far higher, and poverty is a fact of life for many. If a woman stays in school just one additional year, her earnings can increase by 10% to 20% over a lifetime, and her children are more likely to survive (Bokova and Bush 2012). In some poor Global South countries in Southeast Asia and sub-Saharan Africa, the literacy rate (those who have basic reading skills) among adults is less than 50% (UNESCO Institute for Statistics 2012). Countries with the lowest literacy rates are mostly in sub-Saharan Africa: Burkina Faso (23.6%), Mali (24%), and Chad (25.7%) (Infoplease 2013). (See Map 11.1 on page 314.)

Education can be studied at each level of analysis: micro, meso, and macro. The next section provides a summary of how various theories offer different perspectives for understanding education in society.

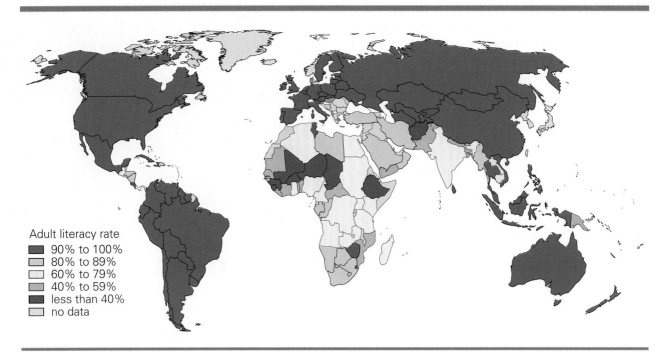

Map 11.1 Adult Literacy Rates by Country

Source: Friedrich Huebler, http://huebler.blogspot.com/2012/05/literacy.html, UNESCO Institute for Statistics.

While Ethiopia shares the commitment to mass education of all young people, its resources are very meager, as we can see from this photo of a crowded impoverished school in an Ethiopian village.

Who Does What? Micro-Level Interactions in Educational Organizations

The process of education takes place at the micro level in the classrooms and corridors of local schools, with key players who enact the everyday drama of teaching and learning. Schools are important organizations in local communities as well. The school is a source of pride and a unifying symbol of identity. Local communities rally around the success of their school. Moreover, in many communities, the school system is a large employer with real importance to the economic vitality of the area. At the micro level, much sociological analysis has focused on interpersonal exchanges within a classroom and on the school as a social setting within a community. At this level, sociologists look at roles and statuses in educational settings and the informal norms and interaction patterns that evolve in those settings. Let us begin by reviewing two micro-level theories, and then some common in-school interactions.

Micro-Level Theories: Individuals Within Schools

Symbolic Interaction Perspective and the Classroom. Symbolic interaction theory focuses on how people interact based on the meaning they have assigned to various traits, behaviors, or symbols (e.g., clothing). Children actively create distinctions among individuals and groups, becoming agents in determining the social reality in which they live. Popularity is a major issue for many children, especially in middle school years; it refers to being noticed and liked and having everyone know who you are. Students may increase their popularity by being attractive, representing the school in an athletic contest, or being seen in a leadership position. The difficulty is that there are few such positions, leading to a competition in which some individuals are losers. In the United States, the losers are more likely to be children from families who cannot afford to purchase popular clothing or other status symbols or to send their children to sports training or music camp. Winners have access to material and symbolic resources that give them high visibility. They are given special privileges in the school and are more likely to develop leadership skills and to feel good about themselves—forms of social and cultural capital (Vijayakumar 2012).

Classrooms are small societies of peers that reflect the interaction patterns and problems of the larger world. One's sense of self—an intensely personal experience—is shaped by the micro interactions of the school. Thus, for young people from 6 to 18 years old, the extensive time spent in school means the status of student has enormous impact on how individuals see themselves. The image that is reflected back to someone—as student or as teacher, for example—can begin to mold one's sense of competence, intelligence, and likability. The symbolic interaction perspective considers how symbols affect sense of self or shape social hierarchies (Eder, Evans, and Parker 1995).

The larger school organization creates a structure that influences how individuals make sense of their reality and interact with others. Some symbolic interaction theorists, including those representing the Iowa School, emphasize the link between the self and meso-level positions or statuses (Stryker 2000). Official school positions—such as president of the student council or senior class president or varsity team member—become important elements of one's *self*.

Thinking Sociologically

How do you think teachers affect the sense of self of students? How do students affect the sense of self, the confidence, and the effectiveness of each other and of teachers?

Rational Choice Theory and Educational Settings. Rational choice theory focuses on the cost-benefit analysis that individuals undertake in virtually everything they do. What are the costs—in terms of money, relationships, self-esteem, or other factors—and what are the benefits? If benefits outweigh costs, the individual is likely to decide to continue the rewarding activities, but if costs outweigh benefits, the individual is likely to seek other courses of action.

How might weighing costs and benefits influence decisions about education? One example is teachers making rational choices about staying in the teaching profession. In a given year, approximately 85% of all teachers in the United States stayed in the same school, 7% moved to new schools, and 8% left teaching entirely (Keigher and Cross 2010).

Males have many ways of becoming known and respected. Male athletic competitions draw bigger crowds than female athletics, and one can become a local celebrity based on one's skill on the field or court.

Rational choice theorists explain teacher retention by looking at perceived benefits—rewarding professional practice, working with children or adolescents, time off in summers—and perceived costs, such as poor salary for a college graduate; lack of respect from parents, students, and administrators; 12- to 14-hour days for nine months of the year; and lack of professionalism in treatment of teachers. The costs today are seen by teachers in some countries as higher than they used to be for professionals in teaching, so the turnover rate in the profession is high.

Thinking Sociologically

Think of a teacher you know or have observed. What seem to be the costs and benefits of the various roles teachers fulfill? Do you think most teacher behavior is shaped by this kind of rational choice calculation?

Statuses and Roles in the Educational System

Students, teachers, staff, and administrators hold major statuses in educational systems. The roles associated with each status in educational organizations bring both obligations and inherent problems. When the status holders agree on expected behaviors (role expectations), schools function smoothly. When they do not agree, conflicts can arise. Let us look at several statuses and accompanying roles in schools.

Students and the Peer Culture of Schools. In a private Rwandan secondary school, 45 students are crowded onto benches. They are quiet, respectful, and very hardworking. They know they are in a privileged position, and many students are lined up to take their place on the bench should they not carry out their roles, work hard, and succeed. Although they have no written texts, students write down the lectures in their notebooks and memorize the material. In some countries such as Rwanda, going to high school is a privilege. In others such as the United States, it is a necessary part of life that many students resist.

While many experts acknowledge that girls and boys have different experiences in school, a recent debate in Britain and the United States focuses on whether boys and girls should be taught in separate classrooms. Those who argue for separate classrooms, especially in the middle school years, point out the different interests, opportunities for involvement and recognition, and learning styles of girls and boys at these early adolescent ages. Others argue that equality requires mixed-gender classes. Some parochial schools have long been single-sex, and now public school districts are experimenting with single-sex classes. Research such as that presented in the next "Sociology in Our Social

In Rwandan secondary schools as many as 45 students may be in a classroom with little more than wooden benches and tables.

World" discusses concerns that have been raised about gender differences in U.S. schools (Weil 2008).

Another gender issue in peer culture is sexual harassment in schools. In Grades 7 to 12 in 2010–2011, 48% of students experienced some form of sexual harassment and reported negative effects. Abuse was verbal, physical, and electronic, with over 30% experiencing harassment through electronic media such as Twitter and Facebook. Girls reported more harassment than boys: in person 52% to 35%, and electronic 36% to 24%. However, few students reported harassment to parents or school personnel (Hill and Kearl 2011; Munsey 2012).

Compared to boys, girls experience "hostile hallways" in more physically and psychologically harmful ways, and students who identified themselves as gay, lesbian, bisexual, or transgendered experienced high levels of bullying and assaults as well (Gay, Lesbian, and Straight Education Network 2006). While trying to deal with all the challenges of being a teenager, lesbian, gay, bisexual, and/or transgender (LGBT) teens additionally have to deal with harassment, threats, and violence directed at them on a daily basis. They hear antigay slurs such as "homo," "faggot," and "sissy" about 26 times a day or once every 14 minutes. Even more troubling, a study found that 31% of gay youth had been threatened or injured at school in the last year alone (Mental Health America 2011).

The environment outside the school also powerfully affects students' achievement and behavior within the school. Disorganization in the community and family is related to lack of school commitment and is reflected in delinquent behavior (Ogbu 1998). The students at highest risk for dropping out of school in Global North countries are also at higher risk for joining gangs and committing violent crimes. They often feel the system is stacked against them (Noguera 1996, 2011; Willis 1979). Educators are deeply concerned about disruptive students, not only because they disrupt learning and make school unsafe for others but because many are at risk of dropping out of school and becoming burdens to society.

Teachers: The Front Line. Teachers in the classroom occupy the front line in implementing the goals of the school, community, and society. Teachers are those role partners who serve as gatekeepers, controlling the flow of students, activities, resources, and privileges. One scholar estimated that teachers have more than a thousand interchanges a day in their roles as classroom managers (Jackson 1968).

As primary socializers and role models for students, teachers are expected to support and encourage students and at the same time to judge their performance—giving grades and recommendations as part of the selection and allocation functions of education. This creates role strain, which can interfere with the task of teaching and contribute

Sociology in Our Social World

Where the Boys Are: And Where Are the Boys?

"The Fragile Girl"; "The War Against Boys"; "Failing at Fairness: How America's Schools Cheat Girls"; and "At Colleges, Women Are Leaving Men in the Dust" are just a few article titles in a debate about whether girls or boys have the biggest advantage or disadvantage in schools. For many years, concern focused on factors that inhibited minorities' educational attainment in school. Recently, some authors are turning the tables and focusing their concern on gender.

Statistics indicate that the state of educational achievement varies greatly by sex, age, race or ethnicity, and socioeconomic status. Why is this so? Among the many reasons for the differences, researchers point to the incredible gains made by women and the fact that women tend to study more. In the United States, African American, Hispanic, and low-income males lag behind all other groups, including females from their own ethnic group. On the other hand, Asians and Pacific Islanders have the highest high school completion rate—96.6% compared to whites (96.2%), blacks (90.1%), Hispanics (82.3%), and Native Americans (86.4%) (Stillwell 2010).

One analysis concludes that "more than 60% of the people in prison are now racial and ethnic minorities. For Black males in their 30s, 1 in every 10 is in prison or jail on any given day," further reducing their chances for education, good jobs, and a stable family life (Sentencing Project 2013). The reasons are many, but the bottom line is that these young men feel disconnected from a society that helps women with children but ignores the vulnerabilities of men (Mincy 2006). They often feel alienated from their society. The following figures provide a partial picture:

- An estimated 2 million to 3 million youth ages 16 through 24 are without postsecondary education and are disconnected—neither in school nor employed (Mincy 2006).

- Black teens have not witnessed education as a path to better jobs for their parents, siblings, and neighbors: In January 2011, unemployment for African Americans aged 20 or older was 14.6% compared to an 8.4% unemployment rate for whites of the same age (Allegretto, Amerikaner, and Pitts 2011).

- A review of college attendance statistics shows that women are attending and graduating at a higher rate than men, and black men are at the bottom of the graduation rates. Table 11.1 compares these groups.

Table 11.1 College Attendance Rates and Graduation Rates by Ethnicity and Gender

Race	College Attendance Rate (2012)
White, non-Hispanic	61%
Hispanic	13%
African American	14%
Males	38% (full-time)
Females	62% (full-time)

Source: National Center for Education Statistics (2012a).

(Continued)

(Continued)

One result of lower high school graduation rates and disillusion with education among males is that higher education is experiencing "feminization." Women have surpassed men in college completion with a 58% completion rate in 6 years, while males had a 53% rate of completion (National Center for Education Statistics 2012c; Pollard 2011). Men, regardless of race or class, get lower grades, take more time to graduate, and are less likely to get a bachelor's degree (Lewin 2006). However, men from the highest income group attend college at a slightly higher rate than women in that group, and men from low-income families— disproportionately African American and Hispanic—are the most underrepresented in higher education. The gender gap in favor of females has been most pronounced among low-income whites and Hispanics.

The gender gap in college admissions favors females, and by 2020 is predicted to be 58.6% women and 41.4% men (Hennigan 2012). However, it is actually harder for women to get into college since many more women than men are applying. This trend has been most pronounced among low-income whites, Hispanics, and black males. The imbalance is of such concern to college admissions officers that some colleges are turning away more qualified females in favor of males (Britz 2006). Some colleges are even adding activities such as football to attract more male students ("Colleges' Gender Gap" 2010).

What is the big deal? The issue is the changing job market and who will have the training to get the jobs. As more high tech and white collar workers are needed, those without higher education lose. Boys are not getting the education they need to advance themselves and to help the society. Concern about boys is a relatively new twist in the equity issue. Ultimately, educators hope to create an educational system that equally benefits all groups.

to teacher burnout. U.S. teachers are held accountable for students' progress as measured on standardized tests, as well as being tested on their own competency to determine their knowledge and skills (Dworkin and Tobe 2012).

In Japan, where education is considered extremely important for training future generations, teachers are treated with great respect and honor. They receive salaries competitive with those in industry and professions such as law and medicine (Ballantine and Hammack 2012). In Europe, many high schools are organizationally like universities. Teachers think of themselves as akin to professors. By contrast, studies in Australia and the United States show teachers feel they are unappreciated (Saha and Dworkin 2006). In the United States, secondary teachers think of themselves as more like middle school teachers than like university professors (Legters 2001). The organizational context of the teachers' work is a key source of problems. Overcoming poor social standing and lack of respect for teaching require better recruiting, training, and upgrading the status of teachers (Ingersoll and Merrill 2012).

Thinking Sociologically

Who should enforce high teacher standards—the federal, state, or local government? Teacher unions? Community interest groups? Who should decide what these standards are?

Administrators: The Managers of the School System. Key administrators—superintendents, assistant superintendents, principals and assistant principals, and headmasters and headmistresses—hold the top positions in the educational hierarchy of local schools. They are responsible for a long list of tasks: issuing budget reports; engaging in staff negotiations; hiring, firing, and training staff members; meeting with parents; carrying out routine approval of projects; managing public relations; preparing reports for boards of directors, local education councils, legislative bodies, and national agencies; keeping up with new regulations; making recommendations regarding the staff; and many other tasks.

Status holders in schools follow many rules and norms, some written and some not. The informal system is as important a part of the educational organization as formal rules, as we will see.

The Informal System: What Really Happens Inside Schools?

The informal system of schooling includes the unspoken, unwritten, implicit norms of behavior that we learn in classrooms and from peers, whether in kindergarten or in college. We will discuss schools as complex formal organizations below, but every organization also has an informal system. The informal system does not appear in written goal statements or course syllabi but nevertheless influences our experiences in school in important ways. Dimensions of the

Dropouts

Schools have a formal structure and a culture that affect the classroom. Note the arrangement of desks and the norm of raising a hand before a student may speak. Yet this is far from a universal pattern in schools in North America or around the globe. The formal system is only part of the classroom environment, for every school and classroom also has an informal culture.

Four-year-old preschoolers recite the Pledge of Allegiance. Developing patriotism is part of the implicit and informal curriculum of schools.

informal system include the educational climate, the value climate, and the hidden curriculum within a classroom. Here we focus on the hidden curriculum.

The *hidden curriculum* refers to the implicit "rules of the game" that students learn in school (Snyder 1971). It includes everything the student learns in school that is not explicitly taught, such as unstated social and academic norms. Students have to learn and respond to these to be socially acceptable and to succeed in the education system (Snyder 1971).

Children worldwide begin learning what is expected of them in preschool and kindergarten, providing the basis for schooling in the society (Neuman 2005). For example, Gracey describes early school socialization as "academic boot camp." Kindergarten teachers teach children to follow rules, to cooperate with each other, and to accept the teacher as the boss who gives orders and controls how time is spent (Gracey 1967). All of this is part of what young children learn; lessons are instilled in students even though it is not yet the formal curriculum of reading, writing, and arithmetic. These less formal messages form the hidden curriculum, an alternative set of "three Rs"—rules, routines, and regulations. Sometimes being tardy has a bigger impact on grades than whether one has actually learned the material—as some children can face failure for being late more than five times even if they score 90% on the exams.

For conflict theorists, the hidden curriculum is a social and economic agenda that maintains class differences. More is expected of elites, and they are given greater responsibility and opportunities for problem solving that result in higher

achievement (Brookover and Erickson 1975). Many working-class schools stress order and discipline, teaching students to obey rules and to accept their lot as responsible, punctual workers (Willis 1979). All of this brings us to a consideration of the formal organizational aspects of education—the rules, routines, regulations, and statuses.

Thinking Sociologically

What examples of the informal system can you see in the courses you are currently taking? How do these norms and strategies affect your learning experience?

After the School Bell Rings: Meso-Level Analysis

Schools can be like mazes, with passages to negotiate, hallways lined with pictures and lockers, and classrooms that set the scene for the educational process. Schools are mazes in a much larger sense as well. They involve complex interwoven social systems at the meso level where we encounter the formal organization of the school bureaucracy. The following sections focus on the formal systems, bureaucracy, and decision making in educational institutions.

Formal Education Systems

Formal education came into being in the Western world in 16th-century Europe when other social, political, economic, and religious institutions required new skills and knowledge

Hidden Curriculum

that families did not necessarily possess. Schools were seen as a way for Catholics to indoctrinate people to religious faith and for Lutherans to teach people to read so they could interpret the Bible for themselves. The first compulsory education system was in a Lutheran monastery in Germany in 1619. By the 19th century, schooling was seen as necessary to teach the European lower classes better agricultural methods, skills for the rapidly growing number of factory jobs, national loyalty, and obedience to authorities (Gatto 2003).

After 1900, national school systems were common in Europe and its colonial outposts. These systems shared many common organizational structures, curricula, and methods, as nations borrowed ideas from other countries. The Prussian model, with strict discipline and ties to the military, became popular in Europe in the 1800s, for example, and the two-track system of education that developed—one for the rich and one for the poor—existed worldwide.

Industrializing societies required workers with reading and math skills; today this includes electronic and technological skills. Schooling that formerly served only the elite gradually became available to the masses, and some societies began to require schooling for basic literacy (usually third-grade level). Schools emerged as major formal organizations and eventually developed extensive bureaucracies. The postwar period from 1950 to 1970 brought about a rapid rise in education worldwide with worldwide enrollment in primary schooling jumping from 36% to 84% and secondary enrollments going from 13% to 36% (Boli 2002). Figure 11.1 shows trends since 1970, with worldwide primary schooling up to 90% by 2009 and secondary schooling reaching 68% (UNESCO Institute for Statistics 2012).

Sometimes, differing goals for educational systems lead to conflict. What need, for example, does a subsistence farmer in Nigeria or Kenya have for Latin? Yet, Latin was often imposed as part of the standard curriculum in colonized nations. Many countries have revised curricula based on goals and needs of agriculturally based economies.

The Bureaucratic School Structure

The meso-level formal bureaucratic atmosphere that permeates many schools arose because it was cost-effective, efficient, and productive. Bureaucracy provided a way to document and process masses of students coming from different backgrounds. Recall Weber's bureaucratic model of groups and organizations, discussed in Chapter 5:

1. Schools have a *division of labor* among administrators, teachers, students, and support personnel. The roles associated with the statuses are part of the school structure. Individual teachers or students hold these roles for a limited time and are replaced by others coming into the system.

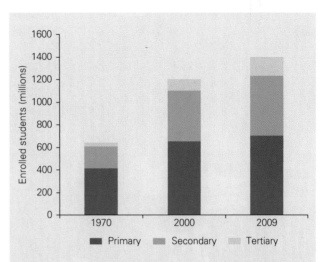

Figure 11.1 Number of Students (in Millions) Worldwide Enrolled in School From Primary to Tertiary Education, 1970, 2000, and 2009

Source: United Nations Educational, Scientific and Cultural Organization. 2012. *World Atlas of Gender Equality in Education* (p. 9). Retrieved January 27, 2013 (http://www .uis.unesco.org/Education/Documents/unesco-world-atlas-gender-education-2012.pdf).

2. The *administrative hierarchy* incorporates a chain of command and channels of communication.

3. Specific *rules and procedures* in a school cover everything from course content to discipline in the classroom and use of the schoolyard.

4. Personal relationships are downplayed in favor of *formalized relations* among members of the system, such as placement on the basis of tests and grading.

5. *Rationality* governs the operations of the organization; people are hired and fired on the basis of their qualifications and how well they do their jobs (Weber 1947).

One result of bureaucracy is that impersonal rules can lock people into rigid behavior patterns, leading to apathy and alienation (Kozol 2006; Sizer 1984; Waters 2012). Children like Tomás in the opening example do not fit into neat cubbyholes that bureaucratic structures invariably create. These children view school not as a privilege but as a requirement imposed by an adult world. Caught between the demands of an impersonal bureaucracy and goals for their students, teachers cannot always give every child the personal help she or he needs. Thus, we see that organizational requirements of educational systems at a meso level can influence the personal student-teacher relationship at the micro level.

 Educational Stratification   Bureaucracy

These chairs represent the bureaucracy or hierarchy of the school, with every student treated alike and facing the teacher. Look through other photos in this chapter, especially photos from Global South countries. Do you notice anything about the arrangement of students that suggests differences in relationships in the school?

Educational Decision Making at the Meso Level

Who should have the power to make decisions about what children learn? In Africa, Asia, Japan, Latin America, and many European countries, centralized national ministries of education determine educational standards and funding for the whole country. By contrast, some heterogeneous societies, such as Canada, Israel, and the United States, with many different racial, ethnic, regional, and religious subcultures, have more local autonomy in decision making. Teachers, administrators, school boards, parents, and interest groups all claim the right to influence the curriculum. Consider the following example of influences from micro and macro levels on the meso-level educational organization.

Local-Level Influences. In U.S. communities, curriculum conflicts occur routinely over the selection of reading materials and sex education courses as well as over any content thought to contain obscenity, sex, nudity, political or economic bias, profanity, slang or nonstandard English, racism or racial hatred, and antireligious or presumed anti-American sentiment (Delfattore 2004; Goodman and Gonzalez 2012). For example, Family Friendly Libraries, an online grassroots interest group that started in Virginia, argues that the popular *Harry Potter* books should be banned from school libraries because the members of this group believe the series promotes the religion of witchcraft (DeMitchell and Carney 2005).

Banned book classics in the past have included the *Wizard of Oz* series, *Rumpelstiltskin*, *Anne Frank: The Diary of a Young Girl*, *Madame Bovary*, *The Grapes of Wrath*, *The Adventures of Huckleberry Finn*, Shakespeare's *Hamlet*, Chaucer's *The Miller's Tale*, and Aristophanes's *Lysistrata* (Ballantine and Hammack 2012). Table 11.2 shows the most frequently challenged books in 2012. Off the list that

Table 11.2 The 10 Most Challenged Books of 2012

	Title	*Reason for Banning*
1	*Captain Underpants* (series) by Dav Pilkey	Offensive language, unsuited for age group
2	*The Absolutely True Diary of a Part-Time Indian* by Sherman Alexie	Offensive language, racism, sexually explicit, unsuited for age group
3	*Thirteen Reasons Why* by Jay Asher	Drugs/alcohol/smoking, sexually explicit, suicide, unsuited for age group
4	*Fifty Shades of Grey* by E. L. James	Offensive language, sexually explicit
5	*And Tango Makes Three* by Peter Parnell and Justin Richardson	Homosexuality, unsuited for age group
6	*The Kite Runner* by Khaled Hosseini	Homosexuality, offensive language, religious viewpoint, sexually explicit
7	*Looking for Alaska* by John Green	Offensive language, sexually explicit, unsuited for age group
8	*Scary Stories* (series) by Alvin Schwartz	Unsuited for age group, violence
9	*The Glass Castle* by Jeannette Walls	Offensive language, sexually explicit
10	*Beloved* by Toni Morrison	Sexually explicit, religious viewpoint, violence

Source: American Library Association (2013).

Note: For the top 100 banned books, go to http://www.ala.org/bbooks/bannedbooksweek.

Trading Schools

year but on for several years past were *The Catcher in the Rye* by J. D. Salinger and *Of Mice and Men* by John Steinbeck (American Library Association 2013).

National-Level Influences. Whether or not the national government should control education is a question in all societies. Because the U.S. Constitution leaves education in the hands of each state, the involvement of the federal government has been more limited than in most countries. Yet, the federal government wields enormous influence through its power to make federal funds available for special programs, such as mathematics and science, reading, special education, or school lunch programs. The government may withhold funds from schools that are not in compliance with federal laws and the U.S. Constitution. For example, the federal government, courts, and public opinion forced all-male military academies to become coeducational, despite the schools' resistance to such change. School changes as a result of the Civil Rights Act and the Americans with Disabilities Act are other examples of federal government influence on local schools through the enforcement of federal laws. Schools have had to accommodate people with various disabilities—people who in the past would have been left out of the system. With their classroom experiences and working with other teachers and children, the differently abled can participate fully in society. However, as the next "Sociology in Our Social World" shows, this process is not always smooth.

Thinking Sociologically

The discussion in this section demonstrates that educational needs at the micro (individual) level, the meso (institutional or ethnic group) level, and the macro (national) level can be very different. This raises the question of who makes decisions and whether individual needs or societal needs take precedence. Where do you think the primary authority for decision making should be—at the local, state, or national level? Why?

In addition to the structural features of schools as organizations and part of the institutional structure of society, education interplays with national and global forces in interesting and complex ways. We turn next to a macro-level analysis.

Education, Society, and the Road to Opportunity: The Macro Level

In Dalton, Georgia, Latinos make up over half the school-age population. In the school that researcher Hector Tobar visited there, 80% of the student body was Hispanic. The town has been unable to recruit bilingual teachers to this rural community, so the community sends the teachers to Mexico to

Sociology in Our Social World

Disability and Inequality

by Robert M. Pellerin

Living with a visual disability for over 40 years has provided me with lived experience. I also did research on experiences of others with disabilities as part of my PhD research. My results show that having a disability puts people at a disadvantage in education, employment, attitudes of others toward those with disabilities, and personal relationships. Technologies for those with disabilities have advanced, legislation has been introduced and sometimes passed, and advocacy for rights abound, but I still have to remind others, including professionals, that due to my visual impairment some methods of communication, such as print media, do not work. Additionally, most of the technology from which those with visual impairment could benefit is unaffordable, and most mainstream companies do not include features that would make products disability-friendly. The bottom line is that many of us are ready, willing, and able to be productive citizens, but we are often precluded from positions because of our disabilities and difficulty obtaining accommodation.

 Special Education

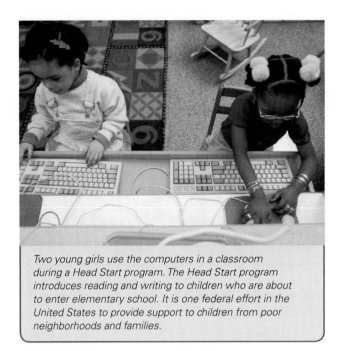

Two young girls use the computers in a classroom during a Head Start program. The Head Start program introduces reading and writing to children who are about to enter elementary school. It is one federal effort in the United States to provide support to children from poor neighborhoods and families.

learn Spanish. The principal at the elementary school admits that it is expensive, but the people in Dalton think it is important for their children to be bilingual and for everyone to be educated. The teachers do instruction in both English and Spanish. Dalton spends more than $7,400 per student, and it funds its schools entirely through income from the town's carpet factories (more than 100 of them) where most of the parents work. The cofounder of the Georgia Project, which assists new immigrants in their adjustment, believes that "the factories need the workers, and the workers come with families . . . Without good schools for the workers' children, the county would leave itself wide open to a whole host of social problems down the road. Giving Dalton's Mexican kids a decent education was the sensible thing to do, 'pure self-interest'" (Diggs 2011:59–60).

Other states have not been so accommodating—or pragmatic—with Mexican immigrants. In 2000, voters in Arizona approved the most restrictive English-only education law in the country, and since that time non-English speakers in Arizona public schools have been part of an English-only program, with no Spanish spoken in school. Mexican students start behind and stay behind according to teachers (Diggs 2011).

Educational decisions made by states and national governments affect individual families and their kids and the communities, states, and national economic and educational systems. Let us look at some implications of education for societies. This section focuses on the role of education in the stratification system. Although it has implications regarding individual families' chances to succeed, the reality is that education is deeply interwoven into the macro-level inequalities of the society.

Why Societies Have Education Systems: Macro-Level Theories

Wherever it takes place and whatever the content, education gives individuals the information and skills that their society regards as important and prepares them to live and work in their society. Education plays a more major role in the lives of children in some societies. For example, village children in Global South countries around the world go to the community school, tablets in hand, but when the family needs help in the fields or with child care, older children often stay at home. Even though attending several years of school is mandated by law in most countries, not all people become literate. Even transportation to schools can be an issue, with children in Myanmar crowding onto a gondola and youngsters in school buses in India having four passengers per small bench. Learning to survive—how to grow crops, care for the home, treat diseases, and make clothing—takes most of an individual's available time and energy.

Functionalist Perspective on the Purposes of Education. Functional theorists argue that both formal and informal education serve certain crucial purposes in society, especially as societies modernize. The functions of education as a social institution are summarized in Figure 11.2 on page 324. Note that some functions are planned and formalized (manifest functions) whereas others are not planned—informal results of the educational process (latent functions).

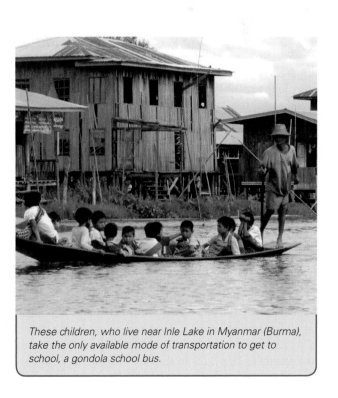

These children, who live near Inle Lake in Myanmar (Burma), take the only available mode of transportation to get to school, a gondola school bus.

 Immigration and Education School Reform

Manifest Functions (Planned and formalized)

- Socialize children to be productive members of society.
- Select and train individuals for positions in society.
- Promote social participation, change, and innovation.
- Enhance personal independence and social development.

Latent Functions (unplanned and informal)

- Confine and supervise underage citizens.
- Weaken parental controls over youths.
- Provide opportunities for peer cultures to develop.
- Provide contexts for the development of friendships and mate selection.

Figure 11.2 Key Functions of Education

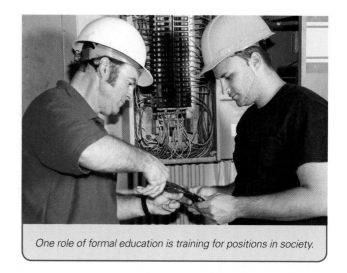

One role of formal education is training for positions in society.

Let us consider several manifest functions of education:

1. *Socialization: Teaching Children to Be Productive Members of Society.* Societies use education to pass on essential information of a culture—especially the values, skills, and knowledge necessary for survival. This process occurs sometimes in formal classrooms and other times in informal places. In postindustrial societies, family members cannot teach all the skills necessary for survival. Formal schooling emerged as a meso-level institution to meet the needs of macro-level industrial and postindustrial societies, furnishing the specialized training required by rapidly growing and changing technology.

2. *Selecting and Training Individuals for Positions in Society.* Students take standardized tests, receive grades at the end of the term or the year, and ask teachers to write recommendation letters. These activities are part of the selection process prevalent in competitive societies with formal educational systems. Individuals accumulate *credentials*—grade point averages, standardized test scores, and degrees that determine the colleges or job opportunities available to them, the fields of study or occupations they can pursue, and ultimately their positions in society. In some societies, educational systems enact this social function through tracking, ability grouping, grade promotion and retention, high-stakes and minimum-competency testing, and pull-out programs that contribute to job training, such as vocational education and service learning.

Thus, education outfits people for making a living in their society and contributing to the economy. Individual, family, community, state, and national income and standard of living are linked to the level of education of the citizenry. For example, Map 11.2 in the next "Engaging Sociology"

indicates the distribution of college degrees in the United States, a macro-level factor.

3. *Promoting Change and Innovation.* In multicultural societies such as Israel, France, and England, schools help assimilate immigrants by teaching them the language and customs, along with strategies for reducing intergroup tensions. In Israel, for example, many recent Jewish immigrants from Africa and Russia work hard to master Hebrew and to move successfully through the Israeli educational system. In most societies, providing educational opportunity to all groups is a challenge, but effective social participation requires education.

Institutions of higher education are expected to generate new knowledge, technology, and ideas and to produce students with up-to-date skills and knowledge to lead industry and other key institutions in society. In our high-tech age, critical thinking and analytical skills are more essential for problem solving than rote memorization, and this fact is reflected in curriculum change.

India has top-ranked technology institutes, and the highly skilled graduates are employed by multinational companies around the world. Companies in Europe and the United States send information to India for processing and receive it back the next morning because of the time difference. Well-trained, efficient engineers and computer experts working in India for lower wages than workers in many highly developed countries have become an important part of the global economy (Friedman 2005).

4. *Enhancing Personal and Social Development.* Do you remember your first day of elementary school? For many it marks a transition between the intimate world of the family and an impersonal school world that emphasized discipline, knowledge and skills, responsibility, and obedience. In school, children learn that they are no longer accepted

Engaging Sociology

Consequences of High or Low Numbers of Bachelor's Degrees

Study the map below and answer the following questions.

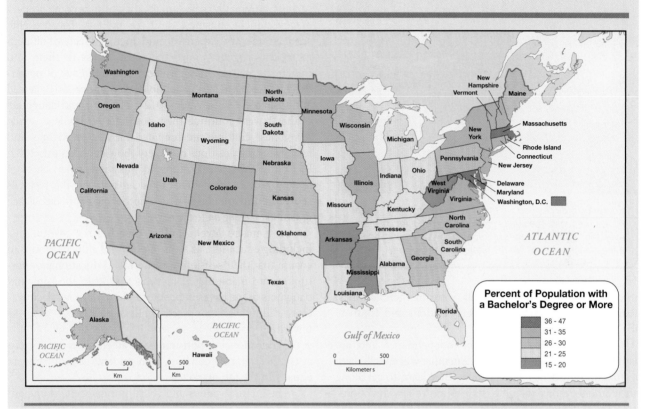

Map 11.2   Percentage of the U.S. Population Holding a Bachelor's Degree or Higher

Source: StateMaster.com (2013).

Engaging With Sociological Data

1. How does your region and your state rank on the number of bachelor's degrees awarded?

2. How might the economy of a state be affected when an especially low percentage of the population has a college degree?

3. What kinds of businesses, industries, or professionals are more likely to locate in a state with a very high percentage of its population having a college education?

4. How might the politics, the health care system, or scientific research be influenced by high or low levels of education within the state?

5. Look at the states that have especially high or especially low levels of the population with college degrees. What might be some causes of these high or low rates of college graduation? Some results? Check the statistics on your state or province.

6. What else can we learn or do you notice when studying the map? What questions does this map raise?

Education provides hope in this refugee camp in the Central African Republic. The adults created this school for children, even though families often lack food. They view education as a functional necessity for the future of their children.

unconditionally as they typically were in their families. Rather, they must meet certain expectations and compete for attention and rewards.

In school, children develop independence and are taught social skills and ethical conduct that will enable them to function in society. For example, they learn to get along with others, resolve disputes, stay in line, follow directions, obey the rules, take turns, be kind to others, be neat, tell the truth, listen, plan ahead, work hard, meet deadlines, and so on. Children worldwide begin learning what is expected of them in family, preschool, and kindergarten, providing the basis for schooling in each society (Neuman 2005).

Latent functions may be just as important to the society as manifest functions. Schools keep children off the streets until they can be absorbed into productive roles in society. They provide young people with a place to congregate and interact among themselves, fostering a "youth culture" of music, fashion, slang, dances, dating, and cliques or gangs. At the ages when social relationships are being established, especially with the opposite sex, schools are the central meeting place for the young—a kind of mate selection market. Education also weakens parental control over youths, helps them begin the move toward independence, and provides experience in large, impersonal secondary groups.

Conflict Perspective on Education and Stratification.
A small percentage of fortunate students around the world receive elite educations, but many others do not. Critics of functionalism emphasize the role of education in social stratification and competition between groups. They focus

on the impact education or lack thereof has on children's life chances and unequal opportunity in society.

Attendance at elite high schools is a means of attaining high social status. Graduates of British "public" schools (similar to U.S. private or preparatory schools), American preparatory (prep) schools, and private international high schools attend the best universities and become leaders of government, business, and the military. Because elite schools are very expensive and highly selective, affluent members of society have the most access to them and thereby perpetuate class privilege and influence of powerful elites (Howard and Gaztambide-Fernandez 2010; Persell and Cookson 1985; Wade 2012). The sons and daughters of the "haves" continue their positions of privilege, while lower-class children are prepared for less prestigious and less rewarding positions in society (Bowles and Gintis 2002; R. Collins 2004). According to this view, when elites of society protect their educational advantages, the result is **reproduction of class**—*the socioeconomic positions of one generation passing on to the next.*

At a macro level, conflict theorists see institutions, including education, as tools of powerful affluent groups to ensure that their self-interests are met. Educational opportunities are manipulated in ways that keep the sons and daughters of the haves in positions of privilege, while lower-class children are prepared for less prestigious and less rewarding positions in society. If schools do not provide equal educational opportunities for all children in a society, as conflict theorists contend, then students cannot compete equally in the job market.

The cultural values and social norms of the dominant group, such as ideas of etiquette, proper ways of speaking and writing, and notions of deference to superiors, are transmitted to all social classes and legitimated through formal schooling. Other definitions of reality from other ethnic or socioeconomic groups are marginalized. Studies comparing working-class schools with upper-middle-class schools and private schools with public schools support this view, revealing structural differences in the ways schools are organized that reinforce class differences, especially among the poorest children (Kozol 2005, 2012). According to conflict theorists, this process enhances power and confirms the privileges of the dominant group. The education system is not equally beneficial to all or even to the majority of citizens in society. In addition, private schools sometimes become sanctuaries for those who do not want race- and class-integrated schools, perpetuating religious, economic, and racial segregation.

With elite school and choice plans in some schools, critics fear that public schools might be left with the least capable students and teachers, further stratifying an already troubled system. This issue was at the root of the Chicago teachers' union strike in September 2012 that closed down the schools for over a week (Chubb and Moe 1990; Tareen and Keyser 2012).

Zimbabwe once had one of the best education systems in Africa, but after severe economic crises in the country, educational conditions have declined rapidly. Still, some children are privileged over other children, who do not get any education. This system that provides education only for the privileged protects the interests of the elite, according to conflict theorists.

Having explored some lenses through which sociologists analyze educational systems, we now focus on the problem of equal opportunity in schools.

Thinking Sociologically

Consider the community in which you went to high school. Do you think the education there enhances upward social mobility and serves all students and the community or serves the affluent, reproducing social Class and training people to fulfill positions at the same level as their parents, or some combination? Explain.

Can Schools Bring About Equality in Societies?

Equal opportunity exists when all people have an equal chance of achieving high socioeconomic status in society regardless of their class, ethnicity or race, or gender (Riordan 2004). James Coleman describes the meaning and goals of equal educational opportunity:

- To provide a common curriculum for all children regardless of background
- To ensure that children from diverse backgrounds attend the same school
- To provide equality within a given locality (Coleman 1968, 1990)

Equal opportunity means that children are provided with equal facilities, financing, and access to school

programs. Schools in poor neighborhoods or in rural villages in the United States and around the world, however, often lack the basics—safe buildings, school supplies and books, and funds to operate. Lower-class minority students who live in poor areas fall disproportionately at the bottom of the educational hierarchy. Many children face what seem to be insurmountable barriers to educational success: poverty, lack of health care and immunizations, and other disadvantages that result in increased school absences or dropping out (Kozol 2012; Noguera 2011). These conditions at home and in neighborhoods affect children's achievement in school and test scores (Boger and Orfield 2009; Coleman 1990). Integration of schools, often achieved by busing students to other schools and magnet school programs, became the controversial methods of providing equal opportunity. However, many scholars agree that schools alone cannot create equal opportunity (Jencks 1972).

Who Gets Ahead and Why? The Role of Education in Stratification

Education is supposed to be a *meritocracy*, a social group or organization in which people are allocated to positions according to their abilities and credentials as in level of education attained. This, of course, is consistent with the principles of a meritocratic social system where the most qualified person is promoted and decisions are impersonal and based on "credentials" (Charles, Roscigno, and Torres 2007). Still, in societies around the world, we see evidence that middle-class and elite children, especially boys in the Global South, receive more and better education than equally qualified children of a lower class. Children do not attend school on an equal footing, and in many cases, meritocracy does not exist. Conflict theorists, in particular, maintain that education creates and perpetuates inequality. The haves hold the power to make sure that institutions, including schools, serve their own needs and protect their access to privileges (Sadovnik 2007). Elite parents have social and cultural capital—language skills, knowledge of how the social system works, and networks—to ensure that their children succeed (Kao 2004).

Sources of Inequality. Three sources of inequality in schools—testing, tracking, and funding—illustrate how schools reproduce and perpetuate social stratification. They also give clues as to what might be done to minimize the repetitious pattern of poverty.

1. *Assessing Student Achievement.* Testing is one means of placing students in schools according to their achievement and merit and determining their progress. Yet many scholars including sociologists of education argue that standardized test questions, the vocabulary employed, and testing situations disadvantage lower-class, minority, and

Reproduction of Class

immigrant students, resulting in lower scores and relegating these students to lower tracks in the educational system. In addition, in the case of IQ tests, scientists know that intelligence is complex and that paper-and-pencil tests measure only selected types of intelligence (Gardner 1987, 1999; Smith 2008). Other scholars question whether the tests have hidden biases based on socioeconomic backgrounds. Higher-class students with strong schooling and enriched backgrounds generally score higher on achievement tests.

Nonetheless, testing is the means used to evaluate student achievement locally, nationally, and internationally. The U.S. Obama administration has broadened assessment to include factors in addition to test scores for placement of students. Table 11.3 in the next "Engaging Sociology" shows differences in ACT (American College Test) and SAT (Scholastic Assessment Test) scores depending on sex, race, and ethnic group. Answer the questions that are posed as you engage with the sociological data presented.

Engaging Sociology

Test Score Variations by Gender and Ethnicity

Evaluate your testing experiences and compare them to those of other groups.

Table 11.3   ACT and SAT Scores by Sex and Race/Ethnicity

ACT Scores: 2010	Average	SAT Scores: 2011	Average
Composite, total scores	21	SAT Writing, all students	489
Male	21.2	Male	482
Female	20.9	Female	496
White	22.3	White	516
Black/African American	16.9	Black/African American	417
American Indian/Alaska Native	19.0	American Indian/Alaska Native	465
Hispanic	18.6	Hispanic	444
Asian/Pacific Islander	23.4	Asian/Pacific Islander	528
SAT Scores: 2011	**Average**		
SAT Critical Reading, all students	497	SAT Math, all students	514
Male	500	Male	531
Female	495	Female	500
White	528	White	535
Black/African American	428	Black/African American	427
Hispanic	451	Hispanic	463
Asian/Pacific Islander	517	Asian/Pacific Islander	595
American Indian/Alaska Native	484	American Indian/Alaska Native	488

Source: National Center for Education Statistics (2011, 2012b).

Sociological Data Analysis:

1. Were your scores an accurate measure of your ability or achievement? Why or why not?

2. What other factors such as your gender or ethnicity enter in?

3. Have your scores affected your life chances? Are there ways in which you have been privileged or disprivileged in the testing process?

4. What might be some causes of the variation in test scores between groups or categories of students?

2. *Student Tracking. Tracking* (sometimes called *streaming*) places students in ability groups, presumably to allow educators to address students who have similar attainment in math, reading, or other subjects, or who have individual learning needs. It also contributes to the stratification process that perpetuates inequality. Research finds that tracking levels correlate directly with factors such as the child's class background and ethnic group, language skills, appearance, and other socioeconomic variables (Rosenbaum 1999; Wells and Oakes 1996). In other words, track placement is not always a measure of a student's ability but can be based on teachers' impressions or questionable test results. Over time, differences in children's achievement become reinforced. Research shows that students from lower social classes and minority groups are clustered in the lower tracks and complete fewer years of school, resulting in school failure in early adolescence (Oakes et al. 1997; Chen and Kaplan 2003; Zehr 2009).

3. *School Funding.* The amount of money available to fund schools and the sources providing it affect the types of programs offered, an important issue for nations that must compete in the global social and economic system. Money for education comes in some societies from central governments and in others from a combination of federal, state, and local government and private sources, such as tuition, religious denominations, and philanthropies. In Uganda, for example, the government runs the schools, but most funding comes from tuition paid by each student or by the student's family. Whatever the source, schools sometimes face budget crises and must trim programs.

In the United States, unequal public school spending results from reliance on unequal local property taxes as well as state and federal funds. On average, local governments provide 44% of education funding for elementary and secondary school budgets from income taxes, corporate taxes, sales taxes, and fees. States provide about 47%, mostly from property taxes; however, this percentage is dropping with tight state budgets. About 10% of education funding comes from the federal government (New America Foundation 2012).

Spending is closely related to the racial and class composition of schools and to student achievement levels. Schools in low-income communities are particularly disadvantaged by smaller tax bases and fewer local resources (Condron and Roscigno 2003). Wealthier districts, on the other hand, can afford better education for their children because more money is collected from property taxes. Higher-class students have advantages not available in poor districts (*Education Week* 2011; Kozol 2005). Controversies over equitable school funding in the United States have reached the courtroom in a number of states (Reyes and Rodriguez 2004).

This is a somewhat affluent school in South Africa. Children like this, whose parents can afford to send them to school, will likely grow up with enough education to have better economic prospects.

Education and Social Policy Issues

What path should nations take to improve their education systems? In the United States there is constant debate about fair and equitable funding policies, about the best methods of teaching children, and about accountability. At the core of these issues lies the question of who should make decisions about education. Should the centralized leadership of the federal government be dominant so that there is some coherence and consistency in educational policy across states? Should states that provide the majority of funding for schools determine educational policies? Should local districts have most power since they know the local situation and needs?

Since 1965 and the establishment of the Department of Education in the United States, each president has put his mark on the U.S. education system. Although the federal government pays only about 10% of school funding, federal policies have a major impact on local school decisions.

The greatest barrier to equal education in the 21st century, both within and between countries, may prove to be socioeconomic, with many minorities falling into the lower classes. The value of early childhood education for low-income children has been established, but access is far from universal. Still, applied sociologist Geoffrey Canada has had success with implementing programs for poor children in Harlem, from preschool to high school, as discussed in the next "Sociologists in Action" on page 330.

Global Policy Issues in Education

Most societies view the education and training of young people as an economic investment in the future. Countries

Sociologists in Action   Geoffrey Canada and the Harlem Children's Zone

The United States is "the land of opportunity," but not for residents of Harlem, according to Geoffrey Canada. In Harlem the goal is to avoid being beaten, shot, or raped. Canada has an ambitious agenda—to break the cycle of poverty and have all young people in the Harlem Children's Zone graduate from college.

Canada's life experience prepared him to work as a social activist and educator. He grew up in the South Bronx, was raised by a single mom, and then had a lucky break. He moved to the suburbs with his grandparents, and from there he received a college degree from Bowdoin College and a master's from the Harvard Graduate School of Education.

Having been given an opportunity for education, he is now giving back to the community. As president and CEO of the Harlem Children's Zone in New York, he works with students to increase high school and college graduation rates. The Harlem Children's Zone started out as a 24-block area of Harlem, but has grown to 97 blocks due to its success. In the 97-block neighborhood, his center follows the academic careers of youth, providing social, medical, and educational services that are free to the 10,000 children who live in the Zone. He has built his own charter school, the Promise Academy, with 1,200 students in grades K–10, soon to be K–12. Tuition to the school is free, and admission is done by lottery. For those who do not win the school's admissions lottery, Harlem Children's Zone still provides services to most people in the Zone, including parenting classes, preschool language classes, school preparation classes, and SAT tutoring.

The Promise Academy has long days and a short summer vacation, a dress code, and strict discipline. The student-teacher ratio is 6 to 1. For students who work hard and achieve, there are rewards. Canada is not apologetic about "buying" the students' cooperation. Some get free trips to Disneyland for good grades, and others get paid for good high school grades.

The Zone is not cheap to run, but Canada points out that the costs of a child ending up in the criminal justice system are much greater, for if a child fails, the community and society have also failed. Therefore, he believes the investment is sound. The program costs $76 million a year, or $5,000 per child. Much of the funding comes from the business community and Wall Street. That may sound like a lot of money, but the national average in 2006 was over $9,000 per student, and the average expenditure per student for the state of New York was nearly $15,000 (U.S. Census Bureau 2008). To test the effectiveness of the school and program, a Harvard economics professor studied the data from tests of achievement and other academic indicators. He found that the Promise Academy elementary school had closed the gap in math and reading between its students and students in white or mixed schools, and outperformed many of the comparison schools. Those middle school students who started the Promise Academy were behind, but they caught up to students in comparison schools. According to this evaluator, the results were "stunning." However, recent evaluations indicate that in addition to the creative teaching and learning, some classrooms are subdued with students reading from textbooks. While the graduation rate is 98%, only 46% of students are deemed college ready (Insideschools 2013).

The project has been called "one of the biggest social experiments of our time" (Tough 2004, 2008). Because of the proven success of the Harlem Children's Zone, President Obama has taken notice and plans to replicate the model in 20 other cities across the nation.

Geoffrey Canada received his undergraduate degree from Bowdoin College and his master's in education from Harvard. He has written several books and articles, including Reaching Up for Manhood: Transforming the Lives of Boys in America (1998).

with capitalist economic systems are more likely to have an educational system that stresses individualism and competition, pitting students against one another for the best grades and the best opportunities. The elites often ensure that their own children get a very different education than the children of the laboring class. Socialist and traditional economic systems often encourage cooperation and collaboration among students, with the collective needs of society viewed as more important than the needs of individuals. The social economic values of the society are reflected

in approaches to learning and in motivation of students (Rankin and Aytaç 2006).

Political and economic trends outside of a country can also have an impact on the educational system within the country. Examples of external influences include world educational and technological trends, new inventions, and new knowledge.

Education of Girls Around the Globe. In rich Global North countries, girls generally have the same chance to obtain an education as boys. The picture is different in Global South countries. An important factor in access to education is where one lives. In the country of Niger, Africa, 68% of boys and 57% of girls attend primary school (UNESCO Institute for Statistics 2011), but only 12% of girls in rural areas are in primary school, compared to 83% in the capital city, Niamey (Sperling 2005).

The availability of clean drinking water is a major issue in the Global South. Because women and girls must spend as much as six hours a day carrying water to their homes (26% of a woman's day in Africa), the daughters are needed to care for children. When wells were built so that usable water was more accessible, the school attendance of girls immediately increased by 11% because of better sanitation and local access to water. Indeed, research by WaterAid estimates that in the Global South, 443 million school days are lost each year due to water-related diseases. Water is just one of the many impediments to girls' education (Foundation Source Access 2013; WaterAid 2013).

What is clear is that when girls are educated, the consequences are great: "What is striking is the breadth of benefits derived from educating girls—not only economic benefits in terms of higher wages, greater agricultural productivity, and faster economic growth, but also health benefits" (Sperling 2006:274). More educated girls and women tend to be healthier; have lower fertility rates that provide for lower maternal, infant, and child mortality; have greater protection against HIV/AIDS; have increased labor force participation and earnings; provide better health care and education to their children; lift households out of poverty; and have a greater ability to pass on these benefits to the next generation (National Security Network 2011; World Bank 2012).

Thinking Sociologically

How can education of girls improve the lives of others in society? How might education be affected by global events, such as a war or a worldwide economic recession?

The Future of Education in the Global System. The search for the best model of education is never-ending. School systems around the world are under pressure to meet the diverse needs of both the societies as a whole and their individual citizens. A major concern in Global North countries as they move into the information age is this: What will become of those students who do not complete enough education to fit into the technological and economic needs in the 21st century? High school used to prepare most young people for a job and marriage. By the 1990s, in the Global North high school was preparation for college, which was itself necessary to find a decent job

Computer and Internet skills are essential to success in college and most jobs in this globalized social world. Many courses, even degrees, can now be done online.

In Liberia, as elsewhere around the world, an education is necessary as the economy is globalized and skills in literacy and numeracy become critical to hopes of prosperity. Students work in this school by candlelight.

in the globalizing world. Although the value of going into debt in the United States to receive a college education is debated today, most studies show that those with college degrees receive much higher salaries and lifelong earnings (McArdle 2012). In the United States, educators, corporations, wealthy individuals, and philanthropies—concerned that minority groups are falling behind—support special programs to reduce the technological divide between the haves and have-nots, the latter composed of poor and minority families (Attewell 2001).

The role of technology in the future of education is expanding, and the technological cybergap may be closing in some parts of the world. However, there are differences in the implementation of new innovations and ways computers are used. Global South countries will need to invest in Internet

bandwidth and other technologies to allow citizens to close the gap, and this is slowly being achieved as fiber-optic cable is laid various places around the world (Science Daily 2011a). Some predict that e-texts will replace most paper texts within five years in Global South countries (TechWench 2010).

In the process of governments developing their educational policies, we again see the interconnections of our social world. Curricula respond to global events and international markets and are also shaped by micro-level effectiveness or ineffectiveness of teachers and students in individual classrooms. Another core institution that also socializes individuals, answers the question of "why," and provides hope for the future is focused mostly in addressing the question of meaning in life. We turn now to a sociological perspective on religion.

Religion: The Search for Meaning

Abu Salmaan, a Muslim father and shopkeeper in Syria, prays frequently in keeping with the commands of the holy book of this faith. Like his neighbors, when the call to prayer is heard, he comes to the village square, faces Mecca, and prostrates himself, with his head to the ground, to honor God and to pray for peace. Doing this five times a day is a constant reminder of his ultimate loyalty to God—whom he calls Allah. As part of the larger Abrahamic religious tradition (which includes Judaism, Christianity, and Islam), he believes in one God and accepts the Hebrew Bible and the authority of Jeremiah, Isaiah, Amos, and Jesus as prophets. He believes that God also revealed Truth in another voice—that of Muhammad. He is devoted, worships daily, gives generously to charities, and makes business decisions based on moral standards of a God-loving Muslim.

Trevor Weaver is a Presbyterian living in Louisville, Kentucky. He attends worship and prays to God in church and in emergencies when he feels helpless. Trevor had theological studies at a church-related college, and he has a strong knowledge of the scriptures. When he makes daily decisions, he thinks about the ethical implications of his behavior as "a member of the larger family of God." He opposes prayer in schools because this would make some children feel ostracized; he values diversity and acceptance of other traditions, and he believes each person needs to "work out his own theology." He thinks of himself as a person of faith, but his evangelical neighbor thinks he is a fallen soul.

Tuneq, knowledgeable Netsilik Eskimo hunter that he is, apologizes to the soul of the seal he has just killed. He shares the meat and blubber with his fellow hunters, and he makes sure that every part of the seal is used or consumed—skin, bones, eyes, tendons, brain, and muscles. If he fails to honor the seal by using every morsel, or if he violates a rule of hunting etiquette, an invisible vapor will come from his body and sink through the ice, snow, and water. This vapor will collect in the hair of Nuliajuk, goddess of the sea. In revenge, she will call the sea mammals to her so the people living on the ice above will starve. Inuit religion provides rules that help enforce an essential ecological ethic among these arctic hunters to preserve the delicate natural balance.

These are but three examples from the world's many and varied religious systems. What they have in common is that each system provides directions for appropriate and expected behaviors and serves as a form of social control for individuals within that society. Indeed, these directions are made *sacred,* a realm of existence different from mundane

Religion takes many forms and is expressed in many ways, but it is always about a sense of meaning. That sense of meaning generates sacredness and makes other aspects of life meaningful. Here a Jewish girl reads the Torah during her bat mitzvah, the initiation ceremony into the faith.

everyday life. Religion, according to Andrew M. Greeley, the well-known Catholic priest and sociologist, pervades the lives of people of faith. It cannot be separated from the rest of the social world (Greeley 1989). Sociologists are interested in these relationships—in the way social relationships and structures affect religion and in the consequences of religion for individuals and for society as a whole.

In this part of the chapter, we explore religion as a complex social phenomenon, one that is interrelated with other processes and institutions of society. We investigate what religion does for individuals, how individuals become religious, and how religion and modern societies interact.

What Does Religion Do for Us?

We began this section on religion by looking at examples of daily experiences in which religion and society have enormous power over people. Why do people engage in religious practices, beliefs, and organizations? In short, they find that religion meets some very basic needs.

Human questions about the meaning of life, the finality of death, or whether injustice and cruelty will ever be ended cannot normally be answered by science or by everyday experience. Religion helps explain the meaning of life, death, suffering, injustice, and events beyond our control. As sociologist Émile Durkheim pointed out, humans generally view such questions as belonging to a realm of existence different from the mundane or profane world of experience. He called this separate dimension the *sacred realm.* This sacred realm elicits feelings of awe, reverence, and even fear. It is viewed as being above normal inquiry and doubt. Religious guidelines, beliefs, and values dictate "rights and wrongs," provide answers to the big questions of life, and instill moral codes and ideas about the world in members of each society or subculture. For that reason, religions are extremely important in controlling everyday behavior of individuals (Ammerman 2009; Durkheim [1915] 2002, 1947).

Thus, religion is more than a set of beliefs about the supernatural. It often *sacralizes* (makes sacred and unquestionable) the culture in which we live, the class or caste position to which we belong, the attitudes we hold toward other people, and the morals to which we adhere. Religion is a part of our lifestyle, our gender roles, and our place in society. We are often willing to defend it with our lives. Many different people around the world believe quite as strongly as we do that they have found the Truth—and are willing to die for their faith.

Although the root causes of various wars such as those between Hindus and Muslims in India, Catholics and Protestants in Northern Ireland, and Sunnis and Shiites in several Muslim countries are often political and economic, religious differences help polarize we-versus-they sentiments. Such conflicts are never exclusively about religion, but religion can convince each antagonist that God is on its side. Religion is an integral part of most societies and is important in helping individuals define reality and answer difficult questions.

Thinking Sociologically

Consider your own religious tradition. Which of the purposes or functions of religion mentioned above does your religious faith address? If you are not part of a faith community or do not hold religious beliefs of a particular group, are there other beliefs or groups that fulfill these functions for you?

Components of Religion

Religion normally involves at least three components: a faith or worldview that provides a sense of meaning and purpose in life (which we will call the *meaning system*), a set of interpersonal relationships and friendship networks (which we will call the *belonging system*), and a stable pattern of roles, statuses, and organizational practices (which we will call the *structural system*) (Roberts and Yamane 2012).

Meaning System

The meaning system of a religion includes the ideas and symbols it uses to provide a sense of purpose in life and

to help explain why suffering, injustice, and evil exist. It provides a big picture to explain events that would otherwise seem chaotic and irrational. For example, although the loss of a family member through death may be painful, many people find comfort and hope and a larger perspective on life or on the idea of life after death.

Because each culture has different problems to solve, the precise needs reflected in the meaning system vary. Hence, different societies have developed different ways of answering questions and meeting needs. In agricultural societies, the meaning systems revolve around growing crops and securing the elements necessary for crops—water control, sunlight, and good soil. Among the Zuni of New Mexico and the Hopi of Arizona, water for crops is a critical concern. These Native American people typically grow corn in a climate that averages roughly 10 inches of rain per year, so it is not surprising that the central focus of the dances and the supernatural beings—*kachinas*—is to bring rain. In many societies, the death rate is so high that high fertility has been necessary to perpetuate the group. Thus, fertility goddesses take on great significance. In other societies, strong armies and brave soldiers have been essential to preserve the group from invading forces; hence, gods or rituals of war have been popular. Over time, meaning systems of religion have reflected needs of the societies in which the religion is practiced.

Belonging System

Belonging systems are profoundly important in most religious groups. Many people remain members of religious groups not so much because they accept the meaning system of the group but because that is where their belonging system—their friendship and kinship network—is found. Their religious group is a type of extended family. A prayer group may be the one area in their lives in which people can be truly open about their personal pain and feel safe to expose their vulnerabilities (Wuthnow 1994). Irrespective of the meaning system, a person's sense of identity may be very much tied up with being a Buddhist, a Christian, a Muslim, or a follower of some other faith tradition (Kosmin and Keysar 2009; C. Smith 2009).

The religious groups that grow the fastest are those that have devised ways to foster friendship networks within the group, including emphasis on *endogamy,* marrying within one's group. If a person is a member of a small group in which interpersonal ties grow strong—a church bridge club or a Quran study group—he or she is likely to feel a stronger commitment to the entire organization. The success of megachurches is due in part to their attention to the belonging system, making people feel they belong to smaller groups within the larger organization. In short, the belonging system refers to the interpersonal networks and

Faith

Burmese students from 5 to 11 years old pray together in Myawadi, Myanmar (formerly Burma). The sense of belonging and conforming to the group helps make the meaning system seem real.

the emotional ties that develop among adherents to a particular faith community.

Structural System

A religion involves a group of people who share a common meaning system. However, if each person interprets the beliefs in his or her own way and if each attaches his or her own meanings to the symbols, the meaning system becomes so individualized that *sacralization* (making sacred) of common values can no longer occur. Therefore, some system of control and screening of new revelations must be developed. Religious leaders in designated statuses must have the authority to interpret the theology and define the essentials of the faith. The group also needs methods of designating leaders, of raising funds to support their programs, and of ensuring continuation of the group. To teach the next generation the meaning system, members need to develop a formal structure to determine the content and form of their educational materials, and then they must produce and distribute them. If the religion is to survive past the death of a charismatic leader, it must undergo institutionalization. In other words, a *structural system* of established statuses, norms, ways to access resources, and routine procedures for addressing problems must be set up.

Religious institutions embrace several interrelated components: the meaning system, mostly operating at the micro level; the belonging system, critical at the micro level but also part of various meso-level organizations; and the structural system, which tends to have its major impact at the meso and macro levels. These may reinforce one another

and work in harmony toward common goals, or there may be conflict between them. When change occurs, it usually occurs because of disruption in one of the systems. A group cannot survive in the modern world unless it undergoes *routinization of charisma*. That is, the religious organization must develop established roles, statuses, groups, and routine procedures for making decisions and obtaining resources (Weber 1947).

At the local level, too, a formal religious structure develops, with committees doing specific tasks, such as overseeing worship, maintaining the building, recruiting religious educators, and raising funds. These committees report to an administrative board that works closely with the clergy (the ordained ministers) and has much of the final responsibility for the life and continued existence of the congregation. The roles, statuses, and committees make up the structural system. The structure is every bit as important as the meaning system if the group is to thrive. Most religious organizations are, among other things, bureaucracies, with the same sort of dysfunctions of any formal organization (as discussed in Chapter 5).

The three components of religion—meaning, belonging, and structure—are interconnected and interdependent. One member of a faith community may be committed to the meaning system, another to the belonging system through strong friendship networks, and a third to the structural system, making large financial donations to a congregation even though he or she rarely attends services. In most cases, however, commitment to one of these systems will reinforce commitment to the others. They usually go together. (See Figure 11.3.)

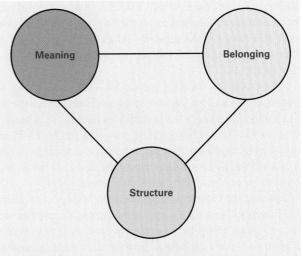

Figure 11.3 Three Components of Religion

Note: Religious commitment can involve any one or more of these dimensions of religion.

Thinking Sociologically

Think about the meaning, belonging, and structural systems of a religion with which you are familiar. How do these elements influence—and how are they influenced by—the larger social world, from the individual to national and global systems?

Becoming Part of a Faith Community: Micro-Level Analysis

We are not born religious, although we may be born into a religious group. We learn our religious beliefs through socialization, just as we learn our language, customs, norms, and values. Our family usually determines the religious environment in which we grow up, whether it is an all-encompassing message or a one-day-a-week lesson in religious socialization. We start imitating religious practices such as prayer before we understand these practices intellectually. Then, as we encounter the unexplainable events of life, religion is there to provide meaning. Gradually, religion becomes an ingrained part of many people's lives.

It is unlikely that we will adopt a religious belief that falls outside the religions of our society. For instance, if we are born in India, we will be raised in and around the Hindu, Muslim, and Sikh faiths. In most Arab countries, we will become Muslim; in South American countries, Catholic; and in many Southeast Asian countries, Buddhist. Indeed, although our religious affiliation may seem normal and typical to us, none of us is part of a religion that is held by a majority of the world's people, and we may in fact be part of a rather small minority religious group when we think in terms of the global population. Table 11.4 shows this vividly.

Learning the meaning system of a religious group is both a formal and an informal process. Formal teaching in most religions takes place primarily in the temple, church, or mosque. The formal teaching may take the form of bar or bat mitzvah classes, Sunday school, or parochial school in a madrassa. Informal religious teaching occurs when we observe others "practicing what they preach."

Again, the meaning (believing) and belonging systems are linked in important ways. Most people do not belong to a religious group because they believe, at least initially. Rather, they come to believe because they want to belong and are socialized to feel they are an integral part of the group (Greeley 1972; Roberts and Yamane 2012). People generally accept the explanation about death or injustice or suffering or gay rights provided by the religious group.

Table 11.4   Religious Membership Around the Globe

Religion	Membership (in millions)	Percentage of World Population
Christian (Total)	2,280.6	33.0
Roman Catholic	1,150.7	16.7
Independent	419.8	6.1
Protestant	370.7	5.4
Orthodox	270.2	3.9
Anglican	86.1	1.2
Unaffiliated	119.0	1.7
Muslim	1,553.2	22.5
Hindu	942.9	13.6
Nonreligious	659.8	9.6
Buddhist	462.6	6.7
Chinese Folk Religion	454.4	6.6
Atheist	137.6	2.0
Sikh	23.7	0.3
Jewish	14.8	0.2
Spiritist	13.7	0.2
Taoist	8.4	0.1
Baha'i	7.3	0.1
Confucianist	6.5	0.1
Jain	5.3	0.1
Shintoist	2.8	a
Zoroastrian	.2	a

Source: Barrett, Johnson, and Crossing. 2011. "2010 Annual Megacensus of Religion." *Time Almanac 2011.* Reprinted with permission from *Encyclopedia Britannica Almanac* 2011 Copyright © 2011 by Encyclopedia Britannica, Inc.

Note: Numbers add up to more than the total world population because many people identify themselves with more than one religious tradition. Thus, the percentages will also add up to more than 100%. Percentages are rounded.

a = Less than 0.05%.

They feel comfortable sharing similar feelings and beliefs with other believers.

Research on people who switch religious affiliations or join new religious movements indicates that loyalty to a friendship network usually comes first, followed by commitment to the meaning and structural systems. In many cases, accepting a new meaning system is the final stage rather than the initial stage of change (Roberts and Yamane 2012).

There is more fluidity in religious membership now than at any time in human history. Historically, most people stayed part of the same religious group for a lifetime. Studies show that 28% of U.S. citizens have left the faith in which they were raised, and 44% of Americans will change their religious affiliation in their lifetime, just as a very high percentage will change their place of residence, their jobs, and even their spouses (Pew Forum on Religion and Public Life 2012). In fact, the increase in cross-religious marriages is a factor in the religious switching, as 37% of current marriages involve spouses with different religious affiliations (Pew Forum on Religion and Public Life 2012). Change is becoming part of the norm in North America, particularly since World War II, and this is affecting religious affiliation as well. Still, the change is likely to be to a new branch of the same religion rather than to an entirely different religious tradition, and when it does involve a more major shift, it is usually because of the increased diversity of our society so that we know someone personally from the other faith tradition.

Because changing religious groups occurs most often through change of friendship networks, religious groups frequently try to control the boundaries and protect their members from outside influences. The Amish in the United States have done this by living in their own communities and attempting to limit schooling of their children by outside authorities. To help perpetuate religious beliefs and practices, most religious groups encourage endogamy, marrying within the group. For example, Orthodox Jews have food taboos and food preparation requirements that limit the likelihood they will share a meal with "outsiders."

Religious groups also try to socialize members to make sacrifices of time, energy, and financial resources on behalf of their faith. If one has sacrificed and has devoted one's resources and energy for a cause, one is likely to feel a commitment to the organization—the structural system (Kanter 2005; Sherkat and Ellison 1999). Many young men in the Church of Jesus Christ of Latter-day Saints (Mormons) devote two years of their lives to being missionaries, and young women devote one to one-and-a-half years. They must save money in advance to support themselves. This sacrifice of other opportunities and investment of time, energy, and resources in the church creates an intense commitment to the organization. Few of these young people later feel that they have wasted those years or that the investment was unwise. So commitment to the structural system is connected to strong commitment to the meaning and belonging systems.

The survival of a religious group depends in part on how committed its members are and whether they share freely of their financial and time resources. Most religious groups try, therefore, to socialize their members into commitment to the meaning system, the belonging system, and the structural system of their religion.

Thinking Sociologically

How did you or individuals you know become committed to a faith community? Did you or they think about the process as it occurred, or were you/they born into it?

Symbols and the Creation of Meaning: A Symbolic Interactionist Perspective

Dina is appalled as she looks around the Laundromat. The *gaje* (the term Roma use to refer to non-Roma) just do not seem to understand cleanliness. These middle-class North American neighbors of hers are very concerned about whether their clothes are *melalo*—dirty with dirt. By contrast, they pay no attention to whether they are *marime*—defiled or polluted in a spiritual sense. She watches in disgust as a woman not only places the clothing of men, women, and children in a single washing machine but also includes clothing from the upper and lower halves of bodies together. No respectable Roma (sometimes called Gypsies by outsiders) would allow such mixing, and if it did occur, the cloth could be used only as rags. The laws of spiritual purity make clear that the lower half of the body is defiled. Anything that comes in contact with the body below the waist or that touches the floor becomes *marime* and can never again be considered *wuzho*—truly "clean." Food that touches the floor becomes filthy and inedible.

Ideally, a Roma woman would have five separate washtubs for men's and women's upper-body and lower-body

A Romanian Roma woman uses different tubs to wash upper- and lower-body clothing and men's and women's apparel separately so they will not become spiritually defiled.

Biblical Law

clothing and children's clothing. Roma know too well that the spirit of Mamioro brings illness to homes that are *marime.* The lack of spiritual cleanliness of non-Roma causes Roma to minimize their contact with *gaje,* to avoid sitting on a chair used by a *gaje,* and generally to recoil at the thought of assimilation into the larger culture (Southerland 1986; Sway 1988). How we make sense of the world takes place through meaning systems, as illustrated in the above example. For the Roma, things have meaning in ways that differ from the ideas that are prominent in the larger society, and the different meanings result in different behaviors and sometimes separation between groups.

Symbolic interaction theory focuses on how people make sense of the meaning of things and how we construct our worlds. In an ambiguous situation, we seek help from others: Is the situation funny, scary, bizarre, normal, or mysterious? Think about how you feel attracted to, or perhaps put off by, someone who wears a cross as a necklace, an Orthodox Jewish man who wears a yarmulke to cover the crown of his head, or a Muslim woman with a head scarf. Symbols affect the way we feel about people and whether we are inclined to form a relationship. Symbols affect micro-level interaction. Note that a Muslim woman may wear a head scarf, and while she finds it a reassuring reminder of her family's long tradition, others may view it as a symbol of women's oppression or even find it a cause for hatred of the "other."

It is the meaning system that most interests symbolic interactionists—the worldview or conceptual framework by which people make sense of life and cope with suffering and injustice. Religious meaning systems are made up of three elements: myths, rituals, and symbols.

Myths are *stories that transmit values and embody ideas about life and the world.* When sociologists of religion use the word *myth,* they are not implying that the story is untrue. A myth may relate historical incidents that actually occurred, it may involve fictional events, or it may communicate abstract ideas such as reincarnation. Regardless of the literal truth or fiction of these stories, myths transmit values and a particular outlook on life. If a story such as the exodus from Egypt by ancient Hebrew people elicits some sense of sacredness, communicates certain values, and helps life make sense, then it is a myth. The Netsilik Eskimo myth of the sea goddess Nuliajuk (explained earlier in the chapter) reinforces and makes sacred the value of conservation in an environment of scarce resources. It provides messages for appropriate behavior in that group. Thus, whether a myth is factual or not is irrelevant. Myths are always "true" in some deeper metaphorical sense. Indeed, stories that are not true—in some deeper sense—are simply not "myths."

Rituals are *ceremonies or repetitive practices, often to invoke a sense of awe of the sacred and to make certain ideas sacred.* The ceremonies may include music, dancing, kneeling, praying, chanting, storytelling, and other symbolic acts. A number of religions, such as Islam, emphasize devotion to orthopraxy (conformity of behavior in rituals and in morality) more than orthodoxy (conformity to beliefs or doctrine) (D. Preston 1988; Tipton 1990). Praying five times a day while facing Mecca, mandated for the Islamic faithful, is an example of orthopraxy.

Often, rituals involve an enactment of myths. In some Christian churches, the symbolic cleansing of the soul is enacted by actually immersing people in water during baptism. Likewise, Christians frequently reenact the last supper of Jesus (Communion or Eucharist) as they accept their role as modern disciples. Among the Navajo, rituals enacted by a medicine man may last as long as five days. An appropriate myth is told, and sand paintings, music, and dramatics lend power and unique reality to the myths.

The group environment of the ritual is important. Ethereal music, communal chants, and group actions such as kneeling or taking off one's shoes when entering the shrine or mosque create an aura of separation from the everyday world and a mood of awe so that the beliefs seem eternal and beyond question. They become sacralized. Rituals also make ample use of symbols, discussed in Chapter 4.

A **symbol** is an *object or an action that represents something else and therefore has meaning beyond its own existence; flags and wedding rings are examples.* Because religion deals with a transcendent realm, a realm that cannot be experienced or proven with the five senses, sacred symbols are a central part of religion. They have a powerful emotional impact on the faithful and reinforce the sacredness of myths.

Muslims pray to God (whom they call Allah) five times a day, removing their shoes and prostrating themselves as they face Mecca. This is an important ritual, and it illustrates that orthopraxy is central for Muslims. Personal devotion, which is expressed in actions, is emphasized in Islam.

The yarmulke (skullcap or kippah) has been worn by Jewish men since roughly the second century CE. It symbolizes respect for and fear of God and serves to remind the wearer of the need for humility: There is always some distance between him and God. These caps are also a sign of belonging and commitment to the Jewish community.

Sacred symbols are in some ways comparable to computer chips, in that they both store an enormous amount of information and can deliver it with powerful immediacy (Leach 1979). Seeing a cross can flood a Christian's consciousness with a whole series of images, events, and powerful emotions concerning Jesus and his disciples. Tasting the bitter herb during a Jewish Seder service may likewise elicit memories of the story of slavery in Egypt, recall the escape under the leadership of Moses, and send a moral message to the celebrant to work for freedom and justice in the world today. The mezuzah, a plaque consecrating a house on the doorpost of a Jewish home, is a symbol reminding the occupants of their commitment to obey God's commandments and reaffirming God's commitment to them as a people. Because symbols are often heavily laden with emotion and can elicit strong feelings, they are used extensively in rituals to represent myths.

Myths, rituals, and symbols are usually interrelated and interdependent (see Figure 11.4). Together, they form the meaning system—a set of ideas about life or about the cosmos that seem uniquely realistic and compelling. They reinforce rules of appropriate behavior and even political and economic systems by making them sacred. They can also control social relationships between different groups. The Gypsy revulsion at the filthy *marime* practices of non-Gypsies, like the kosher rules for food preparation among the Jews, create boundaries between "us" and "them" that greatly reduce prospects of marriage outside of the religious community. Some scholars think these rituals and symbolic meanings are the key reason why Gypsies and Jews have survived for millennia as distinct groups without being assimilated or absorbed into dominant cultures. The symbols and meanings created barriers that prevented the obliteration of their cultures.

When symbolic interactionists study religion, they tend to focus on how symbols influence people's perception of reality and on the role rituals and myths play in defining what is "really real" for people. Symbolic interactionists

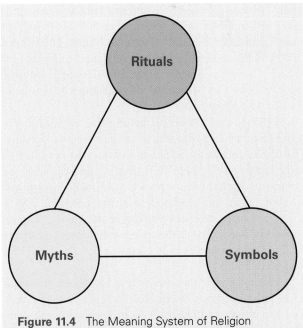

Figure 11.4 The Meaning System of Religion Is Composed of Three Interrelated Elements

These shoes outside a mosque are a symbol of awe for the holy. Removal of shoes is an expression of sacred respect for God among Muslims.

stress that humans are always trying to create, determine, and interpret the meaning of events. Clearly, no other institution focuses as explicitly on determining the meaning of life and its events as religion.

Thinking Sociologically

In a tradition with which you are familiar, how do symbols and sacred stories reinforce a particular view of the world or a particular set of values and social norms?

Seeking Eternal Benefits: A Rational Choice Perspective

Rational choice theorists maintain that people decide whether or not they should join or leave a religious group by asking, "What are the benefits, and what are the costs? Do the benefits outweigh the costs?" The benefits, of course, are nonmaterial when it comes to religious choices—feeling that life has meaning, confidence in an afterlife, sense of communion with God, and so forth (Finke and Stark 2005; Warner 1993). This approach views churchgoers as consumers who are out to meet their needs or obtain a "product." It depicts churches as entrepreneurial establishments, or "franchises," in a competitive market, with "entrepreneurs" (ministers) as leaders. Competition for members leads churches to "market" their religion to consumers. Converts and religious people generally are thus regarded as active and rational agents pursuing self-interests, and growing churches are those that meet "consumer demand" (Finke and Stark 2005; Jelen 2002). Religious groups produce religious "commodities" (rituals, meaning systems, sense of belonging, symbols, etc.) to meet the "demands" of consumers (Christiano, Swatos, and Kivisto 2008).

Rational choice theorists believe that aggressive religious entrepreneurs who seek to produce religious products that appeal to a target audience will reap the benefits of a large congregation. Churches, temples, and mosques are competitive enterprises, and each must make investments of effort, time, and resources to attract potential buyers. There are many religious entrepreneurs seeking to meet individual needs. The challenge is for the various groups to beat the competition by better meeting the demand (Finke and Stark 2005).

Rational choice theorists believe that when more religious groups compete for the hearts and minds of members, concern about spiritual matters is invigorated, and commitment is heightened. Religious pluralism and spiritual diversity increase rates of religious activity as each group seeks its market share and as more individual needs are met in the society (Finke and Stark 2005; Iannaccone and Bainbridge 2010).

Thinking Sociologically

Does the rational choice approach seem to you to make sense of religious behavior? Is religious behavior similar to self-interested economic behavior?

Religion and Modern Life: Meso-Level Analysis

As we think of religion at the meso level, two categories come to mind. First, religion is an institution, as described in the introduction to institutions. Second, the institution of religion is composed of many real organizations at the meso level—our denominational affiliation (Lutheran, Presbyterian), regional Catholic diocese, or Jewish movement (Hasidic, Orthodox, Conservative, Reform). The next section gives an overview of types of religious organizations.

Types of Religious Associations

The unique history of religious organizations in the United States has led one observer to describe America as the "denominational society" (Greeley 1972). Although religious establishments existed in the American colonies, the United States as a nation is religiously diverse in two senses: multiple religious groups living side-by-side with no single faith tradition being dominant, and church and state given their own autonomous realms by the U.S. Constitution (Stark and Finke 2000).

Denominations and Denominationalism. In the United States and most other Western countries, local congregations are part of larger centralized organizations. These *centralized coordinating bodies or associations that link local congregations with a similar history and theology* are called **denominations**.

In the long history of human society, denominationalism is a unique and rather recent way of organizing religion (Bass 2012). For most of human history, religion and the rest of life had been seamless and undifferentiated. Over time, religion gradually became distinct from other social institutions, in particular the political or governmental structures. The result is that specifically religious organizations arose. Initially, a single religious organization dominated a particular geographic area, so that for several centuries the Roman Catholic Church was the dominant religious group in Europe. Eventually, however, the religious sphere itself came to be diverse as various regional movements arose, some of them within Catholicism (the Dominicans, the Jesuits, and so forth). The Reformation Era (1517–1648), however, launched Protestantism and brought about the emergence of different Christian groups that were distinct in beliefs and organization. Most of them were splinter groups from Catholicism, such as the Lutherans (Gorski 2000).

Although this spawned some religious pluralism, each religious group attempted to become the official and government-approved church in its territory. Conflict rather than peaceful coexistence came to characterize Europe, and many people were forced out of their own countries because of their faith.

Some of those driven out of Europe for religious reasons were followers of the Calvinist Puritan movement who were seeking to reform the Church of England. They ended up founding the New England colonies and creating religious establishments of their own. Four of the colonies (Rhode Island, Delaware, New Jersey, and Pennsylvania) were religiously very diverse and had no state-sponsored church. As a result, no single religious group established dominance or control in North America. This led to necessary peaceful coexistence: religious pluralism and official separation of church and state.

Freedom of religion and prohibition of a state-endorsed church are key conditions for denominationalism. When scholars have referred to the United States as "the denominational society," they mean a society that is characterized by religious congregations united into denominations that are presumed equal under the law and that generally treat other bodies with an attitude of mutual respect (Greeley 1972). As a consequence of this organizational pattern of religious pluralism, there are hundreds of denominations in the United States (Mead, Hill, and Atwood 2005). Indeed, the *Handbook of Denominations in the United States* lists 31 Baptist denominations alone (Mead, Hill, and Atwood 2005). This denominationalism has also become a global phenomenon; the *World Christian Encyclopedia* reports 33,830 denominations within Christianity worldwide (Barrett, Kurian, and Johnson 2001; Roberts and Yamane 2012).

Although diversity within Protestantism was a key force for denominationalism, it has become fully incorporated by all major religious groups in the United States. Some scholars have even identified Jewish "denominationalism" in reference to the four branches of Judaism—Orthodox, Conservative, Reform, and Reconstructionist (Lazerwitz et al. 1998). The Nation of Islam and American Society of Muslims are distinctively American Islamic denominations (though the former is often viewed negatively by traditional Muslims). If this pattern continues, we might eventually see Sunni and Shite Islamic organizations develop as distinctive Islamic denominations. Buddhism and Hinduism also have different branches or schools, though like Islam they were brought to America in large numbers only recently, so time will tell whether there will be an evolution of those branches into recognizable denominations.

Denominational Structures and the Micro-Meso Connection. Denominations have organizational structures, but they are not all alike. Three types of denominational

There were 10 Lutheran denominations in the United States as of 2010, and most of the splits have been based on immigration and ethnicity patterns rather than race or doctrinal differences. This congregation, St. Pedro's, began as a Danish congregation, but is now affiliated with the largest of the Lutheran groups, the Evangelical Lutheran Church in America. The ELCA is the largest because of a series of consolidations. So denominationalism is characterized by fission (splits) and by fusion (mergers).

structures prevail: congregational, episcopal, and presbyterian (DiMaggio and Powell 1983; Roberts and Yamane 2012). Note that these are *not* the same as churches by those names, but rather the organizational structure (or "polity") of a number of churches.

In a *congregational* polity or structure, the authority of the local congregation is supreme. For example, the thousands of Baptist and United Church of Christ congregations in the United States hire and fire their own ministers, control their own finances, own their own property, decide whether to ordain women, and make other decisions about the congregation (Ammerman 1990, 2009).

The *episcopal*—also called "hierarchical"—pattern of governance places ultimate authority over local churches in the centralized hands of bishops (the word *episcopal* means "governed by bishops"). All of the Roman Catholic Church's nearly 20,000 U.S. congregations (or "parishes") are geographically defined. They are clustered into a "diocese," which is under the authority of the local bishop and, ultimately, under the authority of the bishop of Rome—the pope. In an episcopal structure, a bishop and his or her executive staff decides who will be the priest or minister of the local church. A committee of the local congregation may be consulted, but the bishop has the final say. Christian churches that have some form of episcopal organization include Anglican, Episcopalian, Eastern Orthodox, Methodist, African Methodist Episcopal, AME Zion, and *some* Lutherans. So, the local United Methodist church building in your community is actually *owned* by the larger denomination and is only maintained by the local congregation, and a bishop decides who will be the minister.

Presbyterian polity, quite simply, is a middle ground between episcopal (with a bishop having tremendous power) and congregational (where the congregation has total authority). In presbyterian polity, authority is shared so that neither a single local congregation nor the hierarchy can trump the other. The Presbyterian church is the best example of this compromise position. Presbyterian structure usually involves a local board in a congregation that can make decisions—called Sessions. There are also organizations comprising groups of congregations at regional and national levels that, in order of regional to national, are typically called Presbyteries, Synods, and then the National Assembly. Almost all Reformed churches use this approach: Dutch Reformed, Swiss Reformed, and Presbyterian, which was an offshoot of the Scottish Reformed tradition. Table 11.5 provides some examples of which churches tend to follow which polity.

Both denominations and congregations from all religious traditions are susceptible to influence from the larger social system. Hence, they have a tendency to become like each other. Scholars recognize a tendency for organizations to morph into similar forms (DiMaggio and Powell 1983). The point is that while denominational structure or polity strongly affects the structure of a local congregation and how it works, the social environment can also cause a certain amount of adaptation.

Although the idea of a congregational authority emerged from the study of Christianity, this organizational form is not limited to the Christian tradition. Further, the tendency to assimilate to the pattern in the social environment happens to religious groups as much as it does to individuals, as shown in the next "Sociology in Our Social World."

New Religious Movements or Cults

New religious movements (NRMs) are protest or splinter groups. They arise to meet specific needs that people have not met through traditional religious organizations. However, unlike sects, if NRMs survive for several generations, become established, and gain some legitimacy, they become new religions rather than a new denomination of an existing faith. *Cult* was once the common term for this kind of movement, but the media and the public have so completely misused the word that its meaning has become unclear and often negative. The term *cult*, as sociologists have historically used it, is simply descriptive, not judging the group as good, bad, or kooky. Most sociologists of religion now prefer to use the term *NRM* to describe these religious forms (Christiano, Swatos, and Kivisto 2008; "New Religious Movement" 2012).

NRMs are either imported into a country as immigrants enter from other lands or are founded on a new revelation (or insight) by a charismatic leader. They are usually out of the mainstream religious system, at least in their early days. Christianity, Buddhism, and Islam all began as NRMs or cults. The estimated number of NRMs in North America at the beginning of the 21st century was between 1,500 and 2,000 (Melton 1992; Nichols, Mather, and Schmidt 2006). There could be 10,000 more NRMs in Africa and an undetermined but large number in Asia (Hadden 2006; Religious Worlds 2007).

An NRM is often started by a charismatic leader, someone who claims to have received a new insight, often directly from God. For example, Reverend Sun Myung Moon founded an NRM called the Unification Church, the members of which are often referred to as *Moonies*. While claiming to be a part of Christianity, the Unification Church has its own additional scripture to complement the Bible, and Reverend Moon has a standing in the Unification Church equal to Jesus—an idea offensive to most Christian groups.

Some sensational NRMs have ended in tragedy: Reverend Jim Jones led his devoted followers to a retreat in Guyana, South America, and ultimately to their suicides in the belief that heaven was awaiting them (Lacayo 1993; S. Wright 1995). A group suicide also occurred in 1997 in California by a band called Heaven's Gate, whose members thought supernatural beings were coming to take them away in a flying saucer (Wessinger 2000).

Table 11.5 Polity or Organizational Structures of Selected Churches

Congregational Polity	Episcopal Polity	Presbyterian Polity
United Church of Christ (Congregationalists)	Roman Catholic Church	Reformed Churches
National Baptist	Episcopal Church	Dutch Reformed
Southern Baptist	Anglican Church	Swiss Reformed
Christian Church (Disciples of Christ)	United Methodist	French Reformed
Churches of Christ	African Methodist Episcopal	Church of Scotland
Unitarian Universalists	Evangelical Lutheran	Presbyterian Church USA

Cults

Sociology in Our Social World

Islam, Mosques, and Organizational Structure

Most mosques in the United States are relatively new, with 87% having been founded since 1970 and 62% of those since 1980. The number of mosques is up 74% since 2000. At the turn of the century, there were 1,209 mosques in the United States, and by 2010 there were 2,106 (Grossman 2012).

Christian congregations tend to be somewhat autonomous entities: supported by members but linked organizationally to a denomination. According to one Islamic scholar, "Most of the world's mosques are simply a place to pray. . . . A Muslim cannot be a member of a particular mosque" because mosques belong to God, not to the people (Bagby 2003:115). The role of the imam—the minister—is simply to lead prayers five times a day and to run the services on the Sabbath, including delivery of a sermon. Unlike many Christian and Jewish leaders in the United States, the imam does not run an organization and does not need formal training at a seminary. In some countries, mosques are government supported, so imams had to make major changes in how they operate when they started congregations in North America. Because they could not depend on government funding, Islamic mosques needed to adapt to the congregational model: recruiting members who were loyal to a particular local mosque and would support it. They also began to put more emphasis on religious education (which had been managed largely by extended families in the "old country"), religious holidays are celebrated at the mosque rather than with families, and life cycle celebrations (births and marriages) became events for the congregation. This is a major change in the role of the mosque and the imam for many Muslims.

Bagby reports that there are two main categories of mosques: (1) those attended primarily by African Americans and (2) those attended primarily by immigrants. African American mosques represent only 27% of the total number of mosques, and they are in some important ways different in organizational structure from those attended by immigrants (28% of the remaining American Muslims being from South Asia, 15% being Arab, and 30% having a mixed background). So even the makeup of mosques is unlike anything most Americans might expect. Only 28% of American mosques depend on an imam as the final authority, whereas the majority are led by an executive committee or board of directors (called the *majlis*). More important, 93% of African American mosques are led by an imam, compared with only 38% of immigrant-attended mosques.

About 33% of all mosques in the United States have a paid, full-time imam, and 16% of those imams need to hold a second job. In comparison, 89% of other congregations (Christian and Jewish) have paid ministers. Only 13% of imams have a master's degree in theology, which is the standard expected for most mainstream Christian and Jewish clergy. So despite having exceptionally high levels of adherents in management and the professions, with exceptionally high incomes, and having 58% of adherents with college degrees, Islamic mosques are less bureaucratized, with less emphasis on professional credentials, membership roles, or denominational connections. It is likely that mosques will begin to assimilate to the religious organizational pattern of the larger society.

Most new religious groups are not dangerous to members. Furthermore, most religious groups that are now accepted and established were stigmatized as weird or evil when they started. Early Christians were characterized by Romans as dangerous cannibals, and in the 19th century and early decades of the 20th century in the United States, Roman Catholics were depicted in the media as dangerous, immoral, and anti-American (Bromley and Shupe 1981). When we encounter media reports about NRMs,

we should listen to and read these with a good dose of skepticism and recognize that not all cults are like the sensational ones.

NRMs tend to be hard to study because the members feel they might be persecuted for their faith and beliefs. Witchcraft (or Wicca) is one example of a religion that has been forced to remain secretive, and the next "Sociology in Our Social World" explores the strategies of one sociologist to examine this interesting religious community.

Sociology in Our Social World

Witchcraft in the United States

Wiccans participate in a lunar ritual in Illinois.

In *A Community of Witches: Contemporary Neo-Paganism and Witchcraft in the United States*, Helen Berger applies sociological analysis to conduct a fascinating study of contemporary Wicca (H. Berger 1999). She did participant observation in a newly formed coven in New England. A coven is a small congregation of witches, usually having no more than 10 or 12 members. It took considerable effort to establish trust with the members, but this method of gathering data allowed her to experience firsthand the close-knit support group and the actual behaviors and interactions within the group. A national organization provided her with a wealth of printed material produced by Neo-Pagans and allowed her entry to several national Neo-Pagan festivals, where she observed the rituals. She also did in-depth, open-ended interviews with 40 members from a number of covens. By using a variety of methods, Berger was able to gain in-depth information, but she was also able to get an idea of whether her experiences were generalizable to all parts of the country.

Although Berger found Wicca to be a rather healthy and vibrant movement, she also found that it experiences some of the same dilemmas as any other religious congregation. Wicca is feminist, believing in a goddess and emphasizing gender equality. It also celebrates the spiritual unity of humans with nature and therefore has a strong ecology ethic. The religion encourages an intuitive approach to decision making (rather than using logic) and celebrates the senses. This sensuousness embraces sexuality, fertility, and being at one with the universe.

Berger finds that Wicca is a product of the globalized world, for the religion involves bits and pieces selected from religions around the world. It has spread with modern technology, including Internet communication, desktop publishing, and fax machines. Wicca is a fast-growing religion, especially among women (Religious Tolerance 2012). Furthermore, it is a religion about self-fulfillment, in keeping with a contemporary emphasis on self-awareness and self-transformation. In a more recent book, *Teenage Witches*, Berger worked with an Australian scholar, Douglas Ezzy, to explore the expansion of witchcraft among teenagers in the English-speaking world (Berger and Ezzy 2007). The book is based on interviews that Berger and Ezzy did with 90 young people in the United States, the United Kingdom, and Australia (30 from each country). Young people, even more than the generation before them, are attracted by the emphasis on self-transformation. Many of the past generation found their politics, particularly their belief in environmentalism and gender equity, mirrored in Wicca. Unlike the past generation, the new generation of witches is more likely to practice alone—that is, outside the covens. These individuals learn about the religion through books and magazines and online. They may interact with others on websites, through blogs, or in Wiccan chat rooms, but they remain solitary practitioners.

With the increase in the number of teenagers becoming interested in supernatural ideas from *Harry Potter* to the *Twilight* series, witches are in part a product of the growth of positive media representations of magic and supernaturalism. The expansion in Wiccan covens may be one result of this shift in media depictions. However, Berger and Ezzy found that many more young people search online for information about witchcraft or read books about it than actually become witches. Although the media may stimulate interest, it does not cause young people to join. Those who do become witches tend to find that the religion speaks to their personal needs. They are more likely to already have had an interest in the occult and to have felt themselves to be different from their peers. The influx of young people has the potential to significantly change the face of the religion, particularly because so few of them seek coven training and have the traditional ideas and practices passed on to them.

Thinking Sociologically

What factors might cause the birth and success of NRMs?

Religion in Society: Macro-Level Analysis

As an integral part of society, religion meets the needs of individuals and of the society. In this section, we explore structural-functional and conflict theories as we consider some functions of religion in society and the role of religion in stratification systems of society.

The Contribution of Religion to Society: A Structural-Functional Perspective

Regardless of their personal belief or disbelief in the supernatural, sociologists of religion acknowledge that religion has important social consequences. Structural-functionalists contend that religion has some positive consequences—helping people answer questions about the meaning of life and providing part of the glue that helps hold a society together. Let us look at some of the social functions of religion, keeping in mind that the role of religion varies depending on the structure of the society and the time period.

Social Cohesion. Religion helps individuals feel a sense of belonging and unity with others, a common sense of purpose with those who share the same beliefs. Durkheim's widely cited study of suicide stresses the importance of belonging to a group such as a congregation (Durkheim [1897] 1964). Research shows that a high rate of congregational membership and religious homogeneity in a community is associated with lower rates of suicide. This lower suicide rate among the highly religious appears to hold in Muslim societies as well as in the United States (Ellison, Burr, and McCall 1997; Lotfi, Ayar, and Shams 2012). Thus, religion serves society well as long as religious views are consistent with other values of society (Bainbridge and Stark 1981).

In complex and heterogeneous societies, however, no single religion can provide the core values of the culture. In such circumstances, a **civil religion**—*the cultural beliefs, practices, and symbols that relate a nation to the ultimate conditions of its existence*—entails a shared public faith in the nation and what the nation stands for based on a country's history, social institutions, set of beliefs, symbols, and rituals that pervade secular life and institutions. It provides a theology of the nation that serves to bless the nation and to enhance conformity and loyalty. Civil religion is based on a set of beliefs, symbols, and rituals that pervade many

aspects of secular life and institutions: pledging allegiance, saluting the flag, and singing the national anthem. This civil religion often serves as an alternative religion to Christianity or to whatever religion is most dominant. It involves a shared public faith in the nation and what that nation stands for. Civil religion is supported by various types of patriotic groups that legitimate the governmental system (Bellah 1992; Roberts and Yamane 2012).

Legitimating Social Values and Norms. The values and norms in a culture must be seen as compelling to members of the society. Religion often sacralizes social

Civil religion blends reverence for the nation with more traditional symbols of faith. Pictured is the chapel at Punchbowl, the Pacific cemetery for U.S. military personnel, located in Hawaii. Note that two U.S. flags are inside the altar area and are more prominent than two of the three religious symbols that also adorn the chancel: the Christian cross, the Jewish Star of David, and the Buddhist Wheel of Dharma.

Civil Religion

norms—grounds them in a supernatural reality or a divine command that makes them beyond question. Whether those norms have to do with care for the vulnerable, the demand to work for peace and justice, the sacredness of a monogamous heterosexual marriage, or proper roles of men and women, foundations of morality from scripture create guidelines and feelings of absoluteness. This, in turn, lends stability to the society. Of course, the absoluteness of the norms also makes it more difficult to change them as the society evolves. This inflexibility is precisely what pleases religious conservatives and distresses theological liberals, the latter often seeking new ways to interpret the old norms. Note also that what people say they believe and how they behave are not always compatible, as the next "Sociology in Our Social World" makes clear.

Social Change. Religion can work for or against social change, depending on the time and place. Some religions fight to maintain the status quo or return to simpler times. This is true of many fundamentalist religions, be they branches of Christian, Jewish, Hindu, or Islamic faiths, that seek to simplify life in the increasingly complex industrial world. Other religious traditions support or encourage change. Japan was able to make tremendous strides in industrialization and growth of business in a short time following World War II, in part because the Shinto, Confucian, and Buddhist religions provided no obstacles and, in fact, supported the changes. In the United States, the central figures in the civil rights movement were nearly all African American religious leaders. As the first nationwide organizations controlled by black people, African American religious organizations established networks and communication channels that were used by those interested in change (Farley 2010; Lincoln and Mamiya 1990; McAdam 1999, 2003).

Thinking Sociologically

Which religious groups in your community have a stabilizing influence, and which ones seem to have a disruptive influence? Which ones make the existing system seem sacred and beyond question? Which push for more social equality and less ethnocentrism toward others? Are there mosques, temples, or churches that oppose the government's policies, or do they foster unquestioning loyalty?

The Link Between Religion and Stratification: A Conflict Perspective

Our religious ideas and values and the way we worship are shaped not only by the society into which we are born but also by our family's position in the stratification system.

Religion serves different primary purposes for individuals, depending on their positions in the society. People of various social statuses differ in the type and degree of their involvement in religious groups. At times, religions reinforce socially defined differences between people, giving sacred legitimacy to racial, gender, and sexual bias and inequality. Conflict theory considers ways in which religion relates to stratification and the status of minority groups.

The Class Base of Religion. Conflict theorist Karl Marx states clearly his view of the relationship between religion and class—that religion helps perpetuate the power structure. For the proletariat or working class, religion is a sedative, he asserts, a narcotic that dulls people's sensitivity to and understanding of their desperate situations. He calls religion the "opiate of the people." It keeps people in line and provides an escape from suffering in everyday life. At the same time, it helps those in power keep other people in line because it promises that if laborers serve well in this life, then life in the hereafter or the next incarnation will be better. Some religions justify the positions of those who are better off by saying they have earned it (Marx [1844] 1963).

Because the needs and interests of socioeconomic groups differ, religion is class based in most Global North societies. In the United States, religious affiliation is highly correlated with social class measures such as education, occupation, and income (Pyle 2006; Smith and Faris 2005). The specific links between denominational affiliation and socioeconomic measures in the United States at the beginning of the 21st century are indicated in Table 11.6 on page 348. Sects tend to attract lower- and working-class

This religious procession in Bolivia is a community-uniting event that supports tradition and stability. Marx felt that when religion unites people who have different self-interests, it is not a positive thing. It serves as the opiate of the masses.

Iran

Sociology in Our Social World

Red Sex, Blue Sex

Even sex has political-religious guidelines and implications. Reactions at the 2008 Republican convention to the pregnancy of Sarah Palin's unmarried evangelical 17-year-old daughter were far from what some people might have expected. One delegate said, "I think it's great that she instilled in her daughter the values to have the child and not to sneak off someplace and have an abortion." Another added that "even though young children are making that decision to become pregnant, they've also decided to take responsibility for their actions and . . . get married and raise this child" (Talbot 2008).

For social liberals in the U.S. "blue states," sex education is the key. They are not particularly bothered by teens having sex before marriage but would regard a teenage daughter's pregnancy as devastating news. On the other hand, social conservatives in "red states" generally advocate abstinence-only education and denounce sex before marriage. However, they are relatively unruffled when a teenager does become pregnant, as long as she does not choose to have an abortion.

From a national survey of 3,400 teens between 13 and 17 years old and from a government study of adolescent sexual behavior, the authors of the National Longitudinal Study of Adolescent Health conclude that "religion is a good indicator of attitudes toward sex, but a poor one of sexual behavior, and that this gap is especially wide among teenagers who identify themselves as evangelical" (Regnerus 2007; Sessions 2012). The vast majority of white evangelical adolescents—74%—say that they believe in abstaining from sex before marriage. (Only half of mainline Protestants and a quarter of Jews say that they believe in abstinence.) Moreover, among the major religious groups, evangelical virgins are the least likely to anticipate that sex will be pleasurable and the most likely to believe that having sex will cause their partners to lose respect for them. Yet the adolescent health research indicated that evangelical teenagers are more sexually active than Mormons, mainline

Protestants, and Jews. On average, white evangelical Protestants make their "sexual debut" shortly after turning 16; 80% of unmarried evangelicals are having sex, and 30% of their pregnancies end in abortion (Regnerus 2007; Sessions 2012; Shriver 2007). It is interesting to note that states with comprehensive sex education programs in schools have half the teen birthrates as those in the evangelical South that ban sex education in schools (Sessions 2012). Some sociologists argue that teens used to get married at earlier ages, but now wait to marry until they are economically secure, demanding that evangelical young people remain sexless during their young adulthood. This may not be realistic.

Another key difference between evangelical and other teens "is that evangelical protestant teenagers are significantly less likely than other groups to use contraception. This could be because evangelicals are also among the most likely to believe that using contraception will send the message that they are looking for sex" or that condoms will not really protect them from pregnancy or venereal disease (Talbot 2008).

The disconnect between belief ideals and actual behavior is obvious when we examine the outcomes of abstinence-pledge movements. Roughly 2.5 million people have taken a pledge to remain celibate until marriage, usually under the auspices of religiously based movements such as True Love Waits or the Silver Ring Thing. However, more than half of those who take such pledges end up having sex before marriage—and not usually with their future spouse. While those who take the pledge tend to delay their first sexual intercourse for 18 months longer than nonpledgers and have fewer partners, communities with high rates of pledging also have very high rates of sexually transmitted diseases. This could be because fewer people in these communities use condoms when they break the pledge (Regnerus 2007; Talbot 2008).

The main point is that sexual attitudes and behaviors can be linked to our religious beliefs and affiliations but perhaps not in the ways we expect.

worshippers because they focus on the problems and life situations faced by people in lower social classes. People with higher social status attend worship more regularly and know more about the scriptures, but people with lower socioeconomic status are more likely to pray daily (Albrecht and Heaton 1984; Roberts and Yamane 2012).

Table 11.6   Socioeconomic Profiles of American Religious Groups

| Religious Group | Educational Level (in percentage) | | Annual Household Income (in $) |
	% with Least a College Degree	No High School	% Over 100,000
Hindu	74	4	43
Jewish	59	3	46
Episcopal Church in USA	57	1	35
Unitarian	51	3	26
Buddhist	48	3	22
Presbyterian USA	47	7	28
Orthodox	46	6	28
United Church of Christ (Congregationalists)	42	4	18
Atheist	42	8	28
United Methodist	35	8	22
Disciples of Christ	35	10	20
Evangelical Lutheran in America	30	6	17
Nondenominational	29	6	18
Latter-Day Saint (Mormon)	28	8	15
Catholic	26	17	19
Muslim	24	21	16
Southern Baptist	21	15	15
Seventh Day Adventist	21	24	11
Religious but Unaffiliated	17	21	12
American Baptist	14	23	8
Assemblies of God	12	24	8
Other Pentecostal	11	26	7
Jehovah's Witness	9	19	9
Black Baptist	8	19	8

Source: Pew Forum on Religion and Public Life (2008:78–80, 84–86).

Max Weber referred to this pattern of people belonging to religious groups that espouse values and characteristics compatible with their social status as *elective affinity* (Weber 1946). For example, people in laboring jobs usually find that obeying rules of the workplace and adhering to the instructions of the employer or supervisor are essential for success on the job (Bowles and Gintis 1976; MacLeod 2008). The faith communities of the poor and the working class tend to stress obedience, submission to "superiors," and the absoluteness of religious standards. The values of the workplace are reenacted and legitimated in the churches and help socialize children to adapt to laboring jobs with strict standards and expectations.

Many people in affluent congregations are paid to be divergent thinkers, to be problem solvers, and to break the mold of conventional thinking. They will not do well professionally if they merely obey rules. Instead, they are expected to be rule makers while trying to solve organizational or management problems (Bowles and Gintis 1976). It is not surprising, then, that the denominations of the affluent are more likely to value tolerance of other perspectives, religions, or values and to view factors that limit individual opportunity (e.g., institutional racism and sexism) as evil. They embrace tolerance of differences and condemn rigidity, absolutism, and conventionalism. Critical thinking, creativity, and even a streak of independence are valuable characteristics. Their religious communities are likely to encourage each member to work out his or her own theology, within limits (Roberts and Yamane 2012; Roof 1999).

Thinking Sociologically

How do the social class and religious affiliation of people you know relate to the discussion here? How do denominations with higher-than-average levels of college education and income (Unitarians, Jews, Episcopalians, Presbyterians, and Congregationalists) in your community differ from those with less education and income?

Racial, Gender, and Sexual Biases in Religion. Most religious groups profess to welcome all comers, yet most have practiced discrimination against some group at some time, often related to political, economic, and other social class factors in the society. In fact, some studies show positive relationships among religion, prejudice, and discrimination. However, it is important to recognize that religion has multiple and even contradictory effects on societies. For example, most Christian denominations have formal statements that reject racial and ethnic prejudice as un-Christian. The meaning system often teaches tolerance.

Worship

However, informal group norms in a local congregation—the belonging system—can foster distrust of certain racial and ethnic groups (Roberts and Yamane 2012; Woodberry and Smith 1998). Despite the content of the morning message at worship, attitudes of bigotry can be fostered among members of the congregation at the church picnic.

The structural system of religion can also play a role. Promotions to larger churches or temples are usually awarded to those clergy who are well liked, who have growing and harmonious congregations, and who have maintained financially sound organizations. Ministers are sometimes reluctant to speak out forcefully on controversial issues or for racial equality for fear of offending their parishioners. Bishops may not promote a minister to a larger church if his or her current congregation is racked with dissention and donations have declined. Even though the denomination's meaning system may oppose prejudice, the structural system may reward clergy who do not defend that meaning system (Campbell and Pettigrew 1959; Roberts and Yamane 2012). The result is ministers who are sometimes reluctant to speak out about bigotry, and this silence allows it to continue.

Women have often been the main volunteers and the most faithful attendees in Christian congregations, and in some denominations, they hold leadership positions (Chaves 2004). This curious phenomenon that women are more spiritual or religious than men is discussed in the next "Engaging Sociology" on page 350. Despite their involvement, women have often been denied entrance into many statuses within religious organizations and are kept separated. In some Christian, Islamic, and Jewish worship services, women must cover their heads or sit separately. This symbolizes and communicates the presumed differences between women and men before God as laid out in 1 Corinthians 11:2–16. Ordination of women is a newly won right in several denominations (Chaves 2004; Religious Tolerance 2012).

Similarly, religious groups have often constructed barriers to equal treatment of women. For example, men within Islam have more power, although women must be treated with respect. Within this faith tradition, many adherents see this stratification as providing protection for both groups to worship without distraction. All worshippers remove their shoes, and women must cover their heads and sometimes their faces, and they cannot enter certain areas of the mosque when men are present. Literal teachings of many religions legitimate treating women differently, often in ways that disallow leadership opportunities and imply inferiority. This is true of certain groups within all of the Abrahamic religious traditions: Judaism, Christianity, and Islam.

Many deeply religious women have been concerned over the lack of significant roles for women and have fought for reformation within their religions. In recent decades, Roman Catholic nuns have had considerable authority to take leadership and to address issues that they think are

central to the faith. However, the Leadership Conference of Women Religious, the umbrella group that represents the majority of American nuns, is in deep conflict with the new pope as he tries to limit the autonomy relative to engagement in justice issues.

By the beginning of the 21st century, three fourths of the public in the United States favored having women as pastors, ministers, priests, or rabbis, compared to 42% in 1977 (Lyons 2002). The Vatican of the Roman Catholic Church has taken a strong position as recently as 2010, threatening excommunication and categorizing any attempt by woman to be ordained to be a grave crime against the church—in the same category as priests who sexually abuse children. Yet in 2012, 59% of American Catholics supported ordination of women priests according to a *New York Times*/CBS poll (J. Levitt 2012). Still, even a very small percentage of Protestants report that they actually have a woman as senior pastor (Chaves 2004). Because such leadership statuses are important symbolic positions, many women feel that this refusal helps sacralize the social stereotype of women as less capable human beings.

While most mainline Christian denominations now have official statements on the equality of women and formal policies against discrimination in ordaining or hiring

A Presbyterian minister blesses the cup before offering the sacrament of Communion.

Engaging Sociology

Women and Spirituality

Figure 11.5 indicates that there is a spirituality gap.

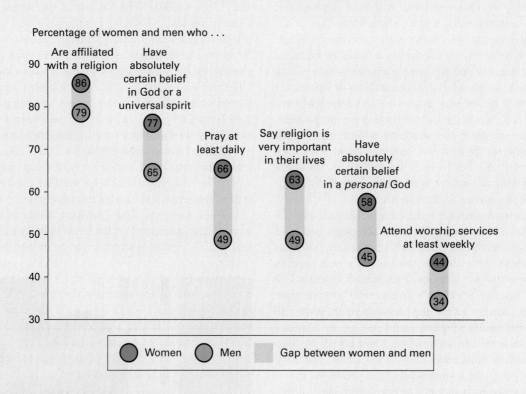

Figure 11.5 The Gender Gap in Spirituality

Source: Pew Forum on Religion and Public Life (2009).

Sociological Data Analysis:

1. Are you convinced by the evidence in Figure 11.5 that women are more spiritual than men? Why or why not?

2. Do these findings agree with your observations? If so, why do you think this is the case? If not, why do the data seem to suggest less involvement of men?

3. Is the message of religious communities and faith traditions (altruism, self-sacrifice, trusting others) less in tune with the everyday experiences of men than of women?

women pastors, the official meaning system does not tell the whole story. Again, religious structures play a role. Local congregational search committees that screen and hire new ministers care deeply about the survival and health of the local church. Studies show that members of these committees are themselves usually not personally opposed to women in the pulpit, but they believe that others in their church would be offended and would stop coming and giving money to the church. Thus, local belonging and structural systems of the religion may perpetuate unequal treatment of clergywomen, even if the meaning system says they are equal (Chaves 1999; Lehman 1985).

Given these frustrations, some women have been uncomfortable working for reform from within and have left traditional religions to form new structures in which they can worship as equals, including NRMs. Indeed, women in the Western world have, throughout history, been more likely than men to opt for unconventional forms of religion (McGuire 2002).

Gays in the church, ordination of gay and lesbian ministers, and same-sex marriage in churches make for heated debate over church policy and even threaten to split some denominations. Most established religious groups assume the normality of heterosexuality. Marriage is sanctified by religious ceremony in all major religious groups, but recently, some religious bodies have openly debated the possibility of recognizing officially sanctioned weddings for gays and lesbians. Opposition to homosexuality is especially strong among religious fundamentalists. Liberals in the churches tend to see this issue as one of prejudice against people for a characteristic that is an inborn trait and therefore not a sin. Conservatives argue that homosexuality is a choice that has moral implications. Conservatives see liberal notions about homosexuality and gender roles as a threat to society, family, and the moral order. Liberals typically see no moral issue and no threat to society when sexuality is expressed within a committed relationship. Bigotry—lack of tolerance of other lifestyles—is what is offensive. Thus, conservatives and liberals construct the core of morality differently.

In some instances, religion may reinforce and legitimate social prejudices toward racial groups, women, or gays and lesbians. In others, religion may be a powerful force for change and for greater equality in a society. Seldom does religion take a passive or entirely disinterested position on these matters. Consider conflicts around the world, many of which are based on religious and class differences. People are fighting and dying for their religious beliefs. In Belfast, Ireland, bombs sent Catholics and Protestants to their graves or to hospitals, maimed for life. In India, Muslims and Hindus continue to massacre each other. Protestant against Catholic, Shiite Muslim against Sunni Muslim, Jew against Muslim, Christian against Jew—religion elicits strong emotions

and influences people's definition of reality. Ethnocentric attitudes can be reinforced by religious beliefs. Religion has been the apparent cause of wars and social strife, but it has also been the motivation for altruism and service to others and a major contributor to social solidarity.

Thinking Sociologically

From what you know about the status of racial, gender, and sexual groups, how are problems they face in religion and other institutions (family, education, politics, economics, health) similar?

Religion and Secularization: Micro-, Meso-, and Macro-Level Discord

Secularization refers to *the diminishing influence and role of religion in everyday life.* Instead of religion being the dominant institution, it is but one of many. Secularization involves a movement away from supernatural and sacred interpretations of the world and toward decisions based on empirical evidence and logic. Before modern scientific explanations and technology, religion helped explain the unexplainable. However, the scientific method, emphasis on logical reasoning, and the belief that there are many different religious interpretations rather than one have challenged religious and spiritual approaches to the world. Although religion is still strong in the lives of many individuals, it does not have the extensive control over other institutions of education, health, politics, or family that it once did. In most Global North countries, it is an institution among others rather than being the dominant one. Whereas in 1957, 69% of the population thought religion was increasingly important in U.S. society, in 2013 77% felt it was declining in importance (M. Brown 2013).

Some scholars have argued that secularization is an inevitable and unstoppable force in the modern postindustrial world (Gorski and Altinordu 2008; Dobbelaere 2000). Others argue that secularization is far from inevitable and has almost reached its limit (Stark 2000; Warner 1993). Our social world model helps us understand that, like religion, secularization is a complex phenomenon that occurs at several levels and affects each society differently (Chaves and Gorski 2001; Yamane 1997).

Secularization may be occurring at the societal level, but evidence suggests that secularization is not so pervasive at the individual level in North America (Bellah et al. 1996; Chaves and Gorski 2001). According to a 2011 Gallup poll, 92% of Americans believe in God or a universal spirit, although

Despite the process of secularization in some parts of the world, the sense of awe before the holy remains strong for many people. This enormous Buddha at the Yungang Buddhist caves at Wuzhou Mountain in China was built out of a sense of sacredness for Buddha, and it then became a source of veneration for subsequent generations. Secularization may have occurred in many societies at the macro level, but religious faith is strong at the individual micro level.

other research has found that 12% to 15% of Americans do not identify with any specific religious tradition (Newport 2012; Pew Forum on Religion and Public Life 2010). Still, 63% claim membership in a local congregation, and 61% say religion is very important in their lives (Newport 2009). Moreover, religious membership has increased over the past three centuries (Finke and Stark 2005). In the "good old days" of American colonialism, only about 17% of the population belonged to a church. Religious membership rose fairly steadily from the 1770s until the 1960s. Although there has been a modest decline in the past 50 years, membership in mosques, synagogues, or churches was has consistently been reported above 60% of the adult population (Newport 2006). In Canada, two thirds of the population expresses a belief in God, but only 42% indicates that religion is a really important part of their lives (Boswell 2007). Still,

half the Canadian population reports having had a personal religious experience, three out of four claim to pray at least occasionally, and overall religious membership in Canada has continued to increase every decade (Bibby 2002; Clark and Schellenberg 2008). When religious faith guides people's everyday lives—their conduct on the job, their political choices, their sexual behavior, their behavior in the science classroom, or their attitudes toward racial relations—then secularization at the micro level is weak. Faith still matters to many people.

Within religiously affiliated organizations (Baptist hospitals, Presbyterian colleges, Jewish social service foundations), the decisions about how to deliver services or who will be hired or fired are based on systematic policies designed for organizational efficiency. In other words, meso-level secularization is present even within many religious organizations. Likewise, policies in the society at large are made with little discussion of theological implications, decisions being based on human rights arguments rather than on what is sinful, again suggesting that society has become secular at the macro level (Chaves 1993; Roberts and Yamane 2012; Yamane 1997). Debates about prayer in schools and involvement of religious leaders in political issues suggest that societal-level secularization is a continuing point of controversy in the United States. Still, few will deny that the bureaucratic structures of the United States and virtually every other postindustrial nation are thoroughly secularized. Processes of secularization at the macro, meso, and micro levels do not seem to be consistent or compatible. Table 11.7 indicates what complete secularization might look like at each level.

In short, most sociologists of religion believe that religion continues to be a particularly powerful force at the individual level and has some influence at the meso and macro levels. There is a macro-level trend toward secularization in most Global North societies, but the trend is neither inevitable nor uniform across societies (Roberts and Yamane 2012; Sommerville 2002).

At a global level, no particular theological authority has power to determine policies, religious authority structures are minimal, and secularization is well established. Perhaps this is one reason why conservatives of nearly every religious faith are leery of global processes and global organizations, such as the United Nations. Our global organizations are governed by rational-legal (secular) authority, not religious doctrines.

Thinking Sociologically

What might be the results if a society is secularized at the meso and macro levels but not at the micro level? Why?

Table 11.7 Secularization in the Social World

	Institutional Differentiation (Separation of Religion So It Does Not Dominate Other Institutions)	Decision Making
Macro Level	Institutions in the society, including government, education, and the economy, are independent, separate, and autonomous from religious organizations.	Decision making about social policies uses logic, empirical data, and cost-benefit analysis rather than scripture, theological arguments, or proclamations of religious authorities.
Meso Level	Organizations look to other social associations for accepted practices of how to operate the organization, not to religious organizations and authorities.	Decision making about an organization's policies is based on analyses of possible consequences, rather than on scripture, theological arguments, or proclamations of religious authorities.
Micro Level	Individuals emphasize being "spiritual rather than religious," formulate their own meaning system or theology, and may believe that spirituality has little to do with other aspects of their lives.	Decision making about life decisions is based on individual self-interest without concern for the teachings of the religious group or the clergy.

Religion in the Contemporary Global Context

As the foregoing discussion makes clear, religion affects and is influenced by the larger social context. This is true all the way to the global context with such issues as war and peace and the World Wide Web.

Religion and Peace

Can religion bring peace to the world? Most religious systems advocate living in harmony with other humans and with nature, yet peace is not the reality. Although the meaning system of all the Abrahamic religions embraces a world of peace and justice, the structural system does not always reward those who pay attention to the meaning system, as we see in cases of racism and sexism. Christian denominations often foster nationalistic loyalty—with displays of the flag and even pledges of allegiance to the flag during worship. This endorsement of national pride can actually foster we-versus-they thinking and can undermine peace. Congregations that take peace activities seriously may decline in membership and financial stability, whereas those that stir up chauvinistic sentiments attract large numbers. So the structural system may actually undermine the message of the meaning system because growth and financial vitality is a major concern of many local church leaders. Despite rhetoric, fiscal concerns can actually trump claims to worship the "Prince of Peace." Liberal theologies suggest that God may speak to people through a variety of channels, including the revelations of other religious traditions. While leaders may feel their beliefs provide the fullest and most complete expression of God's Truth, they recognize that other beliefs also provide paths

to Truth. This pluralism has resulted in more tolerance, but it is probably also an indicating of secularization of the theology itself.

Members of fundamentalist groups—be they Orthodox Jews, traditional Muslims, or born-again Christians—generally believe in a literal interpretation of their holy books. They usually believe they have the only Truth, which they defend or try to spread. This generates ethnocentrism and sometimes hatred, and people fight to defend their belief systems and preserve their distinctive identity (Marty and Appleby 1991, 2004). They seldom believe in pluralism or tolerance of other beliefs but rather believe they are the only true religion. Consequently, they resist and defend themselves against modernism, which threatens their beliefs and way of life (Ebaugh 2005; Stern 2003; Wessinger 2000). This means religious groups may engage in violent acts against others. Conflict between religious groups is especially intense if ethnic, economic, and religious differences are present. Where the lines of "we" and "they" are virtually identical on social class, ethnicity, political affiliation, and religious identification, hostilities escalate. Crosscutting social cleavages reduces social hostilities, as Figure 11.6 (page 354) illustrates. When one is in a group that has people of different religions, different ethnicities, and different socioeconomic classes, it becomes much less likely that one will vilify people from those other groups. They no longer—as a category—can be seen as uniformly evil or as the enemy. This is what is meant by crosscutting divisions.

Religion has the greatest potential for reducing hatred between groups when those groups share some type of common identification. If the conflict is over ethnicity and economics, a common religious heritage can lessen the likelihood of violent confrontation. Some religious groups (including Christian, Jewish, and Muslim) have joined together in

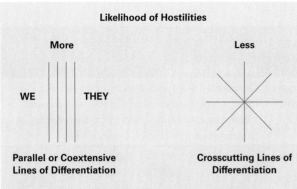

Likelihood of Hostilities

More   Less

WE   THEY

Parallel or Coextensive   Crosscutting Lines of
Lines of Differentiation   Differentiation

Figure 11.6 Lines of Differentiation Between
"We" and "They"

Note: Imagine that each line represents a division in the society between groups based on religion, ethnicity, political party, economic status, language spoken, skin color, or other factors. Parallel lines of differentiation divide people in each conflict along the same lines. *Crosscutting lines* cut the differences so that people who were part of "they" in a previous antagonism become part of "we" in the present discord—lessening the likelihood of deep and permanent hostilities.

peaceful enterprises such as attempts to ban nuclear weapons or address global poverty or climate change. This common purpose provides for cooperation and collaboration, thus lessening animosity and we-versus-they thinking.

Perhaps the core reason that some countries are secular is because of histories of religious hostilities. The conflicts in Europe between religions were very brutal, beginning with the bloodletting in the Hundred Years' War. From that time, "religion was the sixteenth century word for nationalism" (Wallerstein 2005:125). The intense religious in-group loyalties led to a willingness to kill those who were the "other." The horrific religious conflicts in European societies did not reach closure until the Enlightenment. At this time, tolerance of other religions became dominant and a primary foundation for determining national policy (Dobbelaere 1981, 2000; Lambert 2000).

The global rise of *religious nativism*—absolutistic religious groups that insist only their own view of life and the divine is Truth—appears to be a local reaction against global modernization. This seems to be true regardless of whether the religious group is Islamic, Buddhist, Hasidic Jewish, Christian, or Malaysian Dukway (Fernandez 2011; Salzman 2008). Rapid global change has resulted in anomie as people confront change—fear of obliteration of their own culture and religious perspectives, increasing secularization of the society as the supernatural realm shrinks, threat to the material self-interests of religious organizations, and fear of interdependence with powerful nations of the Western world. All of these threats have strengthened religious nativism (Fernandez 2011).

Thinking Sociologically

What specific religious beliefs or behaviors might influence the way in which religions and countries relate to one another? How might religious organizations influence international relations? For example, how might anti-Muslim prejudice by Christians influence U.S. relations with countries that are predominantly Islamic?

Religion, Technology, and the World Wide Web

Technology and the Internet impact not only nations but also religions. From television broadcasts of megachurch services to Muslim chat rooms using technology to communicate, religious messages travel in new ways. Prior to the wide distribution of religious texts to people who were not ordained ministers, the hierarchies of Christendom controlled what was disseminated as Truth. The common (and typically illiterate) member of the local church did not have any basis for challenging the Pope or other church leaders. Those leaders were the authority. However, Martin Luther used the printed word in many powerful ways. He and other reformers claimed that the Bible alone was the ultimate source of Truth and religious authority. The church leaders were to be believed only insofar as they were faithful to the scriptures. Luther himself used the printed word to spread his version of Christian Truth, and he did so with a vengeance. He not only wrote more than other dissenters; he outpublished the entire legion of Vatican defenders. He published in the common languages of the people rather than in Latin, and the Protestant Reformation was launched. It is doubtful that this could have happened without the printing press, which also had similar revolutionary effects within Judaism (Brasher 2004).

Today, television and multimedia worship have enhanced the marketing of religion, including the modification of the product to meet "consumer" demand (Ebaugh 2005; Roberts and Yamane 2012; Sargeant 2000). The Internet is the most recent technology with enormous impacts. Brasher reports that there are more than a million religion websites and they cover an extraordinarily wide range of religious beliefs and practices (Brasher 2004). Even conservative Christians such as Jerry Falwell, who dubbed the Internet "an evil Tower of Babel," have used it to spread their message. The panic over whether the turn of the millennium (Y2K) would result in massive crashes in computers around the world was related to the "end of the world" prophecies by some conservative Christians (Brasher 2004). The computer, in short, was to be the medium to bring an end to life in this world.

The medium of the Internet is fast-paced and oriented to the now (Brasher 2004). Technology is often outdated in a few years if not in a few months, and the past hardly seems a source of authority or of Truth. Yet, traditional religious communities often excel in maintaining and propagating memories of past events that give meaning to life or that define notions of sacredness and Truth as the world around them changes rapidly. It is too early to tell for sure what impacts these most recent technologies might have on religions around the world, but one thing is clear: The Internet allows for instant access to information about religions that otherwise might be obscure or nonexistent for many people.

Religion provides a sense of meaning regarding life's big questions, addressing our spiritual life and our sense of purpose. Humans in the modern world, however, are not just spiritual. They live in states with massive governmental bureaucracies that hold power and resolve conflicts, and they participate in economic systems that produce and distribute the goods and services needed for survival. In the web of interconnected institutions, we now turn to an examination of politics and economics.

What Have We Learned?

Educational systems are typically viewed as the channel for reduction of inequality, the source of upward mobility, the way to improve the economy, and the path for reduction of prejudice in societies. However, institutions such as education also have a vested interest in stability. Schools foster patriotism and loyalty toward the political system, families support schools and education, and education is expected to support the economic vitality of the nation. Institutions and organizations are driven by interest in their own survival, and risk-taking behaviors on behalf of change are not necessarily ones that foster survival. Taking risks may threaten those who have power, privilege, and influence. It should not be surprising, therefore, that education does more to enhance stability than to create change. Still, those who seek to improve the society see tremendous potential in education as an agent of change if its influence can be harnessed. It works largely with young minds in the socialization process—carrying out what powerful policy makers feel is important.

Religion is a powerful force in the lives of people around the world. It typically elicits passions and deep loyalties, and in so doing, it can stimulate people to great acts of self-sacrificing charity or it can elicit horrible atrocities and intergroup bigotries. People's religious affiliation is strongly related to their nationality, ethnic and racial group, and lifestyle. It is the one institution in most societies that consistently professes a desire for peace and goodwill, yet there may be inconsistencies between what people say and what they do. Religion provides a sense of meaning in life regarding the big questions, and that is why religious things come to have sacred meaning. From a sociological perspective,

however, it is important to recognize that systems of meaning, belonging, and structure are interconnected and interdependent components of religion. Humans in the modern world, however, are not just spiritual. They live in states with massive governmental bureaucracies that hold power and resolve conflicts, and they participate in economic systems that produce and distribute the goods and services needed for survival. The next institutions we will examine are politics and economics—how power relations are negotiated at each level in the social world.

Key Points:

- Education is one of the primary institutions of society, focusing on socialization of children and adults into their cultures so they become contributing members. (See pp.313–314.)

- At the micro level, social theory is attentive to interactions in classrooms and local schools, using concepts of symbolic interaction or cost-benefit analysis to understand the climate of learning. (See pp.314–316.)

- At the micro level, various statuses and roles interact within a school, and classrooms develop their own cultures that may or may not enhance learning. (See pp.316–319.)

- What children learn in schools goes far beyond the formal curriculum. The informal system includes implicit messages that can support or sabotage the formal and intended messages. (See p. 319.)

(Continued)

(Continued)

- At the meso level, education can be understood as a formal organization that works toward certain goals (bureaucracy) but that has many of the dysfunctions of other bureaucracies. (See pp. 319–322.)

- Macro-level theories focus on how education supports the social system (functionalism) or on how education serves the interests of the "haves" and reproduces social inequality (conflict theory). (See pp. 322–327.)

- At the macro level, national governments try to see that their national needs are met by shaping educational policy, and their actions often create tension with those administrators and teachers at the meso and micro levels who do the actual work of teaching. (See pp. 328–329.)

- Educating is also a macro-level global concern, with a variety of questions about how to help economic development in the Global South without imposing Western models that are incompatible with the cultures of other countries. (See pp. 329–332.)

- Religion makes our most important values sacred, operating through three interconnected systems: a meaning system, a belonging system, and a structural system. (See pp. 332–336.)

- We become committed to a religious group through these three systems, by our attachment to a reference group that becomes a belonging system, by making investments in the organization (the structural system), and by holding as real the system of ideas (the meaning system). (See pp. 332–336.)

- At the micro level, symbolic interaction theory illuminates how the meaning system works, with an interaction of myths, rituals, and symbols defining reality and making the values and the meaning system sacred. Rational choice theory focuses on costs and benefits that influence how individuals make decisions about religious commitments, but it also examines how religious organizations go about seeking a "market share" in the competition for members. (See pp. 336–340.)

- Denominationalism is a rather modern way to organize religious life, but it arises when there are a plurality of religious groups and when religious authority is separated from governmental authority. New religious movements (NRMs) also arise in pluralistic social contexts. (See pp. 340–345.)

- At the macro level of analysis, functionalists maintain that religions can serve as a kind of glue to help solidify a society and can meet basic needs of individuals. By contrast, conflict theorists focus on ways that religion reinforces conflicts and inequalities in societies, whether socioeconomic, racial, or gender. (See pp. 345–351.)

- In the United States and Canada, secularization is dominant at the meso and macro levels but seems not to be taking place much at the micro level. (See pp. 351–354.)

- At the global level, religion can be involved in issues of war and peace (sometimes undermining peace unwittingly) and is currently experiencing interface with the world of technology and the World Wide Web. (See pp. 354–355.)

Discussion Questions

1. Why is a good system of education important for a democracy? How can gaining a sociological perspective help people become more effective participants in a democratic society?

2. How do structural-functional and conflict theorists describe the "hidden curriculum" in schools? What description best matches your own school experience? Why?

3. How do schools "reproduce and perpetuate social stratification"? If you had the power and desire to use the school system to reduce inequality, what policies would you implement? What do you think the chances are of your policies actually being put into place? Why?

4. If you are a person of faith and affiliated with a religious community, how did you become so? If you are not, why is that so? How did your family members and peers influence your views toward religion?

5. Why is organization of religious groups important? How do systems of meaning, belonging, and structure connect to one another?

6. What do you think might happen to society if religions did not exist? Why? How would an absence of religion impact you personally?

Contributing to Our Social World: What Can We Do?

At the Local Level

- Every college and university provides opportunities for students to *tutor and mentor other students*. Ask the chair of your department how you can help!

- *Campus religious foundations or ministries:* Most colleges and universities, including many of those not affiliated with a religion, have religious groups on campus. If you are not already a member and would like to join such an organization on your campus, contact a student representative or faculty sponsor, attend a meeting, and become involved. Most of these organizations participate in various types of outreach work, including volunteering for soup kitchens, food pantries, or thrift stores for the poor. If you attend a religiously affiliated college or university, you will find many and varied ministries to choose from.

At the Organization or Institutional Level

- Most primary schools welcome *reading and math tutors*, volunteers and service learning students who can read to young students and tutor them in reading and math. Contact a faculty member on your campus who specializes in early childhood education and investigate the opportunities for such volunteer work.

- *Volunteers of America* (www.voa.org) chapters organize to provide low-income and homeless children with school supplies and backpacks every year through "Operation Backpack." You can learn more about the program and how to locate your local VOA chapter at the VOA website or by Googling "VOA and operation backpack" and the name of your state.

- *Denominationally based campus organizations.* Many religious campus organizations such as the Newman Foundation (Roman Catholic; http://newmanfnd.org),

InterVarsity (Christian; www.intervarsity.org), Muslim Students Association (MSA; http://msanational.org), and Hillel Foundation (Jewish; www.hillel.org) are branches of larger organizations. You can find out more about them and how to start or join a chapter by going to their websites.

At the National and Global Levels

- *Teaching abroad* provides an opportunity to make a difference in the lives of children. Consider teaching English abroad through one of many organizations that sponsor teachers. Visit www.globaltesol.com, www.teachabroad.com, www.jetprogramme.org, and related websites.

- *Tikkun Community* (*www.tikkun.org*) is an interreligious organization, started by the Jewish community, to "mend, repair, and transform the world." It is an "international community of people of many faiths calling for social justice and political freedom."

- *The American Friends Service Committee* (*www.afsc.org*) is a Quaker organization that promotes lasting peace with justice, as a practical expression of faith in action."

- *Catholic Relief Services* (www.crs.org) "carries out the commitment of the Bishops of the United States to assist the poor and vulnerable" in more than 100 countries.

- *Lutheran World Relief* (*www.lwr.org*) "extends the hand of Christian love to people overcoming poverty and injustice in fifty countries."

Visit **www.sagepub.com/oswcondensed3e** for online activities, sample tests, and other helpful information. Select "Chapter 11: Education and Religion" for chapter-specific activities.

CHAPTER

12

Politics and Economics

Penetrating Power and Privilege

The phrase in the subtitle of this chapter refers to the fact that power and privilege penetrate every aspect of our lives. The phrase has a double meaning, however, for sociology helps us to penetrate the sources and the consequences of power and privilege—both political and economic.

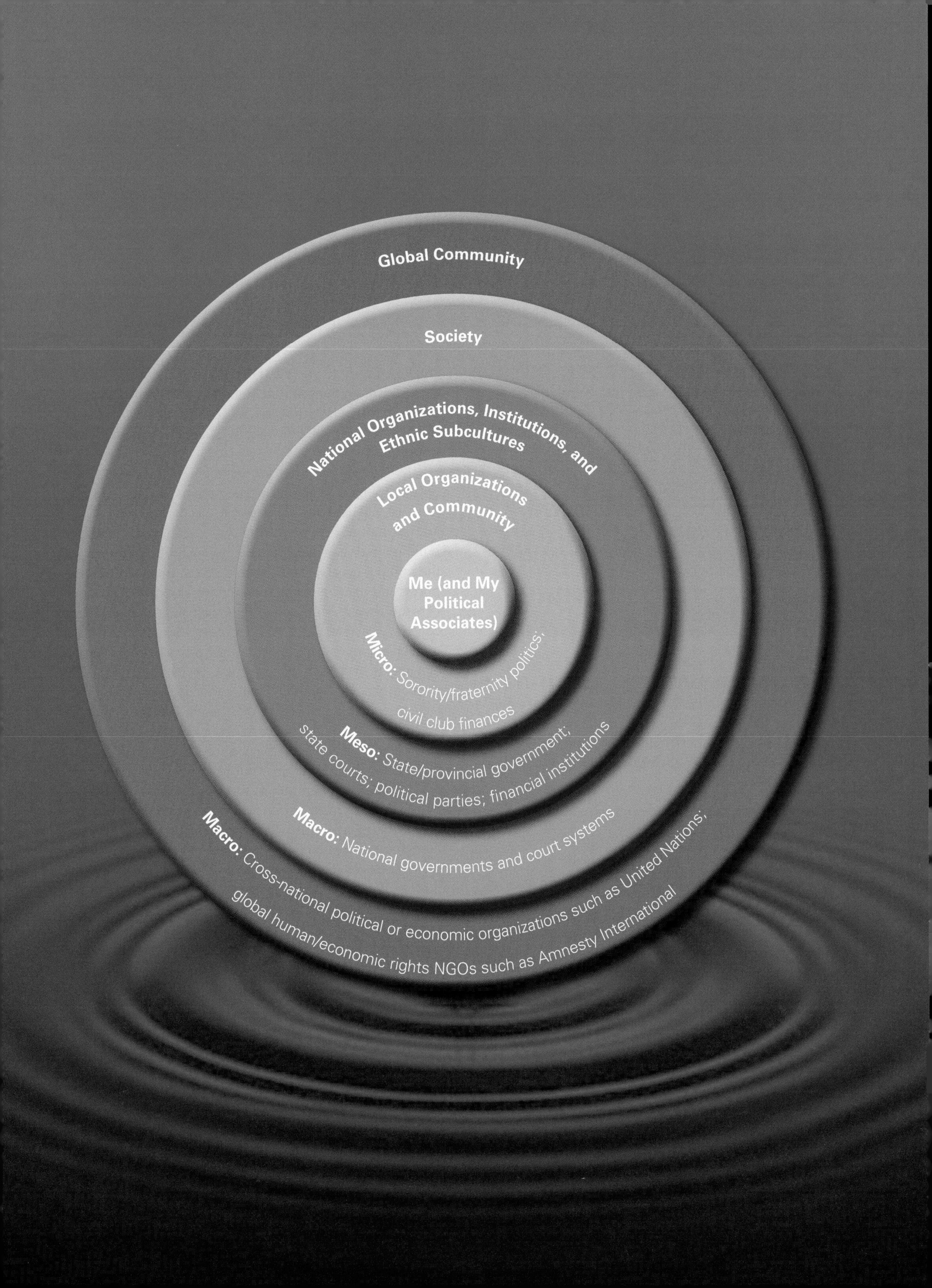

Global Community

Society

National Organizations, Institutions, and Ethnic Subcultures

Local Organizations and Community

Me (and My Political Associates)

Micro: Sorority/fraternity politics; civil club finances

Meso: State/provincial government; state courts; political parties; financial institutions

Macro: National governments and court systems

Macro: Cross-national political or economic organizations such as United Nations; global human/economic rights NGOs such as Amnesty International

Think About It	
Micro: Me (and My Political and Economic Life)	How do political power and economic power penetrate my own life, even in the privacy of my home?
Micro: Local Community	How do people in my local community exercise power in constructive or destructive ways?
Meso: National Institutions; Complex Organizations; Ethnic Groups	How does the political institution interact with the economic institution to affect my life?
Macro: National Society	Why does economic instability threaten a government?
Macro: Global Community	Why do struggles over power and privilege often evolve into war and terrorism?

What's coming in this chapter?

What Is Power?

Power and Privilege in Our Social World

Theoretical Perspectives on Power and Privilege

Micro-Level Analysis: Individuals, Power, and Participation

Meso-Level Analysis: Distributions of Power and Privilege Within a Nation

Macro-Level Analysis: National and Global Systems of Power and Privilege

magine that a nuclear disaster has struck. The mortality rate is stunning. The few survivors gather together for human support and collectively attempt to meet their basic survival needs. They come from varying backgrounds and have diverse skills. Before the disaster some—the

Politics is about power and about mobilizing support to lead. The 2012 presidential primaries generated a lot of interest as these two candidates—Mitt Romney (left) and Barack Obama (right)—battled for the most powerful political office on the planet—the U.S. presidency.

stockbroker and the business executive, for instance—earned more money and held higher social status than the others, but that is in the past. Faced with the new and unfamiliar situation, different skills seem more immediately important for survival.

Where should this group begin? Think about the options. Some sort of organization seems essential, a structure that will help the group meet its needs. Food and shelter are paramount. Those with experience in agriculture and building trades are likely to take leadership roles to provide these initial necessities. As time goes on, the need for clear norms and rules emerges. The survivors decide that all members must work—must contribute their share of effort to the collective survival. At first, these norms are unwritten, but gradually some norms and rules are declared more important and are recorded, with sanctions (penalties) attached for noncompliance. Committees are formed to deal with group concerns, and a semblance of a judicial system emerges. Someone is appointed to coordinate work shifts, and others are chosen to oversee emerging aspects of this small society's life. This scenario could play out in many ways.

What is happening? A social structure is evolving. Not everyone in the group will agree with the structure, and some people will propose alternatives. Whose ideas are adopted? Leadership roles may fall to the physically strongest, perhaps the most persuasive, or those with the most skills and knowledge for survival. Those who are most competent at organizing may become the leaders, but that outcome is by no means ensured. In our world of power and privilege, a war, an invading power, or revolutionary overthrow of an unstable government can change the form of a political system overnight, necessitating rapid reorganization.

The opening scenario and the political activity in our modern society share a common element—power. The concept of power is critical to understanding many aspects of our social world. Our primary focus in this chapter is the political and economic dimensions of society, since both enforce the distribution of power and resources in societies. Political systems involve the relationships between individuals and between the individual and larger social institutions. Economic systems produce and distribute goods and services, and not everyone gets an equal share; thus, some citizens are given privileges that others do not have. While politics and economics are intertwined, we give more attention to political systems in this chapter because we have discussed economics in several other chapters such as those in Part III (on inequality). We consider the nature of power, politics, and economics at each level in our social world; theoretical perspectives on power and privilege; individuals and power; the distribution of power and privilege through economic and political systems; and national and global systems of governance, including international conflicts, war, and terrorism.

Thinking Sociologically

Global climate change has resulted in flooding of many Pacific islands. Only a few people have survived. How would you construct a social system from scratch? What are the issues that would need to be resolved if one were to build a system from scratch?

What Is Power?

Power is an age-old theme in many great scholarly discussions. Social philosophers since Plato, Aristotle, and Socrates have addressed the issue of political systems and power. Machiavelli, an early 16th-century Italian political philosopher, is perhaps best known for his observation that "the ends justify the means." His understanding of how power was exercised in the 15th, 16th, and 17th centuries significantly influenced how monarchs used the powers of the state (the means) to obtain wealth, new territories, and trade dominance (the ends).

The most common definition of power used in social sciences today comes from Max Weber, who saw **power** as *the ability of a person or group to realize its own will in group action, even against resistance of others who disagree* (Weber 1947). Building on Weber's idea of power, one perspective is that there are various *power arenas*. First, the nation-state (national government) attempts to control the behavior of individuals through (a) *physical control* (police force) or *outright coercion* (threats and actual violence), (b) *symbolic control* such as intimidation or manipulation of people, and (c) *rules of conduct* that channel behavior toward desired patterns, such as workplace rules.

Second, Weber's definition explains power as the ability to influence social life. Wherever people interact or participate in activities or organizations, power is a consequence (Olsen 1970). Therefore, individuals who have an understanding of interorganizational dynamics and can

manipulate organization members are likely to have more power than others in organizational settings.

A third perspective focuses on a traditional Marxist approach to class structures, arguing that the control of economic resources and production allows the ruling class to keep ruling (Therborn 1976). People who control economic resources also protect their self-interests by controlling political processes through ideology, economic constraints, and physical coercion or political resources. Among many recent examples, Zimbabwe's leader, Robert Mugabe, used all of these methods of controlling political processes to hold onto power. In the United States, conflict theorists interpret those with power and privilege as using media in their self-interest to convince the public that they will eventually also be super-rich. Therefore, the inequalities seem fair to the public, and the members of the middle and working classes are convinced that further tax breaks and advantages to the wealthy are—in the long run—in their own self-interest. Thus, power is found in all parts of the social world and is an element of every social situation (Domhoff 1998). So how does power work at each level?

Thinking Sociologically

How do you, your family members, your boss, or your professors use power? What kind of power does each of these people have?

Power and Privilege in Our Social World

Power operates at the most micro levels of interaction, from individuals to family groups. In family life, husband-wife relations often involve negotiation and sometimes conflict over how to run a household and spend money. Interactions between parents and children also involve power issues as parents socialize their children. Indeed, the controversy over whether spanking is effective discipline or abusive imposition of pain is a question of how parents use their power to teach their children and control their behavior.

At the meso level, power operates in cities, counties, and states and provinces. Governments make decisions about which corporations receive tax breaks to locate their plants within the region. They pass laws that regulate everything from how long one's grass can be before a fine is imposed to how public schools will be funded. State and provincial governments in Western democracies also can control the

Individuals can work to elect the party—and the candidates—that they think will make their lives better and improve conditions in the world. They work at the micro level to influence who will wield power in meso and macro systems.

Theoretical Perspectives on Power and Privilege

Do you and I have any real decision-making power? Can our voices or votes make a difference, or do leaders hold all the power? Many sociologists and political scientists have studied these questions and found several answers to who holds power and the relationship between the rulers and the ruled.

Micro- and Meso-Level Perspectives: Legitimacy of Power

Interaction theorists focus on symbols and constructions of reality that allow some people to assume power. For symbolic interactionists, a central question is how loyalty to the power of the state is created—a loyalty that is so strong that citizens are willing to die for the state in a war. In the founding years of the United States, loyalty tended to be mostly to individual states. Even as late as the Civil War, Northern battalions fought under the flag of their own state rather than that of the United States. The Federalist Party, which stressed centralized government in early U.S. history, faded from the scene. The Democratic-Republican Party, which evolved into the current Democratic Party, had downplayed the power of the federal government. This has changed. Today, the Democratic Party generally supports a larger role for the federal government than its rival, although Republican president George W. Bush expanded federal powers substantially.

Most people in the United States think of themselves as U.S. citizens more than Virginians or Pennsylvanians or Oregonians, and they are willing to defend the whole country. National symbols such as anthems and flags help create loyalty to nations. The treatment of flags is an interesting issue that illustrates the social construction of meaning around national symbols. The next "Sociology in Our Social World" explores this issue.

Socialization of individuals at the micro level generally instills a strong sense of loyalty to the government in power and loyalty to a flag or another symbol that represents the nation. Individuals learn their political and economic attitudes, values, and behaviors—their political socialization—from family, schools, the media, and their nation. For example, any nation's leaders provide much of the information for newspapers and other media and can spin that information to suit their needs and manage the perceptions of the public. Governments also play a role in what is taught in schools, including attitudes of the citizenry regarding capitalism, socialism, and other economic or political systems (Glasberg and Shannon 2011).

way people live and make their living. Therefore, people have an interest in influencing governments by selecting their leaders, contributing to political campaigns, and helping elect the people who support their views. Interest groups such as ethnic or minority groups and national organizations and bureaucracies also wield power and try to influence the political process at the meso level.

At the macro level, international organizations such as the United Nations and World Bank; nongovernmental organizations such as Doctors Without Borders; and military, political, and economic alliances such as the North Atlantic Treaty Organization are parts of the global system of power. Locally organized groups can force change that influences politics at the local, state/provincial, national, or global level. Provincial or state laws shape what can and cannot be done at the local level. Laws at the national level influence state, province, or county politics and policies. Global treaties affect national autonomy.

Power can be studied in political organizations such as local, state, or federal governments; in political parties—Republican, Democratic, Liberation, or Green; and in other types of organizations such as the auto and banking industries. Power can also be understood in terms of the allocation of economic resources in a society and what factors influence patterns of resource distribution. Both economic and political systems are important in the sociologist's consideration of power distribution in any society. Let us first consider the theoretical lenses that help us understand power and politics.

Sociology in Our Social World

The Flag, Symbolism, and Patriotism

Flags have become pervasive symbols of nations, creating a national identity (Billig 1995). In some countries, loyalty to the nation is taught with daily pledges to the flag at work or school. National loyalty becomes sacred and that sacredness is embedded in the flag as a symbol of patriotism. Émile Durkheim maintained that one's national group elicits loyalty and thereby becomes sacred (Durkheim 1947). He believed that sacredness actually is a form of respect for that which transcends the individual, including the state. In the United States, the flag and its construction illustrate key ideas in symbolic interaction theory. The stars and stripes each have specific meaning related to states and the nation. However, for many decades after the nation was founded, U.S. citizens had more loyalty to their state than to a federal government, but in the aftermath of the Civil War, a sense of nation began to gel (Billig 1995). By the 21st century, loyalty to the nation had become very strong, with many people risking their lives to defend it. The American flag had also became a focal point for that allegiance.

Care of the U.S. flag is an interesting example of symbolism and respect for that symbol. Flag etiquette instructions make it clear that flying a flag that is faded, soiled, or dirty is considered an offense to the flag. We are told to either burn or bury a damaged flag as a way to honor and respect it.

Some citizens and legislators have proposed a constitutional amendment prohibiting burning of the U.S. flag to prevent protesters from using the flag as a statement against certain American policies. Because protests show disrespect, some patriots have a visceral reaction of outrage. As recently as June 2006, the Senate came within one vote of sending the flag burning amendment to the individual states for ratification (CNN.com 2006). Supporters want flag burners punished and disrespect for the flag outlawed. Those who oppose this amendment feel that only tyrannical countries limit freedom of speech. They feel that the principle of free speech, which is central to democracy, must be allowed even if a sacred symbol is at stake. Indeed, opponents of the amendment think passing such a law would be a desecration of what that flag stands for. The two sides have each attached different meanings to what is considered desecration of the national symbol. In the meantime, if you have a tattered or fading flag, burning it is the way you honor that flag—as long as you do so in private!

Other aspects of the U.S. Flag Code, which specifies what is considered official respect for or desecration of the flag, are interesting precisely because many people violate this code while they believe themselves to be displaying their patriotism (Sons of Union Veterans of the Civil War 2010).

1. The flag should *never* be used for advertising in any manner whatsoever. It should not be embroidered on cushions, handkerchiefs, or scarves, nor reproduced on paper napkins, carry-out bags, wrappers, or anything else that will soon be thrown away.

2. No *part* of the flag—depictions of stars and stripes that are in any form other than that approved for the flag design itself—should ever be used as a costume, a clothing item, or an athletic uniform.

3. Displaying a flag after dark should not be done unless it is illuminated, and it should not be left out when it is raining.

4. The flag should *never* be represented flat or horizontally (as many marching bands do). It should *always* be aloft and free.

5. The flag should under no circumstances be used as a ceiling covering.

According to the standards established by U.S. military representatives and congressional action, any of these forms of display may be considered a desecration of the flag, yet the meaning that common people give to these acts is quite different. Symbolic interactionists are interested in the meaning people give to actions and how symbols themselves inform behavior.

This man no doubt feels he is expressing his patriotism, yet technically he is violating the U.S. Flag Code and "desecrating" the American flag. During the Vietnam War, protesters risked attack for dressing this way, which was viewed as disrespect for the flag and the country.

Thinking Sociologically

Is wearing a shirt or sweater with the U.S. stars and stripes in some sort of artistic design an act of desecration of the flag or a statement of patriotism? Does flying a Confederate flag symbolize disrespect for the national U.S. flag? Explain.

Social Construction of Politics: Legitimacy, Authority, and Power

Max Weber distinguished between legitimate and illegitimate power. *Power that people consider legitimate* is called **authority** and is recognized as lawful and just by those subject to it (Weber 1946). Governments have legitimate power when citizens acknowledge that the government has the right to exercise power over them. This is measured by two factors: whether the state can govern without the use or threat of forceful coercion and the degree to which challenges to state authority are processed through channels such as the legal

system rather than overthrow of the government (Jackman 1993). Citizens of Western societies recognize elected officials and laws made by elected bodies as legitimate authority. They adhere to a judge's rulings because they recognize that court decrees are legitimate. In contrast, illegitimate power, or coercion, includes living under force of a military regime or being imprisoned without charge. (See Figure 12.1.) These distinctions between legitimate and illegitimate power are important to our understanding of how leaders or political institutions establish the right to lead. To Weber, illegitimate power is sustained by brute force or coercion. Authority is granted by the people who are subject to the power, which means that no coercion is needed (Weber 1946).

Force + Consent = Power

Force < Consent = Legitimate Power (authority) [force is less than consent]

Force > Consent = Illegitimate Power (e.g., dictatorship) [force is greater than consent]

Figure 12.1   Weber's Formula Regarding Power

How Do Leaders Gain Legitimate Power?

In constitutional democracies, those with power do not have the right to arbitrarily hold people against their will, to take their property, to demand they make unauthorized payments, or to kill them to protect others. Yet, even in democracies, certain people in power have the right to carry out such actions against people who are determined to be threats to society. How do leaders get these rights? Generally, leaders with legitimate power gained their positions in one of three ways:

1. *Traditional authority* is passed on through the generations, usually within a family line, so that positions are inherited. Tribal leaders in African societies pass their titles and power to their sons. Japanese and many European royal lines pass from generation to generation. Authority is seen as "normal" for a family or a person to hold because of tradition. It has always been done that way, so no one challenges it. When authority is granted based on tradition, authority rests with the position rather than the person. The authority is easily transferred to another heir of that status such as a king, a queen, or a tribal chief.

2. *Charismatic authority* is power held by an individual resulting from a claim of extraordinary, even divine, personal characteristics. Charismatic leaders often emerge at times of change when strong, new leadership is needed. Some vivid examples of charismatic religious leaders include Jesus, Muhammad, and the founder of the Mormon Church, Joseph Smith. Charismatic political leaders include Mao Zedong in China, Nelson Mandela in South Africa, and

Executive Branch

Prince William and Kate Middleton are in line eventually to inherit the throne of England as King and Queen, and their positions have legitimacy because the citizenry of England consent to the system. The authority of the throne is traditional.

Mahatma Gandhi in India. These men led their countries to independence and had respect from citizens that bordered on "awe." Some women have also been recognized as charismatic leaders, such as Burma's (Myanmar's) Aung San Suu Kyi, prodemocracy activist, widely recognized prisoner of conscience, leader of the National League for Democracy of Burma, and winner of many awards including the Nobel Peace Prize in 1991.

The key point is that for charismatic leaders, unlike traditional authority leaders, the right to lead rests with the person, not the position. This is a change-oriented and unstable form of leadership because authority resides in a single person and at death the leadership also dies. The most common pattern is that, as stability reemerges, power will become institutionalized—rooted in stable routine patterns of the organization. Charismatic leaders are effective during transitional periods but are often replaced by rational-legal leaders once affairs of state become stable.

3. *Rational-legal authority* is most typical in modern nation-states. Leaders have the expertise to carry out the duties of their positions, and the leadership structure is usually bureaucratic and rule bound. Individuals are granted authority because they have proper training or have proved their merit. This is the form of authority most familiar to individuals living in democracies. The rational-legal form of authority often seems entirely irrational and an invitation to chaos to people in tradition-oriented societies. It is important that authority in this system is divided between the position (which establishes criteria and credentials for the position) and the person (who has achieved those credentials for the position).

Each of these three types of authority is a "legitimate" exercise of power because the people being governed give their consent, at least implicitly, to the leaders (Weber 1947, [1904–1905] 1958). However, on occasion leaders overstep their legitimate bounds and rule by force. Some of these rulers, such as Muammar al-Qaddafi in Libya and Hosni Mubarak in Egypt, are challenged and overthrown.

Self-Interest as a Path to Legitimacy

In the United States, legitimacy to govern is often rooted in ideology—in the dreams and self-image of the nation. However, in contemporary democratic politics, there is often, and perhaps increasingly, explicit reference to self-interests of voters. This reflects the *rational choice perspective* that humans tend to vote for their own self-interests and benefit, regardless of whether the actions of government would be fair to all citizens. Both U.S. Republican and Democratic parties draw support based on self-interests.

Both parties try to convince the public that their own policies will serve the self-interests of each voter. Democrats tend to argue that their government policies benefit citizens directly. For example, the democratic appeals from Vice President Joe Biden tend to be very clear and forceful in support of the self-interests of the working and middle classes.

Republicans stress that less government and more tax breaks to those with wealth creates a greater stimulus to the economy than anything the government can do (though the immediate effect is beneficial to the wealthy), but will have long-term benefits for the entire populace. Again, the appeal is to self-interests. Ronald Reagan appealed to self-interest when he asked in his campaign for the presidency: "Are you better off now than you were four years ago when this administration took office?" (Shirley 2012). This explicit appeal is one path to legitimacy of power, and it is the explanation favored by rational choice theorists.

An issue that interests many theorists is that many people do not understand their own self-interests. This is especially true in the world of politics with propaganda on various sides of any issue and with the complexity of social policies. The result is that people may vote for people who support policies that would actually harm them. To make it even more complex, some people vote based on values—right to life or protection of the environment, for example—because they think it is the right thing to do. The policy may not be in the person's self-interests—unless the person is considering long-term noneconomic interests, such as a desire to please God and to have a good place in the afterlife.

Macro Perspectives: Who Rules?

Power is more often studied at the macro level of nations and global conflicts, but theories set forth two very different views of how power is distributed.

Pluralist Model

The pluralist model holds that power is distributed among various groups so that no one group has complete power. According to pluralists, it is primarily through interest groups that you and I, average people, can influence decision-making processes. Our interests are represented by groups such as unions or environmental organizations that act to keep power from being concentrated in the hands of an elite few (Dahl 1961; Dye and Zeigler 1983).

Politics involves negotiation and compromise between competing groups. Interest groups can block policies that conflict with their own interests by mobilizing large numbers against certain legislative or executive actions. Witness the efforts to influence health care reform in the United States and to reform government and industry practices. Greenpeace, Common Cause, Earth First!, the Christian Coalition, Focus on the Family, the Family Research Council, various labor unions, and other consumer, environmental, religious, and political action groups have had impacts on policy decisions. According to pluralists, shared power is found in each person's ability to join groups and influence policy decisions and outcomes.

National or international nongovernmental organizations (NGOs) can have a major impact on global issues and policy making, as exemplified by the Grameen Bank and other microcredit organizations (Yunus and Jolis 1999). NGOs exert influence on power holders because of the

numbers they represent, the money they control, the issues they address, and the effectiveness of their spokespeople or lobbyists. Sometimes they form coalitions around issues of concern such as the environment, human rights, and women's and children's issues. According to pluralists, multiple power centers offer the best chance to maintain democratic forms of government because no one group dominates and many citizens are involved. Although an interest group may dominate decision making on a specific issue, no one group dictates policy on all issues.

Another major theory counters the pluralists, arguing that the real power centers at the national level are controlled by an elite few and that most individuals like you and me have little power.

Elite Model

The power elite model asserts that it is inevitable that a small group of elite individuals will rule societies. Individuals have limited power through interest groups, but real power is held by the power elite (Domhoff 1998, 2008; Mills 1956). They wield power through their institutional roles and make decisions about war, peace, the economy, wages, taxes, justice, education, welfare, and health issues—all of which have serious impact on citizens. These powerful elites attempt to maintain, perpetuate, and even strengthen their rule. This influence eventually leads to abuse of their power (Michels [1911] 1967).

The social philosopher Vilfredo Pareto expanded on this idea of abuse of power, pointing out that abuse would cause a countergroup to challenge the elite for power. Eventually, as the latter group gains power, its members become corrupt as well, and the cycle—a circulation of the elite—continues. Corruption in many countries illustrates this pattern (Pareto [1911] 1955). Consider the long-lasting regimes in some Middle Eastern and North African countries that have amassed power and money over many years.

C. Wright Mills also argues that there is an invisible but interlocking power elite in U.S. society, consisting of leaders in military, business, and political spheres; they make the key political, economic, and social decisions for the nation and manipulate what the public hears (Mills 1956). For example, in the business sphere, the top corporations control more than half of the nation's industrial assets, transportation, communication, and utilities. They also manage two thirds of the insurance assets. According to the power elite theory, the U.S. upper class provides a cohesive economic/political power structure that represents upper-class interests (Domhoff 1998, 2008).

Private preparatory schools are one example of how elite status is transmitted to the next generation (Howard 2007; Persell and Cookson 1985). Many of those who hold top positions on national committees and boards or in the foreign policy-making agencies of national government

Pluralist models provide one way of understanding patterns of power distribution in society, suggesting that having many sources of power in a society inhibits any one group from dominating. For workers, this usually means uniting to have a strong voice through unions. Here we see several hundred autoworkers and their supporters stage a protest against poor pay and working conditions and violation of labor practices by their company.

attended the same private preparatory schools and Ivy League colleges—Brown, Columbia, Cornell, Harvard, University of Pennsylvania, Princeton, Yale, and Dartmouth.

Key government officials come from positions in industry, finance, law, and universities. They are linked with an international elite that helps shape the world economy. According to the power elite model, Congress ultimately has minimal power. Elite models maintain that government seldom regulates business. Instead, business co-opts politicians to support its interests by providing financial support needed to run political election campaigns.

Pluralists, however, disagree, believing that one reason we have big government is that a very powerful government serves as a balance to the enormous power of the corporate world. Big business and big government are safety checks against tyranny—and each is convinced that the other is too big.

A woman in Libya usually means uniting to have a strong voice through unions. Here we see several hundred autoworkers and their supporters stage a protest against poor pay and working conditions and violation of labor practices by their company.

Thinking Sociologically

Is your national society controlled by pluralist interest groups or a power elite? Can individuals influence the power elite? What evidence supports your view?

Micro-Level Analysis: Individuals, Power, and Participation

Karin signed up for every credit card available in the United States. She would max out one card and move on to the next, always paying just enough to keep the debt collectors from the door—until the day it all came crashing down on her. By then she was $53,000 in debt. She had transferred money from one no-interest card to another to avoid paying the interest. Then the monetary crisis of late 2008 hit, and soon banks were in such serious trouble that they had to tighten policies. Loans were hard to get, credit card companies became more selective, and when she could not pay the minimum due, Karin's interest rate jumped to 26%. She had little choice but to declare bankruptcy, even though it would devastate her credit rating for at least seven years. The bankruptcy provision is governed by laws passed by her government and administered by the courts. Little does Karin know that credit cards did not even exist until the 1950s, but the trajectory of her life for the next few years will be shaped by the innovations of an entrepreneur, by global economic forces, and by legislative and judicial political systems that define her options.

Whether you experience credit or home mortgage problems, have health insurance, or are subject to a military draft depends in part on the political and economic decisions made by the government in power. Political systems influence our personal lives in myriad ways, some of which are readily apparent: health and safety regulations, taxation, military draft, regulations on food and drugs that people buy, and even whether the gallon of gas pumped into one's car is really a full gallon. In this section, we explore the impact individuals have on the government and the variables that influence participation in political and economic policy-making processes. A key issue at the micro level is decisions by individuals to vote or otherwise participate in the political system. This private decision is, in turn, affected by where those individuals fall in the stratification system of society, not just by personal choices.

Participation in Democratic Processes

Citizens in democratic countries have the power to vote. Most countries, even dictatorships, have some form of citizen participation. In only a handful of countries are there no elections. Sociologists ask many questions about voting patterns, such as what influences voting and why some individuals do not participate in the political process at all. Social scientists want to know how participation affects (and is affected by) the individual's perception of his or her power in relationship to the state.

Ideology and Attitudes About Politics and Economics

Political ideology affects how people think about power. Let us consider several ways that our beliefs and attitudes affect our political ideas. First, what do we believe about the power of the individual versus the power of the state? If we believe that individuals are motivated by selfish considerations and desire for power, we may feel as the 17th-century English philosopher Thomas Hobbes did: Humans need to be controlled, and order must be imposed by an all-powerful sovereign. This is more important than individual freedom and liberty. On the other hand, we might believe, as did John Locke, another 17th-century political philosopher, that human nature is perfectible and rational, that we are not born selfish but we learn selfishness through experience with others. Humans, Locke argued, should have their needs and interests met, and among these needs are liberty, ability to sustain life, and ownership of property. He felt the people should decide who governs them. Thus, we can see that support for democracy is influenced by one's core assumptions about what it means to be human.

Second, do we believe in equal distribution of resources—wealth, property, and income—or do we think that those who are most able or who have inherited high status should receive more of the wealth? Some social scientists, politicians, and voters think that individuals have different abilities and are therefore entitled to different rewards. Some people are successful, and some are not. Others think government should facilitate more equal distribution of resources simply because all persons are equally deserving of dignity. Conflict theorists tend to support this view.

In the United States, for example, Republicans (and others on "the right") tend to believe individuals and local communities should take more responsibility for education, health care, welfare, child care, and other areas of common public concern, feeling that this protects rights to local control and prevents creation of a powerful bureaucracy.

Democrats (and those on "the left") are more likely to argue for the federal government's social responsibility to the people. For instance, Democrats have been concerned that leaving policies such as school integration to local communities would perpetuate inequality and discriminatory patterns in some communities. National government involvement, they feel, protects the rights of all citizens. Republicans argue that less government allows for more individual freedom and also stimulates innovation as individuals seek to solve problems and make money by doing so. The ongoing debates about the national welfare system, health care policies, educational and military expenditures, and other government spending in the United States reflect these different philosophies.

Third, do we believe that change is desirable? Generally, these views fall into two camps: change as a potential threat to stability versus policy change to benefit the general population or segments of the population. Views on change affect how people vote.

Voters in many countries are influenced by issues such as the environment or immigration rather than traditional party ideology. Party affiliation based on ideology is becoming relatively weak in the United States, and an increasing number of people are identifying themselves as Independents rather than Democrats or Republicans, either because they do not want to commit themselves to one ideology or because they are more interested in specific issues than in an overriding philosophy of government.

Thinking Sociologically

How might your decision about how to vote (a micro-level decision) be affected by your ideology and attitudes about politics and economics? How might these decisions make a difference in how state/provincial, national, or global systems work?

Levels of Participation in Politics

A key right of most adult citizens in participatory democracies in the world is to elect their leaders. Voting provides many citizens with power when done fairly, although some elections are corrupt or rigged and deny citizens their rights. However, in dictatorships citizens do not have the right to determine the leadership of their nation; rather, it is determined by tyrannical power or birthright (Glasberg and Shannon 2011).

The majority of people in the world are uninvolved in the political process because there are few opportunities for them to meaningfully participate (especially in nondemocratic countries). They feel that involvement can have little relevance for them (apathy) or that they cannot affect the process (alienation from a system that does not value them). However, political decisions may affect people directly, and they may be drawn unwittingly into the political arena. Peasants making a subsistence living may be forced off the land and into refugee camps by wars over issues that have little relevance to them. Their children may be drafted and taken away to fight and be killed in these battles. Religious or ideological factions may force them to help pay for conflicts in which they see no purpose or have no stake. In recent years, such situations have drawn the uninvolved into politics in Guatemala, Colombia, Uganda, Cambodia (Kampuchea), Haiti, Rwanda, Somalia, Sudan, India, Iraq, Lebanon, Gaza, Afghanistan, and North Africa.

Political participation is affected by election laws, including those that enfranchise people, that stress voting as a requirement of citizenship, and that structure elections to facilitate representation by historically underrepresented groups. In some countries, voting is an obligation of citizenship, and voter turnout is above 90%. For example, in Argentina, Australia, Brazil, and Congo, to name a few, it is a violation of the law not to vote (World Factbook 2013g).

 Republicans in America

 Immigration

Fines, community service, and even jail time are penalties for not voting. Elections are held over many days to ensure that people can get to the polls. Some other countries also make sure that ethnic minorities and women have a voice by structuring elections to ensure broad representation. Even inmates in prison are expected to vote in some countries. The next "Sociology Around the World" examines the reasons that an African country—the war-torn nation of Rwanda—emerged early in the 21st century with the highest percentage of women in government of any nation in the world.

Sociology Around the World

Women and Political Change in Postgenocide Rwanda

By Melanie Hughes

In 2003, Rwanda became the new global leader in women's political representation. In 2011, women were elected to over 56% of the seats in Rwanda's Chamber of Deputies, plus the speaker's chair and cabinet positions, making it the most gender balanced of any national legislature in the history of the world (McCrummen 2008; see also Table 9.1 on page 251). For the first time since 1988, a country outside of Scandinavia garnered the top spot in women's political representation, and for the first time in history, the position was held by an African country. From just 10 years earlier, the number of women serving in Rwanda's parliament almost tripled.

Many were particularly surprised about Rwandan women's involvement, given the country's recent history of economic upheaval and civil war. The instability culminated in 1994, when during a span of 100 days, an estimated 800,000 Rwandans died at the hands of their countrymen and women in a horrific ethnic genocide. So, how did Rwanda bounce back within a decade to lead the world in women's political representation?

At the micro level, research suggests that the behavior of individual women during and after the Rwandan genocide generated support for their empowerment (Hughes 2004). During the civil war, women served on the front lines with men, led military actions, and worked as mediators to help end the insurgency. After conflict subsided, women played key roles in the reconstruction effort (UNIFEM 2002). Interviews with Rwandans suggest that the burdens taken on by women during this period generated both the political will and the public support necessary to advance women in politics (Mutamba 2005).

Important changes also occurred at the meso level. Immediately after the killing subsided, women's associations, both new and old, began to step into the void (Longman 2005). Women's organizations took action early on to shape the new state. For example, in 1994, an organization of women's associations drafted a document addressing Rwanda's postconflict problems and suggesting how women could foster reconciliation (Powley 2003). Building up to the adoption of the new constitution in 2003, women's organizations served as a bridge, taking suggestions from women at the grassroots level into meetings with the transitional government.

Women at all levels were supported by international organizations and foreign aid. Rwanda's economic troubles meant that dependence on international funding was unavoidable, and women were well situated to take advantage of foreign monies. The empowerment of women, especially in the Global South, was on the agenda of the United Nations and other global bodies. Therefore, many international organizations helped advance the idea that women's incorporation into political decision-making positions was essential for sustainable peace (Hughes 2004).

Actions by individual women, native women's associations, and international organizations all helped encourage the transitional government to adopt female-friendly political institutions. Women's councils and women-only elections were established to guarantee female representation down to the grassroots level. In addition, the new constitution mandated that women fill 30% of all policy-making posts in Rwanda.

Rwanda today has a democratically elected government, but with a fairly authoritarian leader. However, since the election in 2003, women have still been able to revise inheritance laws, pass a law banning discrimination against women, and strengthen rape laws (Longman 2005). Rwanda has come a long way toward giving women a political voice.

In the United States, voter turnout is rather low, with far fewer than half of eligible voters going to the ballot box during most elections. However, in the 2012 presidential election, 58.7% of eligible voters turned out (Nonprofit Vote 2012; U.S. Election Project 2012). As a result, with Obama winning just over 50% of the votes cast, just under 29% of the eligible voters voted for the president. An even smaller percentage voted for Governor Romney. Presidential-year elections, though, do have a higher turn-out than "off-year" elections, and the numbers have gen-erally been higher in the 21st century than in the three decades from 1970 to 2000 (Information Please Almanac 2008; Lederman 2012; McDonald 2009). Higher African American and Latino participation has been especially important to the increasing numbers of voters (Sherwood 2012; Short 2009).

In off-year elections—when many senators, congres-sional representatives, and state governors are elected—the turnout hovers in the low 40s or even below. If it is a very close election, only slightly more than 20% of the citizenry has supported the new officeholder. Figure 12.2 indicates voter turnout in the United States since 1990.

Participation in elections in the United States is the second lowest of the Western democracies, as indicated in Table 12.1. This means that U.S. citizens are not exer-cising their right to vote. The unusually high number of "inactives" is not an encouraging sign for the vitality of a democracy. Still, there was a resurgence of interest in poli-tics among those under 30 years old during the 2008 and 2012 presidential campaigns with the primary elections for nomination of candidates and the November election for president yielding record-breaking turnouts. This is dis-cussed in the next "Sociology in Our Social World" feature.

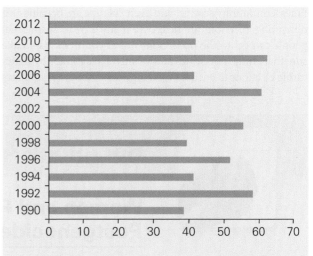

Figure 12.2 Voter Turnout in the United States: 1990-2012 (by percentage of eligible voters)

Source: United States Election Project (2012).

Table 12.1 Average Voter Participation Over 60 Years (all elections) and Most Recent Election

Country	Voter Participation % (all elections for 60 years)	Most recent parliamentary election (year)
Italy	92.5	75.2% (2013)
Iceland	89.5	81.4% (2013)
New Zealand	86.2	74.2% (2011)
South Africa	85.5	77.3% (2009)
Austria	85.1	81.7% (2008)
Netherlands	84.8	74.6% (2012)
Australia	84.4	93.2% (2010)
Denmark	83.6	87.7% (2011)
Sweden	83.3	84.6% (2010)
Germany	80.6	70.8% (2009)
United Kingdom	74.9	65.8% (2010)
Argentina	70.6	79.4% (2011)
Japan	69.0	59.3% (2012)
Canada	68.4	61.4% (2011)
France	67.3	55.4% (2012)
Bolivia	61.4	94.6% (2009)
USA	48.3	58.7% (2012)
Mexico	48.1	62.5% (2012)

Source: International Institute for Democracy and Electoral Assistance (2012).

*The figures are averages of voter participation for all elections over a 60-year period. Note that enfranchisement of women and various eth-nic minorities has changed in some countries during that time, so these should be viewed as very crude overall indicators of voting patterns.

Note: To see the voting participation figures for 172 countries in the world, go to www.idea.int/vt/.

Although election turnouts mean that only about 29% of the total citizenry actively supported President Obama, the outcome has consequences for the direction of the country. In 2012, the Obama family celebrated the reelection of the president.

Political Involvement

Sociology in Our Social World

The 2012 Presidential Election and the Youth Vote

by Jeremiah Castle

The 2012 United States presidential election was a close race between incumbent Barack Obama and challenger Mitt Romney. The election saw the creation or evolution of several trends that impact younger voters. Recognizing that the 18–29 age group was a key part of Obama's coalition in 2008, both campaigns attempted to reach out to this key constituency in debates and advertisements. Social media again played an important role, as the campaigns used platforms like Facebook and Twitter to keep followers updated on news and appearances. Together, these trends suggest that both parties are increasingly realizing the impact of younger voters.

Throughout the campaign both candidates stressed how their policies would improve life for recent graduates. For example, youth-specific issues played an important role in the second presidential debate. During the debate, which was conducted in a "town hall" format where undecided voters asked the candidates questions, a 20-year-old college student asked the candidates what they could do to make sure college students would have jobs after graduation. Romney assured the young voter that he would maintain the Pell Grant and student loan programs, and promised to improve the economy, thereby creating more jobs for recent graduates. Obama emphasized how creating new manufacturing jobs, increasing jobs in green energy, and reducing the deficit would create employment opportunities for younger voters ("Full Transcript of the Second Presidential Debate" 2012). Their responses suggest that both candidates were keenly aware of the impact of economic conditions on the plight of younger voters.

In an effort to appeal to younger voters, both parties explored new ways to use social media in 2012. Obama kicked off his reelection campaign with a video posted on YouTube (Cillizza 2011; "It Begins With Us" 2011). Throughout the campaign, both Obama (@BarackObama) and Romney (@MittRomney) used Twitter accounts to spread news, advocate policies, and keep supporters energized over the course of the campaign. In an effort to attract new followers, the Obama campaign used Facebook to hold drawings for dinner with the president, while the Romney team offered an opportunity to accompany him for a day on the campaign trail (Felix 2012). Facebook also served as a nonpartisan platform to increase civic engagement among users, including offering a tool for users to find their polling places and encouraging them to announce that they voted via a status update on Election Day.

While both campaigns used social media, data suggest that the Obama campaign was able to reach a wider audience. For example, as of November 6, 2012, Obama's Facebook page had 32 million likes, while Romney's page had just 12 million. Obama's advantage appeared to be even greater on Twitter: As of November 6, 2012, Obama had more than 22 million followers, while Romney had just 1.7 million followers. Certainly not all of those who like the page are citizens or can vote in the U.S. election, but it still suggests that Obama had a major advantage in the breadth of his social media following.

Obama also had the advantage among youth voters at the polls. Early exit polls confirmed that, while Obama's advantage among younger voters was not as large as it was in 2008, it remained substantial. In 2012, 60% of voters ages 18–29 supported Obama (down from 66% of younger voters in 2008), while 36% supported Romney. Exit polls also show that younger voters represented about 19% of the total electorate, up roughly a point from 2008 (Kingkade 2012). One study showed that if the votes of those under 30 were not counted, Romney would have won the crucial battleground states of Ohio, Florida, Virginia, and Pennsylvania, thereby giving him the presidency ("At Least 80 Electoral Votes Depended on Youth" 2012). This finding leaves little doubt that younger voters had a significant impact on the outcome of the election.

The pattern of (slightly) increasing turnout from younger voters led experts, including Rock the Vote president Heather Smith, to speculate that higher youth turnout is due to differing norms between the Millennial generation (the current youth generation, born between the 1980s and 2000s) and Generation X (those born between the 1960s and 1980s) (Robillard 2012). However, it remains to be seen whether this trend will continue in the future. Given that Obama is prohibited from seeking another term by the Constitution, both the Republicans and Democrats will be seeking new potential presidential candidates over the coming years. Certainly one criterion that will be used to evaluate candidates will be their appeal to younger voters. While nothing is certain, current evidence suggests that younger voters will continue to play an important role in national politics in the coming years.

* * * * * * *

Jeremiah Castle earned a minor in sociology in college and is now a PhD candidate in political science at the University of Notre Dame.

Thinking Sociologically

How important do you think voting blocs were in the 2008 and 2012 U.S. presidential election—the youth vote, women, African Americans, Latinos, the religious right?

Meso-Level Analysis: Distributions of Power and Privilege Within a Nation

A village within the Bantu society of southern Africa has lost its chief. Bantu societies provide for heirs to take on leadership when a leader dies. However, there is no male heir to the position, so a female from the same lineage is appointed. This woman must assume the legal and social roles of a male husband, father, and chief by acting as a male and taking a "wife." The wife is assigned male sexual partners, who become the biological fathers of her children. This provides heirs for the lineage, but the female chief is their social father because she has socially become a male. This pattern has been common practice in many southern Bantu societies and among many other populations in four separate geographic areas of Africa (D. O'Brien 1977). Ruling groups in society, in this case a meso-level tribal society under the jurisdiction of a nation-state, have mechanisms for ensuring a smooth transition of power and in this case

Among the Bantu of southern Africa, if a chief dies it is possible for a woman within the family lineage to succeed him, but she must take a "wife" and fulfill the leadership role normally established for males.

maintaining male dominance to keep the controlling structure functioning.

Meso-level political institutions include state or provincial governments, national political parties, and large formal organizations within the nation. Meso-level political institutions influence and are influenced by other institutions: family, education, religion, health care, and economics.

What Purposes Do Political and Economic Institutions Serve?

We have learned in earlier chapters that each institution has purposes or functions it serves. Just as family, education, medicine, and religion meet certain societal needs, so do the political and economic systems. The following six activities are typical purposes (functions) of meso-level political and economic institutions. They set the stage for power and privilege carried out at the macro level in national and international arenas:

1. *To maintain social control.* We expect to live in safety, to live according to certain "rules," to be employed in meaningful work, and to participate in other activities prescribed or protected by law. Ideally, governments help clarify expectations and customs and implement laws that express societal values.

2. *To serve as an arbiter in disputes.* When disputes arise over property or the actions of another individual or group, a judicial branch of government can intervene. In some systems, such as tribal groups mentioned earlier, a council of elders or powerful individuals performs judicial functions. In other cases, elected or appointed judges have the right to hear disputes, make judgments, and carry out punishment for infractions.

3. *To protect citizens of the group.* Governments are responsible for protecting citizens from takeover by external powers or disruption from internal sources.

4. *To represent the group in relations with other groups or societies.* Individuals cannot negotiate agreements with foreign neighbors. Official representatives deal with other officials to negotiate arms and trade agreements, protect the world's airways, determine fishing rights, and establish military bases in foreign lands, among other agreements.

The four functions listed thus far are rather clearly political in nature, but the last two are areas of contention between political and economic realms.

5. *To make plans for the future of the group.* As individuals, we have little direct impact on the direction our society takes, but the official governmental body shares responsibility with economic institutions for planning in the society. In some socialist societies, this planning dictates what each individual will contribute to the nation: how many

engineers, teachers, or nurses these societies need. They then train people according to these projections. In capitalist systems, for instance, supply and demand is assumed to regulate the system, and there is less governmental planning—especially in economic matters. The question of who plans for the future is often a source of stress between the political and economic institutions: Are the planners elected politicians or private entrepreneurs?

6. *To provide for the needs of their citizens.* Governments differ greatly in the degree to which they attempt to meet the material needs of citizens. Some provide for many of the health and welfare needs of citizens, whereas others tend to leave this largely to individuals, families, and local community agencies. Not everyone agrees that providing needs is an inherent responsibility of the state. The debates over a health care system and welfare system in the United States point to the conflicts over who should be responsible—the state or private entrepreneurs. Should such services be coordinated by the government or left to "the invisible hand" of market forces?

The ways in which governments carry out these six functions are largely determined by their philosophies of power and political structures. Political and economic institutions, like family and religious institutions, come in many forms. In essence, these variations in political institutions reflect variations in human ideas of power.

Thinking Sociologically

In an era of terrorist threats, how do you think the "protecting the safety of the citizens" function has affected the ability of governments to meet their other functions?

Meso- and Macro-Level Systems of Power and Privilege

While *politics* refers to the social institution that determines and exercises power relations in society, *economics* is the social institution that deals with production and distribution of goods and services. Both politics and economics focus on questions related directly to power relationships among individuals, organizations, nation-states, and societies. These two institutions overlap in part because to have power means one has access to resources. How goods are distributed to the members of society is often determined by who has power.

Getting elected to positions of power requires significant financial resources, so being in political positions means cultivating relationships with leaders in the economic system. Thus, there is a reciprocal relationship between economics and politics. In many countries, the government is the largest employer, purchaser of goods, controller of exports and imports, and regulator of industry and of interest rates. In the United States, many government regulatory agencies, such as the Food and Drug Administration, Department of Agriculture, and Justice Department, watch over the economic sector to protect consumers.

Government officials have a vested interest in the well-being of the economy, for should the economy fail, the state is likely to fail as well. Recessions, depressions, and high rates of inflation put severe strains on governments that need stable economies to run properly. When problems occur, government officials are inclined to increase their roles in the economic sector. Witness the volatile money markets from 2008 to 2012 and measures such as bailouts taken by many governments to stabilize their economies. In September 2008, the Dow Jones index dropped an unprecedented 777 points in a single day and fell another 782 points a week later. The New York Stock Exchange, usually bustling, was nearly empty, and President Bush and Congress immediately began to look for "stimulus packages" to keep the economy from going into a recession. As Obama became president in 2009, turning the economy around became one of the key challenges of his presidency.

A stable economic system is essential to political stability, and extreme fluctuations in the economy are frightening to those in power. On the day the Dow Jones index dropped dramatically, the New York Stock Exchange, usually bustling with activity, was nearly empty.

The problem of a dramatic drop in financial markets is a loss of confidence so that no one invests, lending institutions are not able to loan money easily, business stagnates, unemployment rates skyrocket, and the entire government may be held responsible for lack of economic vitality. When a country goes into a recession, the party in power is often held responsible and will not likely be reelected if the recovery takes too long. Economic recessions can destroy the careers of politicians but can also create such dissatisfaction that the entire government may be at risk of an uprising by citizens. Indeed, Dennis Blair, the U.S. director of national intelligence, in February 2009 declared the global economic crisis to be the most serious national security issue facing the nation, calling it a "bigger threat than Al Qaeda terrorists" (Haniffa 2009).

Recession in countries around the world influence other countries because of trade and international markets. A vivid example in 2012 was the instability of the Greek economy, which has created fear in the rest of the European Union that this one economy might undermine the rest of the countries in that union.

Types of Political Systems

The major political systems in the world range from fascist totalitarianism to democracy. However, each culture puts its own imprint on the system it uses, making for tremendous variation in actual practice. Two broad approaches are discussed next to illustrate the point.

Authoritarian Systems. The government of Saudi Arabia is a hereditary monarchy based on traditional leadership. **Authoritarian political systems** such as this *are controlled by absolute monarchs or dictators who allow limited or no participation of the population in government and control much of what happens in the lives of individuals.* They often have the backing of the military to keep them in power. Authoritarian regimes have been common forms of government in the world. Some are helpful to citizens—benevolent dictators—but most control and discourage dissent. The Castro brothers—Fidel and more recently Raúl—have maintained absolute control of Cuba since 1959, and while they are despised by many Cuban immigrants in the United States and subject to U.S. government embargos, they are admired by many Cubans as ruling in the best interests of the people, even if autocratically.

A **totalitarian government** is *any form of government that almost totally controls people's lives.* Totalitarian states are often based on a specific political ideology and run by a single ruling group or party, referred to as an *oligarchy.* Russia under Joseph Stalin, Germany under Adolf Hitler, and Libya under Muammar al-Qaddafi are examples. The state typically controls the workplace, education, the media, and other aspects of life. All actions revolve around state-established objectives. Dissent and opposition are

The Castro brothers, Fidel and his younger brother Raúl, overthrew a dictatorship in Cuba in 1959, one that was supportive of the wealthy. Although the leadership of the Castros has been more supportive of the common laborer, it is still very much a dictatorship.

discouraged or forcefully eliminated as we have seen in North Korea and Iran in recent years, with violent crackdowns on demonstrators. Interrogation by secret police, imprisonment, and torture are used to quiet dissenters. Terror is used as a tactic to deal with both internal and external dissent, but when it is used by the state to control the citizenry or to terrorize those of another nation, it is called *state terrorism.*

Throughout history, most people have lived under authoritarian or totalitarian systems. Under certain conditions, totalitarian regimes can turn into democratic ones, and of course, democratically elected leaders can become self-proclaimed dictators, as was the case of Robert Mugabe in Zimbabwe, Africa. The next "Sociology Around the World" provides an example of one totalitarian regime.

Democratic Systems. In contrast to totalitarian regimes, **democratic systems** are *characterized by accountability of the government to the citizens and a large degree of control by individuals over their own lives.* Democracies always have at least two political parties that compete in elections for power and that generally accept the outcome of elections. Mechanisms for the smooth transfer of power are laid out in a constitution or another legal document. "Ideal-type" democracies share the following characteristics, although few democracies fit this description exactly:

1. *Citizens participate in selecting the government.* There are free elections with anonymous ballots cast, widespread suffrage (voting rights), and competition

Sociology Around the World

The Khmer Rouge Revolution: A Totalitarian Regime

These skulls are the remains of people massacred by the Khmer Rouge government in the Killing Fields in Cambodia.

When the Khmer Rouge faction took over the government of Cambodia in 1978, it abolished private property; relocated urban dwellers to rural areas; seized personal property; classified some people as peasants, workers, or soldiers—and killed the rest. The group's most amazing feat was the total evacuation of the capital city, Phnom Penh. This was done to remove urban civilization and isolate Cambodia from other political influences, such as democracy.

This complete social and economic revolution under the leadership of Pol Pot was planned in Paris by a small group of intellectual revolutionaries. They believed it would allow Kampuchea, their former name for the country, to rebuild from scratch, eliminating all capitalism, private property, and Western culture and influence.

After urban dwellers were resettled in rural camps, the totalitarian regime tried to break down the family system by prohibiting contact between members, including sexual relations between husbands and wives. Many people, including defeated soldiers, bureaucrats, royalty, businesspeople, intellectuals with opposing views, Muslims, and Buddhist monks, were slaughtered for minor offenses—hence the term *Killing Fields* to describe the execution sites. The death toll is estimated at more than 1.25 million. However, the Cambodian Genocide Program has uncovered meticulous records kept by Khmer Rouge leaders, and combined with evidence from mass graves, these data may double that number (Crossette 1996; Mydans 2009).

Famine followed the killings, causing many Cambodians to flee their land, traveling by night and hiding by day to reach refugee camps across the border in Thailand. Today with increases in global demand for manufacturing, the economy in Cambodia is growing, especially in the areas of garment work and tourism. Thousands of tourists visit Angkor Wat and the Killing Fields each year. Today those working in agriculture have dropped to 36%, with 24.3% in industry and 39.7% in the service sector (World Factbook 2013f).

Cambodia has never been a country at peace, and that seems to be true today. Violence still exists. The Human Rights Center reports chaos, corruption, poverty, and a reign of terror in Cambodia, as the military kills and extorts money from citizens. Killings, violence, and intimidation surrounded elections though the parliamentary elections of 2012 had somewhat fewer problems than in the past (Loy 2012).

between members of different parties running for offices. Those who govern do so by the consent of the majority, but the political minorities have rights, representation, and responsibilities.

2. *Civil liberties are guaranteed.* These usually include freedom of association, freedom of the press, freedom of speech, and freedom of religion. Such individual rights ensure dissent, and dissent creates more ideas about how

to solve problems. These freedoms are therefore essential for a democracy to thrive.

3. *Government powers are limited by constitution.* The government can intrude only into certain areas of individuals' lives. Criminal procedures and police power are clearly defined, thus prohibiting harassment or terrorism by the police. The judicial system helps maintain a balance of power.

4. *Governmental structure and process are spelled out.* Generally, some officials are elected whereas others are appointed, but all are accountable to the citizens. Representatives are given authority to pass laws, approve budgets, and hold the executive officer accountable for activities.

5. *Written documents such as constitutions are the basis for the development of legal systems.* The constitutions describe activities in which the government must—or must not—engage. Constitutions can provide some protection against tyrants and arbitrary actions by government. The two main forms of democratic constitutional government are the parliamentary and presidential systems. In typical parliamentary governments, the head of state is often a monarch, and the head of government is a prime minister, chancellor, or premier. These are two different people. Belgium, Canada, Denmark, Great Britain, Japan, the Netherlands, Norway, and Sweden have this model. Examples of presidential governments include France, Italy, the United States, and Germany. The presidents in these countries tend to have more autonomy than do the heads of parliamentary governments.

Proportional representation means that each party is given a number of seats corresponding to the percentage of votes it received in the election. In winner-takes-all systems, the individual with more than 50% of the votes gets the seat. In the United States, the winner-takes-all presidential

The British system of government is a parliamentary democracy. This is the opening ceremony in 2012 for the Parliament. Note the pomp and circumstance that are used to create a sense of awe for power and authority.

system has come under attack because the winner of the popular vote can lose the electoral vote to an opponent who wins several of the most populous states by narrow margins. This actually happened in a presidential election in the United States: Al Gore received the most votes for president in 2000, but because all but two states (Maine and Nebraska) had a winner-takes-all system for electing the Electoral College, George W. Bush became the next president. Defenders of this system of choosing the president argue that this protects the voice of each state, even if each individual voice is not given the same weight.

Constitutional governments may have from two to a dozen or more parties, as has been the case in Switzerland. Most have four or five viable ones. In European countries, typical parties include Social Democrats, Christian Democrats, Communists, Liberals, and other parties specific to local or state issues, such as green parties.

Technology and Democracy

In the modern world, there are new challenges and issues that face democracies. Electronic technology—the Internet and other telecommunications technologies—can be a boon to democracy, an opportunity for people around the world to gain information necessary to be an informed electorate, or a burden that hinders thoughtful debate and civic engagement in ideas, these being essential ingredients of a functioning democracy (Barber 2006). For example, the 2012 election for U.S. president had unlimited political contributions that funded negative campaign ads. These ads were often deceptive and required good analytical skills to avoid being manipulated by them.

The Internet, fax machines, camcorders, and other telecommunications devices have been major instruments for poor and indigenous people, linking them to the outside world and combating oppressive governments. On the other hand, blogs, talk shows, webpages, and Internet discussions are often known more for sound bites and polemical attacks on opponents than for reasoned debates in which opposing sides express views.

The key contribution that these technologies bring is speed—helping citizens stay in touch with their elected representatives. However, speed is not always good for democracy. Both representative and direct democracy are speed-averse, requiring time and patience to implement laws (Barber 2006). Technology can also undermine democracy by a confounding of information (with which we are sometimes overloaded) with wisdom and by digital media's tendency to reduce everything to simplistic opposites, as though only two choices are possible (Barber 2006).

Representative democracy involves citizens electing officials periodically and then letting them make the decisions. In a direct democracy, the voters make major policy decisions, and citizens work in communities to govern their social life, develop civic trust, and create social capital. This, of course, requires a well-informed electorate, which does not exist in all countries.

Thinking Sociologically

How can the issues of technology enumerated earlier be problems for representative democracy? What positive effect might electronic technology have on direct participatory democracy?

Types of Economic Systems

As societies become industrialized, one of two basic economic systems evolves: a planned system or a market system. Planned or centralized systems involve state-based planning and control of property, whereas market systems/ capitalism stress individual planning and private ownership of property, with much less governmental coordination or oversight. These basic types vary depending on the peculiarities of the country and its economy. For instance, China has a highly centralized planned economy with strict government control, yet some private property and incentive plans exist, and these are expanding. The United States is a market system, yet the government puts many limitations on business enterprises and regulates the flow and value of money. For example, the Federal Reserve is the overseer of the U.S. banking system, which entails a Board of Governors—five economists—who control the flow of money so as to regulate inflation and recession. This is a form of regulation of the economy by "planners."

Distinctions between planned and market systems rest on the degree of centralized planning and the ownership of property. In each type of system, decisions must be made concerning which goods to produce (and in what quantity), what to do in the event of shortages or surpluses, and how to distribute goods. Who has power to make these decisions helps determine what type of system it is.

Market Systems/Capitalism. Market systems/capitalism are *economic systems driven by the balance of supply and demand, allowing free competition to reward the efficient and the innovative with profits; they stress individual planning and private ownership of property.* The goal of capitalism is profit, made through free competition between competitors for the available markets. It assumes that the laws of supply and demand will allow some to profit while others fail. Needed goods will be made, and the best product for the price will win out over the others. No planning is needed by any oversight group because the invisible hand of the market will ensure sufficient quality control, production, and

distribution of goods. This system also rewards innovative entrepreneurs who take risks and solve problems in new ways, resulting in potential growth and prosperity.

The goal of capitalist manufacturers is to bring in more money than they pay out to produce goods and services. Because workers are a production cost, getting the maximum labor output for the minimum wage is beneficial to capitalists. Thus, for example, multinational corporations look for the cheapest world sources of labor with the fewest restrictions on employment and operations. Marx predicted that there would be victims in such a system—those whom the system exploited. This potential for exploitation leads most governments to exercise some control over manufacturing and the market, although the degree of control varies widely.

Capitalism was closest to its pure form during the Industrial Revolution, when some entrepreneurs gained control of the capital and resources to manipulate those who needed work and became laborers. Using available labor and mechanical innovations, these entrepreneurs built industries. Craftspeople such as cobblers could not compete with the efficiency of the new machine-run shops, and many were forced to become laborers in new industries to survive.

Marx predicted that capitalism would cause citizens to split into two main classes: the *bourgeoisie*, capitalists who own the means of production (the "haves"), and the *proletariat*, those who sell their labor to capitalists (the "have-nots"). He argued that institutions such as education, politics, laws, and religion would evolve to preserve the privileges of the elite. Religious ideology often stresses hard work and deference to authority, allowing entrepreneurs to increase profits that benefit the owners. Furthermore, members of the economic and political elite usually encourage patriotism to distract the less privileged from their conflicts with the elite. According to Marx, the elite want the masses to draw the line between "us" and "them" based on national loyalty, not based on lines of economic self-interests (Gellner and Breuilly 2009). So in Marxist thought, even patriotism is a tool of the elite to control the workers. However, Marx believed that ultimately the workers would realize their plight, develop political awareness, and rebel against their conditions. They would overthrow the "haves" and bring about a new and more egalitarian order.

The revolutions that Marx predicted have not occurred in most countries. Labor unions have protected workers from the severe exploitation that Marx witnessed in the early stages of industrialization in England, and capitalist governments have created and expanded a wide array of measures to protect citizens, including social security systems, unemployment compensation, disability programs, welfare systems, and health care systems. Therefore, workers have not been discontent to the point of revolt, but they have expressed frustrations through union walkouts and strikes followed by compromises between workers and capitalist owners.

Economics

One of the major criticisms of pure capitalism is that profit is the only value that drives the system. Human dignity and well-being, environmental protection, rights of ethnic groups, and other social issues are important only as they impact profits. This leaves some people deeply dissatisfied with capitalism.

Planned (or Centralized) Systems.

Planned (or centralized) systems are *economic systems in which the government or another centralized group does planning of production and distribution.* They de-emphasize private ownership of property and have the government do economic planning. All matters of production and labor are, in theory, governed with the "communal" good in mind. There is deep suspicion of the exploitation that can occur when individuals all pursue their own self-interests. Those who hold to this philosophy believe that the market system also results in oligarchy—a system run by the financial elite in the pursuit of their own self-interests. Therefore, the state needs to oversee the total economy. Values other than profits can be protected and affirmed. China, Cuba, and about 24 nations in Africa, Asia, and Latin America have planned economies with industry controlled by the state (Freedom House 2002).

In reality, however, no system is a perfect planned state with the complete elimination of private property or differences in privilege. China, based on a Communist ideology, made rapid progress in tackling hunger, illiteracy,

The Chinese and Vietnamese systems have been highly centralized economies in which the government has done the planning. In recent years, both China and Vietnam have permitted more initiatives by entrepreneurs, rewarding those who would take a risk in the market. This photo is of a bustling street in Ho Chi Minh City, Vietnam.

population growth, drug addiction, and other problems by using its strong central government to establish five-year economic development plans. Today, however, the government is experimenting with new economic plans including limited private entrepreneurship, more imported goods, and trade and development agreements with other countries. Much of China has moved beyond the survival level and can experiment with modifications to the economic system. China has not, however, granted much political freedom to its citizenry.

One key criticism of planned systems is that placing economic power and political power in the hands of the leadership can lead to control by a few leaders, and that can result in tyranny. Multiple power centers in government, the business world, and the military can balance each other and help protect against dictatorships and tyranny (Heilbroner and Milberg 2012).

Mixed Economies.

Mixed economies, sometimes called "democratic socialism," try to balance societal needs and individual freedoms. **Democratic socialism**, for example, *refers to collective or group planning of the development of the society but within a democratic political system.* Private profit is less important than in capitalism, and the good of the whole is paramount. Planning may include goals of creating equality, protecting the environment, or supporting families, but individuals' rights to pursue their own self-interests are also allowed within certain parameters. Mixed economies seek checks and balances so that both political and economic decision makers are accountable to the public. Several countries, including Sweden, Great Britain, Norway, Austria, Canada, France, and Australia, have incorporated some democratic socialist ideas into their governmental policies, especially in public services.

Many Western European democracies redistribute income through progressive tax plans that tax according to people's ability to pay. The government uses this tax money to nationalize education, health plans and medical care, pensions, maternity leaves, and sometimes housing for its citizens. Although much of industry is privately run, the government provides regulations for the industry and assesses high taxes to pay for government programs. Typically, public service industries such as transportation, communications, and power companies are government controlled.

When U.S. president Obama was first elected, he was faced with a huge economic crisis that was extremely complex, but most analysts believe that a major cause had been deregulation of banks and the system of loans for home mortgages and businesses. President Obama—like his Republican predecessor, George W. Bush—pushed a massive ($787 billion) stimulus plan through Congress (Scott 2009). The problem was lack of regulation of the economy, and the solution was massive support for corporations and businesses, actions that some consider socialist.

Note Democratic socialism in the United States includes Social Security, Medicaid, Medicare, farm subsidies, federal unemployment insurance, the national park system that ensures open natural spaces, the idea of public schools to educate the citizenry, policies that limit pollution and protect the environment that all the citizens share, and thousands of other programs that most Americans rely on. So despite hostility to the term *socialism,* any government program that "bails out the economy" (such as rescuing failing banks) or that "protects consumers" is a component of a mixed economy that include some socialist policies. Note that both Republicans and Democratic administrations have supported such policies and the policies have been very popular.

Economic systems that attempt to balance market and planned economies are relatively recent experiments in governance, and they remain an idealized vision that has yet to be fully implemented or understood. In some ways, democratic socialist states outproduce capitalist ones, and in some ways, they can seem cumbersome ways to run a complex society. The bottom line in evaluating which system works best comes down to value priorities: individualism and economic growth for companies versus values such as equality, protection of the most vulnerable (such as the unemployed), and sustaining a healthy environment.

Many theorists believe that democratic socialism is what Karl Marx really had in mind, not the bureaucratic system that evolved in the Soviet Union, China, and elsewhere. Marx, after all, felt that the worst of all governments was *state capitalism*—a system in which the state controlled the economy. His early writings, in particular, put much more emphasis on decentralization and even a withering away of the government (Marx [1844] 1963). Few social democrats today think the government will ever wither away, but they think that the public, not just the elite, should have input into economic as well as governmental decisions and planning. The market system (capitalism) and the planned systems (socialism and communism) both have their advocates, but each system also has its shortcomings. The question, then, is whether there is an economic system that can avoid the dangers of each.

More than two centuries ago, it was widely believed, perhaps rightly at that time, that democracy could not work. The notion of self-governance by the citizenry was discredited as a pipe dream. Yet this experiment in self-governance is continuing, despite some flaws and problems. In a speech to the British House of Commons in 1947, then prime minister Winston Churchill said that "democracy is the worst form of government, except for all those other forms that have been tried" (Langworth 2009:574). Some economists and social philosophers have argued that if the people can plan for self-governance, they certainly should be able to plan for economic development in a way that does not put economic power solely in the hands of a political elite.

The institutions of politics and economics cannot be separated. In the 21st century, new political and economic relationships will emerge as each institution influences the other. Both institutions ultimately have a close connection to power and privilege.

Macro-Level Analysis: National and Global Systems of Power and Privilege

Each nation state develops its own systems of power and privilege in unique ways depending on its history, leaders, needs, and relations with other nations. The macro-level analysis includes both the individual nation-states and international organizations including terrorist groups that cross borders.

Power and the Nation-State

A *nation-state* is a political, geographical, and cultural unit with recognizable boundaries and a system of government. Boundaries of nation-states have been established through wars, conquests, negotiations, and treaties. These boundaries change as disputes over territory are resolved by force or negotiation. For example, Russia and the country of Georgia had a conflict in 2008 over whether two breakaway provinces of Georgia—Ossetia and Abkhazia—belonged within the national boundaries of Georgia.

There are officially 196 nation-states in the world today, 193 of which are represented in the United Nations (Worldometers 2012). This number is increasing as new independent nation-states continue to develop in Europe, Asia, Africa, and other parts of the world. One of the newest countries is South Sudan, which broke away from Sudan in Africa in 2011.

Within each nation-state, power is exerted by the systems that govern people through leaders, laws, courts, tax structure, the military, and the economic system. Different forms of power dominate at different times in history and in different geographical settings.

The notions of the nation-state and of nationalism are so completely internalized in us that we do not stop to think of them as social constructions of reality, created by people to meet group needs. In historical terms, nationalism is a rather recent or modern concept, emerging only after the nation-state (Gellner 1987, 1993; Gellner and Breuilly 2009).

Medieval Europe, for example, knew no nation-states. One scholar writes that "throughout the Middle Ages, the mass of inhabitants living in what is now known as France or England did not think of themselves as 'French' or 'English.' They had little conception of a territorial nation (a 'country') to which they owed an allegiance stronger than life itself" (Billig 1995:21). Some argue that the nation-state has "no precedent in history" prior to the 16th century and perhaps considerably later than that (Giddens 1987:166).

This raises an interesting question: Why did nation-states emerge in Europe and then spread throughout the rest of the world? This puzzle of modern history has to do with the change to rational organizational structures (Billig 1995). It is noteworthy that today every square foot of Earth's land space is thought to be under the ownership of a nation-state. Yet, even today, a sense of patriotism linking one's personal identity to the welfare of a nation is a foreign idea to many. People have loyalty to their region, their ethnic or tribal group, their religious group, or their local community, but a sense of being Pakistani or Kenyan or Afghani is weak at best. Yet, in places like the United States, having a passionate sense of national loyalty for which one would die is so taken for granted that anyone lacking this loyalty is suspect or deviant. Note the earlier discussion of the role of the flag. The nation is largely an imagined reality, something that exists because we choose to believe that it exists (Anderson 2006). Indeed, for some people, belonging to the nation has become a substitute for religious faith or local ethnic belonging (Theroux 2012).

Revolutions and Rebellions

From the 1980s to the present, significant social and political changes have taken place throughout the world. The Berlin Wall was dismantled, leading to unification of East and West Germany and the breakup of the USSR (Union of Soviet Socialist Republics). The Baltic states of Estonia, Latvia, and Lithuania became independent. In Eastern Europe, political and social orders established since World War II underwent radical change. When the Soviet Union and Yugoslavia broke apart, national boundaries were redrawn. Internal strife resulted from ethnic divisions formerly kept under check by the strong centralized governments in these areas. In addition, 2011 and 2012 was the time of the "Arab Spring," during which a number of dictators in the Middle East fell from power.

Were these changes revolutions? *Revolution* refers to social and political transformations of a nation that result when states fail to fulfill their expected responsibilities (Skocpol 1979). Revolutions can be violent and generally result in altered distributions of power in the society. Revolutions typically occur when the government does not respond to citizen needs and when leadership emerges to challenge the existing regime. News from around the world frequently reports on nation-states that have been challenged by opposition groups attempting to overthrow the regimes. This is the case in Syria and other Middle Eastern nations. Today revolutions are enhanced by new technologies, as discussed in the next "Sociology Around the World."

An example of a nonviolent revolution has been the Zapatista movement in southern Mexico (Chiapas). Here we see Zapatista commanders holding a Mexican flag as they attend a mass rally in Mexico City's main square. The Zapatista delegation called for indigenous rights including clean water and schooling for its children through sixth grade. The Zapatistas wore masks so they could not be identified and persecuted by the government, but they are a sophisticated movement that is in communication with other human rights movements around the globe.

Revolutions can be violent overthrow of governments or nonviolent events such as this Burmese monk protest that was violently suppressed by the government in Myanmar. Courageous acts like this did lead to change.

Revolution

Sociology Around the World

Social Media and Political Protests

by Jeremiah Castle

Recent events confirm that social media are playing a significant role in modern political protests. For example, social media have helped maintain news coverage of events going on inside Syria since the civil war began there in 2011. After the Syrian government attempted to restrict nonstate reporters following the outbreak of protests, members of the rebel groups and bystanders tweeted and uploaded YouTube videos of the government-led violence going on there (Mackey 2011). These videos helped bolster support for the rebels both inside Syria and in some parts of the broader international community.

There are a number of potential benefits to social media, the most obvious of which is a nearly limitless audience. Social media websites like Facebook, Twitter, and YouTube make it possible for networks of people with similar opinions to connect across great distances. Social media and text messaging can help large groups of people coordinate actions quickly, and the greater anonymity of the Internet can facilitate communication of political ideologies that might otherwise go unshared (Woods 2011). However, critics point out that social media-based networks are often not as "deep" as more traditional networks like those that provided a foundation for the civil rights movement in the United States (Gladwell 2010).

Crackdowns on protesters in Iran and other countries have provided support for growing fears that governments will use social media to identify and silence dissidents (P. Howard 2011; Morozov 2009). However, the events in Syria are part of a growing pattern that suggests protesters are willing to face the potential costs in order to enjoy the immense organizational benefits of social media. In 2009, protesters in Moldova used Twitter, Facebook, and text messages to mobilize opposition to the Communist Party's recent election wins (Barry 2009). A few months later, citizens and reporters in Iran used social media to keep more traditional media outlets informed of events going on there following the disputed 2009 elections (Landler and Stelter 2009). Protesters used YouTube to distribute videos of police beating crowds, raiding Tehran University,

and shooting women in the streets, causing concerns among the media due to the graphic nature of the videos and the difficultly in verifying their authenticity (Stelter 2009).

In 2011, Twitter, Facebook, and YouTube all played a role in the protests that ended Egyptian president Hosni Mubarak's tenure in office. A Facebook group titled "We are all Khaled Said," dedicated to the memory of an Alexandrian man beaten to death by police, had over 1.8 million subscribers (Preston 2011). In fall 2012, citizens of the Philippines protested a new law that might allow social media users to be prosecuted for libel by replacing their Facebook profile pictures with black silhouettes and making blank posts (Whaley 2012). Widening Internet access, faster connection speeds, and improvements in strategy provide reasons to believe that social media will play an increasing role in the future of political protest.

Interestingly, new evidence suggests that social media can also cause protests in a more direct fashion. Social media have dramatically expanded the marketplace of ideas, and now anyone with a keyboard, phone, or camera can distribute his or her thoughts to a worldwide audience. In one recent case, an American filmmaker who published an anti-Islamic film on YouTube helped spark a series of protests in numerous Muslim countries, including Egypt, Syria, Libya, Pakistan, and Sudan (Mackey and Stack 2012). After an attack on the U.S. Embassy in Libya killed Ambassador Christopher Stevens and several others, some Libyans even used social media to tweet pictures apologizing for the behavior of their fellow nationals (Mackey 2012). This tragic incident serves as a reminder that, with the democratization of ideas brought by social media, one person's actions have the potential to affect the lives of others around the world.

* * * * * * *

Jeremiah Castle is a graduate student working on a PhD in political science at Notre Dame University. He minored in sociology in college.

The Meso-Macro Political Connection

State or provincial governments and national political parties are meso-level organizations that operate beyond the local community, but they are less encompassing in their influence than national or federal governments or global systems. Still, decisions at the state or provincial government level can have major influences in political processes at the national level. For example, in 2012 some state governors refused the federal funds for expanding Medicaid to cover more poor residents, which may impact individuals who are not covered, but also national health care policies and costs. Here we look at another issue: the recent controversies about how to nominate and elect a president within the United States. Although the focus is on the U.S. political system, this discussion should be seen as illustrative of the tensions and peculiarities of the meso-macro link in any complex political system.

In some U.S. states, only members of the party can vote in their selection of candidates for office. In other states, citizens who are registered as Independents can vote in either primary election and help select the party's candidate. In other states, Democrats and Republicans can cross over and vote in the primary for the other party. What are the implications of having different rules in different states about crossover party voting?

In some U.S. states, each political party runs its own caucuses (face-to-face meetings of voters in homes, schools, and other buildings) to discuss policy and to carry out public votes. In caucus states, the political party funds and operates the process of selecting delegates who will nominate the presidential candidate—so the political party rather than the state sets the rules. By contrast, other states have primary elections run by the state government, but even these are not all the same. In most states, delegates are selected based on the proportion of the vote won by a candidate in that state. However, in some states on the Republican side, delegate selection is a winner-takes-all system, even if one candidate wins by a hundred votes. Some states have a formula by which some delegates are elected in the primary based on proportion of the statewide vote while others are chosen based on who wins each congressional district. In short, there is not uniformity. In addition, one state, New Hampshire, has in its state constitution a clause that the state *must* have the first presidential primary, and this means the state has more influence on winnowing down the presidential candidates than other states. (See Table 12.2 [The processes for various states—whether winner-takes-all or proportional—are listed in a table at **www.sagepub.com/oswcondensed3e**].)

Table 12.2   Meso-Level Presidential Nomination Variations in the United States

"Open" Allowing citizens to cross over to vote in the other party's election	Semi-Closed Allowing Independents to vote in either party's election	States With Caucuses Rather Than Primaries Controlled by the political parties rather than the state
AL MN TN AR MS VT ID MO VA IN ND WA MI SC WI	AK IL NH CA IA OH GA MA RI	AK ME NV CO MN ND IA ME WA KS NE WY
Open in the Democratic but closed in the Republican processes in: MT UT WV	Semi-closed in Democratic and closed in the Republican processes in KS	Texas has both a primary and a caucus

Sources: BBC *News* (2008), Bowen (2008), Center for Voting and Democracy (2008), Green Papers (2008a, 2008b), National Archives and Records Administration (2008), *The New York Times* (2008), Project Vote Smart (2008), State of Delaware (2008), Voting and Democracy Research Center (2008).

Note: States not listed have "closed" primaries.

Thinking Sociologically

Is it acceptable that some states never get any say in the nomination of candidates because the process is completed before they vote? Can one state write into its constitution (as New Hampshire has done) that it *must* have the first primary election, or should this be a decision that is somehow made at the national level? Who has the authority to tell a state it cannot put that in its constitution?

This means that some state governments decide when the primaries will be held, while elsewhere the selection of nominees is "owned" by the political parties. With a contentious U.S. election in 2008, several controversial questions were raised. Can a political party tell a state when to have its elections and then punish that state if it does not obey by refusing to seat its delegates at the party convention? This is exactly what happened in Michigan and Florida. In Florida, a Republican-dominated legislature moved the date of the primary election. The Democrats from that state were outvoted in the state legislature, but they still lost the right to represent their state at the Democratic convention where the presidential candidate was nominated. Can a state legislature—a meso-level political entity—tell a national political party—another meso-level political entity—how to run its nomination process? The answers to these questions are not clear, yet they can have profound effects on who becomes the next president of the most powerful nation on Earth.

Finally, in some states, the Republican primary is a "beauty contest" with no binding outcome. The results are purely advisory, and the delegates from that state are free to ignore the outcome of the election. The delegates are selected by the party insiders in that state, not by the voters. The Democratic Party has only recently passed a national policy banning this kind of primary. On the other hand, the Democratic Party has 915 "superdelegates"—party insiders who have not been elected by the populace and who may commit their votes to anyone they please. So both parties allow delegates who are not representing any constituency that elected them to choose the presidential nominee. What are the implications for a democracy?

Even selection of the Electoral College, which actually decides who will be president after the general election, is not uniform in policy across the states. Two states—Nebraska and Maine—have proportional distribution of electors—so that if a candidate takes 40% of the popular vote, he or she would receive 40% of the electoral votes. All the others have winner-takes-all electoral votes, even if the candidate won by half a percentage point. Should there be consistency between the states in the way the Electoral College is selected? Should state elections all be proportional or all be winner-takes-all?

Because the Constitution grants considerable autonomy to states to make these decisions, how does the nation ever get consistency? At the state (meso) level, legislatures are very protective of their right to make their own decisions. Yet, governance of the nation and the nation's relationships with the global community may be at stake. The point is this: Meso-level political power can shape power at the macro level, which then influences policies relevant to individual lives. The three levels are intimately linked. The next "Engaging Sociology" raises questions about where authority for decisions resides at each level in the social system.

Global Interdependencies: Cooperation and Conflicts

Dependency theorists and world systems theorists point out the inequality between rich core countries and dependent "peripheral" countries. The more dependent a country is, the more inequality is likely to exist between that country and core countries. The physical quality of life for citizens in dependent countries is also likely to be poor. For example, permitting a foreign company to mine resources in a Global South country may produce a short-term gain in employment for the country and may make some leaders

Engaging Sociology

Political Decisions: Social Processes at the Micro, Meso, and Macro Levels

Imagine that your state legislature is considering a change in the presidential election process. Your Electoral College state representatives would be selected according to the percentage of the popular vote in your state going to each candidate (Republican, Democratic, Libertarian, and Green Party). (Note: Currently, almost all states distribute their electors on a winner-takes-all basis.)

1. Identify two possible micro-level consequences of this policy change. For example, how might it affect an individual's decision to vote or how the local board of elections does its job?

2. Identify three consequences at the macro level. For example, how might the change affect how presidential candidates spend their resources and time, how might Congress respond to such an initiative, and so forth?

3. How does this illustrate the influence of meso-level organizations on micro and macro levels of the social system? For example, is it a problem for a *national* democracy when the delegate selection system is so completely variable at the meso (state) level, or does this make elections even more democratic because states can make their own autonomous decisions? Explain your answer.

4. Which system—winner-takes-all or percentage of the popular vote—would produce the fairest outcome? Why?

wealthy, but when the exhaustible resources are gone, the dependent country is often left with its natural resources destroyed and an even poorer economy (Haines, Haines, and Sherburne 2013; Wallerstein 1979, 1991).

The most affluent countries in the Global North have democracies, but there is some question about how to create a democratic system in poor countries with different cultural values and systems (Etounga-Manguelle 2000). What are the chances that the United States or another powerful nation-state will be successful in attempts to create democracies elsewhere? The odds are probably not good, according to a number of political analysts. Despite the movement toward political liberalization, democracy, and market-oriented reforms in countries such as Chile, Mexico, Nigeria, Poland, Senegal, Thailand, and Turkey, not all of these societies are ready to adopt democratic forms of governance (Diamond 1992, 2009).

Foreign powers can do little to alter the social structure and cultural traditions of other societies, and as indicated, these structures are key to the successful development of democracy. If the imposed system is premature or incompatible with the society's level of development and other institutional structures, authoritarian dictatorship rather than democracy may emerge as the traditional authority structure breaks down. Some scholars believe certain preconditions are necessary for the emergence of democracy:

- High levels of economic well-being
- The absence of extreme inequalities in wealth and income
- Social pluralism, including a particularly strong and autonomous middle class
- A market-oriented economy
- Influence in the world system of democratic states
- A culture that is relatively tolerant of diversity and can accommodate compromise
- A functioning and impartial media that will hold the government accountable
- A literate population (80% or more) that is informed about issues
- A written constitution with guarantees of free speech and freedom of assembly (Bottomore 1979; Inglehart 1997)

Thinking Sociologically

Why might some analysts believe that Iraq or Afghanistan—where the United States has attempted to set up democracies—may not be ready for a successful democratic government? Can you describe societies with which you are familiar that are—or are not—ready for democratic government?

Socioeconomic development strengthens democracy by contributing to social stability (Diamond 1992, 2003). Thus, an outside power can help establish the structures necessary to support democracy but is seldom successful trying to impose democracy. If countries in the Global North want more democracies around the world, an important strategy is to support economic development in less affluent countries. Again, politics and economics are intertwined.

Some Global South countries see discussions of democracy as a ploy—a cover-up used by dominant affluent nations for advancing their wealth. For example, the Global North nations have combined to form a coalition of nations calling itself the Group of 8 (or the G8—the United States, Japan, Germany, Canada, France, Great Britain, Italy, and Russia). The G8 uses its collective power to regulate global economic policies to ensure stability (and thereby ensure that its members' interests are secure). The G8 has the power to control world markets through the World Trade Organization, the World Bank, and the International Monetary Fund (Brecher, Costello, and Smith 2012; Kaiser Family Foundation 2010). This is discussed further in Chapter 14. Global South nations have responded to the G8 with an organization of poor countries that they call the G77. They are attempting to create collective unity so they will have some power to determine their own destinies (Brecher, Costello, and Smith 2012; Eitzen and Zinn 2012; Hearn 2012). Map 12.1 shows where the G8 and G77 nations are located.

Political systems can face threats from internal sources such as disaffected citizens, the military, and interest groups vying for power, or they can be challenged by external sources such as other nations wanting land or resources or by coalitions of nations demanding change. This is the situation for North Korea and Iran as coalitions of nations demand that they drop their nuclear enrichment programs. Sometimes these power struggles erupt into violence. The following section discusses how war, terrorism, and rebellion challenge existing systems.

Violence on the Global Level

Once upon a time, gallant knights in shining armor went forth to battle with good luck tokens from their ladies and the cause of their religion or their monarch to spur them on. They seldom died in these battles, and the daily life of the society went on as usual. By contrast, since the invention of modern weaponry, no one has been safe from death and destruction in war. Weapons can destroy whole civilizations. A malfunctioning computer, a miscalculation, a deranged person, a misunderstanding between hostile factions, or a terrorist attack could kill millions of people.

War is *armed conflict occurring within, between, or among societies or groups.* It is sometimes called "organized mass

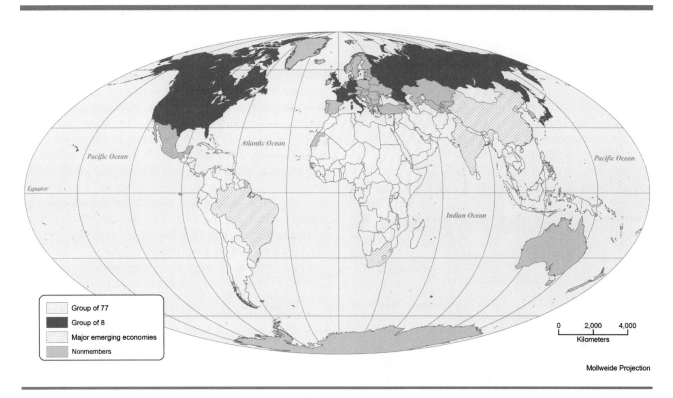

Map 12.1 Countries of the Group of 8, Major Emerging Economies, and Countries of the Group of 77

Source: www.g77.org. Map by Anna Versluis.

Palestinian schoolchildren take cover under their desks in their classroom during an emergency drill. This exercise to prepare for war is stimulated by the government's fear of attacks by neighboring enemies.

violence" (Nolan 2002:1803). War is a frequent but not inevitable condition of human existence. Many countries are now engaged in wars that are debilitating and detrimental to their economies and morale. Some of these wars (between India and Pakistan, in the Sudan, between Palestine and Israel, and between rival factions in the Congo) have lasted for years. Others have been short and decisive. In 2011 there were 26 active armed conflicts, 2 more than in 2010 (Ploughshares 2013). Table 12.3 on page 386 lists ongoing world conflicts as of 2010.

Why Do Nations Go to War?

Leaders use moral, religious, or political ideology to legitimize war, although the cause may be conflicts over economic resources or ethnic tensions. Wars have been waged to support religions through crusades and jihads; to liberate a country from domination by a foreign power; to protect borders, resources, and cultural customs; and to capture resources, including slaves, land, and oil. War can also distract citizens from other problems in their country, and politicians intent on staying in power may therefore use it to their advantage. On the other hand, there are cultures

Table 12.3 Significant Ongoing Armed Conflicts, 2010

Main Warring Parties Middle East	Year Began[1]
Libya and Syria	2012
United States and United Kingdom vs. Iraq	2003
Israel vs. Palestine	1948
Yemen: government forces vs. the rebel group Shabab al-Moumineen (The Youthful Believers)	2004
Turkey: government forces vs. the Kurdistan Workers' Party (PKK)	1999
Asia	
Afghanistan: U.S., U.K., and coalition forces vs. al-Qaeda and Taliban	2001
India vs. Kashmiri separatist groups/Pakistan	1948
India vs. Assam insurgents (various)	1979
Philippines vs. Mindanaoan separatists (MILF/ASG)	1971
Sri Lanka vs. Tamil Eelam[2]	1978
Africa	
Algeria vs. Armed Islamic Group (GIA)	1991
Somalia vs. rival clans and Islamist groups	1991
Sudan vs. Darfur rebel groups	2003
Uganda vs. Lord's Resistance Army (LRA)	1986
Europe	
Russia vs. Chechen separatists	1994
Latin America	
Colombia vs. National Liberation Army (ELN)	1978
Colombia vs. Revolutionary Armed Forces of Colombia (FARC)	1978
Colombia vs. United Self-Defense Forces of Colombia (AUC)	1990

Sources: Information Please Database (2010); Ploughshares (2013).

Note: As of October 2009.

1. Where multiple parties and long-standing but sporadic conflict are concerned, date of first combat deaths is given.

2. A 2002 cease-fire collapsed in 2006.

where war is virtually unknown. Groups, often isolated, live in peace and cooperation, with little competition for land and resources. The bottom line is that war is a product of societies, created by societies, and learned in societies.

Two familiar sociological theories attempt to explain the social factors that can lead to war. Functional theorists think underlying social problems cause disruptions to the system, including war, terrorism, and revolution. If all parts of the system were working effectively, they contend, these problems would not occur. Agents of social control and a smooth-running system would prevent disruptions. However, some functionalists also argue that war brings a population together behind a cause, resulting in social solidarity.

Conflict theorists see war, terrorism, and revolution as the outcome of oppression by the ruling elite and an attempt to overthrow that oppression. Many businesses profit from wars because their manufacturing power is put to full use. In fact, more money is spent on war than on prevention of disease, illiteracy, hunger, and other human problems. Citizens from the lower classes and racial minorities join the military, fight, and die in disproportionate numbers. They are more likely to join the military as an avenue to job training. They join as enlistees who serve on the front lines and are more at risk.

Some nations are more war-prone than others, and one cannot tell simply by paying attention to the rhetoric about war and peace. U.S. politicians give much vocal support to peace, but the country has been at war 193 of the 233 years since the colonies declared independence. Indeed, during the entire 20th century, there were only six years when the United States was not engaged in some sort of military action around the world (M. Brandon 2005; Noguera and Cohen 2006).

The conclusion is that war is not a natural or biological necessity. It is in large part a social construction that forms because of the values of a particular culture (Stoessinger 1993). If this is true, war might not be inevitable, but avoidable.

A soldier, just back from Iraq after finishing his service, looks at the boots of nearly 2,000 U.S. soldiers and thousands of Iraqi civilians killed during the Iraq War. The display was at Military Park in Newark, New Jersey. Those who have served in wartime know better than anyone the agonies and costs of war that tables and pie charts cannot convey.

How Might Nations Avoid War?

Deterrence is one approach to discourage and perhaps avoid war. Some government officials argue that if a nation is militarily strong, no one will dare attack it, the country will be secure, and leaders can "negotiate from strength." Believers in this approach argue nations should become superior to others or maintain a balance with other militaristic nations. However, evidence from ongoing statistical analyses of militarization concludes that deterrence has not been effective in reducing the chance of war. The more militarized a country becomes, the more likely the country is to enter into war. Continual buildup of weapons increases mistrust and raises the potential for misunderstandings, mistakes, or disaster. Furthermore, military personnel often have a vested interest in war—that is what the military is trained to do and what proves its competence. Business interests and economies may also profit from supporting war.

Deterrence is extremely expensive. As countries develop their military power, the spiral toward bigger, more sophisticated, and expensive technological weaponry continues. Figure 12.3 shows military spending around the world, giving rise to what is often called the military-industrial complex. The question is whether *brinkmanship*, expending money and pushing the potential for conflict to the brink, works to deter others. The question has been applied to many international conflicts including North Korea. Two classic experiments—replicated numerous times—studied strategies leading up to brinkmanship and how to reduce threats (Deutsch and Krauss 1960; Deutsch and Lewicki 1970). The results indicate that parties with similar power or wealth usually do not lock themselves into positions they cannot reverse, especially if they will continue to have interaction with their opponents. Brinkmanship is a high-risk strategy.

World military expenditures in 2011 were $1.75 trillion and rising (Ritholtz 2013). The United States accounted for over 41% of world military spending, China was responsible for 8.2%, and Russia 4.1% (Shah 2012). In 2012 the United States spent an estimated $682.5 billion.

Military expenditures are outpacing the GDP (gross domestic product) of world countries, the equivalent of $236 for each person in the world (Shah 2012). This is usually at the expense of social programs such as education and health care (Hinton 2010). Spending for weapons widens the gap between rich and poor countries and diverts money from social causes at home and abroad (Isaacs 2011). Still, many people feel that protection of the citizenry is the government's most essential responsibility, and brinkmanship is the way to achieve security.

Negotiation is the second approach to avoiding war and resolving conflicts by discussion to reach agreement. For example, diplomacy and treaties have set limits on nuclear weapons and their use. Due to negotiations, stockpiles of U.S. weapons have been reduced from 10,000 long- and

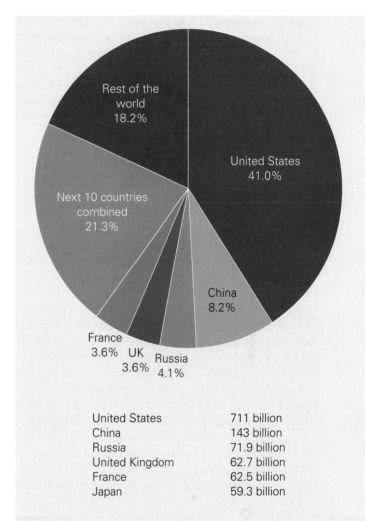

United States	711 billion
China	143 billion
Russia	71.9 billion
United Kingdom	62.7 billion
France	62.5 billion
Japan	59.3 billion

Figure 12.3   U.S. Military Spending Versus the World, 2011 (in billions of U.S. dollars and percentage of total global)

short-range nuclear weapons in 2010 to approximately 8,500 warheads—still enough to annihilate the human race several times over (Isaacs 2011; Stockholm International Peace Research Institute Yearbook 2010, 2012). The debate is over whether such preparations are essential or actually create the possibility for violence as a way to solve problems. President Obama has pointed out that maintaining Cold War–era weapons systems is expensive and can drain a weakened economy (Zeleny 2009).

In the 1990s, the superpowers made major efforts to move into a new peaceful era through negotiation between adversaries. Peace talks were held in the Middle East, Cambodia, Rwanda, the former Yugoslavia and Bosnia, Ireland, and other countries threatened by tensions and war. Leaders of the United Nations were often involved in diplomatic attempts to resolve conflicts. The inherent problem, however, is that more positive negotiation means a partial win—and a partial loss—for each side. Each gives

Working for Peace

a little, and each gets a little. Both sides tend to want a win-lose resolution—with the other side losing. Commitment to a win-lose perspective can lead to a lose-lose situation with neither side really winning.

Some citizens are not satisfied to leave peacekeeping efforts to their government leaders. Strong grassroots peace movements in Europe, the Middle East, the United States, South Africa, and other countries are aimed at lessening tensions and conflicts around the world. The widespread demonstrations in many European and U.S. cities by people opposed to the wars in Iraq and Afghanistan are examples.

Many peace groups sponsor educational programs and museum displays. The horrors depicted in the Hiroshima Peace Memorial Museum in Japan; the Killing Fields in Cambodia; the Holocaust Memorial Museum in Washington, D.C.; the Anne Frank Museum in Amsterdam, Netherlands; the Kigali (Rwanda) Genocide Memorial Centre; and the Korean War and Vietnam War veterans' memorials in Washington, D.C., all help sensitize the public and politicians to the effects of war. Interestingly, most war memorials in the United States glorify the wars and lionize the heroes who fought in them. In Europe, many memorials stress the pathos and agony of war. However, the Vietnam Veterans Memorial sends a different message about the sorrows of war. Peace advocates and veterans of the war often stand and weep together in front of that memorial.

Scholars draw several conclusions from studies of war in the past century: (a) No nation that began a major war in the 20th century emerged a clear winner; (b) in the nuclear age, war between nuclear powers could be suicidal; and (c) a victor's peace plan is seldom lasting. Those peace settlements that are negotiated on the basis of equality are much more permanent and durable. War is often stimulated by inequitable distribution of resources. Therefore, peace that is lasting also requires attention to at least semi-equitable distribution of resources. So economics are also at the heart of war and peace issues

In the long run, people around the world would seem to benefit when there is peace, yet many leaders and citizens hold bitter hatred against their neighbors. Obviously, this is not a climate for peace. As long as there is discrimination, hunger, and poverty in the world, the roots of violence are present. The world is a complex interdependent system. When the linkages between peoples are based on ideologies that stress we-they polarities and power differentials that alienate people, then war, terrorism, and violence will not disappear from the globe.

Terrorism

"Geronimo! Bin Laden, mastermind of 9/11, is dead!" was the headline on May 2, 2011. For the 10 years since September 11, 2001, the search had been on. That was when three commercial airplanes became the missiles of terrorists, two crashing into the Twin Towers of the World Trade Center in New York City and one crashing into the Pentagon in Washington, D.C., killing more than 3,025 people from 68 nations and injuring countless others. This was an act of terrorists. Why did they do it?

Terrorism refers to *the planned use of random, unlawful (or illegal) violence or threat of violence against civilians to create (or raise) fear and intimidate citizens in order to advance the*

The Vietnam Veterans Memorial in Washington, D.C., is more like many European war memorials than most U.S. war memorials. It expresses and elicits a sense of the anguish of war—loss, pain, and suffering. This man mourns the loss of close a friend and comrade as he leans into the wall of names of those killed in the Vietnam War.

Activists of the International Solidarity Movement protest against the construction of the Israeli security fence near a Palestinian village. American Rachel Corrie, a member of the ISM, was run over and killed by an Israeli bulldozer in 2003, when she tried to stop it from destroying a family's home.

Terrorism

terrorist group's political or ideological goals (U.S. Department of Defense 2012). Terrorism usually refers to acts of violence by private nonstate groups to advance revolutionary political goals, but *state terrorism*—government use of terror to control people—also proliferates. Terrorists are found at all points on the political continuum: anarchists, nationalists, religious fundamentalists, and members of ethnic groups. There were 11,604 terrorist attacks in 72 countries in 2010, resulting in 49,901 victims and 13,186 deaths. This is a 5% rise in attacks over the previous year, but a drop in deaths (U.S. Department of State 2011).

What makes terrorism effective? Terrorists strike randomly and change tactics so that governments have no clear or effective way of dealing with them. This unpredictability causes public confidence in the ability of government to protect citizens and deal with crises to waver. Terrorists seldom attack targets in oligarchic or dictatorial societies because these countries ignore their demands for money or release of prisoners despite the risk to innocent civilians and hostages' lives (Frey 2004).

Security officers in Bulgaria look at a damaged bus carrying Israeli tourists after it was hit by a bomb explosion in 2012. This was identified as an act of terrorism against Israel.

Why do terrorists commit hostile acts? We cannot address terrorism if we do not understand its root causes. In our anger against terrorists, we sometimes fail to look at why they commit these atrocities. Who are the terrorists, and what have they to gain? Without understanding the underlying causes of terrorism, we can do little to prevent it.

Few terrorists act alone. They are members of groups that are highly committed to an ideology or a cause—religious, political, or both. Terrorists are willing to die to support their groups' cause. Class, ethnic, racial, or religious alienation often lies at the roots of terrorism. The ideology of terrorist groups stresses *we*-versus-*they* perceptions of the world, with *they* being "evil." Those committing terrorist acts often feel they are the victims of more powerful forces, and sometimes, they see their only weapon to fight back as the ultimate sacrifice—their lives. Some feel their situation is so bad that they have nothing to lose by committing terrorist acts or even suicide. Thus we can say that one person's terrorist is someone else's freedom fighter, which is in the eye of the beholder.

Founders of terrorist groups are often charismatic and preach a message that appeals to followers. Osama bin Laden was one such leader of the terrorist network al-Qaeda. His death in May 2011 by U.S. commandos has altered the command structure of al-Qaeda, and maybe even the organization itself. Yet al-Qaeda and organizations that claim an al-Qaeda affiliation are still considered the biggest threat to the United States and other nations (U.S. Department of Defense 2011).

Ahmad is a 20-year-old terrorist. When he was very young, his family's home was taken away, and the residents of his town scattered to other locations. He began to resent those who he thought had dislocated his family and separated him from friends and relatives. Ahmad sees little future for himself or his people, little hope for education or a career of his choosing. He feels he has nothing to lose by joining a resistance organization to fight for what he sees as justice.

Ahmad puts the "greater good" of his religious and political beliefs and his group above his individual well-being. When he agrees to commit a terrorist act, he truly believes it is right and is the only way he can retaliate and bring attention to the suffering of his people. If killed, he knows he will be praised and become a martyr within his group. His family may even receive compensation for his death.

Continued frustration by those who are alienated has been expressed by a long string of violent, sophisticated, bloody acts. Those who are attacked feel that they are the real victims and have done nothing to deserve the brutality.

Religious and political beliefs are usually at the root of what leads some terrorists to commit violent acts. Timothy McVeigh and Terry Nichols were charged with bombing the Alfred P. Murrah Federal Building in Oklahoma City, Oklahoma. Research on their backgrounds shows connections to paramilitary, antigovernment militia groups. These patriot groups are white supremacists and antigovernment (despite their fanatic pro-Americanism). Most patriot paramilitary groups consider themselves to be devoutly Christian, and they believe their acts are justified by their religion and their "good intentions." They are scattered throughout the United States as shown in Map 8.2 on page 221. Structural explanations help predict when conditions are right for terrorism. Terrorism and war are unlikely to exist unless there is conflict and strife within and between societal systems. Ahmad learned his attitudes, hatreds, and stereotypes from his family, friends, charismatic leaders, and media such as the Internet. These beliefs were reinforced by his leaders, religious beliefs, and schools. However, their origin was often economic despair.

Conflict theory's explanations of terrorism lie in the unequal distribution of world resources and the oppression of groups in the social world. Wealthy countries such as Germany, Japan, and the United States control resources and capital and have considerable economic influence and power over peripheral nations. Citizens of poor countries work for multinational corporations, often for very low wages, and the profits are returned to wealthy countries, helping perpetuate their elite status. The result is that the rich get richer and the poor get poorer. This inequity results in feelings of alienation, hostilities, and sometimes acts of

terrorism against the more powerful country. The attack on the New York City World Trade Center was carried out in part to terrorize and punish the United States.

Reactions to terrorism range from demands for immediate retaliation to frustration with the lack of power and control to fight a "hidden" enemy. People disagree over whether governments should negotiate with the terrorists and try to understand their demands or hold firm by not negotiating or giving in to such coercion.

Terrorism, then, is the means by which the powerless can attempt to receive attention to their cause and gain some power in the global system, even if it involves hijackings, bombings, suicides, kidnappings, and political assassinations. Terrorists feel they are justified in their actions. The victims of these acts are understandably outraged.

Democracy comes in many forms and structures. If you want to live in a society where you have a voice, get involved in the political system and stay well informed about the policies that your government is considering or has

recently enacted. Healthy political systems need diverse voices and critics—regardless of what party is currently in power—to create vibrant societies that represent the citizens. The following two chapters focus on processes of change in societies.

What Have We Learned?

The most direct source of power is the political system, with the ability to influence decisions about how society is run. The most direct source of privilege is the economic system, though these two institutions are highly interlinked. There is no one right way to organize a political or an economic system, for each approach has shortcomings. However, some systems do a better job of distributing power and privilege, ensuring accountability, and providing checks on abuses of power.

Key Points:

- The study of political and economic processes and systems involves penetrating power—in the sense that we try to penetrate the meanings and consequences of power and that power penetrates every aspect of our lives. Power involves ability to realize one's will, despite resistance. (See pp. 360–361.)

- Power and economics penetrate our intimate (micro-level) lives, our (meso-level) organizations and institutions, and our (macro-level) national and global structures and policies. (See pp. 361–362.)

- Leadership facilitates getting things done in any social group. It can be accomplished through raw power (coercion) or through authority (granted by the populace). Different types of leadership invest authority in the person, the position, or both. (See pp. 360–365.)

- Various theories illuminate different aspects of political power and view the nation's policy-making processes very differently—as dominance of the power elite or as pluralistic centers of power. (See pp. 365–367.)

- At the micro level, a key issue is each citizen's decision to vote or participate in politics. These decisions are not just individualist choices but are shaped by culture and structures of the society. (See pp. 367–372.)

- At the meso level, the political institution (when it functions well) works to resolve conflicts and to address social needs within the political system, and this may be done with authoritarian or democratic structures. Within nations, meso-level policies can also have major implications for national power distribution. (See pp. 372–374.)

- The economic system ensures production and distribution of goods in the society, and the type of political and economic system in a society determines who has the power to plan for the future and who has access to resources. (See pp. 374–377.)

- Three types of economic systems—market, planned, and mixed—can be found in industrial societies, each with its own set of pros and cons. (See pp. 377–379.)

- At the macro level, nation-states have emerged only in the past four or five centuries as part of modernity. (See pp. 379–383.)

- At the global level, issues of power, access to resources, alienation, and ideology shape economic policies, war, terrorism, and the prospects for lives of peace and prosperity for citizens around the planet. (See pp. 383–390.)

Discussion Questions

1. As you were growing up, did your parents encourage you to try to influence your local community or society? Why or why not? Was their perspective on power more like the pluralist or the elite theoretical perspective? Explain. How have their views about power influenced your own?

2. Is your family of origin part of what William G. Domhoff refers to as the "power elite"? What makes you think so? Are you a member of the power elite? Why or why not? If you are not, what do you think your chances are of becoming a member of the power elite? Why?

3. Do you think that large corporations have undue influence over the U.S. government? Why or why not?

4. If you had the choice, would you rather live in a society with a planned/centralized or a market/capitalist economic system? Why?

5. How do conflict theorists explain terrorism? Do you agree? Why or why not? How would you suggest the U.S. government try to stem terrorism? What theoretical perspective do you think is most helpful in terms of understanding and dealing with terrorism? Why?

Contributing to Our Social World: What Can We Do?

At the Local Level

- Consider getting involved in the *student government* on your campus. If you would like to see something changed on your campus, establish relationships with key administrators and organize other students. Consider running for a leadership position in a student club or the student government association. Doing so will help you to learn how to gain and use power (the ability to act) and learn the basic principles of the democratic process.

- *Model legislature or Model UN programs* can be found on most campuses, and are usually administered through the department of political science. Consider joining yours and gain valuable knowledge and skills in debating and governing.

- *Arrange a campus visit by a local political candidate or office holder.* This could be done through a sociology club. It would be especially appropriate to have the visitor discuss the political system as a social institution.

At the Organizational or Institutional Level

- *Government internships.* Consider doing an internship in your *state/provincial legislature* (www.ncsl.org/legislative-staff.aspx?tabs=856,33,816) *or in Congress* (www.senate.gov/reference/Index/Employment.htm and www.house.gov/content/educate/internships.php) with a state/provincial legislator, the governor's office (Google "governor's office," "internship," and the name of your state), or a court judge (Google "court judge," the name of your district, and "internship").

- *Special-interest parties.* Become involved in a special-interest political group such as the Green Party (www.gp.org), the Libertarian Party (www.lp.org), the Socialist Party (www.sp-usa.org), the Tea Party (www.teaparty.org), Occupy Together (www.occupytogether.org), or any number of others.

At the National and Global Levels

- *Internships at the White House or one of the executive offices, such as the Departments of State, Agriculture, Commerce, and so on.* You can learn about the White House internship program and how to apply at www.whitehouse.gov/about/internships. Google the name of a cabinet office to obtain contact information for the other executive offices.

- Several agencies of the *United Nations* hire interns. The general contact for relevant information is www.un.org/Depts/OHRM/sds/internsh.

Visit **www.sagepub.com/oswcondensed3e** for online activities, sample tests, and other helpful information. Select "Chapter 12: Politics and Economics" for chapter-specific activities.

PART V

Social Dynamics

Social structures such as institutions—family, education, religion, health, politics, and economics—tend to resist change. Yet, this entire book shows that societies are dynamic and changing. Institutions and organizations come alive with *processes* that are fluid and vibrant. Globalization, a major theme in this book, is a process bringing transformation to our social world. We do not live in the same sort of world our grandparents inhabited. The macro- and meso-level dimensions of the world have become increasingly powerful, which is exactly why we need a sociological perspective (imagination) to understand how the events in our own micro worlds are influenced by the larger society.

This section looks at some of those dynamic, fluid, and vibrant processes—population changes, expansion of technology, social movements, and more. When we are in periods of rapid change, understanding how that change occurs and what processes are involved is key to influencing change. For example, from global climate change to terrorism and from new digital technologies to immigrants in our communities, we need to understand what the actual facts are regarding causes and consequences before we can respond constructively. We live in exciting and challenging times, and we will thrive best if we understand the micro-, meso-, and macro-level dimensions of change in our lives and the linkages between parts of our social world.

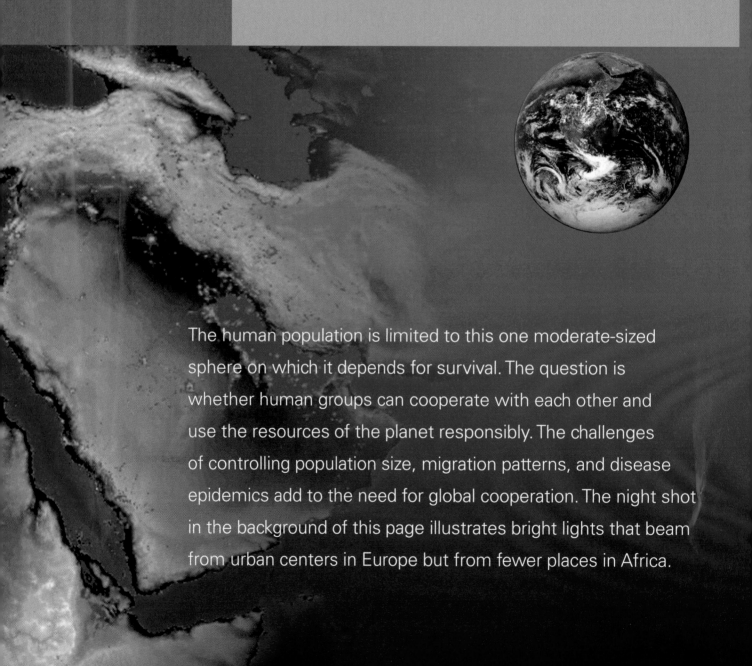

CHAPTER 13

Population and Health

Living on Spaceship Earth

The human population is limited to this one moderate-sized sphere on which it depends for survival. The question is whether human groups can cooperate with each other and use the resources of the planet responsibly. The challenges of controlling population size, migration patterns, and disease epidemics add to the need for global cooperation. The night shot in the background of this page illustrates bright lights that beam from urban centers in Europe but from fewer places in Africa.

Global Community

Society

National Organizations, Institutions, and Ethnic Subcultures

Local Organizations and Community

Me (and My Neighbors)

Micro: Your local school and community

Meso: Institutions affected by population trends

Macro: National policies on population: birth incentives, birth control, and abortion

Macro: Global migrations, epidemics, wars

Think About It

Micro: Self and Inner Circle	Why is your family the size it is?
Micro: Local Community	What characterizes the population composition of your hometown? Where do you fit into that composition?
Meso: National Institutions; Complex Organizations; Ethnic Groups	Why do people move from rural areas to urban areas? What problems does this movement pattern create?
Macro: National Society	How might immigration affect the makeup of a nation, and what effect could this have on a nation's policies?
Macro: Global Community	How do global issues relating to urbanization, the environment, and technology affect your family and your local community?

What's coming in this chapter?

Macro-Level Patterns in World Population Growth

Meso-Level Institutional Influences on Population Change

Micro-Level Population Patterns and Our Everyday Lives

Environmental and Demographic Policy Issues

Table 13.1   Population Clock, 2012 (in thousands)

	World	Global South (Less Developed)	Global North (More Developed)
Population	7,057,075	5,814,057	1,234,018
Births per day	385	347	38
Births per year	140,542	126,618	13,924
Deaths per day	154	121	33
Deaths per year	56,238	44,046	12,192
Infant deaths per day	15.8	15.6	0.2
Natural annual increase	84,304	82,572	81,185

Source: Population Reference Bureau (2012).

W hen Sally Ride, the first U.S. woman in space, looked down at the earth, she saw a beautiful green and blue spherical object drifting through space. She described the view at night when parts of the sphere glow with lights while other parts are dark. In 2012 Rider died of pancreatic cancer. Her mission in life was to share part of that awesome experience with young people, especially girls, and encourage them to explore sciences.

That relatively small planet that Ride viewed from afar is home to earthlings. The controlling inhabitants of the planet are humans, more than 7.1 billion of them. In the United States the population is increasing by one birth every 8 seconds, one death every 12 seconds, and one international migrant every 44 seconds for a net gain of one person every 13 seconds (U.S. Census Bureau 2013). In the world, the increase is approximately 211,090 people daily (U.S. Census Bureau 2013). The topic of this chapter is the life, death, spread, and distribution of those humans living on spaceship earth (J. Diamond 2005).

Since the emergence of *Homo sapiens* in East Africa, human populations have grown in uneven surges and declines due to births, deaths, and migrations. The World Population Clock (see Table 13.1) illustrates the current state of the human population.

The world's human population has grown sporadically over the millennia, so the explosion of human beings on the planet in the past two and a half centuries is stunning. If we collapsed all of human history into one 24-hour day, the period since 1750 would consume one minute. Yet, 25%

of all humans have lived during this one-minute period. In the 200 years between 1750 and 1950, the world's population mushroomed from 800 million to 2.5 billion. On October 12, 1999, the global population reached 6 billion. It has now expanded to more than 7 billion, with most growth in the Global South (Haub 2012). This means the world is growing each year by the number of people in Germany, the Philippines, or Vietnam. Every minute in 2012, 267 children were born and 107 people die around the world, resulting in a net increase of 160 people per minute (Population Reference Bureau 2012). Between 2000 and 2050, virtually all of the world's growth will occur in Africa, Asia, and Latin America.

Let us start by focusing on one area of our world: Kenya. We begin here partly because East Africa, where Kenya and Tanzania are located, was home to spaceship earth's earliest human inhabitants. Scientists believe bones found in the dry

Changes in the environment and in the global economy make it difficult for this Kenyan family to provide for itself. Some of these children and their cousins may find it necessary to move to urban centers, a worldwide migration trend. Much of the socialization they receive in villages will not be relevant to their adult urban lives.

Olduvai Gorge area are the oldest remains of *Homo sapiens* ever found. We also focus here because today Kenya is making human history for another reason. With a population of nearly 40 million people and a growth rate of 2.44% annually, Kenya has one of the most rapidly growing populations on earth (World Factbook 2013g). Kenya is made up of many tribal groups of people. With different religions and value systems, the people have clashed in power struggles in recent years. Still, there are several themes that pervade most Kenyan subcultures, as illustrated by the following example.

Wengari, like Kenyan girls of most tribal affiliations, married in her teens. She has been socialized to believe that her main purpose in life is to bear children, to help with the farming, and to care for her parents in their old age. Children are seen as an asset in Kenya. Religious beliefs and cultural value systems encourage large families. However, the population of Kenya is 45.2% *dependent*: people younger than 15 or older than 64 in societies where the population is living longer, who rely on working-age citizens to support them (World Factbook 2013g). The working-age population is becoming scarce and cannot continue to feed the growing dependent population. Further, severe droughts ravage parts of the country—droughts that are killing animal herds and preventing growth of crops. These facts, however, have little meaning to young women like Wengari, who have been socialized to conform to the female role within their society.

By contrast, far to the north of Kenya—in the industrialized, urbanized countries of Europe—birthrates are below population replacement levels, meaning population size eventually will begin to drop. Germany, Hungary, and Latvia, for instance, are losing population. While Asia's share of world population may continue to hover around 60% through the next century, Europe's portion has declined sharply and is likely to drop even more during the

21st century, although immigrant populations are growing. Africa and Latin America each will gain part of Europe's portion. By 2100, Africa is expected to capture the greatest share. Countries growing by less than 1% annually include Japan, Australia, New Zealand, Russia, and much of Europe (Population Reference Bureau 2013).

In industrialized and postindustrial societies, children in the middle class and above are dependent until they leave home. Typical European young people wait until their late 20s or even 30s to start a family, postponing children until their education is complete and a job is in hand. Many limit their family size because societal values support small families. It is difficult to house large families in small urban apartments where the majority of the population lives. Workers must support and feed their families on earned wages rather than through farming. Both mother and father often work, and unlike many children in the Global South, most children born in Europe will survive to old age. **Life expectancy**, the *average number of years a person in a particular society can expect to live*, is 63 years in Kenya (IndexMundi 2012; World Factbook 2013g). In Japan and some European countries, it is older than 81 years.

On yet another continent, China, the country with the largest population in the world (about 1.35 billion people), had the greatest drop in population growth in the late 20th century due to strict governmental family planning practices (World Factbook 2013c). India, the second-largest country, has a population growth rate (increase in a country's population during a specified time) of 1.31% a year, just over replacement level (World Factbook 2013f).

Hanoi, Vietnam, is a crowded Asian city. The overcrowding in some cities means that governments have a difficult time providing the infrastructure and services needed for the growing urban population.

Although some countries have birthrates below population replacement levels, the world's population continues to grow because of the skyrocketing growth rate in other countries and because of *population momentum* caused by the large number of individuals of childbearing age having children. Even though birthrates per couple are dropping, the number of women of childbearing age is still very high, resulting in continued growth in population size. Unfortunately, most of the countries with the highest growth rates are in the Global South, where there are fewer resources to support the additional population.

What we have been discussing is called **demography**, *the study of human populations*. When demographers speak of **populations**, they mean *all permanent societies, states, communities, adherents of a common religious faith, racial or ethnic groups, kinship or clan groups, professions, and other identifiable categories of people*. The size, geographical location, and spatial movement of the population; its concentration in certain geographical areas including urban areas; and changing characteristics of the population are important elements in the study of demography. With growing populations and limited farmland to support the population, hungry people move to cities in hopes of finding jobs. This *pattern of movement from rural areas to cities* is called **urbanization**.

The previous chapters have been organized by moving from micro- to macro-level analysis. Because demographic work has focused on societies and global trends, we will reverse the order and discuss macro-level patterns in world population growth first, followed by meso-level institutional influences on population, and finally micro-level factors affecting population patterns.

Thinking Sociologically

Do you have a choice in how many children you have? What factors go into your decision? How might your decision differ if you were in a different country? Should macro-level global patterns—which include food shortages and climate change—be a consideration in the size of your family and your neighbors' families? Why or why not?

Macro-Level Patterns in World Population Growth

Early humans roamed the plains of Africa for thousands of years, their survival and growth depending on the environment in which they lived. They mastered fire and tools, then domesticated animals and invented agriculture, and with these skills slowly increased control over the environment, allowing their numbers to expand. This evolution in the growth patterns of human populations is worth closer examination.

Patterns of Population Growth Over Time

Members of the small band of early *Homo sapiens* who inhabited the Olduvai Gorge moved gradually, haltingly, from this habitat into what are now other parts of Africa, Asia, and Europe. The process took thousands of years. At times, births outnumbered deaths and populations grew, but at other times, plagues, famines, droughts, and wars decimated populations. From the beginning of human existence, estimated from perhaps one million years ago until modern times, the number of births and deaths balanced each other over the centuries (J. Diamond 2005). The large population we see today results from population evolution that consisted of three phases:

1. Humans, because of their thinking ability, competed satisfactorily in the animal kingdom to obtain the basic necessities for survival of the species.

2. With the agricultural revolution that occurred about 10,000 years ago and the resulting food surplus, mortality rates declined, and the population grew as more infants survived and people lived longer.

3. The biggest increase came with the Industrial Revolution, beginning about 300 years ago. Improved medical knowledge and sanitation helped bring the death rate down.

When industrialization made its debut, it brought the social and economic changes discussed in Chapter 3 (e.g., machines replaced human labor, and mass production used resources in new ways), but it also augmented urbanization of societies. The population explosion began with industrialization in Europe and spread to widely scattered areas of the globe. With trade and migrations came the diffusion of ideas and better medical care, influencing population growth rates in all parts of the world by keeping people alive longer. Figure 13.1 shows population growth throughout history. The worldwide *rate* of population growth, or how fast the population increases, reached its peak in the 1960s. Although it has dropped to a current rate of about 1.1% per year, the population will continue to increase until fertility levels drop further (World Factbook 2013j).

Migration

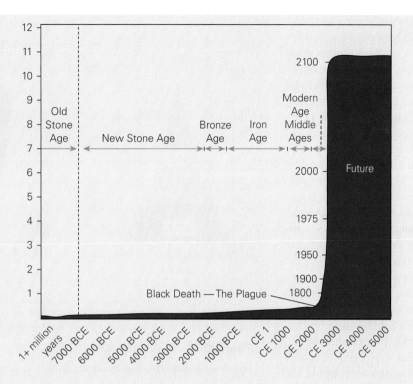

Figure 13.1 The Exponential World Population Growth From About 8000 BCE to 21st Century

Source: Abu-Lughod (2001:50).

In the urban Global South, overcrowding is so severe that many people are homeless and must bathe every day in public in whatever water supply they can find. Here in Kolkata (Calcutta), India, even some people with homes do not have their own water supply and have to use fire hydrants on the streets, as this family is doing.

Predictors of Population Growth

In some villages in sub-Saharan and East African countries, which have the highest rates of HIV/AIDS in the world, children are forced to fend for themselves. With large percentages of the working-age population dead (or dying) from AIDS, orphaned children take care of their younger siblings. In some villages in Uganda, for instance, social workers visit periodically to bring limited food for survival and see that children are planting crops. These children must learn survival skills and gender roles at a very young age. They have little chance to experience a childhood typical in other places or to receive an education.

Think for a moment about the impact that your age and sex have on your position in society and your activities. Are you of childbearing age? Are you dependent on others for most of your needs, or are you supporting others? Your status is largely due to your age and sex and what they mean in your society. In analyzing the impact of age and sex on human behavior, three concepts can be very useful: youth and age dependency ratios, sex ratios, and age-sex population pyramids.

The *youth dependency ratio* is the number of children younger than the age 15 compared to the number between

15 and 64. The number of those older than 64 compared to those between 15 and 64 is called the *age dependency ratio*. Although many of the world's young people younger than 15 help support themselves and their families and many older than 64 are likewise economically independent, these figures have been taken as the general ages when individuals are not contributing to the labor force. They represent the economic burden (especially in wealthy countries) of people in the population who must be supported by the working-age population. The **dependency ratio**, then, is *the ratio of those in both the young and aged groups compared to the number of people in the productive age groups between 15 and 64 years old.*

In several resource-poor countries nearly half of the population is younger than 15 years of age. These include Niger (49% under age 15), Uganda (49.9%), Congo (44.4%), and Afghanistan (42.3) (IndexMundi 2012). Working adults in less privileged countries have a tremendous burden to support the dependent population, especially if a high percentage of the population is urban and not able to be self-supporting through farming.

Similarly, high percentages of dependent people older than 64 are found in most Global North countries. In the European countries of Norway, Sweden, Denmark, Germany, and the United Kingdom, between 15% and 20% of the population is in the age group older than 64. These countries have low death rates, resulting in the average life expectancy at birth being as high as 83.75 years for women in Sweden (World Factbook 2013h). Using fertility and death rates to make projections based on current patterns, Josef Wöss predicts that from 2010 to 2050 the dependency ratio will increase by 92% (Wöss 2012).

Consider the case of Japan, which faces the problem of its "graying" or aging population. In 2013 24.8% of its population was 65 or older, and the average life expectancy was 84.19 years (World Factbook 2013m). Those young people up to 15 years old who would be expected to support the older population in the future make up only 13.4% of the population (World Factbook 2013m). The Japanese population is graying nearly twice as fast as the population in many other nations, in large part because the birthrate is low, 8.4 births per 1,000 in the population; with a death rate of 9.2 per 1,000, there is a negative growth rate each year—the population is shrinking. There simply are not enough replacement workers to support the aging population (Pearce 2010). Japan provides a glimpse into the future for other rapidly aging societies, including Germany, the United States, and China. (See Figure 13.2 for a vivid depiction of the expected transformation in the age composition of Japan in one century.)

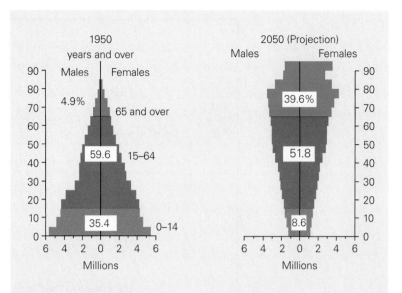

Japan's percentage of population older than 65 is growing faster than that of any other nation and in one century will have become transformed.

Figure 13.2 Japan Grows Old

Source: Statistical Handbook of Japan (2010).

Japan is an aging society, with life expectancy exceeding 84 years and 24.8% of the population over age 65. Ninety-two-year-old Toshi Uechi practices a traditional Japanese dance in Okinawa. An active lifestyle and a Spartan diet have helped make Okinawa the home of an exceptionally high percentage of centenarians (those older than 100 years).

Aging

The *sex ratio* refers to the ratio of males to females in the population. For instance, the more females there are, especially in their fertile years, the more potential there is for population growth. The sex ratio also affects population growth patterns by determining the supply of eligible spouses. Economic cycles, wars in which the proportion of males to females may decrease, and migrations that generally take males from one area and add them to another affect marriage patterns. **Population pyramids** *are pyramid-shaped diagrams that illustrate sex ratios and dependency ratios* (see Figure 13.3).

The graphic presentation of the age and sex distribution of a population tells us a great deal about that population. The structures are called pyramids because that is the shape they took until several decades ago. By looking up and down the pyramid, we can see the proportion of population at each age level. Looking to the right and left of the centerline tells us the balance of males to females at each age. The bottom line shows us the total population at each age.

The first pyramid shows populations that have fairly low birth- and death rates, typical of Global North countries. The second pyramid illustrates populations with high birthrates and large dependent youth populations, typical of the Global South. The world population has been getting both younger (the Global South) *and* older (the Global North), resulting in large numbers of dependent people.

As Global South nations have more and more children, they are creating more potential parents in later years, adding momentum to the world's population growth. Fewer deaths of infants and children, which can be credited to immunizations and disease control, result in lower mortality rates, younger populations, and higher potential numbers of births in the future. Ask yourself what might change rapid population growth in some countries.

Thinking Sociologically

Consider your own country's population pyramid. You can find it at www.census.gov/population/international. What can you tell about your country's level of development by studying the population pyramid? How might societies differ if they have a young population versus an old one?

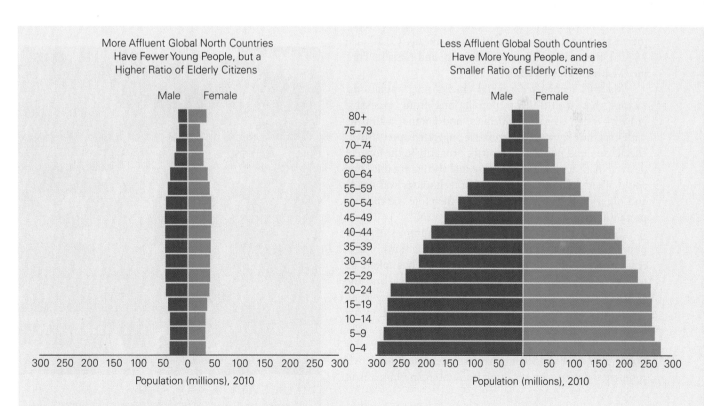

Figure 13.3 Population Pyramids, by Level of Affluence, 2009

Source: Bremner et al. (2009). Reprinted with permission.

Population Patterns: Theoretical Explanations

Interest in population size and growth began with the earliest historical writings. Scriptures such as the Quran and the Bible have supported population growth to increase the ranks of the faithful. Of course, population expansion made sense at the time these holy tracts were written. Government leaders throughout the ages have adopted various philosophies about the best size of populations. The ancient Greek philosopher Plato argued that the city-state should have 5,040 citizens and that measures should be taken to increase or decrease the population to bring it in line with this figure (Plato [circa 350 BCE] 1960). However, the first significant scholarly analysis that addressed global population issues came from Thomas Malthus (1766–1834), an English clergyman and social philosopher.

Malthus's Theory of Population

In *An Essay on the Principle of Population*, Malthus argued that humans are driven to reproduce and will multiply without limits if no checks are imposed. An unchecked population increases geometrically: 2 parents could have 4 children, 16 grandchildren, 64 great-grandchildren, and so forth—and that is simply with a continuous average family size of 4 children. Because the means of subsistence (food) increases at best only arithmetically or lineally (5, 10, 15, 20, 25), the end result is a food shortage and possible famine (Malthus [1798] 1926).

Malthus recognized several checks on populations, factors that would keep populations from excessive growth—wars, disease, epidemics, and famine (a drastic, wide-reaching shortage of food). He suggested "preventive" checks on rapid population growth, primarily in the form of delayed marriage and practice of sexual abstinence until one could afford a family. Contraception technology was crude and often unrealistic in his day, and therefore, he did not present it as an option for population control.

Looking at the world today, we see examples of these population checks. War decimated the populations of several countries during the world wars and has taken its toll on other countries in Eastern Europe, Africa, and the Middle East since then. The AIDS virus, SARS (severe acute respiratory syndrome), Ebola, and bird flu have raised fears of new plagues (epidemics of often fatal diseases). Waterborne diseases such as cholera and typhus strike after floods, and the floods themselves are often caused by environmental destruction resulting from too many humans in a geographic area.

Food shortages necessitating food aid due to impending famines were found in many countries in 2010, including North Korea, Afghanistan, Congo, Burundi, Eritrea, Sudan, Angola, Chad, Liberia, Zimbabwe, Bangladesh, Ethiopia, and Somalia (World Famine Timeline 2011). Famines are caused in part by erosion and stripping the earth of natural protections such as forests and grasslands by people in need of firewood to cook or more land to cultivate crops or to graze animals. Today, economic factors are also affecting populations as imported cheap food is driving local farmers out of business in some areas, resulting in food shortages and farmers with no income.

Four main criticisms have been raised about Malthus's theory. First, Malthus did not anticipate the role capitalism would play in exploiting raw materials and encouraging excessive consumption patterns in wealthy industrial nations, escalating the environmental impact (Robbins 2011). Second, Malthus's idea that food production would grow arithmetically and could not keep up with population growth must be modified in light of current agricultural techniques that increase yields, at least in some parts of the world. Third, Malthus saw abstinence from sex, even among the married, as the main method of preventing births and did not recognize the potential for contraception. Fourth, poverty has not always proven to be an inevitable result of population growth.

Two neo-Malthusian scientists accept much of his theory but make modifications based on current realities. Garrett Hardin, a biologist, argues that individuals' personal goals are not always consistent with societal goals

Malthus predicted that if left unchecked, population increases would result in massive famine and disease. Actress/activist Mia Farrow took this photo of food distribution in famine-plagued Sudan, Africa.

Scarcity of freshwater and other resources threatens survival. Women walk long distances to find water, as in these two water sources near Alem Ketema in Ethiopia. In the 19th century, Malthus predicted shortages of food and water due to population increases.

for population constraint. If people act solely on their own and have many children, social tragedy may well ensue (Hardin 1968). Paul Ehrlich added to the formula of "too many people and too little food" the additional problem of a "dying planet"—caused by environmental damage. To hold on to economic gains, population must be checked, and to check population, family planning is necessary (Ehrlich and Ehrlich 1990). The Ehrlichs' ideas can be summed up as follows:

> America and other rich nations have a clear choice today. They can continue to ignore the population problem and their own massive contributions to it. Then they will be trapped in a downward spiral that may well lead to the end of civilization in a few decades. More frequent droughts, more damaged crops and famines, more dying forests, more smog, more international conflicts, more epidemics . . . will mark our course. (Ehrlich and Ehrlich 1990:23)

The neo-Malthusians favor contraception rather than simple reliance on the moral restraint that Malthus proposed. They also acknowledge that much of the environmental damage is caused by corporate pollution and excessive consumption habits in affluent areas such as the United States, Canada, and Europe (Weeks 2012).

Thinking Sociologically

What are contemporary examples of Malthus's population checks of war, disease, and famine? Are family planning and contraception sufficient to solve the problem of global overpopulation by humans? Can you think of other alternatives?

Demographic Transition: Explaining Population Growth and Expansion

Why should a change in the economic structure such as industrialization and movement from rural agricultural areas to urban cities have an impact on population size? One explanation is found in the **demographic transition theory**, which *links trends in birth- and death rates with patterns of economic and technological development.* It is used to determine how changes in economic structure and movement from agricultural areas to urban areas can have an impact on population size.

The idea of demographic transition involves comparing countries' stages of economic development with trends in birth- and death rates. Three stages of development are identified in this theory:

Stage 1:   Populations have high birth- and death rates that tend to balance each other over time. Births may outpace deaths until some disaster diminishes the increase. This has been the pattern for most of human history.

Stage 2:   Populations still have high birthrates, but death rates decline (i.e., more people live longer) because of improvements in health care and sanitation, establishment of public health programs, disease control and immunizations, and food availability and distribution. This imbalance between continuing high births and declining deaths means that the population growth rate is very high.

Stage 3:   Populations level off at the bottom of the chart with low birthrates and low death rates. Most industrial and postindustrial societies are in this stage. Population growth rates in these countries are very low because Global North urban nuclear families are small.

These stages are illustrated in Figure 13.4 on page 404.

Demographic transition theory helps explain the developmental stage and population trends in countries around the world, but it does not consider some other important

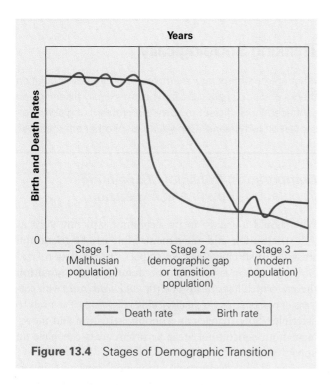

Years

Stage 1
(Malthusian
population)

Stage 2
(demographic gap
or transition
population)

Stage 3
(modern
population)

— Death rate   — Birth rate

Figure 13.4   Stages of Demographic Transition

factors that affect the size of populations: (a) People's age at marriage influences how many childbearing years they have (late marriage means fewer years until menopause); (b) contraceptive availability determines whether families can control their number of children; (c) a country's resources and land may determine how much population a country can support; (d) the economic structure of a country, religious beliefs, and political philosophies affect attitudes toward birth control and family size; and (e) economic expansion rates influence a country's need for labor.

Critics argue that there is a built-in assumption that modernization in the second and third stages will result in rational choices about family size. Yet, as long as women gain status by having large families, they are likely to continue to have large families (Robbins 2011). Economic development and education of girls generally result in a decline in the birthrate. The process of modernization that parallels economic development puts pressure on extended families to break apart into smaller nuclear family units, especially as families move to crowded urban areas. Urban families tend to have fewer children because children are a liability and cannot help support the family. Economic development, modernization, and urbanization did not occur together in all parts of the world, so the outcome of the three-stage transition has not always occurred as predicted in the theory.

The wealth flow theory suggests that two strategies are operating in couples' personal decisions about their family size. When wealth flows from children to parents—that is, when children are an asset working on the family farm or laboring—parents have larger families. When wealth flows from parents to children, families are likely to have fewer

children (Caldwell 1982). To raise a child to 18 years in the United States, for instance, costs on average more than $222,360, and that figure does not include the cost of college (Belkin 2011).

Conflict Theorists' Explanations of Population Growth

Karl Marx and Friedrich Engels did not agree with Malthus's idea that population growth outstrips food and resources because of people's fertility rates, resulting in poverty. They felt that social and structural factors built into the economic system were the cause of poverty. Capitalist structures resulted in wealth for the capitalists and created overpopulation and poverty for those at the periphery of the system. Workers were expendable, kept in competition for low wages, used when needed, and let go when unprofitable to capitalists. In short, for conflict theorists, inequitable distribution and control of resources are at the heart of poverty.

Socialist societies, Marx argued, could absorb the growth in population so the problem of overpopulation would not exist. In a classless society, all would be able to find jobs, and the system would expand to include everyone. Engels asserted that population growth in socialist societies could be controlled by the central government. This regulation is, in fact, what is happening in most present-day socialist countries through such methods as strict family planning and liberal abortion policies. In China, for instance, a couple is not supposed to marry until their combined age is 50.

Another aspect of conflict theory is the impact that wealthy areas have on poor areas, as exemplified by toxic waste from industries and landfills for wastes. Environmental racism is directly related to the social status differences of groups in society. People of color are 2 to 3 times more likely to live in communities with hazardous waste problems. It has become a pressing issue in many neighborhoods, especially poor minority areas where housing has knowingly been built on contaminated land (Bell 2012). Toxic dumps and burns, hazardous waste sites, landfills on which people must live because of lack of space, dumping waste in indigenous "First Nation" lands, and abandoned chemical plants and mines occur not only in poor countries but also in poor areas of Global North countries. Regulations in the United States to prevent housing being built on contaminated land are controversial because they require testing and delay development. Conflict between haves and have-nots is clear in such an issue.

From these problems has come the *environmental justice movement.* Prominent on the agenda of many environmental groups is concern about contamination near poor, often minority neighborhoods. Race and social class often go together when justice is of concern, and that is true of environmental issues as well. Consider these

Indigenous Medicine

examples: In Los Angeles, minority schools are located in areas with high levels of airborne toxins; in Missouri, industrial-scale hog farms are located in counties with low income; in Massachusetts, communities with high proportions of low-income minorities are 10 times more likely to experience chemical releases from industries than high-income communities. Other quality-of-life indicators like poor-quality drinking water and noise pollution from highways are common in low-income and minority neighborhoods (Bell 2012). One classic study in Chicago focused on efforts to have a more eco-friendly or "green" city by doing more recycling. However, there were substantial problems of pollution, disease risk, and other costs to the neighborhoods where this recycling was done. It is sobering to realize that environmentally friendly policies have often been implemented at a cost to those who have

fewest resources—people living in poverty and minorities (Pellow 2002).

Meso-Level Institutional Influences on Population Change

Meso-level analysis focuses on institutions and ethnic subcultures within a country. In this section we examine how birthrates and other population patterns are influenced by institutions within a society.

Populations change in three main ways: (1) size (overall number of people), (2) composition (the makeup of the population, including sex ratio, age distribution, and religious or ethnic representation in the population), and (3) distribution (density or concentration in various places, especially urban areas). The key demographic variables that cause changes in these areas are (1) **fertility** (*the birthrate*), (2) **mortality** (*the death rate*), and (3) **migration** (*movement of people from one place to another*). Populations change when births and deaths are not evenly balanced or when significant numbers of people move from one area to another. Migration does not change the size or composition of the world as a whole but can affect size or makeup in a local micro-level community or national macro-level population. The most unpredictable yet potentially controllable population factor is fertility.

Institutional Factors Affecting Fertility Rates

Jeanne, one of the coauthors of this book, was riding in the back of a "mammy wagon," a common means of transport in West Africa. Crowded in with the chickens and pigs and people, she did not expect the conversation that ensued. The man in his late 20s asked if she was married and for how long. Jeanne responded, "Yes, for three years." The man continued, "How many children do you have?" Jeanne answered, "None." The man commented, "Oh, I'm sorry!" Jeanne replied, "No, don't be sorry. We planned it that way!" This man had been married for 10 years to a woman three years younger than he and had eight children. The ninth was on the way. In answer to his pointed questions, Jeanne explained that she was not being cruel to her husband and that birth control was what prevented children, and no, it did not make sex less enjoyable. He expressed surprise that limiting the number of children was possible and rather liked the idea. He jumped at the suggestion that he visit the family planning clinic in the city. With his meager income, he and his wife were finding it hard to feed all the little

Overpopulation presents a challenge to food and water resources, and large populations damage the environment and provide little ecological recovery time. The top photo shows pollution of a stream in Yunnan, China. The bottom photo pictures a billboard in Shanghai advertising China's "One Child Only" policy.

mouths. The point is that knowledge of and access to family planning options is not always available. Institutions affect that knowledge and access.

Demographers consider micro-, meso-, and macro-level factors in attempting to understand fertility rates around the world. We know that individuals' personal decisions are key. People deciding to marry, couples' decisions to use contraception, their ideas about the acceptability of abortion, and whether they choose to remain childless can have an impact on national and global rates of population change. So choices at the micro level do make a difference at the macro level.

Economic Factors and Population Patterns

Fertility also fluctuates with what is happening in meso-level institutions such as economic and political systems. During depressions, for example, the rate of fertility tends to drop. Thus, meso-level structural factors—including level of economic prosperity within the nation, the government's commitment to providing (or restricting) contraception, changes in norms and values about sexuality within a society, and health care factors—all influence decisions within families about fertility.

We know that one of the most significant distinguishing characteristics between rich Global North and poor Global South countries is their fertility rates. The worldwide fertility rate has fallen in every major world region, but the rate in some places still remains very high. Thirty-three Global South countries in sub-Saharan Africa and 14 in Asia have especially low incomes and thus high economic vulnerability. These countries with weak economic systems are growing at the fastest rate in the world—2.4% per year. The average number of children per woman in sub-Saharan Africa is 5.1. In the Global North, the number of children per woman fell to 1.3 in many countries, although government subsidies for child care and tax relief for having children have kept the rate at about 2.0 in France, Norway, and some other countries (Population Reference Bureau 2012). Figure 13.5 compares population increases in the Global North regions of the world—the one's with the strongest economies—with the poor Global South regions—where poverty is widespread.

The key point is that the economic system does affect fertility rates.

Thinking Sociologically

What does Figure 13.5 (fertility rates by development levels) tell you about the lives of individuals in these different regions of the world?

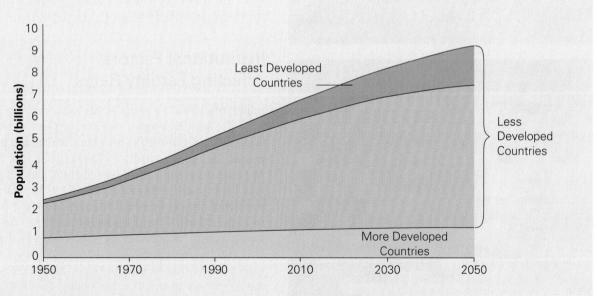

Nearly All Future Population Growth Will Be in the World's Less Developed Countries.

Figure 13.5 Comparison of Regions of Greatest Population Growth From 1950 to 2050

Source: Haub (2012). Reprinted with permission.

Note: Fertility rates have fallen in every major world region but are still highest in sub-Saharan Africa.

Health

Extremely dense populations are often found in poverty-stricken areas. This slum in Kolkata (Calcutta), India, houses many rural migrants who are the lucky ones, having found a spot in the overpopulated sliver of land by a highway where they put up a shelter of whatever materials are available. Others sleep on sidewalks and highway medians.

Political Systems and Population Patterns

When institutions of government establish policies, these can be *pronatalist* (those that encourage fertility) or *antinatalist* (those that discourage fertility). Government policies take several forms: (1) manipulating contraceptive availability; (2) promoting change in factors that affect fertility such as the status of women, education, and degree of economic development; (3) using propaganda for or against having children; (4) creating incentives (maternity leaves, benefits, and tax breaks) or penalties (such as fines); and (5) passing laws governing age of marriage, size of family, contraception, and abortion.

Antinatalist policies arise out of concern over available resources and differences in birthrates among population subgroups. Singapore, a country in Asia located off the Malay Peninsula, consists of one main island and many smaller islands. It is one of the most crowded places on earth, with 7,405 people per square kilometer. This is compared to 34 in the United States, 4 in Canada, and 351 in Japan (World Bank 2013a). The entire population of Singapore is urban, and 90% live in the capital city. The country has little unemployment and one of the highest per capita incomes in Asia. However, it is dependent on imports from other countries for most of its raw materials and food.

Some years ago, the central government in Singapore started an aggressive antinatalist plan. Birth control was made available, and residents of Singapore who had more than one or two children were penalized with less health care, smaller housing, and higher costs for services such as education. Singapore now claims one of the lowest natural increase rates (the birthrate minus the death rate) in Southeast Asia, at 0.5% a year. Singapore's governmental policies have controlled the natural increase rate (Population Reference Bureau 2011).

China's antinatalist policy has been in effect since 1962. The government discourages traditional preferences for early marriage, large families, and many sons by using group pressure, privileges for small families, and easy availability of birth control and abortion. The government has reduced the fertility rate to 1.55 children per family. The government plan is to keep the rate at or below 1.8, the replacement level. Unfortunately, there are side effects to such a stringent policy among a people who value male children. There has been an increase in selective abortions by couples hoping to have sons, and there are instances of female infanticide—killing of female infants when they are born—so that families can try for a male child.

In Eastern Europe, governments are worried about the drop in birthrates, so they take a pronatalist approach to managing the population. There are fewer young people to pay taxes and to do jobs needed in the society. Incentives established to bring the society to a replacement level of population include giving workers a day off to "have sex"; free summer camps for young couples—without condoms; cars and monetary gifts for new parents; and additional benefits for parents and their children. Abortions and even birth control have been banned in some Eastern European countries (Reproductive Health Matters 2011).

In the United States, citizens like to think that decisions about fertility are entirely a private matter left to the couple. Indeed, it is sometimes hard to pin a simple label of antinatalist or pronatalist on the administration in power. Presidents Ronald Reagan, George W. Bush, and George H. W. Bush each implemented a "gag rule" that limited the availability of birth control for teens in the United States unless parents were informed that the teen had applied for contraception. Presidents Bill Clinton and Barack Obama each eliminated the gag policy. Many experts argue that the gag rule has contributed to the increased teen pregnancy rates in the United States. Others argue that it is a parent's responsibility, not the government's, to deal with such matters.

Both limits to contraceptive availability and prohibitions on abortion are pronatalist because they increase fertility. While promoting births may not be the intention of those who oppose birth control and abortion, the policy has the latent consequence of population increases. Other governmental policies that might encourage larger families, such as family tax breaks or access to day care centers, are much less available in the United States. Each new administration brings its own policy initiatives.

A condom mascot offers leaflets to teenagers in Bangkok, Thailand, during a promotional campaign to educate Thai youths on how to use condoms. The issue is related partially to birth control and partially to HIV/AIDS prevention. The effect is an antinatalist effort to lower the fertility rate.

Thinking Sociologically

Do you think it is appropriate for governments to use enticements or penalties to encourage or discourage fertility decisions by couples? Why or why not? Identify several positive factors and several problems with either pronatalist or antinatalist policies that have been discussed above.

Religion and Population Patterns

Religion is a primary shaper of morality and values in most societies. Norms and customs of a society or subculture also influence fertility. In some cultures, pronatalist norms support a woman having a child before she is married so she can prove her fertility. In other societies, a woman can be stoned to death for having a child or even sex out of wedlock.

Some religious groups oppose any intervention (birth control or abortion) in the natural processes of conception and birth. Roman Catholicism, for example, teaches that large families are a blessing from God and that artificial birth control is a sin. The Roman Catholic Church officially advocates the rhythm method to regulate conception, a less reliable method in lessening birthrates than contraception technology. However, there are many Catholics in the Western world who are not following these teachings (Rodricks 2012).

Education and Population

"Women with secondary schooling have smaller families— substantially smaller than those of women lacking that level of education. In other words, the higher women's status in society—as measured by education level and job opportunities—the lower their fertility" (Population Reference Bureau 2013). If a country wants to control population growth, providing better access to schools and raising the education level of women is a key to success. Figure 13.6 shows the relationship between education and family size in five Global South countries (Haub 2012). Note that the higher the educational level, the lower the fertility rate and population growth. So, again, education and reduction of poverty are major variables contributing to population moderation.

Moreover, while family planning programs and contraceptive use have increased in much of the world, availability and use in sub-Saharan Africa remains low. Global use of modern contraception was 57% in 2012, but 222 million Global South women who would like to control family size are not using contraception because of limited access, fear of side effects, cultural or religious opposition, and gender-based barriers (World Health Organization 2012). The consequence is more than 76 million unplanned births in recent years (Medical News Today 2009).

As seen earlier, many factors affect fertility rates. Lower population growth means less pressure on governments to provide emergency services for booming populations and more attention to services such as schools, health care, and jobs. Most population experts encourage governments and other meso-level institutions in fast-growing countries to act aggressively to control population size. There are consequences of population fluctuations

In Indonesia, Nur Azizah binti Hanafiah, 22, receives a caning, having been found by a citizen having illegal sex with her boyfriend at her house. This Aceh region of Indonesia has practiced Islamic Sharia law since 2001. In some societies, she would have been stoned to death for having premarital sex.

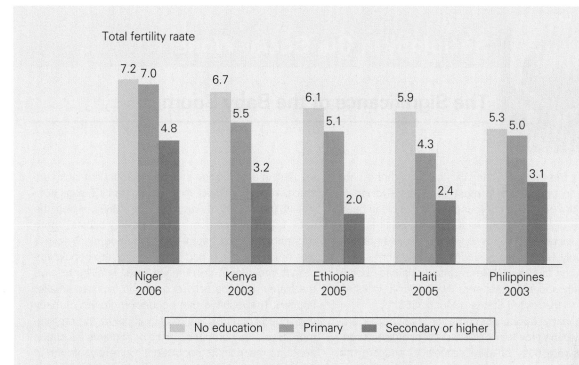

Total fertility raate

Figure 13.6 Lifetime Births per Woman by Highest Level of Education

Source: Haub (2012).

for affluent parts of the world as well as for poor parts. The impact of the baby boom in the United States illustrates this, as discussed in the next "Sociology in Our Social World" on page 410.

Thinking Sociologically

After reading the essay on the significance of the baby boom, discuss what impact the baby boom and the baby boomlet have had on your opportunities for education and a career. How will retirement of baby boomers affect your opportunities?

Mortality Rates: Social Patterns of Health, Illness, and Death

Health is *a state of physical, mental, and social well-being or the absence of disease.* **Illness**, or *lack of health*, affects the way we perform our individual responsibilities in the social world and our life expectancy, or mortality rates. When, where, and how illness and diseases are treated are shaped by each society's cultural values, demographic makeup, beliefs, financial status, laws, and decisions of powerful people. In the West African country of Nigeria, for example, some fundamentalist religious leaders refuse

to allow international medical teams to immunize children against polio. They have little trust in the motives of Western medical teams. However, when an epidemic of this crippling disease broke out and children began dying, some leaders relented and allowed Western medicine to be utilized, although convincing the public is still difficult (Padden 2009). Thus, both individual decisions and institutional norms have an effect on health and mortality in a community or a nation.

Life Expectancy and Infant Mortality

What causes the stark contrast in life expectancy and infant mortality rates between Global South and Global North countries? *Life expectancy* refers to the average number of years a person in a particular society can expect to live. It reflects the overall health conditions in a country. Imagine living in Chad, Africa, where the life expectancy at birth is 49.07 years and the average number of children for each mother is 4.8. Of every 1,000 babies born alive, 91.94 will die within the first year (World Factbook 2013b). At 24, life is half over. More than 72% of men and women live in rural areas where most are subsistence farmers, working small plots that may not provide enough food to keep their families from starving (World Factbook 2013a). When one plot is overfarmed and the soil is depleted so that plants will no longer grow, the family moves to another plot and clears the land, depleting more arable land. Shortages of food result in malnutrition, making the population susceptible to illnesses

 Infant Mortality   Mental Illness

Sociology in Our Social World

The Significance of the Baby Boom

At the end of World War II, the birthrate shot up temporarily in most countries involved in the war, as many young people who had been forced to delay marriage made up for lost time. The postwar economy was growing, people were employed in relatively well-paying positions, and the norms supported large families. While in Britain this baby boom lasted only about 3 years after World War II, it lasted 17 years in the United States: 1946 to 1963.

The baby boom phenomenon has had many impacts. During the late 1960s, school boards and contractors were busy building schools to educate the growing number of children. By the 1980s, student numbers declined, and towns were consolidating schools and closing buildings. When the baby boomers entered the job market starting in the mid-1960s, there were great numbers of applicants for jobs, and employers could pay less. The supply was so great they were assured that someone would take the job.

Two decades later, it was much easier for young people to find jobs because there were fewer of them in that age range looking for starting-level positions. However, that generation is finding it hard to get promotions because the baby boomers have dominated so many of the high-level positions. In addition, trends in marketing and advertising have, for years, been dictated by the baby boom generation because they are such a large segment of the consumer public.

By the 1960s, people's views of the ideal family size and the proper age for marriage changed. The zero-population-growth movements and environmental concerns slowed the rate of growth. The period from the late 1960s to the early 1970s has been referred to as a "baby bust" or the "birth dearth." (This fluctuation resulted in a population structure that did not look very much like a pyramid, as shown in Figure 13.3, page 401.)

In the mid-1970s and into the 1980s, when the baby boom generation started having babies, there was another baby boom—or "baby boomlet"—but it was much smaller, in part because the zero-population-growth movement encouraged small families to save the planet, and the baby boomers in fact had smaller families. The result is that population growth in many developed countries has remained below the replacement level (the number of births or migrants a location needs to maintain its population). Currently, growth in the overall size of populations in the Global North is due largely to immigration. Otherwise, many populations would be declining more significantly.

Population change also triggers cultural and social change. Each generation—the G.I. generation (1900–1924), the silent generation (1925–1945), the baby boomers (1946–1964), Generation X (1965–1979), Millennials or Generation Y (1980–2000), and Generation Z (2000–present)—faces new and different political environments, ethnic group changes, and societal changes (Pew Research Center 2011). Gen Xers (or the children of the baby boomers) now look at careers as transient, and they often move from job to job to advance instead of working up the internal labor market of one firm or organization. Similarly, Millennials are experiencing "delayed adulthood" (Furstenberg 2003). Unlike their parents, who saw having a family as the major rite of passage for growing up, Millenials spend more time attaining education and delay partnering and parenting until they achieve fiscal security. These are two strategies societies have made to adapt to population shifts. The point is that extreme fluctuations in fertility rates can affect societies in a number of ways.

and disease. What medical care is available is mostly in urban areas. In this section we consider the demographics of countries and the effect on health, illness, life expectancy, and mortality.

Low life expectancy is a complex matter involving malnutrition, lack of access to basic resources and health care, exploitation of natural resources by foreign companies, the state of the world economic system, and corruption within national or regional governments. In many poor countries, rural families have no access to doctors or medicine, such as antibiotics. They rely on local healers and herbal remedies that are effective for some illnesses but cannot cure other

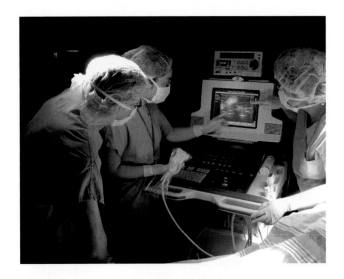

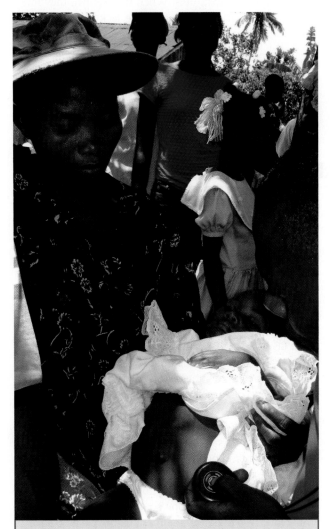

High-tech medical equipment is expensive (top), but in places like Haiti (bottom), physicians must use what little technology they have available.

medical problems. People frequently die from problems that are easily cured in affluent countries. Polluted water also spreads diseases as seen in the 2008–2009 cholera epidemic in Zimbabwe and the 2010 epidemic in Haiti.

There are significant differences in the causes of death in affluent Global North versus poor Global South countries. In the past, people in the Global North died from heart attacks and bad infections. Today many who suffer heart attacks and have bad infections can be kept alive, even cured, extending life expectancy into the 80s. Other than coronary heart disease, which is a prime cause of death everywhere, the major causes of death in affluent countries today are stroke and various forms of cancer. In less affluent countries, the major causes of mortality include lower respiratory infections, HIV/AIDS, perinatal diseases, diarrhea, malaria, and tuberculosis, reducing life expectancy in some regions to only 40 years (World Health Organization 2011).

Infant mortality refers to the number of deaths within the first year of life divided by the number of live births in the same year times 1,000. Even in the Global North country of the United States, some groups have less access to medical insurance and health care including prenatal care. They are at higher risk for problem births and infant deaths: those younger than 18, the unmarried, African Americans, Hispanics, people of low socioeconomic status, and women with little education and lack of prenatal care. Infants born to minority teenage mothers living in poverty are of particular concern in the United States. These infants come into the world with many strikes against them, and their mortality rate is especially high. They often have low birth weight, the most common direct or indirect cause of infant mortality. The U.S. infant mortality rate improved from 12.5 deaths per 1,000 births in 1980 to an estimated 5.9 per 1,000 in 2013, but it is still higher than the rate in many other Global North countries (World Factbook 2013i). For example, Canada's rate in 2013 was 4.8 deaths per 1,000 births (World Factbook 2013a).

The infant mortality rates in various regions of the world are shown in Table 13.2 on page 412.

Mortality From the Spread of Diseases and Plagues

Modern diseases such as HIV/AIDS, avian influenza (bird flu), tuberculosis, malaria, cholera, and SARS have claimed hundreds of lives this decade, but due to advanced medicine and global interventions to prevent their spread, combined they still do not come close to the deaths from the bubonic plague in the 1600s. That is because today global organizations including the World Health Organization are monitoring diseases such as bird flu and SARS to make sure the impact never reaches the tragic levels of the bubonic plague that killed one quarter of the European population. The next "Sociology Around the World" feature illustrates

Alternative Medicine   Malnutrition

Table 13.2   Infant Mortality Rates Around the World

Region	Infant Mortality Rate*
World	41
More affluent (Global North) countries	5
Less affluent (Global South) countries	49
Least affluent (the very poor Global South)	72
Africa	67
North America	6
Latin America	20
Asia	37
Europe	5

Source: Population Reference Bureau (2012).

Note: The infant mortality rate indicates deaths of children under one year per 1,000 births.

the effect that the bubonic plague, or Black Death, had on world population trends.

The largest modern-day plague is HIV/AIDS, a disease that has spread to the far corners of the globe. In 2011, the HIV/AIDS pandemic and related illnesses took the lives of 1.7 million people in the world. Of the 70 million people who have been infected with the virus, about 35 million people have dies of AIDS. Thirty-four million people were living with HIV as of the end of 2011. Sub-Saharan Africa had the highest infection rate at 1 in every 20 adults, or 5 percent of the population (World Health Organization 2013).

In just one country—South Africa—the HIV-infected population is 1 in every 10 people for a total of over 5 million infected. Average life expectancy is 59 years (September 2013). Local traditions contribute to the spread of AIDS. For example, men travel to urban areas for work and contract AIDS from prostitutes. When they return, they infect their wives. A major problem is the lack of resources for contraception and medications.

Sociology Around the World

"Ring Around the Rosie" and the Plague

Ring around the Rosie, Pockets full of posies, Ashes, ashes, We all fall down!

Remember this nursery school rhyme? You probably did not understand the meaning of the rhyme as a child. Some interpretations say it refers to the bubonic plague (Black Death), which ravaged England and Europe in the early to mid-1600s, leaving dead and dying people in its wake. People infected with the plague got red circular sores that smelled very bad. People would put flowers (posies) in their pockets or on their bodies somewhere to cover up the smell. Because people were dying so rapidly, it was difficult to keep up with burials, and the dead were burned to reduce the spread of the disease (ashes, ashes). So many people were sick and dying that "we all fall down." Although there are variations on this story, it is probably true that the rhyme was related to a major plague in London (Snopes.com 2007).

From 1603 to 1849, the clergy had the task of recording the deaths, the causes of deaths, and the burials in a community. These were circulated weekly, with a summary put out before Christmas. This process is one of the earliest records of vital statistics. In 1662, John Graunt from London analyzed the records for the first known statistical analysis of demographic data. Among his findings was that for every 100 people born in London at the time, 16 survived to age 36 and 3 to age 66 (Weeks 2012). The bubonic plague had an impact on social relationships, too. Many citizens avoided anyone who was a stranger, and some who contracted the disease died miserable lonely deaths because of others' fears of the disease.

As the Industrial Revolution advanced, so did income, housing, sanitation, and nutrition. All of these improvements in people's lives reduced the incidence of plague and increased life expectancy. Today, cases of the bubonic plague can be found in several places, including India and the rural southwest United States. Antibiotics are effective treatment for people who have access to them, but many poor people cannot afford expensive medications from affluent countries, and the disease can still be fatal.

Thinking Sociologically

How might global diseases such as AIDS and bird flu affect your life including the foods available for your dinner, the economy of your country and your community, the vacation or business travel plans you might have, and so forth? In other words, to rephrase Martin Luther King Jr.'s statement about injustice, how might disease anywhere mean disease everywhere?

The treatment of health and illness varies a great deal from one country to another and even on the same continent. Canada, for example, has a system that tries to provide health service to its entire citizenry, unlike the United States where health care is based largely on ability to pay.

The next "Sociology Around the World" on page 414 discusses health care in Canada, which has better health indicators of life expectancy and infant mortality than the United States while the costs are significantly less (National Coalition on Health Care 2008).

No system is perfect, including the Canadian one. The issue is to provide better and affordable care to citizenry, for it has a major impact on demographic variables like infant mortality and life expectancy. This in turn influences the productivity and the quality of life of the entire country.

Globalization and the Mobility of Disease

When the West Nile virus—a deadly mosquito-borne disease—was first discovered in New York City, it killed seven people before any action could be taken. Within a year, it had spread to 12 states, and within two years, it was found not only in mosquitoes but in 60 species of birds and a dozen different types of mammals. By mid-2013, 9 U.S. states reported new infections (Centers for Disease Control and Prevention [CDC] 2013). Although health officials acted rapidly to stem the spread of this disease, other pandemics are a constant threat. The world is highly connected, and diseases anywhere in the world can quickly spread to other continents, overpowering the medical community's ability to diagnose, isolate, and treat diseases. Because both people and infection are highly mobile today, the problem is global.

The density and mobility of the world's population, the use of land and space that determines the number of rodents and insects, the quality of water supplies, and the direct contact people have with one another influence the spread of disease. Currently, about half of the world's people live in urban areas, many in slums surrounding major cities. Problems such as open sewers, inadequate sanitation, lack of electricity, and polluted water pervade these slums. Most infectious diseases spread more readily where there is a population of at least 150,000 and increase dramatically with more than one million (M. Wilson 2006). Our globe

AIDS is a huge problem in Africa. This roadside billboard in Kitwe, Zambia, is part of an educational campaign to help get control of the pandemic.

This woman has just acquired new bed nets, which her family will use to protect itself from malaria-causing mosquitoes. Often, people are bitten and infected while they sleep, bites that result in high mortality rates.

 International Healthcare

The Medicated Child

Sociology Around the World

Comparing Health Care Systems: The Canadian Model

Two principles underlie Canada's system: All Canadians should have the right to health care, and financial barriers to care should be eliminated. After World War II, the Canadian government established a group of health insurance plans ("socialized insurance") that provided universal health insurance to improve the health of all Canadians. The costs are shared by federal and provincial governments with 70% paid by public funds and 30% by private funding. The government, in consultation with medical professionals, sets prices for services (Commonwealth Fund 2011).

Infant mortality and life expectancy are two key measures of a country's health status. Comparing these major indicators in Canada and the United States, Canada has lower infant mortality (4.8 deaths per 1,000 live births in Canada vs. 5.9 in the United States in 2011) (World Factbook 2013a, 2013i). Canada also has higher life expectancy—81.57 years in Canada vs. 78.62 years in the United States (World Factbook 2013a, 2013i). Canada pays for its health care system—Canadians' taxes are 10% to 15% higher than those in the United States—but total cost per capita (per person) is 33% less for health care. In other words, the overall cost to consumers means higher taxes but lower costs overall. Canada spent 11.3% of its gross domestic product (GDP) on health care, while the United States spent 17.4% of its GDP on health care (*Huffington Post* 2012a). Comparing Canada and the United States with 16 developed countries, the United States spent the most per capita ($7,960 in 2011). Norway is second in cost per citizen at $5,352, and Canada is only about half as expensive at $4,478. Table 13.3 provides comparative data on six Global North nations.

Problems of care denied because of lack of insurance, discrimination against certain groups, and

Table 13.3   Health Expenditures in the Most Expensive Countries and Life Expectancy Outcomes

	Cost per Citizen	% of Gross Domestic Product	Average Life Expectancy
Denmark	$4,438	11.5%	79.0 yrs
Canada	$4,478	11.3%	81.5 yrs
Netherlands	$4,914	12.0%	80.6 yrs
Switzerland	$5,344	11.6%	82.3 years
Norway	$5,352	9.6%	81.0 yrs
United States	$7,960	17.4%	78.5 yrs

Note: Switzerland has the closest health care system to the newly passed U.S. Affordable Care Act.

Source: Huffington Post (2012a).

geographic maldistribution—major issues in the U.S. system—have been largely solved in Canada and most other Global North countries (Reid 2009). In a comparison of access in the U.S. and Canadian systems, 13% of Americans are unable to get needed care, many for financial reasons. In Canada, 3.7% cannot get care, almost none for financial reasons (HealthReform.gov 2010; Hiebert-White 2010).

In addition, controls by insurance companies result in hospital stays in the United States that are 20% to 40% shorter than in most other countries for similar procedures. Some attribute this to the profit motive, which undermines attention to services and to client needs as foremost. Yet, in Canada, waiting periods for nonessential procedures are longer, and tests such as MRIs are given less often. However, individuals can sometimes pay.

has increasing numbers of cities that exceed one million people, many with crowded slums.

Most diseases are transmitted by direct contact with infected people. A World Health Organization study indicates that of the infections leading to death, 65% are due to person-to-person contact. Another 22% come from

food, water, or soil contamination; 13% are transmitted by insects; and just 0.3% are acquired directly from animals (bird flu, rabies, etc.). Because people are moving around the globe for job opportunities, business, and tourism much more today than in the past, they are exposed to more people in more environments. More than 5,000 airports

Comparative Health Systems

Smoking

now host international travelers, and more than one million people cross international borders each day, counting only commercial airline travel (M. Wilson 2006).

Health as a global issue is not limited to diseases and their treatment. Use of tobacco is a major issue, with perhaps a trillion "sticks"—mostly American and Chinese made—being smuggled and sold into countries around the world each year. The top U.S. tobacco companies now earn more from cigarette sales abroad than at home (Schapiro 2006). These companies have a vested interest in the globalization of their product. Some governments have mixed reactions to this importation: They gain tremendous revenue from taxes and tariffs on tobacco products, but health care costs also increase due to tobacco-related diseases (CDC 2012).

We will all die. The question for demographers is how and at what age. Both our place of birth and our social status in our country affect our life expectancy. Those lucky enough to be in Global North countries or in cities with adequate health facilities are likely to live longest. That leaves millions to fend for themselves when it comes to

health care, and early deaths are likely. Mortality, then, is a major variable in understanding population dynamics. When we compare it with birthrates in countries, we can tell if the population is growing or declining.

Migration: Where and Why People Move

Most of us have moved one or more times in our lives. Perhaps, we have moved to a larger house down the block, maybe to another area of our country for a job opportunity or school, or even to another country altogether. The process of changing one's place of residence is called *geographic mobility*. Over the history of the human race, people have migrated to the far reaches of the globe. Because of adaptability to climatic and geographic barriers, humans have dispersed to more areas of the globe than any other species. Even inhospitable locations such as the Arctic North and the South Pole have human settlements.

The *push-pull* model points out that some people are pushed from their original locations by wars, plagues, famine, political or religious conflicts, economic crises, or other factors and pulled to new locations by economic opportunities or political and religious tolerance. Most people do not leave a location unless they have been forced out or they have a viable alternative in the new location. They weigh the benefits of moving versus the costs (Weeks 2012). In some cases, the push factors are especially strong; in others, the pull factors dominate.

Migration is often initiated at the micro level: A lucrative job offer in another location requires a move, the family dwelling becomes too small, a relative needs help, or a family member's health requires a different climate. If an opportunity is present, the individual or family may move. However, if the risks are high, if the information about migration is scarce, or if negative factors such as leaving family behind are present, individuals may decide not to move. For rational choice theorists, assessment of costs and benefits by individuals are the driving forces in migration.

Although the decision to move is often a personal or family one, it is also influenced by the sociocultural environment. History is replete with examples of large groups of people who left an area because of aspirations to improve their life chances; hopes of retaining a way of life; or expulsion by political, economic, or religious forces. Chinese railroad workers came to the United States for economic reasons. Amish and Mennonite settlers from Europe sought religious freedom and preservation of their way of life. Italian immigration to the United States took place in a collective manner. When a family left Italy, it would usually move to a U.S. city where a relative or previous acquaintances lived. Thus, residents of entire apartment buildings in the North End of Boston were from the same extended family, or entire city blocks of people came from the same town or region of southern Italy (Gans 1962). Also, former

Many people around the world engage in tobacco use, a serious health hazard that brings many risks. This is also a concern to the society as a whole because it means lowered productivity and increased health care costs for all.

 Healthcare Costs   The Future of Medicine

colonial powers have numerous immigrants from colonized countries. This has helped make many European cities, such as London and Paris, the multicultural environments they are today.

Those living at the receiving end have not always been welcoming and in fact have often tried to isolate the newcomers in ghettos, preventing them from moving into neighborhoods. Job opportunities are sometimes limited, especially in difficult economic times when competition for jobs is greatest (Foner 2005). Immigration laws in the United States, for example, reflect the nation's attitudes toward immigrants at different time periods. The Chinese Exclusion Act of 1882 ended Chinese immigration; the national origin system in 1921 targeted Southern Europeans and reduced immigration from Greece and Italy; the Immigration and Naturalization Act of 1965 and the Immigration Reform and Control Act of 1986 aimed to keep out less skilled and illegal immigrants but facilitated entry of skilled workers and relatives of U.S. residents (Schaefer 2012). Current debates in the U.S. Congress over immigration reform show the contentious nature of policies related to immigration, especially illegal immigration.

Immigrants seeking a better life often struggle in their new locations. Mohammed, who is from Senegal, traverses the streets of Verona, Italy, during the day selling children's books and trying to make enough to live on, hoping he might have some money left to send back to his family. Mohammed speaks five languages and has a high school education, but opportunities in his homeland are limited, and he is an undocumented immigrant in Italy. Most Global North countries are desirable destinations for those seeking economic opportunities. European countries, especially former colonies, have large populations of immigrants from North Africa and the Middle East. These immigrants often face great peril in their attempts to gain entry into more prosperous nations, yet many find themselves in crowded, unsanitary housing with little economic opportunity.

Social science studies of the impact of immigration counter some of the negative stereotypes, pointing out that there is a significant economic gain for receiving countries. Yet some U.S. states and European cities are burdened with newcomers who are not yet self-sufficient. California Proposition 187, for example, illustrated anger about illegal immigration. Known as "Save Our State" (SOS), this bill denied education, welfare, and nonemergency health care to undocumented immigrants (Schaefer 2012). It was struck down by the federal district court (American Civil Liberties Union 1999). These policies often make life difficult for immigrants, even if they do have official papers.

Interestingly, scholars who study migration—especially long-distance migration that involves crossing into another country—point out that migrants are usually among the most hardworking, ambitious, optimistic, healthy, and well-adjusted people, for it takes considerable courage and motivation to undertake a migration to a new land. Wilkerson summarizes:

> Any migration takes some measure of energy, planning, and forethought. It requires not only the desire for something better but the willingness to act on that desire to achieve it. Thus the people who undertake such a journey are more likely to be either among the more educated of their homes of origin or those most motivated. (Wilkerson 2010:261)

African Americans who migrated from the South to the North in the United States during the 20th century, for example, tended to have more education, more entrepreneurial spirit, and more stable family ties than those left behind (Wilkerson 2010). Immigrants are usually not the dregs of the society they come from, but often the "cream of the crop."

Moves from rural farm communities to urban areas are a common internal migration pattern found around the world. International moves are often influenced by political unrest or discrimination against a group of people such as the Nazi persecutions of the Jewish population. For people who depend on the land, drought and other adverse environmental conditions force relocation.

International Migration

An amazing 3.1% of the world's population is "on the go" each year. That is 214 million international migrants, or 1 out of every 33 persons in the world. Half are women. These migrants change the size and characteristics of populations around the world, from those being expanded to those being left behind (International Organization for Migration 2012). From 1995 to 2000, 2.6 million migrants left the Global South for Global North countries, and more than half of them entered the United States or Canada. However, with the great recession starting around 2008, fewer immigrants are entering the United States. In Mexico, there has been an economic rebound and a decline in birthrates. With the anti-immigrant environment and tighter border controls, fewer Mexicans are making the trip to the United States, and more in the United States are returning to Mexico.

International migration is especially common where political turmoil, wars, famines, or natural disasters ravage a country. *Refugees,* those "who flee in search of refuge in times of war, political oppression, or religious persecution," numbered 43.7 million in 2011, half of them children. This is a 15-year high (United Nations High Commissioner for Refugees 2012). The ongoing crises in Syria and South Sudan will add significantly to the numbers. Roughly 27.5 million citizens are also *internally displaced,* forcibly relocated within their own countries by

Push-Pull Factors   Earthquakes and Megacities

violent conflict or environmental disaster. In 2011, the countries with the most refugees were Afghanistan and Iraq, accounting for 45% of all refugees under United Nations responsibility (Koleth 2012). Displacement can also occur because of natural disasters—such as tsunamis and hurricanes. All of these people are victimized by push factors, and that means they need a new place to live.

Economic opportunities and the demand for cheap labor have brought many guest workers from the Global South to European nations and the Persian Gulf states, where foreign workers make up the majority of the labor force. The migrants experience the pull of job opportunities, and the receiving nations need people willing to do hard but low-paying labor.

Prior to 1914, when World War I began, it was not standard practice for nations to require a passport to enter a country (Friedman 2005). Because most people could not afford intercontinental travel, controlling the flow of people was not an issue. During most of the past century—until the 1980s—the United States had a more restrictive stance than Canada or most European countries regarding immigration, but regulation eased in the 1980s (Farley 2010). By

2011, the total number of foreign-born people in the United States was 39.9 million (or 12.9%) (Center for American Progress Immigration Team 2012; Passel and Cohn 2012). The United States is and continues to be a nation populated largely by immigrants or recent descendants of immigrants.

Thinking Sociologically

Think about your own grandparents or great-grandparents. How long have your ancestors occupied the same land or lived in the same community? Do they go back more than one generation on the same property? If they have been mobile, what factors were critical in their decision to move? How has their mobility or stability influenced your family's experiences? How were they received in their new home?

Porous U.S. borders have been highly divisive as the U.S. Congress and state legislatures struggle to find appropriate immigration policies. The lack of agreement stems from conflicts over how the country feels about immigrants. Some favor the diversity and new ideas brought by skilled, highly educated immigrants, as well as the labor brought by low-skilled immigrants, who work at jobs not filled by U.S. citizens. Conflicts focus on who the migrants are, their religions, economic impact, settlement patterns, political loyalties, moral values, and work habits. Research finds that, for the most part, immigrants are industrious, innovative, and hardworking. They pay taxes and contribute to their communities. However, 9/11 affected attitudes about immigration, with a 20% increase in U.S. citizens favoring policies restricting immigration. Policy proposals include a fence along a length of the Mexican-U.S. border, an increase in border patrols, and use of drones to patrol the border. While the Bush and Obama administrations have pushed for immigration reform in Congress, this is a controversial topic on which agreement is hard to reach (Migration Information Source 2011). By the time this text is published, there will likely be a new immigration law as Congress nears action in 2013.

Internal Migration in the United States

The rate of internal migration in the United States is high compared with that in most places in the world. Patterns of migration have primarily involved individual "pull" migration to economic opportunities and better housing. Almost half report housing as the main reason for their relocation: A better apartment or house, owning rather than renting, cheaper housing, and a better neighborhood with less crime are primary reasons for moving. Table 13.4 on page 418 provides reasons for moving in the United States that fall into several categories.

This ship containing more than 300 immigrants from Eritrea, East Africa, was spotted by an Italian customs police helicopter. Every year, thousands of illegal immigrants departing from the Mediterranean coasts of Africa try to reach Europe through Lampedusa or Sicily. The commute is dangerous, and many immigrants are found dead on the Sicilian shoreline, but the desire for a better future keeps the masses coming.

Table 13.4   Movers by Type of Move and Reasons for Moving, 2010 (in percentages)

Reasons for Mobility	All Movers	Type of Mobility		
		Intracounty	Intercounty	From Abroad
Family-related reasons	30.3	30.2	30.7	28.3
Change in marital status	7.3	7.5	7.2	5.0
To establish own household	11.2	12.6	8.3	5.7
Other family reasons	11.7	10.1	15.3	17.5
Housing reasons	43.7	52.8	24.4	8.4
Wanted to own home	4.6	5.4	3.1	0.3
New/better house/apartment	15.5	19.2	7.3	4.3
Cheaper housing	10.8	13.0	6.2	1.7
Work-related reasons	16.4	9.6	31.1	40.7
New job/job transfer	7.8	2.7	18.9	23.8
To look for work/lost job	2.6	1.3	5.1	8.8
Closer to work/easier commute	4.2	4.2	4.5	1.4
Retired	0.5	0.3	0.8	2.4
Other job-related reasons	1.3	1.0	1.9	4.3
Other reasons (college, health, climate, natural disaster)	9.5	7.4	13.8	22.6

Source: U.S. Census Bureau (2012i).

During different historical periods, movement directions have varied. For many years, rural residents in the United States moved to higher-income urban areas. Until the 1950s, people moved out of the South and into the North, especially north-central states. Then the pattern reversed, and the flow started south and west. Movement since the 1960s has been toward the Sunbelt, especially to California, Arizona, Texas, and Florida. Movement to the Pacific Coast and even Alaska has also increased due to economic opportunities in these locations.

Thinking Sociologically

What are the benefits and costs for individuals and governments of extensive internal migration? Do you observe any of these costs or benefits in your community or in your region of the country?

One major form of internal migration is **urbanization**—*the process by which an increasing percentage of the population moves from rural areas to more densely populated cities.* For people who are seeking economic opportunity, excitement, and anonymity, they are "pulled" to cities.

The urbanization process involves a change of lifestyle for individuals that results from living in cities. The problem is that in many areas of the world the poor, who come to cities to find opportunities, live with no running water, electricity, or sewage disposal and lack basic services including health care and education. They set up makeshift shelters of any materials available. Some live on the streets. Countries and cities have little money to provide needed services to the migrants, and migrants often lack the skills needed for success in urban areas. Yet the world continues to become more urbanized as rural areas and farmland cannot support the growing populations.

Urban areas of 10 million or more residents, called *megacities,* dot the globe. In the 1950s, New York City was the only place in the world that had 10 million people. At that time, there were 75 cities in the world with 1 million to 5 million residents, mostly in the Global North. Table 13.5 shows the rapid change in this pattern with half of the 10 largest population centers in 2000 and 2011. By 2020, data projections predict even more changes in the order of the 10 largest population centers: Tokyo would retain the number one position, followed by Delhi, Mumbai, São Paulo, Mexico City, New York/ Newark, Shanghai, Dhaka, Kolkata, and Karachi. The issue of world urbanization trends is discussed in the next "Engaging Sociology" on pages 420 and 421.

Immigration   Homicide and Urbanization

Table 13.5 The 10 Largest Population Centers (population in millions)

2000 Rank	Urban Center	Population	2011 Rank	Urban Center	Population
1	Tokyo, Japan	34,450	1	Tokyo, Japan	37,200
2	Mexico City, Mexico	18,066	2	Delhi, India	22,700
3	New York/Newark, USA	17,846	3	Mexico City, Mexico	20,400
4	São Paulo, Brazil	17,099	4	New York/Newark, USA	20,400
5	Mumbai (Bombay), India	16,086	5	Shanghai, China	20,200
6	Kolkata (Calcutta), India	13,058	6	São Paulo, Brazil	19,900
7	Shanghai, China	12,887	7	Mumbai (Bombay), India	19,700
8	Buenos Aires, Argentina	12,583	8	Beijing, China	15,600
9	Delhi, India	12,441	9	Dhaka, Bangladesh	15,400
10	Los Angeles, USA	11,814	10	Kolkata (Calcutta), India	14,400

Source: United Nations, Department of Economic and Social Affairs, Population Division (2012).

In Mumbai (Bombay) many children have no choice but to sleep on the streets each night.

Thinking Sociologically

How might your own life be affected by urbanization trends? Even if you live in a rural area, how might the movement of the population toward cities impact politics, popular culture, and other dimensions of your life?

Micro-Level Population Patterns and Our everyday lives

You might get the impression that population studies are mostly about other places and problems that do not affect your country. However, understanding demography can be extremely important for comprehending social processes very close to your everyday life. While most Global North countries do not have massive famines or population explosions, population fluctuations influence them in many ways. Consider the life choice decisions you as an individual will be making regarding education, employment, and retirement.

In 1969, Keith, one of the coauthors of this book, lived in Boston, and his wife taught in a suburban school system there. The elementary school where she taught had four first-grade classrooms, with 28 children per room—112 first graders in the school. By the next year, the decline

Urbanization

420   Social Dynamics

Engaging Sociology

World Urbanization Trends

World Urbanization Prospects are reports published by the United Nations Population Division. They provide valuable data on past, present, and future urbanization trends in regions and subregions of the world. They also provide data on individual cities and urban areas. Consider the impact of major migration trends on the environment, friends and relatives left behind, dual-career families, maintaining one's culture, the impact of new cultural ideas spreading, and many more impacts. The major findings of the most recent edition follow in Figures 13.7 through 13.9.

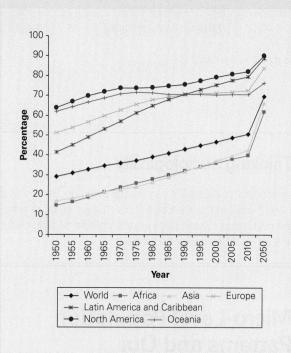

Figure 13.7 Percentage of Population Residing in Urban Areas

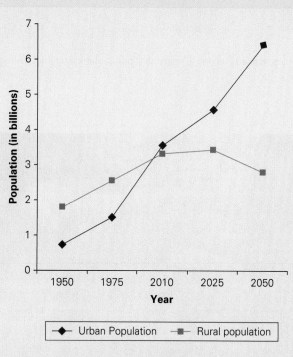

Figure 13.8 Urban and Rural Population of the World, 1950–2050

Sociological Data Analysis of Figure 13.7:

1. What do you learn from this graph about world urbanization trends? Which continents seem to be urbanizing most rapidly?

2. How might these trends affect people moving to urban areas?

3. What might be some effects on global climate change, the possibilities of globally transmitted diseases, political stability or instability, or the global economy?

4. How might the global trend toward urbanization affect your own life?

Sociological Data Analysis of Figure 13.8:

1. When the size of the rural population declines, how might it affect the culture of a nation?

2. Identify two positive and two negative consequences of this urbanization trend for a nation.

Source: United Nations Department of Economic and Social Affairs, Population Division, 2012.

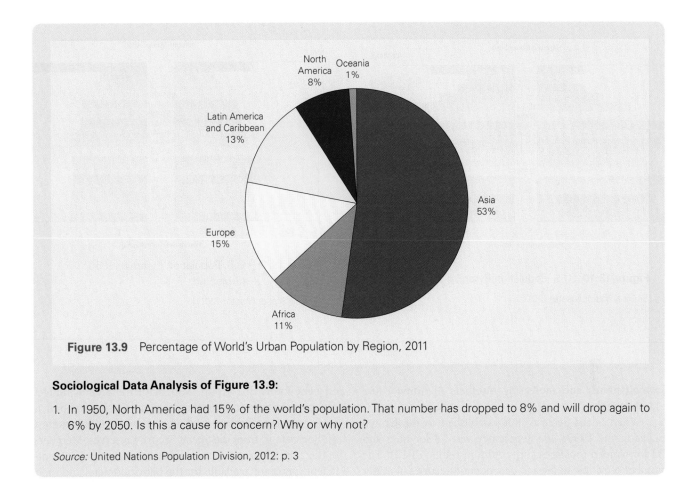

Figure 13.9 Percentage of World's Urban Population by Region, 2011

Sociological Data Analysis of Figure 13.9:

1. In 1950, North America had 15% of the world's population. That number has dropped to 8% and will drop again to 6% by 2050. Is this a cause for concern? Why or why not?

Source: United Nations Population Division, 2012: p. 3

in the fertility rate six years earlier was being felt, and the number of first graders declined. Within four years, the number of first graders in her school was reduced to 40, with two classrooms and only 20 students per class. Some school systems lost half their student population in a few years. One year, first-grade teachers were losing their jobs or having to move to another grade, and the next year, it was second-grade teachers who were scrambling. The third year, third-grade teachers were in oversupply, and so forth. With low demand, these were not times for college students to be pursuing teaching careers. A personal decision was being influenced by population trends—and this pattern continues.

We have already mentioned the impact of the baby boom (the high fertility rates from 1946 to about 1963) and the following baby bust (the drop in fertility for more than a decade following the baby boom). The impact on the population is graphically represented in the population pyramid of the United States (see Figure 13.10 on page 422). Figure 13.11 demonstrates other patterns of age and sex distribution in the country as current 40-year-olds become 80-year-olds. As you can see in both cases, the U.S. population no longer looks anything like a pyramid, yet from it we can tell a great deal about job prospects, retirement security, career

decisions, and deviance rates, to name only a few of the outcomes. As that bulge for the baby boomer group moves into the senior citizens category, it is likely to have a real impact on the society.

The decision about your career choice is deeply personal, but population trends also shape that decision. For example, if a business that produces baby products expands its production shortly after a dip in fertility rates, the timing of the business expansion may cause severe financial hardships or even bankruptcy for the company. Smart businesspeople pay a great deal of attention to characteristics of the population. That same information might be relevant to an individual deciding on a career. For example, this is an incredibly good time for students who enjoy working with older people or in the medical field to think about a career in gerontology or health care.

Retirement is another topic for which population patterns are critical. Most countries in the Global North are struggling with how young working people are going to support the nonworking aging populations. The number of working people contributing to pensions compared to retirees who depend on support is changing dramatically. Systems in many countries are in trouble because of

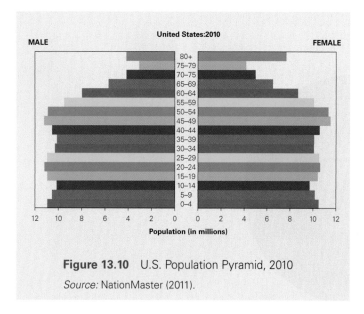

Figure 13.10 U.S. Population Pyramid, 2010

Source: NationMaster (2011).

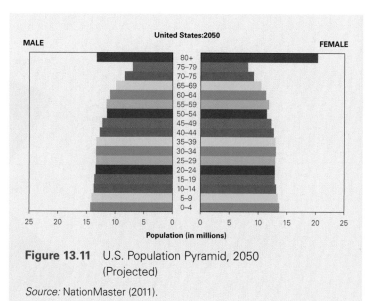

Figure 13.11 U.S. Population Pyramid, 2050 (Projected)

Source: NationMaster (2011).

low birthrates and increasing numbers of nonworking elderly people.

When Social Security was established in the United States in the 1930s, life expectancy was 58 for men and 62 for women (Social Security Administration 2013). The number of people in the age-dependent categories of under 15 and over 65 was low. For each person who received Social Security in 1945, 42 paid into the federal coffers (Social Security Administration 2012a). Forty people each paying $255 a year could easily support a retired person receiving $10,000 per year. However, the average life expectancy has shifted, and the age-dependent population has increased. Currently in the United States, nearly 14% of the population is over the age of 65, as opposed to 4% in the 1930s (World Factbook 2013i). Moreover, predictions are that by 2035, 20% of the population will be older than 65. When the baby boomers are collecting Social Security, the people born during the birth dearth will be the ones in their prime earning years, but there are far fewer of them paying into the system. When commentators and politicians say Social Security is in trouble, therefore, they are not generally saying it has been mismanaged. They are pointing to problems created by changes in the composition of the U.S. population.

In the 1980s, the U.S. administration and Congress saw the problem coming and for the first time began to save funds in a Social Security account for the baby boomers. They also passed laws requiring baby boomers to work longer before they qualify for Social Security. That there are so many baby boomers—and that an extremely high percentage of citizens older than the age of 65 vote—makes it unlikely that Congress or the president would cut back

on benefits to this group. Still, with the federal budget squeezed by war and natural disasters causing the deficit to grow, some members of Congress have voiced interest in "borrowing" from the Social Security reserves. Members of the younger generations will be the ones to pay if insufficient funds are available for the baby boomers, and their future pensions may be in jeopardy. The aging population and need for funds could have a profound influence on your own family budget and retirement.

Rates of deviance and juvenile delinquency in a local community are also influenced by population patterns. In the 1960s and 1970s, these rates climbed precipitously. When the rates of juvenile delinquency began to decline in the 1980s and 1990s, members of both major U.S. political parties claimed it was their policies that made the difference. However, most deviant acts are committed by young people in their mid-teens to early 20s. Thus, when the baby boomers were in their teens and early 20s, the overall rates of deviance were higher. Many of those same delinquents became upright citizens—even law-and-order conservatives—once they had families and careers. When the birth dearth group members reached their teens, overall rates of crime dropped because there were fewer teenagers. So private and personal decisions by thousands of couples (micro level) may result in a rise or fall of the crime rates for the entire country 15 years later.

Because population trends will shape your life, understanding those trends can help you use that knowledge to your advantage. To illustrate the power of demographic trends on individual decisions, the next "Engaging Sociology" provides an exercise in problem solving using information from population pyramids of U.S. cities.

 Aging

Social Security

Engaging Sociology

Population Pyramids and Predicting Community Needs and Services

Study these three population pyramid graphs. Based on what you see, answer the following questions:

1. Which community would be likely to have the lowest crime rate? Explain.

2. Which would be likely to have the most cultural amenities (theaters, art galleries, concert halls, etc.)? Explain.

3. Imagine you were an entrepreneur planning on starting a business in one of these communities.

   a. Name three businesses that you think would be likely to succeed in each community. Explain.

   b. Name one business that you think would be unlikely to succeed in each community. Explain.

Norfolk, Virginia

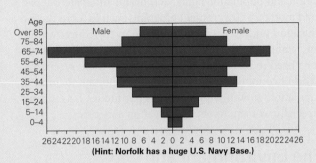

(Hint: Norfolk has a huge U.S. Navy Base.)

Bloomington, Indiana

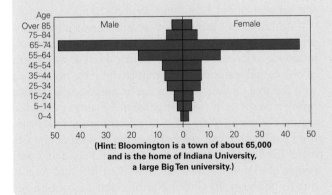

(Hint: Bloomington is a town of about 65,000 and is the home of Indiana University, a large Big Ten university.)

Naples, Florida

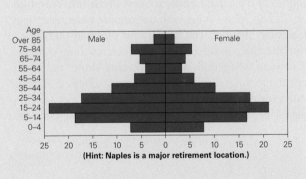

(Hint: Naples is a major retirement location.)

Source: Tables adapted from Nationmaster (2011). "United States Population Pyramids," www.nationmaster.com/country/us/Age_distribution.

Environmental and Demographic Policy Issues

Does rapid population growth retard the economic development of a country? This question has been a subject of debate among demographers and policy makers for many years. It is important because the beliefs of decision makers affect the policies and solutions they advocate. For instance, if policy makers feel that population growth retards economic development, family planning efforts are more likely.

Population Patterns and Economic Development

The issue of population growth has caused heated debate at several world population conferences. Some socialist and Catholic countries argue that capitalistic economic exploitation and political control, not population growth, cause poverty in Global South countries. They point out that multinational companies and foreign countries exploit poor countries' resources, sometimes with corruption and payoffs to government officials. This leaves poor people with no gains. High population growth contributes to global

 Fertility   Fertility

problems and policy challenges; countries cannot adjust quickly enough to provide the infrastructure (housing, health care, sanitation, education) for so many additional people. The largest impacts of high fertility and resulting additional people are in five areas: food security and distribution of food sources; contribution of humans to climate change; ability of governments to reduce poverty; demographic shifts that affect populations such as urbanization and population aging; and health and maternal and child mortality. Government programs such as reproductive education and accessible contraception to reduce fertility but retain reproductive choice can help, but local traditions need to be considered for programs to be acceptable (World Economic Forum 2012). Also important to limiting population growth is providing opportunities for citizens, especially women, to obtain education and jobs.

The Environment and Urban Ecosystems

The mountains rise from the sea, dotted with pastel-colored shanties. On the drive from the port city of La Guaira up into the mountains to the capital city of Caracas, Venezuela, one sees settlements nestled into the hillsides. The poor, who have come from throughout the country to find opportunities in the capital, make shelters in the hills surrounding Caracas, often living with no running water, electricity, or sewage disposal. The laundry list of urban problems is overwhelming: excessive size and overcrowding; shortages of services, education, and health care; slums and squatters; traffic congestion; unemployment; and effects of global restructuring, including loss of agricultural land, environmental degradation, and resettlement of immigrants and

The hills surrounding Caracas, the capital of Venezuela, are densely packed with migrants from rural areas looking for opportunities in the urban area. Many of these areas lack the most basic services.

refugees (Brunn, Williams, and Zeigler 2003). This section considers several of the many problems facing urban areas such as Caracas.

In the past three decades, the urban populations in Africa, Asia, and Latin America have grown rapidly, and many of the largest cities in the world are now in the Global South. Rural-to-urban migration and development of megacities dominate the economic and political considerations in many countries. The newcomers spill out into the countryside, engulfing towns along the way.

Ecosystems—streams, rivers, inland and coastal wetlands, grasslands, and forests—provide critical resources and services that sustain human health and well-being (EcoSummit 2012). Yet our ecosystems are under stress, much of it caused by human activity. Extinction of species, lack of water and water pollution, resource exploitation, collapse of some global fisheries, and new diseases are the likely results of this breakdown. Urbanization by 2050 will stretch resources to their limits. Cities will have difficulty disposing of wastes, resulting in possible epidemics due to poor sanitation. Humans are contributing to the problems that are killing people now and will kill many in the future. The problems are exacerbated by an increase in natural disasters (e.g., hurricanes), which scientists believe to be a result of global climate change. An increase in quality of life in some regions of the world is actually magnifying the problems and hastening the demise of the environments that support cities ("Ecosystems Report" 2006).

Additional infrastructure problems threaten to immobilize cities in the Global South. Traffic congestion and pollution are so intense in some cities that the slow movement of people and goods reduces productivity, jobs, health, and vital services. Pollution of the streets and air is a chronic problem, especially with expansion of automobile use around the world. Older cities face deteriorating infrastructures, with water, gas, and sewage lines in need of replacement. Even in affluent cities like Tokyo and London, many people are forced to wear face masks in July and August due to pollution. In Global North countries, concern for these problems has brought some action and relief, but in impoverished countries where survival issues are pressing, environmental contamination is a low priority. Thus, the worst air pollution is now found in major cities in the Global South. This air pollution, in turn, contributes to global climate change that has the potential to have devastating effects on life on this planet.

The reality is that the demographic migration pattern of urbanization is connected to the health and illness of a population—and ultimately to mortality. Millions of individual decisions to move to cities have resulted in meso and macro problems—which then impact the individuals who moved. In demography as in all other areas of our social world, the micro, meso, and macro levels are inextricably linked.

Many factors create change in a society. Some of them contribute to change in a particular direction, and others retard change. The next chapter examines the larger picture of social transformation in our complex and multileveled social world.

What Have We Learned?

Population trends, including migration resulting in urbanization, provide a dynamic force for change in societies. Whether one is interested in understanding social problems such as environmental degradation, social policy, or factors that may affect one's own career, demographic processes are critical forces. We ignore them at our peril—as individuals and as a society. Family businesses can be destroyed, retirement plans obliterated, and the health of communities sabotaged by population factors if they are overlooked. If they are considered, however, they can enhance planning that leads to prosperity and enjoyment of our communities.

Key Points:

- Population analysis (called demography) looks at the makeup of a population and how the trends and the composition of a population affect the society at each level of analysis. (See pp. 396–398.)

- The planet-wide increase in the human population's fertility is stunning. Implications for adequate resources to support life are illustrated in the population pyramids. (See pp. 398–401.)

- Various theories explain causes of the rapid growth, ranging from medical technology to cultural factors, but the demographic transition is key. (See pp. 402–405.)

- Many institutions affect and are affected by fertility and mortality rates at the meso level—especially health care issues such as infant mortality, spread of various diseases, and life expectancy. (See pp. 405–415.)

- Migration is also an important issue for the society—whether the migration is international or internal—for it can change the size, distribution, and composition of a nation's citizenry. (See pp. 415–419.)

- Population patterns can also affect individual decisions at the micro level, from career choices to business decisions to programs that will affect retirement possibilities. (See pp. 419–423.)

- The migration pattern that causes urbanization has created a series of problems that are related to health, mortality, environmental destruction, and global climate change, yet cities remain a draw because of prospects for jobs. (See pp. 423–424.)

Discussion Questions

1. Why is it important for policy makers to understand the demographic trends in their nation? Why should *you* be interested in such knowledge? How might it impact your understanding of and positions on issues related to (a) immigration, (b) education, (c) health care, and (d) Social Security legislation?

2. How many children (if any) do you think you would (ideally) like to have? Why? What might make this (ideal) number change?

3. What are some examples of (a) pronatalist and (b) antinatalist policies? Do you approve of such policies? Why or why not? How might your perspective differ depending on the demographics of your particular nation?

4. How is the social status of girls and women related to a society's ability to control population growth? How might you use this information to promote gender equality in your country if you were a male leader in the government of an overcrowded nation? A female leader?

5. What are some of the major reasons people leave their country of origin and move to another? Have you ever done so? Why? If not, under what circumstances would you be willing to leave the country in which you were born and move to another?

Contributing to Our Social World: What Can We Do?

At the Local Level

- The *U.S. Census Bureau* is always at work collecting, analyzing, and disseminating demographic information. It is a great source of data, ranging from information on your block to the whole nation. Invite a representative to your campus to discuss the bureau's activities. You can check internship and job opportunities with the Census Bureau at www.census.gov/hrd/www/jobs/student.html.

- Check out your *local department of urban planning, urban and regional development, or community development* by Googling those terms and the name of your town, county, or province. Invite a representative to campus or visit one's office. Discuss how population information is used in planning and service delivery contexts. Consider an internship with one of the organizations you find in your area.

At the Organizational or Institutional Level

- *The Population Association of America (PAA)* "is a nonprofit, scientific, professional organization that promotes research on population issues," according to its website. At www.populationassociation.org, you can find information on demographic issues and ways to get involved in efforts to promote legislation promoted by the PAA.

At the National and Global Levels

- The *Population Reference Bureau* (www.prb.org/About.aspx) "informs people around the world about population, health, and the environment, and empowers them to use that information to advance the well-being of current and future generations."

- *Planned Parenthood* (www.plannedparenthood.org) promotes family planning education and outreach programs throughout the United States. Planned Parenthood International (www.ippf.org) works in 180 nations. The organizations use volunteers and interns, as well as providing long-term employment opportunities.

- *The Population Council* (www.popcouncil.org) promotes family planning in order to reduce poverty, create healthier populations and communities, empower women, and improve lives across the globe. You can find fact sheets and other information at the organization's website. You can also look for possible job and internship opportunities at www.popcouncil.org/employment/index.asp.

Visit **www.sagepub.com/oswcondensed3e** for online activities, sample tests, and other helpful information. Select "Chapter 13: Population and Health" for chapter-specific activities.

The Process of Change

Can We Make a Difference?

Humans are profoundly influenced by the macro structures around them, but people are also capable of creating change, especially if they band together with others and approach change in an organized way. Social movements such as those depicted in the photos are powerful ways to bring about change.

Global Community

Society

National Organizations, Institutions, and Ethnic Subcultures

Local Organizations and Community

Me Facilitating Change

Micro: Unemployment and business scandals causing personal losses

Meso: Family instability; ethnic protests against discrimination

Macro: National government decisions about war, trade, or tariffs

Macro: United Nations hunger, poverty, and women's programs; International Monetary Fund debt relief programs

Think About It	
Micro: Self and Inner Circle	Can you as an individual bring about change in the world?
Micro: Local Community	What do you think needs to change in your community?
Meso: National Institutions; Complex Organizations; Ethnic Groups	What about your community (organizational or ethnic community factors) influence the possibility and type of change?
Macro: National Society	How does the training and support for technological innovation affect the process of change in your country?
Macro: Global Community	How do global changes—such as educating women—impact people and societies at each level?

What's coming in this chapter?

The Complexity of Change in Our Social World

Social Change: Process and Theories

Collective Behavior: Micro-Level Behavior and Change

Planned Change in Organizations: Meso-Level Change

Social Movements: Macro-Level Change

Technology, Environment, and Change

Our planet is in peril, according to evidence from the Asian subcontinent to the Arctic and from Africa to the Americas (Tollefson 2012; United Nations Climate Change Conference 2009). A major part of the problem is the waste humans create. Wet, dry, smelly, and sometimes recyclable, garbage is a problem, and we are running out of space to dispose of our refuse. We dump it in the ocean and see garbage surfacing on beaches and killing fish and birds (Heyes 2012). We bury it in landfills, and the surrounding land and water resources become toxic. We sort and recycle it, creating other problems such as where to dispose of recycled materials (Bell 2012). Perhaps your community or campus has separate bins for glass, cans, paper, and garbage. Recycling is a relatively new movement in response to the urgent pleas from environmentalists and policy makers about our garbage and trash that pollute water sources, cause areas of the oceans to die from trash dumping, and deplete renewable resources.

Recycling, salvaging items that can be reused, is part of a social reform movement—the environmental movement. However, few issues have simple solutions. The dumping and recycling have to take place somewhere. Many of the recycling plants and trash dumps are located in areas where poor people and minorities live. Some have referred to this pattern of placing polluting industries and garbage dumps as *environmental racism,* in which ethnic minorities are put at

risk by the diseases and pollutants that recycling entails (Bell 2012; Pellow 2002). This illustrates the complexity of solving global problems. At the micro level, individuals can help the environmental movement to save the planet through responsible personal actions. At the meso level, the environmental movement can help local and regional governments enact policies and plans to reduce the garbage problem, while groups organized to address environmental racism can help ensure that poor and minority groups are not harmed in the process. At the macro level, world leaders need to find responsible ways to dispose of environmental wastes. Our social world is, indeed, complex and interdependent.

Turn on the morning or evening news, and there are lessons about other aspects of our changing social world. We see headlines of medical advances and cures for disease; biological breakthroughs in cloning and the DNA code; terrorist bombings in Afghanistan, Israel, Iraq, Pakistan, Chechnya, and other parts of the world; famine in drought-afflicted sub-Saharan Africa; disasters such as earthquakes, hurricanes, tsunamis, and floods; and social activists calling for boycotts of chocolate, coffee, oil companies, Walmart, or other multinational corporations. Some events seem far away and hard to imagine: thousands killed by a tidal wave in India, hundreds swept away by mud from an erupting volcano in Colombia, or a rise in terrorism reflecting divisions in world economic, political, and religious ideologies. Others may impact you directly—having affordable access to health insurance, living in an area suffering from the results of a drought or severe storm, or accessing financial aid for increasing college costs. Some of these are natural events; others are due to human actions.

Social change is *variations or alterations over time in the structure, culture (including norms and values), and behavior patterns of a society.* Some change is controllable, and some is out of our hands, but change is inevitable and ever present. Change can be rapid, caused by some disruption to the existing system, or it can be gradual and evolutionary. Very often, change at one level in the social world occurs because of change at another level. Micro, meso, and macro levels of society often work together in the change process, but are sometimes out of sync.

Environmental Justice

News War

In this chapter, we explore the process of change, causes of change, and some strategies for bringing about desired change. We consider the complexity of change in our social world; explanations and theories of social change; the role of collective behavior in bringing about change; planned change in organizations; and macro-level social movements, technology, and environment as they affect and are affected by change.

Our social world model is based on the assumption that change, whether evolutionary or revolutionary, is inevitable and ever present in the social world. The impetus for change may begin at the micro, meso, or macro level of analysis. Studies of the change process are not complete, however, until the level under study is understood in relation to other levels in the model, for each level affects the others in multiple ways.

Thinking Sociologically

In what ways do you take actions to lessen your impact on the environment? Might your activities be linked to improving conditions for the planet or to worsening conditions for ethnic minorities?

The Complexity of Change in Our Social World

The Yir Yoront, a group of Australian Aborigines, have long believed that if their own ancestors did not do something, then they must not do it. It would be wrong and might cause evil to befall the group (Sharp 1990). Obviously, this is not a people who favor change or innovation. By contrast, *progress* is a positive word in much of Australia and in other countries where change is seen as normal, even desirable. The traditions, cultural beliefs of a society, and internal and external pressures all affect the degree and rate of change in society (Berman 2011).

Change at the Individual Level: Micro-Level Analysis

One of the nation's top entrepreneurs, Microsoft's Bill Gates, combines intelligence, business acumen, and philanthropy, qualities that appeal to American individualism. Gates has power to influence others because of his fame, wealth, and personal organizational skills. He is able to bring about

Mother Teresa, a nun who devoted her life to helping the dying and destitute in India, established the orphanage shown here in Kolkata (Calcutta). In the photo at the right, Bill Gates holds a child who is receiving a trial malaria vaccine at a medical research center in Mozambique. Gates, who supports many health initiatives, announced a grant of $168 million to fight malaria, a disease that kills more than 1 million people a year in Africa, 90% of them children (Gates 2013). Sometimes social change occurs because of individual initiatives.

Wal-Mart

change in organizations through his ability to motivate people and set wheels in motion. Some people have persuasive power to influence decision making, based on expertise, wealth, privileged positions, access to information, or the ability to use coercive force. On the other hand, common people, if they feel strongly about an issue, can rally others and bring about change in a society. Each individual in society has potential to be an agent of change.

Individuals are active agents, and they can either stimulate or resist change. Sometimes they prod organizations to change, insisting on more family-supportive policies (like an on-site day care center), better safety precautions for employees, or more environmentally friendly buildings and programs. Colleges may develop more recycling programs, more energy-efficient buildings or transportation systems, and more degree programs that involve study of the environment.

Sometimes individuals are not eager to change. They must be enticed or manipulated into change by organizations. When this does occur, most organizations—schools, businesses, volunteer associations—use one or more of the following strategies to persuade individuals to accept change: They appeal to individuals' values, they use persuasion by presenting hard data and logic, they convince individuals that the existing benefits of change outweigh the costs, they remove uncooperative individuals from the organization ("addition by subtraction"), they provide rewards or sanctions for acceptance of change to alter the cost-benefit ratio, or they compel individuals to change by an order from authority figures. In any case, individuals are a critically important part of any understanding of social change.

Change at the Institutional Level: Meso-Level Analysis

Meso-level change involves actions by institutions, formal organizations, and ethnic groups that are smaller than the nation, but more encompassing than local groups. One social problem that affects people at all levels in the social system is global climate change, an issue that is connected to pollution and use of the earth's natural resources. In response, many meso-level organizations have developed policies and practices to reduce emission of pollutants and change the way they use resources. For example, many denominations have developed programs to be more "green" or "earth-friendly." The United Church of Christ is one such group, passing a resolution in July 2009 encouraging local churches to become "Earthwise Congregations." An example of one congregation within this meso-level denomination follows.

Mayflower United Church of Christ in Minneapolis was one of the first in the nation to seek this designation. The church has an action team that works on ways to help members have more energy-efficient homes, but it also brought a resolution to the congregation that by 2030, the church would be entirely carbon-neutral. The resolution was approved, and fundraising began to change the heating system to solar energy. The roof of the church is now covered with solar panels. Within 18 months, the church reported a reduction of carbon emission of almost 50% (Mayflower Church 2013). Members of the congregation have also begun lobbying the state legislature to have more public transit, and especially more transportation that runs on electricity rather than oil-based fuels. Other United Church of Christ congregations are also taking actions, as are other communities of faith—inspired by denominational resolutions at the meso level.

Another interesting example is the way many universities—under pressure from college students—have changed their polices about production of clothing. Multinational corporations like the Gap and Nike had been fostering the growth of sweatshops in the Global South because it was highly profitable. Professors, students, and concerned citizens in Europe, Japan, and the United States began to insist that these companies establish acceptable labor and human rights conditions in their factories in the Global South. Their efforts gradually grew into an antisweatshop movement with strong labor and religious support and tens of thousands of active participants. College students on hundreds of campuses in the United States took up the antisweatshop cause, ultimately holding sit-ins on many campuses to force their colleges to ban the use of college logos on products not produced under acceptable labor conditions (Brecher, Costello, and Smith 2012). This meant that universities in the United States began to influence production of clothing on other continents.

State governments, the American Medical Association, the American Farm Bureau, the U.S. Chamber of Commerce, and the National Association for the Advancement of Colored People are meso-level organizations. Any one of them can implement policies that could impact local branches of the larger organization and have ripple effects across the country—influencing individuals' lives (micro level) or the national and global situation (macro level).

Change at the National and Global Levels: Macro-Level Analysis

Change often occurs as well at the macro level. It may begin at the national level in response to some concern, or it may be stimulated by a global organization (like the United Nations or the World Bank) or by a global concern, like climate change. We will discuss national and then global forces that can bring change.

Society-Level Change

Take a look at the impact of humans on the global environment and the constant change we are bringing to our planet.

To illustrate the increasingly complex and biologically interdependent social world, consider that pollution of the environment by any one country now threatens other countries. Carcinogens, acid rain, and other airborne chemicals carry across national boundaries (Brecher, Costello, and Smith 2012). Heat-trapping gases have risen dramatically in the past several years, causing pessimism about reversing the effects (Borenstein 2013). People in the United States comprise about 5% of the world's population but emit almost a fourth of the heat-trapping gases ("Global Warming and Climate Change" 2013).

In the past century, scientists claim, the earth's surface has warmed by one degree. That does not sound like much until one considers that during the last ice age, the earth's surface was only seven degrees cooler than it is today. Small variations can make a huge difference, and those consequences are likely to be dire if the Earth's surface temperature increases by another two or three degrees. Currently, massive blocks of sea ice are melting each year at a rate that equals the size of Maryland and Delaware combined (Cousteau 2008; "Global Warming and Climate Change" 2013). It is alarming to visit the glaciers on the South Island of New Zealand (closest to Antarctica) and realize that glaciers there are melting so fast that they have receded by as much as 10 or 12 miles in just a couple of decades. In the Northern Hemisphere, Greenland is home to many glaciers such as the Petermann Glacier. Warming recently caused the Petermann Glacier to calve an iceberg twice the size of Manhattan (BBC News 2012).

In a warmer world, there is less snowfall, smaller mountain icecaps, and a resultant smaller spring runoff of crucial freshwater. In fact, 80% of the world's population today lives in areas with shortages of water for human use (Environment 911 2012). While some of the environmental change may be rooted in natural causes, the preponderance of evidence suggests that human activity—the way we consume and the way we live our lives—is the primary cause (Gore 2012). Even if humans were not a significant cause, global climate change would have consequences at many levels of the social world.

Thinking Sociologically

What do you think happens when people do not have enough water in their current location to survive? What happens when they try to move into someone else's territory to gain access to needed resources such as land and water?

Obviously, this is a global issue with implications for nations that must work together for change. Yet, some nations do not want to change because they feel controls will impede progress. The Kyoto Protocol on global warming requires commitment by nations to curb carbon dioxide and other emissions, but U.S. President George W. Bush rejected it because it "does not make economic sense" (Lindsay 2006:310–11). As of September 2013, 192 countries and the European Union had approved the treaty. One notable exception is the United States (United Nations Framework Convention on Climate Change 2013). The Obama administration has indicated support for dramatic efforts to curb climate change and global warming, but passage of a bill in Congress is still pending.

Fixing the environmental issues will be expensive, it may temporarily hinder the economy and slow the rate of growth, and it may even contribute to continuation of the recession. Because recessions are terrifying for any elected politician who aims to keep the public happy, change is not easy. Still, most of the rest of the world's nations have signed the Kyoto Protocol, and there is continuing pressure on the United States to get on board. Because nations are still the most powerful units for allocating resources and for setting policy, changes in national policies that address the issues of a shared environment are of critical importance. The two big quandaries are (a) the costs and benefits to various nations of participating in a solution and (b) the matter of time—will nations respond before it is too late to make a difference? Currently, most of the cost and consequences of pollution are accruing to impoverished countries. Rich nations have benefited from the status quo, but it is becoming increasingly clear that the rich will also pay a price. Not only will they have to face pollution, increasingly severe weather and intense storms, and contaminated food supplies from around the world, but if Global South countries cannot support their populations, there will be increasing pressure from immigration (legally or not) to affluent nations.

Due to the well-documented phenomenon of global climate change, polar bears are only one of many species that are endangered because of a disappearing habitat. This is an issue that no one nation can address on its own.

Global Systems and Change

As the world becomes increasingly interconnected and interdependent, impetus for change comes from global organizations, national and international organizations and governments, and multinational corporations. New and shifting alliances between international organizations and countries link together nations, form international liaisons, and create changing economic and political systems. The following international alliances between countries, for example, are based primarily on economic ties:

- SADC: Southern African Development Community
- NAFTA: North American Free Trade Agreement
- CAFTA-DR: Dominican Republic–Central America Free Trade Agreement
- WIPO: World Intellectual Property Organization
- G8: Group of Eight—the most affluent and most powerful countries in the world
- OPEC: Organization of the Petroleum Exporting Countries
- APEC: Asia-Pacific Economic Cooperation
- EU: European Union

Consider NAFTA, which was initiated in 1993 to establish a free trade area between Canada, the United States, and Mexico to facilitate trade in the region. Promoters, including many global corporations, promised the agreement would create thousands of new high-wage jobs, raise living standards in each of the countries, improve environmental conditions, and transform Mexico from a poor developing country into a booming new market. Opponents (including labor unions, environmental organizations, consumer groups, and religious communities) argued the opposite—that NAFTA would reduce wages; destroy jobs, especially in the United States; undermine democratic policy making in North America by giving corporations free rein; and threaten health, environment, and food safety (U.S. Trade Representative 2012).

Analyses of the agreement show mixed results. There is some indication that tariffs are down and U.S. exports have increased. The treaty countries trade $2.7 billion, and trade tripled between 1993 and 2011 from $288 billion to $1 trillion (U.S. Trade Representative 2012). NAFTA has been more effective in increasing trade in agricultural commodities than in nonagricultural products. Some analysts argue that there is improvement in areas of environmental protection and labor rights. The truth is hard to determine, but there are probably both gains and losses.

In the preceding discussion of changes at different levels of analysis, the principle is that change at one level leads to change in other levels as it has done in the global cases of terrorism, climate change, and NAFTA. Changes at the macro level affect individuals, just as change at the micro level has repercussions at the meso and macro levels.

Social Change: Process and Theories

●━━━━━━━━━━━━━━━━━━━━━━━━━━●

Something always triggers a social change. The impetus may come from within the organization or society, a source of change known as *strain*. Sometimes, it comes from outside the organization, in what sociologists call *stress*. Strain may be caused by conflicting goals or by contrasting belief systems within the organization. There is constant impetus for change as we see in the following discussion.

The Process of Social Change

Conflicting goals are seen in the case of the platinum mining industry and its union workers. In the Lonmin South African platinum mines (providing materials for catalytic converters and jewelry), 44 workers died in August 2012 during strikes demanding pay hikes. Individual miners work in difficult, dangerous conditions to try to meet their basic needs for food and shelter for their families. Sometimes they must live at the mines away from their families for many months, but when jobs are scarce one does what one must. Company goals focus on the bottom line, being profitable in a competitive environment. The company argues that it cannot afford to raise wages and still be competitive (Herskovitz 2012). This conflict and others like it demonstrate how the needs of the workers can be at odds with those of the company.

Contrasting belief systems (political, religious, economic, and social) within a society can also have a major effect on the type and rate of change. For example, some religious groups oppose stem cell research, which often uses cells of fetuses created in test tubes. Others within the same congregation believe this research will alleviate suffering of loved ones and save lives. Although both sides believe they are pro-life, the internal strain in the religious group emanates from events and forces in science, medicine, and other institutions (Religious Tolerance 2010).

Stresses, those pressures for change that come from the organization's external environment, can be traced to several sources: the natural environment and natural disasters, population dynamics, actions of leaders, new technologies, changes in other institutions, and major historical events.

The natural environment can bring about either slow or dramatic change in a society. Natural disasters such as floods, hurricanes, tsunamis, heavy snows, earthquakes, volcanic eruptions, mudslides, tornadoes, and other sudden events are not planned occurrences, but they can have dramatic consequences. Disease epidemics are often unpredictable, such as the 2008–2009 cholera outbreak in Zimbabwe, Africa, that killed more than 4,000 people and the one in Haiti that has killed thousands since 2011 and resulted in more than 110,000 cases in 2012 (Nichols 2012; Rusere

Global Food Crisis

Natural disasters—floods, hurricanes, tornadoes, earthquakes, volcanic eruptions—can be the cause of major social changes in a community. As shown in this photo from a community on Lake Pontchartrain near New Orleans, Hurricane Katrina took its toll on Mississippi and Louisiana.

2009). Epidemics such as the SARS (severe acute respiratory syndrome) threat have brought about change in the World Health Organization, global medical reporting systems, and response networks. For instance, the Global Public Health Intelligence Network now scans Internet communications for rumors and reports of suspicious diseases. This way, health organizations from the local to global levels can act quickly to contain the spread of deadly epidemics.

Population dynamics—birth- and death rates, size of populations, age distribution, and migration patterns—can be important contributors to external stress on organizations. Where populations are growing at extremely rapid rates, strains on government systems result in inability to meet basic needs of the people. Values and beliefs regarding childbearing, knowledge of birth control, and the position of women in society are some of the crucial social variables in addressing the ability to meet needs. Immigration due to political upheavals or motivated by anticipated economic opportunities creates stress on the societies that receive the newcomers as they attempt to meet the immigrants' needs. For example, many refugees from the conflict in Syria are fleeing to camps in the nearby countries of Turkey and Lebanon. Map 14.1 shows the global hot spots for refugees entering other countries.

Leaders influence change through their policy decisions or the social movements they help generate. Mohandas K. (Mahatma) Gandhi in India taught the modern world nonviolent methods of bringing about change in political

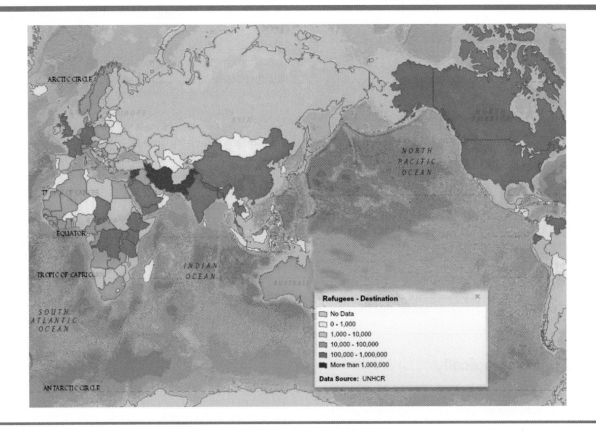

Map 14.1   Countries Receiving Refugees, Asylum Seekers, and Internally Displaced People, 2010

Source: National Geographic Society (2013).

New arrivals at Al Salaam camp, in Sudan's Darfur region, make temporary shelters out of household goods they were able to carry with them. A USAID-supported program at this one site is helping register more than 10,000 people who were displaced by violence in their home regions. Migration is a major factor in social change, and in cases like this, it is associated with great suffering and hardship.

systems. Policies of Charles Taylor, former military dictator of Liberia, created long-term war that resulted in thousands of deaths. President Robert Mugabe of Zimbabwe locked his country in a downward spiral of economic turmoil and disease, killing thousands. These leaders' actions created internal strains in their own countries and external stressors resulting in discussions and sometimes change in the international community.

Technology also influences societal change. William F. Ogburn compiled a list of 150 social changes in the United States that resulted from the invention of the radio, such as instant access to information (Ogburn 1933). Other lists could be compiled for the telephone, television, automobile, computer, and new technologies such as iPhones. Some of these changes give rise to secondary changes. For example, automobile use led to the development of paved highways, complex systems of traffic patterns and rules, and need for gasoline stations. The next "Sociology in Our Social World" explores several issues involving the automobile and change.

Thinking Sociologically

What might be some long-term social consequences for our individual lives and societies of the expanded use of the computer, cell phones and iPhones, the microwave oven, and cars that can navigate themselves and warn us of hazards around us?

The diffusion or spread of the technology throughout the world is likely to be uneven, especially in the early stages of the new technology. For example, computer technology is advancing rapidly, but those advances began in corporate boardrooms, on military bases, and in university laboratories. Policies of governing bodies—such as funding for school computers—determine the rate of public access. Thus, only gradually are computers reaching the world's citizenry through schools, libraries, and eventually private homes.

Major historical events—wars, economic crises, assassinations, political scandals, and catastrophes—can change the course of world events. For instance, the triggering event that actually started World War I was the assassination of Archduke Franz Ferdinand of the Austro-Hungarian empire. This assassination resulted in the German invasion of several other countries and the beginning of the war. So a micro-level act, the murder of an individual, had global ramifications. Clearly, internal strains and external stressors give impetus to the processes of change. The question is, How do these processes take place?

Theories of Social Change

Social scientists seek to explain the causes and consequences of social change, sometimes with the hope that change can be controlled or guided. Theories of change often reflect the events and belief systems of particular historical time periods. For example, conflict theory developed during periods of change in Europe. It began to gain adherents in the United States during the 1960s when intense conflict over issues of race and ethnic relations, the morality of the Vietnam War, and changes in social values peaked. Theories such as structural-functionalism that focused on social harmony were of little help.

Major social change theories tend to focus on the micro level (symbolic interaction and rational choice theories) or the meso and macro levels (evolutionary, functional, conflict, and world systems theories). As we review these theories, many will be familiar from previous chapters. However, here they are related to the process of change.

Micro-Level Theories of Change

Symbolic Interactionism. According to symbolic interaction theory, a micro-level theory, human beings are always trying to make sense of the things they experience, figure out what an event or interaction means, and determine what action is required of them. Humans construct meanings that agree with or diverge from what others around them think. This capacity to define one's situation, such as concluding that one is oppressed even though others have accepted the circumstances as normal, can be a powerful impetus to change. It can be the starting point of social movements, cultural changes, and revolutions.

Social Movements

Sociology in Our Social World

Technology and Change: The Automobile

Only a century ago, a newfangled novelty was spreading quickly from urban areas to the countryside: the automobile. At the turn of the 20th century, this strange horseless carriage was often referred to in rural areas as the "devil wagon." The introduction of this self-propelled vehicle was controversial, and in the 1890s and early 1900s, some cities and counties had rules forbidding motorized vehicles. In Vermont, a walking escort had to precede the car by an eighth of a mile with a red warning flag, and in Iowa, motorists were required to telephone ahead to a town they planned to drive through to warn the community lest their horses be alarmed (M. Berger 1979; Clymer 1953; Glasscock 1937; Morris 1949). In most rural areas, motorists were expected to pull their cars to a stop or even to shut down the motor when a horse-drawn buggy came near. "Pig and chicken legal clauses" meant the automobile driver was liable for any injury that occurred when passing an animal near the road, even if the injury was due to the animal running away (Scott-Montagu 1904).

Automobiles were restricted to cities for nearly a decade after their invention because roads were inadequate outside of the urban areas and they often slid off muddy roads into ditches. These conditions had not deterred horses. In 1915, Owen G. Roberts invented a seat belt because on a daylong 80-mile drive westward from Columbus, Ohio, Mary Roberts was knocked unconscious when the rough roads caused her head to smack the roof of the car. Paving of roads became a necessity for automobile travel and, of course, made automobile travel much faster and more common. The expansion was stunning. Roughly 85,000 motored vehicles were in use in the United States in 1911. By 1930, the number was nearly 10 million, and in 2007 the estimated number of registered passenger vehicles was 254.4 million (M. Berger 1979; Tilley 2009).

Forms of entertainment began to change when people were able to be more mobile. As the Model T made cars affordable, families no longer had only each other for socializing, and entertainment became available virtually any night of the week (M. Berger 1979; McKelvie 1926). Thus, dependence on family was lessened, possibly weakening familial bonds and oversight (M. Berger 1979). Even courting was substantially changed, as individuals could go farther afield to find a possible life partner, couples could go more places on dates, and two people could find more privacy.

Transportation that made traversing distances more possible changed how people related to a number of other institutions as well. Motorized buses made transportation to schools possible, and attendance rates of rural children increased substantially (U.S. Department of Interior Office of Education 1930). Because people could drive farther to churches, they often chose to go to city churches, where the preachers were more skilled public speakers and the music was of higher quality. Some people found that a country drive was a more interesting way to spend Sunday mornings, and preachers often condemned cars for leading people away from church (Berger 1979). Many country churches consolidated or closed. Still, once pastors could afford cars, rural people received new services such as pastoral calls (W. H. Wilson 1924). The automobile was also a boon to the mental health

(Continued)

(Continued)

of isolated farm women, allowing them to visit with neighbors (M. Berger 1979; McNall and McNall 1983).

As people could live in less congested areas but still get to work in a reasonable amount of time via an automobile or public transport, the suburbs began to develop around major cities. No longer did people locate homes close to shopping, schools, and places of worship. Still, a dispersed population needs to use more gasoline, thereby creating pollution. As the wealthy moved to expensive suburbs and paid higher taxes to support

outstanding schools, socioeconomic and ethnic stratification between communities increased.

When Owen G. Roberts built one of the first automobiles in Ohio and established a large automobile dealership, it was not his intent to heighten segregation, to create funding problems for poor inner-city areas, or to pollute the environment. Yet, these are some of the *unintended consequences* of the spread of the automobile. It sometimes takes decades before we can identify the consequences of the technologies we develop and adopt.

Some sociologists believe that individuals are always at the core of any social trends or movements, even if those movements are national or global (Blumer 1986; Giddens 1986; Simmel [1902–1917] 1950). After all, it is individuals who act, make decisions, and take action. There are a number of leaders, for example, who have changed the world for better (Mahatma Gandhi) or worse (Adolf Hitler). Neither corporations nor nations nor bureaucracies make decisions—people do. The way in which an individual defines the reality he or she is experiencing makes a huge difference in how that person will respond.

Social institutions and structures are always subject to maverick individuals "thinking outside the box" and changing how others see things. Individual actions can cause riots, social movements, planned change in organizations, and a host of other actions that have the potential to transform the society. That people may construct reality in new ways can be a serious threat to the status quo, and those who want to protect the status quo try to ensure that people will see the world the same way they do. If change feels threatening to some members who have a vested interest in the current arrangements, those individuals who advocate change may face resistance.

Leaders often provide opportunities for group members to participate in suggesting, planning, and implementing

change to help create acceptance and positive attitudes toward change. This collaborative process is often used when a firm or a public agency is planning a major project, such as the development of a shopping mall or a waste disposal site, and cooperation and support by other parts of the community become essential. Symbolic interactionists would see this as an effort to build a consensus about what the social changes mean and to implement change in a way that is not perceived as threatening to the members.

Rational Choice. To rational choice theorists, behaviors are largely driven by individuals seeking rewards and limiting costs. Because of this, most individuals engage in those activities that bring positive rewards and try to avoid the negative. A group seeking change can attempt to set up a situation in which desired behavior is rewarded. The typology presented in Figure 14.1 shows the relationship between behaviors and sanctions.

Bringing about change may not require a change in costs or rewards. It may be sufficient simply to change the people's perception of the advantages and disadvantages of certain actions. Sometimes, people do not know all the rewards, or they have failed to accurately assess the costs of an action. For example, few citizens in the United States realize all the financial, health, and legal benefits

Behavior		**Sanction**	
		Formal	**Informal**
	Positive	Bonuses, advances, fringe benefits, recognition	Praise, smile, pat on the back
	Negative	Demotion, loss of salary	Ridicule, exclusion, talk behind back

Figure 14.1 Relationship Between Behaviors and Sanctions

of marriage. To change marriage rates, we may not need more benefits to encourage marriage. We may do just as well to change the population's appraisal of the benefits already available.

Meso- and Macro-Level Theories of Change

Social Evolutionary Theories. Social evolutionary theories at the macro level assume that societies change slowly from simple to more complex forms. Early unilinear theories maintained that all societies moved through the same steps and that advancement or progress was desirable and would lead to a better society. These theories came to prominence during the Industrial Revolution when European social scientists sought to interpret the differences between their own societies and the "primitive societies" of other continents. Europe was being stimulated by travel, exposure to new cultures, and a spawning of new philosophies, a period called the Enlightenment. Europeans witnessed the developments of mines, railroads, cities, educational systems, and rising industries, which they defined as "progress" or "civilization." World travelers reported that other peoples and societies did not seem to have these developments.

In recent versions of evolutionary theory, scholars identify five stages through which societies progress: hunter-gatherer, horticultural, agrarian, industrial, and postindustrial (Nolan and Lenski 2010; see Chapter 3). This does *not* mean that some stages are "better" than others; it means that this is the typical pattern of change due to new technologies and more efficient harnessing of energy.

Many modern cases do not fit this pattern because they skip steps or are selective about what aspects of technology they wish to adopt. Countries such as India and China are largely agricultural but are importing and developing the latest technology that allows them to skip over developmental steps. Most African countries will not see landlines for phones, but instead will have cell phones even in the more remote areas. Furthermore, advocates of some religious, social, and political ideologies question the assumption that "material progress" (which is what technology fosters) is desirable.

Even the phrase *developing countries* has been controversial with some scholars because it might imply that all societies are moving toward the type of social system characterized by the affluent or "developed" societies. Many now use the term *Global South* because poor countries are disproportionately south of the 20th parallel North whereas affluent nations are typically north of that latitude. Note that the term is a metaphor for all poor countries, north or south. The term is meant to avoid an assumption of inevitable evolution toward Western cultures.

Contemporary evolutionary theories acknowledge that change takes place in multiple ways and not just in a straight line. The rapid spread of ideas and technologies means that societies today may move quickly from simple to complex, creating modern states. Consider the mass of contradictions of the Middle East today. Due to the world demand for their oil, several countries in this region now have the highest per capita incomes (income for each person) in the world. For example, in 2012, Qatar had an income of $103,900 for each individual, while the average for the United States was $50,700 (World Factbook 2012d). The urban elite in these countries have access to modern conveniences such as the latest technology, jets, and cell phones. Yet other Middle Eastern people still live traditional lives as nomads or herders in small villages or earn their living from the desert. Not all segments of society change at the same rate, making categorization of some societies difficult. A single nation may be both postindustrial and pastoral.

Functional Theories. Functional theorists assume that societies are basically stable systems held together by the shared norms and values of their members. The interdependent parts work together to make the society function smoothly. A change in one part of the society affects all the

The efficiency and speed of modes of transportation for goods and people vary around the world, often reflecting the level of development of the region or country. "Premodern" modes of transportation leave less pollution and sometimes move more easily through congested streets than do trucks. Sometimes, technological progress has high costs including pollution, and resistance to that "progress" may make sense.

other parts, each changing in turn until the system resumes a state of equilibrium. Change can come from external or internal sources, from stresses in contact with other societies, or from strains within.

Slow, nondisruptive change occurs as societies become more complex, but any change may be seen as threatening to the equilibrium of a system. Rapid change is seen as especially dysfunctional or disruptive. Because sudden, disruptive change is difficult to explain using functional theory and because any major change is viewed with some suspicion, some sociologists have turned to conflict theories to help explain change, especially rapid or violent changes.

Conflict Theories. Conflict theorists assume that societies are dynamic and that change and conflict are inevitable. According to Karl Marx, socioeconomic class conflict is the major source of tension leading to change in any society. Karl Marx and Friedrich Engels argued that the antagonistic relationship they saw developing between the workers (proletariat) and the owners of the production systems (bourgeoisie) in 19th-century England would lead to social revolution. From this, they thought a new world order would emerge in which the workers themselves would own the means of production. Thus, conflict between the owners and the workers would be the central factor driving social change (Marx and Engels [1848] 1969).

Other conflict theorists study variables such as gender, religion, politics, and ethnic or interest group problems in their analyses, feeling that these factors can also be the grounds for oppression and "we" versus "they" differences (Dahrendorf 1959). Some see conflict as useful for society because it forces societies to adapt to new conditions and leads to healthy change (Coser 1956). Conflict over slavery or over gender inequality is an example of a problem that causes stresses and strains, often resulting in improved society. The current conflict over health care in the United States may also eventually lead to a better system.

World Systems Theory of Global Change. World systems theorists focus on the historical development of the whole world and how that development has influenced individual countries today. Capitalist economies first appeared about 1500. Since then, except for a few isolated tribal groupings, almost all societies have been at least indirectly influenced by dominant capitalist world economic and political systems (Wallerstein 1974).

This theory divided the world system into three main parts: the core, semiperipheral, and peripheral areas (see Figure 14.2). The core areas are economically and politically powerful. Core countries include most European states, Australia and New Zealand, Japan, Canada, the United States, and a few others (Wallerstein 1974). Historically, they have controlled global decision making, received the largest share of the profits from the world economic system,

In this typical situation, these South African miners are all black and work for low wages, whereas the supervisors and managers are white. These gold miners from poor peripheral countries are part of a multinational corporation and the larger world economic system, with stockholders from the core capitalist world system.

and dominated peripheral areas politically, economically, and culturally by controlling the flow of technology and capital into those countries. Peripheral countries, many of which are in Africa and Asia, provide cheap labor and raw materials for the core countries' needs.

The semiperipheral countries are in an intermediate position, trading with both the core and the peripheral countries. The Baltic regions of Eastern Europe, Brazil, Argentina, South Africa, India, the Philippines, Iran, and Mexico are among the semiperipheral areas. Because most semiperipheral countries are industrializing, they serve as areas to which core-country businesses and multinational corporations can move for continued growth, often in partnerships, as semiperipheral states aspire to join the core countries. The core and semiperipheral countries process raw materials, often from peripheral countries, and may

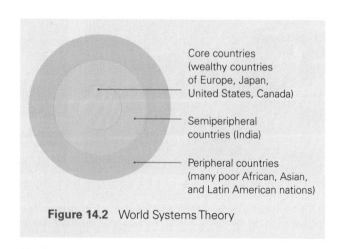

Core countries (wealthy countries of Europe, Japan, United States, Canada)

Semiperipheral countries (India)

Peripheral countries (many poor African, Asian, and Latin American nations)

Figure 14.2 World Systems Theory

sell the final products back to the peripheral countries. The semiperipheral countries and the peripheral countries need the trade and the resources of the core countries, but they are also at a severe disadvantage in competition and are exploited by those at the core, resulting in an uneasy relationship.

In one sense, world systems theory is a conflict theory that is global in nature, with core countries exploiting the poor countries. As we might expect from conflict theory, some groups of noncore countries have increased their collective power by forming alliances such as OPEC (Organization of the Petroleum Exporting Countries), African Union, and SEATO (Southeast Asia Treaty Organization). These alliances present challenges to the historically core countries of the world system because of their combined economic and political power. For example, the price we pay at the gas pump reflects, in part, the power of OPEC to set prices.

When we understand international treaties and alliances as part of larger issues of conflict over resources and economic self-interests, the animosity by noncore countries toward core countries such as the United States begins to make sense. Likewise, the mistrust of the United States toward countries that seem to be getting U.S. jobs is not entirely unfounded. The problem is an extraordinarily complex system that always leaves the most vulnerable more at risk and the wealthiest even richer (Gibler 2012; Rothkopf 2012; Stiglitz 2012).

We have discussed examples of planned change, but sometimes behavior that results in change is unplanned and even spontaneous as described in the following section.

Thinking Sociologically

Where is your clothing made? Did a multinational corporation have it assembled in the Global South? Who benefits from companies buying cheap labor from the Global South: You? The workers? Governments? The companies that manufacture the products? Who, if anyone, is hurt?

Collective Behavior: Micro-Level Behavior and Change

Flash mobs, political demonstrations, and stock market sell-offs are all forms of collective behavior and can stimulate change. In this section we introduce a form of change that has uncertain outcomes.

A flash mob is a group of people who assemble suddenly in a public place and perform an unusual act of short duration, often for the purposes of entertainment, satire, or artistic expression. They are often fun and sometimes have a message critiquing the society or calling for change. This church-based flash mob in Minnehaha Park (in Minneapolis) sang and danced shortly before the November 2012 elections to encourage voters to support same-sex marriages.

Collective behavior refers to *actions that are spontaneous, unstructured, and disorganized and that may violate norms; this behavior arises when people are trying to cope with stressful situations and unclear or uncertain conditions* (Goode 1992; Smelser 1963, 1988). Collective behavior falls into two main types: crowd behavior and mass behavior. It often starts as a response to an event or a stimulus. It could begin with a shooting or beating, a speech, a sports event, or a rumor. The key is that as individuals try to make sense of the situations they are in and respond based on their perceptions, collective social actions emerge.

Crowd behaviors—mobs, panics, riots, and demonstrations—are all forms of collective behavior in which a crowd acts, at least temporarily, as a unified group (LeBon [1895] 1960). Crowds are often made up of individuals who see themselves as supporting a just cause. Because the protesters are in such a large group, they may not feel bound by the normal social controls—either internal (normal moral standards) or external (fear of police sanctions).

Mass behavior occurs when individual people communicate or respond in a similar manner to ambiguous or uncertain situations, often based on common information from the news or on the Internet. Examples include public opinion, rumors, fads, and fashions. Unlike social movements, these forms of collective behavior generally lack a hierarchy of authority and clear leadership, a division of labor, and a sense of group action.

Theories of Collective Behavior

Social scientists studying group and crowd dynamics find that most members of crowds are respectable, law-abiding citizens, but faced with specific situations, they act out (Berk 1974; Ritzer 2013a; Turner and Killian 1993). Several explanations of individual involvement dominate the modern collective behavior literature.

Based on principles of rational choice theory, the *minimax strategy* suggests that individuals try to minimize their losses or costs and maximize their benefits (Berk 1974). People are more likely to engage in behavior if they feel the rewards outweigh the costs. Individuals may become involved in a riot if they feel the outcome—drawing attention to their plight, the possibility of improving conditions, solidarity with neighbors and friends, looting goods—will be more rewarding than the status quo or the possible negative sanctions.

Emergent norm theory points out that individuals in crowds have different emotions and attitudes that guide their decisions and behaviors than if they act alone. The theory addresses the unusual situations and breakdown of norms in which most collective behavior takes place. Unusual situations may call for the development of new norms and even new definitions of what is acceptable behavior. The implication of this theory is that in ambiguous situations, people look to others for clues about what is happening or what is acceptable, and norms emerge in ambiguous contexts that may be considered inappropriate in other contexts (Turner and Killian 1993). This really is the most widely used approach to understanding collective behavior (Ritzer 2013a).

Imagine that you were in a situation at an athletic event where someone in the crowd with a very loud voice began to taunt a referee or a player from the visiting team. Initially some people around you laughed, but as the initiator began to chant an insult, your friends and others around you began to join in. Chances are good that in the camaraderie of the moment, you followed suit and joined the cheer—even if it was very disrespectful. Normally you would not make such an insulting remark to someone's face, but in this situation where you were anonymous, the pattern of behavior emerged, and you joined the crowd. This would be an example of an emergent norm affecting an entire crowd.

Value-added theory (sometimes called structural stain theory) describes conditions for crowd behavior and social movements. Key elements are necessary for collective behavior, with each new variable adding to the total situation until conditions are sufficient for individuals to begin to act in common. At this point collective behavior emerges (Smelser 1963). These are the six factors Smelser identified that can result in collective behavior:

1. *Structural conduciveness:* Existing problems create a climate that is ripe for change (e.g., tensions between religious and ethnic groups in Iraq).

2. *Structural strain:* The social structure is not meeting the needs and expectations of the citizens, which creates widespread dissatisfaction with the status quo—the current arrangements (the Iraqi government is unable to control violence and provide basic services).

3. *Spread of a generalized belief:* Common beliefs about the cause, effect, and solution of the problem evolve, develop, and spread (U.S. troops begin to leave; militias are killing members of other groups).

4. *Precipitating factor:* A dramatic event or incident occurs to incite people to action (groups of men from different religious groups are kidnapped, bound, and shot).

5. *Mobilization for action:* Leaders emerge and set out a path of action, or an emergent norm develops that stimulates common action (citizens gather to protest the killings, and angry spokespersons enrage the crowd).

6. *Social controls are weak:* If police, military, or political or religious leaders are unable to counter the mobilization, a social movement or other crowd behavior (e.g., a riot or mob) is likely to develop. (Some analysts have argued that civil war has erupted in Iraq because of a lack of a trained police force.)

When all six factors are present, some form of collective behavior will emerge. Those trying to control crowds that are volatile must intervene to alter one or more of these six conditions (Kendall 2004; Smelser 1963).

On the southern outskirts of Basra in Iraq, British soldiers monitor a checkpoint leading into the city, checking people for weapons. A young Iraqi girl experiences the tense and hostile realities of war. This kind of military presence is often scary for residents and is very dangerous work for soldiers. This is an example of the precariousness of maintaining social control in volatile situations.

Thinking Sociologically

Think of an example of crowd behavior or a social movement, preferably one in which you have been involved. Try to identify each of the six factors from Smelser's theory to help explain your example.

Types of Collective Behavior

Collective behavior ranges from spontaneous violent mobs to temporary fads and fashions. Figure 14.3 shows the range of actions.

Mobs are *emotional crowds that engage in violence against a specific target. Examples include lynchings, killings, and hate crimes.* Near the end of the U.S. Civil War, self-appointed vigilante groups roamed the countryside in the South looking for army deserters, torturing and killing both those who harbored deserters and the deserters themselves. There were no courts and no laws, just "justice" in the eyes of the vigilantes. Members of these groups constituted mobs. The film *Cold Mountain* depicts these scenes vividly. Unless curbed, mobs often damage or destroy their target.

Riots—*an outbreak of illegal violence committed by individuals expressing frustration or anger against people, property, or both*—begin when certain conditions occur. Often, a sense of frustration or deprivation sets the stage for a riot—hunger, poverty, poor housing, lack of jobs, discrimination, poor

education, or an unresponsive or unfair judicial system. If the conditions for collective behavior are present, many types of incidents can be the precipitating factor setting off a riot. For example, in late 2010 as a response to the rumor that Nepalese United Nations soldiers brought the cholera epidemic from Nepal, frustrated Haitian citizens rioted, wounding a number of UN peacekeeping troops. The distinction between riots and mobs is illustrated in Figure 14.4.

Panic *occurs when a large number of individuals become fearful or try to flee threatening situations that are beyond their control, sometimes putting their lives in danger.* Panic can occur in a crowd situation, such as a restaurant or theater in which someone yells, "Fire," or it can occur following rumors or information spread by the media. Panic started by rumors set off the run on the stock market in October 1929. A large number of actions by individuals caused the stock market crash in the United States and repercussions around the world. In 2008, the collapse of global investment banking and securities trader Bear, Stearns, and Co. resulted in turmoil in the financial markets. Only with radical intervention by the federal government was the immediate panic abated. Panics can result in collapse of an organization, destruction, or even death as a result of the group action.

Rumors *are forms of mass behavior in which unsupported or unproven reports about a problem, an issue, or a concern circulate widely throughout the public.* Rumors may spread only in a local area, but with electronic means available, rumors are spreading more widely and rapidly. Without authoritative information, ambiguous situations can produce faulty information on which decisions are made and actions are

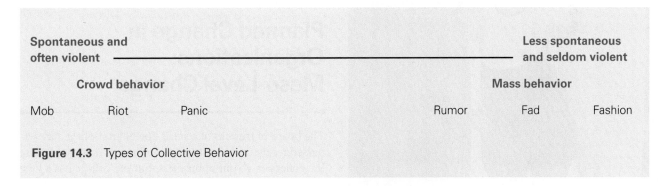

Spontaneous and often violent						Less spontaneous and seldom violent
Crowd behavior				**Mass behavior**		
Mob	Riot	Panic		Rumor	Fad	Fashion

Figure 14.3 Types of Collective Behavior

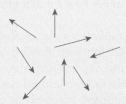

Riots involve dispersed actions expressing frustration (e.g., urban riots over poor conditions).

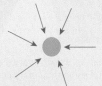

Mobs involve a group collectively focusing their action on a single individual or location (e.g., a lynch mob).

Figure 14.4 The Difference Between Riots and Mobs

Mob Mentality

based. *Urban legends,* one example of widely spread but unverified messages, are unsubstantiated stories that sound plausible and become widely circulated. People telling them usually believe them (Mikkelson and Mikkelson 2013). Go to www.snopes.com/college/college.asp for some entertaining urban legends about professors, exam scams, embarrassments, and other college pranks.

Fads are *temporary behaviors, activities, or material objects that spread rapidly and are copied enthusiastically by large numbers of people.* Body modification, especially tattooing, appeals mostly to young people of all social classes. Tattoo artists emblazon IDs, secret society and organization emblems, fraternity symbols, and decorations to order on all parts of the customers' bodies. Body modification has taken place for centuries, but it goes through fads (University of Pennsylvania 2010). Sometimes, fads become institutionalized—that is, they gain a permanent place in the culture. Other fads die out, replaced by the next hot item.

Fashions are established largely at fashion shows, where designers introduce new clothing styles. Fashions cannot occur unless there is a very high level of affluence, where people can afford to throw away perfectly good clothing for something more stylish. For many people in the Global South, it is a gift just to have clean, warm clothing, and the very existence of such displays of consumerism is amazing, appealing, and sometimes appalling.

Fashions refer to a *style of appearance and behavior that is temporarily favored by a large number of people.* Clothing styles, music genres, color schemes in home décor, types of automobiles, and architectural designs are examples. Fashions typically last longer than fads but sometimes survive only a season, as can be seen in the clothing industry. Music styles such as "hardcore techno," "acid," "alternative hip-hop," and "UK 2-step garage" were popular among some groups as the previous edition of this book was being written, but two years later, the fads were "dub step," "indie," "electropop," "screamo," and "Latin-pop." These styles will probably be passé by the time you read this, replaced by new fads emerging in mass behavior.

Each of these forms of collective behavior involves micro-level individual actions that cumulatively become collective responses to certain circumstances. However, ripples are felt in other levels of the social world. Insofar as these various types of collective activity upset the standard routines of the society and the accepted norms, they can unsettle the entire social system and cause lasting change.

The separation of each of the forms of change into levels is somewhat artificial, of course, for individuals are also acting in organizations and in national social movements. However, when we move to meso- and macro-level analyses, the established structures and processes of the society become increasingly important. Much of the change at these levels is planned change.

Planned Change in Organizations: Meso-Level Change

The board of trustees of a small liberal arts college has witnessed recent drops in student enrollments that could cause the college to go out of business, but the college has a long tradition of fine education and devoted alumni. How does the college continue to serve future students and current alumni? The problem is how to plan change to keep the college solvent.

A company manufactures silicon chips for computers. Recently, the market has been flooded with inexpensive chips, primarily from Asia, where they are made more cheaply than this North American firm can possibly make them. Does the company succumb to the competition, figure out ways to meet it, or diversify its products? What steps should be taken to facilitate the change? Many companies in Silicon Valley, California, face exactly this challenge.

Rumors

A Native American nation within the United States faces unemployment among its people due in large measure to discrimination by Anglos in the local community. Should the elders focus their energies and resources on electing sympathetic politicians, boycotting racist businesses, filing lawsuits, becoming entrepreneurs as a nation so they can hire their own people, or beginning a local radio station so they will have a communication network for a social movement? What is the best strategy to help this proud nation recover from centuries of disadvantage?

All these are real problems faced by real organizations. Anywhere we turn, organizations face questions involving change, questions that arise because of internal strains and external stresses. How organizational leaders and public sociologists deal with change will determine the survival and well-being of the organizations.

How Organizations Plan for Change

When working for an organization, you will engage in the process of planning for change. Some organizations spend time and money writing long-range strategic plans and doing self-studies to determine areas for ongoing change. Sometimes change is desired, and sometimes it is forced on the organization by stresses from society, more powerful organizations, or individuals (Kanter 1983, 2001a, 2001b; Olsen 1968). Moreover, a problem solved in one area can create unanticipated problems someplace else.

Planned change such as strategic planning is the dream of every organizational leader. It involves deliberate, structured attempts, guided by stated goals, to alter the status quo of the social unit (Bennis, Benne, and Chin 1985; Ferhansyed 2008). There are several important considerations as we think about planned change: How can we identify what needs to be changed? How can we plan or manage the change process successfully? What kind of systems adapt well to change? Here, we briefly touch on the topic and outline three approaches advocated by experts to plan change. Keep in mind the levels of analysis as you read about change models.

Models for Planning Organizational Change

Change models fall into two main categories: closed system models, which deal with the internal dynamics of the organization, and open system models (e.g., our social world model), which consider the organization and its environment. Let us sample a couple of these models.

Closed system models, often called classical or mechanistic models, focus on the internal dynamics of the organization. The goal of change using closed models is to move the organization closer to the ideal of bureaucratic efficiency and effectiveness. An example is time and motion studies, which analyze how much time it takes a worker to do a certain task and how it can be accomplished more efficiently. Each step in the McDonald's process of getting a hamburger to you, the customer, has been planned and timed for greatest efficiency (Ritzer 2013b). In some closed system models, change is legislated from the top executives and filters down to workers.

By contrast, the organizational development approach claims that participants in the organization should be involved in decision making leading to change. The leadership is more democratic and supportive of workers, and the atmosphere is transparent— open, honest, and accountable to workers and investors. This model emphasizes that change comes about through adjusting workers' values, beliefs, and attitudes regarding new demands on the organization. Many variations on this theme have evolved, with current efforts including team building and change of the organizational culture to improve worker morale. Closed system models tend to focus on group change that occurs from within the organization.

Open system models combine both internal processes and the external environment. The latter provides the organization with inputs (workers and raw materials) and feedback (acceptability of the product or result). In turn, the organization has outputs (products) that affect the larger society. There are several implications of this model: (a) Change is an ever-present and ongoing process, (b) all parts of the organization and its immediate environment are linked, and (c) change in one part has an effect on other parts. The model in Figure 14.5 illustrates the open system.

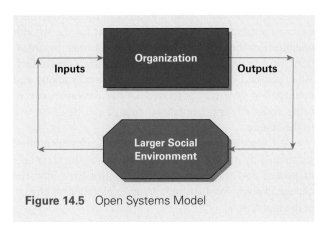

Figure 14.5   Open Systems Model

Thinking Sociologically

Using the model in Figure 14.5, fill in the parts as they relate to your college or university. For example, inputs might include students, federal student aid grants, new knowledge, and technology.

The Process of Planned Change

A huge issue causing conflict in the Global South is the lack of availability of clean drinking water. Nongovernmental organizations (NGOs) plan ways to improve the lives of individuals in many parts of the world. For example, in parts of Africa, women must spend as much as six hours a day carrying water to the home. Because daughters are needed to care for younger siblings while the mother is away, many girls are unable to attend school. This, in turn, has implications for the continuation of poverty (WaterAid 2008, 2012).

With global climate change, the glaciers on top of mountains like Mount Kenya are melting. Although that mountain peak has been snow-covered for more than 10,000 years, the glaciers are expected to be completely gone in perhaps 20 years (Cousteau 2008). When the mountaintop snow disappears, the water supply for hundreds of thousands of people and animals will disappear. An example of one British nongovernmental organization that is bringing about change in this area is WaterAid. It has grown to become an international NGO that focuses entirely on water and sanitation issues, including hygiene. Communities in poor countries throughout the world are assisted in developing the most appropriate technologies for clean water, given the geographical features and resources of the area.

This example shows one of the many types of organizations that both change within themselves to meet new conditions and bring about change in the world, adding to our understanding of change. The process of planned change is like a puzzle with a number of pieces that differ for each organization but must fit together for the smooth operation of the organization. The goal of most organizations is to maintain balance and avoid threats or conflict. Slow, planned reform of the system by organizations and countries is generally perceived as the desirable way to bring about change. Unplanned change can be disruptive to the system.

At the societal and global macro levels, change is often stimulated by individuals and events outside the chambers of power, and there is much less control over how the change evolves. We turn next to an exploration of change at the macro level.

Social Movements: Macro-Level Change

Beijing, China, hosted the prestigious summer 2008 Olympics, athletic games that promote peace and goodwill around the globe. The Olympic torch traversed the globe to prepare for and celebrate the event. However, its travels and the opening of the games were far from peaceful and full of goodwill. Protests about Chinese human rights and autonomy for Tibet (now a part of China) dogged the torch, and major political leaders refused to attend the opening ceremonies. A social movement was spurred by an uprising in Tibet, a region that was an independent country until the 1950s. The issues—human rights violations by China and autonomy of Tibet—created protests and demonstrations around the world. Will this social movement bring about change in the status of Tibetans or in human rights in China? Worldwide attention may aid the cause of those in Tibet seeking improved life conditions, or it may not. However, those people who raised these issues at the games in China are hoping to change more serious life and death policies for people. The point is that a social movement tries to bring about change. Let us explore several questions: What is a social movement, what brings it about, and what might be the results?

What Is a Social Movement?

From human rights and women's rights to animal rights and environmental protection, individuals seek ways to express their concerns and frustrations. **Social movements** are *consciously organized attempts outside of established institutions to enhance or resist change through group action.* Movements focus on a common interest of members, such as abortion policy. They have an organization, a leader, and one or more goals that aim to correct some perceived wrongs existing in the society or even around the globe. Social movements are most often found in industrial or postindustrial societies, although they can occur anyplace groups of people have a concern or frustration. Social movements entail large groups of people who hold little power individually, but do have power as united groups that promote or resist social change. The problems leading to social movements often result from the way resources—human rights, jobs, income, housing, money for education and health care, and power—are distributed. In turn, countermovements—social movements against the goals of the original movement—may develop, representing other opinions (McCarthy and Zald 1977).

Many individuals join social movements to change the world or their part of the world and affect the direction of

Human Rights

Social movements are attempts to foster or resist change through group action—usually done outside of the existing institutional structures. This group staffs a "prayer and protest vigil" outside the office of their congressional representative in Eden Prairie, Minnesota. It is part of a larger social movement on immigration reform—internested in creating a path to citizenship for undocumented immigrants.

history. In fact, some social movements have been successful in doing just that. Consider movements around the world that have protected lands, forests, rivers, and oceans, seeking environmental protection for the people whose survival depends on those natural resources. For example, the Chipko movement in a number of areas of India has been fighting the logging of forests by commercial industries. Villagers, mostly women who depend on the forests, use Gandhi-style nonviolent methods to oppose the deforestation. These women have set an example for environmentalists in many parts of the world who wish to save trees (Scribd 2011). Another example is a movement by local peasants in Bihar, India, that fought efforts by government officials to control their fishing rights in the Ganges River. Those controls would have limited their livelihoods, but the citizens organized themselves and successfully stood up against the power of the state.

Types of Social Movements

Stonewall is a gay, lesbian, and bisexual rights movement that began when patrons of a gay bar fought back against a police raid in New York in 1969. After that incident, the concern about gay rights erupted from a small number of activists into a widespread movement for rights and acceptance. Stonewall now has gone global, with chapters in other countries and continents.

Proactive social movements advocate moving forward with a new initiative—proposing something that did not

exist before. One example is the gay rights movement, which promotes change in a new direction for the society. The 2010 lifting of the ban on openly gay and lesbian soldiers in the military and marriage rights in some states are examples of recent victories for the gay rights movement.

Reactive social movements resist change reacting against something that exists or against new trends or new social policies—like same-sex marriage initiatives. For example, Focus on the Family has organized lobbying efforts and rallies against legalizing same-sex marriages. The reactive movement had success in the 1990s with the Defense of Marriage Act (DOMA) that allowed states to honor same-sex marriages that were contracted in another state. However, the U.S. Supreme Court ruled in 2013 that key parts of DOMA are unconstitutional—a violation of rights of citizens in that it "disparages and injures" part of the population. This ruling means that more than a thousand federal rights may be restored to gays and lesbians in those states where they can legally marry. The ruling does affect state laws that govern marriage, so those rights are limited in states where same-sex marriage is not legal. At this point the question of states honoring marriages in another state has also not been resolved (*Huffington Post* 2013; Liptak 2013b).

Note that both liberals and conservatives can be involved in reactive movements. When businesses want to build a corporation or plant in an area that will wipe out a native forest or destroy a historic area, liberals can be at the forefront of fighting "progress." Whether proactive or reactive, there are five main types of social movements: expressive, social reform, revolutionary, resistance or regressive, and globalized.

Expressive movements *take place in groups, but they focus on changing individuals and saving people from corrupt lifestyles.* Many expressive movements are religious, such as the born-again Christian movements, Zen Buddhism, Scientology, the Christian Science Church, and Transcendental Meditation. Expressive movements also include secular psychotherapy movements and self-help or self-actualization groups.

Social reform movements *seek to change some specific dimension of society, usually involving legislative policy modification or appeals to the courts.* Movement members generally are concerned about specific social issues but support the society as a whole. These movements focus on a major issue such as environmental protection, women's rights, same-sex marriage, "just and fair" globalization, reducing the national debt, or national abortion policy. Typically, these movements are not interested in disrupting the functioning of the entire society: They have one issue they think needs reform.

The Sojourners Community was started in the early 1970s by highly committed theology students at Trinity Evangelical Divinity School in Deerfield, Illinois. Their group was theologically evangelical and conservative Christian, but wanted their faith to engage the social crisis that surrounded them, including civil rights, poverty, and the Vietnam War.

Many environmental and peace groups use nonviolent protest, legislative means, and appeals to the public or to the courts to accomplish the desired goals. This is a silent protest on the beach in Santa Monica, California, where protesters set up crosses to represent all of the deaths of U.S. soldiers in Iraq.

They began a newspaper that eventually became known as *Sojourners* magazine. They advocate for a consistent pro-life policy (antiabortion, antiwar, and anti–death penalty). Their widely known and charismatic leader, Jim Wallis, writes and speaks around the country, arguing that on matters of faith and social policy, "the right gets it wrong and the left doesn't get it" (Wallis 2005, 2013). They have been a voice from the evangelical community, but they are also highly critical of many on the political "left." They advocate for policies they believe stem from the compassion and love of the Christian message, and they are also unapologetic about their traditional stance on the core of the faith.

Revolutionary movements *attempt to transform society, to bring about total change in society by overthrowing existing power structures and replacing them with new ones.* These movements often resort to violent means to achieve their goals, as has been the case with many revolutions throughout history. When we read in the paper that there has been a coup, we are learning about a revolutionary movement that has ousted the government in power. Although it was not violent, Nelson Mandela's African National Congress succeeded in taking power in South Africa in 1994, rewriting the constitution, and purging a racially segregated apartheid social system that had oppressed four fifths of the South African population.

Resistance or regressive movements *try to protect an existing system, protect a part of that system, or return to what a system had been by overthrowing current laws and practices. Members of such movements see societal change as a threat to values or practices and wish to maintain the status quo or return to a former status by reversing the change process* (Eitzen and Zinn 2012a; Inglehart and Baker 2001). The Taliban

religious movement in Afghanistan is a regressive movement against modernization, especially against the Western pattern of giving freedom and autonomy to women. The movement was successful in gaining power in the 1990s, imposing a harsh brand of Islamic law in the sections of Afghanistan under its control. The Taliban insists that its version of Islam is pure in that it follows a literal understanding of the Muslim holy book. This means that someone believed to have committed adultery should be stoned to death, the hands or arms of thieves should be amputated, and women who deviate from the Taliban's interpretation of Muslim law should be mutilated, publically beaten, and sometimes executed (Antonowicz 2002).

Global transnational movements *are mobilized groups that take place across societies as international organizations seek change in the status of women, child labor, rights of indigenous peoples, environmental degradation, global warming, disease pandemics, and other issues that affect the global community.* An example is Free the Slaves, a global antislavery organization started by sociologist Kevin Bales. This organization has researched, written about, and acted to alleviate the plight of millions of indentured people, the 27 million slaves in the world, "forced to work without pay, under threat of violence and unable to walk away" (Bales 2007; Bales and Soodalter 2010; Bales, Trodd, and Williamson 2009; Free the Slaves 2013).

Another example of a transnational or global protest against a multinational corporation is the autoworkers' conflict with General Motors in Colombia. A group of 68 autoworkers at a GM assembly plant outside of Bogotá formed a protest movement in May 2011. The issue was that a number of workers were fired when they could no longer perform their jobs due to severe workplace injuries, including severe impairments to backs and rotator cuffs. Some of

These are three of the men who were so desperate they went on a hunger strike—even sewing their lips together—outside the U.S. Embassy in Bogotá, Colombia. A nonprofit organization learned of the protest involving General Motors firing the injured men, apparently without disability compensation, and it became an issue in the United States.

the workers will never be able to work again. Medical records were changed to read "injuries unrelated to occupation," and a labor inspector who authorized the firings is now in jail, but compensation was still not forthcoming. After 15 months of protests, 13 protesters began a hunger strike, 8 of them sewing their mouths shut. International supporters began solidarity actions to put pressure on GM to enter into negotiations, and American supporters were sending money, writing letters, and even engaging in fasting or hunger strikes themselves (Witness for Peace 2012). This is a local issue in Colombia that has mobilized people in other parts of the world.

Figure 14.6 summarizes the types of movements and focus of each, from the micro to the macro level.

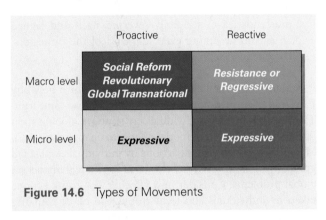

	Proactive	Reactive
Macro level	*Social Reform Revolutionary Global Transnational*	*Resistance or Regressive*
Micro level	*Expressive*	*Expressive*

Figure 14.6 Types of Movements

Thinking Sociologically

Consider a social movement with which you are familiar. What type of movement is it, and what was or is it trying to accomplish?

Globalization and Social Movements

Social movements are about people trying to improve their situations within their societies. They are intriguing because they provide compelling evidence that humans make choices and are capable of countering macro- and meso-level forces. As Eitzen and Zinn put it,

> Powerful social structures constrain what we do, but they can never control [us] entirely. Human beings are not passive actors . . . Individuals acting alone, or with others, can shape, resist, challenge, and sometimes change the social structures that impinge on them. These actions constitute *human agency.* (Eitzen and Zinn 2012a:269)

Since World War II, power in the global system has been dominated by a group of industrial giants recently calling themselves the Group of 8 (or the "G8"). These nations

control world markets and regulate economic and trading policies (International Encyclopedia of the Social Sciences 2008). Included among these elites are the dominant three (Japan representing the East, Germany representing Central Europe, and the United States representing the American continents) and five other important but less dominating powers (Canada, France, Great Britain, Italy, and Russia). The G8 are the core countries that have the most power in the World Trade Organization, the World Bank, the International Monetary Fund (IMF), and other regulatory agencies that preside over the global economy. These agencies have often required that poor countries adhere to their demands or lose the right to loans and other support.

These policies imposed from above have sometimes been disastrous for poor countries, causing situations in which a debt burden is created that can never be paid off due to World Bank and IMF policies. The IMF points out that the loans are the only way poor countries can meet the United Nations Millennium Development Goals (IMF 2013). Critics argue that the loans make poor countries dependent on wealthy countries and that the loans should be forgiven. They argue that if these were individuals rather than countries, we would call them indentured servants or slaves (Brecher, Costello, and Smith 2012; Weller and Hersh 2006). This creates nations where hopelessness would seem to reign supreme, yet social movements are arising in precisely these places and are often joining forces across national boundaries (Eitzen and Zinn 2012a; Ferree 2012; Muchhala 2012). Even some groups within the G8 nations—labor unions, college student groups, and religious bodies concerned about social justice—are joining the movements.

Some of the poorest nations have now formed their own organization to counter what was then called the G7 (now the G8). Calling themselves the G77, these countries are now uniting, rather like a labor union seeking collective unity among workers, in attempts to gain some power and determine their own destinies (Brecher, Costello, and Smith 2012; Hayden 2006). Map 12.1 on page 385 displays the location of G8 and G77 countries.

In the competition to find cheaper labor for higher profits, there is a "race to the bottom," as communities must lower standards or else lose jobs to some other part of the world that is even more impoverished. Globalization as it now exists—with corporate profits as the ruling principle of most decision making—has lessened environmental standards, consumer protection, national sovereignty and local control of decisions, and safety protections for workers. Yet when jobs move elsewhere, the people who had come to depend on those jobs are devastated and often thrust into poverty and homelessness, and the country loses tax revenue.

Although workers risk losing jobs by participating in protests for higher wages and better working conditions, one result of globalization has been a rise in countermovements. "Globalization from below" refers to the efforts by common people in small groups and protest movements to fight back (Della Porta et al. 2006; Eitzen and Zinn 2012a). Rather than globalization being controlled solely by the pursuit of profits, these countermovements seek to protect workers, to defend the environment, and to combat the bone-crunching poverty that plagues so much of the Global South. The argument goes like this:

> It is the activity of people—going to work, paying taxes, buying products, obeying government officials, staying off private property—that continually re-creates the power of the powerful. . . . [The system, for all its power and resources, is dependent on common people to do the basic jobs that keep the society running.] This dependency gives people a potential power over the society—but one that can be realized only if they are prepared to reverse their acquiescence. . . . Social movements can be understood as the collective withdrawal of consent to established institutions. (Brecher, Costello, and Smith 2012:279)

The movement against globalization can be understood as withdrawing consent for such globalization. There are thousands of small resistance actions to the oppressive policies of G8 transnational corporations (Brecher, Costello, and Smith 2012; Hearn 2012). They involve micro-level actions to bring change at the macro level. Consider the following example:

Under heavy pressure from the World Bank, the Bolivian government sold off the public water system of its third-largest city, Cochabamba, to a subsidiary of the San Francisco–based Bechtel Corporation, which promptly doubled the price of water for people's homes. Early in 2000, the people of Cochabamba rebelled, shutting down the city with general strikes and blockades. The government declared a state of siege, and a young protester was shot and killed. Word spread all over the world from the remote Bolivian highlands via the Internet. Hundreds of e-mail messages poured into Bechtel from all over the world, demanding that it leave Cochabamba. In the midst of local and global protests, the Bolivian government, which had said that Bechtel must not leave, suddenly reversed itself and signed an accord accepting every demand of the protestors. (Brecher, Costello, and Smith 2012:284)

Many concerned citizens in the Global North now buy Fair Trade Certified goods such as coffee, cacao, and fruit. This is an effort by individuals to support globalization from below—a different model of how to change the world. Many activists believe that actions by individuals and small groups, globalization from below, can have a real impact on global problems. Consider how effective you think actions taken by individuals and local groups can be by thinking about the issues in the next "Engaging Sociology."

Engaging Sociology

Micro to Macro: Change From the Bottom Up

The idea of globalization "from the bottom up" suggests that actions of lots of people at the micro or local level can have a significant impact on how things develop at the most macro level of the social world we inhabit. Think about that process and what forces can enhance or retard that kind of change.

1. Are you familiar with cases in which "globalization from below" has made a difference in local, national, or international events? If so, what are those? If not, do a Google search and find two examples of "globalization from below" online.

2. Identify three structural challenges that might make it hard for people at the micro level to change the national and global forces that interfere with the quality of their lives.

3. Identify three reasons to be optimistic about why change from the bottom up can be successful.

4. To examine a specific example of a group that approaches globalization from below, do a Google search of the Zapatistas or of their leader, Subcomandante Marcos. What are the pros and the cons of this movement? Do you think the Zapatistas have any chance of bringing change to the poor disfranchised people of southern Mexico? Why or why not?

In summary, some social change is planned by organizations, some is initiated by groups that are outside the organizational structure (social movements), and some is unplanned and spontaneous (collective behavior). The most important point, however, is that actions by individuals can affect the larger social world, sometimes even having global ramifications. Likewise, national and international changes and social movements influence the lives of individuals.

Antiglobalization

Technology, Environment, and Change

At the edge of the town of Bhopal, India, looms a subsidiary plant of the U.S.-based Union Carbide Corporation. The plant provides work for many of the town's inhabitants. However, on December 3, 1984, things did not go as normal. A storage tank from the plant, filled with the toxic chemical liquid methyl isocyanate, overheated and turned to gas, which began to escape through a pressure-relief valve. The gas formed a cloud and drifted away from the plant. By the time the sirens were sounded, it was too late for many people. The deadly gas had done its devastating work: More than 3,000 were dead and thousands ill, many with permanent injuries from the effects of the gas. Put in perspective, the number of casualties was about equal to the

Global protests often focus on actions of Western multinational corporations. Women demonstrators, including Bhopal gas victims in India, hold a "Wanted" poster of former Union Carbide chairman Warren Anderson, arguing that he should be tried for crimes for the deaths of more than 3,000 people and the injuries of tens of thousands in Bhopal.

number in the terrorist attack on the Twin Towers of New York City on September 11, 2001.

This example illustrates change at multiple levels of analysis. We see a global multinational company (Union Carbide) in a society (India) that welcomed the jobs for its citizens. A community within that larger society benefited from the jobs until many residents were killed or disabled, leaving shattered families and devastated individual lives. The accident also spawned a number of forms of collective behavior. The immediate aftermath of the accident at Bhopal included panic, as people tried to flee the deadly gas. Later it resulted in several social movements as activists demanded accountability and safety measures. In 1989, Union Carbide paid $470 million in damages, but that did not begin to cover the cleanup and payment to victims. A New York federal court recently rendered a decision after 25 years, dismissing all further claims by Indian plaintiffs against the U.S. parent company, arguing that Union Carbide India was responsible. Meanwhile, the town of Bhopal and its residents have not received what they feel is fair compensation (Bhattacharya 2012). The disaster did bring about planned change in the way Union Carbide does business and protects workers and citizens.

Technology refers to *the practical application of tools, skills, and knowledge to meet human needs and extend human abilities.* Technology and environment cannot be separated as we see at Bhopal. The raw products that fuel technology come from the environment, the wastes return to the environment, and technological mistakes affect the environment. This section discusses briefly the development and process of technology, the relationship between technology and environment, and the implications for change at each level of analysis.

Throughout human history, there have been major transition periods when changes in the material culture brought about revolutions in human social structures and cultures (Toffler and Toffler 1980). For example, the agricultural revolution resulted in the plow to till the soil, establishing new social arrangements and eventually resulting in food surpluses that allowed cities to flourish. The Industrial Revolution brought machines powered by steam and petrol, resulting in mass society, divisions of labor in manufacturing, and socialist and capitalist political-economic systems. Today, postindustrial technology, based on the microchip, is fueling the spread of information, communication, and transportation on a global level to explore space and analyze, store, and retrieve masses of information in seconds. However, each wave affects only a portion of the world, leaving other people and countries behind and creating divisions between the Global North and the Global South.

Sociologist William Ogburn has argued that change is brought about through three processes: discovery, invention, and diffusion. *Discovery* is a new way of seeing reality. The material objects or ideas have been present, but they are seen in a new light when the need arises or conditions are conducive to the discovery. It is usually accomplished by an individual or a small group, a micro-level activity (Ogburn [1922] 1938, 1961, 1964).

Invention refers to combining existing parts, materials, or ideas to form new ones. There was no light bulb or combustion engine lying in the forest waiting to be discovered. Human ingenuity was required to put together something that had not previously existed. Technological innovations often result from research institutes and the expansion of science, increasingly generated at the meso level of the social system.

Diffusion is the spread of an invention or a discovery from one place to another. The spread of ideas such as capitalism, democracy, and religious beliefs has brought changes in human relationships around the world. Likewise, the spread of various types of music, film technology, telephone systems, and computer hardware and software across the globe has had important ramifications for global interconnectedness. Diffusion often involves expansion of ideas across the globe, but it also requires individuals to adopt ideas at the micro level.

Technology and Science

The question "How do we know what we know?" is often answered, "It's science." **Science** is *the systematic process of producing human knowledge; it uses empirical research methods to discover facts and test theories.* Whether social, biological,

Scientists have developed technologies to ease the looming energy crisis and climate change. Solar panels at this restaurant in Portugal provide independence from other sources of energy.

or physical, science provides a systematic way to approach the world and its mysteries. It uses empirical research methods to discover facts and test theories. Technology applies scientific knowledge to solve problems. Early human technology was largely a result of trial and error, not scientific knowledge or principles. Humans did not understand why boats floated or fires burned. Since the Industrial Revolution, many inventors and capitalists have seen science and technology as routes to human betterment and happiness. Science has become a major social institution in industrial and postindustrial societies, providing the bases of information and knowledge for sophisticated technology.

Indeed, one of the major transformations in modern society is due to science becoming an institution. Prior to the 18th century, science was an avocation. People like Benjamin Franklin experimented in their backyards with whatever spare cash they had to satisfy their own curiosity.

Science in the contemporary world is both a structure and a social process. Institutionalization means creation of the organized, patterned, and enduring sets of social structures that provide guidelines for behavior and help the society meet its needs. Within these structures, actions are taken—the processes within the structure—that accomplish a goal such as conducting research. Modern science involves mobilizing financial resources and employing the most highly trained people (which in turn has required the development of educational institutions). Innovation resulting in change will be very slow until a society has institutionalized science—providing extensive training and paying some people simply to do research. Specialization in science speeds up the rates of discovery. A researcher focuses in one area and gets much more in-depth understanding. Effective methods of communication across the globe mean that we do not need to wait six years for a research manuscript to cross the ocean and to be translated into another language. Competition in science means that researchers move quickly on their findings. Delaying findings may mean that the slowpoke does not get a permanent position, called tenure, at his or her university; promotion in the research laboratory; or awards for innovation.

We would not have automobiles, planes, missiles, space stations, computers, the Internet, and many of our modern conveniences without the institutionalization of science and without scientific application (technology). Science is big business, funded by industry and political leaders. University researchers and some government-funded science institutes engage in *basic research* designed to discover new knowledge, often on topics that receive funding. Industry and some governmental agencies such as the military and the Department of Agriculture employ scientists to do *applied research* and to discover practical uses for existing knowledge.

Scientific knowledge is usually cumulative, with each study adding to the existing body of research. However,

Thomas Edison had more than a thousand patented inventions, including the lightbulb, recorded sound, and movies, but perhaps his most influential invention was the research lab—in which people were paid to invent and to conduct research at Menlo Park in New Jersey. This was the seminal step in the institutionalization of science.

radical new ideas can result in scientific revolutions (Kuhn 1970). Galileo's finding that the Earth revolves around the Sun and Darwin's theory of evolution are two examples of radical new ideas that changed history. More recently, cumulative scientific knowledge has resulted in energy-efficient engines that power cars and computer technology that has revolutionized communication.

Thinking Sociologically

Imagine what your life would have been like before computers, email, and the Internet. What would be different? (Note that you are imagining the world from only 10 to 20 years ago.) Ask your parents or grandparents what this past world was like.

Technology and Change

The G8 countries have yearly meetings to regulate global economic policy and markets. The group's power enables those eight countries to dominate technology by controlling many raw products—from natural gas to sugarcane. In the process, powerful government leaders profoundly influence which countries will be rich or poor. Although some politicians like to tell us they believe in a free market economy, uninhibited by governmental interference, they actually intervene regularly in the global market.

New technological developments can be a force for world integration but also for economic and political disintegration (Schaeffer 2003). For example, research and development (R&D) is a measure of countries' investment in the future. For many years the biggest investors have been the European Union, the United States, and Japan. However, since 2007, China has increased its R&D while the top research countries reduced their share. In fact, in 2002 Global North countries provided 83% of the research and development, but today the European Union, the United States, and China each provide 20% of the world's researchers, with Japan at 10% and Russia at 7% (UNESCO Institute for Statistics 2010).

The technological revolution in communications has resulted in fiber-optic cable and wireless microwave cell phones and satellite technologies that make it easier to communicate with people around the world. We now live in a global village, a great boon for those fortunate enough to have the education and means to take advantage of it (Drori 2006; Howard and Jones 2004).

Technology has had some unexpected consequences, including a staggering increase in the amount of trash generated in the society. Depicted here is trash from the fast-food industry in Egypt. The volume of trash has created problems of disposal and pollution control.

However, the changes in technology do not always have a positive effect on less affluent countries. For example, by substituting fiber-optic cable for old technologies, the demand for copper, used for more than 100 years to carry electrical impulses for telephones and telegraphs, has bottomed out. Countries such as Zambia and Chile, which depended on the copper trade, have seen major negative impacts on their economies. New developments resulting in artificial sweeteners reduced demand for sugar, the major source of income for 50 million people who work in the beet and cane sugar industries around the globe. As new technologies bring substantial benefits to many in the world, their results can also harm people in other parts of the interconnected world. Changes in technology and the economy have forced many individuals to leave their native villages in search of paid labor positions in urban factories and the tourism industry, disrupting family lives.

Rapid technological change has affected generational relationships as well. It is not uncommon for younger generations to have more technological competence than their elders, and this sometimes creates a generational digital divide in competencies regarding use of computers, cell phones, and other electronic devices. In some settings younger people are looked to for their expertise, whereas in the past the elders were the source of knowledge and wisdom. Often the older members of a business or group feel devalued and demoralized late in their careers because those with technical competence view the older members of the group as "outdated has-beens." Even networks and forms of entertainment such as the Wii-U and Nintendo 3DS further the social distance between generations. With the changes brought about by technology come changes in the nonmaterial culture—the values, political ideologies, and human relationships. Clearly technology can have a variety of social impacts—both positive and negative.

In the opening questions, we asked whether you as an individual can make a difference in your community, country, or world. In closing, we present in the final "Engaging Sociology" a plan you can follow to make a difference.

Thinking Sociologically

First, read "Engaging Sociology," *Making a Difference*. Then use the steps to plan how you would bring about a change that would make a difference in your community, in your country, or in the world. Go to *Contributing to Our Social World: What Can We Do?* at the end of this and other chapters to find ways that you could be actively involved in bettering the society.

Engaging Sociology

Making a Difference

If you want to bring about social change, consider the following steps used by public/applied sociologists. Because bringing about change requires cooperation, working in a group context is often essential. Flexibility, openness to new ideas, and willingness to entertain alternative suggestions are also key factors in successful change. The following steps provide a useful strategy for planning change:

1. *Identify the issue:* Be specific and focus on what is to be changed. Without clear focus, your target for change can get muddied or lost in the attempt.
2. *Research the issue and use those findings:* Learn as much as you can about the situation or problem to be changed. Use informants, interviews, written materials, observation, existing data (such as Census Bureau statistics), or anything that helps you understand the issues. That will enable you to find the most effective strategies to bring about change.
3. *Find out what has already been done and by whom:* Other individuals or groups may be working on the same issue. Be sure you know what intervention has already taken place. This can also help determine whether attempts at change have been tried, what has been successful, and whether further change is needed.
4. *Change must take into account each level of analysis:* When planning a strategy, you may focus on one level of analysis, but be sure to consider what interventions are needed at other levels to make the change effective or to anticipate the effects of change on other levels.
5. *Determine the intervention strategy:* Map out the intervention and the steps to carry it out. Identify resources needed, and plan each step in detail.
6. *Evaluate the plan:* Get feedback on the plan from those involved in the issue and from unbiased colleagues. If possible, involve those who will be affected by the intervention in the planning and evaluation of the change. When feasible, test the intervention plan before implementing it.
7. *Implement the intervention:* Put the plan into effect, watching for any unintended consequences. Ask for regular feedback from those affected by the change.
8. *Evaluate the results:* Assess what is working, what is not, and how the constituents that experience the change are reacting. Sociological knowledge and skills should help guide this process.

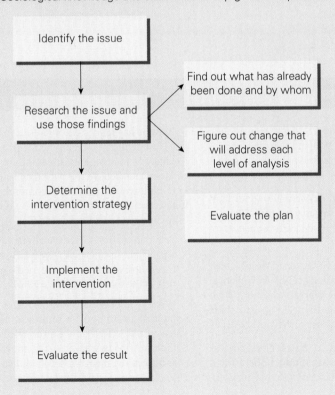

What Have We Learned?

Can you change the world? The underlying message of this chapter and the text is that choices we make facilitate change at each level in our social world. Sociology helps us to learn how to work with groups to make a difference. One of the founders of sociology, Émile Durkheim, argued that sociology is not worth a single hour's work if it does not help change the world for the better.

As you face individual challenges to bring about change in your social world, keep in mind this message: Change at one level affects all others. Sociology as a discipline is focused on gathering accurate information about the society in which we live. Sociologists often use their knowledge to advocate for changes that they think will make a better society. We hope that through this book and this course you have gained important sociological insights that will help you contribute to the dialogue about how to make our social world a better, more humane place.

Key Points:

- Social change—variation or alteration over time in behavior patterns, culture, or structure in a society—typically involves change at one level of the social system that ripples through the other levels, micro, meso, and macro. (See pp. 430–433.)

- Strains within an organization or a group can induce change—as can stress that is imposed from the outside environment. (See pp. 433–436.)

- Sociological theories—whether micro or macro—offer explanations for the causes of change. (See pp. 436–441.)

- At the micro level, change is often initiated through collective behavior, which can take several forms: crowds, mobs, riots, rumors, fads, and fashions. (See pp. 441–444.)

- At the meso level, change of organizations is often managed through a planned process. (See pp. 444–446.)

- Social movements often provide impetus for change at the macro level. Social changes can be induced at the micro level, but they have implications even at the global level. (See pp. 446–450.)

- Science and technology can also stimulate change, but science has its greatest impact for change when it is institutionalized. (See pp. 450–454.)

- Social structures constrain what we do, but individuals, especially when acting in concert with others, can challenge, resist, and change the social systems that constrain them. We can change our society because of *human agency.* (See p. 455.)

Discussion Questions

1. How old were you on September 11, 2001? How did the terrorist attacks that day affect you and your perspective on terrorism? How do you think the 9/11 attacks impacted people in different ways depending on their age?

2. What is the latest technological device you or your family has acquired? How has it changed your life? What are the (a) intended and (b) unintended consequences of your having it?

3. Every organization must adapt to change. Describe how an organization to which you belong coped with change. Was the adaptation successful? Why or why not? What was your role? Did you feel as though you had some influence over the adaptation strategy? Why or why not?

4. Were you aware that the United States gives far less than the 0.7% of gross national product the United

Nations has requested of nations in order to achieve the UN Millennium Development Goals to decrease poverty, illiteracy, famine, and disease? Why do you think most Americans believe the nation contributes more? Do you think it would be in the self-interest of the United States to contribute more? Why or why not?

5. What sociological theory best explains what has happened in many Arab countries that gave rise to the Arab Spring and its aftermath? Why? How might you use this theory to explain what happened—and what might happen in the future—in this region?

6. What type of social movement has led to the dramatic increase in support for same-sex marriage over the past few years? Why? How do the results of this movement indicate the power of social movements to influence society at the micro, meso, and macro levels?

Contributing to Our Social World: What Can We Do?

At the Local Level

- *Campus-wide movements:* A wide range of social issues, including international peace, environmental issues, human rights, and specific student concerns such as campus safety and the rising cost of higher education, may have movements represented on your campus. Consider participating in such activities. If you feel strongly about an issue for which no movement exists, consider organizing one with a few like-minded students. You can find tools to create a campus movement at www.campus activism.org/index.php, www.campusactivism.org/display resource-471.htm, and www.thetaskforce.org/reports_ and_research/campus_manual.

- Many *community movements* bring about change at the local level, sometimes with national and even international effects. Check with your professors, service learning and campus activities offices, and chambers of commerce to find these.

At the Organizational or Institutional Level

- *Invite a movement leader to campus.* Consider inviting movement leaders to your campus for a lecture, or organize a conference that features several experts in a particular field. Environment, civil rights, and modern slavery are topics that have wide appeal. Professors who teach classes that cover these issues will be able to help you find a good speaker. Work with your sociology club or student government to provide funding for the speaker.

- *Volunteer Match* seeks to connect individuals with movements of interest to them. Its website (www.volunteer-match.org) has suggestions for getting involved in your local area.

At the National and Global Levels

- *The Jubilee Movement* promotes international debt forgiveness for the world's poorest countries—a solution that the U.S. government has embraced in principle and for whose implementation it has appropriated billions of dollars in funding. A major obstacle to improvement in living conditions in the less developed countries is the enormous amount of money they owe to the World Bank and International Monetary Fund, as well as governments in the industrialized nations for past-due, development-oriented loans. Named for the principle offered in the Hebrew Scriptures that creditors are to cancel all debt owed to them every jubilee year (once every 49 years), the organization sponsors legislative programs, research work, and educational outreach activities throughout the world. The website of Jubilee USA (www.jubileeusa.org/about-us) provides information on ways in which you can get involved, and includes information about international debt, activities, and the history of the movement.

Visit **www.sagepub.com/oswcondensed3e** for online activities, sample tests, and other helpful information. Select "Chapter 14: The Process of Change" for chapter-specific activities.

References

AAANativeArts. 2013. "Facts About Alaskan Natives." Retrieved August 26, 2013 (www.aaanativearts.com/alaskan-natives/index.html).

Abu-Lughod, Janet L. 2001. *New York, Chicago, Los Angeles: America's Global Cities.* Minneapolis: University of Minnesota Press.

Adler, Patricia A. and Peter Adler. 1991. *Backboards and Blackboards: College Athletes and Role Engulfment.* New York: Columbia University Press.

Adler, Patricia A. and Peter Adler. 2004. "The Gloried Self." Pp. 117–26 in *Inside Social Life,* 4th ed., edited by Spencer E. Cahill. Los Angeles: Roxbury.

Afghanistan Opium Survey. 2011. Retrieved April 13, 2012 (www.unodc.org/documents/crop-monitoring/Afghanistan/Executive_Summary_2011_web.pdf).

Aguirre, Adalberto and David V. Baker. 2007. *Structured Inequality in the United States,* 2nd ed. Englewood Cliffs, NJ: Prentice Hall.

Aguirre, Adalberto, Jr., and Jonathan H. Turner. 2011. *American Ethnicity: The Dynamics and Consequences of Discrimination,* 7th ed. Boston: McGraw-Hill.

Ahmad, Nehaluddin. 2009. "Sati Tradition—Widow Burning in India: A Socio-legal Examination." *Web Journal of Current Legal Issues,* 2 WEB JCLI. Retrieved April 7, 2011 (http://webjcli.ncl.ac.uk-/2009/issue2/almad2/html).

Alarcon, Arthur L. and Paula M. Mitchell. 2011. "Executing the Will of the Voters? A Roadmap to Mend or End the California Legislature's Multi-Billion Dollar Death Penalty Debacle." *Loyola of Los Angeles Law Review* 44(June):S41.

Alatas, Syed Farid. 2006. "Ibn Khaldun and Contemporary Sociology." *International Sociology* 21(6):782–95.

Albrecht, Stan L. and Tim B. Heaton. 1984. "Secularization, Higher Education, and Religiosity." *Review of Religious Research* 26(September):43–58.

Alexander, Michelle. 2010. *The New Jim Crow: Mass Incarceration in the Age of Color Blindness.* New York: The New Press.

Alexander, Michelle. 2011. "More Black Men Are in Prison Today Than Were Enslaved in 1850." October 13. Retrieved April 15, 2012 (www.huffingtonpost.com/2011/10/12/michelle-alexander-more-Black-men-are-in-prison-today-than-were-enslaved-in-1850_n_1007368.html).

Alexander, Victoria D. 2003. *Sociology of the Arts: Exploring Fine and Popular Forms.* Malden, MA: Blackwell.

Alger, Jonathan R. 2003. "*Gratz/Grutter* and Beyond: the Diversity Leadership Challenge." University of Michigan. Retrieved August 7, 2011 (http://www.vpcomm.umich.edu/admissions/overview/challenge.html).

Allegretto, Sylvia, Ary Amerikaner, and Steven Pitts. 2011. "Black Employment and Unemployment: Teen Employment Population Ratios by Race." Chart 14, p. 14. *Work in the Black Community,* February 4. University of California at Berkeley Labor Center. Retrieved April 17, 2011 (http://laborcenter.berkeley.edu/blackworkers/monthly/bwreport_2011-02-04_27.pdf).

Amato, Paul R. 2000. "The Consequences of Divorce for Adults and Children." *Journal of Marriage and the Family* 62(November):1269–87.

American Civil Liberties Union. 1999, July 29. "CA's Anti-immigrant Proposition 187 Is Voided, Ending State's Five-Year Battle With ACLU, Rights Groups." Retrieved September 7, 2013 (https://www.aclu.org/immigrants-rights/cas-anti-immigrant-proposition-187-voided-ending-states-five-year-battle-aclu-righ).

American Library Association. 2013. "Top Ten Challenged Books Lists by Year: 2001–2012." Retrieved August 30, 2013 (http://www.ala.org/bbooks/frequentlychallengedbooks/top10#2012).

American Sociological Association. 2006. "'What Can I Do with a Bachelor's Degree in Sociology?' A National Survey of Seniors Majoring in Sociology." Washington DC: American Sociological Association Research and Development Department.

American Sociological Association. 2009. *21st Century Careers With an Undergraduate Degree in Sociology.* Washington, DC: Author.

Ammerman, Nancy. 1990. *Baptist Battles: Social Change and Religious Conflict in the Southern Baptist Convention.* New Brunswick, NJ: Rutgers University Press.

Ammerman, Nancy. 2009. "Congregations: Local, Social, and Religious." Pp. 562–80 in *Oxford Handbook of the Sociology of Religion,* edited by Peter Clarke. New York, Oxford: Oxford University Press.

Amnesty International. 2006. "Facts and Figures on the Death Penalty." Retrieved August 8, 2006 (http://web.amnesty.org/pages/deathpenalty-facts-eng, http://web.amnesty.org/pages/deathpenaltycountries-eng).

Amnesty International. 2013. "Abolish the Death Penalty: Death Penalty in 2012." Retrieved August 21, 2013 (http://www.amnesty.org/en/death-penalty).

Ancestry.co.uk. 2013. "UK Parish Baptism, Marriage and Burial Records." Retrieved August 29, 2013 (http://search.ancestry.co.uk/search/grouplist.aspx?group=EPR).

Anderson, Benedict. 2006. *Imagined Communities: Reflections on the Origin and Spread of Nationalism,* Rev. ed. London: Verso.

Anderson, Margaret and Patricia Hill Collins. 2006. *Race Class and Gender: An Anthology,* 6th ed. Belmont: Wadsworth.

Anti-Defamation League. 2010. "ADL Audit: 1,211 Anti-Semitic Incidents Across the Country in 2009." Retrieved April 7, 2011 (www.adl.org/PresRele/ASUS_12/5814_12.htm).

Anti-Violence Resource Guide. 2012. "Facts About Violence." *Feminist.com.* Retrieved May 26, 2012 (www.feminist.com/antiviolence/facts.html).

Antonowicz, Anton. 2002. "Zarmina's Story." *Daily Mirror,* June 19. Retrieved February 7, 2013 (www.freerepublic.com/focus/news/702415/posts).

Arnold, David O., ed. 1970. *The Sociology of Subcultures.* Berkeley, CA: Glendessary.

Arrighi, Barbara A. 2000. *Understanding Inequality: The Intersection of Race, Ethnicity, Class, and Gender.* Lanham, MD: Rowman & Littlefield.

Arulampalam, Wiji, Alison L. Booth, and Mark L. Bryan. 2007. "Is There a Glass Ceiling Over Europe? Exploring the Gender Pay Gap Across the Wages Distribution." *Industrial and Labor Relations Review* 60(2):163–86.

ASA Task Force on Institutionalizing Public Sociologies. 2005. *Public Sociology and the Roots of American Sociology: Re-Establishing our Connection to the Public.* Washington, DC: American Sociological Association. Retrieved August 15, 2013 (www.asanet.org/images/asa/docs/pdf/TF%20on%20PS%20Rpt%20(54448).pdf).

Aseltine, Robert H., Jr. 1995. "A Reconsideration of Parental and Peer Influences on Adolescent Deviance." *Journal of Health and Social Behavior* 36(2):103–21.

Ashley, David and David Michael Orenstein. 2009. *Sociological Theory,* 7th ed. Boston: Allyn & Bacon.

Association for Applied and Clinical Sociology. 2013. "Mission." Retrieved August 19, 2013 (http://www.aacsnet.net/).

"At Least 80 Electoral Votes Depended on Youth." 2012. Center for Information & Research on Civic Learning and Engagement. Retrieved November 1, 2012 (www.civicyouth.org/at-least-80-electoral-votes-depended-on-youth/).

Attewell, Paul. 2001. "The First and Second Digital Divides." *Sociology of Education* 74(3):252–59.

Aulette, Judy Root. 2010. *Changing American Families.* Boston: Allyn & Bacon.

Ayers, Dennis. 2010. "Top 50 Favorite Gay Films!" *Afterelton,* September 20. Retrieved May 27, 2012 (www.afterelton.com/movies/2010/9/favorite-gay-films?page=0%20).

Bagby, Ihsan. 2003. "Imams and Mosque Organization in the United States: A Study of Mosque Leadership and Organizational Structure in American Mosques." Pp. 113–34 in *Muslims in the United States,* edited by Philippa Strum and Danielle Tarantolo. Washington, DC: Woodrow Wilson International Center for Scholars.

Bahney, Anna. 2009. "Don't Talk to Invisible Strangers." *New York Times,* March 9. Retrieved August 13, 2009 (www.nytimes.com/2006/03/09/fashion/thursdaystyles/09parents.html).

Bainbridge, William S. and Rodney Stark. 1981. "Suicide, Homicide, and Religion: Durkheim Reassessed." *Annual Review of the Social Sciences of Religion* 5:33–56.

Bakalian, Anny and Medhi Bozorgmehr. 2009. *Backlash 9/11: Middle Eastern and Muslim Americans Respond.* Berkeley: University of California Press.

Bales, Kevin. 1999. *Disposable People: New Slavery in the Global Economy,* Updated ed. Berkeley: University of California Press.

Bales, Kevin. 2000. *New Slavery: A Reference Handbook,* 2nd ed. Santa Barbara, CA: ABC-CLIO.

Bales, Kevin. 2004. *Disposable People: New Slavery in the Global Economy,* 2nd ed. Berkeley: University of California Press.

Bales, Kevin. 2007. *Ending Slavery: How We Free Today's Slaves.* Berkeley: University of California Press.

Bales, Kevin. 2012. *Disposable People: New Slavery in the Global Economy,* 3rd ed. Berkeley: University of California Press.

Bales, Kevin. 2013. "Confronting Slavery With the Tools of Sociology." In *Sociologists in Action: Race, Class, and Gender,* edited by Shelley White, Jonathan White, and Kathleen Odell Korgen. Thousand Oaks, CA: Sage.

Bales, Kevin and Ron Soodalter. 2010. *The Slave Next Door: Human Trafficking and Slavery in America Today.* Berkeley: University of California Press.

Bales, Kevin and Zoe Trodd. 2008. *To Plead Our Own Cause: Personal Stories by Today's Slaves.* Ithaca, NY: Cornell University Press.

Bales, Kevin, Zoe Trodd, and Alex Kent Williamson. 2009. *Modern Slavery: The Secret World of 27 Million People.* Oxford, UK: Oneworld Press.

Ballantine, Jeanne H. and Floyd M. Hammack. 2012. *The Sociology of Education: A Systematic Analysis,* 7th ed. Upper Saddle River, NJ: Prentice Hall.

Bankston, Carl L., III. 2004. "Social Capital, Cultural Values, Immigration, and Academic Achievement: The Host Country Context and Contradictory Consequences." *Sociology of Education* 77(2):176–80.

Barash, David. 2002. "Evolution, Males, and Violence." *The Chronicle Review* (May 24):B7.

Barber, Benjamin R. 2006. "The Uncertainty of Digital Politics: Democracy's Relationship with Information Technology." Pp. 61–69 in *Globalization: The Transformation of Social Worlds,* edited by D. Stanley Eitzen and Maxine Baca Zinn. Belmont, CA: Wadsworth.

Barr, Colin and David Goldman. 2010 "20 Highest Paid CEOs." April 6. Retrieved March 11, 2011 (http://money.cnn.com/galleries/2010/news/1004/gallery.top_ceo_pay/).

Barrett, David B., Todd M. Johnson, and Peter F. Crossing. 2011. "2010 Annual Megacensus of Religion." *Time Almanac.* Chicago: Encyclopedia Britannica, Inc.

Barrett, David, George Kurian, and Todd Johnson, eds. 2001. *World Christian Encyclopedia,* 2 vols. New York: Oxford University Press.

Barry, Ellen. 2009. "Protests in Moldova Explode, With Help of Twitter." *New York Times,* April 8: A1. Retrieved October 6, 2012 (www.nytimes.com).

Basso, Keith H. 1979. *Portraits of the Whiteman: Linguistic Play and Cultural Symbols Among the Western Apache.* Cambridge, UK: Cambridge University Press.

Basu, Moni. 2012. "Census: More People Identify as Mixed Race." CNN, September 27. Retrieved April 28, 2013 (http://inamerica.blogs.cnn.com/2012/09/27/census-more-people-identify-as-mixed-race/).

Bass, Diana Butler. 2012. *Christianity After Religion.* New York: Harper One.

BBC News. 2008. "U.S. Elections Map: State by State Guide." Retrieved February 8, 2013 (http://news.bbc.co.uk/2/hi/in_depth/629/629/7223461.stm).

BBC News. 2012. "Iceberg Breaks Off From Greenland's Petermann Glacier." July 19. Retrieved February 8, 2013 (www.bbc.co.uk/news/world-europe-18896770).

BBC's Science and Nature. 2009. "The Ghost in Your Genes." Retrieved November 12, 2009 (www.bbc.co.uk/sn/tvradio/programmes/horizon/ghostgenes.shtml).

Beckwith, Carol. 1983. "Niger's Wodaabe: People of the Taboo." *National Geographic* 164(4):483–509.

Beckwith, Carol. 1993. *Nomads of Niger.* New York: Harry N. Abrams.

Belding, Theodore C. 2004. "Nobility and Stupidity: Modeling the Evolution of Class Endogamy." Retrieved August 7, 2008 (http://arxiv.org/abs/nlin.AO/0405048).

Belkin, Lisa. 2011. "The Cost of Raising a Child." *New York Times,* July 27.

Bell, Daniel. 1973. *The Coming of Post-Industrial Society: A Venture in Social Forecasting.* New York: Basic Books.

Bell, Daniel. 1999. *The Coming of Post-Industrial Society: A Venture in Social Forecasting,* Special anniversary edition. New York: Basic Books.

Bell, Michael Mayerfeld. 2012. *An Invitation to Environmental Sociology,* 4th ed. Thousand Oaks, CA: Sage/Pine Forge.

Bellah, Robert N. 1992. *The Broken Covenant: American Civil Religion in Time of Trial.* Chicago: University of Chicago Press.

Bellah, Robert N., Richard Madsen, William M. Sullivan, Ann Swindler, and Steven M. Tipton. 1996. *Habits of the Heart: Individualism and Commitment in American Life,* Updated ed. Berkeley: University of California Press.

Bellisari, Anna. 1990. *Biological Bases of Sex Differences in Cognitive Ability and Brain Function.* Unpublished paper.

Bennis, Warren G., Kenneth D. Benne, and Robert Chin. 1985. *The Planning of Change,* 4th ed. New York: Holt, Rinehart Winston.

Benokraitis, Nijole V. 2008. *Marriages and Families: Changes, Choices, and Constraints,* 6th ed. Englewood Cliffs, NJ: Prentice Hall.

Benokraitis, Nijole V. 2012. *Marriages and Families: Changes, Choices, and Constraints—2010 Census Update,* 7th ed. Englewood Cliffs, NJ: Prentice Hall.

Berger, Helen A. 1999. *A Community of Witches: Contemporary Neo-Paganism and Witchcraft in the United States.* Columbia: University of South Carolina Press.

Berger, Helen A. and Douglas Ezzy. 2007. *Teenage Witches: Magical Youth and the Search for the Self.* New Brunswick, NJ: Rutgers University Press.

Berger, Michael L. 1979. *The Devil Wagon in God's Country: The Automobile and Social Change in Rural America, 1893–1929.* Hamden, CT: Archon.

Berger, Peter L. and Thomas Luckmann. 1966. *The Social Construction of Reality.* Garden City, NY: Doubleday.

Berk, Richard A. 1974. *Collective Behavior.* Dubuque, IA: Brown.

Berman, Bruce J. 2011. "Of Magic, Invisible Hands and Elfs: How Not to Study Ethnicity in Africa." Presented at the ECAS4, Uppsala, Sweden, June 14–18.

Berman, Carol. 2010. "Glass Ceiling Is Still Solid." March 15. Retrieved May 25, 2012 (http://jobs.aol.com/articles/2010/03/15/glass-ceiling-is-still-solid-especially-if-you-have-an-mba/).

Better Factories. 2012. *Better Factories Cambodia Newsletter* 9(March). (Retrieved May 28, 2012 (www.betterfactories.org/content/docu ments/1/Newsletter%20No.%2019_Eng.pdf).

Bettie, Julie. 2003. *Women Without Class: Girls, Race, and Identity.* Berkeley: University of California Press.

Bhattacharya, Prasenjit. 2012. "Court Rules Union Carbide Not Liable in Bhopal Case." *The Wall Street Journal,* June 28. Retrieved June 21, 2013 (http://online.wsj.com/article/SB1000142405270230356150 4577493).

Bibby, Reginald W. 2002. *Restless Gods: The Renaissance of Religion in Canada.* Toronto, Canada: Stoddard.

Billig, Michael. 1995. *Banal Nationalism.* Thousand Oaks, CA: Sage.

Birdwhistell, Raymond L. 1970. *Kinesics and Context: Essays on Body Motion Communication.* Philadelphia: University of Pennsylvania Press.

Bjelopera, Jerome P. and Kristin M. Finklea. 2012. "Organized Crime: An Evolving Challenge for U.S. Law Enforcement." Congressional Research Service. Retrieved April 13, 2012 (www.fas.org/sgp/crs/ misc/R41547.pdf).

Blau, Peter M. 1956. *Bureaucracy in Modern Society.* New York: Random House.

Blau, Peter M. 1964. *Exchange and Power in Social Life.* New York: John Wiley.

Blau, Peter and Otis Dudley Duncan. 1967. *The American Occupational Structure.* New York: John Wiley.

Blee, Kathleen M. 2008. "White Supremacy as Extreme Deviance." Pp. 108–17 in *Extreme Deviance,* edited by Erich Goode and D. Angus Vail. Thousand Oaks, CA: Pine Forge.

Blumer, Herbert. 1969. *Symbolic Interactionism: Perspective and Method.* Englewood Cliffs, NJ: Prentice Hall.

Blumer, Herbert. 1986. *Symbolic Interactionism: Perspective and Method.* Berkeley: University of California Press.

Boger, John Charles and Gary Orfield. 2009. *School Resegregation: Must the South Turn Back?"* University of North Carolina Press.

Bokova, Irina and Laura Bush. 2012. "Literacy Is Key to Unlocking the Cycle of Poverty." *Houston Chronicle,* September 7. Retrieved January 28, 2013 (www.chron.com/opinion/outlook/article/Literacy-is-key-to-unlocking-the-cycle-of-poverty-3848564.php).

Boli, John. 2002. "Globalization." Pp. 307–13 in *Education and Sociology: An Encyclopedia,* edited by David L. Levinson, Peter W. Cookson, Jr., and Alan R. Sadovnik. New York: RoutledgeFalmer.

Bonacich, Edna and Jake B. Wilson. 2005. "Hoisted by Its Own Petard: Organizing Wal-Mart's Logistics Workers." *New Labor Forum* 14:67–75.

Bond, Jeff. 2010. "The Anthropology of Garbage." *Columns,* March. Retrieved August 15, 2013 (www.washington.edu/alumni/columns/ march10/garbage.html).

Bonilla-Silva, Eduardo. 2003. *Racism Without Racists: Color-Blind Racism and the Persistence of Racial Inequality in the United States.* Berkeley: University of California Press.

Borenstein, Seth. 2013. "U.S. Scientists Report Big Jump in Heat-Trapping CO2." March 5. Retrieved June 20, 2013 (phys.org/news/2013-03-scientists-big-heat-trapping-co2.html).

Boston Globe. 2012 "Where the States Stand on Gay Marriage." June 10. Retrieved June 10, 2012 (www.boston.com/business/articles/2012/06/10/ where_the_states_stand_on_gay_marriage/).

Boswell, Randy. 2007. "Religion Not Important to Most Canadians, Although Majority Believe in God: Poll" *National Post,* December 4. Retrieved June 20, 2013 (http://life.nationalpost.com/2012/04/07/ religion-not-important-to-most-canadians-although-majority-be-lieve-in-god-poll/).

Bottomore, Tom. 1979. *Political Sociology.* New York: Harper & Row.

Boulding, Elise with Jennifer Dye. 2002. "Women and Development." In *Introducing Global Issues,* 2nd ed., edited by Michael T. Snarr and D. Neil Snarr. Boulder, CO: Lynne Rienner.

Bourdieu, P. and J. C. Passeron. 1977. *Reproduction in Education, Society and Culture.* London: Sage.

Bowen, Debra. 2008. "History Behind California's Primary Election System." Retrieved March 21, 2008 (www.sos.ca.gov/elections/ elections_decline.htm).

Bowles, Samuel and Herbert Gintis. 1976. *Schooling in Capitalist America.* New York: Basic Books.

Bowles, Samuel and Herbert Gintis. 2002. "Schooling in Capitalist America Revisited." *Sociology of Education* 75(1):1–18.

Boy, Angie and Andrzej Kulczycki. 2008. "What We Know About Intimate Partner Violence in the Middle East and North Africa." *Violence Against Women* 14(1):53–70.

Brandon, Emily. 2012. "65-and-Older Population Soars." *US News Money,* January 9. Retrieved March 31, 2012 (http://money.usnews.com/ money/retirement/articles/2012/01/09/65-and-older-population-soars).

Brandon, Mark E. 2005. "War and American Constitutional Order." In *The Constitution in Wartime: Beyond Alarmism and Complacency,* edited by Mark Tushner. Durham, NC: Duke University Press.

Brasher, Brenda E. 2004. *Give Me That On-Line Religion.* New Brunswick, NJ: Rutgers University Press.

Brecher, Jeremy, Tim Costello, and Brendan Smith. 2012. "Globalization and Social Movements." Pp. 272–90 in *Globalization: The Transformation of Social Worlds,* 3rd ed., edited by D. Stanley Eitzen and Maxine Baca Zinn. Belmont, CA: Wadsworth.

Bremner, Jason, Carl Haub, Marlene Lee, Mark Mather, and Eric Zuehlke. 2009. "World Population Highlights." *Population Bulletin* 64(3):3. Population Reference Bureau. Retrieved January 10, 2010 (www.prb .org/pdf09/64.3highlights.pdf).

Brettell, Caroline B., and Carolyn F. Sargent. 2009. *Gender in Cross-Cultural Perspective.* 5th ed. Pearson.

Bridgeland, John M., John J. Dilulio, and Karen Burke Morison. 2006. *The Silent Epidemic: Perspectives of High School Dropouts.* March. Retrieved July 11, 2011 (http://www.civicenterprises.net/pdfs/thesilent epi-demic3–06.pdf).

Brier, Noah Rubin. 2004. "Coming of Age." *American Demographics* 26(9):16.

British Columbia Ministry of Labour & Citizens' Services. 2006. *B.C. Stats Infoline* 6(40). October 6. Retrieved April 17, 2010 (www.bcstats.gov .bc.ca/releases/info2006/in0647.pdf).

Britton, Dana M. 2000. "The Epistemology of the Gendered Organization." *Gender and Society* 14(3):418–34.

Britz, Jennifer Delahunty. 2006. "Are Today's Girls Too Successful?" *Dayton Daily News* (March 31):A7.

Bromley, David G. and Anson D. Shupe, Jr. 1981. *Strange Gods: The Great American Cult Scare.* Boston: Beacon.

Brookover, Wilbur B. and Edsel L. Erickson. 1975. *Sociology of Education.* Homewood, IL: Dorsey.

Broom, Leonard and Philip Selznick. 1963. *Sociology: A Text With Adapted Readings,* 3rd ed. New York: Harper & Row.

Brown, Dee. 2001. *Bury My Heart at Wounded Knee: An Indian History of the American West,* 30th anniversary ed. New York: Holt.

Brown, Donald E. 1991. *Human Universals.* Philadelphia: Temple University Press.

Brown, Matthew. 2013. "Influence of Faith: Americans Say Religion Is Good But Faith Is Losing Its Influence." Deseret News, June 1. Retrieved June 20, 2013 (www.deseretnews.com/article/865580938/ Influence-of-faith-Americans-say-religion-is-good-but-faith-is-losing-its-influence.html?pg=all).

Bruner, Jerome. 1996. *The Culture of Education.* Cambridge, MA: Harvard University Press.

Brunn, Stanley D., Jack F. Williams, and Donald J. Zeigler. 2003. *Cities of the World: World Regional Urban Development,* 3rd ed. Lanham, MD: Rowman & Littlefield.

Buechler, Steven. 2008. "What Is Critical About Sociology?" *Teaching Sociology* 36(4):318–30.

Bullas, Jeff. 2012. "20 Interesting Facts, Figures and Statistics Revealed by Facebook." Jeffbullas.com. Retrieved September 25, 2012 (www .jeffbullas.com/2012/04/30/20-interesting-facts-figures-and-statis tics-revealed-by-facebook/).

Burawoy, Michael. 2005. "For Public Sociology." *American Sociological Review* 56(2):4–28.

Burn, Shawn Meghan. 2011. *Women Across Cultures: A Global Perspective,* 3rd ed. New York: McGraw-Hill.

Cainkar, Louise A. 2009. *Homeland Insecurity: The Arab American and Muslim American Experience After 9/11.* New York: Russell Sage Foundation.

Caldwell, John C. 1982. *Theory of Fertility Decline.* New York: Academic Press.

Calhoun, Craig, ed. 2007. *Sociology in America: A History.* Chicago: University of Chicago Press.

Campbell, Ernest Q. and Thomas F. Pettigrew. 1959. *Christians in Racial Crisis.* Washington, DC: Public Affairs Press.

Canada, Geoffrey. 1998. *Reaching Up for Manhood: Transforming the Lives of Boys in America.* Boston: Beacon Press.

Cancian, Francesca M. 1992. "Feminist Science: Methodologies That Challenge Inequality." *Gender and Society* 6(4):623–42.

Carroll, Lizz. 2010. "Interracial Marriage: Which Groups Are More Likely to Wed?" *DiversityInc,* May 27. Retrieved April 10, 2011 (www.diversityinc.com/article/7719/Interracial-Marriage-Which-Groups-Are-More-Likely-to-Wed/).

Carrothers, Robert M. and Denzel E. Benson. 2003. "Symbolic Interactionism in Introductory Textbooks: Coverage and Pedagogical Implications." *Teaching Sociology* 31(2):162–81.

Casasanto, Daniel. 2008. "Who's Afraid of the Big Bad Whorf? Crosslinguistic Differences in Temporal Language and Thought." *Language Learning* 58(1):63–79.

Cashell, Brian W. 2007. "CRS Report for Congress: Who Are the 'Middle Class'?" Retrieved February 28, 2008 (http://opencrs.cdt.org/rpts/RS22627_20070320.pdf).

Casteel, Chris. 2011. "New Survey on Hunger in America Measures Problems, Perceptions." March 11. Retrieved March 18, 2011 (http://newsok.com/new-survey-on-hunger-in-america-measures-problems-perceptions.article/3547666).

Castiello, Umberto, Cristina Becchio, Stefania Zoia, Cristian Nelini, Luisa Sartori, Laura Blason, Giuseppina D'Ottavio, Maria Bulgheroni, and Vittorio Gallese. 2010. "Wired to Be Social: The Ontogeny of Human Interaction." *PLoS ONE* 5(10). Retrieved October 19, 2010 (www.plosone.org/article/info%3Adoi%2F10.1371%2Fjournal.pone.0013199).

Catalyst. 2013. "Women's Earnings and Income." March 21. Retrieved May 2, 2013 (www.catalyst.org/knowledge/womens-earnings-and-income).

CBS News. 2010. "The Cost of Dying." *60 Minutes,* December 3. Retrieved July 16, 2012 (www.cbsnews.com/2100-18560_162-5711689.html?tag=contentMain;contentBody).

CBC News. 2010. "Four in 10 First Marriages End in Divorce." October 4. Retrieved June 27, 2012 (www.cbc.ca/news/canada/story/2010/10/04/vanier-study004.html).

Center for American Progress Immigration Team. 2012. "The Facts on Immigration Today." July 6. Retrieved July 30, 2012 (www.americanprogress.org/issues/2012/07/immigration_facts.html).

Center for American Women and Politics. 2013. "Women in the U.S. Congress 2013." Retrieved August 26, 2013 (www.cawp.rutgers.edu/fast_facts/levels_of_office/documents/cong.pdf).

Center for Voting and Democracy. 2008. "Understanding Super Tuesday: State Rules on February 5 and Lessons for Reform." Retrieved March 21, 2008 (www.fairvote.org/?page=27&pressmode=showspecific&showarticle=185).

Centers for Disease Control and Prevention. 2009. "Overweight and Obesity." July 27–29. Retrieved November 4, 2009 (www.cdc.gov/obesity/index.html).

Centers for Disease Control and Prevention. 2012. "Economic Facts About U.S. Tobacco Production and Use." Retrieved August 3, 2012 (www.cdc.gov/tobacco/data_statistics/fact_sheets/economics/econ_facts/).

Centers for Disease Control and Prevention. 2013. "West Nile Virus: Preliminary Maps and Data for 2013." Retrieved June 10, 2013 (www.cdc.gov/westnile/statsMaps/preliminaryMapsData/index.html).

Centers for Disease Control and Prevention/National Center for Health Statistics. 2013. "National Marriage and Divorce Rate Trends." National Vital Statistics System. Retrieved August 27, 2013 (http://www.cdc.gov/nchs/nvss/marriage_divorce_tables.htm).

Chambliss, William J. 1973. "The Saints and the Roughnecks." *Society* 11(December):24–31.

Charles, Camille Z., Vincent J. Roscigno, and Kimberly C. Torres. 2007. "Racial Inequality and College Attendance: The Mediating Role of Parental Investments." *Social Science Research* 36(1):329–52.

Charon, Joel. 2010. *Symbolic Interactionism: An Introduction, and Interpretation, an Integration,* 10th ed. Englewood Cliffs, NJ: Prentice Hall.

Chase-Dunn, Christopher and E. N. Anderson. 2006. *The Historical Evolution of World-Systems.* New York: Palgrave Macmillan.

Chaves, Mark. 1993. "Denominations as Dual Structures: An Organizational Analysis." *Sociology of Religion* 54(20):147–69.

Chaves, Mark. 1999. *Ordaining Women: Culture and Conflict in Religious Organizations.* Cambridge, MA: Harvard University Press.

Chaves, Mark. 2004. *Congregations in America.* Cambridge, MA: Harvard University Press.

Chaves, Mark and Philip S. Gorski. 2001. "Religious Pluralism and Religious Participation." *Annual Review of Sociology* 27:261–81.

Chen, Zeng-Yin and Howard B. Kaplan. 2003. "School Failure in Early Adolescence and Status Attainment in Middle Adulthood: A Longitudinal Study." *Sociology of Education* 76(2):110–27.

Cheng, Cecilia. 2005. "Processes Underlying Gender-Role Flexibility: Do Androgynous Individuals Know More or Know How to Cope?" *Journal of Personality* 73(3):645–73.

Cherlin, Andrew. 1978. "Remarriage as an Incomplete Institution." *American Journal of Sociology* 84(3):634–50.

Cherlin, Andrew J. 2010. *The Marriage-Go-Round: The State of Marriage and the Family in America Today.* New York: Random House.

Cherry, Kendra. 2012. "Understanding Body Language." *About.com Psychology.* Retrieved September 25, 2012 (http://psychology.about.com/od/nonverbalcommunication/ss/understanding-body-language.htm).

"Children and Watching TV." 2011. *American Academy of Child and Adolescent Psychiatry* 54(December). Retrieved May 24, 2012 (www.aacap.org/cs/root/facts_for_families/children_and_watching_tv).

Christiano, Kevin J., William H. Swatos, Jr., and Peter Kivisto. 2008. *Sociology of Religion: Contemporary Developments,* Rev. ed. Walnut Creek, CA: AltaMira.

Chubb, John E. and Terry M. Moe. 1990. *Politics, Markets, and America's Schools.* Washington, DC: Brookings Institution.

Cillizza, Chris. 2011. "Facebook, President Obama, and the Youth Vote in 2012." *The Washington Post,* April 20. Retrieved November 1, 2012 (www.washingtonpost.com/blogs/the-fix/post/facebook-president-obama-and-the-youth-vote-in-2012/2011/04/20/AF9zCwCE_blog.html).

Clark, Warren and Grant Schellenberg. 2008. "Who's Religious?" *Statistics Canada.* Retrieved January 30, 2013 (http://www.statcan.gc.ca/pub/11-008-x/2006001/9181-eng.htm#half).

Clarkson, Lamar. 2011. "Divorce Rates Falling, Report Finds." *CNN Living,* May 19. Retrieved June 6, 2012 (http://articles.cnn.com/2011-05-19/living/divorce.rates.drop_1_divorce-rate-divorce-laws-marriage?_s=PM:LIVING).

Clausen, John A. 1986. *The Life Course: A Sociological Perspective.* Englewood Cliffs, NJ: Prentice Hall.

Clinard, Marshall B. and Robert F. Meier. 2004. *Sociology of Deviant Behavior,* 12th ed. Belmont, CA: Wadsworth/Thomson Learning.

Clymer, Floyd. 1953. *Those Wonderful Old Automobiles.* New York: Bonanza.

CNBC. 2010. "Mob Money: An American Greed." July 7. Retrieved February 8, 2013 (www.cnbc.com/id/37593299/mob_money).

CNN.com. 2006. "Flag-Burning Amendment Fails by a Vote." June 28. Retrieved August 16, 2008 (www.cnn.com/2006/POLITICS/06/27/flag.burning).

Cohen, Jessica and Wendy D. Manning. 2010. "The Relationship Context of Premarital Serial Cohabitation." *Social Science Research* 39(September):766–76.

Coleman, James. 1990. *Equality and Achievement in Education.* Boulder, CO: Westview.

Coleman, James S. 1968. "The Concept of Equality of Educational Opportunity." *Harvard Education Review* 38(Winter):7–22.

Coleman, James William. 2006. *The Criminal Elite: Understanding White Collar Crime,* 6th ed. New York: Worth.

Coleman-Jensen, Alisha, Mark Nord, Margaret Andrews, and Steven Carlson. 2011. "Household Food Security in the United States in 2010." ERR-125, U.S. Department of Agriculture, Economic Research Service, September. Retrieved May 17, 2012 (www.cbpp.org/cms/index.cfm?fa=view&id=2226).

"Colleges' Gender Gap." 2010. *Los Angeles Times,* January 25. Retrieved September 12, 2012 (http://articles.latimes.com/2010/jan/25/opinion/la-ed-gender25-2010jan25).

Collins, Patricia Hill. 2000. *Black Feminist Thought: Knowledge, Consciousness, and the Politics of Empowerment,* 2nd ed. New York: Routledge.

Collins, Patricia Hill. 2009. *Black Feminist Theory: Knowledge, Consciousness, and Politics of Empowerment,* 2nd ed., Revised 10th Anniversary Edition. New York: Routledge.

Collins, Randall. 1971. "A Conflict Theory of Sexual Stratification." *Social Problems* 19(Summer):2–21.

Collins, Randall. 2004. "Conflict Theory of Educational Stratification." *American Sociological Review* 36:47–54.

Commonwealth Fund. 2011, November. "International Profiles of Health Care Systems, 2011." Pp. 21–31. Retrieved September 7, 2013 (www.commonwealthfun.org/~/media/Files/Publications/Fund%20Report/2011/Nov/1562_Squires_Intl_Profiles_2011_11_10.pdf).

ComScore. 2010. "Social Networking Sites Reach a Higher Percentage of Women Than Men Worldwide." July 28. Retrieved May 25, 2012 (www.comscore.com/Press_Events/Press_Releases/2010/7/Social_Networking_Sites_REach_a -Higher_Percentage_of_Women_than_Men_).

Condron, Dennis J. and Vincent J. Roscigno. 2003. "Disparities Within: Unequal Spending and Achievement in an Urban School District." *Sociology of Education* 76(January):18–36.

Consumer Rankings. 2012. "The 5 Best Dating Sites of 2012." June 2. Retrieved June 3, 2012 (www.consumer-rankings.com/dating/).

Cook, Karen S., Jodi O'Brien, and Peter Kollock. 1990. "Exchange Theory: A Blueprint for Structure and Process." Pp. 158–81 in *Frontiers of Social Theory: The New Syntheses,* edited by George Ritzer. New York: Columbia University Press.

Cooley, Charles Horton. 1902. *Human Nature and the Social Order.* New York: Scribner.

Cooley, Charles Horton. [1909] 1983. *Social Organization: A Study of the Larger Mind.* New York: Schocken Books.

Coontz, Stephanie. 2005. *Marriage, a History: From Obedience to Intimacy, or How Love Conquered Marriage.* New York: Viking.

Coontz, Stephanie. 2011a. "On Marriage." January 4. Retrieved February 25, 2012 (www.youtube.com/watch?v=gwtb7jz8G4k).

Coontz, Stephanie. 2011b. "What Is the 'Traditional American Family'? Interview With Stephanie Coontz." *The Mother Company,* November 22. Retrieved May 25, 2012 (www.themotherco.com/2011/1/what-is-the-traditional-family/).

Coser, Lewis A. 1956. *The Functions of Social Conflict.* New York: Free Press.

Cousteau, Jacques-Yves. 2008. "The Great Ocean Adventure." Lecture at Hanover College, January 15.

Cowen, Nick and Nigel Williams. 2012. "Comparisons of Crime in OECD Countries." *Civitas Crime.* Retrieved May 2, 2013 (www.civitas.org.uk/crime/crime_stats_oecdjan2012.pdf).

Crary, David and Denise Lavoie. 2013. "Brothers Were Radicalized Via Internet." *Minneapolis Star Tribune* (April 24):A1, A4.

Creswell, John W. 2009. *Research Design: Qualitative, Quantitative, and Mixed Methods Approaches,* 3rd ed. Thousand Oaks, CA: Sage.

Crime Library. 2012. "Worst Cases of Bullying." Retrieved October 5, 2012 (www.gtrutv.com/library/crime/photogallery/worst-cases-of-bullying.html?curPhoto=3).

Cronkite, Walt. 2012. "Romney Says He's 'Fine' With Gay Couples Adopting Children." *CBS News,* May 10. Retrieved June 3, 2012 (www.cbsnews.com/8301-503544_162-57432292-503544/romney-says-hes-fine-with-gay-couples-adopting-children/).

Crosby, Faye J. 2004. *Affirmative Action Is Dead; Long Live Affirmative Action.* New Haven, CT: Yale University Press.

Crossette, Barbara. 1996. "Angkor Emerges From the Jungle." *The New York Times,* January 28. Retrieved September 9, 2008 (http://query.nytimes.com/gst/fullpage.html?res=9500e0d91139f93ba15752c0a960958260&sec=travel&spon=&pagewanted=1).

Crummey, Robert O. 1970. *The Old Believers and the World of Antichrist: The Vyg Community and the Russian State, 1694–1855.* Madison: University of Wisconsin Press.

Curtiss, S. 1977. *Genie: A Psycholinguistic Study of a Modern-Day "Wild Child."* New York: Academic Press.

Cushman, Thomas and Stjepan G. Mestrovic. 1996. *This Time We Knew: Western Responses to Genocide in Bosnia.* New York: New York University Press.

Cuzzort, R. P. and Edith W. King. 2002. *Social Thought Into the Twenty-First Century,* 6th ed. Belmont, CA: Wadsworth.

DaCosta, Kimberly McClain. 2007. *Making Multiracials: State, Family, and Market in the Redrawing of the Color Line.* Stanford, CA: Stanford University Press.

Dahl, Robert A. 1961. *Who Governs?* New Haven, CT: Yale University Press.

Dahlberg, Frances. 1981. *Woman the Gatherer.* New Haven, CT: Yale University Press.

Dahrendorf, Ralf. 1959. *Class and Class Conflict in Industrial Societies.* Palo Alto, CA: Stanford University Press.

Dalit Liberation Education Trust. 1995. *10th Anniversary Newsletter* (May). Madras: Human Rights Education Movement of India.

Dalton, Harlon. 2012. "Failing to See." Pp. 15–18 in *White Privilege,* edited by Paula S. Rothenberg. New York: Worth.

Data360. 2012. "U.S. Life Expectancy Rates." Retrieved March 31, 2012 (http://www.data360.org/dsg.aspx?Data_Set_Group_Id=195).

Davis, Kingsley. 1940. "Extreme Social Isolation of a Child." *American Journal of Sociology* 45:554–65.

Davis, Kingsley. 1947. "A Final Note on a Case of Extreme Isolation." *American Journal of Sociology* 52:432–37.

Davis, Kingsley. 1960. "Legitimacy and the Incest Taboo." Pp. 398–402 in *A Modern Introduction to the Family,* edited by Norman W. Bell and Ezra F. Vogel. Glencoe, IL: The Free Press.

Davis, Kingsley and Wilbert Moore. 1945. "Some Principles of Stratification." *American Sociological Review* 10(April):242–45.

Day, Jennifer Cheeseman. 2011. "Population Profile of the U.S.: Percentage of the Population, by Race and Hispanic Origin." U.S. Census Bureau, Population Division. Retrieved April 19, 2011 (http://www.census.gov/population/www/pop-profile/natproj.html).

Death Penalty Information Center. 2012. "Facts About the Death Penalty." April 13. Retrieved April 16, 2012 (www.deathpenaltyinfo.org/documents/FactSheet.pdf).

DeBoskey, Bruce. 2012. "Women Changing the Face of Philanthropy." July 22. *The Denver Post.* Retrieved April 25, 2013 (www.denverpost.com/business/ci_21124380/women-changing-face-philanthropy).

DeCarlo, Scott. 2012. "CEO Pay." *Forbes.com,* April 4. Retrieved May 14, 2012 (www.forbes.com/forbes/2012/0423/ceo-compensation-12-company-earnings-highest-gravity-defying-pay.html).

DeGenova, Mary Kay, Nick Stinnett, and Nancy Stinnett. 2011. *Intimate Relationships, Marriages, and Families,* 8th ed. New York: McGraw-Hill.

Delfattore, Joan. 2004. "Romeo and Juliet Were Just Good Friends." Pp. 177–83 in *Schools and Society,* 2nd ed., edited by Jeanne H. Ballantine and Joan Z. Spade. Belmont, CA: Wadsworth.

Della Porta, Donatella, Massimillano Andretta, Lorenzo Mosca, and Herbert Reiter. 2006. *Globalization From Below: Transnational Activists and Protest Networks.* Minneapolis: University of Minnesota Press.

DeMartini, Joseph R. 1982. "Basic and Applied Sociological Work: Divergence, Convergence, or Peaceful Coexistence?" *Journal of Applied Behavioral Science* 18(2):205–206.

DeMitchell, Todd A. and John J. Carney. 2005. "Harry Potter and the Public School Library." *Phi Delta Kappan* (October):159–65.

Denali Commission. 2001. *Telecommunications Services Inventory of Rural Alaska: Final Database and Report.* Juneau, Alaska: McDowell Group.

Denali Commission. 2011. *Annual Report 2011: Transforming Alaskan Communities.* Retrieved August 26, 2013 (www.denali.gov/images/documents/annual_reports/2011DenaliAnnualReport.pdf).

DePalma, Anthony. 1995. "Racism? Mexico's in Denial." *The New York Times,* June 11, p. E4.

Deutsch, M. and R. M. Krauss. 1960. "The Effect of Threat on Interpersonal Bargaining." *Journal of Abnormal and Social Psychology* 61:181–89.

Deutsch, Morton and Roy J. Lewicki. 1970. "'Locking-In' Effects During a Game of Chicken." *Journal of Conflict Resolution* 14(3):367–78.

Dews, C. L. Barney and Carolyn Leste Law, eds. 1995. *This Fine Place So Far From Home: Voices of Academics From the Working Class.* Philadelphia: Temple University Press.

Diamond, Jared. 1999. *Guns, Germs, and Steel: The Fates of Human Societies.* New York: W. W. Norton.

Diamond, Jared. 2005. *Collapse: How Societies Choose to Fail or Succeed.* New York: Viking.

Diamond, Larry. 1992. "Introduction: Civil Society and the Struggle for Democracy." Pp. 1–28 in *The Democratic Revolution: Struggles for Freedom and Pluralism in the Developing World,* edited by Larry Diamond. New York: Freedom House.

Diamond, Larry. 2003. "Universal Democracy?" *Policy Review* (June/July). Retrieved August 28, 2008 (www.hoover.org/publications/poicyreview/3448571.html).

Diamond, Larry. 2009. *The Spirit of Democracy: The Struggle to Build Free Societies Throughout the World.* New York: Times Books/Henry Holt & Co.

Diep, Francie. 2011. "Fast Facts About the Japan Earthquake and Tsunami." *Scientific American,* March 14. Retrieved May 13, 2012 (www.scientificamerican.com/article.cfm?if=fast-facts-japan).

Diggs, Nancy Brown. 2011. *Hidden in the Heartland.* East Lansing: Michigan State University Press.

Dilon, Michele. 2009. *Introduction to Sociological Theory: Theorists, Concepts, and Their Applicability to the Twenty-First Century.* Malden, MA: Wiley-Blackwell.

DiMaggio, Paul and Walter Powell. 1983. "The Iron Cage Revisited: Institutional Isomorphism and Collective Rationality in Organizational Fields." *American Sociological Review* 48:147–60.

Diouf, Jacques. 2010–2011. *Women—Key to Food Security.* Food and Agriculture Organization of the United Nations. Retrieved August 21, 2013 (www.fao.org/docrep/014/am719e/am719e00.pdf).

Divorce Rate. 2011. "Divorce Updates and Divorce Rate in 2011." Retrieved June 6, 2012 (http://divorcerate2011.com/divorce-updates).

Dixon, Patrick. 2011. "Steroid Use." *Global Change.* Retrieved May 23, 2012 (www.globalchange.com/steroids.htm).

Dobbelaere, Karel. 1981. *Secularization: A Multidimensional Concept.* Beverly Hills, CA: Sage.

Dobbelaere, Karel. 2000. "Toward an Integrated Perspective of the Processes Related to the Descriptive Concept of Secularization." Pp. 21–39 in *The Secularization Debate,* edited by William H. Swatos, Jr. and Daniel V. A. Olson. Lanham, MD: Rowman & Littlefield.

"Doing Gender." 2011. *Creative Sociology.* August 10. Retrieved September 5, 2013 (http://creativesociology.blogspot.com/2011/08/doing-gender.html).

Domestic Violence Resource Center. 2012. "Domestic Violence Statistics." Retrieved June 21, 2012 (www.dvrc-or.org/domestic/violence/resources/C61).

Domhoff, G. William. 1998. *Who Rules America? Power and Politics in the Year 2000,* 3rd ed. Mountain View, CA: Mayfield.

Domhoff, G. William. 2005. "The Class-Domination Theory of Power." *Who Rules America,* 6th ed. Retrieved May 16, 2012 (www2.ucsc.edu/whorulesamerica/power/class_domination.html).

Domhoff, G. William. 2008. "Who Rules America.net: Power, Politics, and Social Change." Retrieved March 24, 2008 (http://sociology.ucsc.edu/whoruleeesamerica).

Domhoff, G. William. 2009. *Who Rules America: Challenges to Corporate and Class Dominance.* Upper Saddle River, NJ: Prentice Hall.

Domina, Thurston. 2005. "Leveling the Home Advantage: Assessing the Effectiveness of Parental Involvement in Elementary School." *Sociology of Education* 78(3):233–49.

Drafke, Michael. 2008. *The Human Side of Organizations.* Englewood Cliffs, NJ: Prentice Hall.

Drori, Gili S. 2006. *Global E-Litism: Digital Technology, Social Inequality, and Transnationality.* New York: Worth.

Du Bois, W. E. B. [1899] 1967. *The Philadelphia Negro: A Social Study.* New York: Schocken.

Dufur, Mikaela J. and Seth L. Feinberg. 2007. "Artificially Restricted Labor Markets and Worker Dignity in Professional Football." *Journal of Contemporary Ethnography* 36(5):505–36.

Durkheim, Émile. [1893] 1947. *The Division of Labor in Society,* translated by George Simpson. New York: Free Press.

Durkheim, Émile. [1897] 1964. *Suicide.* Glencoe, IL: Free Press.

Durkheim, Émile. [1915] 2002. In *Classical Sociological Theory,* edited by Craig Calhoun. Malden, MA: Blackwell.

Durkheim, Émile. 1947. *Elementary Forms of Religious Life.* Glencoe, IL: Free Press.

Dusenbery, Maya and Jaeah Lee. 2012. "Charts: The State of Women's Athletics, 40 Years After Title IX." *Mother Jones,* June 22. Retrieved May 2, 2013 (www.motherjones.com/politics/2012/06/chasrts-womens-athletics-title-nine-ncaa).

Dworkin, Anthony Gary and Rosalind J. Dworkin. 1999. *The Minority Report: An Introduction to Racial, Ethnic, and Gender Relations,* 3rd ed. Fort Worth, TX: Harcourt Brace.

Dworkin, Anthony Gary and Pamela F. Tobe. 2012. "Teacher Burnout in Light of School Safety, Student Misbehavior, and Changing Accountability Standards." Pp. 199–211 in *Schools and Society: A Sociological Approach to Education,* edited by Jeanne H. Ballantine and Joan Z. Spade. Thousand Oaks, CA: Sage Pine Forge.

Dye, Thomas R. 2002. *Who's Running America? The Bush Restoration.* Englewood Cliffs, NJ: Prentice Hall.

Dye, Thomas and Harmon Zeigler. 1983. *The Irony of Democracy.* North Scituate, MA: Duxbury Press.

Dyer, Richard. 2012. "The Matter of Whiteness." Pp. 9–14 in *White Privilege,* edited by Paula S. Rothenberg. New York: Worth.

Earls, Felton M. and Albert J. Reiss. 1994. *Breaking the Cycle: Predicting and Preventing Crime.* Washington, DC: National Institute of Justice.

"Eating Disorder Statistics." 2008. South Carolina Department of Mental Health. Retrieved May 27, 2012 (www.state.sc.us/dmh/anorexia/statistics/htm).

Ebaugh, Helen Rose Fuchs. 2005. *Handbook of Religion and Social Institutions*. New York: Springer.

Eckert, Penelope. 1989. *Jocks and Burnouts: Social Categories and Identity in High School*. New York: Teacher's College Press.

EcoSummit. 2012. "Ecological Sustainability: Restoring the Planet's Ecosystem Services." *Fourth International Ecosummit*. Retrieved July 31, 2012 (www.ecosummit2012.org/).

"Ecosystems Report Links Human Well-Being With Health of Planet." 2006. *Popline* 28(January/February):1.

Eder, Donna, Catherine Colleen Evans, and Stephen Parker. 1995. *School Talk: Gender and Adolescent Culture*. New Brunswick, NJ: Rutgers University Press.

Education Week. 2011. "School Finance." June 20. Retrieved September 14, 2012 (www.edweek.org/ew/issues/school-finance/).

Edwards, Harry. 2000. "Crisis of the Black Athlete on the Eve of the 21st Century." *Society* 37(3):9–13.

eHarmony. 2012. "Information." Retrieved February 9, 2013 (http://advice.eharmony.com/information).

Ehrenreich, Barbara. 2001. *Nickel and Dimed: On (Not) Getting By in America*. New York: Henry Holt.

Ehrenreich, Barbara. 2005. *Bait and Switch: The (Futile) Pursuit of the American Dream*. New York: Henry Holt.

Ehrlich, Paul and Ann Ehrlich. 1990. *The Population Explosion*. New York: Simon and Schuster.

Eitzen Stanley and Maxine Baca Zinn. 1998. *In Conflict and Order*, 8th ed. Boston: Allyn & Bacon.

Eitzen, D. Stanley and Maxine Baca Zinn. 2012a. "Changing Global Structures: Resistance and Social Movements." Pp. 269–71 in *Globalization: The Transformation of Social Worlds*, 3rd ed., edited by D. Stanley Eitzen and Maxine Baca Zinn. Belmont, CA: Wadsworth.

Eitzen, D. Stanley and Maxine Baca Zinn, eds. 2012b. *Globalization: The Transformation of Social Worlds*, 3rd ed. Belmont, CA: Wadsworth.

Eitzen, D. Stanley, Maxine Baca Zinn, and Kelly Eitzen Smith. 2013. *In Conflict and Order: Understanding Society*, 13th ed. Upper Saddle River, NJ: Pearson.

Elam, Jerome. 2011. "Pedophiles and Pimps Score at Large Sporting Events Like Super Bowl XLVI." *The Washington Times*, January 17. Retrieved January 21, 2013 (http://communities.washingtontimes.com/neighborhood/heart-without-compromise-children-and-children-wit/2012/jan/17/pedophiles-and-pimps-score-large-sporting-events-s/).

Ellison, Christopher G., J. A. Burr, and P. L. McCall. 1997. "Religious Homogeneity and Metropolitan Suicide Rates." *Social Forces* 76(1):273–99.

Ellison, Christopher G. and Daniel A. Powers. 1994. "The Contact Hypothesis and Racial Attitudes Among Black Americans." *Social Science Quarterly* 75(2):385–400.

Emerson, Michael O. and Christian Smith. 2000. *Divided by Faith: Evangelical Religion and the Problem of Race in America*. New York: Oxford University Press.

Emerson, Michael O., with Rodney Woo. 2006. *People of the Dream: Multiracial Congregations in the United States*. Princeton, NJ: Princeton University Press.

Engels, Friedrich. [1884] 1942. *The Origin of the Family, Private Property, and the State*. New York: International Publishing.

Enloe, Cynthia. 2006. "Daughters and Generals in the Politics of the Globalized Sneaker." In *Beyond Borders: Thinking Critically About Global Issues*, edited by Paula S. Rothenberg. New York: Worth.

Environment 911. 2012. "Causes of Water Shortages." Retrieved February 8, 2013 (www.environment911.org/221.Causes_of_Water_Shortages).

Environmental Defense Fund. 2012. "Climate: Facts, Dangers and What You Can Do." Retrieved September 8, 2012 (www.edf.org/climate-facts-dangers-and-what-climatechange&gclid).

Erikson, Erik H. 1950. *Childhood and Society*. New York: Norton.

Eshleman, J. Ross and Richard A. Bulcroft. 2010. *The Family*, 12th ed. Boston: Allyn & Bacon.

Esperitu, Yen Le. 1992. *Asian American Panethnicity: Bridging Institutions and Identities*. Philadelphia: Temple University Press.

Ethnic Majority. 2012. "African, Hispanic (Latino), and Asian American Members of Congress." Retrieved April 22, 2011 (www.ethnicmajority.com/congress.htm).

Etounga-Manguelle, Daniel. 2000. "Does Africa Need a Cultural Adjustment Program?" Pp. 65–77 in *Culture Matters: How Values Shape Human Progress*, edited by Lawrence E. Harrison and Samuel P. Huntington. New York: Basic Books.

Etzioni, Amitai. 1975. *A Comparative Analysis of Complex Organizations*. New York: Free Press.

Evans, Martin. 2012. "First Case of People Trafficking for Organs Uncovered in UK." *The Telegraph*, April 25. Retrieved January 19, 2013 (http://www.telegraph.co.uk/news/uknews/crime/9227137/First-case-of-people-trafficking-for-organs-uncovered-in-UK.html).

Evans, Tom. 2010. "Bosnian Leader: 'Ethnic Cleansing' Continues 15 Years after War." *CNN World*, March 1. Retrieved May 6, 2012 (http://articles.cnn.com/2010-03-01/world/bosnia.herzegovina_1_ethnic-cleansing-serb-bosnian-leader?_s=PM:WORLD).

Facebook.com. 2013. "Key Facts." Retrieved August 20, 2013 (https://newsroom.fb.com/Key-Facts).

Fackler, Martin. 2007. "Career Women in Japan Find a Blocked Path." *The New York Times*, August 6. Retrieved November 8, 2009 (www.nytimes.com/2007/08/06/world/asia/06equal.html).

Farley, John E. 2010. *Majority-Minority Relations*, 6th ed. Englewood Cliffs, NJ: Prentice Hall.

Farrer, Claire R. 2011. *Thunder Rides a Black Horse: Mescalero Apaches and the Mythic Present*, 3rd ed. Long Grove, IL: Waveland.

Fathi, David C. 2009. "Prison Nation." Human Rights Watch, April 9. Retrieved April 15, 2009 (www.hrw.org/en/news/2009/04/09/prison-nation).

Fausto-Sterling, Anne. 1992. *Myths of Gender: Biological Theories About Women and Men*, 2nd ed. New York: Basic Books.

Fausto-Sterling, Anne. 2000. "The Five Sexes, Revisited." *Sciences* 40(July/August):118.

Federal Bureau of Investigation. 2006. "2006 Financial Crime Report." Retrieved February 8, 2008 (www.fbi.gov/publications/financial/fcs_report2006/financial_crime_2006.htm).

Federal Bureau of Investigation. 2009. "Crime in the United States: Expanded Homicide Data." Retrieved June 3, 2012 (www2.fbi.gov/ucr/cius2009/offenses/expanded_information/homicide.html).

Federal Bureau of Investigation. 2012. "Crime Rates Are Down." *Uniform Crime Report*, June 11. Retrieved October 6, 2012 (www.fbi.gov/news/stories/2012/june/crimes_061112/crimes_061112).

Feagin, Joe R. and Clairece Booher Feagin. 1986. *Discrimination American Style: Institutional Racism and Sexism*. Malabar, FL: Krieger.

Feagin, Joe R. and Clairece Booher Feagin. 2010. *Racial and Ethnic Relations*, 9th ed. Englewood Cliffs, NJ: Prentice Hall.

Featherman, David L. and Robert Hauser. 1978. *Opportunity and Change*. New York: Academic Press.

Fedotov, Yury. 2012. "Briefing: Fight Against Transnational Organized Crime and Drug Trafficking." Retrieved April 18, 2013 (www.unodc.org/unodc/en/speeches/briefing-to-member-states-toc-7-february-2012.html).

Felix, Samantha. 2012. "Side by Side: How Obama and Romney's Social Media Battle Stacks Up." *Business Insider*, September 23. Retrieved November 1, 2012 (www.businessinsider.com/winner-of-the-obamaromney-social-media-campaign-2012-9?op=1).

Feller, Avi and Chad Stone. 2009. "Top 1% of Americans Reaped Two-Thirds of Income Gains in Last Economic Expansion." Center on Budget and Policy Priorities, September 9. Retrieved January 7, 2010 (www.cbpp.org/cms/index.cfm?fa=view&id=2908).

Ferhansyed. 2008. "Fundamental Terminology of Planned Change." Retrieved December 21, 2009 (http://organizationdevelopment. wordpress.com/2008/08/10/fundamental-terminology-of-organization-development).

Fernandez, Eleazar S. 2011 Burning *Center, Porous Borders: The Church in a Globalized World.* Eugene, OR: Wipf and Stock.

Ferree, Myra Marx. 2012. "Globalization and Feminism: Opportunities and Obstacles for Activism in a Global Arena." Pp. 291–320 in in *Globalization: The Transformation of Social Worlds*, 3rd ed., edited by D. Stanley Eitzen and Maxine Baca Zinn. Belmont, CA: Wadsworth.

Fine, Gary Alan. 1990. "Symbolic Interactionism in the Post-Blumerian Age." Pp. 117–57 in *Frontiers of Social Theory: The New Synthesis*, edited by George Ritzer. New York: Columbia University Press.

Finke, Roger and Rodney Stark. 2005. *The Churching of America, 1776–1990: Winners and Losers in Our Religious Economy*, 2nd ed. New Brunswick, NJ: Rutgers University Press.

"First Born Children." 2008. Retrieved June 29, 2008 (http://social.jrank .org/pages/261/Firstborn-children.html).

Fitch, Catherine, Ron Goeken, and Steven Ruggles. 2005. "The Rise of Cohabitation in the United States: New Historical Estimates." Retrieved July 14, 2011 (http://www.hist.umn.edu/~ruggles/cohab-revised2.pdf).

Fitzpatrick, Laura. 2010. "Why Do Women Still Earn Less Than Men?" Time, April 20. Retrieved March 18, 2011 (www.time.com/time/nation/article/0,8599,1983185,00.html).

"Five Rules for Online Networking." 2005. CNN, April 1. Retrieved July 25, 2006 (www.cnn.com/2005/US/Careers/03/31/online.networking).

Flavin, Jeanne. 2004. "Employment, Counseling, Housing Assistance . . . and Aunt Yolanda? How Strengthening Families' Social Capital Can Reduce Recidivism." *Fordham Urban Law Journal* 3(2):209–16.

Florida, Richard. 2002. *The Rise of the Creative Class.* New York: Basic Books.

Florida, Richard. 2004. *Cities and the Creative Class.* New York: Routledge.

Florida, Richard. 2012a. "Creative Class Group." March 2. Retrieved March 5, 2012 (www.creativeclass.com/richard_florida).

Florida, Richard. 2012b. "The Joys of Urban Tech." *The Wall Street Journal*, August 31. Retrieved September 25, 2012 (www.creativeclass.com/rfcgdb/articles/WSJ%20The%20Joys%20of%20Urban%20Tech.pdf).

Foner, Nancy. 2005. *In a New Land: A Comparative View of Immigration.* New York: New York University Press.

Forbes. 2012. "The World's Billionaires." May 5. Retrieved May 16, 2012 (http://www.forbes.com/billionaires/).

Ford, Clennan S. 1970. *Human Relations Area Files: 1949–1969—A Twenty Year Report.* New Haven, CT: Human Relations Area Files.

Foundation Source Access. 2013. "Children and WaterAid." Retrieved February 9, 2013 (http://access.foundationsource.com/project/children-and-wateraid).

Foundation for Women. 2012. "Eliminating Global Poverty through Microcredit." Retrieved May 21, 2012 (www.foundationforwomen .org/).

France 24 International News. 2009. "Increase in Number of Billionaires Despite Credit Crisis." October 13. Retrieved November 11, 2009 (www.france24.com/en/20091013-global-crisis-china-billionaires-economy-asia-wealthy-rich-list).

Frank, Mark G. and Thomas Gilovich. 1988. "The Dark Side of Self- and Social Perception: Black Uniforms and Aggression in Professional Sports." *Journal of Personality and Social Psychology* 54(1):74–85.

Free the Slaves. 2013. "Our Mission." Retrieved January 19, 2013 (www .freetheslaves.net).

Freedom House. 2002. *Freedom in the World 2001–2002.* New York: Author.

Freedom to Marry. 2013. "States." Retrieved September 3, 2013 (http:// www.freedomtomarry.org/states).

Freese, J., B. Powell, and L. C. Steelman. 1999. *Rebel Without a Cause or Effect: Birth Order and Social Attitudes.* Washington, DC: American Sociological Association.

Freud, Sigmund. [1923] 1960. *The Ego and the Id.* New York: Norton.

Frey, Bruno S. 2004. *Dealing With Terrorism: Stick or Carrot?* Cheltenham, UK: Edward Elgar.

Friedman, Thomas L. 2005. *The World Is Flat: A Brief History of the Twenty-First Century.* New York: Farrar, Straus, & Giroux.

Friedman, Thomas L. 2008. *Hot, Flat and Crowded: Why We Need a Green Revolution—and How It Can Renew America.* New York: Farrar, Straus & Giroux.

"Full Transcript of the Second Presidential Debate." 2012. *New York Times*, October 16. Retrieved November 1, 2012 (www.nytimes .com/2012/10/16/us/politics/transcript-of-the-second-presidential-debate-in-hempstead-ny.html?pagewanted=all&_r=0).

Furstenberg, F. F. 2003. "Growing Up in American Society: Income, Opportunities, and Outcomes." Pp. 211–33 in *Social Dynamics of the Life Course: Transitions, Institutions, and Interrelations*, edited by W. R. Heinz and V. W. Marshall. New York: A. deGruyter.

Future for All. 2013. "Future Technology and Society." Retrieved August 20, 2013 (www.futureforall.org).

Gaijinpot. 2010. "Japanese Women Stand Low on the Corporate Ladder." August 30. Retrieved May 27, 2012 (http://injapan.gaijinpot.com/work-tips/2010/08/30/japanese-women-stand-low-on-the-corporate-ladder/).

Gallagher, Charles. 2004. "Transforming Racial Identity Through Affirmative Action." Pp. 153–70 in *Race and Ethnicity: Across Time, Space and Discipline*, edited by Rodney D. Coates. Leiden, Holland: Brill.

Gallup. 2011. "More Than 9 in 10 Americans Continue to Believe in God." June 3. Retrieved July 14, 2011 (www.gallup.com/poll/147887/ americans-continue-believe-god.aspx).

Gallup Center for Muslim Studies. 2010. *In U.S., Religious Prejudice Stronger Against Muslims.* Retrieved January 22, 2013 (www.gallup.com/ poll/125312/religious-prejudice-stronger-against-muslims.aspx).

Gallup, George and Roger E. Hern'ndez. 2005. "Friends, Cliques, and Peer Pressure." Pp. 71–85 in *Teens and Relationships*, edited by Roger Hernandez. Philadelphia: Mason Crest Publishers.

Gannon, Shane Patrick. 2009. *Translating the Hijra: The Symbolic Reconstruction of the British Empire in India.* PhD thesis, University of Alberta.

Gans, Herbert J. 1962. *The Urban Villagers: Group and Class in the Life of Italian-Americans.* New York: Free Press.

Gans, Herbert J. 1971. "The Uses of Poverty: The Poor Pay All." *Social Policy* 2(2):20–24.

Gans, Herbert J. 1995. *The War Against the Poor.* New York: Basic Books.

Gans, Herbert J. 2007. "No, Poverty Has Not Disappeared." Reprinted in *Sociological Footprints*, edited by Leonard Cargan and Jeanne Ballantine. Belmont, CA: Wadsworth.

Gardner, Howard. 1987. "The Theory of Multiple Intelligences." *Annual Dyslexia* 37:19–35.

Gardner, Howard. 1999. *Intelligence Reframed: Multiple Intelligences for the 21st Century.* New York: Basic Books.

Gates, Bill. 2013. "Annual Letter." Retrieved February 5, 2013 (www.gates foundation.org/annualletter).

Gatto, John Taylow. 2003. *The Prussian Connection.* New York: The Odysseus Group.

Gay, Lesbian, and Straight Education Network (GLSEN). 2006. "GLSEN's 2005 National School Climate Survey Sheds New Light on Experiences of Lesbian, Gay, Bisexual and Transgendered (LGBT) Students." Retrieved August 8, 2008 (www.glsen.org/cgi-bin/iowa/ all/library/record/1927.html).

Gellner, Ernest. 1987. *Culture, Identity, and Politics.* Cambridge: Cambridge University Press.

Gellner, Ernest. 1993. "Nationalism." Pp. 409–11 in *Blackwell Dictionary of Twentieth Century Thought,* edited by William Outhwaite and Tom Bottomore. Oxford, UK: Basil Blackwell.

Gellner, Ernest and John Breuilly. 2009. *Nations and Nationalism,* 2nd ed. Ithaca, NY: Cornell University Press.

"Gender Stereotypes Easing More for Girls than Boys." 2011. *USA Today.* Retrieved May 21, 2012 (www.usatoday.com/news/health/wellness/teen-ya/story/2011/05/Gender-stereotypes-easing-more-for-girls-than-boys/46886846/1).

Gendercide: The War on Baby Girls." March 4, 2010. Retrieved May 2, 2010 (www.economist.com/node/15606229)

"Getting Married in Japan." 2013. Retrieved January 24, 2013 (http://japanese.about.com/library/weekly/aa080999.htm).

Gibbs, Jack P. 1989. *Control: Sociology's Central Notion.* Urbana: University of Illinois Press.

Gibler, John. 2012. "Mexico's Ghost Towns." Pp. 68–72 in *Globalization: The Transformation of Social Worlds,* 3rd ed., edited by D. Stanley Eitzen and Maxine Baca Zinn. Belmont, CA: Wadsworth.

Giddens, Anthony. 1986. *The Constitution of Society.* Berkeley: University of California Press.

Giddens, Anthony. 1987. *Social Theory and Modern Sociology.* Cambridge, UK: Polity Press.

Gilbert, Dennis. 2011. *The American Class Structure in an Age of Growing Inequality,* 8th ed. Thousand Oaks, CA: Sage.

Gilligan, Carol. 1982. *In a Different Voice: Psychological Theory and Women's Development.* Cambridge, MA: Harvard University Press.

Girls Health. 2009. "Bullying." *Girlshealth.gov.* Retrieved May 21, 2012 (www.girlshealth.gov/bullying/).

Givens, David B. 2012. "Nonverbal Communication." *Center for Nonverbal Studies.* Retrieved September 25, 2012 (http://center-for-nonverba-studies.org/nvcom.htm).

Gladwell, Malcolm. 2010. "Small Change: Why the Revolution Will Not Be Tweeted." *The New Yorker,* October 4. Retrieved October 9, 2012 (http://www.newyorker.com).

Glasberg, Davita Silfen and Deric Shannon. 2011. *Political Sociology: Oppression, Resistance, and the State.* Thousand Oaks, CA: Sage.

Glasscock, C. B. 1937. *The Gasoline Age: The Story of the Men Who Made It.* Indianapolis, IN: Bobbs-Merrill.

Global Fund for Women. 2012. "Status of Women Fact Sheet." Retrieved October 1, 2012 (www.globalfundforwomen.org/impact/media-center/fact-sheets/status-of-women-fact-sheet).

Global Issues. 2012. "World Military Spending." Retrieved July 27, 2012 (www.globalissues.org/print/article/75#WorldMilitarySpending).

"Global Opium Production." 2011. *The Economist,* June 24. Retrieved April 13, 2012 (www.economist.com/node/16432922).

Global Security. 2009. "Guantanamo Bay Detainees." Retrieved April 14, 2012 (www.globalsecurity.org/military/facility/guantanamo-bay_detainees.htm).

"Global Warming and Climate Change." 2013. *The New York Times,* January 8. Retrieved February 5, 2013 (http://topics.nytimes.com/top/news/science/topics/globalwarming/index.html).

Globe Women. 2013. "WEXPO: Women's Online Marketplace." Retrieved January 23, 2013 (http://www.wexpo.biz/).

Goffman, Erving. [1959] 2001. *Presentation of Self in Everyday Life.* New York: Harmondsworth, UK: Penguin.

Goffman, Erving. 1961. *Asylums: Essays on the Social Situation of Mental Patients and Other Inmates.* New York: Anchor.

Goffman, Erving. 1967. *Interaction Ritual.* New York: Anchor.

Goode, Erich. 1992. *Collective Behavior.* New York: Harcourt Brace Jovanovich.

Goode, Erich. 2012. *Drugs in American Society,* 8th ed. Boston: McGraw-Hill.

Goode, William J. 1970. *World Revolution and Family Patterns.* New York: Free Press.

Goodman, Amy and Juan Gonzalez. 2012. "Debating Tucson School District's Book Ban after Suspension of Mexican American Studies Program." *Democracy Now,* January 18. Retrieved January 28, 2013 (www.democracynow.org/2012/1/18/debating_tucson_school_district_book_ban).

Goodstein, Laurie. 2012. "Ugandan Gay Rights Group Sues U.S. Evangelist." *The New York Times,* March 14. Retrieved May 27, 2012 (www.nytimes.com/2012/03/15/us/ugandan-gay-rights-group-sues-scott-lively-an-american-evangelist.html).

Gordon, Milton. 1970. "The Subsociety and the Subculture." Pp. 150–63 in *The Sociology of Subcultures,* edited by David O. Arnold. Berkeley, CA: Glendessary.

Gore, Al. 2012. "Global Warming Is Real." *EarthSky,* April 30. Retrieved September 7, 2012 (http://earthsky.org/human-world/al-gore-at-hampshire-college-global-warming-is-real).

Gorski, Phillip S. 2000. "Historicizing the Secularization Debate: Church, State, and Society in Late Medieval and Early Modern Europe, ca 1300 to 1700." *Social Forces*(February):138–67.

Gorski, Philip and Ates Altinordu. 2008. "After Secularization." *Annual Review of Sociology* 34:55–85.

Gottfredson, Michael R. and Travis Hirschi. 1990. *A General Theory of Crime.* Palo Alto, CA: Stanford University Press.

Gouldner, Alvin W. 1960. "The Norm of Reciprocity: A Preliminary Statement." *American Sociological Review* 25(2):161–78.

Gracey, Harry L. 1967. "Learning the Student Role: Kindergarten as Academic Boot Camp." Pp. 215–26 in *Readings in Introductory Sociology,* 3rd ed., edited by Dennis Wrong and Harry L. Gracey. New York: Macmillan.

Grandpa Junior. 2006. "If You Were Born Before 1945." Retrieved July 20, 2006 (www.grandpajunior.com/1945.shtml).

Granovetter, Mark. 2007. "Introduction for the French Reader." *Sociologica* 1(Suppl.):1–10.

Gray, Emma. 2012. "Women and Poverty In the United States: 18 Essential Facts and Statistics." August 29. *The Huffington Post.* Retrieved May 5, 2013 (www.huffingtonpost.com/2012/08/29/women-and-poverty-united-states-facts-statistics_n_1838384.html#slide=more247419).

Greeley, Andrew M. 1972. *The Denominational Society.* Glenview, IL: Scott, Foresman.

Greeley, Andrew M. 1989. *Religious Change in America.* Cambridge, MA: Harvard University Press.

The Green Papers. 2008a. "Presidential Primaries, Caucuses, and Conventions." Retrieved March 21, 2008 (www.thegreenpapers.com/P08/CO-R.phtml).

The Green Papers. 2008b. "Presidential Primaries 2008: Republican Delegate Selection and Voter Eligibility." Retrieved March 21, 2008 (www.thegreenpapers.com/P08/R-DSVE.phtml?sort=a).

Greensboro Justice Fund. 2005. "Courage From the Past." *GJF Newsletter* (17, Summer):1.

Grossman, Cathy Lynn. 2012. "Number of U.S. Mosques Up 74% Since 2000." *USA Today,* February 29. Retrieved June 7, 2012 (www.usatoday.com/news/religion/story/2012-02-29/islamic-worship-growth-us/53298792/1).

Guarino-Ghezzi, S. and B. Carr. 1996. "Juvenile Offenders Versus the Police: A Community Dilemma." *Caribbean Journal of Criminology and Social Psychology* 1(2):24–43.

Guarino-Ghezzi, S. and L. Kimball. 1996, April. *Transitioning Youth From Secure Treatment to the Community.* Boston, MA: Department of Youth Services.

Guerino, Paul, Paige M. Harrison, and William J. Sabol. 2011. "Prisoners in 2010 (Revised)." December 15. Retrieved April 15, 2012 (http://bjs.ojp.usdoj.gov/index.cfm?ty=tp&tid=13).

Gumperz, John J. and Stephen C. Levinson, eds. 1996. *Rethinking Linguistic Relativity.* Cambridge, UK: Cambridge University Press.

Hadden, Jeffrey K. 2006. "New Religious Movements." Retrieved August 14, 2008 (www.hirr.hartsem.edu/denom/new_religious_movements.html).

Hagan, Frank E. 2011. *Introduction to Criminology,* 7th ed. Thousand Oaks, CA: Sage.

Haines, J. T., Tommy Haines, and Andrew Sherburne [Directors]. 2013. *Gold Fever.* St. Paul, MN: Northland Films.

Hall, Edward T. 1959. *The Silent Language.* New York: Doubleday.

Hall, Edward T. 1983. *The Dance of Life.* Garden City, NY: Anchor Books/Doubleday.

Hall, Edward T. and Mildred Reed Hall. 1992. *An Anthropology of Everyday Life.* New York: Doubleday.

Hall, Richard H. 2002. *Organizations: Structures, Processes, and Outcomes,* 7th ed. Englewood Cliffs, NJ: Prentice Hall.

Hamilton, Rebecca. 2012. "Factbox: Which States Allow Same-Sex Marriage?" *Reuters,* February 13. Retrieved May 27, 2012 (www.reuters.com/article/2012/02/13/us-usa-gaymarriage-states-idUSTRE81C1YH2020213).

Handel, Gerald, Spencer Cahill, and Frederick Elkin. 2007. *Children and Society: The Sociology of Children and Childhood Socialization.* New York: Oxford University Press.

Handwerk, Brian. 2004. "Female Suicide Bombers: Dying to Kill." *National Geographic News,* December 13. Retrieved July 5, 2008 (http://news.nationalgeographic.com/news/2004/12/1213_041213_tv_suicide_bombers.html).

Haniffa, Aziz. 2009. "Financial Crisis Bigger Than Al Qaeda, Says U.S. Intelligence Czar." *Rediff India Abroad,* February 13. Retrieved March 17, 2009 (www.rediff.com/money/2009/feb/15bcrisis-financial-crisis-bigger-threat-than-al-qaeda-says-us-intel-chief.htm).

Hansen, Randall and Katharine Hansen. 2003. "What Do Employers Really Want? Top Skills and Values Employers Seek From Job-Seekers" (Quintessential Careers). Retrieved June 23, 2008 (www.quintcareers.com/job_skills_values.html).

Hardin, Garrett. 1968. "The Tragedy of the Commons." *Science* 162(3859):1243–48.

Harris, Judith Rich. 2009. *The Nurture Assumption: Why Children Turn Out the Way They Do,* Revised and updated ed. New York: Free Press.

Harris, Marvin. 1989. *Cows, Pigs, War, and Witches: The Riddles of Culture.* New York: Random House.

Harris, Paul. 2011. "The Decline and Fall of the American Middle Class." September 13. Retrieved May 17, 2012 (www.guardian.co.uk/commentisfree/cifamerica/2011/sep/13/american-middle-class-poverty).

Harris Interactive. 2009. "Most Prestigious Occupations: Firefighters, Scientists Top List: Prestige of 23 Professions and Occupations." *Marketing Charts.* Retrieved May 17, 2012 (www.marketingcharts.com/topics/behavior-marketing/most-prestigious-occupations-firefighters-scientist-top-list-10045/harris-interactive).

Hart, Betty and Todd R. Risley. 2003. "The Early Catastrophe: The 30 Million Word Gap by Age 3." *American Educator* 27(1):4–9.

Haub, Carl. 2012. "Fact Sheet: World Population Trends 2012." Population Reference Bureau. Retrieved August 25, 2012 (www.prb.org/Publications/Datasheets/2012/world-population-data-sheet/fact-sheet-world-population.aspx).

Hayden, Tom. 2006. "Seeking a New Capitalism in Chiapas." Pp. 348–54 in *Globalization: The Transformation of Social Worlds,* edited by D. Stanley Eitzen and Maxine Baca Zinn. Belmont, CA: Wadsworth.

HealthReform.gov. 2010. "Coverage Denied: How the Current Health Insurance System Leaves Millions Behind." Retrieved January 10, 2010 (www.healthreform.gov/reports/denied_coverage/index.html).

Hearn, Kelly. 2012. "Big Oil Wreaks Havoc in the Amazon, but Communities Are Fighting Back." Pp. 313–16 in *Globalization: The Transformation of Social Worlds,* 3rd ed., edited by D. Stanley Eitzen and Maxine Baca Zinn. Belmont, CA: Wadsworth.

Heilbroner, Robert L. and William Milberg. 2012. *The Making of Economic Society.* Upper Saddle River, NJ: Pearson.

Helgeson, Baird and Jim Ragsdale. 2013. "Same Sex Marriage Prevails." *Minneapolis Star Tribune* (May 14):1.

Henley, Nancy, Mykol Hamilton, and Barrie Thorne. 2000. "Womanspeak and Manspeak: Sex Differences in Communication, Verbal and Nonverbal." Pp. 111–15 in *Sociological Footprints,* edited by Leonard Cargan and Jeanne Ballantine. Belmont, CA: Wadsworth.

Hennigan, Ashley. 2012. "Missing Men: Addressing the College Gender Gap." *Higher Ed Live.* Retrieved September 12, 2012 (http://higheredlive.com/missing-men/).

Herskovitz, Jon. 2012. "Militant South African Union Tells Lonmin to Pay Up." Reuters, September 7. Retrieved September 8, 2012 (www.reuters.com/article/2012/09/07/us-safrica-mines-idUSBRE8860U820120907).

Hertsgaard, Mark. 2003. *The Eagle's Shadow: Why America Fascinates and Infuriates the World.* New York: Picador.

Hesse-Biber, Sharlene Nagy. 2007. *The Cult of Thinness,* 2nd ed. New York: Oxford University Press.

Hewitt, John P. 2007. *Self and Society: A Symbolic Interactionism Social Psychology,* 10th ed. Boston: Allyn & Bacon.

Hewitt, John P. and David Shulman. 2011. *Self and Society: A Symbolic Interactionist Approach to Social Psychology,* 11th ed. Englewood Cliffs, NJ: Prentice Hall.

Heyes, J. D. 2012. "Plastic Waste Garbage Floating in Pacific Ocean Has Increased 100-Fold." *NaturalNews.com,* May 15. Retrieved September 7, 2012 (www.naturalnews.com/035866_garbage_floating_Pacific_Ocean.html).

Hiebert-White, Jane. 2010. "Uninsured Expected to Rise to 52 Million by 2010." *Health Affairs,* June 2. Retrieved January 10, 2010 (http://healthaffairs.org/blog/2009/06/02/52-million-uninsured-americans-by-2010/).

Hill, Catherine and Holly Kearl. 2011. "Crossing the Line: Sexual Harassment at School." Washington, DC: AAUW. November. Retrieved September 20, 2012 (www.aauw.org/learn/research/upload/CrossingTheLine.pdf).

Hinton, Christopher. 2010."Global Military Spending to Outpace GDP Growth in 2010." *Market Watch,* June 18. Retrieved May 10, 2011 (www.marketwatch.com/story/worlds-militaries-see-another-budget-busting-year-2010-06-18).

Hirschi, Travis. [1969] 2002. *Causes of Delinquency.* New Brunswick, NJ: Transaction Publishers.

Hispanic-Americans.com. 2011. "Mexico Leader Likens Drug Battle to Fight Against French." May 6. Retrieved May 9, 2011 (http://hispanic-americans.com/blog/mexiconews/mexican-leader-likens-drug-battle-to-fight-against-french.aspx).

Hochschild, Arlie. 1989. *The Second Shift: Working Parents and the Revolution at Home.* New York: Viking.

Homans, George C. 1974. *Social Behavior: Its Elementary Forms.* New York: Harcourt, Brace Jovanovich.

Horn, Jordana. 2011. "US Sees Slight Increase in Anti-Semitic Incidents." *The Jerusalem Post,* October 4. Retrieved February 9, 2013 (www.jpost.com/JewishWorld/JewishFeatures/Article.aspx?id=240522).

Houlis, Anna Marie. 2011. "Gender Stereotypes in Picture Books are Blamed for Affecting Children." June 13. Retrieved May 23, 2012 (http://annamariehoulis.wordpress.com/2011/06/13/gender-stereotypes-in-picture-books-are-blamed-for-affecting-children/).

House, James S. 1994. "Social Structure and Personality: Past, Present, and Future." Pp. 77–102 in *Sociological Perspectives on Social Psychology,* edited by Karen Cook, Gary Fine, and James S. House. Boston: Allyn & Bacon

Howard, Adam. 2007. *Learning Privilege: Lessons of Power and Identity in Affluent Schooling.* New York: Taylor and Francis.

Howard, Adam and Ruben Gaztambide-Fernandez, eds. 2010. *Educating Elites: Class Privilege and Educational Advantage.* Lanham, MD: Rowman and Littlefield.

Howard, Philip. 2011. "The Upside Downside of Social Media." *Reuters*, August 23. Retrieved October 3, 2012 (http://blogs.reuters.com).

Howard, Philip N. and Steve Jones, eds. 2004. *Society On-Line: The Internet in Context*. Thousand Oaks, CA: Sage.

Hozien, Muhammad. N.d. "Ibn Khaldun: His Life and Work." Retrieved May 7, 2009 (www.muslimphilosophy.com/ik/klf.htm).

Huddy, Leonie and Stanley Feldman. 2006. "Worlds Apart: Blacks and Whites React to Hurricane Katrina." *Du Bois Review* 3(1):97–113. Retrieved July 7, 2011 (http://journals.cambridge.org/action/display Abstract?fromPage=online&aid=462978).

Huebler, Friedrich. 2012. "Adult and Youth Literacy in 2010." *International Education Statistics,* May 31. Retrieved January 27, 2013 (http://huebler .blogspot.com/2012/05/literacy.html)

Huffington Post. 2012a. "10 Countries Spending the Most on Health Care: 24/7 Wall St." March 29. Retrieved August 1, 2012 (www.huffington-post.com/2012/03/29/healthcare-spending-countries_n_1388306. html#s825346&title=1_United_States).

Huffington Post. 2012b. "Shaken By USC Shooting, Chinese Students Still Seek US Colleges." June 4. Retrieved June 4, 2012 (www .huffingtonpost.com/2012/04/12/shaken-by-usc-shooting-ch_n_ 1420171.html).

Huffington Post. 2013. "Supreme Court DOMA Decision Rules Federal Same-Sex Marriage Ban Unconstitutional." Retrieved June 26, 2013 (www.huffingtonpost.com/2013/06/26/supreme-court-doma-decision_n_3454811.html?ref=topbar).

Hughes, Melanie M. 2004. "Armed Conflict, International Linkages, and Women's Parliamentary Representation in Developing Nations." Master's thesis, Department of Sociology, Ohio State University.

Huizinga, David, Rolf Loeber, and Terence P. Thornberry. 1994. "Urban Delinquency and Substance Abuse: Initial Findings." OJJDP Research Summary. Washington, DC: Government Printing Office.

Human Rights Campaign. 2013. "Parenting Laws: Joint Adoption." Retrieved September 3, 2013 (http://www.hrc.org/files/assets/ resources/parenting_joint-adoption_082013.pdf).

"Human Trafficking: Trafficking by the Numbers." 2012. WGBH, October 8. Retrieved October 8, 2012 (www.wgbh.org/articles/Human-Trafficking-Trafficking-by-the-numbers-285).

Humes, Karen R., Nicholas A. Jones, and Roberto R. Ramirez. 2011. "2010 Census Briefs: Overview of Race and Hispanic Origins: 2010." March, p. 1. Retrieved April 7, 2011 (http://www.census.gov/prod/ cen2010/briefs/c2010br-02.pdf).

Hurst, Charles E. 2013. *Social Inequality: Forms, Causes, and Consequences,* 8th ed. Pearson.

Iannaccone, Laurence and William S. Bainbridge. 2010. "Economics of Religion." Pp. 461–75 in *The Routledge Companion to the Study of Religion*, 2nd ed., edited by John Hinnells. New York: Routledge.

IndexMundi. 2012. "Countries." Retrieved February 7, 2013 (http://www .indexmundi.com/factbook/countries).

Infographics. 2012. "What's Happening? Twitter Facts and Figures." Retrieved September 25, 2012 (www.infographicsarchive.com/social-media/twitter-facts-and-figures/).

Infoplease. 2012. "Most Widely Spoken Languages in the World." Retrieved September 30, 2012 (www.Infoplease.com/ipa/A0775272.html).

Infoplease. 2013. "Lowest Literacy Rates." Retrieved August 28, 2013 (www.infoplease.com/world/countries/lowest-literacy-rates.html).

Information Please Database. 2008. "National Voter Turnout in Federal Elections: 1960–2008." Retrieved March 17, 2009 (www.infoplease .com/ipa/A0781453.html/).

Information Please Database. 2010. "Significant Ongoing Armed Conflicts." Retrieved August 5, 2011 (www.infoplease.com/ipa/ A0904550.html).

Ingersoll, Richard M. and Elizabeth Merrill. 2012. "The Status of Teaching as a Profession." In *Schools and Society: A Sociological Approach to Education*, edited by Jeanne H. Ballantine and Joan Z. Spade. Thousand Oaks, CA: Sage Pine Forge.

Inglehart, Ronald. 1997. *Modernization and Postmodernization: Cultural, Economic, and Political Change in 43 Societies*. Princeton, NJ: Princeton University Press.

Inglehart, Ronald and Wayne E. Baker. 2001. "Modernization's Challenge to Traditional Values: Who's Afraid of Ronald McDonald?" *The Futurist* 35(2):16–22.

Inniss, Janis Prince. 2010. "A Closer Look at Interracial Marriage Statistics." *Everyday Sociology*, August 2. Retrieved April 10, 2011 (nortonbooks. typepad.com/everydaysociology/2010/08/a-closer-look-at-inter racial-marriage-statistics.html).

Innocence Project. 2013. "311 Exonerated." Retrieved August 25, 2013 (www.innocenceproject.org/).

Insideschools. 2013. "Harlem Children's Zone Promise Academy Charter School." Retrieved June 16, 2013 (Insideschools.org/high/browse/ school/1393).

International Beliefs and Values Institute. 2012. "Mission." Staunton, VA: Mary Baldwin College. Retrieved March 23, 2012 (www .ibavi.org).

"The International Digital Divide." 2011. *Science Daily*, February 8. Retrieved May 18, 2012 (www.sciencedaily.com/releases/2011/02/ 110208121345.htm).

International Encyclopedia of the Social Sciences. 2008. Retrieved December 21, 2009 (www.encyclopedia.com/doc/1G2-3045300884 .html).

International Institute for Democracy and Electoral Assistance. 2012. "Voter Turnout." Retrieved June 2, 2013 (www.idea.int/vt/).

International Monetary Fund. 2013. "Debt Relief Under the Heavily Indebted Poor Countries (HIPC) Initiative." January 10. Retrieved February 7, 2013 (http://www.imf.org/external/np/exr/facts/hipc .htm).

International Organization for Migration. 2012. "Global Estimates and Trends." Retrieved July 30, 2012 (www.iom.int/jahia/Jahia/about-migration/facts-and-figures/lang/en).

Internet World Stats. 2010. "Internet World Users by Language." Retrieved May 18, 2012 (www.internetworldstats.com/stats7.htm).

Internet World Stats. 2013. "Internet Usage Statistics." Retrieved April 9, 2013 (www.internetworldstats.com/stats.htm).

Inter-Parliamentary Union. 2013. "Women in National Parliaments." Retrieved August 26, 2013 (www.ipu.org/wmn-e/classif.htm).

Inter-university Consortium for Political and Social Research. 2011. "Voting Behavior: The 2008 Election." Retrieved May 16, 2012 (http://www .icpsr.umich.edu/icpsrweb/SETUPS2008/voting.jsp).

Irvine, Leslie. 2004. *If You Tame Me: Understanding Our Connection With Animals*. Philadelphia: Temple University Press.

Irwin, John and Barbara Owen. 2007. *The Warehouse Prison: Disposal of the New Dangerous Class*. New York: Oxford University Press.

Isaacs, John. 2011. "Current U.S. and Russian Nuclear Weapons Stockpiles." Retrieved December 21, 2011 (http://armscontrolcenter. org/policy/nuclearweapons/articles/031009_current_nuclear_weap-ons_stockpiles/).

"It Begins With Us." 2011. YouTube. Retrieved November 1, 2012 (www .youtube.com/watch?v=f-VZLvVF1FQ).

Jackman, Robert W. 1993. *Power Without Force: The Political Capacity of Nation-States*. Ann Arbor: University of Michigan Press.

Jackson, Philip W. 1968. *Life in Classrooms*. New York: Holt, Rinehart & Winston.

James, Susan Donaldson. 2011. "Census 2010: One-quarter of Gay Couples Raising Children." *ABC News,* June 23. Retrieved June 5, 2012 (http://abcnews.go.com/Health/sex-couples-census-data-trick-les-quarter-raising-children/story?id=13850332).

James, William. [1890] 1934. *The Principles of Psychology*. Mineola, NY: Dover.

Japan Institute for Labour Policy and Training. 2009. "The Gender Gap in the Japanese Labor Market." February 26. Retrieved November 8, 2009 (www.ikjeld.com/en/news/91/the-gender-gap-in-the-labor -market).

Jarrett, R. L., P. J. Sullivan, and N. D. Watkins. 2005. "Developing Social Capital Through Participation in Organized Youth Programs: Qualitative Insights From Three Programs." *Journal of Community Psychology* 33(1):41–55.

Jay, Meg. 2012. "The Downside of Cohabiting Before Marriage." *The New York Times Sunday Review,* April 14. Retrieved June 5, 2012 (www.nytimes.com/2012/04/15/opinion/sunday/the-downside-of-cohabiting-before-marriage.html?pagewanted=all).

Jayson, Sharon. 2011. "Cohabitation Numbers Jump 13%, Linked to Job Losses." *USA Today.* Retrieved June 5, 2012 (www.usatoday.com/news/nation/census/2010-09-24-cohabitation24ONLINE_ST_N.htm).

Jelen, Ted, ed. 2002. *Sacred Markets, Sacred Canopies: Essays on Religious Markets and Religious Pluralism*: New York: Rowman & Littlefield.

Jencks, Christopher. 1972. *Inequality: A Reassessment of the Effects of Family and Schooling in America.* New York: Basic Books.

Jencks, Christopher, ed. 1979. *Who Gets Ahead? The Determinants of Economic Success in America.* New York: Harper & Row.

Jencks, Christopher. 1992. *Rethinking Social Policy: Race, Poverty, and the Underclass.* Cambridge, MA: Harvard University Press.

Johnson, David. 2011. "Income Gap: Is It Widening?" U.S. Census Bureau, September 15. Retrieved May 17, 2012 (http://blogs.census.gov/2011/09/15/income-gap-is-it-widening/).

Johnson, David W. and Frank P. Johnson. 2006. *Joining Together: Group Theory and Group Skills,* 9th ed. Boston: Allyn & Bacon.

Johnson, Paul. 2005. "Majority of Americans Believe Homosexuality Should Not Be Illegal, Support Partner Rights: Gallup Poll." Retrieved August 22, 2006 (www.sodomylaws.org/usa/usnews141.htm).

Johnson, Robert. 2002. *Hard Time: Understanding and Reforming the Prison.* Belmont, CA: Wadsworth/Thompson Learning.

Johnson, Steven. 2009. "How Twitter Will Change the Way We Live (in 140 Characters or Less)." *Time,* June 15, pp. 32–37.

Kain, Edward. 2005. "Family Change and the Life Course: Cohorts and Social Change in the Year 2050." Paper presented at the annual meetings of the Southern Sociological Society, Charlotte, NC.

Kaiser Family Foundation. 2010. "G8 leaders to Discuss Economic Policy, Developing World, Maternal and Child Health, Haitian Rebuilding." June 25. Retrieved July 13, 2012 (http://globalhealth.Kff.org/Daily-Reports/2010/June/25/GH-062510-G8-G20-Summits.aspx).

Kalmijn, Matthijs and Gerbert Kraaykamp. 1996. "Race, Cultural Capital, and Schooling: An Analysis of Trends in the United States." *Sociology of Education* 69(1):22–34.

Kan, Man Yee, Oriel Sullivan, and Jonathan Gershuny. 2011. "Gender Convergence in Domestic Work: Discerning the Effects of Interactional and Institutional Barriers from Large-Scale Data" *Sociology* 45(2):234–51.

Kanter, Rosabeth Moss. 1977. *Men and Women of the Corporation.* New York: Basic Books.

Kanter, Rosabeth Moss. 1983. *The Change Masters: Innovation for Productivity in the American Corporation.* New York: Simon & Schuster.

Kanter, Rosabeth Moss. 2001a. "Creating the Culture for Innovation." In *Leading for Innovation: Managing for Results,* edited by Frances Hesselbein, Marshall Goldsmith, and Iain Somerville. San Francisco: Jossey-Bass.

Kanter, Rosabeth Moss. 2001b. "From Spare Change to Real Change: The Social Sector as Beta Site for Business Innovation." *Harvard Business Review on Innovation* 77(3):122–33.

Kanter, Rosabeth Moss. 2005. *Commitment and Community.* Cambridge, MA: Harvard University Press.

Kao, Grace. 2004. "Social Capital and Its Relevance to Minority and Immigrant Populations." *Sociology of Education* 77:172–76.

Kaplan, Howard B. and Robert J. Johnson. 1991. "Negative Social Sanctions and Juvenile Delinquency: Effects of Labeling in a Model of Deviant Behavior." *Social Science Quarterly* 72(1):117.

Karthikeyan, D. 2011. "Dalits Pay the Price for Their Political Assertion." *The Hindu: Tamil Nadu,* February 18, p. 1.

Kean, Sam. 2007. "What's in a Name?" *The New York Times,* October 28. Retrieved May 21, 2012 (www.nytimes.com/2007/10/28/magazine/28wwln-idealab-t.html).

Keigher, Ashley and Freddie Cross. 2010. "Teacher Attrition and Mobility." School and Staffing Survey. IES. NCES. Retrieved April 17, 2011 (http://nces.ed.gov/pubs2010/2010353.pdf).

Kelber, Harry. 2012. "Manufacturers Are Hiring Workers in America, But Offer a Sharp Drop in Wages and Benefits." *The Labor Educator,* January 2. Retrieved May 28, 2012 (www.laboreducator.org/lt120102.htm).

Kendall, Diane. 2004. *Sociology in Our Times: The Essentials,* 4th ed. Belmont, CA: Wadsworth.

Kephart, William M. 1977. *The Family, Society, and the Individual,* 4th ed. Boston: Houghton-Mifflin.

Kerbo, Harold R. 2008. *Social Stratification and Inequality,* 7th ed. Boston: McGraw-Hill.

Kessler, Sarah. 2011. "Study: 80% of Children Under 5 Use Internet Weekly." *Technology Live,* March 15. Retrieved April 9, 2013 (http://content.usatoday.com/communities/technologylive/post/2011/03/study-80-percent-of-children-under-5-use-internet-weekly/)

Khazaleh, Lorenz. 2009. "Internet Fatwas Cautiously Support Divorce Among Women" *CULCOM,* October 29. Retrieved January 4, 2010 (www.culcom.uio.no/english/news/2009/bogstad.html).

Kids Count Data Center. 2010. "Children in Single-Parent Families by Race-2010." *The Annie E. Casey Foundation.* Retrieved June 6, 2012 (http://datacenter.kidscount.org/data/acrosstates/Rankings.aspx?ind=107).

Killian, Caitlin. 2006. *North African Women in France: Gender, Culture, and Identity.* Palo Alto, CA: Stanford University Press.

Kim, Min-Sun, Katsuya Tasaki, In-Duk Kim, and Hye-ryeon Lee. 2007. "The Influence of Social Status on Communication Predispositions Focusing on Independent and Interdependent Self-Construals." *Journal of Asian Pacific Communication* 17(2):303–329.

Kindlon, Dan and Michael Thompson. 2000. *Raising Cain: Protecting the Emotional Life of Boys.* New York: Ballantine Books.

Kingkade, Tyler. 2012. "Youth Vote 2012 Turnout: Exit Polls Show Greater Share of Electorate Than in 2008." *Huffington Post,* November 7. Retrieved November 8, 2012 (www.huffingtonpost.com/2012/11/07/youth-vote-2012-turnout-exit-polls_n_2086092.html).

Kitano, Harry H., Pauline Aqbayani, and Diane de Anda. 2005. *Race Relations,* 6th edition. Englewood Cliffs, NJ: Prentice Hall.

Knapp, Mark L. and Judith A. Hall. 1997. *Nonverbal Communication in Human Interaction,* 4th ed. Fort Worth: Harcourt Brace.

Kodish, Bruce I. 2003. "What We Do With Language—What It Does With Us." *ETC: A Review of General Semantics* 60:383–95.

Kohlberg, Lawrence. 1971. "From Is to Ought." Pp. 151–284 in *Cognitive Development and Epistemology,* edited by T. Mischel. New York: Academic Press.

Kohn, Melvin. 1989. *Class and Conformity: A Study of Values,* 2nd ed. Chicago: University of Chicago Press.

Koleth, Elsa. 2012. "Asylum Seekers: An Update: Briefing Paper No. 1/2012." NSW Parliamentary Library. Retrieved July 30, 2012 (www.parliament.nsw.gov.au/prod/parment/publications.OD189A/SFile/Asylum%20seekers%20Final%20March%20202012.pdf).

Konrad, Walicia. 2012. "As Medicare Fraud Evolves, Vigilance is Required." *The New York Times,* September 11. Retrieved April 18, 2013 (www.nytimes.com/2012/09/12/business/retirementspecial/medicare-fraud-victimizes-patients-and-taxpayers.html?_r=0)

Korgen, Kathleen Odell, Jonathan M. White, and Shelley K. White. 2013. *Sociologists in Action: Sociology, Social Change, and Social Justice,* 2nd ed. Thousand Oaks, CA: Sage.

Korte, Charles and Stanley Milgram. 1970. "Acquaintance Networks Between Racial Groups." *Journal of Personality and Social Psychology* 15:101–108.

Kosmin, Barry and Ariela Keysar. 2009. *American Religious Identification Survey (ARIS 2008) Summary Report.* March. Hartford, CT: Trinity College.

Kottak, Conrad Phillip. 2010. *Prime-Time Society: An Anthropological Analysis of Television and Culture,* Updated edition. Walnut Creek, CA: Left Coast Press.

Kozol, Jonathan. 2005. "Confections of Apartheid: A Stick-and-Carrot Pedagogy for the Children of Our Inner-City Poor." *Phi Delta Kappan* (December):265–75.

Kozol, Jonathan. 2006. *The Shame of the Nation: The Restoration of Apartheid Schooling in America.* New York: Crown.

Kozol, Jonathan. 2012. *Fire in the Ashes: Twenty-five Years Among the Poorest Children in America.* New York: Random House Crown Publishing Group.

Kramer, Laura. 2010. *The Sociology of Gender: A Brief Introduction,* 3rd ed. New York: Oxford University Press.

Kreider, Rose M. 2010. "Increase in Opposite-Sex Cohabiting Couples From 2009 to 2010 in the Annual Social and Economic Supplement to the Current Population Survey." U.S. Census Bureau, September 15. Retrieved April 11, 2011 (www.census.gov/population/www/socdemo/Inc-Opp-sex-2009-to-2010.pdf).

Kreider, Rose M. and Diana B. Elliott. 2009. "America's Families and Living Arrangements: 2007." U.S. Census Bureau *Current Population Reports,* P20-561. Retrieved January 24, 2013 (http://www.census.gov/prod/2009pubs/p20-561.pdf).

Kreider, Rose M. and Renee Ellis. 2011. "Living Arrangements of Children: 2009." *U.S. Census Bureau,* June. Retrieved May 4, 2013 (www.census.gov/prod/2011pubs/p70-126.pdf).

Kristof, Nicholas and Sheryl WuDunn. 2009. *Half the Sky: Turning Oppression into Opportunity for Women Worldwide.* New York: Alfred A. Knopf.

Kübler-Ross, Elizabeth. 1997. *Death, the Final Stage of Growth,* Rev. ed. New York: Scribner.

Kuhn, Manford. 1964. "Major Trends in Symbolic Interaction Theory in the Past Twenty-Five Years." *Sociological Quarterly* 5:61–84.

Kuhn, Thomas. 1970. *The Structure of Scientific Revolutions,* 2nd ed. Chicago: University of Chicago Press.

Kumlin, Johanna. 2006. "The Sex Wage Gap in Japan and Sweden: The Role of Human Capital, Workplace Sex Composition, and Family Responsibility." *European Sociological Review* (advance access published online on December 18). Retrieved April 17, 2010 (http://esr.oxfordjournals.org/cgi/content/abstract/23/2/203).

Kurtz, Lester R. 2007. *Gods in the Global Village,* 2nd ed. Thousand Oaks, CA: Pine Forge Press.

Lacayo, Richard. 1993. "Cult of Death." *Time* (March 15):36.

Lake, Robert. 1990. "An Indian Father's Plea." *Teacher Magazine* 2(September):48–53.

Lamanna, Mary Ann and Agnes Riedmann. 2010. *Marriages and Families: Making Choices Throughout the Life Cycle,* 11th ed. Belmont, CA: Wadsworth.

Lambert, Yves. 2000. "Religion in Modernity as a New Axial Age: Secularization or New Religious Forms?" Pp. 95–125 in *The Secularization Debate,* edited by William H. Swatos, Jr. and Daniel V. A. Olson. Lanham, MD: Rowman & Littlefield.

Landau, Elizabeth. 2009. "Life Expectancy Could Be Topic in Health Care Debate." June 11. Retrieved April 17, 2010 (www.cnn.com/2009/HEALTH/06/ . . . /life.expectancy.health.care).

Landler, Mark and Brian Stelter. 2009. "Washington Taps Into a Potent New Force in Diplomacy." *New York Times,* June 17, p. A12. Retrieved December 22, 2009 (www.nytimes.com).

Langworth, Richard, ed. 2009. *Churchill by Himself: The Definitive Collection of Quotations.* Jackson, TN: Public Affairs.

Lareau, Annette. 2003. *Unequal Childhoods: Class, Race, and Family Life.* Berkeley: University of California Press.

Larsen, Jensine. 2013. "The Day Women of the Congo Seized Control of the Internet." *The Huffington Post,* March 5. Retrieved May 3, 2013 (www.huffingtonpost.com/news/congo-rape-weapon-of-war).

Lazare, Aaron. 2004. *On Apology.* New York: Oxford University Press.

Lazaridis, Gabriella. 2011. *Security, Insecurity and Migration in Europe.* Farnham, UK: Ashgate Publishing, Ltd.

Lazerwitz, Bernard, J. Alan Winter, Arnold Dashefsky, and Ephraim Tabory. 1998. *Jewish Choices: American Jewish Denominationalism.* Albany: SUNY Press.

Leach, Edmund R. 1979. "Ritualization in Man in Relation to Conceptual and Social Development." Pp. 333–37 in *Reader in Comparative Religion,* 3rd ed., edited by William A. Lessa and Evon Z. Vogt. New York: Harper & Row.

LeBon, Gustave. [1895] 1960. *The Crowd: A Study of the Popular Mind.* New York: Viking.

Lechner, Frank J. and John Boli. 2005. *World Culture: Origins and Consequences.* Malden, MA: Blackwell.

Lederer, Edith M. 2012. "Human Trafficking Victims: 2.4 Million People Across the Globe Are Trafficked for Labor, Sex." *Huff Post World,* April 3. Retrieved January 21, 2013 (www.huffingtonpost.com/2012/04/03/human-trafficking-victims_n_1401673.html).

Lederman, Josh. 2012. "Voter Turnout Shaping Up to Be Lower Than 2008." *Huffington Post,* November 7. Retrieved November 11, 2012 (http://www.huffingtonpost.com/2012/11/07/voter-turnout_n_2088810.html).

Lee, Jennifer and Frank D. Bean. 2004. "America's Changing Color Lines: Immigration, Race/Ethnicity, and Multiracial Identification." *Annual Review of Sociology* 30(August):222–42.

Lee, Jennifer and Frank D. Bean. 2007. "Redrawing the Color Line?" *City and Community* 6(1):49–62.

Legters, Nettie E. 2001. "Teachers as Workers in the World System." Pp. 417–26 in *Schools and Society: A Sociological Approach to Education,* edited by Jeanne H. Ballantine and Joan Z. Spade. Belmont, CA: Wadsworth.

Lehman, Edward C., Jr. 1985. *Women Clergy: Breaking Through Gender Barriers.* New Brunswick, NJ: Transaction.

Leit, R. A., J. J. Gray, and H. G. Pope. 2002. "The Media's Representation of the Ideal Male Body." *International Journal of Eating Disorders* 31(3):334–38.

Lemert, Edwin M. 1951. *Social Pathology.* New York: McGraw-Hill.

Lemert, Edwin M. 1972. *Human Deviance, Social Problems, and Social Control,* 2nd ed. Englewood Cliffs, NJ: Prentice Hall.

Lenski, Gerhard E. 1966. *Human Societies.* New York: McGraw-Hill.

Lerner, Richard M. 1992. "Sociobiology and Human Development: Arguments and Evidence." *Human Development* 35(1):12–51.

Leslie, Gerald R. and Sheila K. Korman. 1989. *The Family in Social Context,* 7th ed. New York: Oxford University Press.

Leung, K., S. Lau, and W. L. Lam. 1998. *Parenting Styles and Academic Achievement: A Cross-Cultural Study.* Detroit, MI: Wayne State University Press.

Levin, Jack and Jack McDevitt. 2003. *Hate Crimes Revisited: America's War on Those Who Are Different.* Boulder, CO: Westview.

Levinson, Stephen C. 2000. "Yeli Dnye and the Theory of Basic Color Terms." *Journal of Linguistic Anthropology* 1:3–55.

Levitt, Judith. 2012. "Women as Priests." *New York Times,* September 29. Retrieved June 20, 2013 (www.nytimes.com/2012/09/30/opinion/sunday/women-as-priests.html).

Levitt, Peggy. 2001. *The Transnational Villagers.* Berkeley: University of California Press.

Levitt, Peggy. 2007. *God Needs No Passport: Immigrants and the Changing American Religious Landscape.* New York: New Press.

Levitt, Peggy and Mary Waters, eds. 2006. *The Changing Face of Home: The Transnational Lives of the Second Generation.* Russell Sage Foundation. Retrieved June 27, 2011 (www.russellsage.org/publications/changing-face-home).

Lewin, Tamar. 2006. "At Colleges, Women Are Leaving Men in the Dust." *The New York Times*, July 9, pp. A1, 18.

Lewin, Tamar. 2012. "At the University of Texas, Admissions as a Mystery." *The New York Times*, April 1. Retrieved June 24, 2013 (/www.nytimes.com/2012/04/02/education/university-of-texas-mysterious-admissions-process.html?_r=0).

Lewis, Maureen A. and Marlaine E. Lockheed. 2006. *Inexcusable Absence: Why 60 Million Girls Still Aren't in School and What to Do About It.* Washington, DC: Center for Global Development.

Library of Congress. 2010. "Margaret Mead: Human Nature and the Power of Culture." July 27. Retrieved March 7, 2012 (www.loc.gov/exhibits/mead/field-sepik.html).

Lichter, Daniel T., Richard N. Turner, and Sharon Sassler. 2010. "Marriage and Family in the New Millennium: Papers in Honor of Steven L. Nock." *Social Science Research* 39(5):754–65. Retrieved April 11, 2011 (doi:10.1016/j.ssresearch.2009.11.002).

Lincoln, Erik and Laurence Mamiya. 1990. *The Black Church in the African American Experience.* Durham, NC: Duke University Press.

Lindberg, Richard and Vesna Markovic. N.d. "Organized Crime Outlook in the New Russia: Russia Is Paying the Price of a Market Economy in Blood." Retrieved January 4, 2001 (www.search-international.com/Articles/crime/russiacrime.htm).

Lindow, Megan. June 20, 2009. "South Africa's Rape Crisis: 1 in 4 Men Say They've Done It." *Time/World.* Retrieved February 27, 2012 (www.time.com/time/world/article/0,8599,1906000,00.html).

Lindsay, James M. 2006. "Global Warming Heats Up." Pp. 307–13 in *Globalization: The Transformation of Social Worlds,* edited by D. Stanley Eitzen and Maxine Baca Zinn. Belmont, CA: Wadsworth.

Lindsey, Linda L. 2011. *Gender Roles: A Sociological Perspective,* 5th ed. Englewood Cliffs, NJ: Prentice Hall.

Linton, Ralph. 1937. *The Study of Man.* New York: D. Appleton-Century.

Lips, Hilary M. 2010. *Sex and Gender: An Introduction,* 9th ed. Boston: McGraw-Hill.

Liptak, Adam. 2008. "U.S. Prison Population Dwarfs that of Other Nations." *The New York Times,* April 23. Retrieved April 15, 2012 (www.nytimes.com/2008/04/23/world/americas/23iht-23prisons.12253738.html).

Liptak, Adam. 2012. "Justices Take Up Race as a Factor in College Entry." *The New York Times,* February 21. Retrieved May 12, 2012 (www.nytimes.com/2012/02/22/us/justices-to-hear-case-on-affirmative-action-in-higher-education.html?pagewanted=all).

Liptak, Adam. 2013a. "Justices Step Up Scrutiny of Race in College Entry" *The New York Times,* June 24. Retrieved June 24, 2013 (www.nytimes.com/2013/06/25/us/affirmative-action-decision.html?pagewanted=all&_r=0).

Liptak, Adam. 2013b. "Supreme Court Bolsters Gay Marriage With Two Major Rulings." *The New York Times,* June 27. Retrieved June 27, 2013 (www.nytimes.com/2013/06/27/us/politics/supreme-court-gay-marriage.html?nl=todaysheadlines&emc=edit_th_20130627&_r=0).

Liska, Allen E. 1999. *Perspectives in Deviance,* 3rd ed. Englewood Cliffs, NJ: Prentice Hall.

Lofgren, Orvar. 1999. *On Holiday: A History of Vacationing.* Berkeley: University of California Press.

Lofgren, Orvar. 2010. "The Global Beach." Pp. 37–55 in *Tourists and Tourism,* 2nd ed., edited by Sharon Bohn Gmelch. Long Grove, IL: Waveland Press.

Lofquist, Daphne. 2011. "Same-Sex Couple Households." *American Community Survey Briefs* (September). Retrieved August 27, 2013 (http://www.census.gov/prod/2011pubs/acsbr10-03.pdf).

Loftsdottir, Kristin. 2004. "When Nomads Lose Cattle: Wodaabe Negotiations of Ethnicity." *African Sociological Review* 8(2): 55–76.

Longman, Timothy. 2005. "Rwanda: Achieving Equality or Serving an Authoritarian State?" Pp. 133–150 in *Women in African Parliaments,* edited by Gretchen Bauer and Hannah Britton. Boulder, CO: Lynne Reinner.

Lopez, Ian F. Haney. 1996. *White by Law.* New York: New York University Press.

Lopez-Garza, Marta. 2002. "Convergence of the Public and Private Spheres: Women in the Informal Economy." *Race, Gender, and Class* 9(3):175–92.

Lopreato, Joseph. 2001. "Sociobiological Theorizing: Evolutionary Sociology" Pp. 405–33 in *Handbook of Sociological Theory.* Secaucus, NJ: Springer.

Lorber, Judith. 1998. "Reinventing the Sexes: The Biomedical Construction of Femininity and Masculinity." *Contemporary Society* 27(5): 498–99.

Lorber, Judith. 2009. *Gender Inequality: Feminist Theories and Politics.* New York: Oxford University Press.

Lorber, Judith and Lisa Jean Moore. 2007. *Gendered Bodies.* Los Angeles, CA: Roxbury.

Lorber, Judith and Lisa Jean Moore. 2011. *Gendered Bodies: Feminist Perspectives,* 2nd ed. New York: Oxford University Press.

Lorillard, Didi. 2011. "What's Going on With the Venerable State of Marriage?" *GoLocal Lifestyle.* Retrieved June 4, 2012 (www.golocalprov.com/lifestyle/modern-manners-etiquette-sharing-household-chores/).

Lotfi Yaser, Ali Ayar, and Simin Shams. 2012. "The Relation Between Religious Practice and Committing Suicide: Common and Suicidal People in Darehshahr, Iran." *Procedia—Social and Behavioral Sciences* July 16–18(50):1051–60.

Loy, Irwin. 2012. "Observers: Cambodian Vote Improved but Problems Remain." *Voice of America.* Retrieved July 25, 2012 (www.voanews.com/content/observers-cambodian-elections-improved-but-problems-remain/1146999.html).

Luhby, Tami. 2012. "Worsening Wealth Inequality by Race." *CNN Money,* June 21. Retrieved April 28, 2013 (http://money.cnn.com/2012/06/21/news/economy/wealth-gap-race/index.htm)

Luhman, Reid and Stuart Gilman. 1980. *Race and Ethnic Relations: The Social and Political Experience of Minority Groups.* Belmont, CA: Wadsworth.

Lumsden, Charles J. and Edward O. Wilson. 1981. *Genes, Mind, and Culture: The Coevolutionary Process.* Cambridge, MA: Harvard University Press.

Luscombe, Belinda. 2010. "Marriage: What's It Good For?" *Time* 176(November 29):48–56.

Lyons, Linda. 2002. "Church Reform: Women in the Clergy." Gallup, May 7. Retrieved August 8, 2011 (http://www.gallup.com/poll/indicators/indreligion.asp).

Machalek, Richard and Michael W. Martin. 2010. "Evolution, Biology, and Society: A Conversation for the 21st Century Classroom." *Teaching Sociology* 38(1):35–45.

Macionis, John. 2012. *Sociology,* 14th ed. Upper Saddle River, NJ: Prentice Hall.

Mackey, Robert. 2011, April 23. "Social Media Accounts of the Protests in Syria." The Lede Weblog, *New York Times.* Retrieved October 3, 2012 (thelede.blogs.nytimes.com).

Mackey, Robert. 2012. "Update on Rage Over Anti-Islam Film." The Lede Weblog, *New York Times,* September 12. Retrieved October 2, 2012 (thelede.blogs.nytimes.com).

Mackey, Robert and Liam Stack. 2012. "Obscure Film Mocking Muslim Prophet Sparks Anti-U.S. Protests in Egypt and Libya." The Lede Weblog, *New York Times,* September 11. Retrieved October 2, 2012 (thelede.blogs.nytimes.com).

MacLeod, Jay. 2008. *Ain't No Makin' It: Aspirations and Attainment in a Low-Income Neighborhood,* 3rd ed. Boulder, CO: Westview.

Madden, Mary and Kathryn Zickuhr. 2011. "65% of Online Adults Use Social Networking Sites." *Pew Internet.* Retrieved May 25, 2012 (http://pewinternet.org/Reports/2011/Social-Networking-Sites.aspx).

Maglaty, Jeanne. 2011. "When Did Girls Start Wearing Pink?" Retrieved May 9, 2013 (www.smithsonianmag.com/arts-culture/When-Did-Girls-Start-Wearing-Pink.html).

Mahoney, Brian. 2012. "NBA 'Set The Tone' With Black Coaches." *Athletic Business Daily* E-News, April 27. Retrieved May 10, 2012 (http://athleticbusiness.com/articles/lexisnexis.aspx?Inarticleid=16545818 46&Intopicid=136030023).

"Male Dominance Causes Rape." 2008. *Journal of Feminist Insight*, December 8. Retrieved April 8, 2011 (http://journaloffeministinsight.blogspot.com/2008/12/male-dominance-causes-rape.html).

Malthus, Thomas R. [1798] 1926. *An Essay on the Principle of Population.* London: Macmillan.

Manning, Wendy D., Monica A. Longmore, and Peggy C. Giordano. 2007. "The Changing Institution of Marriage: Adolescents' Expectations to Cohabit and to Marry." *Journal of Marriage and Family* 69(August):559–75.

Marger, Martin N. 2012. *Race and Ethnic Relations: American and Global Perspectives,* 9th ed. Belmont, CA: Wadsworth.

Markoff, John and Somini Sengupta. 2011. "Separating You and Me? 4.74 Degrees." *The New York Times,* November 21. Retrieved September 25, 2012 (www.nytimes.com/2011/11/22/technolgoy/between-you-and-me-4-74-degrees.html).

Marti, Geraldo. 2009. "Affinity, Identity, and Transcendence: The Experience of Religious Racial Integration in Diverse Congregations" *Journal for the Scientific Study of Religion* 48(March):54–96.

Martin, Michel and Gwen Thompkins. 2009. "Proposed Uganda Law: If You See a Homosexual, Call The Police." National Public Radio: "Tell Me More," December 18. Retrieved April 12, 2011 (www.npr.org/templates/story/story.php?storyId=121605525).

Martin, Patricia Yancey and Robert A. Hummer. 1989. "Fraternities and Rape on Campus." *Gender and Society* 3(4):457–73.

Martineau, Harriet. [1837] 1962. *Society in America.* Garden City, NY: Doubleday.

Martineau, Harriet. 1838. *How to Observe Manners and Morals.* London: Charles Knight & Co.

Marty, Martin E. and R. Scott Appleby, eds. 1991. *Fundamentalism Observed.* Chicago: University of Chicago Press.

Marty, Martin E. and R. Scott Appleby, eds. 2004. *Accounting for Fundamentalism: The Dynamic Character of Movements.* Chicago: University of Chicago Press.

Marx, Karl. [1844] 1963. "Contribution to the Critique of Hegel's Philosophy of Right." Pp. 43–59 in *Karl Marx: Early Writings,* translated and edited by T. B. Bottomore. New York: McGraw-Hill.

Marx, Karl. [1844] 1964. *The Economic and Philosophical Manuscripts of 1844.* New York: International Publishers.

Marx, Karl and Friedrich Engels. [1848] 1969. *The Communist Manifesto.* Baltimore: Penguin.

Marx, Karl and Friedrich Engels. 1955. *Selected Work in Two Volumes.* Moscow: Foreign Language Publishing House.

Massey, Douglas S. 2007. *Categorically Unequal: The American Stratification System.* New York: Russell Sage.

Massey, Douglas S. and Nancy A. Denton. 1998. *American Apartheid: Segregation and the Making of the Underclass.* Cambridge, MA: Harvard University Press.

Mattingly, Marybeth and Liana C. Sayer. 2006. "Under Pressure: Trends and Gender Differences in the Relationship Between Free Time and Feeling Rushed." *Journal of Marriage and Family* 68(1):205–21.

Mayflower Church. 2013. "An Earthwise Congregation." Retrieved September 7, 2013 (http://www.mayflowermpls.org/social-justice/earthwise).

McAdam, Doug. 1999. *Political Process and the Development of Black Insurgency, 1930–1970,* 2nd ed. Chicago: University of Chicago Press.

McAdam, Doug. 2003. "Beyond Structural Analysis: Toward a More Dynamic Understanding of Social Movements." Pp. 281–198 in *Social Movements and Networks: Relational Approaches to Collective Action,* edited by Mario Diani and Doug McAdam. New York: Oxford University Press.

McArdle, Megan 2012. "The College Bubble: Is College a Lousy Investment?" *Newsweek,* September 17, pp. 22–26.

McCaghy, Charles H., Timothy A. Capron, J. D. Jamieson, and Sandra Harley Carey. 2006. *Deviant Behavior: Crime, Conflict, and Interest Groups,* 7th ed. Boston: Allyn & Bacon.

McCarthy, John D. and Mayer N. Zald. 1977. "Resource Mobilization and Social Movements: A Partial Theory." *American Journal of Sociology* 82(6):1212–41.

McCrummen, Stephanie. 2008. "Women Run the Show in a Recovering Rwanda." *The Washington Post,* October 27. Retrieved May 6, 2011 (www.washingtonpost.com/wp-dyn/content/article/2008/10/26/AR2008102602197.html).

McDonald, Michael. 2009. "2008 General Election Turnout Rates." Retrieved July 11, 2009 (http://elections.gmu.edu/Turnout_2008G.html).

McEvoy, Alan W. and Jeff B. Brookings. 2008. *If She Is Raped: A Guidebook for the Men in Her Life,* 4th ed., abridged. Tampa, FL: Teal Ribbon Books.

McGuire, Meredith. 2002. *Religion: The Social Context,* 5th ed. Belmont, CA: Wadsworth.

McIntosh, Peggy. 1992. "White Privilege and Male Privilege: A Personal Account of Coming to See Correspondences through Work in Women's Studies." Pp. 70–81 in *Race, Class, and Gender: An Anthology,* edited by Margaret A. Anderson and Patricia Hill Collins. Belmont, CA: Wadsworth.

McIntosh, Peggy. 2002. "White Privilege: Unpacking the Invisible Knapsack." Pp. 97–101 in *White Privilege: Essential Readings on the Other Side of Racism,* edited by Paula S. Rothenberg. New York: Worth.

McKelvie, Samuel R. 1926. "What the Movies Meant to the Farmer." *Annals of the American Academy of Political and Social Science* 128(November):131.

McKie, Linda and Samantha Callan. 2012. *Understanding Families: A Global Introduction.* Thousand Oaks: Sage.

McNall, Scott G. and Sally Allen McNall. 1983. *Plains Families: Exploring Sociology Through Social History.* New York: St. Martin's Press.

McPhail, Deborah, Brenda Beagan, and Gwen E. Chapman. 2012. "'I Don't Want to Be Sexist But . . .' Denying and Re-Inscribing Gender Through Food." *Food, Culture & Society* 15(3):473–89.

McVey, G., S. Tweed, and E. Blackmore. 2004. "Dieting Among Preadolescent and Young Adolescent Females." *CMAJ*(May 11):1559–61. Retrieved May 23, 2012 (www.ncbi.nlm.nih.gov/pubmed/15136549).

Mead, Frank, Samuel Hill, and Craig Atwood, eds. 2005. *Handbook of Denominations in the United States,* 12th ed. Nashville, TN: Abingdon Press.

Mead, George Herbert. [1934] 1962. *Mind, Self, and Society.* Chicago: University of Chicago Press.

Mead, Margaret. [1935] 1963. *Sex and Temperament in Three Primitive Societies.* New York: William Morrow.

Medical News Today. 2009. "Women's Health." September 4. Retrieved January 6, 2010 (www.medicalnewstoday.com/articles/162997.php).

Mehan, Hugh. 1992. "Understanding Inequality in Schools: The Contribution of Interpretive Studies." *Sociology of Education* 65(1):1–20.

Mehra, Bharat, Cecelia Merkel, and Ann P. Bishop. 2004. "The Internet for Empowerment of Minority and Marginalized Users." *New Media and Society* 6:781–802.

Melton, J. Gordon. 1992. *Encyclopedic Handbook of Cults in America,* Revised and updated ed. London: Routledge.

Meltzer, B. 1978. "Mead's Social Psychology." Pp. 15–27 in *Symbolic Interactionism: A Reader in Social Psychology,* 3rd ed., edited by J. Manis and B. Meltzer. Boston: Allyn & Bacon.

Mental Health America. 2011. "Bullying in Schools: Harassment Puts Gay Youth at Risk." Retrieved April 17, 2011 (www.nmha.org/index.cfm?objectid=CA866DCF-1372-4D20-C8EB26EEB30B9982).

Menzel, Peter and Faith D'Aluisio. 1998. *Man Eating Bugs.* Berkeley, CA: Ten Speed Press.

Merton, Robert K. 1938. "Social Structure and Anomie." *American Sociological Review* 3(October):672–82.

Merton, Robert K. [1942] 1973. *The Sociology of Science: Theoretical and Empirical Investigations.* Chicago: University of Chicago Press.

Merton, Robert K. 1949. "Discrimination and the American Creed." Pp. 99–126 in *Discrimination and American Welfare,* edited by Robert M. MacIver. New York: Harper.

Merton, Robert K. 1968a. "Social Structure and Anomie." *American Sociological Review* 3(October):672–82.

Merton, Robert K. 1968b. *Social Theory and Social Structure,* 2nd ed. New York: Free Press.

Metropolitan Community Churches. 2013. "Our Churches." Retrieved August 27, 2013 (http://mccchurch.org/ourchurches).

Michael, John. N.d. "Pros and Cons of Private Prisons." Retrieved February 9, 2012 (www.ehow.com/info_8110862_pros-cons-private-prisons.html).

Michels, Robert. [1911] 1967. *Political Parties.* New York: Free Press.

Michon, Kathleen. 2013. "Federal Marriage Benefits Denied to Same-Sex Couples." NOLO. Retrieved May 3, 2013 (www.nolo.com/lega-ency-clopedia/same-sex-couples-federal -marriage-benefits-30326.html).

Migration Information Source. 2011. Retrieved May 15, 2011 (www.migrationinformation.org/Resources/unitedstates.cfm).

Mikkelson, Barbara and David P. Mikkelson. 2013. "Urban Legends." Retrieved January 1, 2012 (www.snopes.com/college/college.asp).

Milgram, Stanley. 1967. "The Small World Problem." *Psychology Today* 1:61–67.

Mills, C. Wright. 1956. *The Power Elite.* New York: Oxford University Press.

Mills, C. Wright. 1959. *The Sociological Imagination.* New York: Oxford University Press.

Mills, Theodore M. 1984. *The Sociology of Small Groups,* 2nd ed. Englewood Cliffs, NJ: Prentice Hall.

Milner, Murray. 2006. *Freaks, Geeks, and Cool Kids: American Teenagers, Schools, and The Culture of Consumption.* London: Routledge.

Mincy, Ronald B. 2006. *Black Males Left Behind.* Washington, DC: Urban Institute Press.

Minkoff, Debra C. 1995. *Organizing for Equality.* New Brunswick, NJ: Rutgers University Press.

"Misery of the Maquiladoras." 2011. *Socialist Worker,* November 18. Retrieved May 27, 2012 (http://socialistworker.org/2011/11/18/misery-of-the-maquiladoras).

Moore, Valerie Ann. 2001. "Doing Racialized and Gendered Age to Organize Peer Relations: Observing Kids in Summer Camp." *Gender and Society* 15(6):835–58.

Morey, Peter and Amina Yaqin. 2011. *Framing Muslims: Stereotyping and Representation After 9/11.* Cambridge, MA: Harvard University Press.

Morris, Joan M. and Michael D. Grimes. 1997. *Caught in the Middle: Contradictions in the Lives of Sociologists From Working Class Backgrounds.* Westport, CT: Praeger.

Morris, Lloyd R. 1949. *Not So Long Ago.* New York: Random House.

Morrison, Maureen. 2010. "New Data Shed Light on Women's Internet Usage." *Ad Age,* August 3. Retrieved May 25, 2012 (http://adage.com/article/adagestat/data-research-women-s-internet-usage/145224/).

Morozov, Evgeny. 2009. "How Dictators Watch Us on the Web." *Prospect.* Retrieved October 9, 2012 (http://www.prospectmagazine.co.uk/magazine/how-dictators-watch-us-on-the-web/).

Mou, Yi and Wei Peng. 2009. "Gender and Racial Stereotypes in Popular Video Games." IGI Global OnDemand.

Muchhala, Bhumika. 2012. "Students Against Sweat Shops." Pp. 303–12 in *Globalization: The Transformation of Social Worlds,* 3rd ed., edited by D. Stanley Eitzen and Maxine Baca Zinn. Belmont, CA: Wadsworth.

Munsey, Christopher. 2012. "Hostile Hallways." *American Psychological Association: Monitor on Psychology* 43(February):58.

Murdock, George Peter. 1967. *Ethnographic Atlas.* Pittsburgh: University of Pittsburgh Press.

Murstein, Bernard I. 1987. "A Clarification and Extension of the SVR Theory of Dyadic Pairing." *Journal of Marriage and the Family* 49(November):929–33.

"Muslims and Multicultural Backlash." 2011, July. Retrieved March 23, 2012 (http://harvardpress.typepad.com/hup_publicity/2011/07/framing-muslims-morey-yaqin.html).

Mutamba, John. 2005. "Strategies for Increasing Women's Participation in Government." Expert Group Meeting on Democratic Governance in Africa, Nairobi, Kenya, December 6–8.

Mydans, Seth. 2009. "For Khmer Rouge Guard, It Was Kill or Be Killed." March 1. Retrieved July 11, 2009 (www.nytimes.com/2009/03/01/world/asia/01iht-guard.1.20501994.html).

Myrdal, Gunnar. 1964. *An American Dilemma.* New York: McGraw-Hill.

Nagel, Joane. 1994. "Constructing Ethnicity: Creating and Recreating Ethnic Identity and Culture." *Social Problems* 41(1):152–76.

Nakamura, Lisa. 2004. "Interrogating the Digital Divide: The Political Economy of Race and Commerce in the New Media." Pp. 71–83 in *Society On-Line: The Internet in Context,* edited by Philip N. Howard and Steve Jones. Thousand Oaks, CA: Sage.

Nall, Jeff. 2012. "Combating Slavery in Coffee and Chocolate Production." *Toward Freedom,* January 5. Retrieved May 1, 2012 (http://www.towardfreedom.com/labor/2673-combating-slavery-in-coffee-and-chocolate-production).

National Archives and Records Administration. 2008. "What Is the Electoral College?" Retrieved March 21, 2008 (www.archives.gov/federal-register/electoral-college/about.html).

National Center for Education Statistics. 2011. "ACT Score Averages and Standard Deviations, by Sex and Race/Ethnicity, and Percentage of ACT Test Takers, by Selected Composite Score Ranges and Planned Fields of Study: Selected Years, 1995 through 2010" (Table 155). *Digest of Education Statistics.* Retrieved September 14, 2012 (http://nces.ed.gov/programs/digest/d10/tables/dt10_155.asp).

National Center for Education Statistics. 2012a. "Do You Have Information On Postsecondary Enrollment Rates?" Institute of Education Sciences. Retrieved June 16, 2013 (Nces.ed.gov/fastfacts/display.asp?id=98).

National Center for Education Statistics. 2012b. "Higher Education: Gaps in Assess and Persistence Study." Indicator 24: College Entrance Exams. Retrieved September 14, 2012 (http://nces.ed.gov/pubs2012/2012046/chapter 4_8.asp).

National Center for Education Statistics. 2012c. "What Are the Graduation Rates for Students Obtaining a Bachelor's Degree?" Retrieved September 6, 2013 (http://nces.ed.gov/programs/coe/indicator_pgr.asp).

National Center for Injury Prevention and Control. 2011. "The National Intimate Partner and Sexual Violence Survey: 2010." Atlanta, GA: Centers for Disease Control and Prevention, November. Retrieved May 29, 2012 (www.cdc.gov/ViolencePrevention/pdf/NISVS_Executive_Summary-a.pdf).

National Center for Victims of Crime. 2011. "Terrorism." August 25. Retrieved April 13, 2012 (www.ncvc.org/ncvc/main.aspx?dbName=DocumentViewer&DocumentID=47702).

National Coalition on Health Care. 2008. "Health Insurance Cost." Retrieved April 17, 2010 (www.nchc.org OR www.whitehouse2.org/ . . . /305-facts-from-the-national-coalition-on-health-care).

National Conference of State Legislatures. 2012. "Defining Marriage: Defense of Marriage Acts and Same-Sex Marriage Laws." Retrieved June 10, 2012 (www.ncsl.org/issues-research/human-services/same-sex-marriage-overview.aspx).

National Conference of State Legislatures. 2013. "State Laws Regarding Marriages Between First Cousins." Retrieved April 21, 2013 (www.ncsl.org/issues-research/human-services/state-laws-regarding-marriages-between-first-cousi.aspx).

National Geographic Society. 2011, December 8. "7 Billion." Retrieved February 25, 2012 (http://itunes.apple.com/us/aoo/7-billion/id473524096?mt=8).

National Geographic Society. 2013. "Mapping Displaced People Around the World." Retrieved September 7, 2013 (http://education.nationalgeographic.co.uk/education/maps/mapping-displaced-people-around-the-world/?ar_a=1).

National Institutes of Health. 2012. "Stem Cell Information: Stem Cell Basics." February 13. Retrieved March 7, 2012 (http://stemcells.nih.gov/info/basics/basics4.asp).

National Opinion Research Center. 2010. "More Than 60% of Marriages Break Up Because of Adultery." Retrieved February 28, 2011 (www.norc.uchicago.edu/).

National Public Radio. 2008. "Poppy Growing in Afghanistan." *Morning Edition,* February 9.

National Public Radio. 2010. "Affirmative Action: How Far Have We Come?" *All Things Considered,* August 15. Retrieved May 12, 2012 (www.npr.org/templates/story/story.php?storyId=129216337).

National Public Radio. 2011. "Closing Digital Divide." June 29. Retrieved May 18, 2012 (www.npr.org/2011/06/29/137499299/closing-digital-divide-expanding-digital-literacy).

National Science Foundation. 2005. *Children, TV, Computers and More Media: New Research Shows Pluses, Minuses.* Retrieved July 20, 2006 (www.eurekalert.org/pub_releases/2005-02/nsf-ctc021005.php).

National Security Network. 2011. "Where Girls Are Educated 'The Standard of Living Goes Up.'" January 31. Retrieved April 17, 2011 (www.nsnetwork.org/node/1850).

National Vital Statistics System, Centers for Disease Control and Prevention. 2011. "National Marriage and Divorce Rate Trends." Retrieved April 12, 2011 (www.cdc.gov/nchs/nvss/marriage_divorce_tables.htm).

Nationmaster. 2011. "United States Population Pyramids." Retrieved May 19, 2011 (www.nationmaster.com/country/us/Age_distribution).

Neuman, Michelle J. 2005. "Global Early Care and Education: Challenges, Responses, and Lessons." *Phi Delta Kappan* (November):188–92.

New America Foundation. 2012. "School Finance: Federal, State, and Local K–12 School Finance Overview." Federal Education Budget Project. Retrieved June 16, 2013 (Febp.newamerica.net/background-analysis/school-finance).

"New Federal Report: Sexual Abuse Plagues U.S. Prisons and Jails." 2010. *Just Detention,* August 26. Retrieved March 8, 2011 (www.businesswire.com/).

Newman, David. 2009. *Families: A Sociological Perspective.* New York: McGraw-Hill.

Newman, Matthew L., Carla J. Groom, Lori D. Handelman, and James W. Pennebaker. 2008. "Gender Differences in Language Use: An Analysis of 14,000 Text Samples." *Discourse Process* 45:211–36.

Newport, Frank. 2006. "Mormons, Evangelical Protestants, Baptists Top Church Attendance List." Gallup. Retrieved April 17, 2010 (www.gallup.com/ . . . /mormons-evangelical-protestants-baptists-top-church-attendance-list.aspx).

Newport, Frank. 2009. "This Christmas, 78% of Americans Identify as Christian." Gallup, December 24. Retrieved September 26, 2012 (www.gallup.com/poll/124793/This-Christmas-78-Americans-Identify-Christian.aspx).

Newport, Frank. 2012. "More Than Nine in Ten Americans Continue to Believe in God." Gallup. Retrieved September 26, 2012 (www.gallup.com/poll/147887/americans-continue-believe-god.aspx).

Newport, Frank and Elizabeth Mendes. 2009. "About One in Six U.S. Adults Are Without Health Insurance." Gallup, July 22. Retrieved April 7, 2011 (http://www.gallup.com/poll/121820/one-six-adults-without-health-insurance.aspx).

"New Religious Movement (NRM)." 2012. *Encyclopedia Britannica.* Retrieved September 21, 2012 (www.britannica.com/EBchecked/topic/1007307/new-religious-movement-NRM).

The New York Times. 1893, July 23. "Finery for Infants." Retrieved May 8, 2012 (http://query.nytimes.com/mem/archive-free/pdf?res=F20E17FB3B5F1A738DDDAA0A94DF405B8385F0D3).

The New York Times. 2008. "Primary Calendar: Democratic Nominating Contests." Retrieved March 30, 2008 (http://politics.nytimes.com/election-guide/2008/primaries/democraticprimaries/index.html).

News of Future. 2012. "1 Million Hydrogen-Fueled Cars in U.S." Retrieved March 7, 2012 (www.newsoffuture.com/million_hydrogen_fueled_cars_in_us_future_energy.html).

Nichols, Larry A., George A. Mather, and Alvin J. Schmidt. 2006. *Encyclopedic Dictionary of Cults, Sects, and World Religions,* Revised and updated ed. Grand Rapids, MI: Zondervan.

Nichols, Michelle. 2012 "U.N. Says Haiti Struggling to Cope with Cholera as Aid Withdrawn." *Chicago Tribune,* August 31. Retrieved September 10, 2012 (http://articles.chicagotribune.com/2012-08-31/news/sns-rt-us-haiti-unbre87u1b5-20120831_1_cholera-cases-cholera-out break-cholera-epidemic).

Noel, Donald. 1968. "A Theory of the Origin of Ethnic Stratification." *Social Problems* 16(Fall):157–72.

Noguera, Pedro A. 1996. "Preventing and Producing Violence: A Critical Analysis of Responses to School Violence." *Sociology of Education* 56(3):189–212.

Noguera, Pedro A. 2011. "A Broader and Bolder Approach Uses Education to Break Cycle of Poverty." *Phi Delta Kappan* 93(3):9–14.

Noguera, Pedro and Robby Cohen. 2006. "Patriotism and Accountability: The Role of Educators in the War on Terrorism." *Phi Delta Kappan* 87(8):573–78.

Nolan, Cathal J. 2002. "War." P. 1803 in *The Greenwood Encyclopedia of International Relations.* London: Greenwood.

Nolan, Patrick and Gerhard Lenski. 2010. *Human Societies: An Introduction to Macrosociology,* 11th ed. Boulder, CO: Paradigm.

Nolan, Patrick D., Jennifer Triplett, and Shannon McDonough. 2010. "Sociology's Suicide: A Forensic Autopsy." *The American Sociologist* 41:292–305.

Nonprofit Vote. 2012. "America Goes to the Polls 2012." Retrieved June 2, 2013 (www.nonprofitvote.org).

Oakes, Jeannie, Amy Stuart Wells, Makeba Jones, and Amanda Datnow. 1997. "Detracking: The Social Construction of Ability, Cultural Politics, and Resistance to Reform." *Teacher's College Record* 98(3):482–510.

O'Brien, Denise. 1977. "Female Husbands in Southern Bantu Societies." In *Sexual Stratification: A Cross-Cultural View,* edited by Alice Schlegel. New York: Columbia University Press

O'Brien, Jody. 2011. *The Production of Reality,* 5th ed. Thousand Oaks, CA: Sage

O'Connel, Sanjida. 1993. "Meet My Two Husbands." *Guardian,* March 4, Sec. 2, p. 12.

OECD Family Database. 2010. "Cohabitation Rate and Prevalence of Other Forms of Partnership." Retrieved June 5, 2012 (www.oecd.org/dataoecd/52/27/41920080/pdf).

Ogbu, John U. 1998. "Understanding Cultural Diversity and Learning." *Educational Researcher* 21(8):5–14.

Ogburn, William F. [1922] 1938. *Social Change, With Respect to Culture and Original Nature.* New York: Viking.

Ogburn, William F. 1933. *Recent Social Trends.* New York: McGraw-Hill.

Ogburn, William F. 1961. "The Hypothesis of Cultural Lag." Pp. 1270–73 in *Theories of Society: Foundations of Modern Sociological Theory,* Vol. 2, edited by Talcott Parsons, Edward Shils, Kaspar D. Naegele, and Jesse R. Pitts. New York: Free Press.

Ogburn, William F. 1964. In *On Culture and Social Change: Selected Papers,* edited by Otis Dudley Duncan. Chicago: University of Chicago Press.

Ogunwole, Stella U., Malcolm P. Drewery, Jr., and Merarys Rios-Vargas. 2012. "The Population with a Bachelor's Degree or Higher by Race and Hispanic Origin: 2006–2010." American Community Survey Briefs, U.S. Census, May. Retrieved February 10, 2013 (http://www.census.gov/prod/2012pubs/acsbr10-19.pdf).

Olsen, Marvin E. 1968. *The Process of Social Organization.* New York: Holt, Rinehart, & Winston.

Olsen, Marvin E. 1970. "Power as a Social Process." Pp. 2–10 in *Power in Societies,* edited by Marvin Olsen. New York: Macmillan.

One in Four, Inc. N.d. Retrieved November 6, 2009 (www.oneinfourusa .org).

One Laptop per Child. 2011. Retrieved March 18, 2011 (http:// laptop .org/en/vision/).

Oswald, Ramona Faith. 2000. "A Member of the Wedding? Heterosexism and Family Ritual." *Journal of Social and Personal Relationships* 17(June):349–68.

Oswald, Ramona Faith. 2001. "Religion, Family, and Ritual: The Production of Gay, Lesbian, and Transgendered Outsiders-Within." *Review of Religious Research* 43(December):39–50.

Padden, Brian. 2009. "Nigeria Still Fighting False Rumors About Polio Vaccine." February 17. Retrieved August 6, 2011 (http://www.voanews .com/english/news/a-13-2009-02-17-voa48-68672337.html).

Palmer, Craig. 1989. "Is Rape a Cultural Universal? A Re-examination of the Ethnographic Data." *Ethnology* 28(Jan):1–16.

Papalia, Diane E. and Ruth Duskin Feldman. 2011. *Experience Human Development.* 12th ed. Boston: McGraw-Hill.

Pareto, Vilfredo. [1911] 1955. "Mathematical Economics." In *Encyclopedie des Sciences Mathematique.* New York: Macmillan.

Parsons, Talcott. 1951. *Toward a General Theory of Action.* New York: Harper & Row.

Parsons, Talcott and Robert F. Bales. 1953. *Family, Socialization, and Interaction Process.* Glencoe, IL: Free Press.

Passel, Jeffrey and D'Vera Cohn. 2012. "U.S. Foreign-Born Population: How Much Change from 2009 to 2010?" Pew Research Center, January 9. Retrieved July 30, 2012 (www.pewhispanic.org/2012/01/09/u-s-foreign-born-population-how-much-change-from-2009-to-2010/).

PBS. 2012. "World's Biggest Congregation" *Religion and Ethics Newsweekly,* August 10. Retrieved October 3, 2012 (www.pbs.org/wnet/reli gionandethics/episodes/january-27-2012/worlds-biggest-congrega tion/10162/).

Pearce, Fred. 2010. "As Longevity Grows, The World Might Become a Better Place." *Washington Post,* May 25. Retrieved July 28, 2011 (www.washingtonpost.com/wp-dyn/content/article/2010/05/24/ AR2010052402607.html).

Peek, Lori. 2011. *Behind the Backlash: Muslim Americans After 9/11.* Philadelphia: Temple University Press.

Pellow, David Naguib. 2002. *Garbage Wars: The Struggle for Environmental Justice in Chicago.* Cambridge, MA: MIT Press.

People's Daily Online. 2011, March 11. Retrieved May 15, 2012 (http:// english.peopledaily.com.cn/90001/98649/7315789.html).

Perez, Miguel. 2011. "The Latino Backlash Is Coming Sooner Than Republicans Expected." April 6. Retrieved April 7, 2011 (http://www .paragoulddailypress.com/articles/2011/04/06/opinion/doc4d9ba4c 6c2ef4312670875.txt).

Persell, Caroline Hodges. 2005. "Race, Education, and Inequality." Pp. 286–24 in *Blackwell Companion to Social Inequalities,* edited by M. Romero and E. Margolis. Oxford, UK: Blackwell.

Persell, Caroline Hodges and Peter W. Cookson, Jr. 1985. "Chartering and Bartering: Elite Education and Social Reproduction." *Social Problems* 33(2):114–29.

Pescosolido, Bernice A. and Sharon Georgianna. 1989. "Durkheim, Suicide, and Religion: Toward a Network Theory of Suicide." *American Sociological Review* 54(February):33–48.

Pettigrew, Thomas F. and Linda R. Tropp. 2000. "Does Intergroup Contact Reduce Prejudice? Recent Meta-Analytic Findings." Pp. 93–114 in *Reducing Prejudice and Discrimination,* edited by Stuart Oskamp. London: Psychology Press, Taylor and Francis Group.

Pew Center on the States. 2011. "State of Recidivism: The Revolving Door of American Prisons." The Pew Charitable Trusts, April 3, p. 2. Retrieved April 16, 2012 (www.pewcenteronthestates.org/ initiatives_detail.aspx?initiativeID).

Pew Forum on Religion and Public Life. 2008. "U.S. Religious Landscape Survey, 2008." Retrieved March 2, 2008 (http://religions.pewforum .org/pdf/report-religious-landscape-study-full.pdf).

Pew Forum on Religion and Public Life. 2009. "Most Latino Evangelicals Pray Every Day." June 11. Retrieved September 26, 2012 (www .pewforum.org/Frequency-of-Prayer/Most-Latino-Evangelicals-Pray-Every-Day.aspx).

Pew Forum on Religion and Public Life. 2010. "U.S. Religious Landscape Survey." Retrieved January 1, 2010 (http://religions.pewforum.org/ reports).

Pew Forum on Religion and Public Life. 2012. "U.S. Religious Landscape Survey." September 18. Retrieved September 18, 2012 (http://reli gions.pewforum.org/reports).

Pew Hispanic Center. 2011. "Hispanics Account for 56% of Nation's Growth in Past Decade." Retrieved April 7, 2011 (http://pewhis panic.org/).

Pew Internet and American Life Project. 2012. "Demographics of Internet Users." Retrieved March 5, 2012 (http://www.pewinternet.org/Static-Pages/trend-Data/Whos-Online.aspx).

Pew Research Center. 2010. "The Decline of Marriage and Rise of New Families." *Pew Social & Demographic Trends,* November 18. Retrieved March 8, 2012 (www.pewsocialtrends.org/2010/11/18/the-decline-of-marriage-and-rise-of-new-families/).

Pew Research Center. 2011. "The Generation Gap and the 2012 Election." November 3. Retrieved July 29, 2012 (www.people-press. org/2011/11/03/section-1-how-generations-have-changed/).

Phillips, Richard. 2013. "Animal Communication." Lecture at *Tuesdays With a Liberal Arts Scholar,* University of Minnesota, May 6.

Phipher, Mary. 1994. *Reviving Ophelia: Saving the Selves of Adolescent Girls.* New York: Ballantine Books.

Piaget, Jean. 1989. *The Child's Conception of the World.* Savage, MD: Littlefield, Adams Quality Paperbacks.

Piaget, Jean and Barbel Inhelder. [1955] 1999. *Growth of Logical Thinking.* London: Routledge & Kegan Paul.

Pickard, Ruth and Daryl Poole. 2007. "The Study of Society and the Practice of Sociology." Previously unpublished essay.

Pieterse, Jan Nederveen. 2004. *Globalization and Culture.* Lanham, MD: Rowman & Littlefield.

Plato. [ca. 350 BCE] 1960. *The Laws.* New York: Dutton.

Ploughshares. 2013. "2012 Armed Conflicts Report Summary." Retrieved August 31, 2013 (http://ploughshares.ca/pl_publications/2012-armed-conflicts-report-summary/).

PolitiFact.com. 2009. "Coburn Says 20% of Every Medicare Dollar Goes to Fraud." Retrieved April 13, 2012 (www.politifact.com/truth-o-meter/statements/2009/aug/27/tom-coburn/coburn-says-20-percent-of-every-medicare-dollar-goes-to-fraud).

Pollard, Kelvin. 2011. "The Gender Gap in College Enrollment and Graduation." *Population Reference Bureau.* Retrieved September 12, 2012 (www.prb.org/Articles/2011/gender-gap-in-education.aspx).

"Polygamy in France: Many Wives' Tales." 2010. *The Economist,* May 6. Retrieved May 3, 2013 (www.economist.com/node/16068972).

Popenoe, David. 2002. "Debunking Divorce Myths." *National Marriage Project.* New Brunswick, NJ: Rutgers. Retrieved November 30, 2009 (health.discovery.com/centers/loverelationships/articles/divorce .html).

Population Reference Bureau. 2007a. "World Population Data Sheet." Retrieved July 22, 2009 (http://www.prb.org/Publications/Datashee ts/2007/2007WorldPopulationDataSheet.aspx).

Population Reference Bureau. 2007b. "World Population Highlights." *Population Bulletin* 62(3):2.

Population Reference Bureau. 2011. "Rate of Natural Increase." Retrieved June 9, 2013 (www.prb.org/DataFinder/Topic/Rankings. aspx?ind=16).

Population Reference Bureau. 2012. "2012 World Population Data Sheet." Retrieved August 25, 2012 (www.prb.org/pdf12/2012-population-data-sheet_eng.pdf).

Population Reference Bureau. 2013. "Total Fertility Rate." Retrieved September 2, 2013 (www.prb.org/DataFinder/Topic/Rankings.aspx?ind=17).

Potok, Mark. 2012. "The 'Patriot' Movement Explodes." *Intelligence Report* 145(Spring). Southern Poverty Law Center.

Powell, Andrea D. and Arnold S. Kahn. 1995. "Racial Differences in Women's Desires to Be Thin." *International Journal of Eating Disorders* 17(2):191–95.

Powley, Elizabeth. 2003. "Strengthening Governance: The Role of Women in Rwanda's Transition." In *Women Waging Peace,* edited by S. N. Anderlini. Washington, DC: Hunt Alternatives Fund.

Preston, David L. 1988. *The Social Organization of Zen Practice: Constructing Transcultural Reality.* Cambridge, UK: Cambridge University Press.

Preston, Jennifer. 2011. "The Year in Media: Social Media and Egypt's Revolution." Media Decoder Weblog, *New York Times,* December 21. Retrieved October 6, 2012 (http://mediadecoder.blogs.nytimes.com).

Project Vote Smart. 2008. "State Presidential Primary and Caucus Dates." Retrieved April 17, 2010 (www.votesmart.org/election_president_state_primary_dates.php).

Proudman, Charlotte Rachael. 2012 "Sex and Sharia: Muslim Women Punished for Failed Marriages." *The Independent,* April 2. Retrieved May 24, 2012 (http://blogs.independent.co.uk/2012/04/02/sex-and-sharia-muslim-women-punished-for-failed-marriages/).

Pyle, Ralph E. 2006. "Trends in Religious Stratification: Have Religious Group Socioeconomic Distinctions Declined in Recent Decades?" *Sociology of Religion* 67(Spring):61–79.

Quinney, Richard. 2002. *Critique of Legal Order: Crime Control in Capitalist Society.* New Brunswick, NJ: Transaction.

Radcliffe-Brown, A. R. 1935. "On the Concept of Functional in Social Science." *American Anthropologist* 37(3):394–402.

Radelet, Michael L. and Traci L. Lacock. 2009. "Do Executions Lower Homicide Rates? The Views of Leading Criminologists." *The Journal of Criminal Laws and Criminology* 99(2).

Rani, M., S. Bonu, and N. Diop-Sidibe. 2004. "An Empirical Investigation of Attitudes Towards Wife-beating Among Men and Women in Seven Sub-Saharan African Countries." *African Journal of Reproductive Health* 8(3):116–36.

Rankin, Bruce H. and Is̡ik A. Aytaç. 2006. "Gender Inequality in Schooling: The Case of Turkey." *Sociology of Education* 79(1):25–43.

Rappoport, Leon. 2003. *How We Eat: Appetite, Culture and the Psychology of Food.* Toronto, Ontario, Canada: ECW Press.

Read, Kristen. 2011. "Number of Internet Users Worldwide Climbs to 2 Billion." UN International Telecommunications Union, January 28. Retrieved March 18, 2011 (http://graphicartsmag.com/news/2011/01/number-of-internet-users-worldwide).

Reason. 2011. "In-Depth Study: After Divorce, 44% of Women Fell Into Poverty." *Family Research Council,* May 31. Retrieved June 6, 2012 (http://primacyofreason.blogspot.com/2011/05/in-depth-study-after-divorce-44-of_31.html).

Regnerus, Mark D. 2007. *Forbidden Fruit: Sex and Religion in the Lives of American Teenagers.* New York: Oxford University Press.

Reid, Scott A. and Sik Hung Ng. 2006. "The Dynamics of Intragroup Differentiation in an Intergroup Social Context." *Human Communication Research* 32:504–525.

Reid, T. R. 2009. *The Healing of America: A Global Quest for Better, Cheaper and Fairer Health Care.* New York: Penguin Press.

Reilly, Ryan J. 2013. "Guantanamo Hunger Strike Numbers Continue to Rise." April 17. Retrieved April 18, 2013 (www.huffingtonpost.com/2012/04/17/guantanamo-hunger-strike_n_3099856.html).

Reiman, Jeffrey and Paul Leighton. 2010a. *The Rich Get Richer and the Poor Get Prison: Ideology, Class, and Criminal Justice,* 9th ed. Boston: Pearson.

Reiman, Jeffrey and Paul Leighton. 2010b. *The Rich Get Richer and the Poor Get Prison: A Reader.* Boston: Allyn & Bacon.

Religious Tolerance. 2009. "U.S. Divorce Rates for Various Faith Groups, Age Groups, and Geographic Areas." Retrieved April 17, 2010 (www.religioustolerance.org/chr_dira.htm).

Religious Tolerance. 2010. "Stem Cell Research: All Viewpoints." Retrieved September 8, 2012 (www.religioustolerance.org/res_stem.htm).

Religious Tolerance. 2012. "The Status of Women, Currently and Throughout History." Retrieved November 30, 2012 (http://www.religioustolerance.org/women.htm).

Religious Worlds. 2007. "New Religious Movements." Retrieved August 14, 2008 (www.religiousworlds.com/newreligions.html).

Renick, Oliver. 2011. "Disconnected: 70 Percent of World Doesn't Have Internet, Despite Rising Phone Usage." *Laptop,* October 31. Retrieved May 18, 2012 (http://blog.laptopmag.com/disconnected-70-percent-of-world-doesn%E2%80%99t-have-internet-despite-rising-phone-usage).

Reproductive Health Matters 2011. "Pro-Natalist Policies in Eastern Europe Hit Young Women Hard." August 19. Retrieved July 28, 2012 (www.rhmjournal.org.uk/news.php?newsID=952).

Reyes, A. H., and G. M Rodriguez. 2004. "School Finance: Raising Questions for Urban Schools." *Education and Urban Society* 37(3):3–21.

Rideout, Victoria J., Ulla G. Foehr, and Donald F. Roberts. 2010. "Generation M2: Media in the Lives of 8- to 18-Year-Olds." A Kaiser Family Foundation Study, January. Retrieved March 2, 2011 (www.kff.org/entmedia/upload/8010.pdf).

Riordan, Cornelius. 2004. *Equality and Achievement: An Introduction to the Sociology of Education.* Upper Saddle River, NJ: Prentice Hall.

Ritholtz, Barry. 2013. "US Military Spending vs. World." April 17. Retrieved June 2, 2013 (www.ritholtz.com/blog/2012/04/us-military-spending-vs-world/).

Ritzer, George. 2007. *The Globalization of Nothing,* 5th ed. Thousand Oaks, CA: Pine Forge.

Ritzer, George. 2013a. *Introduction to Sociology.* Thousand Oaks, CA: Sage.

Ritzer, George. 2013b. *The McDonaldization of Society,* 20th anniversary ed. Thousand Oaks, CA: Sage.

Ritzer, George and Douglas J. Goodman. 2004. *Sociological Theory,* 6th ed. New York: McGraw-Hill.

Roach, Ronald. 2004. "Survey Reveals 10 Biggest Trends in Internet Use." *Black Issues in Higher Education,* October 21.

Robbins, Richard H. 2011. *Global Problems and the Culture of Capitalism,* 5th ed. Upper Saddle River NJ: Prentice Hall.

Roberts, Keith A. and Karen A. Donahue. 2000. "Professing Professionalism: Bureaucratization and Deprofessionalization in the Academy," *Sociological Focus* 33(4):365–83.

Roberts, Keith A. and David Yamane. 2012. *Religion in Sociological Perspective,* 5th ed. Thousand Oaks, CA: SAGE/Pine Forge Press.

Robertson, Roland. 1997. "Social Theory, Cultural Relativity and the Problem of Globality." Pp. 69–90 in *Culture, Globalization and the World System,* edited by Anthony King. Minneapolis: University of Minnesota Press.

Robillard, Kevin. 2012. "Study: Youth Vote Was Decisive." *Politico,* November 7. Retrieved November 1, 2012 (www.politico.com/news/stories/1112/83510.html).

Rodricks, Dan. 2012. "Catholics, Contraception and the Heretic Faithful." *The Baltimore Sun,* February 8. Retrieved Feb. 5, 2013 (http://articles.baltimoresun.com/2012-02-08/news/bs-ed-rodricks-catholics-20120208_1_cafeteria-catholics-church-leaders-protest-catholic-identity).

Rodriguez, Eric M. and S. C. Ouellette. 2000. "Gay and Lesbian Christians: Homosexual and Religious Identity Integration in the Members of a Gay-Positive Church." *Journal for the Scientific Study of Religion* 39(3):333–47.

Roethlisberger, Fritz J. and William J. Dickson. 1939. *Management and the Worker.* Cambridge, MA: Harvard University Press.

Roof, Wade Clark. 1999. *Spiritual Marketplace: Baby Boomers and the Remaking of American Religion.* Princeton, NJ: Princeton University Press.

Rosenbaum, James E. 1999. "If Tracking Is Bad, Is Detracking Better? A Study of a Detracked High School." *American Schools* (Winter):24–47.

Rosenberg, Matt. 2012. "Maquiladoras in Mexico: Export Assembly Plants for the United States." *About.com Geography.* Retrieved May 28, 2012 (http://geography.about.com/od/urbaneconomicgeography/a/maquiladoras.htm).

Rossi, Alice S. 1984. "Gender and Parenthood." *American Sociological Review* 49(February):1–19.

Rossides, Daniel W. 1997. *Social Stratification: The Interplay of Class, Race, and Gender.* Englewood Cliffs, NJ: Prentice Hall.

Rothenberg, Paula S. 2010. *Race, Class, and Gender in the United States: An Integrated Study,* 8th ed. New York: Worth.

Rothenberg, Paula S. 2011. *White Privilege: Essential Readings on the Other Side of Racism,* 3rd ed. New York: Worth Publishers.

Rothkopf, David. 2012. "Two Septembers." Pp. 100–103 in *Globalization: The Transformation of Social Worlds,* 3rd ed., edited by D. Stanley Eitzen and Maxine Baca Zinn. Belmont, CA: Wadsworth.

Rothman, Robert A. 2005. *Inequality and Stratification: Race, Class, and Gender,* 5th ed. Englewood Cliffs, NJ: Prentice Hall.

Rubenstein, Grace. 2007. "Computers for Peace: The $100 Laptop." Retrieved April 21, 2009 (www.edutopia.org/computers-peace).

Rusere, Patience. 2009. "Rainy Season Brings New Cholera Outbreaks in Zimbabwe, Five Deaths Reported." *Voice of America News,* November 16. Retrieved December 20, 2009 (www1.voanews.com/zimbabwe/news/a-13-56-74-2009-11-16-voa48-70422597.html).

Rydgren, Jens. 2004. Mechanisms of Exclusion: Ethnic Discrimination in the Swedish Labour Market." *Journal of Ethnic and Migration Studies* 30(4):687–716.

Saad, Lydia. 2010. "Americans' Acceptance of Gay Relations Crosses 50% Threshold." Gallup Politics, May 25. Retrieved May 27, 2012 (www.gallup.com/poll/135764/americans-acceptance-gay-relations-crosses-threshold.aspx).

Sadovnik, Alan R. 2007. *Sociology of Education: A Critical Reader.* New York: Routledge.

Safdar, Khadeeja. 2012. "Median Income Falling, Even as More Find Jobs." *The Huffington Post,* March 7. Retrieved May 16, 2012 (www.huffingtonpost.com/2012/03/07/media-income-2011_n_1324859.html).

Sage, George H. and D. Stanley Eitzen, 2012. *Sociology of North American Sport* 9th ed. New York: Oxford University Press.

Sager, Ira, Ben Elgin, Peter Elstrom, Faith Keenan, and Pallavi Gogoi. 2006. "The Underground Web." Pp. 261–70 in *Globalization: The Transformation of Social Worlds,* edited by D. Stanley Eitzen and Maxine Baca Zinn. Belmont, CA: Wadsworth.

Saha, Lawrence and A. Gary Dworkin. 2006. "Educational Attainment and Job Status: The Role of Status Inconsistency on Occupational Burnout." Paper presented at the International Sociological Association, July 23–29, Durban, South Africa.

Saharan Vibe. 2007. "Wodaabe Beauty Ceremony." February 19. Retrieved November 6, 2009 (saharanvibe.blogspot.com/2007/02/wodaabe-beauty-ceremony.html).

Salzman, Michael B. 2008. "Globalization, Religious Fundamentalism and the Need for Meaning." *International Journal of Intercultural Relations* 32(July):318–27.

Samovar, Larry A. and Richard E. Porter. 2003. *Intercultural Communication.* Belmont, CA: Wadsworth.

Sanday, Peggy Reeves. 1996. *A Woman Scorned: Acquaintance Rape on Trial.* Berkeley: University of California Press.

Sanday, Peggy Reeves. 2007. *Fraternity Gang Rape: Sex, Brotherhood, and Privilege on Campus.* New York: New York University Press.

Sanday, Peggy and Ruth Gallagher Goodenough, eds. 1990. *Beyond the Second Sex.* Philadelphia: University of Pennsylvania Press.

Sandberg, Sheryl. 2013. *Lean In: Women, Work, and the Will to Lead.* New York: Alfred A. Knopf.

Sang-Hun, Choe. 2013. "As Families, Change, Korea's Elderly Are Turning to Suicide." *The New York Times,* February 18. Retrieved April 12, 2013 (www.nytimes.com/2013/02/17/world/asia/in-korea-changes-in-society-and-family-dynamics-drive-rise-in-elderly-suicides.html?hp&_r=0).

Sapir, Edward. 1929. "The Status of Linguistics as a Science." *Language* 5:207–214.

Sapir, Edward. 1949. In *Selected Writings of Edward Sapir in Language, Culture, and Personality,* edited by David G. Mandelbaum. Berkeley: University of California Press.

Sapiro, Virginia. 2003. *Women in American Society: An Introduction to Women's Studies,* 5th ed. Mountain View, CA: Mayfield.

Sapolsky, Robert. 2011. "The Trouble with Testosterone." In *The Kaleidoscope of Gender,* 3rd ed., edited by Joan Z. Spade and Catherine G. Valentine. Thousand Oaks: Pine Forge.

Sargeant, Kimon Howland. 2000. *Seeker Churches: Promoting Traditional Religion in a Nontraditional Way.* New Brunswick, NJ: Rutgers University Press.

Sassler, Sharon and Amanda J. Miller. 2011. "Waiting to Be Asked: Gender, Power, and Relationship Progression Among Cohabiting Couples." *Journal of Family Issues* 32(April):482–506.

Saxbe, Darby E., Rena L Repetti, and Anthony P. Graesch. 2011. "Time Spent in Housework and Leisure: Links With Parents' Physiological Recovery From Work." *Journal of Family Psychology* 25(April):271–81.

Schaefer, Richard T. 2012. *Racial and Ethnic Groups,* 13th ed. Upper Saddle River, NJ: Prentice Hall.

Schaefer, Richard T. and Jenifer Kunz. 2007. *Racial and Ethnic Groups.* Upper Saddle River, NJ: Pearson/Prentice Hall.

Schaeffer, Robert K. 2003. *Understanding Globalization: The Social Consequences of Political, Economic, and Environmental Change,* 2nd ed. Lanham, MD: Rowman & Littlefield.

Schapiro, Mark. 2006. "Big Tobacco." Pp. 271–84 in *Globalization: The Transformation of Social Worlds,* edited by D. Stanley Eitzen and Maxine Baca Zinn. Belmont, CA: Wadsworth.

Schmalleger, Frank. 2006. *Criminology Today: An Integrative Introduction,* 4th ed. Upper Saddle River, NJ: Pearson Prentice Hall.

Schmalleger, Frank. 2012. *Criminology Today: An Integrative Introduction,* 6th ed. Upper Saddle River, NJ: Prentice Hall.

Schneider, Barbara and James S. Coleman. 1993. *Parents, Their Children, and Schools.* Boulder, CO: Westview.

Schneider, Linda and Arnold Silverman. 2006. *Global Sociology,* 4th ed. Boston: McGraw-Hill.

Schoepflin, Todd. 2011. "Doing Gender." *Creative Sociology,* August 10. Retrieved May 25, 2012 (http://creativesociology.blogspot.com/2011/08/doing-gender.html).

Science Daily. 2011a. "The International Digital Divide." February 8. Retrieved September 14, 2012 (www.sciencedaily.com/releases/2011/02/110208121345.htm).

Science Daily. 2011b. "Prison Education Programs Reduce Inmate Prison Return Rate, Study Shows." October 4. Retrieved April 16, 2012 (www.sciencedaily.com/releases/2011/10/111004180121.htm).

Scott, Ellen K., Andrew S. London, and Nancy A. Myers. 2002. "Dangerous Dependencies: The Intersection of Welfare Reform and Domestic Violence." *Gender and Society* 16(6):878–97.

Scott, Mark. 2009. "Politicians Urge for Global Stimulus." *BusinessWeek,* March 9. Retrieved July 22, 2009 (http://www.businessweek.com/executivesummary/archives/2009/03/politicians_urg.html).

Scott-Montagu, John. 1904. "Automobile Legislation: A Criticism and Review." *North American Review* 179(573):168–77.

Scribd. 2011. "Chipko Movement." Retrieved January 1, 2012 (www.scribd.com/doc/27513230/Chipko-Movement).

Sentencing Project. 2012a. "Facts About Prisons and Prisoners." Retrieved May 30, 2012 (www.sentencingproject.org/doc/publications/publications/inc_factsAboutPrisons_jan2012.pdf).

Sentencing Project. 2012b. "Rate of Incarceration per 100,000, by Gender and Race, 2010." Retrieved September 12, 2012 (www.sentencingproject.org/template/page.cfm?id=122).

The Sentencing Project. 2012c. "Trends in U.S. Corrections." Retrieved August 25, 2013 (http://sentencingproject.org/doc/publications/inc_Trends_in_Corrections_Fact_sheet.pdf).

Sentencing Project. 2013. "Racial Disparity." Retrieved September 3, 2013 (http://www.sentencingproject.org/template/page.cfm?id=122).

September, Chanel. 2013. "10% of S. Africans Infected with HIV." *Eye Witness News*, May 14. Retrieved June 10, 2013 (Ewn.co.za/2013/05/14/More-people-infected-with-HIV)

Sernau, Scott. 2010. *Social Inequality in a Global Age*. Thousand Oaks, CA: SAGE/Pine Forge Press.

Sessions, David. 2012. "Evangelicals Struggle to Address Premarital Sex and Abortion." *The Daily Beast,* July 13. Retrieved September 20, 2012 (www.thedailybeast.com/articles/2012/07/13/evangelicals-struggle-to-address-premarital-sex-and-abortion.html).

Shade, Leslie Regan. 2004. "Bending Gender Into the Net: Feminizing Content, Corporate Interests, and Research Strategy." Pp. 57–70 in *Society On-Line: The Internet in Context,* edited by Philip N. Howard and Steve Jones. Thousand Oaks, CA: Sage.

Shah, Anup. 2012. "World Military Spending: Expenditures in 2011." Retrieved February 10, 2013 (www.globalissues.org/print/article/75=WorldMilitarySpending).

Shah, Taimoor and Alissa J. Rubin. 2012. "In Poppy War, Taliban aim to Protect a Cash Crop." *The New York Times,* April 12. Retrieved April 14, 2012 (www.nytimes.com/2012/04/12/world/asia/taliban-poppy-war-targets-tractors-and -police.html).

Sharp, Henry S. 1991. "Memory, Meaning, and Imaginary Time: The Construction of Knowledge in White and Chipewayan Cultures." *Ethnohistory* 38(2):149–73.

Sharp, Lauriston. 1990. "Steel Axes for Stone-Age Australians." Pp. 410–24 in *Conformity and Conflict,* 7th ed., edited by James P. Spradley and David W. McCurdy. Glenview, IL: Scott Foresman.

Shaw, Susan M. and Janet Lee. 2005. *Women's Voices, Feminist Visions: Classic and Contemporary Readings,* 3rd ed. Boston: McGraw-Hill.

Sherif, Muzafer and Carolyn Sherif. 1953. *Groups in Harmony and Tension.* New York: Harper & Row.

Sherkat, Darren E. and Christopher G. Ellison. 1999. "Recent Developments and Current Controversies in the Sociology of Religion." *Annual Review of Sociology* 25:363–94.

Shirley, Craig. 2012. "Better Off Circa 2012." *Politico,* September 5. Retrieved October 11, 2012 (www.politico.com/news/stories/0912/80719.html).

Shriver, Eunice Kennedy. 2007. *Add Health Study.* Washington, DC: National Institute of Child Health and Human Development. Retrieved December 24, 2009 (www.nichd.nih.gov/health/topics/add_health_study.cfm).

Siegel, Dina and Hans Nelen, eds. 2008. "Organized Crime: Culture, Markets, and Policies." *Series: Studies in Organized Crime* 7. New York: Springer.

Siegel, Larry J. 2013. *Criminology: Theories, Patterns, and Typologies,* 11th ed. Belmont, CA: Thomson/Wadsworth.

Simmel, Georg. [1902–1917] 1950. *The Sociology of Georg Simmel,* translated by Kurt Wolff. Glencoe, IL: Free Press.

Simmel, Georg. 1955. *Conflict and the Web of Group Affiliation,* translated by Kurt H. Wolff. New York: Free Press.

Simmons, Rachel. 2002. *Odd Girl Out: The hidden culture of aggression in girls.* Orlando, FL: Harcourt.

"6.7% of World Has a College Degree." 2010. Retrieved March 11, 2011 (www.huffingtonpost.com/2010/05/19/percent-of-world-with-col_n_581807.html).

Sizer, Theodore R. 1984. *Horace's Compromise: The Dilemma of the American High School.* Boston: Houghton Mifflin.

Skocpol, Theda. 1979. *States and Social Revolutions: A Comparative Analysis of France, Russia, and China.* Cambridge, UK: Cambridge University Press.

Smelser, Neil J. 1963. *Theory of Collective Behavior.* New York: Free Press.

Smelser, Neil J. 1988. "Social Structure." Pp. 103–29 in *Handbook of Sociology,* edited by Neil J. Smelser. Newbury Park, CA: Sage.

Smelser, Neil J. 1992. "The Rational Choice Perspective: A Theoretical Assessment." *Rationality and Society* 4:381–410.

Smith, Christian and Robert Faris. 2005. "Socioeconomic Inequality in the American Religious System: An Update and Assessment." *Journal for the Scientific Study of Religion* 44(1):95–104.

Smith, Christian, with P. Snell. 2009. *Souls in Transition: The Religious and Spiritual Lives of Emerging Adults.* New York: Oxford University Press.

Smith, Mark K. 2008. "Howard Gardner and Multiple Intelligences." *The Encyclopedia Of Informal Education.* Retrieved April 17, 2011 (http://www.infed.org/thinkers/gardner.htm).

Smith, Phillip. 2009. "Prohibition: UN Drug Chief Says Black Market Drug Profits Propped Up Global Banking System Last Year." *Drug War Chronicle,* January 30. Retrieved June 30, 2011 (http://stopthedrugwar.org/chronicle/570/costa_UNODC_drug_trade_banks).

Snarr, Michael T. and D. Neil Snarr. 2008. *Introducing Global Issues,* 4th ed. Boulder, CO: Lynne Rienner Publishers.

Snopes.com. 2007. "Ring Around the Rosie." Retrieved July 31, 2012 (www.snopes.com/language/literary/rosie.asp).

Snyder, Benson R. 1971. *The Hidden Curriculum.* New York: Alfred A. Knopf.

Social Security Administration. 2012a. "Social Security History." Retrieved September 3, 2013 (http://www.socialsecurity.gov/history/index.html).

Social Security Administration. 2012b. "Top 10 Baby Names for 2012." Retrieved September 3, 2013 (http://www.socialsecurity.gov/OACT/babynames/).

Social Security Administration. 2013. "Social Security History: Life Expectancy for Social Security." Retrieved February 6, 2013 (www.ssa.gov/history/lifeexpect.html).

Sommerville, C. John. 2002. "Stark's Age of Faith Argument and the Secularization of Things: A Commentary." *Review of Religious Research* (Fall):361–72.

Son, Young-ho. 1992. "Korean Response to the 'Yellow Peril' and Search for Racial Accommodation in the United States." *Korean Journal* 32(2):58–74.

Sons of Union Veterans of the Civil War. 2010. "The United States' Flag Code." Retrieved December 212, 2011 (http://suvcw.org/flag.htm).

Southerland, Anne. 1986. *Gypsies: The Hidden Americans.* Prospect Heights, IL: Waveland.

Southern Poverty Law Center. 2012. "FBI: Dramatic Spike in Hate Crimes Targeting Muslims." *Intelligence Report.* Spring. Retrieved May 1, 2013 (www.splcenter.org/get-informed/intelligence-report/browse-all-issues/2012/spring/fbi-dramatic-spike-in-hate-crimes-targetin)

Sowell, Thomas. 1994. *Race and Culture: A World View.* New York: Basic Books.

Spacey, John. 2012. "Japan's Crime Rate." June 30. *Japan Talk.* Retrieved April 18, 2013 (www.japan-talk.com/jt/new/japans-crime-rate).

Sperling, Gene B. 2005, November. "The Case for Universal Basic Education for the World's Poorest Boys and Girls." *Phi Delta Kappan.* Retrieved September 3, 2013 (http://www.cfr.org/education/case-universal-basic-education-worlds-poorest-boys-girls/p9739).

Sperling, Gene B. 2006. "What Works in Girls' Education." PBS Wide Angle. Retrieved July 11, 2009 (www.pbs.org/wnet/wideangle/episodes/time-for-school-series/essay-what-works-in-girls-education/274).

Spero News. 2009. "China: Good News From Beijing, the Number of Billionaires Is Rising, So Is the Economy." October 13. Retrieved November 11, 2009 (www.speronews.com/a/20830/china—good-news-from-beijing-the-number-of-billionaires-is-rising-so-is-the-economy).

Stanley, Scott M. and Galena K. Rhoades. 2009. "Marriages at Risk: Relationship Formation and Opportunities for Relationship Education." Pp. 21–44 in *What Works in Relationship Education,* edited by Harry Benson and Samantha Callan. Doha, Qatar: Doha International Institute for Family Studies and Development.

Staples, Brent. 2001. "Black Men and Public Space." Pp. 244–46 in *The Production of Reality,* edited by Jodi O'Brien and Peter Kollock. Thousand Oaks, CA: Pine Forge Press.

Staples, Robert. 1999. *The Black Family: Essays and Studies,* 6th ed. Belmont, CA: Wadsworth.

Stark, Rodney. 2000. "Secularization, R.P.I." Pp. 41–66 in *The Secularization Debate,* edited by William H. Swatos, Jr., and Daniel V. A. Olson. Lanham, MD: Rowman & Littlefield.

Stark, Rodney and Roger Finke. 2000. *Acts of Faith: Explaining the Human Side of Religion.* Berkeley: University of California Press.

State of Alaska. 2006. "Workplace Alaska: How to Apply." Retrieved July 5, 2006 (http://notes3.state.ak.us/WA/MainEntry.nsf/WebData/HTMLHow+to+Apply/?open).

State of Delaware. 2008. "Presidential Primary Election." Retrieved March 21, 2008 (http://elections.delaware.gov/information/elections/presidential_2008.shtml).

StateMaster.com. 2013. "Bachelor's Degree or Higher, by Percentage (Most Recent) by State." Retrieved June 30, 2013. (www.statemaster.com/graph/edu_bac_deg_or_hig_by_per-bachelor-s-degree-higher-percentage)

Statistical Handbook of Japan. 2010. "Population." Retrieved May 13, 2011 (www.stat.go.jp/english/data/handbook/c02cont.htm#cha2_2).

Stelter, Brian. 2009. "In Coverage of Iran, Amateurs Take the Lead." Mediadecoder Weblog, *New York Times,* June 17. Retrieved December 22, 2009 (http://mediadecoder.blogs.nytimes.com).

Stern, Jessica. 2003. *Terror in the Name of God: Why Religious Militants Kill.* New York: HarperCollins.

Stewart, Susan D. 2007. *Brave New Stepfamilies: Diverse Paths Toward Stepfamily Living.* Thousand Oaks, CA: Sage.

Stiglitz, Joseph E. 2012. "A Real Cure for the Global Economic Crackup." Pp. 104–109 in *Globalization: The Transformation of Social Worlds,* 3rd ed., edited by D. Stanley Eitzen and Maxine Baca Zinn. Belmont, CA: Wadsworth.

Stillwell, Robert. 2010. "Public School Graduates and Dropouts From the Common Core of Data: School Year 2007–08." Retrieved July 14, 2011 (nces.ed.gov/pubs2010/2010341.pdf).

Stockholm International Peace Research Institute Yearbook. 2010. "World Military Expenditures Increase Despite Financial Crisis." June 2. Retrieved May 10, 2011 (www.sipri.org/media/pressreleases/2010/100602yearbooklaunch).

Stockholm International Peace Research Institute Yearbook. 2012. "World Nuclear Forces: Summary." Retrieved June 2, 2012 (www.sipri.org/yearbook/2012/07)

Stoessinger, John. 1993. *Why Nations Go to War.* New York: St. Martin's Press.

Stone, Brad and Noam Cohen. 2009. "Social Networks Spread Defiance Online." *The New York Times,* June 16. Retrieved June 30, 2009 (www.nytimes.com/2009/06/16/world/middleeast/16media.html?_r=1&ref=world).

Stop Child Trafficking Now. 2012. "Child Trafficking Statistics." Retrieved May 1, 2012 (http://sctnow.org/contentpages.aspx?parentnavigationid=5827-4e7a-bde1-f61690fa44a8).

Stout, David. 2009. "Violent Crime Fell in 2008, F.B.I. Report Says." *The New York Times,* September 14. Retrieved November 4, 2009 (www.nytimes.com/2009/09/15/us/15crime.html).

Straus, Murray A., Richard J. Gelles, and Suzanne K. Steinmetz. 2006. *Behind Closed Doors: Violence in the American Family.* New Brunswick, NJ: Transaction.

Stringer, Donna M. 2006. "Let Me Count the Ways: African American/European American Marriages." Pp. 170–76 in *Intercultural Communication: A Reader,* edited by Larry A. Samovar, Richard E. Porter, and Edwin R. McDaniel. Belmont, CA: Wadsworth.

Stryker, Sheldon. 1980. *Symbolic Interactionism: A Social Structural Version.* Menlo Park, CA: Benjamin Cummings.

Stryker, Sheldon. 2000. "Identity Competition: Key to Differential Social Involvement." Pp. 21–40 in *Identity, Self, and Social Movements,* edited by Sheldon Stryker, Timothy Owens, and Robert White. Minneapolis: University of Minnesota Press.

Stryker, Sheldon and Anne Stratham. 1985. "Symbolic Interaction and Role Theory." Pp. 311–78 in *Handbook of Social Psychology,* edited by Gardiner Lindsey and Eliot Aronson. New York: Random House.

Stutz, Fredrick P. and Barney Warf. 2005. *The World Economy.* Upper Saddle River, NJ: Prentice Hall.

Sutherland, Edwin H., Donald R. Cressey, and David Luckenbil. 1992. *Criminology.* Dix Hills, NY: General Hall.

Sway, Marlene. 1988. *Familiar Strangers: Gypsy Life in America.* Urbana: University of Illinois Press.

Szymanski, Linda A., Ann Sloan Devlin, Joan C. Chrisler, and Stuart A. Vyse. 1993. "Gender Role and Attitude Toward Rape in Male and Female College Students." *Sex Roles* 29:37–55.

Talbot, Margaret. 2008. "Red Sex, Blue Sex." *The New Yorker,* November 3. Retrieved December 24, 2009 (www.newyorker.com/reporting/2008/11/03/081103fa_fact_talbot).

Tamney, Joseph B. 1992. *The Resilience of Christianity in the Modern World.* Albany: State University of New York Press.

Tanenhaus, Sam. 2012. "History vs. the Tea Party." *The New York Times,* January 14. Retrieved July 15, 2012 (www.nytimes.com/2012/01/15/sunday-review/gop-history-vs-the-tea-party.html?pagewanted=all).

Tapscott, Don. 1998. *Growing Up Digital: The Rise of the Net Generation.* New York: McGraw Hill.

Tareen, Sophia and Jason Keyser. 2012. "Chicago Teachers Strike: No Deal Reached Yet, Talks Continue on Day 5." *Huffington Post,* September 14. Retrieved September 14, 2012 (www.huffingtonpost.com/2012/09/14/chicago-teachers-strike-n_0_n_1883626.html).

Taub, Diane E. and Penelope A. McLorg. 2010. "Influences of Gender Socialization and Athletic Involvement on the Occurrence of Eating Disorders." Pp. 73–82 in *Sociological Footprints: Introductory Readings in Sociology,* 11th ed., edited by Leonard Cargan and Jeanne H. Ballantine. Belmont, CA: Wadsworth Cengage Learning.

Tea Party Patriots. 2012. "About Tea Party Patriots." Retrieved June 13, 2012 (http://www.teapartypatriots.org/about/?gclid=CIyk15G6y7ACFcIUKgod00KPXw).

TechWench. 2010. "Physical Books to Be Overshadowed by E-Books Within 5 Years." October 19. Retrieved April 17, 2011 (www.techwench.com/physical-books-to-be-overshadowed-by-e-books-within-5-years/).

Therborn, Goran. 1976. "What Does the Ruling Class Do When It Rules?" *Insurgent Sociologist* 6:3–16.

Theroux, David J. 2012. "Secular Theocracy: The Foundations and Folly of Modern Tyranny." *The Independent Institute,* January 11. Retrieved July 13, 2012 (www.independent.org/newsroom/article.asp?id=3206).

Thiagaraj, Henry. 2007. *Minority and Human Rights From the Dalits' Perspective.* Chennai, India: Oneworld Educational Trust.

Thio, Alex D., Jim D. Taylor, and Martin D. Schwartz. 2012. *Deviant Behavior,* 11th ed. Boston: Pearson.

Thompson, A. C. 2009. "Katrina's Hidden Race War." *The Nation,* January 5. Retrieved July 7, 2011 (www.thenation.com/article/katrinas-hidden-race-war).

Thompson, Derek. 2011. "How Women in the Workforce Are Changing America." *The Atlantic,* March 9. Retrieved June 9, 2012 (www.theatlantic.com/business/archive/2011/03/how-women-in-the-workforce-are-changing-america/72235/).

Thorne, Barrie. 1993. *Gender Play: Girls and Boys in School.* New Brunswick, NJ: Rutgers University Press.

Thumma, Scott and Dave Travis. 2007. *Beyond Megachurch Myths: What We Can Learn From America's Largest Churches.* Hoboken, NJ: Jossey-Bass.

Tichenor, Veronica Jaris. 1999. "Status and Income as Gendered Resources: The Case of Marital Power." *Journal of Marriage and the Family* 61(August):638–50.

Tilley, Michael. 2009. "Power Shift? Proponents Again Push for Natural Gas-Powered Vehicles." Retrieved January 17, 2011 (www.thecity-wire.com/index.php?q=node/5479).

Tipton, Steven M. 1990. "The Social Organization of Zen Practice: Constructing Transcultural Reality." *American Journal of Sociology* 96(2):488–90.

Toffler, Alvin and Heidi Toffler. 1980. *The Third Wave.* New York: Morrow.

Tolbert, Pamela S. and Richard H. Hall. 2009. *Organizations: Structures, Processes, and Outcomes,* 10th ed. Englewood Cliffs, NJ: Prentice Hall.

Tollefson, Jeff. 2012. "Heatwaves Blamed on Global Warming." *Nature.* Retrieved September 7, 2012 (www.nature.com/news/heatwaves-blamed-on-global-warming-1.11130).

Topix.com. 2010. "Fired for Being Gay? It's Legal in 29 States." Retrieved July 10, 2011 (www.topix.com/forum/state/de/TP9N5JVK30FRS3NLO).

TopTenz.net. 2011. "Top 10 Most Spoken Languages." March 29. Retrieved September 30, 2012 (www.toptenz.net/top-10-most-spoken-languages.php).

Tough, Paul. 2004. "The Harlem Project." *The New York Times,* June 20. *Retrieved* September 6, 2013 (www.nytimes.com/2004/06/20/magazine/the-harlem-project.html?pagewanted=all&src=pm).

Tough, Paul. 2008. *Whatever It Takes: Geoffrey Canada's Quest to Change Harlem and America.* Boston: Houghton Mifflin Harcourt.

"Transnational Crime in the Developing World." 2011. Cited in "The 12 Most Profitable International Crimes." Retrieved April 13, 2012 (http://247wallst.com/2011/02/10/the-12-most-profitable-international -crimes/).

Transparency International. 2012. "Global Corruption Barometer 2010/11." Retrieved October 6, 2012 (http://gcb.transparency.org/gcb201011/infographic/).

Travers, Jeffrey and Stanley Milgram. 1969. "An Experimental Study of the Small World Problem." *Sociometry* 32:425–43.

Truman, Jennifer L. 2011a. "Criminal Victimization, 2010." National Crime Victimization Survey, U.S. Department of Justice, September. Retrieved May 26, 2012 (www.bjs.gov/content/pub/pdf/cv10.pdf).

Truman, Jennifer L. 2011b. "Rate of Total Violent Crime Victimization Declined by 13% in 2010." U.S. Bureau of Justice Statistics, September 15. Retrieved April 13, 2012 (www.bjs.ojp.usdoj.gov/index.cfm?ty=pbdetail&iid=2224).

Truman, Jennifer L. and Michael Planty. 2012. "Criminal Victimization, 2011." October, NCJ 239437. Retrieved August 25, 2013 (http://www.bjs.gov/content/pub/pdf/cv11.pdf).

Tumin, Melvin M. 1953. "Some Principles of Social Stratification: A Critical Analysis." *American Sociological Review* 18(August):387–94.

Turnbull, Colin M. 1962. *The Forest People.* New York: Simon & Schuster.

Turner, Bryan S. 1991a. "Politics and Culture in Islamic Globalism." Pp. 161–81 in *Religion and Global Order,* edited by Roland Robertson and William R. Garrett. New York: Paragon.

Turner, Bryan S. 1991b. *Religion and Social Theory.* London: Sage.

Turner, Jonathan H. 2003. *The Structure of Sociological Theory,* 7th ed. Belmont, CA: Wadsworth

Turner, Ralph H. and Lewis M. Killian. 1993. "The Field of Collective Behavior." Pp. 5–20 in *Collective Behavior and Social Movements,* edited by Russell L. Curtis, Jr. and Benigno E. Aguirre. Boston: Allyn & Bacon.

UNESCO Institute for Statistics. 2010. "World Science Report 2010." November 17. Retrieved December 2, 2010 (www.uis.unesco.org/ev_en.php?ID=8167_201&ID2=DO_TOPIC).

UNESCO Institute for Statistics. 2011. "Education Profile—Niger." Retrieved September 3, 2013 (http://stats.uis.unesco.org/unesco/TableViewer/document.aspx?ReportId=121&IF_Language=en&BR_Country=5620).

UNESCO Institute for Statistics. 2012. "Primary School Curricula on Reading and Mathematics in Developing Countries." *Technical Paper* 8. Retrieved January 28, 2013 (www.uis.unesco.org/Education/ . . . tp8-education-curriculum-reading-math-2012-en3.pdf).

UNIFEM. 2002. "Report of the Learning Oriented Assessment of Gender Mainstreaming and Women's Empowerment Strategies in Rwanda." Retrieved April 7, 2008 (www.unifem.org/attachments/products/rwanda_assessment_report_eng.pdf).

United Church of Christ. 2013. "Twenty-Seventh General Synod—Grand Rapids." Retrieved June 24, 2013 (www.ucc.org/environmental-ministries/about-us.html).

United Nations. 2010. "Violence Against Women." Ch. 6 in *The World's Women: Trends and Statistics.* Retrieved April 11, 2012 (http://unstats.un.org/unsd/demographic/products/Worldswomen/WW2010%20Report_by%20chapter(pdf)/Vnce%20against%20women.pdf).

United Nations Climate Change Conference. 2009. Retrieved December 22, 2009 (http://en.cop15.dk/about+cop15).

United Nations, Department of Economic and Social Affairs, Population Division. 2008, February. *Economic & World Urbanization Prospects: The 2007 Revision.* Retrieved April 27, 2009 (http://www.un.org/esa/population/publications/wup2007/2007WUP_Highlights_web.pdf).

United Nations, Department of Economic and Social Affairs, Population Division. 2010. *World Urbanization Prospects: The 2009 Revision.* Retrieved July 26, 2011 (http://esa.un.org/unpd/wup/index.htm).

United Nations, Department of Economic and Social Affairs, Population Division. 2012. "Data on Cities and Urban Agglomerations." *World Urbanization Prospects: The 2011 Revision.* Retrieved December 22, 2012 (http://esa.un.org/unpd/wup/CD-ROM/Urban-Agglomerations.htm).

United Nations, Department of Economic and Social Affairs, Population Division. 2012. "World Urbanization Prospects, the 2011 Revision." Retrieved October 13, 2013 (http://esa.un.org/unpd/wup/index.htm)

United Nations, Department of Economic and Social Affairs, Population Division. 2012. "World Urbanization Prospects: The 2011 Revision," March 2012. Retrieved October 22, 2013 (http://esa.un.org/unup/pdf/WUP2011_Highlights.pdf)

United Nations Framework Convention on Climate Change. 2013. "Status of Ratification of the Kyoto Protocol." Retrieved September 7, 2013 (http://unfccc.int/kyoto_protocol/status_of_ratification/items/2613.php).

United Nations High Commissioner for Refugees. 2012. "UNHCR Report Shows Highest Number of Refugees in 15 Years." June 19. Retrieved July 30, 2012 (www.euronews.com/2012/06/19/unhrc-report-shows-highest-number-of-refugees-in-15-years/).

United Nations Population Division, 2012. "World Urbanization Prospects: The 2011 Revision" March 2012. Retrieved October 22, 2013 (http://esa.un.org/unup/pdf/WUP2011_Highlights.pdf).

United Nations Department of Economic and Social Affairs, Population Division. 2012. "World Urbanization Prospects, the 2011 Revision" Retrieved October 13, 2013 (http://esa.un.org/unpd/wup/index.htm)

University of Pennsylvania. 2010. "Body Modification." Retrieved November 18, 2010 (penn.museum/sites/body_modification/bod-modpierce.shtml).

UN News Centre. 2010. "Senior UN Official Cites Evidence of Growing Support for Abolishing Death Penalty." February 24. Retrieved March 8, 2011 (www.un.org/apps/news/story.asp?NewsID=33877&Cr=death+penalty&Cr1=).

UN News Centre. 2012. "Millions of Children in Cities Face Poverty and Exclusion—UN Report." Retrieved August 23, 2013 (http://www.un.org/apps/news/story.asp?NewsID=41395#.Uhex_WTTVXg).

UPI.com. 2010. "12 Percent in U.S. Foreign Born." October 19. Retrieved May 5, 2012 (www.upi.com/Top_News/US/2010/10/19/12-percent-in-US-foreign-born/UPI-87261287522622/).

U.S. Bureau of Justice Statistics. 2003. *Sourcebook of Criminal Justice Statistics.* Washington, DC: U.S. Department of Justice.

U.S. Bureau of Labor Statistics. 2008. "Marriage and Divorce Rates by Country: 1980–2008." Retrieved June 6, 2012 (www.census.gov/compendia/statab/2011/tables/11s1335.pdf).

U.S. Bureau of Labor Statistics. 2012. "Women's Earnings as a Percent of Men's in 2010." January 10. Retrieved May 25, 2012 (www.bls.gov/opub/ted/2012/ted_20120110.htm).

U.S. Bureau of Labor Statistics. 2013. "American Time Use Survey—2012 Results." Retrieved August 27, 2013 (http://www.bls.gov/news.release/atus.nr0.htm).

U.S. Census Bureau. 2007. "America's Families and Living Arrangements: 2007." Retrieved February 21, 2009 (http://www.census.gov/prod/2009pubs/p20-561.pdf).

U.S. Census Bureau. 2008. *Public Education Finances: 2006.* Retrieved January 7, 2010 (www2.census.gov/govs/school/06f33pub.pdf).

U.S. Census Bureau. 2009a. "Fact Sheet: Alaska." Retrieved August 8, 2011 (http://factfinder.census.gov/servlet/ACSSAFFFacts?_event=Search&_state=04000US02).

U.S. Census Bureau. 2009b. "Historical Income Tables—Households." Retrieved April 26, 2009 (www.census.gov/hhes/www/income/histinc/h02AR.html).

U.S. Census Bureau. 2010. "Income, Poverty, and Health Insurance Coverage in the United States, 2010." Report P60, n. 238, Table B-2, pp. 68–73.

U.S. Census Bureau. 2011a. "Alaska QuickFacts." Retrieved April 7, 2011 (quickfacts.census.gov/qfd/states/02000.html).

U.S. Census Bureau. 2011b. "Custodial Parents Becoming Less Likely to Received Full Amount of Child Support, Census Bureau Reports." Dec. 7. Retrieved June 6, 2012 (www.census.gov/newsroom/releases/archives/children/cb11-206.html).

U.S. Census Bureau. 2012a. "Current Population Survey Definitions." Retrieved August 27, 2013 (http://www.census.gov/cps/about/cpsdef.html).

U.S. Census Bureau. 2012b. "Educational Attainment by Race and Hispanic Origin." Table 229 Retrieved May 5, 2012 (www.census.gov/compendia/statab/2012/tables/12s0229.pdf).

U.S. Census Bureau. 2012c. "Hispanic Origin: The Hispanic Population in the United States: 2011." Retrieved August 26, 2013 (http://www.census.gov/population/hispanic/data/2011.html).

U.S. Census Bureau. 2012d. "Marriage and Divorce Rates by Country: 1980–2008." *Statistical Abstract of the United States:* Retrieved June 28, 2012 (www.census.gov/compendia/statab/2012/tables/12s1336.pdf).

U.S. Census Bureau. 2012e. "Mean Earnings of Full-Time Year-Round Workers in Current Dollars by Educational Attainment, Sex, and Age: 2009." *Statistical Abstract of the United States: 2012.* Retrieved May 8, 2013. (www.census.gov/compendia/statab/2012/tables/12s0703.pdf).

U.S. Census Bureau. 2012f. "Table 231. Educational Attainment by Selected Characteristics: 2010." *Statistical Abstract of the United States: 2012.* Retrieved August 19, 2013 (http://www.census.gov/compendia/statab/2012/tables/12s0231.pdf).

U.S. Census Bureau. 2012g. "Table 232. Mean Earnings by Highest Degree Earned." Retrieved February 21, 2013. (www.census.gov/compendia/statab/2012/tables/12s0232.pdf)

U.S. Census Bureau. 2012h. "Table 703: Mean Earnings of Full-Time Year-Round Workers in Current Dollars by Educational Attainment, Sex, and Age: 2009 [Excel version]." *Statistical Abstract of the United States: 2012.* Retrieved May 8, 2013 (www.census.gov/compendia/statab/cats/income_expenditures_poverty_wealth/income_for_persons.html).

U.S. Census Bureau. 2012i. "Table 31. Movers by Type of Move and Reason for Moving: 2010." Retrieved September 7, 2013 (http://www.census.gov/compendia/statab/2012/tables/12s0031.pdf).

U.S. Census Bureau. 2013. "U.S. and World Population Clock." Retrieved June 9, 2013 (www.census.gov/popclock/).

U.S. Census Bureau, Population Division, International Programs Center. 2011. "International Data Base." Retrieved August 6, 2011 (www.census.gov/ipo/www/idbnew.html).

U.S. Department of Defense. 2011. *Dictionary of Military and Associated Terms,* January 31. Retrieved January 19, 2013 (http://ra.defense.gov/documents/rtm/jp1_02.pdf).

U.S. Department of Defense. 2012. "Department of Defense Antiterrorism Program Memo: Instruction No. 2000.12, March 1. Retrieved July 28, 2012 (www.dtic.mil/whs/directives/corres/pdf/200012p.pdf).

U.S. Department of Education, National Center for Education Statistics. 2012. *The Condition of Education 2011* (NCES 2012-045), Indicator 45. Retrieved January 27, 2013 (http://nces.ed.gov/fastfacts/display.asp?id=40).

U.S. Department of Interior Office of Education. 1930. *Availability of Public School Education in Rural Communities* (Bulletin No. 34, edited by Walter H. Gaummitz). Washington, DC: Government Printing Office.

U.S. Department of Justice. 2011a. "Crime Clock Statistics." Retrieved August 21, 2013 (http://www.fbi.gov/about-us/cjis/ucr/crime-in-the-u.s/2011/crime-in-the-u.s.-2011/offenses-known-to-law-enforcement/crime-clock).

U.S. Department of Justice. 2011b. "Hate Crimes Remain Steady: 2010 FBI Report Released." Retrieved April 18, 2013 (www.fbi.gov/news/stories/2011/november/hatecrimes_111411/hatecrimes_111411).

U.S. Department of Justice. 2011c. "Violent Crime." *Crime in the United States 2011.* Retrieved August 21, 2013 (http://www.fbi.gov/about-us/cjis/ucr/crime-in-the-u.s/2011/crime-in-the-u.s.-2011/violent-crime/violent-crime).

U.S. Department of Labor. 2011. "Highlights of Women's Earnings in 2010." *Report 1031.* Retrieved June 5, 2012 (www.bls.gov/cps/cpswom2010.pdf).

U.S. Department of Labor, Bureau of Labor Statistics. 2012, October. "Report 1038: Highlights of Women's Earnings in 2011." Retrieved September 3, 2013 (http://www.bls.gov/cps/cpswom2011.pdf).

U.S. Department of State. 2011. *Country Reports on Terrorism 2010.* Retrieved July 14, 2012 (www.state.gov/documents/organization/170479.pdf).

U.S. Department of State. 2013. "Country Reports on Terrorism." National Consortium for the Study of Terrorism and Responses to Terrorism. Retrieved August 25, 2013 (www.state.gov/documents/organization/210288.pdf).

U.S. Election Project. 2012, March 31. "General Election Turnout Rates." Retrieved August 31, 2013 (http://elections.gmu.edu/Turnout_2008G.html).

U.S. General Accounting Office. 2004. "Defense of Marriage Act: Update to Prior Report." GAO-04-353R, January 23. Retrieved June 30, 2012 (http://www.gao.gov/products/GAO-04-353R).

U.S. Senate. 2013. "Ethnic Diversity in the Senate." Retrieved February 21, 2013 (www.senate.gov/artandhistory/history/common/briefing/minority_senators.htm).

U.S. Trade Representative. 2012. "Joint Stats From 2012 NAFTA Commission Meeting." Retrieved September 8, 2012 (www.ustr.gov/).

Veblen, Thorstein. 1902. *The Theory of the Leisure Class: An Economic Study of Institutions.* New York: Macmillan.

Verbeek, Stjin and Rinus Penninx. 2009. "Employment Equity Policies in Work Organisations." Pp. 69–94 in *Equal Opportunity and Ethnic Inequality in European Labour Markets: Discrimination, Gender, and Policies of Diversity,* edited by Karen Kraal, Judith Roosblad, and John Wrench. Amsterdam: University of Amsterdam Press.

Vervaeck, Armand and James Daniell. 2011. "Japan Tohoku Tsunami and Earthquake: The Death Toll Is Climbing Again." Earthquake Report, August 15. Retrieved May 13, 2012 (Httlp://earthquake-report.com/2011/08/04/japan-tsunami-following-up-the-aftermath-part-16-june/).

Victor, Barbara. 2003. *Army of Roses: Inside the World of Palestinian Women Suicide Bombers.* Emmaus, PA: Rodale Books.

Vijayakumar, Gowri. 2012. "Girls and Education: A Global Approach." May 20. Retrieved January 28, 2013 (www.socwomen.org/web/images/stories/resources/fact_sheets/fact_2_2012-girlseducation.pdf).

Vivat International. 2012. "Poverty." Retrieved January 23, 2013 (vivatinternational.org/our-work/poverty-eradication/).

Voting and Democracy Research Center. 2008. "Primaries: Open and Closed." Retrieved March 21, 2008 (www.fairvote.org/?page=1801).

Wade, Lisa. 2012. "The New Elite: Attributing Privilege and Class vs. Merit." *Sociological Images: Inspiring Sociological Imaginations Everywhere,* June 21. Retrieved September 14, 2012 (http://thesocietypages.org/socimages/2012/06/21/the-new-elite-attributing-privilege-to-class-vs-merit/).

Waite, Linda J. and Maggie Gallagher. 2000. *The Case for Marriage: Why Married People Are Happier, Healthier, and Better Off Financially.* New York: Doubleday.

Walby, Sylvia. 1990. *The Historical Roots of Materialist Feminism.* Paper presented at the International Sociological Association, Madrid, Spain.

The Wall Street Journal. 2009. "The Madoff Case: A Timeline." March 12. Retrieved November 5, 2009 (http://online.wsj.com/article/SB1129669 54231272304.html?mod=googlenews.wsj).

Wallerstein, Immanuel. 1974. *The Modern World System.* New York: Academic Press.

Wallerstein, Immanuel. 1979. *The Capitalist World Economy.* London: Cambridge University Press.

Wallerstein, Immanuel. 1991. *Geopolitics and Geoculture: Essays on the Changing World-System.* Cambridge, MA: Cambridge University Press.

Wallerstein, Immanuel. 2004. *World Systems Analysis: An Introduction.* Durham, NC: Duke University Press.

Wallerstein, Immanuel. 2005. "Render Unto Caesar? The Dilemmas of a Multicultural World." *Sociology of Religion* 66(2):121–33.

Wallerstein, Judith S. and Sarah Blakeslee. 1996. *The Good Marriage: How and Why Love Lasts.* New York: Warner Books.

Wallis, Jim. 2005. *God's Politics: Why the Right Gets It Wrong and the Left Doesn't Get It.* New York: HarperCollins.

Wallis, Jim. 2013. *On God's Side: What Religion Forgets and Politics Hasn't Learned About Serving the Common Good.* Grand Rapids, MI: Brazos Press.

War Child. 2013. "Child Soldier: Some Words Don't Belong Together." Retrieved April 9, 2013 (www.warchild.org.uk/issues/child-soldiers?gclid=CJ_78cL7bYCFSdgMgod11wAmQ).

Ward, Martha C. and Monica Edelstein. 2009. *A World Full of Women,* 5th ed. Boston: Allyn & Bacon.

Warner, R. Stephen. 1993. "Work in Progress Toward a New Paradigm for the Sociological Study of Religion in the United States." *American Journal of Sociology* 98(5):1044–1093.

Washington, Jesse. 2011. "The Disappearing Black Middle Class." *Chicago Sun Times,* July 10. Retrieved May 4, 2012 (www.suntimes.com/news/nation/6397110-418/the-disappearing-black-middle-class.html).

WaterAid. 2008. "WaterAid's Key Facts and Statistics." Retrieved February 25, 2008 (www.wateraid.org/international/what_we_do/statistics/default.asp).

WaterAid. 2012. "Annual Review 2010/11." Retrieved September 9, 2012 (www.wateraid.org/uk/about_us/annual_report/default.asp).

WaterAid. 2013. "Precipitation for Education." Retrieved February 10, 2013 (www.wateraid.org/other/Print.asp).

Waters, Tony. 2012. *Schooling, Childhood, and Bureaucracy: Bureaucratizing the Child.* Basingstoke, England: Palgrave Macmillan.

Way, Niobe. 2011 *Deep Secrets: Boys' Friendships and the Crisis of Connection.* Cambridge, MA: Harvard University Press.

Weaver, Janelle. 2010. "Social Life Starts in the Womb." *Science*Shot, October 12. Retrieved October 19, 2010 (http://news.science mag.org/sciencenow/2010/10/scienceshot-social-life-starts-in .html?rss=1&utm_source=twitterfeed&utm_medium=twitter).

Weber, Max. [1904–1905] 1958. *The Protestant Ethic and the Spirit of Capitalism,* translated by Talcott Parsons. New York: Scribner.

Weber, Max. 1946. *From Max Weber: Essays in Sociology,* translated and edited by Hans H. Gerth and C. Wright Mills. New York: Oxford University Press.

Weber, Max. 1947. *The Theory of Social and Economic Organization,* translated and edited by A. M. Henderson and Talcott Parsons. New York: Oxford University Press.

WebSiteOptimization.com. 2010. "U.S. Broadband Penetration Jumps to 45.2%—U.S. Internet Access Nearly 75%." April 13. Retrieved March 1, 2011 (www.websiteoptimization.com/bw/0403/).

Webster's Unabridged English Dictionary. 1989. New York: Gramercy Books.

Weeks, John R. 2012. *Population: An Introduction to Concepts and Issues,* 11th ed. Belmont, CA: Wadsworth.

Weil, Elizabeth. 2008. "Teaching to the Testosterone." *The New York Times Magazine,* March 2, p. 38.

Weller, Christian E. and Adam Hersh. 2006. "Free Markets and Poverty." Pp. 69–73 in *Globalization: The Transformation of Social Worlds,* edited by D. Stanley Eitzen and Maxine Baca Zinn. Belmont, CA: Wadsworth.

Wells, Amy Stuart and Jeannie Oakes. 1996. "Potential Pitfalls of Systemic Reform: Early Lessons From Research on Detracking." *Sociology of Education* 69(Extra Issue):135–43.

Wessinger, Catherine. 2000. *How the Millennium Comes Violently: From Jonestown to Heaven's Gate.* New York: Seven Bridges.

West, Heather C., William J. Sabol, and Sarah J. Greenman. 2009. "Prisoners in 2009." U.S. Department of Justice, Bureau of Justice Statistics. Retrieved July 7, 2011 (http://bjs.ojp.usdoj.gov/content/pub/pdf/p09.pdf).

Whaley, Floyd. 2012. "New Internet Law in Philippines Takes Effect, Raising Fears." *New York Times,* October 3. Retrieved October 6, 2012 (http://www.nytimes.com).

White House. 2011. "Fact Sheet: New Actions on Guantanamo and Detainee Policy." March 7. Retrieved April 14, 2012 (www.white house.gov/sites/default/files/Fact_Sheet_--_Guantanamo_and_Detainee_Policies.pdf).

Whitney, Lance. 2012. "2011 Ends with Almost 6 Billion Mobile Phone Subscriptions." CNET News. Retrieved May 18, 2012 (http://news .cnet.com/8301-1023_3-57352095-93/2011-ends-with-almost-6-billion-mobile-phone-subscriptions/).

Whorf, Benjamin Lee. 1956. *Language, Thought, and Reality.* New York: John Wiley.

Whyte, William H. 1956. *The Organization Man.* New York: Simon and Schuster.

Wilcox, Norma and Tracey Steele. 2003. "Just the Facts: A Descriptive Analysis of Inmate Attitudes Toward Capital Punishment." *The Prison Journal* 83(4):464–82.

Wilkerson, Isabel. 2010. *The Warmth of Other Suns: The Epic Story of America's Great Migration.* New York: Vintage/Random House

Williams, Brian K., Stacey C. Sawyer, and Carl M. Wahlstrom. 2013. *Marriages, Families, and Intimate Relationships,* 3rd ed. Boston: Allyn & Bacon.

Williams, Christine L. 2006. *Inside Toyland: Working, Shopping, and Social Inequality.* Berkeley: University of California Press.

Williams, Gregory H. 1996. *Life on the Color Line: The True Story of a White Boy Who Discovered He Was Black.* New York: Dutton.

Williams, Robin Murphy, Jr. 1970. *American Society: A Sociological Interpretation,* 3rd ed. New York: Alfred Knopf.

Willie, Charles Vert. 2003. *A New Look at Black Families,* 5th ed. Walnut Creek, CA: AltaMira.

Willis, Paul. 1979. *Learning to Labor: How Working Class Kids Get Working Class Jobs.* Aldershot, Hampshire, England: Saxon House.

Wilson, Edward O. 1980. *Sociobiology.* Cambridge, MA: Belknap.

Wilson, Edward O. 1987. *The Coevolution of Biology and Culture.* Cambridge, MA: Harvard University Press.

Wilson, Edward O., Michael S. Gregory, Anita Silvers, and Diane Sutch. 1978. "What Is Sociobiology?" *Society* 15(6):1–12.

Wilson, K. 1993. *Dialectics of Consciousness: Problems of Development, the Indian Reality.* Madras: Oneworld Educational Trust.

Wilson, Mary E. 2006. "Infectious Concerns: Modern Factors in the Spread of Disease." Pp. 313–19 in *Globalization: The Transformation of Social Worlds,* edited by D. Stanley Eitzen and Maxine Baca Zinn. Belmont, CA: Wadsworth.

Wilson, Warren H. 1924. "What the Automobile Has Done to and for the Country Church." *Annals of the American Academy of Political and Social Science* 116(November):85–86.

Wilson, William Julius. 1978. *The Declining Significance of Race: Blacks and Changing American Institutions.* Chicago: University of Chicago Press.

Wilson, William Julius. 1984. "The Black Underclass." *The Wilson Quarterly* (Spring):88–89.

Wilson, William Julius. 1993a. *The Ghetto Underclass: Social Science Perspectives.* Newbury Park, CA: Sage.

Wilson, William Julius. 1993b. "The New Urban Poverty and the Problem of Race." *The Tanner Lecture on Human Values,* October 22 (printed in *Michigan Quarterly Review,* 247–73).

Wilson, William Julius. 1996. *When Work Disappears.* New York: Alfred A. Knopf.

Winders, Bill. 2004. "Changing Racial Inequality: The Rise and Fall of Systems of Racial Inequality in the U.S." Paper presented at the Annual Meeting of the American Sociological Association, San Francisco.

Winkler, Karen J. 1991. "Revisiting the Nature vs. Nurture Debate: Historian Looks Anew at Influence of Biology on Behavior." *Chronicle of Higher Education,* May 22, pp. A5, A8.

Winslow, Robert W. and Sheldon X. Zhang. 2008. *Criminology: A Global Perspective.* Upper Saddle River, NJ: Pearson Prentice Hall.

Witness for Peace. 2012. "Mediation With GM Fails, Workers Re-Start Hunger Strike." September 3. Retrieved October 14, 2012 (http://witnessforpeace.org/).

Witt, Susan D. 2000. "The Influence of Television on Children's Gender Role Socialization." *Childhood Education* 76. Retrieved May 24, 2012 (www.eric.ed.gov/ERICWebPortal/recordDetail?accno=EJ610307).

Wolf, Richard. 2010. "Number of uninsured Americans Rises to 50.7 Million." *USA Today,* September 17. Retrieved April 7, 2011 (www.usatoday.com/news/nation/2010-09-17-uninsured17_ST_N.htm).

Wong, Adrienne. 2012. "Chinese Applications to U.S. Schools Skyrocket." *NBC Nightly News.* Retrieved May 15, 2012 (http://behindthewall.msnbc.msn.com/_news/2012/01/11/9679479-chinese-applicatons-to-us-schools-skyrocket?lite).

Wood, Julia T. 2008. *Gendered Lives: Communication, Gender, and Culture,* 8th ed. Belmont, CA: Wadsworth.

Woodberry, Robert D. and Christian S. Smith. 1998. "Fundamentalism et al: Conservative Protestants in America." *Annual Review of Sociology* 24:25–26.

Woods, Andrew K. 2011. "These Revolutions Are Not All Twitter (Op-Ed)." *New York Times,* February 1. Retrieved October 6, 2012 (http://www.nytimes.com).

The World Almanac and Book of Facts. 2013. New York: Infobase Publishing.

World Bank. 2011. *World Development Report 2012: Gender Equality and Development.* Retrieved August 21, 2013 (http://siteresources.worldbank.org/INTWDR2012/Resources/7778105-1299699968583/7786210 1315936222006/Complete-Report.pdf).

World Bank. 2012. "Girls' Education: Learning for All." Retrieved September 14, 2012 (http://web.worldbank.org/WBSITE/EXTERNAL/TOPICS/EXTEDUCATION/o,,contentMDK:20298916~menuPK:617572~pagePK:148956~piPK:216618~theSitePK:282386,00.html).

World Bank. 2013a. "Population Density (People Per Square KM of Land Area)." Retrieved June 9, 2013 (http://data.worldbank.org/indicator/EN.POP.DNST).

World Bank. 2013b. "Ratio of Female to Male Secondary Enrollment (%)." Retrieved June 15, 2013 (http://data.worldbank.org/).

World Coalition. 2012. "World Database." World Coalition Against the Death Penalty. Retrieved May 29, 2012 (http://www.worldcoalition.org/worldwide-database.html).

World Development Report. 2012. *World Development Report: Gender Equality and Development.* World Bank. Retrieved October 1, 2012 (http://go.worldbank.org/6R2KGVEXPO).

World Economic Forum. 2012. "Seven Billion and Growing: A 21st-Century Perspective on Population." Retrieved July 28, 2012 (http://reports.weforum.org/global-agenda-council-2012/councils/population-growth/).

World Factbook. 2012a. "Country Comparison: GDP Per Capita." Retrieved February 9, 2013 (https://www.cia.gov/library/publications/the-world-factbook/rankorder/2004rank.html).

World Factbook 2012b. "Country Comparison: Life Expectancy at Birth." Retrieved August 30, 2012 (www.cia.gov/library/publications/the-world-factbook/rankorder/2102rank.html).

World Factbook. 2012c. "Field Listing: Literacy." Retrieved January 28, 2013 (https://www.cia.gov/library/publications/the-world-factbook/fields/2103.html).

World Factbook. 2012d. "GDP Per Capita." Retrieved August 30, 2012 (https://www.cia.gov/library/publications/the-world-factbook/rankorder/2004rank.html).

World Factbook. 2012e. "Infant Mortality Rate." Retrieved August 30, 2012 (www.cia.gov/library/publications/the-world-factbook/rankorder/2091rank.html).

World Factbook. 2013a. "Canada." Retrieved September 2, 2013 (https://www.cia.gov/library/publications/the-world-factbook/geos/ca.html).

World Factbook. 2013b. "Chad." Retrieved September 2, 2013 (https://www.cia.gov/library/publications/the-world-factbook/geos/cd.html).

World Factbook. 2013c. "China." Retrieved September 2, 2013 (https://www.cia.gov/library/publications/the-world-factbook/geos/ch.html).

World Factbook. 2013d. "Country Comparison: Infant Mortality Rate." Retrieved August 23, 2013 (https://www.cia.gov/library/publications/the-world-factbook/rankorder/2091rank.html).

World Factbook. 2013e. "Country Comparison: Life Expectancy at Birth." Retrieved August 23, 2013 (https://www.cia.gov/library/publications/the-world-factbook/rankorder/2102rank.html).

World Factbook. 2013f. "India." Retrieved September 2, 2013 (https://www.cia.gov/library/publications/the-world-factbook/geos/in.html).

World Factbook. 2013g. "Kenya." Retrieved September 2, 2013 (https://www.cia.gov/library/publications/the-world-factbook/geos/ke.html).

World Factbook. 2013h. "Sweden." Retrieved September 2, 2013 (https://www.cia.gov/library/publications/the-world-factbook/geos/sw.html).

World Factbook. 2013i. "United States." Retrieved September 2, 2013 (https://www.cia.gov/library/publications/the-world-factbook/geos/us.html).

World Factbook. 2013j. "World Population Growth Rate." Retrieved September 2, 2013 (https://www.cia.gov/library/publications/the-world-factbook/geos/xx.html).

World Factbook. 2013k. "Cambodia." Retrieved August 31, 2013 (https://www.cia.gov/library/publications/the-world-factbook/geos/cb.html).

World Factbook. 2013l. "Suffrage." Retrieved August 31, 2013 (https://www.cia.gov/library/publications/the-world-factbook/fields/2123.html).

World Factbook. 2013m. "Japan." Retrieved September 7, 2013 (https://www.cia.gov/library/publications/the-world-factbook/geos/ja.html).

World Famine Timeline. 2011. "World Disasters: Famine Timeline in 21st Century." Retrieved May 13, 2011 (www.mapreport.com/subtopics/d/0.html#2010).

World Health Organization. 2011. "The Top 10 Causes of Death." Retrieved August 29, 2012 (www.who.int/mediacentre/factsheets/fs310/en/index.html).

World Health Organization. 2012. "Family Planning: Fact Sheet No. 351." July. Retrieved July 29, 2012 (www.who.int/mediacentre/factsheets/fs351/en/index.html).

World Health Organization. 2013. "Global Health Observatory: HIV/AIDS." Retrieved June 10, 2013 (www.who.int/gho/hiv/en/).

World Hunger Education Service. 2011a. "World Child Hunger Facts." December 18. Retrieved May 10, 2012 (www.worldhunger.org/articles/Learn/child_hunger_facts.htm).

World Hunger Education Service. 2011b. "World Hunger and Poverty Facts and Statistics." Retrieved April 12, 2011 (www.worldhunger.org/articles/Learn/world%20hunger%20facts%202002.htm#).

World Hunger Education Service. 2012a. "Hunger in America: 2012 United States Hunger and Poverty Facts." Retrieved May 17, 2012 (www.worldhunger.org/articles/Learn/us_hunger_facts.htm).

World Hunger Education Service. 2012b. "World Child Hunger Facts." Retrieved August 26, 2013 (http://www.worldhunger.org/articles/Learn/child_hunger_facts.htm).

World Hunger Education Service. 2012c. "World Hunger and Poverty Facts and Statistics." Retrieved May 16, 2012 (www.worldhunger.org/articles/Learn/world%20hunger%20facts%20202002.htm).

World Hunger Education Service. 2013a. "Hunger in America: 2013 United States Hunger and Poverty Facts" Retrieved August 24, 2013 (http://www.worldhunger.org/articles/Learn/us_hunger_facts.htm).

World Hunger Education Service. 2013b. "World Hunger and Poverty Facts and Statistics." Retrieved August 24, 2013 (http://www.worldhunger.org/articles/Learn/world%20hunger%20facts%202002.htm#).

World Hunger Facts. 2009. Retrieved November 11, 2009 (www.worldhunger.org/articles/Learn/world%20hunger%20facts%20202002.htm).

Worldometers: World Statistics Updated in Real Time. 2012. "United Nations Member States." Retrieved July 13, 2012 (www.worldometers.info/united-nations/).

WorldWideLearn. 2007. "Guide to College Majors in Sociology." Retrieved June 23, 2008 (www.worldwidelearn.com/online-education-guide/social-science/sociology-major.htm).

Wöss, Josef. 2012. "Tackling the Ageing Challenge: The Labour Market as a Key Determinant." Retrieved August 25, 2012 (www.esip.org/files/RT2_Josef%20W%C3%B6ss.pdf).

Wright, Erik Olin. 2000. *Class Counts: Comparative Studies in Class Analysis,* Student ed. Cambridge, MA: Cambridge University Press.

Wright, Stuart A. 1995. *Armageddon in Waco: Critical Perspectives on the Branch Davidian Conflict.* Chicago: University of Chicago Press.

Wuthnow, Robert, ed. 1994. *"I Come Away Stronger": How Small Groups Are Shaping American Religion.* Grand Rapids, MI: William B. Eerdmans.

Yablonski, Lewis. 1959. "The Gang as a Near-Group." *Social Problems* 7(Fall):108–117.

Yamane, David. 1997. "Secularization on Trial: In Defense of a Neosecularization Paradigm." *Journal for the Scientific Study of Religion* 36(1):109–122.

Yinger, J. Milton. 1960. "Contraculture and Subculture." *American Sociological Review* 25(October):625–35.

Yoon, Mi Yung. 2011a. "More Women in the Tanzanian Legislature: Do Numbers Matter?" *Journal of Contemporary African Studies* 29(January):83–98.

Yoon, Mi Yung. 2011b. "Factors Hindering 'Larger' Representation of Women in Parliament: The Case of Seychelles." *Commonwealth and Comparative Politics* 49(February):98–114.

Yunus, Muhammad and Alan Jolis. 1999. *Banker to the Poor: Micro-Lending and the Battle Against World Poverty.* New York: Public Affairs.

Zehr, Mary Ann. 2009. "The Problem of Tracking in Middle Schools." *Education Week,* June 4. Retrieved April 17, 2011 (http://blogs.edweek.org/edweek/curriculum/2009/06/the_problem_of_tracking_in_mid.html).

Zeleny, Jeff. 2009. "Obama Vows, 'We Will Rebuild' and 'Recover.'" *The New York Times,* February 25. Retrieved February 25, 2009 (www.nytimes.com/2009/02/25/us/politics/25obama.html?scp=1&sq=obama%20vows%20we%20will%20rebuild&st=cse).

Zimbardo, Philip. 2009. "The Stanford Prison Experiment: A Simulation of the Psychology of Imprisonment Conducted at Sanford University." Video (www.prisonexp.org).

Zimbardo, Philip C., Craig Haney, Curtis Banks, and David Jaffe. 1973. "The Mind Is a Formidable Jailer: A Pirandellian Prison." *The New York Times* (April 8):38–60.

Zull, James E. 2002. *The Art of Changing the Brain: Enriching the Practice of Teaching by Exploring the Biology of Learning.* Sterling, VA: Stylus.

Credits

Image, "How Do We Know?" features. © iStockphoto.com.

Image, "What Have We Learned?" features. © iStockphoto.com.

Image, "Sociology Around the World" features. © iStockphoto.com.

Image, "Sociology in Our Social World" features. © iStockphoto.com.

Chapter 1

Photo 1.1 CO, page 2. © iStockphoto.com
Photo 1.2 CO, page 2. © iStockphoto.com/Judy Foldetta
Photo 1.3 CO, page 2. © Keith Roberts
Photo 1.4 CO, page 2. © iStockphoto.com/Jessica Liu
Photo 1.1, page 4. © Keith Roberts
Photo 1.2, page 5. © Peter Turnley/Corbis
Photo 1.3, page 6. © Keith Roberts
Photo 1.4, page 7. © PhotoStock-Israel/Alamy
Photo 1.5, page 8. © Dan Lundberg/Wikipedia
Photo 1.6, page 9. © iStockphoto.com/Jessica Liu
Photo 1.7, page 11. © Image Source/Corbis
Photo 1.8, page 11. © iStockphoto.com/Pascal Genes
Photo 1.9, page 12. Photo courtesy of Hanover College
Photo 1.10, page 13. © Thinkstock
Photo 1.11, page 17. Image courtesy Central Asia Institute
Photo 1.12, page 18. © Peter Turnley/CORBIS
Photo 1.13, page 21. © Benjamin J. Myers/Corbis
Photo 1.14, page 25. © iStockphoto.com/Sylvie Fourgeot

Chapter 2

Photo 2.1 CO, page 28. © iStockphoto.com/ Vicktor Pryymachuk
Photo 2.2 CO, page 28. © iStockphoto.com
Photo 2.3 CO, page 28. © iStockphoto.com/ mikeuk
Photo 2.4 CO, page 28. © iStockphoto.com/ Laurence Gough
Photo 2.1, page 30. © Sean Sprague/The Image Works
Photo 2.2, page 31. © iStockphoto.com/Monte Wilson
Photo 2.3, page 34. © Keith Roberts

Photo 2.4, page 36. © Digital Vision/Christopher Robbins/Thinkstock
Photo 2.5, page 36. © Keith Roberts
Photo 2.6, page 37. © Jeanne Ballantine
Photo 2.7, page 37. © Keith Roberts
Photo 2.8, page 38. © istockphoto.com/David H. Lewis
Photo 2.9, page 42. © Charles Marville/The Bridgeman Art Library/Getty Images
Photo 2.10, page 44. © Keith Roberts
Photo 2.11, page 47. © Karen Porter
Photo 2.12, page 48. © Jeanne Ballantine
Photo 2.13, page 49. © Bettmann/CORBIS
Photo 2.14, page 49. © N/A
Photo 2.15, page 49. © Bettmann/CORBIS
Photo 2.16, page 51. © Courtesy of the American Sociological Association
Photo 2.17, page 51. © SAUL LOEB/Getty Images

Chapter 3

Photo CO 3.1, page 56. © Jared Embree
Photo CO 3.2, page 56. © Peter Menzel/ menzelphoto.com
Photo CO 3.3, page 56. © Peter Menzel/ menzelphoto.com
Photo CO 3.4, page 56. © Jared Embree
Photo CO 3.5, page 56. © Peter Menzel/ menzelphoto.com
Photo 3.1, page 59. © Peter Menzel/menzelphoto. com
Photo 3.2, page 59. © Canstock
Photo 3.3, page 60. © Keith Roberts
Photo 3.4, page 61. © Olivier Martel/Corbis
Photo 3.5, page 61. © istockphoto.com/Britta Kasholm-Tengve
Photo 3.6, page 62. © Ben Penner
Photo 3.7, page 62. © iStockphoto.com/Richard Stamper
Photo 3.8, page 63. © Lifesize/Thinkstock
Photo 3.9, page 67. © Bettmann/CORBIS
Photo 3.10, page 67. © istockphoto.com/Paige Falk
Photo 3.11, page 69. © istockphoto.com/Paige Falk
Photo Essay 3.1, page 71. © Keith Roberts
Photo Essay 3.2, page 71. © Keith Roberts
Photo Essay 3.3, page 71. © Jared Embree
Photo Essay 3.4, page 71. © Keith Roberts
Photo Essay 3.5, page 71. © Jared Embree
Photo Essay 3.6, page 71. © Elise Roberts

Photo 3.12, page 75. © istockphoto.com/Andrew Leve
Photo 3.13, page 76. © iStockphoto.com
Photo 3.14, page 76. © Sarah Jolly
Photo 3.15, page 76. © iStockphoto.com
Photo 3.16, page 77. © Courtesy of Hanover College
Photo 3.17, page 79. © Andy Aitchison/Corbis
Photo 3.18, page 82. © iStockphoto/Thinkstock
Photo 3.19, page 84. N/A
Photo 3.20, page 84. N/A
Photo 3.21, page 85. © Daniel Berehulak/Getty

Chapter 4

Photo 4.1 CO, page 88. © Yang Liu/Corbis
Photo 4.3 CO, page 88. © Ariel Skelley/Corbis
Photo 4.4 CO, page 88. © iStockphoto.com/Sean Locke
Photo 4.5 CO, page 88. Image courtesy Central Asia Institute
Photo 4.1, page 90. © iStockphoto.com/Ben German
Photo 4.2, page 92. © iStockphoto.com/Peeter Viisimaa
Photo 4.3, page 95. © Keith Roberts
Photo 4.4, page 97. © Keith Roberts
Photo 4.5, page 98. © iStockphoto.com/ Christopher Knittel
Photo 4.6, page 99. © Digital Vision/ Thinkstock
Photo 4.7, page 100. © istockphoto.com/Carsten Brandt
Photo 4.8, page 100. © Jehad Nga/Corbis
Photo 4.9, page 100. © iStockphoto.com/Alan Eisen
Photo 4.10, page 100. © ©ZHAO ZP/EPA/Landov
Photo 4.11, page 101. © Comstock/Jupiterimages/ Thinkstock
Photo 4.12, page 104. © Everett Kennedy Brown/ epa/Corbis
Photo 4.13, page 105. © Digital Vision/Jeff Randall/ Thinkstock

Chapter 5

Photo 5.1 CO, page 112. © BananaStock/ Thinkstock
Photo 5.2 CO, page 112. © iStockphoto.com/ Aaron Kohr
Photo 5.3 CO, page 112. © iStockphoto.com/Sean Locke

Photo 5.4 CO, page 112. © Tim Pannell/Corbis
Photo 5.5 CO, page 112. © iStockphoto.com
Photo 5.1, page 114. © Keith Roberts
Photo 5.2, page 118. © iStockphoto.com /Jacob Wackerhausen
Photo 5.3, page 119. © iStockphoto.com /Mark Coffey
Photo 5.4, page 119. © Michael Westhoff/ iStockphoto.com
Photo 5.5, page 119. © iStockphoto.com/Julie Deshaies
Photo 5.6, page 119. © iStockphoto.com
Photo 5.7, page 119. © iStockphoto.com/ Stephanie Phillips
Photo 5.8, page 120. © istockphoto.com/Sean Locke
Photo 5.10, page 122. © Jeanne Ballantine
Photo 5.11, page 122. © Bruno Morandi/Corbis
Photo 5.12, page 122. © Jeanne Ballantine
Photo 5.13, page 122. © Kate Ballantine
Photo 5.14, page 124. © iStockphoto.com/Nancy Louie
Photo 5.15, page 125. © Frank Hammer
Photo 5.16, page 126. © Elise Roberts
Photo 5.17, page 127. © iStockphoto/Thinkstock
Photo 5.18, page 128. © Steve Starr/Corbis
Photo 5.19, page 131. © iStockphoto.com/Sean Locke
Photo 5.20, page 133. © USAID
Photo 5.21, page 136. © Clay Ballantine
Photo 5.22, page 136. © Clay Ballantine
Photo 5.23, page 136. © FAO/Giulio Napolitano

Chapter 6

Photo 6.1 CO, page 140. © Mark Goddard/ iStockphoto.com
Photo 6.2 CO, page 140. © Stephanie Phillips/ iStockphoto.com
Photo 6.3 CO, page 140. © Ryan McVay
Photo 6.4 CO, page 140. © Carson Ganci/Design Pics/Corbis
Photo 6.5 CO, page 140. © iStockphoto.com/ Jennifer Matthews
Photo 6.1, page 144. © Jose Fuste Raga/Corbis
Photo 6.2, page 144. © iStockphoto.com/Eva Serrabassa
Photo 6.3, page 144. © Keith Roberts
Photo 6.4, page 144. © DAVE MARTIN/ AP Images
Photo 6.5, page 145. © iStockphoto.com/Frances Twitty
Photo 6.6, page 145. © iStockphoto.com/Jerry Koch
Photo 6.7, page 146. © Jupiterimages/ Pixland/ Thinkstock
Photo 6.8, page 147. © Keith Roberts
Photo 6.9, page 148. © N/A
Photo 6.10, page 149. © iStockphoto.com
Photo 6.11, page 151. © Polka Dot/Jupiterimages/ Thinkstock
Photo 6.12, page 152. © Ta'izz, Yemen/ Corbis
Photo 6.13, page 153. © MICHAEL REYNOLDS/ epa/Corbis
Photo 6.14, page 154. © AP Images
Photo 6.15, page 156. © blueskybcn/ istock

Photo 6.16, page 157. © Adam Mastoon/CORBIS
Photo 6.17, page 157. © Moviestore collection Ltd / Alamy
Photo 6.18, page 158. © Ron Sachs/CNP/Corbis
Photo 6.19, page 160. © Jupiterimages/ Thinkstock
Photo 6.20, page 161. © istockphoto.com/Slobo Mitic
Photo 6.21, page 163. © Jupiterimages/ Thinkstock
Photo 6.22, page 165. © istockphoto.com/Slobo Mitic

Chapter 7

Photo 7.1 CO, page 172. © Keith Roberts
Photo 7.3 CO, page 172. © Jeanne Ballantine
Photo 7.4 CO, page 172. © Jeanne Ballantine
Photo 7.5 CO, page 172. © iStockphoto.com/Juan Collado
Photo 7.6 CO, page 172. © Elise Roberts
Photo 7.7 CO, page 172. © iStockphoto.com/Skip O'Donnell
Photo 7.1, page 174. © epa european pressphoto agency b.v. / Alamy
Photo 7.2, page 175. © Keith Roberts
Photo 7.3, page 175. © Keith Roberts
Photo 7.4, page 175. © USAID
Photo 7.5, page 176. © iStockphoto.com/Thania Navarro
Photo 7.6, page 177. © iStockphoto.com/Thomas Hottner
Photo 7.7, page 178. © iStockphoto.com/Tomaz Levstek
Photo 7.8, page 180. © Jeanne Ballantine
Photo 7.9, page 180. © iStockphoto.com/GYI NSEA
Photo 7.10, page 182. © **Paul** Almasy/CORBIS
Photo 7.11, page 183. © USAID
Photo 7.12, page 186. © Wendy Stone/CORBIS
Photo 7.13, page 189. © iStockphoto.com/ Fernando Caceres
Photo 7.14, page 189. © Jeanne Ballantine
Photo 7.15, page 191. © Keith Roberts
Photo 7.16, page 193. © Elise Roberts
Photo 7.17, page 195. © Keith Roberts
Photo 7.18, page 197. © iStockphoto.com/ peeterv
Photo 7.19, page 197. © iStockphoto.com/Pgiam
Photo 7.20, page 197. © iStockphoto.com/M
Photo 7.21, page 200. © iStockphoto.com
Photo 7.22, page 200. © Emma Rian/zefa/Corbis
Photo 7.23, page 201. © Jeanne Ballantine
Photo 7.24, page 204. © Keith Roberts

Chapter 8

Photo 8.1 CO, page 208. © iStockphoto.com
Photo 8.2 CO, page 208. © Jeanne Ballantine
Photo 8.3 CO, page 208. © Jeanne Ballantine
Photo 8.4 CO, page 208. © Jiang Dao Hua/ iStockphoto.com
Photo 8.5 CO, page 208. © Elise Roberts
Photo 8.1, page 210. © Zana Briski and Kids with Cameras. Used with permission from "Kids with Cameras."

Photo 8.2, page 211. © Sophie Elbaz/Sygma/ Corbis
Photo 8.3, page 211. © N/A
Photo 8.4, page 215. © Bettmann/CORBIS
Photo 8.5, page 217. © istockphoto.com /Jerry Moorman
Photo 8.6, page 219. © Bettmann/Corbis
Photo 8.7, page 222. © Andrew Holbrooke/ Corbis
Photo 8.8, page 224. © Phil Schermeister/ CORBIS
Photo 8.9, page 226. © N/A
Photo 8.10, page 227. © MOHAMED NURELDIN ABDALLAH/Reuters/Landov
Photo 8.11, page 228. © Keith Roberts
Photo 8.12, page 229. © Keith Roberts
Photo 8.13, page 230. © Josef Scaylea/CORBIS
Photo 8.14, page 231. © William Campbell/ Sygma/Corbis
Photo 8.15, page 233. © Bettmann/CORBIS
Photo 8.16, page 234. © SEAN GARDNER/Reuters /Landov
Photo 8.17, page 235. © TOUHIG SION/CORBIS SYGMA
Photo 8.17, page 238. © TOUHIG SION/CORBIS SYGMA

Chapter 9

Photo 9.1 CO, page 242. © Kazuyoshi Nomachi/ Corbis
Photo 9.2 CO, page 242. © iStockphoto.com/Zsolt Nyulaszi
Photo 9.3 CO, page 242. © Mansir Petrie
Photo 9.4 CO, page 242. © Mansir Petrie
Photo 9.5 CO, page 242. © iStockphoto.com/Jo Ann Snover
Photo 9.1, page 245. © Atlantide Phototravel/ Corbis
Photo 9.2, page 246. © Thomas Strange/ iStockphoto.com
Photo 9.3, page 249. © iStockphoto.com/GYI NSEA
Photo 9.4, page 249. © iStockphoto.com/GYI NSEA
Photo 9.5, page 249. © Rebecca Blackwell/ AP Images
Photo 9.6, page 253. © Jostein Hauge/iStockphoto. com
Photo 9.7, page 255. © N/A
Photo 9.8, page 256. © iStockphoto.com/GYI NSEA
Photo 9.9, page 257. © Photo by Joe Robbins; Courtesy of Hanover College
Photo 9.10, page 257. © Wesley Hitt/ Getty Images
Photo 9.11, page 261. © iStockphoto.com/Aldo Murillo
Photo 9.12, page 261. © iStockphoto.com/ Pathathai Chungyam
Photo 9.13, page 262. © USAID
Photo 9.14, page 264. © Trinette Reed/Brand X/ Corbis
Photo 9.15, page 266. © istock.com/kali9
Photo 9.16, page 267. © Jeanne Ballantine

Photo 9.17, page 267. © Nadeem Khawer/epa/Corbis

Photo 9.18, page 270. © Narendra Shrestha /epa/Corbis

Photo 9.19, page 272. © goodshot/thinkstock

Photo 9.20, page 273. © thomsonreuters/Sohel Ahmed

Photo 9.21, page 273. © UNESCO; Photo by Dominique Rogers

Chapter 10

Photo 10.1 CO, page 284. © Akram Saleh/Reuters/Corbis

Photo 10.2 CO, page 284. © iStockphoto.com/Sandra Gligorijevic

Photo 10.3 CO, page 284. © iStockphoto.com/Radu Razvan

Photo 10.4 CO, page 284. © iStockphoto.com/Nancy Louie

Photo 10.5 CO, page 284. © istockphoto.com/Fred Palmieri

Photo 10.1, page 286. © Elena Korenbaum

Photo 10.2, page 287. © Kate Ballantine

Photo 10.3, page 289. © Kate Ballantine

Photo 10.4, page 289. © iStockphoto.com/ Glenda Powers

Photo 10.5, page 290. © Kate Ballantine

Photo 10.6, page 291. © Wolfgang Kaehler/CORBIS

Photo 10.7, page 292. © Carla Howery

Photo 10.8, page 293. © Photodisc/ Barbara Penoyar/ Thinkstock

Photo 10.9, page 296. © iStock.com/GYI NSEA

Photo 10.10, page 299. © Comstock/ Jupiter Images/ Thinkstock

Photo 10.11, page 299. © China Photos/Getty Images

Photo 10.12, page 300. © Elise Roberts

Photo 10.13, page 303. © Mark Savage/Corbis

Photo 10.14, page 305. © David Adame/Getty Images

Photo 10.15, page 306. © Hemera/Thinkstock

Photo 10.16, page 306. © iStockphoto.com

Chapter 11

Photo 11.1 CO, page 310. © Jared Embree

Photo 11.2 CO, page 310. © Jeanne Ballantine

Photo 11.3 CO, page 310. Keith Roberts

Photo 11.4 CO, page 310. © Keith Roberts

Photo 11.1, page 313. © Father Celse Hakuziyaremye

Photo 11.2, page 314. © Jared Embree

Photo 11.3, page 315. © iStockphoto.com/Brandon Laufenberg

Photo 11.4, page 316. © Jeanne Ballantine

Photo 11.5, page 317. © Najlah Feanny/Corbis

Photo 11.6, page 319. © Keith Roberts

Photo 11.7, page 319. © Keith Roberts

Photo 11.8, page 321. © N/A

Photo 11.9, page 323. © miafarrow.org

Photo 11.10, page 323. © Gideon Mendel/Corbis

Photo 11.11, page 324. © Karen Kasmauski/Corbis

Photo 11.12, page 326. © Anthony Bannister/Corbis

Photo 11.13, page 327. © Najlah Feanny/Corbis

Photo 11.14, page 329. © Elise Roberts

Photo 11.15, page 331. © miafarrow.org

Photo 11.16, page 331. Courtesy of Hanover College

Photo 11.17, page 333. istockphoto.com/Steven Allen

Photo 11.18, page 335. © Paula Bronstein/Getty Images

Photo 11.19, page 337. © Peter Turnley/CORBIS

Photo 11.20, page 338. © Antoine Gyori/CORBIS SYGMA

Photo 11.21, page 339. © Keith Roberts

Photo 11.22, page 339. © istockphoto.com/kevin miller

Photo 11.23, page 341. © Keith Roberts

Photo 11.24, page 344. © Virginia Caudill

Photo 11.25, page 345. © Keith Roberts

Photo 11.26, page 346. © Elise Roberts

Photo 11.27, page 346. © Keith Roberts

Photo 11.28, page 346. © Elise Roberts

Chapter 12

Photo 12.1 CO, page 358. © iStockphoto.com/Tony Tremblay

Photo 12.2 CO, page 358. © USAID

Photo 12.3 CO, page 358. © istockphoto.com/Ann Steer

Photo 12.1, page 360. © Larry W. Smith/epa/Corbis

Photo 12.2, page 362. © Eric Thayer/Getty Images

Photo 12.3, page 364. © iStockphoto.com

Photo 12.4, page 365. © istock.com/ EdStock2

Photo 12.5, page 366. © ANDREW ROSS/AFP/Getty Images

Photo 12.6, page 367. © Paula Bronstein/Getty Images

Photo 12.7, page 370. © Ralf-Finn Hestoft/Corbis

Photo 12.8, page 372. © Ernst Haas/Ernst Haas/Getty Images

Photo 12.9, page 373. © Mario Tama/Getty Images

Photo 12.10, page 374. © PRENSA LATINA/Reuters /Landov

Photo 12.11, page 375. © Elise Roberts

Photo 12.12, page 376. © Steve Parsons/AFP/Getty Images

Photo 12.13, page 378. © Keith Roberts

Photo 12.14, page 380. © JORGE UZON/AFP/Getty Images

Photo 12.15, page 380. © AFP/AFP/Getty Images

Photo 12.16, page 385. © AHMAD GHARABLI/AFP/Getty Images

Photo 12.17, page 386. © Mia Song/Star Ledger/Corbis

Photo 12.18, page 388. © Ursillo Catherine/Getty

Photo 12.19, page 388. © David Silverman/Getty Images

Photo 12.20, page 389. © NIKOLAY DONCHEV/Corbis

Chapter 13

Photo 13.1 CO, page 394. © iStockphoto.com/Bart Sadowski

Photo 13.2 CO, page 394. © NASA

Photo 13.1, page 397. © USAID

Photo 13.2, page 397. © Elise Roberts

Photo 13.3, page 399. © Jeanne Ballantine

Photo 13.4, page 400. © Reuters/CORBIS

Photo 13.5, page 402. © Alain Keler/Sygma/Corbis

Photo 13.6, page 403. © 2006 World Health Organization

Photo 13.7, page 405. © Kate Ballantine

Photo 13.8, page 405. © Wolfgang Kaehler/CORBIS

Photo 13.9, page 407. © Jeanne Ballantine

Photo 13.10, page 408. © PORNCHAI KITTIWONGSAKUL/AFP/Getty Images

Photo 13.11, page 408. © Nani Afrida/epa/Corbis

Photo 13.12, page 411. © iStockphoto.com/ David Elfstrom

Photo 13.13, page 411. © Jared Embree

Photo 13.14, page 413. © Jared Embree

Photo 13.15, page 413. © USAID

Photo 13.16, page 415. © 2009 Jupiter images Corporation

Photo 13.17, page 417. © Mimi Mollica/Corbis

Photo 13.18, page 419. © Louie Psihoyos/CORBIS

Photo 13.19, page 424. © iStockphoto.com/Loic Bernard

Chapter 14

Photo 14.1, page 428. © Bart Sadowski/iStockphoto.com

Photo 14.2 CO, page 428. © Brave New Films

Photo 14.3 CO, page 428. © Keith Binns

Photo 14.1, page 431. © Jeanne Ballantine

Photo 14.2, page 431. © Jon Hrusa/epa/Corbis

Photo 14.3, page 433. © istockphoto.com/ Erlend Kvalsvik

Photo 14.4, page 435. © iStockphoto.com

Photo 14.5, page 436. © USAID

Photo 14.6, page 437. © Keith Roberts

Photo 14.7, page 439. © Keith Roberts

Photo 14.8, page 439. © Keith Roberts

Photo 14.9, page 439. © Keith Roberts

Photo 14.10, page 440. © Gideon Mendel/Corbis

Photo 14.11, page 441. © Peter Turnley/The Denver Post/Corbis

Photo 14.12, page 442. © N/A

Photo 14.13, page 444. © istockphoto.com/bgwalker

Photo 14.14, page 447. Courtesy of Witness for Peace

Photo 14.15, page 448. © TEKEE TANWAR/AFP/Getty Images

Photo 14.16, page 448. © Jeanne Ballantine

Photo 14.17, page 451. © Keith Roberts

Photo 14.18, page 452. © Jeanne Ballantine

Photo 14.19, page 453. © Claudio Peri/ Corbis

Photo 14.20, page 453. © Kate Ballantine

Glossary

Absolute poverty. Not having resources to meet basic needs, 200

Achieved status. Social status that is chosen or earned by decisions one makes and sometimes by personal ability, 122

Achieved stratification systems. Societal systems that allow individuals to earn positions through their ability, efforts, and choices, 193

Agents of socialization. The transmitters of culture—the people, organizations, and institutions that help us define our identity and teach us how to thrive in our social world, 101

Agricultural societies. Societies that rely primarily on raising crops for food but make use of technological advances such as the plow, irrigation, animals, and fertilization to continuously cultivate the same land, 61

Alienation. Feeling uninvolved, uncommitted, unappreciated, and unconnected to the group or the society, 133

Anomie. The state of normlessness that occurs when rules for behavior in society break down under extreme stress from rapid social change or conflict, 125

Arranged marriages. A pattern of mate selection in which someone other than the couple—elder males, parents, a matchmaker—selects the marital partners, 295

Ascribed statuses. Social statuses that are often assigned at birth and that do not change during an individual's lifetime; gender, race, and ethnic status group are examples, 122

Ascribed stratification system. A societal system in which characteristics beyond the control of the individual—such as family background, age, sex, and race—determine one's position in society, 193

Assimilation. The structural and cultural merging of minority and majority groups in society, 228

Authoritarian political systems. Controlled by absolute monarchs or dictators who allow limited or no participation of the population in government and control much of what happens in the lives of individuals, 374

Authority. Power that people consider legitimate, 364

Beliefs. Ideas about life, the way society works, and where one fits in, 72

Bureaucracies. Specific types of large formal organizations that have the purpose of maximizing efficiency; they are characterized by formal relations between participants, clearly laid-out procedures and rules, and pursuit of shared goals, 130

Caste systems. The most rigid ascribed stratification systems; individuals are born into a status, which they retain throughout life, and that status is deeply embedded in religious, political, and economic norms and institutions, 193

Cause-and-effect relationships. Occur when there is a relationship between variables so that one variable stimulates a change in another, 35

Civil religion. The cultural beliefs, practices, and symbols that relate a nation to the ultimate conditions of its existence, 345

Class systems. Allow individuals the possibility to earn positions through their ability, efforts, and choices, 194

Collective behavior. Actions that are spontaneous, unstructured, and disorganized and that may violate norms; this behavior arises when people are trying to cope with stressful situations and unclear or uncertain conditions, 441

Conflict theory. Theory that focuses on societal groups competing for scarce resources, 48

Content analysis. Entails the systematic categorizing and recording of information from written or recorded sources—printed materials, videos, radio broadcasts, or artworks, 38

Control group. In a controlled experiment, the group in which the subjects are not exposed to the variable the experiment wants to test, 37

Controls. Steps used by researchers to eliminate all variables except those related to the hypothesis—especially those variables that might be spurious, 35

Correlation. A relationship between variables in which change in one variable is associated with change in another, 35

Counterculture. Groups with expectations and values that contrast sharply with the dominant values of a particular society, 79

Crime. Deviant actions for which there are severe formal penalties imposed by the government, 142

Cultural capital. The language patterns, values, experiences, and knowledge that children learn at home and bring with them to school, 178

Cultural relativism. Requires setting aside cultural and personal beliefs and prejudices to understand another group or society through the eyes of members of that community using its own standards, 69

Culture. The way of life shared by a group of people—the knowledge, beliefs, values, rules or laws, language, customs, symbols, and material products within a society that help meet human needs, 58

Democratic socialism. Collective or group planning of the development of society, but within a democratic political system; the good of the whole is paramount, 378

Democratic systems. Political forms characterized by accountability of the government to the citizens and a large degree of control by individuals over their own lives, 374

Demographic transition theory. Links trends in birth and death rates with patterns of economic and technological development, 403

Demography. The study of human populations, 398

Denominations. Centralized coordinating bodies or associations that link local congregations with a similar history and theology, 340

Dependency ratio. The ratio of those in both the young and aged groups compared with the number of people in the productive age groups between 15 and 64 years old, 400

Dependent variable. The variable in a cause-and-effect relationship that is affected by and comes after the independent variable in time sequence, 35

Deviance. The violation of social norms, 142

Discrimination. Differential treatment and harmful actions against minorities, 219

Dysfunctions. Actions that undermine the stability or equilibrium of society, 47

Empirical knowledge. Involves use of the five senses to gather facts that have been objectively (without opinion or bias) observed and carefully measured; this is done so that the reality of what is being measured should be the same for all the people who observe it, 31

Endogamy. Norms that require individuals to marry inside certain human boundaries, whatever the societal members see as protecting the homogeneity of the group, 295

Environment. The setting in which the social unit operates, including everything that influences the social unit, such as its physical surroundings and technological innovations, 19

Ethnic group. A group within the human species that is based on cultural factors: language, religion, dress, foods, customs, beliefs, values, norms, a shared group identity or feeling, and sometimes loyalty to a homeland, monarch, or religious leader, 217

Ethnocentrism. The tendency to view one's own group and its cultural expectations as right, proper, and superior to others, 67

Evidence. Facts and information that are confirmed through systematic processes of testing, using the five senses, sometimes enhanced with research tools, 32

Existing sources. Materials that already exist but are being employed in a new way or analyzed to understand a different research question, 37

Exogamy. Norms governing the choice of a mate that require individuals to marry outside of their own immediate group, 294

Experiments. All variables except the one being studied are controlled so researchers can study the effects of the variable under study, 37

Experimental group. In a controlled experiment, the group in which people are exposed to the variable being studied to test its effect, 37

Expressive movements. Group phenomena that focus on changing individuals and saving people from corrupt lifestyles; religious movements, secular psychotherapy movements, and self-help or self-actualization groups are examples, 447

Extended family. Two or more adult generations that share tasks and living quarters. This may include brothers, sisters, aunts, uncles, cousins, and grandparents, 300

Fads. Temporary behaviors, activities, or material objects that spread rapidly and are copied enthusiastically by large numbers of people, 444

Family of orientation. The family into which we are born, 287

Family of procreation. The family we create ourselves, 287

Fashions. A style of appearance and behavior that is temporarily favored by a large number of people, 444

Feminist theory. Critiques the hierarchical power structures, which feminists argue treat women and other minorities unequally, 51

Fertility. Demographic processes referring to the birth rate, 405

Formal agents of socialization. Official or legal agents (e.g., families, school, teachers, religious training) whose purpose it is to socialize the individual into the values, beliefs, and behaviors of the culture, 102

Formal organizations. Modern rational organizations comprised of complex secondary groups deliberately formed to pursue and achieve certain goals, 129

Formal sanctions. Rewards or punishments conferred by recognized officials to enforce the most important norms, 75

Free-choice marriage. A pattern of mate selection in which the partners select each other based primarily on romance and love, 296

Functional theory (also called structural-functional theory). Assumes that all parts of the social structure (including groups, organizations, and institutions), the culture (values and beliefs), and social processes (e.g., social change or child rearing) work together to make the whole society run smoothly and harmoniously, 47

Game stage. Stage in the process of developing a social self when a child develops the ability to take the role of multiple others concurrently (norms, values, and expectations of the generalized other) and conform to societal expectations, 98

Gender. A society's notions of masculinity and femininity—socially constructed meanings associated with male or female—and how individuals construct their identity in terms of gender within these constraints, 246

Gender roles. Those commonly assigned tasks or expected behaviors linked to an individual's sex-determined statuses, 247

Generalized other. A composite of societal expectations that a child learns from family, peers, and other organizations, 98

Genocide. The systematic effort of one group, usually the dominant group, to destroy a minority group, 226

Global culture. Behavioral standards, symbols, values, and material objects that have become common across the globe, 82

Globalization. The process by which the entire world is becoming a single interdependent sociocultural entity, more uniform, more integrated, and more interdependent, 82

Global transnational movements. Mobilized groups that take place across societies as international organizations seek change in the status of women, child labor, rights of indigenous peoples, environmental degradation, global warming, disease pandemics, and other issues that affect the global community, 448

Goal displacement. Occurs when the original motives or goals of the organization are displaced by new secondary goals, 134

Groups. Units involving two or more people who interact with each other because of shared common interests, goals, experiences, and needs, 125

Hate crimes. Criminal offenses committed against a person, property, or a group that are motivated by the offender's bias against a religious, ethnic, or racial group; national origin; gender; or sexual orientation, 156

Health. A state of physical, mental, and social well-being or the absence of disease, 409

Herding society. Society in which the food-producing strategy is based on the society's domestication of animals, whose care is the central focus of their activities, 61

Horticultural societies. Societies in which the food-producing strategy is based on domestication of plants, using digging sticks and wooden hoes to cultivate small gardens, 61

Hunter-gatherer society. A society in which people rely on the vegetation and animals occurring naturally in their habitat to sustain life, 61

Hypothesis. An educated guess about how variables are related to each other, including causal relationships; the speculations do not yet have supporting data, 34

I. The spontaneous, unpredictable, impulsive, and largely unorganized aspect of the self, 95

Ideal culture. Consists of practices, beliefs, and values that are regarded as most desirable in society and are consciously taught to children, 72

Illness. Lack of health, 409

Imitation stage. A period when children under 3 years old are preparing for role-taking by observing others and imitating their behaviors, sounds, and gestures, 97

Independent variable. The variable in a cause-and-effect relationship that comes first in a time sequence and causes a change in another variable, 35

Industrial societies. Rely primarily on mechanized production for subsistence, resulting in greater division of labor based on expertise, 62

Informal agents of socialization. Unofficial forces that shape values, beliefs, and behaviors in which socialization is not the express purpose; examples are the media, books, advertising, and the Internet, 102

Informal sanctions. Unofficial rewards or punishments such as smiles, frowns, or ignoring unacceptable behaviors, 75

In-group. A group to which an individual feels a sense of loyalty and belonging; it also may serve as a reference group, 128

Institutions. Social units in societies through which organized social activities take place that provide the rules, roles, and relationships set up to meet human needs and direct and control human behavior. They provide the setting for activities essential to human and societal survival, 278

Labeling theory. Symbolic interaction view that labels people carry affect their own and others' perceptions, directing behavior to conformity or deviance, 149

Language. Conveys verbal and nonverbal messages among members of society; the foundation of every culture, 75

Latent functions. Unplanned or unintended consequences of actions or of social structures, 47

Levels of analysis. Social groups from the largest to the smallest, 16

Life expectancy. The average number of years a person in a particular society can expect to live, 397

Lifestyle. Includes attitudes, values, beliefs, behavior patterns, and other aspects of one's place in the world, shaped by socialization, 184

Looking-glass self. A reflective process that develops our *self* based on our interpretations and internalization of the reactions of others to us, 94

Macro-level analysis. Analysis of the largest social units in the social world, including entire nations, global forces, and international social trends, 20

Manifest functions. The planned outcomes of interactions, social organizations, or institutions, 47

Market systems/capitalism. An economic system driven by the balance of supply and demand, allowing free competition to reward the efficient and innovators with profits; stresses individual planning and private ownership of property, 377

Master status. An individual's social status that becomes most important and takes precedence over other statuses, 123

Material culture. Includes all the objects we can see or touch; all the artifacts of a group of people, 70

Me. The part of the self that has learned the rules of society through interaction and role-taking, and it controls the *I* and its desires, 97

Means of production. Property, machinery, and cashed owned by capitalists, 48

Mechanical solidarity. Social cohesion and integration based on the similarity of individuals in the group, including shared beliefs and values, and emotional ties between people, 60

Meritocracy. A social group or organization in which people are allocated to positions according to their abilities and credentials, as in level of education attained, 188

Meso-level analysis. Analysis of intermediate-size social units, smaller than the nation but large enough to encompass more than the local community or region, 20

Microcultures. Groups that affect only a small segment of one's life or influence a limited period of one's life, 78

Micro-level analysis. Analysis with a focus on individual or small group interaction in specific situations, 20

Migration. In terms of demographic processes, refers to the movement of people from one place to another, 405

Minority groups. Groups in a population that differ from others in some characteristics and are therefore subject to less power, fewer privileges, and discrimination, 213

Mobs. Emotional crowds that engage in violence against a specific target; lynchings, killings, and hate crimes are examples, 443

Monogamy. The most familiar form of marriage in industrial and postindustrial societies; refers to marriage of two individuals, 299

Mortality. In terms of demographic processes, refers to the death rate, 405

Myths. Stories, true or not, that transmit values and embody ideas about life and the world, 338

National culture. Refers to common values and beliefs that tie citizens of a nation together, 82

National society. A population of people usually living within a specified geographic area, who are connected by common ideas, cooperate for the attainment of common goals, and are subject to a particular political authority, 82

Nonmaterial culture. The thoughts, language, feelings, beliefs, values, and attitudes that make up much of our culture, 70

Nonverbal communication. Interactions without words using facial expressions, the head, eye contact, body posture, gestures, touch, walk, status symbols, and personal space, 118

Norms. Rules of behavior shared by members of a society and rooted in the value system, 72

Nuclear family. Consists of two parents and their children—or any two of the three, 300

Objectivity. Entails steps taken to ensure that one's personal opinions or values do not bias or contaminate data collection and analysis, 32

Observation studies (also called field research). Involve systematic, planned observation and recording of interactions or human behavior in natural settings, 37

Oligarchy. The concentration of power in the hands of a small group, 134

Organic solidarity. Refers to cohesion and integration based on differences of individuals in the group so that they are interdependent. The society has a substantial division of labor, with each member playing a highly specialized role in the society and each person being dependent on others due to interdependent, interrelated tasks, 60

Organized crime. Ongoing criminal enterprises by an organized group whose ultimate purpose is economic gain through illegitimate means, 157

Out-group. A group to which an individual does not belong and a group that is often in competition with or in opposition to an in-group, 128

Panic. Occurs when a large number of individuals become fearful or try to flee threatening situations that are beyond their control, sometimes putting their lives in danger, 443

Past-in-present discrimination. Practices from the past that may no longer be allowed but that continue to have consequences for people in the present, 225

Peer group. A group of people who are roughly equal in some status within the society, such as the same age or the same occupation, 93

Planned (or centralized) systems. Economic systems in which the government or another centralized group does planning of production and distribution, 378

Play stage. Involves a child having the ability to see things (role-take) from the perspective of one person at a time; simple role-taking or play-acting, 97

Pluralism. Occurs when each ethnic or racial group in a country maintains its own culture and separate set of institutions but has recognized equity in the society, 228

Polyandry. A marital system in which a wife can have more than one husband, 300

Polygamy. Marriage of one person to more than one partner at the same time, 299

Polygyny. A marital system in which a husband can have more than one wife, 299

Population pyramids. Pyramid-shaped diagrams that illustrate sex ratios and dependency ratios, 401

Population transfer. The removal, often forced, of a minority group from a region or country, 227

Populations. Permanent societies, states, communities, adherents of a common religious faith, racial or ethnic groups, kinship or clan groups, professions, and other identifiable categories of people, 398

Postindustrial societies. Societies that have moved from human labor and manufacturing to automated production and service jobs, largely processing information, 63

Power. Ability of a person or group to realize its own will in groups, even against the resistance of others, 196

Power elite model. Power held by top leaders in corporations, politics, and military; this interlocking elite makes major decisions guiding the nation, 196

Pluralist model of power. Hold that power is not held exclusively by an elite group but is shared among many power centers, each of which has its own self-interests to protect, 197

Prejudice. Attitudes that prejudge a group, usually negatively and not based on facts, 219

Prestige. The esteem, recognition, and respect one receives, based on wealth, position, or accomplishments, 197

Primary deviance. A violation of a norm that may be an isolated act, or an initial act of rule breaking, 149

Primary groups. Groups characterized by close, intimate, long-term contacts, cooperation, and relationships, 127

Public sociologists. Strive to better understand how society operates and to make practical use of their sociological findings, 43

Race. A socially created concept that identifies a group as "different" based on certain biologically inherited physical characteristics, which allows them to be singled out for dissimilar treatment, 213

Racism. Any meso-level institutional arrangement that favors one racial group over another; this favoritism may result in intentional or unintentional consequences for minority groups, 223

Rational choice (exchange) theory. A theory that focuses on humans as fundamentally concerned with self-interests, making rational decisions based on weighing costs and rewards of the projected outcome, 46

Rationalization of social life. The attempt to maximize efficiency by creating rules and procedures focused solely on accomplishing goals, 129

Real culture. The way things in society are actually done, 72

Recidivism rates. The likelihood that someone who is arrested, convicted, and imprisoned will later be a repeat offender, 164

Reference groups. Groups comprised of members who act as role models and establish standards against which members evaluate their conduct, 128

Relative poverty. Occurs when one's income falls below the poverty line, resulting in an inadequate standard of living relative to others in the individual's country, 200

Reproduction of class. The socioeconomic positions of one generation passing on to the next, 326

Resistance or regressive movements. Try to protect an existing system, protect part of that system, or return to what a system had been by overthrowing current laws and practices. They see societal change as a threat to values or practices and wish to maintain the status quo or return to a former status by reversing the change process, 448

Resocialization. The process of shedding one or more positions and taking on others; it involves learning new norms, behaviors, and values suitable to the newly acquired status, 101

Revolutionary movements. Attempt to transform society to bring about a total change in society by overthrowing existing power structures and replacing them with new ones; these movements often resort to violent means to achieve goals, 448

Riots. Outbreaks of illegal violence against random or shifting targets committed by crowds expressing frustration or anger against people, property, or groups in power, 443

Rituals. Ceremonies or repetitive practices, often to invoke a sense of awe of the sacred and to make certain ideas sacred, 338

Role conflict. Conflict between the roles of two or more social statuses, 124

Role strain. Tension between roles within one of the social statuses, 124

Role-taking. The process by which individuals take others into account by imagining themselves in the position of the other, 95

Roles. The expected behaviors, rights, obligations, responsibilities, and privileges assigned to a social status, 123

Rumors. Forms of mass behavior in which unsupported or unproven reports about a problem, an issue, or a concern circulate widely throughout the public, 444

Sample. A small group of systematically chosen people in survey research who represent a much larger group, 38

Sanctions. Rewards and penalties that reinforce norms, 75

Science. The systematic process of producing human knowledge; it uses empirical research methods to discover facts and test theories, 452

Secondary analysis. Uses existing data, information that has already been collected by other researchers in other studies, 37

Secondary deviance. Occurs when an individual continues to violate a norm and begins to take on a deviant identity *because* of being labeled as deviant, 149

Secondary groups. Groups characterized by formal, impersonal, and businesslike relationships; often temporary, based on a specific limited purpose or goal, 127

Secularization. The diminishing influence and role of religion in everyday life; involves a movement away from supernatural and sacred interpretations of the world and toward decisions based on empirical evidence and logic, 351

Self. Refers to the perceptions we have of who we are, 94

Self-fulfilling prophecy. A belief or a prediction that becomes a reality, in part because of the prediction, 179

Sex. A biological term referring to ascribed genetic, anatomical, and hormonal differences between males and females, 246

Sexuality. Refers to culturally shaped meanings both of sexual acts and of how we experience our own bodies—especially in relation to the bodies of others, 247

Side-effect discrimination. Refers to practices in one institutional area that have a negative impact because they are linked to practices in another institutional area; because institutions are interdependent, discrimination in one results in unintentional discrimination in others, 223

Significant others. Parents, guardians, relatives, siblings, or important individuals whose primary and sustained interactions with the individual are especially influential, 97

Social change. Variations or alterations over time in the behavior patterns, culture (including norms and values), and structure of society, 430

Social class. The wealth, power, and prestige rankings that individuals hold in society; a large group with similar rankings, 104

Social construction of reality. The process by which individuals and groups shape reality through social interaction, 83

Social institutions. Organized, patterned, and enduring sets of social structures that provide guidelines for behavior and help each society meet its basic survival needs, 18

Social interaction. Consists of two or more individuals purposefully relating to each other, 118

Social mobility. The extent of individual movement up or down in the class system, changing one's social position in society—especially relative to one's parents, 186

Social movements. Consciously organized attempts outside of established institutional mechanisms to enhance or resist change through group action, 447

Social networks. Refer to individuals linked together by one or more social relationships, connecting them to the larger society, 115

Social processes. Take place through actions of people in institutions and other social units or structures, 19

Social reform movements. Seek to change some specific dimension of society, usually involving legislative policy modification or appeals to the courts, 447

Social status. *A social position in society,* 121

Social stratification. How individuals and groups are layered or ranked in society according to how many valued resources they possess, 176

Social structure. The stable patterns of interactions, statuses, roles, and institutions that provide stability for the society and bring order to individuals' lives, 18

Social units. Interconnected parts of the social world ranging from small groups to societies, 18

Social world model. Refers to the levels of analysis in our social surroundings as an interconnected series of small groups, organizations, institutions, and societies, 17

Socialization. The lifelong process of learning to become a member of the social world, beginning at birth and continuing until death, 90

Society. An organized and interdependent group of individuals who live together in a specific geographical area and who interact more with each other than they do with outsiders; they cooperate for the attainment of common goals and share a common culture over time, 58

Sociological imagination. The recognition of the complex and interactive relationship between micro-level individual experiences and macro-level public issues, 10

Sociology. The scientific study of social life, social change, and the social causes and consequences of human behavior, 6

Spurious relationships. Occur when there is no causal relationship between the independent and dependent variables, but they vary together, often due to a third variable affecting both of them, 35

Stigma. Disapproval attached to disobeying the expected norms so that a person is discredited as less than normal, 160

Subculture. The culture of a meso-level subcommunity that distinguishes itself from the dominant culture of the larger society, 78

Subjugation. The subordination of one group to another that holds power and authority, 227

Survey method. Research method used by sociologists who want to gather information directly from a number of people regarding how they think or feel or what they do; two common survey forms are the interview and the questionnaire, 34

Symbolic interaction theory. Sees humans as active agents who create shared meanings of symbols and events and then interact on the basis of those meanings, 44

Symbols. Actions or objects that represent something else and therefore have meaning beyond their own existence; flags and wedding rings are examples, 44

Technology. The practical application of tools, skills, and knowledge to meet human needs and extend human abilities, 63

Terrorism. The planned use of random, unlawful (or illegal) violence or threat of violence against civilians to create (or raise) fear and intimidate citizens in order to advance the terrorist group's political or ideological goals, 159

Theoretical perspective. Basic view of society that guides sociologists' ideas and research; theoretical perspectives are the broadest theories in sociology, providing overall approaches to understanding the social world and social problems, 44

Theories. Statements or explanations regarding how and why two or more facts are related to each other and the connections between these facts, 32

Total institution. A place that cuts people off from the rest of society and totally controls their lives in the process of resocialization; examples are prisons and boot camps, 101

Totalitarian government. Form of government that almost totally controls people's lives, 374

Transnationalism. The process by which immigrants create multinational social relations that link together their original societies with their new locations; this usually entails national loyalty to more than one country, 107

Triangulation. The utilization of two or more methods of data collection to enhance the amount and type of data for analysis and the accuracy of the findings, 38

Urbanization. The process by which an increasing percentage of the population moves from rural areas to more densely populated cities, 398

Values. Nonmaterial shared judgments about what is desirable or undesirable, right or wrong, good or bad; they express the basic ideals of any culture, 72

Variables. Concepts (ideas) that can vary in frequency of occurrence from one time, place, or person to another, 34

Victimless crimes (public order crimes). Acts committed by or between consenting adults, 156

War. Armed conflict occurring within, between, or among societies or groups, 384

Wealth. One's income, property, and total assets, 196

White-collar (or occupational) crime. The violation of law by an individual or a group in the course of a legitimate, respected occupation or financial activity, 158

Index

Absolute poverty, 200
Acceptance strategy, 232
Achieved status, 122–123
Achieved stratification systems, 193
Administrator role in education, 318–319
Adolescence, 99, 246
Adoption by gay couples, 286, 286 (photo)
Affirmative action, 235–238
Afghanistan, 158, 228, 245–246, 448
African Americans
    "Black Men and Public Space" (Staples), 96
    class and, 213
    cohabitation and, 302
    incarceration and, 164
    migration by, 416
    racism and discrimination against, 215–216, 223
Age dependency ratio, 400
Agency, human
    institutions and, 283
    symbolic interaction and, 44, 95, 120, 264
Agents of socialization, 101–107, 254–258
Aggression, 233
Agricultural societies, 61–62
Alaska Natives, 224
Alienation, 133
Alliances, international, 434, 441
Al-Qaeda, 389
Altruistic suicide, 126
Ambedkar, B. R., 195
American Friends Service Committee, 357
American Sign Language, 76, 80
American Sociological Association (ASA), 27
American Sociological Association code of ethics, 39
AmeriCorps, 206
Amish, 79, 81
Amnesty International, 238, 240
Analysis levels. See Levels of analysis; Macro-level analysis; Meso-level analysis; Micro-level analysis
Anderson, Warren, 451 (photo)
Anomic suicide, 126
Anomie, 125, 150–152
Anthropology, 11
Anti-Defamation League (ADL), 235, 240
"Anti-Muslim Sentiments in the United States" (Selod), 220
Antinatalist policies, 407
Anti-Slavery International, 212
Apartheid in South Africa, 215
Applied research, 452
Applied sociologists, 43, 455
Arapesh of New Guinea, 67
Aristotle, 42

Arranged marriages, 295–296
Ascribed statuses, 122
Ascribed stratification systems, 193–194
Al-Assad, Bashar, 227
Assimilation, 228, 232
Association for Applied and Clinical Sociology (AACS), 54
Athletes, professional, 95, 186, 232
Attachment, 147
Attitudes toward achievement, 185
Aung San Suu Kyi, 365
Australian Aborigines, 431
Authoritarian political systems, 374
Authority, 364. See also Power and privilege
Automobiles, 437–438
Avoidance strategy, 232–233

Baby boomers, 410, 422
Bachelet, Michelle, 136
Back-to-Africa movement, 232
Bales, Kevin, 212, 448
Bangalore, India, 204
Bantu of southern Africa, 372, 372 (photo)
Barber, Bonnie, 13
Basic research, 452
Basques in Spain, 228
Bates, Bill, 431–432, 431 (photo)
Behaviors and sanctions, 438 (figure)
Beliefs
    change and, 434
    common-sense, 7–9
    defined, 72
    as nonmaterial culture, 72
    in social control theory, 147
Bell, Daniel, 63
Belonging system, 334–335
Bergdahl, Jacqueline, 265
Berger, Helen, 344
Bible, 257
Bigotry, racial, 222
Bin Laden, Osama, 388, 389
Biosocial theories, 91
Birth control, 407, 408 (photo)
Black Death (bubonic plague), 412
"Black Men and Public Space" (Staples), 96
Blackness, associations with, 77
Blair, Dennis, 374
Body image, 246, 256 (photo), 272, 272 (photo)
Books, banned and challenged, 321–322, 321 (table)
Boston Marathon bombings, 105
Bourgeoisie, 49, 377
The boy code, 253–254

Boys and Girls Clubs, 110, 170
Brasher, Brenda E., 354
Brinkmanship, 387
Bubonic plague (Black Death), 412
Buffett, Warren, 192
Bullying, 90, 254, 316
Burawoy, Michael, 43
Bureaucracies
    characteristics of, 131–132
    defined, 130
    evolution of modern organizations, 129–130
    issues in, 132–134
    schools and, 320
    Weber on, 50
    See also Organizations
Burma (Myanmar), 365, 380 (photo)
Burnouts and Jocks in a Public High School, 13
Bush, George H. W., 407
Bush, George W., 376, 378, 407, 433

Calvinist Protestantism, 281–282
Cambodia, 375
Canada, Geoffrey, 329, 330
Canadian health care system, 413, 414
Capitalism
    deviance and, 152
    market systems, 377–378
    Marx on, 48–49, 180, 377
    Weber's The Protestant Ethic and the Spirit of Capitalism, 50–51,
        281–282
    See also Conflict theory; Marx, Karl
Capitalist class, 181
Caracas, Venezuela, 424, 424 (photo)
CARE International, 110, 249
Caste systems, 193, 195, 204
Castle, Jeremiah, 371, 381
Castro, Fidel, 374, 374 (photo)
Castro, Raúl, 374, 374 (photo)
Catholic Relief Services, 357
Cause-and-effect relationships, 35
Cell phone users, 203
Census Bureau, U.S., 54, 426
Centralized (planned) systems, 378
Chad, 409
Chambliss, William J., 150
Change. See Social change
Charismatic authority, 364–365
Chicago school of symbolic interaction theory, 45, 99
Childhood and children
    adoption by gay couples, 286, 286 (photo)
    cultural capital and, 178
    day care, 309
    gender socialization and, 252–254, 262, 264
    isolated and abused children, 92
    "long childhood," 92
    rites of passage and, 99
    See also Education; Socialization
Child slavery, 211
China
    billionaires in, 192
    classes in, 181
    education and, 182
    literacy in, 9 (photo)

male preference system in, 247
Olympics and Tibet protests, 446
planned system in, 378
polyandry in, 299 (photo)
population and, 397, 405 (photo), 407
R&D and, 453
Yungang Buddhist caves, 352 (photo)
Chinese railway workers, 230 (photo)
Churchill, Winston, 379
Cigarettes, 415
Civil religion, 345, 345 (photo)
Civil Rights Commission, U.S., 235
Class consciousness, 180
Class systems, 178, 194–197. See also Social class; Stratification
Climate change, global, 433, 446
Clinton, Bill, 407
Closed system model, 445
Cochabamba, 450
Code of ethics (American Sociological Association), 39
Cohabitation, 301–302, 301 (figure)
Collective behavior, 441–444
Colleges and universities
    attendance, by social class, 188 (table)
    bachelor's degrees in U.S., 325 (map)
    cultural capital, social capital, and first-generation college
        students, 190–191
    Human Language and the Marvel of a College Classroom, 45
    Oberlin College as counterculture, 81
    preference policies, 236, 237
    rape on U.S. college campuses, 268
    See also Education
Collins, Patricia Hill, 51–52, 51 (photo)
Colombia, 448–449
Color-blind prejudice, 222
Commitment, 147
Common sense, 7–9
Communication
    nonverbal, 76, 118–119, 119 (photo)
    norms and, 75
    See also Language
Communist Manifesto (Marx and Engels), 49
Community movements, 457
Community of Peace People, 194
Community organizations, 138
Competitive perspective, 52 (figure)
Computer technology. See Internet and computers
Comte, Auguste, 42, 43
Conflict theory
    about, 48–50
    on change, 440
    on criminal justice system, 163, 164
    cultural theory, 85–86
    defined, 48
    on deviance, 153
    on education, 319, 326
    on family, 293
    on gender stratification, 266
    on institutions, 282–283
    on minority groups, 230–231
    on population growth, 404–405
    on poverty, 201
    on socialization, 93
    on stratification, 179–181

on terrorism, 390
on war, terrorism, and revolution, 386
Conformity, 152
"Confronting Slavery With the Tools of Sociology" (Bales), 212
Congregational polity, 341
Congress, U.S., 231, 231 (table)
Conspicuous consumption, 178
Constitutions, 376
Content analysis, 38
Control groups, 37
Controls, 35
Cooley, Charles H., 94, 127, 151
Cooperative perspective, 52 (figure)
Core countries, 162, 162 (map), 383, 440, 440 (figure)
Corporations and gender socialization, 254–255, 273
Correlation, 35
Corrie, Rachel, 388 (photo caption)
Corrigan, Mairead, 194
Coser, Lewis, 50
Cost-benefit determinations. *See* Rational choice (exchange) theory
Countercultures, 79, 81
Creative class, 65
Credentials, 324
Crime
    cross-national comparison of, 160–161, 161 (table), 168
    defined, 142
    as deviance, 145–146
    fraudulent organizations, 157
    global, 161–162
    measurement of, 154–155
    occupational, 158–159
    organized, 157–158
    police and delinquent youth, 167
    policy and control of, 162–168
    terrorism and state-organized crime, 159–160
    types of, 155–157
Crime prevention programs, 170
Criminal justice system, 163–166, 170, 224
Cross-Cultural Differences in Family Dissolution, 307
Cross-cultural mobility, 192
Crowd behaviors, 441
Cults, 342
Cultural capital, 176, 178
Cultural relativism, 69–70
Cultural Survival, 240
Culture
    characteristics of, 66
    class and, 198
    counterculture, 79, 81
    defined, 58
    ethnocentrism, 67–69
    ideal vs. real, 72
    material, 70, 71
    microcultures, 78
    national and global cultures, 81–83
    nonmaterial, 70–77
    as software, 58, 86
    subcultures and countercultures, 78–79
    theories of, 83–86
Cybercrimes, 159

Dahrendorf, Ralf, 49–50
Dalits of India, 193, 195, 200

Darwin, Charles, 453
Data analysis, 38–39
Data collection methods, 34–38
Davis, Kingsley, 92, 179
Day care, 309
Deaf Subculture in the United States, 80
Death, socialization and, 100–101. *See also* Mortality
Death penalty, 165–166, 166 (map)
Death rituals, 100 (photo)
Debt bondage, 211
"Debunking Misconceptions About Divorce" (Popenoe), 304
Decision making, educational, 321–322
Defense of Marriage Act (DOMA), 447
Definition of a situation, 289
DeGeneres, Ellen, 303 (photo)
Degradation, 163
Delayed gratification, 179
Democratic Party, 364, 365, 368, 383
Democratic-Republican Party, 364
Democratic socialism, 378–379
Democratic systems
    characteristics of, 374–376
    defined, 374
    legitimacy and, 364–365
    participation and, 367–371
    technology and, 376–377
Demographic transition theory, 403–404, 404 (figure)
Demography, 398. *See also* Populations and population trends
Denominations, 340–341
Dependency ratio, 399–400
Dependent variables, 35
de Rossi, Portia, 303 (photo)
Deterrence, 387
"Developing countries," 439
Deviance
    definitions of, 142–146
    law, violation of, 145–146
    meso- and macro-level explanations for, 150–154
    micro-level explanations for, 146–150
    population patterns and, 422
    See also Crime
Differential association theory, 148–149
Diffusion, 452
Digital divide, 201–204, 203 (table)
Dineh, 69
"Disability and Inequality" (Pellerin), 322
Disasters. *See* Natural disasters
Discovery, 451–452
Discrimination
    defined, 219
    effects of, 231–232
    meso-level analysis of, 223–226
    minority reactions to, 232–234
    See also Racism
Disease. *See* Illness
Dissatisfaction in bureaucracies, 133
Distance, social, 119
Divorce, 9, 303–306, 305 (table), 307 (table)
Domestic violence, 20–22, 293 (photo), 294
Dominican Republic, 227
Dramaturgical analysis, 120–121
Drug trade, 158
Du Bois, W. E. B., 49, 49 (photo)

Durkheim, Émile
    on anomie, 150
    functionalism and, 47
    on mechanical and organic solidarity, 60, 264
    on patriotism, 363
    on the sacred realm, 333–334
    scientific sociology and, 43
    on suicide, 125–126
Dyads, 6, 18 (photo)
Dysfunctions, 47

Eccles, Jacquelynne, 13
Eckert, Penelope, 13
Economic development, 313, 423–424
Economics, defined, 373
Economic stratification. *See* Stratification
Economic systems
    family and, 281, 292
    global economic crisis, 279
    institutional impacts at levels of analysis, 280 (table)
    purposes of economic institutions, 372–373
    religion, linkage with, 281–282
    types of, 377–379
    See also Power and privilege
Economic vitality, 189
Economists, 12
Ecosystems, 424
Edison, Thomas, 453 (photo caption)
Education
    bachelor's degrees in U.S., 325 (map)
    boys and, 317–318
    bureaucratic structure and, 320
    Burnouts and Jocks in a Public High School, 13
    cultural capital, social capital, and, 190–191
    decision making in, 321–322
    family, linkage with, 280–281
    formal systems, 319–320
    gender socialization and, 103, 256–257
    Human Language and the Marvel of a College Classroom, 45
    informal system, 319
    institutional impacts at levels of analysis, 280 (table)
    literacy, 9 (photo), 313, 314 (map)
    Oberlin College as counterculture, 81
    policy issues, 329–332
    population and, 408–409, 409 (figure)
    private preparatory schools and elite status, 366–367
    rape on U.S. college campuses, 268
    schools as local organizations, 314
    social status and access to, 182–183
    statuses and roles in, 315–319
    stratification and, 179, 326–329
    theoretical perspectives on, 314–315, 323–326
    upward mobility and, 188–189, 188 (table)
    women and, 267
    world education, state of, 313
Egoistic suicide, 126
Ehrlich, Paul, 403
Eitzen, D. Stanley, 449
Elderly, 100
Elections
    participation in, 368–370, 370 (figure), 370 (table)
    selection systems, 376, 382–383
    "The 2012 Presidential Election and the Youth Vote" (Castle), 371
Elective affinity, 348

Electoral College, 383
Elite theory. *See* Power elite model
Elrod, Leslie, 151
Emergent norm theory, 442
Emotional support and protection in families, 292
Empirical knowledge, 31, 32–33
Endogamy, 295, 334
Engaging Sociology
    bachelor's degrees, consequences of number of, 325 (map)
    change from the bottom up, 450
    cultural capital, social capital, and 1st-generation college students, 190–191
    household tasks by gender, 298
    ideal family, 288
    Internet users, demographics of, 64
    life expectancy, per capita income, and infant mortality, 184
    making a difference, 455
    masculinity and femininity in your social world, 259
    micro-meso-macro social units, 23
    political decisions, 383
    population pyramids and predicting community needs and services, 423
    preference policies at the University of Michigan, 237
    research tables, how to read, 40–41
    social networks, examining, 117
    test score variations by gender and ethnicity, 328
    world urbanization trends, 420
Engels, Friedrich, 49, 266, 293, 404, 440
Environment
    garbage and recycling, 430
    global climate change, 433, 446
    human impact on, 432–433
    natural disasters, 21, 21 (map), 21 (photo), 434–435
Environmental justice movement, 404–405
Environmental policy, 424
Environmental racism, 430
Environments, 19
Episcopal polity, 341–342
Equal Employment Opportunity Commission, U.S., 235
Equality Now, 276
Equal opportunity, 327
Essay on the Principle of Population (Malthus), 402
Estate systems, 193–194
Ethical issues is social research, 39
Ethnic groups
    defined, 217
    education and, 317, 317 (table)
    environmental racism and, 430
    organizations and clubs, 87
    organized crime and, 158
    panethnicity, 217
    social construction of, 217–218
    social mobility and, 191
    test score variations by ethnicity, 328
    See also Minority groups
Ethnocentrism, 67–69, 128
Evangelicals, 347
Evidence, 32
Evolutionary psychology, 91
Evolutionary theories, social, 439
Evolutionary theory of stratification, 181–182
Exchange theory. *See* Rational choice (exchange) theory
Existing sources, 37–38
Exogamy, 294–295

Experimental groups, 37
Experiments, 37
Expressive movements, 447
Extended family, 300
Ezzy, Douglas, 344

Facebook, 116
Fads, 444
Fair Trade Certified label, 211 (figure), 450
Falwell, Jerry, 354
Families of orientation, 287, 289
Families of procreation, 287, 289
Family
    in agricultural vs. industrial societies, 62
    authority and household tasks in marriage, 297–299
    cohabitation issue, 301–302, 301 (table)
    definitions of, 287
    divorce, 303–306, 305 (table), 307, 307 (table)
    education and economy, linkage with, 280–281
    extended and nuclear, 300
    global patterns and policies, 306–307
    "ideal," 288
    as institution, 278, 299–300
    institutional impacts at levels of analysis, 280 (table)
    mate selection, 294–297
    same-sex relationships, 302–303
    socialization and, 102, 104, 188, 291–292
    theoretical perspectives on, 289–294
    variations in, 286
Famines, 402–403
Farrow, Mia, 402 (photo)
Fashions, 444
FBI Index Crimes, 155
Federalist Party, 364
Federal Reserve, 377
Femininity. *See* Gender
Feminist theory
    about, 51–52
    on class, race, and gender, 269
    defined, 51
    on deviance, 153
    on family, 293–294
    on gender stratification, 266–267
Fernández de Kirchner, Cristina, 249 (photo)
Fertility, 189, 405–409
Field research (observation studies), 37
Films, 157, 158 (photo), 219, 255
Filter theory, 297 (figure)
First Nations peoples, 72, 226
Flags, 363
Florida, Richard, 64, 65
Focus on the Family, 447
Folkways, 73, 74 (table), 75
Food, 58, 265
Food shortages, 402–403
Formal agents of socialization, 102
Formal organizations, 129
Formal sanctions, 74–75
Franklin, Benjamin, 452
Franz Ferdinand, Archduke, 436
Fraud, 157, 159
Free-choice marriage, 296
Free the Children, 110, 206
Free the Slaves, 212, 448

Frustration-aggression theory, 221
Functionalism. *See* Structural-functional (or functional) theory
Fundamentalism, 353

Galileo, 453
Game stage, 98
Gandhi, Mohandas K. (Mahatma), 145, 233, 233 (photo),
    365, 435–436, 438
Gang rape, 268, 269
Garbage, 430, 453 (photo)
Garvey, Marcus, 232
Gastarbeiter (guest workers), 230
Gates, Bill, 192
Gay people. *See* Homosexuality and LGBT individuals
Gender
    boys and education, 317–318
    class and race, interaction with, 269
    common-sense beliefs on, 8–9
    costs and consequences of stratification, 271–273
    definitions of sex, gender, and sexuality, 246–247
    feminization of poverty, 200–201
    "Gender and Food" (Bergdahl), 265
    homosexuality, minority status, and, 269–271
    household tasks and, 297–299
    levels of analysis on, 247–252
    peer culture in schools and, 316
    policy and, 273–274
    rape and, 268
    religion and, 348–351
    socialization, 103, 247, 252–258
    social mobility and, 191
    stratification, 258–264
    test score variations by, 328
    theoretical perspectives on, 263–269
    variations around the world, 244–246
    Wodaabe society and, 8 (photo)
    See also Feminist theory; Women
Gender roles
    change in, 252
    defined, 247
    deviance and, 154
    results of, 272
    socialization into, 103, 247, 252–258
Gender stratification. *See* Gender
Generalized other, 98
General Motors, 448–449
Generation X, 371, 410
Genocide, 226–227
Geographic mobility, 415. *See also* Migration
Georgia project, 323
Gibson, William, 114
The Girl With the Dragon Tattoo (film), 255
Glass ceiling, 258, 272–273
Global climate change, 433, 446
Global crimes, 161–162
Global culture, 82–83
Global economic crisis, 279
Global economies, interdependent, 191
Globalization
    defined, 82
    "from below," 449–450
    mobility of disease and, 411–413
    as process, 393
    social movements and, 449–450

women and, 134–137
See also Sociology Around the World
Global North
    democracy and, 384
    education in, 313, 330–331
    environmental issues, 424
    family in, 292
    fertility rates in, 406
    gender inequality and, 260–261
    gender role expectations in, 272
    life expectancy and, 409, 411
    migration and, 416
    population and, 400, 401 (figure)
    serial monogamy in, 300
    world systems theory and, 162
Global Public Health Intelligence Network, 435
Global South
    clean drinking water issue, 331, 446
    crime and, 162
    democracy and, 384
    "developing countries" vs., 439
    education in, 313, 323, 327, 331
    fertility rates in, 406, 408
    infant mortality rates in, 412 (table)
    infrastructure and pollution in, 424
    life expectancy and, 409, 411
    migration and, 416–417
    population and, 396, 399 (photo), 401, 401 (figure)
    social mobility and, 192
    sweatshops in, 273, 432
    world systems theory and, 162
Global transnational movements, 448
Goal displacement, 134
Gomez, Selena, 180 (photo)
Gore, Al, 376
Government. *See* Political systems; Power and privilege
Gracey, Harry L., 319
Grameen Bank, 206
Graunt, John, 412
Greeley, Andrew M., 333
Group of 8 (G8), 384, 385 (map), 449, 453
Group of 77 (G77), 384, 385 (map), 449
Groups
    Burnouts and Jocks in a Public High School, 13
    defined, 125
    deviance and, 144–145
    formation of, 125
    importance of, for individuals, 125–126
    types of, 126–127, 128 (table)
Guantánamo Bay, 159–160, 160 (photo), 164
Guarino-Ghezzi, Susan, 167
Guatemala, 73

Habitat for Humanity, 206, 309
Haiti, 21 (photo), 177
Haiti and subjugation, 227
Hante, Barber G. S., 219 (photo)
Hardin, Garrett, 403
Harlem Children's Zone, 330
Hasidic Jews, 79, 79 (photo)
Hate crimes, 156–157
Hate groups, 221, 221 (map)
Hausa of West Africa, 294
Head Start, 110, 323 (photo)

Health, defined, 409. *See also* Illness
Health care. *See* Medicine
Heaven's Gate, 342
Helú, Carlos Slim, 192
Herding societies, 61
Heterosexism, 269–270
Hidden curriculum, 319
Higher education. *See* Colleges and universities; Education
Hijras, 270
Hinduism, 193, 258
Hitler, Adolf, 226–227, 438
HIV/AIDS, 412
Hochschild, Arlie, 297
Hofstra University, 309
Holocaust, 226, 238
Homogamy, 295
Homophobia, 270
Homo sapiens, spread of, 214 (map)
Homosexuality and LGBT individuals
    adoption by gay couples, 286, 286 (photo)
    assimilation and, 232
    bullying and assault in schools, 316
    gay rights movement, 447
    gender, minority status, and, 269–271
    hate crimes and, 156–157
    LGBT groups, 170
    religion and, 351
    rights and, 270–271
    same-sex relationships and civil unions, 302–303, 351
Horejes, Thomas P., 80
Horizontal mobility, 187
Horticultural societies, 61
Hospital microculture, 78
Hostility between groups, 230
Household tasks, 297–299
Hughes, Melanie, 369
Humanistic sociology, 43
Human Language and the Marvel of a College Classroom, 45
Human rights movements, global, 238
Human trafficking, 210–211
The Hunger Games (film), 255
Hunger in the world, 199, 199 (table)
Hunter-gatherer societies, 60–61, 279
Hypotheses, 34

I, 95–97, 99
Ibn Khaldun, 41–42
Ideal culture, 72
Ideal-type bureaucracies, 132
Ideology, 368
Illness
    defined, 409
    epidemics, 435
    globalization and mobility of disease, 413–415
    mortality from, 411–413
    population and, 402
Imitation stage, 97
Immigrant aid groups, 87
Immigration, 217–218, 415–418
Immigration laws, 416
Impression management, 121
Incest taboos, 74, 74 (table), 295
Income gap, 198
Independent variables, 35

India
  caste system in, 193, 195, 204
  population and, 397–398
  "sacred cow" in, 85
  Union Carbide gas disaster (Bhopal), 451
Indonesia, 408 (photo)
Industrial Revolution, 60, 439
Industrial societies, 62–63
Inequality, 171, 322, 327–329. *See also* Stratification
Infant mortality, 184, 411, 412 (table), 414
Informal agents of socialization, 102
Informal sanctions, 75
Information societies, 63–66
In-group, 128
Innovation, 152
Institutionalized privilege or disprivilege, 251
Institutions
  crimes involving, 157–159
  defined, 278–279
  development of modern institutions, 279
  interconnections between, 279–282
  levels of analysis, impact at, 280 (table)
  social institutions, defined, 18
  structure vs. process, 277
  theories on, 282–283
  See also Organizations; *specific institutions, such as* family
Interaction, social, 117–121. *See also* Groups; Social networks
Interest groups, 365
Intergenerational mobility, 186–187
Internally displaced persons, 416–417
International Monetary Fund (IMF), 449
International Sociological Association (ISA), 27
International Solidarity Movement, 388 (photo)
Internet and computers
  cybercrimes, 159
  cyberspace, 114
  democracy and, 376–377
  demographics of Internet users, 64 (table)
  digital divide, national and global, 201–204, 203 (table)
  discrimination and, 224
  e-Romance, 296
  gender and, 262–263
  Internet users and access (map), 108
  religion and, 354–355
  socialization and, 105–107
  "Social Media and Political Protests" (Castle), 381
  social networks and sites, 116
Internships, 391
Intersectionality, 52
Intersex people, 246
Interview method, 34
Intimate distance, 119
Intragenerational mobility, 187
Invention, 452
"Invisible escalator," 258
Involvement, 147
Iowa school of symbolic interaction theory, 45–46, 99
Islam and Muslims
  arranged marriage and, 295
  gender and, 245 (photo), 258
  mosques and organizational structure, 343
  prayer, 33 (photo)
  sentiments against, 220
  Israel, 389 (photo)

Jails, 163–164
James, LeBron, 95, 186
Japan
  crime and, 160–161
  marriage in, 295, 296 (photo)
  population and, 400 (figure)
  women workers in, 272
Jesus, 364
Jews and Judaism
  branches of Judaism, 341
  gender and, 248, 257–258
  scapegoating and, 226
  Touro Synagogue, Rhode Island, 229
  yarmulke, 339 (photo)
Jim Crow laws, 215–216
Johnson, Lyndon, 235
Jones, Jim, 342
Jubilee Movement, 457

Katz, Jackson, 253
Kenya, 396–397
The Khmer Rouge Revolution, 375
Kindlon, Dan, 253–254
King, Martin Luther, Jr., 145, 233
Kiva.org, 250
Ku Klux Klan (KKK), 221, 222 (photo)
Kyoto Protocol, 433

Labeling theory, 148, 149–150
Labor pool, cheap, 229, 449
Labor unions, 138, 365 (photo), 377
Language
  defined, 75
  development of, 76 (photo)
  gender and, 248
  Human Language and the Marvel of a College Classroom, 45
  linguistic relativity theory, 77
  as nonmaterial culture, 75–77
  spoken, written, and nonverbal, 76
  symbolic interaction theory and, 44–45
Latent functions, 47, 324 (figure), 326
Laws, 74, 145–146
Leadership Conference of Women Religious, 349
Leadership Conference on Civil and Human Rights, 240
Least interest, principle of, 121
Legitimacy of power, 362–365
Lenski, Gerhard E., 181–182
Lesbians. *See* Homosexuality and LGBT individuals
Levels of analysis
  defined, 16
  distinctions among, 22
  engaging sociology, 23
  social world model and, 16–17
  structure of society and, 19, 20 (table)
  theoretical perspectives and, 44–52
  See also Macro-level analysis; Meso-level analysis; Micro-level
    analysis
LGBT groups, 170. *See also* Homosexuality and LGBT individuals
Life and Death in a Guatemalan Village, 73
Life chances, 183
Life cycle, socialization through, 99–101
Life expectancy, 183–184, 397, 409–411, 414 (table)
Lifestyle, 184–185
Linguistic relativity theory, 77

Literacy, 9 (photo), 313, 314 (map)
Local service organizations, 54
Locke, John, 368
Lonmin mines, South Africa, 434
Looking-glass self, 94–95, 151
Lower middle class, 198
Luther, Martin, 303, 354
Lutheran World Relief, 357

Maathai, Wangari, 194
Machiavelli, 42
Machiavelli, Niccolo, 361
Macro-level analysis
    change, 432–434
    crime, 159–162
    cultures, 81–83
    defined, 20–21
    deviance, 150–154
    education, 322–329
    family, 301–306
    institutional impacts, 280 (table)
    networks, 116, 134
    nonviolent resistance, 233–234
    population growth, 398–405
    power and privilege, 362, 379–390
    religion, 345–351
    sex, gender and sexuality, 250–252, 258–263
    socialization and, 93, 107–108
    stratification, 177, 193–198
    theoretical perspectives and, 47–52
    See also Conflict theory; Feminist theory; Levels of analysis;
        Structural-functional (or functional) theory
Madoff, Bernard (Bernie), 159
MADRE, 276
Make Peace With Police (MPWP) program, 167
Male body, ideal, 246, 272
Malthus, Thomas, 402–403
Manager class, 181
Mandela, Nelson, 364, 448
Manifest functions, 47, 324–326, 324 (figure)
Manning, Peyton, 186
Mao Zedong, 364
Maquiladoras, 273
Market systems/capitalism, 377–378
Marriage
    authority and household tasks in, 297–299
    divorce, 9, 303–306, 305 (table), 307, 307 (table)
    mate selection, 294–297
    same-sex, 270, 302–303, 351
    types of, 299–300
    See also Family
Martineau, Harriet, 49, 49 (photo)
Marx, Karl, 49 (photo)
    on capitalism and class, 377
    on change, 440
    conflict theory and, 48–49
    feminist theory and, 266
    on population, 404
    power elite model and, 196
    on religion and class, 346
    socialism and, 379
    on stratification, 180–181, 230
    Weber on, 50–51
Masculinity. See Gender

Massachusetts Department of Youth Services (DYS), 167
Mass behavior, 441
Mass media, 255–256, 270. See also Internet and computers
Master status, 123
Material culture, 70
Mate selection, 294–297
Matriarch, 297
Mayflower United Church of Christ, Minneapolis, 432
Mayoux, Linda, 249
The McDonaldization of Society, 130
McDonald's, 445
McVeigh, Timothy, 389
Me, 97, 99
Mead, George Herbert, 44, 95, 97–98
Mead, Margaret, 67
"Mean girls," 90
Meaning system, 334
Means of production, 48, 180
Mechanical solidarity, 60, 264
Medicare fraud, 157
Medicine
    access to health care, 183
    Canadian health care system, 413, 414
    divorce and, 305
    as institution, 279
    institutional impacts at levels of analysis, 280 (table)
    world health care expenditures and life expectancy, 414 (table)
Megacities, 418
Menchú Tum, Rigoberta, 73, 194
Mentoring, 110, 138
Meritocracy, 188
Merton, Robert, 47, 152
Meso-level analysis
    change, 432, 444–446
    crime and organizations, 157–159
    defined, 20
    deviance, 150–154
    discrimination, 223–226
    education, 319–322
    family, 299–300
    institutional impacts, 280 (table)
    networks, 116
    nonviolent resistance, 233–234
    population change, 405–418
    power and privilege, 361–362, 372–379
    religion and modern life, 340–345
    sex, gender and sexuality, 248–250, 254–263
    socialization and, 93, 104–107
    stratification, 177
    subcultures and countercultures, 78–81
    theoretical perspectives and, 44–52
    See also Conflict theory; Feminist theory; Levels of analysis;
        Structural-functional (or functional) theory
Mexico, 434
Michels, Robert, 133
Microcredit, 206, 249–250
Microcultures, 78
Microfinance organizations, 138
Micro-level analysis
    change, 431–432
    collective behavior, 441–444
    defined, 20
    deviance, 146–150
    discrimination, 232–233

education, 314–319
family dynamics, 294–299
institutional impacts, 280 (table)
microcultures, 78
networks, 115
population patterns, 419–422
power and privilege, 361, 367–372
religious affiliation and membership, 336–337, 336 (table)
self-development, 94–99
sex, gender and sexuality, 247–248, 252–254
social interaction, 117–125
socialization and, 93, 102–104
social status, 182–186
stratification, 176
theoretical perspectives and, 44–46
See also Levels of analysis; Rational choice (exchange) theory;
Symbolic interaction theory
Middle class, 190, 198
Middleton, Kate, Duchess of Cambridge, 174, 174 (photo)
Middleton, Pippa, 174
Migration, 217–218, 405, 415–418 418 (table)
Milgram, Stanley, 115
Military expenditures, 387, 387 (figure)
Millennial generation, 371, 410
Mills, C. Wright, 10, 366
Mini-max strategy, 442
Minority groups ·
characteristics of, 213–218
defined, 213
discrimination, analysis of, 223–226
dominant–minority group relations, 226–231, 227 (figure)
education and, 317, 317 (table)
effects of prejudice, racism, and discrimination, 231–232
incarceration and, 164
key concepts, using and relating, 225 (figure)
LGBT (lesbian, gay, bisexual, and transgender), 269–271
organizations and, 133, 138
policies, 234–238
prejudice, analysis of, 219–222
reactions to prejudice, racism, and discrimination, 232–234
slavery, human trafficking, and, 210–213
See also Ethnic groups; Race
Mixed economies, 378–379
Mobs, 443, 443 (figure)
Model legislature and Model UN programs, 391
Monogamy, 299
Moon, Sun Myung, 342
Moore, Valerie Ann, 103
Moore, Wilbert, 179
More, Thomas, 42
Mores, 73–74, 74 (table)
Mortality
defined, 405
from diseases and plagues, 411–413
globalization and mobility of disease, 413–415
life expectancy and infant mortality, 409–411, 412 (table)
world rates of, 412 (table)
Mortification, 163
Mother Teresa, 175, 431 (photo)
Mubarak, Hosni, 381
Mugabe, Robert, 361, 436
Muhammad, 364
Murdock, George, 299
Muslims. *See* Islam and Muslims

Myanmar (Burma), 365, 380 (photo)
Myrdal, Gunnar, 72
Myths, 338

NAFTA (North American Free Trade Agreement), 434
National culture, 82
National Incident-Based Reporting System (NIBRS), 155
National Organization for Women (NOW), 276
National Relief Charities, 240
National Security Entry-Exit Registration System, 220
National society, 82
Nation-states, 379–380
Native Americans
avoidance and, 232–233
ethnocentrism and, 69
religion and, 334
as social construction, 217
"Trail of Tears," 227–228
value of cooperation among, 72
Natural disasters, 21, 21 (map), 21 (photo), 434–435
Nature vs. nurture, 91
Negotiation, 387–388
Neo-Malthusians, 403
Neo-Pagans, 344
Networks, social, 115–117, 115 (figure). *See also* Social interaction
Newport, Rhode Island, 174, 175 (photo)
New religious movements (NRMs), 342–345
Nichols, Terry, 389
Nigeria, 409
Nolan, Patrick, 182
Nongovernmental organizations (NGOs), 87, 365, 446
Nonmaterial culture
beliefs, 72
defined, 70, 72
language as, 75–77
norms, 72–75
values, 72
Nonverbal communication, 76, 118–119, 119 (photo)
Nonviolent resistance, 233–234, 448 (photo)
Norms
defined, 72
homosexuality and, 270
informal, 132
mate selection and, 294–295
as nonmaterial culture, 72–75
religion and, 343–344
social interaction and, 118
See also Deviance
Nuclear family, 300
Nudity, 74–75

Obama, Barak, 222, 225, 360 (photo), 370, 370 (photo), 371,
378, 407
Obama, Michelle, 51 (photo), 370 (photo)
Oberlin College, 81
Obesity, 151, 265
Objectivity, 32
Observation studies (field research), 37
Occupational (white-collar) crime, 158–159
Occupy Wall Street, 233, 234 (photo)
Ogburn, William F., 436, 451–452
Oklahoma City bombing, 389
Oligarchy, 134
One Laptop per Child foundation, 204

Open class systems, 187
Open system model, 445, 445 (figure)
Organic solidarity, 60, 264
Organizational development approach, 445
Organizations
    crimes involving, 157–159
    gendered, 260–262, 260 (figure)
    modern, evolution of, 129–130
    modern life and, 131
    planned change in, 444–446
    schools as local organizations, 314
    See also Bureaucracies
Organized crime, 157–158
Outcastes of India, 195
Out-group, 128

Palin, Sarah, 347
Panethnicity, 217
Panic, 443–444
Pareto, Vilfredo, 366
Parra, Jorge, 126 (photo)
Parsons, Talcott, 47
Passing, 232
Past-in-present discrimination, 225–226, 262
Patil, Pratibha, 249 (photo)
Patriarchy, 297
Peace
    grassroots movements for, 388
    negotiation and, 387
    religion and, 353–354
    war and, 386, 388
Peace Corps, 206
Peek, Lori, 220
Peer culture in schools, 316
Peer groups, 93
Pellerin, Robert M., 322
Per capita income, 184
Peripheral countries, 162, 162 (map), 383, 440, 440 (figure)
Permanent Forum on Indigenous Issues, UN, 240
Personal space and distance, 118–119
Petty bourgeoisie, 181
Piaget, Jean, 215
Plague, 412
Planned Parenthood, 426
Planned (centralized) systems, 378
Plato, 42, 402
Play stage, 97
Pluralism, 228, 229, 340–341, 353
Pluralist model of power (pluralist theory), 197, 365, 367
Polaris Project, 170
Police and delinquent youth, 167
Policy
    crime, 162–168
    digital divide, global, 204
    education, 329–332
    environmental and demographic, 423–424
    family, 306
    gender, 273–274
    minority groups, 234–238
    population, 407
    socialization, 108
Political behavior and social status, 185
Political science, 11–12
Political systems

authoritarian, 374
democratic, 364–365, 367–372, 374–376
the flag, symbolism, and patriotism, 363
ideology and, 368
institutional impacts at levels of analysis, 280 (table)
political parties and selection of candidates, 382–383, 382 (table)
politics, defined, 373
population patterns and, 407
purposes of economic institutions, 372–373
sexual attitudes and, 347
See also Elections; Power and privilege
Pollack, William, 253
Pol Pot, 375
Polyandry, 299 (photo), 300
Polygamy, 299–300
Polygyny, 299
Ponzi, Charles, 159
Ponzi schemes, 159
Popenoe, David, 304
Population Association of America (PAA), 426
Population clock, 396 (table)
Population Council, 426
Population pyramids, 401, 401 (figure), 422 (figure), 423 (figure)
Population Reference Bureau, 426
Populations and population trends
    as change trigger, 435
    economic development and, 423–424
    environment and, 424
    everyday lives and, 418–422
    fertility rates, institutional factors affecting, 405–409
    fertility rates and upward mobility, 189
    growth patterns over time, 398, 399 (table)
    largest world population centers, 419 (table)
    migration, 415–418 418 (table)
    mortality rates, 409–415
    percentage by world region, 421 (figure)
    populations, defined, 398
    predictors of, 399–401
    theoretical explanations for, 402–405
    urbanization and, 418, 419 (table), 420
Population transfer, 227–228
Postindustrial societies, 63–66
Poverty
    absolute vs. relative, 200
    feminization of, 200–201
    functions of, 202
    hunger, 199, 199 (table)
    sociological study and, 30–31
    See also Social class
Power and privilege
    G8 and G77, 384, 385 (map)
    global inequality and, 383–384
    ideology and, 368
    institutionalized privilege or disprivilege, 251
    legitimacy and, 362–365
    levels of analysis and, 361–362
    marriage, authority in, 297–299
    nation-states and, 379–380
    political parties and selection of candidates, 382–383, 382 (table)
    power, defined, 196, 361
    purpose of political and economic institutions, 372–373
    revolutions and rebellions, 380–381
    stratification and, 181
    systems of, 373–379

terrorism and, 388–390
  theoretical perspectives on, 362–367
  voter participation, 368–371, 370 (figure), 370 (table)
  war and, 384–388, 386 (table)
Power elite model, 196, 366–367
Predatory crimes, 155–156
Preference policies, 236, 237
Prejudice
  color-blind, 222
  defined, 219
  effects of, 231–232
  explanations of, 221–222
  in-groups and, 128
  minority reactions to, 232–234
  nature of, 219–221
  See also Stratification
Presbyterian polity, 342
Prestige, 181, 197
Primary deviance, 149
Primary groups, 127, 128 (table)
Prisons, 163–164, 165 (table)
Privilege. *See* Power and privilege; Stratification
Proactive social movements, 447
Processes. *See* Social processes
Professionals in bureaucracies, 132–133
Proletariat, 49, 377
Promise Academy (Harlem), 330
Pronatalist policies, 407
Property (wealth), 181, 194–196
Proportional representation, 376
Prostitution, 210 (photo), 211
The Protestant Ethic and the Spirit of Capitalism (Weber), 50–51,
    281–282
Psychology, 12, 91
Public distance, 119
Public order crimes, 156
Public sociologists, 43, 455
Punishment
  death penalty, 165–166, 166 (map)
  for law violations, 145
  in rational choice theory, 147, 167
  sanctions, 75, 102, 438 (figure)
  social class and, 104
  See also Crime
Push-pull model, 415

Al-Qaddafi, Muammar, 374
Qualitative research, 36
Quantitative research, 36
Questionnaires, 36
Quota systems, 236
Quran, 258

Race
  biracial and multiracial populations, 217–218
  "Black Men and Public Space" (Staples), 96
  class and, 216, 216 (table)
  death penalty and, 165–166
  defined, 213
  education and, 317, 317 (table)
  environmental justice movement and, 404–405
  gender, class, and, 269
  incarceration and, 164
  marriages, interracial, 295

  origins of concept of, 214–215
  religion and, 348–349
  social construction of, 215–216
  See also Minority groups
Racism
  bigotry, racial, 222
  color associations and, 77
  costs of, 231–232
  defined, 223
  environmental, 430
  minority reactions to, 232–234
Random samples, 38
Rape, 21–22, 268, 269
Rational choice (exchange) theory
  about, 46
  defined, 46
  on deviance, 146–147
  on education, 315
  on family, 290–291
  on interaction, 121
  mini-max strategy, 442
  on religion, 340
  on self-interest, 365
  on stratification, 178–179
Rationalization of social life, 129, 130
Rational-legal authority, 365
Reactive social movements, 447
Reagan, Ronald, 365, 407
Real culture, 72
Rebellion, 153
Recidivism rates, 164, 166–167, 168
Reciprocity, 60–61, 121, 290
Recycling, 430
Reference groups, 128
Refugees, 435, 435 (map)
Regressive movements, 448
Relative poverty, 200
Religion
  affiliation and membership, 336–337, 336 (table)
  caste systems and, 193
  civil religion, 345, 345 (photo)
  denominations and denominationalism, 340–341
  environment and, 19
  expressive movements and, 447
  function of, 333–334
  gender socialization and, 257–258
  homosexuality and, 271, 303
  institutional impacts at levels of analysis, 280 (table)
  Internet, technology, and, 354–355
  learning meaning systems in, 336
  marriage and, 295, 303
  meaning, belonging, and structural components of, 334–335,
    335 (figure)
  megachurches, 127
  myths, rituals, and symbols in meaning systems of, 337–340
  new religious movements (NRMs), 342–345
  organizational structures in, 341–342, 342 (table), 343
  peace and, 353–354
  population and, 408
  rational choice and, 340
  secularization, 351–352, 353 (table)
  sexual attitudes and, 347
  social change and, 346
  social cohesion and, 345

social status and, 185
stratification and, 346–351, 348 (table)
values and norms, legitimation of, 345–346
Weber's *Protestant Ethic* and, 281–282
Religious nativism, 354
Representative samples, 38
Reproduction and replacement, family and, 291
Reproduction of class, 326
Republican Party, 364, 365, 368, 383
Research, sociological
causality and, 35
data analysis, 38–39
data collection methods, 34–38
ethical issues in, 39
how to read a research table, 40–41
planning a study, 33–34
scientific approach, 31–32
social theory and, 32–33
See also Theories
Research and development (R&D), 453
Resistance or regressive movements, 448
Resocialization, 101, 163
Resources, access to, 177. *See also* Stratification
Resource theory, 297
Retirement, 22, 100, 244, 421–422
Retreatism, 152
Revolutionary movements, 380, 381, 448
"Ring Around the Rosie" and the Plague, 412
Riots, 443, 443 (figure)
Rites of passage, 99, 248
Ritualism, 152
Rituals, 338
Ritzer, George, 130
Roberts, Mary, 437
Roberts, Owen G., 437, 438
Role conflict, 124, 124 (figure)
Roles, 123, 123 (table), 315–319
Role strain, 124, 124 (figure)
Role-taking, 95, 97–98
Roma, 337
Roman Catholic Church, 349
Romantic love, 296
Romney, Mitt, 360 (photo), 370, 371
Roosevelt, Franklin D., 219 (photo caption)
Rossi, Alice, 91
Rumors, 444
Rumsfeld, Donald, 107
Rwanda, 369

Sacralization, 334, 335
Sacred realm, 333–334
Said, Khaled, 381
Saint-Simon, Henri, 42
Samples, 38
Sanctions, 75, 102, 145, 438 (figure)
Scapegoating, 202, 221–222, 226
Schools. *See* Education
Science
defined, 452
development of sociology as, 39–44
ideas underlying, 31–32
as institution, 279
social change and, 452–453

Scientific sociology, 43
Secondary analysis, 37
Secondary deviance, 149
Secondary groups, 127, 128 (table)
Second shift, 297
Secularization, 351–352, 353 (table)
Segregation
by gender, 248, 266
past-in-present discrimination and, 225
poverty and, 216
slums and, 215 (photo)
South African apartheid, 215, 448
as subjugation, 227
Seldo, Saher, 220
Self
defined, 94
global societies and, 107–108
I and Me as parts of, 95–97
looking-glass self and role taking, 94–95
socialization and development of, 94–99
Self-fulfilling prophecies, 179
Self-interest, 365
Semiperipheral countries, 162, 162 (map), 440–441,
440 (figure)
September 11, 2001, attacks, 4–5, 219–221, 238
Serial monogamy, 300
Service learning, 110
Sex, 246, 247–248. *See also* Gender
Sex ratio, 401
Sexual assault, 21–22, 164, 268, 269. *See also* Violence against
women
Sexuality, 72, 247–248, 347. *See also* Gender
Sexual orientation. *See* Homosexuality and LGBT individuals
Sexual regulation by family, 291
Shepard, Matthew, 156, 157 (photo)
Sherif, Carolyn, 235
Sherif, Muzafer, 235
Side-effect discrimination, 223–225, 224 (figure), 261
Significant others, 97–98
Simmel, Georg, 85
Simputer Trust, 204
Singapore, 407
Sirleaf, Ellen Johnson, 249 (photo)
Slavery, 210–213, 227
Smith, Joseph, 364
Smoking, 415
Social capital, 138, 166–167, 176
Social change
the automobile and technological change,
437–438
collective behavior, 441–444, 443 (figure)
defined, 430
education and, 324
family and, 292
levels of analysis on, 431–434
making a difference, 455
organizations, planned change in, 444–446
process of, 434–436
religion and, 346
social movements, 446–450
as social process, 19
technology, environment, and, 451–454
theories of, 436–441

Social class
    capitalism and, 377
    class consciousness, 180
    class systems, 194–197
    college attendance by, 188 (table)
    death penalty and, 165–166
    defined, 104
    environmental justice movement and, 404–405
    gender, race, and, 269
    race and, 216, 216 (table)
    religion and, 346–348, 348 (table)
    reproduction of class, 326
    socialization and, 104
    in United States, 197–198, 199 (figure)
    See also Social mobility; Stratification
Social cohesion, 345
Social construction of reality
    defined, 83–84
    deviance and, 144
    family and, 289
    gender, 246–247
    politics and, 364
    race and, 215–216
Social control theory, 146, 147
Social disorganization, 150–152
Social distance, 119
Social dynamics (Comte), 42
Social evolutionary theories, 439
Social institutions, defined, 18. *See also* Institutions
Social interaction, 117–121. *See also* Groups; Social networks
Socialism, 378–379
Socialization
    agents of, 101–107
    defined, 90
    education and, 319, 324
    elements of, 90–91
    family and, 102, 104, 188, 291–292
    of gender, 103, 247, 252–258
    government and, 364
    importance of, 91–92
    in life cycle, 99–101
    nature vs. nurture and, 91
    policy and practice, 108
    resocialization, 101
    self, development of, 94–99
    as social process, 19
    the social world and, 93
    transnationalism and, 107–108
"Social Media and Political Protests" (Castle), 381
Social mobility
    cross-cultural mobility, 192
    defined, 186
    factors affecting, 188–192
    measurement of, 187–188, 187 (table)
    types of, 186–187
Social movements, 446–450, 449 (table)
Social networks, 115–117, 115 (figure). *See also* Social interaction
Social policy. *See* Policy
Social processes
    of change, 434–436
    Comte's social dynamics, 42
    defined, 19
    institutions and structure vs. process, 277

    in social world model, 19
    See also Populations and population trends
Social reform movements, 447
Social sciences, 11–12
Social Security, 422
Social statics, 42
Social status. *See* Status
Social stratification. *See* Stratification
Social structures
    Comte's social statics, 42
    defined, 18
    institutions and structure vs. process, 277
    levels of analysis and, 19, 20 (table)
    in social world model, 18
    structural stain theory, 442–443
    structural system in religion, 335
    See also Bureaucracies; Groups; Organizations; Structural-
        functional (or functional) theory
Social units, 18. *See also* Groups
Social world model
    defined, 17
    environment, 19
    levels of analysis and, 16–17, 19–22
    social processes, 19
    social structures, 18
    See also specific topics
Society
    defined, 58
    evolution of societies, 59–66
    as hardware, 58–59, 86
    structure of, 59
Sociobiology, 91
Sociological associations, 27
Sociological imagination, 10
Sociologists for Women in Society (SWS), 276
Sociologists in Action
    creativity, community, and applied sociology, 65
    Harlem Children's Zone, 330
    international travel and intercultural education, 135
    microfinance, sociology students engaging with, 250
    police and delinquent youth, 167
    slavery in the 21st century, stopping, 212
Sociologists Without Borders (SSF), 238
Sociology
    common sense beliefs and, 7–9
    defined, 6
    employment in, 14–15, 14 (table), 15 (table), 16 (table)
    humans, social nature of, 4, 7
    ideas underlying, 6–7
    occupational categories in, 14 (table)
    questions sociologists ask, 10–11
    reasons for studying, 12–14
    as science, development of, 39–44
    scientific, humanistic, and public, 43–44
    social sciences and, 11–12
    See also Engaging Sociology
Sociology Around the World
    Cross-Cultural Differences in Family Dissolution, 307
    The Khmer Rouge Revolution, 375
    Life and Death in a Guatemalan Village, 73
    The McDonaldization of Society, 130
    Outcastes of India, 195
    "Ring Around the Rosie" and the Plague, 412

"Social Media and Political Protests" (Castle), 381
Tunisian Village Meets the Modern World, 24
"Women and Political Change in Postgenocide Rwanda" (Hughes), 369
Sociology in Our Social World
    "Anti-Muslim Sentiments in the United States" (Selod), 220
    Being Clear About Causality, 35
    "Black Men and Public Space" (Staples), 96
    The Boy Code, 253–254
    Burnouts and Jocks in a Public High School, 13
    Deaf Subculture in the United States, 80
    "Debunking Misconceptions About Divorce" (Popenoe), 304
    "Disability and Inequality" (Pellerin), 322
    The Flag, Symbolism, and Patriotism, 363
    The Functions of Poverty, 202
    "Gender and Food" (Bergdahl), 265
    Gender Socialization in American Public Schools, 103
    Human Language and the Marvel of a College Classroom, 45
    Islam, Mosques, and Organizational Structure, 343
    The Significance of the Baby Boom, 410
    "Stigmatizing Fatness" (Elrod), 151
    "The 2012 Presidential Election and the Youth Vote" (Castle), 371
    Where the Boys Are: And Where Are the Boys?, 317–318
    Witchcraft in the United States, 344
Sojourners Community, 447–448
Solidarity, mechanical vs. organic, 60
South Africa, 215, 412, 434, 440 (photo), 448
Southern Poverty Law Center, 235, 240
Southside Up global map, 68 (map)
Sowell, Thomas, 230
Space, personal, 118–119
Sports
    gender and, 257
    professional athletes, 95, 186, 232
Spurious relationships, 35
Stalin, Joseph, 374
Staples, Brent, 95, 96
"Starbuckization," 130
State capitalism, 379
State-organized crime, 159–160
State terrorism, 374, 389
Status
    ascribed vs. achieved, 122–123
    defined, 121
    deviance and, 144–145
    in educational system, 315–319
    family and, 292
    groups, link to, 121–123
    high schools and, 256–257
    individual social status, 182–186
    power elite theory on, 366–367
    role, relationship with, 123, 123 (table)
Status inconsistency, 185–186, 194
Stereotyping, 96, 219. See also Gender
Stigma, 150, 151, 160, 232
"Stigmatizing Fatness" (Elrod), 151
Stone, Margaret, 13
Stonewall movement, 447
Strain as trigger of change, 434–436
Strain theory, 152–153
Stratification
    achieved systems of, 194–197
    ascribed systems of, 193–194

assumptions in, 176
cultural capital and social capital, 190–191
digital divide, national and global, 201–204, 203 (table)
"Disability and Inequality" (Pellerin), 322
education and, 326–329
importance of, 176–177
individual social status, 182–186
population and, 406, 406 (figure)
poverty and, 199–201, 202
religion and, 346–351
social classes in the U.S., 197–198, 199 (table)
social mobility, 186–192
social stratification. defined, 176
theoretical explanations for, 177–182
See also Gender; Minority groups
Street crimes, 155–156
Stress as trigger of change, 434–436
Strict affirmative action, 235–236
Structural-functional (or functional) theory
    about, 47–48
    on change, 439–440
    cultural theory, 84–85
    defined, 47
    on deviance, 150–153
    on education, 323–326
    on family, 291–292
    on gender stratification, 264–266
    on institutions, 282
    on minority groups, 229–230
    on religion, 343–344
    on socialization, 93
    on stratification, 179
    on terrorism, 389–390
    on war, terrorism, and revolution, 386
Structural strain theory, 442–443
Structural system in religion, 335
Structured interviews, 34
Student government, 391
Student movements, 457
Student organizations, 27, 240, 357
Subcultures, 78–79, 80
Subjugation, 227
Suicide, 125–126, 345
Survey method, 34–36
Sweatshops, 273, 432
Symbolic interaction theory
    about, 44–46
    on change, 436–438
    cultural theory, 83–84
    defined, 44
    on deviance, 148–150
    on education, 314–315
    on family, 289–290
    on gender stratification, 263–264
    on institutions, 283
    on interaction, 120–121
    looking-glass self and role-taking in, 94–95
    on race, 215–216
    on religion and creation of meaning, 337–340
    self-development and, 99
    on stratification, 178

Symbols
   defined, 44
   flags and, 363
   in religious meaning systems, 338–339
   socialization and, 95

Taboos, 74, 74 (table), 295
Taliban, 158, 228, 251, 448
Taylor, Charles, 436
Tchambuli (Chambri) of New Guinea, 245
Teachers, role of, 316–318
Teaching Tolerance program (Southern Poverty Law Center), 235, 240
Tea Party Patriots, 233–234
Technology
   automobiles and technological change, 437–438
   cell phone users, 203
   defined, 63, 451
   democracy and, 376–377
   postindustrial societies and, 63–66
   uneven diffusion of, 436
   See also Internet and computers
Television, 105, 255–256, 354
Terrorism
   Boston Marathon bombings, 105
   defined, 159, 388–389
   explanations for, 389–390
   as global counterculture, 83
   September 11, 2001, attacks, 4–5, 219–221, 238
   state terrorism, 374, 389
   types of terrorist groups, 160 (table)
Testing and test scores, 327–328
Theories
   biosocial, 91
   cooperative vs. competitive perspectives, 52 (figure)
   cultural, 83–86
   defined, 32
   differential association, 148–149
   emergent norm, 442
   empirical research and, 32–33
   evolutionary theory of stratification, 181–182
   filter, 297 (figure)
   frustration-aggression, 221
   labeling, 148, 149–150
   linguistic relativity, 77
   major theoretical perspectives in sociology, 44–52
   pluralist, 197, 365, 367
   power elite model, 196, 366–367
   resource, 297
   social control, 146, 147
   social evolutionary, 439
   strain, 152–153
   structural strain, 442–443
   theoretical perspective, defined, 44
   using, 52
   value-added, 442–443
   wealth flow, 404
   of Weber, 50–51
   world systems, 162, 440–441, 440 (figure)
   See also Conflict theory; Feminist theory; Rational choice (exchange) theory; Structural-functional (or functional) theory; Symbolic interaction theory

Thiagaraj, Henry, 195
Thompson, Michael, 253–254
Thorne, Barrie, 103, 264
Tibet, 446
Tikkun Community, 357
Time and motion studies, 445
Title IX, 257
Tobacco use, 415
Tobar, Hector, 322
Total institution, 101, 163
Totalitarian government, 374, 375
Touro Synagogue, Rhode Island, 229
Toys and gender, 255
Traditional authority, 364
Transgender, 247, 270. *See also* Homosexuality and LGBT individuals
Transnationalism, 107
Transportation technology, 437–438, 439 (photo)
Triangulation, 38
Tsarnaev, Tamerlan and Dzhokhar, 105
Tuareg, 59, 60 (photo)
Tunisian Village Meets the Modern World, 24
Tutoring, 110, 138
Twins, 4
Twitter, 116
"The 2012 Presidential Election and the Youth Vote" (Castle), 371
Type I and Type II offenses, 155

Underclass, 181
UNESCO (UN Educational, Scientific and Cultural Organization), 110, 313
Unification Church, 342
Uniform Crime Reports (UCRs), 155
Union Carbide Corporation, 451
Unions, 138, 365 (photo), 377
United Church of Christ, 432
United Nations (UN)
   Inter-Agency Network on Women and Gender Equality, 276
   internships with, 391
   Permanent Forum on Indigenous Issues, 87, 240
   "Statement on Race," 214
   Universal Declaration of Human Rights, 238
   women's status and, 136
   World Urbanization Prospects, 420
Universal Declaration of Human Rights, 238
Universities. *See* Colleges and universities; Education
University of Michigan, 236, 237
Upper middle class, 198
Upward mobility. *See* Social mobility
Urbanization, 398, 418, 419 (table), 420
Urban legends, 444
USA PATRIOT Act, 220
U.S. Flag Code, 363

Value-added theory, 442–443
Values, 72, 343–344
Van Gogh, Vincent, 145
Variables, 34
Verstehen, 50, 293
Vertical mobility, 187
Victimization surveys, 155
Victimless crimes, 156
Video games and gender, 255

Vietnam Veterans Memorial (Washington, D.C.), 388, 388 (photo)
Violence against women, 20–22, 154, 267, 293 (photo), 294
Voices, 309
Volunteer Match, 457
Volunteers of America, 357
Voter participation, 368–370, 370 (figure), 370 (table)
Voting rights and women, 251

Wallis, Jim, 448
War, 384–388, 386 (table)
Ward, Lester, 43
Washington, George, 229
Way, Niobe, 254
Wealth, 194–196
Wealth flow theory, 404
Weber, Max
    on bureaucracies, 131–132
    on elective affinity, 348
    on power and authority, 361, 364, 364 (figure)
    The Protestant Ethic and the Spirit of Capitalism, 50–51, 281–282
    rationalization of social life, 129, 130
    on status inconsistency, 185
    theoretical contributions of, 50–51
    on three Ps (property, power, prestige), 181, 194
    Verstehen concept, 50, 293
Welfare programs, 201
White-collar (occupational) crime, 158–159
Wicca, 343–345
William, Prince, 174, 174 (photo), 365 (photo)
William Paterson, University, 250
Williams, Betty, 194
Wilson, William Julius, 213
Winner-takes-all system, 376
Witchcraft (Wicca), 343–345
Wodaabe of Niger, 8 (photo), 245, 245 (photo)

Women
    in abusive relationships, 290
    body image and, 256 (photo), 272, 272 (photo)
    common-sense beliefs on development and, 9
    deviance and, 154
    education of girls around the globe, 330–331
    empowerment of, 249–250
    globalization and, 134–137
    in government leadership, 249 (photo), 251–252,
        251 (table)
    obesity and, 151
    organizations and, 133
    religion and, 349–351
    violence against, 20–22, 154, 267, 293 (photo), 294
    voting rights and, 251
    work and, 258, 260 (figure), 272–273
    See also Gender
"Women and Political Change in Postgenocide Rwanda"
    (Hughes), 369
Women's movements, 274
Worker class, 181
World Bank, 449, 450
World Education, 110
World Health Organization (WHO), 435
World of Warcraft (WoW), 255
World systems theory, 162, 440–441, 440 (figure)
World Urbanization Prospects (UN Population Division), 420

Yir Yoront of Australia, 431
Youth dependency ratio, 399–400
Yunus, Muhammad, 206

Zimbardo, Philip, 163
Zinn, Maxine Baca, 449
Zuckerberg, Mark, 116